Organizational Behaviour

Stephen P. Robbins
San Diego State University

Timothy A. Judge
University of Florida

Timothy T. Campbell
University of Dubai

**Financial Times
Prentice Hall**
is an imprint of

Harlow, England • London • New York • Boston • San Francisco • Toronto • Sydney • Singapore • Hong Kong
Tokyo • Seoul • Taipei • New Delhi • Cape Town • Madrid • Mexico City • Amsterdam • Munich • Paris • Milan

Pearson Education Limited
Edinburgh Gate
Harlow
Essex CM20 2JE
England

and Associated Companies throughout the world

Visit us on the World Wide Web at:
www.pearsoned.co.uk

First published 2010

ISBN: 978-0-273-71939-7

British Library Cataloguing-in-Publication Data
A catalogue record for this book is available from the British Library

Library of Congress Cataloging-in-Publication Data
Robbins, Stephen P., 1943–
 Organizational behaviour / Stephen P. Robbins, Timothy A. Judge, Tim Campbell. – 1st ed.
   p. cm.
  ISBN 978-0-273-71939-7 (pbk.)
  1. Organizational behavior. 2. Personnel management. 3. Psychology, Industrial. 4. Leadership. I. Judge, Tim. II. Campbell, Tim. III. Title.
HD58.7.R6223 2010
302.3′5–dc22
                                                              2010004227

10 9 8 7 6 5 4 3
14 13 12 11

Typeset in 9.5/12pt Minion by 35
Printed and bound by Grafos S. A., Barcelona, Spain

Organizational Behaviour

Visit the *Organizational Behaviour, first edition* Companion Website at **www.pearsoned.co.uk/robbins** to find a wealth of valuable **student** learning material. Including:

- Exam-style questions with answer guidance to prepare for exam success.
- Multiple-choice quizzes on the main topics in organizational behaviour.
- Flashcards to help you revise.
- Online glossary for quick reference to key terms in organizational behaviour.

Brief contents

Contents

Chapter 1 What is organizational behaviour?

Chapter 2 Foundations of individual behaviour

Chapter 3 Attitudes and job satisfaction

Chapter 4 Personality and values

Chapter 5 Perception and individual decision making

Chapter 6 Motivation concepts

Chapter 7 Motivation: from concepts to applications

Chapter 8 Emotions and moods

Chapter 9 Foundations of group behaviour

Chapter 10   Understanding work teams

Chapter 11   Communication

Chapter 12 Basic approaches to leadership

Chapter 13 Contemporary issues in leadership

Chapter 16 Foundations of organization structure

Chapter 17 Organizational culture

Chapter 18 Human resource policies and practices

Chapter 19 Organizational change and stress management

Supporting resources

Visit **www.pearsoned.co.uk/robbins** to find valuable online resources

Companion Website for students:

- Exam-style questions with answer guidance to prepare for exam success.
- Multiple-choice quizzes on the main topics in organizational behaviour.
- Flashcards to help you revise.
- Online glossary for quick reference to key terms in organizational behaviour.

For instructors

- Complete, downloadable Instructor's Manual
- PowerPoint slides that can be downloaded and used for presentations
- Testbank of question material

For more information please contact your local Pearson Education sales representative or visit **www.pearsoned.co.uk/robbins**

Preface

Organizational behaviour (OB) is concerned with understanding the behaviour of people at work. Because it is people who are ultimately responsible for the success, or even survival, of an organization, OB is an essential field of study. Questions such as what motivates employees to provide performance beyond expectations? Why do some employees love their job and others in exactly the same role hate it? What is the secret to great organizational leadership? Should employees have any say in what they do? And many other questions have been asked for generations. Traditionally, the answers to these questions were often dealt with through a manager's own preconceived ideas or 'hunches'. *Organizational Behaviour* helps to answer these questions by comprehensive systematic study.

This book draws on previous work by Stephen Robbins and Tim Judge, that has long been considered the standard for all organizational behaviour textbooks, to produce a particularly European OB textbook without losing sight of the global context. It continues the Robbins and Judge tradition of making current, relevant research come alive for students while maintaining its hallmark features – clear writing style, cutting-edge content and compelling pedagogy, whilst dealing with the variability of organizational behaviour across Europe.

The features of the book

Writing style: a particular feature of the book is the conversational and 'student friendly' writing style. Concepts are carefully explained in an understandable fashion without compromising the more complex theoretical aspects.

Examples: an important method of supporting students understanding of concepts is to relate what is being learnt to the real world. This book is packed full of recent examples drawn primarily from Europe, but also globally, and from a wide variety of organizations.

The three-level model of analysis: this book presents OB at three levels of analysis. It begins with individual behaviour and then moves to group behaviour. Finally it adds the organization system to capture the full complexity of organizational behaviour.

Opening vignettes: each chapter begins with an introduction to the topic by using a real-world illustration. The intention is to provide an example students can relate back to as the topic is explored and perhaps question their initial assumptions.

'Myth or science?' boxes: this feature presents a commonly accepted 'fact' about human behaviour, followed by confirming or disproving research evidence. Some examples include 'You can't teach an old dog new tricks'; 'Happy workers are productive workers'; and 'It's not what you know, it's who you know'. These boxes provide repeated evidence that common sense can often lead us astray in the attempt to understand human behaviour, and that behavioural research offers a means for testing the validity of common-sense notions.

'OB in the news': OB concepts regularly appear in the media, such as job satisfaction, employee loyalty, and workplace conflict. This feature prepares students to recognise and evaluate these issues when presented with them in newspapers, magazines, TV, etc.

'Face the facts': these boxes highlight interesting facts from recent surveys that emphasise key aspects of the texts. For example, the extent of teleworking and how it varies across Europe and the popularity of working in teams. Students should be encouraged to further explore the validity, implications, and reasons for the results.

Experiential exercises: an experiential, hands-on, in-class exercise is included in each chapter, along with material in the Instructor's Manual that will make for unique and entertaining exercises to highlight a key chapter concept.

Ethical dilemma: each chapter has an associated ethical dilemma. The recognition of ethical issues when dealing with people has risen significantly over the past decade. For instance, is it O.K. to lie during negotiations? Is it acceptable to force people to work as a part of a team? Is fudging parts of your C.V. acceptable because 'everybody else does it'? Are large bonuses acceptable for top management when the company has posted huge financial losses? This feature helps students to recognise ethical issues and think about how they would resolve them.

Case incidents: there are two case incidents at the end of each chapter that are devised to apply what has been learnt in the chapter to short, interesting real world events.

Point/counterpoint dialogues: an important skill for students is the ability to formulate supported arguments rather than simply describe concepts. These dialogues allow students to see two sides of an OB controversy and to stimulate their critical thinking. They are especially useful to stimulate class discussions.

Further pedagogy: each chapter has a structure that makes it easy for students to follow. Chapter Outlines provide a list of contents for each chapter. Learning Objectives are provided at the outset of each chapter and linked to the text throughout in marginal annotations. These objectives are then linked to the *questions for review* at the end of the chapter. There is also a running glossary of key terms and definitions in the margin adjacent to the point at which the term is first discussed at length.

Supplements

Companion website

This website serves as a student study and review site. The site includes chapter quizzes and an online glossary.

Self-assessment library (S.A.L.)

S.A.L. is a unique learning tool that allows the assessment of personal knowledge, beliefs, feelings, and actions in regard to a wide range of skills, abilities, and interests. Self-Assessments have been integrated into each chapter including a self-assessment at the beginning of each chapter. S.A.L. helps students better understand their interpersonal and behavioural skills as they relate to the theoretical concepts presented in each chapter.

Instructor's resources

Instructor's Manual: the manual includes expanded outlines of the topics in the chapter, teaching tips to accompany the boxed text and exercises, and answers to all question material.

PowerPoint slides: each chapter is accompanied by a PowerPoint presentation.

Test Bank: the test bank allows lecturers to create customised tests from over 2,500 questions including multiple choice, true/false and essay questions.

Guided Tour

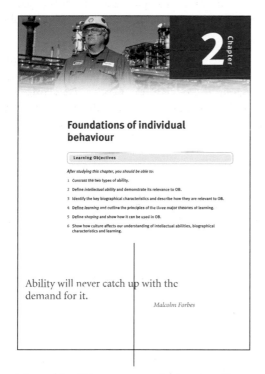

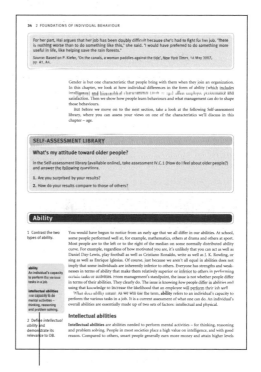

Learning objectives open each chapter. They enable you to focus on what you should have achieved and help structure your learning. Each learning objective is highlighted throughout the text to help you navigate your way through each chapter.

Margin definitions pick out key terms and ideas and explain them fully.

The **ethical dilemma** box separates out controversial themes helping stimulate discussion and debate regarding possible ethical pitfalls.

Each chapter comes with two **case incidents**. These present key research and theory and answering the questions encourages you to think critically about the evidence presented.

Questions for review will test your understanding and help track your progress.

Each chapter comes with an engaging **experiental exercise.** Use these in a group and see how your results compare with those of your classmates.

The book is full of small **case studies** which encourage debate and stimulate class discussion.

Myth *or* science takes on popular pre-conceptions about organizational behaviour looking at the truth behind the myths.

The **global** box highlights cultural differences in organizational behaviour across countries and continents to illustrate diversity across the globe.

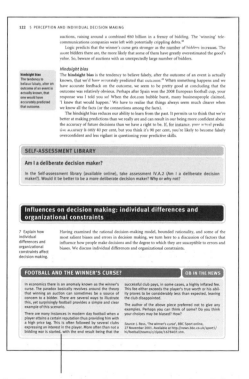

Exhibits take you out of the main text to explore various theoretical concepts and enhance your understanding of the chapter.

These snappy **Point/counterpoint** boxes improve your understanding by providing different perspectives.

OB in the news contains extracts and articles from a variety of sources in the media and promotes discussion of real examples of organizational behaviour in practice.

Acknowledgements

Textbooks are a very labour-intensive exercise that require the participation of numerous people. I would particularly like to acknowledge the excellent contributions by the team of reviewers and their suggestions for improvement that have helped shape this book:

Alexandra Beauregard, London School of Economics, UK

Frans M. van Eijnatten, Eindhoven University of Technology, Netherlands

Gabriele Jacobs-Belschak, Erasmus University Rotterdam, Netherlands

Iain Lauder, Edinburgh Business School, Heriot-Watt University, UK

Mohammad Latifi, University of Uppsala, Sweden

John Roscoe, Thames Valley University, UK

I would also like to whole-heartedly acknowledge the team at Pearson Education for their many efforts in getting this book to print and into the hands of students and faculty.

My gratitude to the commitment and dedication of the OB research community, without which there would be no textbook. And finally, to Joanne, the unwavering support of Helen and David, and the inspiration of Sam and Leo to further understand human behaviour.

Publisher's acknowledgements

We are grateful to the following for permission to reproduce copyright material:

Figures

Figure 1.1 after *Real Managers*, Cambridge, MA: Ballinger (Luthans, F., Hodgetts, R. M. and Rosenkrantz, S. A. 1988), with permission from Fred Luthans; Figure 3.2 adapted from *How Engaged are British Employees?*, CIPD (2006) Figure 12, Figure 13, with the permission of the publisher, the Chartered Institute of Personnel and Development, London (www.cipd.co.uk); Figure 3.3 from When bureaucrats get the blues: Responses to dissatisfaction among federal employees, *Journal of Applied Social Psychology*, 15, No.1, July, p. 83 (Rusbult, C. and Lowery, B. 2006), Copyright © 2006, 1985 V. H. Winston, reprinted with permission from John Wiley & Sons, Inc; Figure 4.2 from *Atlas of European Values*, Brill (Halman, L. ed. 2005) p. 55, with permission from Koninklijke Brill NV and Dr. Loek Halman; Figure 4.3 from *Making Vocational Choices: A Theory of Vocational Personalities and Work Environments* (Holland, J. L. 1992), Reproduced by special permission of the Publisher, Psychological Assessment Resources, Inc., from *Making Vocational Choices*, Third Edition, copyright 1973, 1985, 1992, 1997 by Psychological Assessment Resources, Inc. All rights reserved; Figure 5.3 from Motivating creativity in organizations: On doing what you love and loving what you do, pp. 39–58 (Amabile, T. M. 1997), Copyright © 1997, by The Regents of the University of California. Reprinted from the *California Management Review*, Vol. 40, No. 1. By permission of The Regents; Figure 6.1 adapted from Maslow, Abraham H.; Frager, Robert D. (Editor); Fadiman, James (Editor), *Motivation and Personality*, 3rd, © 1987. Electronically reproduced by permission of Pearson Education, Inc., Upper Saddle River, New Jersey; Figure 6.2 reprinted by permission of Harvard Business School Press. From *One More Time: How Do You Motivate Employees?* by F. Herzberg. Boston, MA 2003. Copyright © 2003 by the Harvard Business School Publishing Corporation; all rights reserved; Figure 6.4 from *The Wall Street Journal*, permission Cartoon Features Syndicate; Figure 6.6 adapted from Building a practically useful theory of goal setting and task motivation: a 35-year odyssey, *American Psychologist*, September, pp. 705–717 (Locke, E. A. and Latham, G. P. 2002), APA, adapted with permission; Figure 7.1 adapted Hackman, J. R./Oldham, G. R., *Work Redesign*, © 1980, p. 77. Adapted by permission of Pearson Education, Inc., Upper Saddle River, New Jersey; Figure 7.2 from *Improving Life at Work*, Glenview, IL: Scott Foresman (Hackman, J. R. and Suttle, J. L. eds 1977) p. 138, reprinted by permission of J. Richard Hackman and J. Lloyd Suttle; Figure 8.5 after Emotion in the workplace: The new challenge for managers, *Academy of Management Executive*, February, p. 77 (Ashkanasy, N. M. and Daus, C. S. 2002), reproduced with permission of Academy of Management (NY); permission conveyed through Copyright Clearance Center, Inc; Figure 9.4 from Erez, A., Elms, H. and Fong, E., Lying, Cheating, Stealing: Groups and the Ring of Gyges, paper presented at the Academy of Management Annual Meeting, Honolulu, HI, August 8, 2005, with permission from Amir Erez; Figure 9.6 from *Build a Better Life by Stealing Office Supplies*, Kansas City, MO: Andrews & McMeal (Adams, S. 1991) p. 31, 'Group writing' cartoon, Dilbert reprinted by permission of Knight Features Limited; Figure 10.4 from Team-Role Descriptions from Belbin Team-Role Summary Sheet handout © e-interplace, Belbin Associates, UK. 2001, reproduced with permission from Belbin Associates; Figure 11.3 from Daft, *Organizational Behavior*, 1E. © 2001 South-Western, a part of Cengage Learning, Inc. Reproduced by permission. www.cengage.

com/permissions; Figure 14.1 from Leo Cullum, *New Yorker* cartoon 1/6/1986, © Leo Cullum/Condé Nast Publications/www.cartoonbank.com; Figure 15.2 from *Handbook of Industrial and Organizational Psychology*, 2nd ed., Vol. 3, Consulting Psychologists Press (Dunnette, M. D. and Hough, L. M. eds 1992) p. 668, K. Thomas 'Conflict and Negotiation Processes in Organizations', with permission from Nicholas Brealey Publishing; Figure 17.1 adapted from *Understanding Organizations*, by Charles Handy (Penguin Books 1976, Fourth Edition 1993) p. 183, p. 185, p. 187, p. 190, Copyright © Charles Handy, 1976, 1981, 1985, 1993, 1999, reproduced by permission of Penguin Books Ltd.

Tables

Table 1.1 adapted from Mintzberg, Henry, *The Nature of Managerial Work*, 1st Edition, © 1980. Reprinted by permission of Pearson Education, Inc., Upper Saddle River, NJ. Reprinted by permission; Table 2.2 adapted from *HR Magazine*, reprinted with the permission of *HR Magazine*, published by the Society for Human Resource Management, Alexandria, VA; Table 4.1 this article was published in *Business Ethics: Research Issues and Empirical Studies*, Frederick, W. C. and Weber, J., The Values of Corporate Managers and Their Critics: An Empirical Description and Normative Implications, pp. 123–144, Copyright Elsevier 1990; Table 4.3 from Geert Hofstede, *Culture's Consequences: Comparing Values, Behaviors, Institutions and Organizations Across Nations*, Second Edition. Thousand Oaks, California: Sage Publications, 2001, Copyright © Geert Hofstede BV, reproduced with permission; Table on page 165 from *Quality of Working Life in the Czech Republic*, Eurofound (Vaskova, R. and Kroupa, A. 28 February 2005) ID: CZ0502SR01, © European Foundation for the Improvement of Living and Working Conditions, 2010, Wyattville Road, Loughlinstown, Dublin 18, Ireland, www.eurofound.europa.eu; Table on page 193 adapted from Hackman, J. R./Oldham, G. R., *Work Redesign*, © 1980, p. 317. Adapted by permission of Pearson Education, Inc., Upper Saddle River, New Jersey; Table 9.1 adapted from A Typology of Deviant Workplace Behaviors: A Multidimensional Scaling Study, *Academy of Management Journal*, April, p. 565 (Robinson, S. L. and Bennett, R. J. 1995), reproduced with permission of Academy of Management (NY); permission conveyed through Copyright Clearance Center, Inc; Table 11.1 after When 'No' Means 'Yes', *Marketing*, October, pp. 7–9 (Kiely, M. 1993), Reproduced from *Marketing* magazine with permission of the copyright owner, Haymarket Business Publications Ltd; Table 13.1 after Substitutes for leadership: Their meaning and measurement, *Organizational Behavior and Human Performance*, December, p. 378 (Kerr, S. and Jermier, J. M. 1978), Copyright 1978, with permission from Elsevier.

Text

Extract on page 58 adapted from Success can be a game with many players, *Financial Times*, 28 May 2008 (Murray, S.), reprinted with permission from Sarah Murray; Extract on page 66 from Job satisfaction secret of happiness, *The Scotsman*, 30 June 2006 (Urquhart, F.), Scotsman Publications Ltd; Extract on pages 75–76 from The Inspector's Dilemma, The Open University, http://www.ibe.org.uk/teaching/The%20Inspectordilemma.pdf, reprinted with permission of Institute of Business Ethics; Extract on page 76 adapted from Money isn't everything in life, *Financial Times*, 28 May 2008 (Richards, H.), reprinted with permission from Huw Richards, Freelance Journalist; Extract on page 77 adapted from Drawing back from extreme jobs, *The Sunday Times*, 3 December 2006 (Millard, R.), © The Sunday Times 3 December 2006/nisyndication.com; Extract on page 110 from Shazia Mirza speaking at the launch of Moving on up? the way forward, House of Commons, March 2007, reprinted with permission from Shazia Mirza; Exhibit 5.2 from Robbins, Stephen P., *Decide and Conquer: Make Winning Decisions and Take Control of Your Life*, 1st, © 2004. Electronically reproduced by permission of Pearson Education, Inc., Upper Saddle River, New Jersey; Extract on page 218 from Crying game; Waterworks at the water cooler, *The Times*, 13 October 2004, © The Times 13 October 2004/nisyndication.com; Extract on page 222 adapted from Emotions as Strategic Game in a Hostile Workplace: An Exemplar Case, *Employee Responsibilities and Rights Journal*, Special

Issue: The Traumatised Worker, Vol. 16, No. 3, pp. 167–78 (Perrone, J. and Vickers, M. H. 2004), with kind permission from Springer Science and Business Media; Extract on page 281 adapted from Volvo Cars Ghent: A self-managing team model, *Workplace Innovation: Four Case Examples*, Box 1: Overview, p. 1 (EMCC Company Network 2005) © European Foundation for the Improvement of Living and Working Conditions, 2005, © European Foundation for the Improvement of Living and Working Conditions, 2010, Wyattville Road, Loughlinstown, Dublin 18, Ireland, www.eurofound.europa.eu; Extract on pages 281–82 adapted from Sociable Climbing, *Financial Management*, pp. 16–19 (Orton-Jones, C. 2008), Copyright © 2008, reproduced with permission of Blackwell Publishing Ltd; Exhibit 11.1 adapted from *Cutting Back*, Jossey-Bass (Hirschhorn, L. 1983) pp. 54–56, with permission from Larry Hirschhorn; Extract on page 310 adapted from Go gets to grips with communications, *Employers Law*, 1 September 2001, with permission from Reed Business Information; Extract on page 318 from You need to be popular, or well-liked to be an effective leader, http://www.work911.com/leadership-development/faq/mythpopular.htm, Copyright 2007–2008 Robert Bacal/Bacal & Associates, reproduced with permission from Bacal & Associates; Exhibit 13.1 after *Charismatic Leadership in Organizations*, Thousand Oaks, CA: Sage (Conger, J. A. and Kanungo, R. N. 1998) p. 94, reproduced with permission of Sage Publications, Inc. Books; permission conveyed through Copyright Clearance Center, Inc; Exhibit 13.2 from From transactional to transformational leadership: Learning to share the vision, *Organizational Dynamics*, Vol. 18, No. 3, Winter, p. 22 (Bass, Bernard M. 1990), Copyright 1990, with permission from Elsevier; Extract on page 363 from Siemens AG vision statement, with permission from Siemens AG; Extract on page 363 from Toshiba vision statement, with permission from Toshiba Corporation; Exercise on page 392 adapted from A Simple – But Powerful - Power Simulation, *Exchange: The Organizational Behavior Teaching Journal*, 4, pp. 38–42 (Bolman, L. and Deal, T. F. 1979), reproduced with permission of Sage Publications, Inc. Journals; permission conveyed through Copyright Clearance Center, Inc; Extract on page 393 from Out of the typing pool into career limbo, *BusinessWeek*, Issue 3471, p. 93 (Linda Bernier 1996), 'I don't want to fight anymore', reprinted from 15 April 1996 issue of Bloomberg BusinessWeek by special permission, copyright © 1996 by Bloomberg LP; Extract on page 428 from This organization is dis-organization, *Fast Company*, 18 December 2007 (LaBarre, P.), http://www.fastcompany.com/magazine/03/oticon.html?page=0%2C1, with permission from Fast Company Copyright © 2010. All rights reserved; Exercise on page 450 adapted from An exercise of authority, *Organizational Behavior Teaching Review*, 14, no. 2, 1989–1990, 28–42 (Kahn, W. A.), reproduced with permission of Sage Publications, Inc. Journals; permission conveyed through Copyright Clearance Center, Inc; Extract on page 451 from What is the right organization design?, *Organizational Dynamics*, Vol. 36, No. 4, pp. 340–41 (Anand, N. and Daft, R. 2007), Copyright 2007, with permission from Elsevier; Extract on pages 451–52 from Organizational structure, *Journal of Accountancy*, Vol. 123, 1, pp. 84–86 (Kion, S. and Markstein, D. 1967), Copyright 1967 American Institute of Certified Public Accountants, Inc. All rights reserved. Used with permission; Epigraph on page 454 from Jim Collins, *Good to Great and the Social Sectors*. Copyright © 2005 by Jim Collins. Reprinted with permission from Jim Collins; Extract on page 480 after A New Odd Couple: Google, P&G Swap Workers to Spur Innovation, *Wall Street Journal (Eastern edition)*, p. A1 (Byron, E. 2008), Reprinted by permission of Wall Street Journal, Copyright © 2008 Dow Jones & Company, Inc. All Rights Reserved Worldwide. License number 2344221482972; Epigraph on page 484 from Jack F. Welch, with permission from Jack F. Welch; Extract on page 500 from Performance review takes a page from Facebook, *BusinessWeek*, 12 March (McGregor, J. 2009), reprinted from 12 March 2009 issue of Bloomberg BusinessWeek by special permission, copyright © 2009 by Bloomberg LP; Exhibit 19.2 adapted from *Leading Change* (Kotter, J. P. 1996), Reprinted by permission of Harvard Business School Press. From Leading Change by J. P. Kotler. Boston, MA 1996. Copyright © 1996 by the Harvard Business School Publishing Corporation; all rights reserved; Exercise on page 543 after Power and the changing environment, *Journal of Management Education*, Vol. 24, No. 2, April, pp. 295–296 (Barbuto, Jr., John E. 2000), reproduced with permission of Sage Publications, Inc. Journals; permission conveyed through Copyright Clearance Center, Inc.

The Financial Times

Extract on page 40 adapted from City banker alleges race discrimination, *FT.com*, 12 September 2007 (Tait, N.), http://www.ft.com/cms/s/0/bae5a9e6-60c7-11dc-8ec0-0000779fd2ac.html?nclick_check=1; Extract on page 417 from Bristol mediation, *FT.com*, 30 March 2007 (Baker, D.), http://www.ft.com/cms/s/2/af72973e-de38-11db-afa7-000b5df10621.html; Extract on page 479 from European Special Award – Piscines Ideales, *FT.com*, 28 May 2008, http://www.ft.com/cms/s/0/0557a05c-2c50-11dd-9861-000077b07658.html; Extract on page 515 adapted from Profile: Slovak success story respected across Europe, *FT.com*, 18 November 2005 (Tieman, R.), http://www.ft.com/cms/s/1/bd7114d4-582c-11da-948f-00000e25118c.html.

Photographs

(Key: b-bottom; c-centre; l-left; r-right; t-top)

Alamy Images: Alvey & Towers Picture Library 488, Eddie Gerald 457, Extreme Sports Photo 171, 172, Jeff Morgan Education 184, Libby Welch 200, 214, Malcolm Case-Green 211, MBI 109, 115, Robert Convery 491, Stephen Dorey 439, UpperCut Images 398, 399; **AT&T Archives and History Center:** 237; **Corbis:** Bob Daemmrich 232, Michael Christopher Brown 466, Redlink 243, Reuters 118, 150, Shen Bohan / Xinhua Press 427, 430; **Doug Mindell Photography:** 205; **Dreamstime.com:** 286, 287; **DVLA:** 436; **Getty Images:** 82l, 83, 228, 229, AFP 71, 124, 352, 411, 415, 454, 455, 493, Dave M Bennett 145, David Levenson 339, 340, Djamilla Rosa Cochran 359, Film Magic / Jason Kempin 314, 316, Foodpix 514, 528, Franck Prevel 91, Iconica 485, Image Bank 8, Jim Spellman 464, Justin Sullivan 261, M J Kim 186, Mark Allen 110, Max Whittaker 139, Michael Porro 57, 62, Mike Clarke 408, Paula Bronstein 303, Philippe Wojazer 315, Pool 1, 2, Roland Magunia 371, Sean Gallup 82r, 89, Shaun Curry 291, Stan Honda 86, Stephen Jaffe 234, Torsten Silz 370, 383, Toru Yamanaka / AFP 43; **iStockphoto:** 403, Vetta Collections 48; **Kobal Collection Ltd:** New Line Cinema 443; **Press Association Images:** Aijaz Rahi / AP 201, Antonio Calanni 159, AP Archive 321, Daniel Maurer / AP 181, Douglas C Pizac / AP 343t, Gorassini Giancario / ABACA 138, 154, Harry Cabluck / Associated Press 16, John Giles / PA Archive 153, Justin Williams 428, MARTIAL TREZZINI / AP 374, Robert F Bukaty / AP 274, Schnoerrer / DPA 13; **Q-Cells:** 289; **Reaktor Innovations:** 61; **Redux:** Eros Hoagland 58, Jim Wilson / NY Times 272, Patrick Allard / REA 325, Ruth Fremson 260, 269; **Reuters:** Kimberley White 376, Manuel Silvestri 33, Mel Langsdon 343cl, Michael Dalder 320, Nathalie Koulischer 380, Russell Boyce 348, STR New 515; **Rex Features:** Sipa Press 264, 484, 498; **Shell International:** 32, 37; **TopFoto:** 526, 526.

In some instances we have been unable to trace the owners of copyright material, and we would appreciate any information that would enable us to do so.

What is organizational behaviour?

Learning Objectives

After studying this chapter, you should be able to:

1 Demonstrate the importance of interpersonal skills in the workplace.

2 Describe the manager's functions, roles and skills.

3 Define *organizational behaviour* (*OB*).

4 Show the value to OB of systematic study.

5 Identify the major behavioural science disciplines that contribute to OB.

6 Demonstrate why there are few absolutes in OB.

7 Identify the challenges and opportunities managers have in applying OB concepts.

8 Compare the three levels of analysis in this book's OB model.

For many people, one of the most frustrating aspects of life is not being able to understand other people's behaviour.

Richard Carlson[1]

Trust, pride and camaraderie at Ferrari

Pool/Getty Images

Since 1947, the year Ferrari's 125 S first triumphed in competition, the Italian car manufacturer with the prancing horse logo has become one of the world's most respected luxury brands. No one knows this better than the company's 2,850 employees. 'We are aware that we are working to perpetuate a myth,' says one employee. 'Ferrari is unique in the world.'

One of the keys to the company's outstanding success has been its high-quality work environment. This is no accident. Ferrari invests time and resources in creating a comfortable and stimulating organizational climate, where people feel motivated and involved, and where they can make the most of themselves while working as part of a team.

Ferrari is home to several distinctive employee development programmes, including Learning Point, an e-learning centre; and Creativity Club, which stimulates employees' original thinking through meetings with artists, theatrical actors, chefs and other creative souls. 'Ferrari offers growth opportunities that I never found in my previous work experiences,' comments one employee. 'Managers are my friends. Here people say hello to each other with a smile.'

Ferrari's leaders also pay careful attention to maintaining a clean, safe working environment; the factory and offices are designed with temperature controls, natural lighting and noise control. 'We work in a serene and very clean environment, where passion and perseverance are rewarded,' says one employee.

The company provides incentives through innovative reward programmes, many tied to the car-racing theme. Through the 'Grand Quality Prix' programme, employees 'race' around a metaphorical track by offering ideas, suggestions and innovative solutions that, if approved and implemented, increase their individual scores. Employees who reach either of two 'pit stops' or the finish line receive an award.

Of course, one of the greatest perks of working at Ferrari is the opportunity to take pride in the company's strong tradition and indulge a passion for automobiles. To this end, every employee receives two tickets to the Imola and Monza F1 races, and to the GT championship. They also get to see new Formula 1 and GT cars before they are shown to the public.

'Many people here wear the Ferrari logo. That means a great attachment to the company and to its values,' says one employee. 'I am proud to be part of this company, where we are all one family, part of a team of excellent people working well together. We work for a common, important, and unique objective: to help Ferrari to continue to be a part of history.'

Source: Based on '100 Best Workplaces in Europe 2007' Great place to work institute/Financial Times *see* http://www.greatplacetowork.com/ and http://www.ft.com/reports/bestwork2007.

Ferrari is a company that recognises the key to its success is people. If its people are effectively managed, they are more likely to deliver a quality product and service, constantly improve existing offerings, and provide performance that is beyond expectations. Ferrari's approach to managing its people doesn't derive from common sense but from knowledge gained through systematic study. This is where organizational behaviour comes into play.

To see how far common sense gets you, try the following Self-assessment library.

SELF-ASSESSMENT LIBRARY

How much do I know about organizational behaviour?

In the Self-assessment library (available online), take assessment IV.G.1 (How much do I know about OB?) and answer the following questions.

1. How did you score? Are you surprised by your score?

2. How much of effective management do you think is common sense? Did you score on the test change your answer to this question?

The importance of interpersonal skills

1 Demonstrate the importance of interpersonal skills in the workplace.

Although practising managers have long understood the importance of interpersonal skills to managerial effectiveness, business schools have been slower to get the message. Until the late 1980s, business school curricula emphasised the technical aspects of management, specifically focusing on economics, accounting, finance and quantitative techniques. Course work in human behaviour and people skills received minimal attention relative to the technical aspects of management. Over the past two decades, however, business faculty have come to realise the importance that an understanding of human behaviour plays in determining a manager's effectiveness, and required courses on people skills have been added to many curricula. A UK graduate employer survey revealed that candidates are normally academically proficient, but lacking in so-called 'soft skills' such as team working, communicating effectively, leadership and cultural awareness. Employers claim that developing these interpersonal skills is essential for managerial effectiveness.[2]

Recognition of the importance of developing managers' interpersonal skills is closely tied to the need for organizations to get and keep high-performing employees. Regardless of labour market conditions, outstanding employees are always in short supply.[3] Companies with reputations as good places to work – such as Ferrari, 3M, Cisco Systems, Microsoft, Accenture, Google, Procter & Gamble, Randstad, Hugo Boss, SAP[4] – have a big advantage. Research demonstrates that wages and fringe benefits are not the main reasons people like their jobs or stay with an employer. Often it is the quality of the employee's job and the supportiveness of the work environment that is more important.[5] So having managers with good interpersonal skills is likely to make the workplace more pleasant, which, in turn, makes it easier to hire and keep qualified people. In addition, creating a pleasant workplace appears to make good economic sense. For instance, companies with reputations as good places to work have been found to generate superior financial performance.[6]

We have come to understand that technical skills are necessary, but they are not enough to succeed in management. In today's increasingly competitive and demanding workplace, managers can't succeed on their technical skills alone. They also have to have good people skills. This book has been written to help both managers and potential managers develop those people skills.

What managers do

managers
Individuals who achieve goals through other people.

organization
A consciously coordinated social unit, composed of two or more people, that functions on a relatively continuous basis to achieve a common goal or set of goals.

planning
A process that includes defining goals, establishing strategy, and developing plans to coordinate activities.

organizing
Determining what tasks are to be done, who is to do them, how the tasks are to be grouped, who reports to whom and where decisions are to be made.

leading
A function that includes motivating employees, directing others, selecting the most effective communication channels and resolving conflicts.

controlling
Monitoring activities to ensure that they are being accomplished as planned and correcting any significant deviations.

Let's begin by briefly defining the terms *manager* and *organization* – the place where managers work. Then let's look at the manager's job; specifically, what do managers do?

Managers get things done through other people. They make decisions, allocate resources and direct the activities of others to attain goals. Managers do their work in an **organization**, which is a consciously coordinated social unit, composed of two or more people, that functions on a relatively continuous basis to achieve a common goal or set of goals. On the basis of this definition, manufacturing and service firms are organizations, and so are schools, hospitals, churches, military units, retail stores, police departments and government agencies. The people who oversee the activities of others and who are responsible for attaining goals in these organizations are managers (although they're sometimes called *administrators*, especially in not-for-profit organizations).

Management functions

In the early part of the twentieth century, a French industrialist by the name of Henri Fayol wrote that all managers perform five management functions: planning, organizing, commanding, coordinating and controlling.[7] Today, we have condensed these to four: planning, organizing, leading and controlling.

Because organizations exist to achieve goals, someone has to define those goals and the means for achieving them; management is that someone. The **planning** function encompasses defining an organization's goals, establishing an overall strategy for achieving those goals, and developing a comprehensive set of plans to integrate and coordinate activities. Evidence indicates that this function is the one that increases the most as managers move from lower-level to mid-level management.[8]

Managers are also responsible for designing an organization's structure. We call this function **organizing**. It includes determining what tasks are to be done, who is to do them, how the tasks are to be grouped, who reports to whom and where decisions are to be made.

Every organization contains people, and it is management's job to direct and coordinate those people. This is the **leading** function. When managers motivate employees, direct the activities of others, select the most effective communication channels or resolve conflicts among members, they're engaging in leading.

The final function managers perform is **controlling**. To ensure that things are going as they should, management must monitor the organization's performance. Actual performance is then compared with the previously set goals. If there are any significant deviations, it is management's job to get the organization back on track. This monitoring, comparing and potential correcting is what is meant by the controlling function.

So, using the functional approach, the answer to the question 'What do managers do?' is that they plan, organize, lead and control.

Management roles

In the late 1960s, Henry Mintzberg, a graduate student at Massachusetts Institute of Technology, undertook a careful study of five executives to determine what those managers did on their jobs. On the basis of his observations, Mintzberg concluded that managers perform 10 different,

Table 1.1	Mintzberg's managerial roles

Role	Description
Interpersonal	
Figurehead	Symbolic head; required to perform a number of routine duties of a legal or social nature
Leader	Responsible for the motivation and direction of employees
Liaison	Maintains a network of outside contacts who provide favours and information
Informational	
Monitor	Receives a wide variety of information; serves as nerve centre of internal and external information of the organization
Disseminator	Transmits information received from outsiders or from other employees to members of the organization
Spokesperson	Transmits information to outsiders on organization's plans, policies, actions and results; serves as expert on organization's industry
Decisional	
Entrepreneur	Searches organization and its environment for opportunities and initiates projects to bring about change
Disturbance handler	Responsible for corrective action when organization faces important, unexpected disturbances
Resource allocator	Makes or approves significant organizational decisions
Negotiator	Responsible for representing the organization at major negotiations

Source: Mintzberg, Henry, *The Nature of Managerial Work.*, 1st edition, © 1980. Reprinted by permission of Pearson Education, Inc., Upper Saddle River, NJ.

highly interrelated roles – or sets of behaviours – attributable to their jobs.[9] As shown in Table 1.1 these 10 roles can be grouped as being primarily (1) interpersonal, (2) informational and (3) decisional.

Interpersonal roles

All managers are required to perform duties that are ceremonial and symbolic in nature. For instance, when the Dean of a University hands out degrees at graduation or a factory supervisor gives a group of high school students a tour of the premises, he or she is acting in a *figurehead* role. All managers also have a *leadership* role. This role includes hiring, training, motivating and disciplining employees. The third role within the interpersonal grouping is the *liaison* role. Mintzberg described this activity as contacting outsiders who provide the manager with information. These may be individuals or groups inside or outside the organization. The sales manager who obtains information from the quality-control manager in their own company has an internal liaison relationship. When that sales manager has contacts with other sales executives through a marketing trade association, they have an outside liaison relationship.

Informational roles

All managers, to some degree, collect information from outside organizations and institutions. Typically, they obtain it by reading magazines and talking with other people to learn of changes in the public's tastes, what competitors may be planning and the like. Mintzberg called this the *monitor* role. Managers also act as a conduit to transmit information to organizational members. This is the *disseminator* role. In addition, managers perform a *spokesperson* role when they represent the organization to outsiders.

Decisional roles

Mintzberg identified four roles that revolve around making choices. In the *entrepreneur* role, managers initiate and oversee new projects that will improve their organization's performance. As *disturbance handlers*, managers take corrective action in response to unforeseen problems. As *resource allocators*, managers are responsible for allocating human, physical and monetary resources. Finally, managers perform a *negotiator* role, in which they discuss issues and bargain with other units to gain advantages for their own unit.

Management skills

Still another way of considering what managers do is to look at the skills or competencies they need to achieve their goals. Robert Katz has identified three essential management skills: technical, human and conceptual.[10]

Technical skills

technical skills
The ability to apply specialised knowledge or expertise.

Technical skills encompass the ability to apply specialised knowledge or expertise. When you think of the skills of professionals such as civil engineers or oral surgeons, you typically focus on their technical skills. Through extensive formal education, they have learned the special knowledge and practices of their field. Of course, professionals don't have a monopoly on technical skills, and not all technical skills have to be learned in schools or other formal training programmes. All jobs require some specialised expertise, and many people develop their technical skills on the job.

Human skills

human skills
The ability to work with, understand and motivate other people, both individually and in groups.

The ability to work with, understand and motivate other people, both individually and in groups, defines **human skills**. Many people are technically proficient but interpersonally incompetent. They might be poor listeners, unable to understand the needs of others, or have difficulty managing conflicts. Because managers get things done through other people, they must have good human skills to communicate, motivate and delegate.

Conceptual skills

conceptual skills
The mental ability to analyse and diagnose complex situations.

Managers must have the mental ability to analyse and diagnose complex situations. These tasks require **conceptual skills**. Decision making, for instance, requires managers to identify problems, develop alternative solutions to correct those problems, evaluate those alternative solutions, and select the best one. Managers can be technically and interpersonally competent yet still fail because of an inability to rationally process and interpret information.

Effective versus successful managerial activities

Fred Luthans and his associates looked at the issue of what managers do from a somewhat different perspective.[11] They asked the question 'Do managers who move up the quickest in an organization do the same activities and with the same emphasis as managers who do the best job?' You would tend to think that the managers who are the most effective in their jobs would also be the ones who are promoted the fastest. But that's not what appears to happen.

Luthans and his associates studied more than 450 managers. What they found was that these managers all engaged in four managerial activities:

1. **Traditional management.** Decision making, planning and controlling
2. **Communication.** Exchanging routine information and processing paperwork
3. **Human resource management.** Motivating, disciplining, managing conflict, staffing and training
4. **Networking.** Socialising, politicking and interacting with outsiders

The 'average' manager in the study spent 32 per cent of their time in traditional management activities, 29 per cent communicating, 20 per cent in human resource management activities and 19 per cent networking. However, the amount of time and effort that different managers spent on those four activities varied a great deal. Specifically, as shown in Figure 1.1, managers who were *successful* (defined in terms of the speed of promotion within their organization) had a very different emphasis from managers who were *effective* (defined in terms of the quantity and quality of their performance and the satisfaction and commitment of their employees). Among successful managers, networking made the largest relative contribution to success, and human resource management activities made the least relative contribution. Among effective managers, communication made the largest relative contribution and networking the least. More recent studies, conducted in a variety of countries (Australia, Israel, Italy, Japan and the United States), further confirm the link between networking and success within an organization.[12] For example,

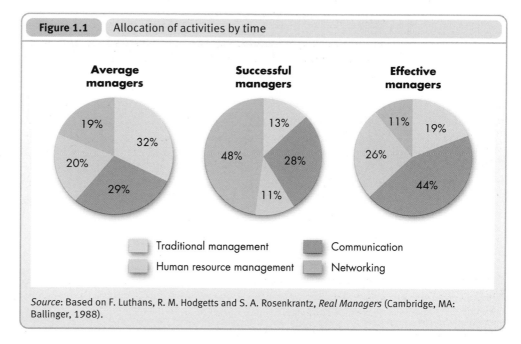

Figure 1.1   Allocation of activities by time

Average managers

Successful managers

Effective managers

- Traditional management
- Human resource management
- Communication
- Networking

Source: Based on F. Luthans, R. M. Hodgetts and S. A. Rosenkrantz, *Real Managers* (Cambridge, MA: Ballinger, 1988).

one study found that Australian managers who actively networked received more promotions and enjoyed other rewards associated with career success. And the connection between communication and effective managers is also clear. A study of 410 US managers indicates that managers who seek information from colleagues and employees – even if it's negative – and who explain their decisions are the most effective.[13]

This research adds important insights to our knowledge of what managers do. On average, managers spend approximately 20 to 30 per cent of their time on each of the four activities: traditional management, communication, human resource management and networking. However, successful managers don't give the same emphasis to each of those activities as do effective managers. In fact, their emphases are almost the opposite. This finding challenges the historical assumption that promotions are based on performance, and it illustrates the importance of networking and political skills in getting ahead in organizations.

A review of the manager's job

One common thread runs through the functions, roles, skills, activities and approaches to management: Each recognises the paramount importance of managing people. Regardless of whether it is called 'the leading function', 'interpersonal roles', 'human skills', or 'human resource management, communication and networking activities', it's clear that managers need to develop their people skills if they're going to be effective and successful.

organizational behaviour (OB)
A field of study that investigates the impact that individuals, groups and structure have on behaviour within organizations, for the purpose of applying such knowledge toward improving an organization's effectiveness.

Enter organizational behaviour

3 Define *organizational behaviour (OB)*.

We've made the case for the importance of people skills. But neither this book nor the discipline on which it is based is called 'people skills'. The term that is widely used to describe the discipline is *organizational behaviour*.

Organizational behaviour (often abbreviated OB) is a field of study that investigates the impact that individuals, groups and structure have on behaviour within organizations, for the purpose of applying such knowledge toward improving an organization's effectiveness. That's a mouthful, so let's break it down.

Organizational behaviour is a field of study, meaning that it is a distinct area of expertise with a common body of knowledge. What does it study? It studies three determinants of behaviour

Image Bank/Getty Images

Microsoft understands how organizational behaviour affects an organization's performance. The company has been consistently ranked the best workplace in Europe. Microsoft maintains good employee relationships by providing a great work environment, generous benefits and challenging jobs. Microsoft is constantly seeking to maintain high levels of job satisfaction. For example, Microsoft Netherlands launched a programme called 'The New World of Work', in which employees helped to redesign their work lives by using the company's IT and mobile devices to make their work lives more flexible. At Microsoft, employee loyalty and productivity are high, contributing to the company's growth to around €27 billion in revenues since its founding in 1975.

Source: 'Best workplaces', *Financial Times*, special report, 28 May 2008. www.ft.com/bestworkplaces2008.

in organizations: individuals, groups and structure. In addition, OB applies the knowledge gained about individuals, groups and the effect of structure on behaviour in order to make organizations work more effectively.

To sum up our definition, OB is concerned with the study of what people do in an organization and how their behaviour affects the organization's performance. And because OB is concerned specifically with employment-related situations, you should not be surprised to find that it emphasises behaviour as related to concerns such as jobs, work, absenteeism, employment turnover, productivity, human performance and management.

There is increasing agreement as to the components or topics that constitute the subject area of OB. Although there is still considerable debate as to the relative importance of each, there appears to be general agreement that OB includes the core topics of motivation, leader behaviour and power, interpersonal communication, group structure and processes, learning, attitude development and perception, change processes, conflict, work design and work stress.[14]

Complementing intuition with systematic study

4 Show the value to OB of systematic study.

Each of us is a student of behaviour. Since our earliest years, we've watched the actions of others and have attempted to interpret what we see. Whether or not you've explicitly thought about it before, you've been 'reading' people almost all your life. You watch what others do and try to explain to yourself why they have engaged in their behaviour. In addition, you've attempted to predict what they might do under different sets of conditions. Unfortunately, your casual or commonsense approach to reading others can often lead to erroneous predictions.

However, you can improve your predictive ability by supplementing your intuitive opinions with a more systematic approach.

The systematic approach used in this book will uncover important facts and relationships and will provide a base from which more accurate predictions of behaviour can be made. Underlying this systematic approach is the belief that behaviour is not random. Rather, there are certain fundamental consistencies underlying the behaviour of all individuals that can be identified and then modified to reflect individual differences.

'PRECONCEIVED NOTIONS VERSUS SUBSTANTIVE EVIDENCE'   MYTH *OR* SCIENCE?

Assume that you signed up to take an introductory university course in finance. On the first day of class, your tutor asks you to take out a piece of paper and answer the following question: 'What is the net present value at a discount rate of 12 per cent per year of an investment made by spending €1,000,000 this year on a portfolio of shares, with an initial dividend next year of €100,000 and an expected rate of dividend growth thereafter of 4 per cent per year?' It's unlikely you'd be able to answer that question without some instruction in finance.

Now, change the scenario. You're in an introductory course in organizational behaviour. On the first day of class, your tutor asks you to write the answer to the following question: 'What's the most effective way to motivate employees at work?' At first you might feel a bit of reluctance, but once you began writing, you'd likely have no problem coming up with suggestions on motivation.

That's one of the main challenges of teaching, or taking, a course in OB. You enter an OB course with a lot of *preconceived notions* that you accept as *facts*. You think you already know a lot about human behaviour.[15] That's not typically true in finance, accounting or even marketing. So, in contrast to many other disciplines, OB not only introduces you to a comprehensive set of concepts and theories; it has to deal with a lot of commonly accepted 'facts' about human behaviour and organizations that you've acquired over the years. Some examples might include: 'You can't teach an old dog new tricks'; 'leaders are born, not made' and 'two heads are better than one'. But these 'facts' aren't necessarily true. So one of the objectives of a course in organizational behaviour is to *replace* popularly held notions, often accepted without question, with science-based conclusions.

As you'll see in this book, the field of OB is built on decades of research. This research provides a body of substantive evidence that is able to replace preconceived notions. Throughout this book, we've included boxes titled 'Myth or Science?' They call your attention to some of the most popular of these notions or myths about organizational behaviour. We use the boxes to show how OB research has disproved them or, in some cases, shown them to be true. Hopefully, you'll find these boxes interesting. But more importantly, they'll help remind you that the study of human behaviour at work is a science and that you need to be vigilant about 'off-the-top-of-your-head' explanations of work-related behaviours.

These fundamental consistencies are very important. Why? Because they allow predictability. Behaviour is generally predictable, and the *systematic study* of behaviour is a means to making reasonably accurate predictions. When we use the phrase **systematic study**, we mean looking at relationships, attempting to attribute causes and effects, and basing our conclusions on scientific evidence – that is, on data gathered under controlled conditions and measured and interpreted in a reasonably rigorous manner.

An approach that complements systematic study is evidence-based management. **Evidence-based management (EBM)** involves basing managerial decisions on the best available scientific evidence. We'd want doctors to make decisions about patient care based on the latest available evidence, and EBM argues that we want managers to do the same. That means managers must become more scientific in how they think about management problems. For example, a manager might pose a managerial question, search for the best available evidence, and apply the relevant information to the question or case at hand. You might think it's difficult to argue against this (what manager would argue that decisions shouldn't be based on evidence?), but the vast majority of management decisions are still made spontaneously, with little or no systematic study of available evidence.[16]

Systematic study and EBM add to **intuition**, or those instincts about 'why I do what I do' and 'what makes others tick'. Of course, a systematic approach does not mean that the things you have come to believe in an unsystematic way are necessarily incorrect. The trick is to know when to go with your instincts. If we make all decisions with intuition we're likely to be making

systematic study
Looking at relationships, attempting to attribute causes and effects and drawing conclusions based on scientific evidence.

evidence-based management (EBM)
Basing managerial decisions on the best available scientific evidence.

intuition
A gut feeling not necessarily supported by research.

decisions with incomplete information – a bit like making an investment decision with only half the data.

The limits of relying on intuition are made worse by the fact that we tend to overestimate the accuracy of what we think we know. A recent survey revealed that 86 per cent of managers thought their organization was treating their employees well. However, only 55 per cent of the employees thought they were well treated.

We find a similar problem when relying on business press and popular media for management wisdom. The business press tends to be dominated by fads. As one writer put it, 'Every few years, new companies succeed, and they are scrutinised for the underlying truths they might reveal. But often there is no underlying truth; the companies just happened to be in the right place at the right time.'[17] Although we try to avoid it, we might also fall into this trap. It's not that the business press stories are all wrong; it's that without a systematic approach, it's hard to separate the wheat from the chaff.

Some of the conclusions we make in this text, based on reasonably substantive research findings, will only support what you always knew was true. But you'll also be exposed to research evidence that runs counter to what you may have thought was common sense. One of the objectives of this text is to encourage you to enhance your intuitive views of behaviour with a systematic analysis, in the belief that such analysis will improve your accuracy in explaining and predicting behaviour.

We're not advising that you throw your intuition, or all the business press, out the window. Nor are we arguing that research is always right. Researchers make mistakes, too. What we are advising is to use evidence as much as possible to inform your intuition and experience. That is the promise of OB.

Disciplines that contribute to the OB field

5 Identify the major behavioural science disciplines that contribute to OB.

Organizational behaviour is an applied behavioural science that is built on contributions from a number of behavioural disciplines. The predominant areas are psychology and social psychology, sociology and anthropology. As you shall learn, psychology's contributions have been mainly at the individual or micro level of analysis, while the other disciplines have contributed to our understanding of macro concepts such as group processes and organization. Figure 1.2 is an overview of the major contributions to the study of organizational behaviour.

Psychology

psychology
The science that seeks to measure, explain and sometimes change the behaviour of humans and other animals.

Psychology is the science that seeks to measure, explain and sometimes change the behaviour of humans and other animals. Psychologists concern themselves with studying and attempting to understand individual behaviour. Those who have contributed and continue to add to the knowledge of OB are learning theorists, personality theorists, counselling psychologists, and, most important, industrial and organizational psychologists.

Early industrial/organizational psychologists concerned themselves with the problems of fatigue, boredom and other factors relevant to working conditions that could impede efficient work performance. More recently, their contributions have been expanded to include learning, perception, personality, emotions, training, leadership effectiveness, needs and motivational forces, job satisfaction, decision-making processes, performance appraisals, attitude measurement, employee-selection techniques, work design and job stress.

Social psychology

social psychology
An area of psychology that blends concepts from psychology and sociology and that focuses on the influence of people on one another.

Social psychology blends concepts from both psychology and sociology, though it is generally considered a branch of psychology. It focuses on peoples' influence on one another. One major area receiving considerable investigation from social psychologists has been *change* – how to implement it and how to reduce barriers to its acceptance. In addition, we find social psychologists making significant contributions in the areas of measuring, understanding and changing

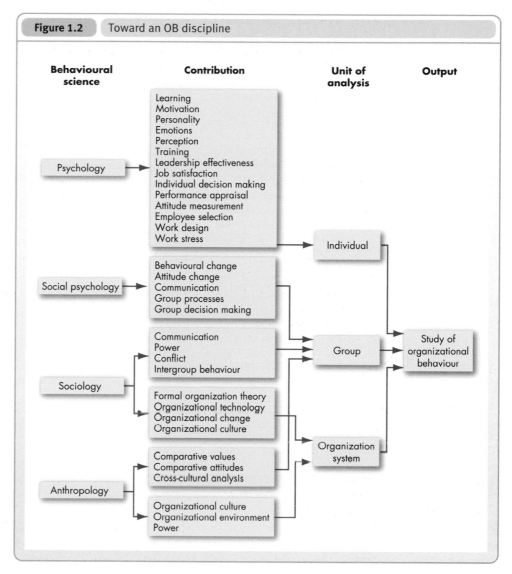

Figure 1.2   Toward an OB discipline

attitudes; communication patterns; and building trust. Finally, social psychologists have made important contributions to our study of group behaviour, power and conflict.

Sociology

sociology
The study of people in relation to their social environment or culture.

While psychology focuses on the individual, **sociology** studies people in relation to their social environment or culture. Sociologists have contributed to OB through their study of group behaviour in organizations, particularly formal and complex organizations. Perhaps most importantly, sociology has contributed to research on organizational culture, formal organization theory and structure, organizational technology, communications, power and conflict.

Anthropology

anthropology
The study of societies to learn about human beings and their activities.

Anthropology is the study of societies to learn about human beings and their activities. For instance, anthropologists' work on cultures and environments has helped us understand differences in fundamental values, attitudes and behaviour between people in different countries and within different organizations. Much of our current understanding of organizational culture, organizational environments and differences between national cultures is a result of the work of anthropologists or those using their methods.

OTHER DISCIPLINES MAKE USE OF OB CONCEPTS **OB IN THE NEWS**

It may surprise you to learn that, increasingly, other business disciplines are employing OB concepts.

Of the business disciplines, marketing has the closest overlap with OB. One of the primary areas of marketing is consumer research, and trying to predict consumer behaviour is not that different from trying to predict employee behaviour. Both require an understanding of the dynamics and underlying causes of human behaviour, and there's a lot of correspondence between the disciplines.

What's perhaps more surprising is the degree to which the so-called hard disciplines are making use of soft OB concepts. Behavioural finance, behavioural accounting and behavioural economics (also called *economic psychology*) all have grown in importance and interest in the past several years.

On reflection, this shouldn't be so surprising. Your common sense will tell you that humans are not perfectly rational creatures, and in many cases, our actions don't conform to a rational model of behaviour. Although some elements of irrationality are incorporated into economic thought, increasingly, finance, accounting and economics researchers find it useful to draw from OB concepts.

For example, investors have a tendency to place more weight on private information (information that only they, or a limited group of people, know) than on public information, even when there is reason to believe that the public information is more accurate. To understand this phenomenon, finance researchers use OB concepts. In addition, behavioural accounting research might study how feedback influences auditors' behaviour, or the functional and dysfunctional implications of earnings warnings on investor behaviour.

The point is that while you take separate courses in various business disciplines, the lines between them are increasingly being blurred as researchers draw from common disciplines to explain behaviour. We think that's a good thing because it more accurately matches the way managers actually work, think and behave.

Source: Based on W. Chuang and B. Lee, 'An empirical evaluation of the overconfidence hypothesis,' *Journal of Banking and Finance*, September 2006, pp. 2489–515; and A. R. Drake, J. Wong and S. B. Salter, 'Empowerment, motivation, and performance: examining the impact of feedback and incentives on nonmanagement employees', *Behavioural Research in Accounting*, 19 (2007), pp. 71–89.

There are few absolutes in OB

6 Demonstrate why there are few absolutes in OB.

There are few, if any, simple and universal principles that explain organizational behaviour. There are laws in the physical sciences – chemistry, astronomy, physics – that are consistent and apply in a wide range of situations. They allow scientists to generalise about the pull of gravity or to be confident about sending astronauts into space to repair satellites. But as a noted behavioural researcher aptly concluded, 'God gave all the easy problems to the physicists.' Human beings are complex. Because we are not alike, our ability to make simple, accurate and sweeping generalisations is limited. Two people often act very differently in the same situation, and the same person's behaviour changes in different situations. For instance, not everyone is motivated by money, and you are not likely to behave the same way in classes on Monday as you did at a party the night before.

That doesn't mean, of course, that we can't offer reasonably accurate explanations of human behaviour or make valid predictions. However, it does mean that OB concepts must reflect situational, or contingency, conditions. We can say that *x* leads to *y*, but only under conditions specified in *z* – the **contingency variables**. The science of OB was developed by applying general concepts to a particular situation, person or group. For example, OB scholars would avoid stating that everyone likes complex and challenging work (the general concept). Why? Because not everyone wants a challenging job. Some people prefer the routine over the varied or the simple over the complex. In other words, a job that is appealing to one person may not be to another, so the appeal of the job is contingent on the person who holds it.

As you proceed through this book, you'll encounter a wealth of research-based theories about how people behave in organizations. But don't expect to find a lot of straightforward cause-and-effect relationships. There aren't many! Organizational behaviour theories mirror the subject matter with which they deal. People are complex and complicated, and so too must be the theories developed to explain their actions.

contingency variables
Situational factors: variables that moderate the relationship between two or more other variables.

Challenges and opportunities for OB

7 Identify the challenges and opportunities managers have in applying OB concepts.

Understanding organizational behaviour has never been more important for managers than it is today. A quick look at a few of the dramatic changes now taking place in organizations supports this claim. For instance, the typical employee is getting older; more and more women are in the workplace; corporate downsizing and the heavy use of temporary workers are severing the bonds of loyalty that historically tied many employees to their employers; and global competition is requiring employees to become more flexible and to learn to cope with rapid change.

In short, there are a lot of challenges and opportunities today for managers to use OB concepts. In this section, we review some of the most critical issues confronting managers for which OB offers solutions – or at least some meaningful insights toward solutions.

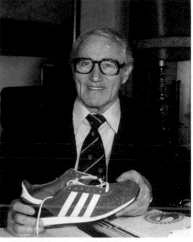

In his workshop at Herzogenaurach near Nuremberg in Germany, Adi Dassler made his first training shoe for runners in 1920. Today, the Adidas product range extends from shoes, apparel and accessories for basketball, soccer, fitness and training to adventure, trail and golf. The Adidas Group has over 25,000 employees worldwide and more than 150 subsidiaries that guarantee a marketplace presence for Adidas around the world. Adidas is a truly global organization.

Source: http://www.adidas-group.com/ en/overview/history/Historye.pdf.

Responding to globalisation

Organizations are no longer constrained by national borders. The quintessentially British Rolls Royce cars are owned by the German firm BMW. The famous Dutch brewing company Heineken owns over 100 breweries in more than 60 countries. ExxonMobil, an American company, receives almost 75 per cent of its revenues from sales outside the United States. New employees at Finland-based phone maker Nokia are increasingly being recruited from India, China and other developing countries – with non-Finns now outnumbering Finns at Nokia's renowned research centre in Helsinki. And all major automobile manufacturers now build cars outside their borders; for instance, Honda builds cars in the US, Ford in Brazil, Volkswagen in Mexico, Toyota in England and both Mercedes and BMW in South Africa.

These examples illustrate that the world has become a global village. In the process, the manager's job is changing.

Increased foreign assignments

If you're a manager, you are increasingly likely to find yourself in a foreign assignment – transferred to your employer's operating division or subsidiary in another country. Once there, you'll have to manage a workforce that is likely to be very different in needs, aspirations and attitudes from those you are used to back home.

Working with people from different cultures

Even in your own country, you're going to find yourself working with bosses, peers and other employees who were born and raised in different cultures. What motivates you may not motivate them. Or your style of communication may be straightforward and open, but they may find this approach uncomfortable and threatening. To work effectively with people from different cultures, you need to understand how their culture, geography and religion have shaped them and how to adapt your management style to their differences.

Coping with anticapitalism backlash

Capitalism's focus on efficiency, growth and profits may be generally accepted in, for example, the United Kingdom, the United States, Australia and Hong Kong, but these capitalistic values aren't nearly as popular in places like France, the Middle East and the Scandinavian countries. For instance, because Finland's egalitarian values have created a 'soak the rich' mentality among politicians, traffic fines are based on the offender's income rather than the severity of the offense.[18] So when one of Finland's richest men (he is heir to a sausage fortune), who was making close to €5 million a year, was ticketed for doing 80 kilometres per hour through a 40-kilometre per hour zone in central Helsinki, the Finnish court hit him with a fine of €130,000!

Managers at global companies such as McDonalds, Nestlé, and Coca-Cola have come to realise that economic values are not universally transferable. Management practices need to be modified to reflect the values of the different countries in which an organization operates.

Overseeing movement of jobs to countries with low-cost labour

It's increasingly difficult for managers in advanced nations, where minimum wages are typically €7 or more an hour, to compete against firms who rely on workers from China and other developing nations where labour is available for about 40 cents an hour. It's not by chance that a good portion of Europeans wear clothes made in China and work on computers whose microchips came from Taiwan. Further, in the European Union cost differentials have meant a migration of jobs from West to East. In Germany, hourly labour costs are about €28, compared with some €8 in the Czech Republic, €7.50 in Poland and €4 in Romania.[19] In a global economy, jobs tend to flow to places where lower costs provide business firms with a comparative advantage. Such practices, however, are often strongly criticised by trade unions, politicians, local community leaders and others who see this exporting of jobs as undermining the job markets in developed countries. Managers must deal with the difficult task of balancing the interests of their organization with their responsibilities to the communities in which they operate.

Managing workforce diversity

One of the most important and broad-based challenges currently facing organizations is adapting to people who are different. The term we use for describing this challenge is *workforce diversity*. Whereas globalisation focuses on differences between people *from* different countries, workforce diversity addresses differences among people *within* given countries.

Workforce diversity means that organizations are becoming a more heterogeneous mix of people in terms of gender, age, race, ethnicity and sexual orientation. A diverse workforce, for instance, includes women, the physically disabled and senior citizens. Managing this diversity has become a global issue. For instance, managers in Canada and Australia are finding it necessary to adjust to large influxes of Asian workers. Women, long confined to low-paying temporary jobs in Japan, are moving into managerial positions. In Europe, since the foundation of the European Union (EU) in 1957, it has been enlarged five times to create a membership of 27 states over 50 years later. The EU guarantees the freedom of movement of people between the states. The effect has been to create considerably more diverse workforces in EU member countries in terms of nationalities, cultures, languages and religions.

> **workforce diversity**
> The concept that organizations are becoming more heterogeneous in terms of gender, age, race, ethnicity, sexual orientation and inclusion of other diverse groups.

Embracing diversity

We used to take a melting-pot approach to differences in organizations, assuming that people who were different would somehow automatically want to assimilate. But we now recognise that employees don't set aside their cultural values, lifestyle preferences and differences when they come to work. The challenge for organizations, therefore, is to make themselves more accommodating to diverse groups of people by addressing their different lifestyles, family needs and work styles. The melting-pot assumption is being replaced by one that recognises and values differences.[20]

Haven't organizations always included members of diverse groups? Yes, but they were a small per centage of the workforce and were, for the most part, ignored by large organizations. Moreover, it was assumed that these minorities would seek to blend in and assimilate. For instance, the bulk of the pre-1980s UK workforce were male Caucasians working full-time to support their non-employed wives and school-aged children. Now such employees are the true minority![21]

Changing European demographics

There have been two particularly significant demographic changes in the European labour market: age and gender. Europe's ageing population officially makes it the 'oldest continent'.[22] In the EU in 2000, 36 per cent of people in the workplace were over 50, just six years later, the figure was 44 per cent and the trend is predicted to continue. Concomitantly, the number of workers under 35 is decreasing.[23] By the middle of the twenty-first century, it has been predicted that two people in work will support every pensioner – half of the current ratio. The Scandinavian countries and the Netherlands have the highest rates of older workers in the EU and will see a substantial proportion of their workforce retiring over the next 10 years.[24] This trend will mean rethinking how companies can motivate and retain younger workers and how they value older workers by making better use of their skills and experience. Increasing older worker participation and delaying the exit from the labour force will be essential to support economic growth and ease the mounting pressure on social protection systems, in particular regarding pensions and healthcare systems.[25]

In the same way that older workers are changing the profile of the labour market, so too have women. Eighty per cent of the growth in the UK workforce between 2004 to 2010 was forecast to be women.[26] The increase in the number of female workers has similarly been evident across Europe and North America.

Implications

Workforce diversity has important implications for management practice. Managers have to shift their philosophy from treating everyone alike to recognising differences and responding to those differences in ways that ensure employee retention and greater productivity while, at the same time, not discriminating. This shift includes, for instance, providing diversity training and revamping benefits programmes to accommodate the different needs of different employees. Diversity, if positively managed, can increase creativity and innovation in organizations as well as improve decision making by providing different perspectives on problems.[27] When diversity is not managed properly, there is a potential for higher turnover, more difficult communication and more interpersonal conflicts.

FACE THE FACTS

Demographic ageing is one of the main challenges facing the EU in the coming years. By 2050 almost one in three citizens in the EU will be aged over 65, up from the current level of around one in six.

- Of the EU member states, the Czech Republic, Estonia, Germany, Greece, Hungary, Italy, Latvia, Lithuania, Poland, Portugal, Slovenia, Slovakia and Spain will face the most substantial declines in the working age population of between 20–30 per cent by 2050 and

almost all will also see a marked rise in the share of older workers.

- People live on average a further 20 years or more after withdrawing from active work life.
- 45 per cent of EU citizens aged 15 or older believe that their fellow citizens retire too early.

Source: Employment in Europe 2007 *European Commission*.

Improving quality and productivity

In the 1990s, organizations around the world added capacity in response to increased demand. Companies built new facilities, expanded services and added staff. The result? Today, almost every industry suffers from excess supply. Automobile factories can build more cars than consumers can afford. The telecom industry is drowning in debt from building capacity that might take 50 years to absorb, and most cities and towns now have far more restaurants than their communities can support.

Excess capacity translates into increased competition. And increased competition is forcing managers to reduce costs and, at the same time, improve their organizations' productivity and the quality of the products and services they offer. Management guru Tom Peters claimed almost all quality improvement comes via simplification of design, manufacturing, layout, processes and procedures. To achieve these ends, managers are implementing programmes such as quality management and process reengineering – programmes that require extensive employee involvement.

Today's managers understand that the success of any effort at improving quality and productivity must include their employees. These employees will not only be a major force in carrying out changes but increasingly will actively participate in planning those changes. OB offers important insights into helping managers work through these changes.

Improving customer service

Today, the majority of employees in developed countries work in service jobs. For instance, In the United Kingdom, Germany and Japan, the percentages working in service industries are 69, 68 and 65, respectively. Examples of these service jobs include technical support representatives, fast-food counter workers, sales clerks, waiters or waitresses, nurses, automobile repair technicians, consultants, credit representatives, financial planners and flight attendants. The common characteristic of these jobs is that they require substantial interaction with an organization's customers. And because an organization can't exist without customers – whether that organization is the BBC, KPMG, Nokia, a law firm, a museum, a school or a government agency – management needs to ensure that employees do what it takes to please customers.[28] For example, at Patagonia – a retail outfitter for climbers, mountain bikers, skiers and boarders, and other outdoor fanatics – managers are held directly responsible for customer service. In fact, customer service is the store manager's most important general responsibility: 'Instil in your employees the meaning and importance of customer service as outlined in the retail philosophy, "our store is a place where the word 'no' does not exist"; empower staff to "use their best judgement" in all customer service matters.'[29] OB can help managers at Patagonia achieve this goal and, more generally, can contribute to improving an organization's performance by showing managers how employee attitudes and behaviour are associated with customer satisfaction.

Many an organization has failed because its employees failed to please customers. Management needs to create a customer-responsive culture. OB can provide considerable guidance in helping managers create such cultures – cultures in which employees are friendly and courteous, accessible, knowledgeable, prompt in responding to customer needs and willing to do what's necessary to please the customer.[30]

Harry Cabluck/Associated Press

It's an annual tradition for Michael Dell to work the phone lines, helping customers in Dell, Inc.'s consumer department. Dell models the customer-responsive culture he created in founding Dell Computer Corporation in 1984 with the idea of building relationships directly with customers. He attributes his company's climb to market leadership as the world's top computer systems company to a persistent focus on the customer. Dell employees deliver superior customer service by communicating directly with customers via the Internet or by phone.

Improving people skills

We opened this chapter by demonstrating how important people skills are to managerial effectiveness. We said that 'this book has been written to help both managers and potential managers develop those people skills'.

As you proceed through the chapters, we'll present relevant concepts and theories that can help you explain and predict the behaviour of people at work. In addition, you'll gain insights into specific people skills that you can use on the job. For instance, you'll learn ways to design motivating jobs, techniques for improving your listening skills and how to create more effective teams.

Stimulating innovation and change

Today's successful organizations must foster innovation and master the art of change, or they'll become candidates for extinction. Victory will go to the organizations that maintain their flexibility, continually improve their quality, and beat their competition to the marketplace with a constant stream of innovative products and services. Domino's single-handedly brought on the demise of thousands of small pizza parlours whose managers thought they could continue doing what they had been doing for years. Amazon.com is putting a lot of independent bookstores out of business as it proves you can successfully sell books from an Internet website. Dell has become the world's largest seller of computers by continually reinventing itself and outsmarting its competition.

An organization's employees can be the impetus for innovation and change, or they can be a major stumbling block. The challenge for managers is to stimulate their employees' creativity and tolerance for change. The field of OB provides a wealth of ideas and techniques to aid in realising these goals.

Coping with 'temporariness'

With change comes temporariness. Globalisation, expanded capacity and advances in technology have combined in recent years to make it imperative that organizations be fast and flexible if they are to survive. The result is that most managers and employees today work in a climate best characterised as 'temporary'.

Evidence of temporariness is everywhere in organizations. Jobs are continually being redesigned; tasks are increasingly being done by flexible teams rather than individuals; companies are relying more on temporary workers; jobs are being subcontracted out to other firms; and pensions are being redesigned to move with people as they change jobs.

Workers need to continually update their knowledge and skills to perform new job requirements. For example, production employees at companies such as Bosch and Dunlop Tyres now need to know how to operate computerised production equipment. That was not part of their job descriptions 20 years ago. Work groups are also increasingly in a state of flux. In the past, employees were assigned to a specific work group, and that assignment was relatively permanent. There was a considerable amount of security in working with the same people day in and day out. That predictability has been replaced by temporary work groups, teams that include members from different departments and whose members change all the time, and the increased use of employee rotation to fill constantly changing work assignments. Finally, organizations themselves are in a state of flux. They continually reorganize their various divisions, sell off poor-performing businesses, downsize operations, subcontract noncritical services and operations to other organizations and replace permanent employees with temporary workers.

Today's managers and employees must learn to cope with temporariness. They have to learn to live with flexibility, spontaneity and unpredictability. The study of OB can provide valuable guidance into helping you better understand a work world of continual change, how to overcome resistance to change, and how best to create an organizational culture that thrives on change.

Working in networked organizations

Computerisation, the Internet, and the ability to link computers within organizations and between organizations have created a different workplace for many employees – a networked organization. These technology changes allow people to communicate and work together even though they may be thousands of miles apart. They also allow people to become independent contractors, who can telecommute via computer to workplaces around the globe and change employers as the demand for their services changes. Software programmers, graphic designers, systems analysts, technical writers, photo researchers, book editors and medical transcribers are just a few examples of people who can work from home or other non-office locations.

The manager's job is different in a networked organization, especially when it comes to managing people. For instance, motivating and leading people and making collaborative decisions 'online' requires different techniques than are needed in dealing with individuals who are physically present in a single location.

As more and more employees do their jobs linked to others through networks, managers need to develop new skills. OB can help with honing those skills.

Helping employees balance work–life conflicts

The typical employee in the 1960s or 1970s showed up at the workplace Monday through Friday and did their job in 8- or 9-hour blocks of time. The workplace and hours were clearly specified. That's no longer true for a large segment of today's workforce. Employees are increasingly complaining that the line between work and nonwork time has become blurred, creating personal conflicts and stress.[31] At the same time, however, today's workplace presents opportunities for workers to create and structure their work roles.

A number of forces have contributed to blurring the lines between employees' work life and personal life. First, the creation of global organizations means their world never sleeps. At any time and on any day, for instance, thousands of General Electric employees are working somewhere. The need to consult with colleagues or customers 8 or 10 time zones away means that many employees of global firms are 'on call' 24 hours a day. Second, communication technology allows employees to do their work at home, in their cars or on the beach in Dubai. This lets many people in technical and professional jobs do their work any time and from any place. Third, organizations are asking employees to put in longer hours. This is particularly notable in the United Kingdom where the number of people working over 48 hours has more than doubled since 1998 and one in six of all workers is doing more than 60 hours.[32] Finally, fewer families have only a single breadwinner. Today's married employee is typically part of a dual-career couple. This makes it increasingly difficult for married employees to find the time to fulfil commitments to home, spouse, children, parents and friends.

Employees are increasingly recognising that work is infringing on their personal lives, and they're not happy about it. For example, recent studies suggest that employees want jobs that give them flexibility in their work schedules so they can better manage work–life conflicts.[32] In fact, evidence indicates that balancing work and life demands now surpasses job security as an employee priority.[34] In addition, the next generation of employees is likely to show similar concerns.[35] A majority of university students say that attaining a balance between personal life and work is a primary career goal. They want 'a life' as well as a job. Organizations that don't help their people achieve work–life balance will find it increasingly difficult to attract and retain the most capable and motivated employees.

As you'll see in later chapters, the field of OB offers a number of suggestions to guide managers in designing workplaces and jobs that can help employees deal with work–life conflicts.

Creating a positive work environment

Although competitive pressures on most organizations are stronger than ever, we've noticed an interesting turn in both OB research and management practice, at least in some organizations. Instead of responding to competitive pressures by 'turning up the heat', some organizations are trying to realise a competitive advantage by fostering a positive work environment. For example, Wales-based motor insurance company Admiral chief executive Henry Engelhardt encourages a positive work environment by meeting every employee within three weeks of joining. This reinforces the senior management's commitment to engaging with all members of the organization. Engelhardt also has an online blog accessible by staff and senior management regularly 'walk the floor' to ensure they stay in touch with issues affecting front-line staff.[36]

positive organizational scholarship
An area of OB research that concerns how organizations develop human strength, foster vitality and resilience, and unlock potential.

At the same time, a real growth area in OB research has been **positive organizational scholarship** (also called *positive organizational behaviour*), which concerns how organizations develop human strengths, foster vitality and resilience and unlock potential. Researchers in this area argue that too much of OB research and management practice has been targeted toward identifying what's wrong with organizations and their employees. In response, these researchers try to study what's *good* about organizations.[37]

For example, positive organizational scholars have studied a concept called 'reflected best-self' – asking employees to think about situations in which they were at their 'personal best' in order to understand how to exploit their strengths. These researchers argue that we all have things at which we are unusually good, yet too often we focus on addressing our limitations and too rarely think about how to exploit our strengths.[38]

Although positive organizational scholarship does not deny the presence (or even the value) of the negative (such as critical feedback), it does challenge researchers to look at OB through a new lens. It also challenges organizations to think about how to exploit their employees' strengths rather than dwell on their limitations.

Improving ethical behaviour

In an organizational world characterised by cutbacks, expectations of increasing worker productivity and tough competition in the marketplace, it's not altogether surprising that many employees feel pressured to cut corners, break rules and engage in other forms of questionable practices.

ethical dilemmas
Situations in which individuals are required to define right and wrong conduct.

Members of organizations are increasingly finding themselves facing **ethical dilemmas**, situations in which they are required to define right and wrong conduct. For example, should they 'blow the whistle' if they uncover illegal activities taking place in their company? Should they follow orders with which they don't personally agree? Do they give an inflated performance evaluation to an employee whom they like, knowing that such an evaluation could save that employee's job? Do they allow themselves to 'play politics' in the organization if it will help their career advancement?

What constitutes good ethical behaviour has never been clearly defined, and, in recent years, the line differentiating right from wrong has become even more blurred. Employees see people all around them engaging in unethical practices – elected officials are accused of taking bribes; corporate executives inflate company profits so they can cash in lucrative share options; and managers 'looking the other way' when their sales team mislead customers to win orders. When caught, these people give excuses such as 'everyone does it' or 'you have to seize every advantage nowadays'. Is it any wonder that employees are expressing decreased confidence and trust in management and that they're increasingly uncertain about what constitutes appropriate ethical behaviour in their organizations?[39]

Managers and their organizations are responding to this problem from a number of directions.[40] They're writing and distributing codes of ethics to guide employees through ethical dilemmas. They're offering seminars, workshops and other training programmes to try to improve ethical behaviours. They're providing in-house advisors who can be contacted, in many cases anonymously, for assistance in dealing with ethical issues, and they're creating protection mechanisms for employees who reveal internal unethical practices.

Today's manager needs to create an ethically healthy climate for their employees, where they can do their work productively and confront a minimal degree of ambiguity regarding what constitutes right and wrong behaviours. In upcoming chapters, we'll discuss the kinds of actions managers can take to create an ethically healthy climate and help employees sort through ethically ambiguous situations. We'll also present ethical-dilemma exercises at the end of each chapter that will allow you to think through ethical issues and assess how you would handle them.

Coming attractions: developing an OB model

8 Compare the three levels of analysis in this book's OB model.

We conclude this chapter by presenting a general model that defines the field of OB, stakes out its parameters, and identifies its primary dependent and independent variables. The end result will be a 'coming attraction' of the topics in the remainder of this book.

An overview

model
An abstraction of reality. A simplified representation of some real-world phenomenon.

A **model** is an abstraction of reality, a simplified representation of some real-world phenomenon. A mannequin in a retail store is a model. So, too, is the accountant's formula Assets + Liabilities = Owners' Equity. Figure 1.3 presents the skeleton on which we will construct our OB model. It proposes that there are three levels of analysis in OB and that, as we move from the individual level to the organization systems level, we add systematically to our understanding of behaviour in organizations. The three basic levels are analogous to building blocks; each level is constructed on the previous level. Group concepts grow out of the foundation laid in the individual section; we overlay structural constraints on the individual and group in order to arrive at organizational behaviour.

dependent variable
A response that is affected by an independent variable.

The dependent variables

productivity
A performance measure that includes effectiveness and efficiency.

A **dependent variable** is the key factor that you want to explain or predict and that is affected by some other factor. What are the primary dependent variables in OB? Scholars have historically tended to emphasise productivity, absenteeism, turnover and job satisfaction. More recently, two more variables – deviant workplace behaviour and organizational citizenship behaviour – have been added to this list. We'll briefly discuss each of these variables to ensure that you understand what they mean and why they have achieved their level of distinction.

effectiveness
Achievement of goals.

Productivity

efficiency
The ratio of effective output to the input required to achieve it.

An organization is productive if it achieves its goals and does so by transferring inputs to outputs at the lowest cost. As such, **productivity** implies a concern for both **effectiveness** and **efficiency**.

A hospital, for example, is *effective* when it successfully meets the needs of its clientele. It is *efficient* when it can do so at a low cost. If a hospital manages to achieve higher output from its present staff by reducing the average number of days a patient is confined to a bed or by increasing the number of staff–patient contacts per day, we say that the hospital has gained productive efficiency. A business firm is effective when it attains its sales or market share goals, but its productivity also depends on achieving those goals efficiently. Popular measures of organizational efficiency include return on investment, profit per euro of sales and output per hour of labour.

We can also look at productivity from the perspective of the individual employee. Take the cases of Sam and Leo, who are both long-distance lorry drivers. If Sam is supposed to drive his fully loaded lorry from London to Cardiff in four hours or less, he is effective if he makes the 150-mile trip within that time period. But measures of productivity must take into account the costs incurred in reaching the goal. That's where efficiency comes in. Let's assume that, with

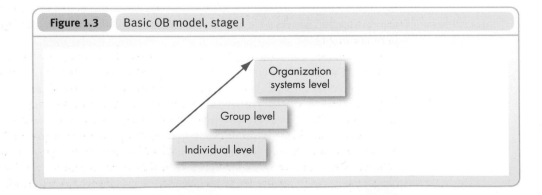

| Figure 1.3 | Basic OB model, stage I |

Organization systems level

Group level

Individual level

identical lorries and loads, Sam made the London-to-Cardiff run in 3.5 hours and averaged 2 miles per litre. Leo, however, made the trip in 3.5 hours also but averaged 3 miles per litre. Both Sam and Leo were effective – they accomplished their goal – but Leo was more efficient than Sam because his lorry consumed less petrol and, therefore, he achieved his goal at a lower cost.

Organizations in service industries need to include attention to customer needs and requirements in assessing their effectiveness. Why? Because in these types of businesses, there is a clear chain of cause and effect running from employee attitudes and behaviour to customer attitudes and behaviour to an organization's productivity. Sears, the American-based department stores, has carefully documented this chain.[41] The company's management found that a 5 per cent improvement in employee attitudes leads to a 1.3 per cent increase in customer satisfaction, which in turn translates into a 0.5 per cent improvement in revenue growth. More specifically, Sears found that by training employees to improve the employee–customer interaction, it was able to improve customer satisfaction by 4 per cent over a 12-month period, which generated an estimated €120 million in additional revenues.

In summary, one of OB's major concerns is productivity. We want to know what factors will influence the effectiveness and efficiency of individuals, of groups and of the overall organization.

Absenteeism

absenteeism
The failure to report to work.

Absenteeism is defined as the failure to report to work. Absenteeism is a huge cost and disruption to employers. A recent survey revealed the average cost of absence to United Kingdom employers was nearly €800 per employee per year.[42] The Confederation for British Industry (CBI) believes that absenteeism levels are the main reason why United Kingdom productivity lags behind the United States and some parts of Europe.[43] Across Europe, absence is particularly high in the Netherlands, United Kindgom, Sweden, Norway and Iceland. For these countries reducing absence would provide a substantial boost to the labour supply.[44]

It's obviously difficult for an organization to operate smoothly and to attain its objectives if employees fail to report to their jobs. The work flow is disrupted, and often important decisions must be delayed. In organizations that rely heavily on assembly-line production, absenteeism can be considerably more than a disruption; it can result in a drastic reduction in the quality of output, and, in some cases, it can bring about a complete shutdown of the production facility. Levels of absenteeism beyond the normal range in any organization have a direct impact on that organization's effectiveness and efficiency.

Are *all* absences bad? Probably not. Although most absences have a negative impact on the organization, we can conceive of situations in which the organization may benefit by an employee's voluntarily choosing not to come to work. For instance, in jobs in which an employee needs to be alert – consider surgeons and airline pilots, for example – it may be better for the organization if an ill or fatigued employee does *not* report to work. An accident in such jobs could be disastrous. But these examples are clearly atypical. For the most part, we can assume that organizations benefit when employee absenteeism is low.

Turnover

turnover
Voluntary and involuntary permanent withdrawal from an organization.

Turnover is the voluntary and involuntary permanent withdrawal from an organization. A high turnover rate results in increased recruiting, selection and training costs. What are those costs? They're higher than you might think. For instance, one survey put the average cost per employee at €9,000, rising to €13,000 for senior managers or directors.[45] In addition, a high rate of turnover can disrupt the efficient running of an organization when knowledgeable and experienced personnel leave and replacements must be found and prepared to assume positions of responsibility.

All organizations, of course, have some turnover. This average varies a lot by industry, for example, surveys consistently identify the highest levels of turnover in hotels, catering and leisure, whilst lower levels occur in central government and education services.[46] If the 'right' people are leaving the organization – the marginal and submarginal employees – turnover can actually be positive. It can create an opportunity to replace an underperforming individual with someone who has higher skills or motivation, open up increased opportunities for promotions and add new and fresh ideas to the organization.[47] In today's changing world of work, reasonable levels of employee-initiated turnover facilitate organizational flexibility and employee independence, and they can lessen the need for management-initiated layoffs.

But turnover often involves the loss of people the organization doesn't want to lose. For instance, a study covering 900 employees who had resigned from their jobs found that 92 per cent earned performance ratings of 'satisfactory' or better from their superiors.[48] So when turnover is excessive, or when it involves valuable performers, it can be a disruptive factor that hinders the organization's effectiveness.

Deviant workplace behaviour

Given the cost of absenteeism and turnover to employers, more and more OB researchers are studying these behaviours as indicators or markers of deviant behaviour. Deviance can range from someone playing his music too loudly to violence. Managers need to understand this wide range of behaviours to address any form of employee dissatisfaction. If managers don't understand *why* an employee is acting up, the problem will never be solved.

deviant workplace behaviour
Voluntary behaviour that violates significant organizational norms and, in so doing, threatens the well-being of the organization or its members.

We can define **deviant workplace behaviour** (also called *antisocial behaviour* or *workplace incivility*) as voluntary behaviour that violates significant organizational norms and, in doing so, threatens the well-being of the organization or its members. What are organizational norms in this context? They can be company policies that prohibit certain behaviours such as using company resources for personal use. They also can be unspoken rules that are widely shared, such as not playing loud music in one's workspace. Consider, for example, an employee who plays U2 at work with the speakers amped up. Yes, he may be showing up at work, but he may not be getting his work done, and he could also be irritating co-workers or customers (unless they are U2 fans themselves). But deviant workplace behaviours can be much more serious than an employee playing loud music. For example, an employee may insult a colleague, steal, gossip excessively or engage in sabotage, all of which can wreak havoc on an organization.

Managers want to understand the source of workplace deviance in order to avoid a chaotic work environment, and workplace deviance can also have a considerable financial impact. Although the annual costs are hard to quantify, US estimates are that deviant behaviour costs employers dearly, from €2.5 billion for violence to €4 billion for corporate security against cyberattacks to over €100 billion for theft.[49]

Deviant workplace behaviour is an important concept because it's a response to dissatisfaction, and employees express this dissatisfaction in many ways. Controlling one behaviour may be ineffective unless one gets to the root cause. The sophisticated manager will deal with root causes of problems that may result in deviance rather than solve one surface problem (excessive absence) only to see another one crop up (increased theft or sabotage).

TRANSFER PRICING AND INTERNATIONAL CORPORATE DEVIANCE   GLOBAL

Workplace deviance isn't limited to the harmful behaviours of employees within one location. There are cases of corporate deviance that extend across country borders. Consider transfer pricing, which is the price that one part of a company charges another part of the same company for a product or service. What happens with transfer pricing if various parts of a company are located in different countries, which is becoming increasingly common as more and more companies extend their operations across the globe to become multinational businesses?

Tax rates on company profits differ – sometimes greatly – from country to country. Transfer pricing, when used to shift income from high-tax countries to low-tax countries, can be a deviant corporate policy if it is abused. One way to increase overall profit – that is, the combined profit of the multinational's headquarters and its subsidiaries – is to take profits in the country with the lower taxes.

Take the case of a multinational firm whose headquarters sold toothbrushes to a subsidiary for €3,500 – each. The subsidiary, with the higher tax of the two, claimed a loss (after all, it paid €3,500 per toothbrush). The multinational firm, with the lower tax of the two, took the profit and paid the tax on it. Because the two firms were part of the same organization, they combined the results of the transaction, and the company made a staggering profit.

Transfer pricing, according to a survey by the international auditing firm Ernst & Young, has become a heated issue among multinational companies. Why? Because governments are losing a lot of tax income.

Source: Based on 'Case of the U.S. $5000 Toothbrush,' *Finance Week*, 27 April 2005, pp. 45–46.

Organizational citizenship behaviour

organizational citizenship behaviour (OCB)
Discretionary behaviour that is not part of an employee's formal job requirements, but that nevertheless promotes the effective functioning of the organization.

Organizational citizenship behaviour (OCB) is discretionary behaviour that is not part of an employee's formal job requirements but that nevertheless promotes the effective functioning of the organization.[50]

Successful organizations need employees who will do more than their usual job duties – who will provide performance that is *beyond* expectations. In today's dynamic workplace, where tasks are increasingly done in teams and where flexibility is critical, organizations need employees who will engage in 'good citizenship' behaviours such as helping others on their team, volunteering for extra work, avoiding unnecessary conflicts, respecting the spirit as well as the letter of rules and regulations, and gracefully tolerating occasional work related impositions and nuisances.

Organizations want and need employees who will do those things that aren't in any job description. And the evidence indicates that organizations that have such employees outperform those that don't.[51] As a result, OB is concerned with OCB as a dependent variable.

Job satisfaction

job satisfaction
A positive feeling about one's job resulting from an evaluation of its characteristics.

The final dependent variable we will look at is **job satisfaction**, which we define as a positive feeling about one's job resulting from an evaluation of its characteristics. Unlike the previous five variables, job satisfaction represents an attitude rather than a behaviour. Why, then, has it become a primary dependent variable? For two reasons: its demonstrated relationship to performance factors and the value preferences held by many OB researchers.

The belief that satisfied employees are more productive than dissatisfied employees has been a basic tenet among managers for years, though only now has research begun to support this theory after decades of questions about the satisfaction–performance relationship.[52] Recently, a study of more than 2,500 business units found that units scoring in the top 25 per cent on the employee opinion survey were, on average, 4.6 per cent *above* their sales budget for the year, while those scoring in the bottom 25 per cent were 0.8 per cent *below* budget. In real numbers, this was a difference of €60 million in sales per year between the two groups.[53]

Moreover, it can be argued that advanced societies should be concerned not only with the quantity of life – that is, concerns such as higher productivity and material acquisitions – but also with its quality. Researchers with strong humanistic values argue that satisfaction is a legitimate objective of an organization. Not only is satisfaction negatively related to absenteeism and turnover, but, they argue, organizations have a responsibility to provide employees with jobs that are challenging and intrinsically rewarding. Therefore, although job satisfaction represents an attitude rather than a behaviour, OB researchers typically consider it an important dependent variable.

The independent variables

What are the major determinants of productivity, absenteeism, turnover, deviant workplace behaviour, OCB and job satisfaction? Our answer to that question brings us to the independent variables. An **independent variable** is the presumed cause of some change in a dependent variable.

independent variable
The presumed cause of some change in a dependent variable.

Consistent with our belief that organizational behaviour can best be understood when viewed essentially as a set of increasingly complex building blocks, the base, or first level, of our model lies in understanding individual behaviour.

Individual-level variables

It has been said that 'managers, unlike parents, must work with used, not new, human beings – human beings whom others have gotten to first.'[54] When individuals enter an organization, they are a bit like used cars. Each is different. Some are 'low mileage' – they have been treated carefully and have had only limited exposure to the realities of the elements. Others are 'well worn', having been driven over some rough roads. This metaphor indicates that people enter organizations with certain intact characteristics that will influence their behaviour at work. The most obvious of these are personal or biographical characteristics such as age, gender, marital status;

personality characteristics; an inherent emotional framework; values and attitudes; and basic ability levels. These characteristics are essentially in place when an individual enters the workforce, and, for the most part, there is little management can do to alter them. Yet they have a very real impact on employee behaviour. Therefore, each of these factors – biographical characteristics, ability, values, attitudes, personality, and emotions – will be discussed as independent variables in Chapters 2 through 4 and 8.

There are four other individual-level variables that have been shown to affect employee behaviour: perception, individual decision making, learning and motivation. Those topics will be introduced and discussed in Chapters 2, 5, 6 and 7.

Group-level variables

The behaviour of people in groups is more than the sum total of all the individuals acting in their own way. The complexity of our model is increased when we acknowledge that people's behaviour when they are in groups is different from their behaviour when they are alone. Therefore, the next step in the development of an understanding of OB is the study of group behaviour.

Chapter 9 lays the foundation for an understanding of the dynamics of group behaviour. The chapter discusses how individuals in groups are influenced by the patterns of behaviour they are expected to exhibit, what the group considers to be acceptable standards of behaviour, and the degree to which group members are attracted to each other. Chapter 10 translates our understanding of groups to the design of effective work teams. Chapters 11 through 15 demonstrate how communication patterns, leadership, power and politics, and levels of conflict affect group behaviour.

Organization system-level variables

Organizational behaviour reaches its highest level of sophistication when we add formal structure to our previous knowledge of individual and group behaviour. Just as groups are more than the sum of their individual members, so organizations are more than the sum of their member groups. The design of the formal organization; the organization's internal culture; and the organization's human resource policies and practices (that is, selection processes, training and development programmes, performance evaluation methods) all have an impact on the dependent variables. These are discussed in detail in Chapters 16 through 18.

Toward a contingency OB model

Our final model is shown in Figure 1.4. It shows the six key dependent variables and a large number of independent variables, organized by level of analysis, that research indicates have varying effects on the former. As complicated as this model is, it still doesn't do justice to the complexity of the OB subject matter. However, it should help explain why the chapters in this book are arranged as they are and help you to explain and predict the behaviour of people at work.

For the most part, our model does not explicitly identify the vast number of contingency variables because of the tremendous complexity that would be involved in such a diagram. Rather, throughout this book we will introduce important contingency variables that will improve the explanatory linkage between the independent and dependent variables in our OB model.

Note that we have included the concepts of change and stress in Figure 1.4, acknowledging the dynamics of behaviour and the fact that work stress is an individual, group, and organizational issue. Specifically, in Chapter 19, we will discuss the change process, ways to manage organizational change, key change issues currently facing managers, consequences of work stress, and techniques for managing stress.

Also note that Figure 1.4 includes linkages between the three levels of analysis. For instance, organizational structure is linked to leadership. This link is meant to convey that authority and leadership are related; management exerts its influence on group behaviour through leadership. Similarly, communication is the means by which individuals transmit information; thus, it is the link between individual and group behaviour.

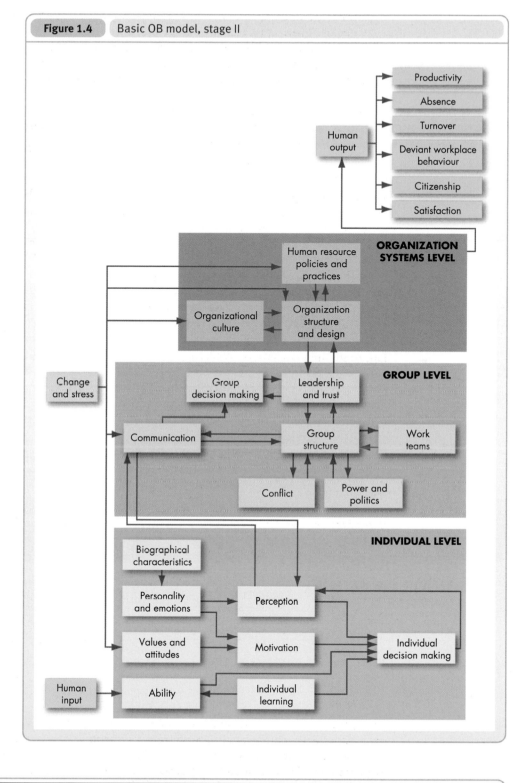

Figure 1.4 Basic OB model, stage II

Global implications

We've already discussed how globalisation presents challenges and opportunities for OB. We want to draw your attention to this spot in the chapter, though, because in every subsequent chapter, we will have a section at this point – titled 'Global implications' – that discusses how some of the things we know about OB are affected by cultural differences within and between countries. Most OB research has been conducted in Western cultures (especially the United

States). That is changing, however, and compared to even a few years ago, we're now in a much better position to answer the question 'How does what we know about OB vary based on culture?' You'll find that some OB principles don't vary much across cultures, but others vary a great deal from culture to culture.

Summary and implications for managers

Managers need to develop their interpersonal, or people, skills if they are going to be effective in their jobs. Organizational behaviour (OB) is a field of study that investigates the impact that individuals, groups and structure have on behaviour within an organization, and it applies that knowledge to make organizations work more effectively. Specifically, OB focuses on how to improve productivity; reduce absenteeism, turnover and deviant workplace behaviour; and increase organizational citizenship behaviour and job satisfaction.

We all hold generalisations about the behaviour of people. Some of our generalisations may provide valid insights into human behaviour, but many are erroneous. Organizational behaviour uses systematic study to improve predictions of behaviour that would be made from intuition alone. But because people are different, we need to look at OB in a contingency framework, using situational variables to moderate cause-and-effect relationships.

Organizational behaviour offers both challenges and opportunities for managers. It offers specific insights to improve a manager's people skills. It recognises differences and helps managers to see the value of workforce diversity and practices that may need to be changed when managing in different countries. It can improve quality and employee productivity by showing managers how to empower their people, design and implement change programmes, improve customer service and help employees balance work–life conflicts. It provides suggestions for helping managers meet chronic labour shortages. It can help managers to cope in a world of temporariness and to learn ways to stimulate innovation. Finally, OB can offer managers guidance in creating an ethically healthy work climate.

POINT/COUNTERPOINT

In search of the quick fix

POINT ➡

Walk into your nearest major bookstore. You'll undoubtedly find a large section of books devoted to management and managing human behaviour. A close look at the titles will reveal that there is certainly no shortage of popular books on topics related to organizational behaviour. To illustrate the point, consider the following popular books that are currently available on the topic of leadership:

- *If Harry Potter Ran General Electric: Leadership Wisdom from the World of Wizards* (Currency/Doubleday, 2006)
- *Catch! A Fishmonger's Guide to Greatness* (Berrett-Koehler, 2003)
- *Bhagavad Gita on Effective Leadership* (iUniverse, 2006)

- *Power Plays: Shakespeare's Lessons on Leadership and Management* (Simon & Schuster, 2000)
- *The Leadership Teachings of Geronimo* (Sterling House, 2002)
- *Leadership Wisdom from the Monk Who Sold His Ferrari* (Hay House, 2003)
- *The 21 Irrefutable Laws of Leadership* (Maxwell, 1998)

Organizations are always looking for leaders; and managers and aspiring managers are continually looking for ways to hone their leadership skills. Publishers respond to this demand by offering hundreds of titles that promise insights into the subject of leadership. Books like these can provide people with the secrets to leadership that others know about.

COUNTERPOINT ⬅

Beware of the quick fix! We all want to find quick and simple solutions to our complex problems. But here's the bad news: For problems related to organizational behaviour, quick and simple solutions are often wrong because they fail to consider the diversity among organizations, situations and individuals. As Einstein said, 'everything should be made as simple as possible, but not simpler.'

When it comes to trying to understand people at work, there is no shortage of simplistic ideas and books and consultants to promote them. And these books aren't just about leadership. Consider three recent bestsellers. *Who Moved My Cheese?* is a metaphor about two mice that is meant to convey the benefits of accepting change. *Fish!* tells how a fish market made its jobs more motivating. And *Whale Done!* proposes that managers can learn a lot about motivating people from techniques used by whale trainers at Sea World in San Diego, US. Are the 'insights' from these books generalisable to people working in hun-

dreds of different countries, in a thousand different organizations, doing a million different jobs? It's very unlikely.

Popular books on organizational behaviour often have cute titles and are fun to read. But they can be dangerous. They make the job of managing people seem much simpler than it really is. They are also often based on the author's opinions rather than substantive research.

Organizational behaviour is a complex subject. Few, if any, simple statements about human behaviour are generalisable to all people in all situations. Should you really try to apply leadership insights you got from a book about Shakespeare or Harry Potter to managing software engineers in the twenty-first century?

QUESTIONS FOR REVIEW

1. What is the importance of interpersonal skills?
2. What do managers do in terms of functions, roles and skills?
3. What is organizational behaviour (OB)?
4. Why is it important to complement intuition with systematic study?
5. What are the major behavioural science disciplines that contribute to OB?
6. Why are there few absolutes in OB?
7. What are the challenges and opportunities for managers in using OB concepts?
8. What are the three levels of analysis in this book's OB model?

Experiential exercise

WORKFORCE DIVERSITY

Purpose

To learn about the different needs of a diverse workforce.

Time required

Approximately 40 minutes.

Participants and roles

Divide the class into six groups of approximately equal size. Assign each group one of the following roles:

Nancy is 28 years old. She is a divorced mother of three children, ages 3, 5 and 7. She is the department head. She earns €30,000 per year on her job and receives another €1,800 per year in child support from her ex-husband.

Ethel is a 72-year-old widow. She works 25 hours per week to supplement her €4,000 annual pension. Including her hourly wage of €6.25, she earns €11,500 per year.

John is a 34-year-old black male born in Trinidad. He is married and the father of two small children. John attends university at night and is within a year of earning his bachelor's degree. His salary is €13,500 per year. His wife is a lawyer and earns approximately €35,000 per year.

Fu is a 26-year-old physically impaired male Asian. He is single and has a master's degree in education. Fu is

paralysed and confined to a wheelchair as a result of a car accident. He earns €16,000 per year.

Mike is a 16-year-old white male high school student who works 15 hours per week after school and during holidays. He earns €4.20 per hour, or approximately €3,000 per year.

The members of each group are to assume the character consistent with their assigned role.

Background

The six participants work for a company that has recently installed a flexible benefits programme. Instead of the traditional 'one benefit package fits all', the company is allocating an additional 25 per cent of each employee's annual pay to be used for discretionary benefits. Those benefits and their annual cost are as follows:

- Supplementary health care for employee:
  Plan A (no deductible and pays 90 per cent) = €1,500
  Plan B (€100 deductible and pays 80 per cent) = €1,000
  Plan C (€500 deductible and pays 70 per cent) = €250

- Supplementary health care for dependents (same deductibles and percentages as above):
  Plan A = €1,000
  Plan B = €750
  Plan C = €250

- Supplementary dental plan = €250
- Life insurance:
  Plan A (€12,500 coverage) = €250
  Plan B (€25,000 coverage) = €500
  Plan C (€50,000 coverage) = €1,000
  Plan D (€125,000 coverage) = €1,500
- Mental health plan = €250
- Prepaid legal assistance = €150
- Vacation = 2 per cent of annual pay for each week, up to 6 weeks a year
- Pension at retirement equal to approximately 50 per cent of final annual earnings = €750
- Four-day workweek during the 3 summer months (available only to full-time employees) = 4 per cent of annual pay
- Day-care services (after company contribution) = €1,000 for all of an employee's children, regardless of number
- Company-provided transportation to and from work = €375
- College tuition reimbursement = €500
- Language class tuition reimbursement = €250

The task

1. Each group has 15 minutes to develop a flexible benefits package that consumes 25 per cent (and no more!) of their character's pay.

2. After completing step 1, each group appoints a spokesperson who describes to the entire class the benefits package the group has arrived at for their character.

3. The entire class then discusses the results. How did the needs, concerns and problems of each participant influence the group's decision? What do the results suggest for trying to motivate a diverse workforce?

Source: Special thanks to Professor Penny Wright (San Diego State University) for her suggestions during the development of this exercise.

Ethical dilemma

LYING IN BUSINESS

Do you think it's ever okay to lie? If you were negotiating for the release of hostages, most people would probably agree that if lying would lead to the hostages' safety, it's okay. What about in business, where the stakes are rarely life or death? Business executives have gone to jail for lying. Calisto Tanzi, founder of Italian firm Parmalat presided over one of the biggest corporate scandals in history. After being caught embezzling an estimated €800 million from his own firm, he found himself in Milan prison. The career of one of the world's most respected business leaders crashed to an ignominious end when Lord Browne, chief executive of BP, resigned immediately after revelations that he had lied to a high court judge.

But what about less extreme cases? Tony Wells had 30 years' experience of working in information technology, in jobs ranging from programming to senior management. The 49-year-old decided to look for a new job and began sending his CV to recruitment agencies. In the year that followed, not a single agency called him back. As an experiment, he changed his age on his CV to 30 and had five phone calls within three days. Perhaps you wouldn't lie on your CV, but would you omit facts?

Questions

1. In a business context, is it ever okay to lie? If yes, what are those situations? Why is it okay to lie in these situations?

2. A recent survey revealed that 24 per cent of managers said they have fired someone for lying. Do you think it's fair to fire an employee who lies, no matter what the nature of the lie? Explain.

3. In business, is withholding information for your own advantage the same as lying? Why or why not?

4. In a business context, if someone has something to gain by lying, what percentage of people, do you think, would lie?

Source: Based on 'Lying at work could get you fired', *UPI*, 5 March 2006; 'Brain scans detect more activity in those who lie', Reuters, 29 November 2004; www.msnbc.msn.com/id/6609019; P. Ekman and E. L. Rosenberg, *What the Fact Reveals: Basic and Applied Studies of Spontaneous Expression Using the Facial Action Coding System (CAPS)*, 2nd edn (New York: Oxford University Press, 2004); E. Crooks, C. Hoyos and N. Tait, 'Browne quits BP after lying to court', *Financial Times*, 1 May 2007; K. Thomas, 'Why IT workers are lying about their age', *Financial Times*, 30 March 2005.

CASE INCIDENT 1

A great place to work

Which companies have been recognised as among the best places to work in Europe? You would probably guess Google, Microsoft, Cisco or 3M, and you would be right. However, you probably wouldn't guess that on the same list is a small swimming pool manufacturer in Athens. What makes it such a great place to work?

Piscines Ideales employees are embraced from the moment they arrive: they are welcomed by the CEO himself, and receive a welcome book that includes the story of the company, pictures of colleagues and descriptions of company practices and policies. They are also given the CEO's mobile phone number as soon as they are recruited, and they learn the company's basic values: respect, camaraderie, teamwork, pride, focus on quality and learning and personal development.

Piscines Ideales also celebrates every birthday in the company with a company-bought birthday cake; people gather together almost daily to sing the birthday song and blow out candles. The CEO frequently invites employees to his house to celebrate the New Year, and they go out for dinner and dancing to celebrate his birthday.

Employees who get married receive a month's worth of salary as a bonus; those who have children receive three extra days off, plus a financial bonus. When employees' children start their studies at a university, the company gives them a personal computer. The Piscines 'family' even goes on vacations together: every year, the company sponsors a trip abroad to an exotic destination for all employees.

Above all, Piscines Ideales managers regard all employees as potential business leaders; everyone is given opportunities for career development, and no fewer than one third of the company's current 21 franchisees were formerly Piscines employees.

The family treatment has created a sense of devotion to the company's future. As one employee explained, 'We have all loved each other truly. We work with fun and we help each other with our heart. We all want to continue like this, and we all want to take our family company even higher.'

Source: Based on 'Best workplaces' *Financial Times* Special Report, 28 May 2008 www.ft.com/bestworkplaces2008; 'Special award winners', best places to work Europe, 2007.

Questions

1. What makes Piscines Ideales a great place to work?

2. Would you be satisfied working for this company? Why or why not? Would this work environment suit everybody?

3. Would this approach to managing people work for all organizations? Why or why not?

4. Is there evidence that being regarded as a 'great place to work' generates superior financial performance?

CASE INCIDENT 2

Rage and violence in the workplace

According to recent research as many as 8 in 10 employees suffer from 'work rage' triggered by anything from lazy colleagues to ill-defined job roles. As many as 7 in 10 report that verbal abuse and shouting is common in their place of work.

Seeing a colleague hurl their BlackBerry at the wall or square-up to an unpopular boss may be diverting at the time, but according to one employee relations advisor, a persistently angry colleague can be highly disruptive in a team.

'Anger makes people say hurtful things and it triggers insecurity and lack of trust. Staff may become tentative in their approach to a colleague with anger problems, obstructing the work process and flow, and in the case of explosive anger, may become fearful of violence.'

The advisor advocates a zero-tolerance approach when the red mist comes down. 'Line management should directly confront any individual who exhibits anger in the workplace and HR should not hesitate to deal with it in a disciplinary context.'

Although most flare-ups at work are minor – an oath, a phone banged down or a slammed desk drawer – work rage can, on occasions, be dramatic. A senior anger management instructor talks of the two senior surgeons referred to him after they set upon one another with scalpels and knives in an operating theatre. An occupational psychologist remembers seeing a colleague coolly smash every single window pane in his office with a metal waste basket.

Anger that turns violent is a serious issue across Europe. A European Foundation for the Improvement of Living and Working Conditions survey of more than 30,000 workers in 31 countries found that the highest incidence of workplace violence was in the Netherlands where 10 per cent of workers reported being the victims of violence, closely followed by France and the UK with 9 per cent. Across the EU the figure is 5 per cent. The incidence of threats of violence is far higher prompting the UK Trades Union Congress (TUC) to claim, 'Violent assaults and threats are the fastest growing health and safety concern in the workplace.'

TUC general secretary John Monks said: 'Too many workers face the threat of violence when they go to work, and in some jobs, the only question is "when" will you get attacked, not "whether". Workers are facing a rising tide of violence and employers haven't got to grips with the threat. Individual acts of violence are random, but violence itself is all too predictable in some jobs. That means the risk of violence can and should be assessed, managed and reduced.'

Source: Based on V. Matthews, 'Anger management in the workplace: Raging bull', *Personnel Today*, 1 September 2008; Q. Reade, 'Violence and threats pack a punch in workplace woes top five', *Personnel Today*, 5 November 2002; K. Redford, 'Spotlight on: violence in the workplace', *Personnel Today*, 18 April 2006.

Questions

1. Is 'work rage' simply an inevitable part of working life? Would you find it acceptable?

2. How might work rage affect an organization's productivity?

3. When rage turns to violence, how liable should companies be for violent acts committed during work by their own employees?

4. Can companies completely prevent workplace violence? If not, what steps can they take to reduce it?

5. Very few companies have formal antiviolence policies. Why do you think this is?

Endnotes

1 Cited J. Bailey and M. Burch, *25 Essential Skills and Strategies for the Professional Behavior Analysts* (New York, NY: Routledge, 2009), p. 153.

2 See Association of Graduate Recruiters http://www.agr.org.uk. Accessed 8 July 2009.

3 See, for instance, C. Penttila, 'Hiring hardships', *Entrepreneur*, October 2002, pp. 34–35.

4 See: www.greatplacetowork.com; *Sunday Times* '100 best companies to work for'; 'Best workplaces' *Financial Times*, special report, 28 May 2008 www.ft.com/bestworkplaces2008.

5 *The 2002 National Study of the Changing Workforce* (New York: Families and Work Institute, 2002).

6 I. S. Fulmer, B. Gerhart and K. S. Scott, 'Are the 100 best better? An empirical investigation of the relationship between being a "great place to work" and firm performance,' *Personnel Psychology*, Winter 2003, pp. 965–93.

7 H. Fayol, *Industrial and General Administration* (Paris: Dunod, 1916).

8 A. I. Kraut, P. R. Pedigo, D. D. McKenna and M. D. Dunnette, 'The role of the manager: what's really important in different management jobs', *Academy of Management Executive*, 19, 4 (2005), pp. 122–29.

9 H. Mintzberg, *The Nature of Managerial Work* (Upper Saddle River, NJ: Prentice Hall, 1973).

10 R. L. Katz, 'Skills of an effective administrator,' *Harvard Business Review*, September–October 1974, pp. 90–102.

11 F. Luthans, 'Successful vs. effective real managers', *Academy of Management Executive*, May 1988, pp. 127–32; and F. Luthans, R. M. Hodgetts and S. A. Rosenkrantz, *Real Managers* (Cambridge, MA: Ballinger, 1988). See also F. Shipper and J. Davy, 'A model and investigation of managerial skills, employees' attitudes and managerial performance', *Leadership Quarterly* 13 (2002), pp. 95–120.

12 P. H. Langford, 'Importance of relationship management for the career success of Australian managers', *Australian Journal of Psychology*, December 2000, pp. 163–69; and A. M. Konrad, R. Kashlak, I. Yoshioka, R. Waryszak and N. Toren, 'What do managers like to do? A five-country study', *Group & Organization Management*, December 2001, pp. 401–33.

13 A. S. Tsui, S. J. Ashford, L. St. Clair and K. R. Xin, 'Dealing with discrepant expectations: response strategies and managerial effectiveness', *Academy of Management Journal*, December 1995, pp. 1515–43.

14 See, for instance, C. Heath and S. B. Sitkin, 'Big-B versus Big-O: what is *organizational* about organizational behavior?' *Journal of Organizational Behavior*, February 2001, pp. 43–58. For a review of what one eminent researcher believes *should* be included in organizational behavior, based on survey data, see J. B. Miner, 'The rated importance, scientific validity, and practical usefulness of organizational behavior theories: a quantitative review', *Academy of Management Learning & Education*, September 2003, pp. 250–68.

15 See L. A. Burke and J. E. Moore, 'A perennial dilemma in OB education: engaging the traditional student', *Academy of Management Learning & Education*, March 2003, pp. 37–52.

16 D. M. Rousseau and S. McCarthy, 'Educating managers from an evidence-based perspective', *Academy of Management Learning & Education*, 6, 1 (2007), pp. 84–101.

17 J. Surowiecki, 'The fatal-flaw myth', *The New Yorker*, 31 July 2006, p. 25.

18 'In Finland, fine for speeding sets record', *International Herald Tribune*, 11 February 2004, p. 2.

19 J. Cienski, K. Eddy, T. Escritt and S. Wagstyl, 'Gone west: why Eastern Europe is labouring under an abundance of jobs', *Financial Times* (Asia Edition), London (UK), 17 January 2008, p. 7.

20 O. C. Richard, 'Racial diversity, business strategy, and firm performance: a resource-based view', *Academy of Management Journal*, April 2000, pp. 164–77.

21 'Bye-Bye, Ozzie and Harriet', *American Demographics*, December 2000, p. 59.

22 G. Beets, 'EU demographics: living longer and reproducing less', *Pharmaceuticals Policy and Law*, 9 (2007), pp. 29–40.

23 C. Lindsay, 'A century of labour market change: 1900 to 2000', *Labour Market Trends*, March 2003, pp. 133–44.

24 'Fourth European working conditions survey', *European Foundation for the Improvement of Living and Working Conditions*, 2007.

25 'Employment in Europe 2007', *European Commission* http://www.igfse.pt/upload/docs/gabdoc/2008/01-Jan/keah07001_en.pdf. Accessed 7 August 2009.

26 'Britain in 2010', *Department of Work and Pensions*, 2001.

27 See M. E. A. Jayne and R. L. Dipboye, 'Leveraging diversity to improve business performance: research findings and recommendations for organizations', *Human Resource Management*, Winter 2004, pp. 409–24; S. E. Jackson and A. Joshi, 'Research on domestic and international diversity in organizations: a merger that works?', in N. Anderson, D. S. Ones, H. K. Sinangil and C. Viswesvran (eds), *Handbook of Industrial, Work & Organizational Psychology*, vol. 2 (Thousand Oaks, CA: Sage, 2001), pp. 206–31; and L. Smith, 'The business case for diversity,' *Fortune*, 13 October 2003, pp. S8–S12.

28 See, for instance, S. D. Pugh, J. Dietz, J. W. Wiley and S. M. Brooks, 'Driving service effectiveness through employee-customer linkages', *Academy of Management Executive*, November 2002, pp. 73–84; and H. Liao and A. Chuang, 'A multilevel investigation of factors influencing employee service performance and customer outcomes', *Academy of Management Journal*, February 2004, pp. 41–58.

29 See http://www.patagonia.com; and 'Patagonia sets the pace for green business', *Grist Magazine*, 22 October 2004, www.grist.org.

30 See, for instance, M. Workman and W. Bommer, 'Redesigning computer call center work: a longitudinal field experiment', *Journal of Organizational Behavior*, May 2004, pp. 317–37.

31 See, for instance, V. S. Major, K. J. Klein and M. G. Ehrhart, 'Work time, work interference with family, and psychological distress', *Journal of Applied Psychology*, June 2002, pp. 427–36; D. Brady, 'Rethinking the rat race', *BusinessWeek*, 26 August

2002, pp. 142–43; J. M. Brett and L. K. Stroh, 'Working 61 plus hours a week: why do managers do it?' *Journal of Applied Psychology*, February 2003, pp. 67–78.

32 M. Bunting (2004) *Willing Slaves: How the Overwork Culture is Ruling Our Lives*, London: Harper Collins.

33 See, for instance, *The 2002 National Study of the Changing Workforce* (New York: Families and Work Institute, 2002).

34 Cited in S. Armour, 'Workers put family first despite slow economy, jobless fears', *USA Today*, 6 June 2002, p. 3B.

35 S. Shellenbarger, 'What job candidates really want to know: will I have a life?' *Wall Street Journal*, 17 November 1999, p. B1; and 'U.S. employers polish image to woo a demanding new generation', *Manpower Argus*, February 2000, p. 2.

36 'Best workplaces', *Financial Times*, special report, 28 May 2008, www.ft.com/bestworkplaces2008.

37 F. Luthans and C. M. Youssef, 'Emerging positive organizational behavior', *Journal of Management*, June 2007, pp. 321–49; and J. E. Dutton and S. Sonenshein, 'Positive organizational scholarship', in C. Cooper and J. Barling (eds), *Encyclopedia of Positive Psychology* (Thousand Oaks, CA: Sage, 2007).

38 L. M. Roberts, G. Spreitzer, J. Dutton, R. Quinn, E. Heaphy and B. Barker, 'How to play to your strengths', *Harvard Business Review*, January 2005, pp. 1–6; and L. M. Roberts, J. E. Dutton, G. M. Spreitzer, E. D. Heaphy and R. E. Quinn, 'Composing the reflected best self portrait: becoming extraordinary in work organizations', *Academy of Management Review*, 30, 4 (2005), pp. 712–36.

39 J. Merritt, 'For MBAs, soul-searching 101', *BusinessWeek*, 16 September 2002, pp. 64–66; and S. Greenhouse, 'The mood at work: anger and anxiety', *New York Times*, 29 October 2002, p. E1.

40 See, for instance, G. R. Weaver, L. K. Trevino and P. L. Cochran, 'Corporate ethics practices in the mid-1990's: an empirical study of the Fortune 1000,' *Journal of Business Ethics*, February 1999, pp. 283–94; and C. De Mesa Graziano, 'Promoting ethical conduct: a review of corporate practices', *Strategic Investor Relations*, Fall 2002, pp. 29–35.

41 A. J. Rucci, S. P. Kirn and R. T. Quinn, 'The employee–customer–profit chain at Sears,' *Harvard Business Review*, January–February 1998, pp. 83–97.

42 CIPD (2007) *Recruitment, Retention and Turnover*, Survey report 2007, London: CIPD. Available at http://www.cipd.co.uk/surveys.

43 Confederation for British Industry (www.CBI.org.uk).

44 L. Lusinyan and L. Bonato (2007) 'Work absence in Europe', *IMF Staff Papers*, 54, 3

45 CIPD (2007) *Recruitment, Retention and Turnover 2007*. Survey report, London: CIPD. (Survey report). Available at: http://www.cipd.co.uk/surveys.

46 L. Lusinyan and L. Bonato (2007) 'Work absence in Europe', *IMF Staff Papers*, 54, 3.

47 See, for example, M. C. Sturman and C. O. Trevor, 'The implications of linking the dynamic performance and turnover literatures', *Journal of Applied Psychology*, August 2001, pp. 684–96.

48 Cited in 'You often lose the ones you love', *IndustryWeek*, 21 November 1988, p. 5.

49 R. J. Bennett and S. L. Robinson, 'Development of a measure of workplace deviance', *Journal of Applied Psychology*, 85, 3 (2000), pp. 349–60; A. M. O'Leary-Kelly, M. K. Duffy and R. W. Griffin, 'Construct confusion in the study of antisocial work behavior', *Research in Personnel and Human Resources Management*, 18 (2000), pp. 275–303; and C. Porath, C. Pearson and D. L. Shapiro, 'Turning the other cheek or an eye for an eye: targets' responses to incivility', paper interactively presented at the annual meeting of the National Academy of Management, Chicago, Illinois, August 1999.

50 D. W. Organ, *Organizational Citizenship Behavior: The Good Soldier Syndrome* (Lexington, MA: Lexington Books, 1988), p. 4; and J. A. LePine, A. Erez and D. E. Johnson, 'The nature and dimensionality of organizational citizenship behavior: a critical review and meta-analysis', *Journal of Applied Psychology*, February 2002, pp. 52–65.

51 P. M. Podsakoff, S. B. MacKenzie, J. B. Paine and D. G. Bachrach, 'Organizational citizenship behaviors: a critical review of the theoretical and empirical literature and suggestions for future research', *Journal of Management*, 26, 3 (2000), pp. 543–48; and M. C. Bolino and W. H. Turnley, 'Going the extra mile: cultivating and managing employee citizenship behavior', *Academy of Management Executive*, August 2003, pp. 60–73.

52 T. A. Judge, C. J. Thoresen, J. E. Bono and G. R. Patton, 'The job satisfaction–job performance relationship: a qualitative and quantitative review', *Psychological Bulletin*, 127 (2001), pp. 376–407.

53 M. Buckingham and C. Coffman, *First, Break All the Rules: What the World's Greatest Managers Do Differently* (New York: Simon & Schuster, 1999).

54 H. J. Leavitt, *Managerial Psychology*, rev. edn (Chicago: University of Chicago Press, 1964), p. 3.

Foundations of individual behaviour

Learning Objectives

After studying this chapter, you should be able to:

1 Contrast the two types of ability.

2 Define *intellectual ability* and demonstrate its relevance to OB.

3 Identify the key biographical characteristics and describe how they are relevant to OB.

4 Define *learning* and outline the principles of the three major theories of learning.

5 Define *shaping* and show how it can be used in OB.

6 Show how culture affects our understanding of intellectual abilities, biographical characteristics and learning.

Ability will never catch up with the demand for it.

Malcolm Forbes

Paddling against the tide

Manuel Silvestri/Reuters

Meet Alexandra Hai, the first woman to operate a gondola in Venice.

For more than a millennium, gondolas have been navigating the canals of Italy's most fabled city. And for more than a millennium, they've been operated by men. Until 2007, when Hai won her right to operate one. But it didn't come without a fight. Hai, a 40-year-old of German and Algerian descent, had to go to court. The court ruled in her favour but restricted her operations to transporting the guests of a local hotel.

Whenever Hai is out, people stop, stare, take pictures and shout ('Brava, Gondoliera! Brava!' shouted one resident from his balcony). Not all the reactions are so positive, though.

Roberto Luppi, president of the Venice gondoliers' association, said that Hai has been proven incapable of operating a gondola, having failed four tests. He says the court's decision to allow her to operate is a publicity stunt. He defends the threats she's received from some male gondoliers, arguing, 'After a person accuses gondoliers of being racists and sexists, what does she expect?' he said. 'That they are supposed to give her kisses?'

Compared to the United Kingdom and especially the Scandinavian countries, Italy differentiates markedly between gender roles (though, of course, there is a lot of individual variation within Italy, as within most countries). In Venice, the first woman was allowed to wait on tables in St Mark's Square only 8 years ago at the Aurora Café. However, next door, the Firoian Café allows women to wait on tables only indoors.

Even though Hai continues to operate her gondola, locals still dispute her right to be on the water. Hai maintains that she failed the tests because they were rigged against her. Luppi and many other Venetians see it differently. 'She needs to look in the mirror and accept that she cannot drive', he said. To most of the gondoliers, the job is fit only for a man since it requires strength and the ability to navigate currents and paddle in reverse, and even for aesthetic reasons (relating to the traditional garb of the gondoliers). Says one gondolier, 'Let's leave just one tradition intact. Being a gondolier is a tradition and it is very difficult work.'

▶

For her part, Hai argues that her job has been doubly difficult because she's had to fight for her job. 'There is nothing worse than to do something like this,' she said. 'I would have preferred to do something more useful in life, like helping save the rain forests.'

Source: Based on P. Kiefer, 'On the canals, a woman paddles against the tide', *New York Times*, 14 May 2007, pp. A1, A4.

Gender is but one characteristic that people bring with them when they join an organization. In this chapter, we look at how individual differences in the form of ability (which includes intelligence) and biographical characteristics (such as age) affect employee performance and satisfaction. Then we show how people learn behaviours and what management can do to shape those behaviours.

But before we move on to the next section, take a look at the following Self-assessment library, where you can assess your views on one of the characteristics we'll discuss in this chapter – age.

SELF-ASSESSMENT LIBRARY

What's my attitude toward older people?

In the Self-assessment library (available online), take assessment IV.C.1 (How do I feel about older people?) and answer the following questions.

1. Are you surprised by your results?

2. How do your results compare to those of others?

Ability

1 Contrast the two types of ability.

You would have begun to notice from an early age that we all differ in our abilities. At school, some people performed well at, for example, mathematics, others at drama and others at sport. Most people are to the left or to the right of the median on some normally distributed ability curve. For example, regardless of how motivated you are, it's unlikely that you can act as well as Daniel Day-Lewis, play football as well as Cristiano Ronaldo, write as well as J. K. Rowling, or sing as well as Enrique Iglesias. Of course, just because we aren't all equal in abilities does not imply that some individuals are inherently inferior to others. Everyone has strengths and weaknesses in terms of ability that make them relatively superior or inferior to others in performing certain tasks or activities. From management's standpoint, the issue is not whether people differ in terms of their abilities. They clearly do. The issue is knowing *how* people differ in abilities and using that knowledge to increase the likelihood that an employee will perform their job well.

ability
An individual's capacity to perform the various tasks in a job.

intellectual abilities
The capacity to do mental activities – thinking, reasoning and problem solving.

What does *ability* mean? As we will use the term, **ability** refers to an individual's capacity to perform the various tasks in a job. It is a current assessment of what one can do. An individual's overall abilities are essentially made up of two sets of factors: intellectual and physical.

Intellectual abilities

2 Define *intellectual ability* and demonstrate its relevance to OB.

Intellectual abilities are abilities needed to perform mental activities – for thinking, reasoning and problem solving. People in most societies place a high value on intelligence, and with good reason. Compared to others, smart people generally earn more money and attain higher levels

Table 2.1 Dimensions of intellectual ability

Dimension	Description	Job example
Number aptitude	Ability to do speedy and accurate arithmetic	Accountant: Computing the sales tax on a set of items
Verbal comprehension	Ability to understand what is read or heard and the relationship of words to each other	Plant manager: Following corporate policies on hiring
Perceptual speed	Ability to identify visual similarities and differences quickly and accurately	Fire investigator: Identifying clues to support a charge of arson
Inductive reasoning	Ability to identify a logical sequence in a problem and then solve the problem	Market researcher: Forecasting demand for a product in the next time period
Deductive reasoning	Ability to use logic and assess the implications of an argument	Supervisor: Choosing between two different suggestions offered by employees
Spatial visualisation	Ability to imagine how an object would look if its position in space were changed	Interior decorator: Redecorating an office
Memory	Ability to retain and recall past experiences	Salesperson: Remembering the names of customers

of education. Smart people are also more likely to emerge as leaders of groups. Intelligence quotient (IQ) tests, for example, are designed to ascertain a person's general intellectual abilities. So, too, are school and university admission tests, such as the graduate admission test in business (GMAT). Testing firms don't make the argument that their tests assess intelligence, but experts know that they do.[1] The seven most frequently cited dimensions making up intellectual abilities are number aptitude, verbal comprehension, perceptual speed, inductive reasoning, deductive reasoning, spatial visualisation and memory.[2] Table 2.1 describes these dimensions.

Intelligence dimensions are positively related, so that high scores on one dimension tend to be positively correlated with high scores on another. If you score high on verbal comprehension, for example, you're more likely to score high on spatial visualisation. The correlations aren't perfect, meaning that people do have specific abilities. However, the correlations are high enough that for some time, researchers have recognised a general factor of intelligence, called **general mental ability (GMA)**. GMA doesn't deny that there are specific abilities, but it suggests that it makes sense to talk about overall, or general, intelligence.

general mental ability (GMA)
An overall factor of intelligence, as suggested by the positive correlations among specific intellectual ability dimensions.

Jobs differ in the demands they place on incumbents to use their intellectual abilities. The more complex a job is in terms of information-processing demands, the more general intelligence and verbal abilities will be necessary to perform the job successfully.[3] Of course, a high IQ is not a requirement for all jobs. For jobs in which employee behaviour is highly routine and there are little or no opportunities to exercise discretion, a high IQ is not as important to performing well. However, that does not mean that people with high IQs cannot have an impact on jobs that are traditionally less complex.

Testing has been used for more than 50 years, but there has been a significant rise in use in the last decade. The selection process has also become more sophisticated and so testing has assumed an increasingly prominent role for a number of organizations. General mental ability tests are used by around 75 per cent of companies. However, questions have been raised regarding, for example, the validity of some tests, the use of online testing and problems posed by cultural differences.[4]

An interesting study investigated IQ levels across Europe. A 'normal' IQ ranges from 85 to 115, but exceptionally gifted people have scores starting at 145. The results found that Germans came out on top with an average IQ of 107, followed by the Netherlands, Poland, Sweden, Italy, Austria and Switzerland, with Britons in eighth place and the French nineteenth.[5] There are, of course, significant variations within the countries.

THE BENEFITS OF CULTURAL INTELLIGENCE `GLOBAL`

Have you ever noticed that some individuals seem to have a knack for relating well to people from different cultures? Some researchers have labelled this skill *cultural intelligence*, which is an outsider's natural ability to interpret an individual's unfamiliar gestures and behaviours in the same way that others from the individual's culture would. Cultural intelligence is important because, when conducting business with people from different cultures, misunderstandings can often occur, and, as a result, cooperation and productivity may suffer.

Consider the following example: An American manager was meeting with his fellow design team engineers, two of whom were German. As ideas floated around the table, his German colleagues quickly rejected them. The American thought the feedback was harsh and concluded that his German colleagues were rude. However, they were merely critiquing the ideas, not the individual – a distinction that the American was unable to make, perhaps due to a lack of cultural intelligence. As a result, the American became wary of contributing potentially good ideas. Had the American been more culturally intelligent, he likely would have recognised the true motives behind his colleagues' remarks and thus may have been able to use those remarks to improve his ideas.

It is unclear whether the notion of cultural intelligence is separate from other forms of intelligence, such as emotional intelligence, and even whether cultural intelligence is different from cognitive ability. However, it is clear that the ability to interact well with individuals from different cultures is a key asset in today's global business environment.

Source: Based on C. Earley and E. Mosakowski, 'Cultural Intelligence', *Harvard Business Review*, October 2004, pp. 139–46.

While intelligence is a big help in performing a job well, it doesn't make people happier or more satisfied with their jobs. The correlation between intelligence and job satisfaction is about zero. Why? Research suggests that although intelligent people perform better and tend to have more interesting jobs, they are also more critical in evaluating their job conditions. Thus, smart people have it better, but they also expect more.[6]

Physical abilities

physical abilities
The capacity to do tasks that demand stamina, dexterity, strength, and similar characteristics.

Though the changing nature of work suggests that intellectual abilities are becoming increasingly important for many jobs, **physical abilities** have been, and will remain, important for successfully doing certain jobs. Research on the requirements needed in hundreds of jobs has identified nine basic abilities involved in the performance of physical tasks.[7] These are described in Table 2.2. Individuals differ in the extent to which they have each of these abilities. Not

Table 2.2	Nine basic physical abilities

Ability	Description
Strength factors	
1. Dynamic strength	Ability to exert muscular force repeatedly or continuously over time
2. Trunk strength	Ability to exert muscular strength using the trunk (particularly abdominal) muscles
3. Static strength	Ability to exert force against external objects
4. Explosive strength	Ability to expend a maximum of energy in one or a series of explosive acts
Flexibility factors	
5. Extent flexibility	Ability to move the trunk and back muscles as far as possible
6. Dynamic flexibility	Ability to make rapid, repeated flexing movements
Other factors	
7. Body coordination	Ability to coordinate the simultaneous actions of different parts of the body
8. Balance	Ability to maintain equilibrium despite forces pulling off balance
9. Stamina	Ability to continue maximum effort requiring prolonged effort over time

Source: Reprinted with the permission of *HR Magazine*, published by the Society for Human Resource Management, Alexandria, VA.

surprisingly, there is also little relationship among them: A high score on one is no assurance of a high score on others. High employee performance is likely to be achieved when management has ascertained the extent to which a job requires each of the nine abilities and then ensures that employees in that job have those abilities.

Biographical characteristics

3 Identify the key biographical characteristics and describe how they are relevant to OB.

biographical characteristics
Personal characteristics such as age, gender, race, and length of tenure – that are objective and easily obtained from personnel records.

As discussed in Chapter 1, this textbook is essentially concerned with finding and analysing the variables that have an impact on employee productivity, absence, turnover, deviance, citizenship and satisfaction. The list of those variables – as shown in Figure 1.4 – is long and contains some complicated concepts. Many of the concepts – motivation, say, or power and politics or organizational culture – are hard to assess. It might be valuable, then, to begin by looking at factors that are easily definable and readily available – data that can be obtained, for the most part, simply from information available in an employee's personnel file. What factors would these be? Obvious characteristics would be an employee's age, gender, race and length of service with an organization. Fortunately, a sizeable amount of research has specifically analysed many of these **biographical characteristics**.

Age

The relationship between age and job performance is likely to be an issue of increasing importance during the next decade for two primary reasons. First, there is a widespread belief that job performance declines with increasing age. Regardless of whether this is true, a lot of people believe it and act on it. Second, as noted in Chapter 1, the workforce is ageing. By 2050 the average age of Europe's population will be 49 years and one in three Europeans will be retired.

Shell International

Shell believes that having the right staff with the right skills at the right time is critical. The older worker phenomenon is of vital importance to Shell as the more experienced workers have a huge amount of knowledge and expertise and many are reaching retirement age. Retaining these skilled individuals has become a strategic imperative for the company.

Source: CIPD 'Managing an ageing workforce: the role of total reward', February 2008.

What is the perception of older workers? Evidence indicates that employers hold mixed feelings.[8] They see a number of positive qualities that older workers bring to their jobs, such as experience, judgement, a strong work ethic and commitment to quality. But older workers are also perceived as lacking flexibility and as being resistant to new technology; and in a time when organizations are actively seeking individuals who are adaptable and open to change, the negatives associated with age clearly hinder the initial hiring of older workers and increase the likelihood that they will be let go during cutbacks. Now let's take a look at the evidence. What effect does age actually have on turnover, absenteeism, productivity and satisfaction?

The older you get, the less likely you are to quit your job. That conclusion is based on studies of the age–turnover relationship.[9] Of course, this shouldn't be too surprising. As workers get older, they have fewer alternative job opportunities. In addition, older workers are less likely to resign than are younger workers, because their long tenure tends to provide them with higher wage rates, longer paid holidays and more attractive pension benefits.

It's tempting to assume that age is also inversely related to absenteeism. After all, if older workers are less likely to quit, won't they also demonstrate higher stability by coming to work more regularly? Not necessarily. Most studies do show an inverse relationship, but close examination finds that the age–absence relationship is partially a function of whether the absence is avoidable or unavoidable.[10] In general, older employees have lower rates of avoidable absence than do younger employees. However, they have higher rates of unavoidable absence, probably due to the poorer health associated with ageing and the longer recovery period that older workers need when injured.

How does age affect productivity? There is a widespread belief that productivity declines with age. It is often assumed that an individual's skills – particularly speed, agility, strength and coordination – decay over time and that prolonged job boredom and lack of intellectual stimulation contribute to reduced productivity. The evidence, however, contradicts that belief and those assumptions. For instance, during a three-year period, a large hardware chain staffed one of its stores solely with employees over 50 and compared its results with those of five stores with younger employees. The store staffed by the over-50 employees was significantly more productive (measured in terms of sales generated against labour costs) than two of the other stores and held its own with the other three.[11] Other reviews of the research find that age and job performance are unrelated.[12] Moreover, this finding seems to be true for almost all types of jobs, professional and nonprofessional. The natural conclusion is that the demands of most jobs, even those with heavy manual labour requirements, are not extreme enough for any declines in physical skills attributable to age to have an impact on productivity; or, if there is some decay due to age, it is offset by gains due to experience.[13]

Our final concern is the relationship between age and job satisfaction. On this issue, the evidence is mixed. Most studies indicate a positive association between age and satisfaction, at least up to the age of 60.[14] Other studies, however, have found a U-shaped relationship.[15] Several explanations could clear up these results, the most plausible being that these studies are intermixing professional and nonprofessional employees. When the two types are separated, satisfaction tends to continually increase among professionals as they age, whereas it falls among nonprofessionals during middle age and then rises again in the later years.

Gender

Few issues initiate more debates, misconceptions and unsupported opinions than whether women perform as well on jobs as men do. In this section, we review the research on that issue.

The evidence suggests that the best place to begin is with the recognition that there are few, if any, important differences between men and women that will affect their job performance. There are, for instance, no consistent male–female differences in problem-solving ability, analytical skills, competitive drive, motivation, sociability or learning ability.[16] Psychological studies have found that women are more willing to conform to authority and that men are more aggressive and more likely than women to have expectations of success, but those differences are minor. Given the significant changes that have taken place in the past 40 years in terms of increasing female participation rates in the workforce and rethinking what constitutes male and female roles, you should operate on the assumption that there is no significant difference in job productivity between men and women.[17]

One issue that does seem to differ between genders, especially when the employee has preschool-age children, is preference for work schedules.[18] Working mothers are more likely to prefer part-time work, flexible work schedules and telecommuting in order to accommodate their family responsibilities.

But what about absence and turnover rates? Are women less stable employees than men? First, on the question of turnover, the evidence indicates no significant differences.[19] Women's quit rates are similar to those for men. The research on absence, however, consistently indicates that women across Europe and US have higher rates of absenteeism than men do.[20] Scandinavian countries and the US demonstrate particularly noticeable differences.[21] The most logical explanation for this finding is that European and North American cultures have historically placed home and family responsibilities on the woman. When a child is ill or someone needs to stay home to wait for a plumber, it has been the woman who has traditionally taken time off from work. However, this research is undoubtedly time bound.[22] The historical role of the woman in caring for children and as secondary breadwinner has definitely changed in the past generation, and a large proportion of men nowadays are as interested in day care and the problems associated with child care in general as are women.

Race

Race is a controversial issue. It can be so contentious that it's tempting to avoid the topic. A complete picture of individual differences in OB, however, would be incomplete without a discussion of race.

What is race? Before we can discuss how race matters in OB, first we have to reach some consensus about what race is, and that's not easily done. Some scholars argue that it's not productive to discuss race for policy reasons (it's a divisive issue), for biological reasons (a large percentage of us are a mixture of races), or for genetic and anthropological reasons (many anthropologists and evolutionary scientists reject the concept of distinct racial categories). However, if you look around the streets of London, Brussels, Dublin or any city, you will see a variety of skin tones, hair textures and other physical characteristics. It is these characteristics, along with culture and ethnic origins, that people may use to group themselves and others into 'races'.[23] Commonly considered as racial groups include White, Pakistani, Black African, Black Caribbean, Romany Gypsy and many others. For our purposes we will define race as the biological heritage people use to identify themselves. This definition allows each individual to define their race. Tiger Woods, for example, refuses to place himself into a single racial category, emphasising his multi-ethnic roots.

Race has been studied quite a bit in OB, particularly as it relates to employment outcomes such as personnel selection decisions, performance evaluations, pay and workplace discrimination. Doing justice to all of this research isn't possible here, so let's summarise a few points.

First, research has consistently demonstrated that race is a factor in some selection decisions. Experiments in countries including Belgium, England, France and the Netherlands have detected that non-white racial minorities were discriminated against in more than 25 per cent of the occasions when interviews or jobs were offered.[24] Second, there is evidence to suggest that there is a tendency for individuals to favour colleagues of their own race in performance evaluations and promotion decisions.[25] This has been implicated as one of the reasons why senior management positions across Europe are under-represented by minority racial groups.[26] As a consequence, racial minorities are comparatively disadvantaged in terms of pay.[27]

The major dilemma faced by employers who use mental ability tests for selection, promotion, training and similar personnel decisions is concern that they may have a negative impact on racial and ethnic groups.[28] For instance, some minority groups score, on average, as much as 1 standard deviation lower than whites on verbal, numeric and spatial ability tests, meaning that only 10 per cent of minority group members score above the average for whites. However, after reviewing the evidence, researchers have concluded that 'despite group differences in mean test performance, there is little convincing evidence that well-constructed tests are more predictive of educational, training, or occupational performance for members of the majority group than for members of minority groups'.[29] The issue of racial differences in cognitive ability tests continues to be hotly debated.[30]

CITY BANKER ALLEGES RACE DISCRIMINATION   OB IN THE NEWS

A senior City banker yesterday launched a highly unusual race discrimination claim against Dresdner Kleinwort, alleging that he was treated less favourably – and eventually made redundant – because he was neither German nor a German speaker. The unfair dismissal and race discrimination claim could be worth close to €12 million if it succeeds.

Australian-born Malcolm Perry, a former global head of fixed income and credit at DrK, told an employment tribunal that he became increasingly concerned about being excluded from key decision-making after the bank – owned by insurer Allianz – decided to merge its corporate and investment banking businesses in late 2005 under a new chief executive, Stefan Jenztsch. 'From the moment Stefan was appointed, there was speculation, both internally and externally over Allianz's agenda,' he said. 'There was a general feeling that the hidden objective was the creation of a niche German investment bank servicing Dresdner's German corporate clients to the detriment of [its] international franchise.'

Mr Perry went on to tell the London-based tribunal: 'This left non-German and non-German speaking employees based outside Frankfurt and not aligned to the German business nervous about the outcome of Stefan's restructuring plans.' 'As it transpired, those concerns were entirely justified,' he claimed. In a witness statement, Mr Perry said that the bank's capital market committee had comprised 14 executives at the time of Mr Jenztsch's arrival, five of whom were German and nine who were non-German or non-German speaking. But he claimed that by early 2007, none of the non-German/non-German speakers had retained their jobs, in contrast to the position of their German counterparts.

Mr Perry was made redundant in June 2006 after being told he was no longer required in his existing role and was not going to be given a key position in the bank's new structure. He is suing DrK for both unfair dismissal and race discrimination.

Eventually, the bank conceded the unfair dismissal element. But it hit back strongly at the discrimination charge, saying it totally rejected Mr Perry's allegations. 'We are a committed equal opportunity employer and will defend ourselves vigorously from Mr Perry's claims,' it said. A bank official stressed that it was not the case that employees had to be German or speak German to advance their careers, and pointed out that of DrK's 6,000 employees, less than half – 2,300 – were in Germany.

Source: Adapted from N. Tait, City banker alleges race discrimination, FT.com, 12 September 2007.

Other biographical characteristics: tenure and religion

The last set of biographical characteristics we'll look at are tenure and religion.

Employment tenure

With the exception of gender and racial differences, few issues are more subject to misconceptions and speculations than the impact of seniority on job performance. Employment tenure refers to the length of time that a worker has spent with the same employer.

Extensive reviews have been conducted of the seniority–productivity relationship.[31] If we define *seniority* as time on a particular job, we can say that the most recent evidence demonstrates a positive relationship between seniority and job productivity. So tenure, expressed as work experience, appears to be a good predictor of employee productivity. Across Europe, a positive relationship has been demonstrated between increases in the average tenure level in an economy and the rate of labour productivity growth.[32]

The research relating tenure to absence is quite straightforward. Studies consistently demonstrate seniority to be negatively related to absenteeism.[33] In fact, in terms of both frequency of absence and total days lost at work, tenure is the single most important explanatory variable.[34]

Tenure is also a potent variable in explaining turnover. The longer a person is in a job, the less likely they are to quit.[35] Moreover, consistent with research that suggests that past behaviour is the best predictor of future behaviour,[36] evidence indicates that tenure on an employee's previous job is a powerful predictor of that employee's future turnover.[37]

The evidence indicates that tenure and job satisfaction are positively related.[38] In fact, when age and tenure are treated separately, tenure appears to be a more consistent and stable predictor of job satisfaction than is chronological age.

Religion

The effects of religion in the workplace has greatly increasing in prominence over the past decade. A wave of high-profile religious bias lawsuits is testing the limits of anti-discrimination laws and forcing businesses to reconsider how they approach deep-rooted beliefs. About 600 religious belief discrimination complaints were filed in the United Kingdom between March 2007 and April 2008, according to employment tribunal statistics. British Airways, for example, triggered a storm of criticism after barring a check-in worker from visibly wearing a crucifix around her neck at work, a policy the airline later amended. Similar battles have been fought over Muslim employees' right to wear a hijab, or headscarf and other overtly religious attire.[39] Other issues include, For example, employees not being able to serve alcohol, having to leave early or not be able to work on certain religious days, and premises having to provide prayer rooms. Religion is clearly having an effect in the workplace, however, there has not been a great deal of research into these affects to date. What is known is that workers who are the victims of religious discrimination have higher levels of health problems, absence and turnover.[40]

Learning

4 Define *learning* and outline the principles of the three major theories of learning.

All complex behaviour is learned. If we want to explain and predict behaviour, we need to understand how people learn. In this section, we define *learning*, present three popular learning theories, and describe how managers can facilitate employee learning.

A definition of *learning*

> **learning**
> A relatively permanent change in behaviour that occurs as a result of experience.

What is **learning**? A psychologist's definition is considerably broader than the layperson's view that 'it's what we did when we went to school'. In actuality, each of us is continuously 'going to school'. Learning occurs all the time. Therefore, a generally accepted definition of *learning* is 'any relatively permanent change in behaviour that occurs as a result of experience'.[41] Ironically, we can say that changes in behaviour indicate that learning has taken place and that learning is a change in behaviour.

The previous definition suggests that we can see changes taking place, but we can't see the learning itself. The concept is theoretical and, hence, not directly observable:

> *You have seen people in the process of learning, you have seen people who behave in a particular way as a result of learning and some of you (in fact, probably the majority of you) have 'learned' at some time in your life. In other words, we infer that learning has taken place if an individual behaves, reacts, responds as a result of experience in a manner different from the way he formerly behaved.*[42]

Our definition has several components that deserve clarification. First, learning involves change. Change may be good or bad from an organizational point of view. People can learn unfavourable behaviours – to hold prejudices or to shirk their responsibilities, for example – as well as favorable behaviours. Second, the change must become ingrained. Immediate changes may be only reflexive or a result of fatigue (or a sudden burst of energy) and thus may not represent learning. Third, some form of experience is necessary for learning. Experience may be acquired directly through observation or practice, or it may be acquired indirectly, as through reading. The crucial test still remains: Does this experience result in a relatively permanent change in behaviour? If the answer is 'yes', we can say that learning has taken place.

Theories of learning

> **classical conditioning**
> A type of conditioning in which an individual responds to some stimulus that would not ordinarily produce such a response.

How do we learn? Three theories that have been offered to explain the process by which we acquire patterns of behaviour are classical conditioning, operant conditioning and social learning.

Classical conditioning

Classical conditioning grew out of experiments to teach dogs to salivate in response to the ringing of a bell, conducted in the early 1900s by Russian physiologist Ivan Pavlov.[43] A simple surgical procedure allowed Pavlov to measure accurately the amount of saliva secreted by a dog.

When Pavlov presented the dog with a piece of meat, the dog exhibited a noticeable increase in salivation. When Pavlov withheld the presentation of meat and merely rang a bell, the dog did not salivate. Then Pavlov proceeded to link the meat and the ringing of the bell. After repeatedly hearing the bell before getting the food, the dog began to salivate as soon as the bell rang. After a while, the dog would salivate merely at the sound of the bell, even if no food was offered. In effect, the dog had learned to respond – that is, to salivate – to the bell. Let's review this experiment to introduce the key concepts in classical conditioning.

In Pavlov's experiment, the meat was an *unconditioned stimulus*; it invariably caused the dog to react in a specific way. The reaction that took place whenever the unconditioned stimulus occurred was called the *unconditioned response* (or the noticeable increase in salivation, in this case). The bell was an artificial stimulus, or what we call the *conditioned stimulus*. Although it was originally neutral, after the bell was paired with the meat (an unconditioned stimulus), it eventually produced a response when presented alone. The last key concept is the *conditioned response*. This describes the behaviour of the dog; it salivated in reaction to the bell alone.

Using these concepts, we can summarise classical conditioning. Essentially, learning a conditioned response involves building up an association between a conditioned stimulus and an unconditioned stimulus. When the stimuli, one compelling and the other one neutral, are paired, the neutral one becomes a conditioned stimulus and, hence, takes on the properties of the unconditioned stimulus.

Classical conditioning can be used to explain why Christmas carols often bring back pleasant memories of childhood; the songs are associated with the festive holiday spirit and evoke fond memories and feelings of euphoria. In an organizational setting, we can also see classical conditioning operating. For example, at one manufacturing plant, every time the top executives from the head office were scheduled to make a visit, the plant management would clean up the administrative offices and wash the windows. This went on for years. Eventually, employees would turn on their best behaviour and dress smartly whenever the windows were cleaned – even in those occasional instances when the cleaning was not paired with a visit from the top executives. People had learned to associate the cleaning of the windows with a visit from the head office.

Classical conditioning is passive. Something happens, and we react in a specific way. It is elicited in response to a specific, identifiable event. As such, it can explain simple reflexive behaviours. But most behaviour – particularly the complex behaviour of individuals in organizations – is emitted rather than elicited. That is, it's voluntary rather than reflexive. For example, employees *choose* to arrive at work on time, ask their boss for help with problems, or surf the Internet when no one is watching. The learning of those behaviours is better understood by looking at operant conditioning.

Operant conditioning

operant conditioning
A type of conditioning in which desired voluntary behaviour leads to a reward or prevents a punishment.

Operant conditioning argues that behaviour is a function of its consequences. People learn to behave to get something they want or to avoid something they don't want. Operant behaviour means voluntary or learned behaviour in contrast to reflexive or unlearned behaviour. The tendency to repeat such behaviour is influenced by the reinforcement or lack of reinforcement brought about by the consequences of the behaviour. Therefore, reinforcement strengthens a behaviour and increases the likelihood that it will be repeated.

What Pavlov did for classical conditioning, the Harvard psychologist B. F. Skinner did for operant conditioning.[44] Skinner argued that creating pleasing consequences to follow specific forms of behaviour would increase the frequency of that behaviour. He demonstrated that people will most likely engage in desired behaviours if they are positively reinforced for doing so; that rewards are most effective if they immediately follow the desired response; and that behaviour that is not rewarded, or is punished, is less likely to be repeated. For example, we know a professor who places a mark by a student's name each time the student makes a contribution to class discussions. Operant conditioning would argue that this practice is motivating because it conditions a student to expect a reward (earning class credit) each time they demonstrate a specific behaviour (speaking up in class). The concept of operant conditioning was part of Skinner's broader concept of **behaviourism**, which argues that behaviour follows stimuli in a relatively unthinking manner. In Skinner's form of radical behaviourism, concepts such as feelings, thoughts and other states of mind are rejected as causes of behaviour. In short, people

behaviourism
A theory which argues that behaviour follows stimuli in a relatively unthinking manner.

Toru Yamanaka/AFP/Getty Images

Toyota Motor Corporation applies social learning theory in teaching employees skills they need to meet the company's high standards of quality and efficiency. At its new Global Production Center training facility in Toyota City, Japan, employees from factories around the world learn production techniques through observation and direct experience. Trainees first watch computerised 'visual manuals' to learn basic skills. Then, under the tutelage of an experienced production master, they practise the skills. In this photo, a trainer (left) models a spray-painting technique while a trainee practises the skill.

learn to associate stimulus and response, but their conscious awareness of this association is irrelevant.[45]

You see apparent illustrations of operant conditioning everywhere. For example, any situation in which it is either explicitly stated or implicitly suggested that reinforcements are contingent on some action on your part involves the use of operant learning. Your instructor says that if you want a high grade in the course, you must supply correct answers on the test. A commissioned salesperson wanting to earn a sizeable income finds that doing so is contingent on generating high sales in their territory. Of course, the linkage can also work to teach the individual to engage in behaviours that work against the best interests of the organization. Assume that your boss tells you that if you will work overtime during the next three-week busy season, you'll be compensated for it at your next performance appraisal. However, when performance-appraisal time comes, you find that you are given no positive reinforcement for your overtime work. The next time your boss asks you to work overtime, what will you do? You'll probably decline! Your behaviour can be explained by operant conditioning: If a behaviour fails to be positively reinforced, the probability that the behaviour will be repeated declines.

Social learning

Individuals can learn by observing what happens to other people and just by being told about something, as well as through direct experiences. For example, much of what we have learned comes from watching models – parents, teachers, peers, motion picture and television performers, bosses and so forth. This view that we can learn through both observation and direct experience is called **social-learning theory**.[46]

social-learning theory
The view that people can learn through observation and direct experience.

Although social-learning theory is an extension of operant conditioning – that is, it assumes that behaviour is a function of consequences – it also acknowledges the existence of observational learning and the importance of perception in learning. People respond to how they perceive and define consequences, not to the objective consequences themselves.

The influence of models is central to the social-learning viewpoint. Four processes have been found to determine the influence that a model will have on an individual:

1. **Attentional processes.** People learn from a model only when they recognise and pay attention to its critical features. We tend to be most influenced by models that are attractive, repeatedly available, important to us or similar to us in our estimation.

2. **Retention processes.** A model's influence depends on how well the individual remembers the model's action after the model is no longer readily available.

3. **Motor reproduction processes.** After a person has seen a new behaviour by observing the model, the watching must be converted to doing. This process then demonstrates that the individual can perform the modelled activities.

4. **Reinforcement processes.** Individuals are motivated to exhibit the modelled behaviour if positive incentives or rewards are provided. Behaviours that are positively reinforced are given more attention, learned better and performed more often.

Shaping: a managerial tool

5 Define *shaping* and show how it can be used in OB.

Because learning takes place on the job as well as prior to it, managers are concerned with how they can teach employees to behave in ways that most benefit the organization. When we attempt to mould individuals by guiding their learning in graduated steps, we are **shaping behaviour**.

Consider a situation in which an employee's behaviour is significantly different from that sought by management. If management rewarded the individual only when he showed desirable responses, there might be very little reinforcement taking place. In such a case, shaping offers a logical approach toward achieving the desired behaviour.

shaping behaviour
Systematically reinforcing each successive step that moves an individual closer to the desired response.

We *shape* behaviour by systematically reinforcing each successive step that moves the individual closer to the desired response. If an employee who has chronically been a half-hour late for work comes in only 20 minutes late, we can reinforce that improvement. Reinforcement would increase as responses more closely approximated the desired behaviour.

'YOU CAN'T TEACH AN OLD DOG NEW TRICKS!'   MYTH *OR* SCIENCE?

This statement is false. It reflects the widely held stereotype that older workers have difficulty adapting to new methods and techniques. Studies consistently demonstrate that older employees are perceived as being relatively inflexible, resistant to change and less willing and able to be trained than their younger counterparts.[47] But these perceptions are mostly wrong.

Evidence does indicate that older workers (typically defined as people aged 50 and over) are less confident of their learning abilities (perhaps due to acceptance of societal stereotypes). Moreover, older workers do seem to be somewhat less efficient in acquiring complex or demanding skills, and, on average, they are not as fast in terms of reaction time or in solving problems. That is, they may take longer to train. However, once trained, research indicates that older workers actually learn more than their younger counterparts, and they are better at transferring what they have learned to the job.[48] And age actually improves some intellectual abilities,

such as verbal ability, and older brains are packed with more so-called expert knowledge – meaning they tend to have better outlines for how to solve problems.[49]

The ability to acquire the skills, knowledge or behaviour necessary to perform a job at a given level – that is, trainability – has been the subject of much research. And the evidence indicates that there are differences between people in their trainability. A number of individual-difference factors (such as low ability and reduced motivation) have been found to impede learning and training outcomes. However, age has not been found to influence these outcomes. In fact, older employees actually benefit more from training. Still, the stereotypes persist.

Source: K. A. Wrenn and T. J. Maurer, 'Beliefs about older workers' learning and development behavior in relation to beliefs about malleability of skills, age-related decline, and control', *Journal of Applied Social Psychology*, 34, 2 (2004), pp. 223–42.

Methods of shaping behaviour

There are four ways to shape behaviour: through positive reinforcement, negative reinforcement, punishment and extinction.

Following a response with something pleasant is called *positive reinforcement*. This would describe, for instance, a boss who praises an employee for a job well done. Following a response by the termination or withdrawal of something unpleasant is called *negative reinforcement*. If your instructor asks a question and you don't know the answer, looking through your lecture notes is likely to preclude your being called on. This is a negative reinforcement because you have learned that looking busily through your notes prevents the instructor from calling on you. *Punishment* is causing an unpleasant condition in an attempt to eliminate an undesirable behaviour. Giving an employee a two-day suspension from work without pay for showing up drunk is an example of punishment. Eliminating any reinforcement that is maintaining a behaviour is called *extinction*. When the behaviour is not reinforced, it tends to be gradually extinguished. Instructors who wish to discourage students from asking questions in class can eliminate this behaviour in their students by ignoring those who raise their hands to ask questions. Hand raising will become extinct when it is invariably met with an absence of reinforcement.

Both positive and negative reinforcement result in learning. They strengthen a response and increase the probability of repetition. In the preceding illustrations, praise strengthens and increases the behaviour of doing a good job because praise is desired. The behaviour of 'looking busy' is similarly strengthened and increased by its terminating the undesirable consequence of being called on by the teacher. However, both punishment and extinction weaken behaviour and tend to decrease its subsequent frequency. In shaping behaviour, a critical issue is the timing of reinforcements. This is an issue we'll consider now.

SELF-ASSESSMENT LIBRARY

How good am I at disciplining others?

In the Self-assessment library (available online), take assessment II.B.5 (How good am I at disciplining others?).

---

continuous reinforcement
Reinforcing a desired behaviour each time it is demonstrated.

intermittent reinforcement
Reinforcing a desired behaviour often enough to make the behaviour worth repeating but not every time it is demonstrated.

fixed-interval schedule
Spacing rewards at uniform time intervals.

variable-interval schedule
Distributing rewards in time so that reinforcements are unpredictable.

Schedules of reinforcement

The two major types of reinforcement schedules are *continuous* and *intermittent*. A **continuous reinforcement** schedule reinforces the desired behaviour each and every time it is demonstrated. Take, for example, the case of someone who historically has had trouble arriving at work on time. Every time that person is not late, their manager might compliment them on their desirable behaviour. With **intermittent reinforcement**, on the other hand, not every instance of the desirable behaviour is reinforced, but reinforcement is given often enough to make the behaviour worth repeating. This latter schedule can be compared to the workings of a slot machine, which people will continue to play even when they know it is adjusted to give a considerable return to the casino. The intermittent payoffs occur just often enough to reinforce the behaviour of slipping in coins and pulling the handle. Evidence indicates that the intermittent, or varied, form of reinforcement tends to promote more resistance to extinction than does the continuous form.[50]

An intermittent reinforcement can be of a ratio or interval type. *Ratio schedules* depend on how many responses the subject makes. The individual is reinforced after giving a certain number of specific types of behaviour. *Interval schedules* depend on how much time has passed since the previous reinforcement. With interval schedules, the individual is reinforced on the first appropriate behaviour after a particular time has elapsed. A reinforcement can also be classified as fixed or variable.

When rewards are spaced at uniform time intervals, the reinforcement schedule is a **fixed-interval schedule**. The critical variable is time, which is held constant. This is the predominant schedule for most salaried workers in Europe. When you get your pay on a weekly, semi-monthly, monthly or other predetermined time basis, you're rewarded on a fixed-interval reinforcement schedule.

If rewards are distributed in time so that reinforcements are unpredictable, the schedule is a **variable-interval schedule**. When an instructor advises their class that pop quizzes will be given during the term (the exact number of which is unknown to the students) and the quizzes will

Table 2.3   Schedules of reinforcement

Reinforcement schedule	Nature of reinforcement	Effect on behaviour	Example
Continuous	Reward given after each desired behaviour	Fast learning of new behaviour but rapid extinction	Compliments
Fixed-interval	Reward given at fixed time intervals	Average and irregular performance with rapid extinction	Weekly paychecks
Variable-interval	Reward given at variable time intervals	Moderately high and stable performance with slow extinction	Pop quizzes
Fixed-ratio	Reward given at fixed amounts of output	High and stable performance attained quickly but with rapid extinction	Piece-rate pay
Variable-ratio	Reward given at variable amounts of output	Very high performance with slow extinction	Commissioned sales

account for 20 per cent of the term grade, they are using a variable-interval schedule. Similarly, a series of randomly timed unannounced visits to a company office by the corporate audit staff is an example of a variable-interval schedule.

In a **fixed-ratio schedule**, after a fixed or constant number of responses are given, a reward is initiated. For example, a piece-rate incentive plan is a fixed-ratio schedule; the employee receives a reward based on the number of work pieces generated. If the piece rate for a zipper installer in a dressmaking factory is €5 per dozen, the reinforcement (money in this case) is fixed to the number of zippers sewn into garments. After every dozen is sewn in, the installer has earned another €5.

When the reward varies relative to the behaviour of the individual, they are said to be reinforced on a **variable-ratio schedule**. Salespeople on commission are examples of individuals on such a reinforcement schedule. On some occasions, they may make a sale after only two calls on a potential customer. On other occasions, they might need to make 20 or more calls to secure a sale. The reward, then, is variable in relation to the number of successful calls the salesperson makes. Table 2.3 summarises the schedules of reinforcement.

fixed-ratio schedule
Initiating rewards after a fixed or constant number of responses.

variable-ratio schedule
Varying the reward relative to the behaviour of the individual.

Reinforcement schedules and behaviour

Continuous reinforcement schedules can lead to early satiation, and under this schedule, behaviour tends to weaken rapidly when reinforcers are withheld. However, continuous reinforcers are appropriate for newly emitted, unstable or low-frequency responses. In contrast, intermittent reinforcers preclude early satiation because they don't follow every response. They are appropriate for stable or high-frequency responses.

In general, variable schedules tend to lead to higher performance than fixed schedules (see Figure 2.1). For example, as noted previously, most employees in organizations are paid on fixed-interval schedules. But such a schedule does not clearly link performance and rewards. The reward is given for time spent on the job rather than for a specific response (performance). In contrast, variable-interval schedules generate high rates of response and more stable and consistent behaviour because of the high correlation between performance and reward and because of the uncertainty involved – the employee tends to be more alert because there is a surprise factor.

Behaviour modification

A now-classic study took place a number of years ago with freight packers at Emery Air Freight (now part of FedEx).[51] Emery's management wanted packers to use freight containers for shipments whenever possible because of specific economic savings. When packers were asked about the percentage of shipments contained, the standard reply was 90 per cent. An analysis by Emery

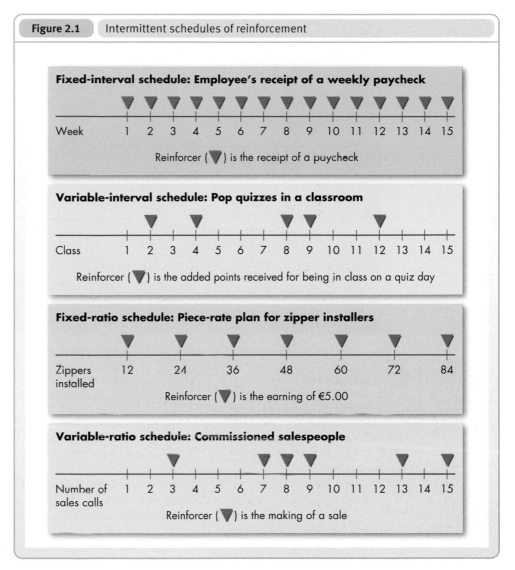

Figure 2.1 Intermittent schedules of reinforcement

found, however, that the actual container utilisation rate was only 45 per cent. In order to encourage employees to use containers, management established a programme of feedback and positive reinforcements. Each packer was instructed to keep a checklist of daily packings, both containerised and noncontainerised. At the end of each day, the packer computed the container utilisation rate. Almost unbelievably, container utilisation jumped to more than 90 per cent on the first day of the programme and held at that level. Emery reported that this simple programme of feedback and positive reinforcements saved the company around €1.5 million over a three-year period.

This programme at Emery Air Freight illustrates the use of behaviour modification, or what has become more popularly called **OB Mod**.[52] It represents the application of reinforcement concepts to individuals in the work setting. The typical OB Mod programme follows a five-step problem-solving model: (1) identify critical behaviours; (2) develop baseline data; (3) identify behavioural consequences; (4) develop and implementing an intervention strategy; and (5) evaluate performance improvement.[53]

Everything an employee does on the job is not equally important in terms of performance outcomes. The first step in OB Mod, therefore, is to identify the critical behaviours that make a significant impact on the employee's job performance. These are those 5 to 10 per cent of behaviours that may account for up to 70 or 80 per cent of each employee's performance. Freight packers using containers whenever possible at Emery Air Freight is an example of a critical behaviour.

OB Mod
The application of reinforcement concepts to individuals in the work setting.

Vetta Collections/iStockphoto

An investigation was conducted into the usefulness of OB Mod techniques in improving safety in the offshore oil drilling industry. The research revealed impressive results. Before the OB Mod interventions, the percentage of employees working safely averaged 76 per cent. At the end of the study the average was over 90 per cent. Results also demonstrated a marked decrease in injury incidence rates.

Source: Z. Zhu, J. Wallin and R. Reber 'Safety improvements: an application of behaviour modification techniques', *Journal of Applied Management Studies*, 9, 1 (2000), pp. 135–40.

The second step requires the manager to develop some baseline performance data. This is obtained by determining the number of times the identified behaviour is occurring under present conditions. In the Emery freight-packing example, this was the revelation that 45 per cent of all shipments were containerised.

The third step is to perform a functional analysis to identify the behavioural contingencies or consequences of performance. This tells the manager the antecedent cues that emit the behaviour and the consequences that are currently maintaining it. At Emery Air Freight, social norms and the greater difficulty in packing containers were the antecedent cues. This encouraged the practice of packing items separately. Moreover, the consequences for continuing the behaviour, prior to the OB Mod intervention, were social acceptance and escaping more demanding work.

Once the functional analysis is complete, the manager is ready to develop and implement an intervention strategy to strengthen desirable performance behaviours and weaken undesirable behaviours. The appropriate strategy will entail changing some elements of the performance–reward linkage – structure, processes, technology, groups or the task – with the goal of making high-level performance more rewarding. In the Emery example, the work technology was altered to require the keeping of a checklist. The checklist plus the computation, at the end of the day, of a container-utilisation rate acted to reinforce the desirable behaviour of using containers.

The final step in OB Mod is to evaluate performance improvement. In the Emery intervention, the immediate improvement in the container-utilisation rate demonstrated that behavioural change took place. That it rose to 90 per cent and held at that level further indicates that learning took place. That is, the employees underwent a relatively permanent change in behaviour.

A number of organizations have used OB Mod to improve employee productivity; to reduce errors, absenteeism, tardiness and accident rates; and to improve friendliness toward customers.[54] For instance, a clothing manufacturer saved over €40,000 in one year due to fewer absences. A packing firm improved productivity 16 per cent, cut errors by 40 per cent, and reduced accidents by more than 43 per cent – resulting in savings of over €½ million. A bank successfully used OB Mod to increase the friendliness of its tellers, which led to a demonstrable improvement in customer satisfaction.

Problems with OB Mod and reinforcement theory

Although the effectiveness of reinforcements in the form of rewards and punishments has a lot of support in the literature, that doesn't necessarily mean that Skinner was right or that OB Mod is the best way to reward people. What if the power of reinforcements isn't due to operant conditioning or behaviourism? One problem with behaviourism is, as research shows, that thoughts and feelings immediately follow environmental stimuli, even those explicitly meant to shape behaviour. This is contrary to the assumptions of behaviourism and OB Mod, which assume that people's innermost thoughts and feelings in response to the environment are irrelevant.

Think about praise from a supervisor. For example, assume your course instructor compliments you for asking a good question. A behaviourist would argue that this shapes your behaviour because you find the stimulus (the compliment) pleasant and therefore respond by attempting to ask other questions that will generate the same reward. However, imagine, for example, that you had to weigh the pleasant feelings produced by your instructor's praise against the whispers of jealous classmates. Your choice of what to do would likely be dictated by weighing the value of these stimuli, which may be a rather complex mental process involving thinking and feeling.

Also, is it really shaping if the compliment was given without an intention of moulding behaviour? Isn't it perhaps overly restrictive to view all stimuli as motivated to obtain a particular response? Is the only reason we tell someone we love them because we wish to obtain a reward or to mould their behaviour?

Because of these problems, among others, operant conditioning and behaviourism have been superseded by other approaches that emphasise cognitive processes.[55] There is no denying, though, the contribution of these theories to our understanding of human behaviour.

FACE THE FACTS

A study of OB Mod in a variety of manufacturing, service and not-for-profit organizations over 20 years demonstrated that:

- When OB Mod has been systematically applied using both monetary and nonmonetary reinforcers, performance on average increased 17 per cent.
- The average increase in performance was significantly higher for manufacturing companies (33 per cent) compared with service organizations (13 per cent).

- Interestingly, when monetary OB Mod reinforcers (in comparison to nonmonetary reinforces) were used in combination with performance feedback and social attention and recognition, performance improvement in the service organizations decreased from 30 to 9 per cent.

Source: F. Luthans and A. Stajkovic (1999) 'Reinforce for performance: the need to go beyond pay and even rewards', *Academy of Management Executive*, 13, 2; pp. 49–57.

Global implications

6 Show how culture affects our understanding of intellectual abilities, biographical characteristics and learning.

As you will see, there may be no global or cross-cultural research on some of the topics we discuss in a chapter, and this chapter is no exception. We therefore confine our comments here to areas where there has been the most cross-cultural research: (1) How does research on intellectual abilities generalise across cultures? (2) Do biographical characteristics such as gender and age operate similarly across cultures? and (3) Do the principles of learning work in different cultures?

Intellectual abilities

Evidence strongly supports the ideas that the structures and measures of intellectual abilities generalise across cultures. Thus, someone in Venezuela or Sudan does not have a different set of mental abilities than a Dutch or UK worker. Moreover, data from across many cultures support the finding that specific mental abilities indicate a higher-order factor we call general mental ability (GMA). There is some evidence that IQ scores vary to some degree across cultures, but those differences are much smaller when we consider educational and economic differences.[56]

Biographical characteristics

Obviously, some biographical characteristics vary across cultures. Some cultures are more racially homogenous than others, and the average age of citizens varies across countries (for example, in Italy and Japan, a far greater percentage of the population is over 65 than in India or China). That doesn't mean, however, that the relationships we've described between age and performance, or between gender and turnover, are different across cultures. Frankly, we do not have a great deal of good scientific evidence on whether, for example, gender or age affects absenteeism similarly across cultures. One Accenture survey of US managers in eight countries revealed some surprising differences. Compared to British managers, female managers in the Philippines believed that their country was more supportive of women's advancement into leadership positions.[57] While such survey results are interesting, they don't substitute for systematic study. Thus, we really don't know the degree to which gender (or other biographical factors) varies in importance in predicting OB outcomes in different countries.

Learning

There is little research on how theories of learning generalise to organizations and employees in different cultures. This is due in part to the fact that much of the research on learning theories is fairly old, conducted before there was a lot of cross-cultural research. For example, two major recent reviews of cross-cultural research in OB did not mention learning theories, reinforcement theory or behavioural modification. That doesn't mean these theories are necessarily culturally bound; it means we really don't yet know one way or the other.

Summary and implications for managers

This chapter looked at three individual variables – ability, biographical characteristics and learning. Let's now try to summarise what we found and consider their importance for a manager who is trying to understand organizational behaviour.

Ability

Ability directly influences an employee's level of performance. Given management's desire to get high-performing employees, what can be done?

First, an effective selection process will improve the fit. A job analysis will provide information about jobs currently being done and the abilities that individuals need to perform the jobs adequately. Applicants can then be tested, interviewed and evaluated on the degree to which they possess the necessary abilities.

Second, promotion and transfer decisions affecting individuals already in the organization's employ should reflect the abilities of candidates. As with new employees, care should be taken to assess critical abilities that incumbents will need in the job and to match those requirements with the organization's human resources.

Third, the fit can be improved by fine-tuning the job to better match an incumbent's abilities. Often, modifications can be made in the job that, while not having a significant impact on the job's basic activities, better adapt it to the specific talents of a given employee. Examples would be changing some of the equipment used or reorganising tasks within a group of employees.

Biographical characteristics

Biographical characteristics are readily observable to managers. However, just because they're observable doesn't mean they should be explicitly used in management decisions. We also need to be aware of implicit biases we or other managers may have.

Learning

Any observable change in behaviour is *prima facie* evidence that learning has taken place. Positive reinforcement is a powerful tool for modifying behaviour. By identifying and rewarding performance-enhancing behaviours, management increases the likelihood that those behaviours will be repeated. Our knowledge about learning further suggests that reinforcement is a more effective tool than punishment. Although punishment eliminates undesired behaviour more quickly than negative reinforcement does, punished behaviour tends to be only temporarily suppressed rather than permanently changed. And punishment may produce unpleasant side effects, such as lower morale and higher absenteeism or turnover. In addition, the recipients of punishment tend to become resentful of the punisher. Managers, therefore, are advised to use reinforcement rather than punishment.

POINT/COUNTERPOINT

All human behaviour is learned[58]

POINT →

Human beings are essentially blank slates that are shaped by their environment. B. F. Skinner, in fact, summarised his belief in the power of the environment to shape behaviour when he said, 'Give me a child at birth and I can make him into anything you want.'

Following are some of the societal mechanisms that exist because of this belief in the power of learned behaviour:

Role of parenting. We place a great deal of importance on the role of mothers and fathers in the raising of children. We believe, for instance, that children raised without fathers will be hindered by their lack of a male role model. And parents who have continual run-ins with the law risk having government authorities take their children from them. The latter action is typically taken because society believes that irresponsible parents don't provide the proper learning environment for their children.

Importance of education. Most advanced societies invest heavily in the education of their young. They typically provide 10 or more years of free education. And in Europe, going on to higher education after finishing high school has become the norm rather than the exception. This investment in education is undertaken because it is seen as a way for young people to learn knowledge and skills.

Job training. For individuals who don't go on to university, most will pursue job-training programmes to develop specific work-related skills. They'll take courses to become proficient as auto mechanics, medical assistants and the like. Similarly, people who seek to become skilled trades workers will pursue apprenticeships as carpenters, electricians or pipe fitters. In addition, business firms invest billions of euros each year in training and education to keep current employees' skills up-to-date.

Manipulation of rewards. Organizations design complex compensation programmes to reward employees fairly for their work performance. But these programmes are also designed with the intention to motivate employees. They are designed to encourage employees to engage in behaviours that management desires and to extinguish behaviours that management wants to discourage. Salary levels, for instance, typically reward employee loyalty, encourage the learning of new skills and motivate individuals to assume greater responsibilities in the organization.

These mechanisms all exist and flourish because organizations and society believe that people can learn and change their behaviour.

COUNTERPOINT ←

Although people can learn and can be influenced by their environment, far too little attention has been paid to the role that evolution has played in shaping human behaviour. Evolutionary psychology tells us that human beings are basically hardwired at birth. We arrive on Earth with ingrained traits, honed and adapted over millions of years, that shape and limit our behaviour.

All living creatures are 'designed' by specific combinations of genes. As a result of natural selection, genes that produce faulty design features are eliminated. Characteristics that help a species survive tend to endure and get passed on to future generations. Many of the characteristics that helped early *Homo sapiens* survive live on

today and influence the way we behave. Here are a few examples:

Emotions. Stone Age people, at the mercy of wild predators and natural disasters, learned to trust their instincts. Those with the best instincts survived. Today, emotions remain the first screen to all information we receive. We know we are supposed to act rationally, but our emotions can never be fully suppressed.

Risk avoidance. Ancient hunter-gatherers who survived were not big risk takers. They were cautious. Today, when we're comfortable with the status quo, we typically see any change as risky and, thus, tend to resist it.

▶

Stereotyping. To prosper in a clan society, Early humans had to quickly 'size up' whom they could trust or not trust. Those who could do this quickly were more likely to survive. Today, like our ancestors, we naturally stereotype people based on very small pieces of evidence, mainly their looks and a few readily apparent behaviours.

Male competitiveness. Males in early human societies frequently had to engage in games or battles in which there were clear winners and losers. Winners attained high status, were viewed as more attractive mates, and were more likely to reproduce. The ingrained male desire to do public battle and display virility and competence persists today.

Evolutionary psychology challenges the notion that people are free to change their behaviour if trained or motivated. It doesn't say that we can't engage in learning or exercise free will. What it does say is that nature predisposes us to act and interact in particular ways in particular circumstances. As a result, we find that people in organizational settings often behave in ways that don't appear to be beneficial to themselves or their employers.

QUESTIONS FOR REVIEW

1. What are the two types of ability?

2. What is intellectual or cognitive ability, and how is it relevant to OB?

3. What are the key biographical characteristics, and why are they relevant to OB?

4. What is learning, and what are the major theories of learning?

5. What is shaping, and how can it be used as a management tool?

6. How does culture affect our understanding of intellectual abilities, biographical characteristics and learning?

Experiential exercise

POSITIVE REINFORCEMENT VERSUS PUNISHMENT

Exercise overview (Steps 1–4)

This 10-step exercise takes approximately 20 minutes.

1. Two volunteers are selected to receive reinforcement or punishment from the class while performing a particular task. The volunteers leave the room.

2. The instructor identifies an object for the student volunteers to locate when they return to the room. (The object should be unobstructed but clearly visible to the class. Examples that have worked well include a small triangular piece of paper that was left behind when a notice was torn off a classroom bulletin board, a smudge on the whiteboard and a chip in the plaster of a classroom wall.)

3. The instructor specifies the actions that will be in effect when the volunteers return to the room. For punishment, students should hiss or boo when the first volunteer is moving away from the object. For positive reinforcement, they should cheer and applaud when the second volunteer is getting closer to the object.

4. The instructor should assign a student to keep a record of the time it takes each of the volunteers to locate the object.

Volunteer 1 (Steps 5 and 6)

5. Volunteer 1 is brought back into the room and is told, 'Your task is to locate and touch a particular object in the room, and the class has agreed to help you. You cannot use words or ask questions. Begin.'

6. Volunteer 1 continues to look for the object until it is found, while the class engages in the punishing behaviour.

Volunteer 2 (Steps 7 and 8)

7. Volunteer 2 is brought back into the room and is told, 'Your task is to locate and touch a particular object in the room, and the class has agreed to help you. You cannot use words or ask questions. Begin.'

8. Volunteer 2 continues to look for the object until it is found, while the class assists by giving positive reinforcement.

Class review (Steps 9 and 10)

9. The timekeeper will present the results of how long it took each volunteer to find the object.

10. The class will discuss: What was the difference in behaviour of the two volunteers? What are the implications of this exercise to shaping behaviour in organizations?

Source: Adapted from an exercise developed by Larry Michaelsen of the University of Oklahoma.

Ethical dilemma

DROP THAT WEIGHT OR YOU'RE FIRED!

Can your boss put you on a diet? No, but she can make it worth your while to lose pounds. Half of the 463 companies surveyed in a US report by the National Business Group on Health are using financial rewards to persuade employees to join programmes to improve their health. It saves health-care money and boosts productivity: a 2005 analysis of 42 studies found that such programmes could achieve a 25 to 30 per cent reduction in medical and absenteeism costs within 3.6 years.

Now companies are wondering just how far they can go. Can they require participation? Punish those who don't get optimal results? But it's a slippery slope, says Peter Cappelli, director of the Center for Human Resources at the Wharton

School of Business. There are big legal and ethical issues with pushing employees to change their behaviour. And big costs if they don't.

Source: Based on J. Barrett, Drop that weight or you're fired! (Periscope: workplace) (Brief article) *Newsweek*, 14 April 2008.

Questions

1. Do you think it is right to reward employees for losing weight? Why? Why not?

2. OB Mod is essentially a technique to shape the behaviours' of employees to those that the organization desires. Does that mean it is unethical?

CASE INCIDENT 1

The Flynn Effect

Given that a substantial amount of intellectual ability (up to 80 per cent) is inherited, it might surprise you to learn that intelligence test scores are rising. In fact, scores have risen so dramatically that today's great-grandparents seem mentally deficient by comparison.

First, let's review the evidence for rising test scores. Then, we'll review explanations for the results.

On an IQ scale where 100 is the average, scores have been rising about 3 points per decade, meaning that if your grandparent scored 100, the average score for your generation would be around 115. That's a pretty big difference – about a standard deviation – meaning that someone whose from your grandparent's generation whose score was at the 84th percentile would only be average (50th) percentile by today's norms.

James Flynn is a New Zealand-based researcher credited with first documenting the rising scores. He first reported the results in 1984, when he found that almost everyone who took a well-validated IQ test in the 1970s did better than those who took it in the 1940s.

The results appear to hold up across cultures. Test scores are rising in not only Germany, the Netherlands, Belgium, Britain and the US, but in most other countries in which the effect has also been tested.

What explains the Flynn Effect? Researchers are not entirely sure, but some of the explanations offered are:

1. **Education.** Students today are better educated than their ancestors, and education leads to higher test scores.

2. **Smaller families.** In 1900, the average couple had four children; today the number is less than two. We know

firstborns tend to have higher IQs than other children, probably because they receive more attention than their later-born siblings.

3. **Test-taking know-how.** Today's children are tested so often that they are test savvy: They know how to take tests and how to do well on them.

4. **Genes.** Although smart couples tend to have fewer, not more, children, it's possible that due to better education, tracking and testing, those who do have the right genes are better able to exploit those advantages. Some genetics researchers also have argued that if two people of different intelligence mate, because the gene of the more intelligent mate is stronger, it wins out, meaning the child's IQ will be closer to the IQ of the smarter parent.

Questions

1. Do you believe people are really getting smarter? Why or why not?

2. Which of the factors explaining the Flynn Effect do you agree with?

3. Are there any societal advantages or disadvantages to the Flynn Effect?

Source: F. Greve, 'Rise in average IQ scores makes kids today exceptional by earlier standards,' *Jewish World Review*, 14 February 2006, pp. 1–3; J. R. Flynn (1994) 'IQ gains over time', in R. J. Sternberg (ed.), *Encyclopedia of Human Intelligence* (pp. 617–23). New York: Macmillan; and M. A. Mingroni, 'Resolving the IQ paradox: heterosis as a cause of the Flynn Effect and other trends', *Psychological Review*, July 2007, pp. 806–29.

CASE INCIDENT 2

Professional sports: rewarding and punishing the same behaviour?

Enthusiasts say the Tour de France is the biggest, hardest, most gruelling race there is, a prize so precious that cyclists will do anything to win. And they have. In the past, riders have scattered broken glass and fans have tossed nails on the road to confound rivals. And that's just for starters. In the 1960s, riders attempted to gain a competitive edge with amphetamines and alcohol. In doing so, Britain's Tom Simpson lost his life during the 1967 Tour. Some say cycling faced a near death following the 1998 doping scandal in which French officials caught an employee of the Festina cycling team with a carload of performance-enhancing drugs, including erythropoietin (EPO) – a hormone that helps the blood carry more oxygen, letting you go faster and longer on your two wheels. Following an arrest in the case, six of Festina's nine riders conceded they had used performance-enhancing drugs, including current Crédit Agricole team leader Christophe Moreau. Later that year, he tested positive for anabolic steroids. The drugs controversies continued into the new millennium.

In early 2002, Italy's Stefano Garzelli, leader of the Vini Caldirola team, tested positive for traces of probenecid, a diuretic that can be used to mask other drugs. And Spanish cyclist Igor Gonzalez de Galdeano was banned after a test during the 2002 event found excessive levels of an anti-asthma drug. In January 2004, French police seized male hormones, EPO, amphetamines and arrested two cyclists in the anti-doping investigation involving Cofidis, one of France's top teams and home to three world champions. The 2006 tour was rocked by a drugs scandal before it even started, and the 2007 tour was marred by drugs controversies throughout.

But here's the problem: The same system that punishes those who take performance-enhancing drugs may also reinforce such behaviour. The risk of a ban may not serve as a strong deterrent compared to the fame and fortune of winning. And the rewards of winning are not limited to the riders. Revenues from sales and merchandising are incentives for riders to perform at high levels and for team owners to reward them.

Cycling is not alone in being embroiled in drug controversies. It appears that professional sports may be trying to have their cake and eat it, too. As we have seen, behaviour that may lead individuals and teams to fame and fortune may also be behaviour that demands punishment.

Source: CBC Sports http://www.cbc.ca/sports/indepth/drugs/stories/top10.html#7. Accessed 17 June 2008; http://nbcsports.msnbc.com/id/13559903/. Accessed 17 June 2008; R. Kammerer, 'Documents link Tour winner to doping, says German expert', *The Guardian*, 1 August 2007.

Questions

1. What type of reinforcement schedule does random drug testing represent? Is this type of schedule typically effective or ineffective?

2. What are some examples of behaviours in typical organizations that managers reward but that may actually be detrimental to others or to the organization as a whole? As a manager, what might you do to try to avoid this quandary?

3. If you were the Director of the Tour de France, what steps would you take to try to reduce the use of drugs? Is punishment likely to be the most effective deterrent? Why or why not?

4. Is it ever okay to allow potentially unethical behaviours, which on the surface may benefit organizations, to persist? Why or why not?

Endnotes

1 L. S. Gottfredson, 'The challenge and promise of cognitive career assessment', *Journal of Career Assessment*, 11, 2 (2003), pp. 115–35.

2 M. D. Dunnette, 'Aptitudes, abilities, and skills', in M. D. Dunnette (ed.), *Handbook of Industrial and Organizational Psychology* (Chicago, IL: Rand McNally, 1976), pp. 478–83.

3 J. F. Salgado, N. Anderson, S. Moscoso, C. Bertua, F. de Fruyt and J. P. Rolland, 'A meta-analytic study of general mental ability validity for different occupations in the European Community', *Journal of Applied Psychology*, December 2003, pp. 1068–81; and F. L. Schmidt and J. E. Hunter, 'Select on intelligence', in E. A. Locke (ed.), *Handbook of Principles of Organizational Behavior* (Malden, MA: Blackwell, 2004).

4 *See* M. Frase, 'Smart selections', *HRMagazine*, 52, 12 (2007), pp. 63–67; A. Furnham, J. Crump and T. Chamorro-Premuzic, 'Managerial level, personality and intelligence', *Journal of Managerial Psychology*, 22, 8 (2007), p. 805; CIPD (2006) *Recruitment, Retention and Turnover Survey 2006*. London: CIPD. Available at: http://www.cipd.co.uk/surveys; J. Pickard, 'Testing times', *People Management*, 10, 2 (2004), pp. 43–44.

5 H. Nugent, 'Germans are brainiest (but at least we're smarter than the French)', *The Times*, 27 March 2006.

6 Y. Ganzach, 'Intelligence and job satisfaction', *Academy of Management Journal*, 41, 5 (1998), pp. 526–39; and Y. Ganzach, 'Intelligence, education, and facets of job satisfaction', *Work and Occupations*, 30, 1 (2003), pp. 97–122.

7 E. A. Fleishman, 'Evaluating physical abilities required by jobs', *Personnel Administrator*, June 1979, pp. 82–92.

8 K. Greene, 'Older workers can get a raw deal – some employers admit to promoting, challenging their workers less', *Wall Street Journal*, 10 April 2003, p. D2; and K. A. Wrenn and T. J.

Maurer, 'Beliefs about older workers' learning and development behavior in relation to beliefs about malleability of skills, age-related decline, and control', *Journal of Applied Social Psychology*, 34, 2 (2004), pp. 223–42.

9 D. R. Davies, G. Matthews and C. S. K. Wong, 'Ageing and work', in C. L. Cooper and I. T. Robertson (eds), *International Review of Industrial and Organizational Psychology*, vol. 6 (Chichester: Wiley, 1991), pp. 183–87.

10 R. D. Hackett, 'Age, tenure, and employee absenteeism', *Human Relations*, July 1990, pp. 601–19.

11 Cited in K. Labich, 'The new unemployed', *Fortune*, 8 March 1993, p. 43.

12 See G. M. McEvoy and W. F. Cascio, 'Cumulative evidence of the relationship between employee age and job performance', *Journal of Applied Psychology*, February 1989, pp. 11–17; and F. L. Schmidt and J. E. Hunter, 'The validity and utility of selection methods in personnel psychology: practical and theoretical implications of 85 years of research findings', *Psychological Bulletin*, 124, pp. 262–74.

13 See, for instance, F. J. Landy, *Alternatives to Chronological Age in Determining Standards of Suitability for Public Safety Jobs* (University Park, PA: Center for Applied Behavioral Sciences, Pennsylvania State University, 1992).

14 R. Lee and E. R. Wilbur, 'Age, education, job tenure, salary, job characteristics, and job satisfaction: a multivariate analysis', *Human Relations*, August 1985, pp. 781–91.

15 K. M. Kacmar and G. R. Ferris, 'Theoretical and methodological considerations in the age-job satisfaction relationship', *Journal of Applied Psychology*, April 1989, pp. 201–07; and W. A. Hochwarter, G. R. Ferris, P. L. Perrewe, L. A. Witt and C. Kiewitz, 'A note on the nonlinearity of the age–job satisfaction relationship', *Journal of Applied Social Psychology*, June 2001, pp. 1223–37.

16 See E. M. Weiss, G. Kemmler, E. A. Deisenhammer, W. W. Fleischhacker and M. Delazer, 'Sex differences in cognitive functions', *Personality and Individual Differences*, September 2003, pp. 863–75; and A. F. Jorm, K. J. Anstey, H. Christensen and B. Rodgers, 'Gender differences in cognitive abilities: the mediating role of health state and health habits', *Intelligence*, January 2004, pp. 7–23.

17 See M. M. Black and E. W. Holden, 'The impact of gender on productivity and satisfaction among medical school psychologists', *Journal of Clinical Psychology in Medical Settings*, March 1998, pp. 117–31.

18 S. Shellenbarger, 'More job seekers put family needs first', *Wall Street Journal*, November 15, 1991, p. B1.

19 R. W. Griffeth, P. W. Hom and S. Gaertner, 'A meta-analysis of antecedents and correlates of employee turnover: update, moderator tests, and research implications for the next millennium,' *Journal of Management*, 26, 3 (2000), pp. 463–88.

20 See, for instance, K. D. Scott and E. L. McClellan, 'Gender differences in absenteeism', *Public Personnel Management*, Summer 1990, pp. 229–53; and A. VandenHeuvel and M. Wooden, 'Do explanations of absenteeism differ for men and women?' *Human Relations*, November 1995, pp. 1309–29.

21 L. Lusinyan and L. Bonato, 'Work absence in Europe', *IMF Staff Papers*, 54, 3 (2007), p. 475

22 See, for instance, M. Tait, M. Y. Padgett, and T. T. Baldwin, 'Job and life satisfaction: a reevaluation of the strength of the relationship and gender effects as a function of the date of the study', *Journal of Applied Psychology*, June 1989, pp. 502–07; and M. B. Grover, 'Daddy stress', *Forbes*, 6 September 1999, pp. 202–08.

23 M. Bamshad and S. Olson, 'Does race exist?', *Scientific American Magazine*, November 2003, p. 10

24 P. Riach and J. Rich, 'Field experiments of discrimination in the market place', *Economic Journal*, November 2002, pp. F480–F518.

25 J. M. Sacco, C. R. Scheu, A. M. Ryan and N. Schmitt, 'An investigation of race and sex similarity effects in interviews: a multilevel approach to relational demography', *Journal of Applied Psychology*, 88, 5 (2003), pp. 852–65; and G. N. Powell and D. A. Butterfield, 'Exploring the influence of decision makers' race and gender on actual promotions to top management', *Personnel Psychology*, 55, 2 (2002), pp. 397–428.

26 'Businesses urged to shape up on race', *Equal Opportunities Review*, 90, March–April (2000).

27 National Audit Office, 'Ethnic minority employment gap costs economy £8.6 billion', *Equal Opportunities Review*, 174, March 2008, p. 44.

28 P. Bobko, P. L. Roth and D. Potosky, 'Derivation and implications of a meta-analytic matrix incorporating cognitive ability, alternative predictors, and job performance', *Personnel Psychology*, Autumn 1999, pp. 561–89.

29 M. J. Ree, T. R. Carretta and J. R. Steindl, 'Cognitive ability', in N. Anderson, D. S. Ones, H. K. Sinangil and C. Viweswaran (eds) *Handbook of Industrial, Work, and Organizational Psychology*, Vol. 1 (London: Sage, 2001), pp. 219–32.

30 See J. P. Rushton and A. R. Jenson, 'Thirty years of research on race differences in cognitive ability', *Psychology, Public Policy, and the Law*, 11, 2 (2005), pp. 235–95; and R. E. Nisbett, 'Heredity, environment, and race differences in IQ: a commentary on Rushton and Jensen (2005)', *Psychology, Public Policy, and the Law*, 11, 2 (2005), pp. 302–10.

31 M. A. Quinones, J. K. Ford and M. S. Teachout, 'The relationship between work experience and job performance: a conceptual and meta-analytic review', *Personnel Psychology*, Winter 1995, pp. 887–910.

32 P. Auer, J. Berg and I. Coulibaly, (2005) 'Is a stable workforce good for productivity?', *International Labour Review*, 144, 3 (2005), pp. 319–43.

33 I. R. Gellatly, 'Individual and group determinants of employee absenteeism: test of a causal model', *Journal of Organizational Behavior*, September 1995, pp. 469–85.

34 P. O. Popp and J. A. Belohlav, 'Absenteeism in a low status work environment', *Academy of Management Journal*, September 1982, p. 681.

35 R. W. Griffeth, P. W. Hom and S. Gaertner, 'A meta-analysis of antecedents and correlates of employee turnover.'

36 R. D. Gatewood and H. S. Field, *Human Resource Selection* (Chicago, IL: Dryden Press, 1987).

37 J. A. Breaugh and D. L. Dossett, 'The effectiveness of biodata for predicting turnover', paper presented at the National Academy of Management Conference, New Orleans, August 1987.

38 W. van Breukelen, R. van der Vlist and H. Steensma, 'Voluntary employee turnover: combining variables from the "traditional" turnover literature with the theory of planned behavior', *Journal of Organizational Behavior*, 25, 7 (2004), pp. 893–914.

39 M. Murphy, 'Employers face legal tests over religious beliefs', *Financial Times*, 25 May 2008.

40 *Fourth European Working Conditions Survey*, European Foundation for the Improvement of Living and Working Conditions, 2007. Available at http://www.eurofound.europa.eu; see CIPD, *Race, Religion, and Employment Factsheet, 2007*; and CIPD, Diversity: An Overview. Available at: http://www.cipd.co.uk/subjects/dvsequl/general.

41 See H. M. Weiss, 'Learning theory and industrial and organizational psychology', in M. D. Dunnette and L. M. Hough (eds), *Handbook of Industrial & Organizational Psychology*, 2nd edn, vol. 1 (Palo Alto, CA: Consulting Psychologists Press, 1990), pp. 172–73.

42 W. McGehee, 'Are we using what we know about training? Learning theory and training', *Personnel Psychology*, Spring 1958, p. 2.

43 I. P. Pavlov, *The Work of the Digestive Glands*, trans. W. H. Thompson (London: Charles Griffin, 1902). See also the special issue of *American Psychologist*, September 1997, pp. 933–72, commemorating Pavlov's work.

44 B. F. Skinner, *Contingencies of Reinforcement* (East Norwalk, CT: Appleton-Century-Crofts, 1971).

45 J. A. Mills, *Control: A History of Behavioral Psychology* (New York: New York University Press, 2000).

46 A. Bandura, *Social Learning Theory* (Upper Saddle River, NJ: Prentice Hall, 1977).

47 T. Maurer, K. Wrenn and E. Weiss, 'Toward understanding and managing stereotypical beliefs about older workers' ability and desire for learning and development', *Research in Personnel and Human Resources Management*, 22 (2003), pp. 253–85.

48 J. A. Colquitt, J. A. LePine and R. A. Noe, 'Toward an integrative theory of training motivation: a meta-analytic path analysis of 20 years of research', *Journal of Applied Psychology*, 85, 5 (2000), pp. 678–707.

49 S. Begley, 'The upside of Aging', *New York Times*, 16 February 2007, pp. W1, W4.

50 A. D. Stajkovic and F. Luthans, 'A meta-analysis of the effects of organizational behavior modification on task performance, 1975–95', *Academy of Management Journal*, October 1997, pp. 1122–49.

51 'At Emery Air Freight: positive reinforcement boosts performance', *Organizational Dynamics*, Winter 1973, pp. 41–50.

52 F. Luthans and R. Kreitner, *Organizational Behavior Modification and Beyond: An Operant and Social Learning Approach* (Glenview, IL: Scott, Foresman, 1985); A. D. Stajkovic and F. Luthans, 'A meta-analysis of the effects of organizational behavior modification on task performance, 1975–95'; and A. D. Stajkovic and F. Luthans, 'Behavioral management and task performance in organizations: conceptual background, meta-analysis, and test of alternative models', *Personnel Psychology*, Spring 2003, pp. 155–92.

53 A. D. Stajkovic and F. Luthans, 'A meta-analysis of the effects of organizational behavior modification on task performance', p. 1123.

54 See F. Luthans and A. D. Stajkovic, 'Reinforce for performance: the need to go beyond pay and even rewards', *Academy of Management Executive*, May 1999, pp. 49–57; and A. D. Stajkovic and F. Luthans, 'Differential effects of incentive motivators on work performance', *Academy of Management Journal*, 44, 3 (2001), pp. 580–90.

55 E. A. Locke, 'Beyond determinism and materialism, or isn't it time we took consciousness seriously?' *Journal of Behavior Therapy & Experimental Psychiatry*, 26, 3 (1995), pp. 265–73.

56 N. Barber, 'Educational and ecological correlates of IQ: a cross-national investigation', *Intelligence* (May–June 2005), pp. 273–84.

57 S. Falk, 'The anatomy of the glass ceiling,' *Accenture*, 2006, www.accenture.com.

58 Points in this argument are based on N. Nicholson, 'How hardwired is human behavior?' *Harvard Business Review*, July–August 1998, pp. 135–47; and B. D. Pierce and R. White, 'The evolution of social structure: why biology matters', *Academy of Management Review*, October 1999, pp. 843–53.

Attitudes and job satisfaction

> ### Learning Objectives
>
> *After studying this chapter, you should be able to:*
>
> 1 Contrast the three components of an attitude.
>
> 2 Summarise the relationship between attitudes and behaviour.
>
> 3 Compare and contrast the major job attitudes.
>
> 4 Define *job satisfaction* and show how it can be measured.
>
> 5 Summarise the main causes of job satisfaction.
>
> 6 Identify four employee responses to dissatisfaction.
>
> 7 Show whether job satisfaction is an important concept globally.

For success, attitude is equally important as ability.

Walter Scott

Google: what a place to work!

Eros Hoagland/Redux

One of the side effects of the free food for Google staff is what is known as the 'Google 15' – the number of pounds that employees typically gain after joining the Internet company. But whether it is providing snacks and gourmet meals in the canteen, annual skiing trips or games rooms at the office, the philosophy behind such perks is the same – encouraging staff to meet each other, interact in informal settings and encourage teamwork.

Another way the company does this is to hold competitions in everything from office decorating to dancing and football, with prizes for the winners. Managers also receive a quarterly 'celebratory fund' either to reward accomplishments, or to build teamwork by going bowling, go-carting or dining out. In the Paris office, sales teams end each quarter with some kind of outing, such as an evening of cocktails and dancing or a team dinner at a restaurant.

Google's also aims to make its workplace feel fun. Massage chairs, table tennis tables, video games, lava lamps, hammocks, beanbags, bicycles, large rubber balls, couches and scooters are all part of the furniture.

Flexibility and empowerment are actively encouraged. Employees have a large degree of independence in deciding how to work – both in terms of the hours they work and how they do their jobs.

Google recognises the importance of creating positive employee attitudes and satisfied employees. And the company is good at it. Google consistently ranks as one of the best workplaces in Europe and was number 1 in France, Italy and the UK in 2008. At Google Italy, 100 per cent of staff agreed that 'this is a friendly place to work' and 96 per cent agreed that 'there is a "family" or "team" feeling here'.

One of the most popular office events reflects another of the reasons Google employees rank their workplace as a successful one: giving back. When Larry Brilliant, director of Google.org – the company's philanthropic arm – gave a talk in the London office recently, there was a 95 per cent turn-out at the event. As well as corporate philanthropy activities, the company is also launching a volunteering initiative. 'To individual employees, it's very important,' according to Google manager Nick Creswell, 'And as an organization, it is as well.'

Source: Adapted from S. Murray 'Success can be a game with many players', *Financial Times*, special report, 28 May 2008, p. 7; Great Place to Work Institute http://www.greatplacetowork.co.uk.

Like Google, many other organizations are very concerned with the attitudes of their employees. In this chapter, we look at attitudes, their link to behaviour, and how employees' satisfaction or dissatisfaction with their jobs affects the workplace.

What are your attitudes toward your job? Use the following Self-assessment library to determine your level of satisfaction with your current or past jobs.

SELF-ASSESSMENT LIBRARY

How satisfied am I with my job?

In the Self-assessment library (available online), take assessment I.B.3 (How satisfied am I with my job?) and then answer the following questions. If you currently do not have a job, answer the questions for your most recent job.

1. How does your job satisfaction compare to that of others in your class who have taken the assessment?

2. Why do you think your satisfaction is higher or lower than average?

Attitudes

attitudes
Evaluative statements or judgements concerning objects, people or events.

Attitudes are evaluative statements – either favourable or unfavourable – about objects, people or events. They reflect how we feel about something. When I say 'I like my job', I am expressing my attitude to my work.

Attitudes are complex. If you ask people about their attitude toward religion, their political leaders or the organization they work for, you may get a simple response, but the reasons underlying the response are probably complex. In order to fully understand attitudes, we need to consider their fundamental properties or components.

What are the main components of attitudes?

1 Contrast the three components of an attitude.

Typically, researchers have assumed that attitudes have three components: cognition, affect and behaviour.[1] Let's look at each.

The statement 'my pay is low' is a description. It is the **cognitive component** of an attitude – the aspect of an attitude that is a description of or belief in the way things are. It sets the stage for the more critical part of an attitude – its **affective component**. Affect is the emotional or feeling segment of an attitude and is reflected in the statement 'I am angry over how little I'm paid.' Finally, and we'll discuss this issue at considerable length later in this section, affect can lead to behavioural outcomes. The **behavioural component** of an attitude refers to an intention to behave in a certain way toward someone or something (to continue the example, 'I'm going to look for another job that pays better.').

cognitive component
The opinion or belief segment of an attitude.

affective component
The emotional or feeling segment of an attitude.

behavioural component
An intention to behave in a certain way toward someone or something.

Viewing attitudes as being made up of three components – cognition, affect and behaviour – is helpful in understanding their complexity and the potential relationship between attitudes and behaviour. Keep in mind that these components are closely related, and cognition and affect in particular are inseparable in many ways. For example, imagine you concluded that someone had just treated you unfairly. Aren't you likely to have feelings about that, occurring virtually instantaneously with the thought? Thus, cognition and affect are intertwined.

Figure 3.1 illustrates how the three components of an attitude are related. In this example, an employee didn't get a promotion he thought he deserved; a co-worker got it instead. The employee's attitude toward his supervisor is illustrated as follows: the employee thought he deserved the promotion (cognition), the employee strongly dislikes his supervisor (affect) and the employee is looking for another job (behaviour). As we previously noted, although we often think that cognition causes affect, which then causes behaviour, in reality these components are often difficult to separate.

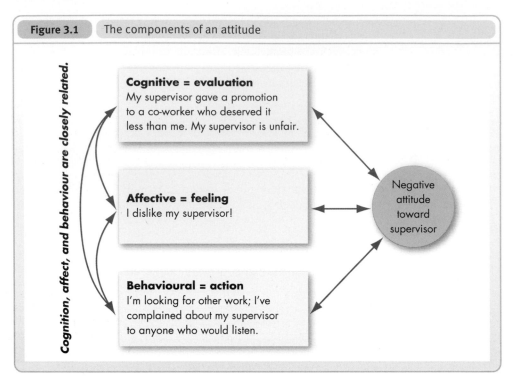

Figure 3.1 The components of an attitude

In organizations, attitudes are important for their behavioural component. If workers believe, for example, that supervisors, auditors and bosses are all in conspiracy to make employees work harder for the same or less money, it makes sense to try to understand how these attitudes formed, their relationship to actual job behaviour, and how they might be changed.

Does behaviour always follow from attitudes?

2 Summarise the relationship between attitudes and behaviour.

Early research on attitudes assumed that they were causally related to behaviour; that is, the attitudes people hold determine what they do. Common sense, too, suggests a relationship. Isn't it logical that people watch television programmes they like, or that employees try to avoid assignments they find distasteful?

However, in the late 1960s, this assumed effect of attitudes on behaviour was challenged by a review of the research.[2] One researcher – Leon Festinger – argued that attitudes *follow* behaviour. Did you ever notice how people change what they say so it doesn't contradict what they do? Perhaps a friend of yours has consistently argued that the quality of French cars isn't up to that of German cars. But his dad gives him a late-model Renault, and suddenly French cars aren't so bad. Festinger argued that these cases of attitude following behaviour illustrate the effects of **cognitive dissonance**.[3] *Cognitive dissonance* refers to any incompatibility an individual might perceive between two or more attitudes or between behaviour and attitudes. Festinger argued that any form of inconsistency is uncomfortable and that individuals will attempt to reduce the dissonance and, hence, the discomfort. They will seek a stable state, in which there is a minimum of dissonance.

cognitive dissonance
Any incompatibility between two or more attitudes or between behaviour and attitudes.

Research has generally concluded that people seek consistency among their attitudes and between their attitudes and their behaviour.[4] They do this by altering either the attitudes or the behaviour or by developing a rationalisation for the discrepancy. Tobacco executives provide an example.[5] How, you might wonder, do these people cope with the ongoing barrage of data linking cigarette smoking and negative health outcomes? They can deny that any clear causation between smoking and cancer, for instance, has been established. They can brainwash themselves by continually articulating the benefits of tobacco. They can acknowledge the negative consequences of smoking but rationalise that people are going to smoke and that tobacco companies merely promote freedom of choice. They can accept the research evidence and begin actively working to make less dangerous cigarettes or at least reduce their availability to more vulnerable groups, such as teenagers. Or they can quit their job because the dissonance is too great.

Reaktor Innovations

Reaktor Innovations is a privately owned software and technology consulting company based in Helsinki that employs around 80 people, the company is highly successful in moulding positive employee attitudes through a strong focus on professional development, empowerment and employee coaching. Employees must be positive about working for Reaktor – only two have left since it started in 2000.

Source: 'Best Workplaces', *Financial Times*, special report, 28 May 2008.

No individual, of course, can completely avoid dissonance. You know that cheating on your income tax is wrong, but you 'fiddle' the numbers a bit every year and hope you're not audited. Or you tell your children to floss their teeth every day, but *you* don't. So how do people cope? Festinger would propose that the desire to reduce dissonance depends on the *importance* of the elements creating it and the degree of *influence* the individual believes he has over the elements; individuals will be more motivated to reduce dissonance when the attitudes or behaviour are important or when they believe that the dissonance is due to something they can control. A third factor is the *rewards* of dissonance; high rewards accompanying high dissonance tend to reduce the tension inherent in the dissonance.

These moderating factors suggest that just individuals who experience dissonance will not necessarily move directly toward reducing it. If the issues underlying the dissonance are of minimal importance, if individuals perceive the dissonance is externally imposed and substantially uncontrollable, or if rewards are significant enough to offset it, an individual will not be under great tension to reduce the dissonance.

While Festinger questioned the attitudes–behaviour relationship by arguing that, in many cases, attitudes follow behaviour, other researchers asked whether there was any relationship at all. More recent research shows that attitudes predict future behaviour and confirmed Festinger's original belief that certain 'moderating variables' can strengthen the link.[6]

Moderating variables

The most powerful moderators of the attitudes–behaviour relationship are the *importance* of the attitude, its *correspondence to behaviour*, its *accessibility*, whether there exist *social pressures*, and whether a person has *direct experience* with the attitude.[7]

Important attitudes reflect fundamental values, self-interest, or identification with individuals or groups that a person values. Attitudes that individuals consider important tend to show a strong relationship to behaviour.

The more closely the attitude and the behaviour are matched or correspond, the stronger the relationship. Specific attitudes tend to predict specific behaviours, whereas general attitudes tend to best predict general behaviours. For instance, asking someone specifically about their intention to stay with an organization for the next six months is likely to better predict turnover for that person than if you asked them how satisfied they were with their job overall. On the other

Michael Porro/Getty Images

The 'Fifteen' restaurants in London, Coventry, Amsterdam and Melbourne, founded by the celebrity chef Jamie Oliver, have strong values. Operated by the Fifteen Foundation, the restaurants exist to inspire disadvantaged young people – homeless, unemployed, overcoming drug or alcohol problems – to believe that they can create for themselves great careers in the restaurant industry. Fifteen is an enterprise where behaviours and attitudes are closely aligned. The attitude is that disadvantaged young people deserve help and the restaurants mission is to achieve this.

Source: http://www.fifteen.net.

hand, overall job satisfaction would better predict a general behaviour such as whether the individual was engaged in their work or motivated to contribute to their organization.[8]

Attitudes we remember easily are more likely to predict our behaviour. Interestingly, you're more likely to remember attitudes you frequently express. So the more you talk about your attitude on a subject, the more you're likely to remember it, and the more likely it is to shape your behaviour.

Discrepancies between attitudes and behaviour are more likely to occur when social pressures to behave in certain ways hold exceptional power. This situation tends to characterise behaviour in organizations. It may explain why an employee who holds strong anti-union attitudes attends pro-union organizing meetings or why tobacco executives, who are not smokers themselves and who tend to believe the research linking smoking and cancer, don't actively discourage others from smoking.

Finally, the attitude–behaviour relationship is likely to be much stronger if an attitude refers to something with which the individual has direct personal experience. Asking university students with no significant work experience how they would respond to working for an authoritarian supervisor is far less likely to predict actual behaviour than asking that same question of employees who have actually worked for such an individual.

What are the major job attitudes?

3 Compare and contrast the major job attitudes.

A person can have thousands of attitudes, but OB focuses our attention on a very limited number of work-related attitudes. These tap positive or negative evaluations that employees hold about aspects of their work environment. Most of the research in OB has looked at three attitudes: job satisfaction, job involvement and organizational commitment.[9] A few other attitudes attracting attention from researchers include perceived organizational support and employee engagement; we'll also briefly discuss these.

job satisfaction
A positive feeling about one's job resulting from an evaluation of its characteristics.

job involvement
The degree to which a person identifies with a job, actively participates in it and considers performance important to self-worth.

psychological empowerment
Employees' belief in the degree to which they affect their work environment, their competence, the meaningfulness of their job and their perceived autonomy in their work.

organizational commitment
The degree to which an employee identifies with a particular organization and its goals and wishes to maintain membership in the organization.

affective commitment
An emotional attachment to an organization and a belief in its values.

Job satisfaction

The term **job satisfaction** describes a positive feeling about a job, resulting from an evaluation of its characteristics. A person with a high level of job satisfaction holds positive feelings about their job, while a dissatisfied person holds negative feelings. When people speak of employee attitudes, they usually mean job satisfaction. In fact, the two are frequently used interchangeably. Because of the high importance OB researchers have given to job satisfaction, we'll review this attitude in detail later in this chapter.

Job involvement

Related to job satisfaction is **job involvement**.[10] Job involvement measures the degree to which people identify psychologically with their job and consider their perceived performance level important to self-worth.[11] Employees with a high level of job involvement strongly identify with and really care about the kind of work they do. Another closely related concept is **psychological empowerment**, which is employees' beliefs in the degree to which they influence their work environment, their competence, the meaningfulness of their job and the perceived autonomy in their work.[12] For example, one study of nursing managers in Singapore found that good leaders empower their employees by involving them in decisions, making them feel their work is important and giving them discretion to 'do their own thing'.[13]

High levels of both job involvement and psychological empowerment are positively related to organizational citizenship and job performance.[14] In addition, high job involvement has been found to be related to a reduced number of absences and lower resignation rates.[15]

Organizational commitment

The third job attitude we'll discuss is **organizational commitment**, a state in which an employee identifies with a particular organization and its goals and wishes to maintain membership in the organization.[16] So, high job involvement means identifying with your specific job, while high organizational commitment means identifying with your employing organization.

There are three separate dimensions to organizational commitment:[17]

1. **Affective commitment.** An **affective commitment** is an emotional attachment to the organization and a belief in its values. For example, an RSPCA employee may be affectively committed to the organization because of its involvement with animals.

2. **Continuance commitment.** A **continuance commitment** is the perceived economic value of remaining with an organization compared to leaving it. An employee may be committed to an employer because they are paid well and feels it would hurt their family to quit.

3. **Normative commitment.** A **normative commitment** is an obligation to remain with the organization for moral or ethical reasons. For example, an employee who is spearheading a new initiative may remain with an employer because they feel they would 'leave the employer in the lurch' if they left.

CHINESE EMPLOYEES AND ORGANIZATIONAL COMMITMENT   GLOBAL

Are employees from different cultures committed to their organizations in similar ways? A 2003 study explored this question and compared the organizational commitment of Chinese employees to that of Canadian and South Korean workers. Although results revealed that the three types of commitment – normative, continuance, and affective – are present in all three cultures, they differ in importance.

Normative commitment, an obligation to remain with an organization for moral or ethical reasons, was higher in the Chinese sample of employees than in the Canadian and South Korean samples. Affective commitment, an emotional attachment to the organization and a belief in its values, was also stronger in China than in Canada and South Korea. Chinese culture may explain why. The Chinese emphasise loyalty to one's group, and in this case, one's 'group' may be the employer, so employees may feel a certain loyalty from the start and become more emotionally attached as their time with the organization grows. To the extent that the Chinese view their organization as part of their group and

▶

become emotionally attached to that group, they will be more committed to their organization. Perhaps as a result of this emphasis on loyalty, the normative commitment of Chinese employees strongly predicted intentions to maintain employment with an organization.

Continuance commitment, the perceived economic value of remaining with an organization compared to leaving it, was lower in the Chinese sample than in the Canadian and South Korean samples. One

reason is that Chinese workers value loyalty toward the group more than individual concerns.

So, although all three countries experience normative, continuance and affective commitment, the degree to which each is important differs across countries.

Source: Based on Y. Cheng and M. S. Stockdale, 'The validity of the three-component model of organizational commitment in a Chinese context', *Journal of Vocational Behavior*, June 2003, pp. 465–89.

---

continuance commitment
The perceived economic value of remaining with an organization compared to leaving it.

normative commitment
An obligation to remain with an organization for moral or ethical reasons.

A positive relationship appears to exist between organizational commitment and job productivity, but it is a modest one.[18] A review of 27 studies suggested that the relationship between commitment and performance is strongest for new employees, and it is considerably weaker for more experienced employees.[19] And, as with job involvement, the research evidence demonstrates negative relationships between organizational commitment and both absenteeism and turnover.[20] In general, affective commitment seems more strongly related to organizational outcomes such as performance and turnover than the other two commitment dimensions. One study found that affective commitment was a significant predictor of various outcomes (perception of task characteristics, career satisfaction, intent to leave) in 72 per cent of the cases, compared to only 36 per cent for normative commitment and 7 per cent for continuance commitment.[21] The weak results for continuance commitment make sense in that it really isn't a strong commitment at all. Rather than an allegiance (affective commitment) or an obligation (normative commitment) to an employer, a continuance commitment describes an employee who is 'tethered' to an employer simply because there isn't anything better available.

There is reason to believe that the concept of commitment may be less important to employers and employees today than it once was. The unwritten loyalty contract that existed 30 years ago between employees and employers has been seriously damaged, and the notion of employees staying with a single organization for most of their career has become increasingly irrelevant. Given that, 'measures of employee–firm attachment, such as commitment, are problematic for new employment relations.'[22] This suggests that *organizational commitment* is probably less important as a work-related attitude than it once was. In its place, we might expect something akin to *occupational commitment* to become a more relevant variable because it better reflects today's fluid workforce.[23]

Perceived organizational support

perceived organizational support (POS)
The degree to which employees believe an organization values their contribution and cares about their well-being.

Perceived organizational support (POS) is the degree to which employees believe the organization values their contribution and cares about their well-being (for example, an employee believes their organization would accommodate them if they had a child-care problem or would forgive an honest mistake on their part). Research shows that people perceive their organization as supportive when rewards are deemed fair, when employees have a voice in decisions, and when their supervisors are seen as supportive.[24] Although less research has linked POS to OB outcomes than is the case with other job attitudes, some findings suggest that employees with strong POS perceptions are more likely to have higher levels of organizational citizenship behaviours and job performance.[25]

Employee engagement

employee engagement
An individual's involvement and satisfaction with, and enthusiasm for, the work he or she does.

A new concept is **employee engagement**, an individual's involvement with, satisfaction with, and enthusiasm for, the work they do. For example, we might ask employees about the availability of resources and the opportunities to learn new skills, whether they feel their work is important and meaningful, and whether their interactions with co-workers and supervisors are rewarding.[26] Highly engaged employees have a passion for their work and feel a deep connection to their company, disengaged employees do not. These workers put time but not energy or attention into their work. Employee engagement has become increasingly important over the past decade as research evidence has emerged to strongly support the concept for organizational success. A recent study of nearly 8,000 business units in 36 companies found that compared to other companies, those whose employees had high-average levels of engagement had higher levels of customer satisfaction, were more productive, had higher profits, and had lower levels of turnover and accidents.[27] Another study of over 664,000 employees from 71 companies around the world found an almost 52 per cent difference in one-year performance improvement in operating income between companies with highly engaged employees as compared to those companies with low engagement scores. Research has also demonstrated that organizations which foster high levels of engagement are more likely to retain high-performing employees.[28] Engagement becomes a real concern for most organizations because surveys indicate that few employees – between 17 per cent and 29 per cent – are highly engaged by their work. Caterpillar set out to increase employee engagement and concluded that its initiative resulted in an 80 per cent drop in grievances and a 34 per cent increase in highly satisfied customers.[29]

Because of some of these promising findings, employee engagement has attracted quite a following in many business organizations and management consulting firms. However, the concept is relatively new, so we have a lot to learn about how engagement relates to other concepts, such as job satisfaction, organizational commitment, job involvement or intrinsic motivation to do one's job well. Engagement may be broad enough that it captures the intersection of these variables. In other words, it may be what these attitudes have in common.

SELF-ASSESSMENT LIBRARY

Am I engaged?

In the Self-assessment library (available online), take assessment IV.B.1 (Am I engaged?). (Note: If you do not currently have a job, answer the questions for your most recent job.)

Are these job attitudes really all that distinct?

You might wonder whether these job attitudes are really distinct. After all, if people feel deeply involved in their job (high job involvement), isn't it probable that they like it (high job satisfaction)? Similarly, won't people who think their organization is supportive (high perceived organizational support) also feel committed to it (strong organizational commitment)? Evidence suggests that these attitudes are highly related, perhaps to a troubling degree. For example, the correlation between perceived organizational support and affective commitment is very strong.[30] The problem is that a strong correlation means the variables may be redundant (so, for example, if you know someone's affective commitment, you basically know their perceived organizational support).

But why is this redundancy so troubling? Why have two steering wheels on a car when you need only one? Why have two concepts – going by different labels – when you need only one? Redundancy is inefficient and confusing. Although we OB researchers like proposing new attitudes, often we haven't been good at showing how they compare and contrast with each other. There is some measure of distinctiveness among these attitudes, but they overlap greatly. The overlap may exist for various reasons, including the employee's personality. Some people are predisposed to be positive or negative about almost everything. If someone tells you they love their company, it may not mean a lot if they are positive about everything else in their life. Or the overlap may mean that some organizations are just all-around better places to work than others. This may mean that if you as a manager know someone's level of job satisfaction, you know most of what you need to know about how the person sees the organization.

JOB SATISFACTION KEY TO HAPPINESS

Job satisfaction is the key to happiness and wellbeing – ranking above family life, health and wealth – according to research by a team of economists at a Scottish university. The researchers at Aberdeen University, in a European-wide study, have also uncovered evidence of a dramatic increase of stress-related illnesses in recent years among employees working in demanding jobs with tight deadlines.

Professor Ioannis Theodossiou, who led the research team at the Centre for European Labour Market Research at the university's business school, said the three-year study had highlighted a number of key findings which demonstrated the link between job satisfaction and an individual's quality of life.

He said the link between working patterns on an employee's quality of life and wellbeing was now of major concern. Prof Theodossiou said:

Employers increasingly demand that their employees have versatile skills, working-time flexibility and a willingness to relocate. It is widely accepted that European workers are becoming more stressed by time constraints and deadlines, and since work is an overwhelmingly important part of most of our lives, the satisfaction we derive from our jobs is a major factor in how happy we are as individuals.

He said the researchers found that satisfaction with the amount of leisure time, with the environment and with housing comes last in the pecking order of happiness and wellbeing. 'Career fulfilment provides workers with the means to maintain life satisfaction, according to our results.'

Source: F. Urquhart 'Job satisfaction secret of happiness,' *The Scotsman* 30 June 2006.

Additional activities designed to change attitudes include arranging for people to do volunteer work in community or social service centres to meet individuals and groups from diverse backgrounds and using exercises that let participants feel what it's like to be different. For example, when people participate in the exercise *Blue Eyes–Brown Eyes*, in which people are segregated and stereotyped according to their eye colour, participants see what it's like to be judged by something over which they have no control. Evidence suggests that this exercise reduces participants' negative attitudes toward individuals who are different from them.[31]

Job satisfaction

We have already discussed job satisfaction briefly. Now let's dissect the concept more carefully. How do we measure job satisfaction? How satisfied are employees in their jobs? What causes an employee to have a high level of job satisfaction? How do dissatisfied and satisfied employees affect an organization?

Measuring job satisfaction

4 Define *job satisfaction* and show how it can be measured.

We've defined job satisfaction as a positive feeling about a job resulting from an evaluation of its characteristics. This definition is clearly a very broad one.[32] Yet breadth is inherent in the concept. Remember, a person's job is more than just the obvious activities of shuffling papers, writing programme code, waiting on customers or driving a lorry. Jobs require interacting with co-workers and bosses, following organizational rules and policies, meeting performance standards, living with working conditions that are often less than ideal and the like.[33] This means that an employee's assessment of how satisfied they are with the job is a complex summation of a number of discrete job elements. How, then, do we measure the concept?

The two most widely used approaches are a single global rating and a summation score made up of a number of job facets. The single global rating method is nothing more than a response to one question, such as 'All things considered, how satisfied are you with your job?' Respondents circle a number between 1 and 5 that corresponds to answers from 'highly satisfied' to 'highly dissatisfied'. The other approach – a summation of job facets – is more sophisticated. It identifies key elements in a job and asks for the employee's feelings about each. Typical elements here are the nature of the work, supervision, present pay, promotion opportunities and relations with co-workers.[34] Respondents rate them on a standardised scale, and researchers add the ratings to create an overall job satisfaction score.

Is one of these approaches superior to the other? Intuitively, summing up responses to a number of job factors seems likely to achieve a more accurate evaluation of job satisfaction. The research, however, doesn't support the intuition.[35] This is one of those rare instances in which simplicity seems to work as well as complexity, and comparisons of the two methods indicate that one is essentially as valid as the other. The best explanation for this outcome is that the concept of job satisfaction is inherently so broad that the single question captures its essence. Another explanation may be that some important facets are left out of the summation of job facets. Both methods are helpful. For example, the single global rating method isn't very time-consuming, which frees managers to address other workplace issues and problems. And the summation of job facets helps managers zero in on where problems exist, making it easier to deal with unhappy employees and solve problems faster and more accurately.

How satisfied are people in their jobs?

Are most people satisfied with their jobs? The answer seems to be a qualified 'yes' across Europe and in most other developed countries. European Commission research asserts that a vast majority of European Union workers are satisfied with their jobs. In Austria, Denmark, France, Ireland and the Netherlands over 90 per cent of workers reported being satisfied with their jobs. Although in Greece, Italy and Spain workers were more dissatisfied (over 20 per cent), the majority were still positive.[36] However, two caveats need to be mentioned. First, there is at least some evidence to suggest that there has been a decline in levels of reported job satisfaction, for example in the UK, Germany and the US.[37]

Second, research shows that satisfaction levels vary a lot, depending on which facet of job satisfaction you're talking about. For example, as shown in Figure 3.2 British workers are, on average, satisfied with their jobs overall, variety in the job, and with their fellow workers. However, they tend to be less satisfied with their pay and with promotion opportunities.[38] It's not really clear why people dislike their pay and promotion possibilities more than other aspects of their jobs.

What causes job satisfaction?

5 Summarise the main causes of job satisfaction.

Think about the best job you've ever had. What made it so? Chances are you probably liked the work you did. In fact, of the major job-satisfaction facets (work itself, pay, advancement opportunities, supervision, co-workers), enjoying the work is almost always the one most strongly correlated with high levels of overall job satisfaction. Interesting jobs that provide training, variety, independence and control satisfy most employees.[39] Jobs involving solving unforeseen problems, performing complex tasks and learning new things have been associated with higher levels of work satisfaction. In other words, most people prefer work that is challenging and stimulating over work that is predictable and routine. A Europe-wide survey demonstrated that education, job security, job autonomy, work/life balance and employee participation are all strongly correlated with increased job satisfaction. Conversely, a clear relation with the level of job satisfaction did not emerge in terms of employment sector, age, gender or marital status. However, other studies demonstrate that these factors may have an influence on job satisfaction at a national level. Which jobs have the highest levels of satisfaction? One study claimed that around 70 per cent of hairdressers record high overall job satisfaction scores, yet only around 25 per cent of bus drivers do so.[40]

You've probably noticed that pay comes up often when people discuss job satisfaction. There is an interesting relationship between salary and job satisfaction. For people who are poor (for example, living below the poverty line) or who live in poor countries, pay does correlate with job satisfaction and with overall happiness. There is some discussion surrounding whether people in low paid jobs are less satisfied than those in high paid jobs, but this does appear to be the case. Interestingly, a study of 14 countries in the EU supported this relationship in all countries apart from the United Kingdom where lower paid workers were more satisfied than higher paid workers. The implication was that British low pay workers may obtain compensating differences

Figure 3.2	British job satisfaction levels by facet

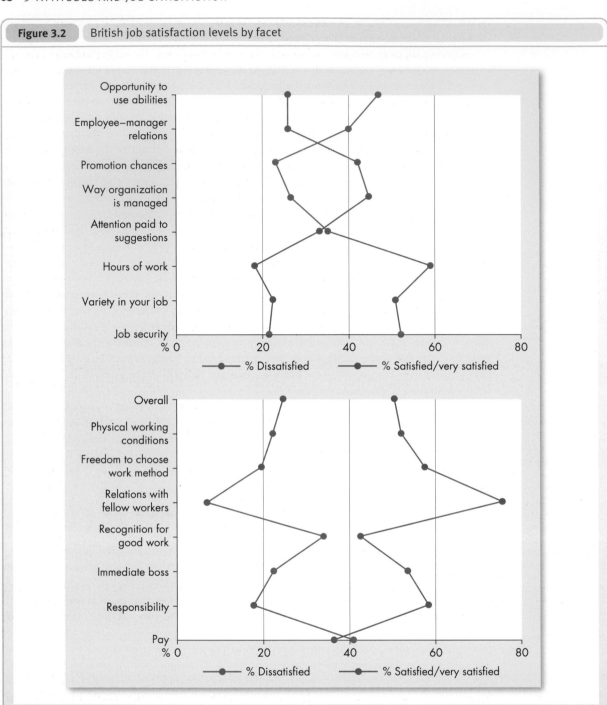

Source: Adapted from CIPD, *How Engaged are British Employees?* (London: CIPD, 2006), Figure 12, Figure 13. With the permission of the publisher, the Chartered Institute of Personnel and Development, London (www.CIPD.co.uk).

in the form of non-monetary benefits.[41] There is also some evidence that the influence of wages on job satisfaction varies across European countries. It appears to be more important in countries where wages are lower.[42]

But, once an individual reaches a level of comfortable living, the relationship virtually disappears. In other words, people who earn €40,000 are, on average, no happier with their jobs than those who earn close to €20,000. Jobs that are compensated handsomely have average job satisfaction levels no higher than those that are paid much less.[43] To further illustrate this point, one researcher even found no significant difference when he compared the overall well-being of the richest people on the Forbes 400 list with that of Maasai herdsmen in East Africa.[44] As we saw in the Google example at the beginning of the chapter, good benefits do appear to satisfy employees, but high pay levels much less so.

Money does motivate people, as we will discover in Chapter 6. But what motivates us is not necessarily the same as what makes us happy. Career changes are becoming more common where workers will exchange a high paying job for a lesser paying job that gives them greater job satisfaction, for example, bankers retraining as teachers, journalists turned gym instructors and TV producers as forest rangers. A senior analyst for an investment fund who quit to become an acupuncturist commented that, 'I had a job that paid me very well, good friends, paid back my student loan, wasn't working long hours, had pretty nice colleagues, but I got to the point where I never wanted to get up to go to work, so I thought something needed to change, and work seemed to be the obvious thing to change'.[45] Maybe your goal isn't to be happy. But if it is, money's probably not going to do much to get you there.[46]

Job satisfaction is not just about job conditions. Personality also plays a role. People who are less positive about themselves are less likely to like their jobs. Research has shown that people who have positive **core self-evaluations** – who believe in their inner worth and basic competence – are more satisfied with their jobs than those with negative core self-evaluations. Not only do they see their work as more fulfilling and challenging, they are more likely to gravitate toward challenging jobs in the first place. Those with negative core self-evaluations set less ambitious goals and are more likely to give up when confronting difficulties. Thus, they're more likely to be stuck in boring, repetitive jobs than those with positive core self-evaluations.[47]

> **core self-evaluations**
> Bottom-line conclusions individuals have about their capabilities, competence and worth as a person.

'HAPPY WORKERS ARE PRODUCTIVE WORKERS'　　MYTH *OR* SCIENCE?

This statement is generally true. The idea that 'happy workers are productive workers' developed in the 1930s and 1940s, largely as a result of findings drawn by researchers conducting the Hawthorne studies at Western Electric. Based on those conclusions, managers worked to make their employees happier by focusing on working conditions and the work environment. Then, in the 1980s, an influential review of the research suggested that the relationship between job satisfaction and job performance was not particularly high. The authors of that review even went so far as to label the relationship as 'illusory'.[48]

More recently, a review of more than 300 studies corrected some errors in that earlier review. It estimated that the correlation between job satisfaction and job performance is moderately strong. This conclusion also appears to be generalisable across international contexts. The correlation is higher for complex jobs that provide employees with more discretion to act on their attitudes.[49]

The reverse causality might be true: Productive workers are likely to be happy workers, or productivity might lead to satisfaction.[50] In other words, if you do a good job, you intrinsically feel good about it. In addition, your higher productivity should increase your recognition, your pay level and your likelihood of promotion. Cumulatively, these rewards, in turn, increase your level of satisfaction with the job.

Both arguments are probably right: Satisfaction can lead to high levels of performance for some people, while for others, high performance is satisfying.

The impact of satisfied and dissatisfied employees on the workplace

> 6 Identify four employee responses to dissatisfaction.

There are consequences when employees like their jobs and when they dislike their jobs. One theoretical model – the exit–voice–loyalty–neglect framework – is helpful in understanding the consequences of dissatisfaction. Figure 3.3 illustrates the framework's four responses, which differ from one another along two dimensions: constructive/destructive and active/passive. The responses are defined as follows:[51]

> **exit**
> Dissatisfaction expressed through behaviour directed toward leaving the organization.

- **Exit.** The **exit** response involves directing behaviour toward leaving the organization, including looking for a new position as well as resigning.
- **Voice.** The **voice** response involves actively and constructively attempting to improve conditions, including suggesting improvements, discussing problems with superiors and undertaking some forms of union activity.
- **Loyalty.** The **loyalty** response involves passively but optimistically waiting for conditions to improve, including speaking up for the organization in the face of external criticism and trusting the organization and its management to 'do the right thing'.

| Figure 3.3 | Responses to job satisfaction |

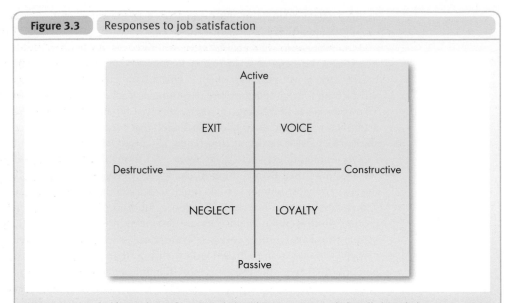

Source: Reprinted with permission from C. Rusbult and D. Lowery, *Journal of Applied Psychology*, 15, 1, 2006 p. 83.

voice
Dissatisfaction expressed through active and constructive attempts to improve conditions.

loyalty
Dissatisfaction expressed by passively waiting for conditions to improve.

neglect
Dissatisfaction expressed through allowing conditions to worsen.

- **Neglect.** The **neglect** response involves passively allowing conditions to worsen, including chronic absenteeism or lateness, reduced effort and increased error rate.

Exit and neglect behaviours encompass our performance variables – productivity, absenteeism, and turnover. But this model expands employee response to include voice and loyalty – constructive behaviours that allow individuals to tolerate unpleasant situations or to revive satisfactory working conditions. It helps us to understand situations, such as those sometimes found among unionised workers, for whom low job satisfaction is coupled with low turnover.[52] Union members often express dissatisfaction through the grievance procedure or through formal contract negotiations. These voice mechanisms allow them to continue in their jobs while convincing themselves that they are acting to improve the situation.

As helpful as this framework is in presenting the possible consequences of job dissatisfaction, it's quite general. We now discuss more specific outcomes of job satisfaction and dissatisfaction in the workplace.

Job satisfaction and job performance

As the 'Myth or Science?' box concludes, happy workers are more likely to be productive workers, although it's hard to tell which way the causality runs. Some researchers used to believe that the relationship between job satisfaction and job performance was a management myth. But a review of 300 studies suggested that the correlation is pretty strong.[53] As we move from the individual level to that of the organization, we also find support for the satisfaction–performance relationship.[54] When satisfaction and productivity data are gathered for the organization as a whole, we find that organizations with more satisfied employees tend to be more effective than organizations with fewer satisfied employees.

Job satisfaction and OCB

It seems logical to assume that job satisfaction should be a major determinant of an employee's organizational citizenship behaviour (OCB).[55] Satisfied employees would seem more likely to talk positively about the organization, help others, and go beyond the normal expectations in their job. Moreover, satisfied employees might be more prone to go beyond the call of duty because they want to reciprocate their positive experiences. Consistent with this thinking, evidence suggests that job satisfaction is moderately correlated with OCBs, such that people who are more satisfied with their jobs are more likely to engage in OCBs.[56] More recent evidence suggests that satisfaction influences OCB through perceptions of fairness.

Why do those satisfied with their jobs contribute more OCBs? Research indicates that fairness perceptions explain the relationship, at least in part.[57] What does this mean? Basically, job satisfaction comes down to conceptions of fair outcomes, treatment, and procedures.[58] If you don't feel that your supervisor, the organization's procedures, or pay policies are fair, your job satisfaction is likely to suffer significantly. However, when you perceive organizational processes and outcomes to be fair, trust develops. And when you trust your employer, you're more willing to voluntarily engage in behaviours that go beyond your formal job requirements.

Job satisfaction and customer satisfaction

As we noted in Chapter 1, employees in service jobs often interact with customers. Since the management of service organizations should be concerned with pleasing those customers, it is reasonable to ask: Is employee satisfaction related to positive customer outcomes? For frontline employees who have regular contact with customers, the answer is 'yes'.

The evidence indicates that satisfied employees increase customer satisfaction and loyalty.[59] Why? In service organizations, customer retention and defection are highly dependent on how frontline employees deal with customers. Satisfied employees are more likely to be friendly, upbeat and responsive – which customers appreciate. And because satisfied employees are less prone to turnover, customers are more likely to encounter familiar faces and receive experienced service. These qualities build customer satisfaction and loyalty. The relationship also seems to apply in reverse: Dissatisfied customers can increase an employee's job dissatisfaction. Employees who have regular contact with customers report that rude, thoughtless or unreasonably demanding customers adversely affect the employees' job satisfaction.[60]

A number of companies are acting on this evidence. Businesses such as Virgin Atlantic, Enterprise Rent-A-Car, Ritz-Carlton Hotels, Lexus and John Lewis fixate on pleasing their customers. Toward that end, they also focus on building employee satisfaction – recognising that employee satisfaction will go a long way toward contributing to their goal of having happy customers. These firms seek to hire upbeat and friendly employees, train employees in the

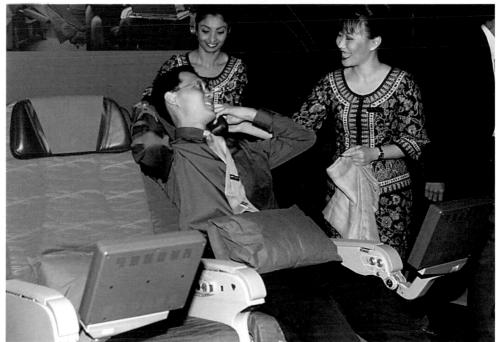

AFP/Getty Images

Service organizations know that satisfied and loyal customers depend on how front-line employees deal with customers. Singapore Airlines has earned a reputation among world travellers for outstanding customer service. The airline's 'putting people first' philosophy applies to both its employees and customers. In recruiting flight attendants, the airline selects people who are warm, hospitable and happy to serve others. Through extensive training, Singapore shapes recruits into attendants focused on complete customer satisfaction.

importance of customer service, reward customer service, provide positive employee work climates and regularly track employee satisfaction through attitude surveys.

Job satisfaction and absenteeism

We find a consistent negative relationship between satisfaction and absenteeism, but the correlation is moderate to weak.[61] While it certainly makes sense that dissatisfied employees are more likely to miss work, other factors have an impact on the relationship and reduce the correlation coefficient. For example, organizations that provide liberal sick leave benefits are encouraging all their employees – including those who are highly satisfied – to take days off. Assuming that you have a reasonable number of varied interests, you can find work satisfying and yet still want to take off to enjoy a 3-day weekend or relax on a warm summer day if those days come free with no penalties.

An excellent illustration of how satisfaction directly leads to attendance, when there is minimal impact from other factors, is a study done at Sears, Roebuck the fourth largest American retailer.[62] Sears had a policy of not permitting employees to be absent from work for avoidable reasons without penalty. The occurrence of a freak 2 April snowstorm in Chicago created the opportunity to compare employee attendance at the Chicago office with attendance in New York, where the weather was quite nice. (Satisfaction data were available on employees at both locations.) The storm crippled Chicago's transportation system and individuals knew they could miss work this day with no penalty. If satisfaction leads to attendance when there are no outside factors, the more satisfied employees should have come to work in Chicago, while dissatisfied employees should have stayed home. The study found that on this particular 2 April, absenteeism rates in New York were just as high for satisfied groups of workers as for dissatisfied groups. But in Chicago, the workers with high satisfaction scores did indeed have much higher attendance than did those with lower satisfaction levels, exactly what we would have expected if satisfaction is negatively correlated with absenteeism.

Job satisfaction and turnover

Satisfaction is also negatively related to turnover, but the correlation is stronger than what we found for absenteeism.[63] Yet, again, other factors, such as labour-market conditions, expectations about alternative job opportunities and length of tenure with the organization, are important constraints on an employee's decision to leave their current job.[64]

Evidence indicates that an important moderator of the satisfaction–turnover relationship is the employee's level of performance.[65] Specifically, level of satisfaction is less important in predicting turnover for superior performers. Why? The organization typically makes considerable efforts to keep these people. They get pay raises, praise, recognition, increased promotional opportunities and so forth. Just the opposite tends to apply to poor performers. The organization makes few attempts to retain them. There may even be subtle pressures to encourage them to quit. We would expect, therefore, that job satisfaction is more important in influencing poor performers to stay than in influencing superior performers to stay. Regardless of level of satisfaction, the latter are more likely to remain with the organization because the receipt of recognition, praise and other rewards gives them more reasons to do so.

Job satisfaction and workplace deviance

Job dissatisfaction predicts a lot of specific behaviours, including substance abuse, stealing at work, undue socialising and tardiness. Researchers argue that these behaviours are indicators of a broader syndrome that we would term *deviant behaviour in the workplace* (or *employee withdrawal*).[66] The key is that if employees don't like their work environment, they'll respond somehow. It is not always easy to forecast exactly *how* they'll respond. One worker's response might be to quit. Another might take work time to surf the Internet, take work supplies home for personal use and so on. In short, evidence indicates that workers who don't like their jobs 'get even' in various ways – and because employees can be quite creative in the ways they do that, controlling one behaviour, such as having an absence control policy, leaves the root cause untouched. If employers want to control the undesirable consequences of job dissatisfaction, they should attack the source of the problem – the dissatisfaction – rather than try to control the different responses.

Managers often 'don't get it'

Given the evidence we've just reviewed, it should come as no surprise that job satisfaction can affect the bottom line. One study by a management consulting firm separated large organizations into high morale (where more than 70 per cent of employees expressed overall job satisfaction) and medium or low morale (where fewer than 70 per cent did so). The share prices of companies in the high morale group grew 19.4 per cent, compared to 10 per cent for the medium or low morale group. Despite these results, many managers are unconcerned about job satisfaction of their employees. Still others overestimate the degree to which their employees are satisfied with their jobs, so they don't think there's a problem when there is. One study of 262 large employers found that 86 per cent of senior managers believed their organization treated its employees well, but only 55 per cent of the employees agreed. Another study found 55 per cent of managers thought morale was good in their organization, compared to only 38 per cent of employees.[67] Managers first need to care about job satisfaction, and then they need to measure it, rather than just assume that everything is going well.

FACE THE FACTS

- According to one study, the highest average levels of job satisfaction in Europe were observed in Denmark (95 per cent), Ireland (94 per cent) and the Netherlands (88 per cent). The lowest average job satisfaction was reported by workers in the southern European countries of Portugal (80 per cent), Spain (77 per cent) and Greece (69 per cent).

- Companies with strong reputations as 'great places to work' attract more applicants than other companies. In 2007, SAP Germany received 340,000 job applications, equivalent to 43 applications per staff member, and Google in France received more than 23,000 applications. With only 125 people, that is 184 per employee.

- A recent survey ranked the five best large workplaces in Europe as Microsoft, Google, Cisco, 3M and Impuls Finanzmanagement.

Sources: T. K. Bauer, *High Performance Workplace Practices and Job Satisfaction. Evidence from Europe*, Discussion Paper No. 1265, Institute for the Study of Labour (IZA), 2004. Available at: http://ftp.iza.org/dp1265.pdf; 'Best workplaces', *Financial Times*, special report, 28 May 2008.

Global implications

7 Show whether job satisfaction is an important concept globally.

Most of the research on job satisfaction has been conducted in the United States and to a lesser extent western Europe. So, we might ask: Is job satisfaction a Western concept? The evidence strongly suggests that this is *not* the case; people in other cultures can and do form judgements of job satisfaction. Moreover, it appears that similar factors cause, and result from, job satisfaction across cultures. For example, we noted earlier that pay is positively, but relatively weakly, related to job satisfaction. This relationship appears to hold in all industrialised nations.

Although job satisfaction appears to be a relevant concept across cultures, that doesn't mean there are no cultural differences in job satisfaction. Evidence suggests that employees in Western cultures have higher levels of job satisfaction than those in Eastern cultures.[68] Is the reason that employees in Western cultures have better jobs? Or are individuals in Western cultures simply more positive (and less self-critical)? Although both factors are probably at play, evidence suggests that individuals in Eastern cultures value negative emotions more than do individuals in Western cultures, whereas those in Western cultures tend to emphasise positive emotions and individual happiness.[69] That may be why employees in Western cultures are more likely to have higher levels of satisfaction.

Summary and implications for managers

Managers should be interested in their employees' attitudes because attitudes give warnings of potential problems and because they influence behaviour. Satisfied and committed employees, for instance, have lower rates of turnover, absenteeism and withdrawal behaviours. They also perform better on the job. Given that managers want to keep resignations and absences down – especially among their most productive employees – they'll want to do things that generate positive job attitudes. As one review put it, 'A sound measurement of overall job attitude is one of the most useful pieces of information an organization can have about its employees.'[70]

The most important thing managers can do to raise employee satisfaction is focus on the intrinsic parts of the job, such as making the work challenging and interesting. Although paying employees poorly will likely not attract high-quality employees to the organization, or keep high performers, managers should realise that high pay alone is unlikely to create a satisfying work environment. Creating a satisfied workforce is hardly a guarantee of successful organizational performance, but evidence strongly suggests that whatever managers can do to improve employee attitudes will likely result in heightened organizational effectiveness.

POINT/COUNTERPOINT

Managers can create satisfied employees

POINT ➡

A review of the evidence has identified four factors conducive to high levels of employee job satisfaction: Mentally challenging work, equitable rewards, supportive working conditions and supportive colleagues.[71] Management is able to control each of these factors:

Mentally challenging work. Generally, people prefer jobs that give them opportunities to use their skills and abilities and offer a variety of tasks, freedom and feedback on how well they're doing. These characteristics make work mentally challenging.

Equitable rewards. Employees want pay systems that they perceive as just, unambiguous and in line with their expectations. When pay is seen as fair – based on job demands, individual skill level and community pay standards – satisfaction is likely to result.

Supportive working conditions. Employees want their work environment both to be safe and personally comfortable and to facilitate their doing a good job. In addition, most prefer working relatively close to home, in clean and relatively modern facilities, with adequate tools and equipment.

Supportive colleagues. People get more out of work than merely money and other tangible achievements. For most employees, work also fulfils the need for social interaction. Not surprisingly, therefore, having friendly and supportive co-workers leads to increased job satisfaction. The boss's behaviour is also a major determinant of satisfaction. Studies find that employee satisfaction is increased when the immediate supervisor is understanding and friendly, offers praise for good performance, listens to employees' opinions and shows a personal interest in employees.

COUNTERPOINT ⬅

The notion that managers and organizations can control the level of employee job satisfaction is inherently attractive. It fits nicely with the view that managers directly influence organizational processes and outcomes. Unfortunately, a growing body of evidence challenges the notion that managers control the factors that influence employee job satisfaction. The most recent findings indicate that it is largely genetically determined.[72]

Whether a person is happy or not is essentially determined by gene structure. Approximately 50 to 80 per cent of people's differences in happiness, or subjective well-being, has been found to be attributable to their genes. Identical twins, for example, tend to have very similar careers, report similar levels of job satisfaction and change jobs at similar rates.

Analysis of satisfaction data for a selected sample of individuals over a 50-year period found that individual results were stable over time, even when the subjects changed employers and occupations. This and other research suggests that an individual's disposition toward life – positive or negative – is established by genetic makeup, holds over time and carries over into a disposition toward work.

Given these findings, there is probably little most managers can do to influence employee satisfaction. Despite the fact that managers and organizations go to extensive lengths to try to improve employee job satisfaction by manipulating job characteristics, working conditions and rewards, people will inevitably return to their own 'set point'. A bonus may temporarily increase the satisfaction level of a negatively disposed worker, but it is unlikely to sustain it. Sooner or later, a dissatisfied worker will find new areas of fault with the job.

The only place managers will have any significant influence is in the selection process. If managers want satisfied workers, they need to screen out negative people who derive little satisfaction from their jobs, irrespective of work conditions.

QUESTIONS FOR REVIEW

1. What are the main components of attitudes? Are these components related or unrelated?

2. Does behaviour always follow from attitudes? Why or why not? Discuss the factors that affect whether behaviour follows from attitudes.

3. What are the major job attitudes? In what ways are these attitudes alike? What is unique about each?

4. How do we measure job satisfaction?

5. What causes job satisfaction? For most people, is pay or the work itself more important?

6. What outcomes does job satisfaction influence? What implications does this have for management?

7. Does job satisfaction appear to vary by country?

Experiential exercise

WHAT FACTORS ARE MOST IMPORTANT TO YOUR JOB SATISFACTION?

Most of us probably want a job we think will satisfy us. But because no job is perfect, we often have to trade off job attributes. One job may pay well but provide limited opportunities for advancement or skill development. Another may offer work we enjoy but have poor benefits. The following is a list of 21 job factors or attributes:

- Autonomy and independence
- Benefits
- Career advancement opportunities
- Career development opportunities
- Compensation/pay
- Communication between employees and management
- Contribution of work to organization's business goals
- Feeling safe in the work environment
- Flexibility to balance life and work issues
- Job security
- Job-specific training

- Management recognition of employee job performance
- Meaningfulness of job
- Networking
- Opportunities to use skills/abilities
- Organization's commitment to professional development
- Overall corporate culture
- Relationship with co-workers
- Relationship with immediate supervisor
- The work itself
- The variety of work

On a sheet of paper, rank-order these job factors from top to bottom, so that number 1 is the job factor you think is most important to your job satisfaction, number 2 is the second most important factor to your job satisfaction and so on.

Now gather in teams of three or four people and try the following:

1. Appoint a spokesperson who will take notes and report the answers to the following questions, on behalf of your group, back to the class.
2. Averaging across all members in your group, generate a list of the top five job factors.

3. Did most people in your group seem to value the same job factors? Why or why not?
4. Your instructor will provide you with the results of a study of a random sample of 600 employees conducted by the Society for Human Resource Management (SHRM). How do your group's rankings compare to the SHRM results?
5. The chapter says that pay doesn't correlate all that well with job satisfaction, but in the SHRM survey, people say it is relatively important. Can your group suggest a reason for the apparent discrepancy?
6. Now examine your own list again. Does your list agree with the group list? Does your list agree with the SHRM study?

Ethical dilemma

THE INSPECTOR'S DILEMMA

A newly promoted inspector of police is appointed to a post in a British urban police station. The inspector is a graduate and subscribes wholeheartedly to the police force's adoption of 'Fair treatment and equal opportunities for all'. In the new job, the inspector has the management of a shift of 10 constables and two sergeants. Both the latter are older than the inspector and have been police officers for longer. About half the con-

stables have served for longer, but the other five include two probationer-constables. Each of these probationer-constables is being mentored by a long-serving constable. Shifts work closely together. There is a culture of mutual support.

The bulk of the area's older inhabitants are migrants from the Indian sub-continent or from the Caribbean, though the younger people are likely to have been born in the UK. All the officers in the station are white. The inspector notices that dismissive, derogatory remarks about ethnic groups are part of the common currency of the station. The superintendent in charge of the station is within five years of retirement and is proud of being 'of the old school'.

Questions

1. What factors do you think may have caused these attitudes towards migrants to have developed?

2. Do you think these attitudes may affect the officers behaviour? What factors may moderate this?

3. Do you think age is a factor in the development of these attitudes?

4. Suggest methods that the inspector can use to help change the attitudes of the officers.

Source: Open University. Available at the *Institute of Business Ethics*, http://www.ibe.org.uk/teaching/The%20Inspectordilemma.pdf.

CASE INCIDENT 1

Money isn't everything in life

Changing attitudes towards salaries and job satisfaction

Working lives and labour markets may have changed radically over the past quarter century, but some values remain the same. The modern worker might not express it in quite the same terms, but he or she would be sure to recognise the aspiration implicit in the old trade union demand for 'a fair day's pay for a fair day's work'. This is not, it should be noted, the same as wanting the highest possible day's pay. Very few workers conform to the maximise-at-all costs model of classical economic theory, least of all in countries where markets are run in closest conformity to those theories.

When Monster, the employment and careers website, polled users in 2008 as to whether they would 'take a pay cut for the job of [their] dreams', they received more than 34,000 responses from 18 countries in Europe and North America. The sample is by definition self-selecting rather than scientific – Monster reckons its identikit user is 34 years old, has 13 years' work experience and earns €40,000 annually – but since 87 per cent of their users are seeking new employment, it is a fair assumption that such questions are uppermost in their minds. 'Dream job' is also a matter of definition. Nevertheless it was intriguing to note that the vast majority of respondents (76 per cent) said 'yes'. There were variations across the sample, however, with 84 per cent in Ireland responding 'yes' and Switzerland, Italy and the US close behind at 82 per cent. Whereas workers in Germany (73 per cent), France (66 per cent) and Hungary (62 per cent) were the most cautious.

Andrea Bertone, co-head of Monster Europe, says: 'The countries where the "yes" score was highest were those with very flexible labour markets and low unemployment rates [at the time of the survey], where people are willing to take more risks in order to go for a new opportunity.' He would expect to see higher scores in future: 'Over the next nine years we will see the baby boomers reaching retirement age and the workforce will then be dominated by Generations X and Y, who look at work less as a life focus than as a life enriching experience.'

These insights are reflected in Sir George Bain's comment when he moved from heading the London Business School to become vice chancellor of Queen's University, Belfast, taking a pay cut of around a quarter. Sir George said then: 'I have always taken the view that you are a fool if you change jobs or refuse them, purely on the grounds

of money. But I'm well aware that attitude is a middle-class luxury. My father could not possibly have taken a substantial pay cut or given up one job with no certainty of another.'

Palle Ellemann, managing director of Great Place to Work (GPTW) Institute Europe, suggests that the emphasis on money is greatest in the first two years of an appointment: 'After that, other things about the job matter more.' Nor are winners in the GPTW Europe awards necessarily the highest payers. Artti Aurasmaa, chief executive of Finland's 3 Step IT, reckons its basic rates 'would not be above average rates. In some cases they may be below.' Guido Wallraff, human resources manager for Cisco Germany, says his company's pay rates may be slightly above average, because it benchmarks against comparable employers. What they share is a philosophy emphasising fairness, transparency and rewarding good work.

Each also acknowledges wider influences – Mr Wallraff at Cisco Germany says that much of its practice echoes that elsewhere in Cisco and that Germany's system of works councils encourages fairness and openness. Meanwhile Mr Aurasmaa has his own theory for Finnish traditions: 'Where it is cold, people had to make sure they looked after each other in order to survive, and that has remained part of our culture.' Mr Wallraff suggests: 'We don't have much in the way of fixed assets. Our main asset is our people and their ideas, so we have to look after them.'

Questions

1. Do you think you would take a pay cut for your dream job? Why? Why not?

2. What other factors are important to you?

3. Pay doesn't seem to be a major reason for the satisfaction of workers at 3 Step IT and Cisco, what other factors might be important to workers in these companies?

4. How generalisable is the relationship between job satisfaction and productivity?

Source: Adapted from H. Richards, 'Money isn't everything in life', in 'Best workplaces', *Financial Times, 28 May 2008*; 15 May 2008, Monster poll reports majority of workers worldwide willing to take a pay cut for their 'dream job'. Available at http://www.about-monster.com/content/monster-poll-reports-majority-workers-worldwide-willing-take-pay-cut-their-dream-job. Accessed 11 July 2009.

CASE INCIDENT 2

Extreme jobs

You've probably heard of extreme sports; snowboarding, freestyle skiing, skydiving. Activities that attract admiration, demand the ultimate in endurance, deliver an adrenaline rush. Well, make way for 'extreme jobs', a similar phenomenon taking place in offices across the globe.

The word was first coined in 2002 by a senior banker in London who worked a 70-hour week with frequent travel requirements across time zones, and constant pressure on performance. Rather than resent her hours in the office, however, she felt as exhilarated by it, as if she were bungee jumping, or mountaineering. 'Work hard, play hard' is an awful cliché. Yet lots of people in the financial industry use it as a great accolade. Add on ambitious professionals in the media, medicine, law and consulting, and you will gather that a lot of people are holding down extreme jobs.

Sylvia Ann Hewlett, a professor at Columbia University, New York, spent a year 'mapping' the world of extreme workers, with two surveys of high-earning professionals, one in large multinational corporations in Europe, India and China and another in the US.

She defines an extreme job as a job that entails at least 60 hours a week and at least five of the following characteristics:

- Physical presence at the office at least 10 hours a day
- Tight deadlines and a fast pace
- Unpredictable flow of work
- Inordinate scope of responsibility
- Large amount of travel

- After-hours work events
- 24/7 availability to clients
- Responsibility for profit and loss
- Responsibility for mentoring and recruiting

What does a 60-hour week mean? With an hour-long commute each way, it means leaving the house at 7am and returning at 9pm, five days a week.

She concludes that extreme jobs are dangerously alluring. 'We didn't find it unexpected that jobs have become more intense. The surprise was that people love their jobs to death. They really do feel fulfilled by them'. And yet, she says, extreme jobs come at a price, '. . . the fallout is wreaking havoc in private lives'. Relationships with partners and children are suffering, and particularly women are leaving extreme jobs in droves.

Questions

1. Do you think only certain individuals are attracted to these types of jobs, or is it the characteristics of the jobs themselves that are satisfying?

2. What characteristics of these jobs might contribute to increased levels of job satisfaction?

3. Would you be satisfied in an extreme job? Why or why not? Would it depend on the stage of your career and/or personal life?

4. How might extreme jobs relate to job performance, citizenship behaviour, customer satisfaction and turnover?

Source: Adapted from R. Millard, 'Drawing back from extreme jobs', 3 December 2006, *The Sunday Times*. © The Sunday Times 3 December 2006 nisyndication.com

Endnotes

1 S. J. Breckler, 'Empirical validation of affect, behavior, and cognition as distinct components of attitude', *Journal of Personality and Social Psychology*, May 1984, pp. 1191–205; and S. L. Crites, Jr., L. R. Fabrigar and R. E. Petty, 'Measuring the affective and cognitive properties of attitudes: conceptual and methodological issues', *Personality and Social Psychology Bulletin*, December 1994, pp. 619–34.

2 A. W. Wicker, 'Attitude versus action: The relationship of verbal and overt behavioral responses to attitude objects', *Journal of Social Issues*, Autumn 1969, pp. 41–78.

3 L. Festinger, *A Theory of Cognitive Dissonance* (Stanford, CA: Stanford University Press, 1957).

4 See, for instance, I. R. Newby-Clark, I. McGregor and M. P. Zanna, 'Thinking and caring about cognitive consistency: when and for whom does attitudinal ambivalence feel uncomfortable?', *Journal of Personality & Social Psychology*, February 2002, pp. 157–66; and D. J. Schleicher, J. D. Watt and G. J. Greguras, 'Reexamining the job satisfaction-performance

relationship: the complexity of attitudes', *Journal of Applied Psychology*, 89, 1 (2004), pp. 165–77.

5 See, for instance, J. Nocera, 'If it's good for Philip Morris, can it also be good for public health?' *New York Times*, 18 June 2006 (www.nytimes.com).

6 See L. R. Glasman and D. Albarracín, 'Forming attitudes that predict future behavior: a meta-analysis of the attitude–behavior relation', *Psychological Bulletin*, September 2006, pp. 778–822.; I. Ajzen, 'The directive influence of attitudes on behavior', in M. Gollwitzer and J. A. Bargh (eds), *The Psychology of Action: Linking Cognition and Motivation to Behavior* (New York: Guilford, 1996), pp. 385–403; and I. Ajzen, 'Nature and operation of attitudes', in S. T. Fiske, D. L. Schacter and C. Zahn-Waxler (eds), *Annual Review of Psychology*, vol. 52 (Palo Alto, CA: Annual Reviews, Inc., 2001), pp. 27–58.

7 Ibid.

8 D. A. Harrison, D. A. Newman and P. L. Roth, 'How important are job attitudes? Meta-analytic comparisons of

integrative behavioral outcomes and time sequences', *Academy of Management Journal* 49, 2 (2006), pp. 305–25.

9 P. P. Brooke, Jr., D. W. Russell and J. L. Price, 'Discriminant validation of measures of job satisfaction, job involvement, and organizational commitment', *Journal of Applied Psychology*, May 1988, pp. 139–45; and R. T. Keller, 'Job involvement and organizational commitment as longitudinal predictors of job performance: A study of scientists and engineers', *Journal of Applied Psychology*, August 1997, pp. 539–45.

10 See, for example, S. Rabinowitz and D. T. Hall, 'Organizational research in job involvement', *Psychological Bulletin*, March 1977, pp. 265–88; G. J. Blau, 'A multiple study investigation of the dimensionality of job involvement', *Journal of Vocational Behavior*, August 1985, pp. 19–36; C. L. Reeve and C. S. Smith, 'Refining Lodahl and Kejner's job involvement scale with a convergent evidence approach: applying multiple methods to multiple samples', *Organizational Research Methods*, April 2000, pp. 91–111; and J. M. Diefendorff, D. J. Brown and A. M. Kamin, 'Examining the roles of job involvement and work centrality in predicting organizational citizenship behaviors and job performance', *Journal of Organizational Behavior*, February 2002, pp. 93–108.

11 Based on G. J. Blau and K. R. Boal, 'Conceptualizing how job involvement and organizational commitment affect turnover and absenteeism', *Academy of Management Review*, April 1987, p. 290.

12 K. W. Thomas and B. A. Velthouse, 'Cognitive elements of empowerment: an "interpretive" model of intrinsic task motivation,' *Academy of Management Review*, 15, 4 (1990), pp. 666–81; G. M. Spreitzer, 'Psychological empowerment in the workplace: dimensions, measurement, and validation', *Academy of Management Journal*, 38, 5 (1995), pp. 1442–65; G. Chen and R. J. Klimoski, 'The impact of expectations on newcomer performance in teams as mediated by work characteristics, social exchanges, and empowerment', *Academy of Management Journal*, 46, 5 (2003), pp. 591–607; A. Ergeneli, G. Saglam and S. Metin, 'Psychological empowerment and its relationship to trust in immediate managers', *Journal of Business Research*, January 2007, pp. 41–49; and S. E. Seibert, S. R. Silver and W. A. Randolph, 'Taking empowerment to the next level: a multiple-level model of empowerment, performance, and satisfaction', *Academy of Management Journal*, 47, 3 (2004), pp. 332–49.

13 B. J. Avolio, W. Zhu, W. Koh and P. Bhatia, 'Transformational leadership and organizational commitment: mediating role of psychological empowerment and moderating role of structural distance', *Journal of Organizational Behavior*, 25, 8, 2004, pp. 951–68.

14 J. M. Diefendorff, D. J. Brown, A. M. Kamin and R. G. Lord, 'Examining the roles of job involvement and work centrality in predicting organizational citizenship behaviors and job performance,' *Journal of Organizational Behavior*, February 2002, pp. 93–108.

15 G. J. Blau, 'Job involvement and organizational commitment as interactive predictors of tardiness and absenteeism', *Journal of Management*, Winter 1986, pp. 577–84; K. Boal and R. Cidambi, 'Attitudinal correlates of turnover and absenteeism: A meta analysis', paper presented at the meeting of the American Psychological Association, Toronto, Canada, 1984; and M. R. Barrick, M. K. Mount and J. P. Strauss, 'Antecedents of involuntary turnover due to a reduction in force,' *Personnel Psychology*, 47, 3 (1994), pp. 515–35.

16 Blau and Boal, 'Conceptualizing,' p. 290.

17 J. P. Meyer, N. J. Allen and C. A. Smith, 'Commitment to organizations and occupations: extension and test of a three-component conceptualization', *Journal of Applied Psychology*, 78, 4 (1993), pp. 538–51.

18 M. Riketta, 'Attitudinal organizational commitment and job performance: a meta-analysis', *Journal of Organizational Behavior*, March 2002, pp. 257–66.

19 T. A. Wright and D. G. Bonett, 'The moderating effects of employee tenure on the relation between organizational commitment and job performance: a meta-analysis', *Journal of Applied Psychology*, December 2002, pp. 1183–90.

20 See, for instance, W. Hom, R. Katerberg and C. L. Hulin, 'Comparative examination of three approaches to the prediction of turnover', *Journal of Applied Psychology*, June 1979, pp. 280–90; H. Angle and J. Perry, 'Organizational commitment: individual and organizational influence', *Work and Occupations*, May 1983, pp. 123–46; J. L. Pierce and R. B. Dunham, 'Organizational commitment: pre-employment propensity and initial work experiences', *Journal of Management*, Spring 1987, pp. 163–78; and T. Simons and Q. Roberson, 'Why managers should care about fairness: the effects of aggregate justice perceptions on organizational outcomes', *Journal of Applied Psychology*, 88, 3 (2003), pp. 432–43.

21 R. B. Dunham, J. A. Grube and M. B. Castañeda, 'Organizational commitment: the utility of an integrative definition', *Journal of Applied Psychology*, 79, 3 (1994), pp. 370–80.

22 D. M. Rousseau, 'Organizational behavior in the new organizational era', in J. T. Spence, J. M. Darley and D. J. Foss (eds), *Annual Review of Psychology*, vol. 48 (Palo Alto, CA: Annual Reviews, 1997), p. 523.

23 Ibid.; K. Lee, J. J. Carswell and N. J. Allen, 'A meta-analytic review of occupational commitment: relations with person- and work-related variables', *Journal of Applied Psychology*, October 2000, pp. 799–811; G. Blau, 'On assessing the construct validity of two multidimensional constructs: occupational commitment and occupational entrenchment', *Human Resource Management Review*, Fall 2001, pp. 279–98; and E. Snape and T. Redman, 'An evaluation of a three-component model of occupational commitment: dimensionality and consequences among United Kingdom human resource management specialists', *Journal of Applied Psychology*, 88, 1 (2003), pp. 152–59.

24 L. Rhoades, R. Eisenberger and S. Armeli, 'Affective commitment to the organization: the contribution of perceived organizational support', *Journal of Applied Psychology*, 86, 5 (2001), pp. 825–36.

25 Z. X. Chen, S. Aryee and C. Lee, 'Test of a mediation model of perceived organizational support', *Journal of Vocational Behavior*, June 2005, pp. 457–70; and J. A. M. Coyle-Shapiro and N. Conway, 'Exchange relationships: examining psychological contracts and perceived organizational support', *Journal of Applied Psychology*, July 2005, pp. 774–81.

26 D. R. May, R. L. Gilson and L. M. Harter, 'The psychological conditions of meaningfulness, safety and availability and the engagement of the human spirit at work', *Journal of Occupational and Organizational Psychology*, 77, 1 (2004), pp. 11–37.

27 J. K. Harter, F. L. Schmidt and T. L. Hayes, 'Business-unit-level relationship between employee satisfaction, employee engagement, and business outcomes: a meta-analysis', *Journal of Applied Psychology*, 87, 2 (2002), pp. 268–79.

28 See V. Furness 'Employee management: engagement defined', *Employee Benefits*, (London: Centaur Media, 2008), p. 56; Chartered Institute of Personnel and Development's (CIPD), *How Engaged are British Employees?*, November 2006; 'Engaged employees help boost the bottom line: ISR study reveals that employers with an engaged workforce deliver improved financial results', Washington DC, *SHRM conference*, 27 June 2006 www.isrinsight.com.

29 N. R. Lockwood, *Leveraging Employee Engagement for Competitive Advantage* (Alexandria, VA: Society for Human Resource Management, 2007); and R. J. Vance, *Employee Engagement and Commitment* (Alexandria, VA: Society for Human Resource Management, 2006).

30 L. Rhoades and R. Eisenberger, 'Perceived organizational support: a review of the literature', *Journal of Applied Psychology*, 87, 4 (2002), pp. 698–714; and R. L. Payne and D. Morrison, 'The differential effects of negative affectivity on measures of well-being versus job satisfaction and organizational commitment', *Anxiety, Stress & Coping: An International Journal*, 15, 3 (2002), pp. 231–44.

31 T. L. Stewart, J. R. LaDuke, C. Bracht, B. A. M. Sweet and K. E. Gamarel, 'Do the "Eyes" have it? A program evaluation of Jane Elliott's "Blue-eyes/brown-eyes" diversity training exercise', *Journal of Applied Social Psychology*, 33, 9 (2003), pp. 1898–921.

32 For problems with the concept of job satisfaction, see R. Hodson, 'Workplace behaviors', *Work and Occupations*, August 1991, pp. 271–90; and H. M. Weiss and R. Cropanzano, 'Affective events theory: a theoretical discussion of the structure, causes and consequences of affective experiences at work', in B. M. Staw and L. L. Cummings (eds), *Research in Organizational Behavior*, vol. 18 (Greenwich, CT: JAI Press, 1996), pp. 1–3.

33 The Wyatt Company's 1989 national WorkAmerica study identified 12 dimensions of satisfaction: work organization, working conditions, communications, job performance and performance review, co-workers, supervision, company management, pay, benefits, career development and training, job content and satisfaction, and company image and change.

34 See E. Spector, *Job Satisfaction: Application, Assessment, Causes, and Consequences* (Thousand Oaks, CA: Sage, 1997), p. 3.

35 J. Wanous, A. E. Reichers and M. J. Hudy, 'Overall job satisfaction: how good are single-item measures?', *Journal of Applied Psychology*, April 1997, pp. 247–52.

36 European Commission, *Employment in Europe 2003: Recent Trends and Prospects*, Luxembourg, Office for Official Publications of the European Communities, 2003. Available at: http://europa.eu.int/comm/employment_social/news/2003/oct/eie2003_en.pdf.

37 See: *Measuring Job Satisfaction in Surveys – Comparative Analytical Report*, European Foundation for the Improvement of Living and Working Conditions, 2007; and F. Green and N. Tsitsianis, 'An investigation of national trends in job satisfaction in Britain and Germany', *British Journal of Industrial Relations*, 43, 3 (September 2005), pp. 410–29; 'US Job Satisfaction Declines', *USA Today*, 9 April 2007, p. 1B.

38 Chartered Institute of Personnel and Development (CIPD) *How Engaged are British Employees?*, published in November 2006.

39 J. Barling, E. K. Kelloway and R. D. Iverson, 'High-quality work, job satisfaction, and occupational injuries', *Journal of Applied Psychology*, 88, 2 (2003), pp. 276–83; F. W. Bond and D. Bunce, 'The role of acceptance and job control in mental health, job satisfaction, and work performance', *Journal of Applied Psychology*, 88, 6 (2003), pp. 1057–67.

40 See Fourth European Working Conditions Survey, *European Foundation for the Improvement of Living and Working Conditions*, 2007; Measuring job satisfaction in surveys – Comparative analytical report European Foundation for the Improvement of Living and Working Conditions, 2007; M. Rose, (2003) 'Good deal, bad deal? Job satisfaction in occupations', *Work Employment Society*, 17, pp. 503–30; and N. Ahn and J. Garcia (2004) Job Satisfaction in Europe. FEDEA working paper series 2004–16. Available at http://www.fedea.es/pub/Papers/2004/dt2004–16.pdf.

41 J. Vieira and L. Diaz-Serrano (2005) 'Low pay, higher pay and job satisfaction within the European Union: empirical evidence from fourteen countries', *Discussion Paper No. 1558*. Institute for the Study of Labor. Available at ftp://repec.iza.org/RePEc/Discussion paper/dp1558.pdf.

42 S. Gazioglu and A. Tanselb 'Job satisfaction in Britain: individual and job related factors', *Applied Economics*, 38 (2006), pp. 1163–71; M. Rose (2003) Good deal, bad deal? Job satisfaction in occupations, *Work Employment Society*, 17, pp. 503–30.

43 See, for example, T. A. Judge, R. F. Piccolo, N. P. Podsakoff, J. C. Shaw and B. L. Rich, 'Can happiness be "earned"?: The relationship between pay and job satisfaction', working paper, University of Florida, 2005.

44 E. Diener, E. Sandvik, L. Seidlitz and M. Diener, 'The relationship between income and subjective well-being: relative or absolute?', *Social Indicators Research*, 28 (1993), pp. 195–223.

45 See careershifters.org http://www.careershifters.org/node/513, accessed 19 June 2008.

46 E. Diener and M. E. P. Seligman, 'Beyond money: toward an economy of well-being', *Psychological Science in the Public Interest*, 5, 1 (2004), pp. 1–31; and A. Grant, 'Money=happiness? That's rich: here's the science behind the axiom', *The (South Mississippi) Sun Herald*, 8 January 2005.

47 T. A. Judge and C. Hurst, 'The benefits and possible costs of positive core self-evaluations: a review and agenda for future research', in D. Nelson and C. L. Cooper (eds), *Positive Organizational Behaviour* (London, UK: Sage Publications, 2007), pp. 159–74.

48 M. T. Iaffaldano and M. Muchinsky, 'Job satisfaction and job performance: a meta-analysis', *Psychological Bulletin*, March 1985, pp. 251–73.

49 T. A. Judge, C. J. Thoresen, J. E. Bono and G. K. Patton, 'The job satisfaction–job performance relationship: a qualitative and quantitative review', *Psychological Bulletin*, May 2001, pp. 376–407; T. Judge, S. Parker, A. E. Colbert, D. Heller and R. Ilies, 'Job satisfaction: a cross-cultural review', in N. Anderson, D. S. Ones, H. K. Sinangil and C. Viswesvaran (eds), *Handbook of Industrial, Work, & Organizational Psychology*, vol. 2 (Thousand Oaks, CA: Sage, 2001), p. 11.

50 C. N. Greene, 'The satisfaction–performance controversy', *Business Horizons*, February 1972, pp. 31–41; E. E. Lawler, III, *Motivation in Organizations* (Monterey, CA: Brooks/Cole, 1973); and M. M. Petty, G. W. McGee and J. W. Cavender, 'A meta-analysis of the relationship between individual job satisfaction and individual performance', *Academy of Management Review*, October 1984, pp. 712–21.

51 See D. Farrell, 'Exit, voice, loyalty, and neglect as responses to job dissatisfaction: a multidimensional scaling study', *Academy of Management Journal*, December 1983, pp. 596–606; C. E. Rusbult, D. Farrell, G. Rogers and A. G. Mainous, III, 'Impact of exchange variables on exit, voice, loyalty, and neglect: an integrative model of responses to declining job satisfaction', *Academy of Management Journal*, September 1988, pp. 599–627; M. J. Withey and W. H. Cooper, 'Predicting exit, voice, loyalty, and neglect', *Administrative Science Quarterly*, December 1989, pp. 521–39; J. Zhou and J. M. George, 'When job dissatisfaction leads to creativity: encouraging the expression of voice', *Academy of Management Journal*, August 2001, pp. 682–96; J. B. Olson-Buchanan and W. R. Boswell, 'The role of employee loyalty and formality in voicing discontent', *Journal of Applied Psychology*, December 2002, pp. 1167–74; and A. Davis-Blake, J. P. Broschak and E. George, 'Happy together? How using nonstandard workers affects exit, voice, and loyalty among standard employees', *Academy of Management Journal*, 46, 4 (2003), pp. 475–85.

52 R. B. Freeman, 'Job satisfaction as an economic variable', *American Economic Review*, January 1978, pp. 135–41.

53 T. A. Judge, C. J. Thoresen, J. E. Bono and G. K. Patton, 'The job satisfaction–job performance relationship: a qualitative and quantitative review', *Psychological Bulletin*, May 2001, pp. 376–407.

54 C. Ostroff, 'The relationship between satisfaction, attitudes, and performance: an organizational level analysis', *Journal of Applied Psychology*, December 1992, pp. 963–74; A. M. Ryan, M. J. Schmit and R. Johnson, 'Attitudes and effectiveness: examining relations at an organizational level', *Personnel Psychology*, Winter 1996, pp. 853–82; and J. K. Harter, F. L. Schmidt and T. L. Hayes, 'Business-unit level relationship between employee satisfaction, employee engagement, and business outcomes: a meta-analysis', *Journal of Applied Psychology*, April 2002, pp. 268–79.

55 See T. S. Bateman and D. W. Organ, 'Job satisfaction and the good soldier: the relationship between affect and employee "citizenship",' *Academy of Management Journal*, December 1983, pp. 587–95; P. Podsakoff, S. B. MacKenzie, J. B. Paine and D. G. Bachrach, 'Organizational citizenship behaviors: a critical review of the theoretical and empirical literature and suggestions for future research', *Journal of Management*, 26, 3 (2000), pp. 513–63.

56 B. J. Hoffman, C. A. Blair, J. P. Maeriac and D. J. Woehr, 'Expanding the criterion domain? A quantitative review of the OCB literature', *Journal of Applied Psychology*, 92, 2, 2007, pp. 555–66; D. W. Organ and K. Ryan, 'A meta-analytic review of attitudinal and dispositional predictors of organizational citizenship behavior', *Personnel Psychology*, Winter 1995, pp. 775–802; and J. A. LePine, A. Erez and D. E. Johnson, 'The nature and dimensionality of organizational citizenship behavior: a critical review and meta-analysis', *Journal of Applied Psychology*, February 2002, pp. 52–65.

57 J. Fahr, P. M. Podsakoff and D. W. Organ, 'Accounting for organizational citizenship behavior: leader fairness and task scope versus satisfaction', *Journal of Management*, December 1990, pp. 705–22; R. H. Moorman, 'Relationship between organization justice and organizational citizenship behaviors: do fairness perceptions influence employee citizenship?', *Journal of Applied Psychology*, December 1991, pp. 845–55; and M. A. Konovsky and D. W. Organ, 'Dispositional and contextual determinants of organizational citizenship behavior', *Journal of Organizational Behavior*, May 1996, pp. 253–66.

58 D. W. Organ, 'Personality and organizational citizenship behavior', *Journal of Management*, Summer 1994, p. 466.

59 See, for instance, B. Schneider and D. E. Bowen, 'Employee and customer perceptions of service in banks: replication and extension', *Journal of Applied Psychology*, August 1985, pp. 423–33; D. J. Koys, 'The effects of employee satisfaction, organizational citizenship behavior, and turnover on organizational effectiveness: a unit-level, longitudinal study', *Personnel Psychology*, Spring 2001, pp. 101–14; and J. Griffith, 'Do satisfied employees satisfy customers? support-services staff morale and satisfaction among public school administrators, students, and parents', *Journal of Applied Social Psychology*, August 2001, pp. 1627–58.

60 M. J. Bitner, B. H. Booms and L. A. Mohr, 'Critical service encounters: the employee's viewpoint', *Journal of Marketing*, October 1994, pp. 95–106.

61 E. A. Locke, 'The nature and causes of job satisfaction', in M. D. Dunnette (ed.), *Handbook of Industrial and Organizational Psychology* (Chicago, IL: Rand McNally, 1976), p. 1331; R. D. Hackett and R. M. Guion, 'A reevaluation of the absenteeism–job satisfaction relationship', *Organizational Behavior and Human Decision Processes*, June 1985, pp. 340–81; K. D. Scott and G. S. Taylor, 'An examination of conflicting findings on the relationship between job satisfaction and absenteeism: a meta-analysis', *Academy of Management Journal*, September 1985, pp. 599–612; R. Steel and J. R. Rentsch, 'Influence of cumulation strategies on the long-range prediction of absenteeism', *Academy of Management Journal*, December 1995, pp. 1616–34; and Johns, 'The psychology of lateness, absenteeism, and turnover', p. 237.

62 F. J. Smith, 'Work attitudes as predictors of attendance on a specific day', *Journal of Applied Psychology*, February 1977, pp. 16–19.

63 W. Hom and R. W. Griffeth, *Employee Turnover* (Cincinnati, OH: South-Western Publishing, 1995); R. W. Griffeth, P. W. Hom and S. Gaertner, 'A meta-analysis of antecedents and correlates of employee turnover: update, moderator tests, and research implications for the next millennium', *Journal of Management*, 26, 3 (2000), p. 479; Johns, 'The psychology of lateness, absenteeism, and turnover', p. 237; Hom and Griffeth, *Employee Turnover*; R. W. Griffeth, P. W. Hom and S. Gaertner, 'A meta-analysis of antecedents and correlates of employee turnover: update, moderator tests, and research implications for the next millennium', *Journal of Management*, 26, 3 (2000), p. 479; and G. Johns, 'The psychology of lateness, absenteeism, and turnover', p. 237.

64 See, for example, C. L. Hulin, M. Roznowski and D. Hachiya, 'Alternative opportunities and withdrawal decisions: empirical and theoretical discrepancies and an integration', *Psychological Bulletin*, July 1985, pp. 233–50; and J. M. Carsten and P. E. Spector, 'Unemployment, job satisfaction, and employee turnover: a meta-analytic test of the Muchinsky Model', *Journal of Applied Psychology*, August 1987, pp. 374–81.

65 D. G. Spencer and R. M. Steers, 'Performance as a moderator of the job satisfaction–turnover relationship', *Journal of Applied Psychology*, August 1981, pp. 511–14.

66 K. A. Hanisch, C. L. Hulin and M. Roznowski, 'The importance of individuals' repertoires of behaviors: the scientific appropriateness of studying multiple behaviors and general attitudes', *Journal of Organizational Behavior*, 19, 5 (1998), pp. 463–80.

67 K. Holland, 'Inside the minds of your employees', *New York Times* (28 January 2007), p. B1; 'Study sees link between morale and stock price', *Workforce Management* (27 February 2006), p. 15; and 'The workplace as a solar system', *New York Times* (28 October 2006), p. B5.

68 M. J. Gelfand, M. Erez and Z. Aycan, 'Cross-cultural organizational behavior', *Annual Review of Psychology* 58, 2007, pp. 479–514; A. S. Tsui, S. S. Nifadkar and A. Y. Ou, 'Cross-national, cross-cultural organizational behavior research: advances, gaps, and recommendations', *Journal of Management*, June 2007, pp. 426–78.

69 M. Benz and B. S. Frey, 'The value of autonomy: evidence from the self-employed in 23 countries', Working paper 173, Institute for Empirical Research in Economics, University of Zurich, November 2003. (http://ssrn.com/abstract=475140); and P. Warr, *Work, Happiness, and Unhappiness* (Mahwah, NJ: Laurence Erlbaum, 2007).

70 D. A. Harrison, D. A. Newman and P. L. Roth, 'How important are job attitudes? Meta-analytic comparisons of integrative behavioral outcomes and time sequences', *Academy of Management Journal*, 49, 2 (2006), pp. 305–26.

71 Judge, *et al.*, 'Job satisfaction: a cross-cultural review'; T. A. Judge and A. H. Church, 'Job satisfaction: research and practice', in C. L. Cooper and E. A. Locke (eds), *Industrial and Organizational Psychology: Linking Theory with Practice* (Oxford, UK: Blackwell, 2000), pp. 166–198; L. Saari and T. A. Judge, 'Employee attitudes and job satisfaction', *Human Resource Management*, 43, 4 (2004), pp. 395–407.

72 See, for instance, R. D. Arvey, B. McCall, T. J. Bouchard, Jr. and P. Taubman, 'Genetic influences on job satisfaction and work values', *Personality and Individual Differences*, July 1994, pp. 21–33; D. Lykken and A. Tellegen, 'Happiness is a stochastic phenomenon', *Psychological Science*, May 1996, pp. 186–89; and D. Lykken and M. Csikszentmihalyi, 'Happiness – stuck with what you've got?' *Psychologist*, September 2001, pp. 470–72; and 'double take,' *UNH Magazine*, Spring 2000 (www.unhmagazine.unh.edu/sp00/twinssp00.html).

Personality and values

> ### Learning Objectives
>
> *After studying this chapter, you should be able to*:
>
> 1 Define *personality*, describe how it is measured and explain the factors that determine an individual's personality.
>
> 2 Describe the Myers-Briggs Type Indicator personality framework and assess its strengths and weaknesses.
>
> 3 Identify the key traits in the Big Five personality model.
>
> 4 Demonstrate how the Big Five traits predict behaviour at work.
>
> 5 Identify other personality traits relevant to OB.
>
> 6 Define *values*, demonstrate the importance of values and contrast terminal and instrumental values.
>
> 7 Identify the dominant values in today's workforce.
>
> 8 Identify Hofstede's five value dimensions of national culture.

Without commonly shared and widely entrenched moral values and obligations, neither the law, nor democratic government, nor even the market economy will function properly.

Vaclav Havel, writer and former president of the Czech Republic

You're fired!

Getty Images

Surely Sir Alan Sugar's Mr Angry turn on the UK version of the *Apprentice* television show is an act. In reality, as with many celebrities, he will be different from his primetime persona, searing *Apprentice* contestants over a high heat, then eliminating one after a firestorm of abusive language with a finger jab and 'You're fired', or is he?

Interviews with *The Times* newspaper give an indication of Sugar's personality and whether he is as rude in business as he appears on screen. 'What you see on screen is me, there's no question of that,' Sir Alan says. 'But it is the side of me the BBC chooses to show. There is more light-hearted banter, which hits the cutting-room floor because it doesn't put bums on seats. It's a one-way portrayal, not the whole of me.'

Sugar grew up in working-class Hackney in London, sold vegetables to greengrocers, then sold car radio aerials and electrical goods, and set up his first company at 21. Home computing and electricals made him very rich. His company, Amstrad, was sold in 2007 to BSkyB for nearly €150 million. With his interests now focused on construction, property and aviation, his personal wealth is valued at around €950 million.

If he's not Mr Angry, who is he? 'You've got to be able to laugh at yourself, at disaster, in the business world. It keeps you sane. I'm sarcastic when things go wrong, that's what you don't see. But it's right to show me angry . . .' The voice rises again.

Sir Alan is one of a group of business chiefs who advised Prime Minister Gordon Brown on enterprise, and is proud to be 'the rough diamond, the streetwise member of the mob'. Sugar has also dabbled in football when he became chairman of Tottenham Hotspur in 1991. It was not a winning combination. He described his decade at the helm, during which the club got through five managers, as 'a waste of my time' and condemned football players generally as 'total scum', most of whom would be in prison were it not for the sport.

Andy Hasoon, CEO of Fifty Lessons, a digital media company, claims 'Sir Alan Sugar is stuck in the dark ages of management practice when it was seen as OK to shout at people and humiliate them.'

But, as Sir Alan is so fond of saying, 'I am what I am.'

Source: *The Times*, 26 March 2008 'Sir Alan Sugar: talking tough', *The Times*, 27 April 2008; 'The Rich List: Alan Sugar', *The Times*, 20 April 2006 'Sir Alan Sugar's style is outdated'.

Our personalities shape our behaviours. So if we want to better understand the behaviour of someone in an organization, it helps if we know something about their personality. In the first half of this chapter, we review the research on personality and its relationship to behaviour. In the latter half, we look at how values shape many of our work-related behaviours.

One of the personality traits we'll discuss is narcissism. Like many other CEOs and celebrities, Sir Alan Sugar might be described as relatively narcissistic. Check out the Self-assessment library to see how you score on narcissism (remember: be honest!).

SELF-ASSESSMENT LIBRARY

Am I a narcissist?

In the Self-assessment library (available online), take assessment IV.A.1 (Am I a narcissist?) and answer the following questions.

1. How did you score? Did your scores surprise you? Why or why not?
2. On which facet of narcissism was your highest score? Your lowest?
3. Do you think this measure is accurate? Why or why not?

Personality

Why are some people quiet and passive, while others are loud and aggressive? Are certain personality types better adapted than others for certain job types? Before we can answer these questions, we need to address a more basic one: What is personality?

What is personality?

1 Define *personality*, describe how it is measured and explain the factors that determine an individual's personality.

When we talk of personality, we don't mean that a person has charm, a positive attitude toward life or a smiling face. When psychologists talk of personality, they mean a dynamic concept describing the growth and development of a person's whole psychological system. Rather than looking at parts of the person, personality looks at some aggregate whole that is greater than the sum of the parts.

Defining Personality

personality
The sum total of ways in which an individual reacts and interacts with others.

The definition of *personality* we most frequently use was produced by Gordon Allport nearly 70 years ago. He said personality is 'the dynamic organization within the individual of those psychophysical systems that determine his unique adjustments to his environment.'[1] For our purposes, you should think of **personality** as the sum total of ways in which an individual reacts to and interacts with others. We most often describe it in terms of the measurable traits a person exhibits.

Measuring personality

The most important reason managers need to know how to measure personality is that research has shown that personality tests are useful in hiring decisions. Scores on personality tests help managers forecast who is the best bet for a job.[2] And some managers want to know how people score on personality tests to better understand and more effectively manage the people who work for them. By far the most common means of measuring personality is through self-report surveys, with which individuals evaluate themselves by rating themselves on a series of factors such as 'I worry a lot about the future.' Though self-report measures work well when well constructed, one weakness of these measures is that the respondent might lie or practise impression management – that is, the person could fake answers on the test to create a good impression. This is especially a concern when the survey is the basis for employment. Another problem is accuracy. In other words, a perfectly good candidate could have just been in a bad mood when the survey was taken.

Observer-ratings surveys provide an independent assessment of personality. Instead of self-reporting, a co-worker or another observer does the rating (sometimes with the subject's knowledge and sometimes not). Even though the results of self-report surveys and observer-ratings surveys are strongly correlated, research suggests that observer-ratings surveys are a better predictor of success on the job.[3] However, each can tell us something unique about an individual's behaviour in the workplace.

Personality determinants

An early debate in personality research centred on whether an individual's personality was the result of heredity or of environment. Was the personality predetermined at birth, or was it the result of the individual's interaction with their surroundings? Clearly, there's no simple black-and-white answer. Personality appears to be a result of both hereditary and environmental factors. However, it might surprise you that research in personality development has tended to better support the importance of heredity over the environment.

Heredity refers to factors determined at conception. Physical stature, facial attractiveness, gender, temperament, muscle composition and reflexes, energy levels and biological rhythms are generally considered to be either completely or substantially influenced by who your parents are – that is, by their biological, physiological and inherent psychological makeup. The heredity approach argues that the ultimate explanation of an individual's personality is the molecular structure of the genes, located in the chromosomes.

Studies of young children lend strong support to the power of heredity.[4] Evidence demonstrates that traits such as shyness, fear and aggression can be traced to inherited genetic characteristics. This finding suggests that some personality traits may be built into the same genetic code that affects factors such as height and hair colour.

Researchers in many different countries have studied thousands of sets of identical twins who were separated at birth and raised separately.[5] If heredity played little or no part in determining personality, you would expect to find few similarities between the separated twins. But the researchers found a lot in common. For almost every behavioural trait, a significant part of the variation between the twins turned out to be associated with genetic factors. For instance, one set of twins who had been separated for 39 years and raised 70 kilometres apart were found to drive the same model and colour car. They chain-smoked the same brand of cigarette, owned dogs with the same name, and regularly holidayed within a few kilometres of each other in a beach community 2,500 kilometres away. Researchers have found that genetics accounts for about 50 per cent of the personality differences and more than 30 per cent of the variation in occupational and leisure interests.

Interestingly, the twin studies have suggested the parental environment doesn't add much to our personality development. In other words, the personalities of identical twins raised in different households are more similar to each other than to the personalities of the siblings they were actually raised with. Ironically, the most important contribution our parents may have made to our personalities is giving us their genes!

This is not to suggest that personality never changes. Over periods of time, people's personalities do change. Most research in this area suggests that while some aspects of our personalities do change over time, the rank orderings do not change very much. For example, people's scores on measures of dependability tend to increase over time. However, there are still strong individual differences in dependability, and despite the fact that most of us become more responsible over time, people tend to change by about the same amount so that the rank order stays roughly the same.[6] An analogy to intelligence may make this clearer. Children become smarter as they age so that nearly everyone is smarter at age 20 than they were at age 10. Still, if Sam is smarter than Leo at age 10, he is likely to be so at age 20, too. The same holds true with personality: If you are more dependable than your sibling now, that is likely to be true in 20 years, even though you both should become more dependable over time.

Early work on the structure of personality tried to identify and label enduring characteristics that describe an individual's behaviour. Popular characteristics include shy, aggressive, submissive, lazy, ambitious, loyal and timid. When someone exhibits these characteristics in a large number of situations, we call them **personality traits**.[7] The more consistent the characteristic and the more frequently a trait occurs in diverse situations, the more important that trait is in describing the individual.

A number of early efforts tried to identify the primary traits that govern behaviour.[8] However, for the most part, they resulted in long lists of traits that were difficult to generalise from and provided little practical guidance to organizational decision makers. Two exceptions

heredity
Factors determined at conception, one's biological, physiological and inherent psychological makeup.

personality traits
Enduring characteristics that describe an individual's behaviour.

2 Describe the Myers-Briggs Type Indicator personality framework and assess its strengths and weaknesses.

are the Myers-Briggs Type Indicator and the Big Five Model. Over the past 20 years, these two approaches have become the dominant frameworks for identifying and classifying traits.

The Myers-Briggs Type Indicator

Myers-Briggs Type Indicator (MBTI)
A personality test that taps four characteristics and classifies people into 1 of 16 personality types.

The **Myers-Briggs Type Indicator (MBTI)** is the most widely used personality-assessment instrument in the world.[9] More than 3.5 million questionnaires are completed worldwide every year, it is available in 19 languages and there are over 13,000 qualified users in Europe[10]. It's a 100-question personality test that asks people how they usually feel or act in particular situations. On the basis of their answers, individuals are classified as extraverted or introverted (E or I), sensing or intuitive (S or N), thinking or feeling (T or F), and judging or perceiving (J or P). These terms are defined as follows:

- **Extraverted versus introverted.** Extraverted individuals are outgoing, sociable, and assertive. Introverts are quiet and shy.
- **Sensing versus intuitive.** Sensing types are practical and prefer routine and order. They focus on details. Intuitives rely on unconscious processes and look at the 'big picture'.
- **Thinking versus feeling.** Thinking types use reason and logic to handle problems. Feeling types rely on their personal values and emotions.
- **Judging versus perceiving.** Judging types want control and prefer their world to be ordered and structured. Perceiving types are flexible and spontaneous.

Stan Honda/Getty Images

Olli-Pekka Kallasvuo, President and CEO of Nokia, scores high on all personality dimensions of the Big Five model. A previous European Business Leader of the Year award winner, he is described as sociable, agreeable, conscientious, emotionally stable and open to experiences. These personality traits have contributed to Kallasvuo's high job performance and career success at Nokia; he joined the company in 1980 as Corporate Counsel and was promoted through the organization into the firm's top position in 2006.

These classifications together describe 16 personality types. To illustrate, let's take several examples. INTJs are visionaries. They usually have original minds and great drive for their own ideas and purposes. They are sceptical, critical, independent, determined and often stubborn. ESTJs are organizers. They are realistic, logical, analytical and decisive and have a natural head for business or mechanics. They like to organize and run activities. The ENTP type is a conceptualiser. He or she is innovative, individualistic, versatile and attracted to entrepreneurial ideas. This person tends to be resourceful in solving challenging problems but may neglect routine assignments. A book profiling 13 contemporary businesspeople who created super-successful firms including Apple Computer, Honda Motors, Microsoft and Sony found that all were intuitive thinkers (NTs).[11] This result is particularly interesting because intuitive thinkers represent only about 5 per cent of the population.

The MBTI is widely used in practice by organizations including Siemans, Unipart, Ernst & Young, NXP and many hospitals and educational institutions. In spite of its popularity, the evidence is mixed as to whether the MBTI is a valid measure of personality – with most of the evidence suggesting that it isn't.[12] One problem is that it forces a person into either one type or another (that is, you're either introverted or extraverted). There is no in-between, though people can be both extraverted and introverted to some degree. The best we can say is that the MBTI can be a valuable tool for increasing self-awareness and providing career guidance. But because results tend to be unrelated to job performance, managers probably shouldn't use it as a selection test for job candidates.

The Big Five personality model

3 Identify the key traits in the Big Five personality model.

Big Five Model
A personality assessment model that taps five basic dimensions.

The MBTI may lack for strong supporting evidence, but the same can't be said for the five-factor model of personality typically called the the **Big Five Model**, or the 'Big Five'. An impressive body of research supports its thesis that five basic dimensions underlie all others and encompass most of the significant variation in human personality.[13] The Big Five factors are:

- **Extraversion.** The **extraversion** dimension captures one's comfort level with relationships. Extraverts tend to be gregarious, assertive and sociable. Introverts tend to be reserved, timid and quiet.

extraversion
A personality dimension that describes someone who is sociable, gregarious and assertive.

agreeableness
A personality dimension that describes someone who is goodnatured, cooperative and trusting.

conscientiousness
A personality dimension that describes someone who is responsible, dependable, persistent and organized.

emotional stability
A personality dimension that characterises someone as calm, self-confident, secure (positive) versus nervous, depressed and insecure (negative).

openness to experience
A personality dimension that characterises someone in terms of imagination, sensitivity and curiosity.

4 Demonstrate how the Big Five traits predict behaviour at work.

- **Agreeableness.** The **agreeableness** dimension refers to an individual's propensity to defer to others. Highly agreeable people are cooperative, warm and trusting. People who score low on agreeableness are cold, disagreeable and antagonistic.

- **Conscientiousness.** The **conscientiousness** dimension is a measure of reliability. A highly conscientious person is responsible, organized, dependable and persistent. Those who score low on this dimension are easily distracted, disorganized and unreliable.

- **Emotional stability.** The **emotional stability** dimension – often labelled by its converse, neuroticism – taps a person's ability to withstand stress. People with positive emotional stability tend to be calm, self-confident and secure. Those with high negative scores tend to be nervous, anxious, depressed and insecure.

- **Openness to experience.** The **openness to experience** dimension addresses one's range of interests and fascination with novelty. Extremely open people are creative, curious and artistically sensitive. Those at the other end of the openness category are conventional and find comfort in the familiar.

How do the Big Five traits predict behaviour at work?

Research on the Big Five has found relationships between these personality dimensions and job performance.[14] As the authors of the most-cited review put it: 'The preponderance of evidence shows that individuals who are dependable, reliable, careful, thorough, able to plan, organized, hardworking, persistent, and achievement-oriented tend to have higher job performance in most if not all occupations.'[15] In addition, employees who score higher in conscientiousness develop higher levels of job knowledge, probably because highly conscientious people exert greater levels of effort on their jobs. The higher levels of job knowledge then contribute to higher levels of job performance.[16]

Although conscientiousness is the Big Five trait most consistently related to job performance, the other traits are related to aspects of performance in some situation. All five traits also have other implications for work and for life. Let's look at the implications of these traits one at a time. Figure 4.1 summarises the discussion.

People who score high on emotional stability are happier than those who score low. Of the Big Five traits, emotional stability is most strongly related to life satisfaction, job satisfaction and low stress levels. This is probably true because high scorers are more likely to be positive and optimistic in their thinking and experience fewer negative emotions. People low on emotional stability are hyper-vigilant (looking for problems or impending signs of danger), and high scores are associated with fewer health complaints. One upside of low emotional stability, however, is that when in a bad mood, such people make faster and better decisions than emotionally stable people in bad moods.[17]

Compared to introverts, extraverts tend to be happier in their jobs and in their lives as a whole. They experience more positive emotions than do introverts, and they more freely express these feelings. They also tend to perform better in jobs that require significant interpersonal interaction, perhaps because they have more social skills – they usually have more friends and spend more time in social situations than introverts. Finally, extraversion is a relatively strong predictor of leadership emergence in groups; extraverts are more socially dominant, 'take charge' sorts of people, and they generally are more assertive than introverts.[18] One downside of extraversion is that extraverts are more impulsive than introverts; they are more likely to be absent from work and engage in risky behaviour.[19]

Individuals who score high on openness to experience are more creative in science and in art than those who score low. Because creativity is important to leadership, open people are more likely to be effective leaders. Also, open individuals are more comfortable with ambiguity and change than are those who score lower on this trait. As a result, open people cope better with organizational change and are more adaptable in changing contexts.[20]

You might expect agreeable people to be happier than disagreeable people, and they are, but only slightly. When people choose romantic partners, friends or organizational team members, agreeable individuals are usually their first choice. Thus, agreeable individuals are better liked than disagreeable people, which explains why they tend to do better in interpersonally oriented jobs such as customer service. Agreeable people also are more compliant and rule-abiding. Agreeable children do better in school and as adults are less likely to get involved in drugs or

Figure 4.1	Model of how Big Five traits influence OB in the news criteria

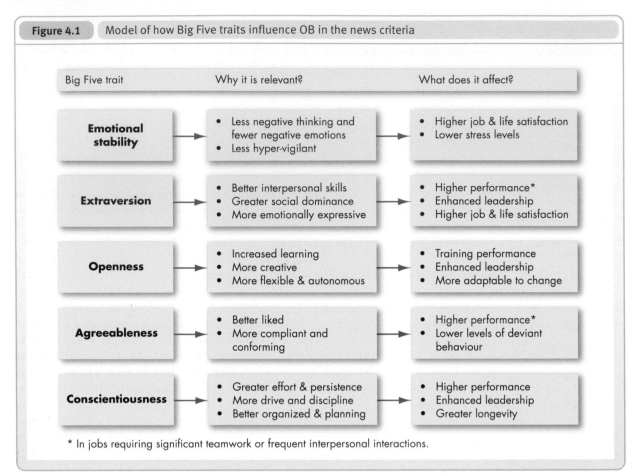

Big Five trait	Why it is relevant?	What does it affect?
Emotional stability	• Less negative thinking and fewer negative emotions • Less hyper-vigilant	• Higher job & life satisfaction • Lower stress levels
Extraversion	• Better interpersonal skills • Greater social dominance • More emotionally expressive	• Higher performance* • Enhanced leadership • Higher job & life satisfaction
Openness	• Increased learning • More creative • More flexible & autonomous	• Training performance • Enhanced leadership • More adaptable to change
Agreeableness	• Better liked • More compliant and conforming	• Higher performance* • Lower levels of deviant behaviour
Conscientiousness	• Greater effort & persistence • More drive and discipline • Better organized & planning	• Higher performance • Enhanced leadership • Greater longevity

* In jobs requiring significant teamwork or frequent interpersonal interactions.

excessive drinking.[21] Thus, agreeable individuals are less likely to engage in organizational deviance. One downside of agreeableness is that it is associated with lower levels of career success (especially earnings). This may occur because agreeable individuals are poorer negotiators; they are so concerned with pleasing others that they often don't negotiate as much for themselves as do others.[22]

Interestingly, conscientious people live longer than less conscientious people because they tend to take better care of themselves (eat better, exercise more) and engage in fewer risky behaviours (smoking, drinking/drugs, or risky driving behaviour).[23] Still, there are downsides to conscientiousness. It appears that conscientious people, probably because they're so organized and structured, don't adapt as well to changing contexts. Conscientious people are generally performance-oriented. They have more trouble than less conscientious people learning complex skills early in the training process because their focus is on performing well rather than on learning. Finally, conscientious people are often less creative than less conscientious people, especially artistically.[24]

FACE THE FACTS

- A research study looking at managerial level and personality revealed that conscientiousness, extraversion and intuition were positively correlated with the respondent's managerial level.
- Another study administered the Myers-Briggs Type Indicator (MBTI) to more than 8,000 participants from 86 countries (although 90 per cent were European). The results revealed one of the main areas of difference between managers and non-managers was in the thinking–feeling dimension. Eighty-five per cent of managers said they made decisions on the basis of

logical objective analysis, compared with 45 per cent of non-managers.

- Interviews with 1,000 managers in charge of recruitment revealed personality as the most important factor in graduate selection.

Source: See J. Moutafi, A. Furnham and J. Crump, 'Is managerial level related to personality?', *British Journal of Management*, 18, 3 (2007), p. 272; M. Carr, 'How managers and non-managers differ in their MBTI personality type', *People Management*, 12, 9 (5 April 2006); Q. Reade, 'Employers look at personality when hiring graduates', *Personnel Today*, 21 May 2002.

5 Identify other personality traits relevant to OB.

Other personality traits relevant to OB

Although the Big Five traits have proven to be highly relevant to OB, they don't exhaust the range of traits we can use to describe someone's personality. Now we'll look at other, more specific, personality attributes that have been found to be powerful predictors of behaviour in organizations. The first relates to one's core self-evaluation. The others are Machiavellianism, narcissism, self-monitoring, propensity for risk taking and the Type A and proactive personalities.

core self-evaluation
The degree to which an individual likes or dislikes himself or herself, whether the person sees himself or herself as capable and effective, and whether the person feels in control of his or her environment or powerless over the environment.

Core self-evaluation

People differ in the degree to which they like or dislike themselves and whether they see themselves as capable and effective. This self-perspective is the concept of **core self-evaluation**. People who have positive core self-evaluations like themselves and see themselves as effective, capable and in control of their environment. Those with negative core self-evaluations tend to dislike themselves, question their capabilities and view themselves as powerless over their environment.[25] We discussed in Chapter 3 that core self-evaluations relate to job satisfaction because people with positive core self-evaluations see more challenge in their job and actually attain more complex jobs.

Machiavellianism
The degree to which an individual is pragmatic, maintains emotional distance and believes that ends can justify means.

But what about job performance? People with positive core self-evaluations perform better than others because they set more ambitious goals, are more committed to their goals and persist longer at attempting to reach these goals. For example, one study of life insurance agents found that core self-evaluations were critical predictors of performance. In life insurance sales, 90 per cent of sales calls end in rejection, so agents have to believe in themselves to persist. In fact, this study showed that the majority of successful salespersons had positive core self-evaluations.[26]

You might wonder whether someone can be *too* positive. In other words, what happens when someone thinks he is capable, but he is actually incompetent? One study of Fortune 500 CEOs, for example, showed that many are overconfident, and their perceived infallibility often causes them to make bad decisions.[27] Teddy Forstmann, chairman of the global sports marketing giant IMG, said of himself, 'I know God gave me an unusual brain. I can't deny that. I have a God-given talent for seeing potential.'[28] One might say that people like Forstmann are overconfident, but very often we humans sell ourselves short and are less happy and effective than we could be because of it. If we decide we can't do something, for example, we won't try, and not doing it only reinforces our self-doubts.

Sean Gallup/Getty Images

A positive core self-evaluation helped Angela Merkel, Germany's first woman Chancellor, meet the daunting challenges and complexity of her job. Only scraping to election victory in 2005, just 6 months later her approval ratings were stratospheric. A nation that had been wallowing in a bout of angst was now so transformed that the newspaper *Der Spiegel* ran a cover calling Germany the 'Land of Smiles.' Merkel could not be described as charismatic, rather, it was her quiet, no-frills confidence and competence that won plaudits.

Source: Based on M. Elliott, 'Angela Merkel', *Time*, 30 April 2006.

Machiavellianism

Kuzi is a young bank manager in Taiwan. He's had three promotions in the past 4 years. Kuzi makes no apologies for the aggressive tactics he's used to propel his career upward. 'I'm prepared to do whatever I have to do to get ahead', he says. Kuzi would properly be called Machiavellian. Marie led her Brussels-based company last year in sales performance. She's assertive and persuasive, and she's effective at manipulating customers to buy her product line. Many of her colleagues, including her boss, also consider Marie as Machiavellian.

The personality characteristic of **Machiavellianism** (often abbreviated Mach) is named after Niccolo Machiavelli, who wrote in the sixteenth century on how to gain and use power. An individual high in Machiavellianism is pragmatic, maintains emotional distance and believes that ends can justify means. 'If it works, use it,' is consistent with a high-Mach perspective. A considerable amount of research has been directed toward relating high- and low-Mach personalities to certain behavioural outcomes.[29] High Machs manipulate more, win more, are persuaded less and persuade others more than do low Machs.[30] Yet high-Mach outcomes are moderated by situational factors. It has been found that high Machs flourish (1) when they interact face-to-face with others rather than indirectly; (2) when the situation has a minimal number of rules and regulations, thus allowing latitude for improvisation; and (3) when emotional involvement with details irrelevant to winning distracts low Machs.[31] Thus, whether high Machs make good employees depends on the type of job. In jobs that require bargaining skills (such as labour negotiation) or that offer substantial rewards for winning (such as commissioned sales), high Machs will be productive. But if the ends can't justify the means, if there are absolute standards of behaviour, or if the three situational factors we noted are not in evidence, our ability to predict a high Mach's performance will be severely curtailed.

Narcissism

narcissism
The tendency to be arrogant, have a grandiose sense of self-importance, require excessive admiration and have a sense of entitlement.

Hans likes to be the centre of attention. He likes to look at himself in the mirror a lot. He has extravagant dreams and seems to consider himself a person of many talents. Hans is a narcissist. The term is from the Greek myth of Narcissus, the story of a man so vain and proud that he fell in love with his own image. In psychology, **narcissism** describes a person who has a grandiose sense of self-importance, requires excessive admiration, has a sense of entitlement and is arrogant. An example of narcissistic personality might be Volvo's Pehr Gyllenhammar. His visionary leadership was initially very popular; however, over time Gyllenhammar felt he could ignore the concerns of his operational managers. He pursued risky and expensive business deals, which he publicised on television and in the press. On one level, you can ascribe Gyllenhammar's falling out of touch with his workforce simply to poor strategy. But it is also possible to attribute it to his narcissistic personality. His overestimation of himself led him to believe that others would want him to be the leader of a multi-national enterprise. In turn, these fantasies led him to pursue a merger with Renault, which was tremendously unpopular with Swedish employees. In the end, Gyllenhammar had no option but to resign.

This example was cited in a study that found while narcissists thought they were *better* leaders than their colleagues, their supervisors actually rated them as *worse* leaders. For example, an Oracle executive described that company's CEO Larry Ellison as follows: 'The difference between God and Larry is that God does not believe he is Larry.'[32] Because narcissists often want to gain the admiration of others and receive affirmation of their superiority, they tend to 'talk down' to those who threaten them, treating others as if they were inferior. Narcissists also tend to be selfish and exploitive, and they often carry the attitude that others exist for their benefit.[33] Studies indicate that narcissists are rated by their bosses as less effective at their jobs than others, particularly when it comes to helping other people.[34]

Self-monitoring

self-monitoring
A personality trait that measures an individual's ability to adjust his or her behaviour to external, situational factors.

Joyce McIntyre is always in trouble at work. Though she's competent, hardworking and productive, her performance reviews tend to rate her no better than average, and she seems to have made a career of irritating bosses. Joyce's problem is that she's politically inept. She's unable to adjust her behaviour to fit changing situations. As she puts it, 'I'm true to myself. I don't remake myself to please others.' We would be correct in describing Joyce as a low self-monitor.

Self-monitoring refers to an individual's ability to adjust their behaviour to external, situational factors.[35] Individuals high in self-monitoring show considerable adaptability in adjusting their behaviour to external situational factors. They are highly sensitive to external cues and can behave differently in different situations. High self-monitors are capable of presenting striking contradictions between their public persona and their private self. Low self-monitors, like Joyce, can't disguise themselves in that way. They tend to display their true dispositions and attitudes in every situation; hence, there is high behavioural consistency between who they are and what they do.

The evidence indicates that high self-monitors tend to pay closer attention to the behaviour of others and are more capable of conforming than are low self-monitors.[36] They also receive better performance ratings, are more likely to emerge as leaders, and show less commitment to their organizations.[37] In addition, high self-monitoring managers tend to be more mobile in their careers, receive more promotions (both internal and cross-organizational), and are more likely to occupy central positions in an organization.[38]

Risk taking

Rogue traders stand out for their willingness to take risks. Jerome Kerviel's highly speculative and unauthorised trading lost the French bank, Société Générale, almost €5 billion. In 1995,

Société Générale, a 141-year-old France-based bank, was plunged into crisis after Rogue trader Jerome Kerviel lost 4.9 billion euros in an unauthorised and highly speculative stock deal. The public prosecutor claimed the 31-year-old, 'wanted to be seen as an exceptional trader, an astute market player,' adding that Kerviel was attracted by the possibility of earning a €300,000 bonus. Kerviel stands out as a risk taker.[39]

Type A personality
Aggressive involvement in a chronic, incessant struggle to achieve more and more in less and less time and, if necessary, against the opposing efforts of other things or other people.

Nick Leeson's unsupervised risky trading caused the collapse of Barings Bank, the United Kingdom's oldest investment bank.

People differ in their willingness to take chances. This propensity to assume or avoid risk has been shown to have an impact on how long it takes managers to make a decision and how much information they require before making a choice. For instance, 79 managers worked on simulated personnel exercises that required them to make hiring decisions.[40] High risk-taking managers made more rapid decisions and used less information in making their choices than did the low risk-taking managers. Interestingly, decision accuracy was the same for both groups.

Although previous studies have shown managers in large organizations to be more risk averse than growth-oriented entrepreneurs who actively manage small businesses, recent findings suggest that managers in large organizations may actually be more willing to take risks than entrepreneurs.[41] For the work population as a whole, there are also differences in risk propensity.[42] As a result, it makes sense to recognise these differences and even to consider aligning risk-taking propensity with specific job demands. For instance, a willingness to take risks might prove a major obstacle to an accountant who performs auditing activities. This job might be better filled by someone with a low risk-taking propensity.

Type A personality

Do you know people who are excessively competitive and always seem to be experiencing a sense of time urgency? If you do, it's a good bet those people have **Type A personalities**. A person with a Type A personality is 'aggressively involved in a chronic, incessant struggle to achieve more and more in less and less time, and, if required to do so, against the opposing efforts of other things or other persons'.[43] Type A's:

1. are always moving, walking and eating rapidly;
2. feel impatient with the rate at which most events take place;
3. strive to think or do two or more things at once;
4. cannot cope with leisure time;
5. are obsessed with numbers, measuring their success in terms of how many or how much of everything they acquire.

In contrast to the Type A personality is the Type B, who is exactly opposite. Type B's are 'rarely harried by the desire to obtain a wildly increasing number of things or participate in an endless growing series of events in an ever-decreasing amount of time'.[44] Type B's never suffer from a sense of time urgency with its accompanying impatience, can relax without guilt and so on.

Type A's operate under moderate to high levels of stress. They subject themselves to more or less continuous time pressure, creating for themselves a life of deadlines. These characteristics result in some rather specific behavioural outcomes. For example, Type A's are fast workers because they emphasise quantity over quality. In managerial positions, Type A's demonstrate their competitiveness by working long hours and, not infrequently, making poor decisions because they make them too fast. Type A's are also rarely creative. Because of their concern with quantity and speed, they rely on past experiences when faced with problems. They will not allocate the time necessary to develop unique solutions to new problems. They rarely vary in their responses to specific challenges in their milieu; hence, their behaviour is easier to predict than that of Type B's.

Do Type A's differ from Type B's in their ability to get hired? The answer appears to be 'yes'.[45] Type A's do better than Type B's in job interviews because they are more likely to be judged as having desirable traits such as high drive, competence, aggressiveness and success motivation.

Proactive personality

Did you ever notice that some people actively take the initiative to improve their current circumstances or create new ones while others sit by passively reacting to situations? The former

proactive personality
People who identify opportunities, show initiative, take action and persevere until meaningful change occurs.

individuals have been described as having **proactive personalities**.[46] Proactives identify opportunities, show initiative, take action and persevere until meaningful change occurs. They create positive change in their environment, regardless of, or even in spite of, constraints or obstacles.[47] Not surprisingly, proactives have many desirable behaviours that organizations covet. For instance, evidence indicates that proactives are more likely than others to be seen as leaders and more likely to act as change agents within an organization.[48] Other actions of proactives can be positive or negative, depending on the organization and the situation. For example, proactives are more likely to challenge the status quo or voice their displeasure when situations aren't to their liking.[49] If an organization requires people with entrepreneurial initiative, proactives make good candidates; however, these are people who are also more likely to leave an organization to start their own businesses.[50] As individuals, proactives are more likely than others to achieve career success.[51] They select, create and influence work situations in their favour. Proactives are more likely than others to seek out job and organizational information, develop contacts in high places, engage in career planning and demonstrate persistence in the face of career obstacles.

'ENTREPRENEURS ARE A BREED APART'   MYTH *OR* SCIENCE?

This statement is true. A review of 23 studies on the personality of entrepreneurs revealed significant differences between entrepreneurs and managers on four of the Big Five: Entrepreneurs scored significantly higher on conscientiousness, emotional stability and openness to experience, and they scored significantly lower on agreeableness. Though of course not every entrepreneur achieves these scores, the results clearly suggest that entrepreneurs are different from managers in key ways.

A fascinating study of MBA students provides one explanation for how entrepreneurs are different from others. Studying male MBA students with either some or no prior entrepreneurial experience, the authors found that those with prior experience had significantly higher levels of testosterone (measured by taking a saliva swab at the beginning of the study) and also scored higher on risk propensity. The authors of this study concluded that testosterone, because it is associated with social

dominance and aggressiveness, energises individuals to take entrepreneurial risks. Because individual differences in testosterone are 80 per cent inherited, this study adds more weight to the conclusion that entrepreneurs are different from others.

What's the upshot of all this? An individual who is considering a career as an entrepreneur or a business owner might consider how they score on the Big Five. To the extent that they are high in conscientiousness, emotional stability and openness and low in agreeableness, such a career might be for them.

Source: R. E. White, S. Thornhill and E. Hampson, 'Entrepreneurs and evolutionary biology: the relationship between testosterone and new venture creation', *Organizational Behavior and Human Decision Processes*, 100 (2006), pp. 21–34; and H. Zhao and S. E. Seibert, 'The Big Five personality dimensions and entrepreneurial state: a meta-analytical review', *Journal of Applied Psychology*, 91, 2 (2006), pp. 259–71.

A GLOBAL PERSONALITY   GLOBAL

Determining which employees will succeed on overseas business assignments is often difficult for an organization's managers because the same qualities that predict success in one culture may not in another. However, researchers are naming personality traits that can help managers zero in on which employees would be suited for foreign assignments.

You might think that of the Big Five traits, openness to experience would be most important to effectiveness in international assignments. Open people are more likely to be culturally flexible – to 'go with the flow' when things are different in another country. Although research is not fully consistent on the issue, most does suggest that managers who score high on openness perform better than others in international assignments.

Among numerous other findings evident in expatriate research, extroversion, agreeableness and emotional stability have been demonstrated as being negatively related to the expatriates desire to terminate the assignment. Conscientiousness has been found to be positively related to performance ratings by supervisors.

What does the research mean for organizations? When it comes to choosing employees for global assignments, personality can make a difference.

Source: Based on M. A. Shaffer, D. A. Harrison and H. Gregersen, 'You can take it with you: individual differences and expatriate effectiveness', *Journal of Applied Psychology*, January 2006, pp. 109–25; E. Silverman, 'The global test', *Human Resource Executive Online*, 16 June 2006, www.hreonline.com/HRE/story.jsp?storyId=5669803; and P. M. Caligiuri, 'The Big Five personality characteristics as predictors of expatriate's desire to terminate the assignment and supervisor-rated performance', *Personnel Psychology*, 53 (2000), pp. 67–88.

Having discussed personality traits – the enduring characteristics that describe a person's behaviour – we now turn to values. Although personality and values are related, they're not the same. Values are often very specific and describe belief systems rather than behavioural tendencies. Some beliefs or values don't say much about a person's personality, and we don't always act in ways that are consistent with our values.

Values

6 Define *values*, demonstrate the importance of values and contrast terminal and instrumental values.

values
Basic convictions that a specific mode of conduct or end-state of existence is personally or socially preferable to an opposite or converse mode of conduct or end-state of existence.

value system
A hierarchy based on a ranking of an individual's values in terms of their intensity.

Is capital punishment right or wrong? If a person likes power, is that good or bad? The answers to these questions are value-laden. Some might argue, for example, that capital punishment is right because it is an appropriate retribution for crimes such as murder and treason. Others might argue, just as strongly, that no government has the right to take anyone's life.

Values represent basic convictions that 'a specific mode of conduct or end-state of existence is personally or socially preferable to an opposite or converse mode of conduct or end-state of existence.'[52] They contain a judgemental element in that they carry an individual's ideas as to what is right, good or desirable. Values have both content and intensity attributes. The content attribute says that a mode of conduct or an end-state of existence is *important*. The intensity attribute specifies *how important* it is. When we rank an individual's values in terms of their intensity, we obtain that person's **value system**. All of us have a hierarchy of values that forms our value system. This system is identified by the relative importance we assign to values such as freedom, pleasure, self-respect, honesty, obedience and equality.

Are values fluid and flexible? Generally speaking, no. They tend to be relatively stable and enduring.[53] A significant portion of the values we hold are established in our early years – from parents, teachers friends and others. As children, we are told that certain behaviours or outcomes are *always* desirable or *always* undesirable, with few grey areas. You were told, for example, that you should be honest and responsible. You were probably never taught to be just a little bit honest or a little bit responsible. It is this absolute, or 'black-or-white,' learning of values that more or less ensures their stability and endurance. The process of questioning our values, of course, may result in a change. More often, our questioning merely acts to reinforce the values we hold.

The importance of values

Values are important to the study of organizational behaviour because they lay the foundation for our understanding of people's attitudes and motivation and because they influence our perceptions. Individuals enter an organization with preconceived notions of what 'ought' and 'ought not' to be. Of course, these notions are not value-free. On the contrary, they contain interpretations of right and wrong. Furthermore, they imply that certain behaviours or outcomes are preferred over others. As a result, values cloud objectivity and rationality.

Values generally influence attitudes and behaviour.[54] Suppose you enter an organization with the view that allocating pay on the basis of performance is right, while allocating pay on the basis of seniority is wrong. How are you going to react if you find that the organization you've just joined rewards seniority and not performance? You're likely to be disappointed – and this can lead to job dissatisfaction and a decision not to exert a high level of effort because 'it's probably not going to lead to more money anyway'. Would your attitudes and behaviour be different if your values aligned with the organization's pay policies? Most likely.

terminal values
Desirable end-states of existence; the goals a person would like to achieve during their lifetime.

Classifying values

Milton Rokeach created the Rokeach Value Survey (RVS).[55] It consists of two sets of values, each containing 18 individual value items. One set, called **terminal values**, refers to desirable

Table 4.1 Mean value ranking of executives, union members and activists (top five only)

EXECUTIVES		UNION MEMBERS		ACTIVISTS	
Terminal	Instrumental	Terminal	Instrumental	Terminal	Instrumental
1. Self-respect	1. Honest	1. Family security	1. Responsible	1. Equality	1. Honest
2. Family security	2. Responsible	2. Freedom	2. Honest	2. A world of peace	2. Helpful
3. Freedom	3. Capable	3. Happiness	3. Courageous	3. Family security	3. Courageous
4. A sense of accomplishment	4. Ambitious	4. Self-respect	4. Independent	4. Self-respect	4. Responsible
5. Happiness	5. Independent	5. Mature love	5. Capable	5. Freedom	5. Capable

Source: Adapted from W. C. Frederick and J. Weber, 'The values of corporate managers and their critics: An empirical description and normative implications', in W. C. Frederick and L. E. Preston (eds), *Business Ethics: Research Issues and Empirical Studies* (Greenwich, CT: JAI Press, 1990), pp. 123–44.

instrumental values
Preferable modes of behaviour or means of achieving one's terminal values.

end-states. These are the goals a person would like to achive during his or her lifetime. These include values such as a comfortable life, a sense of accomplishment, equality, and wisdom. The other set, called **instrumental values**, refers to preferable modes of behaviour, or means of achieving the terminal values. Some examples of these are intellectual, ambitious, courageous, and responsible.

Several studies confirm that RVS values vary among groups.[56] People in the same occupations or categories (for example, corporate managers, union members, parents, students) tend to hold similar values. For instance, one study compared corporate executives, members of a steelworkers' union, and members of a community activist group. Although there was a good deal of overlap among the three groups,[57] there were also some very significant differences (see Table 4.1). The activists had value preferences that were quite different from those of the other two groups. They ranked 'equality' as their most important terminal value; executives and union members ranked this value 12 and 13, respectively. Activists ranked 'helpful' as their second-highest instrumental value. The other two groups both ranked it 14. These differences are important, because executives, union members, and activists all have a vested interest in what corporations do. These differences make things difficult for groups that have to negotiate with each other and can create serious conflicts when they contend with each other over an organization's economic and social policies.[58]

Begun in 1981, and still going, the European Values Study (EVS) is a large-scale research program designed to better understand the values of European people. Insights were gained into how people value, for example, friendship, human rights, hard work, tolerance and honesty. An interesting result was the difference across Europe regarding work ethos (or work ethic) (see Figure 4.2). This represents the degree to which individuals place work at or near the centre of their lives. Persons with a strong work ethic regard hard work as intrinsically good and as almost a moral duty. In contrast, they regard leisure somewhat suspiciously because of its potential to harm both persons and society as a whole.[59] These results have implications for such topics as job satisfaction, commitment, motivation, and work/life balance. Data from the EVS has now been incorporated into the World Values Survey to assess global values and how they change over time.

Contemporary work values

Contemporary work cohorts

7 Identify the dominant values in today's workforce.

As we will see, people's values differ depending on, for example, generation and culture, so it is difficult to give a blanket list of common contemporary work values. However, it is useful to review some recent national research to shed some light on what values are important for today's workers and how they vary between demographic groups. A UK study revealed cooperation was the most highly rated value overall. The research then looked at differences between gender, age, education and occupation. Men saw prosperity as relatively more important, whilst women prioritised working relationships. In terms of age, progression and personal growth declined in

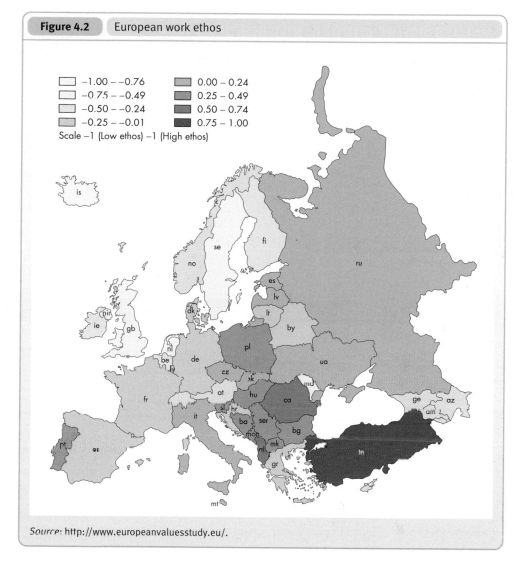

Figure 4.2   European work ethos

☐ −1.00 – −0.76	☐ 0.00 – 0.24
☐ −0.75 – −0.49	☐ 0.25 – 0.49
☐ −0.50 – −0.24	☐ 0.50 – 0.74
☐ −0.25 – −0.01	☐ 0.75 – 1.00

Scale −1 (Low ethos) −1 (High ethos)

Source: http://www.europeanvaluesstudy.eu/.

importance with age whilst younger workers were the most change-oriented and career-driven. Graduates place relatively more importance on work values linked to challenge and advancement such as career progression, job satisfaction, personal growth and autonomy. In contrast, non-graduate employees place importance on more tangible, immediate factors such as salary and rewards, line manager relationships, loyalty and trust. Strong leadership and clear communication are of most importance to managerial, professional and sales groups, with sales groups also prioritising loyalty and trust more than other occupational groups.[60]

Studies in other contexts have revealed that male Norwegian business school students are more oriented towards prosperity than females. A comparison of Polish and German secondary school students also revealed gender differences. The males were more inclined to look for work that was demanding in terms of time and personal commitment and that involved some degree of risk-taking. However, it does seem that gender differences in terms of values are decreasing.[61]

Perhaps the most research into the differences in generational values has been conducted in the United States. These findings suggest that older workers (65+) are hardworking, conservative and conforming. The dominant values of those aged mid-40 to mid-60 include achievement, ambition and dislike of authority. Late-20s to early-40s value work/life balance, relationship, dislike of rules. Whereas under-30s value financial success, confidence and loyalty to self and to relationships.

Whilst it must be recognised that there will be significant variations within groups, it is useful to recognise that groups tend to reflect similar values and this can be a valuable aid in explaining and predicting behaviour.[62]

VALUES DEFINE EUROPE, NOT BORDERS

OB IN THE NEWS

Enlargement is one of the EU's most successful policies and a powerful foreign policy tool. The EU has progressively extended its zone of peace and democracy across the European continent. Following the entry of 10 new members last May, the EU stretches from the Atlantic to the Carpathian mountains, and from northern Lapland down to the coast of the Levant in the eastern Mediterranean.

After this 'big bang', the EU needs to pace itself. Further enlargements must be gradual and carefully managed to ensure that European citizens support them and that the Union maintains its capacity to act. But the EU cannot close its doors. What principles should guide our enlargement policy?

I am often asked where Europe's ultimate borders lie. My answer is that the map of Europe is defined in the minds of Europeans. Geography sets the frame, but fundamentally it is values that make the borders of Europe. Enlargement is a matter of extending the zone of European values, the most fundamental of which are liberty and solidarity, tolerance and human rights, democracy and the rule of law.

Source: O. Rehn, 'Values define Europe, not borders', *Financial Times*, 4 January 2005, p. 15.

Linking an individual's personality and values to the workplace

Thirty years ago, organizations were concerned only with personality because their primary focus was to match individuals to specific jobs. That concern still exists. But, in recent years, that interest has expanded to include how well the individual's personality *and* values match the *organization*. Why? Because managers today are less interested in an applicant's ability to perform a *specific* job than with the *flexibility* to meet changing situations and commitment to the organization.

We'll now discuss person–job fit and person–organization fit in more detail.

Person–job fit

personality–job fit theory
A theory that identifies six personality types and proposes that the fit between personality type and occupational environment determines satisfaction and turnover.

The effort to match job requirements with personality characteristics is best articulated in John Holland's **personality–job fit theory**.[63] Holland presents six personality types and proposes that satisfaction and the propensity to leave a position depend on the degree to which individuals successfully match their personalities to a job. Each one of the six personality types has a congruent occupation. Table 4.2 describes the six types and their personality characteristics and gives examples of congruent occupations.

Holland developed the Vocational Preference Inventory questionnaire, which contains 160 occupational titles. Respondents indicate which of these occupations they like or dislike, and their answers form personality profiles. Research strongly supports the resulting hexagonal diagram shown in Figure 4.3.[64] The closer two fields or orientations are in the hexagon, the more compatible they are. Adjacent categories are quite similar, whereas diagonally opposite ones are highly dissimilar.

What does all this mean? The theory argues that satisfaction is highest and turnover is lowest when personality and occupation are in agreement. Social individuals should be in social jobs, conventional people in conventional jobs, and so forth. A realistic person in a realistic job is in a more congruent situation than a realistic person in an investigative job. A realistic person in a social job is in the most incongruent situation possible. The key points of this model are that (1) there do appear to be intrinsic differences in personality among individuals, (2) there are different types of jobs, and (3) people in jobs congruent with their personality should be more satisfied and less likely to voluntarily resign than people in incongruent jobs.

Person–organization fit

We've noted that researchers in recent years have looked at matching people to *organizations* as well as to jobs. If an organization faces a dynamic and changing environment and requires

| Table 4.2 | Holland's typology of personality and congruent occupations |

Type	Personality characteristics	Congruent occupations
Realistic: Prefers physical activities that require skill, strength, and coordination	Shy, genuine, persistent, stable, conforming, practical	Mechanic, drill press operator, assembly-line worker, farmer
Investigative: Prefers activities that involve thinking, organizing, and understanding	Analytical, original, curious, independent	Biologist, economist, mathematician, news reporter
Social: Prefers activities that involve helping and developing others	Sociable, friendly, cooperative, understanding	Social worker, teacher, counsellor, clinical psychologist
Conventional: Prefers rule-regulated, orderly and unambiguous activities	Conforming, efficient, practical, unimaginative, inflexible	Accountant, corporate manager, bank teller, file clerk
Enterprising: Prefers verbal activities in which there are opportunities to influence others and attain power	Self-confident, ambitious, energetic, domineering	Lawyer, real estate agent, public relations specialist, small business manager
Artistic: Prefers ambiguous and activities that allow creative expression	Imaginative, disorderly, idealistic, emotional, impractical	Painter, musician, writer, interior unsystematic decorator

| Figure 4.3 | Relationships among occupational personality types |

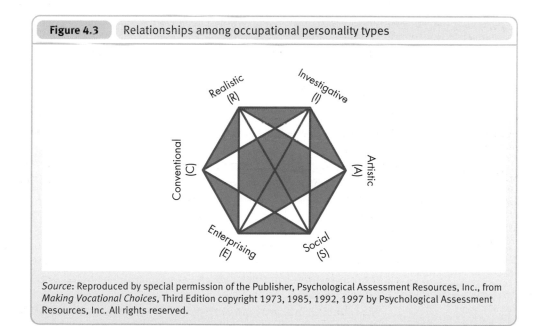

Source: Reproduced by special permission of the Publisher, Psychological Assessment Resources, Inc., from *Making Vocational Choices*, Third Edition copyright 1973, 1985, 1992, 1997 by Psychological Assessment Resources, Inc. All rights reserved.

employees who are able to readily change tasks and move easily between teams, it's more important that employees' personalities fit with the overall organization's culture than with the characteristics of any specific job.

The person–organization fit essentially argues that people are attracted to and selected by organizations that match their values, and they leave organizations that are not compatible with their personalities.[65] Using the Big Five terminology, for instance, we could expect that people high on extraversion fit well with aggressive and team-oriented cultures, that people high on agreeableness match up better with a supportive organizational climate than one that focuses on aggressiveness, and that people high on openness to experience fit better into organizations that emphasise innovation rather than standardisation.[66] Following these guidelines at the time of hiring should lead to selecting new employees who fit better with the organization's culture, which should, in turn, result in higher employee satisfaction and reduced turnover. Research on person–organization fit has also looked at people's values and whether they match the organization's culture. The fit of employees' values with the culture of their organization predicts job satisfaction, commitment to the organization, and low turnover.[67]

Global implications

Personality

8   Identify Hofstede's five value dimensions of national culture.

Do personality frameworks, such as the Big Five model, transfer across cultures? Are dimensions such as the Type A personality relevant in all cultures? Let's try to answer these questions.

The five personality factors identified in the Big Five model appear in almost all cross-cultural studies.[68] These studies have included a wide variety of diverse cultures – such as China, Israel, Germany, Japan, Spain, Nigeria, Norway, Pakistan and the United States. Differences tend to be in the emphasis on dimensions and whether countries are predominantly individualistic or collectivistic. For example, Chinese managers use the category of conscientiousness more often and the category of agreeableness less often than do US managers. And the Big Five appear to predict a bit better in individualistic than in collectivist cultures.[69] But there is a surprisingly high amount of agreement, especially among individuals from developed countries. As a case in point, a comprehensive review of studies covering people from the European Community found that conscientiousness was a valid predictor of performance across jobs and occupational groups.[70]

power distance
A national culture attribute that describes the extent to which a society accepts that power in institutions and organizations is distributed unequally.

individualism
A national culture attribute that describes the degree to which people prefer to act as individuals rather than as members of groups.

collectivism
A national culture attribute that describes a tight social framework in which people expect others in groups of which they are a part to look after them and protect them.

masculinity
A national culture attribute that describes the extent to which the culture favours traditional masculine work roles of achievement, power and control. Societal values are characterised by assertiveness and materialism.

femininity
A national culture attribute that has little differentiation between male and female roles, where women are treated as the equals of men in all aspects of the society.

Values

Because values differ across cultures, an understanding of these differences should be helpful in explaining and predicting behaviour of employees from different countries.

Hofstede's framework for assessing cultures

One of the most widely referenced approaches for analysing variations among cultures was done in the late 1970s by the Dutch writer Geert Hofstede.[71] He surveyed more than 116,000 IBM employees in 40 countries about their work-related values and found that managers and employees vary on five value dimensions of national culture:

- **Power distance. Power distance** describes the degree to which people in a country accept that power in institutions and organizations is distributed unequally. A high rating on power distance means that large inequalities of power and wealth exist and are tolerated in the culture, as in a class or caste system that discourages upward mobility of its citizens. A low power distance rating characterises societies that stress equality and opportunity.

- **Individualism versus collectivism. Individualism** is the degree to which people prefer to act as individuals rather than as members of groups and believe in individual rights above all else. **Collectivism** emphasises a tight social framework in which people expect others in groups of which they are a part to look after them and protect them.

- **Masculinity versus femininity.** Hofstede's construct of **masculinity** is the degree to which the culture favours traditional masculine roles such as achievement, power, and control, as opposed to viewing men and women as equals. A high masculinity rating indicates the culture has separate roles for men and women, with men dominating the society. A high **femininity** rating means the culture sees little differentiation between male and female roles and treats women as the equals of men in all respects.

uncertainty avoidance
A national culture attribute that describes the extent to which a society feels threatened by uncertain and ambiguous situations and tries to avoid them.

long-term orientation
A national culture attribute that emphasises the future, thrift and persistence.

short-term orientation
A national culture attribute that emphasises the past and present, respect for tradition and fulfilment of social obligations.

- **Uncertainty avoidance.** The degree to which people in a country prefer structured over unstructured situations defines their uncertainty avoidance. In cultures that score high on uncertainty avoidance, people have an increased level of anxiety about uncertainty and ambiguity and use laws and controls to reduce uncertainty. Cultures low on **uncertainty avoidance** are more accepting of ambiguity and are less rule oriented, take more risks, and more readily accept change.

- **Long-term versus short-term orientation.** This is the newest addition to Hofstede's typology. It focuses on the degree of a society's long-term devotion to traditional values. People in a culture with **long-term orientation** look to the future and value thrift, persistence, and tradition. In a **short-term orientation**, people value the here and now; they accept change more readily and don't see commitments as impediments to change.

How do different countries score on Hofstede's dimensions? Table 4.3 shows the ratings for the countries for which data are available. For example, power distance is higher in Malaysia than in any other country. Great Britain is very individualistic. Great Britain also tends to be short term in orientation and is low in power distance (people in Great Britain tend not to accept built-in class differences between people). Sweden, Denmark and Ireland are relatively low on uncertainty avoidance, meaning that most adults are relatively tolerant of uncertainty and ambiguity. Germany scores relatively high on masculinity, meaning that most people emphasise traditional gender roles (at least relative to countries such as Denmark, Finland, Norway, and Sweden).

You'll notice regional differences. Western and Northern nations such as Canada and the Netherlands tend to be more individualistic. Compared to other countries, poorer countries such as Mexico and the Philippines tend to be higher on power distance. South American nations tend to be higher than other countries on uncertainty avoidance, and Asian countries tend to have a long-term orientation.

Hofstede's culture dimensions have been enormously influential on OB researchers and managers. Nevertheless, his research has been criticised. First, although the data have since been updated, the original work is more than 30 years old and was based on a single company (IBM). A lot has happened on the world scene since then. Some of the most obvious changes include the fall of the Soviet Union, the transformation of central and eastern Europe, the end of apartheid in South Africa, and the rise of China as a global power. Second, few researchers have read the details of Hofstede's methodology closely and are therefore unaware of the many decisions and judgement calls he had to make (for example, reducing the number of cultural values to just five). Some results are unexpected. For example, Japan, which is often considered a highly collectivist nation, is considered only average on collectivism under Hofstede's dimensions.[72] Despite these concerns, Hofstede has been one of the most widely cited social scientists ever, and his framework has left a lasting mark on OB.

The GLOBE framework for assessing cultures

Begun in 1993, the Global Leadership and Organizational Behaviour Effectiveness (GLOBE) research programme is an ongoing cross-cultural investigation of leadership and national culture. Using data from 825 organizations in 62 countries, the GLOBE team identified nine dimensions on which national cultures differ.[73] Some of these – such as power distance, individualism/collectivism, uncertainty avoidance, gender differentiation (similar to masculinity versus femininity), and future orientation (similar to long-term versus short-term orientation) – resemble the Hofstede dimensions. The main difference in the GLOBE framework is that it added dimensions, such as humane orientation (the degree to which a society rewards individuals for being altruistic, generous, and kind to others) and performance orientation (the degree to which a society encourages and rewards group members for performance improvement and excellence).

Which framework is better? That's hard to say, and each has its adherents. We give more emphasis to Hofstede's dimensions here because they have stood the test of time and the GLOBE study confirmed them. However, researchers continue to debate the differences between these frameworks, and future studies may, in time, favour the more nuanced perspective of the GLOBE study.[74]

Table 4.3	Hofstede's cultural values by nation

Country	Power distance		Individualism versus collectivism		Masculinity versus femininity		Uncertainty avoidance		Long- versus short-term orientation	
	Index	Rank	Index	Rank	Index	Rank	Index	Rank	Index	Rank
Argentina	49	35–36	46	22–23	56	20–21	86	10–15		
Australia	36	41	90	2	61	16	51	37	31	22–24
Austria	11	53	55	18	79	2	70	24–25	31	22–24
Belgium	65	20	75	8	54	22	94	5–6	38	18
Brazil	69	14	38	26–27	49	27	76	21–22	65	6
Canada	39	39	80	4–5	52	24	48	41–42	23	30
Chile	63	24–25	23	38	28	46	86	10–15		
Colombia	67	17	13	49	64	11–12	80	20		
Costa Rica	35	42–44	15	46	21	48–49	86	10–15		
Denmark	18	51	74	9	16	50	23	51	46	10
Ecuador	78	8–9	8	52	63	13–14	67	28		
El Salvador	66	18–19	19	42	40	40	94	5–6		
Finland	33	46	63	17	26	47	59	31–32	41	14
France	68	15–16	71	10–11	43	35–36	86	10–15	39	17
Germany	35	42–44	67	15	66	9–10	65	29	31	22–24
Great Britain	35	42–44	89	3	66	9–10	35	47–48	25	28–29
Greece	60	27–28	35	30	57	18–19	112	1		
Guatemala	95	2–3	6	53	37	43	101	3		
Hong Kong	68	15–16	25	37	57	18–19	29	49–50	96	2
India	77	10–11	48	21	56	20–21	40	45	61	7
Indonesia	78	8–9	14	47–48	46	30–31	48	41–42		
Iran	58	29–30	41	24	43	35–36	59	31–32		
Ireland	28	49	70	12	68	7–8	35	47–48	43	13
Israel	13	52	54	19	47	29	81	19		
Italy	50	34	76	7	70	4–5	75	23	34	19
Jamaica	45	37	39	25	68	7–8	13	52		
Japan	54	33	46	22–23	95	1	92	7	80	4
Korea (South)	60	27–28	18	43	39	41	85	16–17	75	5
Malaysia	104	1	26	36	50	25–26	36	46		
Mexico	81	5–6	30	32	69	6	82	18		
The Netherlands	38	40	80	4–5	14	51	53	35	44	11–12
New Zealand	22	50	79	6	58	17	49	39–40	30	25–26
Norway	31	47–48	69	13	8	52	50	38	44	11–12
Pakistan	55	32	14	47–48	50	25–26	70	24–25	0	34
Panama	95	2–3	11	51	44	34	86	10–15		
Peru	64	21–23	16	45	42	37–38	87	9		
Philippines	94	4	32	31	64	11–12	44	44	19	31–32
Portugal	63	24–25	27	33–35	31	45	104	2	30	25–26
Singapore	74	13	20	39–41	48	28	8	53	48	9
South Africa	49	35–36	65	16	63	13–14	49	39–40		
Spain	57	31	51	20	42	37–38	86	10–15	19	31–32
Sweden	31	47–48	71	10–11	5	53	29	49–50	33	20
Switzerland	34	45	68	14	70	4–5	58	33	40	15–16
Taiwan	58	29–30	17	44	45	32–33	69	26	87	3
Thailand	64	21–23	20	39–41	34	44	64	30	56	8
Turkey	66	18–19	37	28	45	32–33	85	16–17		
United States	40	38	91	1	62	15	46	43	29	27
Uruguay	61	26	36	29	38	42	100	4		
Venezuela	81	5–6	12	50	73	3	76	21–22		
Yugoslavia	76	12	27	33–35	21	48–49	88	8		
Regions:										
Arab countries	80	7	38	26–27	53	23	68	27		
East Africa	64	21–23	27	33–35	41	39	52	36	25	28–29
West Africa	77	10–11	20	39–41	46	30–31	54	34	16	33

Scores range from 0 = extremely low on dimension to 100 = extremely high.

Note: 1 = highest rank. LTO ranks: 1 = China; 15–16 = Bangladesh; 21 = Poland; 34 = lowest.

Source: from Geert Hofstede, *Culture's Consequences: Comparing Values, Behaviors, Institutions and Organizations Across Nations*, Second Edition. Thousand Oaks, California: Sage Publications, 2001. Copyright © Geert Hofstede BV, reproduced with permission.

Summary and implications for managers

Personality

What value, if any, does the Big Five model provide to managers? From the early 1900s through the mid-1980s, researchers sought to find a link between personality and job performance. 'The outcome of those 80-plus years of research was that personality and job performance were not meaningfully related across traits or situations.'[75] However, the past 20 years have been more promising, largely due to the findings surrounding the Big Five. Screening candidates for jobs who score high on conscientiousness – as well as the other Big Five traits, depending on the criteria an organization finds most important – should pay dividends. Each of the Big Five traits has numerous implications for important OB criteria. Of course, managers still need to take situational factors into consideration.[76] Factors such as job demands, the degree of required interaction with others, and the organization's culture are examples of situational variables that moderate the personality–job performance relationship. You need to evaluate the job, the work group, and the organization to determine the optimal personality fit. Other traits, such as core self-evaluation or narcissism, may be relevant in certain situations, too.

Although the MBTI has been widely criticised, it may have a place in organizations. In training and development, it can help employees to better understand themselves and it can help team members to better understand each other. And it can open up communication in work groups and possibly reduce conflicts.

Values

Why is it important to know an individual's values? Values often underlie and explain attitudes, behaviours, and perceptions. So knowledge of an individual's value system can provide insight into what 'makes the person tick'.

Employees' performance and satisfaction are likely to be higher if their values fit well with the organization. For instance, the person who places great importance on imagination, independence, and freedom is likely to be poorly matched with an organization that seeks conformity from its employees. Managers are more likely to appreciate, evaluate positively, and allocate rewards to employees who 'fit in', and employees are more likely to be satisfied if they perceive that they do fit in. This argues for management to strive during the selection of new employees to find job candidates who have not only the ability, experience, and motivation to perform but also a value system that is compatible with the organization's.

POINT/COUNTERPOINT

Traits are powerful predictors of behaviour

POINT ➡

The essence of trait approaches in OB is that employees possess stable personality characteristics that significantly influence their attitudes toward, and behavioural reactions to, organizational settings. People with particular traits tend to be relatively consistent in their attitudes and behaviour over time and across situations.

Of course, trait theorists recognise that all traits are not equally powerful. They tend to put them into one of three categories. *Cardinal traits* are those so strong and generalised that they influence every act a person performs. *Primary traits* are generally consistent influences on behaviour, but they may not show up in all situations. Finally, *secondary traits* are attributes that do not form a vital part of the personality but come into play only in particular situations. For the most part, trait theories have

focused on the power of primary traits to predict employee behaviour.

Trait theorists do a fairly good job of meeting the average person's face-validity test. Think of friends, relatives, and acquaintances you have known for a number of years. Do they have traits that have remained essentially stable over time? Most of us would answer that question in the affirmative. If Cousin Ann was shy and nervous when we last saw her 10 years ago, we would be surprised to find her outgoing and relaxed now.

Managers seem to have a strong belief in the power of traits to predict behaviour. If managers believed that situations determined behaviour, they would hire people almost at random and structure the situation properly. But

▶

the employee selection process in most organizations places a great deal of emphasis on how applicants perform in interviews and on tests. Assume that you're an interviewer and ask yourself 'What am I looking for in job candidates?' If you answered with terms such as *conscientious, hardworking, persistent, confident* and *dependable*, you're a trait theorist.

COUNTERPOINT ←

Few people would dispute that some stable individual attributes affect reactions to the workplace. But trait theorists go beyond that and argue that individual behaviour consistencies are widespread and account for much of the differences in behaviour among people.

Two problems with using traits to explain a large proportion of behaviour in organizations are that the evidence isn't all that impressive, and individuals are highly adaptive so that personality traits change in response to organizational situations.

First, though personality does influence workplace attitudes and behaviours, the effects aren't all that strong; traits explain a minority of the variance in attitudes and behaviour. Why is this so? The effects of traits are likely to be strongest in relatively weak situations and weakest in relatively strong situations. Organizational settings tend to be strong situations because they have rules and other formal regulations that define acceptable behaviour and punish deviant behaviour; and they have informal norms that dictate appropriate behaviours. These formal and informal constraints minimise the effects of personality traits.

By arguing that employees possess stable traits that lead to cross-situational consistencies in behaviours, trait theorists imply that individuals don't really adapt to different situations. But a growing body of evidence suggests that an individual's traits are changed by the organizations the individual participates in. If the individual's personality changes as a result of exposure to organizational settings, in what sense can that individual be said to have traits that persistently and consistently affect their reactions to those very settings? Moreover, people typically belong to multiple organizations that often include very different kinds of members. And they adapt to those different situations, too. Instead of being prisoners of a rigid and stable personality framework, as trait theorists propose, people regularly adjust their behaviour to reflect the requirements of various situations.

Sources: R. Hogan, 'In defense of personality measurement: new wine for old whiners', *Human Performance*, 18, 4 (2005), pp. 331–41; and N. Schmitt, 'Beyond the Big Five: increases in understanding and practical utility', *Human Performance*, 17, 3 (2004), pp. 347–57.

QUESTIONS FOR REVIEW

1. What is personality? How do we typically measure it? What factors determine personality?

2. What is the Myers-Briggs Type Indicator (MBTI), and what does it measure?

3. What are the Big Five personality traits?

4. How do the Big Five traits predict work behaviour?

5. Besides the Big Five, what other personality traits are relevant to OB?

6. What are values, why are they important, and what is the difference between terminal and instrumental values?

7. Do values differ across cultures? How so?

Experiential exercise

WHAT ORGANIZATIONAL CULTURE DO YOU PREFER?

The Organizational Culture Profile (OCP) can help assess whether an individual's values match the organization's.[77] The OCP helps individuals sort their characteristics in terms of importance, which indicates what a person values.

1. Working on your own, complete the OCP that your instructor will provide you with.
2. Your instructor may ask you the following questions individually or as group of three or four students (with a spokesperson appointed to speak to the class for each group):

(a) What were your most preferred and least preferred values? Do you think your most preferred and least preferred values are similar to those of other class or group members?

(b) Do you think there are generational differences in the most preferred and least preferred values?

(c) Research has shown that individuals tend to be happier, and perform better, when their OCP values match those of their employer. How important do you think a 'values match' is when you're deciding where you want to work?

Ethical dilemma

HIRING BASED ON BODY ART

Leonardo's Pizza in Gainesville, Florida, US, regularly employs heavily tattooed workers. Tina Taladge and Meghan Dean, for example, are covered from their shoulders to their ankles in colourful tattoos. So many of the employees at Leonardo's sport tattoos that body art could almost be a qualification for the job. Many employers, however, are not that open to tattoos. Consider Russell Parrish, 29, who lives near Orlando, Florida, and has dozens of tattoos on his arms, hands, torso and neck. In searching for a job, Parrish walked into 100 businesses, and in 60 cases, he was refused an application. 'I want a career,' Parrish says, 'I want same the shot as everybody else.'

Parrish isn't alone. Many other US employers, including Walt Disney World, GEICO, SeaWorld, the US Postal Service and Wal-Mart, have policies against visible tattoos. A survey of employers revealed that 58 per cent indicated that they would be less likely to hire someone with visible tattoos or body piercings. 'Perception is everything when it comes to getting a job,' says Elaine Stover, associate director of career services at Arizona State University. 'Some employers and clients could perceive body art negatively.'

However, other employers – such as Bank of America, Allstate, and IBM – allow tattoos. Bank of America goes so far as to have a policy against using tattoos as a factor in hiring decisions.

Policies toward tattoos vary because, legally, employers can do as they wish. As long as the rule is applied equally to everyone (It would not be permissible to allow tattoos on men but not on women, for example), policies against tattoos are perfectly legal. Though not hiring people with tattoos is discrimination, 'it's legal discrimination,' said Gary Wilson, a Florida employment lawyer.

Thirty-six per cent of those aged 18 to 25, and 40 per cent of those aged 26 to 40, have at least one tattoo, whereas only 15 per cent of those over 40 do, according to a 2006 US survey by the Pew Research Center. One study in *American Demographics* suggested that 57 per cent of senior citizens viewed visible tattoos as 'freakish'.

Clint Womack, like most other people with multiple tattoos, realises there's a line that is dangerous to cross. While the 33-year-old hospital worker's arms, legs and much of his torso are covered with tattoos, his hands, neck and face are clear. 'Tattoos are a choice you make,' he says, 'and you have to live with your choices.'

Questions

1. Why do some employers ban tattoos while others don't mind them?

2. Is it fair for employers to reject applicants who have tattoos? Is it fair to require employees, if hired, to conceal their tattoos?

3. Should it be illegal to allow tattoos to be a factor at all in the hiring process?

Sources: R. R. Hastings, 'Survey: the demographics of tattoos and piercings', *HRWeek*, February 2007, www.shrm.org; and H. Wessel, 'Taboo of tattoos in the workplace', *Orlando (Florida) Sentinel*, 28 May 2007, www.tmcnet.com/usubmit/2007/05/28/2666555.htm.

CASE INCIDENT 1

The rise of the nice CEO?

If asked to describe the traits of an effective CEO, most people would probably use adjectives such as *driven*, *competitive* and *tough*. While it's clear that some hard-nosed CEOs, like AMSTRAD chief executive Alan Sugar (see the chapter opening vignette), are successful, recently some authors have suggested that being 'nice' is really important in today's workplace, even in the CEO suite. In a recent book, management professor Robert Sutton argues that getting along well with others is important to the successful functioning of organizations.

Many companies, such as Google, have developed policies to weed out those who habitually behave in an uncivil manner. Lars Dalgaard, CEO of SuccessFactors, specifically seeks to avoid employing 'nasty' people in his company. Job interviews are lengthy and feature probing questions designed to uncover any browbeating tendencies. Last year, Dalgaard took candidates vying for a chief financial officer vacancy to lunch at a local restaurant to see how they treated the waiting staff. Some got a free lunch but nothing more. When managers and employees are hired, they get a welcome letter from Dalgaard that spells out 15 corporate values, the last of which reminds them to be 'nice'.

Although it's not clear whether they've read Sutton's book, some CEOs of Fortune 500 companies do seem to project the image of a 'kinder, gentler CEO'. Let's consider three examples, all of whom were protégés of Jack Welch when he was CEO of General Electric (GE) and of whom were candidates to be his successor: Bob Nardelli, James McNerney and Jeff Immelt.

Bob Nardelli, former CEO, Home Depot

When Bob Nardelli wasn't chosen to be CEO of GE, he demanded to know why. Didn't he have the best numbers? His bitterness was palpable, say GE insiders. When Nardelli became CEO of Home Depot, in his first few months on the job, he became notorious for his imperious manner and explosive temper. At one meeting, he yelled, 'You guys don't know how to run a f---ing business.' When Nardelli was fired as CEO in 2006, it was due to a combination of factors, including Home Depot's lacklustre stock price, but his abrasive personality played no small part.

BusinessWeek wrote: 'With the stock price recently stuck at just over 40, roughly the same as when Nardelli arrived 6 years ago, he could no longer rely on other sterile metrics to assuage the quivering anger his arrogance provoked within every one of his key constituencies: employees, customers, and shareholders.'

James McNerney, CEO, Boeing

These are heady days at Boeing, which commands record levels of new orders and dominates its European rival Airbus as never before. Most CEOs would take credit for this success. Not James McNerney, who gives the credit to Boeing's engineers and employees. 'I view myself as a value-added facilitator here more than as someone who's crashing through the waves on the bridge of a frigate,' he says. A former GE colleague compared Nardelli and McNerney, saying, 'Jim's problems have been as tough, or tougher, than the ones that Bob had to face. But he has tried to solve them in a much more pleasant way. The guy is loved over there at Boeing.'

Jeff Immelt, CEO, General Electric

Although Jeff Immelt is the first to point out that the nickname 'Neutron Jack' for his predecessor Jack Welch was misleading, and that the differences between him and Welch are not as dramatic as some claim, Immelt is noted for his calm demeanour and trusting approach. In speaking of his approach, he said, 'I want to believe the best in terms of what people can do. And if you want to make a growth culture, you've got to have a way to nurture people and not make them fight so goddamn hard to get any idea through the door.'

Questions

1. Do you think Sutton is wrong and that the contrasting fortunes, and personalities, of Nardelli, McNerney and Immelt are coincidental? Why or why not?

2. Do you think the importance of being 'nice' varies by industry, type of job or country? How so?

3. How comfortable would you be working in a culture like that of SuccessFactors, where a certain level of 'niceness' is part of the job description?

4. Do you think being 'nice' is the same as the Big Five trait of agreeableness? If so, do you think companies should screen out those who score low on agreeableness?

5. Earlier we discussed the fact that entrepreneurs score significantly lower than managers on agreeableness. How would you reconcile this finding with Sutton's point?

Sources: D. Brady, 'Being mean is so last millennium', *BusinessWeek*, 15 January 2007, p. 61; G. Colvin, 'How one CEO learned to fly', *Fortune*, 16 October 2006; B. Grow, 'Out at Home Depot', *BusinessWeek*, 9 January 2007; J. Guynn, 'Crusade against the jerk at work', *San Francisco (California) Chronicle*, 24 February 2007; and 'The Fast Company Interview: Jeff Immelt', *Fast Company*, July 2005, p. 60.

CASE INCIDENT 2

Style and substance have German and French leaders at odds

When former French President Jacques Chirac would come calling on Chancellor Angela Merkel, she seemed charmed by his gallant style, old world sensibility and those light kisses on the hand that got so much media play. But his successor's habit of familiarly kissing and hugging the German leader at their meetings left her cold, even annoyed, according to reports, and this did not help strengthen a relationship that is seen as pivotal within the European Union. Were it just a matter of where to place a kiss, the issue might be solved with the intervention of a protocol officer. But the differences between the two leaders are ones of both style and substance, which make them more difficult to bridge.

When Sarkozy became president, it was thought he and Merkel would be the perfect couple. Both came from parties on the right-hand side of the political spectrum, both have an interest in economic reform and getting an EU reform treaty back on track. They were even born just six months apart. But, on closer examination, the fact that they did not hit it off personally might not be surprising. Their styles could not be more different.

Angela Merkel, a pastor's daughter who grew up in East Germany, is cautious and reserved. She has a down-to-earth style that dispenses with all flash. But she has succeeded in finding a way to communicate her positions – even to foreign leaders on controversial topics like human rights in China or Russian democracy – in a low-key but effective manner. She is the quintessential team player.

Nicolas Sarkozy is a near opposite of that. Brash and in constant movement, he has been called hyperactive by many. Comparisons to Bonaparte have been frequent, given his dismissive behaviour towards his cabinet and his apparent love for showmanship and the spotlight. Observers claim Sarkozy would be wise to calm his style and become more of a player on Team EU, or he could risk alienating more than just Angela Merkel.

The head of the German Bundesbank, Axel Weber, called Sarkozy's understanding of economic realities 'zero' in the wake of the French leader's constant criticism of the European Central Bank. Jean-Claude Juncker, Luxembourg's prime minister, suggested the French leader focus on France's own economic woes instead of constantly carping on the bank's management of the euro. 'On the EU stage, his showmanship will be forgiven once,' said Henrik Uterwedde. 'But if he continues playing this role, he'll have problems.' He says Sarkozy's recent spats with EU leaders and his sometimes contrarian views are a combination of his wanting to score political points at home and his own personality.

'I think the biggest danger for Sarkozy is Sarkozy himself,' he said.

Questions

1. How do you believe Merkel and Sarkozy would score on the Big Five dimensions of personality (extraversion, agreeableness, conscientiousness, emotional stability, openness to experience)? Which ones would they score high on? Which ones might they score low on?

2. What other personality traits do you believe Merkel and Sarkozy exhibit? On what information did you base your decision?

3. Do you think it is possible for the two leaders to work together effectively? How?

Source: Adapted from K. James 'Style and substance have German, French leaders at odds', *European Ties*, 18 September 2007, http://www.dw-world.de/dw/article/0,2144,2786049,00. html.

Endnotes

1 G. W. Allport, *Personality: A Psychological Interpretation* (New York: Holt, Rinehart & Winston, 1937), p. 48. For a brief critique of current views on the meaning of personality, see R. T. Hogan and B. W. Roberts, 'Introduction: personality and industrial and organizational psychology', in B. W. Roberts and R. Hogan (eds), *Personality Psychology in the Workplace* (Washington, DC: American Psychological Association, 2001), pp. 11–12.

2 K. I. van der Zee, J. N. Zaal and J. Piekstra, 'Validation of the multicultural personality questionnaire in the context of personnel selection', *European Journal of Personality*, 17 (2003), pp. S77–S100.

3 T. A. Judge, C. A. Higgins, C. J. Thoresen and M. R. Barrick, 'The Big Five personality traits, general mental ability, and career success across the life span', *Personnel Psychology*, 52, 3 (1999), pp. 621–52.

4 See, for instance, M. B. Stein, K. L. Jang and W. J. Livesley, 'Heritability of social anxiety-related concerns and personality characteristics: a twin study', *Journal of Nervous and Mental Disease*, April 2002, pp. 219–24; and S. Pinker, *The Blank Slate: The Modern Denial of Human Nature* (New York: Viking, 2002).

5 See R. D. Arvey and T. J. Bouchard, Jr., 'Genetics, twins, and organizational behavior', in B. M. Staw and L. L. Cummings (eds), *Research in Organizational Behavior*, vol. 16 (Greenwich, CT: JAI Press, 1994), pp. 65–66; W. Wright, *Born That Way: Genes, Behavior, Personality* (New York: Knopf, 1998); and T. J. Bouchard, Jr. and J. C. Loehlin, 'Genes, evolution, and personality' *Behavior Genetics*, May 2001, pp. 243–73.

6 S. Srivastava, O. P. John and S. D. Gosling, 'Development of personality in early and middle adulthood: set like plaster or persistent change?', *Journal of Personality and Social Psychology*, May 2003, pp. 1041–53.

7 See A. H. Buss, 'Personality as traits', *American Psychologist*, November 1989, pp. 1378–88; R. R. McCrae, 'Trait psychology and the revival of personality and culture studies', *American Behavioral Scientist*, September 2000, pp. 10–31; and L. R. James and M. D. Mazerolle, *Personality in Work Organizations* (Thousand Oaks, CA: Sage, 2002).

8 See, for instance, G. W. Allport and H. S. Odbert, 'Trait names, a psycholexical study', *Psychological Monographs*, 47 (1936); and R. B. Cattell, 'Personality pinned down,' *Psychology Today*, July 1973, pp. 40–46.

9 R. B. Kennedy and D. A. Kennedy, 'Using the Myers-Briggs Type Indicator in career counseling', *Journal of Employment Counseling*, March 2004, pp. 38–44.

10 OPP consultancy http://www.opp.co.uk/MBTI_step_I.aspx. Accessed 23 June 2008.

11 G. N. Landrum, *Profiles of Genius* (New York: Prometheus, 1993).

12 See, for instance, D. J. Pittenger, 'Cautionary comments regarding the Myers-Briggs Type Indicator', *Consulting Psychology Journal: Practice and Research*, Summer 2005, pp. 210–21; L. Bess and R. J. Harvey, 'Bimodal score distributions and the Myers-Briggs Type Indicator: fact or artifact?' *Journal of Personality Assessment*, February 2002, pp. 176–86; R. M. Capraro and M. M. Capraro, 'Myers-Briggs Type Indicator score reliability across studies: a meta-analytic reliability generalization study', *Educational & Psychological Measurement*, August 2002, pp. 590–602; and R. C. Arnau, B. A. Green, D. H. Rosen, D. H. Gleaves and J. G. Melancon, 'Are Jungian preferences really categorical? An empirical investigation using taxometric analysis', *Personality & Individual Differences*, January 2003, pp. 233–51.

13 See, for example, J. M. Digman, 'Personality structure: emergence of the Five-Factor Model', in M. R. Rosenzweig and L. W. Porter (eds), *Annual Review of Psychology*, vol. 41 (Palo Alto, CA: Annual Reviews, 1990), pp. 417–40; R. R. McCrae, 'Special issue: the Five-Factor Model: issues and applications,' *Journal of Personality*, June 1992; D. B. Smith, P. J. Hanges and M. W. Dickson, 'Personnel selection and the five-factor model: reexamining the effects of applicant's frame of reference', *Journal of Applied Psychology*, April 2001, pp. 304–15; and M. R. Barrick and M. K. Mount, 'Yes, personality matters: moving on to more important matters', *Human Performance*, 18, 4 (2005), pp. 359–72.

14 See, for instance, M. R. Barrick and M. K. Mount, 'The Big Five personality dimensions and job performance: a meta-analysis', *Personnel Psychology*, Spring 1991, pp. 1–26; G. M. Hurtz and J. J. Donovan, 'Personality and job performance: the Big Five revisited', *Journal of Applied Psychology*, December 2000, pp. 869–79; J. Hogan and B. Holland, 'Using theory to evaluate personality and job-performance relations: a socio-analytic perspective', *Journal of Applied Psychology*, February 2003, pp. 100–12; and M. R. Barrick and M. K. Mount, 'Select on conscientiousness and emotional stability', in E. A. Locke (ed.), *Handbook of Principles of Organizational Behavior* (Malden, MA: Blackwell, 2004), pp. 15–28.

15 M. K. Mount, M. R. Barrick and J. P. Strauss, 'Validity of observer ratings of the Big Five personality factors,' *Journal of Applied Psychology*, April 1994, p. 272. Additionally confirmed by G. M. Hurtz and J. J. Donovan, 'Personality and job performance: the Big Five revisited'; and M. R. Barrick, M. K. Mount and T. A. Judge, 'The FFM personality dimensions and job performance: meta-analysis of meta-analyses', *International Journal of Selection and Assessment*, 9 (2001), pp. 9–30.

16 F. L. Schmidt and J. E. Hunter, 'The validity and utility of selection methods in personnel psychology: practical and theoretical implications of 85 years of research findings', *Psychological Bulletin*, September 1998, p. 272.

17 M. Tamir and M. D. Robinson, 'Knowing good from bad: the paradox of neuroticism, negative affect, and evaluative processing', *Journal of Personality & Social Psychology*, 87, 6 (2004), pp. 913–25.

18 R. J. Foti and M. A. Hauenstein, 'Pattern and variable approaches in leadership emergence and effectiveness', *Journal of Applied Psychology*, March 2007, pp. 347–55.

19 L. I. Spirling and R. Persaud, 'Extraversion as a risk factor', *Journal of the American Academy of Child & Adolescent Psychiatry*, 42, 2 (2003), p. 130.

20 J. A. LePine, J. A. Colquitt and A. Erez, 'Adaptability to changing task contexts: effects of general cognitive ability, conscientiousness, and openness to experience', *Personnel Psychology* 53 (2000), pp. 563–95.

21 B. Laursen, L. Pulkkinen and R. Adams, 'The antecedents and correlates of agreeableness in adulthood', *Developmental Psychology*, 38, 4 (2002), pp. 591–603.

22 B. Barry and R. A. Friedman, 'Bargainer characteristics in distributive and integrative negotiation,' *Journal of Personality and Social Psychology*, February 1998, pp. 345–59.

23 T. Bogg and B. W. Roberts, 'Conscientiousness and health-related behaviors: a meta-analysis of the leading behavioral contributors to mortality', *Psychological Bulletin*, 130, 6 (2004), pp. 887–919.

24 S. Lee and H. J. Klein, 'Relationships between conscientiousness, self-efficacy, self-deception, and learning over time', *Journal of Applied Psychology*, 87, 6 (2002), pp. 1175–82; G. J. Feist, 'A meta-analysis of personality in scientific and artistic creativity', *Personality and Social Psychology Review*, 2, 4 (1998), pp. 290–309.

25 T. A. Judge and J. E. Bono, 'A rose by any other name . . . are self-esteem, generalized self-efficacy, neuroticism, and locus of control indicators of a common construct?', in B. W. Roberts and R. Hogan (eds), *Personality Psychology in the Workplace* (Washington, DC: American Psychological Association), pp. 93–118.

26 A. Erez and T. A. Judge, 'Relationship of core self-evaluations to goal setting, motivation, and performance', *Journal of Applied Psychology*, 86, 6 (2001), pp. 1270–79.

27 U. Malmendier and G. Tate, 'CEO overconfidence and corporate investment', Research Paper #1799, Stanford Graduate School of Business, June 2004.

28 R. Sandomir, 'Star struck,' *New York Times*, 12 January 2007, pp. C10, C14.

29 R. G. Vleeming, 'Machiavellianism: a preliminary review,' *Psychological Reports*, February 1979, pp. 295–310.

30 R. Christie and F. L. Geis, *Studies in Machiavellianism* (New York: Academic Press, 1970), p. 312; and N. V. Ramanaiah,

A. Byravan and F. R. J. Detwiler, 'Revised neo personality inventory profiles of Machiavellian and Non-Machiavellian people', *Psychological Reports*, October 1994, pp. 937–38.

31 Christie and Geis, *Studies in Machiavellianism*.

32 M. Maccoby, 'Narcissistic leaders: the incredible pros, the inevitable cons', *Harvard Business Review*, January–February 2000.

33 W. K. Campbell and C. A. Foster, 'Narcissism and commitment in romantic relationships: an investment model analysis,' *Personality and Social Psychology Bulletin*, 28, 4 (2002), pp. 484–95.

34 T. A. Judge, J. A. LePine and B. L. Rich, 'The narcissistic personality: relationship with inflated self-ratings of leadership and with task and contextual performance', *Journal of Applied Psychology*, 91, 4 (2006), pp. 762–76.

35 See M. Snyder, *Public Appearances/Private Realities: The Psychology of Self-Monitoring* (New York: W. H. Freeman, 1987); and S. W. Gangestad and M. Snyder, 'Self-monitoring: appraisal and reappraisal', *Psychological Bulletin*, July 2000, pp. 530–55.

36 Snyder, *Public Appearances/Private Realities*.

37 D. V. Day, D. J. Shleicher, A. L. Unckless and N. J. Hiller, 'Self-monitoring personality at work: a meta-analytic investigation of construct validity', *Journal of Applied Psychology*, April 2002, pp. 390–401.

38 M. Kilduff and D. V. Day, 'Do chameleons get ahead? the effects of self-monitoring on managerial careers', *Academy of Management Journal*, August 1994, pp. 1047–60; and A. Mehra, M. Kilduff and D. J. Brass, 'The social networks of high and low self-monitors: implications for workplace performance', *Administrative Science Quarterly*, March 2001, pp. 121–46.

39 'French bank's CEO under fire after rogue trade scandal', *Deutsche-Welle*, 29 January 2008.

40 R. N. Taylor and M. D. Dunnette, 'Influence of dogmatism, risk-taking propensity, and intelligence on decision-making strategies for a sample of industrial managers', *Journal of Applied Psychology*, August 1974, pp. 420–23.

41 I. L. Janis and L. Mann, *Decision Making: A Psychological Analysis of Conflict, Choice, and Commitment* (New York: The Free Press, 1977); W. H. Stewart, Jr. and L. Roth, 'Risk propensity differences between entrepreneurs and managers: a meta-analytic review', *Journal of Applied Psychology*, February 2001, pp. 145–53; J. B. Miner and N. S. Raju, 'Risk propensity differences between managers and entrepreneurs and between low- and high-growth entrepreneurs: a reply in a more conservative vein', *Journal of Applied Psychology*, 89, 1 (2004), pp. 3–13; and W. H. Stewart, Jr. and P. L. Roth, 'Data quality affects meta-analytic conclusions: a response to Miner and Raju (2004) concerning entrepreneurial risk propensity', *Journal of Applied Psychology*, 89, 1 (2004), pp. 14–21.

42 N. Kogan and M. A. Wallach, 'Group risk taking as a function of members' anxiety and defensiveness', *Journal of Personality*, March 1967, pp. 50–63.

43 M. Friedman and R. H. Rosenman, *Type A Behavior and Your Heart* (New York: Alfred A. Knopf, 1974), p. 84.

44 Ibid., pp. 84–85.

45 K. W. Cook, C. A. Vance, and E. Spector, 'The relation of candidate personality with selection-interview outcomes,' *Journal of Applied Social Psychology*, 30 (2000), pp. 867–85.

46 J. M. Crant, 'Proactive behavior in organizations,' *Journal of Management*, 26, 3 (2000), p. 436.

47 S. E. Seibert, M. L. Kraimer and J. M. Crant, 'What do proactive people do? A longitudinal model linking proactive personality and career success', *Personnel Psychology*, Winter 2001, p. 850.

48 T. S. Bateman and J. M. Crant, 'The proactive component of organizational behavior: a measure and correlates', *Journal of Organizational Behavior*, March 1993, pp. 103–18; and J. M. Crant and T. S. Bateman, 'Charismatic leadership viewed from above: the impact of proactive personality', *Journal of Organizational Behavior*, February 2000, pp. 63–75.

49 Crant, 'Proactive behavior in organizations'.

50 See, for instance, R. C. Becherer and J. G. Maurer, 'The proactive personality disposition and entrepreneurial behavior among small company presidents', *Journal of Small Business Management*, January 1999, pp. 28–36.

51 S. E. Seibert, J. M. Crant and M. L. Kraimer, 'Proactive personality and career success,' *Journal of Applied Psychology*, June 1999, pp. 416–27; Seibert, Kraimer and Crant, 'What do proactive people do?'; and J. D. Kammeyer-Mueller and C. R. Wanberg, 'Unwrapping the organizational entry process: disentangling multiple antecedents and their pathways to adjustment', *Journal of Applied Psychology*, 88, 5 (2003), pp. 779–94.

52 M. Rokeach, *The Nature of Human Values* (New York: The Free Press, 1973), p. 5.

53 M. Rokeach and S. J. Ball-Rokeach, 'Stability and change in American value priorities, 1968–1981', *American Psychologist*, 44, 5 (1989), pp. 775–84; and B. M. Meglino and E. C. Ravlin, 'Individual values in organizations: concepts, controversies, and research', *Journal of Management*, 24, 3 (1998), p. 355.

54 See, for instance, Meglino and Ravlin, 'Individual values in organizations', pp. 351–89.

55 Rokeach, *The Nature of Human Values*, p. 6.

56 J. M. Munson and B. Z. Posner, 'The factorial validity of a modified rokeach value survey for four diverse samples', *Educational and Psychological Measurement*, Winter 1980, pp. 1073–79; and W. C. Frederick and J. Weber, 'The values of corporate managers and their critics: an empirical description and normative implications', in W. C. Frederick and L. E. Preston (eds), *Business Ethics: Research Issues and Empirical Studies* (Greenwich, CT: JAI Press, 1990), pp. 123–44.

57 Frederick and Weber, 'The values of corporate managers and their critics'.

58 Ibid., p. 132.

59 European Values Study, http://www.europeanvaluesstudy.eu/

60 'Talentdrain one size does not fit all: demographic differences in work values and employee engagement in the UK', www.talentdrain.com/research.

61 See for a review, P. Gooderham, O. Nordhauga, K. Ringdalb, and G. E. Birkelund (2004) 'Job values among future business leaders: the impact of gender and social background', *Scandinavian Journal of Management*, 20, pp. 277–95.

62 See, for example, J. Levitz, 'Pitching 401(k)s to Generation Y is a tough sell', *Wall Street Journal*, 27 September 2006, pp. B1, B2; P. Paul, 'Global generation gap', *American Demographics*, March 2002, pp. 18–19; N. Watson, 'Generation wrecked', *Fortune*, 14 October 2002, pp. 183–90; K. W. Smola and C. D. Sutton, 'Generational differences:

revisiting generational work values for the new millennium', *Journal of Organizational Behavior*, 23 (2002), pp. 363–82; K. Mellahi and C. Guermat, 'Does age matter? An empirical examination of the effect of age on managerial values and practices in India', *Journal of World Business*, 39, 2 (2004), pp. 199–215; N. A. Hira, 'You raised them, now manage them', *Fortune*, 28 May 2007, pp. 38–46; R. R. Hastings, 'Surveys shed light on generation Y career goals', *SHRM Online*, March 2007, www.shrm.org; and S. Jayson, 'The "millennials" come of age', *USA Today*, 29 June 2006, pp. 1D, 2D.

63 J. L. Holland, *Making Vocational Choices: A Theory of Vocational Personalities and Work Environments* (Odessa, FL: Psychological Assessment Resources, 1997).

64 See, for example, J. L. Holland and G. D. Gottfredson, 'Studies of the hexagonal model: an evaluation (or, the perils of stalking the perfect hexagon)', *Journal of Vocational Behavior*, April 1992, pp. 158–70; T. J. Tracey and J. Rounds, 'Evaluating Holland's and Gati's vocational-interest models: a structural meta-analysis', *Psychological Bulletin*, March 1993, pp. 229–46; J. L. Holland, 'Exploring careers with a typology: what we have learned and some new directions', *American Psychologist*, April 1996, pp. 397–406; and S. X. Day and J. Rounds, 'Universality of vocational interest structure among racial and ethnic minorities', *American Psychologist*, July 1998, pp. 728–36.

65 See B. Schneider, 'The people make the place', *Personnel Psychology*, Autumn 1987, pp. 437–53; B. Schneider, H. W. Goldstein and D. B. Smith, 'The ASA framework: an update,' *Personnel Psychology*, Winter 1995, pp. 747–73; A. L. Kristof, 'Person–organization fit: an integrative review of its conceptualizations, measurement, and implications', *Personnel Psychology*, Spring 1996, pp. 1–49; B. Schneider, D. B. Smith, S. Taylor and J. Fleenor, 'Personality and organizations: a test of the homogeneity of personality hypothesis', *Journal of Applied Psychology*, June 1998, pp. 462–70; W. Arthur, Jr., S. T. Bell, A. J. Villado and D. Doverspike, 'The use of person-organization fit in employment decision-making: an assessment of its criterion-related validity', *Journal of Applied Psychology*, 91, 4 (2006), pp. 786–801; and J. R. Edwards, D. M. Cable, I. O. Williamson, L. S. Lambert and A. J. Shipp, 'The phenomenology of fit: linking the person and environment to the subjective experience of person–environment fit', *Journal of Applied Psychology*, 91, 4 (2006), pp. 802–27.

66 Based on T. A. Judge and D. M. Cable, 'Applicant personality, organizational culture, and organization attraction,' *Personnel Psychology*, Summer 1997, pp. 359–94.

67 M. L. Verquer, T. A. Beehr and S. E. Wagner, 'A meta-analysis of relations between person–organization fit and work attitudes', *Journal of Vocational Behavior*, 63, 3 (2003), pp. 473–89.

68 See, for instance, J. E. Williams, J. L. Saiz, D. L. Formy-Duval, M. L. Munick, E. E. Fogle, A. Adom, A. Haque, F. Neto and J. Yu, 'Cross-cultural variation in the importance of psychological characteristics: a seven-country study', *International Journal of Psychology*, October 1995, pp. 529–50; R. R. McCrae and P. T. Costa, Jr., 'Personality trait structure as a human universal', *American Psychologist*, 1997, pp. 509–16; R. R. McCrae, 'Trait psychology and the revival of personality-and-culture studies', *American Behavioral Scientist*, September 2000, pp. 10–31; S. V. Paunonen, M. Zeidner, H. A. Engvik, P. Oosterveld and R. Maliphant, 'The nonverbal assessment of personality in five cultures', *Journal of Cross-Cultural Psychology*, March 2000, pp. 220–39; H. C. Triandis and E. M. Suh, 'Cultural influences on personality', in S. T. Fiske, D. L. Schacter and C. Zahn-Waxler (eds), *Annual Review of*

Psychology, vol. 53 (Palo Alto, CA: Annual Reviews, 2002), pp. 133–60; R. R. McCrae and J. Allik, *The Five-Factor Model of Personality Across Cultures* (New York: Kluwer Academic/ Plenum, 2002); and R. R. McCrae, P. T. Costa, Jr., T. A. Martin, V. E. Oryol, A. A. Rukavishnikov, I. G. Senin, M. Hrebickova and T. Urbanek, 'Consensual validation of personality traits across cultures', *Journal of Research in Personality*, 38, 2 (2004), pp. 179–201.

69 A. T. Church and M. S. Katigbak, 'Trait psychology in the Philippines', *American Behavioral Scientist*, September 2000, pp. 73–94.

70 J. F. Salgado, 'The five factor model of personality and job performance in the European Community,' *Journal of Applied Psychology*, February 1997, pp. 30–43.

71 G. Hofstede, *Culture's Consequences: International Differences in Work-Related Values* (Beverly Hills, CA: Sage, 1980); G. Hofstede, *Cultures and Organizations: Software of the Mind* (London: McGraw-Hill, 1991); G. Hofstede, 'Cultural constraints in management theories', *Academy of Management Executive*, 7, 1 (1993), pp. 81–94; G. Hofstede and M. F. Peterson, 'National values and organizational practices', in N. M. Ashkanasy C. M. Wilderom and M. F. Peterson (eds), *Handbook of Organizational Culture and Climate* (Thousand Oaks, CA: Sage, 2000), pp. 401–16; and G. Hofstede, *Culture's Consequences: Comparing Values, Behaviors, Institutions, and Organizations Across Nations*, 2nd edn (Thousand Oaks, CA: Sage, 2001). For criticism of this research, see B. McSweeney, 'Hofstede's model of national cultural differences and their consequences: a triumph of faith – a failure of analysis', *Human Relations*, 55, 1 (2002), pp. 89–118.

72 M. H. Bond, 'Reclaiming the individual from Hofstede's ecological analysis'– a 20-year odyssey: comment on Oyserman *et al.* (2002). *Psychological Bulletin*, 128, 1 (2002), pp. 73–77; G. Hofstede, 'The pitfalls of cross-national survey research: a reply to the article by Spector *et al.* on the psychometric properties of the Hofstede values survey module 1994', *Applied Psychology: An International Review*, 51, 1 (2002), pp. 170–

78; and T. Fang, 'A critique of Hofstede's fifth national culture dimension', *International Journal of Cross-Cultural Management*, 3, 3 (2003), pp. 347–68.

73 M. Javidan and R. J. House, 'Cultural acumen for the global manager: lessons from project GLOBE', *Organizational Dynamics*, 29, 4 (2001), pp. 289–305; and R. J. House, P. J. Hanges, M. Javidan and P. W. Dorfman (eds), *Leadership, Culture, and Organizations: The GLOBE Study of 62 Societies* (Thousand Oaks, CA: Sage, 2004).

74 P. C. Early, 'Leading cultural research in the future: a matter of paradigms and taste', *Journal of International Business Studies*, September 2006, pp. 922–31; G. Hofstede, 'What did GLOBE really measure? researchers' minds versus respondents' minds', *Journal of International Business Studies*, September 2006, pp. 882–96; and M. Javidan, R. J. House, P. W. Dorfman, P. J. Hanges and M. S. de Luque, 'Conceptualizing and measuring cultures and their consequences: a comparative review of GLOBE's and Hofstede's approaches', *Journal of International Business Studies*, September 2006, pp. 897–914.

75 L. A. Witt, 'The interactive effects of extraversion and conscientiousness on performance', *Journal of Management*, 28, 6 (2002), p. 836.

76 R. P. Tett and D. D. Burnett, 'A personality trait-based interactionist model of job performance', *Journal of Applied Psychology*, June 2003, pp. 500–17.

77 B. Adkins and D. Caldwell, 'Firm or subgroup culture: where does fitting in matter most?' *Journal of Organizational Behavior*, 25, 8 (2004), pp. 969–78; H. D. Cooper-Thomas, A. van Vianen and N. Anderson, 'Changes in person–organization fit: the impact of socialization tactics on perceived and actual P–O fit', *European Journal of Work & Organizational Psychology*, 13, 1 (2004), pp. 52–78; and C. A. O'Reilly, J. Chatman and D. F. Caldwell, 'People and organizational culture: a profile comparison approach to assessing person–organization fit', *Academy of Management Journal*, 34, 3 (1991), pp. 487–516.

Perception and individual decision making

Learning Objectives

After studying this chapter, you should be able to:

1 Define *perception* and explain the factors that influence it.

2 Explain attribution theory and list the three determinants of attribution.

3 Identify the shortcuts individuals use in making judgements about others.

4 Explain the link between perception and decision making.

5 Apply the rational model of decision making and contrast it with bounded rationality and intuition.

6 List and explain the common decision biases or errors.

7 Explain how individual differences and organizational constraints affect decision making.

8 Contrast the three ethical decision criteria.

9 Define *creativity* and discuss the three-component model of creativity.

Indecision and delays are the parents of failure

George Canning

Perception and reality

Mark Allen/Getty Images

If you are unaware of Shazia Mirza, you would probably not pick her as a stand up comedian. She has won numerous awards and is in international demand, performing sell-out shows in a host of cities worldwide. Mirza gives a glimpse of her experiences as an Asian woman comedian in the following speech that gives us insights into the judgements people make based upon perceptions.

When I first started in comedy people didn't take me seriously. They thought I might not stick at it and might go off and marry my cousin in Pakistan but he didn't want me either. I was a bit of a novelty because even though I was a comedian gigging every night they couldn't imagine me, an Asian woman, doing a white man's job. It took them a lot of time to get used to seeing me in that position and to imagine me doing that job well. And I felt like I had to be twice as funny as everyone else. People sort of expected me to do certain types of material like about arranged marriages and being an Asian woman.

Because I'm an Asian woman they thought that's all I'd have to talk about, they were quite shocked when they saw I could also do jokes about speeding and shoplifting. I only ever want to be defined by good work that I do, not by my race, religion or colour. You do get treated differently when there is only one of you. We should be able to gain jobs and experience in accordance with our aspirations, skills and experience. Not just because you're an Asian woman and 'you might fit the role' or because they need a brown person in the workplace.

Source: Shazia Mirza, speaking at the launch of *Moving on up? The way forward*, House of Commons, March 2007

The chapter-opening story considers perceptions, in this case of an Asian woman. In the following Self-assessment library, consider your perceptions of appropriate gender roles.

SELF-ASSESSMENT LIBRARY

What are my gender role perceptions?

In the Self-assessment library (available online), take assessment IV.C.2. (What are my gender role perceptions?) and answer the following questions.

1. Did you score as high as you thought you would?

2. Do you think a problem with measures like this is that people aren't honest in responding?

3. If others, such as friends, classmates and family members, rated you, would they rate you differently? Why or why not?

4. Research has shown that people's gender role perceptions are becoming less traditional over time. Why do you suppose this is so?

What is perception?

1 Define *perception* and explain the factors that influence it.

perception
A process by which individuals organize and interpret their sensory impressions in order to give meaning to their environment.

Perception is a process by which individuals organize and interpret their sensory impressions in order to give meaning to their environment. However, what we perceive can be substantially different from objective reality. For example, all employees in a firm may view it as a great place to work – favourable working conditions, interesting job assignments, good pay, excellent benefits, understanding and responsible management – but, as most of us know, it's very unusual to find such agreement.

Why is perception important in the study of OB? Simply because people's behaviour is based on their perception of what reality is, not on reality itself. *The world as it is perceived is the world that is behaviourally important.*

Factors that influence perception

How do we explain the fact that individuals may look at the same thing yet perceive it differently? A number of factors operate to shape and sometimes distort perception. These factors can reside in the *perceiver*; in the object, or *target*, being perceived; or in the context of the *situation* in which the perception is made (see Figure 5.1).

When an individual looks at a target and attempts to interpret what he or she sees, that interpretation is heavily influenced by the personal characteristics of the individual perceiver. Personal characteristics that affect perception include a person's attitudes, personality, motives, interests, past experiences and expectations. For instance, if you expect police officers to be authoritative, young people to be lazy, or individuals holding public office to be unscrupulous, you may perceive them as such, regardless of their actual traits.

Characteristics of the target we observe can affect what we perceive. Loud people are more likely to be noticed in a group than quiet ones. So, too, are extremely attractive or unattractive individuals. Because we don't look at targets in isolation, the relationship of a target to its background also influences perception, as does our tendency to group close things and similar things together. For instance, women, people of colour, or members of any other group that has clearly distinguishable characteristics are often perceived as alike in other, unrelated ways as well.

Figure 5.1	Factors that influence perception

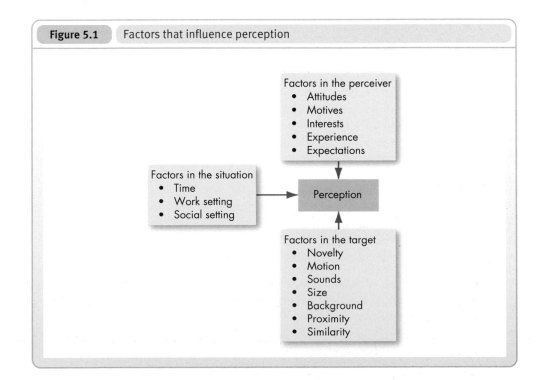

The context in which we see objects or events is also important. The time at which we see an object or event can influence attention, as can location, light, heat or any number of situational factors. For example, at a nightclub on Saturday night, you may not notice a young guest dressed flamboyantly. Yet that same person so attired for your Monday morning management class would certainly catch your attention (and that of the rest of the class). Neither the perceiver nor the target changed between Saturday night and Monday morning, but the situation is different.

Person perception: making judgements about others

2 Explain attribution theory and list the three determinants of attribution.

Now we turn to the most relevant application of perception concepts to OB. This is the issue of *person perception*, or the perceptions people form about each other.

Attribution theory

Non-living objects such as desks, machines and buildings are subject to the laws of nature, but they have no beliefs, motives or intentions. People do. That's why when we observe people, we attempt to develop explanations of why they behave in certain ways. Our perception and judgement of a person's actions, therefore, will be significantly influenced by the assumptions we make about that person's internal state.

attribution theory
An attempt to determine whether an individual's behaviour is internally or externally caused.

Attribution theory tries to explain the ways in which we judge people differently, depending on the meaning we attribute to a given behaviour.[1] It suggests that when we observe an individual's behaviour, we attempt to determine whether it was internally or externally caused. That determination, however, depends largely on three factors: (1) distinctiveness, (2) consensus, and (3) consistency. First, let's clarify the differences between internal and external causation and then we'll elaborate on each of the three determining factors.

Internally caused behaviours are those we believe to be under the personal control of the individual. *Externally* caused behaviour is what we imagine the situation forced the individual to do. For example, if one of your employees is late for work, you might attribute their lateness to their partying into the small hours of the morning and then oversleeping. This is an internal attribution. But if you attribute their arriving late to an automobile accident that tied up traffic, then you are making an external attribution.

Now let's discuss each of the three determining factors. *Distinctiveness* refers to whether an individual displays different behaviours in different situations. Is the employee who arrives late today also the one co-workers say regularly disregards commitments? What we want to know is whether this behaviour is unusual. If it is, we are likely to give it an external attribution. If it's not unusual, we will probably judge the behaviour to be internal.

If everyone who faces a similar situation responds in the same way, we can say the behaviour shows *consensus*. The behaviour of our tardy employee meets this criterion if all employees who took the same route to work were also late. From an attribution perspective, if consensus is high, you would probably give an external attribution to the employee's tardiness, whereas if other employees who took the same route made it to work on time, you would attribute their lateness to an internal cause.

Finally, an observer looks for *consistency* in a person's actions. Does the person respond the same way over time? Coming in 10 minutes late for work is not perceived in the same way for an employee for whom it is an unusual case (they haven't been late for several months) as it is for an employee for whom it is part of a routine pattern (they are late two or three times a week). The more consistent the behaviour, the more we are inclined to attribute it to internal causes.

Figure 5.2 summarises the key elements in attribution theory. It tells us, for instance, that if an employee, Joanne Dickinson, generally performs at about the same level on other related tasks as she does on her current task (low distinctiveness), if other employees frequently perform differently – better or worse – than Joanne does on that current task (low consensus), and if Joanne's performance on this current task is consistent over time (high consistency), you or anyone else judging Joanne's work will be likely to hold her primarily responsible for her task performance (internal attribution).

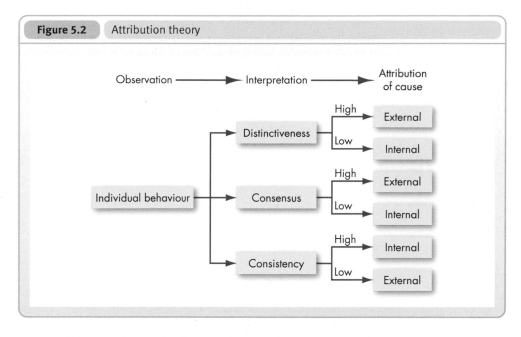

Figure 5.2   Attribution theory

One of the most interesting findings from attribution theory is that errors or biases distort attributions. For instance, substantial evidence suggests that when we make judgements about the behaviour of other people, we tend to underestimate the influence of external factors and overestimate the influence of internal or personal factors.[2] This **fundamental attribution error** can explain why a sales manager is prone to attribute the poor performance of her sales agents to laziness rather than to the innovative product line introduced by a competitor. Individuals and organizations also tend to attribute their own successes to internal factors such as ability or effort, while putting the blame for failure on external factors such as bad luck or unproductive co-workers. This is the **self-serving bias**.[3] For example, when former (and now deceased) Enron CEO Ken Lay was tried for fraud, he blamed former Chief Financial Officer Andrew Fastow, saying, 'I think the primary reason for Enron's collapse was Andy Fastow and his little group of people and what they did.'

Frequently used shortcuts in judging others

We use a number of shortcuts when we judge others. These techniques are frequently valuable: They allow us to make accurate perceptions rapidly and provide valid data for making predictions. However, they are not foolproof. They can and do get us into trouble. Understanding these shortcuts can help you recognise when they can result in significant distortions.

Selective perception

Any characteristic that makes a person, an object or an event stand out will increase the probability that we will perceive it. Why? Because it is impossible for us to assimilate everything we see; we can take in only certain stimuli. This tendency explains why you're more likely to notice cars like your own or why a boss may reprimand some people and not others who are doing the same thing. Because we can't observe everything going on about us, we engage in **selective perception**. A classic example shows how vested interests can significantly influence which problems we see.

Dearborn and Simon performed a perceptual study in which 23 business executives read a comprehensive case describing the organization and activities of a steel company.[4] Six were in sales, five in production, four in accounting, and eight in miscellaneous functions. Each manager was asked to write down the most important problem he found in the case. Eighty-three per cent of the sales executives rated sales important; only 29 per cent of the others did so. The researchers concluded that participants perceived as important the aspects of a situation specifically related to their own unit's activities and goals. A group's perception of organizational activities is selectively altered to align with the vested interests they represent.

fundamental attribution error
The tendency to underestimate the influence of external factors and overestimate the influence of internal factors when making judgements about the behaviour of others.

self-serving bias
The tendency for individuals to attribute their own successes to internal factors and put the blame for failures on external factors.

3 Identify the shortcuts individuals use in making judgements about others.

selective perception
The tendency to selectively interpret what one sees on the basis of one's interests, background, experience and attitudes.

Because we cannot assimilate all that we observe, we take in bits and pieces. But we don't choose them randomly; rather, we select them according to our interests, background, experience and attitudes. Selective perception allows us to 'speed-read' others, but not without the risk of drawing an inaccurate picture. Because we see what we want to see, we can draw unwarranted conclusions from an ambiguous situation.

Halo effect

halo effect
The tendency to draw a general impression about an individual on the basis of a single characteristic.

When we draw a general impression about an individual on the basis of a single characteristic, such as intelligence, sociability, or appearance, a **halo effect** is operating.[5] Consider former Hewlett-Packard CEO Carly Fiorina. Early in her tenure at the global technology solutions company, she was lauded as articulate, decisive, charismatic, savvy, and visionary. At the time of her appointment, *BusinessWeek* said, 'She has it all.' After Fiorina was fired, though, she was described as unproven, egotistical, inflexible and uncompromising. *BusinessWeek* faulted her for her unwillingness to delegate and her inability to execute.[6] So, when Fiorina was deemed effective, everything about her was good. But when she was fired for supposed ineffectiveness, the same people who lauded her before now saw few if any redeeming features. That's both sides of the halo (halo or horns, you might say).

The reality of the halo effect was confirmed in a classic study in which subjects were given a list of traits such as intelligent, skilful, practical, industrious, determined and warm and asked to evaluate the person to whom those traits applied.[7] Subjects judged the person to be wise, humorous, popular, and imaginative. When the same list was modified to include 'cold' instead of 'warm,' a completely different picture emerged. Clearly, the subjects were allowing a single trait to influence their overall impression of the person they were judging.

CAN NEGATIVE PERCEPTIONS DAMPEN INTERNATIONAL BUSINESS RELATIONS?   GLOBAL

Japan and China would seem to be natural economic partners, given that they're geographically so close to each other. However, Japanese companies currently lag behind both Europe and the United States in terms of trade with China. Although the Japanese auto industry has had enormous success in other countries, the top-selling foreign cars in China are produced by Volkswagen (a German company) and GM (a US company). Also, Japan's booming electronics industry currently captures only 5 per cent of the Chinese market.

But who or what is to blame for the dismal business relationship between Japan and China? The perceptions of the public – in both countries – may be the answer. For example, many Chinese citizens are still angered about a report that employees of a Japanese construction company hired Chinese prostitutes for a corporate party. And many Japanese citizens believe that Chinese immigrants are to blame for many of the violent crimes taking place in Japan. In addition to these recent events, historically, relations between the two countries have been strained. Beijing is still upset about Japan's military invasion of China in the 1930s and 1940s, for which Japan refuses to make amends.

These negative perceptions may be difficult to reverse if perceptual errors such as fundamental attribution error and the halo effect are operating. That is, both countries blame each other for their behaviours (internal attribution), and both countries tend to view each other's actions as negative (negative halo effect). Because of these errors, future behaviours, even if they are ambiguous, may be perceived negatively by the other country.

Source: Based on C. Chandler, 'Business is hot, relations are not', *Fortune (Europe)*, 19 April 2004, pp. 20–21; and 'China urges Japan to do more to improve ties', The Associated Press, 14 March 2005.

Contrast effects

contrast effects
Evaluation of a person's characteristics that is affected by comparisons with other people recently encountered who rank higher or lower on the same characteristics.

An old adage among entertainers says, 'Never follow an act that has kids or animals in it.' Why? Audiences love children and animals so much that you'll look bad in comparison. This example demonstrates how **contrast effects** can distort perceptions. We don't evaluate a person in isolation. Our reaction to a person is influenced by other persons we have recently encountered.

In a series of job interviews, for instance, interviewers can make distortions in any given candidate's evaluation as a result of his place in the interview schedule. A candidate is likely to receive a more favourable evaluation if preceded by mediocre applicants and a less favourable evaluation if preceded by strong applicants.

MBI/Alamy

Have you heard stories like the student who gets so drunk that he swallows his door key? Or the undergraduate so smashed that he breaks into a stranger's home thinking it's his friend's? You probably have. What about the one about the student who doesn't drink at all? Perhaps not. It doesn't fit with the Western stereotype about 'binge-drinking students', but there's now significant evidence to show more university students are turning teetotal than have done so for 10 years. Students tend to be stereotyped in the media as hard-drinking hedonists. But that's simply no longer the case.

Source: J. Shepherd, 'The party's over: students tend to be portrayed in the media as hard-drinking hedonists. But that's simply no longer the case', Guardian Education pages, *The Guardian*, 3 June 2008.

Stereotyping

When we judge someone on the basis of our perception of the group to which he or she belongs, we are using the shortcut called **stereotyping**.[8] We saw the problems stereotyping can create at the opening of this chapter.

We rely on generalisations every day because they help us make decisions quickly. They are a means of simplifying a complex world. It's less difficult to deal with an unmanageable number of stimuli if we use heuristics or stereotypes. The problem occurs, of course, when we generalise inaccurately or too much. In organizations, we frequently hear comments that represent stereotypes based on gender, age, race, religion, ethnicity and even weight:[9] 'Women won't relocate for a promotion', 'men aren't interested in child care', 'older workers can't learn new skills', 'overweight people lack discipline'. Stereotypes can be so deeply ingrained and powerful that they influence life-and-death decisions. One US study showed that, controlling for a wide array of factors (such as aggravating or mitigating circumstances), the degree to which black defendants in murder trials looked stereotypically black essentially doubled their odds of receiving a death sentence if convicted.[10]

One specific manifestation of stereotypes is **profiling** – a form of stereotyping in which a group of individuals is singled out, typically on the basis of race or ethnicity, for intensive inquiry, scrutiny, or investigation. Particularly since European and US terrorist attacks in the past decade, the use of ethnic profiling has increased significantly across Europe. However, profiling has been the focus of heated argument. This was vividly illustrated by the deaths of two Muslim youths fleeing police that sparked riots in France.[11] On one side, proponents argue that profiling Muslim youths is necessary in order to prevent terrorism. On the other side, critics argue that profiling is demeaning, discriminatory and an ineffective way to find potential terrorists and that Muslim youths are as law abiding as other citizens. The debate is important and implies the need to balance the rights of individuals against the greater good of society. Organizations need to sensitise employees and managers to the damage that profiling can create.

stereotyping
Judging someone on the basis of one's perception of the group to which that person belongs.

profiling
A form of stereotyping in which a group of individuals is singled out – typically on the basis of race or ethnicity – for intensive inquiry, scrutiny or investigation.

Many have expanded their diversity training programmes, which we discuss in Chapter 18, to particularly address ethnic stereotyping and profiling.

One of the problems of stereotypes is that they *are* widespread and often useful generalisations, despite the fact that they may not contain a shred of truth when applied to a particular person or situation. So, we constantly have to check ourselves to make sure we're not unfairly or inaccurately applying a stereotype in our evaluations and decisions. Stereotypes are an example of the warning, 'The more useful, the more danger from misuse.'

Specific applications of shortcuts in organizations

People in organizations are always judging each other. Managers must appraise their employees' performances. We evaluate how much effort our co-workers are putting into their jobs. When a new person joins a work team, the other members immediately 'size them up'. In many cases, our judgements have important consequences for the organization. Let's briefly look at a few of the most obvious applications.

Employment interview

A major input into who is hired and who is rejected in an organization is the employment interview. It's fair to say that few people are hired without an interview. But evidence indicates that interviewers make perceptual judgements that are often inaccurate.[12] They generally draw early impressions that very quickly become entrenched. Research shows that we form impressions of others within a tenth of a second, based on our first glance at them.[13] If these first impressions are negative, they tend to be more heavily weighted in the interview than if that same information came out later.[14] Most interviewers' decisions change very little after the first 4 or 5 minutes of an interview. As a result, information elicited early in the interview carries greater weight than does information elicited later, and a 'good applicant' is probably characterised more by the absence of unfavourable characteristics than by the presence of favourable characteristics.

Performance expectations

People attempt to validate their perceptions of reality, even when those perceptions are faulty.[15] This characteristic is particularly relevant when we consider performance expectations on the job. The terms **self-fulfilling prophecy** and *Pygmalion effect* have evolved to characterise the fact that an individual's behaviour is determined by other people's expectations. In other words, if a manager expects big things from her people, they're not likely to let her down. Similarly, if a manager expects people to perform minimally, they'll tend to behave so as to meet those low expectations. The expectations become reality. The self-fulfilling prophecy has been found to affect the performance of students in school, soldiers in combat, and even accountants.[16]

Performance evaluation

We'll discuss performance evaluations more fully in Chapter 18, but note for now that they are very much dependent on the perceptual process.[17] An employee's future is closely tied to the appraisal – promotions, pay raises and continuation of employment are among the most obvious outcomes. Although the appraisal can be objective (for example, a salesperson is appraised on how many sales he generates in his territory), many jobs are evaluated in subjective terms. Subjective evaluations of performance, though often necessary, are problematic because of all the errors we've discussed thus far – selective perception, contrast effects, halo effects and so on – affect them. Ironically, sometimes performance ratings say as much about the evaluator as they do about the employee!

self-fulfilling prophecy
A situation in which a person inaccurately perceives a second person, and the resulting expectations cause the second person to behave in ways consistent with the original perception.

decisions
Choices made from among two or more alternatives.

The link between perception and individual decision making

4 Explain the link between perception and decision making.

Individuals in organizations make **decisions**. That is, they make choices from among two or more alternatives. Top managers, for instance, determine their organization's goals, what products or services to offer, how best to finance operations, or where to locate a new manufacturing plant.

Middle- and lower-level managers determine production schedules, select new employees and decide how pay rises are to be allocated. Of course, making decisions is not the sole province of managers. Non-managerial employees also make decisions that affect their jobs and the organizations for which they work. They decide whether to come to work on any given day, how much effort to put forth at work, and whether to comply with a request made by the boss. In recent years, organizations have been empowering their non-managerial employees with job-related decision-making authority that was historically reserved for managers alone. Individual decision making, therefore, is an important part of organizational behaviour. But how individuals in organizations make decisions and the quality of their final choices are largely influenced by their perceptions.

problem
A discrepancy between the current state of affairs and some desired state.

Decision making occurs as a reaction to a **problem**.[18] That is, a discrepancy exists between the current state of affairs and some desired state, requiring us to consider alternative courses of action. For example, if your car breaks down, and you rely on it to get to work, you have a problem that requires a decision on your part. Unfortunately, most problems don't come neatly packaged and labelled 'problem'. One person's *problem* is another person's *satisfactory state of affairs*. One manager may view her division's 2 per cent decline in quarterly sales to be a serious problem requiring immediate action on her part. In contrast, her counterpart in another division of the same company, who also had a 2 per cent sales decrease, might consider that percentage quite acceptable. So the awareness that a problem exists and whether a decision needs to be made is a perceptual issue.

5 Apply the rational model of decision making and contrast it with bounded rationality and intuition.

Moreover, every decision requires us to interpret and evaluate information. We typically receive data from multiple sources and need to screen, process and interpret it. Which data, for instance, are relevant to the decision and which are not? The perceptions of the decision maker will answer that question. We also need to develop alternatives and evaluate the strengths and weaknesses of each. Again, because alternatives don't come with their strengths and weaknesses clearly marked, an individual decision maker's perceptual process will have a large bearing on the final outcome. Finally, throughout the entire decision-making process, perceptual distortions often surface that can bias analysis and conclusions.

Decision making in organizations

rational
Characterised by making consistent, value-maximising choices within specified constraints.

Business schools generally train students to follow rational decision-making models. While these models have considerable merit, they don't always describe how people actually make decisions. This is where OB enters the picture: If we are to improve how we make decisions in organizations, we need to understand the decision-making errors that people commit (in addition to the perception errors just discussed). In the sections that follow, we describe these errors, and we begin with a brief overview of the rational decision-making model.

rational decision-making model
A decision-making model that describes how individuals should behave in order to maximise some outcome.

The rational model, bounded rationality and intuition

Rational decision making

We often think the best decision maker is **rational** and makes consistent, value-maximising choices within specified constraints.[19] These decisions follow a six-step **rational decision-making model**.[20] The six steps are listed in Exhibit 5.1.

EXHIBIT 5.1	**STEPS IN THE RATIONAL DECISION-MAKING MODEL**
1. Define the problem.	4. Develop the alternatives.
2. Identify the decision criteria.	5. Evaluate the alternatives.
3. Allocate weights to the criteria.	6. Select the best alternative.

© Reuters/CORBIS

Operating within the confines of bounded rationality, Rose Marie Bravo revitalised the British retailer Burberry Group PLC when she became CEO. Bravo decided to capitalise on Burberry's quality heritage and trademark plaid design as the solution to the company's stagnant growth. She repositioned Burberry as a global luxury brand by running a celebrity ad campaign to redefine the brand's image as hip for the younger generation and by using the plaid design on new lines of swimwear and children's clothing. Bravo's decisions during her 10 years as CEO transformed a dormant brand into a profitable luxury label.

The rational decision-making model relies on a number of assumptions, including that the decision maker has complete information, is able to identify all the relevant options in an unbiased manner, and chooses the option with the highest utility.[21] As you might imagine, most decisions in the real world don't follow the rational model. For instance, people are usually content to find an acceptable or reasonable solution to a problem rather than an optimal one. Choices tend to be limited to the neighbourhood of the problem symptom and of the current alternative. As one expert in decision making put it, 'Most significant decisions are made by judgement, rather than by a defined prescriptive model.'[22] What's more, people are remarkably unaware of making suboptimal decisions.[23]

Bounded rationality

Most people respond to a complex problem by reducing it to a level at which they can readily understand it. The limited information-processing capability of human beings makes it impossible to assimilate and understand all the information necessary to optimise.[24] So people *satisfice*; that is, they seek solutions that are satisfactory and sufficient.

When you considered which university to attend, did you look at every viable alternative? Did you carefully identify all the criteria that were important in your decision? Did you evaluate each alternative against the criteria in order to find the optimal college? The answers are probably 'no'. Well, don't feel bad. Few people made their university choice this way. Instead of optimising, you probably satisficed.

bounded rationality
A process of making decisions by constructing simplified models that extract the essential features from problems without capturing all their complexity.

Because the human mind cannot formulate and solve complex problems with full rationality, we operate within the confines of **bounded rationality**. We construct simplified models that extract the essential features from problems without capturing all their complexity.[25] We can then behave rationally within the limits of the simple model.

How does bounded rationality work for the typical individual? Once we've identified a problem, we begin to search for criteria and alternatives. But the list of criteria is likely to be far from exhaustive. We identify a limited list of the most conspicuous choices, both easy to find and highly visible, that usually represent familiar criteria and tried-and-true solutions. Next, we begin reviewing them, but our review will not be comprehensive. Instead, we focus on alternatives that differ only in a relatively small degree from the choice currently in effect. Following familiar and well-worn paths, we review alternatives only until we identify one that is 'good enough' – that meets an acceptable level of performance. That ends our search. So the solution represents a satisficing choice – the first *acceptable* one we encounter – rather than an optimal one.

Intuition

intuitive decision making
An unconscious process created out of distilled experience.

Perhaps the least rational way of making decisions is to rely on intuition. **Intuitive decision making** is a nonconscious process created from distilled experience.[26] Its defining qualities are that it occurs outside conscious thought; it relies on holistic associations, or links between disparate pieces of information; it's fast; and it's affectively charged, meaning that it usually engages the emotions.[27]

Intuition is not rational, but that doesn't necessarily make it wrong. And intuition doesn't necessarily operate in opposition to rational analysis; rather, the two can complement each other. And intuition can be a powerful force in decision making. Research on chess playing provides an excellent illustration of how intuition works.[28]

Novice chess players and grand masters were shown an actual, but unfamiliar, chess game with about 25 pieces on the board. After 5 or 10 seconds, the pieces were removed, and each subject was asked to reconstruct the pieces by position. On average, the grand master could put 23 or 24 pieces in their correct squares, while the novice was able to replace only 6. Then the exercise was changed. This time, the pieces were placed randomly on the board. Again, the novice got only about 6 correct, but so did the grand master! The second exercise demonstrated that the grand master didn't have any better memory than the novice. What the grand master *did* have was the ability, based on the experience of having played thousands of chess games, to recognise patterns and clusters of pieces that occur on chessboards in the course of games. Studies also show that chess professionals can play 50 or more games simultaneously, making decisions in seconds, and exhibit only a moderately lower level of skill than when playing one game under tournament conditions, where decisions take half an hour or longer. The expert's experience allows them to recognise the pattern in a situation and draw on previously learned information associated with that pattern to arrive at a decision choice quickly. The result is that the intuitive decision maker can decide rapidly based on what appears to be very limited information.

For most of the twentieth century, experts believed that decision makers' use of intuition was irrational or ineffective. That's no longer the case.[29] There is growing recognition that rational analysis has been overemphasised and that, in certain instances, relying on intuition can improve decision making.[30] But while intuition can be invaluable in making good decisions, we can't rely on it too much. Because it is so unquantifiable, it's hard to know when our hunches are right or wrong. The key is not to either abandon or rely solely on intuition but to supplement it with evidence and good judgement.

Common biases and errors in decision making

6 List and explain the common decision biases or errors.

Decision makers engage in bounded rationality, but an accumulating body of research tells us that decision makers also allow systematic biases and errors to creep into their judgements.[31] These come from attempts to shortcut the decision process. To minimise effort and avoid difficult trade-offs, people tend to rely too heavily on experience, impulses, gut feelings and convenient rules of thumb. In many instances, these shortcuts are helpful. However, they can lead to severe distortions of rationality. Following are the most common biases in decision making.

Overconfidence bias

It's been said that 'no problem in judgement and decision making is more prevalent and more potentially catastrophic than overconfidence'.[32] When we're given factual questions and asked to judge the probability that our answers are correct, we tend to be far too optimistic. For instance, studies have found that, when people say they're 65 to 70 per cent confident that they're right, they are actually correct only about 50 per cent of the time.[33] And when they say they're 100 per cent sure, they tend to be 70 to 85 per cent correct.[34]

From an organizational standpoint, one of the most interesting findings related to over-confidence is that those individuals whose intellectual and interpersonal abilities are *weakest* are most likely to overestimate their performance and ability.[35] So as managers and employees become more knowledgeable about an issue, they become less likely to display overconfidence.[36] And overconfidence is most likely to surface when organizational members are considering issues or problems that are outside their area of expertise.[37]

Anchoring bias

anchoring bias
A tendency to fixate on initial information, from which one then fails to adequately adjust for subsequent information.

The **anchoring bias** is a tendency to fixate on initial information and fail to adequately adjust for subsequent information.[38] The anchoring bias occurs because our mind appears to give a disproportionate amount of emphasis to the first information it receives.[39] This is particularly important when organizations need to make strategic decisions. Individuals must often make initial judgements based upon gathered data and revise those judgements as new information comes in. However, because of anchoring bias the adjustments are typically insufficient.

Anchors are widely used by people in professions where persuasion skills are important – such as advertising, management, politics, real estate and law. Consider the role of anchoring in negotiations. Any time a negotiation takes place, so does anchoring. As soon as someone states a number, your ability to ignore that number has been compromised. For instance, when a prospective employer asks how much you were making in your prior job, your answer typically anchors the employer's offer. You may want to keep this in mind when you negotiate your salary, but remember to set the anchor only as high as you realistically can.

Confirmation bias

confirmation bias
The tendency to seek out information that reaffirms past choices and to discount information that contradicts past judgements.

The rational decision-making process assumes that we objectively gather information. But we don't. We *selectively* gather it. The **confirmation bias** represents a specific case of selective perception. We seek out information that reaffirms our past choices, and we discount information that contradicts them.[40] We also tend to accept at face information value that confirms our preconceived views, while we are critical and sceptical of information that challenges these views. Therefore, the information we gather is typically biased toward supporting views we already hold. This confirmation bias influences where we go to collect evidence because we tend to seek out sources most likely to tell us what we want to hear. It also leads us to give too much weight to supporting information and too little to contradictory information.

Availability bias

Many more people fear flying than fear driving in a car. But if flying on a commercial airline were as dangerous as driving, the equivalent of about 2,000 747s filled to capacity would have to crash globally every year, killing all aboard, to match the risk of being killed in a car accident. Yet the media gives much more attention to air accidents, so we tend to overstate the risk of flying and understate the risk of driving.

availability bias
The tendency for people to base their judgements on information that is readily available to them.

This illustrates the **availability bias**, which is the tendency for people to base their judgements on information that is readily available to them.[41] Events that evoke emotions, that are particularly vivid, or that have occurred more recently tend to be more available in our memory. As a result, we tend to overestimate the chances of unlikely events such as an airplane crash. The availability bias can also explain why managers, when doing annual performance appraisals, tend to give more weight to recent employee behaviours than to behaviours of 6 or 9 months ago.

'NO ONE THINKS THEY'RE BIASED' — MYTH *OR* SCIENCE?

This statement is mostly true. Few of us are truly objective. When Wendelin Wiedeking, chief executive of the Porsche sports car company, became Europe's highest-paid businessman by earning an estimated €67m, the head of a rival German carmaker shook his head in disgust. 'Everyone has the right to earn decent money. But €67m? That is obscene. It goes against every principle of social equality we have', the chief executive said. 'I just cannot understand how he can justify earning so much more than the normal worker.'

Mr Wiedeking says his pay is fully justified: when he took charge of Porsche in 1993 the company was on the verge of bankruptcy. Now it is the world's most profitable carmaker with an operating margin of 80 per cent (though this is mostly due to derivatives trading rather than selling cars). 'I think when the company does well then those who have contributed should share in that,' he says.[42]

This may be an extreme example. But it points to an alarming human tendency that may characterise all of us: Not only do we think we're objective when we evaluate ourselves or others, we don't recognise our biases and lack of objectivity. As one author noted, 'Much of what happens in the brain is not evident in the brain itself, and

thus people are better at playing these sorts of tricks on themselves than at catching themselves in the act.'

A study of doctors, who are often lavished with gifts from pharmaceutical sales representatives, showed this tendency all too well. When asked about whether gifts might influence their prescribing practices, 84 per cent thought that their colleagues were influenced by gifts, but only 16 per cent thought that they were similarly influenced.[43] It may well be that we think others are *less* truthful or objective than they really are and that we think we are *more* truthful or objective than we really are. The lesson? We should recognise the self-serving biases that contaminate our evaluations of others – and of ourselves.

Escalation of commitment

escalation of commitment
An increased commitment to a previous decision in spite of negative information.

Another distortion that creeps into decisions in practice is a tendency to escalate commitment when making a series of decisions.[44] **Escalation of commitment** refers to staying with a decision even when there is clear evidence that it's wrong. For example, consider a friend who has been dating his girlfriend for several years. Although he admits to you that things aren't going too well in the relationship, he says he is still going to marry her. His justification: 'I have a lot invested in the relationship!'

It has been well documented that individuals escalate commitment to a failing course of action when they view themselves as responsible for the failure.[45] That is, they 'throw good money after bad' to demonstrate that their initial decision wasn't wrong and to avoid having to admit that they made a mistake.[46] Escalation of commitment has obvious implications for managerial decisions. Many an organization has suffered large losses because a manager was determined to prove his original decision was right by continuing to commit resources to what was a lost cause from the beginning.

Randomness error

randomness error
The tendency of individuals to believe that they can predict the outcome of random events.

Human beings have a lot of difficulty dealing with chance. Most of us like to believe we have some control over our world and our destiny. Although we undoubtedly can control a good part of our future through rational decision making, the truth is that the world will always contain random events. Our tendency to believe we can predict the outcome of random events is the **randomness error**.

Decision making becomes impaired when we try to create meaning out of random events. One of the most serious impairments occurs when we turn imaginary patterns into super-stitions.[47] These can be completely contrived ('I never make important decisions on Friday the 13th') or evolve from a certain pattern of behaviour that has been reinforced previously (tennis great Bjorn Borg used to grow a beard prior to the Wimbledon tournament because of pre-vious success with a beard). Although many of us engage in some superstitious behaviour, it can be debilitating when it affects daily judgements or biases major decisions. At the extreme, some decision makers become controlled by their superstitions – making it nearly impossible for them to change routines or objectively process new information.

Winner's curse

winner's curse
A decision-making dictum which argues that the winning participants in an auction typically pay too much for the winning item.

The **winner's curse** argues that the winning participants in a competitive auction typically pay too much for the item. Some buyers will underestimate the value of an item, and others will overestimate it, and the highest bidder (the winner) will be the one who overestimated the most. Therefore, unless the bidders dramatically undervalue, there is a good chance that the 'winner' will pay too much. A possible, although still debated, example of the winners curse was the 3G auctions at the turn of the millennium. In the United Kingdom, five licenses for 3G wireless spectrum were auctioned by the government, raising a whopping €25 billion, the equivalent of about €400 per person. Over the next year, a half-dozen other European countries held their own auctions, raising around a combined €60 billion in a frenzy of bidding. The 'winning' tele-communications companies were left with potentially crippling debts.[48]

Logic predicts that the winner's curse gets stronger as the number of bidders increases. The more bidders there are, the more likely that some of them have greatly overestimated the good's value. So, beware of auctions with an unexpectedly large number of bidders.

Hindsight bias

hindsight bias
The tendency to believe falsely, after an outcome of an event is actually known, that one would have accurately predicted that outcome.

The **hindsight bias** is the tendency to believe falsely, after the outcome of an event is actually known, that we'd have accurately predicted that outcome.[49] When something happens and we have accurate feedback on the outcome, we seem to be pretty good at concluding that the outcome was relatively obvious. Perhaps after Spain won the 2008 European football cup, your response was I told you so! When the dot.com bubble burst, many businesspeople claimed, 'I knew that would happen.' We have to realise that things always seem much clearer when we know all the facts (or the connections among the facts).

The hindsight bias reduces our ability to learn from the past. It permits us to think that we're better at making predictions than we really are and can result in our being more confident about the accuracy of future decisions than we have a right to be. If, for instance, your actual predictive accuracy is only 40 per cent, but you think it's 90 per cent, you're likely to become falsely overconfident and less vigilant in questioning your predictive skills.

SELF-ASSESSMENT LIBRARY

Am I a deliberate decision maker?

In the Self-assessment library (available online), take assessment IV.A.2 (Am I a deliberate decision maker?). Would it be better to be a more deliberate decision maker? Why or why not?

Influences on decision making: individual differences and organizational constraints

7 Explain how individual differences and organizational constraints affect decision making.

Having examined the rational decision-making model, bounded rationality, and some of the most salient biases and errors in decision making, we turn here to a discussion of factors that influence how people make decisions and the degree to which they are susceptible to errors and biases. We discuss individual differences and organizational constraints.

FOOTBALL AND THE WINNER'S CURSE?   OB IN THE NEWS

In economics there is an anomaly known as the winner's curse. The paradox basically revolves around the theory that winning an auction can sometimes be a source of concern to a bidder. There are several ways to illustrate this, yet surprisingly football provides a simple and clear example of this scenario.

There are many instances in modern day football when a player attains a certain reputation thus providing him with a high price tag. This is often followed by several clubs expressing an interest in the player. More often than not a bidding war is started, with the end result being that the successful club pays, in some cases, a highly inflated fee. This fee either exceeds the player's true worth or his ability proves to be considerably less than expected, leaving the club disappointed.

The author of the above piece preferred not to give any examples. Perhaps you can think of some? Do you think your choices may be biased? How?

Source: J. Ross, 'The winner's curse', BBC Sport online, 27 November 2001. Available at http://news.bbc.co.uk/sport1/hi/football/teams/c/clyde/1678407.stm.

Individual differences

Decision making in practice is characterised by bounded rationality, common biases and errors and the use of intuition. In addition, individual differences create deviations from the rational model. In this section, we look at two differences: personality and gender.

Personality

There hasn't been much research on personality and decision making. One possible reason is that most researchers who conduct decision-making research aren't trained to investigate personality. However, the studies that have been conducted suggest that personality does influence decision making. Research has considered conscientiousness and self-esteem (both of which we discussed in Chapter 4). Let's look at each in the context of decision making.

Some research has shown that specific facets of conscientiousness – rather than the broad trait itself – affect escalation of commitment.[50] Interestingly, one study revealed that two facets of conscientiousness – achievement striving and dutifulness – actually had opposite effects on escalation of commitment. For example, achievement-striving people were more likely to escalate their commitment, whereas dutiful people were less likely. Why might this be the case? Generally, achievement-oriented people hate to fail, so they escalate their commitment, hoping to forestall failure. Dutiful people, however, are more inclined to do what they see as best for the organization. Second, achievement-striving individuals appear to be more susceptible to the hindsight bias, perhaps because they have a greater need to justify the appropriateness of their actions.[51] Unfortunately, we don't have evidence on whether dutiful people are immune to the hindsight bias.

Finally, people with high self-esteem appear to be especially susceptible to the self-serving bias. Why? Because they are strongly motivated to maintain their self-esteem, so they use the self-serving bias to preserve it. That is, they blame others for their failures while taking credit for successes.[52]

Gender

Recent research on rumination offers insights into gender differences in decision making.[53] Overall, the evidence indicates that women analyse decisions more than men do.

Rumination refers to reflecting at length. In terms of decision making, it means overthinking problems. Women, in general, are more likely than men to engage in rumination. Twenty years of study find that women spend much more time than men analysing the past, present and future. They're more likely to over analyse problems before making a decision and to rehash a decision once it has been made. On the positive side, this is likely to lead to more careful consideration of problems and choices. However, it can make problems harder to solve, increase regret over past decisions and increase depression. On this last point, women are nearly twice as likely as men to develop depression.[54]

Why women ruminate more than men is not clear. Several theories have been suggested. One view is that parents encourage and reinforce the expression of sadness and anxiety more in girls than in boys. Another theory is that women, more than men, base their self-esteem and well-being on what others think of them. A third theory is that women are more empathetic and more affected by events in others' lives, so they have more to ruminate about.

Gender differences surface early. By age 11, for instance, girls are ruminating more than boys. But this gender difference seems to lessen with age. Differences are largest during young adulthood and smallest after age 65, when both men and women ruminate the least.[55]

Organizational constraints

Organizations can constrain decision makers, creating deviations from the rational model. For instance, managers shape their decisions to reflect the organization's performance evaluation and reward system, to comply with the organization's formal regulations, and to meet organizationally imposed time constraints. Previous organizational decisions also act as precedents to constrain current decisions.

Performance evaluation

Managers are strongly influenced in their decision making by the criteria on which they are evaluated. If a division manager believes the manufacturing plants under his responsibility are operating best when he hears nothing negative, we shouldn't be surprised to find his plant managers spending a good part of their time ensuring that negative information doesn't reach him.

Reward systems

The organization's reward system influences decision makers by suggesting to them what choices are preferable in terms of personal payoff. For example, if the organization rewards risk aversion, managers are more likely to make conservative decisions. From the 1930s through the mid-1980s, the world's largest car manufacturer, General Motors, consistently gave out promotions and bonuses to managers who kept a low profile and avoided controversy. The result was that GM managers became very adept at dodging tough issues and passing controversial decisions on to committees.

Formal regulations

Consider a shift manager at a fast food restaurant describing the constraints he faces on his job: 'I've got rules and regulations covering almost every decision I make – from how to make the food to how often I need to clean the restrooms. My job doesn't come with much freedom of choice.' His situation is not unique. All but the smallest of organizations create rules and policies to programme decisions, which are intended to get individuals to act in the intended manner. And of course, in so doing, they limit the decision maker's choices.

System-imposed time constraints

Organizations impose deadlines on decisions. For instance, a report on new-product development may have to be ready for the executive committee to review by the first of the month. Almost all important decisions come with explicit deadlines. These conditions create time pressures on decision makers and often make it difficult, if not impossible, to gather all the information they might like to have before making a final choice.

AFP/Getty Images

At McDonald's restaurants throughout the world, formal regulations shape employee decisions by standardising the behaviour of restaurant crew members. McDonald's requires that employees follow rules and regulations for food preparation and service to meet the company's standards of food quality and safety and reliable and friendly service. For example, McDonald's requires 72 safety protocols to be conducted every day in each restaurant as part of a daily monitoring routine for restaurant managers.

Historical precedents

Decisions aren't made in a vacuum. They have a context. In fact, individual decisions are accurately characterised as points in a stream of decisions. Decisions made in the past are ghosts that continually haunt current choices – that is, commitments that have already been made constrain current options. It's common knowledge that the largest determinant of the size of any given year's budget is last year's budget.[56] Choices made today, therefore, are largely a result of choices made over the years.

What about ethics in decision making?

8 Contrast the three ethical decision criteria.

Ethical considerations should be an important criterion in organizational decision making. This is certainly more true today than at any time in the recent past, given the increasing scrutiny business is under to behave in an ethical and socially responsible way. In this section, we present three different ways to frame decisions ethically.

Three ethical decision criteria

An individual can use three different criteria in making ethical choices.[57] The first is the *utilitarian* criterion, in which decisions are made solely on the basis of their outcomes or consequences. The goal of **utilitarianism** is to provide the greatest good for the greatest number. This view tends to dominate business decision making. It is consistent with goals such as efficiency, productivity and high profits. By maximising profits, for instance, a business executive can argue that he is securing the greatest good for the greatest number – as he hands out dismissal notices to 15 per cent of his employees.

Another ethical criterion is to focus on *rights*. This calls on individuals to make decisions consistent with fundamental liberties and privileges, as set forth in documents such as the European Convention on Human Rights. An emphasis on rights in decision making means respecting and protecting the basic rights of individuals, such as the right to privacy, to free speech and to due process. For instance, this criterion protects **whistle-blowers** when they reveal unethical practices by their organization to the press or government agencies, on the grounds of their right to free speech.

A third criterion is to focus on *justice*. This requires individuals to impose and enforce rules fairly and impartially so that there is an equitable distribution of benefits and costs. Union members typically favour this view. It justifies paying people the same wage for a given job, regardless of performance differences, and using seniority as the primary determination in making layoff decisions.

Each of these criteria has advantages and liabilities. A focus on utilitarianism promotes efficiency and productivity, but it can result in ignoring the rights of some individuals, particularly those with minority representation in the organization. The use of rights as a criterion protects individuals from injury and is consistent with freedom and privacy, but it can create an overly legalistic work environment that hinders productivity and efficiency. A focus on justice protects the interests of the underrepresented and less powerful, but it can encourage a sense of entitlement that reduces risk taking, innovation and productivity.

Decision makers, particularly in for-profit organizations, tend to feel safe and comfortable when they use utilitarianism. A lot of questionable actions can be justified when framed as being in the best interests of 'the organization' and shareholders. But many critics of business decision makers argue that this perspective needs to change.[58] Increased concern in society about individual rights and social justice suggests the need for managers to develop ethical standards based on nonutilitarian criteria. This presents a solid challenge to today's managers because making decisions using criteria such as individual rights and social justice involves far more ambiguities than using utilitarian criteria such as effects on efficiency and profits. This helps to explain why managers are increasingly criticised for their actions. Raising prices, selling products with questionable effects on consumer health, closing down inefficient plants, laying off large numbers of

utilitarianism
A system in which decisions are made to provide the greatest good for the greatest number.

whistle-blowers
Individuals who report unethical practices by their employer to outsiders.

employees, moving production overseas to cut costs, and similar decisions can be justified in utilitarian terms. But that may no longer be the single criterion by which good decisions should be judged.

Improving creativity in decision making

9 Define *creativity* and discuss the three-component model of creativity.

creativity
The ability to produce novel and useful ideas.

Although following the steps of the rational decision-making model will often improve decisions, a rational decision maker also needs **creativity**, that is, the ability to produce novel and useful ideas.[59] These are ideas that are different from what's been done before but that are appropriate to the problem or opportunity presented.

Why is creativity important to decision making? It allows the decision maker to more fully appraise and understand the problem, including seeing problems others can't see. Such thinking is becoming more important. Creativity has become a driving force for economic growth. It takes creativity to, for example, develop new products and services or improve the speed and quality of business processes. 'Creative class' jobs – in science, technology, entertainment, design and entrepreneurship – are growing globally. In Europe, Belgium, the Netherlands, Finland, the UK and Ireland now have a particularly high proportion of these jobs.[60] And both companies and business schools are trying to increase the creative potential of their employees and graduates.[61] For example, L'Oréal puts its managers through creative exercises such as cooking or making music, and Business School courses in creativity have more than doubled since 2000.[62]

Creative potential

Most people have creative potential they can use when confronted with a decision-making problem. But to unleash that potential, they have to get out of the psychological ruts many of us fall into and learn how to think about a problem in divergent ways.

People differ in their inherent creativity, and exceptional creativity is scarce. We all know of creative geniuses in science (Albert Einstein), art (Pablo Picasso) and business (Steve Jobs). But what about the typical individual? People who score high on openness to experience (see Chapter 4), for example, are more likely than others to be creative. Intelligent people also are more likely than others to be creative.[63] Other traits associated with creative people include independence, self-confidence, risk taking, an internal locus of control, tolerance for ambiguity, a low need for structure and perseverance in the face of frustration.[64]

A study of the lifetime creativity of 461 men and women found that fewer than 1 per cent were exceptionally creative.[65] But 10 per cent were highly creative and about 60 per cent were somewhat creative. This suggests that most of us have creative potential; we just need to learn to unleash it.

Three-component model of creativity

three-component model of creativity
The proposition that individual creativity requires expertise, creative thinking skills and intrinsic task motivation.

Given that most people have the capacity to be at least somewhat creative, what can individuals and organizations do to stimulate employee creativity? The best answer to this question lies in the **three-component model of creativity**.[66] Based on an extensive body of research, this model proposes that individual creativity essentially requires expertise, creative thinking skills, and intrinsic task motivation (see Figure 5.3). Studies confirm that the higher the level of each of these three components, the higher the creativity.

Expertise is the foundation for all creative work. The film writer, producer, and director Quentin Tarantino spent his youth working in a video rental store, where he built up an encyclopaedic knowledge of movies. The potential for creativity is enhanced when individuals have abilities, knowledge, proficiencies, and similar expertise in their field of endeavour. For example, you wouldn't expect someone with a minimal knowledge of programming to be very creative as a software engineer.

The second component is *creative-thinking skills*. This encompasses personality characteristics associated with creativity, the ability to use analogies, and the talent to see the familiar in a different light.

Research suggests that we are more creative when we're in good moods, so if we need to be creative, we should do things that make us happy, such as listening to music we enjoy, eating foods we like, watching funny movies or socialising with others.[67]

Figure 5.3	The three components of creativity

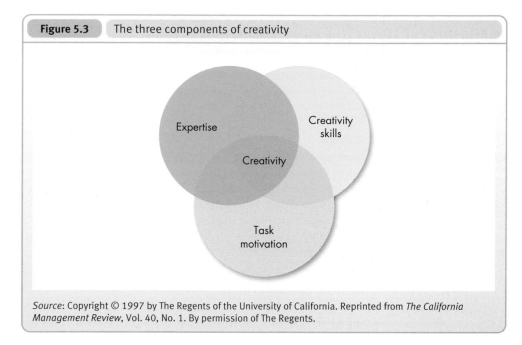

Source: Copyright © 1997 by The Regents of the University of California. Reprinted from *The California Management Review*, Vol. 40, No. 1. By permission of The Regents.

Evidence also suggests that being around others who are creative can actually make us more inspired, especially if we're creatively 'stuck'.[68] One study found that 'weak ties' to creative people – knowing creative people, but not all that closely – facilitates creativity because the people are there as a resource if we need them, but they are not so close as to stunt our own independent thinking.[69]

The effective use of analogies allows decision makers to apply an idea from one context to another. One of the most famous examples in which analogy resulted in a creative breakthrough was Alexander Graham Bell's observation that it might be possible to apply the way the ear operates to his 'talking box'. He noticed that the bones in the ear are operated by a delicate, thin membrane. He wondered why, then, a thicker and stronger piece of membrane shouldn't be able to move a piece of steel. From that analogy, the telephone was conceived.

Some people have developed their creative skills because they are able to see problems in a new way. They're able to make the strange familiar and the familiar strange.[70] For instance, most of us think of hens laying eggs. But how many of us have considered that a hen is only an egg's way of making another egg?

The final component in the three-component model of creativity is *intrinsic task motivation*. This is the desire to work on something because it's interesting, involving, exciting, satisfying or personally challenging. This motivational component is what turns creativity *potential* into *actual* creative ideas. It determines the extent to which individuals fully engage their expertise and creative skills. Creative people often love their work, to the point of seeming obsession. Our work environment can have a significant effect on intrinsic motivation. Stimulants that foster creativity include a culture that encourages the flow of ideas; fair and constructive judgement of ideas; rewards and recognition for creative work; sufficient financial, material and information resources; freedom to decide what work is to be done and how to do it; a supervisor who communicates effectively, shows confidence in others, and supports the work group; and work group members who support and trust each other.[71]

SELF-ASSESSMENT LIBRARY

How creative am I?

In the Self-assessment library (available online), take assessment I.A.5 (How creative am I?).

Global implications

In considering whether there are global differences in the concepts we've discussed in this chapter, let's consider the three areas that have attracted the most research: (1) attributions; (2) decision making; and (3) ethics.

Attributions

Although research on cultural differences in perception is just starting to accumulate, there has been some research on cultural differences in attributions. The evidence is mixed, but most of it suggests that there *are* cultural differences across cultures in the attributions people make.[72] For instance, a study of Korean managers found that, contrary to the self-serving bias, they tended to accept responsibility for group failure 'because I was not a capable leader' instead of attributing failure to group members.[73] Attribution theory was developed largely based on experiments with western European and US workers. But the Korean study suggests caution in making attribution theory predictions in non-Western societies, especially in countries with strong collectivist traditions.

Decision making

The rational model makes no acknowledgment of cultural differences, nor does the bulk of OB research literature on decision making. A 2007 review of cross-cultural OB research covered 25 areas, but cultural influence on decision making was not among them. Another 2007 review identified 15 topics, but the result was the same: no research on culture and decision making.[74] It seems that most OB research assumes that culture doesn't matter to decision making.

But Indonesians, for instance, don't necessarily make decisions the same way New Zealanders do. Therefore, we need to recognise that the cultural background of a decision maker can have a significant influence on the selection of problems, the depth of analysis, the importance placed on logic and rationality and whether organizational decisions should be made autocratically by an individual manager or collectively in groups.[75]

Cultures differ, for example, in terms of time orientation, the importance of rationality, their belief in the ability of people to solve problems and their preference for collective decision making. Differences in time orientation help us understand why managers in Egypt make decisions at a much slower and more deliberate pace than their Dutch counterparts. While rationality is valued in western Europe, that's not necessarily true elsewhere in the world. A German manager might make an important decision intuitively but know it's important to appear to proceed in a rational fashion because rationality is highly valued in the West. In countries such as Iran, where research demonstrates rationality is not as paramount as other factors, efforts to appear rational may not be necessary.

Some cultures emphasise solving problems, while others focus on accepting situations as they are. The United Kingdom falls in the first category; Thailand and Indonesia are examples of the second. Because problem-solving managers believe they can and should change situations to their benefit, UK managers might identify a problem long before their Thai or Indonesian counterparts would choose to recognise it as such. Decision making by Japanese managers is much more group-oriented than in most Western countries. The Japanese value conformity and cooperation. So before Japanese CEOs make an important decision, they collect a large amount of information, which they use in consensus-forming group decisions.

In short, we have reason to believe there are important cultural differences in decision making. Unfortunately, though, there is not yet much research to substantiate these beliefs. OB is a research-based discipline, but research does not always respond quickly to important practical concerns.

Ethics

What is seen as an ethical decision in China may not be seen as such in Ireland. The reason is that there are no global ethical standards.[76] Contrasts between Asia and the West provide an illustration.[77] Because bribery is commonplace in countries such as China, an Irish person working in China might face a dilemma: Should I pay a bribe to secure business if it is an accepted part of that country's culture? A manager of a large US company operating in China caught an employee stealing. Following company policy, she fired him and turned him over to the local authorities. Later, she was horrified to learn that the employee had been summarily executed.[78]

Ethical principles do differ around the globe because of influences such as historical traditions, religious beliefs, and social and political factors. What is considered ethically 'right' in one country may not be considered as such in another. The need for global organizations to establish ethical principles for decision makers and to modify them to reflect cultural norms may be critical if high standards are to be upheld and if consistent practices are to be achieved.

Summary and implications for managers

Perception

Individuals base their behaviour not on the way their external environment actually is but rather on what they see or believe it to be. Whether a manager successfully plans and organizes the work of employees and actually helps them to structure their work more efficiently and effectively is far less important than how employees perceive the manager's efforts. Similarly, employees judge issues such as fair pay for work performed, the validity of performance appraisals, and the adequacy of working conditions in very individual ways; we cannot be assured that they will interpret conditions about their jobs in a favourable light. Therefore, to influence productivity, it's necessary to assess how workers perceive their jobs.

Absenteeism, turnover and job satisfaction are also reactions to an individual's perceptions. Dissatisfaction with working conditions and the belief that an organization lacks promotion opportunities are judgements based on attempts to create meaning out of the job. The employee's conclusion that a job is good or bad is an interpretation. Managers must spend time understanding how each individual interprets reality and, when there is a significant difference between what someone sees and what exists, try to eliminate the distortions.

Individual decision making

Individuals think and reason before they act. This is why an understanding of how people make decisions can be helpful for explaining and predicting their behaviour.

In some decision situations, people follow the rational decision-making model. But few important decisions are simple or unambiguous enough for the rational model's assumptions to apply. So we find individuals looking for solutions that satisfice rather than optimise, injecting biases and prejudices into the decision process and relying on intuition.

Given the evidence we've described on how decisions are actually made in organizations, what can managers do to improve their decision making? We offer four suggestions.

First, analyse the situation. Adjust your decision-making approach to the national culture you're operating in and to the criteria your organization evaluates and rewards. For instance, if you're in a country that doesn't value rationality, don't feel compelled to follow the rational decision-making model or even to try to make your decisions appear rational. Similarly, organizations differ in terms of the importance they place on risk, the use of groups, and the like. Adjust your decision approach to ensure that it's compatible with the organization's culture.

Second, be aware of biases. Then try to minimise their impact. Exhibit 5.2 offers some suggestions.

Third, combine rational analysis with intuition. These are not conflicting approaches to decision making. By using both, you can actually improve your decision-making effectiveness. As you gain managerial experience, you should feel increasingly confident in imposing your intuitive processes on top of your rational analysis.

Finally, try to enhance your creativity. Actively look for novel solutions to problems, attempt to see problems in new ways and use analogies. In addition, try to remove work and organizational barriers that might impede your creativity.

EXHIBIT 5.2	REDUCING BIASES AND ERRORS

Focus on goals

Without goals, you can't be rational, you don't know what information you need, you don't know which information is relevant and which is irrelevant, you'll find it difficult to choose between alternatives, and you're far more likely to experience regret over the choices you make. Clear goals make decision making easier and help you eliminate options that are inconsistent with your interests.

Look for information that disconfirms your beliefs

One of the most effective means for counteracting overconfidence and the confirmation and hindsight biases is to actively look for information that contradicts your beliefs and assumptions. When we overtly consider various ways we could be wrong, we challenge our tendencies to think we're smarter than we actually are.

Don't try to create meaning out of random events

The educated mind has been trained to look for cause-and-effect relationships. When something happens, we ask why. And when we can't find reasons, we often invent them. You have to accept that there are events in life that are outside your control. Ask yourself if patterns can be meaningfully explained or whether they are merely coincidence. Don't attempt to create meaning out of coincidence.

Increase your options

No matter how many options you've identified, your final choice can be no better than the best of the option set you've selected. This argues for increasing your decision alternatives and for using creativity in developing a wide range of diverse choices. The more alternatives you can generate, and the more diverse those alternatives, the greater your chance of finding an outstanding one.

Source: Stephen P. Robbins, *Decide & Conquer: Make Winning Decisions and Take Control of Your Life* , 1st, © 2004. Electronically reproduced by permission of Pearson Education, Inc., Upper Saddle River, New Jersey.

POINT/COUNTERPOINT

When in doubt, do!

POINT →

Life is full of decisions and choices. The real question is not 'To be, or not to be', but rather 'To do, or not to do?' For example, should I confront my lecturer about my course grade? Should I buy a new car? Should I accept a new job? Should I choose this major? Very often, we are unsure of our decision. In such cases, it is almost always better to choose action over inaction. In life, people more often regret inaction than action. Take the following simple example:

	State	
Act	**Rain**	**Shine**
Carry umbrella	Dry (except your feet!)	Inconvenience
Don't carry umbrella	Miserable drenching	Unqualified bliss

Say you carry an umbrella and it doesn't rain, or you don't carry an umbrella and it does rain. In which situation are you worse off? Would you rather experience the mild inconvenience of the extra weight of the umbrella or get drenched? Chances are you'll regret inaction more than action. Research shows that after we make a decision, we regret inaction more than action. Although we often regret actions in their immediate aftermath, over time, regrets over actions decline markedly, whereas regrets over missed opportunities increase. For example, you finally decide to take a trip to New Zealand. You have an amazing time, but a few weeks after you get back, your credit card bill arrives – and it isn't pretty. Unfortunately, you have to work overtime and miss a few dinners out with friends to pay off the bills. A few months down the road, however, you decide to reminisce by looking through your photos from the trip, and you can't imagine not having gone. So, when in doubt, just do!

COUNTERPOINT ←

It's just silly to think that when in doubt, you should always act. People will undoubtedly make mistakes following such simple advice. For example, you're out of work, but you still decide to purchase your dream car – a BMW, fully loaded. Not the smartest idea. So why is the motto 'just do it' dangerous? Because there are two types of regrets: hot regret, in which an individual kicks themselves for having caused something bad, and wistful regret, in which they fantasise about how else things might have turned out. The danger is that actions are more likely to lead to anguish or hot regret, and inaction is more likely to lead to wistful regret. So the bottom line is that we can't apply simple rules such as 'just do it' to important decisions.

Source: Based on T. Gilovich, V. H. Medvec and D. Kahneman, 'Varieties of regret: a debate and partial resolution', *Psychological Review*, 105 (1998), pp. 602–05; see also M. Tsiros and V. Mittal, 'Regret: a model of its antecedents and consequences in consumer decision making', *Journal of Consumer Research*, March (2000), pp. 401–17.

QUESTIONS FOR REVIEW

1. What is perception, and what factors influence our perception?

2. What is attribution theory? What are the three determinants of attribution? What are its implications for explaining organizational behaviour?

3. What shortcuts do people frequently use in making judgements about others?

4. What is the link between perception and decision making? How does one affect the other?

5. What is the rational model of decision making? How is it different from bounded rationality and intuition?

6. What are some of the common decision biases or errors that people make?

7. What are the influences of individual differences, organizational constraints and culture on decision making?

8. Are unethical decisions more a function of an individual decision maker or the decision maker's work environment? Explain.

9. What is creativity, and what is the three-component model of creativity?

Experiential exercise

DECISION MAKING

Consider the two following dilemmas:

1. You are a buyer for a global organization that produces personal care products. The company is a major consumer of palm oil, the production of which has been implicated as having a substantial effect on the natural environment. You want to discontinue the use of palm oil and look for more environmentally friendly alternatives. However, profits from palm oil are crucial for developing countries to fight poverty and cancelling palm oil contracts would have drastic consequences for these suppliers and the communities around them. Will you cancel the contracts or not?

2. You are a manager of a reality TV production company. There has been a small amount of verbal conflict between

participants of the show. Producers want you to purposely highlight the material and, with editing, to make the conflict look as if it was targeted at a disabled person, to increase the exposure of the show. Will you do it?

Discuss:

1. Was your final decision based on intuition or rationality?

2. What biases are evident in the decisions you reached?

3. How did your decisions compare with the rest of the class? Why do you think people made different decisions (assuming that they did)?

4. How might you improve your decision making in the future?

Ethical dilemma

FIVE ETHICAL DECISIONS: WHAT WOULD YOU DO?

How would you respond to each of the following situations?

1. Assume that you're a middle manager in a company with about 1,000 employees. You're negotiating a contract with a very large potential customer whose representative has hinted that you could almost certainly be assured of getting his business if you gave him and his wife an all-expenses-paid cruise to the Caribbean. You know the representative's employer wouldn't approve of such a 'payoff', but you have the discretion to authorise such an expenditure. What would you do?

2. You have an autographed Coldplay CD. You have put the CD up for sale on eBay. So far, the highest bid is €74.50. A friend has offered you €100 for the CD, commenting that he could get €150 for the CD on eBay in a year. You know this is highly unlikely. Should you sell your friend the CD

for what he offered (€100)? Do you have an obligation to tell your friend you have listed your CD on eBay?

3. Your company's policy on reimbursement for meals while travelling on business is that you will be repaid for your out-of-pocket costs, not to exceed €80 per day. You don't need receipts for these expenses – the company will take your word. When travelling, you tend to eat at fast-food places and rarely spend in excess of €20 a day. Most of your colleagues put in reimbursement requests in the range of €55 to €60 per day, regardless of what their actual expenses are. How much would you request for your meal reimbursements?

4. You work for a company that manufactures, markets and distributes various products, including nutritional supplements, to health food and nutrition stores. One of the

company's best-selling products is an herbal supplement called Rosalife. The company advertises that Rosalife 'achieves all the gains of estrogen hormone replacement therapy without any of the side effects'. One day, a research assistant stops by your office with some troubling information. She tells you that while researching another product, she came across a recent study that suggests Rosalife does not offer the benefits the company claims it does. You show this study to your supervisor, who says, 'We're not responsible for validating herbal products, and nobody's hurt anyway.' Indeed, you know this is not the case. What is your ethical responsibility?

5. Assume that you're the manager at a gaming company, and you're responsible for hiring a group to outsource the production of a highly anticipated new game. Because your company is a giant in the industry, numerous companies are trying to get the bid. One of them offers you some kickbacks if you give that firm the bid, but ultimately, it is up to your bosses to decide on the company. You don't mention the incentive, but you push upper management to give the bid to the company that offered you the kickback. Is withholding the truth as bad as lying? Why or why not?

CASE INCIDENT 1

Nestlé: a baby killer?

This case examines how decisions made by Nestlé regarding the marketing of infant formula milk, ironically a vital health resource for some mothers, have been perceived as unethical by some, leading to the longest consumer boycott campaign in history.

Henri Nestlé, founder of the world's largest food and drink company, is credited with being the inventor of formula milk, back in 1867. By the late twentieth century, the formula-milk market had grown into an industry worth billions of euros worldwide, and Nestlé was a major player.

With such a huge market at stake, formula companies were accused of acting in ways calculated to undermine breastfeeding mothers, giving out free samples of their products and targeting women directly through advertising campaigns. The marketing message was that formula was as healthy as breast – even though in some countries the women had no access to clean water to mix up the formula with and no means to sterilise bottles. In some instances, cans of formula were being sold with the instructions in the wrong language for the women being targeted.

These allegations first came to prominence in the late 1970s, in a notorious court case. The charity War on Want had published a pamphlet called 'The Baby Killer' in 1974. When it was released (in amended form) in Switzerland with the title Nestlé Kills Babies, the food giant began a legal suit. It eventually won the case, but it was a Pyrrhic victory: the organization responsible for publishing the booklet in Switzerland was ordered to pay only a token fine.

The following year, 1977, saw the start of calls for a boycott of all Nestlé products in the US; the boycott quickly spread to Europe. In 1981, as a result of the boycott, the World Health Assembly (the decision-making body for WHO) adopted the International Code of Marketing of Breast Milk Substitutes, calling it 'a minimum requirement' to be adopted 'in its entirety'. In 1984, Nestlé agreed to implement the code, and the boycott was officially suspended by the groups who had done most to promote it.

But in 1988 the International Baby Food Action Network (Ibfan) alleged that baby-milk companies were flooding health facilities in the developing world with free and low-cost supplies, and the Nestlé boycott was resumed the following year. In 2000, Nestlé's chief executive said

the company would ensure labels always had instructions in the appropriate language – but campaigners claim many aspects of the code continue to be violated, and argue that consumers should still boycott the company.

No one argues that Nestlé is the only company to have been involved in less-than-perfect practices in developing and developed countries. In 2006, when the UK government launched a new scheme, Healthy Start, to replace the Welfare Food Scheme, two of the biggest producers of formula in Britain – Cow & Gate and Heinz – tried to use it as a marketing opportunity. Cow & Gate produced adverts saying its baby milk was 'closest to breast milk', a claim which is disallowed under the WHO code, until the Department of Health clamped down on them; and Heinz published a graph suggesting its formula was close to breast milk and better than competing brands. Both companies were not only violating the code, but also UK legislation.

So why target Nestlé? Ibfan and the campaigning group Baby Milk Action, say they target the company because they claim it has violated the code more than any other single company worldwide, and also that – as a market leader – it should be setting an example.

Nestlé's response to the alleged violations has tended to rely on denial, arguments about different interpretations of the code, and blaming certain employees. Although it has admitted to making mistakes in the past, the company maintains that it has always abided by the WHO code.

Nestlé is tight-lipped about the effect of the boycott on its sales or public image. But, 30 years on, feelings continue to run high. Users of a parenting website, Netmums, took its founders to task after the site agreed a sponsorship deal with Nestlé, and demonstrators continue to gather outside the company's HQ for a show of strength in favour of a cause that refuses to go away.

Questions

1. What do you think the public's perception is of Nestlé? How was this formed? Have shortcuts beens used to judge Nestlé?

2. Review the section on common biases and errors in decision making. Which of these biases and errors are relevant to Nestlé and why?

3. Do you think Nestlé is making unethical decisions? If so, how could their decisions be improved to be more ethical?

Sources: See 'g2: Milking it: The history of the Nestlé boycott', (Guardian Features pages). *The Guardian* (15 May 2007); A. Crane and D. Matten *Business Ethics: A European Perspective* (Oxford: Oxford University Press, 2009), pp. 299–302; 'g2: Milking it: It was in 1977 that campaigners first called for a boycott of Nestlé because of its aggressive marketing of formula milk in the developing world. Thirty years on, have Nestlé and the other baby-milk firms cleaned up their act? Joanna Moorhead travels to Bangladesh to find out', (Guardian Features pages). *The Guardian* (15 May 2007).

CASE INCIDENT 2

The worst business decisions?

Jeremy Kourdi writes that the worst business decisions are memorable because of their consequences, the ease with which disaster could have been avoided and the tendency for mistake to pile on mistake. These aren't accidents or unfortunate incidents but premeditated decisions that resulted in disaster. The following all made Kourdi's ten worst business decisions list:

IBM

One of the worst decisions occurred when IBM ceded dominance of the software market to Microsoft for €60,000, paying Bill Gates a fee for his operating system and failing to tie him sufficiently to their firm. IBM did not appreciate the potential value of the software market, and were overconfident that they could dominate the hardware market.

Gates realised that if Microsoft's operating system was linked with IBM, it would become the industry standard, with the opportunity to sell compatible software to IBM clones. He was right, with stunning results for Microsoft. The lessons for IBM are clear. Never buy in haste and always think of the future. Decisions set precedents and have consequences.

Dot.com boom

Thousands of flawed decisions were made during the dot.com boom. Issues that would normally affect commercial decisions were overwhelmed by a belief that virtually anything would find a profitable market online. The lessons are clear: common sense matters, don't be afraid to test assumptions and don't be seduced by hype, technology or the promise of the new.

Marks & Spencer

Marks & Spencer's decision not to advertise or even to appoint a marketing director came to characterise its arrogance, complacency, inflexibility and lack of market focus. It was a shocking decision, thankfully now corrected. For years, the firm believed that its culture was geared to the customer. This may have been true for a while, but it could not last forever. The lessons? Avoid complacency, dare to be different and recognise the inevitable: if it ain't broke, then perhaps it should be.

New Coke

Coca-Cola discovered it was losing out to rival Pepsi so it introduced New Coke. Unfortunately, millions of Americans decided they hated New Coke and responded to the change in formula as if the organization had killed off a beloved member of the family. The lessons from Coke's mistake are avoid basing decisions on biased research, stay close to customers and know what makes you or your product special.

Rebranding

The rebranding gaffe has been made by PricewaterhouseCoopers, which renamed its consulting business Monday, and Andersen Consulting, which switched to Accenture. These choices reinforced perceptions of consultants as lacking substance. Other examples are British Airways, when under Robert Ayling, rebranding its fleet with ethnic designs and Royal Mail plumping for Consignia. If an option seems too clever to be true, it probably is. Try to see things from others' viewpoints.

Enron

Enron's decision to resort to financial chicanery and fraud highlights the fact that for decisions to work well, they need to inspire trust. By deciding to go for an illegal, unethical solution to the pressures of rising shareholder expectations, senior executives lost everything. The decisions that work best are honest and compelling. They engage people and gather their own momentum.

According to Kourdi, for every disastrous decision there are many great decisions made every day. While executives should accept that decisions could always be better, what matters is that they make progress, achieve their objectives – and avoid disaster.

Questions

1. For each example, do you think the decision was based more on rational decision making, bounded rationality or intuition?

2. Analyse each example and decide on which biases may have led to the decision.

3. How could the decisions have been improved?

Source: J. Kourdi (2003) *Business Strategy: A Guide to Effective Decision Making*, 1st ed., Profile Books.

Endnotes

1 H. H. Kelley, 'Attribution in social interaction', in E. E. Jones, D. Kanouse, H. H. Kelley, K. E. Nisbett, S. Valins and B. Weiner (eds), *Attribution: Perceiving the Causes of Behavior* (Morristown, NJ: General Learning Press, 1972).

2 See L. Ross, 'The intuitive psychologist and his shortcomings', in L. Berkowitz (ed.), *Advances in Experimental Social Psychology*, vol. 10 (Orlando, FL: Academic Press, 1977), pp. 174–220; and A. G. Miller and T. Lawson, 'The effect of an informational option on the fundamental attribution error', *Personality and Social Psychology Bulletin*, June 1989, pp. 194–204.

3 See, for instance, G. Johns, 'A multi-level theory of self-serving behavior in and by organizations', in R. I. Sutton and B. M. Staw (eds), *Research in Organizational Behavior*, vol. 21 (Stamford, CT: JAI Press, 1999), pp. 1–38; N. Epley and D. Dunning, 'Feeling "holier than thou": are self-serving assessments produced by errors in self- or social prediction?', *Journal of Personality and Social Psychology*, December 2000, pp. 861–75; and M. Goerke, J. Moller, S. Schulz-Hardt, U. Napiersky and D. Frey, '"It's not my fault – but only I can change it": Counterfactual and prefactual thoughts of managers', *Journal of Applied Psychology*, April 2004, pp. 279–92.

4 D. C. Dearborn and H. A. Simon, 'Selective perception: a note on the departmental identification of executives', *Sociometry*, June 1958, pp. 140–44. Some of the conclusions in this classic study have recently been challenged in J. Walsh, 'Selectivity and selective perception: an investigation of managers' belief structures and information processing', *Academy of Management Journal*, December 1988, pp. 873–96; M. J. Waller, G. Huber and W. H. Glick, 'Functional background as a determinant of executives' selective perception', *Academy of Management Journal*, August 1995, pp. 943–74; and J. M. Beyer, P. Chattopadhyay, E. George, W. H. Glick, D. T. Ogilvie and D. Pugliese, 'The selective perception of managers revisited', *Academy of Management Journal*, June 1997, pp. 716–37.

5 See K. R. Murphy and R. L. Anhalt, 'Is halo a property of the rater, the ratees, or the specific behaviors observed?', *Journal of Applied Psychology*, June 1992, pp. 494–500; K. R. Murphy, R. A. Jako and R. L. Anhalt, 'Nature and consequences of halo error: a critical analysis', *Journal of Applied Psychology*, April 1993, pp. 218–25; P. Rosenzweig, *The Halo Effect* (New York: The Free Press, 2007); and C. E. Naquin and R. O. Tynan, 'The team halo effect: why teams are not blamed for their failures', *Journal of Applied Psychology*, April 2003, pp. 332–40.

6 P. Burrows, 'HP's Carly Fiorina: the boss', *BusinessWeek*, 2 August 1999; J. D. Markman, 'Lessons of Carly Fiorina's fall', *TheStreet.com*, 10 February 2005; and C. Edwards, 'Where Fiorina went wrong,' *BusinessWeek*, 9 February 2005.

7 S. E. Asch, 'Forming impressions of personality', *Journal of Abnormal and Social Psychology*, July 1946, pp. 258–90.

8 J. L. Hilton and W. von Hippel, 'Stereotypes', in J. T. Spence, J. M. Darley and D. J. Foss (eds), *Annual Review of Psychology*, vol. 47 (Palo Alto, CA: Annual Reviews Inc., 1996), pp. 237–71.

9 See, for example, G. N. Powell, 'The good manager: business students' stereotypes of Japanese managers versus stereotypes of American managers', *Group & Organizational Management*, March 1992, pp. 44–56; W. C. K. Chiu, A. W. Chan,

E. Snape and T. Redman, 'Age stereotypes and discriminatory attitudes towards older workers: an east–west comparison', *Human Relations*, May 2001, pp. 629–61; C. Ostroff and L. E. Atwater, 'Does whom you work with matter? Effects of referent group gender and age composition on managers' compensation', *Journal of Applied Psychology*, August 2003, pp. 725–40; and M. E. Heilman, A. S. Wallen, D. Fuchs and M. M. Tamkins, 'Penalties for success: reactions to women who succeed at male gender-typed tasks', *Journal of Applied Psychology*, June 2004, pp. 416–27.

10 J. L. Eberhardt, P. G. Davies, V. J. Purdic-Vaughns and S. L. Johnson, 'Looking deathworthy: perceived stereotypicality of black defendants predicts capital-sentencing outcomes', *Psychological Science*, 17, 5 (2006), pp. 383–86.

11 See, for example, J. Wilgoren, 'Struggling to be both Arab and American', *New York Times*, 4 November 2001, p. B1; J. Q. Wilson and H. R. Higgins, 'Profiles in courage', *Wall Street Journal*, 10 January 2002, p. A12; and P. R. Sullivan, 'Profiling', *America*, 18 March 2002, pp. 12–14; O. De Schutter and J. Ringelheim 'Ethnic profiling: a rising challenge for European Human Rights Law', *Modern Law Review*, 71, 3 (May 2008), pp. 358–84; J. Goldston and R. Neild, 'Ethnic profiling fails Europe: targeting terrorists', *International Herald Tribune*, 29 June 2006.

12 H. G. Heneman, III and T. A. Judge, *Staffing Organizations* (Middleton, WI: Mendota House, 2006).

13 J. Willis and A. Todorov, 'First impressions: making up your mind after a 100ms exposure to a face', *Psychological Science*, July 2006, pp. 592–98.

14 See, for example, E. C. Webster, *Decision Making in the Employment Interview* (Montreal: McGill University, Industrial Relations Center, 1964).

15 See, for example, D. Eden, *Pygmalion in Management* (Lexington, MA: Lexington, 1990); D. Eden, 'Leadership and expectations: Pygmalion effects and other self-fulfilling prophecies', *Leadership Quarterly*, Winter 1992, pp. 271–305; D. B. McNatt, 'Ancient Pygmalion joins contemporary management: a meta-analysis of the result', *Journal of Applied Psychology*, April 2000, pp. 314–22; O. B. Davidson and D. Eden, 'Remedial self-fulfilling prophecy: two field experiments to prevent Golem effects among disadvantaged women', *Journal of Applied Psychology*, June 2000, pp. 386–98; and D. Eden, 'Self-fulfilling prophecies in organizations', in J. Greenberg (ed.), *Organizational Behavior: The State of the Science*, 2nd edn (Mahwah, NJ: Erlbaum: 2003), pp. 91–122.

16 D. Eden and A. B. Shani, 'Pygmalion goes to boot camp: expectancy, leadership, and trainee performance', *Journal of Applied Psychology*, April 1982, pp. 194–99; and D. B. McNatt and T. A. Judge, 'Boundary conditions of the Galatea effect: a field experiment and constructive replication', *Academy of Management Journal*, August 2004, pp. 550–65.

17 See, for example, R. D. Bretz, Jr., G. T. Milkovich and W. Read, 'The current state of performance appraisal research and practice: concerns, directions, and implications', *Journal of Management*, June 1992, pp. 323–24; and S. E. DeVoe and S. S. Iyengar, 'Managers' theories of subordinates: a cross-cultural examination of manager perceptions of motivation and appraisal of performance', *Organizational Behavior and Human Decision Processes*, January 2004, pp. 47–61.

18 R. Sanders, *The Executive Decisionmaking Process: Identifying Problems and Assessing Outcomes* (Westport, CT: Quorum, 1999).

19 See H. A. Simon, 'Rationality in psychology and economics', *Journal of Business*, October 1986, pp. 209–24; and E. Shafir and R. A. LeBoeuf, 'Rationality', in S. T. Fiske, D. L. Schacter and C. Zahn-Waxler (eds), *Annual Review of Psychology*, vol. 53 (Palo Alto, CA: Annual Reviews, 2002), pp. 491–517.

20 For a review of the rational model, see E. F. Harrison, *The Managerial Decision-Making Process*, 5th ed. (Boston: Houghton Mifflin, 1999), pp. 75–102.

21 J. G. March, *A Primer on Decision Making* (New York: The Free Press, 1994), pp. 2–7; and D. Hardman and C. Harries, 'How rational are we?' *Psychologist*, February 2002, pp. 76–79.

22 M. Bazerman, *Judgment in Managerial Decision Making*, 3rd edn (New York: Wiley, 1994), p. 5.

23 J. E. Russo, K. A. Carlson and M. G. Meloy, 'Choosing an inferior alternative', *Psychological Science*, 17, 10 (2006), pp. 899–904.

24 D. Kahneman, 'Maps of bounded rationality: psychology for behavioral economics', *American Economic Review*, 93, 5 (2003), pp. 1449–75; J. Zhang, C. K. Hsee and Z. Xiao, 'The majority rule in individual decision making', *Organizational Behavior and Human Decision Processes*, 99 (2006), pp. 102–11.

25 See H. A. Simon, *Administrative Behavior*, 4th edn (New York: The Free Press, 1997); and M. Augier, 'Simon says: bounded rationality matters', *Journal of Management Inquiry*, September 2001, pp. 268–75.

26 See T. Gilovich, D. Griffin and D. Kahneman, *Heuristics and Biases: The Psychology of Intuitive Judgment* (New York: Cambridge University Press, 2002).

27 E. Dane and M. G. Pratt, 'Exploring intuition and its role in managerial decision making', *Academy of Management Review*, 32, 1 (2007), pp. 33–54.

28 As described in H. A. Simon, 'Making management decisions: the role of intuition and emotion', *Academy of Management Executive*, February 1987, pp. 59–60.

29 See, for instance, L. A. Burke and M. K. Miller, 'Taking the mystery out of intuitive decision making,' *Academy of Management Executive*, November 1999, pp. 91–99; N. Khatri and H. A. Ng, 'The role of intuition in strategic decision making', *Human Relations*, January 2000, pp. 57–86; J. A. Andersen, 'Intuition in managers: are intuitive managers more effective?', *Journal of Managerial Psychology*, 15, 1–2 (2000), pp. 46–67; D. Myers, *Intuition: Its Powers and Perils* (New Haven, CT: Yale University Press, 2002); and L. Simpson, 'Basic Instincts', *Training*, January 2003, pp. 56–59.

30 See, for instance, Burke and Miller, 'Taking the mystery out of intuitive decision making'.

31 S. P. Robbins, *Decide & Conquer: Making Winning Decisions and Taking Control of Your Life* (Upper Saddle River, NJ: Financial Times/Prentice Hall, 2004), p. 13.

32 S. Plous, *The Psychology of Judgment and Decision Making* (New York: McGraw-Hill, 1993), p. 217.

33 S. Lichtenstein and B. Fischhoff, 'Do those who know more also know more about how much they know?', *Organizational Behavior and Human Performance*, December 1977, pp. 159–83.

34 B. Fischhoff, P. Slovic and S. Lichtenstein, 'Knowing with certainty: the appropriateness of extreme confidence', *Journal of Experimental Psychology: Human Perception and Performance*, November 1977, pp. 552–64.

35 J. Kruger and D. Dunning, 'Unskilled and unaware of it: how difficulties in recognizing one's own incompetence lead to inflated self-assessments', *Journal of Personality and Social Psychology*, November 1999, pp. 1121–34.

36 Fischhoff, Slovic and Lichtenstein, 'Know with certainty: the appropriateness of extreme confidence'.

37 Kruger and Dunning, 'Unskilled and unaware of it: how difficulties in recognizing one's own incompetence lead to inflated self-assessments'.

38 See, for instance, A. Tversky and D. Kahneman, 'Judgment under uncertainty: heuristics and biases', *Science*, September 1974, pp. 1124–31.

39 J. S. Hammond, R. L. Keeney and H. Raiffa, *Smart Choices* (Boston: HBS Press, 1999), p. 191.

40 See R. S. Nickerson, 'Confirmation bias: a ubiquitous phenomenon in many guises', *Review of General Psychology*, June 1998, pp. 175–220; and E. Jonas, S. Schultz-Hardt, D. Frey and N. Thelen, 'Confirmation bias in sequential information search after preliminary decisions', *Journal of Personality and Social Psychology*, April 2001, pp. 557–71.

41 See A. Tversky and D. Kahneman, 'Availability: a heuristic for judging frequency and probability', in D. Kahneman, P. Slovic and A. Tversky (eds), *Judgment Under Uncertainty: Heuristics and Biases* (Cambridge: Cambridge University Press, 1982), pp. 163–78; and B. J. Bushman and G. L. Wells, 'Narrative impressions of literature: the availability bias and the corrective properties of meta analytic approaches', *Personality and Social Psychology Bulletin*, September 2001, pp. 1123–30.

42 J. Thornhill, R. Milne and M. Steen, 'Accent on égalité', *Finanical Times*, 9 June 2008.

43 J. Thornhill, R. Milne and M. Steen, 'Accent on égalité', *Financial Times*, 9 June 2008; D. Gilbert, 'I'm O.K., you're biased', *New York Times*, 16 April 2006, p. 12; and J. Dana and G. Loewenstein, 'A social science perspective on gifts to physicians from industry', *Journal of the American Medical Association*, July 2003, pp. 252–55.

44 See B. M. Staw, 'The escalation of commitment to a course of action', *Academy of Management Review*, October 1981, pp. 577–87; K. Fai, E. Wong, M. Yik and J. Y. Y. Kwong, 'Understanding the emotional aspects of escalation of commitment: the role of negative affect', *Journal of Applied Psychology*, 91, 2 (2006), pp. 282–97; H. Moon, 'Looking forward and looking back: integrating completion and sunk-cost effects within an escalation-of-commitment progress decision', *Journal of Applied Psychology*, February 2001, pp. 104–13; and A. Zardkoohi, 'Do real options lead to escalation of commitment? comment', *Academy of Management Review*, January 2004, pp. 111–19.

45 B. M. Staw, 'Knee-deep in the big muddy: a study of escalating commitment to a chosen course of action', *Organizational Behavior and Human Performance*, 16 (1976), pp. 27–44.

46 K. F. E. Wong and J. Y. Y. Kwong, 'The role of anticipated regret in escalation of commitment', *Journal of Applied Psychology*, 92, 2 (2007), pp. 545–54.

47 See, for instance, A. James and A. Wells, 'Death beliefs, superstitious beliefs and health anxiety', *British Journal of Clinical Psychology*, March 2002, pp. 43–53.

48 C. Anderson, 'Winner's curse: the 3G auctions were the last party of an old regime', *Wired*, May 2002, http://www.wired.com/wired/archive/10.05/change.html.

49 R. L. Guilbault, F. B. Bryant, J. H. Brockway and E. J. Posavac, 'A meta-analysis of research on hindsight bias', *Basic and Applied Social Psychology*, September 2004, pp. 103–17; and L. Werth, F. Strack and J. Foerster, 'Certainty and uncertainty: the two faces of the hindsight bias', *Organizational Behavior and Human Decision Processes*, March 2002, pp. 323–41.

50 H. Moon, J. R. Hollenbeck, S. E. Humphrey and B. Maue, 'The tripartite model of neuroticism and the suppression of depression and anxiety within an escalation of commitment dilemma', *Journal of Personality*, 71 (2003), pp. 347–68; and H. Moon, 'The two faces of conscientiousness: duty and achievement striving in escalation of commitment dilemmas', *Journal of Applied Psychology*, 86 (2001), pp. 535–40.

51 J. Musch, 'Personality differences in hindsight bias', *Memory*, 11 (2003), pp. 473–89.

52 W. K. Campbell and C. Sedikides, 'Self-threat magnifies the self-serving bias: a meta-analytic integration,' *Review of General Psychology*, 3 (1999), pp. 23–43.

53 This section is based on S. Nolen-Hoeksema, J. Larson and C. Grayson, 'Explaining the gender difference in depressive symptoms', *Journal of Personality & Social Psychology*, November 1999, pp. 1061–72; S. Nolen-Hoeksema and S. Jackson, 'Mediators of the gender difference in rumination', *Psychology of Women Quarterly*, March 2001, pp. 37–47; S. Nolen-Hoeksema, 'Gender differences in depression', *Current Directions in Psychological Science*, October 2001, pp. 173–76; and S. Nolen-Hoeksema, *Women Who Think Too Much* (New York: Henry Holt, 2003).

54 H. Connery and K. M. Davidson, 'A survey of attitudes to depression in the general public: a comparison of age and gender differences', *Journal of Mental Health*, 15, 2 (April 2006), pp. 179–89.

55 M. Elias, 'Thinking it over, and over, and over', *USA Today*, 6 February 2003, p. 10D.

56 A. Wildavsky, *The Politics of the Budgetary Process* (Boston: Little, Brown, 1964).

57 G. F. Cavanagh, D. J. Moberg and M. Valasquez, 'The ethics of organizational politics', *Academy of Management Journal*, June 1981, pp. 363–74.

58 See, for example, T. Machan (ed.), *Commerce and Morality* (Totowa, NJ: Rowman & Littlefield, 1988).

59 T. M. Amabile, 'A model of creativity and innovation in organizations', in B. M. Staw and L. L. Cummings (eds), *Research in Organizational Behavior*, vol. 10 (Greenwich, CT: JAI Press, 1988), p. 126; and J. E. Perry-Smith and C. E. Shalley, 'The social side of creativity: a static and dynamic social network perspective,' *Academy of Management Review*, January 2003, pp. 89–106.

60 R. Florida and I. Tinagli, 'Europe in the creative age', Febuary 2004, Carnegie Mellon/Demos http://creativeclass.com/rfcgdb/articles/Europe_in_the_Creative_Age_2004.pdf.

61 R. Florida, 'A search for jobs in some of the wrong places', *USA Today*, 13 February 2006, p. 11A; and R. Alsop, 'Schools find fun a worthy teacher to foster creativity', *Wall Street Journal*, 12 September 2006, p. B8.

62 'Creativity comes to B-school', *Businessweek*, 26 March 2006, http://www.businessweek.com/bschools/content/mar2006/bs20060326_8436_PG2_bs001.htm.

63 G. J. Feist and F. X. Barron, 'Predicting creativity from early to late adulthood: intellect, potential, and personality', *Journal of Research in Personality*, April 2003, pp. 62–88.

64 R. W. Woodman, J. E. Sawyer and R. W. Griffin, 'Toward a theory of organizational creativity', *Academy of Management Review*, April 1993, p. 298; J. M. George and J. Zhou, 'When openness to experience and conscientiousness are related to creative behavior: an interactional approach', *Journal of Applied Psychology*, June 2001, pp. 513–24; and E. F. Rietzschel, C. K. W. de Dreu and B. A. Nijstad, 'Personal need for structure and creative performance: the moderating influence of fear of invalidity', *Personality and Social Psychology Bulletin*, June 2007, pp. 855–66.

65 Cited in C. G. Morris, *Psychology: An Introduction*, 9th edn (Upper Saddle River, NJ: Prentice Hall, 1996), p. 344.

66 This section is based on T. M. Amabile, 'Motivating creativity in organizations: on doing what you love and loving what you do', *California Management Review*, 40, 1 (1997), pp. 39–58.

67 A. M. Isen, 'Positive affect', in T. Dalgleish and M. J. Power (eds), *Handbook of Cognition and Emotion* (New York: Wiley, 1999), pp. 521–39.

68 J. Zhou, 'When the presence of creative co-workers is related to creativity: role of supervisor close monitoring, developmental feedback, and creative personality', *Journal of Applied Psychology*, 88, 3 (June 2003), pp. 413–22.

69 J. E. Perry-Smith, 'Social yet creative: the role of social relationships in facilitating individual creativity', *Academy of Management Journal*, 49, 1 (2006), pp. 85–101.

70 W. J. J. Gordon, *Synectics* (New York: Harper & Row, 1961).

71 See T. M. Amabile, *KEYS: Assessing the Climate for Creativity* (Greensboro, NC: Center for Creative Leadership, 1995); N. Madjar, G. R. Oldham and M. G. Pratt, 'There's no place like home? the contributions of work and nonwork creativity support to employees' creative performance', *Academy of Management Journal*, August 2002, pp. 757–67; and C. E. Shalley, J. Zhou and G. R. Oldham, 'The effects of personal and contextual characteristics on creativity: where should we go from here?', *Journal of Management*, November 2004, pp. 933–58.

72 See, for instance, G. R. Semin, 'A gloss on attribution theory', *British Journal of Social and Clinical Psychology*, November 1980, pp. 291–300; M. W. Morris and K. Peng, 'Culture and cause: American and Chinese attributions for social and physical events', *Journal of Personality and Social Psychology*, December 1994, pp. 949–71; and D. S. Krull, M. H.-M. Loy, J. Lin, C.-F. Wang, S. Chen and X. Zhao, 'The fundamental attribution error: correspondence bias in individualistic and collectivist cultures', *Personality & Social Psychology Bulletin*, October 1999, pp. 1208–19.

73 S. Nam, 'Cultural and managerial attributions for group performance', unpublished doctoral dissertation; University of Oregon. Cited in R. M. Steers, S. J. Bischoff, and L. H. Higgins, 'Cross-cultural management research', *Journal of Management Inquiry*, December 1992, pp. 325–26.

74 M. J. Gelfand, M. Erez and Z. Aycan, 'Cross-cultural organizational behavior', *Annual Review of Psychology*, January 2007, pp. 479–514; and A. S. Tsui, S. S. Nifadkar and A. Y. Ou, 'Cross-national, cross-cultural organizational behavior research: advances, gaps, and recommendations', *Journal of Management*, June 2007, pp. 426–78.

75 N. J. Adler, *International Dimensions of Organizational Behavior*, 4th edn (Cincinnati, OH: SouthWestern Publishing, 2002), pp. 182–89.

76 T. Jackson, 'Cultural values and management ethics: a 10-nation study', *Human Relations*, October 2001, pp. 1267–302; see also J. B. Cullen, K. P. Parboteeah and M. Hoegl, 'Cross-national differences in managers' willingness to justify ethically suspect behaviors: a test of institutional anomie theory', *Academy of Management Journal*, June 2004, pp. 411–21.

77 W. Chow Hou, 'To bribe or not to bribe?', *Asia, Inc.*, October 1996, p. 104.

78 P. Digh, 'Shades of gray in the global marketplace', *HRMagazine*, April 1997, p. 91.

Motivation concepts

After studying this chapter, you should be able to:

1 Describe the three key three elements of motivation.

2 Identify four early theories of motivation and evaluate their applicability today.

3 Apply the predictions of cognitive evaluation theory to intrinsic and extrinsic rewards.

4 Compare and contrast goal-setting theory and management by objectives

5 Contrast reinforcement theory and goal-setting theory.

6 Demonstrate how organizational justice is a refinement of equity theory.

7 Apply the key tenets of expectancy theory to motivating employees.

8 Compare contemporary theories of motivation.

9 Explain to what degree motivation theories are culture bound.

Motivation will almost always beat mere talent

Norman Ralph Augustine

Arnold power

Max Whittake / Getty Images

Arnold Schwarzenegger, bodybuilder, actor, businessman and politician is a man of tremendous ambition and astonishing will. Motivated early on by a strict childhood in Austria and by dreams of grandeur that would be labelled delusional – except that he achieved them.

He decided early on that 'the bigger you are and the more impressive you look physically, the more people listen and the better you can sell yourself or anything else'. A brutal training regime of up to five hours each day meant he reached his first goal, to become Mr. Universe, by age 19. Over the next eight years, he won 13 more championships.

He made it to America by age 21 and was a millionaire before his Hollywood career even began. He has been successful with many business ventures and investments, starting with a bricklaying business he co-founded. He has investments that now include high-value properties, companies, stocks and bonds.

Schwarzenegger took the same approach with Hollywood that he'd taken with bodybuilding and business: Nothing was going to stop him from being successful. 'One of the great differences about him was that he had a professional business attitude about being a star', says Ivan Reltman, who produced and directed him in *Twins* and *Kindergarten Cop*. Schwarzenegger says he was always thinking, 'How can I convince the world . . . to get out of their home and go watch me?' He was a tireless promoter of everything he was involved in – his movies, his books, his volunteer projects. He did a 30-city book tour for his *Encyclopedia of Modern Bodybuilding*, visited 64 countries to promote the Special Olympics, met every governor in the country as chairman of the first President Bush's Commission on Physical Fitness.

He learned to turn a deaf ear on doubters. 'Other people would say, "This can never happen. There's the talent problem. There's the language problem. The name itself – Schwarzenegger – no one can pronounce it"' he recalls. 'Those were their obstacles, not mine.' If his name was difficult to pronounce, he told himself, then it would be unforgettable.

Being a hugely successful bodybuilder, actor and businessman would probably be enough for most people. Not Schwarzenegger. Elected Governor of California for the first time in 2003, a new era as a politician began. When you've spent your life visualising success, who knows what's coming next.

Sources: B. Morris, 'Arnold power', *Fortune*, 150, 3 (2004), pp. 77–83; www.policalbase.com. Accessed 20 October 2008.

What motivates people like Arnold Schwarzenegger to excel? Is there anything organizations can do to encourage that sort of motivation in their employees? Before we answer that question, try a self-assessment of your confidence in your ability to succeed.

SELF ASSESSMENT LIBRARY

How confident am I in my abilities to succeed?

In the Self-assessment library (available online), take assessment IV.A.3 (How confident am I in my abilities to succeed?) and answer the following questions.

1. How did you score relative to other class members? Does that surprise you?

2. Do you think self-confidence is critical to success? Can a person be too confident?

Motivation is one of the most frequently researched topics in OB.[1] One reason for its popularity is revealed by survey evidence that tells us the majority of the workforce in leading Western economies is not engaged. For example, in Germany around 82 per cent of employees report not being committed to their jobs with 18 per cent of these being actively disengaged. In the United Kingdom, 7 out of 10 employees have no 'passion for work', defined as feeling positive about their job, as well as being prepared to go the extra mile to make sure the job is performed to the best of the worker's ability.[2] Moreover, another study suggested that, by workers' own reports, they waste roughly 2 hours per day, not counting lunch and scheduled breaks (the biggest time-wasters were Internet surfing and talking with co-workers).[3] Clearly, motivation seems to be an issue. The good news is that all this research provides us with considerable insights into how to improve motivation.

In this chapter, we'll review the basics of motivation, assess a number of motivation theories, and provide an integrative model that shows how the best of these theories fit together.

FACE THE FACTS

A survey of 15,000 employees across Europe found:

- Only 15 per cent of workers were highly motivated and willing to put extra effort into their jobs.
- The majority of workers (65 per cent) were moderately interested in their jobs.
- One in five was completely uninterested in their job.

- The most common reasons cited were: lack of interest and care from management; an inability of workers to influence decision-making; senior management failing to demonstrate its value; and a perceived lack of fairness in determining pay levels.

Source: P. Yandall, 'Staff willing to go the extra mile are in the minority', *Personnel Today*, 27 May 2004.

Defining motivation

1 Describe the three key elements of motivation.

What is motivation? It's the result of the interaction between an individual and a situation. Certainly, some individuals, such as Arnold Schwarzenegger, seem to be driven to succeed. But the same student who finds it difficult to read a textbook for more than 20 minutes may devour a Harry Potter book in a day. For this student, the difference in motivation is driven by the situation. So as we analyse the concept of motivation, keep in mind that the level of motivation varies both between individuals and within individuals at different times.

We define **motivation** as the processes that account for an individual's intensity, direction and persistence of effort toward attaining a goal.[4] While general motivation is concerned with effort toward *any* goal, we'll narrow the focus to *organizational* goals in order to reflect our singular interest in work-related behaviour.

The three key elements in our definition are intensity, direction and persistence. *Intensity* is concerned with how hard a person tries. This is the element most of us focus on when we talk about motivation. However, high intensity is unlikely to lead to favourable job-performance

motivation
The processes that account for an individual's intensity, direction and persistence of effort toward attaining a goal.

outcomes unless the effort is channelled in a *direction* that benefits the organization. Therefore, we have to consider the quality of effort as well as its intensity. Effort that is directed toward, and consistent with, the organization's goals is the kind of effort that we should be seeking. Finally, motivation has a *persistence* dimension. This is a measure of how long a person can maintain effort. Motivated individuals stay with a task long enough to achieve their goal.

Early theories of motivation

2 Identify four early theories of motivation and evaluate their applicability today.

The 1950s were a fruitful period in the development of motivation concepts. Four specific theories were formulated during this period, which although heavily attacked and now questionable in terms of validity, are probably still the best-known explanations for employee motivation. As you'll see later in this chapter, we have since developed more valid explanations of motivation, but you should know these early theories for at least two reasons: (1) They represent a foundation from which contemporary theories have grown, and (2) practising managers still regularly use these theories and their terminology in explaining employee motivation.

Hierarchy of needs theory

hierarchy of needs theory
A hierarchy of five needs – physiological, safety, social, esteem and self-actualisation – in which, as each need is substantially satisfied, the next need becomes dominant.

lower-order needs
Needs that are satisfied externally, such as physiological and safety needs.

self-actualisation
The drive to become what a person is capable of becoming.

higher-order needs
Needs that are satisfied internally, such as social, esteem and self-actualisation needs.

It's probably safe to say that the best-known theory of motivation is Abraham Maslow's **hierarchy of needs theory**.[5] Maslow hypothesised that within every human being, there exists a hierarchy of five needs:

1. **Physiological.** Includes hunger, thirst, shelter, sex and other bodily needs
2. **Safety.** Security and protection from physical and emotional harm
3. **Social.** Affection, belongingness, acceptance and friendship
4. **Esteem.** Internal factors such as self-respect, autonomy and achievement, and external factors such as status, recognition and attention
5. **Self-actualisation.** Drive to become what one is capable of becoming; includes growth, achieving one's potential and self-fulfilment

As each of these needs becomes substantially satisfied, the next need becomes dominant. In terms of Figure 6.1, the individual moves up the steps of the hierarchy. From the standpoint of motivation, the theory would say that although no need is ever fully gratified, a substantially satisfied need no longer motivates. So if you want to motivate someone, according to Maslow, you need to understand what level of the hierarchy that person is currently on and focus on satisfying the needs at or above that level.

Maslow separated the five needs into higher and lower orders. Physiological and safety needs were described as **lower-order needs** and social, esteem and **self-actualisation** as **higher-order**

| **Figure 6.1** | Maslow's hierarchy of needs |

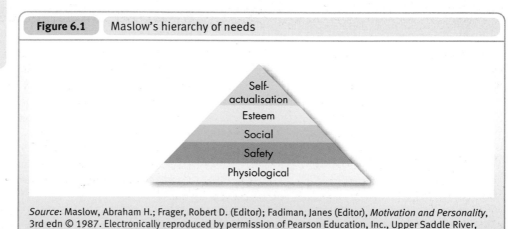

Source: Maslow, Abraham H.; Frager, Robert D. (Editor); Fadiman, Janes (Editor), *Motivation and Personality*, 3rd edn © 1987. Electronically reproduced by permission of Pearson Education, Inc., Upper Saddle River, New Jersey.

needs. The differentiation between the two orders was made on the premise that higher-order needs are satisfied internally (within the person), whereas lower-order needs are predominantly satisfied externally (by things such as pay, union contracts and tenure).

Maslow's needs theory has received wide recognition, particularly among practising managers. This can be attributed to the theory's intuitive logic and ease of understanding. Unfortunately, however, research does not validate the theory. Maslow provided no empirical substantiation, and several studies that sought to validate the theory found no support for it.[6]

Clayton Alderfer attempted to rework Maslow's need hierarchy to align it more closely with empirical research. His revised need hierarchy is labelled **ERG theory**.[7] Alderfer argued that there are three groups of core needs – *existence* (similar to Maslow's physiological and safety needs), *relatedness* (similar to Maslow's social and status needs) and *growth* (similar to Maslow's esteem needs and self-actualisation). Unlike Maslow, Alderfer didn't assume that these needs existed in a rigid hierarchy. An individual could be focusing on all three need categories simultaneously. Despite these differences, empirical research hasn't been any more supportive of ERG theory than of the need hierarchy.[8]

Old theories, especially ones that are intuitively logical, apparently die hard. Although the need hierarchy theory and its terminology have remained popular with practising managers, there is little evidence that need structures are organized along the dimensions proposed by Maslow or Alderfer, that unsatisfied needs motivate, or that a satisfied need activates movement to a new need level.[9]

ERG theory
A theory that posits three groups of core needs: existence, relatedness and growth.

Theory X
The assumption that employees dislike work, are lazy, dislike responsibility and must be coerced to perform.

Theory Y
The assumption that employees like work, are creative, seek responsibility and can exercise self-direction.

Theory X and Theory Y

Douglas McGregor proposed two distinct views of human beings: one basically negative, labelled **Theory X**, and the other basically positive, labelled **Theory Y**.[10] After viewing the way in which managers dealt with employees, McGregor concluded that managers' views of the nature of human beings are based on a certain grouping of assumptions and that managers tend to mould their behaviour toward employees according to these assumptions.

'WOMEN ARE MORE MOTIVATED TO GET ALONG, AND MEN ARE MORE MOTIVATED TO GET AHEAD'

MYTH *OR* SCIENCE?

This statement is generally true. Compared to women, men are relatively more motivated to excel at tasks and jobs. Compared to men, women are more motivated to maintain relationships.

Before proceeding any further, though, it is important to note that these gender differences do not mean that every man is more motivated by his career than every woman. There are differences, but think of it like gender and longevity. Women, on average, live longer than men, but in a significant percentage of couples (roughly 45 per cent), a husband will outlive his wife. So, there are differences, but you need to resist the human tendency to turn a group difference into a broad generalisation or stereotype.

Research indicates that men are more likely to be described by what are called 'agentic traits', such as *active*, *decisive* and *competitive*. Women are more likely to be described by what are termed 'communal' traits, such as *caring*, *emotional* and *considerate*. This evidence, however, might reflect gender stereotypes. We might hold stereotypes of the traits of men and women, but that doesn't necessarily prove that men and women are motivated by different things.

Other evidence, though, suggest that this is not just a gender stereotype. A study of 1,398 working Germans revealed that men were more motivated by agentic strivings and women more by communal strivings, and these gender differences did not change over the 17-month course of the study. As a result of these differences, men had higher levels of 'objective' career success (income, occupational status) than women. Women, however, were more involved in their families than were men.

We don't know whether these differences are ingrained or socialised. If they are socialised, though, evidence suggests that it begins early. A study of the stories that children aged 4 through 9 told about their lives revealed that girls were more likely to emphasise communion (friendships, helping others, affectionate contact) than were boys.

Sources: A. E. Abele, 'The dynamics of masculine-agentic and feminine-communal traits: Findings from a prospective study', *Journal of Personality and Social Psychology*, October 2003, pp. 768–76; and R. Ely, G. Melzi and L. Hadge, 'Being brave, being nice: Themes of agency and communion in children's narratives', *Journal of Personality*, April 1998, pp. 257–84.

Under Theory X, managers believe that employees inherently dislike work and must therefore be directed or even coerced into performing it. In contrast to these negative views about the nature of human beings, under Theory Y, managers assume that employees can view work as being as natural as rest or play, and therefore the average person can learn to accept, and even seek, responsibility.

To understand Theory X and Theory Y more fully, think in terms of Maslow's hierarchy. Theory Y assumes that higher-order needs dominate individuals. McGregor himself held to the belief that Theory Y assumptions were more valid than Theory X. Therefore, he proposed such ideas as participative decision making, responsible and challenging jobs, and good group relations as approaches that would maximise an employee's job motivation.

Unfortunately, there is no evidence to confirm that either set of assumptions is valid or that accepting Theory Y assumptions and altering one's actions accordingly will lead to more motivated workers. OB theories need to have empirical support before we can accept them. Such empirical support is lacking for Theory X and Theory Y as it is for the hierarchy of needs theories.

Two-factor theory

two-factor theory
A theory that relates intrinsic factors to job satisfaction and associates extrinsic factors with dissatisfaction. Also called motivation-hygiene theory.

Psychologist Frederick Herzberg proposed the **two-factor theory** – also called *motivation-hygiene theory*.[11] Believing that an individual's relation to work is basic and that one's attitude toward work can very well determine success or failure, Herzberg investigated the question 'What do people want from their jobs?' He asked people to describe, in detail, situations in which they felt exceptionally *good* or *bad* about their jobs. The responses were then tabulated and categorised.

From the categorised responses, Herzberg concluded that the replies people gave when they felt good about their jobs were significantly different from the replies given when they felt bad. As shown in Figure 6.2, certain characteristics tend to be consistently related to job satisfaction and others to job dissatisfaction. Intrinsic factors, such as advancement, recognition, responsibility and achievement seem to be related to job satisfaction. Respondents who felt good about their work tended to attribute these factors to themselves. On the other hand, dissatisfied respondents tended to cite extrinsic factors, such as supervision, pay, company policies and working conditions.

The data suggest, said Herzberg, that the opposite of satisfaction is not dissatisfaction, as was traditionally believed. Removing dissatisfying characteristics from a job does not necessarily make the job satisfying. As illustrated in Figure 6.3, Herzberg proposed that his findings indicated the existence of a dual continuum: The opposite of 'satisfaction' is 'no satisfaction', and the opposite of 'dissatisfaction' is 'no dissatisfaction'.

According to Herzberg, the factors that lead to job satisfaction are separate and distinct from those that lead to job dissatisfaction. Therefore, managers who seek to eliminate factors that can create job dissatisfaction may bring about peace but not necessarily motivation. They will be placating their workforce rather than motivating workers. As a result, Herzberg characterised conditions surrounding the job such as quality of supervision, pay, company policies, physical working conditions, relations with others and job security as **hygiene factors**. When they're adequate, people will not be dissatisfied; neither will they be satisfied. If we want to motivate people on their jobs, Herzberg suggested emphasising factors associated with the work itself or with outcomes directly derived from it, such as promotional opportunities, opportunities for personal growth, recognition, responsibility and achievement. These are the characteristics that people find intrinsically rewarding.

hygiene factors
Factors – such as company policy and administration, supervision and salary – that, when adequate in a job, placate workers. When these factors are adequate, people will not be dissatisfied.

The two-factor theory has not been well supported in the literature, and it has many detractors.[12] The criticisms of the theory include the following:

1. The procedure that Herzberg used is limited by its methodology. When things are going well, people tend to take credit themselves. Contrarily, they blame failure on the extrinsic environment.

2. The reliability of Herzberg's methodology is questioned. Raters have to make interpretations, so they may contaminate the findings by interpreting one response in one manner while treating a similar response differently.

3. No overall measure of satisfaction was utilised. A person may dislike part of a job yet still think the job is acceptable overall.

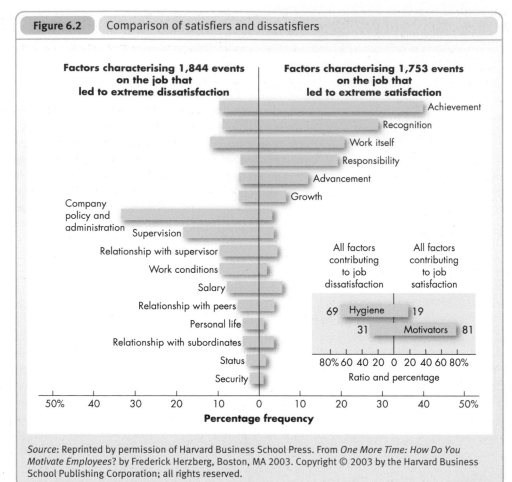

| Figure 6.2 | Comparison of satisfiers and dissatisfiers |

Source: Reprinted by permission of Harvard Business School Press. From *One More Time: How Do You Motivate Employees*? by Frederick Herzberg, Boston, MA 2003. Copyright © 2003 by the Harvard Business School Publishing Corporation; all rights reserved.

| Figure 6.3 | Contrasting views of satisfaction and dissatisfaction |

Traditional view

Satisfaction   Dissatisfaction

Herzberg's view

Motivators

Satisfaction   No satisfaction

Hygiene factors

No dissatisfaction   Dissatisfaction

4. Herzberg assumed a relationship between satisfaction and productivity, but the research methodology he used looked only at satisfaction and not at productivity. To make such research relevant, one must assume a strong relationship between satisfaction and productivity.

Regardless of the criticisms, Herzberg's theory has been widely read, and few managers are unfamiliar with its recommendations.

It's important to realise that even though we may intuitively *like* a theory, that does not mean that we should accept it. Many managers find need theories intuitively appealing, but remember

Natalie Massenet, founder and chairperson of the world's premier luxury fashion retailer, NET-A-PORTER.COM., is a high achiever. As a former fashion editor for international high profile publications *W*, *WWD* and *Tatler*, Massenet's original idea for NET-A-PORTER was to create an online magazine which would allow women to buy 'must-have' designer clothes straight from the page. This idea has grown into a profitable business that delivers more than 200 leading international fashion brands to a global audience. NET-A-PORTER is referred to as the 'barometer of fashion' by the *Financial Times* and is credited by *Vogue* as 'revolutionising the way we buy designer clothes.'

Source: 'European Business Leader Awards 2008'. Available at http://www.ebla2008.com/winners2008.html. Accessed 20 October 2008.

that at one time, the world seemed intuitively flat. Sometimes science backs up intuition, and sometimes it doesn't. In the case of the two-factor theory – as with the need hierarchy and Theory X/Theory Y – it doesn't.

McClelland's theory of needs

You have one beanbag, and there are five targets set up in front of you. Each one is progressively farther away and, hence, more difficult to hit. Target A is easy. It sits almost within arm's reach. If you hit it, you get €2. Target B is a bit farther out, but about 80 per cent of the people who try can hit it. It pays €4. Target C pays €8, and about half the people who try can hit it. Very few people can hit Target D, but the payoff is €16 for those who do. Finally, Target E pays €32, but it's almost impossible to achieve. Which target would you try for? If you selected C, you're likely to be a high achiever. Why? Read on.

McClelland's theory of needs was developed by David McClelland and his associates.[13] The theory focuses on three needs, defined as follows:

- **Need for achievement (nAch)** is the drive to excel, to achieve in relation to a set of standards, to strive to succeed.
- **Need for power (nPow)** is the need to make others behave in a way in which they would not have behaved otherwise.
- **Need for affiliation (nAff)** is the desire for friendly and close interpersonal relationships.

Of the three needs, McClelland and subsequent researchers focused most of their attention on nAch. High achievers perform best when they perceive their probability of success as 0.5 – that is, when they estimate that they have a 50–50 chance of success. They dislike gambling with high odds because they get no achievement satisfaction from success that comes by pure chance. Similarly, they dislike low odds (high probability of success) because then there is no challenge to their skills. They like to set goals that require stretching themselves a little.

Relying on an extensive amount of research, we can make some reasonably well-supported predictions of the relationship between achievement need and job performance. Although less research has been done on power and affiliation needs, there are consistent findings there, too. First, when jobs have a high degree of personal responsibility and feedback and an intermediate degree of risk, high achievers are strongly motivated. High achievers, for example, are successful in entrepreneurial activities such as running their own businesses and managing self-contained units within large organizations.[14] Second, a high need to achieve does not necessarily make someone a good manager, especially in large organizations. People with a high achievement need are interested in how well they do personally and not in influencing others to do well. High-nAch salespeople do not necessarily make good sales managers, and the good general manager in a large organization does not typically have a high need to achieve.[15] Third, the needs for affiliation and power tend to be closely related to managerial success. The best managers are high in their need for power and low in their need for affiliation.[16] In fact, a high power motive may be a requirement for managerial effectiveness.[17]

As you might have gathered, of the early theories of motivation, McClelland's has had the best research support. Unfortunately, it has less practical effect than the others. Because McClelland

---

McClelland's theory of needs
A theory which states that achievement, power and affiliation are three important needs that help explain motivation.

need for achievement (nAch)
The drive to excel, to achieve in relationship to a set of standards and to strive to succeed.

need for power (nPow)
The need to make others behave in a way in which they would not have behaved otherwise.

need for affiliation (nAff)
The desire for friendly and close interpersonal relationships.

argued that the three needs are subconscious – meaning that we may be high on these needs but not know it – measuring them is not easy. In the most common approach, a trained expert presents pictures to individuals, asks them to tell a story about each, and then scores their responses in terms of the three needs. However, because measuring the needs is time-consuming and expensive, few organizations have been willing to invest time and resources in measuring McClelland's concept.

Contemporary theories of motivation

The previously described theories are well known but, unfortunately, have either not held up well under close examination or fallen out of favour. However, there are a number of contemporary theories, and they have one thing in common: Each has a reasonable degree of valid supporting documentation. Of course, this doesn't mean that the theories we are about to introduce are unquestionably right. We call them 'contemporary theories' not because they were all developed recently but because they represent the current state of thinking in explaining employee motivation.

JOBS THAT OFFER THE 'FEEL GOOD' FACTOR   OB IN THE NEWS

Drenching actor Colin Firth in cold coffee to draw public attention to trade injustice was probably not what Raakhi Shah imagined she would end up doing when she joined Oxfam more than two years ago.

As Oxfam's artist liaison manager, Raakhi arranges for celebrities to support the charity's campaigns. 'It could be organizing photo shoots, briefing artists on campaigns or issues, organizing trips abroad, actually going on a trip, or talking to celebrity agents', says Raakhi. Graduate careers in the charity sector are by no means all as glamorous as Raakhi's, but the Trendence survey shows that students are taking a keen interest in non-corporate employers. These non-traditional, altruistic vocations are unable to compete with the likes of Goldman Sachs or GlaxoSmithKline on pay, perks or glamour, but what they offer instead is the opportunity to 'make a difference'.

It is a phrase that is liable to induce a bout of eye-rolling among graduates determined to climb the corporate ladder. But for others, the chance to have an impact on society – to give something back and be paid for your time – makes perfect sense.

'They can see the impact of their work on the environment and how that impacts on us all and future generations', says Janice Hawkins, national recruitment manager for the Environment Agency. 'You can see how much of a difference your work is making. That's a big motivation for people.'

Source: C. Bryant, 'Jobs that offer the "feel good" factor', *Financial Times*, 1 May 2007. Available at: http://search.ft.com/ftArticle?queryText=oxfam+employee+motivation&aje=true&id=070501000465&ct=0. Accessed 10 September 2008.

Cognitive evaluation theory

3 Apply the predictions of cognitive evaluation theory to intrinsic and extrinsic rewards.

Consider this scenario. 'It's strange,' said Jean-François. 'I started work at a community leisure centre as a volunteer. I put in 10 hours a week supervising children's games. I loved coming to work. Then, 3 months ago, they hired me full-time at €10 an hour. I'm doing the same work I did before. But I'm not finding it as much fun.'

There's an explanation for Jean-François' reaction. It's called **cognitive evaluation theory**, which proposes that the introduction of extrinsic rewards, such as pay, for work effort that was previously intrinsically rewarding due to the pleasure associated with the content of the work itself tends to decrease overall motivation.[18] Cognitive evaluation theory has been extensively researched, and a large number of studies have supported it.[19] As we'll show, the major implications of this theory relate to work rewards.

Historically, motivation theorists generally assumed that intrinsic rewards such as interesting work were independent of extrinsic rewards such as high pay. But cognitive evaluation theory suggests otherwise. It argues that when extrinsic rewards are used by organizations as payoffs for superior performance, the intrinsic rewards, which are derived from individuals doing what they like, are reduced. In other words, when extrinsic rewards are given to someone for performing an interesting task, it causes intrinsic interest in the task itself to decline.

cognitive evaluation theory
A theory which states that allocating extrinsic rewards for behaviour that had been previously intrinsically rewarding tends to decrease the overall level of motivation.

Why would such an outcome occur? The popular explanation is that an individual experiences a loss of control over her own behaviour so that the previous intrinsic motivation diminishes. Furthermore, the elimination of extrinsic rewards can produce a shift – from an external to an internal explanation – in an individual's perception of causation of why she works on a task. If you're reading an OB book a month because your instructor requires you to, you can attribute your reading behaviour to an external source. However, after the course is over, if you find yourself continuing to read OB books each month, your natural inclination is to say, 'I must enjoy reading OB books because I'm still reading one a month.'

If the cognitive evaluation theory is valid, it should have major implications for managerial practices. It has been a truism among compensation specialists for years that if pay or other extrinsic rewards are to be effective motivators, they should be made contingent on an individual's performance. But cognitive evaluation theorists would argue that this will only tend to decrease the internal satisfaction that the individual receives from doing the job. In fact, if cognitive evaluation theory is correct, it would make sense to make an individual's pay *noncontingent* on performance in order to avoid decreasing intrinsic motivation.

We noted earlier that the cognitive evaluation theory has been supported in a number of studies. Yet it has also been met with attacks, specifically on the methodology used in these studies[20] and in the interpretation of the findings.[21] But where does this theory stand today? Can we say that when organizations use extrinsic motivators such as pay and promotions and verbal rewards to stimulate workers' performance, they do so at the expense of reducing intrinsic interest and motivation in the work being done? The answer is not a simple 'yes' or a simple 'no'.

Extrinsic rewards that are verbal (for example, receiving praise from a supervisor or co-worker) or tangible (for example, money) can actually have different effects on individuals' intrinsic motivation. That is, verbal rewards increase intrinsic motivation, whereas tangible rewards undermine it. When people are told they will receive a tangible reward, they come to

---

Figure 6.4

"What do you *mean* money isn't everything? This is a bank!"

Source: From the *Wall Street Journal*, 8 February 1995. Reprinted with permission of Cartoon Features Syndicate.

self-concordance
The degree to which a person's reasons for pursuing a goal is consistent with the person's interests and core values.

count on it and focus more on the reward than on the task.[22] Verbal rewards, however, seem to keep people focused on the task and encourage them to do it better.

A recent outgrowth of the cognitive evaluation theory is **self-concordance**, which considers the degree to which peoples' reasons for pursuing goals are consistent with their interests and core values. For example, if individuals pursue goals because of an intrinsic interest, they are more likely to attain their goals and are happy even if they do not attain them. Why? Because the process of striving toward them is fun. In contrast, people who pursue goals for extrinsic reasons (money, status, or other benefits) are less likely to attain their goals and are less happy even when they do achieve them. Why? Because the goals are less meaningful to them.[23] OB research suggests that people who pursue work goals for intrinsic reasons are more satisfied with their jobs, feel like they fit into their organizations better, and may perform better.[24]

What does all of this mean? It means choose your job carefully. Make sure you're choosing to do something for reasons other than extrinsic rewards. For organizations, managers need to provide intrinsic rewards in addition to extrinsic incentives. In other words, managers need to make the work interesting, provide recognition, and support employee growth and development. Employees who feel that what they do is within their control and a result of free choice are likely to be more motivated by their work and committed to their employers.[25]

HOW MANAGERS EVALUATE THEIR EMPLOYEES DEPENDS ON CULTURE — GLOBAL

A recent study found interesting differences in managers' perceptions of employee motivation. The study examined managers from three distinct cultural regions: North America, Asia and Latin America. The results of the study revealed that North American managers perceive their employees as being motivated more by extrinsic factors (for example, pay) than intrinsic factors (for example, doing meaningful work). Asian managers perceive their employees as being motivated by both extrinsic and intrinsic factors, while Latin American managers perceive their employees as being motivated by intrinsic factors.

Even more interesting, these differences affected evaluations of employee performance. As expected, Asian managers focused on both types of motivation when evaluating their employees' performance, and Latin American managers focused on intrinsic motivation. Oddly, North American managers, though believing that employees are motivated primarily by extrinsic factors, actually focused more on

intrinsic factors when evaluating employee performance. Why the paradox? One explanation is that North Americans value uniqueness, so any deviation from the norm – such as being perceived as being unusually high in intrinsic motivation – is rewarded.

Latin American managers focus on intrinsic motivation when evaluating employees may be related to a cultural norm termed *simpatía*, a tradition that compels employees to display their internal feelings. Consequently, Latin American managers are more sensitised to these displays and can more easily notice their employees' intrinsic motivation.

So, from an employee perspective, the cultural background of your manager can play an important role in how you are evaluated.

Source: Based on S. E. DeVoe and S. S. Iyengar, 'Manager's theories of subordinates: a cross-cultural examination of manager perceptions of motivation and appraisal of performance', *Organizational Behavior and Human Decision Processes*, January 2004, pp. 47–61.

Goal-setting theory

4 Compare and contrast goal-setting theory and management by objectives.

goal-setting theory
A theory which says that specific and difficult goals, with feedback, lead to higher performance.

Jerome David, coach of the Thomas School swimming team, gave his squad these last words of advice before they approached the national finals: 'We've trained hard for this. Just do your best. That's all anyone can ask for.'

You've probably heard the sentiment a number of times yourself: 'Just do your best. That's all anyone can ask for.' But what does 'do your best' mean? Do we ever know if we've achieved that vague goal? Would the swimmers have recorded faster times if Coach David had given each a specific goal to aim for? Might you have done better in your high school mathematics class if your parents had said, 'You should strive for 85 per cent or higher on all your work in mathematics' rather than telling you to 'do your best'? The research on **goal-setting theory** addresses these issues, and the findings, as you'll see, are impressive in terms of the effect that goal specificity, challenge and feedback have on performance.

In the late 1960s, Edwin Locke proposed that intentions to work toward a goal are a major source of work motivation.[26] That is, goals tell an employee what needs to be done and how much effort will need to be expended.[27] The evidence strongly supports the value of goals. More to the point, we can say that specific goals increase performance; that difficult goals, when accepted, result in higher performance than do easy goals; and that feedback leads to higher performance than does nonfeedback.[28]

Specific goals produce a higher level of output than does the generalised goal of 'do your best'. Why? The specificity of the goal itself seems to act as an internal stimulus. For instance, when a courier commits to making four round-trips between Brussels and Munich each week, this intention gives him a specific objective to try to attain. We can say that, all things being equal, the courier with a specific goal will outperform a counterpart operating with no goals or the generalised goal of 'do your best'.

If factors such as acceptance of the goals are held constant, we can also state that the more difficult the goal, the higher the level of performance. Of course, it's logical to assume that easier goals are more likely to be accepted. But once a hard task is accepted, the employee can be expected to exert a high level of effort to try to achieve it.

But why are people motivated by difficult goals?[29] First, difficult goals direct our attention to the task at hand and away from irrelevant distractions. Challenging goals get our attention and thus tend to help us focus. Second, difficult goals energise us because we have to work harder to attain them. For example, think of your study habits. Do you study as hard for an easy exam as you do for a difficult one? Probably not. Third, when goals are difficult, people persist in trying to attain them. Finally, difficult goals lead us to discover strategies that help us perform the job or task more effectively. If we have to struggle for a way to solve a difficult problem, we often think of a better way to go about it.

People do better when they get feedback on how well they are progressing toward their goals because feedback helps to identify discrepancies between what they have done and what they want to do; that is, feedback acts to guide behaviour. But all feedback is not equally potent. Self-generated feedback — for which employees are able to monitor their own progress — has been shown to be a more powerful motivator than externally generated feedback.[30]

If employees have the opportunity to participate in the setting of their own goals, will they try harder? The evidence is mixed regarding the superiority of participative over assigned goals.[31] In some cases, participatively set goals elicited superior performance, while in other cases, individuals performed best when assigned goals by their boss. But a major advantage of participation may be in increasing acceptance of the goal itself as a desirable one toward which to work.[32] As we'll note shortly, commitment is important. If participation isn't used, then the individual assigning the goal needs to clearly explain the purpose and importance of the goal.[33]

Are there any contingencies in goal-setting theory, or can we take it as a universal truth that difficult and specific goals will *always* lead to higher performance? In addition to feedback, three other factors have been found to influence the goals–performance relationship: goal commitment, task characteristics and national culture.

Goal-setting theory presupposes that an individual is committed to the goal; that is, an individual is determined not to lower or abandon the goal. Behaviourally, this means that an individual (1) believes they can achieve the goal and (2) wants to achieve it.[34] Goal commitment is most likely to occur when goals are made public, when the individual has an internal locus of control (see Chapter 4), and when the goals are self-set rather than assigned.[35] Research indicates that goal-setting theory doesn't work equally well on all tasks. The evidence suggests that goals seem to have a more substantial effect on performance when tasks are simple rather than complex, well learned rather than novel, and independent rather than interdependent.[36] On interdependent tasks, group goals are preferable.

Finally, goal-setting theory is culture bound. Although more cross-cultural research is needed, goal-setting theory appears to be well adapted to countries such as Ireland and the United Kingdom because its key components align reasonably well with these cultures. It assumes that employees will be reasonably independent (that is, not too high a score on power distance), that managers and employees will seek challenging goals (that is, low in uncertainty avoidance), and that performance is considered important by both (that is, high in achievement). Conversely, we can't expect goal setting to necessarily lead to higher employee performance in countries such as Portugal or France, where the opposite conditions tend to exist.

© Reuters/CORBIS

Hasso Plattner, co-founder of the German software firm SAP, motivates employees by setting stretch goals. Plattner set a shockingly optimistic goal of 15 per cent annual growth for SAP's software license revenues. Employees responded by achieving an even higher growth rate of 18 per cent. Plattner set another stretch goal by announcing a bonus plan that would pay €287 million to hundreds of managers and key employees if they could double the company's market capitalisation, from a starting point of €43 billion, by the end of 2010. For Plattner, setting stretch goals is a way to inject entrepreneurial energy into the 35-year-old company.

Our overall conclusion is that intentions – as articulated in terms of difficult and specific goals – are a potent motivating force. The motivating power of goal-setting theory has been demonstrated on more than 100 tasks involving more than 40,000 participants in many different kinds of industries – from timber, to insurance, to automobiles. Basically, setting specific, challenging goals for employees is the best thing managers can do to improve performance.

SELF-ASSESSMENT LIBRARY

What are my course performance goals?

In the Self-assessment library (available online), take assessment I.C.5 (What are my course performance goals?).

Implementing goal-setting

Goal-setting theory has an impressive base of research support. But as a manager, how do you make it operational? That's often left up to the individual manager or leader. Some managers explicitly set aggressive performance targets – what General Electric called 'stretch goals'. For example, some CEOs such as Procter & Gamble's A. G. Laffey and SAP's Hasso Plattner, are known for the demanding performance goals they set. The problem with leaving it up to the individual manager is that, in many cases, managers don't set goals. A recent survey revealed that when asked whether their job had clearly defined goals, only a minority of employees agreed.[37]

A more systematic way to utilise goal setting is with a management by objectives programme. **Management by objectives (MBO)** emphasises participatively set goals that are tangible, verifiable, and measurable. As depicted in Figure 6.5, the organization's overall objectives are translated into specific objectives for each succeeding level (that is, divisional, departmental,

management by objectives (MBO)
A programme that encompasses specific goals, participatively set, for an explicit time period, with feedback on goal progress.

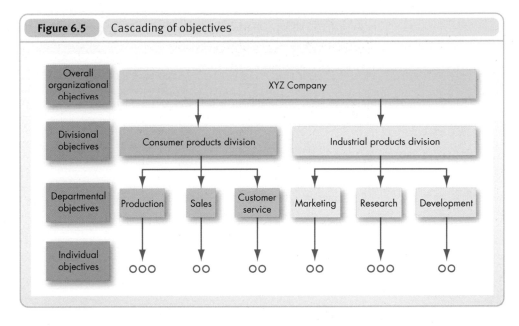

Figure 6.5 Cascading of objectives

individual) in the organization. But because lower-unit managers jointly participate in setting their own goals, MBO works from the 'bottom up' as well as from the 'top down'. The result is a hierarchy that links objectives at one level to those at the next level. And for the individual employee, MBO provides specific personal performance objectives.

Four ingredients are common to MBO programmes: goal specificity, participation in decision making (including participation in the setting of goals or objectives), an explicit time period and performance feedback.[38] Many of the elements in MBO programmes match propositions of goal-setting theory. For example, having an explicit time period to accomplish objectives matches goal-setting theory's emphasis on goal specificity. Similarly, we noted earlier that feedback about goal progress is a critical element of goal-setting theory. The only area of possible disagreement between MBO and goal-setting theory relates to the issue of participation: MBO strongly advocates it, whereas goal-setting theory demonstrates that managers assigning goals is usually just as effective.

You'll find MBO programmes in many business, health care, educational, government and nonprofit organizations.[39] MBO's popularity should not be construed to mean that it always works. There are a number of documented cases in which MBO has been implemented but failed to meet management's expectations.[40] When MBO doesn't work, the culprits tend to be factors such as unrealistic expectations regarding results, lack of commitment by top management, and an inability or unwillingness of management to allocate rewards based on goal accomplishment. Failures can also arise out of cultural incompatibilities. For instance, Fujitsu recently scrapped its MBO-type programme because management found it didn't fit well with the Japanese culture's emphasis on minimising risk and emphasising long-term goals.

Self-efficacy theory

5 Contrast reinforcement theory and goal-setting theory.

self-efficacy
An individual's belief that they are capable of performing a task.

Self-efficacy (also known as *social cognitive theory* or *social learning theory*) refers to an individual's belief that he or she is capable of performing a task.[41] The higher your self-efficacy, the more confidence you have in your ability to succeed in a task. So, in difficult situations, people with low self-efficacy are more likely to lessen their effort or give up altogether, while those with high self-efficacy will try harder to master the challenge.[42] In addition, individuals high in self-efficacy seem to respond to negative feedback with increased effort and motivation, while those low in self-efficacy are likely to lessen their effort when given negative feedback.[43] How can managers help their employees achieve high levels of self-efficacy? By bringing together goal-setting theory and self-efficacy theory.

Goal-setting theory and self-efficacy theory don't compete with one another; rather, they complement each other. As Figure 6.6 shows, when a manager sets difficult goals for employees,

| Figure 6.6 | Joint effects of goals and self-efficacy on performance |

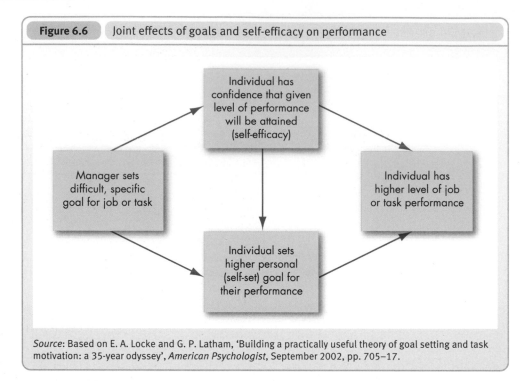

Source: Based on E. A. Locke and G. P. Latham, 'Building a practically useful theory of goal setting and task motivation: a 35-year odyssey', *American Psychologist*, September 2002, pp. 705–17.

this leads employees to have a higher level of self-efficacy and also leads them to set higher goals for their own performance. Why is this the case? Research has shown that setting difficult goals for people communicates confidence. For example, imagine that your boss sets a high goal for you, and you learn it is higher than the goals she has set for your co-workers. How would you interpret this? As long as you didn't feel you were being picked on, you would probably think, 'Well, I suppose my boss thinks I'm capable of performing better than others.' This then sets into motion a psychological process in which you're more confident in yourself (higher self-efficacy) and you set higher personal goals, causing you to perform better both in the workplace and outside it.

The researcher who developed self-efficacy theory, Albert Bandura, argues that there are four ways self-efficacy can be increased:[44]

1. Enactive mastery
2. Vicarious modelling
3. Verbal persuasion
4. Arousal

According to Bandura, the most important source of increasing self-efficacy is what he calls *enactive mastery* – that is, gaining relevant experience with the task or job. If you've been able to do the job successfully in the past, then you're more confident you'll be able to do it in the future.

The second source is *vicarious modelling* – or becoming more confident because you see someone else doing the task. For example, if your friend loses weight, then it increases your confidence that you can lose weight, too. Vicarious modelling is most effective when you see yourself similar to the person you are observing. Watching Tiger Woods play a difficult golf shot might not increase your confidence in being able to play the shot yourself, but if you watch a golfer with a handicap similar to yours, it's persuasive.

The third source is *verbal persuasion*, which is becoming more confident because someone convinces you that you have the skills necessary to be successful. Motivational speakers use this tactic a lot.

Finally, Bandura argues that *arousal* increases self-efficacy. Arousal leads to an energised state, which drives a person to complete a task. The person gets into a heightened mental state and

The Humber Rescue team illustrate the importance of enactive mastery in increasing self-efficacy. The River Humber in the North of England is said to be one of the most dangerous navigable rivers in the world. Humber Rescue is an independent charity responsible for the provision of a fast-response rescue boat on the rivers of the Humber Estuary. The crew is entirely voluntary and comes from all walks of life. Training is vital as it increases the crews confidence to succeed in their tasks and turns the volunteers into lifesavers.

performs better. But when arousal is not relevant, then arousal hurts performance. In other words, if the task is something that requires a steady, lower-key perspective (say, carefully editing a manuscript), arousal may in fact hurt performance.

What are the OB implications of self-efficacy theory? Well, it's a matter of applying Bandura's sources of self-efficacy to the work setting. Training programmes often make use of enactive mastery by having people practise and build their skills. In fact, one of the reasons training works is because it increases self-efficacy.[45]

The best way for a manager to use verbal persuasion is through the *Pygmalion effect* or the *Galatea effect*. As discussed in Chapter 5, the Pygmalion effect is a form of a self-fulfilling prophecy in which believing something to be true can make it true. In the Pygmalion effect, self-efficacy is increased by communicating to an individual's teacher or supervisor that the person is of high ability. For example, studies were done in which teachers were told their students had very high IQ scores (when in fact they had a range of IQs – some high, some low and some in between). Consistent with a Pygmalion effect, the teachers spent more time with the students they *thought* were smart, gave them more challenging assignments, and expected more of them – all of which led to higher student self-efficacy and better student grades.[46] This also has been used in the workplace.[47] The Galatea effect occurs when high performance expectations are communicated directly to an employee. For example, sailors who were told, in a convincing manner, that they would not get seasick in fact were much less likely to get seasick.[48]

Note that intelligence and personality are absent from Bandura's list. A lot of research shows that intelligence and personality (especially conscientiousness and emotional stability) can increase self-efficacy.[49] Those individual traits are so strongly related to self-efficacy (people who are intelligent, conscientiousness and emotionally stable are much more likely to have high self-efficacy than those who score low on these characteristics) that some researchers would argue that self-efficacy does not exist.[50] What this means is that self-efficacy may simply be a by-product in a smart person with a confident personality, and the term *self-efficacy* is superfluous and unnecessary. Although Bandura strongly disagrees with this conclusion, more research on the issue is needed.

Reinforcement theory

6 Demonstrate how organizational justice is a refinement of equity theory.

reinforcement theory
A theory which says that behaviour is a function of its consequences.

A counterpoint to goal-setting theory is **reinforcement theory**. The former is a cognitive approach, proposing that an individual's purposes direct his action. Reinforcement theory takes a behaviouristic approach, arguing that reinforcement conditions behaviour. The two theories are clearly at odds philosophically. Reinforcement theorists see behaviour as being environmentally caused. You need not be concerned, they would argue, with internal cognitive events; what controls behaviour is reinforcers – any consequences that, when immediately following responses, increase the probability that the behaviour will be repeated.

Reinforcement theory ignores the inner state of the individual and concentrates solely on what happens to a person when he or she takes some action. Because it does not concern itself with what initiates behaviour, it is not, strictly speaking, a theory of motivation. But it does provide a powerful means of analysis of what controls behaviour, and this reason, it is typically considered in discussions of motivation.[51]

We discussed the reinforcement process in detail in Chapter 2. Although it's clear that so-called reinforcers such as pay can motivate people, it's just as clear that for people, the process is much more complicated than stimulus–response. In its pure form, reinforcement theory ignores feelings, attitudes, expectations and other cognitive variables that are known to affect behaviour. In fact, some researchers look at the same experiments that reinforcement theorists use to support their position and interpret the findings in a cognitive framework.[52]

Reinforcement is undoubtedly an important influence on behaviour, but few scholars are prepared to argue that it is the only influence. The behaviours you engage in at work and the amount of effort you allocate to each task are affected by the consequences that follow from your behaviour. For instance, if you're consistently reprimanded for outproducing your colleagues,

Gorassini Giancario/ABACA/Press Association Images

In perceiving inequity in pay, Paris's Louvre museum attendants used an *other–inside* referent comparison when comparing their pay to that of other categories of museum staff. Some of the attendants went on strike, demanding a bonus they say other categories of staff have been offered, because they suffer more stress being on the floor looking after the Mona Lisa and other popular masterpieces.

Source: BBC News, Wednesday 14 February 2007. Available at http://news.bbc.co.uk/1/hi/world/europe/6362303.stm.

you'll likely reduce your productivity. But your lower productivity may also be explained in terms of goals, inequity or expectancies.

Equity theory

7 Apply the key tenets of expectancy theory to motivating employees.

Jane Pearson graduated from university last year with a degree in accounting. After interviews with a number of organizations on campus, she accepted a position with a top public accounting firm. Jane was very pleased with the offer she received: challenging work with a prestigious firm, an excellent opportunity to gain valuable experience and the highest salary any accounting major from her university was offered last year – €3,540 per month. But Jane was the top student in her class; she was articulate and mature, and she fully expected to receive a commensurate salary.

Twelve months have passed since Jane joined her employer. The work has proved to be as challenging and satisfying as she had hoped. Her employer is extremely pleased with her performance; in fact, Jane recently received a €150-per-month raise. However, Jane's motivational level has dropped dramatically in the past few weeks. Why? Her employer has just hired a fresh graduate from Jane's former university, who lacks the one-year experience Jane has gained, for €3,740 – €50 more than Jane now makes! Jane is irate. She is even talking about looking for another job.

Jane's situation illustrates the role that equity plays in motivation. Employees make comparisons of their job inputs (for example, effort, experience, education, competence) and outcomes (for example, salary levels, raises, recognition) relative to those of others. We perceive what we get from a job situation (outcomes) in relation to what we put into it (inputs), and then we compare our outcome–input ratio with the outcome–input ratios of relevant others. This is shown in Figure 6.7. If we perceive our ratio to be equal to that of the relevant others with whom we compare ourselves, a state of equity is said to exist; we perceive our situation as fair and that justice prevails. When we see the ratio as unequal, we experience equity tension. When we see ourselves as underrewarded, the tension creates anger; when we see ourselves as overrewarded, the tension creates guilt. J. Stacy Adams has proposed that this negative state of tension provides the motivation to do something to correct it.[53]

equity theory
A theory which says that individuals compare their job inputs and outcomes with those of others and then respond to eliminate any inequities.

The referent that an employee selects adds to the complexity of **equity theory**.[54] There are four referent comparisons that an employee can use:

1. **Self–inside.** An employee's experiences in a different position inside the employee's current organization

2. **Self–outside.** An employee's experiences in a situation or position outside the employee's current organization

3. **Other–inside.** Another individual or group of individuals inside the employee's organization

4. **Other–outside.** Another individual or group of individuals outside the employee's organization

Figure 6.7	Equity theory

Ratio Comparisons*	Perception
$\frac{O}{I_A} < \frac{O}{I_B}$	Inequity due to being underrewarded
$\frac{O}{I_A} = \frac{O}{I_B}$	Equity
$\frac{O}{I_A} > \frac{O}{I_B}$	Inequity due to being overrewarded

*Where $\frac{O}{I_A}$ represents the employee; and $\frac{O}{I_B}$ represents relevant others

Employees might compare themselves to friends, neighbours, co-workers or colleagues in other organizations or compare their present job with past jobs they themselves have had. Which referent an employee chooses will be influenced by the information the employee holds about referents as well as by the attractiveness of the referent. This has led to focusing on four moderating variables: gender, length of tenure, level in the organization, and amount of education or professionalism.[55]

Research shows that both men and women prefer same-sex comparisons. The research also demonstrates that women are typically paid less than men in comparable jobs and have lower pay expectations than men for the same work.[56] Although narrowing, the pay gap persists between women and men in all European Union Member States, to the detriment of women.[57] So a woman who uses another woman as a referent tends to calculate a lower comparative standard. This leads us to conclude that employees in jobs that are not sex segregated will make more cross-sex comparisons than those in jobs that are either male or female dominated. This also suggests that if women are tolerant of lower pay, it may be due to the comparative standard they use. Of course, employers' stereotypes about women (for example, the belief that women are less committed to the organization or that 'women's work' is less valuable) also may contribute to the pay gap.[58]

Employees with short tenure in their current organizations tend to have little information about others inside the organization, so they rely on their own personal experiences. However, employees with long tenure rely more heavily on co-workers for comparison. Upper-level employees, those in the professional ranks, and those with higher amounts of education tend to have better information about people in other organizations. Therefore, these types of employees will make more other–outside comparisons.

Based on equity theory, when employees perceive inequity, they can be predicted to make one of six choices:[59]

1. Change their inputs (for example, exert less effort)

2. Change their outcomes (for example, individuals paid on a piece-rate basis can increase their pay by producing a higher quantity of units of lower quality)

3. Distort perceptions of self (for example, 'I used to think I worked at a moderate pace, but now I realise that I work a lot harder than everyone else.')

4. Distort perceptions of others (for example, 'Alric's job isn't as desirable as I previously thought it was.')

5. Choose a different referent (for example, 'I may not make as much as my brother-in-law, but I'm doing a lot better than my Dad did when he was my age.')

6. Leave the field (for example, quit the job)

The theory establishes the following propositions relating to inequitable pay:

A. **Given payment by time, overrewarded employees will produce more than will equitably paid employees.** Hourly and salaried employees will generate high quantity or quality of production in order to increase the input side of the ratio and bring about equity.

B. **Given payment by quantity of production, overrewarded employees will produce fewer, but higher-quality, units than will equitably paid employees.** Individuals paid on a piece-rate basis will increase their effort to achieve equity, which can result in greater quality or quantity. However, increases in quantity will only increase inequity because every unit produced results in further overpayment. Therefore, effort is directed toward increasing quality rather than increasing quantity.

C. **Given payment by time, underrewarded employees will produce less or poorer quality of output.** Effort will be decreased, which will bring about lower productivity or poorer-quality output than equitably paid subjects.

D. **Given payment by quantity of production, underrewarded employees will produce a large number of low-quality units in comparison with equitably paid employees.** Employees on piece-rate pay plans can bring about equity because trading off quality of output for quantity will result in an increase in rewards, with little or no increase in contributions.

Some of these propositions have been supported, but others haven't.[60] First, inequities created by overpayment do not seem to have a very significant impact on behaviour in most work situations. Apparently, people have a great deal more tolerance of overpayment inequities than of underpayment inequities or are better able to rationalise them. It's pretty damaging to a theory when one-half of the equation (how people respond to overreward) falls apart. Second, not all people are equity sensitive.[61] For example, there is a small part of the working population who actually prefer that their outcome–input ratios be less than the referent comparison's. Predictions from equity theory are not likely to be very accurate with these 'benevolent types'.

It's also important to note that while most research on equity theory has focused on pay, employees seem to look for equity in the distribution of other organizational rewards. For instance, it has been shown that the use of high-status job titles as well as large and lavishly furnished offices may function as outcomes for some employees in their equity equation.[62]

Finally, recent research has been directed at expanding what is meant by *equity*, or *fairness*.[63] Historically, equity theory focused on **distributive justice**, which is the employee's perceived fairness of the *amount and allocation* of rewards among individuals. But increasingly equity is thought of from the standpoint of **organizational justice**, which we define as an overall perception of what is fair in the workplace. Employees perceive their organizations as just when they believe the outcomes they have received and the way in which the outcomes were received are fair. One key element of organizational justice is an individual's *perception* of justice. In other words, under organizational justice, fairness or equity can be subjective, and it resides in the perception of the person. What one person may see as unfair another may see as perfectly appropriate. In general, people have an egocentric, or self-serving, bias. They see allocations or procedure favouring themselves as fair.[64] For example, in a recent poll, 61 per cent of respondents said that they are personally paying their fair share of taxes, but an almost equal number (54 per cent) of those polled felt the system as a whole is unfair, saying that some people abuse the system.[65] Fairness often resides in the eye of the beholder, and we tend to be fairly self-serving about what we see as fair.

Beyond its focus on perceptions of fairness, the other key element of organizational justice is the view that justice is multidimensional. Organizational justice argues that distributive justice is important. For example, how much we get paid relative to what we think we should be paid (distributive justice) is obviously important. But, according to justice researchers, *how* we get paid is just as important. Figure 6.8 shows a model of organizational justice.

Beyond distributive justice, the key addition under organizational justice was **procedural justice** – which is the perceived fairness of the *process* used to determine the distribution of rewards. Two key elements of procedural justice are process control and explanations. *Process control* is the opportunity to present one's point of view about desired outcomes to decision makers. *Explanations* are clear reasons for the outcome that management gives to a person. Thus, for employees to see a process as fair, they need to feel that they have some control over the outcome and feel that they were given an adequate explanation about why the outcome occurred. Also, for procedural fairness, it's important that a manager is *consistent* (across people and over time), is *unbiased*, makes decisions based on *accurate information*, and is *open to appeals*.[66]

Research shows that the effects of procedural justice become more important when distributive justice is lacking. This makes sense. If we don't get what we want, we tend to focus on *why*. For example, if your supervisor gives a spacious office to a co-worker instead of to you, you're much more focused on your supervisor's treatment of you than if you had gotten the office. Explanations are beneficial when they take the form of post hoc excuses (for example, admitting that the act is unfavourable but denying sole responsibility for it) rather than justifications (for example, accepting full responsibility but denying that the outcome is unfavourable or inappropriate).[67] In the office example, an excuse would be 'I know this is bad. I wanted to give you the office, but it was not my decision' and a justification would be 'Yes, I decided to give the office to Sam, but having the corner office is not that big of a deal.'

A recent addition to research on organizational justice is **interactional justice**, which is an individual's perception of the degree to which they are treated with dignity, concern and respect. When people are treated in an unjust manner (at least in their own eyes), they respond by retaliating (for example, criticising a supervisor).[68] Because interactional justice or injustice is

distributive justice
Perceived fairness of the amount and allocation of rewards among individuals.

organizational justice
An overall perception of what is fair in the workplace, composed of distributive, procedural and interactional justice.

procedural justice
The perceived fairness of the process used to determine the distribution of rewards.

interactional justice
The perceived degree to which an individual is treated with dignity, concern and respect.

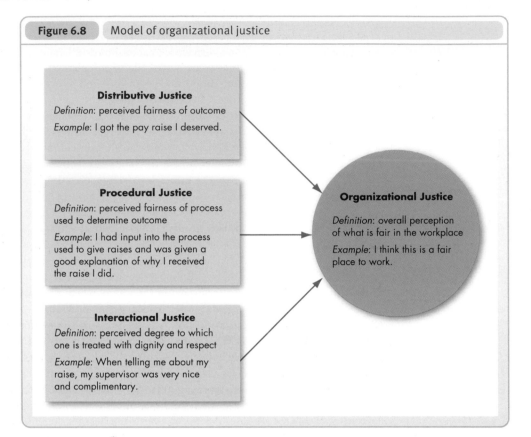

Figure 6.8 Model of organizational justice

Distributive Justice

Definition: perceived fairness of outcome

Example: I got the pay raise I deserved.

Procedural Justice

Definition: perceived fairness of process used to determine outcome

Example: I had input into the process used to give raises and was given a good explanation of why I received the raise I did.

Interactional Justice

Definition: perceived degree to which one is treated with dignity and respect

Example: When telling me about my raise, my supervisor was very nice and complimentary.

Organizational Justice

Definition: overall perception of what is fair in the workplace

Example: I think this is a fair place to work.

intimately tied to the conveyer of the information (usually one's supervisor), whereas procedural injustice often results from impersonal policies, we would expect perceptions of injustice to be more closely related to one's supervisor. Generally, that's what the evidence suggests.[69]

Of these three forms of justice, distributive justice is most strongly related to satisfaction with outcomes (for example, satisfaction with pay) and organizational commitment. Procedural justice relates most strongly to job satisfaction, employee trust, withdrawal from the organization, job performance and citizenship behaviours. There is less evidence on interactional justice.[70]

Managers can take several steps to foster employees' perceptions of fairness. First, they should realise that employees are especially sensitive to unfairness in procedures when bad news has to be communicated (that is, when distributive justice is low). Thus, when managers have bad news to communicate, it's especially important to openly share information about how allocation decisions are made, follow consistent and unbiased procedures, and engage in similar practices to increase the perception of procedural justice. Second, when addressing perceived injustices, managers need to focus their actions on the source of the problem.[71]

8 Compare contemporary theories of motivation.

expectancy theory
A theory which says that the strength of a tendency to act in a certain way depends on the strength of an expectation that the act will be followed by a given outcome and on the attractiveness of that outcome to the individual.

Expectancy theory

Currently, one of the most widely accepted explanations of motivation is Victor Vroom's **expectancy theory**.[72] Although it has its critics, most of the evidence supports the theory.[73]

Expectancy theory argues that the strength of a tendency to act in a certain way depends on the strength of an expectation that the act will be followed by a given outcome and on the attractiveness of that outcome to the individual. In more practical terms, expectancy theory says that employees will be motivated to exert a high level of effort when they believe that effort will lead to a good performance appraisal; that a good appraisal will lead to organizational rewards such as bonuses, salary increases, or promotions; and that the rewards will satisfy the employees' personal goals. The theory, therefore, focuses on three relationships (see Figure 6.9):

1. **Effort–performance relationship.** The probability perceived by the individual that exerting a given amount of effort will lead to performance.

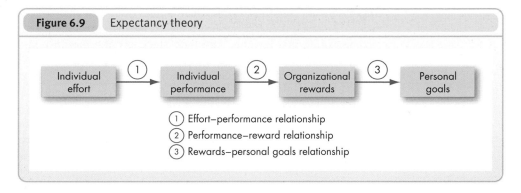

Figure 6.9   Expectancy theory

2. **Performance–reward relationship.** The degree to which the individual believes that performing at a particular level will lead to the attainment of a desired outcome.

3. **Rewards–personal goals relationship.** The degree to which organizational rewards satisfy an individual's personal goals or needs and the attractiveness of those potential rewards for the individual.[74]

Expectancy theory helps explain why a lot of workers aren't motivated on their jobs and do only the minimum necessary to get by. This is evident when we look at the theory's three relationships in a little more detail. We present them as questions employees need to answer in the affirmative if their motivation is to be maximised.

First, *if I give a maximum effort, will it be recognised in my performance appraisal?* For a lot of employees, the answer is 'no'. Why? Their skill level may be deficient, which means that no matter how hard they try, they're not likely to be high performers. The organization's performance appraisal system may be designed to assess nonperformance factors such as loyalty, initiative, or courage, which means more effort won't necessarily result in a higher evaluation. Another possibility is that employees, rightly or wrongly, perceive that the boss doesn't like them. As a result, they expect to get a poor appraisal, regardless of level of effort. These examples suggest that one possible source of low employee motivation is the belief by employees that no matter how hard they work, the likelihood of getting a good performance appraisal is low.

Second, *if I get a good performance appraisal, will it lead to organizational rewards?* Many employees see the performance–reward relationship in their job as weak. The reason is that organizations reward a lot of things besides just performance. For example, when pay is allocated to employees based on factors such as seniority, being cooperative, or flattering the boss, employees are likely to see the performance–reward relationship as being weak and demotivating.

Finally, *if I'm rewarded, are the rewards ones that I find personally attractive?* The employee works hard in the hope of getting a promotion but gets a pay raise instead. Or the employee wants a more interesting and challenging job but receives only a few words of praise. Or the employee puts in extra effort to be relocated to the company's Paris office but instead is transferred to Singapore. These examples illustrate the importance of the rewards being tailored to individual employee needs. Unfortunately, many managers are limited in the rewards they can distribute, which makes it difficult to individualise rewards. Moreover, some managers incorrectly assume that all employees want the same thing, thus overlooking the motivational effects of differentiating rewards. In either case, employee motivation is submaximised.

As a vivid example of how expectancy theory can work, consider the case of stock analysts. Analysts make their living by trying to forecast the future of a stock's price; the accuracy of their buy, sell or hold recommendations is what keeps them in work or gets them fired. But it's not quite that simple. For example, Mike Mayo, 42, is one of the few US Wall Street analysts willing to put sell recommendations on stocks. Why do analysts place so few sell ratings on stocks? After all, in a steady market, by definition, as many stocks are falling as are rising. Expectancy theory provides an explanation: Analysts who place a sell rating on a company's stock have to balance the benefits they receive by being accurate against the risks they run by drawing the company's ire. What are these risks? They include public rebuke, professional blackballing and exclusion from information. As Mayo said, 'There is no recourse for analysts.' When analysts place a buy rating on a stock, they face no such trade-off because, obviously, companies love that they are recommending that investors buy their stock. So, the incentive structure suggests that the expected outcome of buy ratings is higher than the expected outcome of sell ratings, and that's why buy ratings vastly outnumber sell ratings.[75]

Does expectancy theory work? Attempts to validate the theory have been complicated by methodological, criterion, and measurement problems. As a result, many published studies that purport to support or negate the theory must be viewed with caution. Importantly, most studies have failed to replicate the methodology as it was originally proposed. For example, the theory proposes to explain different levels of effort from the same person under different circumstances, but almost all replication studies have looked at different people. Correcting for this flaw has greatly improved support for the validity of expectancy theory.[76] Some critics suggest that the theory has only limited use, arguing that it tends to be more valid for predicting in situations in which effort–performance and performance–reward linkages are clearly perceived by the individual.[77] Because few individuals perceive a high correlation between performance and rewards in their jobs, the theory tends to be idealistic. If organizations actually rewarded individuals for performance rather than according to criteria such as seniority, effort, skill level and job difficulty, then the theory's validity might be considerably greater. However, rather than invalidating expectancy theory, this criticism can be used in support of the theory because it explains why a significant segment of the workforce exerts low levels of effort in carrying out job responsibilities.

Integrating contemporary theories of motivation

9 Explain to what degree motivation theories are culture bound.

We've looked at a lot of motivation theories in this chapter. The fact that a number of these theories have been supported only complicates the matter. It would be simpler if, after presenting half a dozen theories, only one was found valid. But the theories we presented are not all in competition with one another. Because one is valid doesn't automatically make the others invalid. In fact, many of the theories presented in this chapter are complementary. The challenge is now to tie these theories together to help you understand their interrelationships.[78]

Figure 6.10 presents a model that integrates much of what we know about motivation. Its basic foundation is the expectancy model shown in Figure 6.9. Let's work through Figure 6.10. (We will look at job design closely in Chapter 7.)

We begin by explicitly recognising that opportunities can either aid or hinder individual effort. The individual effort box also has another arrow leading into it. This arrow flows out of the person's goals. Consistent with goal-setting theory, this goals–effort loop is meant to remind us that goals direct behaviour.

Expectancy theory predicts that employees will exert a high level of effort if they perceive that there is a strong relationship between effort and performance, performance and rewards, and rewards and satisfaction of personal goals. Each of these relationships, in turn, is influenced by certain factors. For effort to lead to good performance, the individual must have the requisite ability to perform, and the performance appraisal system that measures the individual's performance must be perceived as being fair and objective. The performance–reward relationship will be strong if the individual perceives that it is performance (rather than seniority, personal favourites, or other criteria) that is rewarded. If cognitive evaluation theory were fully valid in the actual workplace, we would predict here that basing rewards on performance should decrease the individual's intrinsic motivation. The final link in expectancy theory is the rewards–goals relationship. Motivation would be high to the degree that the rewards an individual received for high performance satisfied the dominant needs consistent with individual goals.

A closer look at Figure 6.10 also reveals that the model considers achievement motivation, job design, reinforcement and equity theories/organizational justice. A high achiever is not motivated by an organization's assessment of performance or organizational rewards, hence the jump from effort to personal goals for those with a high nAch. Remember, high achievers are internally driven as long as the jobs they are doing provide them with personal responsibility,

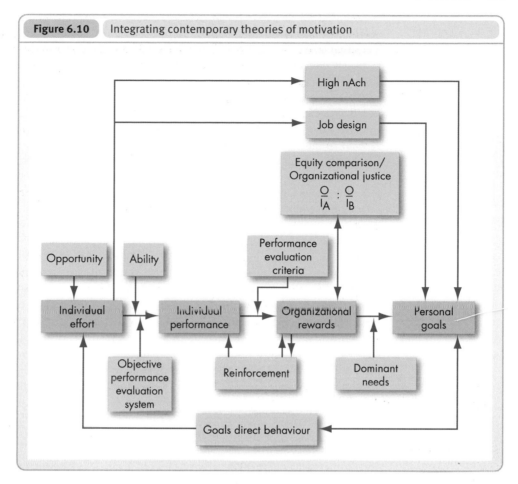

Figure 6.10   Integrating contemporary theories of motivation

feedback, and moderate risks. They are not concerned with the effort–performance, performance–rewards, or rewards–goal linkages.

Reinforcement theory enters the model by recognising that the organization's rewards reinforce the individual's performance. If management has designed a reward system that is seen by employees as 'paying off' for good performance, the rewards will reinforce and encourage continued good performance. Rewards also play the key part in organizational justice research. Individuals will judge the favourability of their outcomes (for example, their pay) relative to what others receive but also with respect to how they are treated: When people are disappointed in their rewards, they are likely to be sensitive to the perceived fairness of the procedures used and the consideration given to them by their supervisor.

Global implications

Caveat emptor: motivation theories are often culture bound

In our discussion of goal-setting theory, we said that care needs to be taken in applying this theory because it assumes cultural characteristics that are not universal. This is true for many of the theories presented in this chapter because many motivation theories were developed in the United States by and about US adults.[79] However, that is not to say that there are not commonalities. For instance, both goal-setting and expectancy theories emphasise goal accomplishment as well as rational and individual thought – characteristics broadly consistent with, among others, US, British, Irish, German and New Zealand cultures. Let's take a look at several motivation theories and consider their global cross-cultural transferability.

Maslow's needs hierarchy argues that people start at the physiological level and then move progressively up the hierarchy in this order: physiological, safety, social, esteem and self-actualisation. This hierarchy, if it has any application at all, aligns with UK and US cultures. In countries such as Japan, Greece and Mexico, where uncertainty-avoidance characteristics are strong, security needs would be on top of the need hierarchy. Countries that score high on nurturing characteristics – such as Denmark, Sweden, Norway, the Netherlands and Finland – would have social needs on top.[80] We would predict, for instance, that group work will motivate employees more when the country's culture scores high on the nurturing criterion.

Another motivation concept that clearly has a US bias is the achievement need. The view that a high achievement need acts as an internal motivator presupposes two cultural characteristics – a willingness to accept a moderate degree of risk (which excludes countries with strong uncertainty avoidance characteristics) and a concern with performance (which applies almost singularly to countries with strong achievement characteristics). This combination is found in Anglo-American countries such as the United States, Canada and Great Britain.[81] However, these characteristics are relatively absent in countries such as Chile and Portugal.

Equity theory has gained a relatively strong following in the United States and the United Kingdom. That's not surprising because US-style reward systems are based on the assumption that workers are highly sensitive to equity in reward allocations. And in the United States, equity is meant to closely tie pay to performance. However, evidence suggests that in collectivist cultures, especially in the former socialist countries of central and eastern Europe, employees expect rewards to reflect their individual needs as well as their performance.[82] Moreover, consistent with a legacy of communism and centrally planned economies, employees exhibited an entitlement attitude – that is, they expected outcomes to be *greater* than their inputs.[83] These findings suggest that US-style pay practices may need modification, especially in Russia and former communist countries, in order to be perceived as fair by employees.

But don't assume there are *no* cross-cultural consistencies. For instance, the desire for interesting work seems important to almost all workers, regardless of their national culture. In a study of seven countries, employees in Belgium, Britain, Israel and the United States ranked 'interesting work' number one among 11 work goals. And workers in Japan, the Netherlands and Germany ranked this factor either second or third.[84] Similarly, in a study comparing job-preference outcomes among graduate students in Canada, Australia, Singapore and the United States, growth, achievement and responsibility were rated the top three and had identical rankings.[85] Both of these studies suggest some universality to the importance of intrinsic factors in the two-factor theory.

Summary and implications for managers

The theories we've discussed in this chapter address different outcome variables. Some, for instance, are directed at explaining turnover, while others emphasise productivity. The theories also differ in their predictive strength. In this section, we (1) review the most established motivation theories to determine their relevance in explaining the dependent variables, and (2) assess the predictive power of each.[86]

Need theories
We introduced four theories that focused on needs: Maslow's hierarchy, ERG, McClelland's needs and the two-factor theory. None of these theories has found widespread support, although the strongest of them is probably McClelland's theory, particularly regarding the relationship between achievement and productivity. In general, need theories (Maslow and ERG) are not very valid explanations of motivation.

Goal-setting theory
There is little dispute that clear and difficult goals lead to higher levels of employee productivity. This evidence leads us to conclude that goal-setting theory provides one of the most powerful

explanations of this dependent variable. The theory, however, does not address absenteeism, turnover, or satisfaction.

Reinforcement theory

This theory has an impressive record for predicting factors such as quality and quantity of work, persistence of effort, absenteeism, tardiness and accident rates. It does not offer much insight into employee satisfaction or the decision to quit.

Equity theory/organizational justice

Equity theory deals with productivity, satisfaction, absence and turnover variables. However, its strongest legacy probably is that it provided the spark for research on organizational justice, which has more support in the literature.

Expectancy theory

Our final theory, expectancy theory, focuses on performance variables. It has proved to offer a relatively powerful explanation of employee productivity, absenteeism and turnover. But expectancy theory assumes that employees have few constraints on their decision discretion. It makes many of the same assumptions that the rational model makes about individual decision making (see Chapter 5), and this limits its applicability. Expectancy theory has some validity because for many behaviours, people consider expected outcomes. However, the rational model goes only so far in explaining behaviour.

POINT/COUNTERPOINT

Failure motivates!

POINT ➡

It's sad but true that many of the best lessons we learn in life are from our failures. Often when we're riding on the wings of success, we coast – until we crash to earth.

Take the example of Dan Doctoroff. Doctoroff is a successful New York investment banker who spent 5 years obsessed with bringing the 2012 Olympics to New York. In his efforts, he used €3 million of his own money, travelled half a million miles, worked 100-hour weeks, and staked his reputation on achieving a goal many thought was foolhardy.

What happened? New York wasn't selected, and all Doctoroff's efforts were in vain. His immediate reaction? He felt 'emotionally paralysed'. But Doctoroff is not sorry he made the effort. He said he learned a lot about himself in trying to woo Olympic decision makers in 78 countries. Colleagues had once described him as brash and arro-

gant. As a result of his efforts, Doctoroff said, he learned to listen more and talk less. He also said that losing made him realise how supportive his wife and three teenage children could be.

Not only does failure bring perspective to people such as Doctoroff, it often provides important feedback on how to improve. The important thing is to learn from the failure and to persist. As Doctoroff says, 'The only way to ensure you'll lose is not to try.'

One of the reasons successful people fail so often is that they set their own bars so high. Harvard's Rosabeth Moss Kanter, who has spent her career studying executives, says, 'Many successful people set the bar so high that they don't achieve the distant goal. But they do achieve things that wouldn't have been possible without that bigger goal.'[87]

COUNTERPOINT ⬅

Do people learn from failure? We've seen that one of the decision-making errors people make is escalation of commitment: They persist in a failed venture just because they think persistence is a virtue or because their ego is involved, even when logic suggests they should move on. One research study found that managers often illogically persist in launching new products, even when the evidence becomes clear that the product is going nowhere. As the authors note, 'It sometimes takes more courage to kill a product that's going nowhere than to sustain it.' So,

the thought of learning from failure is a nice ideal, but most people are too defensive to do that.

Moreover, there is ample evidence that when people fail, they often rationalise their failures to preserve their self-esteem and thus don't learn at all. Although the example of Dan Doctoroff is interesting, it's not clear he's done anything but rationalise his failure. It's human nature. Research shows that when we fail, we often engage in external attributions – blaming the failure on bad luck or powerful others – or we devalue what we failed to get

▶

('It wasn't that important to me anyway,' we may tell ourselves). These rationalisations may not be correct, but that's not the point. We engage in them not to be right but to preserve our often fragile self-esteem. We need to believe in ourselves to motivate ourselves, and because failing undermines that self-belief, we have to do what we can to recover our self-confidence.[88]

In sum, although it is a nice story that failure is actually good, as one songwriter wrote, 'the world is not a song'. Failure hurts, and to either protect ourselves or recover from the pain, we often do *not* learn from failure – we rationalise it away.

QUESTIONS FOR REVIEW

1. Define *motivation*. What are the key elements of motivation?

2. What are the early theories of motivation? How well have they been supported by research?

3. What is cognitive evaluation theory? What does it assume about the effects of intrinsic and extrinsic rewards on behaviour?

4. What are the major predictions of goal-setting theory? Have these predictions been supported by research?

5. What is reinforcement theory? How is it related to goal-setting theory? Has research supported reinforcement theory?

6. What is equity theory? Why has it been supplanted by organizational justice?

7. What are the key tenets of expectancy theory? What has research had to say about this theory?

8. How do the contemporary theories of work motivation complement one another?

9. Do you think motivation theories are often culture bound? Why or why not?

Experiential exercise

GOAL-SETTING TASK

Purpose

This exercise will help you learn how to write tangible, verifiable, measurable and relevant goals that might evolve from an MBO programme.

Time

Approximately 20 to 30 minutes.

Instructions

1. Break into groups of three to five.

2. Spend a few minutes discussing your class instructor's job. What does he or she do? What defines good performance? What behaviours lead to good performance?

3. Each group is to develop a list of five goals that, although not established participatively with your instructor, you believe might be developed in an MBO programme at your college. Try to select goals that seem most critical to the effective performance of your instructor's job.

4. Each group will select a leader who will share the group's goals with the entire class. For each group's goals, class discussion should focus on the goals' (a) specificity, (b) ease of measurement, (c) importance, and (d) motivational properties.

Ethical dilemma

IS GOAL-SETTING MANIPULATION?

Managers are interested in the subject of motivation because they're concerned with learning how to get the most effort from their employees. Is this ethical? For example, when managers set hard, specific goals for employees, aren't they manipulating them?

Manipulate is defined as '(1) to handle, manage, or use, especially with skill, in some process of treatment or performance; (2) to manage or influence by artful skill; (3) to adapt or change to suit one's purpose or advantage'. Aren't these

definitions compatible with the notion of managers skillfully seeking to influence employee productivity for the benefit of the manager and the organization?

Do managers have the right to seek control over their employees? Does anyone, for that matter, have the right to control others? Does control imply manipulation? And if so, is there anything wrong with managers manipulating employees through goal setting or other motivational techniques?

CASE INCIDENT 1

Gender differences in performance motivation

Men and women differ in their perceptions of what is important and motivating for good work performance, a Czech survey reveals.

Employees in the Czech Republic consider financial compensation, in the form of basic pay, as the most important factor motivating good performance. Positive inter-personal relations in the workplace are ranked in second place, followed by respectful treatment by the employer.

From a gender perspective, men place a higher value than women do on the so-called 'instrumental values' (basic salary and bonuses) as motivational factors in their work performance and identification with the employer. Women, on the other hand, place more importance than men do on inter-personal relationships at the workplace, respectful treatment by the employer and the possibility of reconciling work and family life.

The full results are presented below:

Gender gap in key drivers of motivation and commitment

		Extremely/Very important (%)	Important (%)	Not very important/ Not important at all (%)
Flexible working arrangements	Men	44.5	43.5	11.9
	Women	43.7	43.3	13.0
Bonuses**	Men	58.2	34.9	7.0
	Women	52.7	37.4	9.9
Benefits	Men	56.8	35.6	7.6
	Women	55.1	34.8	10.1
Work-life balance**	Men	59.1	36.3	4.5
	Women	65.8	31.1	3.1
Nature of work	Men	63.1	33.8	3.1
	Women	61.8	34.3	3.8
Providing good service to customers/colleagues**	Men	63.4	33.0	3.6
	Women	69.1	28.9	2.0
Being treated with respect**	Men	69.4	28.0	2.6
	Women	76.3	22.3	1.4
People you work with**	Men	78.1	20.4	1.5
	Women	83.4	15.8	0.9
Basic pay*	Men	85.0	14.2	0.8
	Women	80.4	18.7	0.9

Chi squared test: Statistically, significant differences exist between men and women at confidence level:
* $p \leq 0.05$; ** $p \leq 0.01$

Questions

1. Do these results surprise you? Why or why not?

2. What are the implications of these results for the distribution of rewards?

3. Do you think these gender differences in performance motivation occur in your country?

4. Which theory or theories of motivation help explain the overall results that employees in the Czech Republic consider financial compensation, in the form of basic pay, as the most important factor motivating good performance followed by positive inter-personal relations in the workplace, and thirdly respectful treatment by the employer?

Source: R. Vašková and A. Kroupa (2005) *Quality of Working Life in the Czech Republic. Available at*: http://www.eurofound.europa.eu/ewco/surveys/CZ0502SR01/CZ0502SR01.htm.

8 C. P. Schneider and C. P. Alderfer, 'Three studies of measures of need satisfaction in organizations', *Administrative Science Quarterly*, December 1973, pp. 489–505; and I. Borg and M. Braun, 'Work values in East and West Germany: different weights, but identical structures', *Journal of Organizational Behavior*, 17 special issue (1996), pp. 541–55.

9 M. A. Wahba and L. G. Bridwell, 'Maslow reconsidered: a review of research on the need hierarchy theory', *Organizational Behavior and Human Performance*, April 1976, pp. 212–40.

10 D. McGregor, *The Human Side of Enterprise* (New York: McGraw-Hill, 1960). For an updated analysis of Theory X and Theory Y constructs, see R. J. Summers and S. F. Cronshaw, 'A study of McGregor's Theory X, Theory Y and the influence of Theory X, Theory Y assumptions on causal attributions for instances of worker poor performance', in S. L. McShane (ed.), Organizational Behavior, *ASAC 1988 Conference Proceedings*, vol. 9, Part 5. Halifax, Nova Scotia, 1988, pp. 115–23.

11 F. Herzberg, B. Mausner and B. Snyderman, *The Motivation to Work* (New York: Wiley, 1959).

12 R. J. House and L. A. Wigdor, 'Herzberg's dual-factor theory of job satisfaction and motivations: a review of the evidence and criticism', *Personnel Psychology*, Winter 1967, pp. 369–89; D. P. Schwab and L. L. Cummings, 'Theories of performance and satisfaction: a review', *Industrial Relations*, October 1970, pp. 403–30; and J. Phillipchuk and J. Whittaker, 'An inquiry into the continuing relevance of Herzberg's motivation theory,' *Engineering Management Journal*, 8 (1996), pp. 15–20.

13 D. C. McClelland, *The Achieving Society* (New York: Van Nostrand Reinhold, 1961); J. W. Atkinson and J. O. Raynor, *Motivation and Achievement* (Washington, DC: Winston, 1974); D. C. McClelland, *Power: The Inner Experience* (New York: Irvington, 1975); and M. J. Stahl, *Managerial and Technical Motivation: Assessing Needs for Achievement, Power, and Affiliation* (New York: Praeger, 1986).

14 D. C. McClelland and D. G. Winter, *Motivating Economic Achievement* (New York: The Free Press, 1969); and J. B. Miner, N. R. Smith and J. S. Bracker, 'Role of entrepreneurial task motivation in the growth of technologically innovative firms: interpretations from follow-up data', *Journal of Applied Psychology*, October 1994, pp. 627–30.

15 D. C. McClelland, *Power*; D. C. McClelland and D. H. Burnham, 'Power is the great motivator', *Harvard Business Review*, March–April 1976, pp. 100–10; and R. E. Boyatzis, 'The need for close relationships and the manager's job', in D. A. Kolb, I. M. Rubin and J. M. McIntyre, *Organizational Psychology: Readings on Human Behavior in Organizations*, 4th edn (Upper Saddle River, NJ: Prentice Hall, 1984), pp. 81–86.

16 D. G. Winter, 'The motivational dimensions of leadership: power, achievement, and affiliation', in R. E. Riggio, S. E. Murphy and F. J. Pirozzolo (eds), *Multiple Intelligences and Leadership* (Mahwah, NJ: Lawrence Erlbaum, 2002), pp. 119–38.

17 J. B. Miner, *Studies in Management Education* (New York: Springer, 1965).

18 R. de Charms, *Personal Causation: The Internal Affective Determinants of Behavior* (New York: Academic Press, 1968).

19 E. L. Deci, *Intrinsic Motivation* (New York: Plenum, 1975); J. Cameron and W. D. Pierce, 'Reinforcement, reward, and intrinsic motivation: a meta-analysis', *Review of Educational Research*, Fall 1994, pp. 363–423; S. Tang and V. C. Hall, 'The overjustification effect: a meta-analysis,' *Applied Cognitive Psychology*, October 1995, pp. 365–404; E. L. Deci, R. Koestner and R. M. Ryan, 'A meta-analytic review of experiments examining the effects of extrinsic rewards on intrinsic motivation', *Psychological Bulletin*, 125, 6 (1999), pp. 627–68; R. M. Ryan and E. L. Deci, 'Intrinsic and extrinsic motivations: classic definitions and new directions', *Contemporary Educational Psychology*, January 2000, pp. 54–67; and N. Houlfort, R. Koestner, M. Joussemet, A. Nantel-Vivier and N. Lekes, 'The impact of performance-contingent rewards on perceived autonomy and competence', *Motivation & Emotion*, 26, 4 (2002), pp. 279–95.

20 W. E. Scott, 'The effects of extrinsic rewards on "intrinsic motivation": a critique', *Organizational Behavior and Human Performance*, February 1976, pp. 117–19; B. J. Calder and B. M. Staw, 'Interaction of intrinsic and extrinsic motivation: some methodological notes', *Journal of Personality and Social Psychology*, January 1975, pp. 76–80; and K. B. Boal and L. L. Cummings, 'Cognitive evaluation theory: an experimental test of processes and outcomes', *Organizational Behavior and Human Performance*, December 1981, pp. 289–310.

21 G. R. Salancik, 'Interaction effects of performance and money on self-perception of intrinsic motivation', *Organizational Behavior and Human Performance*, June 1975, pp. 339–51; and F. Luthans, M. Martinko and T. Kess, 'An analysis of the impact of contingency monetary rewards on intrinsic motivation', *Proceedings of the Nineteenth Annual Midwest Academy of Management*, St. Louis, 1976, pp. 209–21.

22 Deci, Koestner and Ryan, 'A meta-analytic review of experiments examining the effects of extrinsic rewards on intrinsic motivation'.

23 K. M. Sheldon, A. J. Elliot and R. M. Ryan, 'Self-concordance and subjective well-being in four cultures', *Journal of Cross-Cultural Psychology*, 35, 2 (2004), pp. 209–23.

24 J. E. Bono and T. A. Judge, 'Self-concordance at work: toward understanding the motivational effects of transformational leaders', *Academy of Management Journal*, 46, 5 (2003), pp. 554–71.

25 J. P. Meyer, T. E. Becker and C. Vandenberghe, 'Employee commitment and motivation: a conceptual analysis and integrative model', *Journal of Applied Psychology*, 89, 6 (2004), pp. 991–1007.

26 E. A. Locke, 'Toward a theory of task motivation and incentives', *Organizational Behavior and Human Performance*, May 1968, pp. 157–89.

27 P. C. Earley, P. Wojnaroski and W. Prest, 'Task planning and energy expended: exploration of how goals influence performance', *Journal of Applied Psychology*, February 1987, pp. 107–14.

28 See M. E. Tubbs, 'Goal setting: a meta-analytic examination of the empirical evidence', *Journal of Applied Psychology*, August 1986, pp. 474–83; E. A. Locke and G. P. Latham, 'Building a practically useful theory of goal setting and task motivation', *American Psychologist*, September 2002, pp. 705–17; and E. A. Locke and G. P. Latham, 'New directions in goal-setting theory', *Current Directions in Psychological Science*, 15, 5 (2006), pp. 265–68.

29 E. A. Locke and G. P. Latham, 'Building a practically useful theory of goal setting and task motivation: a 35-year odyssey', *American Psychologist*, 57, 9 (2002), pp. 705–17.

30 J. M. Ivancevich and J. T. McMahon, 'The effects of goal setting, external feedback, and self-generated feedback on

outcome variables: a field experiment', *Academy of Management Journal*, June 1982, pp. 359–72; and E. A. Locke, 'Motivation through conscious goal setting', *Applied and Preventive Psychology*, 5 (1996), pp. 117–24.

31 See, for example, G. P. Latham, M. Erez and E. A. Locke, 'Resolving scientific disputes by the joint design of crucial experiments by the antagonists: application to the Erez-Latham dispute regarding participation in goal setting', *Journal of Applied Psychology*, November 1988, pp. 753–72; T. D. Ludwig and E. S. Geller, 'Assigned versus participative goal setting and response generalization: managing injury control among professional pizza deliverers', *Journal of Applied Psychology*, April 1997, pp. 253–61; and S. G. Harkins and M. D. Lowe, 'The effects of self-set goals on task performance', *Journal of Applied Social Psychology*, January 2000, pp. 1–40.

32 M. Erez, P. C. Earley and C. L. Hulin, 'The impact of participation on goal acceptance and performance: a two-step model', *Academy of Management Journal*, March 1985, pp. 50–66.

33 E. A. Locke, 'The motivation to work: what we know', *Advances in Motivation and Achievement*, 10 (1997), pp. 375–412; and Latham, Erez and Locke, 'Resolving scientific disputes by the joint design of crucial experiments by the antagonists'.

34 H. J. Klein, M. J. Wesson, J. R. Hollenbeck, P. M. Wright and R. D. DeShon, 'The assessment of goal commitment: a measurement model meta-analysis', *Organizational Behavior and Human Decision Processes*, 85, (2001), pp. 32–55.

35 J. R. Hollenbeck, C. R. Williams and H. J. Klein, 'An empirical examination of the antecedents of commitment to difficult goals', *Journal of Applied Psychology*, February 1989, pp. 18–23. See also J. C. Wofford, V. L. Goodwin and S. Premack, 'Meta-analysis of the antecedents of personal goal level and of the antecedents and consequences of goal commitment', *Journal of Management*, September 1992, pp. 595–615; M. E. Tubbs, 'Commitment as a moderator of the goal-performance relation: a case for clearer construct definition', *Journal of Applied Psychology*, February 1993, pp. 86–97; and J. E. Bono and A. E. Colbert, 'Understanding responses to multi-source feedback: the role of core self-evaluations', *Personnel Psychology*, Spring 2005, pp. 171–203.

36 See R. E. Wood, A. J. Mento and E. A. Locke, 'Task complexity as a moderator of goal effects: a meta-analysis', *Journal of Applied Psychology*, August 1987, pp. 416–25; R. Kanfer and P. L. Ackerman, 'Motivation and cognitive abilities: an integrative/aptitude-treatment interaction approach to skill acquisition', *Journal of Applied Psychology (monograph)*, vol. 74, 1989, pp. 657–90; T. R. Mitchell and W. S. Silver, 'Individual and group goals when workers are interdependent: effects on task strategies and performance', *Journal of Applied Psychology*, April 1990, pp. 185–93; and A. M. O'Leary-Kelly, J. J. Martocchio and D. D. Frink, 'A review of the influence of group goals on group performance', *Academy of Management Journal*, October 1994, pp. 1285–301.

37 'Key group survey finds nearly half of all employees have no set performance goals', *IPMA-HR Bulletin*, March 10, 2006, p. 1; S. Hamm, 'SAP dangles a big, fat carrot', *Business Week*, 22 May 2006, pp. 67–68; and 'P&G CEO wields high expectations but no whip', *USA Today*, 19 February 2007, p. 3B.

38 See, for instance, S. J. Carroll and H. L. Tosi, *Management by Objectives: Applications and Research* (New York: Macmillan, 1973); and R. Rodgers and J. E. Hunter, 'Impact of management by objectives on organizational productivity', *Journal of Applied Psychology*, April 1991, pp. 322–36.

39 See, for instance, R. C. Ford, F. S. MacLaughlin and J. Nixdorf, 'Ten questions about MBO', *California Management Review*, Winter 1980, p. 89; T. J. Collamore, 'Making MBO work in the public sector', *Bureaucrat*, Fall 1989, pp. 37–40; G. Dabbs, 'Nonprofit businesses in the 1990s: models for success', *Business Horizons*, September–October 1991, pp. 68–71; R. Rodgers and J. E. Hunter, 'A foundation of good management practice in government: management by objectives', *Public Administration Review*, January–February 1992, pp. 27–39; T. H. Poister and G. Streib, 'MBO in municipal government: variations on a traditional management tool', *Public Administration Review*, January/February 1995, pp. 48–56; and C. Garvey, 'Goalsharing scores', *HRMagazine*, April 2000, pp. 99–106.

40 See, for instance, C. H. Ford, 'MBO: an idea whose time has gone?', *Business Horizons*, December 1979, p. 49; R. Rodgers and J. E. Hunter, 'Impact of management by objectives on organizational productivity', *Journal of Applied Psychology*, April 1991, pp. 322–36; R. Rodgers, J. E. Hunter and D. L. Rogers, 'Influence of top management commitment on management program success', *Journal of Applied Psychology*, February 1993, pp. 151–55; and M. Tanikawa, 'Fujitsu decides to backtrack on performance-based pay', *New York Times*, 22 March 2001, p. W1.

41 A. Bandura, *Self-Efficacy: The Exercise of Control* (New York: Freeman, 1997).

42 A. D. Stajkovic and F. Luthans, 'Self-efficacy and work-related performance: a meta-analysis', *Psychological Bulletin*, September 1998, pp. 240–61; and A. Bandura, 'Cultivate self-efficacy for personal and organizational effectiveness', in E. Locke (ed.), *Handbook of Principles of Organizational Behavior* (Malden, MA: Blackwell, 2004), pp. 120–36.

43 A. Bandura and D. Cervone, 'Differential engagement in self-reactive influences in cognitively-based motivation', *Organizational Behavior and Human Decision Processes*, August 1986, pp. 92–113.

44 A. Bandura, *Self-Efficacy: The Exercise of Control* (New York: Freeman, 1997).

45 C. L. Holladay and M. A. Quiñones, 'Practice variability and transfer of training: the role of self-efficacy generality', *Journal of Applied Psychology*, 88, 6 (2003), pp. 1094–103.

46 R. C. Rist, 'Student social class and teacher expectations: the self-fulfilling prophecy in ghetto education', *Harvard Educational Review*, 70, 3 (2000), pp. 266–301.

47 D. Eden, 'Self-fulfilling prophecies in organizations', in J. Greenberg (ed.), *Organizational Behavior: The State of the Science*, 2nd edn (Mahwah, NJ: Erlbaum, 2003), pp. 91–122.

48 Ibid.

49 T. A. Judge, C. L. Jackson, J. C. Shaw, B. Scott and B. L. Rich, 'Self-efficacy and work-related performance: the integral role of individual differences', *Journal of Applied Psychology*, 92, 1 (2007), pp. 107–27.

50 Ibid.

51 J. L. Komaki, T. Coombs and S. Schepman, 'Motivational implications of reinforcement theory', in R. M. Steers, L. W. Porter and G. Bigley (eds), *Motivation and Work Behavior*, 6th edn (New York: McGraw-Hill, 1996), pp. 87–107.

52 E. A. Locke, 'Latham vs. Komaki: a tale of two paradigms', *Journal of Applied Psychology*, February 1980, pp. 16–23.

53 J. S. Adams, 'Inequity in social exchanges', in L. Berkowitz (ed.), *Advances in Experimental Social Psychology* (New York: Academic Press, 1965), pp. 267–300.

54 P. S. Goodman, 'An examination of referents used in the evaluation of pay', *Organizational Behavior and Human Performance*, October 1974, pp. 170–95; S. Ronen, 'Equity perception in multiple comparisons: a field study', *Human Relations*, April 1986, pp. 333–46; R. W. Scholl, E. A. Cooper and J. F. McKenna, 'Referent selection in determining equity perception: differential effects on behavioral and attitudinal outcomes', *Personnel Psychology*, Spring 1987, pp. 113–27; and T. P. Summers and A. S. DeNisi, 'In search of Adams' other: reexamination of referents used in the evaluation of pay', *Human Relations*, June 1990, pp. 497–511.

55 C. T. Kulik and M. L. Ambrose, 'Personal and situational determinants of referent choice', *Academy of Management Review*, April 1992, pp. 212–37.

56 C. Ostroff and L. E. Atwater, 'Does whom you work with matter? effects of referent group gender and age composition on managers' compensation,' *Journal of Applied Psychology*, 88, 4 (2003), pp. 725–40.

57 Fourth European Working Conditions Survey, European Foundation for the Improvement of Living and Working Conditions, 2007. Available at http://www.eurofound.europa.eu.

58 Ostroff and Atwater, 'Does whom you work with matter?'

59 See, for example, E. Walster, G. W. Walster and W. G. Scott, *Equity: Theory and Research* (Boston: Allyn & Bacon, 1978); and J. Greenberg, 'Cognitive reevaluation of outcomes in response to underpayment inequity', *Academy of Management Journal*, March 1989, pp. 174–84.

60 P. S. Goodman and A. Friedman, 'An examination of Adams' theory of inequity', *Administrative Science Quarterly*, September 1971, pp. 271–88; R. P. Vecchio, 'An individual-differences interpretation of the conflicting predictions generated by equity theory and expectancy theory', *Journal of Applied Psychology*, August 1981, pp. 470–81; J. Greenberg, 'Approaching equity and avoiding inequity in groups and organizations', in J. Greenberg and R. L. Cohen (eds), *Equity and Justice in Social Behavior* (New York: Academic Press, 1982), pp. 389–435; R. T. Mowday, 'Equity theory predictions of behavior in organizations', in R. Steers, L. W. Porter and G. Bigley (eds), *Motivation and Work Behavior*, 6th edn (New York: McGraw-Hill, 1996), pp. 111–31; S. Werner and N. P. Mero, 'Fair or foul? The effects of external, internal, and employee equity on changes in performance of major league baseball players', *Human Relations*, October 1999, pp. 1291–312; R. W. Griffeth and S. Gaertner, 'A role for equity theory in the turnover process: an empirical test', *Journal of Applied Social Psychology*, May 2001, pp. 1017–37; and L. K. Scheer, N. Kumar and J.-B. E. M. Steenkamp, 'Reactions to perceived inequity in U.S. and Dutch inter-organizational relationships', *Academy of Management 46*, no. 3 (2003), pp. 303–16.

61 See, for example, R. C. Huseman, J. D. Hatfield and E. W. Miles, 'A new perspective on equity theory: the equity sensitivity construct', *Academy of Management Journal*, April 1987, pp. 222–34; K. S. Sauley and A. G. Bedeian, 'Equity sensitivity: Construction of a measure and examination of its psychometric properties', *Journal of Management*, 26, 5 (2000), pp. 885–910; M. N. Bing and S. M. Burroughs, 'The predictive and interactive effects of equity sensitivity in teamwork-oriented organizations', *Journal of Organizational Behavior*, May 2001, pp. 271–90; and J. A. Colquitt, 'Does the justice of one interact with the justice of many? reactions to procedural justice in teams', *Journal of Applied Psychology*, 89, 4 (2004), pp. 633–46.

62 J. Greenberg and S. Ornstein, 'High status job title as compensation for underpayment: a test of equity theory', *Journal of Applied Psychology*, May 1983, pp. 285–97; and J. Greenberg, 'Equity and workplace status: a field experiment', *Journal of Applied Psychology*, November 1988, pp. 606–13.

63 See, for instance, J. Greenberg, *The Quest for Justice on the Job* (Thousand Oaks, CA: Sage, 1996); R. Cropanzano and J. Greenberg, 'Progress in organizational justice: tunneling through the maze', in C. L. Cooper and I. T. Robertson (eds), *International Review of Industrial and Organizational Psychology*, vol. 12 (New York: Wiley, 1997); J. A. Colquitt, D. E. Conlon, M. J. Wesson, C. O. L. H. Porter and K. Y. Ng, 'Justice at the millennium: a meta-analytic review of the 25 years of organizational justice research', *Journal of Applied Psychology*, June 2001, pp. 425–45; T. Simons and Q. Roberson, 'Why managers should care about fairness: the effects of aggregate justice perceptions on organizational outcomes', *Journal of Applied Psychology*, June 2003, pp. 432–43; and G. P. Latham and C. C. Pinder, 'Work motivation theory and research at the dawn of the twenty-first century,' *Annual Review of Psychology*, 56 (2005), pp. 485–516.

64 K. Leung, K. Tong and S. S. Ho, 'Effects of interactional justice on egocentric bias in resource allocation decisions', *Journal of Applied Psychology*, 89, 3 (2004), pp. 405–15.

65 'Americans feel they pay fair share of taxes, says poll', *NewsTarget.com*, 2 May 2005, www.newstarget.com/007297.html.

66 G. S. Leventhal, 'What should be done with equity theory? New approaches to the study of fairness in social relationships', in K. Gergen, M. Greenberg and R. Willis (eds), *Social Exchange: Advances in Theory and Research* (New York: Plenum, 1980), pp. 27–55.

67 J. C. Shaw, E. Wild and J. A. Colquitt, 'To justify or excuse? A meta-analytic review of the effects of explanations', *Journal of Applied Psychology*, 88, 3 (2003), pp. 444–58.

68 D. P. Skarlicki and R. Folger, 'Retaliation in the workplace: the roles of distributive, procedural, and interactional justice', *Journal of Applied Psychology*, 82, 3 (1997), pp. 434–43.

69 R. Cropanzano, C. A. Prehar and P. Y. Chen, 'Using social exchange theory to distinguish procedural from interactional justice', *Group & Organization Management*, 27, 3 (2002), pp. 324–51; and S. G. Roch and L. R. Shanock, 'Organizational justice in an exchange framework: clarifying organizational justice dimensions', *Journal of Management*, April 2006, pp. 299–322.

70 J. A. Colquitt, D. E. Conlon, M. J. Wesson, C. O. L. H. Porter and K. Y. Ng, 'Justice at the millennium: a meta-analytic review of the 25 years of organizational justice research', *Journal of Applied Psychology*, 86, 3 (2001), pp. 425–45.

71 J. Reb, B. M. Goldman, L. J. Kray and R. Cropanzano, 'Different wrongs, different remedies? Reactions to organizational remedies after procedural and interactional injustice', *Personnel Psychology* 59 (2006), pp. 31–64; and 'Northwest airlines flight cancellations mount as labor woes continue', *Aero-News.net*, 26 June 2007, www.aero-news.net.

72 V. H. Vroom, *Work and Motivation* (New York: Wiley, 1964).

73 For criticism, see H. G. Heneman III and D. P. Schwab, 'Evaluation of research on expectancy theory prediction of employee performance', *Psychological Bulletin*, July 1972, pp. 1–9; T. R. Mitchell, 'Expectancy models of job satisfaction, occupational preference and effort: a theoretical,

methodological and empirical appraisal', *Psychological Bulletin*, November 1974, pp. 1053–77; and W. Van Eerde and H. Thierry, 'Vroom's expectancy models and work-related criteria: a meta-analysis', *Journal of Applied Psychology*, October 1996, pp. 575–86. For support, see L. W. Porter and E. E. Lawler, III, *Managerial Attitudes and Performance* (Homewood, IL: Irwin, 1968); and J. J. Donovan, 'Work motivation', in N. Anderson D. Ones, H. K. Sinangil and C. Viswesvaran (eds), *Handbook of Industrial, Work & Organizational Psychology*, vol. 2 (Thousand Oaks, CA: Sage, 2001), pp. 56–59.

74 Vroom refers to these three variables as expectancy, instrumentality and valence, respectively.

75 J. Nocera, 'The anguish of being an analyst', *New York Times*, 4 March 2006, pp. B1, B12.

76 P. M. Muchinsky, 'A comparison of within- and across-subjects analyses of the expectancy–valence model for predicting effort', *Academy of Management Journal*, March 1977, pp. 154–58; and C. W. Kennedy, J. A. Fossum and B. J. White, 'An empirical comparison of within-subjects and between-subjects expectancy theory models', *Organizational Behavior and Human Decision Process*, August 1983, pp. 124–43.

77 R. J. House, H. J. Shapiro and M. A. Wahba, 'Expectancy theory as a predictor of work behavior and attitudes: a re-evaluation of empirical evidence', *Decision Sciences*, January 1974, pp. 481–506.

78 For other examples of models that seek to integrate motivation theories, see H. J. Klein, 'An integrated control theory model of work motivation', *Academy of Management Review*, April 1989, pp. 150–72; E. A. Locke, 'The motivation sequence, the motivation hub, and the motivation core', *Organizational Behavior and Human Decision Processes*, December 1991, pp. 288–99; and Mitchell, 'Matching motivational strategies with organizational contexts'.

79 N. J. Adler, *International Dimensions of Organizational Behavior*, 4th edn (Cincinnati, OH: South-Western Publishing, 2002), p. 174.

80 G. Hofstede, 'Motivation, leadership, and organization: do American theories apply abroad?', *Organizational Dynamics*, Summer 1980, p. 55.

81 Ibid.

82 J. K. Giacobbe-Miller, D. J. Miller and V. I. Victorov, 'A comparison of Russian and U.S. pay allocation decisions, distributive justice judgments, and productivity under different payment conditions', *Personnel Psychology*, Spring 1998, pp. 137–63.

83 S. L. Mueller and L. D. Clarke, 'Political–economic context and sensitivity to equity: differences between the United States and the transition economies of Central and Eastern Europe', *Academy of Management Journal*, June 1998, pp. 319–29.

84 I. Harpaz, 'The importance of work goals: an international perspective', *Journal of International Business Studies*, First Quarter 1990, pp. 75–93.

85 G. E. Popp, H. J. Davis and T. T. Herbert, 'An international study of intrinsic motivation composition', *Management International Review*, January 1986, pp. 28–35.

86 This section is based on F. J. Landy and W. S. Becker, 'Motivation theory reconsidered,' in L. L. Cummings and B. M. Staw (eds), *Research in Organizational Behavior*, Vol. 9 (Greenwich, CT: JAI Press, 1987), pp. 24–35.

87 J. Zaslow, 'Losing well: how a successful man deals with a rare and public failure', *Wall Street Journal*, 2 March 2006, p. D1.

88 E. Biyalogorsky, W. Boulding and R. Staelin, 'Stuck in the past: why managers persist with new product failures', *Journal of Marketing*, April 2006, pp. 108–21.

Motivation: from concepts to applications

Learning Objectives

After studying this chapter, you should be able to:

1 Describe the job characteristics model and evaluate the way it motivates by changing the work environment.

2 Compare and contrast the three main ways jobs can be redesigned.

3 Identify three alternative work arrangements and show how they might motivate employees.

4 Give examples of employee involvement measures and show how they can motivate employees.

5 Demonstrate how the different types of variable-pay programmes can increase employee motivation.

6 Show how flexible benefits turn benefits into motivators.

7 Identify the motivational benefits of intrinsic rewards.

Knowing is not enough, we must apply. Being willing is not enough, we must do.

Leonardo Da Vinci

The Gore happy family

Extreme Sports Photo/Alamy

Imagine working in an organization where there are no job titles, no managers only job descriptions, associates and leaders. W. L. Gore & Associates Inc is almost as famous for its work environment as it is for its outdoor performance GORE-TEX® fabric. And those who work there love it. The company has been ranked in the top ten Best Places to Work in France, Germany, Italy, Spain, Sweden and the United Kingdom.

The company was founded over 50 years ago by Bill Gore, who was inspired by the Theory Y management philosophy described by Douglas McGregor. Theory Y promotes work environments that foster imagination and creativity, a core Gore belief, rather than basing them on control and punishment.

The firm has no hierarchical chains of command or instruction, there are no managers, directors or secretaries. The company has 'Associates' rather than 'employees' and 'sponsors' instead of 'bosses', who guide the workforce through a general work area. The Associates are given every opportunity to contribute to the success of the enterprise and are rewarded by being given an equal share of the organization's profits, which changes in line with their salary.

The private company is like any other manufacturing business: it produces, markets and sells goods. In Gore's case, the company manufactures fabrics and polymer products. The big difference, however, is the work environment. This is based on Associates' sense of ownership and equal participation. The Associates adhere to four guiding principles: fairness to each other, freedom to encourage, ability to take on commitments, and consultation with other Associates. The unique kind of corporate structure has proven to be a significant contributor to Associate satisfaction and retention.

John Housego, former manufacturing leader of Gore's fabrics plant, says he was impressed by the company's work ethic right from the word go: 'The thing I like about Gore is its culture of putting people first,' he explains. 'I get a sense of ownership within the company by fulfilling a variety of roles while guiding and helping others.'

GORE-TEX®, GORE® and designs are registered trade marks of W. L. Gore & Associates.

Sources: A. Moore (2004) 'Simply the best', *Personnel Today*; www.Gore.com; Dr Peter Troxler: W. L. Gore & Associates – 'The best company to work for', presentation for Society in Sync Conference, Aberdeen, 10 February 2005. Available at http://www.dln.org.uk/downloads/speakersnotes/troxlerspeakersnotes.pdf; Great Place to Work Institute www.greatplacetowork.co.uk. Accessed 21 October 2008.

As the W. L. Gore & Associates experiment shows, companies vary a lot in the practical approach they take to motivating employees. Gore's approach assumes that employees do their best work when given a lot of autonomy in deciding how they go about doing it. The following self-assessment will provide some information on how motivating *your* job might be.

SELF-ASSESSMENT LIBRARY

What's my job's motivating potential?

In the Self-assessment library (available online), take assessment I.C.8 (What's my job's motivating potential?) and answer the following questions. If you currently do not have a job, answer the questions for your most recent job.

1. How did you score relative to your classmates?

2. Did your score surprise you? Why or why not?

3. How might your results affect your career path?

---

1 Describe the job characteristics model and evaluate the way it motivates by changing the work environment.

In Chapter 6, we focused on motivation theories. In this chapter, we focus on applying motivation concepts. We link motivation theories to practices such as employee involvement and skill-based pay. Why? Because it's one thing to be able to know specific motivation theories; it's quite another to see how, as a manager, you can use them.

Motivating by job design: the job characteristics model

job design
The way the elements in a job are organized.

job characteristics model (JCM)
A model that proposes that any job can be described in terms of five core job dimensions: skill variety, task identity, task significance, autonomy and feedback.

skill variety
The degree to which a job requires a variety of different activities.

task identity
The degree to which a job requires completion of a whole and identifiable piece of work.

task significance
The degree to which a job has a substantial impact on the lives or work of other people.

Increasingly, research on motivation is focused on approaches that link motivational concepts to changes in the way work is structured.

Research in **job design** provides stronger evidence that the way the elements in a job are organized can act to increase or decrease effort. This research also offers detailed insights into what those elements are. We'll first review the job characteristics model and then discuss some ways jobs can be redesigned. Finally, we'll explore some alternative work arrangements.

The job characteristics model

Developed by J. Richard Hackman and Greg Oldham, the **job characteristics model (JCM)** proposes that any job can be described in terms of five core job dimensions:[1]

1. **Skill variety. Skill variety** is the degree to which a job requires a variety of different activities so the worker can use a number of different skills and talent. For instance, an example of a job scoring high on skill variety would be the job of an owner-operator of a garage who does electrical repairs, rebuilds engines, does body work and interacts with customers. A job scoring low on this dimension would be the job of a body shop worker who sprays paint 8 hours a day.

2. **Task identity. Task identity** is the degree to which a job requires completion of a whole and identifiable piece of work. An example of a job scoring high on identity would be the job of a cabinetmaker who designs a piece of furniture, selects the wood, builds the object, and finishes it to perfection. A job scoring low on this dimension would be the job of a worker in a furniture factory who operates a lathe solely to make table legs.

3. **Task significance. Task significance** is the degree to which a job has a substantial impact on the lives or work of other people. An example of a job scoring high on significance would

be the job of a nurse handling the diverse needs of patients in a hospital intensive care unit. A job scoring low on this dimension would be the job of a janitor sweeping floors in a hospital.

4. **Autonomy. Autonomy** is the degree to which a job provides substantial freedom, independence, and discretion to the individual in scheduling the work and in determining the procedures to be used in carrying it out. An example of a job scoring high on autonomy is the job of a salesperson who schedules his or her own work each day and decides on the most effective sales approach for each customer without supervision. A job scoring low on this dimension would be the job of a salesperson who is given a set of leads each day and is required to follow a standardised sales script with each potential customer.

5. **Feedback. Feedback** is the degree to which carrying out the work activities required by a job results in the individual obtaining direct and clear information about the effectiveness of his or her performance. An example of a job with high feedback is the job of a factory worker who assembles iPods and tests them to see if they operate properly. A job scoring low on feedback would be the job of a factory worker who, after assembling an iPod, is required to pass it to a quality-control inspector who tests it for proper operation and makes needed adjustments.

Figure 7.1 presents the job characteristics model. Note how the first three dimensions – skill variety, task identity and task significance – combine to create meaningful work. That is, if these three characteristics exist in a job, the model predicts that the incumbent will view the job as being important, valuable and worthwhile. Note, too, that jobs with high autonomy give job incumbents a feeling of personal responsibility for the results and that, if a job provides feedback, employees will know how effectively they are performing. From a motivational standpoint, the JCM says that individuals obtain internal rewards when they learn (knowledge of results) that they personally (experienced responsibility) have performed well on a task that they care about (experienced meaningfulness).[2] The more these three psychological states are present, the greater will be employees' motivation, performance, and satisfaction and the lower their absenteeism and likelihood of leaving the organization. As Figure 7.1 shows, the links between the job dimensions and the outcomes are moderated or adjusted by the strength of the individual's growth need – that is, by the employee's desire for self-esteem and self-actualisation. This means that individuals with a high growth need are more likely to experience the psychological states when their jobs are enriched than are their counterparts with low growth need. Moreover, the

autonomy
The degree to which a job provides substantial freedom and discretion to the individual in scheduling the work and in determining the procedures to be used in carrying it out.

feedback
The degree to which carrying out the work activities required by a job results in the individual obtaining direct and clear information about the effectiveness of their performance.

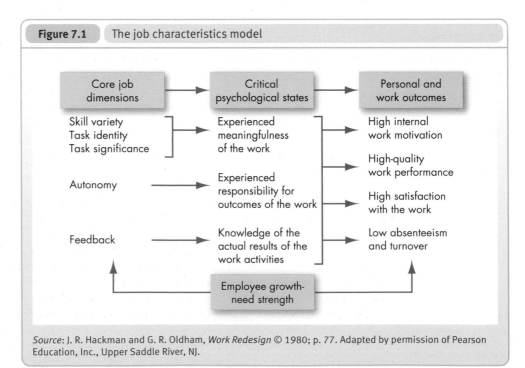

Figure 7.1   The job characteristics model

Source: J. R. Hackman and G. R. Oldham, *Work Redesign* © 1980; p. 77. Adapted by permission of Pearson Education, Inc., Upper Saddle River, NJ.

individuals with a high growth need will respond more positively to the psychological states when they are present than will individuals with a low growth need.

The core dimensions can be combined into a single predictive index, called the **motivating potential score (MPS)**, which is calculated as follows:

motivating potential score (MPS)
A predictive index that suggests the motivating potential in a job.

$$\text{MPS} = \frac{\text{Skill variety} + \text{Task identity} + \text{Task significance}}{3} \times \text{Autonomy} \times \text{Feedback}$$

Jobs that are high on motivating potential must be high on at least one of the three factors that lead to experienced meaningfulness, and they must be high on both autonomy and feedback. If jobs score high on motivating potential, the model predicts that motivation, performance and satisfaction will be positively affected and that the likelihood of absence and turnover will be reduced.

The JCM has been well researched. And most of the evidence supports the general framework of the theory – that is, there is a set of job characteristics, and these characteristics affect behavioural outcomes.[3] But it appears that the MPS model doesn't work – that is, we can better derive motivating potential by adding the characteristics rather than using the complex MPS formula.[4] Beyond employee growth-need strength, other variables, such as the employee's perception of their work load compared to those of others, may also moderate the link between the core job dimensions and personal and work outcomes.[5] Overall, though, it appears that jobs that have the intrinsic elements of variety, identity, significance, autonomy, and feedback are more satisfying and generate higher performance from people than jobs that lack these characteristics.

Take some time to think about your job. Do you have the opportunity to work on different tasks, or is your day pretty routine? Are you able to work independently, or do you constantly have a supervisor or co-worker looking over your shoulder? What do you think your answers to these questions say about your job's motivating potential? Revisit your answers to the self-assessment at the beginning of this chapter and then calculate your MPS from the job characteristics model.

How can jobs be redesigned?

2 Compare and contrast the three main ways jobs can be redesigned.

'Every day was the same thing,' Frank Greer said. 'Stand on that assembly line. Wait for an instrument panel to be moved into place. Unlock the mechanism and drop the panel into the Jeep Liberty as it moved by on the line. Then I plugged in the harnessing wires. I repeated that for eight hours a day. I don't care that they were paying me €20 an hour. I was going crazy. I did it for almost a year and a half. Finally, I just said to my wife that this isn't going to be the way I'm going to spend the rest of my life. My brain was turning to jelly on that Jeep assembly line. So I quit. Now I work in a print shop and I make less than €12 an hour. But let me tell you, the work I do is really interesting. The job changes all the time, I'm continually learning new things, and the work really challenges me! I look forward every morning to going to work again.'

Frank Greer's job at the Jeep plant involved repetitive tasks that provided him with little variety, autonomy, or motivation. In contrast, his job in the print shop is challenging and stimulating. Let's look at some of the ways to put JCM into practice to make jobs more motivating.

Job rotation

job rotation
The periodic shifting of an employee from one task to another.

If employees suffer from overroutinisation of their work, one alternative is to use **job rotation** (or what many now call *cross-training*). We define this practice as the periodic shifting of an employee from one task to another. When an activity is no longer challenging, the employee is rotated to another job, usually at the same level, that has similar skill requirements. Singapore Airlines, one of the best-rated airlines in the world, uses job rotation extensively. For example, a ticket agent may take on the duties of a baggage handler. Job rotation is one of the reasons Singapore Airlines is rated as a highly desirable place to work. Many manufacturing firms have adopted job rotation as a means of increasing flexibility and avoiding layoffs.[6] For instance, Siemens Nederland, the Dutch branch of a large German electronics company, stipulates a maximum time of employment in any one function. Employees doing technical jobs regularly transfer to sales or management, and the other way around.[7] Toyota, a company globally renowned for its human resource practices, rotates production line workers to another job as frequently as every two hours.

The strengths of job rotation are that it reduces boredom, increases motivation through diversifying the employee's activities, and helps employees better understand how their work contributes to the organization. Job rotation also has indirect benefits for the organization because when employees have a wider range of skills, management has more flexibility in scheduling work, adapting to changes, and filling vacancies.[8] However, job rotation is not without drawbacks. Training costs are increased, and productivity is reduced by moving a worker into a new position just when efficiency at the prior job is creating organizational economies. Job rotation also creates disruptions. Members of the work group have to adjust to the new employee. And supervisors may also have to spend more time answering questions and monitoring the work of recently rotated employees.

Job enlargement

> **job enlargement**
> Increasing the number and variety of tasks that an individual performs. Job enlargement results in jobs with more diversity.

More than 35 years ago, the idea of expanding jobs horizontally, or what we call **job enlargement**, grew in popularity. Increasing the number and variety of tasks that an individual performed resulted in jobs with more diversity. Instead of only sorting the incoming mail by department, for instance, a mail sorter's job could be enlarged to include physically delivering the mail to the various departments or running outgoing letters through the postage meter. The difference between job rotation and job enlargement may seem subtle. However, in job rotation, jobs are not redesigned. Employees simply move from one job to another, but the nature of the work does not change. Job enlargement, however, involves actually changing the job.

Efforts at job enlargement have met with less-than-enthusiastic results.[9] One employee who experienced such a redesign on his job remarked, 'Before I had one miserable job. Now, through enlargement, I have three!' However, there have been some successful applications of job enlargement. The housekeeping job in some small hotels, for example, includes not only cleaning bathrooms, making beds, and vacuuming but also replacing burned-out light bulbs, providing turn-down service and restocking mini-bars.

'EVERYONE WANTS A CHALLENGING JOB'   MYTH *OR* SCIENCE?

This statement is false. Many employees do want challenging, interesting, complex work. But, despite all the attention focused by the media, academics, and social scientists on human potential and the needs of individuals, some people prosper in simple, routinised work.[10]

The individual-difference variable that seems to gain the greatest support for explaining who prefers a challenging job and who doesn't is the strength of an individual's higher-order needs.[11] Individuals with high growth needs are more responsive to challenging work. But what percentage of rank-and-file workers actually desires higher-order need satisfaction and will respond positively to challenging jobs? No current data are available, but a study from the 1970s estimated the figure at about 15 per cent.[12] Even after adjusting for technological and economic changes in the nature of work, it seems unlikely that the number today exceeds 40 per cent.

Many employees relish challenging work. But this desire has been overgeneralised to all workers. Organizations increasingly have pushed extra responsibilities on workers, often without knowing whether this is desired or how an employee will handle the increased responsibilities.

Many workers meet their higher-order needs *off* the job. There are 168 hours in every individual's week. Work rarely consumes more than 30 per cent of this time. That leaves considerable opportunity, even for individuals with strong growth needs, to find higher-order need satisfaction outside the workplace.

Job enrichment

> **job enrichment**
> The vertical expansion of jobs, which increases the degree to which the worker controls the planning, execution, and evaluation of the work.

Job enrichment refers to the vertical expansion of jobs. It increases the degree to which the worker controls the planning, execution and evaluation of the work. An enriched job organizes tasks so as to allow the worker to do a complete activity, increases the employee's freedom and independence, increases responsibility and provides feedback so individuals will be able to assess and correct their own performance.[13]

How does management enrich an employee's job? Figure 7.2 offers suggested guidelines based on the job characteristics model. *Combining tasks* takes existing and fractionalised tasks

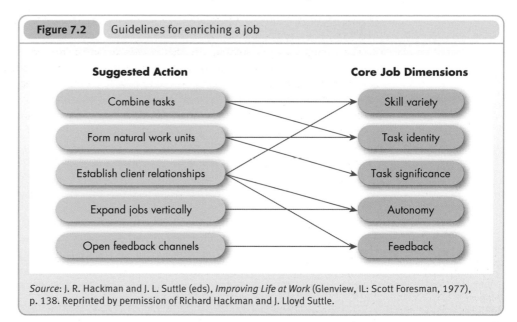

Figure 7.2 Guidelines for enriching a job

Source: J. R. Hackman and J. L. Suttle (eds), *Improving Life at Work* (Glenview, IL: Scott Foresman, 1977), p. 138. Reprinted by permission of Richard Hackman and J. Lloyd Suttle.

and puts them back together to form a new and larger module of work. *Forming natural work units* means that the tasks an employee does create an identifiable and meaningful whole. *Establishing client relationships* increases the direct relationships between workers and their clients (these may be an internal customer as well as someone outside the organization). *Expanding jobs vertically* gives employees responsibilities and control that were formerly reserved for management. *Opening feedback channels* lets employees know how well they are performing their jobs and whether their performance is improving, deteriorating or remaining at a constant level.

One recent study attested to the benefits of establishing direct relationships between employees and the beneficiaries of their work. Researchers found that when university fundraisers briefly interacted with the undergraduate students who would be funded by the scholarships that were the target of the fundraising efforts, they persisted 42 per cent longer, and raised nearly twice as much money, as those who didn't interact with the potential scholarship recipients.[14]

To illustrate job enrichment, let's look at what management at Bank One did with its international trade banking department.[15] The department's chief product is commercial letters of credit – essentially a bank guarantee to stand behind huge import and export transactions. Prior to enriching jobs, the department's 300 employees processed documents in an assembly-line fashion, with errors creeping in at each handoff. Meanwhile, employees did little to hide the boredom they were experiencing from doing narrow and specialised tasks. Management enriched these jobs by making each clerk a trade expert who was able to handle a customer from start to finish. After 200 hours of training in finance and law, the clerks became full-service advisers who could turn around documents in a day while advising clients on such arcane matters as bank procedures in Turkey. The results? Department productivity more than tripled, employee satisfaction soared and transaction volume rose more than 10 per cent per year.

The overall evidence on job enrichment generally shows that it reduces absenteeism and turnover costs and increases satisfaction, but on the critical issue of productivity, the evidence is inconclusive.[16] Some recent evidence suggests that job enrichment works best when it compensates for poor feedback and reward systems.[17]

Alternative work arrangements

3 Identify three alternative work arrangements and show how they might motivate employees.

Beyond redesigning the nature of the work itself and involving employees in decisions, another approach to making the work environment more motivating is to alter work arrangements. We'll discuss three alternative work arrangements: flexitime, job sharing, and teleworking. With the increasing advances in technology, all these alternative work arrangements have become more popular.

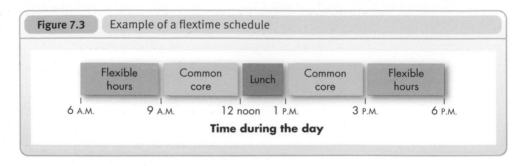

Figure 7.3   Example of a flextime schedule

Flexitime

Susan Ross is the classic 'morning person'. She rises each day at 5 A.M. sharp and full of energy. However, as she puts it, 'I'm usually ready for bed right after the 7 P.M. news.'

Susan's work schedule as a claims processor at The Hartford Financial Services Group is flexible. It allows her some degree of freedom as to when she comes to work and when she leaves. Her office opens at 6 A.M. and closes at 7 P.M. It's up to her how she schedules her 8-hour day within this 13-hour period. Because Susan is a morning person and also has a 7-year-old son who gets out of school at 3 P.M. every day, she opts to work from 6 A.M. to 3 P.M. 'My work hours are perfect. I'm at the job when I'm mentally most alert, and I can be home to take care of my son after he gets out of school.'

Susan Ross's work schedule at The Hartford is an example of **flexitime**. The term is short for 'flexible work time'. It allows employees some discretion over when they arrive at work and when they leave. Employees have to work a specific number of hours a week, but they are free to vary the hours of work within certain limits. As shown in Figure 7.3, each day consists of a common core, usually six hours, with a flexibility band surrounding the core. For example, exclusive of a one-hour lunch break, the core may be 9 A.M. to 3 P.M., with the office actually opening at 6 A.M. and closing at 6 P.M. All employees are required to be at their jobs during the common core period, but they are allowed to accumulate their other 2 hours before and/or after the core time. Some flexitime programmes allow extra hours to be accumulated and turned into a free day off each month.

Flexitime has become a popular scheduling option. For example, in Scandinavian countries almost 60 per cent of all employees benefit from flexitime. In Anglo and continental Europe the figure is about 40 per cent, but the arrangement is less common in eastern Europe, where less than 20 per cent of employees have access to flexitime.[18]

The benefits claimed for flexitime are numerous. They include reduced absenteeism, increased productivity, reduced overtime expenses, reduced hostility toward management, reduced traffic congestion around work sites, improved punctuality and increased autonomy and responsibility for employees that may increase employee job satisfaction.[19] But beyond the claims, what's flexitime's record?

Most of the performance evidence stacks up favourably. Flexitime tends to reduce absenteeism and frequently improves worker productivity,[20] probably for several reasons. Employees can schedule their work hours to align with personal demands, thus improving punctuality and reducing absence, and employees can adjust their work activities to those hours in which they are individually most productive.

Flexitime's major drawback is that it's not applicable to every job. It works well with clerical tasks for which an employee's interaction with people outside their department is limited. It is not a viable option for receptionists, sales personnel in retail stores or similar jobs for which comprehensive service demands that people be at their workstations at predetermined times.

Job sharing

A recent work scheduling innovation is **job sharing**. It allows two or more individuals to split the hours of a job. For example, one person might perform the job from 8 A.M. to noon, while another performs the same job from 1 P.M. to 5 P.M.; or the two could work full, but alternate, days. As a case in point, Sue Manix and Charlotte Schutzman share the title of vice president of

flexitime
Flexible work hours.

job sharing
An arrangement that allows two or more individuals to split a traditional 40-hour-a-week job.

employee communications at Verizon.[21] Schutzman works Monday and Tuesday, Manix works Thursday and Friday, and they alternate Wednesdays. The two women have job-shared for 10 years, acquiring promotions, numerous bonuses and a 20-person staff along the way. With each having children at home, this arrangement allows them the flexibility to better balance their work and family responsibilities.

Job sharing is widely offered in Europe, for example by approximately 30 per cent of employers in Italy and 45 per cent in the UK. However, despite its availability, it doesn't seem to be widely adopted by employees. For example, although 30 per cent of employers offer job sharing in Ireland, only about 6 per cent are personally involved in job sharing.[22] This is probably because of the difficulty of finding compatible partners to share a job and the negative perceptions historically held of individuals not completely committed to their job and employer.

Job sharing allows an organization to draw on the talents of more than one individual in a given job. A bank manager who oversees two job sharers describes it as an opportunity to get two heads but 'pay for one'.[23] It also opens up the opportunity to acquire skilled workers – for instance, women with young children and retirees – who might not be available on a full-time basis.[24] Many Japanese firms are increasingly considering job sharing – but for a very different reason.[25] Because Japanese executives are extremely reluctant to fire people, job sharing is seen as a potentially humanitarian means for avoiding layoffs due to overstaffing.

From the employee's perspective, job sharing increases flexibility. As such, it can increase motivation and satisfaction for those to whom a full-time job is just not practical. But the major drawback from management's perspective is finding compatible pairs of employees who can successfully coordinate the intricacies of one job.[26]

Teleworking

teleworking
People who work mainly in their own home or mainly in different places using home as a base, who use both a telephone and a computer to carry out their work.

It might be close to the ideal job for many people. No commuting, flexible hours, freedom to dress as you please and few or no interruptions from colleagues. It's called **teleworking**, refers to people who work mainly in their own home or mainly in different places using home as a base, who use both a telephone and a computer to carry out their work.[27] Teleworkers are also variously described as mobile workers, remote workers or homeworkers. A closely related term – *the virtual office* – is increasingly being used to describe employees who work out of their home on a relatively permanent basis.

It is estimated that more than 17 million employees telework in the European Union although this figure varies depending on exactly how the term is defined.[28] In the UK, British Telecom has 12,000 employees working from home and the Automobile Association has a virtual call centre consisting of 250 people working where they live.[29]

What kinds of jobs lend themselves to teleworking? Three categories have been identified as most appropriate: routine information-handling tasks, mobile activities and professional and other knowledge-related tasks.[30] Writers, attorneys, analysts and employees who spend the majority of their time on computers or the telephone are natural candidates for teleworking. For instance, telemarketers, customer-service representatives, reservation agents and product-support specialists spend most of their time on the phone. As teleworkers, they can access information on their computers at home as easily as in the company's office.

There are numerous stories of teleworking's success.[31] For instance, nearly a quarter of the staff in Telecom Italia's Info412 call centre operation work full-time from home. They spend 15 per cent less time on calls than other staff and take 3.3 per cent more calls an hour. Employees of the Dutch subsidiary of Oracle claimed the teleworking arrangements have improved their lives. The company says it has gained €23m over five years from the reduction in space, improved productivity and higher staff retention.[32]

The potential pluses of teleworking for management include a larger labour pool from which to select, higher productivity, less turnover, improved morale and reduced office-space costs. The major downside for management is less direct supervision of employees. In addition, in today's team-focused workplace, teleworking may make it more difficult for management to coordinate teamwork.[33] From the employee's standpoint, teleworking offers a considerable increase in flexibility. But not without costs. For employees with a high social need, teleworking can increase feelings of isolation and reduce job satisfaction. And all telecommuters potentially suffer from the 'out of sight, out of mind' effect. Employees who aren't at their desks, who miss meetings and who don't share in day-to-day informal workplace interactions may be at a disadvantage when it comes to raises and promotions. It can be easy for bosses to overlook or undervalue the contribution of employees whom they don't see regularly.

ALTERNATIVE WORK ARRANGEMENTS IN THE EUROPEAN UNION FACE THE FACTS

- In northern European countries, workers can choose to adapt working time to their needs to a large extent (around half of employees say they can do so, with or without certain limits), which is in sharp contrast to southern and eastern European countries, where more than 75 per cent of employees have no possibility whatsoever of adapting their work schedules, as they are set by the company.

- Almost 60 per cent of EU workers work all or almost all the time at company premises leaving a considerable

proportion of people who never or almost never work at company premises (almost 30 per cent).

- The proportion of people teleworking is highest in the Scandinavian countries and the Netherlands and lowest in the southern European countries.

Source: Fourth European Working Conditions Survey *European Foundation for the Improvement of Living and Working Conditions*, 2007.

Ability and opportunity

Clare and Joe both graduated from university a couple years ago, with degrees in education. They both took jobs as primary teachers but in different school districts. Clare immediately confronted a number of obstacles on the job: a large class (42 students), a small and dingy classroom and inadequate supplies. Joe's situation couldn't have been more different. He had only 15 students in his class, plus a teaching aide for 15 hours each week, a modern and well-lighted room, a well-stocked supply cabinet, an iMac computer for every student and a highly supportive principal. Not surprisingly, at the end of their first school year, Joe had been considerably more effective as a teacher than had Clare.

The preceding episode illustrates an obvious but often overlooked fact. Success on a job is facilitated or hindered by the existence or absence of support resources.

A popular, although arguably simplistic, way of thinking about employee performance is as a function (f) of the interaction of ability (A) and motivation (M); that is, Performance = $f(A \times M)$. If either ability or motivation is inadequate, performance will be negatively affected. This helps to explain, for instance, a hard-working athlete or student with modest abilities who consistently outperforms a more gifted, but lazy, rival. So, as noted in Chapter 2, an individual's intelligence and skills (subsumed under the label *ability*) must be considered in addition to motivation if we are to accurately explain and predict employee performance. But a piece of the puzzle is still missing. We need to add **opportunity to perform** (O) to our equation: Performance = $f(A \times M \times O)$.[34] Even though an individual may be willing and able, there may be obstacles that constrain performance.

opportunity to perform Absence of obstacles that constrain the employee. High levels of performance are partially a function of the opportunity to perform.

When you attempt to assess why an employee is not performing to the level at which you believe he or she is capable of performing, take a look at the work environment to see if it's supportive. Does the employee have adequate tools, equipment, materials and supplies? Does the employee have favourable working conditions, helpful co-workers, supportive work rules and procedures, sufficient information to make job-related decisions, adequate time to do a good job and the like? If not, performance will suffer.

Employee involvement

4 Give examples of employee involvement measures and show how they can motivate employees.

What specifically do we mean by **employee involvement**? We define it as a participative process that uses the input of employees to increase their commitment to the organization's success. The underlying logic is that if we involve workers in the decisions that affect them and increase their autonomy and control over their work lives, employees will become more motivated, more committed to the organization, more productive and more satisfied with their jobs.[35]

Daniel Maurer/AP/Press Association Images

Most of the workers at Daimler AG are employed in the company's home country of Germany. But to give employees at other European sites a voice, a European Works Council was established made up of representatives from Spain, France, Italy, Great Britain and the Netherlands. The aim is to promote a Europe-wide exchange of information and opinions between group management and employees.

Examples of employee involvement programmes

Let's look at the three major forms of employee involvement – participative management, representative participation and quality circles – in more detail.

Participative management

employee involvement
A participative process that uses the input of employees and is intended to increase employee commitment to an organization's success.

The distinct characteristic common to all **participative management** programmes is the use of joint decision making. That is, subordinates actually share a significant degree of decision-making power with their immediate superiors. Participative management has, at times, been promoted as a panacea for poor morale and low productivity. But for it to work, the issues in which employees get involved must be relevant to their interests so they'll be motivated, employees must have the competence and knowledge to make a useful contribution, and there must be trust and confidence between all parties involved.[36]

participative management
A process in which subordinates share a significant degree of decision-making power with their immediate superiors.

Dozens of studies have been conducted on the participation–performance relationship. The findings, however, are mixed.[37] A careful review of the research seems to show that participation typically has only a modest influence on variables such as employee productivity, motivation, and job satisfaction. Of course, this doesn't mean that the use of participative management can't be beneficial under the right conditions. What it says, however, is that the use of participation is not a sure means for improving employee performance.

Representative participation

representative participation
A system in which workers participate in organizational decision making through a small group of representative employees.

Almost every country in western Europe has some type of legislation that requires companies to practice **representative participation**. That is, rather than participating directly in decisions, workers are represented by a small group of employees who actually participate. Representative participation has been called 'the most widely legislated form of employee involvement around the world'.[38] The goal of representative participation is to redistribute power within an organization, putting labour on a more equal footing with the interests of management and stockholders.

The two most common forms representative participation takes are works councils and board representatives.[39] Works councils are groups of nominated or elected employees who must be consulted when management makes decisions involving personnel. Board representatives are employees who sit on a company's board of directors and represent the interests of the firm's employees.

The overall influence of representative participation on working employees seems to be minimal.[40] For instance, the evidence suggests that works councils are dominated by management and have little impact on employees or the organization. And although this form of employee involvement might increase the motivation and satisfaction of the individuals who are doing the representing, there is little evidence that this trickles down to the operating employees whom they represent. Overall, 'the greatest value of representative participation is symbolic. If one is interested in changing employee attitudes or in improving organizational performance, representative participation would be a poor choice.'[41]

Quality circles

> **quality circle**
> A work group of employees who meet regularly to discuss their quality problems, investigate causes, recommend solutions and take corrective actions.

Quality circles became popular in Europe and North America during the 1980s.[42] Companies such as Hewlett-Packard, General Electric, Xerox, Procter & Gamble, IBM and Motorola used quality circles. A quality circle is defined as a work group of 8 to 10 employees and supervisors who have a shared area of responsibility and who meet regularly – typically once a week, on company time and on company premises – to discuss their quality problems, investigate causes of the problems, recommend solutions and take corrective actions.

A review of the evidence on quality circles indicates that they tend to show little or no effect on employee satisfaction, and although many studies report positive results from quality circles on productivity, these results are by no means guaranteed.[43] The failure of many quality circle programmes to produce measurable benefits has also led to a large number of them being discontinued. One of the reasons for their failure is that managers deal with employee involvement in only a limited way. 'At most, these programmes operate for one hour per week, with the remaining 39 hours unchanged. Why should changes in 2.5 per cent of a person's job have a major impact?'[44] Basically, quality circles were an easy way for management to get on the employee involvement bandwagon without really involving employees.

Linking employee involvement programmes and motivation theories

Employee involvement draws on a number of the motivation theories discussed in Chapter 6. For instance, Theory Y is consistent with participative management, and Theory X aligns with the more traditional autocratic style of managing people. In terms of two-factor theory, employee involvement programmes could provide employees with intrinsic motivation by increasing opportunities for growth, responsibility, and involvement in the work itself. Similarly, the opportunity to make and implement decisions – and then seeing them work out – can help satisfy an employee's needs for responsibility, achievement, recognition, growth, and enhanced self-esteem. So employee involvement is compatible with ERG theory and efforts to stimulate the achievement need. And extensive employee involvement programmes clearly have the potential to increase employee intrinsic motivation in work tasks.

Using rewards to motivate employees

> 5 Demonstrate how the different types of variable-pay programmes can increase employee motivation.

As we saw in Chapter 3, pay is not a primary factor driving job satisfaction. However, it does motivate people, and companies often underestimate the importance of pay in keeping top talent. A 2006 study found that whereas only 45 per cent of employers thought that pay was a key factor in losing top talent, 71 per cent of top performers indicated that it was a top reason.[45]

Given that pay is so important, we need to understand what to pay employees and how to pay them. To do that, management must make some strategic decisions. Will the organization lead, match or lag the market in pay? How will individual contributions be recognised? In this section, we consider four major strategic rewards decisions that need to be made: (1) what to pay employees (which is decided by establishing a pay structure); (2) how to pay individual employees (which is decided through variable pay plans and skill-based pay plans); (3) what benefits to offer, especially whether to offer employees choice in benefits (flexible benefits); and (4) how to construct employee recognition programmes.

What to pay: establishing a pay structure

There are many ways to pay employees. The process of initially setting pay levels can be rather complex and entails balancing *internal equity* – the worth of the job to the organization (usually established through a technical process called job evaluation) – and *external equity* – the external competitiveness of an organization's pay relative to pay elsewhere in its industry (usually established through pay surveys). Obviously, the best pay system pays the job what it is worth (internal equity) while also paying competitively relative to the labour market.

Some organizations prefer to be pay leaders by paying above the market, while some may lag the market because they can't afford to pay market rates, or they are willing to bear the costs of paying below market (namely, higher turnover as people are lured to better-paying jobs). Wal-Mart, for example, pays less than its competitors and often outsources jobs to China. Chinese workers in Shenzhen earn €100 a month (that's €1,200 per year) to make stereos for Wal-Mart. Of the 6,000 factories that are worldwide suppliers to Wal-Mart, 80 per cent are located in China. In fact, one-eighth of all Chinese exports to the United States go to Wal-Mart.[46]

Pay more, and you may get better-qualified, more highly motivated employees who will stay with the organization longer. But pay is often the highest single operating cost for an organization, which means that paying too much can make the organization's products or services too expensive. It's a strategic decision an organization must make, with clear trade offs.

How to pay: rewarding individual employees through variable-pay programmes

'Why should I put any extra effort into this job?' asked Anne Garcia, a schoolteacher. 'I can excel or I can do the bare minimum. It makes no difference. I get paid the same. Why do anything above the minimum to get by?'

Comments similar to Anne's have been voiced by schoolteachers for decades because pay increases were tied to seniority. Recently, however, a number of countries have begun revamping their schoolteacher compensation systems to motivate people like Anne to strive for excellence in their jobs. For instance, England and Wales have introduced programmes that tie teacher pay partly to the performance of the students in their classrooms.

A number of organizations – business firms as well as school's and other government agencies – are moving away from paying people based solely on credentials or length of service and toward using variable-pay programmes. Piece-rate plans, merit-based pay, bonuses, profit-sharing, gainsharing and employee stock ownership plans are all forms of **variable-pay programmes**. Instead of paying a person only for time on the job or seniority, a variable-pay programme bases a portion of an employee's pay on some individual and/or organizational measure of performance. Earnings therefore fluctuate up and down with the measure of performance.[47]

A recent survey of European pay systems found that over half of the organizations studied used some form of variable pay. The most common variable components of pay were also the most traditional: extra pay for overtime (which is an element of pay for roughly one third of employees) and other forms of extra pay, for example, for poor working conditions. Across Europe, piece rate payment is relatively common in the East, but less so in western Europe. Profit sharing is quite common in Slovakia, France, Luxembourg, the Netherlands, Slovenia and Sweden but is rare in most southern European countries and in Hungary and Romania.[48]

Variable-pay plans have long been used to compensate salespeople and executives. Recently they have begun to be applied to other employees. IBM, Pizza Hut, Cisco and Obiettivo Lavoro are just a few examples of companies using variable pay with rank-and-file employees.[49]

variable-pay programme
A pay plan that bases a portion of an employee's pay on some individual and/or organizational measure of performance.

Jeff Morgan education/Alamy

The England and Wales performance-related pay scheme motivates teachers by basing their pay partly on their performance in raising student achievement rather than on seniority or degrees. The move toward rewarding teachers with bonuses for their individual performance follows the widespread adoption of variable-pay plans in many businesses and government agencies.

Unfortunately, recent survey data indicate that most employees still don't see a strong connection between pay and performance. Only 29 per cent say that when they do a good job, their performance is rewarded.[50]

It is precisely the fluctuation in variable pay that has made these programmes attractive to management. It turns part of an organization's fixed labour costs into a variable cost, thus reducing expenses when performance declines. In addition, when pay is tied to performance, the employee's earnings recognise contribution rather than being a form of entitlement. Low performers find, over time, that their pay stagnates, while high performers enjoy pay increases commensurate with their contributions.

Let's examine the different types of variable-pay programmes in more detail.

Piece-rate pay

> **piece-rate pay plan**
> A pay plan in which workers are paid a fixed sum for each unit of production completed.

Piece-rate wages have been popular for more than a century as a means of compensating production workers. In **piece-rate pay plans**, workers are paid a fixed sum for each unit of production completed. When an employee gets no base salary and is paid only for what they produce, this is a pure piece-rate plan. People who work picking fruit are frequently paid this way. The harder they work and the more fruit they pick, the more they earn. The limitation of these plans is that they're not feasible for many jobs. For example, top football manager's can earn upwards of €5 million per year. That salary is paid regardless of how many games are won. Would it be better to pay, for example, €400,000 for each win? It would be unlikely that a coach would accept such a deal, and it may cause unanticipated consequences as well (such as cheating). So, although incentives are motivating and relevant, for some jobs, it is unrealistic to think they can constitute the only piece of some employees' pay.

Merit-based pay

> **merit-based pay plan**
> A pay plan based on performance appraisal ratings.

Merit-based pay plans pay for individual performance. However, unlike piece-rate plans, which pay based on objective output, **merit-based pay plans** are based on performance appraisal ratings. A main advantage of merit pay plans is that they allow employers to differentiate pay based on performance so that those people thought to be high performers are given bigger raises. The plans can be motivating because, if they are designed correctly, individuals perceive a strong relationship between their performance and the rewards they receive. The evidence supports the importance of this linkage.[51]

Most large organizations have merit pay plans, especially for salaried employees. IBM's merit pay plan, for example, provides increases to employees' base salary based on their annual performance evaluation. Since the 1990s, when the economy stumbled badly, an increasing number of Japanese companies have abandoned seniority-based pay in favour of merit-based pay. Koichi Yanashita, of Takeda Chemical Industries, commented, 'The merit-based salary system is an important means to achieve goals set by the company's top management, not just a way to change wages.'[52]

In an effort to motivate and retain top performers, more companies are increasing the differential between top and bottom performers. The consulting firm Hewitt Associates found that in 2006, employers gave their best performers roughly 10 per cent raises, compared to 3.6 per cent for average performers and 1.3 per cent for below-average performers. They've also found that these differences have increased over time. Martyn Fisher of Imperial Chemical in the United Kingdom said that his company has widened the merit pay gap between top and average performers because, 'as much as we would regret our average performers leaving, we'd regret more an above-target performer leaving'.[53]

Despite the intuitive appeal of pay for performance, merit pay plans have several limitations. One of them is that, typically, such plans are based on an annual performance appraisal. Thus, the merit pay is as valid or invalid as the performance ratings on which it is based. Another limitation of merit pay is that sometimes the pay raise pool fluctuates based on economic conditions or other factors that have little to do with an individual employee's performance. One year, a colleague at a top university who performed very well in teaching and research was given a pay raise of €150. Why? Because the pay raise pool was very small. Yet that is hardly pay-for-performance. Finally, unions typically resist merit pay plans. For example, negotiations over a collective agreement for the ground staff of Austrian Airlines came to a standstill for several months after company management sought to introduce a merit pay scheme. The scheme was strongly opposed by trade unions and by the works council, which threatened to take industrial action.[54]

Bonuses

For many top jobs, annual bonuses are a significant component of the total compensation. For example, Barclays' Bank President Bob Diamond claimed a bonus of €13m in 2006 added to his base salary of €300,000. Deutsche Bank AG former CEO Josef Ackermann received a bonus and shares worth about €12.7 million in 2007. Although a very significant amount, European CEOs are, on average, less well off than their American counterparts. Over the same period, Goldman Sachs Chairman and CEO Lloyd Blankfein took home nearly €53 million in restricted stock, options and cash, making it the largest bonus ever given to a Wall Street CEO at the time.[55] Increasingly, bonus plans are casting a larger net within organizations to include lower-ranking employees. Many companies now reward all employees with bonuses when company profits improve. Following a highly successful 2007–2008 business year, in which Porsche was reported to have made the most profit per car out of all the car makers, the company celebrated its 60th anniversary with a bonus of €6,000 paid to almost every employee working for the sportscar maker.[56]

bonus
A pay plan that rewards employees for recent performance rather than historical performance.

One advantage of bonuses over merit pay is that **bonuses** reward employees for recent performance rather than historical performance. The incentive effects of performance should be higher because, rather than paying people for performance that may have occurred years ago (and was rolled into their base pay), bonuses reward only recent performance. The downside of bonuses is that employees may view them as pay – after all, any worker would choose a €5,000 raise rolled into their base pay over a one-time payment of €5,000. KeySpan Corp., a 9,700-employee utility company, tried to manage this trade-off by combining yearly bonuses with a smaller merit-pay raise. Elaine Weinstein, KeySpan's senior vice president of HR, credits the plan with changing the culture from 'entitlement to meritocracy'.[57]

skill-based pay
A pay plan that sets pay levels on the basis of how many skills employees have or how many jobs they can do.

Skill-based pay

Skill-based pay is an alternative to job-based pay. Rather than having an individual's job title define their pay category, skill-based pay (also called *competency-based* or *knowledge-based pay*) sets pay levels on the basis of how many skills employees have or how many jobs they can do.[58] For instance, New Look, a UK women's fashion retailer, reduced absence of the distribution centre staff by 33 per cent and improved productivity by 53 per cent by introducing skill-based pay. Four levels of pay were created which employees attained by demonstrating competence in core and specialist skills, such as being able to multi-task.[59] For employers, the lure of skill-based pay plans is that they increase the flexibility of the workforce: Filling staffing needs is easier when employee skills are interchangeable. Skill-based pay also facilitates communication across the organization because people gain a better understanding of each others' jobs.

What about the downside of skill-based pay? People can 'top out' – that is, they can learn all the skills the programme calls for them to learn. This can frustrate employees after they've become challenged by an environment of learning, growth and continual pay rises. There is also a problem created by paying people for acquiring skills for which there may be no immediate need. This happened at IDS Financial Services.[60] The company found itself paying people more money even though there was little immediate use for their new skills. IDS eventually dropped its skill-based pay plan and replaced it with one that equally balances individual contribution and gains in work-team productivity. Finally, skill-based plans don't address the level of performance. They deal only with whether someone can perform the skill.

Profit-sharing plans

profit-sharing plan
An organization-wide programme that distributes compensation based on some established formula designed around a company's profitability.

Profit-sharing plans are organization wide programmes that distribute compensation based on some established formula designed around a company's profitability. These can be direct cash outlays or, particularly in the case of top managers, allocations of stock options. When you read about executives like Reuben Mark, the CEO at Colgate-Palmolive, earning €10 million in a year, almost all this comes from cashing in stock options previously granted based on company profit performance. Not all profit-sharing plans, though, need be so grand in scale. Jacob Luke, 13, started his own lawn-mowing business after getting a mower from his uncle. Jacob employs his brother, Isaiah and friend, Marcel Monroe, and pays them each 25 per cent of the profits he makes on each garden.

M J Kim/Getty Images

Securing finance for British films has always been difficult given the risky and fickle nature of the industry. The film adaptation of *The History Boys*, the Alan Bennett play, tested a new business model for British film-making. The budget for *The History Boys* was reduced by more than a half, with almost all cast and crew working for a minimal fee. In exchange everyone was allocated a share in future profits.

Source: M. Carter, 'Profit sharing gives hope for UK film industry', *The Guardian*, Monday 1 May 2006.

Gainsharing

gainsharing
A formula-based group incentive plan.

A variable-pay programme that has gotten a great deal of attention in recent years is **gainsharing**.[61] This is a formula-based group incentive plan. Improvements in group productivity from one period to another determine the total amount of money that is to be allocated. Gainsharing's popularity has traditionally been narrowly focused among large manufacturing companies such as Champion Spark Plug, but is gaining popularity in other sectors, particularly healthcare. Gainsharing is different from profit-sharing in that rewards are tied to productivity gains rather than on profits. Employees in a gainsharing plan can receive incentive awards even when the organization isn't profitable.

Employee stock ownership plans

employee stock ownership plan (ESOP)
A company-established benefits plan in which employees acquire stock, often at below-market prices, as part of their benefits.

Employee stock ownership plans (**ESOPs**) are company-established benefit plans in which employees acquire stock, often at below-market prices, as part of their benefits. Companies as varied as the John Lewis Partnership and Le Monde are now over 50 per cent employee owned. Across Europe ESOPs vary in popularity. About 7 per cent of employees in Germany and Austria own shares of their own companies, whereas the ratio is 20 to 30 per cent in the UK and Ireland, and considerably higher in France.[62]

The research on ESOPs indicates that they increase employee satisfaction.[63] But their impact on performance is less clear. ESOPs have the potential to increase employee job satisfaction and work motivation. But for this potential to be realised, employees need to psychologically experience ownership.[64] That is, in addition to merely having a financial stake in the company, employees need to be kept regularly informed of the status of the business and also have the opportunity to exercise influence over it. The evidence consistently indicates that it takes ownership and a participative style of management to achieve significant improvements in an organization's performance.[65]

Evaluation of variable pay

Do variable-pay programmes increase motivation and productivity? The answer is a qualified 'yes'. For example, studies generally support the idea that organizations with profit-sharing plans have higher levels of profitability than those without them.[66] Similarly, gainsharing has been found to improve productivity in a majority of cases and often has a positive impact on employee attitudes.[67] Another study found that whereas piece-rate pay-for-performance plans stimulated higher levels of productivity, this positive affect was not observed for risk-averse employees. Thus, in general, what economist Ed Lazear has said seems generally right: 'Workers respond to prices just as economic theory predicts. Claims by sociologists and others that monetising incentives may actually reduce output are unambiguously refuted by the data.' But that doesn't mean everyone responds positively to variable-pay plans.[68]

MOST UK EMPLOYEES SAY GREEN BENEFITS WOULD INCREASE THEIR LOYALTY TO EMPLOYERS

OB IN THE NEWS

UK workers would welcome their employers being more environmentally responsible and providing them with more 'green' benefits, a survey has found.

Of 1,000 employees surveyed by HR consultancy Ceridian, 69 per cent said it was important that their employer was environmentally responsible, with more than half wishing their organization would do more. More than a third of all workers surveyed felt that receiving greener benefits would make them more loyal to their employer. Fourteen per cent would change jobs for a greener benefits package.

The top three most attractive 'green' benefits would be incentives to move to sustainable electricity/energy (67 per cent), access to discounts on 'green' recycled products (65 per cent) and discounts on public transport (59 per cent).

Doug Sawers, managing director of Ceridian, said: 'People today recognise they need to do more to ensure the long-term survival of our planet and employees appear to be keen to do their bit when backed by like-minded employers.'

Source: M. Berry, *Personnel Today*, 23 April 2007. Available at http://www.personneltoday.com/articles/2007/04/23/40308/most-uk-employees-say-green-benefits-would-increase-their-loyalty-to-employers.html. Accessed 12 October 2008.

Flexible benefits: developing a benefits package

6 Show how flexible benefits turn benefits into motivators.

Todd Evans and Allison Murphy both work for Citigroup, but they have very different needs in terms of employee benefits. Todd is married and has three young children and a wife who is at home full time. Allison, too, is married, but her husband has a high-paying job with the government and they have no children. Todd is concerned about having a good medical plan and enough life insurance to support his family in case it's needed. In contrast, Allison's husband already has her medical needs covered on his plan, and life insurance is a low priority for both Allison and her husband. Allison is more interested in extra vacation time and long-term financial benefits such as a tax-deferred savings plan.

A standardised benefits package for all employees at Citigroup would be unlikely to satisfactorily meet the needs of both Todd and Allison. Citigroup could, however, cover both sets of needs if it offered flexible benefits.

flexible benefits
A benefits plan that allows each employee to put together a benefits package individually tailored to their own needs and situation.

Flexible benefits allow each employee to put together a benefits package individually tailored to his or her own needs and situation. It replaces the traditional 'one-benefit-plan-fits-all' programmes that dominated organizations for more than 50 years.[69] Consistent with expectancy theory's thesis that organizational rewards should be linked to each individual employee's goals, flexible benefits individualise rewards by allowing each employee to choose the compensation package that best satisfies their current needs. The average organization provides fringe benefits worth approximately 40 per cent of an employee's salary. Traditional benefits programmes were designed for the typical employee of the 1950s – a man with a wife and two children at home. Less than 10 per cent of employees now fit this stereotype. About 25 per cent of today's employees are single, and one-third are part of two-income families with no children. Traditional programmes don't meet their diverse needs, but flexible benefits do. They can be uniquely tailored to accommodate differences in employee needs based on age, marital status, spouses' benefit status, number and age of dependents and the like.

The three most popular types of benefits plans are modular plans, core-plus options and flexible spending accounts.[70] *Modular plans* are predesigned packages of benefits, with each module put together to meet the needs of a specific group of employees. So a module designed for single employees with no dependents might include only essential benefits. Another, designed for single parents, might have additional life insurance, disability insurance and expanded health coverage. *Core-plus plans* consist of a core of essential benefits and a menu-like selection of other benefit options from which employees can select and add to the core. Typically, each employee is given 'benefit credits', which allow the 'purchase' of additional benefits that uniquely meet their needs. *Flexible spending plans* allow employees to set aside up to the euro amount offered in the plan to pay for particular services. It's a convenient way, for example, for employees to pay for health care and dental premiums. Flexible spending accounts can increase employee take-home pay because employees don't have to pay taxes on the euros they spend out of these accounts.

Intrinsic rewards: employee recognition programmes

7 Identify the motivational benefits of intrinsic rewards.

Laura Schendell makes only €8 per hour working at her fast-food and the job isn't very challenging or interesting. Yet Laura talks enthusiastically about her job, her boss and the company that employs her. 'What I like is the fact that Guy [her supervisor] appreciates the effort I make. He compliments me regularly in front of the other people on my shift, and I've been chosen Employee of the Month twice in the past six months. Did you see my picture on that plaque on the wall?'

Organizations are increasingly recognising what Laura Schendell knows: Important work rewards can be both intrinsic and extrinsic. Rewards are intrinsic in the form of employee recognition programmes and extrinsic in the form of compensation systems. In this section, we deal with ways in which managers can reward and motivate employee performance.

Employee recognition programmes range from a spontaneous and private 'thank you' up to widely publicised formal programmes in which specific types of behaviour are encouraged and the procedures for attaining recognition are clearly identified. Some research has suggested that whereas financial incentives may be more motivating in the short term, in the long run, nonfinancial incentives are more motivating.[71]

Nichols Foods Ltd., a British bottler of soft drinks and syrups, has a comprehensive recognition programme.[72] The central hallway in its production area is lined with 'bragging boards', where the accomplishments of various individuals and teams are regularly updated. Monthly awards are presented to people who have been nominated by peers for extraordinary effort on the job. And monthly award winners are eligible for further recognition at an annual off-site meeting for all employees. In contrast, most managers use a far more informal approach. Julia Stewart, president of Applebee's restaurants, frequently leaves sealed notes on the chairs of employees after everyone has gone home.[73] These notes explain how critical Stewart thinks the person's work is or how much she appreciates the completion of a recent project. Stewart also relies heavily on voice mail messages left after office hours to tell employees how appreciative she is for a job well done.

A few years ago, 1,500 employees were surveyed in a variety of work settings to find out what they considered to be the most powerful workplace motivator. Their response? Recognition, recognition and more recognition.[74]

An obvious advantage of recognition programmes is that they are inexpensive (praise, of course, is free!).[75] It shouldn't be surprising, therefore, to find that employee recognition programmes have grown in popularity. A survey of 391 companies found that 84 per cent had some programme to recognise worker achievements and that 4 in 10 said they were doing more to foster employee recognition than they had been just a year earlier.[76]

CULTURAL DIFFERENCES IN JOB CHARACTERISTICS AND JOB SATISFACTION

GLOBAL

How do various factors of one's job contribute to satisfaction in different cultures? A recent study attempted to answer this question in a survey of about 50 countries. The authors of the study distinguished between intrinsic job characteristics (for example, having a job that allows one to use one's skills, frequently receiving recognition from one's supervisor) and extrinsic job characteristics (for example, receiving pay that is competitive within a given industry, working in an environment that has comfortable physical conditions) and assessed differences between the two in predicting employee job satisfaction.

The study found that, across all countries, extrinsic job characteristics were consistently and positively related to satisfaction with one's job. However, countries differed in the extent to which intrinsic job characteristics predicted job satisfaction. Wealthier countries, countries with stronger social security, countries that stress individualism rather than

collectivism, and countries with a smaller power distance (those that value a more equal distribution of power in organizations and institutions) showed a stronger relationship between the presence of intrinsic job characteristics and job satisfaction.

What explains these findings? One explanation is that in countries with greater wealth and social security, concerns over survival are taken for granted, and thus employees have the freedom to place greater importance on intrinsic aspects of the job. Another explanation is that cultural norms that emphasise the individual and have less power asymmetry socialise individuals to focus on the intrinsic aspects of their job. In other words, such norms tell individuals that it is okay to want jobs that are intrinsically rewarding.

Source: Based on X. Huang and E. Van De Vliert, 'Where intrinsic job satisfaction fails to work: national moderators of intrinsic motivation,' *Journal of Organizational Behavior*, 24, 2 (2003), pp. 159–79.

Despite the increased popularity of employee recognition programmes, critics argue that these programmes are highly susceptible to political manipulation by management.[77] When applied to jobs where performance factors are relatively objective, such as sales, recognition programmes are likely to be perceived by employees as fair. However, in most jobs, the criteria for good performance aren't self-evident, which allows managers to manipulate the system and recognise their favourite employees. Abuse of such a system can undermine the value of recognition programmes and lead to demoralising employees.

Global implications

Do the motivational approaches discussed in this chapter vary by culture? Because we've discussed some very different approaches in this chapter, let's break down our analysis by approach. Not every approach has been studied by cross-cultural researchers, so we don't discuss every motivational approach. However, we consider cross-cultural differences in the following approaches: (1) job characteristics and job enrichment, (2) teleworking, (3) variable pay, (4) flexible benefits and (5) employee involvement.

Job characteristics and job enrichment

Although a few studies have tested the job characteristics model in different cultures, the results aren't very consistent. One study suggested that when employees are 'other-oriented' (that is, concerned with the welfare of others at work), the relationship between intrinsic job characteristics and job satisfaction was weaker. As the authors note, because the job characteristics model is relatively individualistic (considering the relationship between the employee and their work), this suggests that job enrichment strategies may not have the same effects in more collectivistic cultures that they do in individualistic cultures.[78] However, another study suggested that the degree to which jobs had intrinsic job characteristics predicted job satisfaction and job involvement equally well for US, Japanese and Hungarian employees.[79]

Teleworking

Does the degree to which employees telecommute vary by nation? Does it effectiveness depend on culture? Slightly more than 8 per cent of all EU workers can be described as, at least some of the time, teleworkers. The proportion of people teleworking is highest in the Scandinavian countries and the Netherlands and lowest in the southern European countries.[80]

This is lower than one study that suggests teleworking in the United States is around 25 per cent of employees. Thus, teleworking appears to be more common in the United States than in Europe. What about the rest of the world? Unfortunately, there is very little data comparing teleworking rates in other parts of the world. Similarly, we don't really know whether teleworking works better in the United States than in other countries. However, the same study that compared telework rates between the EU and the United States determined that employees in Europe appeared to have the same level of interest in telework: Regardless of country, interest is higher among employees than among employers.[81]

Variable pay

You'd probably think that individual pay systems (such as merit pay or pay-for-performance) would work better in individualistic cultures like the United Kingdom, Australia, the Netherlands and the United States than in collectivistic cultures like China or Venezuela. Similarly, you'd probably hypothesise that group-based rewards such as gainsharing or profit-sharing would work better in collectivistic cultures than in individualistic cultures. Unfortunately, there isn't much research on the issue. One recent study did suggest, though, that beliefs about the fairness of a group incentive plan were more predictive of pay satisfaction for employees in the United States than for employees in Hong Kong. One interpretation of these findings is that US employees are more critical in appraising a group pay plan, and therefore it's more critical that the plan be communicated clearly and administered fairly.[82]

Flexible benefits

Today, many major corporations in the United Kingdom and the United States offer flexible benefits, but they are not as common in other parts of the world. One reason is that some countries have more stringent legislation than the UK or US and differences in state benefits that make flexible benefits schemes more difficult to implement. In Italy and France, for example, all benefits are mandated and have to be negotiated with work councils. Cultural differences are also important. Whilst people in the UK are generally appreciative of public recognition, in some Asian cultures people tend to be more low profile and avoid being singled out. However, despite the challenges, the outlook is that flexible benefits are becoming globally more popular.[83]

Employee involvement

Employee involvement programmes differ among countries.[84] For instance, a study comparing the acceptance of employee involvement programmes in Mexico, Poland the United States, and India confirmed the importance of modifying practices to reflect national culture.[85] For example, while US employees readily accepted these programmes, managers in India who tried to empower their employees through employee involvement programmes were rated low by those employees. Employee satisfaction also decreased. These reactions are consistent with India's high power–distance culture, which accepts and expects differences in authority.

Summary and implications for managers

We've presented a number of motivation theories and applications in Chapter 6 and in this chapter. Although it's always dangerous to synthesise a large number of complex ideas into a few simple guidelines, the following suggestions summarise the essence of what we know about motivating employees in organizations.

Recognise individual differences

Managers should be sensitive to individual differences. For example, employees from Asian cultures may prefer not to be singled out as special because it makes them uncomfortable.

Employees have different needs. Don't treat them all alike. Moreover, spend the time necessary to understand what's important to each employee. This allows you to individualise goals, level of involvement and rewards to align with individual needs. Also, design jobs to align with individual needs and therefore maximise the motivation potential in jobs.

Use goals and feedback

Employees should have firm, specific goals, and they should get feedback on how well they are faring in pursuit of those goals.

Allow employees to participate in decisions that affect them

Employees can contribute to a number of decisions that affect them: setting work goals, choosing their own benefits packages, solving productivity and quality problems and the like. This can increase employee productivity, commitment to work goals, motivation and job satisfaction.

Link rewards to performance

Rewards should be contingent on performance. Importantly, employees must perceive a clear linkage between performance and rewards. Regardless of how closely rewards are actually correlated to performance criteria, if individuals perceive this relationship to be low, the results will be low performance, a decrease in job satisfaction, and an increase in turnover and absenteeism.

Check the system for equity

Employees should perceive rewards as equating with the inputs they bring to the job. At a simplistic level, this should mean that experience, skills, abilities, effort and other obvious inputs should explain differences in performance and, hence, pay, job assignments and other obvious rewards.

POINT/COUNTERPOINT

Praise motivates

POINT →

Some of the most memorable, and meaningful, words we've ever heard have probably been words of praise. Genuine compliments mean a lot to people – and can go a long way toward inspiring the best performance. Numerous research studies show that students who receive praise from their teachers are more motivated, and often this motivation lasts well after the praise is given. Too often we assume that simple words of praise mean little, but most of us yearn for genuine praise from people who are in a position to evaluate us.

Companies are starting to learn this lesson. A survey by mobile communications company O_2 reveals that praise is important. If companies were better at acknowledging when staff put extra effort in, 84 per cent of workers would be more loyal to their employers and 71 per cent would be more willing to go the extra mile when required.

Another survey of 11,244 people found workers aged 30 and under were often the least motivated at work, which experts say is a failure of managers to recognise that younger workers require praise. Mark Murray, chief executive of Leadership IQ, says positive reinforcement makes a difference to motivation. 'The reality is they need much more praise and attention than previous generations.'[86]

Praise even seems to be important to long-term relationships. The Gottman Institute, a relationship research and training firm, says its research suggests that the happiest marriages are those in which couples make five times as many positive statements to and about each other as negative ones. Of course, praise is not everything, but it is a very important and often underutilised motivator. And best of all, it's free.

COUNTERPOINT ←

Praise is highly overrated. In theory, it's nice to receive compliments, but in practice, praise has some real pitfalls.

First, a lot of praise is not genuine. Falsely praising people breeds narcissism. Jean Twenge, a researcher who studies narcissism, has said that scores on narcissism have risen steadily since 1982. As she notes, lavishing praise may be the culprit. Told we're wonderful time after time, we start to believe it, even when we aren't.

Second, praise is paradoxical in that the more it's given, the less meaningful it is. If we go around telling everyone they're special, soon it means nothing to those who do achieve something terrific. In the animated film *The Incredibles*, a superhero's mother tells her son, 'Everyone's special!' His reply, 'Which is another way of saying no one is.'

Third, some of the most motivating people are those who are difficult to please. Goran Lindahl, the chief executive

of ABB, the Swiss–Swedish engineering group, or Jack Welch, former CEO of GE. are known for being difficult to please, which means most people will work harder to meet their expectations. Conversely, what happens when you dish out praise for an employee who just shows up? What you've done is send a message that simply showing up is enough. Praise may seem like it's free, but when it's 'dumbing down' performance expectations – so that employees think mediocrity is okay – the price may be huge.

Often what people really need is a gentle kick in the pants. As one management consultant says, 'People want to know how they're doing. Don't sugarcoat it. Just give them the data.'

Source: 'The most praised generation goes to work', *Gainesville (Florida) Sun*, 29 April 2007, pp. 5G, 6G; and J. Zaslow, 'In praise of less praise', *Wall Street Journal*, 3 May 2007, p. D1.

QUESTIONS FOR REVIEW

1. What is the job characteristics model? How does it motivate employees?

2. What are the three major ways that jobs can be redesigned? In your view, in what situations would one of the methods be favoured over the others?

3. What are the three alternative work arrangements of flexitime, job sharing and teleworking? What are the advantages and disadvantages of each?

4. What are employee involvement programmes? How might they increase employee motivation?

5. What is variable pay? What are the variable-pay programmes that are used to motivate employees? What are their advantages and disadvantages?

6. How can flexible benefits motivate employees?

7. What are the motivational benefits of intrinsic rewards?

Experiential exercise

ASSESSING EMPLOYEE MOTIVATION AND SATISFACTION USING THE JOB CHARACTERISTICS MODEL

Purpose

This exercise will help you examine outcomes of the job characteristics model for different professions.

Time

Approximately 30 to 45 minutes.

Background

Data were collected on 6,930 employees in 56 different organizations using the Job Diagnostic Survey. The following table contains data on the five core job dimensions of the job characteristics model for several professions. Also included are growth-needs strength, internal motivation, and pay satisfaction for each profession. The values are averages based on a 7-point scale.

Job Characteristics Averages for Six Professions

Variable	Profession					
	Professional/Technical	Managerial	Sales	Service	Clerical	Machine Trades
Skill variety	5.4	5.6	4.8	5.0	4.0	5.1
Task identity	5.1	4.7	4.4	4.7	4.7	4.9
Task significance	5.6	5.8	5.5	5.7	5.3	5.6
Autonomy	5.4	5.4	4.8	5.0	4.5	4.9
Feedback	5.1	5.2	5.4	5.1	4.6	4.9
Growth needs strength	5.6	5.3	5.7	5.4	5.0	4.8
Internal motivation	5.8	5.8	5.7	5.7	5.4	5.6
Pay satisfaction	4.4	4.6	4.2	4.1	4.0	4.2

Source: Hackman, J. R./Oldham, G. R., *Work Redesign*, © 1980, p. 317. Adapted by permission of Pearson Education, Inc., Upper Saddle River, New Jersey.

Instructions

1. Break into groups of three to five.
2. Calculate the MPS score for each of the professions and compare them. Discuss whether you think these scores accurately reflect your perceptions of the motivating potential of these professions.
3. Graph the relationship between each profession's core job dimensions and its corresponding value for internal

motivation and for pay satisfaction, using the core job dimensions as independent variables. What conclusions can you draw about motivation and satisfaction of employees in these professions?

Source: Adapted from J. R. Hackman and G. R. Oldham, *Work Redesign* (Reading, MA: Addison-Wesley, 1980).

Ethical dilemma

HOW MUCH TO PAY – THE MINIMUM WAGE OR A LIVING WAGE?

The disparity between the wages of workers in different countries has long been recognised and debated. One study compared the wage rates of McDonald's cashiers and crew in 27 different countries. In India the hourly wage was €0.21 compared to €5.67 in Japan. These differences tend to be explained away by the companies involved by referring to vastly different costs of living. Another study gives a richer picture of economic inequality by looking at the proportion of household income that is spent on food. In Denmark, the Netherlands and Switzerland it is less than 20 per cent. In Armenia and Nigeria it is over 80 per cent. Vociferous debate continues on how much organizations should pay in the countries they operate – the minimum wage (if the country has one) or a living wage. Definitions of a living wage differ, but it is generally considered to refer to the amount necessary to provide a basic standard of living. But it is not just across

borders where this is a factor. The group London Citizens is campaigning for a living wage for the people of London. They argue that the cost of living is higher in London compared to other parts of the UK and want employers to pay London staff €8.75 per hour, about two euros above the UK national minimum wage.

Questions

1. Do you believe organizations should pay a living wage rather than the minimum wage? Why?

2. Imagine you are working in a company that wants to pay its employees in Asia a living wage. However, to be able to afford it, it will have to significantly cut the wages of its employees in other parts of the world – yours included.

The firm has decided to let its employees decide by voting for or against. How would you vote?

3. If you were setting the pay scales of a British based company, would you pay Londoners more? What effect on motivation might this have on workers in the rest of the country?

Sources: Ashenfelter, O. and Jurajda, S. (2001) Cross-Country Comparisons of Wage Rates: The Big Mac Index (Mimeo). Princeton University and CERGE-EI/Charles University. (Available at: http://economics.uchicago.edu/download/bigmac.pdf); Global wage report 2008/9 Geneva, International Labour Office, 2008; London Citizens *see* http://www.londoncitizens.org.uk/index.html accessed 16/02/2010.

CASE INCIDENT 1

The most boring job in the world?

Jeremy Campbell loathes his job. He stands on the corner of a busy street in a large city holding a sign that reads 'Golf Sale Today'. The advertisement is for a store located just off the main street that sells, unsurprisingly, golfing equipment. For this store, every working day there is a 'sale'. Nobody knows this more than Jeremy after having held the sign 10 hours a day, six days per week, for almost a year. His day begins at 9am when the store opens and finishes at 8pm when it closes. He is allowed three breaks per day, 15 minutes in the morning, 30 minutes for lunch, and then another 15 minutes in the afternoon. Jeremy is not allowed to listen to music, talk on his mobile phone, or while away the hours in any other manner than hold the sign and try to entice customers into the shop.

'It's awful', moans Jeremy. 'Every day it is the same, boring routine. I seriously don't think I can stand it must longer. If it wasn't for the money I would have packed it in months ago. How much I can actually earn came as quite a shock when I first started. I get €5 for every customer I get into the shop who buys something. On a busy day, I can earn around €300'.

Jeremy's boss, Helen Brosnahan, wants him to stay. 'Before Jeremy came along we had real trouble finding the right person for the job and when we did, they would often leave after only a few days. People don't take the job seriously. But we are a small business and this is one of the few marketing activities we can afford. And besides, it really works. If we just have a sign, people walk past it. But if we have someone holding the sign and talking to people, our sales are much better'.

Helen doesn't want to lose Jeremy but doesn't know what she must do to motivate him. And things have just gotten more complex. Jeremy's first child, Melissa Rose, has just been born.

Questions

1. Analyse Jeremy's job according to the Job Characteristics Model.

2. How can the job be redesigned to make it more motivating?

3. Are there any alternative work arrangements that may help?

4. What pay plan is being used to reward Jeremy? Is it appropriate or is there an alternative that you believe may be more motivating?

5. Does Jeremy's job appeal to you? Why or why not?

CASE INCIDENT 2

A blueprint for Europe

Jussi Itavuori knows all too well the challenges of harmonising national cultures, laws and work practices into a single, cohesive, co-operative universe. As the first group HR director of the multinational, multi-company conglomerate, the European Aeronautic Defence and Space Company (EADS), Itavuori's responsibility could be likened to that of creating a human resources strategy for a united Europe.

A decade ago, Itavuori saw the harmonisation of European social legislation as 'a threat and a straitjacket – more of a straitjacket for business than a positive development for Europe'. Now, however, as he leads HR for Europe's largest aerospace and defence group, he admits to a new perspective. With more than 100,000 employees worldwide, with most based in France, Germany, Spain and the UK, EADS may not yet be a familiar name to the public at large, but its aerospace brands certainly are – companies in which it is either the major partner or the sole owner include Airbus, Eurofighter and Eurocopter.

A Finn, Itavuori joined EADS from lift manufacturer KONE, 14 months after its formation through the merger-integration of a triumvirate of leading European aerospace companies: France's Aerospatiale Matra, Germany's DaimlerChrysler Aerospace (Dasa) and Spain's CASA. A vision for the future corporate culture had already been set, and the merger teams had steadily been putting into place prescribed measures to build a new operational framework. On joining, Itavuori realised he had, among other important tasks, two missions:

1. Developing and establishing the new European industrial relations practice
2. Harmonising managerial compensation and benefits.

This pair proved to be particularly challenging, considering EADS' transnational, transcompany nature, as well as the passionate loyalty to each member company and the products they created.

Itavuori believes the process of becoming a truly European company has many depths and layers, 'and I don't think people always recognise what it really means', he says. As EADS steadily cuts through the jungle-like foliage of issues and bureaucracy that blocks the path to corporate harmonisation, he easily identifies the European social legislative issues he wishes were resolved: taxes, labour law, pensions and benefits such as profit sharing.

The typical multinational does not have as deep a need for harmonisation, as it will not have been built on the premise of integrating such a great variety of different individual cultures, in terms of nations, corporate and products, he says. 'We have to question the level to which we harmonise our ways of working, our ways of compensating people and things like that. We must also recognise that Europe is still made up of national countries and legislations. Being a truly European company means you need to deal with that.'

He compares the challenges of harmonising industrial relations within a European company to the mind-churning folly of trying to match up the multi-coloured layers of blocks on a Rubik's Cube. 'It is a headache,' he admits. 'We have the new layer, which is the European layer, and then you try to change it, and then everything else changes.'

Nevertheless, progress is being made. And one example is the establishment of a European work council within EADS. Describing the pan-national council as 'very active', Itavuori says that, so far, the organization is following in the path of the constructive relationships enjoyed with various unions in France and Germany by EADS forebears. In addition, subcommittees have been formed that serve as work councils for various business units such as Airbus and Eurocopter. 'We have the European, national, business unit, and local levels,' Itavuori says.

Further, in France and Spain, for instance, five trade unions are represented throughout EADS enterprises. 'So you can draw a rather complex matrix on these things,' he says. 'Germany is a bit easier because you have more or less one major trade union which takes care of quite a lot. The UK is a different ball game because the industrial relations tradition is very different from continental Europe. In the UK, it's much less formal and less guided by the system of work councils that operate in continental Europe.'

Under Itavuori's leadership, the other key area of early HR priorities – harmonising compensation and benefits – has also moved on. One element is the harmonisation of the contractual structure for the company's top 1,000 executives and managers, meaning that all enjoy, for instance, the same salary structure of variable and base pay. 'The pay is not necessarily harmonised, but the structure of the pay is,' he says.

The top people are classified in three categories with varying percentages of variable pay per category and by country, with a 'very aggressive' focus on achieving that predates Itavuori's arrival and is linked to EADS' ambitious profit goal. 'It's very results orientated,' says Itavuori. 'Variable pay has been pushed strongly, and it has been pushed by a harmonised structure.'

Describing the intricacies of introducing such a performance management culture to a multicultural environment is a separate story altogether, he says.

'There are deep cultural differences between French and German performance management,' he says, 'and pay philosophies where sometimes people are paid because of the individual, and elsewhere because of their status or job.'

Questions

1. What issues did Itavuori need to deal with when he took charge of EADS?

2. How did he resolve these issues? Do you think they will be successful? Or not?

3. Do you think it is a good idea to harmonise industrial relations practices and managerial compensation and benefits across Europe?

4. As a manager of a Europe-wide organization, what practices would you use to motivate employees?

Source: Adapted from 'A blueprint for Europe', *Personnel Today*, 18 February 2003. Available at: http://www.personneltoday.com/articles/2003/02/18/17535/a-blueprint-for-europe.html. Accessed 20 October 2008.

Endnotes

1 J. R. Hackman and G. R. Oldham, 'Motivation through the design of work: test of a theory', *Organizational Behavior and Human Performance*, August 1976, pp. 250–79; and J. R. Hackman and G. R. Oldham, *Work Redesign* (Reading, MA: Addison-Wesley, 1980).

2 J. R. Hackman, 'Work design', in J. R. Hackman and J. L. Suttle (eds.), *Improving Life at Work* (Santa Monica, CA: Goodyear, 1977), p. 129.

3 See 'Job characteristics theory of work redesign', in J. B. Miner, *Theories of Organizational Behavior* (Hinsdale, IL: Dryden Press, 1980), pp. 231–66; B. T. Loher, R. A. Noe, N. L. Moeller and M. P. Fitzgerald, 'A meta-analysis of the relation of job characteristics to job satisfaction', *Journal of Applied Psychology*, May 1985, pp. 280–89; W. H. Glick, G. D. Jenkins, Jr. and N. Gupta, 'Method versus substance: how strong are underlying relationships between job characteristics and

attitudinal outcomes?', *Academy of Management Journal*, September 1986, pp. 441–64; Y. Fried and G. R. Ferris, 'The validity of the job characteristics model: a review and meta-analysis', *Personnel Psychology*, Summer 1987, pp. 287–322; S. J. Zaccaro and E. F. Stone, 'Incremental validity of an empirically based measure of job characteristics', *Journal of Applied Psychology*, May 1988, pp. 245–52; J. R. Rentsch and R. P. Steel, 'Testing the durability of job characteristics as predictors of absenteeism over a six-year period', *Personnel Psychology*, Spring 1998, pp. 165–90; S. J. Behson, E. R. Eddy and S. J. Lorenzet, 'The importance of the critical psychological states in the job characteristics model: a meta-analytic and structural equations modeling examination', *Current Research in Social Psychology*, May 2000, pp. 170–89; and T. A. Judge, 'Promote job satisfaction through mental challenge', in E. A. Locke (ed.), *Handbook of Principles of Organizational Behavior*, pp. 75–89.

4 T. A. Judge, S. K. Parker, A. E. Colbert, D. Heller and R. Ilies, 'Job satisfaction: a cross-cultural review', in N. Anderson, D. S. Ones (eds.), *Handbook of Industrial, Work and Organizational Psychology*, vol. 2 (Thousand Oaks, CA: Sage Publications, 2002), pp. 25–52.

5 C. A. O'Reilly and D. F. Caldwell, 'Informational influence as a determinant of perceived task characteristics and job satisfaction', *Journal of Applied Psychology*, April 1979, pp. 157–65; R. V. Montagno, 'The effects of comparison of others and prior experience on responses to task design', *Academy of Management Journal*, June 1985, pp. 491–98; and P. C. Bottger and I. K.-H. Chew, 'The job characteristics model and growth satisfaction: main effects of assimilation of work experience and context satisfaction', *Human Relations*, June 1986, pp. 575–94.

6 C. Ansberry, 'In the new workplace, jobs morph to suit rapid pace of change', *Wall Street Journal*, 22 March 2002, p. A1.

7 Siemens, the Netherlands: Flexible working practices, training and development, and exit policy (2005) European Foundation for the Improvement of Living and Working Conditions. Available at: http://www.eurofound.europa.eu/areas/populationandsociety/cases/nl004.htm.

8 J. Ortega, 'Job rotation as a learning mechanism', *Management Science*, October 2001, pp. 1361–70.

9 See, for instance, data on job enlargement described in M. A. Campion and C. L. McClelland, 'Follow-up and extension of the interdisciplinary costs and benefits of enlarged jobs', *Journal of Applied Psychology*, June 1993, pp. 339–51.

10 Hackman, 'Work design,' pp. 115–20.

11 J. P. Wanous, 'Individual differences and reactions to job characteristics', *Journal of Applied Psychology*, October 1974, pp. 616–22; and H. P. Sims and A. D. Szilagyi, 'Job characteristic relationships: individual and structural moderators', *Organizational Behavior and Human Performance*, June 1976, pp. 211–30.

12 M. Fein, 'The real needs and goals of blue-collar workers', *Conference Board Record*, February 1972, pp. 26–33.

13 Hackman and Oldham, *Work Redesign*.

14 A. M. Grant, E. M. Campbell, G. Chen, K. Cottone, D. Lapedis and K. Lee, 'Impact and the art of motivation maintenance: the effects of contact with beneficiaries on persistence behavior', *Organizational Behavior and Human Decision Processes*, 103 (2007), pp. 53–67.

15 Cited in *U.S. News & World Report*, May 31, 1993, p. 63.

16 See, for example, Hackman and Oldham, *Work Redesign*; Miner, *Theories of Organizational Behavior*, pp. 231–66; R. W. Griffin, 'Effects of work redesign on employee perceptions, attitudes, and behaviors: a long-term investigation', *Academy of Management Journal*, 34, 2 (1991), pp. 425–35; and J. L. Cotton, *Employee Involvement* (Newbury Park, CA: Sage, 1993), pp. 141–72.

17 F. P. Morgeson, M. D. Johnson, M. A. Campion, G. J. Medsker and T. V. Mumford, 'Understanding reactions to job redesign: a quasi-experimental investigation of the moderating effects of organizational contact on perceptions of performance behavior', *Personnel Psychology*, 39 (2006), pp. 333–63.

18 European Commission (2007) *Employment in Europe*.

19 D. R. Dalton and D. J. Mesch, 'The impact of flexible scheduling on employee attendance and turnover', *Administrative Science Quarterly*, June 1990, pp. 370–87; K. S. Kush and L. K. Stroh, 'Flextime: myth or reality', *Business Horizons*, September–October 1994, p. 53; and L. Golden, 'Flexible work schedules: what are we trading off to get them?', *Monthly Labor Review*, March 2001, pp. 50–55.

20 See, for example, D. A. Ralston and M. F. Flanagan, 'The effect of flextime on absenteeism and turnover for male and female employees', *Journal of Vocational Behavior*, April 1985, pp. 206–17; D. A. Ralston, W. P. Anthony and D. J. Gustafson, 'Employees may love flextime, but what does it do to the organization's productivity?', *Journal of Applied Psychology*, May 1985, pp. 272–79; J. B. McGuire and J. R. Liro, 'Flexible work schedules, work attitudes, and perceptions of productivity', *Public Personnel Management*, Spring 1986, pp. 65–73; P. Bernstein, 'The ultimate in flextime: from Sweden, by way of Volvo', *Personnel*, June 1988, pp. 70–74; Dalton and Mesch, 'The impact of flexible scheduling on employee attendance and turnover'; and B. B. Baltes, T. E. Briggs, J. W. Huff, J. A. Wright and G. A. Neuman, 'Flexible and compressed workweek schedules: a meta-analysis of their effects on work-related criteria', *Journal of Applied Psychology*, 84, 4 (1999), pp. 496–513.

21 Cited in S. Caminiti, 'Fair shares,' *Working Woman*, November 1999, pp. 52–54.

22 H. Mulligan (2006) 'Attitudes of employers and employees to the changing workplace'; P. Domenico (1998) 'Job-sharing introduced in Italy'; J. Parker (2007) 'Changing work organization results in mixed effects'. All available at European Foundation for the Improvement of Living and Working Conditions, http://www.eurofound.europa.eu/.

23 S. Shellenbarger, 'Two people, one job: it can really work', *Wall Street Journal*, 7 December, 1994, p. B1.

24 'Job-sharing: widely offered, little used', *Training*, November 1994, p. 12.

25 C. Dawson, 'Japan: work-sharing will prolong the pain', *BusinessWeek*, 24 December 2001, p. 46.

26 Shellenbarger, 'Two people, one job'.

27 Y. Ruiz and A. Walling, 'Home-based working using communication technologies', *Labour Market Trends*, 113, 10 (October 2005), pp. 417–26.

28 N. B. Kurland and D. E. Bailey, 'Telework: the advantages and challenges of working here, there, anywhere, and anytime', *Organizational Dynamics*, Autumn 1999, pp. 53–68; and Wells, 'Making telecommuting work', p. 34; European Foundation for the Improvement of Living and Working Conditions (2007) *Telework*. Available at: http://www.

eurofound.europa.eu/areas/industrialrelations/dictionary/definitions/TELEWORK.htm.

29 'Being in remote control; cutting risks', *The Times* (23 June 2008), p. 7.

30 Cited in R. W. Judy and C. D'Amico, *Workforce 2020* (Indianapolis, IN: Hudson Institute, 1997), p. 58.

31 Cited in Wells, 'Making telecommuting work'.

32 A. Maitland, 'Attractions of an out of office experience: MANAGEMENT: A large-scale study shows teleworking offers a range of benefits', *Financial Times* (5 November 2003), p. 12.

33 J. M. Stanton and J. L. Barnes-Farrell, 'Effects of electronic performance monitoring on personal control, task satisfaction, and task performance', *Journal of Applied Psychology*, December 1996, pp. 738–45; B. Pappas, 'They spy', *Forbes*, 8 February 1999, p. 47; S. Armour, 'More bosses keep tabs on telecommuters', *USA Today*, 24 July 2001, p. 1B; and D. Buss, 'Spies like us', *Training*, December 2001, pp. 44–48.

34 L. H. Peters, E. J. O'Connor and C. J. Rudolf, 'The behavioral and affective consequences of performance-relevant situational variables', *Organizational Behavior and Human Performance*, February 1980, pp. 79–96; M. Blumberg and C. D. Pringle, 'The missing opportunity in organizational research: some implications for a theory of work performance', *Academy of Management Review*, October 1982, pp. 560–69; D. A. Waldman and W. D. Spangler, 'Putting together the pieces: a closer look at the determinants of job performance', *Human Performance*, 2 (1989), pp. 29–59; and J. Hall, 'Americans know how to be productive if managers will let them', *Organizational Dynamics*, Winter 1994, pp. 33–46.

35 See, for example, the increasing body of literature on empowerment, such as W. A. Randolph, 'Re-thinking empowerment: why is it so hard to achieve?', *Organizational Dynamics*, 29, 2 (2000), pp. 94–107; K. Blanchard, J. P. Carlos and W. A. Randolph, *Empowerment Takes More Than a Minute*, 2nd edn (San Francisco, CA: Berrett-Koehler, 2001); D. P. Ashmos, D. Duchon, R. R. McDaniel, Jr. and J. W. Huonker, 'What a mess! Participation as a simple managerial rule to "complexify" organizations', *Journal of Management Studies*, March 2002, pp. 189–206; and S. E. Seibert, S. R. Silver and W. A. Randolph, 'Taking empowerment to the next level: a multiple-level model of empowerment, performance, and satisfaction', *Academy of Management Journal*, 47, 3 (2004), pp. 332–49.

36 F. Heller, E. Pusic, G. Strauss and B. Wilpert, *Organizational Participation: Myth and Reality* (Oxford: Oxford University Press, 1998).

37 See, for instance, K. L. Miller and P. R. Monge, 'Participation, satisfaction, and productivity: a meta-analytic review', *Academy of Management Journal*, December 1986, pp. 727–53; J. A. Wagner, III and R. Z. Gooding, 'Shared influence and organizational behavior: a meta-analysis of situational variables expected to moderate participation–outcome relationships', *Academy of Management Journal*, September 1987, pp. 524–41; J. A. Wagner, III, 'Participation's effects on performance and satisfaction: a reconsideration of research evidence', *Academy of Management Review*, April 1994, pp. 312–30; C. Doucouliagos, 'Worker participation and productivity in labor-managed and participatory capitalist firms: a meta-analysis', *Industrial and Labor Relations Review*, October 1995, pp. 58–77; J. A. Wagner, III, C. R. Leana, E. A. Locke and D. M. Schweiger, 'Cognitive and motivational frameworks in U.S. research on participation: a meta-analysis of primary effects', *Journal of Organizational Behavior*, 18

(1997), pp. 49–65; J. S. Black and H. B. Gregersen, 'Participative decision-making: an integration of multiple dimensions', *Human Relations*, July 1997, pp. 859–78; E. A. Locke, M. Alavi and J. A. Wagner, III, 'Participation in decision making: an information exchange perspective', in G. R. Ferris (ed.), *Research in Personnel and Human Resource Management*, vol. 15 (Greenwich, CT: JAI Press, 1997), pp. 293–331; and J. A. Wagner, III and J. A. LePine, 'Effects of participation on performance and satisfaction: additional meta-analytic evidence', *Psychological Reports*, June 1999, pp. 719–25.

38 Cotton, *Employee Involvement*, p. 114.

39 See, for example, M. Gilman and P. Marginson, 'Negotiating european works council: contours of constrained choice', *Industrial Relations Journal*, March 2002, pp. 36–51; J. T. Addison and C. R. Belfield, 'What do we know about the new European Works Council? Some preliminary evidence from Britain', *Scottish Journal of Political Economy*, September 2002, pp. 418–44; and B. Keller, 'The European company statute: employee involvement – and beyond', *Industrial Relations Journal*, December 2002, pp. 424–45.

40 Cotton, *Employee Involvement*, pp. 129–30, 139–40.

41 Ibid., p. 140.

42 See, for example, G. W. Meyer and R. G. Stott, 'Quality circles: panacea or Pandora's box?', *Organizational Dynamics*, Spring 1985, pp. 34–50; E. E. Lawler, III, and S. A. Mohrman, 'Quality circles: after the honeymoon', *Organizational Dynamics*, Spring 1987, pp. 42–54; T. R. Miller, 'The quality circle phenomenon: a review and appraisal', *SAM Advanced Management Journal*, Winter 1989, pp. 4–7; K. Buch and R. Spangler, 'The effects of quality circles on performance and promotions', *Human Relations*, June 1990, pp. 573–82; P. R. Liverpool, 'Employee participation in decision-making: an analysis of the perceptions of members and nonmembers of quality circles', *Journal of Business and Psychology*, Summer 1990, pp. 411–22, E. E. Adams, Jr., 'Quality circle performance', *Journal of Management*, March 1991, pp. 25–39; and L. I. Glassop, 'The organizational benefits of teams', *Human Relations*, 55, 2 (2002), pp. 225–49.

43 T. L. Tang and E. A. Butler, 'Attributions of quality circles' problem-solving failure: differences among management, supporting staff, and quality circle members', *Public Personnel Management*, Summer 1997, pp. 203–25; G. Hammersley and A. Pinnington, 'Quality circles reach end of the line at Land Rover', *Human Resource Management International Digest*, May/June 1999, pp. 4–5; and D. Nagar and M. Takore, 'Effectiveness of quality circles in a large public sector', *Psychological Studies*, January–July 2001, pp. 63–68.

44 Cotton, *Employee Involvement*, p. 87.

45 E. White, 'Opportunity knocks, and it pays a lot better', *Wall Street Journal*, 13 November 2006, p. B3.

46 P. S. Goodman and P. P. Pan, 'Chinese workers pay for Wal-Mart's low prices', *Washington Post*, 8 February 2004; p. A1.

47 Based on J. R. Schuster and P. K. Zingheim, 'The new variable pay: key design issues', *Compensation & Benefits Review*, March–April 1993, p. 28; K. S. Abosch, 'Variable pay: do we have the basics in place?', *Compensation & Benefits Review*, July–August 1998, pp. 12–22; and K. M. Kuhn and M. D. Yockey, 'Variable pay as a risky choice: determinants of the relative attractiveness of incentive plans', *Organizational Behavior and Human Decision Processes*, March 2003, pp. 323–41.

48 Fourth European Working Conditions Survey, European Foundation for the Improvement of Living and Working Conditions, 2007. Available at http://www.eurofound.europa.eu.

49 W. Zellner, 'Trickle-down is trickling down at work', *BusinessWeek*, 18 March 1996, p. 34; and 'Linking pay to performance is becoming a norm in the workplace', *Wall Street Journal*, 6 April 1999, p. A1; D. Coletto (2005) 'Company agreements signed at Manpower and Obiettivo Lavoro european industrial relations observatory on-line'. Available at: http://www.eurofound.europa.eu/eiro/2005/08/feature/it0508201f.htm; 'Best workplaces', *Financial Times*, special report, 28 May 2008, www.ft.com/bestworkplaces2008.

50 Cited in 'Pay programs: few employees see the pay-for-performance connection', *Compensation & Benefits Report*, June 2003, p. 1.

51 M. Fein, 'Work measurement and wage incentives', *Industrial Engineering*, September 1973, pp. 49–51. For updated reviews of the effect of pay on performance, see G. D. Jenkins, Jr., N. Gupta, A. Mitra and J. D. Shaw, 'Are financial incentives related to performance? A meta-analytic review of empirical research', *Journal of Applied Psychology*, October 1998, pp. 777–87; and S. L. Rynes, B. Gerhart and L. Parks, 'Personnel psychology: performance evaluation and pay for performance', *Annual Review of Psychology*, 56, 1 (2005), pp. 571–600.

52 E. Arita, 'Teething troubles aside, merit-based pay catching on', *Japan Times*, 23 April 2004, http://search.japantimes.co.jp/cgi-bin/nb20040423a3.html.

53 E. White, 'The best vs. the rest', *Wall Street Journal*, 30 January 2006, pp. B1, B3.

54 G. Adams (2007) 'Dispute over future pay scheme at Austrian Airlines'. Available at: http://www.eurofound.europa.eu/eiro/2007/06/articles/at0706029i.htm.

55 'Deutsche Bank's CEO to forgo 2008 bonus', *Financial Express*, 18 October 2008. Available at: http://www.financialexpress.com/news/Deutsche-Banks-CEO-to-forgo-2008-bonus/374947/; D. Ellis, 'Goldman's Blankfein collects $68M bonus', 21 December 2007. Available at: http://money.cnn.com/2007/12/21/news/newsmakers/blankfein_bonus/index.htm; G. Fabrikant, 'Executives in Europe seek pay à la U.S.', *International Herald Tribune*, 16 June 2006. Available at: http://www.iht.com/articles/2006/06/15/business/pay.php?page=3; 'Pay survey: bonus league' (*Guardian* financial pages) The *Guardian*, 29 August 2007, p. 23.

56 S. O'Donoghue, 'Porsche pays every employee €6,000 bonus', Available at: http://uk.cars.yahoo.com/29092008/36/porsche-pays-employee-euro-6-000-bonus-0.html. Accessed 20 October 2008.

57 E. White, 'Employers increasingly favor bonuses to raises', *Wall Street Journal*, 28 August 2006, p. B3; and J. S. Lublin, 'Boards tie CEO pay more tightly to performance', *Wall Street Journal*, 21 February 2006, pp. A1, A14.

58 G. E. Ledford, Jr., 'Paying for the skills, knowledge, and competencies of knowledge workers', *Compensation & Benefits Review*, July–August 1995, pp. 55–62; B. Murray and B. Gerhart, 'An empirical analysis of a skill-based pay program and plant performance outcomes', *Academy of Management Journal*, February 1998, pp. 68–78; J. R. Thompson and C. W. LeHew, 'Skill-based pay as an organizational innovation', *Review of Public Personnel Administration*, Winter 2000, pp. 20–40; and J. D. Shaw, N. Gupta, A. Mitra and G. E. Ledford, Jr., 'Success and survival of skill-based pay plans', *Journal of Management*, February 2005, pp. 28–49.

59 S. Weekes, 'Turnover turnaround', *Personnel Today*, 10 February 2004.

60 'Tensions of a new pay plan', *New York Times*, 17 May 1992, p. F5.

61 See, for instance, D.-O. Kim, 'Determinants of the survival of gainsharing programs', *Industrial & Labor Relations Review*, October 1999, pp. 21–42; 'Why gainsharing works even better today than in the past', *HR Focus*, April 2000, pp. 3–5; L. R. Gomez-Mejia, T. M. Welbourne and R. M. Wiseman, 'The role of risk sharing and risk taking under gainsharing', *Academy of Management Review*, July 2000, pp. 492–507; W. Atkinson, 'Incentive pay programs that work in textile', *Textile World*, February 2001, pp. 55–57; M. Reynolds, 'A cost-reduction strategy that may be back', *Healthcare Financial Management*, January 2002, pp. 58–64; and M. R. Dixon, L. J. Hayes and J. Stack, 'Changing conceptions of employee compensation', *Journal of Organizational Behavior management*, 23, 2–3 (2003), pp. 95–116.

62 European Federation of Employee Share Ownership, www.efesonline.org. Accessed 30 October 2008; C. Dougherty 'Europe takes a closer look at employee stock ownership', 31 March.

63 A. A. Buchko, 'The effects of employee ownership on employee attitudes: an integrated causal model and path analysis', *Journal of Management Studies*, 30, 4, pp. 633–57.

64 J. L. Pierce and C. A. Furo, 'Employee ownership: implications for management', *Organizational Dynamics*, 18 (1990), pp. 32–43.

65 See data in D. Stamps, 'A piece of the action', *Training*, March 1996, p. 66.

66 C. G. Hanson and W. D. Bell, *Profit Sharing and Profitability: How Profit Sharing Promotes Business Success* (London: Kogan Page, 1987); M. Magnan and S. St-Onge, 'Profit-sharing and firm performance: a comparative and longitudinal analysis', paper presented at the 58th annual meeting of the Academy of Management, San Diego, CA, August 1998; and D. D'Art and T. Turner, 'Profit sharing, firm performance, and union influence in selected European countries', *Personnel Review*, 33, 3 (2004), pp. 335–50.

67 T. M. Welbourne and L. R. Gomez-Mejia, 'Gainsharing: a critical review and a future research agenda', *Journal of Management*, 21, 3 (1995), pp. 559–609.

68 C. B. Cadsby, F. Song and F. Tapon, 'Sorting and incentive effects of pay for performance: an experimental investigation', *Academy of Management Journal*, 50, 2 (2007), pp. 387–405.

69 See, for instance, M. W. Barringer and G. T. Milkovich, 'A theoretical exploration of the adoption and design of flexible benefit plans: a case of human resource innovation', *Academy of Management Review*, April 1998, pp. 305–24; D. Brown, 'Everybody loves flex', *Canadian HRReporter*, 18 November 2002, p. 1; J. Taggart, 'Putting flex benefits through their paces', *Canadian HR Reporter*, 2 December 2002, p. G3; and N. D. Cole and D. H. Flint, 'Perceptions of distributive and procedural justice in employee benefits: flexible versus traditional benefit plans', *Journal of Managerial Psychology*, 19, 1 (2004), pp. 19–40.

70 D. A. DeCenzo and S. P. Robbins, *Human Resource Management*, 7th edn (New York: Wiley, 2002), pp. 346–48.

71 S. E. Markham, K. D. Scott and G. H. McKee, 'Recognizing good attendance: a longitudinal, quasi-experimental field study', *Personnel Psychology*, Autumn 2002, p. 641; and

S. J. Peterson and F. Luthans, 'The impact of financial and nonfinancial incentives on business unit outcomes over time,' *Journal of Applied Psychology*, 91, no. 1 (2006), pp. 156–65.

72 D. Drickhamer, 'Best plant winners: Nichols Foods Ltd', *IndustryWeek*, 1 October 2001, pp. 17–19.

73 M. Littman, 'Best bosses tell all', *Working Woman*, October 2000, p. 54.

74 Cited in S. Caudron, 'The top 20 ways to motivate employees', *IndustryWeek*, 3 April 1995, pp. 15–16. See also B. Nelson, 'Try praise,' *INC.*, September 1996, p. 115.

75 A. D. Stajkovic and F. Luthans, 'Differential effects of incentive motivators on work performance', *Academy of Management Journal*, June 2001, p. 587. See also F. Luthans and A. D. Stajkovic, 'Provide recognition for performance improvement', in E. A. Locke (ed.), *Handbook of Principles of Organizational Behavior* (Malden, MA: Blackwell, 2004), pp. 166–80.

76 Cited in K. J. Dunham, 'Amid shrinking workplace morale, employers turn to recognition', *Wall Street Journal*, 19 November 2002, p. B8.

77 Ibid.

78 B. M. Meglino and A. M. Korsgaard, 'The role of other orientation in reactions to job characteristics', *Journal of Management*, February 2007, pp. 57–83.

79 M. F. Peterson and S. A. Ruiz-Quintanilla, 'Cultural socialization as a source of intrinsic work motivation', *Group & Organization Management*, June 2003, pp. 188–216.

80 Fourth European Working, Conditions Survey European Foundation for the Improvement of Living and Working Conditions, 2007. Available at http://www.eurofound.europa.eu.

81 P. Peters and L. den Dulk, 'Cross cultural differences in managers' support for home-based telework: a theoretical elaboration', *International Journal of Cross Cultural Management*, December 2003, pp. 329–46.

82 S. C. L. Fong and M. A. Shaffer, 'The dimensionality and determinants of pay satisfaction: a cross-cultural investigation of a group incentive plan', *International Journal of Human Resource Management*, June 2003, pp. 559–80.

83 G. Fuller, 'Flexible benefits: flexing benefits across borders', *Employee Benefits*, 9 October 2008, p. S25.

84 See, for instance, A. Sagie and Z. Aycan, 'A cross-cultural analysis of participative decision-making in organizations', *Human Relations*, April 2003, pp. 453–73; and J. Brockner, 'Unpacking country effects: on the need to operationalize the psychological determinants of cross-national differences', in R. M. Kramer and B. M. Staw (eds.), *Research in Organizational Behavior*, vol. 25 (Oxford, UK: Elsevier, 2003), pp. 336–40.

85 C. Robert, T. M. Probst, J. J. Martocchio, R. Drasgow and J. J. Lawler, 'Empowerment and continuous improvement in the United States, Mexico, Poland, and India: predicting fit on the basis of the dimensions of power distance and individualism', *Journal of Applied Psychology*, October 2000, pp. 643–58.

86 M. Berry, 'Key to staff retention and motivation is recognition of extra effort', *Personnel Today*, 9 November 2006; G. Logan, 'Anatomy of a Gen Y-er', *Personnel Today*, 14 September 2008.

Emotions and moods

After studying this chapter, you should be able to:

1 Differentiate emotions from moods and list the basic emotions and moods.

2 Discuss whether emotions are rational and what functions they serve.

3 Identify the sources of emotions and moods.

4 Show the impact emotional labour has on employees.

5 Describe affective events theory and identify its applications.

6 Contrast the evidence for and against the existence of emotional intelligence.

7 Apply concepts about emotions and moods to specific OB issues.

8 Contrast the experience, interpretation and expression of emotions across cultures.

We know too much and feel too little.

Bertrand Russell

Sweet revenge

Aijaz Rahi/AP/Press Association Images

Can revenge be a motivator? Absolutely. Consider what Terry Garnett says: 'I do hold grudges. Am I motivated by that? Absolutely.'

In the 1990s, Garnett was a senior vice president at Oracle, reporting to Oracle CEO Larry Ellison. The two travelled around the world together, rubbed elbows with media and movie moguls and became friends. The families even holidayed together in Japan. Ellison, an ardent admirer of all things Japanese, invited Garnett to join him in the famed Philosopher's Walk to the Ginkakuji Temple in Kyoto.

A few weeks after returning from their trip to Japan, Ellison called Garnett into his office and summarily fired him. Feeling numb and lacking a clear explanation for his dismissal, Garnett walked the 30 feet from Ellison's office to his own, packed up his things, and left. 'I tried to keep composed,' he said. Privately, though, he was seething, telling himself, 'There will be a day of reckoning.'

Channelling his anger, Garnett started competing directly with Ellison and Oracle by investing in promising start-up projects. A recent example is Ingres, a low-cost software provider that Garnett hopes will compete directly with Oracle's bread-and-butter offering: its high-price database business (together, Oracle and IBM claim 70 per cent of the global database business). Garnett has hired away numerous Oracle employees, forming a small army of engineers and managers to help him take the battle to the enemy. In 2004, Garnett and David Helfrich founded Garnett & Helfrich Capital, a €280 million private equity fund for midsized technology spinouts. Rather than focusing on start-ups or buyouts of well-established companies, Garnett & Helfrich focuses on existing technology businesses or product lines that have struggled.

In reflecting on his successes, Garnett says, 'The simplest way to create a culture is to pick an enemy. We have an enemy. It's Oracle.'

Source: Based on J. McGregor, 'Sweet revenge', *Business Week*, 22 January 2007, pp. 64–70.

As the example of Terry Garnett shows, emotions can spur us to action. Before we delve further into emotions and moods, get an assessment of your mood state right now. Take the following self-assessment to find out what sort of mood you're in.

SELF-ASSESSMENT LIBRARY

How are you feeling right now?

In the Self-assessment library (available online), take assessment IV.D.1 (What is my current mood?) and answer the following questions.

1. What was higher – your positive mood score or negative mood score? How do these scores compare to those of your classmates?

2. Did your score surprise you? Why or why not?

3. What sorts of things influence your positive moods? your negative moods?

Given the obvious role that emotions play in our work and everyday lives, it might surprise you to learn that, until recently, the field of OB has given the topic of emotions little or no attention.[1] How could this be? We can offer two possible explanations.

The first is the *myth of rationality*.[2] From the late nineteenth century and the rise of scientific management until very recently, the protocol of the work world was to keep a damper on emotions. A well-run organization didn't allow employees to express frustration, fear, anger, love, hate, joy, grief and similar feelings. The prevailing thought was that such emotions were the antithesis of rationality. Even though researchers and managers knew that emotions were an inseparable part of everyday life, they tried to create organizations that were emotion free. That, of course, wasn't possible.

The second explanation is that many believed that emotions of any kind are disruptive.[3] When researchers considered emotions, they looked at strong negative emotions – especially anger – that interfered with an employee's ability to work effectively. They rarely viewed emotions as constructive or contributing to enhanced performance.

Certainly some emotions, particularly when exhibited at the wrong time, can hinder employee performance. But this doesn't change the fact that employees bring their emotional sides with them to work every day and that no study of OB would be comprehensive without considering the role of emotions in workplace behaviour.

What are emotions and moods?

1 Differentiate emotions from moods and list the basic emotions and moods.

affect
A broad range of feelings that people experience.

emotions
Intense feelings that are directed at someone or something.

moods
Feelings that tend to be less intense than emotions and that lack a contextual stimulus.

Although we don't want to belabour definitions, before we can proceed with our analysis, we need to clarify three terms that are closely intertwined: *affect*, *emotions* and *moods*.

Affect is a generic term that covers a broad range of feelings that people experience. It's an umbrella concept that encompasses both emotions and moods.[4] **Emotions** are intense feelings that are directed at someone or something.[5] **Moods** are feelings that tend to be less intense than emotions and that often (though not always) lack a contextual stimulus.[6]

Most experts believe that emotions are more fleeting than moods.[7] For example, if someone is rude to you, you'll feel angry. That intense feeling of anger probably comes and goes fairly quickly, maybe even in a matter of seconds. When you're in a bad mood, though, you can feel bad for several hours.

Emotions are reactions to a person (for example, seeing a friend at work may make you feel glad) or event (for example, dealing with a rude client may make you feel angry). You show your emotions when you're 'happy about something, angry at someone, afraid of something'.[8] Moods, in contrast, aren't usually directed at a person or an event. But emotions can turn into moods when you lose focus on the event or object that started the feeling. And, by the same token, good or bad moods can make you more emotional in response to an event. So when a colleague criticises how you spoke to a client, you might become angry at him. That is, you show emotion (anger) toward a specific object (your colleague). But as the specific emotion dissipates,

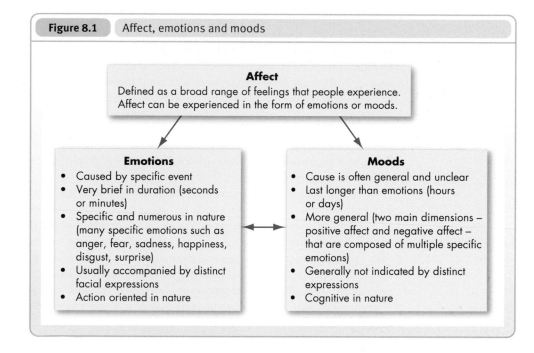

Figure 8.1 Affect, emotions and moods

Affect
Defined as a broad range of feelings that people experience. Affect can be experienced in the form of emotions or moods.

Emotions
- Caused by specific event
- Very brief in duration (seconds or minutes)
- Specific and numerous in nature (many specific emotions such as anger, fear, sadness, happiness, disgust, surprise)
- Usually accompanied by distinct facial expressions
- Action oriented in nature

Moods
- Cause is often general and unclear
- Last longer than emotions (hours or days)
- More general (two main dimensions – positive affect and negative affect – that are composed of multiple specific emotions)
- Generally not indicated by distinct expressions
- Cognitive in nature

you might just feel generally dispirited. You can't attribute this feeling to any single event; you're just not your normal self. You might then overreact to other events. This affect state describes a mood. Figure 8.1 shows the relationships among affect, emotions and mood.

First, as the figure shows, affect is a broad term that encompasses emotions and moods. Second, there are differences between emotions and moods. Some of these differences – that emotions are more likely to be caused by a specific event, and emotions are more fleeting than moods – we just discussed. Other differences are subtler. For example, unlike moods, emotions tend to be more clearly revealed with facial expressions (for example, anger, disgust). Also, some researchers speculate that emotions may be more action-oriented – they may lead us to some immediate action – while moods may be more cognitive, meaning they may cause us to think or brood for a while.[9]

Finally, the figure shows that emotions and moods can mutually influence each other. For example, an emotion, if it's strong and deep enough, can turn into a mood: Getting your dream job may generate the emotion of joy, but it also can put you in a good mood for several days. Similarly, if you're in a good or bad mood, it might make you experience a more intense positive or negative emotion than would otherwise be the case. For example, if you're in a bad mood, you might 'blow up' in response to a co-worker's comment when normally it would have just generated a mild reaction. Because emotions and moods can mutually influence each other, there will be many points throughout the chapter where emotions and moods will be closely connected.

Although affect, emotions and moods are separable in theory, in practice the distinction isn't always crystal clear. In fact, in some areas, researchers have studied mostly moods, and in other areas, mainly emotions. So, when we review the OB topics on emotions and moods, you may see more information on emotions in one area and moods in another. This is simply the state of the research.

Also, the terminology can be confusing. For example, the two main mood dimensions are positive affect and negative affect, yet we have defined affect more broadly than mood. So, although the topic can be fairly dense in places, hang in there. The material is interesting – and applicable to OB.

The basic emotions

How many emotions are there? In what ways do they vary? There are dozens of emotions, including anger, contempt, enthusiasm, envy, fear, frustration, disappointment, embarrassment, disgust, happiness, hate, hope, jealousy, joy, love, pride, surprise and sadness. There have been numerous research efforts to limit and define the dozens of emotions into a fundamental or basic set of emotions.[10] But some researchers argue that it makes no sense to think of basic emotions because even emotions we rarely experience, such as shock, can have a powerful effect on us.[11] Other researchers, even philosophers, argue that there are universal emotions common to all of us. René Descartes, often called the founder of modern philosophy, identified six 'simple and primitive passions' – wonder, love, hatred, desire, joy and sadness – and argued that 'all the others are composed of some of these six or are species of them'.[12] Other philosophers (Hume, Hobbes, Spinoza) identified categories of emotions. Although these philosophers were helpful, the burden to provide conclusive evidence for the existence of a basic set of emotions still rests with contemporary researchers.

In contemporary research, psychologists have tried to identify basic emotions by studying facial expressions.[13] One problem with this approach is that some emotions are too complex to be easily represented on our faces. Take love, for example. Many think of love as the most universal of all emotions,[14] yet it's not easy to express a loving emotion with one's face only. Also, cultures have norms that govern emotional expression, so how we *experience* an emotion isn't always the same as how we *show* it. And many companies today offer anger-management programmes to teach people to contain or even hide their inner feelings.[15]

It's unlikely that psychologists or philosophers will ever completely agree on a set of basic emotions, or even whether it makes sense to think of basic emotions. Still, enough researchers have agreed on six essentially universal emotions – anger, fear, sadness, happiness, disgust and surprise – with most other emotions subsumed under one of these six categories.[16] Some researchers even plot these six emotions along a continuum: happiness–surprise–fear–sadness–anger–disgust.[17] The closer any two emotions are to each other on this continuum, the more likely it is that people will confuse them. For instance, we sometimes mistake happiness for surprise, but rarely do we confuse happiness and disgust. In addition, as we'll see later on, cultural factors can also influence interpretations.

The basic moods: positive and negative affect

One way to classify emotions is by whether they are positive or negative.[18] Positive emotions – such as joy and gratitude – express a favourable evaluation or feeling. Negative emotions – such as anger or guilt – express the opposite. Keep in mind that emotions can't be neutral. Being neutral is being nonemotional.[19]

When we group emotions into positive and negative categories, they become mood states because we are now looking at them more generally instead of isolating one particular emotion. In Figure 8.2, excited is a specific emotion that is a pure marker of high positive affect, while boredom is a pure marker of low positive affect. Similarly, nervous is a pure marker of high negative affect, while relaxed is a pure marker of low negative affect. Finally, some emotions – such as contentment (a mixture of high positive affect and low negative affect) and sadness (a mixture of low positive affect and high negative affect) – are in between. You'll notice that this model does not include all emotions. There are two reasons. First, we can fit other emotions such as enthusiasm or depression into the model, but we're short on space. Second, some emotions, such as surprise, don't fit well because they're not as clearly positive or negative.

So, we can think of **positive affect** as a mood dimension consisting of positive emotions such as excitement, self-assurance, and cheerfulness at the high end and boredom, sluggishness, and tiredness at the low end. **Negative affect** is a mood dimension consisting of nervousness, stress, and anxiety at the high end and relaxation, tranquillity, and poise at the low end. (Note that positive and negative affect *are* moods. We're using these labels, rather than *positive mood* and *negative mood* because that's how researchers label them.)

Positive affect and negative affect play out at work (and beyond work, of course) in that they colour our perceptions, and these perceptions can become their own reality. For example, one flight attendant posted an anonymous blog on the web that said: 'I work in a pressurised aluminium tube and the environment outside my "office" cannot sustain human life. That being said, the human life inside is not worth sustaining sometimes . . . in fact, the passengers can be jerks, and idiots. I am often treated with no respect, nobody listens to me . . . until I threaten to

positive affect
A mood dimension that consists of specific positive emotions such as excitement, self-assurance and cheerfulness at the high end and boredom, sluggishness and tiredness at the low end.

negative affect
A mood dimension that consists of emotions such as nervousness, stress, and anxiety at the high end and relaxation, tranquillity and poise at the low end.

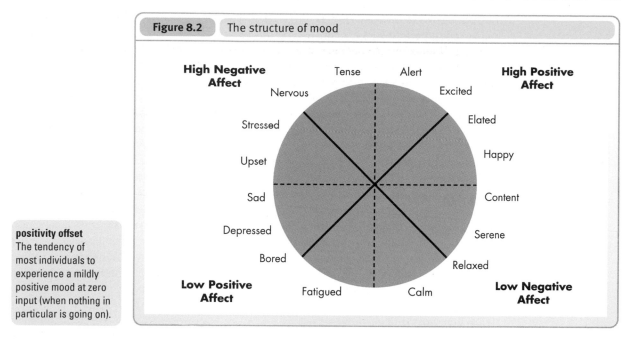

| Figure 8.2 | The structure of mood |

positivity offset
The tendency of most individuals to experience a mildly positive mood at zero input (when nothing in particular is going on).

Doug Mindell Photography

By studying the skull of Phineas Gage, shown here and other brain injuries, researchers discovered an important link between emotions and rational thinking. They found that losing the ability to emote led to the loss of the ability to reason. From this discovery, researchers learned that our emotions provide us with valuable information that helps our thinking process.

2 Discuss whether emotions are rational and what functions they serve.

kick them off the plane.'[20] Clearly, if a flight attendant is in a bad mood, it's going to influence their perceptions of passengers, which will, in turn, influence their behaviour.

Importantly, negative emotions are likely to translate into negative moods. People think about events that created strong negative emotions five times as long as they do about events that created strong positive ones.[21] So, we should expect people to recall negative experiences more readily than positive ones. Perhaps one of the reasons is that, for most of us, they're also more unusual. Indeed, research shows that there is a **positivity offset**, meaning that at zero input (when nothing in particular is going on), most individuals experience a mildly positive mood.[22] So, for most people, positive moods are somewhat more common than negative moods. The positivity offset also appears to operate at work. For example, one study of customer-service representatives in a call centre (probably a job where it's pretty difficult to feel positive) revealed that people reported experiencing positive moods 58 per cent of the time.[23]

The function of emotions

Do emotions make us irrational?

How often have you heard someone say, 'Oh, you're just being emotional'? You might have been offended. The famous philosopher Bertrand Russell wrote 'The degree of one's emotions varies inversely with one's knowledge of the facts'. These observations suggest that rationality and emotion are in conflict with one another and that if you exhibit emotion, you are likely to act irrationally. One team of authors argue that displaying emotions such as sadness, to the point of crying, is so toxic to a career that we should leave the room rather than allow others to witness our emotional display.[24] The author Lois Frankel advises that women should avoid being emotional at work because it will undermine how others rate their competence.[25] These perspectives suggest that the demonstration or even experience of emotions is likely to make us seem weak, brittle, or irrational. However, the research disagrees and is increasingly showing that emotions are actually critical to rational thinking.[26] In fact, there has been evidence of such a link for a long time.

Take the example of Phineas Gage, a railroad worker. One September day in 1848, while Gage was setting an explosive charge at work, a 3'7" iron bar flew into his lower-left jaw and out through the top of his skull. Remarkably, Gage survived his injury. He was still able to read and speak, and he performed well above average on cognitive ability tests. However, it became clear that Gage had lost his ability to experience emotion. He was emotionless at even the saddest misfortunes or the happiest occasions. Gage's inability to express emotion eventually took away his ability to reason. He started making irrational choices about his life, often behaving erratically and against his self-interests. Despite being an intelligent man whose intellectual abilities were unharmed by the accident, Gage drifted from job to job, eventually taking up with a circus. In commenting on Gage's condition, one expert noted, 'Reason may not be as pure as most of us think it is or wish it were . . . emotions and feelings may not be intruders in the bastion of reason at all: they may be enmeshed in its networks, for worse *and* for better.'[27]

The examples of Phineas Gage and many other brain injury studies show us that emotions are critical to rational thinking. We must have the ability to experience emotions to be rational. Why? Because our emotions provide important information about how we understand the world around us. Although we might think of a computer as intellectually superior, a human so void of emotion would be unable to function. Think about a manager making a decision to fire an employee. Would you really want the manager to make the decision without regarding either his or the employee's emotions? The key to good decision making is to employ both thinking *and* feeling in one's decisions.

What functions do emotions serve?

Why do we have emotions? What role do they serve? We just discussed one function – that we need them to think rationally. Charles Darwin, however, took a broader approach. In *The Expression of the Emotions in Man and Animals*, Darwin argued that emotions developed over time to help humans solve problems. Emotions are useful, he said, because they motivate people to engage in actions that are important for survival – actions such as foraging for food, seeking shelter, choosing mates, guarding against predators and predicting others' behaviours. For example, disgust (an emotion) motivates us to avoid dangerous or harmful things (such as rotten foods). Excitement (also an emotion) motivates us to take on situations in which we require energy and initiative (for example, embarking on a new career).

evolutionary psychology
An area of inquiry which argues that we must experience the emotions we do because they serve a purpose.

Drawing from Darwin are researchers who focus on **evolutionary psychology**. This field of study says we must experience emotions – whether they are positive or negative – because they serve a purpose.[28] For example, you would probably consider jealousy to be a negative emotion. Evolutionary psychologists would argue that it exists in people because it has a useful purpose. Mates may feel jealousy to increase the chance that their genes, rather than a rival's genes, are passed on to the next generation.[29] Although we tend to think of anger as being 'bad', it actually can help us protect our rights when we feel they're being violated. For example, a person showing anger when they are double-crossed by a colleague is serving a warning for others not to repeat the same behaviour. Consider another example. Rena Weeks was a secretary at a prominent law firm. Her boss wouldn't stop touching and grabbing her. His treatment of her made her angry. So she did more than quit – she sued, and won a multimillion-euro case.[30] It's not that anger is always good. But as with all other emotions, it exists because it serves a useful purpose. Positive emotions also serve a purpose. For example, a service employee who feels empathy for a customer may provide better customer service than an seemingly unfeeling employee.

But some researchers are not firm believers of evolutionary psychology. Why? Think about fear (an emotion). It's just as easy to think of the harmful effects of fear as it is the beneficial effects. For example, running in fear from a predator increases the likelihood of survival. But what benefit does freezing in fear serve? Evolutionary psychology provides an interesting perspective on the functions of emotions, but it's difficult to know whether this perspective is valid all the time.[31]

Sources of emotions and moods

3 Identify the sources of emotions and moods.

Have you ever said, 'I got up on the wrong side of the bed today'? Have you ever yelled at a co-worker or family member for no particular reason? If you have, it probably makes you wonder where emotions and moods come from. Here we discuss some of the primary influences on moods and emotions.

Personality

Moods and emotions have a trait component – most people have built-in tendencies to experience certain moods and emotions more frequently than others do. Moreover, people naturally differ in how intensely they experience the same emotions. Contrast the former famous tennis player's Jon McEnroe and Bjorn Borg. One was easily moved to anger, while the other was relatively distant and unemotional. McEnroe and Borg probably differ in **affect intensity**, or how strongly they experience their emotions.[32] Affectively intense people experience both positive and negative emotions more deeply – when they're sad, they're really sad, and when they're happy, they're really happy.

> **affect intensity**
> Individual differences in the strength with which individuals experience their emotions.

SELF-ASSESSMENT LIBRARY

What's my affect intensity?

In the Self-assessment library (available online), take assessment IV.D.2 (What's my affect intensity?).

Day of the week and time of the day

Are people in their best moods on the weekends? Well, sort of. As Figure 8.3 shows, people tend to be in their worst moods (highest negative affect and lowest positive affect) early in the week and in their best moods (highest positive affect and lowest negative affect) late in the week.[33]

What about time of the day? (See Figure 8.4.) We often think that people differ, depending on whether they are 'morning' or 'evening' people. However, the vast majority of us follow the same pattern. Regardless of what time people go to bed at night or get up in the morning, levels of positive affect tend to peak around the halfway point between waking and sleeping. Negative affect, however, shows little fluctuation throughout the day.[34] This basic pattern seems to hold whether people describe themselves as morning people or evening people.[35]

What does this mean for organizational behaviour? Monday morning is probably not the best time to ask someone for a favour or convey bad news. Our workplace interactions will probably be more positive from midmorning onward and also later in the week.

Figure 8.3   Our moods are affected by the day of the week

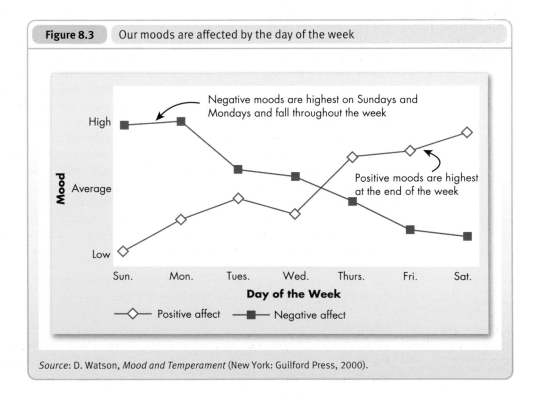

Source: D. Watson, *Mood and Temperament* (New York: Guilford Press, 2000).

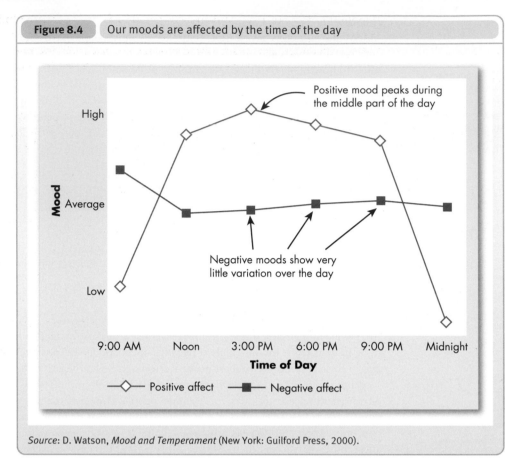

Figure 8.4 Our moods are affected by the time of the day

Positive mood peaks during the middle part of the day

Negative moods show very little variation over the day

Mood: High, Average, Low

Time of Day: 9:00 AM, Noon, 3:00 PM, 6:00 PM, 9:00 PM, Midnight

◇ Positive affect ■ Negative affect

Source: D. Watson, *Mood and Temperament* (New York: Guilford Press, 2000).

Weather

When do you think you would be in a better mood – when it's 30°C and sunny or when it's a gloomy, cold, rainy day? Many people believe their mood is tied to the weather. However, evidence suggests that weather has little effect on mood. One expert concluded, 'Contrary to the prevailing cultural view, these data indicate that people do not report a better mood on bright and sunny days (or, conversely, a worse mood on dark and rainy days).'[36] *Illusory correlation* explains why people tend to *think* that nice weather improves their mood. **Illusory correlation** occurs when people associate two events but in reality there is no connection.

> **illusory correlation**
> The tendency of people to associate two events when in reality there is no connection.

Stress

As you might imagine, stress affects emotions and moods. For example, students have higher levels of fear before an exam, but their fear dissipates once the exam is over.[37] At work, stressful daily events (for example, a nasty e-mail, an impending deadline, the loss of a big sale, being reprimanded by your boss) negatively affect employees' moods. Also, the effects of stress build over time. As the authors of one study note, 'a constant diet of even low-level stressful events has the potential to cause workers to experience gradually increasing levels of strain over time'.[38] Such mounting levels of stress and strain at work can worsen our moods, and we experience more negative emotions. Consider the following entry from a worker's blog: 'i'm in a bit of a blah mood today . . . physically, i feel funky, though and the weather out combined with the amount of personal and work i need to get done are getting to me.' Although sometimes we thrive on stress, for most of us, like this blogger, stress takes a toll on our mood.[39]

Social activities

Do you tend to be happiest when you are at a party with friends? For most people, social activities increase positive mood and have little effect on negative mood. But do people in positive moods seek out social interactions, or do social interactions cause people to be in good moods?

It seems that both are true.[40] And does the *type* of social activity matter? Indeed it does. Research suggests that physical (skiing or hiking with friends), informal (going to a party), or epicurean (eating with others) activities are more strongly associated with increases in positive mood than formal (attending a meeting) or sedentary (watching TV with friends) events.[41]

'PEOPLE CAN'T ACCURATELY FORECAST THEIR OWN EMOTIONS'

MYTH *OR* SCIENCE?

This statement is essentially true. People tend to do a pretty bad job of predicting how they're going to feel when something happens. The research on this topic – called *affective forecasting* – shows that our poor job of affective forecasting takes two forms.

First, we tend to overestimate the pleasure we'll receive from a future positive event. We tend to think we'll be happier with a new car than is actually the case, that owning our own home will feel better than it actually does once we buy it, and even that marriage will make us happier than it will. Research on affective forecasting shows that we overestimate both the intensity (how happy we'll feel) and the duration (how long we'll feel happy) of future positive events.

A second area where we are not very good at affective forecasting is negative events. Just as positive events

tend not to make us feel as good as we think they will, negative events don't make us feel as bad as we think they will.

Many different studies have supported our poor affective forecasting abilities: University students overestimate how happy or unhappy they'll be after being assigned to a good or bad student residence, people overestimate how unhappy they'll be 2 months after a break-up, and women overestimate the emotional impact of unwanted results for a pregnancy test.[42]

So, there is good news and bad news in this story: It's true that the highs aren't as high as we think, but it's also true that the lows aren't as low as we fear. Odds are, the future isn't as bright as you hope, but neither is it as bleak as you fear.

Sleep

Does a lack of sleep make people grumpier? Sleep quality does affect mood. Students and adult workers who are sleep deprived report greater feelings of fatigue, anger and hostility.[43] One of the reasons less sleep, or poor sleep quality, puts people in a bad mood is that it impairs decision making and makes it difficult to control emotions.[44] A recent study suggests that poor sleep the previous night also impairs peoples' job satisfaction the next day, mostly because people feel fatigued, irritable, and less alert.[45]

Exercise

You often hear that people should exercise to improve their mood. But does 'sweat therapy' really work? It appears so. Research consistently shows that exercise enhances peoples' positive mood.[46] It appears that the therapeutic effects of exercise are strongest for those who are depressed. Although the effects of exercise on moods are consistent, they are not terribly strong. So, exercise may help put you in a better mood, but don't expect miracles.

Age

Do you think that young people experience more extreme, positive emotions (so-called 'youthful exuberance') than older people do? If you answered 'yes,' you were wrong. One study of people aged 18 to 94 years revealed that negative emotions seem to occur less as people get older. Periods of highly positive moods lasted longer for older individuals, and bad moods faded for them more quickly than for younger people.[47] The study implies that emotional experience tends to improve with age, so that as we get older, we experience fewer negative emotions.

Gender

The common belief is that women are more emotional than men. Is there any truth to this? The evidence does confirm that women are more emotionally expressive than are men;[48] they experience emotions more intensely, they tend to 'hold onto' emotions longer than men, and they display more frequent expressions of both positive and negative emotions, except anger.[49] Although there may be innate differences between the genders, research suggests that emotional differences also are due to the different ways men and women have been socialised.[50] Men are taught to be tough and brave. Showing emotion is inconsistent with this image. Women, in contrast, are socialised to be nurturing. For instance, women are expected to express more positive emotions on the job (shown by smiling) than men, and they do.[51]

EMOTIONAL RECOGNITION: UNIVERSAL OR CULTURE-SPECIFIC?   GLOBAL

Early researchers studying how we understand emotions based on others' expressions believed that all individuals, regardless of their culture, could recognise the same emotion. So, for example, a frown would be recognised as indicating the emotion sadness, no matter where one was from. However, more recent research suggests that this universal approach to the study of emotions is incorrect because there are subtle differences in the degree to which we can tell what emotions people from different cultures are feeling, based on their facial expressions.

One study examined how quickly and accurately we can read the facial expressions of people of different cultural backgrounds. Although individuals were at first faster at recognising the emotional expression of others from their own culture, when living in a different culture, the speed and accuracy at which they recognised others' emotions increased as they became more familiar with the culture. For example, as Chinese residing in the United States adapted to their surroundings, they were able to recognise the emotions of people native to the United States more quickly. In fact, foreigners are sometimes better at recognising emotions among the citizens in their non-native country than are those citizens themselves.

Interestingly, these effects begin to occur relatively quickly. For example, Chinese students living in the United States for an average of 2.4 years were better at recognising the facial expressions of US citizens than they were at reading the facial expressions of Chinese citizens. Why is this the case? According to the authors of the study, it could be that because they are limited in speaking the language, they rely more on nonverbal communication. What is the upshot for OB? When conducting business in a foreign country, the ability to correctly recognise others' emotions can facilitate interactions and lead to less miscommunication. Otherwise, a slight smile that is intended to communicate disinterest may be mistaken for happiness.

Source: Based on H. A. Elfenbein and N. Ambady, 'When familiarity breeds accuracy: cultural exposure and facial emotion recognition', *Journal of Personality and Social Psychology*, August 2003, pp. 276–90.

Emotional labour

4 Show the impact emotional labour has on employees.

If you've ever had a job working in retail sales or waiting on tables in a restaurant, you know the importance of projecting a friendly demeanour and smiling. Even though there were days when you didn't feel cheerful, you knew management expected you to be upbeat when dealing with customers. So you faked it, and in so doing, you expressed emotional labour.

Every employee expends physical and mental labour when they put their bodies and cognitive capabilities, respectively, into their job. But jobs also require **emotional labour**. Emotional labour is an employee's expression of organizationally desired emotions during interpersonal transactions at work.[52]

emotional labour
A situation in which an employee expresses organizationally desired emotions during interpersonal transactions at work.

emotional dissonance
Inconsistencies between the emotions people feel and the emotions they project.

The concept of emotional labour emerged from studies of service jobs. Airlines expect their flight attendants, for instance, to be cheerful; we expect funeral directors to be sad; and we expect doctors to be emotionally neutral. But really, emotional labour is relevant to almost every job. Your managers expect you, for example, to be courteous, not hostile, in interactions with co-workers. The true challenge arises when employees have to project one emotion while simultaneously feeling another.[53] This disparity is **emotional dissonance**, and it can take a heavy toll on employees. Bottled-up feelings of frustration, anger and resentment can eventually lead to emotional exhaustion and burnout.[54] It's from the increasing importance of emotional labour as a key component of effective job performance that an understanding of emotion has gained heightened relevance within the field of OB.

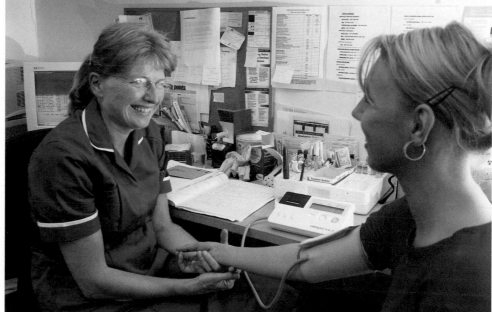

Malcolm Case-Green/Alamy

Many workers were required to display certain emotions as part of their job. This emotional labour sometimes means hiding or suppressing real feelings. For example, nurses are expected to be caring, concerned and helpful regardless of how they actually feel. Emotional labourers often have to bottle up their true feelings until after work.

Emotional labour creates dilemmas for employees. There may be people with whom you have to work that you just don't like. Perhaps you consider their personality abrasive. Maybe you know they've said negative things about you behind your back. Regardless, your job requires you to interact with these people on a regular basis. So you're forced to feign friendliness.

It can help you, on the job especially, if you separate emotions into *felt* or *displayed emotions*.[55] **Felt emotions** are an individual's actual emotions. In contrast, **displayed emotions** are those that the organization requires workers to show and considers appropriate in a given job. They're not innate; they're learned. For example, a police officer is expected to display emotions such as concern, interest and courtesy when dealing with the public. But the emotions the officer actually feels may be frustration and anger.

Effective managers have learned to be serious when giving an employee a negative performance evaluation and to hide their anger when they've been passed over for promotion. And a salesperson who hasn't learned to smile and appear friendly, regardless of her true feelings at the moment, isn't typically going to last long on most sales jobs. How we *experience* an emotion isn't always the same as how we *show* it.[56]

Yet another point is that displaying fake emotions requires us to suppress the emotions we really feel (not showing anger toward a customer, for example). In other words, the individual has to 'act' to keep their job. **Surface acting** is hiding one's inner feelings and forgoing emotional expressions in response to display rules. For example, when a worker smiles at a customer even when they don't feel like it, they are surface acting. **Deep acting** is trying to modify one's inner feelings based on display rules. A health care provider trying to genuinely feel more empathy for his patients is deep acting.[57] Surface acting deals with one's *displayed* emotions, and deep acting deals with one's *felt* emotions. Research shows that surface acting is more stressful to employees than deep acting because it entails feigning one's true emotions.[58]

Interestingly, as important as managing emotions is to many jobs, it seems that the market does not necessarily reward emotional labour. A recent study found that emotional demands matter in setting compensation levels, but only when jobs are already cognitively demanding – such as jobs in law and nursing. But, for instance, child-care workers and waiters – holders of jobs with high emotional demands but relatively low cognitive demands – receive little compensation for the emotional demands of their work.[59]

felt emotions
An individual's actual emotions.

displayed emotions
Emotions that are organizationally required and considered appropriate in a given job.

surface acting
Hiding one's inner feelings and forgoing emotional expressions in response to display rules.

deep acting
Trying to modify one's true inner feelings based on display rules.

Affective events theory

5 Describe affective events theory and identify its applications.

affective events theory (AET)
A model which suggests that workplace events cause emotional reactions on the part of employees, which then influence workplace attitudes and behaviours.

As we have seen, emotions and moods are an important part of our lives, especially our work lives. But how do our emotions and moods influence our job performance and satisfaction? A model called **affective events theory (AET)** has increased our understanding of the links.[60] AET demonstrates that employees react emotionally to things that happen to them at work and that this reaction influences their job performance and satisfaction.

Figure 8.5 summarises AET. The theory begins by recognising that emotions are a response to an event in the work environment. The work environment includes everything surrounding the job – the variety of tasks and degree of autonomy, job demands, and requirements for expressing emotional labour. This environment creates work events that can be hassles, uplifting events, or both. Examples of hassles are colleagues who refuse to carry out their share of work, conflicting directions from different managers, and excessive time pressures. Examples of uplifting events include meeting a goal, getting support from a colleague, and receiving recognition for an accomplishment.[61]

These work events trigger positive or negative emotional reactions. But employees' personalities and moods predispose them to respond with greater or lesser intensity to the event. For instance, people who score low on emotional stability are more likely to react strongly to negative events. And their mood introduces the reality that their general affect cycle creates fluctuations. So a person's emotional response to a given event can change, depending on mood. Finally, emotions influence a number of performance and satisfaction variables, such as organizational citizenship behaviour, organizational commitment, level of effort, intentions to quit and workplace deviance.

In addition, tests of the theory suggest that (1) an emotional episode is actually a series of emotional experiences precipitated by a single event. It contains elements of both emotions and mood cycles. (2) Current emotions influence job satisfaction at any given time, along with the history of emotions surrounding the event. (3) Because moods and emotions fluctuate over time, their effect on performance also fluctuates. (4) Emotion-driven behaviours are typically short in duration and of high variability. (5) Because emotions, even positive ones, tend to be incompatible with behaviours required to do a job, they typically have a negative influence on job performance.[62]

An example might help better explain AET.[63] Say that you work as an aeronautical engineer for Airbus. Because of the downturn in the demand for commercial jets, you've just learned that

---

Figure 8.5   Affective events theory

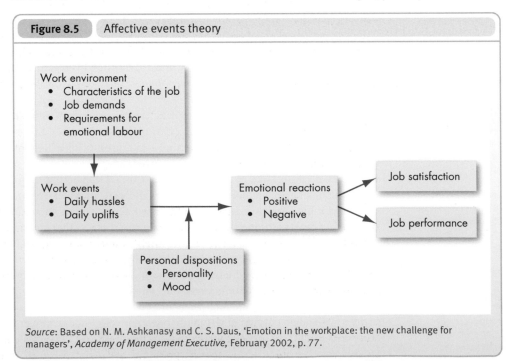

Source: Based on N. M. Ashkanasy and C. S. Daus, 'Emotion in the workplace: the new challenge for managers', *Academy of Management Executive*, February 2002, p. 77.

the company is considering laying off 10,000 employees. This layoff could include you. This event is likely to make you feel negative emotions, especially fear that you might lose your job and primary source of income. And because you're prone to worry a lot and obsess about problems, this event increases your feelings of insecurity. The layoff also puts into place a series of smaller events that create an episode: You talk with your boss, and he assures you that your job is safe; you hear rumours that your department is high on the list to be eliminated; and you run into a former colleague who was laid off 6 months ago and still hasn't found work. These events, in turn, create emotional ups and downs. One day, you're feeling upbeat and that you'll survive the cuts. The next day, you might be depressed and anxious. These emotional swings take your attention away from your work and lower your job performance and satisfaction. Finally, your response is magnified because this is the fourth-largest layoff that Airbus has initiated in the past three years.

In summary, AET offers two important messages.[64] First, emotions provide valuable insights into understanding employee behaviour. The model demonstrates how workplace hassles and uplifting events influence employee performance and satisfaction. Second, employees and managers shouldn't ignore emotions and the events that cause them, even when they appear to be minor, because they accumulate.

Emotional intelligence

6 Contrast the evidence for and against the existence of emotional intelligence.

emotional intelligence (EI)
The ability to detect and to manage emotional cues and information.

Mathilda Mueller is an office manager. Her awareness of her own and others' emotions is almost non-existent. She's moody and unable to generate much enthusiasm or interest in her employees. She doesn't understand why employees get upset with her. She often overreacts to problems and chooses the most ineffectual responses to emotional situations.[65] Mathilda Mueller has low emotional intelligence. **Emotional intelligence (EI)** is a person's ability to (1) be self-aware (to recognise her own emotions when she experiences them), (2) detect emotions in others, and (3) manage emotional cues and information. People who know their own emotions and are good at reading emotion cues – for instance, knowing why they're angry and how to express themselves without violating norms – are most likely to be effective.[66]

Several studies suggest that EI plays an important role in job performance. One study looked at the characteristics of engineers at Lucent Technologies who were rated as stars by their peers. The researchers concluded that stars were better at relating to others. That is, it was EI, not IQ, that characterised high performers. Another study analysed the performance profiles from various positions in 121 companies around the world. The results revealed that EI abilities were more than twice as important, in comparison to technical and cognitive abilities, for excellence.[67]

EI has been a controversial concept in OB. It has supporters and detractors. In the following sections, we review the arguments for and against the viability of EI in OB.

The case for EI

The arguments in favour of EI include its intuitive appeal, the fact that EI predicts criteria that matter, and the idea that EI is biologically based.

Intuitive appeal
There's a lot of intuitive appeal to the EI concept. Almost everyone would agree that it is good to be street-wise and possess social intelligence. People who can detect emotions in others, control their own emotions, and handle social interactions well will have a powerful leg up in the business world, so the thinking goes. As just one example, partners in a multinational consulting firm who scored above the median on an EI measure delivered €1 million more in business than did the other partners.[68]

EI predicts criteria that matter
More and more evidence is suggesting that a high level of EI means a person will perform well on the job. One study found that EI predicted the performance of employees in a cigarette

factory in China.[69]Another study found that being able to recognise emotions in others' facial expressions and to emotionally 'eavesdrop' (that is, pick up subtle signals about peoples' emotions) predicted peer ratings of how valuable those people were to their organization.[70] Finally, a review of 59 studies indicated that, overall, EI correlated moderately with job performance.[71]

EI is biologically based

One study has shown that people with damage to the part of the brain that governs emotional processing (lesions in an area of the prefrontal cortex) score significantly lower than others on EI tests. Even though these brain-damaged people scored no lower on standard measures of intelligence than people without the same brain damage, they were still impaired in normal decision making. Specifically, when people were playing a card game in which there is a reward (money) for picking certain types of cards and a punishment (a loss of money) for picking other types of cards, the participants with no brain damage learned to succeed in the game, while the performance of the brain-damaged group worsened over time. This study suggests that EI is neurologically based in a way that's unrelated to standard measures of intelligence and that people who suffer neurological damage score lower on EI and make poorer decisions than people who are healthier in this regard.[72]

The case against EI

For all its supporters, EI has just as many critics. Its critics say that EI is vague and impossible to measure, and they question its validity.

EI is too vague a concept

To many researchers, it's not clear what EI is. Is it a form of intelligence? Most of us wouldn't think that being self-aware or self-motivated or having empathy is a matter of intellect. So, is EI a misnomer? Moreover, many times different researchers focus on different skills, making it difficult to get a definition of EI. One researcher may study self-discipline. Another may study empathy. Another may look at self-awareness. As one reviewer noted, 'The concept of EI has now become so broad and the components so variegated that . . . it is no longer even an intelligible concept.'[73]

Libby Welch/Alamy

Research found that highly emotionally competent debt collectors recovered over double the amount of revenues compared with their typical co-workers. Two groupings of emotional competencies thought to be essential in successful negotiations were identified as self-awareness and empathy and self-control and adaptability.[74]

EI can't be measured

Many critics have raised questions about measuring EI. Because EI is a form of intelligence, for instance, there must be right and wrong answers about it on tests, they argue. Some tests do have right and wrong answers, although the validity of some of the questions on these measures is questionable. For example, one measure asks you to associate particular feelings with specific colours, as if purple always makes us feel cool and not warm. Other measures are self-reported, meaning there is no right or wrong answer. For example, an EI test question might ask you to respond to the statement, 'I'm good at "reading" other people.' In general, the measures of EI are diverse, and researchers have not subjected them to as much rigorous study as they have measures of personality and general intelligence.[75]

The validity of EI is suspect

Some critics argue that because EI is so closely related to intelligence and personality, once you control for these factors, EI has nothing unique to offer. There is some foundation to this argument. EI appears to be highly correlated with measures of personality, especially emotional stability.[76] But there hasn't been enough research on whether EI adds insight beyond measures of personality and general intelligence in predicting job performance. Still, among consulting firms and in the popular press, EI is wildly popular. For example, one company's promotional materials for an EI measure claimed, 'EI accounts for more than 85 per cent of star performance in top leaders.'[77] To say the least, it's difficult to validate this statement with the research literature.

Weighing the arguments for and against EI, it's still too early to tell whether the concept is useful. It *is* clear, though, that the concept is here to stay.

SELF-ASSESSMENT LIBRARY

What's my emotional intelligence score?

In the Self-assessment library (available online), take assessment I.E.1 (What's my emotional intelligence score?).

OB applications of emotions and moods

7 Apply concepts about emotions and moods to specific OB issues.

In this section, we assess how an understanding of emotions and moods can improve our ability to explain and predict the selection process in organizations, decision making, creativity, motivation, leadership, interpersonal conflict, negotiation, customer service, job attitudes and deviant workplace behaviours. We also look at how managers can influence our moods.

FACE THE FACTS

- 'Professional smilers', such as flight attendants, sales personnel, call centre operators, waiters and others in contact with the public for extended periods of time, are at risk of seriously harming their health according to Professor Dieter Zapf, who led a two-year project at Frankfurt University. His research claims that fake friendliness leads to depression, stress and a lowering of the immune system.

- A study of business leaders revealed 85 per cent agreed emotionally engaging with customers would create loyalty, however, other research shows only 38 per cent of employees receive training on stimulating positive emotions in their customers.

- A survey of call centre staff discovered a strong direct link between performance and emotional intelligence. It also revealed that older staff had higher emotional intelligence scores.

Sources: See M. Berry, 'Enforced smiling in the workplace puts health at risk', *Personnel Today.com*, 16 May 2008; C. Shaw, 'Recruit staff who understand the customer is always right', *Personnel Today*, 26 November 2002; 'Feel your way to success', *Training and Coaching Today*, 1 February 2003; 'Older workers keep cool under pressure', *Personnel Today*, 24 September 2002.

Selection

One implication from the evidence to date on EI is that employers should consider it a factor in hiring employees, especially in jobs that demand a high degree of social interaction. In fact, more and more employers are starting to use EI measures to hire people. For example, it has been claimed that insurance sales agents who scored high on emotional competencies achieved sales figures which were more than twice those of their less emotionally competent colleagues. Others have found that highly emotionally competent debt collectors recovered more than double the amount of revenues compared with their typical co-workers.[78] At L'Oréal, salespersons selected on EI scores outsold those hired using the company's old selection procedure. On an annual basis, salespeople selected on the basis of emotional competence sold €65,000 more than other salespeople did, for a net revenue increase of around €2,000,000.[79]

Decision making

As you saw in Chapter 5, traditional approaches to the study of decision making in organizations have emphasised rationality. More and more OB researchers, though, are finding that moods and emotions have important effects on decision making.

Positive moods and emotions seem to help decision making. People in good moods or those experiencing positive emotions are more likely than others to use heuristics, or rules of thumb,[80] to help make good decisions quickly. Positive emotions also enhance problem-solving skills so that positive people find better solutions to problems.[81]

OB researchers continue to debate the role of negative emotions and moods in decision making. Although one often-cited study suggested that depressed people reach more accurate judgements,[82] more recent evidence has suggested that people who are depressed make poorer decisions. Why? Because depressed people are slower at processing information and tend to weigh all possible options rather than the most likely ones.[83] Although it would seem that weighing all possible options is a good thing, the problem is that depressed people search for the perfect solution when there rarely is any solution perfect.

Creativity

People who are in good moods tend to be more creative than people in bad moods.[84] They produce more ideas, others think their ideas are original, and they tend to identify more creative options to problems.[85] It seems that people who are experiencing positive moods or emotions are more flexible and open in their thinking, which may explain why they're more creative.[86] Supervisors should actively try to keep employees happy because doing so creates more good moods (employees like their leaders to encourage them and provide positive feedback on a job well done), which in turn leads people to be more creative.[87]

Some researchers, however, do not believe that a positive mood makes people more creative. They argue that when people are in positive moods, they may relax ('If I'm in a good mood, things must be going okay, and I must not need to think of new ideas') and not engage in the critical thinking necessary for some forms of creativity.[88] However, this view is controversial.[89] Until there are more studies on the subject, we can safely conclude that for many tasks, positive moods increase our creativity.

Motivation

Two studies have highlighted the importance of moods and emotions on motivation. The first study had two groups of people solve a number of word puzzles. One group saw a funny video clip, which was intended to put the group in a good mood before having to solve the puzzles. The other group was not shown the clip and just started working on solving the word puzzles right away. The results? The positive-mood group reported higher expectations of being able to solve the puzzles, worked harder at them, and solved more puzzles as a result.[90]

The second study found that giving people feedback – whether real or fake – about their performance influenced their mood, which then influenced their motivation.[91] So, a cycle can exist in which positive moods cause people to be more creative, which leads to positive feedback from those observing their work. This positive feedback then further reinforces their positive mood, which may then make them perform even better and so on.

Both of these studies highlight the effects of mood and emotions on motivation and suggest that organizations that promote positive moods at work are likely to have more motivated workers.

Leadership

Effective leaders rely on emotional appeals to help convey their messages.[92] In fact, the expression of emotions in speeches is often the critical element that makes us accept or reject a leader's message. 'When leaders feel excited, enthusiastic, and active, they may be more likely to energise their subordinates and convey a sense of efficacy, competence, optimism, and enjoyment.'[93] Politicians, as a case in point, have learned to show enthusiasm when talking about their chances of winning an election, even when polls suggest otherwise.

Corporate executives know that emotional content is critical if employees are to buy into their vision of their company's future and accept change. When higher-ups offer new visions, especially when the visions contain distant or vague goals, it is often difficult for employees to accept those visions and the changes they'll bring. By arousing emotions and linking them to an appealing vision, leaders increase the likelihood that managers and employees alike will accept change.[94]

Negotiation

Negotiation is an emotional process; however, we often say a skilled negotiator has a 'poker face.' The founder of Britain's Poker Channel, Crispin Nieboer, stated, 'It is a game of bluff and there is fantastic human emotion and tension, seeing who can bluff the longest.'[95] Several studies have shown that a negotiator who feigns anger has an advantage over the opponent. Why? Because when a negotiator shows anger, the opponent concludes that the negotiator has conceded all that they can, so the opponent gives in.[96]

Displaying a negative emotion (such as anger) can be effective, but feeling bad about your performance appears to impair future negotiations. Individuals who do poorly in a negotiation experience negative emotions, develop negative perceptions of their counterpart, and are less willing to share information or be cooperative in future negotiations.[97] Interestingly, then, while moods and emotions have benefits at work, in negotiation, unless we're putting up a false front (feigning anger), it seems that emotions may impair negotiator performance. In fact, a 2005 study found that people who suffered damage to the emotional centres of their brains (damage to the same part of the brain as Phineas Gage) may be the *best* negotiators because they're not likely to overcorrect when faced with negative outcomes.[98]

Customer service

A worker's emotional state influences customer service, which influences levels of repeat business and levels of customer satisfaction.[99] Providing quality customer service makes demands on employees because it often puts them in a state of emotional dissonance. Over time, this state can lead to job burnout, declines in job performance and lower job satisfaction.[100]

emotional contagion
The process by which peoples' emotions are caused by the emotions of others.

In addition, employees' emotions may transfer to the customer. Studies indicate a matching effect between employee and customer emotions, an effect that is called **emotional contagion** – the 'catching' of emotions from others.[101] How does emotional contagion work? The primary explanation is that when someone experiences positive emotions and laughs and smiles at you, you begin to copy that person's behaviour. So when employees express positive emotions, customers tend to respond positively. Emotional contagion is important because when customers catch the positive moods or emotions of employees, they shop longer. But what about negative emotions and moods? Are they contagious, too? Absolutely. When an employee feels unfairly treated by a customer, for example, it's harder for him to display the positive emotions his organization expects of him.[102]

Job attitudes

Ever hear the advice 'Never take your work home with you,' meaning that people should forget about their work once they go home? As it turns out, that's easier said than done. Several studies have shown that people who had a good day at work tend to be in a better mood at home that evening. And people who had a bad day tend to be in a bad mood once they're at home.[103] Evidence also suggests that people who have a stressful day at work have trouble relaxing after they get off work.[104]

Even though people do emotionally take their work home with them, by the next day, the effect is usually gone.[105] So, although it may be difficult or even unnatural to 'never take your work home with you', it doesn't appear that, for most people, a negative mood resulting from a bad day at work carries over to the next day.

Deviant workplace behaviours

Negative emotions can lead to a number of deviant workplace behaviours.

Anyone who has spent much time in an organization realises that people often behave in ways that violate established norms and that threaten the organization, its members, or both. As we saw in Chapter 1, these actions are called *workplace deviant behaviours*.[106] Many of these deviant behaviours can be traced to negative emotions.

For instance, envy is an emotion that occurs when you resent someone for having something that you don't have but that you strongly desire – such as a better work assignment, larger office or higher salary.[107] It can lead to malicious deviant behaviours. An envious employee, for example, could then act hostilely by backstabbing another employee, negatively distorting others' successes, and positively distorting his own accomplishments.[108] Evidence suggests that people who feel negative emotions, particularly those who feel angry or hostile, are more likely than people who don't feel negative emotions to engage in deviant behaviour at work.[109]

How managers can influence moods

In general, you can improve peoples' moods by showing them a funny video clip, giving them a small bag of candy, or even having them taste a pleasant beverage.[110] But what can companies do to improve their employees' moods? Managers can use humour and give their employees small tokens of appreciation for work well done. Also, research indicates that when leaders are in good moods, group members are more positive, and as a result, the members cooperate more.[111]

CRYING AT WORK   OB IN THE NEWS

Crying at work is acceptable for athletes and charity workers and, at opportune moments, politicians. But for everyone else, welling up at work is considered a career-limiting move. Emotion at the office should be controlled, not controlling. And there are now seminars that can help you to learn to deal with potentially fraught issues at the end of the day, and to excuse yourself if the tears well up anyway.

What no course seems to address, however, is how to work with someone who refuses to learn these skills: the workplace weeper. Given the amount of time spent at work, there will be times when personal, emotional events intrude. That's life. What needs confronting, however, is the otherwise reasonable worker who turns on the waterworks at work, and for work-related reasons.

Tears make the observer feel dreadful, but the weeper, curiously, better. A study in the US found that 85 per cent of women and 73 per cent of men admit that they feel lots better after a good cry. Tears flush out stress chemicals. So don't even flinch when that co-worker wells up after discovering that there's no more toner in the copier, or that they've been passed over for promotion. Remember, they are just getting rid of stress. Take one of the following three steps instead. Remove all stray boxes of tissues from the vicinity of your desk – that's just a red rag to the emotional bull. Tilt your head as if empathising and hold that pose for at least 15 minutes. Or, best, say 'I know (halting breath) just (breath) what you mean' as you burst into an even more dramatic flood of your own.

Two can play the crying game.

Source: 'Crying game; waterworks at the water cooler', *The Times*, 13 October 2004. © The Times 13 October 2004/ nisyndication.com.

Finally, selecting positive team members can have a contagion effect as positive moods transmit from team member to team member. One study of professional cricket teams found that players' happy moods affected the moods of their team members and also positively influenced their performance.[112] It makes sense, then, for managers to select team members who are predisposed to experience positive moods.

Global issues

8 Contrast the experience, interpretation and expression of emotions across cultures.

Does the degree to which people *experience* emotions vary across cultures? Do peoples' *interpretations* of emotions vary across cultures? Finally, do the norms for the *expression* of emotions differ across cultures? Let's tackle each of these questions.

Does the degree to which people experience emotions vary across cultures?

Yes. In China, for example, people report experiencing fewer positive and negative emotions than people in other cultures, and the emotions they experience are less intense than what other cultures report. In general, people in most cultures appear to experience certain positive and negative emotions, but the frequency of their experience and their intensity varies to some degree.[113]

Do peoples' interpretations of emotions vary across cultures?

On the whole, people from all over the world interpret negative and positive emotions the same way. We all view negative emotions, such as hate, terror and rage, as dangerous and destructive. And we all desire positive emotions, such as joy, love and happiness. However, some cultures value certain emotions more than others. For example, the Chinese consider negative emotions to be more useful and constructive than do people in the United States. In general, pride is seen as a positive emotion in Western, individualistic cultures, but Eastern cultures such as China and Japan tend to view pride as undesirable.[114]

Do the norms for the expression of emotions differ across cultures?

Absolutely. For example, research has shown that in collectivist countries, people are more likely to believe the emotional displays of another have something to do with their own relationship with the person expressing the emotion, while people in individualistic cultures don't think that another's emotional expressions are directed at them. Friendly customer service clerks are the norm in United States retail stores such as Wal-Mart, however, there are reports that serious German shoppers have been turned off by Wal-Mart's friendly greeters and helpful personnel.[115]

In general, and not surprisingly, it's easier for people to accurately recognise emotions within their own culture than in other cultures. For example, a Chinese businessperson is more likely to accurately label the emotions underlying the facial expressions of a fellow Chinese colleague than those of a foreign colleague.[116]

Interestingly, some cultures lack words for standard emotional terms such as *anxiety*, *depression* and *guilt*. Tahitians, as a case in point, don't have a word directly equivalent to *sadness*. When Tahitians are sad, their peers attribute their state to a physical illness.[117] Our discussion illustrates the need to consider the fact that cultural factors influence what managers think is emotionally appropriate.[118] What's acceptable in one culture may seem extremely unusual or even dysfunctional in another. Managers need to know the emotional norms in each culture they do business in or with so they don't send unintended signals or misread the reactions of others. For example, a UK manager in Japan should know that while UK culture tends to view smiling positively, the Japanese attribute frequent smiling to a lack of intelligence.[119]

Summary and implications for managers

Emotions and moods are similar in that both are affective in nature. But they're also different – moods are more general and less contextual than emotions. And events do matter. The time of day and day of the week, stressful events, social activities, and sleep patterns are some of the factors that influence emotions and moods.

Emotions and moods have proven themselves to be relevant for virtually every OB topic we study. Increasingly, organizations are selecting employees they believe have high levels of emotional intelligence. Emotions, especially positive moods, appear to facilitate effective decision making and creativity. Although the research is relatively recent, research suggests that mood is linked to motivation, especially through feedback, and that leaders rely on emotions to increase their effectiveness. The display of emotions is important to negotiation and customer service, and the experience of emotions is closely linked to job attitudes and behaviours that follow from attitudes, such as deviant behaviour in the workplace.

Can managers control their colleagues' and employees' emotions and moods? Certainly there are limits, practical and ethical. Emotions and moods are a natural part of an individual's makeup. Where managers err is in ignoring their co-workers' and employees' emotions and assessing others' behaviour as if it were completely rational. As one consultant aptly put it, 'You can't divorce emotions from the workplace because you can't divorce emotions from people.'[120] Managers who understand the role of emotions and moods will significantly improve their ability to explain and predict their co-workers' and employees' behaviour.

POINT/COUNTERPOINT

The costs and benefits of organizational display rules

POINT ➡

Organizations today realise that good customer service means good business. After all, who wants to end a shopping trip at the grocery store with a surly cashier? Research clearly shows that organizations that provide good customer service have higher profits than those with poor customer service.[121] An integral part of customer-service training is to set forth display rules to teach employees to interact with customers in a friendly, helpful, professional way – and evidence indicates that such rules work: Having display rules increases the odds that employees will display the emotions expected of them.[122]

As one Starbucks manager says, 'What makes Starbucks different is our passion for what we do. We're trying to provide a great experience for people, with a great product. That's what we all care about.'[123] Starbucks may have good coffee, but a big part of the company's growth has been the customer experience. For instance, the cashiers are friendly and will get to know you by name if you are a repeat customer.

Asking employees to act friendly is good for them, too. Research shows that employees of organizations that require them to display positive emotions actually feel better as a result.[124] And, if someone feels that being asked to smile is bad for him, he doesn't belong in the service industry in the first place.

COUNTERPOINT ⬅

Organizations have no business trying to regulate the emotions of their employees. Companies should not be 'the thought police' and force employees to feel and act in ways that serve only organizational needs. Service employees should be professional and courteous, yes, but many companies expect them to take abuse and refrain from defending themselves. That's wrong. As the philosopher Jean Paul Sartre wrote, we have a responsibility to be authentic – true to ourselves – and within reasonable limits organizations have no right to ask us to be otherwise.

Service industries have no business teaching their employees to be smiling punching bags. Most customers might even prefer that employees be themselves. Employees shouldn't be openly nasty or hostile, of course, but who appreciates a fake smile? Think about trying on an outfit in a store and the clerk automatically says it looks 'absolutely wonderful' when you know it doesn't and you sense the clerk is lying. Most customers would rather talk with a 'real' person than someone enslaved to an organization's display rules. Furthermore, if an employee doesn't feel like slapping on an artificial smile, then it's only going to create dissonance between them and their employer.[125]

Finally, research shows that forcing display rules on employees takes a heavy emotional toll.[126] It's unnatural to expect someone to smile all the time or to passively take abuse from customers, clients, or fellow employees. Organizations can improve their employees' psychological health by encouraging them to be themselves, within reasonable limits.

QUESTIONS FOR REVIEW

1. What are the similarities and differences between emotions and moods? What are the basic emotions and the basic mood dimensions?

2. Are emotions and moods rational? What functions do emotions and moods serve?

3. What are the primary sources of emotions and moods?

4. What is emotional labour, and why is it important to understanding OB?

5. What is affective events theory? Why is it important to understanding emotions?

6. What is emotional intelligence, and what are the arguments for and against its importance?

7. What effect do emotions and moods have on different OB issues? As a manager, what steps would you take to improve your employees' moods?

8. Does the degree to which people *experience* emotions vary across cultures? Do peoples' *interpretations* of emotions vary across cultures, and do different norms across cultures govern the expression of emotions?

Experiential exercise

WHO CAN CATCH A LIAR?

In this chapter, we discussed how people determine emotions from facial expressions. There has been research on whether people can tell whether someone is lying based on facial expression. Let's see who is good at catching liars.

Split up into teams and follow these instructions.

1. Randomly choose someone to be the team organizer. Have this person write down on a piece of paper 'T' for truth and 'L' for lie. If there are, say, six people in the group (other than the organizer), then three people will get a slip with a 'T' and three a slip with an 'L'. It's important that all team members keep what's on their paper a secret.

2. Each team member who holds a T slip needs to come up with a true statement, and each team member who holds

an L slip needs to come up with a false statement. Try not to make the statement so outrageous that no one would believe it (for example, 'I have flown to the moon').

3. The organizer will have each member make his or her statement. Group members should then examine the person making the statement closely to try to determine whether he or she is telling the truth or lying. Once each person has made his or her statement, the organizer will ask for a vote and record the tallies.

4. Each person should now indicate whether the statement was the truth or a lie.

5. How good was your group at catching the liars? Were some people good liars? What did you look for to determine if someone was lying?

Ethical dilemma

ARE WORKPLACE ROMANCES UNETHICAL?

A large percentage of married individuals first met in the workplace. A 2006 survey revealed that 40 per cent of all employees have been in an office romance. Another survey of UK workers reported more than seven out of 10 respondents said they were aware of a romance currently going on in their office. Given the amount of time people spend at work, this isn't terribly surprising. Yet office romances pose sensitive ethical issues for organizations and employees. What rights and responsibilities do organizations have to regulate the romantic lives of their employees?

Take the example of Julie Roehm, senior vice president (VP) of marketing at Wal-Mart, who began dating Sean Womack, VP of communications architecture. When Wal-Mart learned of the relationship, it fired both Roehm and Womack, arguing that the undisclosed relationship violated its policy against workplace romances. After her firing, Roehm sued Wal-Mart, claiming that the company breached her contract and damaged her reputation. Wal-Mart then countersued, alleging that Roehm showed favouritism on Womack's behalf.

The Wal-Mart, Julie Roehm and Sean Womack saga shows that while workplace romances are personal matters, it's hard

to keep them out of the political complexities of organizational life.

Questions

1. Nearly three-quarters of organizations have no policies governing workplace romances. Do you think organizations should have such policies in place?

2. Do you agree with Wal-Mart's policy against workplace romantic relationships? Why or why not?

3. Do you think it is ever appropriate for a supervisor to date an employee under his or her supervision? Why or why not?

4. Some companies, such as Nike, openly try to recruit couples. Do you think this is a good idea? How would you feel working in a department with a 'couple'?

Sources: J. Geenwald, 'Employers are the losers in the dating game', *Workforce Week*, 3 June 2007, pp. 1–2; 'My year at Wal-Mart', *BusinessWeek*, 12 February 2007; M. Crail, 'Research update . . . workplace romance,' *Personnel Today*, 25 July 2006.

CASE INCIDENT 1

The upside of anger?

A researcher doing a case study on emotions in organizations interviewed Laura, a 22-year-old customer-service representative in Australia. The following is a summary of the interview (with some paraphrasing of the interviewer questions):

Interviewer: How would you describe your workplace?

Laura: *Very cold, unproductive, [a] very, umm, cold environment, atmosphere.*

Interviewer: What kinds of emotions are prevalent in your organization?

Laura: *Anger, hatred towards other people, other staff members.*

Interviewer: So it seems that managers keep employees in line using fear tactics?

Laura: *Yeah. [The General Manager's] favourite saying is, 'Nobody's indispensable.' So, it's like, 'I can't do that because I'll get sacked!'*

Interviewer: How do you survive in this situation?

Laura: *You have to cater your emotions to the sort of situation, the specific situation . . . because it's just such a hostile environment, this is sort of the only way you can survive.*

Interviewer: Are there emotions you have to hide?

Laura: *Managers don't like you to show your emotions. . . . They don't like to show that there is anything wrong or anything emotional in the working environment.*

Interviewer: Why do you go along?

Laura: *I feel I have to put on an act because . . . to show your true emotions, especially towards my managers [Laura names two of her senior managers], it would be hatred sometimes. So, you just can't afford to do that because it's your job and you need the money.*

Interviewer: Do you ever rebel against this system?

Laura: *You sort of put on a happy face just so you can annoy [the managers]. I find that they don't like people being happy, so you just annoy them by being happy. So, yeah. It just makes you laugh. You just 'put it on' just because you know it annoys [management].*

It's pretty vindictive and manipulative but you just need to do that.

Interviewer: Do you ever find that this gets to you?

Laura: *I did care in the beginning and I think it just got me into more trouble. So now I just tell myself, 'I don't care.' If you tell yourself something for long enough, eventually you believe it. Yeah, so now I just go 'Oh well.'*

Interviewer: Do you intend to keep working here?

Laura: *It's a means to an end now. So every time I go [to work] and every week I just go, 'Well, one week down, one week less until I go away.' But if I knew that I didn't have this goal, I don't know if I could handle it, or if I would even be there now.*

Interviewer: Is there an upside to working here?

Laura: *I'm so much better at telling people off now than I ever used to be. I can put people in place in about three sentences. Like, instead of, before I would walk away from it. But now I just stand there and fight . . . I don't know if that's a good thing or a bad thing.*

Questions

1. Do you think Laura is justified in her responses to her organization's culture? Why or why not?

2. Do you think Laura's strategic use and display of emotions serve to protect her?

3. Assuming that Laura's description is accurate, how would *you* react to the organization's culture?

4. Research shows that acts of co-workers (37 per cent) and management (22 per cent) cause more negative emotions for employees than do acts of customers (7 per cent).[127] What can Laura's company do to change its emotional climate?

Source: J. Perrone and M. H. Vickers, 'Emotions as strategic game in a hostile workplace: an exemplar case', *Employee Responsibilities and Rights Journal*, 16, 3 (2004), pp. 167–78.

CASE INCIDENT 2

Abusive customers cause emotions to run high

Telephone customer-service representatives have a tough time these days. With automated telephone systems that create a labyrinth for customers, result in long hold times, and make it difficult for them to speak to an actual human being, a customer's frustration often settles in before the representative has had time to say 'hello'. Says Donna Earl, an owner of a customer-service consulting firm, 'By the time you get to the person you need to talk to, you're mad.'

Erin Calabrese knows all too well just how mad customers can get. A customer-service representative at a financial services company, she still vividly recalls one of her worst experiences – with a customer named Jane. Jane called Calabrese over some charges on her credit card and began 'ranting and raving'. 'Your #%#% company, who do you think you are?' yelled Jane. Though Calabrese tried to console the irate customer by offering a refund, Jane only called Calabrese an 'idiot'. The heated conversation continued for almost 10 minutes before Calabrese, shaking, handed the phone to her supervisor and left her desk.

Sometimes customers can be downright racist. One customer-service representative finally quit her job because she constantly heard racial remarks from customers after, she contends, they heard her accent. 'By the time you leave, your head is spinning with all the complaints,' she said.

Unfortunately, these employees have little choice but to take the abuse. Many companies require customer-service employees to display positive emotions at all times to maintain satisfied customers. But the result could be an emotional nightmare that doesn't necessarily end once the calls stop. Calabrese stated that she would frequently take her negative emotions home. The day after she received the abusive call from Jane, Calabrese went home and started a fight with her roommate. It was 'an all-out battle,' recalls Calabrese, 'I just blew up.' The former customer-service representative also recalls the effects of the abusive calls on her family. 'My children would say, "Mom, stop talking about your work. You're home." My husband would say the same thing,' she said.

Emma Parsons, who quit her job as a customer-service representative for the travel industry, was frustrated by the inability to do anything about abusive customers and the mood they'd put her in. 'Sometimes you'd finish a call and you'd want to smash somebody's face. I had no escape, no way of releasing.' She said that if she did retaliate toward an abusive customer, her boss would punish her.

Some companies train their representatives to defuse a customer's anger and to avoid taking abuse personally, but the effort isn't enough. Liz Aherarn of the consulting firm Radclyffe Group, says customer-service employees who work the phones are absent more frequently, are more prone to illness, and are more likely to make stress-related disability claims than other employees. Thus, It is apparent that in the world of customer service, particularly when interactions take place over the phone, emotions can run high, and the effects can be damaging. Although the adage 'the customer comes first' has been heard by many, companies should empower employees to decide when it is appropriate to put the customer second. Otherwise, employees are forced to deal with abusive customers, the effects of which can be detrimental to both the individual and the company.

Questions

1. From an emotional labour perspective, how does dealing with an abusive customer lead to stress and burnout?

2. If you were a recruiter for a customer-service call centre, what personality types would you prefer to hire and why? In other words, what individual differences are likely to affect whether an employee can handle customer abuse on a day-to-day basis?

3. Emotional intelligence is one's ability to detect and manage emotional cues and information. How might emotional intelligence play a role in responding to abusive customers? What facets of emotional intelligence might employees who are able to handle abusive customers possess?

4. What steps should companies take to ensure that their employees are not victims of customer abuse? Should companies allow a certain degree of abuse if that abuse results in satisfied customers and perhaps greater profit? What are the ethical implications of this?

Source: Based on S. Shellenbarger, 'Domino effect: the unintended results of telling off customer-service staff', *Wall Street Journal*, 5 February 2004, p. D.1.

Endnotes

1 See, for instance, C. D. Fisher and N. M. Ashkanasy, 'The emerging role of emotions in work life: an introduction', *Journal of Organizational Behavior*, special issue 2000, pp. 123–29; N. M. Ashkanasy, C. E. J. Hartel and W. J. Zerbe (eds), *Emotions in the Workplace: Research, Theory, and Practice* (Westport, CT: Quorum Books, 2000); N. M. Ashkanasy and C. S. Daus, 'Emotion in the workplace: the new challenge for managers', *Academy of Management Executive*, February 2002, pp. 76–86; and N. M. Ashkanasy, C. E. J. Hartel and C. S. Daus, 'Diversity and emotion: the new frontiers in organizational behavior research', *Journal of Management*, 28, 3 (2002), pp. 307–38.

2 See, for example, L. L. Putnam and D. K. Mumby, 'Organizations, emotion and the myth of rationality', in S. Fineman (ed.), *Emotion in Organizations* (Thousand Oaks, CA: Sage, 1993), pp. 36–57; and J. Martin, K. Knopoff and C. Beckman, 'An alternative to bureaucratic impersonality and emotional labor: bounded emotionality at the Body Shop', *Administrative Science Quarterly*, June 1998, pp. 429–69.

3 B. E. Ashforth and R. H. Humphrey, 'Emotion in the workplace: a reappraisal', *Human Relations*, February 1995, pp. 97–125.

4 S. G. Barsade and D. E. Gibson, 'Why does affect matter in organizations?', *Academy of Management Perspectives*, February 2007, pp. 36–59.

5 See N. H. Frijda, 'Moods, emotion episodes and Emotions', in M. Lewis and J. M. Haviland (eds), *Handbook of Emotions* (New York: Guilford Press, 1993), pp. 381–403.

6 H. M. Weiss and R. Cropanzano, 'Affective events theory: a theoretical discussion of the structure, causes and consequences of affective experiences at work', in B. M. Staw and L. L. Cummings (eds), *Research in Organizational Behavior*, vol. 18 (Greenwich, CT: JAI Press, 1996), pp. 17–19.

7 See P. Ekman and R. J. Davidson (eds), *The Nature of Emotions: Fundamental Questions* (Oxford, UK: Oxford University Press, 1994).

8 Frijda, 'Moods, emotion episodes and Emotions', p. 381.

9 See Ekman and Davidson (eds), *The Nature of Emotions*.

10 See, for example, P. Ekman, 'An argument for basic emotions', *Cognition and Emotion*, May/July 1992, pp. 169–200; C. E. Izard, 'Basic emotions, relations among emotions, and emotion–cognition relations,' *Psychological Bulletin*,

November 1992, pp. 561–55; and J. L. Tracy and R. W. Robins, 'Emerging insights into the nature and function of pride', *Current Directions in Psychological Science*, 16, 3 (2007), pp. 147–50.

11 R. C. Solomon, 'Back to basics: on the very idea of "basic emotions"', *Journal for the Theory of Social Behaviour*, 32, 2 (June 2002), pp. 115–44.

12 R. Descartes, *The Passions of the Soul* (Indianapolis, IN: Hackett, 1989).

13 P. Ekman, *Emotions Revealed: Recognizing Faces and Feelings to Improve Communication and Emotional Life* (New York: Times Books/Henry Holt & Co., 2003).

14 P. R. Shaver, H. J. Morgan and S. J. Wu, 'Is love a "basic" emotion?', *Personal Relationships*, 3, 1 (March 1996), pp. 81–96.

15 Solomon, 'Back to basics'.

16 Weiss and Cropanzano, 'Affective events theory', pp. 20–22.

17 Cited in R. D. Woodworth, *Experimental Psychology* (New York: Holt, 1938).

18 D. Watson, L. A. Clark and A. Tellegen, 'Development and validation of brief measures of positive and negative affect: The PANAS Scales', *Journal of Personality and Social Psychology*, 1988, pp. 1063–70.

19 A. Ben-Ze'ev, *The Subtlety of Emotions* (Cambridge, MA: MIT Press, 2000), p. 94.

20 'Flight attendant war stories . . . stewardess', *AboutMyJob.com*, www.aboutmyjob.com/main.php3?action= displayarticle&artid=2111.

21 Cited in Ben-Ze'ev, *The Subtlety of Emotions*, p. 99.

22 J. T. Cacioppo and W. L. Gardner, 'Emotion', *Annual Review of Psychology*, 50 (1999), pp. 191–214.

23 D. Holman, 'Call centres', in D. Holman, T. D. Wall, C. Clegg, P. Sparrow and A. Howard (eds), *The Essentials of the New Work Place: A Guide to the Human Impact of Modern Working Practices* (Chichester, UK: Wiley, 2005), pp. 111–32.

24 L. M. Poverny and S. Picascia, 'There is no crying in business', *Womensmedia.com*, www.womensmedia.com/new/ Crying-at-Work.shtml.

25 L. P. Frankel, *Nice Girls Don't Get the Corner Office* (New York: Warner Book, 2004).

26 A. R. Damasio, *Descartes' Error: Emotion, Reason, and the Human Brain* (New York: Quill, 1994).

27 Ibid.

28 L. Cosmides and J. Tooby, 'Evolutionary psychology and the emotions', in M. Lewis and J. M. Haviland-Jones (eds), *Handbook of Emotions*, 2nd edn (New York: Guilford Press, 2000), pp. 91–115.

29 D. M. Buss, 'Cognitive biases and emotional wisdom in the evolution of conflict between the sexes', *Current Directions in Psychological Science*, 10, 6 (December 2001), pp. 219–23.

30 K. Hundley, 'An unspoken problem: two-thirds of female lawyers say they have experienced or seen harassment at work. But few want to talk about it', *St. Petersburg (Florida) Times*, 25 April 2004, www.sptimes.com/2005/04/24/ Business/An_unspoken_problem.shtml.

31 K. N. Laland and G. R. Brown, *Sense and Nonsense: Evolutionary Perspectives on Human Behaviour* (Oxford: Oxford University Press, 2002).

32 R. J. Larsen and E. Diener, 'Affect intensity as an individual difference characteristic: a review', *Journal of Research in Personality*, 21 (1987), pp. 1–39.

33 D. Watson, *Mood and Temperament* (New York: Guilford Press, 2000).

34 Ibid.

35 Ibid.

36 Ibid., p. 100.

37 Ibid., p. 73.

38 J. A. Fuller, J. M. Stanton, G. G. Fisher, C. Spitzmüller, S. S. Russell and P. C. Smith, 'A lengthy look at the daily grind: time series analysis of events, mood, stress, and satisfaction', *Journal of Applied Psychology*, 88, 6 (December 2003), pp. 1019–33.

39 See 'Monday blahs,' 16 May 2005, www.ashidome.com/ blogger/housearrest.asp?c=809&m=5&y=2005.

40 A. M. Isen, 'Positive affect as a source of human strength', in L. G. Aspinwall and U. Staudinger (eds), *The Psychology of Human Strengths* (Washington, DC: American Psychological Association, 2003), pp. 179–95.

41 Watson, *Mood and Temperament* (2000).

42 T. D. Wilson and D. T. Gilbert, 'Affective forecasting: knowing what to want', *Current Directions in Psychological Science*, June 2005, pp. 131–34.

43 M. Lavidor, A. Weller and H. Babkoff, 'how sleep is related to fatigue', *British Journal of Health Psychology*, 8 (2003), pp. 95–105; and J. J. Pilcher and E. Ott, 'The relationships between sleep and measures of health and well-being in college students: a repeated measures approach', *Behavioral Medicine*, 23 (1998), pp. 170–78.

44 E. K. Miller and J. D. Cohen, 'An integrative theory of prefrontal cortex function', *Annual Review of Neuroscience*, 24 (2001), pp. 167–202.

45 B. A. Scott and T. A. Judge, 'Tired and cranky? The effects of sleep quality on employee emotions and job satisfaction', working paper, Department of Management, University of Florida, 2005.

46 P. R. Giacobbi, H. A. Hausenblas and N. Frye, 'A naturalistic assessment of the relationship between personality, daily life events, leisure-time exercise, and mood', *Psychology of Sport & Exercise*, 6, 1 (January 2005), pp. 67–81.

47 L. L. Carstensen, M. Pasupathi, M. Ulrich and J. R. Nesselroade, 'Emotional experience in everyday life across the adult life span', *Journal of Personality and Social Psychology*, 79, 4 (2000), pp. 644–55.

48 K. Deaux, 'Sex differences', in M. R. Rosenzweig and L. W. Porter (eds), *Annual Review of Psychology*, vol. 26 (Palo Alto, CA: Annual Reviews, 1985), pp. 48–82; M. LaFrance and M. Banaji, 'Toward a reconsideration of the gender–emotion relationship', in M. Clark (ed.), *Review of Personality and Social Psychology*, vol. 14 (Newbury Park, CA: Sage, 1992), pp. 178–97; and A. M. Kring and A. H. Gordon, 'Sex differences in emotion: expression, experience, and physiology', *Journal of Personality and Social Psychology*, March 1998, pp. 686–703.

49 L. R. Brody and J. A. Hall, 'Gender and emotion', in M. Lewis and J. M. Haviland (eds), *Handbook of Emotions* (New York: Guilford Press, 1993), pp. 447–60; M. G. Gard and A. M. Kring, 'Sex differences in the time course of emotion', *Emotion*, 7, 2 (2007), pp. 429–37; and M. Grossman and W. Wood, 'Sex differences in intensity of emotional experience: a social role interpretation', *Journal of Personality and Social Psychology*, November 1992, pp. 1010–22.

50 N. James, 'Emotional labour: skill and work in the social regulations of feelings', *Sociological Review*, February 1989, pp. 15–42; A. Hochschild, *The Second Shift* (New York: Viking, 1989); and F. M. Deutsch, 'Status, sex, and smiling: the effect of role on smiling in men and women', *Personality and Social Psychology Bulletin*, September 1990, pp. 531–40.

51 A. Rafaeli, 'When clerks meet customers: a test of variables related to emotional expression on the job', *Journal of Applied Psychology*, June 1989, pp. 385–93; and LaFrance and Banaji, 'Toward a reconsideration of the gender–emotion relationship'.

52 See J. A. Morris and D. C. Feldman, 'Managing emotions in the workplace', *Journal of Managerial Issues*, 9, 3 (1997), pp. 257–74; S. Mann, *Hiding What We Feel, Faking What We Don't: Understanding the Role of Your Emotions at Work* (New York: HarperCollins, 1999); and S. M. Kruml and D. Geddes, 'Catching fire without burning out: is there an ideal way to perform emotion labor?', in N. M. Ashkanasy, C. E. J. Hartel and W. J. Zerbe, *Emotions in the Workplace* (New York: Quorum Books, 2000), pp. 177–88.

53 P. Ekman, W. V. Friesen and M. O'Sullivan, 'Smiles when lying', in P. Ekman and E. L. Rosenberg (eds), *What the Face Reveals: Basic and Applied Studies of Spontaneous Expression Using the Facial Action Coding System (FACS)* (London: Oxford University Press, 1997), pp. 201–16.

54 A. Grandey, 'Emotion regulation in the workplace: a new way to conceptualize emotional labor', *Journal of Occupational Health Psychology*, 5, 1 (2000), pp. 95–110; and R. Cropanzano, D. E. Rupp and Z. S. Byrne, 'The relationship of emotional exhaustion to work attitudes, job performance, and organizational citizenship behavior', *Journal of Applied Psychology*, February 2003, pp. 160–69.

55 A. R. Hochschild, 'Emotion work, feeling rules, and social structure', *American Journal of Sociology*, November 1979, pp. 551–75; W.-C. Tsai, 'Determinants and consequences of employee displayed positive emotions', *Journal of Management*, 27, 4 (2001), pp. 497–512; M. W. Kramer and J. A. Hess, 'Communication rules for the display of emotions in organizational settings', *Management Communication Quarterly*, August 2002, pp. 66–80; and J. M. Diefendorff and E. M. Richard, 'Antecedents and consequences of emotional display rule perceptions', *Journal of Applied Psychology*, April 2003, pp. 284–94.

56 Solomon, 'Back to basics'.

57 C. M. Brotheridge and R. T. Lee, 'Development and validation of the emotional labour scale', *Journal of Occupational & Organizational Psychology*, 76, 3 (September 2003), pp. 365–79.

58 A. A. Grandey, 'When "the show must go on": surface acting and deep acting as determinants of emotional exhaustion and peer-rated service delivery', *Academy of Management Journal*, February 2003, pp. 86–96; and A. A. Grandey, D. N. Dickter and H. Sin, 'The customer is not always right: customer aggression and emotion regulation of service employees', *Journal of Organizational Behavior*, 25, 3 (May 2004), pp. 397–418.

59 T. M. Glomb, J. D. Kammeyer-Mueller and M. Rotundo, 'Emotional labor demands and compensating wage differentials', *Journal of Applied Psychology*, 89, 4 (August 2004), pp. 700–14.

60 H. M. Weiss and R. Cropanzano, 'An affective events approach to job satisfaction', *Research in Organizational Behavior*, 18 (1996), pp. 1–74.

61 J. Basch and C. D. Fisher, 'Affective events–emotions matrix: a classification of work events and associated emotions', in N. M. Ashkanasy, C. E. J. Hartel and W. J. Zerbe, (eds), *Emotions in the Workplace* (Westport, CT: Quorum Books, 2000), pp. 36–48.

62 See, for example, H. M. Weiss and R. Cropanzano, 'Affective events theory'; and C. D. Fisher, 'Antecedents and consequences of real-time affective reactions at work', *Motivation and Emotion*, March 2002, pp. 3–30.

63 Based on H. M. Weiss and R. Cropanzano, 'Affective events theory', p. 42.

64 N. M. Ashkanasy, C. E. J. Hartel and C. S. Daus, 'Diversity and emotion: the new frontiers in organizational behavior research', *Journal of Management*, 28, 3 (2002), p. 324.

65 Based on D. R. Caruso, J. D. Mayer and P. Salovey, 'Emotional intelligence and emotional leadership', in R. E. Riggio, S. E. Murphy and F. J. Pirozzolo (eds), *Multiple Intelligences and Leadership* (Mahwah, NJ: Lawrence Erlbaum, 2002), p. 70.

66 This section is based on D. Goleman, *Emotional Intelligence* (New York: Bantam, 1995); P. Salovey and D. Grewal, 'The science of emotional intelligence', *Current Directions in Psychological Science*, 14, 6 (2005), pp. 281–85; M. Davies, L. Stankov and R. D. Roberts, 'Emotional intelligence: in search of an elusive construct', *Journal of Personality and Social Psychology*, October 1998, pp. 989–1015; D. Geddes and R. R. Callister, 'Crossing the line(s): a dual threshold model of anger in organizations', *Academy of Management Review*, 32, 3 (2007), pp. 721–46; and J. Ciarrochi, J. P. Forgas and J. D. Mayer (eds), *Emotional Intelligence in Everyday Life* (Philadelphia, PA: Psychology Press, 2001).

67 D. Goleman, *Working With Emotional Intelligence* (New York Bantam Books, 1998).

68 C. Cherniss, 'The business case for emotional intelligence', *Consortium for Research on Emotional Intelligence in Organizations*, 1999, www.eiconsortium.org/research/business_case_for_ei.pdf.

69 K. S. Law, C. Wong and L. J. Song, 'The construct and criterion validity of emotional intelligence and its potential utility for management studies', *Journal of Applied Psychology*, 89, 3 (2004), pp. 483–96.

70 H. A. Elfenbein and N. Ambady, 'Predicting workplace outcomes from the ability to eavesdrop on feelings,' *Journal of Applied Psychology*, 87, 5 (October 2002), pp. 963–71.

71 D. L. Van Rooy and C. Viswesvaran, 'Emotional intelligence: a meta-analytic investigation of predictive validity and nomological net', *Journal of Vocational Behavior*, 65, 1 (August 2004), pp. 71–95.

72 R. Bar-On, D. Tranel, N. L. Denburg and A. Bechara, 'Exploring the neurological substrate of emotional and social intelligence', *Brain* 126, 8 (August 2003), pp. 1790–800.

73 E. A. Locke, 'Why emotional intelligence is an invalid concept', *Journal of Organizational Behavior*, 26, 4 (June 2005), pp. 425–31.

74 Bachman *et al.* 'Emotional intelligence in the collection of debt'.

75 J. M. Conte, 'A review and critique of emotional intelligence measures', *Journal of Organizational Behavior*, 26, 4 (June 2005), pp. 433–40; and M. Davies, L. Stankov and R. D. Roberts, 'Emotional intelligence: in search of an elusive construct', *Journal of Personality and Social Psychology*, 75, 4 (1998), pp. 989–1015.

76 T. Decker, 'Is emotional intelligence a viable concept?', *Academy of Management Review*, 28, 2 (April 2003), pp. 433–40; and Davies, Stankov and Roberts, 'Emotional intelligence: in search of an elusive construct'.

77 F. J. Landy, 'Some historical and scientific issues related to research on emotional intelligence', *Journal of Organizational Behavior*, 26, 4 (June 2005), pp. 411–24.

78 D. Goleman, *Emotional Intelligence* (New York: Bantam Books, 1995); J. Bachman, S. Stein, K. Campbell and A. Sitarenios 'Emotional intelligence in the collection of debt', *International Journal of Selection and Assessment*, 8, 3 (2000), pp. 14–20.

79 L. M. J. Spencer, D. C. McClelland and S. Kelner, *Competency Assessment Methods: History and State of the Art* (Boston, MA: Hay/McBer, 1997).

80 J. Park and M. R. Banaji, 'Mood and heuristics: the influence of happy and sad states on sensitivity and bias in stereotyping', *Journal of Personality and Social Psychology*, 78, 6 (2000), pp. 1005–23.

81 See A. M. Isen, 'Positive affect and decision making', in M. Lewis and J. M. Haviland-Jones (eds), *Handbook of Emotions*, 2nd edn (New York: Guilford, 2000), pp. 261–77.

82 L. B. Alloy and L. Y. Abramson, 'Judgement of contingency in depressed and nondepressed students: sadder but wiser?', *Journal of Experimental Psychology: General*, 108 (1979), pp. 441–85.

83 N. Ambady and H. M. Gray, 'On being sad and mistaken: mood effects on the accuracy of thin-slice judgments', *Journal of Personality and Social Psychology*, 83, 4 (2002), pp. 947–61.

84 A. M. Isen, 'On the relationship between affect and creative problem solving', in S. W. Russ (ed.), *Affect, Creative Experience and Psychological Adjustment* (Philadelphia, PA: Brunner/Mazel, 1999), pp. 3–17; and S. Lyubomirsky, L. King and E. Diener, 'The benefits of frequent positive affect: does happiness lead to success?', *Psychological Bulletin*, 131, 6 (2005), pp. 803–55.

85 M. J. Grawitch, D. C. Munz and E. K. Elliott, 'Promoting creativity in temporary problem-solving groups: the effects of positive mood and autonomy in problem definition on idea-generating performance', *Group Dynamics*, 7, 3 (September 2003), pp. 200–13.

86 S. Lyubomirsky, L. King and E. Diener, 'The benefits of frequent positive affect: does happiness lead to success?', *Psychological Bulletin*, 13 (2005), pp. 808–55.

87 N. Madjar, G. R. Oldham and M. G. Pratt, 'There's no place like home? The contributions of work and nonwork creativity support to employees' creative performance', *Academy of Management Journal*, 45, 4 (2002), pp. 757–67.

88 J. M. George and J. Zhou, 'Understanding when bad moods foster creativity and good ones don't: the role of context and clarity of feelings', *Journal of Applied Psychology*, 87, 4 (August 2002), pp. 687–97; and J. P. Forgas and J. M. George, 'Affective influences on judgments and behavior in organizations: an information processing perspective', *Organizational Behavior and Human Decision Processes*, 86, 1 (2001), pp. 3–34.

89 L. L. Martin, 'Mood as input: a configural view of mood effects', in L. L. Martin and G. L. Clore (eds), *Theories of Mood and Cognition: A User's Guidebook* (Mahwah, NJ: Lawrence Erlbaum Associates, Publishers, 2001), pp. 135–57.

90 A. Erez and A. M. Isen, 'The influence of positive affect on the components of expectancy motivation', *Journal of Applied Psychology*, 87, 6 (2002), pp. 1055–67.

91 R. Ilies and T. A. Judge, 'Goal regulation across time: the effect of feedback and affect', *Journal of Applied Psychology*, 90, 3 (May 2005), pp. 453–67.

92 K. M. Lewis, 'When leaders display emotion: how followers respond to negative emotional expression of male and female leaders', *Journal of Organizational Behavior*, March 2000, pp. 221–34; and J. M. George, 'Emotions and leadership: the role of emotional intelligence', *Human Relations*, August 2000, pp. 1027–55.

93 J. M. George, 'Trait and state affect', in K. R. Murphy (ed.) *Individual Difference and Behavior in Organizations* (San Fransisco, CA: Jossey-Bass, 1996), pp. 145–71.

94 Ashforth and Humphrey, 'Emotion in the workplace', p. 116.

95 N. Reynolds, 'Whiz-kids gamble on TV channel for poker', *telegraph.co.uk*, 16 April 2005, www.telegraph.co.uk.

96 G. A. Van Kleef, C. K. W. De Dreu and A. S. R. Manstead, 'The interpersonal effects of emotions in negotiations: a motivated information processing approach', *Journal of Personality and Social Psychology*, 87, 4 (2004), pp. 510–28; and G. A. Van Kleef, C. K. W. De Dreu and A. S. R. Manstead, 'The interpersonal effects of anger and happiness in negotiations', *Journal of Personality and Social Psychology*, 86, 1 (2004), pp. 57–76.

97 K. M. O'Connor and J. A. Arnold, 'Distributive spirals: negotiation impasses and the moderating role of disputant self-efficacy', *Organizational Behavior and Human Decision Processes*, 84, 1 (2001), pp. 148–76.

98 B. Shiv, G. Loewenstein, A. Bechara, H. Damasio and A. R. Damasio, 'Investment behavior and the negative side of emotion', *Psychological Science*, 16, 6 (2005), pp. 435–39.

99 W.-C. Tsai and Y.-M. Huang, 'Mechanisms linking employee affective delivery and customer behavioral intentions', *Journal of Applied Psychology*, October 2002, pp. 1001–08.

100 Grandey, 'When "the show must go on"'.

101 See P. B. Barker and A. A. Grandey, 'Service with a smile and encounter satisfaction: emotional contagion and appraisal mechanisms', *Academy of Management Journal*, 49, 6 (2006), pp. 1229–38; and S. D. Pugh, 'Service with a smile: emotional contagion in the service encounter', *Academy of Management Journal*, October 2001, pp. 1018–27.

102 D. E. Rupp and S. Spencer, 'When customers lash out: the effects of customer interactional injustice on emotional labor and the mediating role of emotions', *Journal of Applied*

Psychology, 91, 4 (2006), pp. 971–78; and Tasi and Huang, 'Mechanisms linking employee affective delivery and customer behavioral intentions'.

103 R. Ilies and T. A. Judge, 'Understanding the dynamic relationships among personality, mood, and job satisfaction: a field experience sampling study', *Organizational Behavior and Human Decision Processes*, 89 (2002), pp. 1119–39.

104 R. Rau, 'Job strain or healthy work: a question of task design', *Journal of Occupational Health Psychology*, 9, 4 (October 2004), pp. 322–38; and R. Rau and A. Triemer, 'Overtime in relation to blood pressure and mood during work, leisure, and night time', *Social Indicators Research*, 67, 1–2 (June 2004), pp. 51–73.

105 T. A. Judge and R. Ilies, 'Affect and job satisfaction: a study of their relationship at work and at home', *Journal of Applied Psychology*, 89 (2004), pp. 661–73.

106 See R. J. Bennett and S. L. Robinson, 'Development of a measure of workplace deviance', *Journal of Applied Psychology*, June 2000, pp. 349–60. See also P. R. Sackett and C. J. DeVore, 'Counter productive behaviors at work', in N. Anderson, D. S. Ones, H. K. Sinangil and C. Viswesvaran (eds), *Handbook of Industrial, Work & Organizational Psychology*, vol. 1 (Thousand Oaks, CA: Sage, 2001), pp. 145–64.

107 A. G. Bedeian, 'Workplace envy', *Organizational Dynamics*, Spring 1995, p. 50; and Ben-Ze'ev, *The Subtlety of Emotions*, pp. 281–326.

108 Bedeian, 'Workplace envy', p. 54.

109 K. Lee and N. J. Allen, 'Organizational citizenship behavior and workplace deviance: the role of affect and cognition', *Journal of Applied Psychology*, 87, 1 (2002), pp. 131–42; and T. A. Judge, B. A. Scott and R. Ilies, 'Hostility, job attitudes, and workplace deviance: test of a multilevel model', *Journal of Applied Psychology*, 91, 1 (January 2006), pp. 126–38.

110 A. M. Isen, A. A. Labroo and P. Durlach, 'An influence of product and brand name on positive affect: implicit and explicit measures', *Motivation & Emotion*, 28, 1 (March 2004), pp. 43–63.

111 T. Sy, S. Côté and R. Saavedra, 'The contagious leader: impact of the leader's mood on the mood of group members, group affective tone, and group processes', *Journal of Applied Psychology*, 90, 2 (2005), pp. 295–305.

112 P. Totterdell, 'Catching moods and hitting runs: mood linkage and subjective performance in professional sports teams', *Journal of Applied Psychology*, 85, 6 (2000), pp. 848–59.

113 S. Oishi, E. Diener and C. Napa Scollon, 'Cross-situational consistency of affective experiences across cultures', *Journal of Personality & Social Psychology*, 86, 3 (2004), pp. 460–72.

114 Eid and Diener, 'Norms for experiencing emotions in different cultures'.

115 Ashforth and Humphrey, 'Emotion in the workplace', p. 104; B. Plasait, 'Accueil des touristes dans les grands centres de transit Paris', *Rapport du Bernard Plasait*, 4 October 2004, www.tourisme.gouv.fr/fr/navd/presse/dossiers/att00005767/dp_plasait.pdf; B. Mesquita, 'Emotions in collectivist and individualist contexts', *Journal of Personality and Social Psychology*, 80, 1 (2001), pp. 68–74; and D. Rubin, 'Grumpy German shoppers distrust the Wal-Mart style', *Seattle Times*, 30 December 2001, p. A15.

116 H. A. Elfenbein and N. Ambady, 'When familiarity breeds accuracy: cultural exposure and facial emotional recognition', *Journal of Personality and Social Psychology*, 85, 2 (2003), pp. 276–90.

117 R. I. Levy, *Tahitians: Mind and Experience in the Society Islands* (Chicago, IL: University of Chicago Press, 1973).

118 B. Mesquita and N. H. Frijda, 'Cultural variations in emotions: a review', *Psychological Bulletin*, September 1992, pp. 179–204; and B. Mesquita, 'Emotions in collectivist and individualist contexts', *Journal of Personality and Social Psychology*, January 2001, pp. 68–74.

119 D. Matsumoto, 'Cross-cultural psychology in the 21st century', in J. S. Halonen and S. F. Davis (eds) *The Many Faces of Psychological Research in the 21st Century*, Chapter 5.

120 S. Nelton, 'Emotions in the workplace', *Nation's Business*, February 1996, p. 25.

121 H. Liao and A. Chuang, 'A multilevel investigation of factors influencing employee service performance and customer outcomes', *Academy of Management Journal*, 47, 1 (2004), pp. 41–58.

122 D. J. Beal, J. P. Trougakos, H. M. Weiss and S. G. Green, 'Episodic processes in emotional labor: perceptions of affective delivery and regulation strategies', *Journal of Applied Psychology*, 91, 5 (2006), pp. 1057–65.

123 *Starbucks.com*, 16 May 2005, www.starbucks.com.

124 D. Zapf and M. Holz, 'On the positive and negative effects of emotion work in organizations', *European Journal of Work and Organizational Psychology*, 15, 1 (2006), pp. 1–28.

125 D. Zapf, 'Emotion work and psychological well-being: a review of the literature and some conceptual considerations', *Human Resource Management Review*, 12, 2 (2002), pp. 237–68.

126 J. E. Bono and M. A. Vey, 'Toward understanding emotional management at work: a quantitative review of emotional labor research', in C. E. Härtel and W. J. Zerbe (eds), *Emotions in Organizational Behavior* (Mahwah, NJ: Lawrence Erlbaum Associates, Publishers, 2005), pp. 213–33.

127 Kruml and Geddes, 'Catching fire without burning out'.

Foundations of group behaviour

Learning Objectives

After studying this chapter, you should be able to:

1 Define *group* and differentiate between different types of groups.

2 Identify the five stages of group development.

3 Show how role requirements change in different situations.

4 Demonstrate how norms and status exert influence on an individual's behaviour.

5 Show how group size affects group performance.

6 Contrast the benefits and disadvantages of cohesive groups.

7 Contrast the strengths and weaknesses of group decision making.

8 Compare the effectiveness of interacting, brainstorming, nominal and electronic meeting groups.

9 Evaluate evidence for cultural differences in group status and social loafing, as well as the effects of diversity in groups.

Madness is the exception
in individuals but the rule
in groups.

Friedrich Nietzsche

Brainstorming: A lousy idea for ideas?

Getty Images

You know the routine. Gather a small group of people together. Appoint someone to write the ideas on a flipchart (or type them on a laptop). It's called brainstorming, and it's been around for a long time.

Some brainstorming sessions founder because group members are afraid of saying something stupid. Joe Polidoro, a manager who has worked at several banks, says of brainstorming sessions, 'We sit there looking embarrassed like we're all new to a nudist colony.'

Others struggle with the scheduled nature of such sessions. Some feel as if they're put in a room and told, 'Okay, be creative now.' 'I'm more mercurial than that,' says Kate Lee, a former manager at GE.

Others think the whole idea of brainstorming is fatally flawed, that such sessions rarely produce the creative ideas they are meant to produce. Martha McGuire, senior VP of a bank, argued that the majority of recommendations resulting from brainstorming sessions are obvious. 'You end up with a more pedestrian solution than you would have had, had you not held the session,' she says.

Some argue that the real purpose of brainstorming sessions is not to produce the best idea. Rather, it's to get buy-in for decisions that have already been made. Christopher Holland, a policy analyst for the Australian government, said, 'These things are usually designed to give people the idea that they have input into decisions when the decisions have already been decided.'

One researcher argues that the problems of brainstorming demonstrate the problems of groups. 'If you leave groups to their own devices,' he says, 'they're going to do a very miserable job.'

Source: J. Sondberg, 'Brainstorming works best if people scramble for ideas on their own', *Wall Street Journal*, 13 June 2006, p. B1.

From what you just read, you might think groups are hopeless, but that's not the case. Groups have their place – and their pitfalls. Before we launch into a discussion of these issues, first examine your own attitude toward working in groups. Take the following self-assessment and answer the accompanying questions.

SELF-ASSESSMENT LIBRARY

Do I have a negative attitude toward working in groups?

In the Self-assessment library (available online), take assessment IV.E.1 (What is my attitude toward working in groups?) and answer the following questions.

1. Are you surprised by your results? If yes, why? If not, why not?

2. Do you think it is important to always have a positive attitude toward working in groups? Why or why not?

---

1 Define *group* and differentiate between different types of groups.

The objectives of this chapter and Chapter 10 are to introduce you to basic group concepts, provide you with a foundation for understanding how groups work, and show you how to create effective teams. Let's begin by defining *group* and explaining why people join groups.

Defining and classifying groups

group
Two or more individuals, interacting and interdependent, who have come together to achieve particular objectives.

formal group
A designated work group defined by an organization's structure.

informal group
A group that is neither formally structured nor organizationally determined; such a group appears in response to the need for social contact.

command group
A group composed of the individuals who report directly to a given manager.

task group
People working together to complete a job task.

A **group** is defined as two or more individuals, interacting and interdependent, who have come together to achieve particular objectives. Groups can be either formal or informal. By **formal groups**, we mean those defined by the organization's structure, with designated work assignments establishing tasks. In formal groups, the behaviours that team members should engage in are stipulated by and directed toward organizational goals. Six members making up an airline flight crew are an example of a formal group. In contrast, **informal groups** are alliances that are neither formally structured nor organizationally determined. These groups are natural formations in the work environment that appear in response to the need for social contact. Three employees from different departments who regularly eat lunch or have coffee together are an example of an informal group. These types of interactions among individuals, even though informal, deeply affect their behaviour and performance.

It's possible to further subclassify groups as command, task, interest, or friendship groups.[1] Command and task groups are dictated by formal organization, whereas interest and friendship groups are informal alliances.

A **command group** is determined by the organization chart. It is composed of the individuals who report directly to a given manager. A primary school principal and her 18 teachers form a command group, as do a director of postal audits and his five inspectors.

Task groups, also organizationally determined, represent individuals working together to complete a job task. However, a task group's boundaries are not limited to its immediate hierarchical superior. It can cross command relationships. For instance, if a university student is accused of a campus crime, dealing with the problem might require communication and coordination among the dean of academic affairs, the dean of students, the registrar, the director of security and the student's advisor. Such a formation would constitute a task group. It should be noted that all command groups are also task groups, but because task groups can cut across the organization, the reverse need not be true.

People who may or may not be aligned into common command or task groups may affiliate to attain a specific objective with which each is concerned. This is an **interest group**. Employees who band together to have their holiday schedules altered, to support a peer who has been fired,

EXHIBIT 9.1	WHY DO PEOPLE JOIN GROUPS?

Security. By joining a group, individuals can reduce the insecurity of 'standing alone'. People feel stronger, have fewer self-doubts and are more resistant to threats when they are part of a group.

Status. Inclusion in a group that is viewed as important by others provides recognition and status for its members.

Self-esteem. Groups can provide people with feelings of self-worth. That is, in addition to conveying status to those outside the group, membership can also give increased feelings of worth to the group members themselves.

Affiliation. Groups can fulfil social needs. People enjoy the regular interaction that comes with group membership. For many people, these on-the-job interactions are their primary source for fulfilling their needs for affiliation.

Power. What cannot be achieved individually often becomes possible through group action. There is power in numbers.

Goal achievement. There are times when it takes more than one person to accomplish a particular task – there is a need to pool talents, knowledge or power in order to complete a job. In such instances, management will rely on the use of a formal group.

---

interest group
People working together to attain a specific objective with which each is concerned.

friendship group
People brought together because they share one or more common characteristics.

or to seek improved working conditions represent the formation of a united body to further their common interest.

Groups often develop because the individual members have one or more common characteristics. We call these formations **friendship groups**. Social alliances, which frequently extend outside the work situation, can be based on similar age or ethnic heritage, support for Ajax football team, interest in the same alternative rock band, or the holding of similar political views, to name just a few such characteristics.

There is no single reason why individuals join groups. Because most people belong to a number of groups, it's obvious that different groups provide different benefits to their members. Exhibit 9.1 summarises the most popular reasons people have for joining groups.

Working in groups requires a certain amount of trust. Are you a trusting person? The Self-Assessment feature will help you decide.

Stages of group development

2 Identify the five stages of group development.

Groups generally pass through a standardised sequence in their evolution. We call this sequence the five-stage model of group development. Although research indicates that not all groups follow this pattern,[2] it is a useful framework for understanding group development. In this section, we describe the five-stage general model and an alternative model for temporary groups with deadlines.

The five-stage model

five-stage group-development model
The five distinct stages groups go through: forming, storming, norming, performing and adjourning.

forming stage
The first stage in group development, characterised by much uncertainty.

storming stage
The second stage in group development, characterised by intragroup conflict.

As shown in Figure 9.1, the **five-stage group-development model** characterises groups as proceeding through five distinct stages: forming, storming, norming, performing and adjourning.[3]

The first stage, the **forming stage**, is characterised by a great deal of uncertainty about the group's purpose, structure and leadership. Members 'test the waters' to determine what types of behaviours are acceptable. This stage is complete when members have begun to think of themselves as part of a group.

The **storming stage** is one of intragroup conflict. Members accept the existence of the group, but there is resistance to the constraints that the group imposes on individuality. Furthermore, there is conflict over who will control the group. When this stage is complete, there will be a relatively clear hierarchy of leadership within the group.

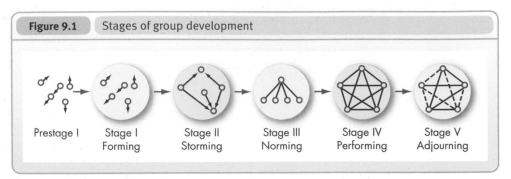

Figure 9.1 Stages of group development

Prestage I | Stage I Forming | Stage II Storming | Stage III Norming | Stage IV Performing | Stage V Adjourning

norming stage
The third stage in group development, characterised by close relationships and cohesiveness.

performing stage
The fourth stage in group development, during which the group is fully functional.

adjourning stage
The final stage in group development for temporary groups, characterised by concern with wrapping up activities rather than task performance.

The third stage is one in which close relationships develop and the group demonstrates cohesiveness. There is now a strong sense of group identity and camaraderie. This **norming stage** is complete when the group structure solidifies and the group has assimilated a common set of expectations of what defines correct member behaviour.

The fourth stage is the **performing stage**. The structure at this point is fully functional and accepted. Group energy has moved from getting to know and understand each other to performing the task at hand.

For permanent work groups, performing is the last stage in the group development. However, for temporary committees, teams, task forces, and similar groups that have a limited task to perform, there is an **adjourning stage**. In this stage, the group prepares for its disbandment. High task performance is no longer the group's top priority. Instead, attention is directed toward wrapping up activities. Responses of group members vary in this stage. Some are upbeat, basking in the group's accomplishments. Others may be depressed over the loss of camaraderie and friendships gained during the work group's life.

Many interpreters of the five-stage model have assumed that a group becomes more effective as it progresses through the first four stages. Although this assumption may be generally true, what makes a group effective is more complex than this model acknowledges.[4] Under some conditions, high levels of conflict may be conducive to high group performance. So we might expect to find situations in which groups in Stage II outperform those in Stage III or IV. Similarly,

© Bob Daemmrich/Corbis

Having passed through the forming, storming and norming phases of group development, this group of women at a Delphi Delco Electronics factory in Mexico now function as a permanent work group in the performing stage. Their structure is functional and accepted and each day they begin their work with a small shift meeting before performing their tasks.

groups do not always proceed clearly from one stage to the next. Sometimes, in fact, several stages go on simultaneously, as when groups are storming and performing at the same time. Groups even occasionally regress to previous stages. Therefore, even the strongest proponents of this model do not assume that all groups follow its five-stage process precisely or that Stage IV is always the most preferable.

Another problem with the five-stage model, in terms of understanding work-related behaviour, is that it ignores organizational context.[5] For instance, a study of a cockpit crew in an airliner found that within 10 minutes, three strangers assigned to fly together for the first time had become a high-performing group. What allowed for this speedy group development was the strong organizational context surrounding the tasks of the cockpit crew. This context provided the rules, task definitions, information and resources needed for the group to perform. They didn't need to develop plans, assign roles, determine and allocate resources, resolve conflicts and set norms the way the five-stage model predicts.

An alternative model for temporary groups with deadlines

Temporary groups with deadlines don't seem to follow the usual five-stage model. Studies indicate that they have their own unique sequencing of actions (or inaction): (1) Their first meeting sets the group's direction; (2) this first phase of group activity is one of inertia; (3) a transition takes place at the end of this first phase, which occurs exactly when the group has used up half its allotted time; (4) a transition initiates major changes; (5) a second phase of inertia follows the transition; and (6) the group's last meeting is characterised by markedly accelerated activity.[6] This pattern, called the **punctuated-equilibrium model**, is shown in Figure 9.2.

> **punctuated-equilibrium model**
> A set of phases that temporary groups go through that involves transitions between inertia and activity.

The first meeting sets the group's direction. A framework of behavioural patterns and assumptions through which the group will approach its project emerges in this first meeting. These lasting patterns can appear as early as the first few seconds of the group's existence. Once set, the group's direction becomes 'written in stone' and is unlikely to be reexamined throughout the first half of the group's life. This is a period of inertia – that is, the group tends to stand still or become locked into a fixed course of action. Even if it gains new insights that challenge initial patterns and assumptions, the group is incapable of acting on these new insights in Phase 1.

One of the most interesting discoveries made in studies of groups[7] was that each group experienced its transition at the same point in its calendar – precisely halfway between its first meeting and its official deadline – despite the fact that some groups spent as little as an hour on their project while others spent six months. It was as if the groups universally experienced a midlife crisis at this point. The midpoint appears to work like an alarm clock, heightening members' awareness that their time is limited and that they need to 'get moving'. This transition ends Phase 1 and is characterised by a concentrated burst of changes, dropping of old patterns

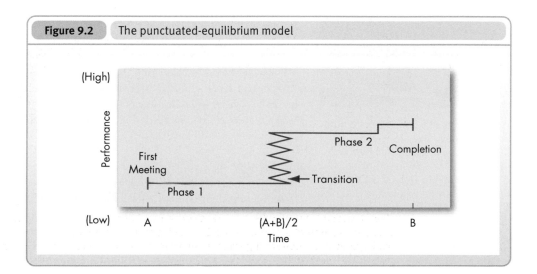

Figure 9.2	The punctuated-equilibrium model

and adoption of new perspectives. The transition sets a revised direction for Phase 2. Phase 2 is a new equilibrium or period of inertia. In this phase, the group executes plans created during the transition period.

The group's last meeting is characterised by a final burst of activity to finish its work. In summary, the punctuated-equilibrium model characterises groups as exhibiting long periods of inertia interspersed with brief revolutionary changes triggered primarily by their members' awareness of time and deadlines. Keep in mind, however, that this model doesn't apply to all groups. It's essentially limited to temporary task groups who are working under a time-constrained completion deadline.[8]

Group properties: roles, norms, status, size and cohesiveness

3 Show how role requirements change in different situations.

Work groups are not unorganized mobs. Work groups have properties that shape the behaviour of members and make it possible to explain and predict a large portion of individual behaviour within the group as well as the performance of the group itself. Some of these properties are roles, norms, status, group size and the degree of group cohesiveness.

Group property 1: roles

role
A set of expected behaviour patterns attributed to someone occupying a given position in a social unit.

Shakespeare said, 'All the world's a stage, and all the men and women merely players.' Using the same metaphor, all group members are actors, each playing a **role**. By this term, we mean a set of expected behaviour patterns attributed to someone occupying a given position in a social unit. The understanding of role behaviour would be dramatically simplified if each of us chose one role and 'played it out' regularly and consistently. Unfortunately, we are required to play a number of diverse roles, both on and off our jobs. As we'll see, one of the tasks in understanding behaviour is grasping the role that a person is currently playing.

For example, David Brosnahan is a plant manager with CF Industries, a large electrical equipment manufacturer in Dublin. He has a number of roles that he fulfils on that job – for instance, CF employee, member of middle management, electrical engineer and primary company spokesperson in the community. Off the job, David Brosnahan finds himself in still more roles: husband, father, Catholic, Rotarian, tennis player, member of the Hornby Country Club and president of his homeowners' association. Many of these roles are compatible; some create conflicts. For instance, how does his religious involvement influence his managerial decisions regarding layoffs, expense account padding and provision of accurate information to government agencies? A recent offer of promotion requires David to relocate, yet his family very much wants to stay in Dublin. Can the role demands of his job be reconciled with the demands of his husband and father roles?

The issue should be clear: Like David Brosnahan, we are all required to play a number of roles, and our behaviour varies with the role we are playing. David's behaviour when he attends work is different from his behaviour at the Rotary club later that same day. So different groups impose different role requirements on individuals.

Paul Hewson, aka Bono, plays a number of diverse roles. As well as being the main vocalist and songwriter for rock band U2, Bono co-owns the Clarence Hotel in Dublin, sits on the board of a private equity firm and has been nominated for the Nobel peace prize three times for his humanitarian work. Each of these positions imposes different role requirements on Bono.

Role identity

Certain attitudes and actual behaviours are consistent with a role, and they create the **role identity**. People have the ability to shift roles rapidly when they recognise that a situation and its demands clearly require major changes. For instance, when trade union stewards were promoted to supervisory positions, it was found that their attitudes changed from pro-union to pro-management within a few months of their promotion. When these promotions had to be rescinded later because of economic difficulties in the firm, it was found that the demoted supervisors had once again adopted their pro-union attitudes.[9]

Role perception

role identity
Certain attitudes and behaviours consistent with a role.

Our view of how we're supposed to act in a given situation is a **role perception**. Based on an interpretation of how we believe we are supposed to behave, we engage in certain types of behaviour. Where do we get these perceptions? We get them from stimuli all around us – friends, books, television. For example, we may form an impression of the work of doctors from watching a hospital based television drama. Of course, the primary reason apprenticeship programmes exist in many trades and professions is to allow beginners to watch an 'expert' so they can learn to act as they are supposed to.

role perception
An individual's view of how he or she is supposed to act in a given situation.

Role expectations

role expectations
How others believe a person should act in a given situation.

Role expectations are defined as the way others believe you should act in a given situation. How you behave is determined to a large extent by the role defined in the context in which you are acting. For instance, the role of a judge at the European Court of Justice is viewed as having propriety and dignity, while a football coach is seen as aggressive, dynamic and inspiring to his players.

psychological contract
An unwritten agreement that sets out what management expects from an employee and vice versa.

In the workplace, it can be helpful to look at the topic of role expectations through the perspective of the **psychological contract** – an unwritten agreement that exists between employees and their employer. This psychological contract sets out mutual expectations – what management expects from workers and vice versa.[10] In effect, this contract defines the behavioural expectations that go with every role. For instance, management is expected to treat employees justly, provide acceptable working conditions, clearly communicate what is a fair day's work, and give feedback on how well an employee is doing. Employees are expected to respond by demonstrating a good attitude, following directions, and showing loyalty to the organization.

What happens when role expectations as implied in the psychological contract are not met? If management is derelict in keeping up its part of the bargain, we can expect negative repercussions on employee performance and satisfaction. When employees fail to live up to expectations, the result is usually some form of disciplinary action up to and including firing.

Role conflict

role conflict
A situation in which an individual is confronted by divergent role expectations.

When an individual is confronted by divergent role expectations, the result is **role conflict**. It exists when an individual finds that compliance with one role requirement may make it difficult to comply with another.[11] At the extreme, it would include situations in which two or more role expectations are mutually contradictory.

Our previous discussion of the many roles David Brosnahan had to deal with included several role conflicts – for instance, David's attempt to reconcile the expectations placed on him as a husband and father with those placed on him as an executive with CF Industries. The former, as you will remember, emphasises stability and concern for the desire of his wife and children to remain in Dublin. CF, on the other hand, expects its employees to be responsive to the needs and requirements of the company. Although it might be in David's financial and career interests to accept a relocation, the conflict comes down to choosing between family and career role expectations.

An experiment: Zimbardo's prison experiment

One of the most illuminating role experiments was done a number of years ago by Stanford University psychologist Philip Zimbardo and his associates.[12] They created a 'prison' in the basement of the Stanford psychology building, hired at the equivalent of about €10 a day two dozen emotionally stable, physically healthy, law-abiding students who scored 'normal average' on extensive personality tests, randomly assigned them the role of either 'guard' or 'prisoner', and established some basic rules.

To get the experiment off to a 'realistic' start, Zimbardo got the cooperation of the local police department. The police went, unannounced, to each future prisoners' home, arrested and handcuffed them, put them in a squad car in front of friends and neighbours, and took them to police headquarters, where they were booked and fingerprinted. From there, they were taken to the Stanford prison.

At the start of the planned two-week experiment, there were no measurable differences between the individuals assigned to be guards and those chosen to be prisoners. In addition, the guards received no special training in how to be prison guards. They were told only to 'maintain law and order' in the prison and not to take any nonsense from the prisoners. Physical violence was forbidden. To simulate further the realities of prison life, the prisoners were allowed visits from relatives and friends. And although the mock guards worked eight-hour shifts, the mock prisoners were kept in their cells around the clock and were allowed out only for meals, exercise, toilet privileges, head-count lineups and work details.

It took the 'prisoners' little time to accept the authority positions of the guards or the mock guards to adjust to their new authority roles. After the guards crushed a rebellion attempt on the second day, the prisoners became increasingly passive. Whatever the guards 'dished out', the prisoners took. The prisoners actually began to believe and act as if they were, as the guards constantly reminded them, inferior and powerless. And every guard, at some time during the simulation, engaged in abusive, authoritative behaviour. For example, one guard said, 'I was surprised at myself . . . I made them call each other names and clean the toilets out with their bare hands. I practically considered the prisoners cattle, and I kept thinking: "I have to watch out for them in case they try something."' Another guard added, 'I was tired of seeing the prisoners in their rags and smelling the strong odours of their bodies that filled the cells. I watched them tear at each other on orders given by us. They didn't see it as an experiment. It was real and they were fighting to keep their identity. But we were always there to show them who was boss.' Surprisingly, during the entire experiment – even after days of abuse – not one prisoner said, 'Stop this. I'm a student like you. This is just an experiment!'

The simulation actually proved *too successful* in demonstrating how quickly individuals learn new roles. The researchers had to stop it after only six days because of the participants' pathological reactions. And remember, these were individuals chosen precisely for their normalcy and emotional stability.

What can we conclude from this prison simulation? The participants in this experiment had, like the rest of us, learned stereotyped conceptions of guard and prisoner roles from the mass media and their own personal experiences in power and powerlessness relationships gained at home (parent–child), in school (teacher–student), and in other situations. This, then, allowed them easily and rapidly to assume roles that were very different from their inherent personalities. In this case, we saw that people with no prior personality pathology or training in their roles could execute extreme forms of behaviour consistent with the roles they were playing.

SELF-ASSESSMENT LIBRARY

Do I trust others?

In the Self-assessment library (available online), take assessment II.B.3 (Do I trust others?). You can also check out assessment 11.B.4 (Do others see me as trustworthy?).

---

4 Demonstrate how norms and status exert influence on an individual's behaviour.

norms
Acceptable standards of behaviour within a group that are shared by the group's members.

Group properties 2 and 3: norms and status

Did you ever notice that golfers don't speak while their partners are putting on the green or that employees usually don't criticise their bosses in public? Why? The answer is norms.

All groups have established **norms** – that is, acceptable standards of behaviour that are shared by the group's members. Norms tell members what they ought and ought not to do under certain circumstances. From an individual's standpoint, they tell what is expected of you in certain situations. When agreed to and accepted by the group, norms act as a means of influencing the behaviour of group members with a minimum of external controls. Different groups, communities and societies have different norms, but they all have them.[13]

Norms can cover virtually any aspect of group behaviour.[14] Probably the most common group norm is a *performance norm*. Work groups typically provide their members with explicit

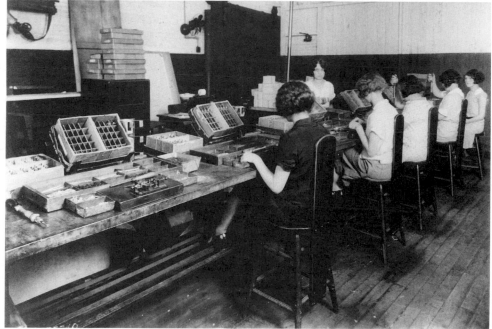

AT&T Archives and History Center

From the Hawthorne studies, observers gained valuable insights into how individual behaviour is influenced by group norms. The group of workers determined the level of fair output and established norms for individual work rates that conformed to the output. To enforce the group norms, workers used sarcasm, ridicule and even physical force to influence individual behaviours that were not acceptable to the group.

cues to how hard they should work, how to get the job done, what their level of output should be, what level of punctuality is appropriate, and the like. These norms are extremely powerful in affecting an individual employee's performance – they are capable of significantly modifying a performance prediction that was based solely on the employee's ability and level of personal motivation. Although arguably the most important, performance norms aren't the only kind. Other types include *appearance norms* (for example, dress codes, unspoken rules about when to look busy), *social arrangement norms* (for example, with whom group members eat lunch, whether to form friendships on and off the job), and *resource allocation norms* (for example, assignment of difficult jobs, distribution of resources like pay or equipment).

The Hawthorne studies

Behavioural scientists generally agree that full-scale appreciation of the importance norms play in influencing worker behaviour did not occur until the early 1930s. This enlightenment grew out of a series of studies undertaken at Western Electric Company's Hawthorne Works in Chicago, US, between 1924 and 1932.[15] Originally initiated by Western Electric officials and later overseen by Harvard professor Elton Mayo, the Hawthorne studies concluded that a worker's behaviour and sentiments were closely related, that group influences were significant in affecting individual behaviour, that group standards were highly effective in establishing individual worker output, and that money was less a factor in determining worker output than were group standards, sentiments, and security. Let us briefly discuss the Hawthorne investigations and demonstrate the importance of these findings in explaining group behaviour.

The Hawthorne researchers began by examining the relationship between the physical environment and productivity. Illumination and other working conditions were selected to represent this physical environment. The researchers' initial findings contradicted their anticipated results.

They began with illumination experiments with various groups of workers. The researchers manipulated the intensity of illumination upward and downward, while at the same time noting changes in group output. Results varied, but one thing was clear: In no case was the increase or decrease in output in proportion to the increase or decrease in illumination. So the researchers introduced a control group: An experimental group was presented with varying intensity of illumination, while the controlled unit worked under a constant illumination intensity. Again, the results were bewildering to the Hawthorne researchers. As the light level was increased in the experimental unit, output rose for both the control group and the experimental group. But to the surprise of the researchers, as the light level was dropped in the experimental group, productivity continued to increase in both groups. In fact, a productivity decrease was observed in the experimental group only when the light intensity had been reduced to that of moonlight. The Hawthorne researchers concluded that illumination intensity was only a minor influence among the many influences that affected an employee's productivity, but they could not explain the behaviour they had witnessed.

As a follow-up to the illumination experiments, the researchers began a second set of experiments in the relay assembly test room at Western Electric. A small group of women was isolated from the main work group so that their behaviour could be more carefully observed. They went about their job of assembling small telephone relays in a room laid out similarly to their normal department. The only significant difference was the placement in the room of a research assistant who acted as an observer – keeping records of output, rejects, working conditions and a daily log sheet describing everything that happened. Observations covering a multiyear period found that this small group's output increased steadily. The number of personal absences and those due to sickness was approximately one-third of those recorded by women in the regular production department. What became evident was that this group's performance was significantly influenced by its status of being a 'special' group. The women in the test room thought that being in the experimental group was fun, that they were in sort of an elite group, and that management was concerned with their interest by engaging in such experimentation. In essence, workers in both the illumination and assembly-test-room experiments were reacting to the increased attention they were receiving.

A third study, in the bank wiring observation room, was introduced to ascertain the effect of a sophisticated wage incentive plan. The assumption was that individual workers would maximise their productivity when they saw that it was directly related to economic rewards. The most important finding to come out of this study was that employees did not individually maximise their outputs. Rather, their output became controlled by a group norm that determined what was a proper day's work. Output was not only being restricted, but individual workers were giving erroneous reports. The total for a week would check with the total week's output, but the daily reports showed a steady level of output, regardless of actual daily production. What was going on?

Interviews determined that the group was operating well below its capability and was levelling output in order to protect itself. Members were afraid that if they significantly increased their output, the unit incentive rate would be cut, the expected daily output would be increased, layoffs might occur or slower workers would be reprimanded. So the group established its idea of a fair output – neither too much nor too little. They helped each other out to ensure that their reports were nearly level.

The norms the group established included a number of 'don'ts'. *Don't* be a rate-buster, turning out too much work. *Don't* be a chiseller, turning out too little work. *Don't* be a squealer on any of your peers. How did the group enforce these norms? Their methods were neither gentle nor subtle. They included sarcasm, name-calling, ridicule and even physical punches to the upper arm of any member who violated the group's norms. Members would also ostracise individuals whose behaviour was against the group's interest.

The Hawthorne studies made an important contribution to our understanding of group behaviour – particularly the significant place that norms have in determining individual work behaviour.

Conformity

As a member of a group, you desire acceptance by the group. Because of your desire for acceptance, you are susceptible to conforming to the group's norms. There is considerable evidence that groups can place strong pressures on individual members to change their attitudes and behaviours to conform to the group's standard.[16]

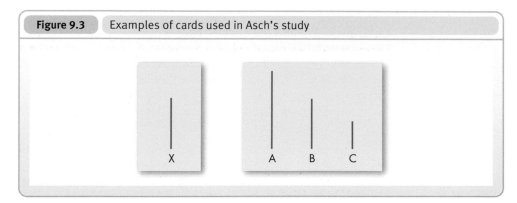

Figure 9.3 Examples of cards used in Asch's study

Do individuals conform to the pressures of all the groups to which they belong? Obviously not, because people belong to many groups, and their norms vary. In some cases, they may even have contradictory norms. So what do people do? They conform to the important groups to which they belong or hope to belong. The important groups have been called **reference groups**, and they're characterised as ones in which a person is aware of other members, defines themselves as a member or would like to be a member, and feels that the group members are significant to them.[17] The implication, then, is that all groups do not impose equal conformity pressures on their members.

The impact that group pressures for **conformity** can have on an individual member's judgement and attitudes was demonstrated in the now classic studies by Solomon Asch.[18] Asch made up groups of seven or eight people, who sat around a table and were asked to compare two cards held by the experimenter. One card had one line, and the other had three lines of varying length. As shown in Figure 9.3, one of the lines on the three-line card was identical to the line on the one-line card. Also as shown in Figure 9.3, the difference in line length was quite obvious; in fact, under ordinary conditions, subjects made fewer than 1 per cent errors. The object was to announce aloud which of the three lines matched the single line. But what happens if the members in the group begin to give incorrect answers? Will the pressures to conform result in an unsuspecting subject (USS) altering an answer to align with the others? That was what Asch wanted to know. So he arranged the group so that only the USS was unaware that the experiment was 'fixed'. The seating was prearranged: The USS was placed so as to be one of the last to announce a decision.

The experiment began with several sets of matching exercises. All the subjects gave the right answers. On the third set, however, the first subject gave an obviously wrong answer – for example, saying 'C' in Figure 9.3. The next subject gave the same wrong answer, and so did the others until it got to the unknowing subject. He knew 'B' was the same as 'X', yet everyone else had said 'C'. The decision confronting the USS was this: Do you publicly state a perception that differs from the preannounced position of the others in your group? Or do you give an answer that you strongly believe is incorrect in order to have your response agree with that of the other group members?

The results obtained by Asch demonstrated that over many experiments and many trials, 75 per cent of the subjects gave at least one answer that conformed – that is, that they knew was wrong but that was consistent with the replies of other group members – and the average for conformers was 37 per cent. What meaning can we draw from these results? They suggest that there are group norms that press us toward conformity. That is, we desire to be one of the group and avoid being visibly different.

The preceding conclusions are based on research that was conducted 50 years ago. Has time altered their validity? And should we consider these findings generalisable across cultures? The evidence indicates that there have been changes in the level of conformity over time; and Asch's findings are culture bound.[19] Specifically, levels of conformity have steadily declined since Asch's studies in the early 1950s. In addition, conformity to social norms is higher in collectivist cultures than in individualistic cultures. Nevertheless, even in individualistic countries, you should consider conformity to norms to still be a powerful force in groups.

reference groups
Important groups to which individuals belong or hope to belong and with whose norms individuals are likely to conform.

conformity
The adjustment of one's behaviour to align with the norms of the group.

Table 9.1	Typology of deviant workplace behaviour

Category	Examples
Production	Leaving early Intentionally working slowly Wasting resources
Property	Sabotage Lying about hours worked Stealing from the organization
Political	Showing favouritism Gossiping and spreading rumours Blaming co-workers
Personal aggression	Sexual harassment Verbal abuse Stealing from co-workers

Source: Adapted from S. L. Robinson and R. J. Bennett, 'A typology of deviant workplace behaviours: a multidimensional scaling study', *Academy of Management Journal*, April 1995, p. 565.

Deviant workplace behaviour

Alexander Andresen is frustrated by a co-worker who constantly spreads malicious and unsubstantiated rumours about him. Debra Hundley is tired of a member of her work team who, when confronted with a problem, takes out his frustration by yelling and screaming at her and other work team members. And Alice Dubois recently quit her job as a dental hygienist after being constantly sexually harassed by her employer.

deviant workplace behaviour
Voluntary behaviour that violates significant organizational norms and, in so doing, threatens the well-being of the organization or its members. Also called antisocial behaviour or workplace incivility.

What do these three episodes have in common? They represent employees being exposed to acts of *deviant workplace behaviour*.[20] **Deviant workplace behaviour** (also called *antisocial behaviour* or *workplace incivility*) is voluntary behaviour that violates significant organizational norms and, in doing so, threatens the well-being of the organization or its members. Table 9.1 provides a typology of deviant workplace behaviours, with examples of each.

Few organizations will admit to creating or condoning conditions that encourage and maintain deviant norms. Yet they exist. Employees report, for example, an increase in rudeness and disregard toward others by bosses and co-workers in recent years. And nearly half of employees who have suffered this incivility report that it has led them to think about changing jobs, with 12 per cent actually quitting because of it.[21]

As with norms in general, individual employees' antisocial actions are shaped by the group context within which they work. Evidence demonstrates that the antisocial behaviour exhibited by a work group is a significant predictor of an individual's antisocial behaviour at work.[22] In other words, deviant workplace behaviour is likely to flourish where it's supported by group norms. What this means for managers is that when deviant workplace norms surface, employee cooperation, commitment, and motivation are likely to suffer. This, in turn, can lead to reduced employee productivity and job satisfaction and increased turnover.

In addition, just being part of a group can increase an individual's deviant behaviour. In other words, someone who ordinarily wouldn't engage in deviant behaviour might be more likely to do so when working in a group. In fact, a recent study suggests that, compared to individuals working alone, those working in a group were more likely to lie, cheat, and steal. As shown in Figure 9.4, in this study, no individual working alone lied, but 22 per cent of those working in groups did. Moreover, individuals working in groups also were more likely to cheat (55 per cent of individuals working in a group cheated on a task versus 23 per cent of individuals working alone) and steal (29 per cent of individuals working in a group stole compared to only 10 per cent working alone).[23] Groups provide a shield of anonymity so that someone who ordinarily might be afraid of getting caught for stealing can rely on the fact that other group members had the same opportunity or reason to steal. This creates a false sense of confidence that may result in more aggressive behaviour. Thus, deviant behaviour depends on the accepted norms of the group – or even whether an individual is part of a group.[24]

| Figure 9.4 | Groups and deviant behaviour |

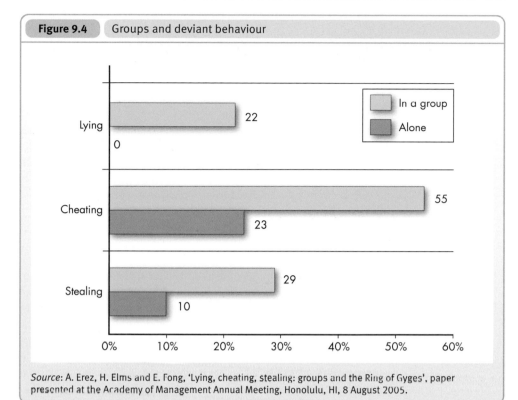

Source: A. Erez, H. Elms and E. Fong, 'Lying, cheating, stealing: groups and the Ring of Gyges', paper presented at the Academy of Management Annual Meeting, Honolulu, HI, 8 August 2005.

Status

status
A socially defined position or rank given to groups or group members by others.

Status – that is, a socially defined position or rank given to groups or group members by others – permeates every society. Even the smallest group will develop roles, rights and rituals to differentiate its members. Status is an important factor in understanding human behaviour because it is a significant motivator and has major behavioural consequences when individuals perceive a disparity between what they believe their status to be and what others perceive it to be.

What determines status?

status characteristics theory
A theory which states that differences in status characteristics create status hierarchies within groups.

According to **status characteristics theory**, status tends to be derived from one of three sources:[25]

1. **The power a person wields over others.** Because they likely control the group's resources, people who control the outcomes of a group through their power tend to be perceived as high status.

2. **A person's ability to contribute to a group's goals.** People whose contributions are critical to the group's success tend to have high status.

3. **An individual's personal characteristics.** Someone whose personal characteristics are positively valued by the group (for example, good looks, intelligence, money, or a friendly personality) typically has higher status than someone who has fewer valued attributes.

Status and norms

Status has been shown to have some interesting effects on the power of norms and pressures to conform. For instance, high-status members of groups are often given more freedom to deviate from norms than are other group members.[26] High-status people are also better able to resist conformity pressures than their lower-status peers. An individual who is highly valued by a group but who doesn't need or care very much about the social rewards the group provides is particularly able to pay minimal attention to conformity norms.[27]

The previous findings explain why many star athletes, celebrities, top-performing sales-people and outstanding academics seem oblivious to appearance or social norms that constrain their peers. As high-status individuals, they're given a wider range of discretion. But this is true only as long as the high-status person's activities aren't severely detrimental to group goal achievement.[28]

Status and group interaction

Interaction among members of groups is influenced by status. We find, for instance, that high-status people tend to be more assertive.[29] They speak out more often, criticise more, state more commands and interrupt others more often. But status differences actually inhibit diversity of ideas and creativity in groups because lower-status members tend to be less active participants in group discussions. In situations in which lower-status members possess expertise and insights that could aid the group, their expertise and insights are not likely to be fully utilised, thus reducing the group's overall performance.

Status inequity

It is important for group members to believe that the status hierarchy is equitable. Perceived inequity creates disequilibrium, which results in various types of corrective behaviour.[30]

The concept of equity presented in Chapter 6 applies to status. People expect rewards to be proportionate to costs incurred. If Dana and Anne are the two finalists for the head nurse position in a hospital, and it is clear that Dana has more seniority and better preparation for assuming the promotion, Anne will view the selection of Dana to be equitable. However, if Anne is chosen because she is the daughter-in-law of the hospital director, Dana will believe an injustice has been committed.

Groups generally agree within themselves on status criteria and, hence, there is usually high concurrence in group rankings of individuals. However, individuals can find themselves in a conflict situation when they move between groups whose status criteria are different or when they join groups whose members have heterogeneous backgrounds. For instance, business executives may use personal income or the growth rate of their companies as determinants of status. Government bureaucrats may use the size of their budgets. Blue-collar workers may use years of seniority. In groups made up of heterogeneous individuals or when heterogeneous groups are forced to be interdependent, status differences may initiate conflict as the group attempts to reconcile and align the differing hierarchies. As we'll see in Chapter 10, this can be a particular problem when management creates teams made up of employees from across varied functions within the organization.

Group property 4: size

5 Show how group size affects group performance.

Does the size of a group affect the group's overall behaviour? The answer to this question is a definite 'yes', but the effect is contingent on what dependent variables you look at.[31] The evidence indicates, for instance, that smaller groups are faster at completing tasks than are larger ones and that individuals perform better in smaller groups than in larger ones.[32] However, for groups engaged in problem solving, large groups consistently get better marks than their smaller counterparts.[33] Translating these results into specific numbers is a bit more hazardous, but we can offer some parameters. Large groups – those with a dozen or more members – are good for gaining diverse input. So if the goal of the group is fact-finding, larger groups should be more effective. On the other hand, smaller groups are better at doing something productive with that input. Groups of approximately seven members tend to be more effective for taking action.

One of the most important findings related to the size of a group has been labelled **social loafing**. Social loafing is the tendency for individuals to expend less effort when working collectively than when working individually.[34] It directly challenges the logic that the productivity of the group as a whole should at least equal the sum of the productivity of the individuals in that group.

A common stereotype about groups is that the sense of team spirit spurs individual effort and enhances the group's overall productivity. But that stereotype may be wrong. In the late 1920s, a German psychologist named Max Ringelmann compared the results of individual and group performance on a rope-pulling task.[35] He expected that the group's effort would be equal to the

social loafing
The tendency for individuals to expend less effort when working collectively than when working individually.

Studies indicate that these employees in Miles, China, collecting harvest grapes for the production of red wine, perform better in a group than when working alone. In collectivist societies such as China, employees show less propensity to engage in social loafing. Unlike individualistic cultures such as the United Kingdom, where people are more likely to be dominated by self-interest, the Chinese are more likely to be motivated by in-group goals.

sum of the efforts of individuals within the group. That is, three people pulling together should exert three times as much pull on the rope as one person, and eight people should exert eight times as much pull. Ringelmann's results, however, didn't confirm his expectations. One person pulling on a rope alone exerted an average of 63 kilograms of force. In groups of three, the per-person force dropped to 53 kilograms. And in groups of eight, it fell to only 31 kilograms per person.

Replications of Ringelmann's research with similar tasks have generally supported his findings.[36] Group performance increases with group size, but the addition of new members to the group has diminishing returns on productivity. So more may be better in the sense that the total productivity of a group of four is greater than that of three people, but the individual productivity of each group member declines.

What causes this social loafing effect? It may be due to a belief that others in the group are not carrying their fair share. If you see others as lazy or inept, you can reestablish equity by reducing your effort. Another explanation is the dispersion of responsibility. Because the results of the group cannot be attributed to any single person, the relationship between an individual's input and the group's output is clouded. In such situations, individuals may be tempted to become 'free riders' and coast on the group's efforts. In other words, there will be a reduction in efficiency when individuals think that their contribution cannot be measured.

The implications for OB of this effect on work groups are significant. When managers use collective work situations to enhance morale and teamwork, they must also provide means by which they can identify individual efforts. If this isn't done, management must weigh the potential losses in productivity from using groups against any possible gains in worker satisfaction.[37]

There are several ways to prevent social loafing: (1) Set group goals so that the group has a common purpose to strive toward; (2) increase intergroup competition, which again focuses the group on the shared outcome; (3) engage in peer evaluation so that each person's contribution to the group is evaluated by each group member; and (4) if possible, distribute group rewards, in part, based on each member's unique contributions.[38] Although none of these actions is a 'silver bullet' that will prevent social loafing in all cases, they should help minimise its effect.

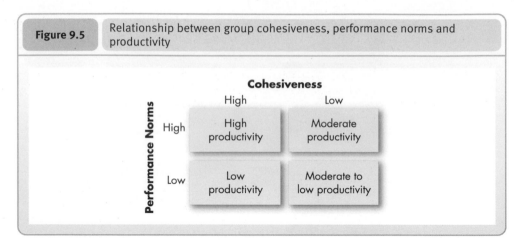

Figure 9.5 Relationship between group cohesiveness, performance norms and productivity

Group property 5: cohesiveness

6 Contrast the benefits and disadvantages of cohesive groups.

cohesiveness
The degree to which group members are attracted to each other and are motivated to stay in the group.

Groups differ in their **cohesiveness** – that is, the degree to which members are attracted to each other and are motivated to stay in the group.[39] For instance, some work groups are cohesive because the members have spent a great deal of time together, or the group's small size facilitates high interaction, or the group has experienced external threats that have brought members close together. Cohesiveness is important because it has been found to be related to group productivity.[40]

Studies consistently show that the relationship between cohesiveness and productivity depends on the performance-related norms established by the group.[41] If performance-related norms are high (for example, high output, quality work, cooperation with individuals outside the group), a cohesive group will be more productive than will a less cohesive group. But if cohesiveness is high and performance norms are low, productivity will be low. If cohesiveness is low and performance norms are high, productivity increases but it increases less than in the high-cohesiveness/high-norms situation. When cohesiveness and performance-related norms are both low, productivity tends to fall into the low-to-moderate range. These conclusions are summarised in Figure 9.5.

What can you do to encourage group cohesiveness? You might try one or more of the following suggestions: (1) Make the group smaller, (2) encourage agreement with group goals; (3) increase the time members spend together, (4) increase the status of the group and the perceived difficulty of attaining membership in the group, (5) stimulate competition with other groups, (6) give rewards to the group rather than to individual members, and (7) physically isolate the group.[42]

GROUP COHESIVENESS ACROSS CULTURES — GLOBAL

A recent study attempted to determine whether motivating work groups by giving them more complex tasks and greater autonomy resulted in increased group cohesiveness. Researchers studied bank teams in the United States, an individualist culture, and in Hong Kong, a collectivist culture. Both teams were composed of individuals from each respective country. The results showed that, regardless of what culture the teams were from, giving teams difficult tasks and more freedom to accomplish those tasks created a more tight-knit group. Consequently, team performance was enhanced.

However, the teams differed in the extent to which increases in task complexity and autonomy resulted in greater group cohesiveness. Teams in individualist cultures responded more strongly than did teams in collectivist cultures, became more united and committed, and, as a result, received higher performance ratings from their supervisors than teams from collectivist cultures. Why do these cultural differences exist? One explanation is that collectivist teams already have a strong predisposition to work together as a group, so there's less need for increased teamwork. What's the lesson? Managers in individualist cultures may need to work harder to increase team cohesiveness. One way to do this is to give teams more challenging assignments and provide them with more independence.

Source: Based on D. Man and S. S. K. Lam, 'The Effects of Job Complexity and Autonomy on Cohesiveness in Collectivist and Individualistic Work Groups: A Cross-Cultural Analysis', *Journal of Organizational Behavior*, December 2003, pp. 979–1001.

Group decision making

7 Contrast the strengths and weaknesses of group decision making.

The belief – characterised by juries – that two heads are better than one has long been accepted as a basic component of many countries' legal systems. This belief has expanded to the point that, today, many decisions in organizations are made by groups, teams or committees.[43] In this section, we discuss group decision making.

Groups versus the individual

Decision-making groups may be widely used in organizations, but does that imply that group decisions are preferable to those made by an individual alone? The answer to this question depends on a number of factors. Let's begin by looking at the strengths and weaknesses of group decision making.[44]

Strengths of group decision making

Groups generate *more complete information and knowledge*. By aggregating the resources of several individuals, groups bring more input into the decision process. In addition to more input, groups can bring heterogeneity to the decision process. They offer *increased diversity of views*. This opens up the opportunity for more approaches and alternatives to be considered. Finally, groups lead to increased *acceptance of a solution*. Many decisions fail after the final choice is made because people don't accept the solution. Group members who participated in making a decision are likely to enthusiastically support the decision and encourage others to accept it.

Weaknesses of group decision making

In spite of the pluses noted, group decisions have their drawbacks. They're time-consuming because groups typically take more time to reach a solution than would be the case if an individual were making the decision. There are *conformity pressures in groups*. The desire by group members to be accepted and considered an asset to the group can result in squashing any overt disagreement. Group discussion can be *dominated by one or a few members*. If this dominant coalition is composed of low- and medium-ability members, the group's overall effectiveness will suffer. Finally, group decisions suffer from *ambiguous responsibility*. In an individual decision, it's clear who is accountable for the final outcome. In a group decision, the responsibility of any single member is watered down.

Effectiveness and efficiency

Whether groups are more effective than individuals depends on the criteria you use to define effectiveness. In terms of *accuracy*, group decisions are generally more accurate than the decisions of the average individual in a group, but they are less accurate than the judgements of the most accurate group member.[45] If decision effectiveness is defined in terms of *speed*, individuals are superior. If *creativity* is important, groups tend to be more effective than individuals. And if effectiveness means the degree of *acceptance* the final solution achieves, the nod again goes to the group.[46]

But effectiveness cannot be considered without also assessing efficiency. In terms of efficiency, groups almost always stack up as a poor second to the individual decision maker. With few exceptions, group decision making consumes more work hours than if an individual were to tackle the same problem alone. The exceptions tend to be the instances in which, to achieve comparable quantities of diverse input, the single decision maker must spend a great deal of time reviewing files and talking to people. Because groups can include members from diverse areas, the time spent searching for information can be reduced. However, as we noted, these advantages in efficiency tend to be the exception. Groups are generally less efficient than individuals. In deciding whether to use groups, then, consideration should be given to assessing whether increases in effectiveness are more than enough to offset the reductions in efficiency.

'ARE TWO HEADS BETTER THAN ONE?' — MYTH *OR* SCIENCE?

Two heads are not necessarily always better than one. In fact, the evidence generally confirms the superiority of individuals over groups when brainstorming. The best individual in a group also makes better decisions than groups as a whole, though groups do tend to do better than the average group member.[47]

Research also indicates that groups are superior only when they meet certain criteria.[48] These criteria include:

1. **The group must have diversity among members.** To get benefits from 'two heads', the heads must differ in relevant skills and abilities.

2. **The group members must be able to communicate their ideas freely and openly.** This requires an absence of hostility and intimidation.

3. **The task being undertaken must be complex.** Relative to individuals, groups do better on complex rather than simple tasks.

Summary

In summary, groups offer an excellent vehicle for performing many of the steps in the decision-making process. They are a source of both breadth and depth of input for information gathering. If the group is composed of individuals with diverse backgrounds, the alternatives generated should be more extensive and the analysis more critical. When the final solution is agreed on, there are more people in a group decision to support and implement it. These pluses, however, can be more than offset by the time consumed by group decisions, the internal conflicts they create, and the pressures they generate toward conformity. Therefore, in some cases, individuals can be expected to make better decisions than groups.

Groupthink and Groupshift

Two byproducts of group decision making have received a considerable amount of attention from researchers in OB. As we'll show, these two phenomena have the potential to affect a group's ability to appraise alternatives objectively and to arrive at quality decision solutions.

The first phenomenon, called **groupthink**, is related to norms. It describes situations in which group pressures for conformity deter the group from critically appraising unusual, minority, or unpopular views. Groupthink is a disease that attacks many groups and can dramatically hinder their performance. The second phenomenon we shall discuss is called **groupshift**. It indicates that in discussing a given set of alternatives and arriving at a solution, group members tend to exaggerate the initial positions they hold. In some situations, caution dominates, and there is a conservative shift. More often, however, the evidence indicates that groups tend toward a risky shift. Let's look at each of these phenomena in more detail.

Groupthink

Have you ever felt like speaking up in a meeting, a classroom or an informal group but decided against it? One reason may have been shyness. On the other hand, you may have been a victim of groupthink, a phenomenon that occurs when group members become so enamoured of seeking concurrence that the norm for consensus overrides the realistic appraisal of alternative courses of action and the full expression of deviant, minority or unpopular views. It describes a deterioration in an individual's mental efficiency, reality testing and moral judgement as a result of group pressures.[49]

We have all seen the symptoms of the groupthink phenomenon:

1. Group members rationalise any resistance to the assumptions they have made. No matter how strongly the evidence may contradict their basic assumptions, members behave so as to reinforce those assumptions continually.

2. Members apply direct pressures on those who momentarily express doubts about any of the group's shared views or who question the validity of arguments supporting the alternative favoured by the majority.

3. Members who have doubts or hold differing points of view seek to avoid deviating from what appears to be group consensus by keeping silent about misgivings and even minimising to themselves the importance of their doubts.

groupthink
A phenomenon in which the norm for consensus overrides the realistic appraisal of alternative courses of action.

groupshift
A change in decision risk between a group's decision and an individual decision that a member within the group would make; the shift can be toward either conservatism or greater risk.

4. There appears to be an illusion of unanimity. If someone doesn't speak, it's assumed that they are in full accord. In other words, abstention becomes viewed as a 'yes' vote.[50]

The *Challenger* and *Columbia* space shuttle disasters and the failure of the main mirror on the *Hubble* telescope have been linked to decision processes at NASA in which groupthink symptoms were evident.[51] And groupthink was found to be a primary factor leading to setbacks at both British Airways and retailer Marks & Spencer as they tried to implement globalisation strategies.[52]

GROUPTHINK FOR AN ENRON JURY?

OB IN THE NEWS

Although Enron has gone down in history as the very symbol of corporate corruption, not every Enron employee behaved unethically. Twenty former Enron employees – most notably Ken Lay, Jeff Skilling and Andrew Fastow – were either convicted of or pleaded guilty to fraudulent behaviour. The conviction of another Enron executive you've probably never heard of – former broadband finance chief Kevin Howard – provides a fascinating, and disturbing, glimpse into how juries use group pressure to reach decisions.

Howard's first trial ended in a hung jury. In the second trial, he was found guilty of conspiracy, fraud and falsifying records. However, shortly after his conviction, two jurors and two alternate jurors said they were pressured by other jurors to reach a unanimous decision even though they believed Howard was innocent. Juror Ann Marie Campbell said, in a sworn statement, 'There was

just so much pressure to change my vote that I felt like we had to compromise and give in to the majority because I felt like there was no other choice.' Campbell said at one point a male juror tried to 'grab her by the shoulders' to convince her, and another 'banged his first on the table during deliberations'. Another jury member said, 'There was an atmosphere of "let's fry them."'

On appeal, a judge threw out Howard's conviction, based, in part, on the earlier judge's instruction to the convicting jury which pressured them to reach a unanimous decision. The Kevin Howard case shows how strong groupthink pressures can be and the degree to which individuals can be pressured to give in to the majority.

Source: K. Hays, 'Judge dismisses Enron convictions', *Houston (Texas) Chronicle*, 1 February 2007.

Groupthink appears to be closely aligned with the conclusions Asch drew in his experiments with a lone dissenter. Individuals who hold a position that is different from that of the dominant majority are under pressure to suppress, withhold or modify their true feelings and beliefs. As members of a group, we find it more pleasant to be in agreement – to be a positive part of the group – than to be a disruptive force, even if disruption is necessary to improve the effectiveness of the group's decisions.

Does groupthink attack all groups? No. It seems to occur most often when there is a clear group identity, when members hold a positive image of their group that they want to protect, and when the group perceives a collective threat to this positive image.[53] So groupthink is not a dissenter-suppression mechanism as much as it's a means for a group to protect its positive image. For NASA, its problems stem from its attempt to confirm its identity as 'the elite organization that could do no wrong'.[54]

What can managers do to minimise groupthink?[55] First, they can monitor group size. People grow more intimidated and hesitant as group size increases and, although there is no magic number that will eliminate groupthink, individuals are likely to feel less personal responsibility when groups get larger than about 10. Managers should also encourage group leaders to play an impartial role. Leaders should actively seek input from all members and avoid expressing their own opinions, especially in the early stages of deliberation. In addition, managers should appoint one group member to play the role of devil's advocate; this member's role is to overtly challenge the majority position and offer divergent perspectives. Still another suggestion is to use exercises that stimulate active discussion of diverse alternatives without threatening the group and intensifying identity protection. One such exercise is to have group members talk about dangers or risks involved in a decision and delaying discussion of any potential gains. Requiring members to first focus on the negatives of a decision alternative makes the group less likely to stifle dissenting views and more likely to gain an objective evaluation.

Groupshift

In comparing group decisions with the individual decisions of members within the group, evidence suggests that there are differences.[56] In some cases, group decisions are more conservative than individual decisions. More often, the shift is toward greater risk.[57]

What appears to happen in groups is that the discussion leads to a significant shift in the positions of members toward a more extreme position in the direction in which they were already leaning before the discussion. So conservative types become more cautious, and more aggressive types take on more risk. The group discussion tends to exaggerate the initial position of the group.

Groupshift can be viewed as actually a special case of groupthink. The decision of the group reflects the dominant decision-making norm that develops during the group's discussion. Whether the shift in the group's decision is toward greater caution or more risk depends on the dominant prediscussion norm.

The greater occurrence of the shift toward risk has generated several explanations for the phenomenon.[58] It has been argued, for instance, that discussion creates familiarisation among the members. As they become more comfortable with each other, they also become more bold and daring. Another argument is that most societies in developed nations value risk, that they admire individuals who are willing to take risks, and that group discussion motivates members to show that they are at least as willing as their peers to take risks. The most plausible explanation of the shift toward risk, however, seems to be that the group diffuses responsibility. Group decisions free any single member from accountability for the group's final choice. Greater risk can be taken because even if the decision fails, no one member can be held wholly responsible.

So how should you use the findings on groupshift? You should recognise that group decisions exaggerate the initial position of the individual members, that the shift has been shown more often to be toward greater risk, and that whether a group will shift toward greater risk or caution is a function of the members' prediscussion inclinations.

Having discussed group decision making and its pros and cons, we now turn to the techniques by which groups make decisions. These techniques reduce some of the dysfunctional aspects of group decision making.

8 Compare the effectiveness of interacting, brainstorming, nominal and electronic meeting groups.

FACE THE FACTS

- 'Groupthink' in the boardrooms of banks has been widely cited as contributing to the recent financial disasters.

- The term 'brainstorming' was originally coined by Alex Osborn in his 1940 work *Applied Imagination*. More recently, the term has been claimed to be insensitive, particularly to those with mental health problems, and alternatives terms such as 'mind showers' have been used. However, a poll of 15 leading mental health charities and campaign bodies found that none of the organizations considered 'brainstorming' as politically incorrect.

- Surveys of students reveal that students' biggest complaint regarding group projects is having to deal with social loafers.

Source: see M. Skapinker, 'Diversity fails to end boardroom "groupthink"', *Financial Times*, London: 26 May 2009. p. 13; M. Millar, 'Ignore the urban myth that brainstorming is insensitive', *Personnel Today*, 25 August 2005; C. Dommeyer (2007), 'Using the diary method to deal with social loafers on the group project: its effects on peer evaluations, group behavior, and attitudes', *Journal of Marketing Education*, 29, 2; pp. 175–86.

Group decision-making techniques

interacting groups
Typical groups in which members interact with each other face-to-face.

brainstorming
An idea-generation process that specifically encourages any and all alternatives while withholding any criticism of those alternatives.

The most common form of group decision making takes place in **interacting groups**. In these groups, members meet face-to-face and rely on both verbal and nonverbal interaction to communicate with each other. But as our discussion of groupthink demonstrated, interacting groups often censor themselves and pressure individual members toward conformity of opinion. Brainstorming, the nominal group technique, and electronic meetings have been proposed as ways to reduce many of the problems inherent in the traditional interacting group.

Brainstorming is meant to overcome pressures for conformity in an interacting group that retard the development of creative alternatives.[59] It does this by utilising an idea-generation process that specifically encourages any and all alternatives while withholding any criticism of those alternatives.

In a typical brainstorming session, five to ten people sit around a table. The group leader states the problem in a clear manner so that it is understood by all participants. Members then

Figure 9.6

Source: S. Adams, *Build a Better Life by Stealing Office Supplies* (Kansas City, MO: Andrews & McMeal, 1991), p. 31. Dilbert reprinted with permission of Knight Features Ltd.

'freewheel' as many alternatives as they can in a given length of time. No criticism is allowed, and all the alternatives are recorded for later discussion and analysis. One idea stimulates others, and judgements of even the most bizarre suggestions are withheld until later to encourage group members to 'think the unusual'.

Brainstorming may indeed generate ideas – but not in a very efficient manner. Research consistently shows that individuals working alone generate more ideas than a group in a brainstorming session. Why? One of the primary reasons is because of 'production blocking'. In other words, when people are generating ideas in a group, there are many people talking at once, which blocks the thought process and eventually impedes the sharing of ideas.[60] The following two techniques go further than brainstorming by offering methods that help groups arrive at a preferred solution.[61]

The **nominal group technique** restricts discussion or interpersonal communication during the decision-making process, hence the term *nominal*. Group members are all physically present, as in a traditional committee meeting, but members operate independently. Specifically, a problem is presented and then the group takes the following steps:

1. Members meet as a group, but before any discussion takes place, each member independently writes down ideas on the problem.

2. After this silent period, each member presents one idea to the group. Each member takes a turn, presenting a single idea, until all ideas have been presented and recorded. No discussion takes place until all ideas have been recorded.

3. The group discusses the ideas for clarity and evaluates them.

4. Each group member silently and independently rank-orders the ideas. The idea with the highest aggregate ranking determines the final decision.

The chief advantage of the nominal group technique is that it permits a group to meet formally but does not restrict independent thinking, as does an interacting group. Research generally shows that nominal groups outperform brainstorming groups.[62]

nominal group technique
A group decision-making method in which individual members meet face-to-face to pool their judgements in a systematic but independent fashion.

Table 9.2	Evaluating group effectiveness			
Effectiveness criteria	**Type of group**			
	Interacting	**Brainstorming**	**Nominal**	**Electronic**
Number and quality of ideas	Low	Moderate	High	High
Social pressure	High	Low	Moderate	Low
Money costs	Low	Low	Low	High
Speed	Moderate	Moderate	Moderate	Moderate
Task orientation	Low	High	High	High
Potential for interpersonal conflict	High	Low	Moderate	Low
Commitment to solution	High	Not applicable	Moderate	Moderate
Development of group cohesiveness	High	High	Moderate	Low

electronic meeting
A meeting in which members interact on computers, allowing for anonymity of comments and aggregation of votes.

The most recent approach to group decision making blends the nominal group technique with sophisticated computer technology.[63] It's called a computer-assisted group, or an **electronic meeting**. Once the required technology is in place, the concept is simple. Up to 50 people sit around a horseshoe-shaped table, empty except for a series of computer terminals. Issues are presented to participants, who type their responses into their computers. Individual comments, as well as aggregate votes, are displayed on a projection screen. The proposed advantages of electronic meetings are anonymity, honesty and speed. Participants can anonymously type any message they want, and it flashes on the screen for all to see at the push of a participant's keyboard key. This technique also allows people to be brutally honest without penalty. And it's supposedly fast because chitchat is eliminated, discussions don't digress and many participants can 'talk' at once without stepping on one another's toes. The early evidence, however, indicates that electronic meetings don't achieve most of their proposed benefits. Evaluations of numerous studies found that electronic meetings actually led to *decreased* group effectiveness, required *more* time to complete tasks, and resulted in *reduced* member satisfaction compared to face-to-face groups.[64] Nevertheless, current enthusiasm for computer-mediated communications suggests that this technology is here to stay and is likely to increase in popularity in the future.

Each of these four group decision techniques has its own set of strengths and weaknesses. The choice of one technique over another depends on what criteria you want to emphasise and the cost–benefit trade-off. For instance, as Table 9.2 indicates, an interacting group is good for achieving commitment to a solution, brainstorming develops group cohesiveness, the nominal group technique is an inexpensive means for generating a large number of ideas, and electronic meetings minimise social pressures and conflicts.

Global implications

9 Evaluate evidence for cultural differences in group status and social loafing, as well as the effects of diversity in groups.

As in most other areas of OB, most of the research on groups has been conducted in North America and to a lesser extent western Europe, but that situation is changing quickly. There are three areas of groups research where cross-cultural issues are particularly important.

Status and culture

Do cultural differences affect status? The answer is a resounding 'yes'.[65]

The importance of status does vary between cultures. Countries also differ on the criteria that create status. For instance, status for Latin Americans and Asians tends to be derived from family position and formal roles held in organizations. In contrast, although status is still important in countries such as the United States and Australia, it is often bestowed more for accomplishments than on the basis of titles and family trees.[66]

The message here is to make sure you understand who and what holds status when interacting with people from a culture different from your own. A German manager who doesn't understand that physical office size is often not a measure of a Japanese executive's position is likely to unintentionally offend his overseas counterparts and, in so doing, lessen his interpersonal effectiveness.

Social loafing

Social loafing appears to have a Western bias. It's consistent with individualistic cultures, such as the United Kingdom, the Netherlands, United States and Canada, that are dominated by self-interest. It is *not* consistent with collective societies, in which individuals are motivated by in-group goals. For instance, in studies comparing employees from the United States with employees from the People's Republic of China and Israel (both collectivist societies), the Chinese and Israelis showed no propensity to engage in social loafing. In fact, the Chinese and Israelis actually performed better in a group than when working alone.

Group diversity

More and more research is being done on how diversity influences group performance. Some of this research looks at cultural diversity, and some of it considers diversity on other characteristics (such as race or gender). Collectively, the research points to both benefits and costs from group diversity.

In terms of costs, diversity appears to lead to increased group conflict, especially in the early stages of a group's tenure. This conflict often results in lower group morale and group members dropping out. One study of groups that were either culturally diverse (composed of people from different countries) or homogeneous (composed of people from the same country) found that on a wilderness survival exercise (not unlike the 'Experiential exercise' in this chapter see p. 253), the diverse and homogenous groups performed equally well, but the diverse groups were less satisfied with their groups, were less cohesive and had more conflict.[67]

In terms of the benefits to diversity, more evidence is accumulating that, over time, culturally and demographically diverse groups may perform better, if they can get over their initial conflicts. Why might this be the case?

Research shows that surface-level diversity – observable characteristics such as national origin, race and gender – actually cues people to possible differences in deep-level diversity – underlying attitudes, values and opinions. One researcher argues, 'The mere presence of diversity you can see, such as a person's race or gender, actually cues a team that there's likely to be differences of opinion.' Although those differences of opinion can lead to conflict, they also provide an opportunity to solve problems in unique ways.

One study of jury behaviour, for example, found that diverse juries were more likely to deliberate longer, share more information and make fewer factual errors when discussing evidence. Interestingly, two studies of MBA student groups found that surface-level diversity led to greater openness even when there was no deep-level diversity. In such cases, the surface-level diversity of a group may subconsciously cue team members to be more open-minded in their views.[68]

In sum, the impact of cultural diversity on groups is a mixed bag. It is difficult to be in a diverse group in the short term. However, if the group members can weather their differences, over time, diversity may help them be more open-minded and creative, thus allowing them to do better in the long run. However, we should realise that even when there are positive effects of diversity on group performance, they are unlikely to be especially strong. As one review stated, 'the business case (in terms of demonstrable financial results) for diversity remains hard to support based on the extant research'.[69]

Summary and implications for managers

Performance

A number of group properties show a relationship with performance. Among the most prominent are role perception, norms, status differences, size of the group and cohesiveness.

There is a positive relationship between role perception and an employee's performance evaluation.[70] The degree of congruence that exists between an employee and the boss in the perception of the employee's job influences the degree to which the boss will judge that employee as an effective performer. To the extent that the employee's role perception fulfils the boss's role expectations, the employee will receive a higher performance evaluation.

Norms control group member behaviour by establishing standards of right and wrong. The norms of a given group can help to explain the behaviours of its members for managers. When norms support high output, managers can expect individual performance to be markedly higher than when group norms aim to restrict output. Similarly, norms that support antisocial behaviour increase the likelihood that individuals will engage in deviant workplace activities.

Status inequities create frustration and can adversely influence productivity and the willingness to remain with an organization. Among individuals who are equity sensitive, incongruence is likely to lead to reduced motivation and an increased search for ways to bring about fairness (for example, taking another job). In addition, because lower-status people tend to participate less in group discussions, groups characterised by high status differences among members are likely to inhibit input from the lower-status members and to underperform their potential.

The impact of size on a group's performance depends on the type of task in which the group is engaged. Larger groups are more effective at fact-finding activities. Smaller groups are more effective at action-taking tasks. Our knowledge of social loafing suggests that if management uses larger groups, efforts should be made to provide measures of individual performance within the group.

Cohesiveness can play an important function in influencing a group's level of productivity. Whether it does depends on the group's performance-related norms.

Satisfaction

As with the role perception–performance relationship, high congruence between a boss and an employee as to the perception of the employee's job shows a significant association with high employee satisfaction.[71] Similarly, role conflict is associated with job-induced tension and job dissatisfaction.[72]

Most people prefer to communicate with others at their own status level or a higher one rather than with those below them.[73] As a result, we should expect satisfaction to be greater among employees whose job minimises interaction with individuals who are lower in status than themselves.

The group size–satisfaction relationship is what one would intuitively expect: Larger groups are associated with lower satisfaction.[74] As size increases, opportunities for participation and social interaction decrease, as does the ability of members to identify with the group's accomplishments. At the same time, having more members also prompts dissension, conflict, and the formation of subgroups, which all act to make the group a less pleasant entity of which to be a part.

POINT/COUNTERPOINT

All jobs should be designed around groups

POINT →

Groups, not individuals, are the ideal building blocks for an organization. There are several reasons for designing all jobs around groups.

First, in general, groups make better decisions than the average individual acting alone.

Second, with the growth in technology, society is becoming more intertwined. Look at the growth of social networking sites such as MySpace, Facebook and YouTube. People are connected anyway, so why not design work in the same way?

Third, small groups are good for people. They can satisfy social needs and provide support for employees in times of stress and crisis. Evidence indicates that social support – both when they provide it and when they receive it – makes people happier and even allows them to live longer.

Fourth, groups are very effective tools for implementation for decisions. Groups gain commitment from their members so that group decisions are likely to be willingly and more successfully carried out.

Fifth, groups can control and discipline individual members in ways that are often extremely difficult through impersonal quasi-legal disciplinary systems. Group norms are powerful control devices.

Sixth, groups are a means by which large organizations can fend off many of the negative effects of increased size.

COUNTERPOINT ←

Capitalistic countries such as Australia, the United States, Canada and the United Kingdom value the individual. Designing jobs around groups is inconsistent with the economic values of these countries. Moreover, as capitalism and entrepreneurship have spread throughout eastern Europe, Asia and other more collective societies, we should expect to see *less* emphasis on groups and *more* on the individual in workplaces throughout the world. Let's look at the United States to see how cultural and economic values shape employee attitudes toward groups.

The United States was built on the ethic of the individual. Its culture strongly values individual achievement and

Groups help prevent communication lines from growing too long, the hierarchy from growing too steep, and individuals from getting lost in the crowd.

The rapid growth of team-based organizations in recent years suggests that we may well be on our way toward a day when almost all jobs are designed around groups.

encourages competition. Even in team sports, people want to identify individuals for recognition. US adults enjoy being part of a group in which they can maintain a strong individual identity. They don't enjoy sublimating their identity to that of the group. When they are assigned to groups, all sorts of bad things happen, including conflict, groupthink, social loafing and deviant behaviour.

Though teams have grown in popularity as a device for employers to organize people and tasks, we should expect resistance to any effort to treat individuals solely as members of a group – especially among workers raised in capitalistic economies.

QUESTIONS FOR REVIEW

1. Define *group*? What are the different types of groups?

2. What are the five stages of group development?

3. Do role requirements change in different situations? If so, how?

4. How do group norms and status influence an individual's behaviour?

5. How does group size affect group performance?

6. What are the advantages and limitations of cohesive groups?

7. What are the strengths and weaknesses of group (versus individual) decision making?

8. How effective are interacting, brainstorming, nominal and electronic meeting groups?

9. What is the evidence for the effect of culture on group status and social loafing? How does diversity affect groups and their effectiveness over time?

Experiential exercise

WILDERNESS SURVIVAL

You are a member of a hiking party. After reaching base camp on the first day, you decide to take a quick sunset hike by yourself. After a few exhilarating miles, you decide to return to camp. On your way back, you realise that you are lost. You have shouted for help, to no avail. It is now dark. And getting cold.

Your task

Without communicating with anyone else in your group, read the following scenarios and choose the best answer. Keep track of your answers on a sheet of paper. You have 10 minutes to answer the 10 questions.

1. The first thing you decide to do is to build a fire. However, you have no matches, so you use the bow-and-drill method. What is the bow-and-drill method?

(a) A dry, soft stick is rubbed between one's hands against a board of supple green wood.

(b) A soft green stick is rubbed between one's hands against a hardwood board.

(c) A straight stick of wood is quickly rubbed back-and-forth against a dead tree.

(d) Two sticks (one being the bow, the other the drill) are struck to create a spark.

2. It occurs to you that you can also use the fire as a distress signal. When signalling with fire, how do you form the international distress signal?

(a) 2 fires

(b) 4 fires in a square

(c) 4 fires in a cross

(d) 3 fires in a line

3. You are very thirsty. You go to a nearby stream and collect some water in the small metal cup you have in you backpack. How long should you boil the water?

(a) 15 minutes

(b) A few seconds

(c) 1 hour

(d) It depends on the altitude.

4. You are very hungry, so you decide to eat what appear to be edible berries. When performing the universal edibility test, what should you do?

(a) Do not eat for 2 hours before the test.

(b) If the plant stings your lip, confirm the sting by holding it under your tongue for 15 minutes.

(c) If nothing bad has happened 2 hours after digestion, eat half a cup of the plant and wait again.

(d) Separate the plant into its basic components and eat each component, one at a time.

5. Next, you decide to build a shelter for the evening. In selecting a site, what do you *not* have to consider?

(a) It must contain material to make the type of shelter you need.

(b) It must be free of insects, reptiles and poisonous plants.

(c) It must be large enough and level enough for you to lie down comfortably.

(d) It must be on a hill so you can signal rescuers and keep an eye on your surroundings.

6. In the shelter that you built, you notice a spider. You heard from a fellow hiker that black widow spiders populate the area. How do you identify a black widow spider?

(a) Its head and abdomen are black; its thorax is red.

(b) It is attracted to light.

(c) It runs away from light.

(d) It is a dark spider with a red or orange marking on the female's abdomen.

7. After getting some sleep, you notice that the night sky has cleared, so you decide to try to find your way back to base camp. You believe you should travel north and can use the North Star for navigation. How do you locate the North Star?

(a) Hold your right hand up as far as you can and look between your index and middle fingers.

(b) Find Sirius and look 60 degrees above it and to the right.

(c) Look for the Big Dipper and follow the line created by its cup end.

(d) Follow the line of Orion's belt.

8. You come across a fast-moving stream. What is the best way to cross it?

(a) Find a spot downstream from a sandbar, where the water will be calmer.

(b) Build a bridge.

(c) Find a rocky area, as the water will be shallow and you will have hand- and footholds.

(d) Find a level stretch where it breaks into a few channels.

9. After walking for about an hour, you feel several spiders in your clothes. You don't feel any pain, but you know some spider bites are painless. Which of these spider bites is painless?

(a) Black widow

(b) Brown recluse

(c) Wolf spider

(d) Harvestman (daddy longlegs)

10. You decide to eat some insects. Which insects should you avoid?

(a) Adults that sting or bite

(b) Caterpillars and insects that have a pungent odour

(c) Hairy or brightly coloured ones

(d) All the above

Group task

Break into groups of five or six people. Now imagine that your whole group is lost. Answer each question as a group, employing a consensus approach to reach each decision. Once the group comes to an agreement, write the decision down on the same sheet of paper that you used for your individual answers. You will have approximately 20 minutes for the group task.

Scoring your answers

Your instructor will provide you with the correct answers, which are based on expert judgements in these situations. Once you have received the answers, calculate (A) your individual score; (B) your group's score; (C) the average individual score in the group; (D) the best individual score in the group. Write these down and consult with your group to ensure that these scores are accurate.

A. Your individual score _____

B. Your group's score _____

C. Average individual score in group _____

D. Best individual score in group _____

Discussion questions

1. How did your group (B) perform relative to yourself (A)?

2. How did your group (B) perform relative to the average individual score in the group (C)?

3. How did your group (B) perform relative to the best individual score in the group (D)?

4. Compare your results with those of other groups. Did some groups do a better job of outperforming individuals than others?

5. What do these results tell you about the effectiveness of group decision making?

6. What can groups do to make group decision-making more effective?

Ethical dilemma

DEALING WITH SHIRKERS

We've noted that one of the most common problems in groups is social loafing, which means group members contribute less than if they were working on their own. We might call such individuals 'shirkers' – those who are contributing far less than other group members.

Most of us have experienced social loafing or shirking, in groups. And we may even admit to times when we shirked ourselves. We discussed earlier in the chapter some ways of discouraging social loafing, such as limiting group size, holding individuals responsible for their contributions, and setting group goals. While these tactics may be effective, in our experience, many students simply work around shirkers. 'We just did it ourselves – it was easier that way,' says one group member.

Consider the following questions for dealing with shirking in groups:

1. If group members end up 'working around' shirkers, do you think this information should be communicated to the instructor so that individual's contribution to the project is judged more fairly? If so, does the group have an ethical responsibility to communicate this to the shirking group member? If not, isn't the shirking group member unfairly reaping the rewards of a 'free ride'?

2. Do you think confronting the shirking group member is justified? Does this depend on the skills of the shirker (whether he is capable of doing good-quality work)?

3. Social loafing has been found to be higher in Western, more individualist nations, than in other countries. Do you think this means we should tolerate shirking in these countries to a greater degree than if it occurred with someone from a more collectivist nation?

CASE INCIDENT 1

Role conflict among telephone service employees

Maggie Becker, 24, is a marketing manager for Kavu, a small chain of coffee shops. Recently, Maggie's wealthy uncle passed away and left to Maggie, his only niece, €100,000. Maggie considers her current salary to be adequate to meet her current living expenses, so she'd like to invest the money so that when she buys a house, she'll have a nice nest egg on which to draw.

One of Maggie's neighbours, Brian, is a financial advisor. Brian told Maggie there was a virtually endless array of investment options. She asked him to present her with two of the best options, and this is what he came up with:

1. **A very low-risk investment bond.** With this option, based on the information Brian provided, Maggie estimates that after 5 years, she stands virtually zero chance of losing money, with an expected gain of approximately €7,000.

2. **A moderate-risk property fund.** Based on the information Brian provided her, Maggie estimates that with this option, she stands a 50 per cent chance of making €40,000 but also a 50 per cent chance of losing €20,000.

Maggie prides herself on being rational and objective in her thinking. However, she's unsure of what to do in this case. Brian refuses to help her, telling her that she's already limited herself by asking for only two options. While driving to her parents' house for the weekend, Maggie finds herself vacillating between the two options. Her older brother is also visiting the folks this weekend, so Maggie decides to gather her family around the table after dinner, lay out the two options, and go with their decision. 'You know the old saying – two heads are better than one,' she says to herself, 'so four heads should be even better.'

Questions

1. Has Maggie made a good decision about the way she is going to make the decision?

2. Which investment would you choose? Why?

3. Which investment do you think most people would choose?

4. Based on what you have learned about groupshift, which investment do you think Maggie's family will choose?

CASE INCIDENT 2

The dangers of groupthink

Sometimes, the desire to maintain group harmony overrides the importance of making sound decisions. When that occurs, team members are said to engage in groupthink. Here are some examples:

- A civilian worker at a large Air Force base recalls a time that groupthink overcame her team's decision-making ability. She was a member of a process improvement team that an Air Force general had formed to develop a better way to handle the base's mail, which included important letters from high-ranking military individuals. The team was composed mostly of civilians, and it took almost a month to come up with a plan. The problem: The plan was not a process improvement. Recalls the civilian worker, 'I was horrified. What used to be 8 steps; now there were 19.' The team had devised a new system that resulted in each piece of mail being read by several middle managers before reaching its intended recipient. The team's new plan slowed down the mail considerably, with an average delay of two weeks. Even though the team members all knew that the new system was worse than its predecessor, no one wanted to question the team's solidarity. The problems lasted for almost an entire year. It wasn't until the general who formed the team complained about the mail that the system was changed.

- During the dot.com boom of the late 1990s, Virginia Turezyn, managing director of Infinity Capital, states that she was a victim of groupthink. At first, Turezyn was sceptical about the stability of the boom. But after continually reading about start-ups turning into multimillion-euro payoffs, she felt different. Turezyn decided to invest millions in several dot.coms, including I-drive, a company that provided electronic data storage. The problem was that I-drive was giving the storage away for free, and as a result, the company was losing money. Turezyn recalls one board meeting at I-drive where she spoke up to no avail. 'We're spending way too much money,' she screamed. The younger executives shook their heads and replied that if they charged for storage, they would lose their customers. Says Turezyn, 'I started to think, "Maybe I'm just too old. Maybe I really don't get it."' Unfortunately, Turezyn did get it. I-drive later filed for bankruptcy.

- Steve Blank, an entrepreneur, also fell victim to groupthink. Blank was a dot.com investor, and he participated on advisory boards of several Internet start-ups. During meetings for one such start-up, a web photo finisher, Blank tried to persuade his fellow board members to change the business model to be more traditional. Recalls Blank, 'I went to those meetings and started saying things like, "Maybe you should spend that €8 million you just raised on acquiring a customer base rather than building a brand." The CEO told me, "Steve, you just don't get it – all the rules have changed."' The team didn't take Blank's advice, and Blank says that he lost hundreds of thousands of euros on the deal.

According to Michael Useem, a professor at the Wharton College of Business, one of the main reasons that groupthink occurs is a lack of conflict. 'A single devil's advocate or whistle-blower faces a really uphill struggle,' he states, 'but if you [the naysayer] have one ally that is enormously strengthening.'

Questions

1. What are some factors that led to groupthink in the cases described here? What can teams do to attempt to prevent groupthink from occurring?

2. How might differences in status among group members contribute to groupthink? For example, how might lower-status members react to a group's decision? Are lower-status members more or less likely to be dissenters? Why might higher-status group members be more effective dissenters?

3. Microsoft CEO Steve Ballmer says that he encourages dissent. Can such norms guard against the occurrence of groupthink? As a manager, how would you try to cultivate norms that prevent groupthink?

4. How might group characteristics such as size and cohesiveness affect groupthink?

Sources: Based on C. Hawn, 'Fear and posing', *Forbes*, 25 March 2002, pp. 22–25; and J. Sandberg, 'Some ideas are so bad that only team efforts can account for them', *Wall Street Journal*, 29 September 2004, p. B1.

Endnotes

1 L. R. Sayles, 'Work group behavior and the larger organization', in C. Arensburg (ed.), *Research in Industrial Human Relations: A Critical Appraisal* (New York: Harper & Row, 1957), pp. 131–45.

2 J. F. McGrew, J. G. Bilotta and J. M. Deeney, 'Software team formation and decay: extending the standard model for small groups', *Small Group Research*, 30, 2 (1999), pp. 209–34.

3 B. W. Tuckman, 'Developmental sequences in small groups,' *Psychological Bulletin*, June 1965, pp. 384–99; B. W. Tuckman

and M. C. Jensen, 'Stages of small-group development revisited', *Group and Organizational Studies*, December 1977, pp. 419–27; and M. F. Maples, 'Group development: extending tuckman's theory', *Journal for Specialists in Group Work*, Fall 1988, pp. 17–23; and K. Vroman and J. Kovacich, 'Computer-mediated interdisciplinary teams: theory and reality', *Journal of Interprofessional Care*, 16, 2 (2002), pp. 159–70.

4 J. F. George and L. M. Jessup, 'Groups over time: what are we really studying?', *International Journal of Human-Computer Studies*, 47, 3 (1997), pp. 497–511.

5 R. C. Ginnett, 'The airline cockpit crew', in J. R. Hackman (ed.), *Groups That Work (and Those That Don't)* (San Francisco, CA: Jossey-Bass, 1990).

6 C. J. G. Gersick, 'Time and transition in work teams: toward a new model of group development', *Academy of Management Journal*, March 1988, pp. 9–41; C. J. G. Gersick, 'Marking time: predictable transitions in task groups', *Academy of Management Journal*, June 1989, pp. 274–309; M. J. Waller, J. M. Conte, C. B. Gibson and M. A. Carpenter, 'The effect of individual perceptions of deadlines on team performance,' *Academy of Management Review*, October 2001, pp. 586–600; and A. Chang, P. Bordia and J. Duck, 'Punctuated equilibrium and linear progression: toward a new understanding of group development,' *Academy of Management Journal*, February 2003, pp. 106–17; see also H. Arrow, M. S. Poole, K. B. Henry, S. Wheelan and R. Moreland, 'Time, change, and development: the temporal perspective on groups', *Small Group Research*, February 2004, pp. 73–105.

7 Gersick, 'Time and transition in work teams'; and Gersick, 'Marking time'.

8 A. Seers and S. Woodruff, 'Temporal pacing in task forces: group development or deadline pressure?', *Journal of Management*, 23, 2 (1997), pp. 169–87.

9 S. Lieberman, 'The effects of changes in roles on the attitudes of role occupants', *Human Relations*, November 1956, pp. 385–402.

10 See D. M. Rousseau, *Psychological Contracts in Organizations: Understanding Written and Unwritten Agreements* (Thousand Oaks, CA: Sage, 1995); E. W. Morrison and S. L. Robinson, 'When employees feel betrayed: a model of how psychological contract violation develops', *Academy of Management Review*, April 1997, pp. 226–56; D. Rousseau and R. Schalk (eds), *Psychological Contracts in Employment: Cross-Cultural Perspectives* (San Francisco, CA: Jossey Bass, 2000); L. Sels, M. Janssens and I. Van den Brande, 'Assessing the nature of psychological contracts: a validation of six dimensions', *Journal of Organizational Behavior*, June 2004, pp. 461–88; and C. Hui, C. Lee and D. M. Rousseau, 'Psychological contract and organizational citizenship behavior in China: investigating generalizability and instrumentality', *Journal of Applied Psychology*, April 2004, pp. 311–21.

11 See M. F. Peterson *et al.*, 'Role conflict, ambiguity, and overload: a 21-nation study', *Academy of Management Journal*, 38, 2 (April 1995), pp. 429–52; and I. H. Settles, R. M. Sellers and A. Damas, Jr., 'One role or two? The function of psychological separation in role conflict', *Journal of Applied Psychology*, June 2002, pp. 574–82.

12 P. G. Zimbardo, C. Haney, W. C. Banks and D. Jaffe, 'The mind is a formidable jailer: a Pirandellian prison', *New York Times*, 8 April 1973, pp. 38–60; and C. Haney and P. G. Zimbardo, 'Social roles and role-playing: observations from the Stanford prison study', *Behavioral and Social Science Teacher*, January 1973, pp. 25–45.

13 For a review of the research on group norms, see J. R. Hackman, 'Group influences on individuals in organizations', in M. D. Dunnette and L. M. Hough (eds), *Handbook of Industrial & Organizational Psychology*, 2nd edn, vol. 3 (Palo Alto, CA: Consulting Psychologists Press, 1992), pp. 235–50. For a more recent discussion, see M. G. Ehrhart and S. E. Naumann, 'Organizational citizenship behavior in work groups: a group norms approach', *Journal of Applied Psychology*, December 2004, pp. 960–74.

14 Adapted from P. S. Goodman, E. Ravlin and M. Schminke, 'Understanding groups in organizations', in L. L. Cummings and B. M. Staw (eds), *Research in Organizational Behavior*, vol. 9 (Greenwich, CT: JAI Press, 1987), p. 159.

15 E. Mayo, *The Human Problems of an Industrial Civilization* (New York: Macmillan, 1933); and F. J. Roethlisberger and W. J. Dickson, *Management and the Worker* (Cambridge, MA: Harvard University Press, 1939).

16 C. A. Kiesler and S. B. Kiesler, *Conformity* (Reading, MA: Addison-Wesley, 1969).

17 Ibid., p. 27.

18 S. E. Asch, 'Effects of group pressure upon the modification and distortion of judgments', in H. Guetzkow (ed.), *Groups, Leadership and Men* (Pittsburgh: Carnegie Press, 1951), pp. 177–90; and S. E. Asch, 'Studies of independence and conformity: a minority of one against a unanimous majority', *Psychological Monographs: General and Applied*, 70, 9 (1956), pp. 1–70.

19 R. Bond and P. B. Smith, 'Culture and conformity: a meta-analysis of studies using Asch's (1952, 1956) line judgment task', *Psychological Bulletin*, January 1996, pp. 111–37.

20 See S. L. Robinson and R. J. Bennett, 'A typology of deviant workplace behaviors: a multidimensional scaling study', *Academy of Management Journal*, April 1995, pp. 555–72; S. L. Robinson and A. M. O'Leary-Kelly, 'Monkey see, monkey do: the influence of work groups on the antisocial behavior of employees', *Academy of Management Journal*, December 1998, pp. 658–72, and R. J. Bennett and S. L. Robinson, 'The past, present, and future of workplace deviance', in J. Greenberg (ed.), *Organizational Behavior: The State of the Science*, 2nd edn (Mahwah, NJ: Erlbaum, 2003), pp. 237–71.

21 C. M. Pearson, L. M. Andersson and C. L. Porath, 'Assessing and attacking workplace civility', *Organizational Dynamics*, 29, 2 (2000), p. 130; see also C. Pearson, L. M. Andersson and C. L. Porath, 'Workplace incivility', in S. Fox and P. E. Spector (eds), *Counterproductive Work Behavior: Investigations of Actors and Targets* (Washington, DC: American Psychological Association, 2005), pp. 177–200.

22 Robinson and O'Leary-Kelly, 'Monkey see, monkey do'.

23 A. Erez, H. Elms and E. Fong, 'Lying, cheating, stealing: it happens more in groups', paper presented at the European Business Ethics Network Annual Conference, Budapest, Hungary, August 30, 2003.

24 S. L. Robinson and M. S. Kraatz, 'Constructing the reality of normative behavior: the use of neutralization strategies by organizational deviants', in R. W. Griffin and A. O'Leary-Kelly (eds), *Dysfunctional Behavior in Organizations: Violent and Deviant Behavior* (Elsevier Science/JAI Press, 1998), pp. 203–20.

25 See R. S. Feldman, *Social Psychology*, 3rd edn (Upper Saddle River, NJ: Prentice-Hall, 2001), pp. 464–65.

26 Cited in Hackman, 'Group influences on individuals in organizations', p. 236.

27 O. J. Harvey and C. Consalvi, 'Status and conformity to pressures in informal groups,' *Journal of Abnormal and Social Psychology*, Spring 1960, pp. 182–87.

28 J. A. Wiggins, F. Dill and R. D. Schwartz, 'On "status-liability"', *Sociometry*, April–May 1965, pp. 197–209.

29 See J. M. Levine and R. L. Moreland, 'Progress in small group research', in J. T. Spence, J. M. Darley, and D. J. Foss (eds), *Annual Review of Psychology*, vol. 41 (Palo Alto, CA: Annual Reviews Inc., 1990), pp. 585–634; S. D. Silver, B. P. Cohen and J. H. Crutchfield, 'Status differentiation and information exchange in face-to-face and computer-mediated idea generation', *Social Psychology Quarterly*, 1994, pp. 108–23; and J. M. Twenge, 'Changes in women's assertiveness in response to status and roles: a cross-temporal meta-analysis, 1931–1993', *Journal of Personality and Social Psychology*, July 2001, pp. 133–45.

30 J. Greenberg, 'Equity and workplace status: a field experiment', *Journal of Applied Psychology*, November 1988, pp. 606–13.

31 E. J. Thomas and C. F. Fink, 'Effects of group size,' *Psychological Bulletin*, July 1963, pp. 371–84; A. P. Hare, *Handbook of Small Group Research* (New York: The Free Press, 1976); and M. E. Shaw, *Group Dynamics: The Psychology of Small Group Behavior*, 3rd edn (New York: McGraw-Hill, 1981).

32 G. H. Seijts and G. P. Latham, 'The effects of goal setting and group size on performance in a social dilemma', *Canadian Journal of Behavioral Science*, 32, 2 (2000), pp. 104–16.

33 Shaw, *Group Dynamics: The Psychology of Small Group Behavior*.

34 See, for instance, D. R. Comer, 'A model of social loafing in real work groups', *Human Relations*, June 1995, pp. 647–67; S. M. Murphy, S. J. Wayne, R. C. Liden and B. Erdogan, 'Understanding social loafing: the role of justice perceptions and exchange relationships', *Human Relations*, January 2003, pp. 61–84; and R. C. Liden, S. J. Wayne, R. A. Jaworski and N. Bennett, 'Social loafing: a field investigation', *Journal of Management*, April 2004, pp. 285–304.

35 W. Moede, 'Die richtlinien der leistungs-psychologie', *Industrielle Psychotechnik*, 4 (1927), pp. 193–207. See also D. A. Kravitz and B. Martin, 'Ringelmann rediscovered: the original article', *Journal of Personality and Social Psychology*, May 1986, pp. 936–41.

36 See, for example, J. A. Shepperd, 'Productivity loss in performance groups: a motivation analysis', *Psychological Bulletin*, January 1993, pp. 67–81; and S. J. Karau and K. D. Williams, 'Social loafing: a meta-analytic review and theoretical integration', *Journal of Personality and Social Psychology*, October 1993, pp. 681–706.

37 S. G. Harkins and K. Szymanski, 'Social loafing and group evaluation', *Journal of Personality and Social Psychology*, December 1989, pp. 934–41.

38 A. Gunnthorsdottir and A. Rapoport, 'Embedding social dilemmas in intergroup competition reduces free-riding', *Organizational Behavior and Human Decision Processes*, 101 (2006), pp. 184–99.

39 For some of the controversy surrounding the definition of cohesion, see J. Keyton and J. Springston, 'Redefining cohesiveness in groups', *Small Group Research*, May 1990, pp. 234–54.

40 B. Mullen and C. Cooper, 'The relation between group cohesiveness and performance: an integration', *Psychological Bulletin*, March 1994, pp. 210–27; P. M. Podsakoff, S. B. MacKenzie and M. Ahearne, 'Moderating effects of goal acceptance on the relationship between group cohesiveness and productivity', *Journal of Applied Psychology*, December 1997, pp. 974–83; and D. J. Beal, R. R. Cohen, M. J. Burke and C. L. McLendon, 'Cohesion and performance in groups: a

meta-analytic clarification of construct relations', *Journal of Applied Psychology*, December 2003, pp. 989–1004.

41 Ibid.

42 Based on J. L. Gibson, J. M. Ivancevich and J. H. Donnelly, Jr., *Organizations*, 8th edn (Burr Ridge, IL: Irwin, 1994), p. 323.

43 N. Foote, E. Matson, L. Weiss and E. Wenger, 'Leveraging group knowledge for high-performance decision-making', *Organizational Dynamics*, 31, 2 (2002), pp. 280–95.

44 See N. R. F. Maier, 'Assets and liabilities in group problem solving: the need for an integrative function', *Psychological Review*, April 1967, pp. 239–49; G. W. Hill, 'Group versus individual performance: are N+1 heads better than one?', *Psychological Bulletin*, May 1982, pp. 517–39; A. E. Schwartz and J. Levin, 'Better group decision making,' *Supervisory Management*, June 1990, p. 4; and R. F. Martell and M. R. Borg, 'A comparison of the behavioral rating accuracy of groups and individuals', *Journal of Applied Psychology*, February 1993, pp. 43–50.

45 D. Gigone and R. Hastie, 'Proper analysis of the accuracy of group judgments', *Psychological Bulletin*, January 1997, pp. 149–67; and B. L. Bonner, S. D. Sillito and M. R. Baumann, 'Collective estimation: accuracy, expertise, and extroversion as sources of intra-group influence', *Organizational Behavior and Human Decision Processes*, 103 (2007), pp. 121–33.

46 See, for example, W. C. Swap and Associates, *Group Decision Making* (Newbury Park, CA: Sage, 1984).

47 D. D. Henningsen, M. G. Cruz and M. L. Miller, 'Role of social loafing in predeliberation decision making', *Group Dynamics: Theory, Research, and Practice*, 4, 2 (June 2000), pp. 168–75.

48 J. H. Davis, *Group Performance* (Reading, MA: Addison-Wesley, 1969); J. P. Wanous and M. A. Youtz, 'Solution diversity and the quality of group decisions', *Academy of Management Journal*, March 1986, pp. 149–59; and R. Libby, K. T. Trotman and I. Zimmer, 'Member variation, recognition of expertise, and group performance', *Journal of Applied Psychology*, February 1987, pp. 81–87.

49 I. L. Janis, *Groupthink: Psychological Studies of Policy Decisions and Fiascoes* (Boston, MA: Houghton Mifflin, 1982); W. Park, 'A review of research on groupthink', *Journal of Behavioral Decision Making*, July 1990, pp. 229–45; J. N. Choi and M. U. Kim, 'The organizational application of groupthink and its limits in organizations', *Journal of Applied Psychology*, April 1999, pp. 297–306; and W. W. Park, 'A comprehensive empirical investigation of the relationships among variables of the groupthink model,' *Journal of Organizational Behavior*, December 2000, pp. 873–87.

50 Janis, *Groupthink*.

51 G. Moorhead, R. Ference and C. P. Neck, 'Group decision fiascos continue: space shuttle Challenger and a revised groupthink framework', *Human Relations*, May 1991, pp. 539–50; E. J. Chisson, *The Hubble Wars* (New York: HarperPerennial, 1994); and C. Covault, '*Columbia* revelations alarming e-mails speak for themselves. But administrator O'Keefe is more concerned about board findings on NASA decision-making', *Aviation Week & Space Technology*, 3 March 2003, p. 26.

52 J. Eaton, 'Management communication: the threat of groupthink', *Corporate Communication*, 6, 4 (2001), pp. 183–92.

53 M. E. Turner and A. R. Pratkanis, 'Mitigating groupthink by stimulating constructive conflict', in C. De Dreu and E. Van de Vliert (eds), *Using Conflict in Organizations* (London: Sage, 1997), pp. 53–71.

54 Ibid., p. 68.

55 See N. R. F. Maier, *Principles of Human Relations* (New York: Wiley, 1952); Janis, *Groupthink: Psychological Studies of Policy Decisions and Fiascoes*; C. R. Leana, 'A partial test of Janis' Groupthink model: effects of group cohesiveness and leader behavior on defective decision making', *Journal of Management*, Spring 1985, pp. 5–17; and N. Richardson Ahlfinger and J. K. Esser, 'Testing the Groupthink model: effects of promotional leadership and conformity predisposition', *Social Behavior & Personality*, 29, 1 (2001), pp. 31–41.

56 See D. J. Isenberg, 'Group polarization: a critical review and meta-analysis', *Journal of Personality and Social Psychology*, December 1986, pp. 1141–51; J. L. Hale and F. J. Boster, 'Comparing effect coded models of choice shifts', *Communication Research Reports*, April 1988, pp. 180–86; and P. W. Paese, M. Bieser and M. E. Tubbs, 'Framing effects and choice shifts in group decision making', *Organizational Behavior and Human Decision Processes*, October 1993, pp. 149–65.

57 See, for example, N. Kogan and M. A. Wallach, 'Risk taking as a function of the situation, the person, and the group', in *New Directions in Psychology*, vol. 3 (New York: Holt, Rinehart & Winston, 1967); and M. A. Wallach, N. Kogan and D. J. Bem, 'Group influence on individual risk taking', *Journal of Abnormal and Social Psychology*, 65 (1962), pp. 75–86.

58 R. D. Clark, III, 'Group-induced shift toward risk: a critical appraisal', *Psychological Bulletin*, October 1971, pp. 251–70.

59 A. F. Osborn, *Applied Imagination. Principles and Procedures of Creative Thinking*, 3rd edn (New York: Scribner, 1963). See also T. Rickards, 'Brainstorming revisited: a question of context', *International Journal of Management Reviews*, March 1999, pp. 91–110; and R. P. McGlynn, D. McGurk, V. S. Effland, N. L. Johll and D. J. Harding, 'Brainstorming and task performance in groups constrained by evidence', *Organizational Behavior and Human Decision Processes*, January 2004, pp. 75–87.

60 N. L. Kerr and R. S. Tindale, 'Group performance and decision-making', *Annual Review of Psychology*, 55 (2004), pp. 623–55.

61 See A. L. Delbecq, A. H. Van deVen and D. H. Gustafson, *Group Techniques for Program Planning: A Guide to Nominal and Delphi Processes* (Glenview, IL: Scott, Foresman, 1975); and P. B. Paulus and H.-C. Yang, 'Idea generation in groups: a basis for creativity in organizations', *Organizational Behavior and Human Decision Processing*, May 2000, pp. 76–87.

62 C. Faure, 'Beyond brainstorming: effects of different group procedures on selection of ideas and satisfaction with the process,' *Journal of Creative Behavior*, 38 (2004), pp. 13–34.

63 See, for instance, A. B. Hollingshead and J. E. McGrath, 'Computer-assisted groups: a critical review of the empirical research', in R. A. Guzzo and E. Salas (eds), *Team Effectiveness and Decision Making in Organizations* (San Francisco, CA: Jossey-Bass, 1995), pp. 46–78.

64 B. B. Baltes, M. W. Dickson, M. P. Sherman, C. C. Bauer and J. LaGanke, 'Computer-mediated communication and group decision making: a meta-analysis', *Organizational Behavior and Human Decision Processes*, January 2002, pp. 156–79.

65 See G. Hofstede, *Cultures and Organizations: Software of the Mind* (New York, McGraw-Hill, 1991).

66 This paragraph is based on P. R. Harris and R. T. Moran, *Managing Cultural Differences*, 5th edn (Houston: Gulf Publishing, 1999).

67 D. S. Staples and L. Zhao, 'The effects of cultural diversity in virtual teams versus face-to-face teams', *Group Decision and Negotiation*, July 2006, pp. 389–406.

68 K. W. Phillips and D. L. Loyd, 'When surface and deep-level diversity collide: the effects on dissenting group members', *Organizational Behavior and Human Decision Processes*, 99 (2006), pp. 143–60; and S. R. Sommers, 'On racial diversity and group decision making: identifying multiple effects of racial composition on jury deliberations', *Journal of Personality and Social Psychology*, April 2006, pp. 597–612.

69 E. Mannix and M. A. Neale, 'What differences make a difference? The promise and reality of diverse teams in organizations,' *Psychological Science in the Public Interest*, October 2005, pp. 31–55.

70 T. P. Verney, 'Role perception congruence, performance, and satisfaction', in D. J. Vredenburgh and R. S. Schuler (eds), *Effective Management: Research and Application*, Proceedings of the 20th Annual Eastern Academy of Management, Pittsburgh, PA, May 1983, pp. 24–27.

71 Ibid.

72 A. G. Bedeian and A. A. Armenakis, 'A path-analytic study of the consequences of role conflict and ambiguity', *Academy of Management Journal*, June 1981, pp. 417–24; and P. L. Perrewe, K. L. Zellars, G. R. Ferris, A. M. Rossi, C. J. Kacmar and D. A. Ralston, 'Neutralizing job stressors: political skill as an antidote to the dysfunctional consequences of role conflict', *Academy of Management Journal*, February 2004, pp. 141–52.

73 Shaw, *Group Dynamics*.

74 B. Mullen, C. Symons, L. Hu and E. Salas, 'Group size, leadership behavior, and subordinate satisfaction', *Journal of General Psychology*, April 1989, pp. 155–70.

Understanding work teams

After studying this chapter, you should be able to:

1 Analyse the growing popularity of using teams in organizations.

2 Contrast groups and teams.

3 Compare and contrast four types of teams.

4 Identify the characteristics of effective teams.

5 Show how organizations can create team players.

6 Decide when to use individuals instead of teams.

7 Show how the understanding of teams differs in a global context.

Teamwork is the fuel that allows common people to attain uncommon results.

Andrew Carnegie

Poaching the whole team

Justin Sullivan/Getty Images

In the competitive search for top talent, it is not unusual for top employees to be hired away from successful companies. Google, for example, has seen a lot of companies hire away its people. And the competition for top talent is set to intensify, according to a European survey of 4,500 chief executives, making finding and retaining talent more difficult.

A new wrinkle in the talent wars is hiring away an entire team. The bank HSBC was left with only a graduate trainee to take charge of analysing media equities after its entire team of media analysts decamped for ABN AMRO. Orrick, Herrington & Sutcliffe, a US-based law firm, recognised Italy as a market ripe for expansion because of the Italian government's strides toward deregulation and privatisation. The firm hired a team of 23 Italian lawyers, including seven partners, from a Milan-based affiliate of Ernst & Young to open its first Italian branch. The advertising giant Interpublic Group brought in 17 creative and sales executives from Saatchi & Saatchi in one of the largest 'lift-outs' in advertising history at the time.

'Lift-outs' have gained a lot of attention in recent years and entail hiring a high-functioning team of people from the same company who have worked well together and can quickly come up to speed in a new environment. Although the practice has been around in industries such as financial services and law, it's becoming increasingly common in other sectors, such as IT, management consulting, medical services and accounting. 'We've even seen it happen between recruiters, which is its own irony,' says one expert.

One factor explaining the rise in lift-outs is speed. When organizations need to enter a competitive market ASAP, they don't have time to spend months hiring and then training team members. Hiring an entire team may be the quickest way to enter a new market or launch a product or service. Another factor is private equity buyouts. Private equity firms seek to turn around a company quickly so that, in most cases, they can resell it for a profit. Time is money, and poaching whole teams can reduce the time necessary to return the company to profitability.

Hiring away whole teams does have disadvantages. One is legality: questions of noncompetition, non-solicitation, confidentiality and intellectual property. These issues are highly contested and vary by country. Another challenge is that the team may act like a team and use its cohesion against the new employer and start to negotiate en masse, for example, to increase benefits. The already expensive team acquisitions may turn out to be very costly indeed.

Sources: J. McGregor, 'I can't believe they took the whole team', *BusinessWeek*, 18 December 2006, pp. 120–22.; B. Sheehan, C. Higgins, T. Dobbins and K. Fitzgerald (2005) 'European conference highlights challenges for human resources managers'. Available at: http://www.eurofound.europa.eu/eiro/2005/06/feature/ie0506202f.htm; B. Groysberg and R. Abrahams (2006) 'Lift outs: how to acquire a high-functioning team', *Harvard Business Review* 84, 12; pp. 133–40.

Teams are increasingly becoming the primary means for organizing work in contemporary business firms. In fact, this trend is so widespread that companies are hiring whole teams. What do you think of your skills in leading and building a team? Take the following self-assessment to find out.

SELF-ASSESSMENT LIBRARY

How good am I at building and leading a team?

In the Self-assessment library (available online), take assessment II.B.6 (How good am I at building and leading a team?) and answer the following questions.

1. Did you score as high as you thought you would? Why or why not?

2. Do you think you can improve your score? If so, how? If not, why not?

3. Do you think there is such a thing as team players? If yes, what are their behaviours?

Why have teams become so popular?

1 Analyse the growing popularity of using teams in organizations.

Decades ago, when companies such as Volvo, W. L. Gore and General Foods introduced teams into their production processes, it made news because no one else was doing it. Today, it's just the opposite. It's the organization that *doesn't* use teams that has become newsworthy. Teams are everywhere.

How do we explain the current popularity of teams? As organizations have restructured themselves to compete more effectively and efficiently, they have turned to teams as a better way to use employee talents. Management has found that teams are more flexible and responsive to changing events than are traditional departments or other forms of permanent groupings. Teams have the capability to quickly assemble, deploy, refocus, and disband. But don't overlook the motivational properties of teams. Consistent with our discussion in Chapter 7 of the role of employee involvement as a motivator, teams facilitate employee participation in operating decisions. So another explanation for the popularity of teams is that they are an effective means for management to democratise their organizations and increase employee motivation.

The fact that organizations have turned to teams doesn't necessarily mean they're always effective. Decision makers, as humans, can be swayed by fads and herd mentality. Are teams truly effective? What conditions affect their potential? How do teams work together? These are some of the questions we'll answer in this chapter.

2 Contrast groups and teams.

Differences between groups and teams

work group
A group that interacts primarily to share information and to make decisions to help each group member perform within his or her area of responsibility.

work team
A group whose individual efforts result in performance that is greater than the sum of the individual inputs.

Groups and teams are not the same thing. In this section, we define and clarify the difference between work groups and work teams.[1]

In Chapter 9, we defined a *group* as two or more individuals, interacting and interdependent, who have come together to achieve particular objectives. A **work group** is a group that interacts primarily to share information and to make decisions to help each member perform within his or her area of responsibility.

Work groups have no need or opportunity to engage in collective work that requires joint effort. So their performance is merely the summation of each group member's individual contribution. There is no positive synergy that would create an overall level of performance that is greater than the sum of the inputs.

A **work team** generates positive synergy through coordinated effort. The individual efforts result in a level of performance that is greater than the sum of those individual inputs. Figure 10.1 highlights the differences between work groups and work teams.

These definitions help clarify why so many organizations have recently restructured work processes around teams. Management is looking for positive synergy that will allow the

| Figure 10.1 | Comparing work groups and work teams |

Work groups → Goal ← **Work teams**

Work groups		Work teams
Share information	◄— Goal —►	Collective performance
Neutral (sometimes negative)	◄— Synergy —►	Positive
Individual	◄— Accountability —►	Individual and mutual
Random and varied	◄— Skills —►	Complementary

organizations to increase performance. The extensive use of teams creates the *potential* for an organization to generate greater outputs with no increase in inputs. Notice, however, that we said *potential*. There is nothing inherently magical in the creation of teams that ensures the achievement of positive synergy. Merely calling a *group* a *team* doesn't automatically increase its performance. As we show later in this chapter, effective teams have certain common characteristics. If management hopes to gain increases in organizational performance through the use of teams, it needs to ensure that its teams possess these characteristics.

FACE THE FACTS

According to European Foundation for the Improvement of Living and Working Conditions surveys:

- 60 per cent of EU workers perform part or all of their work in teams.

- Across the EU teamwork is most common in the UK and Estonia where in both countries 81 per cent of employees report working in teams while the lowest incidence of teamwork is found in Lithuania and Italy at 38 per cent and 41 per cent respectively.

- There is a predominance of teamwork in industrial sectors in contrast to the services sector.

- Although teamwork is more common in larger companies, the incidence of teamwork did not depend on company size in Austria, Finland, Germany, Ireland, the UK and Sweden.

Source: R. Vašková *Teamwork and High Performance Work Organization*, European Foundation for the Improvement of Living and Working Conditions, 2007; *Fourth European Working Conditions Survey*, European Foundation for the Improvement of Living and Working Conditions, 2007. Available at http://www.eurofound.europa.eu.

Types of teams

3 Compare and contrast four types of teams.

problem-solving teams
Groups of 5 to 12 employees from the same department who meet for a few hours each week to discuss ways of improving quality, efficiency and the work environment.

Teams can do a variety of things. They can make products, provide services, negotiate deals, coordinate projects, offer advice, and make decisions.[2] In this section, we'll describe the four most common types of teams you're likely to find in an organization: *problem-solving teams, self-managed work teams, cross-functional teams* and *virtual teams* (see Figure 10.2).

Problem-solving teams

Twenty years ago or so, teams were just beginning to grow in popularity, and most of those teams took a similar form. They were typically composed of 5 to 12 hourly employees from the same department who met for a few hours each week to discuss ways of improving quality, efficiency and the work environment.[3] We call these **problem-solving teams**.

Figure 10.2	Four types of teams

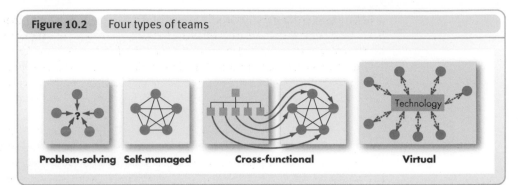

Problem-solving   **Self-managed**   **Cross-functional**   **Virtual**

Sipa Press/Rex Features

At the Louis Vuitton factory in Ducey, France, all employees work in problem-solving teams, with each team focusing on one product at a time. Team members are encouraged to suggest improvements in manufacturing work methods and processes as well as product quality. When a team was asked to make a test run on a prototype of a new handbag, team members discovered that decorative studs were causing the bag's zipper to bunch up. The team alerted managers, who had technicians move the studs away from the zipper, which solved the problem.

In problem-solving teams, members share ideas or offer suggestions on how work processes and methods can be improved; they rarely have the authority to unilaterally implement any of their suggested actions. For instance, Merrill Lynch created a problem-solving team to specifically figure out ways to reduce the number of days it took to open up a new cash management account.[4] By suggesting cuts in the number of steps in the process from 46 to 36, the team was able to reduce the average number of days from 15 to 8.

Self-managed work teams

Although problem-solving teams involve employees in decisions, they 'only' make recommendations. Some organizations have gone further and created teams that can not only solve problems but implement solutions and take responsibility for outcomes.

Self-managed work teams are groups of employees (typically 10 to 15 in number) who perform highly related or interdependent jobs and take on many of the responsibilities of their former supervisors.[5] Typically, these tasks are involved in planning and scheduling work, assigning tasks to members, making operating decisions, taking action on problems and working with

self-managed work teams
Groups of 10 to 15 people who take on responsibilities of their former supervisors.

suppliers and customers. Fully self-managed work teams even select their own members and have the members evaluate each other's performance. As a result, supervisory positions take on decreased importance and may even be eliminated. Maintenance workers at Ireland's Dairygold Cooperative Society Ltd run their function on the basis of a self-managed work team, and have responsibility for budgeting, planning of work and liaising with production. They schedule their own holidays and working hours (within certain constraints), and their team leader negotiates the annual maintenance budget with management.[6]

Business periodicals have been full of articles describing successful applications of self-managed teams. But a word of caution needs to be offered: The overall research on the effectiveness of self-managed work teams has not been uniformly positive.[7] Moreover, although individuals on these teams do tend to report higher levels of job satisfaction compared to other individuals, they also sometimes have higher absenteeism and turnover rates. Inconsistency in findings suggests that the effectiveness of self-managed teams depends on the strength and make-up of team norms, the type of tasks the team undertakes, and the reward structure can significantly influence how well the team performs.

Cross-functional teams

The Boeing Company created a team made up of employees from production, planning, quality, tooling, design engineering and information systems to automate shims on the company's C-17 programme. The team's suggestions resulted in drastically reduced cycle time and cost, as well as improved quality on the C-17 programme.[8]

cross-functional teams
Employees from about the same hierarchical level, but from different work areas, who come together to accomplish a task.

This Boeing example illustrates the use of **cross-functional teams**. These are teams made up of employees from about the same hierarchical level but from different work areas, who come together to accomplish a task.

Many organizations have used horizontal, boundary-spanning groups for decades. For example, IBM created a large task force in the 1960s – made up of employees from across departments in the company – to develop its highly successful System 360. But today cross-functional teams are so widely used that it is hard to imagine a major organizational initiative without one. For instance, all the major automobile manufacturers – including Toyota, Honda, Volkswagen, BMW, GM and Ford – currently use this form of team to coordinate complex projects. And Harley-Davidson relies on specific cross-functional teams to manage each line of its motorcycles. These teams include Harley employees from design, manufacturing and purchasing, as well as representatives from key outside suppliers.[9]

Cross-functional teams are an effective means for allowing people from diverse areas within an organization (or even between organizations) to exchange information, develop new ideas and solve problems, and coordinate complex projects. Of course, cross-functional teams are no picnic to manage. Their early stages of development are often very time-consuming, as members learn to work with diversity and complexity. It takes time to build trust and teamwork, especially among people from different backgrounds with different experiences and perspectives.

Virtual teams

virtual teams
Teams that use computer technology to tie together physically dispersed members in order to achieve a common goal.

The previously described types of teams do their work face-to-face. **Virtual teams** use computer technology to tie together physically dispersed members in order to achieve a common goal.[10] They allow people to collaborate online – using communication links such as wide-area networks, video conferencing or e-mail – whether they're only a room away or continents apart. Virtual teams are so pervasive, and technology has advanced so far, that it's probably a bit of a misnomer to call these teams 'virtual'. Nearly all teams today do at least some of their work remotely.

Despite their ubiquity, virtual teams face special challenges. They may suffer because there is less social rapport and less direct interaction among members. They aren't able to duplicate the normal give-and-take of face-to-face discussion. Especially when members haven't personally met, virtual teams tend to be more task-oriented and exchange less social–emotional information than face-to-face teams. Not surprisingly, virtual team members report less satisfaction with the group interaction process than do face-to-face teams. For virtual teams to be effective, management should ensure that (1) trust is established among team members (research has shown that one inflammatory remark in a team member e-mail can severely undermine team trust); (2) team progress is monitored closely (so the team doesn't lose sight of its goals and no team member 'disappears'); and (3) the efforts and products of the virtual team are publicised throughout the organization (so the team does not become invisible).[11]

GLOBAL VIRTUAL TEAMS   GLOBAL

Years ago, before the vast working public ever dreamed of e-mail, instant messaging or live video conferencing, work teams used to be in the same locations, with possibly one or two members a train or plane ride away. Today, however, the reach of corporations spans many countries, so the need for teams to work together across international lines has increased. To deal with this challenge, multinationals use global virtual teams to gain a competitive advantage. For example, Logitech created a virtual team to take advantage of a pool of global talent. The mechanical engineering and design of the company's new mouse took place in Ireland, electrical engineering in Switzerland, corporate marketing, software engineering and quality assurance at the company's US headquarters. Tooling took place in Taiwan and manufacturing occurred in China.[12]

Global virtual teams have advantages and disadvantages. On the positive side, because team members come from different countries with different knowledge and points of view, they may develop creative ideas and solutions to problems that work for multiple cultures. On the negative side, global virtual teams face more challenges than traditional teams that meet face-to-face. For one thing, miscommunication can lead to misunderstandings, which can create stress and conflict among team members. Also, members who do not accept individuals from different cultures may hesitate to share information openly, which can create problems of trust.

To create and implement effective global virtual teams, managers must carefully select employees whom they believe will thrive in such an environment. Employees must be comfortable with communicating electronically with others, and they must be open to different ideas. When dealing with team members in other countries, speaking multiple languages may also be necessary. Team members also must realise that the values they hold may be different from their teammates' values.

Although global virtual teams face many challenges, companies that implement them effectively can realise tremendous rewards through the diverse knowledge they gain.

Source: Based on N. Zakaria, A. Amelinckx and D. Wilemon, 'Working together apart? Building a knowledge-sharing culture for global virtual teams', *Creativity and Innovation Management*, March 2004, pp. 15–29.

Creating effective teams

4 Identify the characteristics of effective teams.

Many have tried to identify factors related to team effectiveness.[13] However, recent studies have organized what was once a 'veritable laundry list of characteristics'[14] into a relatively focused model.[15] Figure 10.3 summarises what we currently know about what makes teams effective. As you'll see, it builds on many of the group concepts introduced in Chapter 9.

The following discussion is based on the model in Figure 10.3. Keep in mind two caveats before we proceed. First, teams differ in form and structure. Because the model we present attempts to generalise across all varieties of teams, you need to be careful not to rigidly apply the model's predictions to all teams.[16] You should use the model as a guide. Second, the model assumes that it's already been determined that teamwork is preferable to individual work. Creating 'effective' teams in situations in which individuals can do the job better is equivalent to solving the wrong problem perfectly.

The key components of effective teams can be subsumed into four general categories. First are the resources and other *contextual* influences that make teams effective. The second relates to the team's *composition*. The third category is *work design*. Finally, *process* variables reflect those things that go on in the team that influences effectiveness. What does *team effectiveness* mean in this model? Typically, it has included objective measures of the team's productivity, managers' ratings of the team's performance and aggregate measures of member satisfaction.

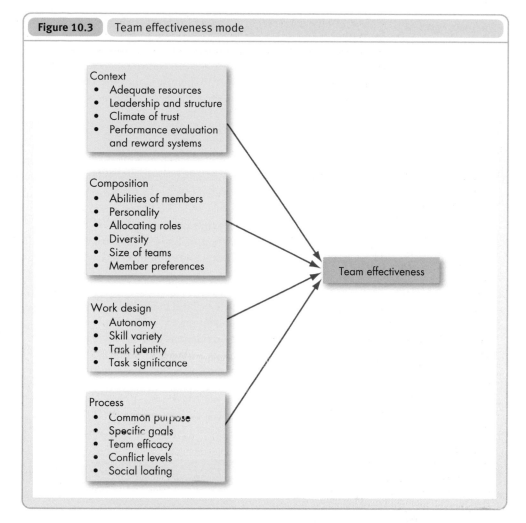

Figure 10.3   Team effectiveness mode

Context
- Adequate resources
- Leadership and structure
- Climate of trust
- Performance evaluation and reward systems

Composition
- Abilities of members
- Personality
- Allocating roles
- Diversity
- Size of teams
- Member preferences

Work design
- Autonomy
- Skill variety
- Task identity
- Task significance

Process
- Common purpose
- Specific goals
- Team efficacy
- Conflict levels
- Social loafing

Team effectiveness

Context: what factors determine whether teams are successful

The four contextual factors that appear to be most significantly related to team performance are the presence of adequate resources, effective leadership, a climate of trust and a performance evaluation and reward system that reflects team contributions.

Adequate resources

Teams are part of a larger organization system. As such, every work team relies on resources outside the group to sustain it. A scarcity of resources directly reduces the ability of a team to perform its job effectively. As one set of researchers concluded, after looking at 13 factors potentially related to group performance, 'perhaps one of the most important characteristics of an effective work group is the support the group receives from the organization'.[17] This support includes timely information, proper equipment, adequate staffing, encouragement and administrative assistance. Teams must receive the necessary support from management and the larger organization if they are to succeed in achieving their goals.

Leadership and structure

Teams can't function if they can't agree on who is to do what and ensure that all members contribute equally in sharing the work load. Agreeing on the specifics of work and how they fit together to integrate individual skills requires team leadership and structure. This can be provided directly by management or by the team members themselves. Although you might think there is no role for leaders in self-managed teams, that couldn't be further from the truth. It is true that in self-managed teams, team members absorb many of the duties typically assumed by managers. However, a manager's job becomes managing *outside* (rather than inside) the team.

Leadership is especially important in **multi-team systems** – where different teams need to coordinate their efforts to produce a desired outcome. In such systems, leaders need to empower teams by delegating responsibility to them, and they need to play the role of facilitator, making sure the teams are coordinating their efforts so that they work together rather than against one another.[18]

Climate of trust

Members of effective teams trust each other. And they also exhibit trust in their leaders.[19] Interpersonal trust among team members facilitates cooperation, reduces the need to monitor each others' behaviour, and bonds members around the belief that others on the team won't take advantage of them. Team members, for instance, are more likely to take risks and expose vulnerabilities when they believe they can trust others on their team. Similarly, as discussed in Chapter 13, trust is the foundation of leadership. Trust in leadership is important in that it allows a team to be willing to accept and commit to its leader's goals and decisions.

Performance evaluation and reward systems

How do you get team members to be both individually and jointly accountable? The traditional, individually oriented evaluation and reward system must be modified to reflect team performance.[20] Individual performance evaluations and incentives may interfere with the development of high-performance teams. So in addition to evaluating and rewarding employees for their individual contributions, management should consider group-based appraisals, profit-sharing, gainsharing, small-group incentives and other system modifications that reinforce team effort and commitment.

SURGICAL TEAMS LACK TEAMWORK   OB IN THE NEWS

Surgery is almost always performed by a team, but in many cases, it's a team in name only. So says a new study of more than 2,100 surgeons, anesthesiologists, and nurses.

When the researchers surveyed these surgery team members, they asked them to 'describe the quality of communication and collaboration you have experienced' with other members of the surgical unit. Perhaps not surprisingly, surgeons were given the lowest ratings for teamwork and nurses the highest ratings. 'The study is somewhat humbling to me,' said Martin Makary, the lead author on the study and a surgeon at the US hospital Johns Hopkins. 'There's a lot of pride in the surgical community. We need to balance out the captain-of-the-ship doctrine.'

The researchers attribute many operating room errors, such as sponges left in patients and operations performed on the wrong part of the body, to poor teamwork. But improving the system is easier said than done. One recent study found that over an 18-month period, there were 174 cases of surgeons operating on the wrong limb or body part. For its part, Johns Hopkins is modelling surgical team training after airline crew training. 'Teamwork is an important component of patient safety,' says Makary.

Sources: E. Nagourney, 'Surgical teams found lacking, in teamwork', *New York Times*, 9 May 2006, p. D6; and 'Nurses give surgeons poor grades on teamwork in OR', *Forbes*, 5 May 2006.

Team composition

The team composition category includes variables that relate to how teams should be staffed. In this section, we address the ability and personality of team members, allocation of roles and diversity, size of the team and members' preference for teamwork.

Abilities of members

Part of a team's performance depends on the knowledge, skills and abilities of its individual members.[21] It's true that we occasionally read about an athletic team composed of mediocre players who, because of excellent coaching, determination and precision teamwork, beats a far more talented group of players. But such cases make the news precisely because they represent

Ruth Fremson/Redux

Senior product scientists Syed Abbas and Albert Post and technology team manager Laurie Coyle functioned as a high-ability team in developing Unilever's new Dove Nutrium bar soap. In solving the complex problems involved in product innovation, the intelligent members of Unilever's research and development teams have advanced science degrees, the ability to think creatively and the interpersonal skills needed to perform effectively with other team members.

an aberration. As the old saying goes, 'The race doesn't always go to the swiftest nor the battle to the strongest, but that's the way to bet.' A team's performance is not merely the summation of its individual members' abilities. However, these abilities set parameters for what members can do and how effectively they will perform on a team.

To perform effectively, a team requires three different types of skills. First, it needs people who have *technical expertise*. Second, it needs people who have the *problem-solving and decision-making skills* to be able to identify problems, generate alternatives, evaluate those alternatives and make competent choices. Finally, teams need people who have good listening, feedback, conflict resolution and other *interpersonal skills*.[22] No team can achieve its performance potential without developing all three types of skills. The right mix is crucial. Too much of one at the expense of others will result in lower team performance. But teams don't need to have all the complementary skills in place at their beginning. It's not uncommon for one or more members to take responsibility for learning the skills in which the group is deficient, thereby allowing the team to reach its full potential.

Research on the abilities of team members has revealed some interesting insights into team composition and performance. First, when the task entails considerable thought (for example, solving a complex problem such as reengineering an assembly line), high-ability teams (that is, teams composed of mostly intelligent members) do better than lower-ability teams, especially when the work load is distributed evenly. (That way, team performance does not depend on the weakest link.) High-ability teams are also more adaptable to changing situations in that they can more effectively adapt prior knowledge to suit a set of new problems.

Second, although high-ability teams generally have an advantage over lower-ability teams, this is not always the case. For example, when tasks are simple (for example, tasks that individual team members might be able to solve on their own), high-ability teams do not perform as well, perhaps because, in such tasks, high-ability teams become bored and turn their attention to other activities that are more stimulating, whereas low-ability teams stay on task. High-ability teams should be 'saved' for tackling the tough problems. So matching team ability to the task is important.

Finally, the ability of the team's leader also matters. Research shows that smart team leaders help less intelligent team members when they struggle with a task. But a less intelligent leader can neutralise the effect of a high-ability team.[23]

Personality of members

We demonstrated in Chapter 4 that personality has a significant influence on individual employee behaviour. This can also be extended to team behaviour. Many of the dimensions identified in the Big Five personality model have been shown to be relevant to team effectiveness. A recent review of the literature suggested that three of the Big Five traits were especially important for team performance.[24] Specifically, teams that rate higher on mean levels of conscientiousness and openness to experience tend to perform better. Moreover, the minimum level of team member agreeableness also matters: Teams did worse when they had one or more highly disagreeable members. Perhaps one bad apple *can* spoil the whole bunch!

Research has also provided us with a good idea about why these personality traits are important to teams. Conscientious people are valuable in teams because they're good at backing up other team members, and they're also good at sensing when that support is truly needed. Open team members communicate better with one another and throw out more ideas, which leads teams composed of open people to be more creative and innovative.[25]

Even if an organization does a really good job of selecting individuals for team roles, most likely they'll find there aren't enough, say, conscientious people to go around. Suppose an organization needs to create 20 teams of 4 people each and has 40 highly conscientious people and 40 who score low on conscientiousness. Would the organization be better off (A) putting all the conscientious people together (forming 10 teams with the highly conscientious people and 10 teams of members low on conscientiousness) or (B) 'seeding' each team with 2 people who scored high and 2 who scored low on conscientiousness?

Perhaps surprisingly, the evidence tends to suggest that option A is the best choice; performance across the teams will be higher if the organization forms 10 highly conscientious teams and 10 teams low in conscientiousness. 'This may be because, in such teams, members who are highly conscientious not only must perform their own tasks but also must perform or re-do the tasks of low-conscientious members. It may also be because such diversity leads to feelings of contribution inequity.'[26]

Allocation of roles

Teams have different needs, and people should be selected for a team to ensure that all the various roles are filled.

Pioneering work on team roles was carried out by Dr Meredith Belbin at Henley Management College, UK in the 1970s. He identified nine clusters of behaviour, termed team roles (see Figure 10.4), each of which has its particular strengths and allowable weaknesses. Successful work teams have people to fill all these roles (on many teams, individuals will play multiple roles.) Manager's can use the Belbin model to help create more balanced teams. Teams can become unbalanced if all team members have similar team roles. If team members have similar weakness, the team as a whole may tend to have that weakness. If team members have similar strengths, they may compete for the team tasks and responsibilities that best suit their natural styles rather than collaborate.[27]

Diversity of members

In Chapter 9, we discussed research on the effect of diversity on groups. How does *team* diversity affect *team* performance?

Many of us hold the optimistic view that diversity should be a good thing – diverse teams should benefit from differing perspectives and do better. Unfortunately, the evidence appears to favour the pessimists. One review concluded, 'Studies on diversity in teams from the last 50 years have shown that surface-level social-category differences such as race/ethnicity, gender, and age tend to . . . have negative effects' on the performance of teams.[28] As in the literature on groups, there is some evidence that the disruptive effects of diversity decline over time, but unlike in the groups literature, there is less evidence that diverse teams perform better eventually.

Figure 10.4	Key roles of teams

Team role	Contribution	Allowable weakness
Plant	Creative, imaginative, unorthodox. Solves difficult problems.	Ignores incidentals. Too preoccupied to communicate effectively.
Resource investigator	Extrovert, enthusiastic, communicative. Explores opportunities. Develops contacts.	Overoptimistic. Loses interest once initial enthusiasm has passed.
Coordinator	Mature, confident, a good chairperson. Clarifies goals, promotes decision-making, delegates well.	Can be seen as manipulative. Offloads personal work.
Shaper	Challenging, dynamic, thrives on pressure. The drive and courage to overcome obstacles.	Prone to provocation. Offends people's feelings.
Monitor evaluator	Sober, strategic and discerning. Sees all options. Judges accurately.	Lacks drive and ability to inspire others.
Teamworker	Co-operative, mild, perceptive and diplomatic. Listens, builds, averts friction.	Indecisive in crunch situations.
Implementer	Disciplined, reliable, conservative and efficient. Turns ideas into practical actions.	Somewhat inflexible. Slow to respond to new possibilities.
Completer finisher	Painstaking, conscientious, anxious. Searches out errors and omissions. Delivers on time.	Inclined to worry unduly. Reluctant to delegate.
Specialist	Single-minded, self-starting, dedicated. Provides knowledge and skills in rare supply.	Contributes on only a narrow front. Dwells on technicalities.

One of the pervasive problems with teams is that while diversity may have real potential benefits, a team is deeply focused on commonly held information. But if diverse teams are to realise their creative potential, they need to focus not on their similarities but on their differences. There is some evidence, for example, that when team members believe others have more expertise, they will work to support those members, leading to higher levels of effectiveness.[29] The key is for diverse teams to communicate what they uniquely know and also what they don't know.

Jim Wilson/NY Times/Redux

Many team members share the common demographic of age at Yahoo!, where more than half of employees are age 34 or younger. Young team members of Yahoo!'s oneSearch team shown here, grew up during the information revolution, are well educated and are results driven. The sharing of these attributes should result in better communication among team members, low turnover and few power struggles.

organizational demography

The degree to which members of a work unit share a common demographic attribute, such as age, sex, race, educational level or length of service in an organization, and the impact of this attribute on turnover.

An offshoot of the diversity issue has received a great deal of attention from group and team researchers. This is the degree to which members of a work unit (group, team or department) share a common demographic attribute, such as age, sex, race, educational level or length of service in the organization, and the impact of that attribute on turnover. We call this variable **organizational demography**. Organizational demography suggests that attributes such as age or the date that someone joins a specific work team or organization should help us to predict turnover. Essentially, the logic goes like this: Turnover will be greater among those with dissimilar experiences because communication is more difficult. Conflict and power struggles are more likely, and they are more severe when they occur. The increased conflict makes unit membership less attractive, so employees are more likely to quit. Similarly, the losers in a power struggle are more apt to leave voluntarily or to be forced out.[30]

Size of teams

The president of AOL Technologies says the secret to a great team is to 'think small. Ideally, your team should have seven to nine people.'[31] His advice is supported by evidence.[32] Generally speaking, the most effective teams have five to nine members. And experts suggest using the smallest number of people who can do the task. Unfortunately, there is a pervasive tendency for managers to err on the side of making teams too large. While a minimum of four or five may be necessary to develop diversity of views and skills, managers seem to seriously underestimate how coordination problems can exponentially increase as team members are added. When teams have excess members, cohesiveness and mutual accountability decline, social loafing increases, and more and more people do less talking relative to others. Moreover, large teams have trouble coordinating with one another, especially when under time pressure. So in designing effective teams, managers should try to keep them at nine or fewer members. If a natural working unit is larger and you want a team effort, consider breaking the group into subteams.[33]

Member preferences

Not every employee is a team player. Given the option, many employees will select themselves *out* of team participation. When people who would prefer to work alone are required to team up, there is a direct threat to the team's morale and to individual member satisfaction.[34] This suggests that, when selecting team members, individual preferences should be considered along with abilities, personalities and skills. High-performing teams are likely to be composed of people who prefer working as part of a group.

'OLD TEAMS CAN'T LEARN NEW TRICKS'   MYTH *OR* SCIENCE?

This statement is true for some types of teams and false for others. Let's look at why.

To study this question, researchers at Michigan State University in the US composed 80 four-person teams from undergraduate business students. The teams engaged in a networked computer simulation that was developed for the US Department of Defense. In the simulation, teams played a command-and-control simulation in which each team member sat at a networked computer connected to his or her other team members' computers. The team's mission was to monitor a geographic area, keep unfriendly forces from moving in and support friendly forces. Performance was measured by both speed (how quickly they identified targets and friendly forces) and accuracy (the number of friendly fire errors and missed opportunities)

Teams were rewarded either cooperatively (in which case team members shared rewards equally) or competitively (in which case team members were rewarded based on their individual contributions). After playing a few rounds, the reward structures were switched, so that the cooperatively rewarded teams were switched to competitive rewards and the competitively rewarded teams were now cooperatively rewarded.

The researchers found that the initially cooperatively rewarded teams easily adapted to the competitive reward conditions and learned to excel. However, the formerly competitively rewarded teams could not adapt to cooperative rewards.

If the results of this study generalise to actual teams, it seems that teams that 'cut their teeth' being cooperative can learn to be competitive, but competitive teams find it much harder to learn to cooperate.

Source· M. D. Johnson, S. E. Humphrey, D. R. Ilgen, D. Jundt and C. J. Meyer, 'Cutthroat cooperation: asymmetrical adaptation to changes in team reward structures', *Academy of Management Journal*, 49, 1 (2006), pp. 103–19.

Work design

Effective teams need to work together and take collective responsibility for completing significant tasks. An effective team must be more than a 'team in name only'.[35] Based on terminology introduced in Chapter 7, the work-design category includes variables such as freedom and autonomy, the opportunity to use different skills and talents (skill variety), the ability to complete a whole and identifiable task or product (task identity), and work on a task or project that has a substantial impact on others (task significance). The evidence indicates that these characteristics enhance member motivation and increase team effectiveness.[36] These work-design characteristics motivate because they increase members' sense of responsibility and ownership of the work and because they make the work more interesting to perform.[37]

Process

The final category related to team effectiveness is process variables. These include member commitment to a common purpose, establishment of specific team goals, team efficacy, a managed level of conflict and minimisation of social loafing.

Why are processes important to team effectiveness? One way to answer this question is to return to the topic of social loafing. We found that $1 + 1 + 1$ doesn't necessarily add up to 3. In team tasks for which each member's contribution is not clearly visible, there is a tendency for individuals to decrease their effort. Social loafing, in other words, illustrates a process loss as a result of using teams. But team processes should produce positive results. That is, teams should create outputs greater than the sum of their inputs. The development of creative alternatives by a diverse group would be one such instance. Figure 10.5 illustrates how group processes can have an impact on a group's actual effectiveness.[38] Research teams are often used in research laboratories because they can draw on the diverse skills of various individuals to produce more meaningful research as a team than could be generated by all the researchers working independently. That is, they produce positive synergy. Their process gains exceed their process losses.

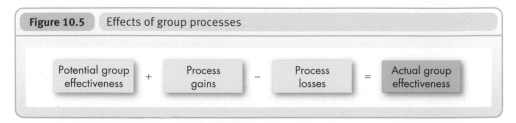

Figure 10.5	Effects of group processes

$$\text{Potential group effectiveness} + \text{Process gains} - \text{Process losses} = \text{Actual group effectiveness}$$

Robert F Bukaty /AP/Press Association Images

Employee teams at New Balance share the common purpose of continuously improving their work processes. In the company's stitching department, shown here, sharing the purpose of quality improvement motivated members of team CS-39 to develop a cross-training programme so all members could learn and perform each other's job skills.

Common plan and purpose

An effective team has a common plan and purpose that provides direction, momentum, and commitment for members.[39] This purpose is a vision, or master plan. It's broader than specific goals.

Members of successful teams put a tremendous amount of time and effort into discussing, shaping, and agreeing on a purpose that belongs to them both collectively and individually. This common purpose, when accepted by the team, becomes the equivalent of what celestial navigation is to a ship captain: It provides direction and guidance under any and all conditions. Like the proverbial ship following the wrong course, teams that don't have good planning skills are doomed; perfectly executing the wrong plan is a lost cause.[40] Effective teams also show **reflexivity**, meaning that they reflect on and adjust their master plan when necessary. A team has to have a good plan, but it also has to be willing and able to adapt when conditions call for it.[41]

reflexivity
A team characteristic of reflecting on and adjusting the master plan when necessary.

Specific goals

Successful teams translate their common purpose into specific, measurable, and realistic performance goals. Just as we demonstrated in Chapter 6 how goals lead individuals to higher performance, goals also energise teams. Specific goals facilitate clear communication. They also help teams maintain their focus on getting results.

Also, consistent with the research on individual goals, team goals should be challenging. Difficult goals have been found to raise team performance on those criteria for which they're set. So, for instance, goals for quantity tend to raise quantity, goals for speed tend to raise speed, goals for accuracy raise accuracy and so on.[42]

Team efficacy

Effective teams have confidence in themselves. They believe they can succeed. We call this *team efficacy*.[43] Success breeds success. Teams that have been successful raise their beliefs about future success, which, in turn, motivates them to work harder. What, if anything, can management do to increase team efficacy? Two possible options are helping the team to achieve small successes and providing skill training. Small successes build team confidence. As a team develops an increasingly stronger performance record, it also increases the collective belief that future efforts will lead to success. In addition, managers should consider providing training to improve members' technical and interpersonal skills. The greater the abilities of team members, the greater the likelihood that the team will develop confidence and the capability to deliver on that confidence.

Mental models

mental models
Team members' knowledge and beliefs about how the work gets done by the team.

Effective teams have accurate and common **mental models** – knowledge and beliefs (a 'psychological map') about how the work gets done. If team members have the wrong mental models, which is particularly likely to happen with teams under acute stress, their performance suffers.[44] The similarity of team members' mental models matters, too. If team members have different ideas about how to do things, the teams will fight over how to do things rather than focus on what needs to be done.[45]

SELF-ASSESSMENT LIBRARY

What's my team efficacy?

In the Self-assessment library (available online), take assessment IV.E.2 (What is my self-efficacy for teamwork?).

Conflict levels

Conflict on a team isn't necessarily bad. As will be discussed in more depth in Chapter 15, teams that are completely void of conflict are likely to become apathetic and stagnant. So conflict can actually improve team effectiveness.[46] But not all types of conflict. Relationship conflicts – those based on interpersonal incompatibilities, tension, and animosity toward others – are almost always dysfunctional. However, on teams performing nonroutine activities, disagreements among members about task content (called *task conflicts*) is not detrimental. In fact, it is often beneficial because it reduces the likelihood of groupthink. Task conflicts stimulate discussion, promote critical assessment of problems and options, and can lead to better team decisions. So effective teams can be characterised as having an appropriate level of conflict.

Social loafing

We talked in Chapter 9 about the fact that individuals can hide inside a group. They can engage in social loafing and coast on the group's effort because their individual contributions can't be identified. Effective teams undermine this tendency by holding themselves accountable at both the individual and team levels. Successful teams make members individually and jointly accountable for the team's purpose, goals, and approach.[47] Therefore, members should be clear on what they are individually responsible for and what they are jointly responsible for.

Turning individuals into team players

5 Show how organizations can create team players.

To this point, we've made a strong case for the value and growing popularity of teams. But many people are not inherently team players. There are also many organizations that have historically nurtured individual accomplishments. Finally, countries differ in terms of how they rate on individualism and collectivism. Teams fit well with countries that score high on collectivism. But what if an organization wants to introduce teams into a work population that is made up largely of individuals born and raised in an individualistic society? A veteran employee of a large company, who had done well working in an individualistic company in an individualist country, described the experience of joining a team: 'I'm learning my lesson. I just had my first negative performance appraisal in 20 years.'[48]

So what can organizations do to enhance team effectiveness – to turn individual contributors into team members? The following are the primary options managers have for trying to turn individuals into team players.

Selection: hiring team players

Some people already possess the interpersonal skills to be effective team players. When hiring team members, in addition to the technical skills required to fill the job, care should be taken to ensure that candidates can fulfil their team roles as well as technical requirements.[49]

Many job candidates don't have team skills. This is especially true for those socialised around individual contributions. When faced with such candidates, managers basically have three options. The candidates can undergo training to 'make them into team players'. If this isn't possible or doesn't work, the other two options are to transfer the individual to another unit within the organization that does not have teams (if this possibility exists) and not to hire the candidate. In established organizations that decide to redesign jobs around teams, it should be expected that some employees will resist being team players and may be untrainable. Unfortunately, such people typically become casualties of the team approach.

Training: creating team players

A large proportion of people raised on the importance of individual accomplishments can be trained to become team players. Training specialists conduct exercises that allow employees to experience the satisfaction that teamwork can provide. They typically offer workshops to help employees improve their problem-solving, communication, negotiation, conflict-management, and coaching skills. Employees also learn the five-stage group development model described in Chapter 9. At Verizon, for example, trainers focus on how a team goes through various stages before it finally gels. And employees are reminded of the importance of patience – because teams take longer to make decisions than do employees acting alone.[50]

When Volkswagen set up the subsidary Auto 5000 GmbH all work was organized into teams with a high degree of autonomy. To facilitate this, special training was provided for the 5,000 new employees in social skills.[51]

Rewarding: providing incentives to be a good team player

An organization's reward system needs to be reworked to encourage cooperative efforts rather than competitive ones.[52] For instance, Hallmark Cards added to its basic individual-incentive system an annual bonus based on achievement of team goals.[53]

Promotions, pay raises and other forms of recognition should be given to individuals who work effectively as collaborative team members. This doesn't mean individual contributions should be ignored; rather, they should be balanced with selfless contributions to the team. Examples of behaviours that should be rewarded include training new colleagues, sharing information with teammates, helping to resolve team conflicts and mastering new skills that the team needs but in which it is deficient.

Finally, don't forget the intrinsic rewards that employees can receive from teamwork. Teams provide camaraderie. It's exciting and satisfying to be an integral part of a successful team. The opportunity to engage in personal development and to help teammates grow can be a very satisfying and rewarding experience for employees.

Beware! Teams aren't always the answer

6 Decide when to use individuals instead of teams.

Teamwork takes more time and often more resources than individual work. For instance, teams have increased communication demands, conflicts to be managed, and meetings to be run. So the benefits of using teams have to exceed the costs. And that's not always the case.[54] In the excitement to enjoy the benefits of teams, some managers have introduced them into situations in which the work is better done by individuals. So before you rush to implement teams, you should carefully assess whether the work requires or will benefit from a collective effort.

How do you know if the work of your group would be better done in teams? It's been suggested that three tests be applied to see if a team fits the situation.[55] First, can the work be done better by more than one person? A good indicator is the complexity of the work and the need for different perspectives. Simple tasks that don't require diverse input are probably better left to individuals. Second, does the work create a common purpose or set of goals for the people in the group that is more than the aggregate of individual goals? For instance, many new-car dealer service departments have introduced teams that link customer-service personnel, mechanics, parts specialists and sales representatives. Such teams can better manage collective responsibility for ensuring that customer needs are properly met. The final test to assess whether teams fit the situation is to determine whether the members of the group are interdependent. Using teams makes sense when there is interdependence between tasks – when the success of the whole depends on the success of each one *and* the success of each one depends on the success of the others. Football, for instance, is an obvious *team* sport. Success requires a great deal of coordination between interdependent players. Conversely, except possibly for relays, swimming teams are not really teams. They're groups of individuals, performing individually, whose total performance is merely the aggregate summation of their individual performances.

Global implications

7 Show how the understanding of teams differs in a global context.

Although research on global considerations in the use of teams is just beginning, three areas are particularly worth mentioning: the extent of teamwork, self-managed teams and team cultural diversity.

Extent of teamwork
Teamworking is widespread across Europe. A major survey put the number of workers across the European Union who do part or all their work in teams at 60 per cent. Whilst prevalent in all EU countries, workings in teams was most common in Slovenia, Netherlands and some Nordic countries, while it was less prevalent in France, Hungary, Italy, Portugal and Spain.[56] In Western European countries, and in particular northern European countries like Sweden, Denmark, United Kingdom and also the Netherlands, the concept of teamwork has been in place for decades, experiencing a surge in the 1980s and 1990s. Conversely, in eastern European countries, new forms of work organization and their influence on company efficiency have only been considered since the start of the 1990s, so their development has so far been comparitively brief.[57] Teamworking is also pervasive in the United States, but some evidence suggests that the extent of teamwork is not as significant in the United States as in other countries. One study comparing US workers to Canadian and Asian workers revealed that 51 per cent of workers in Asia-Pacific and 48 per cent of Canadian employees report high levels of teamwork. But only about one-third (32 per cent) of US employees say their organization has a high level of teamwork.[58] Thus, although teamwork is widely used in the United States, this evidence suggests that there still is a heavy role for individual contributions.

Self-managed teams
Although self-managed teams have not proven to be the panacea many thought they would be, special care needs to be taken when introducing self-managed teams globally. For instance,

evidence suggests that these types of teams have not fared well in Mexico, largely due to that culture's low tolerance of ambiguity and uncertainty and employees' strong respect for hierarchical authority.[59] Thus, in countries that are relatively high in power distance – meaning that roles of leaders and followers are clearly delineated – a team may need to be structured so that leadership roles are spelled out and power relationships are identified.

Team cultural diversity and team performance

Earlier, we discussed research on team diversity in terms of factors such as race or gender. But what about diversity created by national differences? Like the earlier research, evidence indicates that these elements of diversity interfere with team processes, at least in the short term.[60] Cultural diversity does seem to be an asset for tasks that call for a variety of viewpoints. But culturally heterogeneous teams have more difficulty learning to work with each other and solving problems. The good news is that these difficulties seem to dissipate with time. Although newly formed culturally diverse teams underperform newly formed culturally homogeneous teams, the differences disappear after about three months.[61] The reason is that it takes culturally diverse teams a while to learn how to work through disagreements and different approaches to solving problems.

Summary and implications for managers

Few trends have influenced jobs as much as the massive movement to introduce teams into the workplace. The shift from working alone to working on teams requires employees to cooperate with others, share information, confront differences and sublimate personal interests for the greater good of the team.

Effective teams have common characteristics. They have adequate resources, effective leadership, a climate of trust and a performance evaluation and reward system that reflects team contributions. These teams have individuals with technical expertise, as well as problem solving, decision making and interpersonal skills and the right traits, especially conscientiousness and openness. Effective teams also tend to be small – with fewer than 10 people, preferably of diverse backgrounds. They have members who fill role demands and who prefer to be part of a group. And the work that members do provides freedom and autonomy, the opportunity to use different skills and talents, the ability to complete a whole and identifiable task or product, and work that has a substantial impact on others. Finally, effective teams have members who believe in the team's capabilities and are committed to a common plan and purpose, an accurate shared mental model of what is to be accomplished, specific team goals, a manageable level of conflict and a minimal degree of social loafing.

Because individualistic organizations and societies attract and reward individual accomplishments, it is can be difficult to create team players in these environments. To make the conversion, management should try to select individuals who have the interpersonal skills to be effective team players, provide training to develop teamwork skills and reward individuals for cooperative efforts.

POINT/COUNTERPOINT

Sports teams are good models for workplace teams

POINT →

Studies from sports including football, basketball, hockey, volleyball and baseball have found a number of elements of successful sports teams that can be extrapolated to successful work teams.

Successful teams integrate cooperation and competition. Sports teams with the best win–loss record had coaches who promote a strong spirit of cooperation and a high level of healthy competition among their players.

Successful teams score early wins. Early successes build teammates' faith in themselves and their capacity as a team. Research on hockey teams of relatively equal ability found that 72 per cent of the time, the team that was ahead at the end of the first period went on to win. So managers should provide teams with early tasks that are simple and provide 'easy wins'.

Successful teams avoid losing streaks. A couple of failures can lead to a downward spiral if a team becomes demoralised. Managers need to instil confidence in team members that they can turn things around when they encounter setbacks.

Practice makes perfect. Successful sport teams execute on game day but learn from their mistakes in practice. Practice should be used to try new things and fail. A wise manager encourages work teams to experiment and learn.

COUNTERPOINT ←

There are flaws in using sports as a model for developing effective work teams. Here are just four caveats.

All sport teams aren't alike. In baseball, for instance, there is little interaction among teammates. Rarely are more than two or three players directly involved in a play. The performance of the team is largely the sum of the performance of its individual players. In contrast, basketball has much more interdependence among players. Geographic distribution is dense. Usually all players are involved in every play, team members have to be able to switch from offence to defence at a moment's notice, and there is continuous movement by all, not just the player who has the ball. The performance of the team is more than the sum of its individual players. So when using sports teams as a model for work teams, you have to make sure you're making the correct comparison. As one expert noted, 'The problem with sports metaphors is that the meaning you extract from a sports metaphor is entirely dependent on the sport you pick.'

Work teams are more varied and complex than sports teams. In a sports league, the design of the task, the design of the team and the team's context vary relatively little from team to team. But these variables can vary tremendously between work teams. As a result, coaching plays a much more significant part of a sports team's performance than in that of a

Successful teams use half-time breaks. The best coaches in basketball and football use half-time during a game to reassess what is working and what isn't. Managers of work teams should similarly build in assessments at the approximate halfway point in a team project to evaluate what it can do to improve.

Winning teams have stable membership. Stability improves performance. Studies of professional basketball teams have found that when teammates have more time together, they are more able to anticipate one another's moves, and they are clearer about one another's roles.

Successful teams debrief after failures and successes. The best sports teams study the game video. Similarly, work teams should routinely assess their successes and failures and should learn from them.

Sports metaphors are useful. For example, a recent *Harvard Business Review* issue had as the lead story 'Playing to win . . . five killer strategies for trouncing the competition'. The article argues that winners in business play hardball, which means they pick their shots, seek out competitive encounters, set the pace of innovation and test the edges of the possible. Like sports teams, in business you have to play hardball, which means playing to win. That is what the sports model can teach us.

work team. Performance of work teams is a function of getting the team's structural and design variables right. So, in contrast to sports, managers of work teams should focus more on getting the team set up for success than on coaching.

A lot of employees can't relate to sports metaphors. Not everyone on work teams is conversant in sports. Some people aren't as interested in sports as 'sports buffs' and aren't as savvy about sports terminology. And team members from different cultures may not know the sports metaphors you're using. Most Europeans, for instance, are unfamiliar with the rules and terminology of Australian Rules football.

Work team outcomes aren't easily defined in terms of wins and losses. Sports teams typically measure success in terms of wins and losses. Such measures of success are rarely as clear for work teams. When managers try to define success in wins and losses, it tends to infer that the workplace is ethically no more complex than the playing field, which is rarely true.

Source: See N. Katz, 'Sports teams as a model for workplace teams: lessons and liabilities,' *Academy of Management Executive*, August 2001, 15, 3 pp. 56–67; 'Talent Inc.,' *The New Yorker Online Only*, 22 July 2002, www.newyorker.com/online; and D. Batstone, 'HBR Goes CG?', *Worthwhile.com*, 14 April 2004 www.worthwhilemag.com.

QUESTIONS FOR REVIEW

1. How do you explain the growing popularity of teams in organizations?

2. What is the difference between a group and a team?

3. What are the four types of teams?

4. What properties characterise effective teams?

5. How can organizations create team players?

6. When is work performed by individuals preferred over work performed by teams?

7. What are three ways in which our understanding of teams differs in a global context?

Experiential exercise

FIXED VERSUS VARIABLE FLIGHT CREWS

Break into teams of five. Assume that you've been hired by AJet, a start-up airline based in Amsterdam. Your team has been formed to consider the pros and cons of using variable flight crews and to arrive at a recommendation on whether to follow this industry practice at AJet.

Variable flight crews are crews formed when pilots, copilots and flight attendants typically bid for schedules on specific planes (for instance, Boeing 737s, 757s or 767s) based on seniority. Then they're given a monthly schedule made up of 1- to 4-day trips. So any given flight crew on a plane is rarely together for more than a few days at a time. A complicated system is required to complete the schedules. Because of this system, it's not unusual for a senior pilot at a large airline to fly with a different copilot on every trip during any given month. And a pilot and copilot who work together for three days in January may never work together again the rest of the year. (In contrast, a fixed flight crew consists of the same group of pilots and attendants who fly together for a period of time.)

In considering whether to use variable flight crews, your team is to answer the following questions:

1. What are the primary advantages of variable flight crews?

2. If you were to recommend some version of fixed flight crews, drawing from the material in this chapter, on what criteria would you assign AJet crews?

When your team has considered the advantages and disadvantages of variable flight crews and answered these questions, be prepared to present to the class your recommendations and justification.

Ethical dilemma

PRESSURE TO BE A TEAM PLAYER

'Okay, I admit it. I'm not a team player. I work best when I work alone and am left alone,' says Ciaran Murphy.

Ciaran's employer, Broad's Furniture, an office furniture manufacturer, recently reorganized around teams. All production in the company's Dublin factory is now done in teams. And Ciaran's design department has been broken up into three design teams. To Ciaran's dismay, he was assigned to the modular-office design (MOD) team, which does work that Ciaran finds less interesting and challenging than other work he's done. What's worse, Ciaran believes that some low-performing individuals have been put in the team. Maggie Quinn, MOD's new team leader, seems to agree with Ciaran. She told him, 'Ciaran, listen, I know you're not wild about the work MOD is doing, and it's true some weaker individual contributors have been assigned to the team. But that's why we formed the team. We really think that when we work together, the strengths of the team will be magnified and the weaknesses limited.'

Although Ciaran respects Maggie, he's not convinced. 'I've worked here for four years. I'm very good at what I do. And my performance reviews confirm that. I've been rated in the highest performance category every year I've been here. But now everything is changing. My evaluations and pay raises are going to depend on how well the team does. And, get this, 50 per cent of my evaluation will depend on how well the team does – and this isn't a great team. I'm really frustrated and demoralised. They hired me for my design skills. They knew I wasn't a social type. Now they're forcing me to be a team player. This doesn't play to my strengths at all.'

Is it unethical for Ciaran's employer to force him to be a team leader? Is his firm breaking an implied contract that it made with him at the time he was hired? Does this employer have any responsibility to provide Ciaran with an alternative that would allow him to continue to work independently? If you were Ciaran, how would you respond?

CASE INCIDENT 1

Volvo Cars Ghent: A self-managing team model

Since the establishment of the manufacturing plant in 1965, industrial relations at Volvo Cars Ghent, Belgium were characterised by conflict and distrust. A severe crisis in 1978, however, led employers and employees to the conclusion that greater cooperation was necessary to save the plant. The consensus model that arose between management and trade unions at that time became a decisive factor in bringing about growth from the 1980s onwards.

In 1987, the traditional work structure, in which each operator had a fixed workstation and only performed online production tasks, was replaced by a structure of self-steering teams. Within the constraints of line-paced assembly work, groups of approximately 15 operators and a team leader were formed, and were given extended responsibilities with regard to quality, maintenance and material tasks. A job rotation scheme was also implemented. Strong union involvement, a philosophy that regards people as the most valuable asset, and the 'total productive management philosophy' became the cornerstones of teamwork at Volvo Cars Ghent.

During the last decade, some changes have been made to the team model to encourage increased self-management. More specifically, a star-shaped model has been developed, as a means of visualising grouped, indirect and specialised tasks relating to quality, cost, delivery, improvement, safety and the environment. On a voluntary basis, each of these tasks, in turn, becomes the individual responsibility of a single operator in the team, thus creating a greater sense of ownership. In themed group sessions, operators are then given the necessary feedback in relation to their own specialised tasks. Here, the role of the team leader has moved from a supervisory to a more 'coaching' role.

Between 2001 and 2004 the Ghent plant underwent huge expansion when two new models were introduced to the factory. The production capacity almost doubled and 1,400 new employees were hired. This rapid expansion has challenged the distinctive teamwork model that Volvo Cars Ghent has established over time.

The costs of manufacturing in Europe will mean the Ghent plant will continue to face challenges, however, a strong belief in the advantages of working with self-managing teams, both from the point of view of management and of employees, has contributed to the sustainability of the organizational model in the past, and it is claimed, will contribute to meeting the challenges of the future.

Questions

1. What are some advantages and disadvantages of giving teams a lot of autonomy to make decisions?

2. Four contextual factors (adequate resources, leadership and structure, climate of trust and performance evaluation and reward systems) influence team performance. Which of these appear to be present in the above case? If present, are they supportive or unsupportive? How?

3. If you were to compose a team that will be given decision-making responsibility to solve complex problems, what types of members would you select in terms of abilities and personalities?

4. What are some processes losses that are likely to occur in teams such as those at Volvo Cars Ghent? How can these processes losses be avoided?

Source: Adapted from Volvo Cars Ghent: A self-managing team model, *Workplace Innovation: Four Case Examples, Box 1: Overview*, p. 1 (EMCC Company Network 2005).
Published by: European Foundation for the Improvement of Living and Working Conditions.
Available at http://www.eurofound.europa.eu/emcc/publications/2005/ef0550enC.pdf.

CASE INCIDENT 2

Team building: sociable climbing

Outdoor, mud-spattered team-building – the sort involving hiking boots, rain coats and woollen hats – remains an immovable object in the corporate world. When the *Financial Management* magazine asked 50 companies how they turned their workers into cohesive, tight-knit units, there was a deluge of similar responses. From web design firms to pork pie makers came tales of survival weekends with the Parachute Regiment and assaults on Scafell Pike, the highest mountain in England.

But why? Does trudging through mud do any good? And aren't there any better options that boost morale and togetherness without requiring office workers to trudge, half frozen, up a mountain? Bruce Renny, founder of mobile software group Rok, sums up the thoughts of many grumbling employees: 'I went on a residential team-building course about six years ago with a previous company – what a fiasco. It ended up with the two teams loathing each other. Claims and counter-claims of cheating were made, people stormed off in a huff, there were injuries on the road-run and, eventually, a big fight afterwards.'

Outsourced service provider EDS is one company that's searched high and low for something a little more civilised. Its answer? playing with Lego. No joke. In fact, the name of this team-building exercise Is Lego Serious Play and it's endorsed by such strait-laced organizations as Deloitte, IBM and even HM Treasury. Created by two business professors at IMD business school in Lausanne,

▶

it's now offered by dozens of consultancies across Europe and the US. The object of the exercise is to create visual representations of abstract concepts using Lego bricks. Team members might be asked to construct a 3D image of the company's divisions or the reporting structure. When they start scratching their heads and wondering how finance relates to marketing, breakthroughs start occurring. The clients seem impressed. James Johns, of EDS's government industry group, says: 'I'm convinced that we covered more in that one day [of Lego Serious Play] than would have been possible in a week of workshops facilitated by more traditional means.'

But the more physically challenging teambuilding experiences have not yet been overshadowed. When the Royal National Lifeboat Institution (RNLI) wanted to introduce different teams to each other, it booked a day with Go Ape!, a provider of assault courses featuring rope ladders, Tarzan swings and zip slides high in the forest canopy.

Brett Shepherd, the RNLI manager in charge of training and development, explains: 'The "high ropes" course gets the lifeguards to interact with different teams from different beaches in a non-beach environment. Then we set them a challenge: teams of ten lifeguards have to get everyone safely around the course, plus a 70kg manikin. Including the manikin changes the focus of the task. Instead of simply going around as individuals, the lifeguards must become more interactive. The course improves their ability to work in teams and as leaders. We have nothing but positive feedback from our lifeguards about it.' Nestlé, Nokia and Unilever are three of the many blue-chip organizations that keep coming back to Go Ape! for more.

The testimony that Financial Management magazine has received from firms suggests that the traditional company teambuilding outdoor exercises aren't quite so bad after all. One events organizer, Zibrant, measured the effects of its participation (employees, clients and suppliers of the firm were all involved) in the three-peaks challenge. This involves scaling the highest mountains in Scotland (Ben Nevis), England (Scafell Pike) and Wales (Snowdon) on consecutive days and the firm made the following observations:

- There was a reduction in staff turnover from 16 per cent to seven per cent in 2007 (the industry standard is 22 per cent), which could be directly attributed to employee involvement in the challenge.

- The event helped the company to develop shared values with its stakeholders.

- More than 15 per cent of the employees who took part later asked to join the firm's corporate social responsibility committee.

The feedback from employees was pretty encouraging, too: 97 per cent enjoyed the event and said they would take part again; 90 per cent thought that the event was very well organized; and 97 per cent were interested in participating in another charity challenge. 'Words cannot properly describe my sheer delight at being involved in the three-peaks challenge,' says one of the company's climbers, Cecilia Curry. 'The months of training beforehand were demanding and exhausting but, above all, fun. The event itself gave us excitement, fear, pride, pain and an "all in this together" feeling. The atmosphere and sense of bonding with everyone was something that I will never forget.'

The slopes of Scafell Pike won't be falling silent just yet.

Questions

1. Do you believe that team-building activities increase productivity? Why or why not? What other factors might be responsible for increases in profitability following a corporate retreat?

2. What are some other ways besides those described here to build effective teams and increase teamwork among company employees? How might these alternatives be better or worse than those presented?

3. What should companies do about employees who lack athletic talent but are still pressured to participate in physical activities with their colleagues? How might poor performance by those with low athletic ability affect their status within the organization? Are there similar arguments to be made for those who are less cognitively able being pressured to perform the Lego activity?

4. How might you increase teamwork when team members are not often in direct contact with one another? Can you think of any 'electronic' team-building exercises?

Source: Adapted from C. Orton-Jones (2008) 'Sociable climbing', *Financial Management* pp. 16–19.

Endnotes

1 This section is based on J. R. Katzenbach and D. K. Smith, *The Wisdom of Teams* (Cambridge, MA: Harvard University Press, 1993), pp. 21, 45, 85; and D. C. Kinlaw, *Developing Superior Work Teams* (Lexington, MA: Lexington Books, 1991), pp. 3–21.

2 See, for instance, E. Sunstrom, K. DeMeuse and D. Futrell, 'Work teams: applications and effectiveness', *American Psychologist*, February 1990, pp. 120–33.

3 J. H. Shonk, *Team-Based Organizations* (Homewood, IL: Business One Irwin, 1992); and M. A. Verespej, 'When workers get new roles', *IndustryWeek*, 3 February 1992, p. 11.

4 G. Bodinson and R. Bunch, 'AQP's national team excellence award: its purpose, value and process', *Journal for Quality and Participation*, Spring 2003, pp. 37–42.

5 See, for example, S. G. Cohen, G. E. Ledford, Jr. and G. M. Spreitzer, 'A predictive model of self-managing work

team effectiveness', *Human Relations*, May 1996, pp. 643–76; C. E. Nicholls, H. W. Lane and M. Brehm Brechu, 'Taking self-managed teams to Mexico', *Academy of Management Executive*, August 1999, pp. 15–27; and A. Erez, J. A. LePine and H. Elms, 'Effects of rotated leadership and peer evaluation on the functioning and effectiveness of self-managed teams: a quasi-experiment', *Personnel Psychology*, Winter 2002, pp. 929–48.

6 Dobbins, T. (2002) Workplace partnership 'needs to evolve to next stage'. Available at: http://www.eurofound.europa.eu/eiro/2002/08/feature/ie0208203f.htm.

7 See, for instance, J. L. Cordery, W. S. Mueller and L. M. Smith, 'Attitudinal and behavioral effects of autonomous group working: a longitudinal field study', *Academy of Management Journal*, June 1991, pp. 464–76; R. A. Cook and J. L. Goff, 'Coming of age with self-managed teams: dealing with a problem employee', *Journal of Business and Psychology*, Spring 2002, pp. 485–96; and C. W. Langfred, 'Too much of a good thing? Negative effects of high trust and individual autonomy in self-managing teams', *Academy of Management Journal*, June 2004, pp. 385–99.

8 Bodinson and Bunch, 'AQP's national team excellence award.'

9 M. Brunelli, 'How Harley-Davidson uses cross-functional teams', *Purchasing Online*, November 4, 1999.

10 See, for example, J. Lipnack and J. Stamps, *Virtual Teams: People Working Across Boundaries and Technology*, 2nd edn (New York: Wiley, 2000); C. B. Gibson and S. G. Cohen (eds), *Virtual Teams That Work* (San Francisco, CA: Jossey-Bass, 2003); and L. L. Martins, L. L. Gilson and M. T. Maynard, 'Virtual teams: what do we know and where do we go from here?', *Journal of Management*, November 2004, pp. 805–35.

11 A. Malhotra, A. Majchrzak and B. Rosen, 'Leading virtual teams', *Academy of Management Perspectives*, February 2007, pp. 60–70; and J. M. Wilson, S. S. Straus and B. McEvily, 'All in due time: the development of trust in computer-mediated and face-to-face teams', *Organizational Behavior and Human Decision Processes*, 19 (2006), pp. 16–33.

12 B. Bergiel, E. Bergiel, P. Balsmeier, 'Nature of virtual teams: a summary of their advantages and disadvantages', *Management Research News*, 31, 2 (2008), p. 99.

13 See, for instance, J. R. Hackman, 'The design of work teams', in J. W. Lorsch (ed.), *Handbook of Organizational Behavior* (Upper Saddle River, NJ: Prentice Hall, 1987), pp. 315–42; and M. A. Campion, G. J. Medsker and C. A. Higgs, 'Relations between work group characteristics and effectiveness: implications for designing effective work groups', *Personnel Psychology*, Winter 1993, pp. 823–50.

14 D. E. Hyatt and T. M. Ruddy, 'An examination of the relationship between work group characteristics and performance: once more into the breech', *Personnel Psychology*, Autumn 1997, p. 555.

15 This model is based on M. A. Campion, E. M. Papper and G. J. Medsker, 'Relations between work team characteristics and effectiveness: a replication and extension', *Personnel Psychology*, Summer 1996, pp. 429–52; D. E. Hyatt and T. M. Ruddy, 'An examination of the relationship between work group characteristics and performance', pp. 553–85; S. G. Cohen and D. E. Bailey, 'What makes teams work: group effectiveness research from the shop floor to the executive suite', *Journal of Management*, 23, 3 (1997), pp. 239–90; L. Thompson, *Making the Team* (Upper Saddle River, NJ: Prentice-Hall, 2000), pp. 18–33; and J. R. Hackman, *Leading Teams: Setting the Stage for Great Performance* (Boston, MA: Harvard Business School Press, 2002).

16 See M. Mattson, T. V. Mumford and G. S. Sintay, 'Taking teams to task: a normative model for designing or recalibrating work teams', paper presented at the National Academy of Management Conference, Chicago, August 1999; and G. L. Stewart and M. R. Barrick, 'Team structure and performance: assessing the mediating role of intrateam process and the moderating role of task type', *Academy of Management Journal*, April 2000, pp. 135–48.

17 Hyatt and Ruddy, 'An examination of the relationship between work group characteristics and performance', p. 577.

18 P. Balkundi and D. A. Harrison, 'Ties, leaders, and time in teams: strong inference about network structure's effects on team viability and performance', *Academy of Management Journal*, 49, 1 (2006), pp. 49–68; G. Chen, B. L. Kirkman, R. Kanfer, D. Allen and B. Rosen, 'A multilevel study of leadership, empowerment, and performance in teams', *Journal of Applied Psychology*, 92, no. 2 (2007), pp. 331–46; L. A. DeChurch and M. A. Marks, 'Leadership in multiteam systems', *Journal of Applied Psychology*, 91, 2 (2006), pp. 311–29; A. Srivastava, K. M. Bartol and E. A. Locke, 'Empowering leadership in management teams: effects on knowledge sharing, efficacy, and performance', *Academy of Management Journal*, 49, 6 (2006), pp. 1239–51; and J. E. Mathieu, K. K. Gilson and T. M. Ruddy, 'Empowerment and team effectiveness: an empirical test of an integrated model', *Journal of Applied Psychology*, 91, 1 (2006), pp. 97–108.

19 K. T. Dirks, 'Trust in leadership and team performance: evidence from NCAA basketball', *Journal of Applied Psychology*, December 2000, pp. 1004–12; and M. Williams, 'In whom we trust: group membership as an affective context for trust development', *Academy of Management Review*, July 2001, pp. 377–96.

20 See S. T. Johnson, 'Work teams: what's ahead in work design and rewards management', *Compensation & Benefits Review*, March–April 1993, pp. 35–41; and L. N. McClurg, 'Team rewards: how far have we come?', *Human Resource Management*, Spring 2001, pp. 73–86.

21 R. R. Hirschfeld, M. H. Jordan, H. S. Feild, W. F. Giles and A. A. Armenakis, 'Becoming team players: team members' mastery of teamwork knowledge as a predictor of team task proficiency and observed teamwork effectiveness', *Journal of Applied Psychology*, 91, 2 (2006), pp. 467–74.

22 For a more detailed breakdown of team skills, see M. J. Stevens and M. A. Campion, 'The knowledge, skill, and ability requirements for teamwork: implications for human resource management', *Journal of Management*, Summer 1994, pp. 503–30.

23 H. Moon, J. R. Hollenbeck, and S. E. Humphrey, 'Asymmetric adaptability: dynamic team structures as one-way streets', *Academy of Management Journal*, 47, 5 (October 2004), pp. 681–95; A. P. J. Ellis, J. R. Hollenbeck and D. R. Ilgen, 'Team learning: collectively connecting the dots', *Journal of Applied Psychology*, 88, 5 (October 2003), pp. 821–35; C. L. Jackson and J. A. LePine, 'Peer responses to a team's weakest link: a test and extension of LePine and van dyne's model', *Journal of Applied Psychology*, 88, 3 (June 2003), pp. 459–75; and J. A. LePine, 'Team adaptation and post-change performance: effects of team composition in terms of members' cognitive ability and personality', *Journal of Applied Psychology*, 88, 1 (February 2003), pp. 27–39.

24 S. T. Bell, 'Deep-level composition variables as predictors of team performance: a meta-analysis', *Journal of Applied Psychology*, 92, 3 (2007), pp. 595–615; and M. R. Barrick, G. L. Stewart, M. J. Neubert and M. K. Mount, 'Relating member ability and personality to work-team processes and team effectiveness', *Journal of Applied Psychology*, June 1998, pp. 377–91.

25 Ellis, Hollenbeck and Ilgen, 'Team Learning'; C. O. L. H. Porter, J. R. Hollenbeck and D. R. Ilgen, 'Backing up behaviors in teams: the role of personality and legitimacy of need', *Journal of Applied Psychology*, 88, 3 (June 2003), pp. 391–403; A. Colquitt, J. R. Hollenbeck and D. R. Ilgen, 'Computer-assisted communication and team decision-making performance: the moderating effect of openness to experience', *Journal of Applied Psychology*, 87, 2 (April 2002), pp. 402–10; J. A. LePine, J. R. Hollenbeck, D. R. Ilgen and J. Hedlund, 'Effects of individual differences on the performance of hierarchical decision-making teams: much more than G', *Journal of Applied Psychology*, 82, pp. 803–11; Jackson and LePine, 'Peer responses to a team's weakest link'; and LePine, 'Team adaptation and postchange performance'.

26 Barrick, Stewart, Neubert and Mount, 'Relating member ability and personality to work-team processes and team effectiveness', p. 388; and S. E. Humphrey, J. R. Hollenbeck, C. J. Meyer and D. R. Ilgen, 'Trait configurations in self-managed teams: a conceptual examination of the use of seeding for maximizing and minimizing trait variance in teams', *Journal of Applied Psychology*, 92, 3 (2007), pp. 885–92.

27 See www.Belbin.com.

28 E. Mannix and M. A. Neale, 'What differences make a difference: the promise and reality of diverse teams in organizations', *Psychological Science in the Public Interest*, October 2005, pp. 31–55.

29 G. S. Van Der Vegt, J. S. Bunderson and A. Oosterhof, 'Expertness diversity and interpersonal helping in teams: why those who need the most help end up getting the least', *Academy of Management Journal*, 49, 5 (2006), pp. 877–93.

30 K. Y. Williams and C. A. O'Reilly, III, 'Demography and diversity in organizations: a review of 40 years of research', in Staw and Cummings (eds), *Research in Organizational Behavior*, vol. 20, pp. 77–140; and A. Joshi, 'The influence of organizational demography on the external networking behavior of teams', *Academy of Management Review*, July 2006, pp. 583–95.

31 J. Katzenbach, 'What makes teams work?', *Fast Company*, November 2000, p. 110.

32 The evidence in this section is described in Thompson, *Making the Team*, pp. 65–67. See also L. A. Curral, R. H. Forrester and J. F. Dawson, 'It's what you do and the way that you do it: team task, team size, and innovation-related group processes', *European Journal of Work & Organizational Psychology*, 10, 2 (June 2001), pp. 187–204; R. C. Liden, S. J. Wayne and R. A. Jaworski, 'Social loafing: a field investigation', *Journal of Management*, 30, 2 (2004), pp. 285–304; and J. A. Wagner, 'Studies of individualism–collectivism: effects on cooperation in groups', *Academy of Management Journal*, 38, 1 (February 1995), pp. 152–72.

33 'Is your team too big? too small? what's the right number?', *Knowledge@Wharton*, 14 June 2006, pp. 1–5.

34 Hyatt and Ruddy, 'An examination of the relationship between work group characteristics and performance'; J. D. Shaw, M. K. Duffy and E. M. Stark, 'Interdependence

and preference for group work: main and congruence effects on the satisfaction and performance of group members', *Journal of Management*, 26, 2 (2000), pp. 259–79; and S. A. Kiffin-Peterson and J. L. Cordery, 'Trust, individualism, and job characteristics of employee preference for teamwork', *International Journal of Human Resource Management*, February 2003, pp. 93–116.

35 R. Wageman, 'Critical success factors for creating superb self-managing teams', *Organizational Dynamics*, Summer 1997, p. 55.

36 Campion, Papper and Medsker, 'Relations between work team characteristics and effectiveness', p. 430; B. L. Kirkman and B. Rosen, 'Powering up teams', *Organizational Dynamics*, Winter 2000, pp. 48–66; and D. C. Man and S. S. K. Lam, 'The effects of job complexity and autonomy on cohesiveness in collectivist and individualist work groups: a cross-cultural analysis', *Journal of Organizational Behavior*, December 2003, pp. 979–1001.

37 Campion, Papper and Medsker, 'Relations between work team characteristics and effectiveness', p. 430.

38 I. D. Steiner, *Group Processes and Productivity* (New York: Academic Press, 1972).

39 K. Hess, *Creating the High-Performance Team* (New York: Wiley, 1987); Katzenbach and Smith, *The Wisdom of Teams*, pp. 43–64; K. D. Scott and A. Townsend, 'Teams: why some succeed and others fail', *HRMagazine*, August 1994, pp. 62–67; and K. Blanchard, D. Carew and E. Parisi-Carew, 'How to get your group to perform like a team', *Training and Development*, September 1996, pp. 34–37.

40 J. E. Mathieu and W. Schulze, 'The influence of team knowledge and formal plans on episodic team process – performance relationships', *Academy of Management Journal*, 49, 3 (2006), pp. 605–19.

41 A. Gurtner, F. Tschan, N. K. Semmer and C. Nagele, 'Getting groups to develop good strategies: effects of reflexivity interventions on team process, team performance, and shared mental models', *Organizational Behavior and Human Decision Processes*, 102 (2007), pp. 127–42; M. C. Schippers, D. N. Den Hartog and P. L. Koopman, 'Reflexivity in teams: a measure and correlates', *Applied Psychology: An International Review*, 56, 2 (2007), pp. 189–211; and C. S. Burke, K. C. Stagl, E. Salas, L. Pierce and D. Kendall, 'Understanding team adaptation: a conceptual analysis and model', *Journal of Applied Psychology*, 91, 6 (2006), pp. 1189–207.

42 E. Weldon and L. R. Weingart, 'Group goals and group performance', *British Journal of Social Psychology*, Spring 1993, pp. 307–34. See also R. P. DeShon, S. W. J. Kozlowski, A. M. Schmidt, K. R. Milner and D. Wiechmann, 'A multiple-goal, multilevel model of feedback effects on the regulation of individual and team performance', *Journal of Applied Psychology*, December 2004, pp. 1035–56.

43 K. Tasa, S. Taggar and G. H. Seijts, 'The development of collective efficacy in teams: a multilevel and longitudinal perspective', *Journal of Applied Psychology*, 92, 1 (2007), pp. 17–27; C. B. Gibson, 'The efficacy advantage: factors related to the formation of group efficacy', *Journal of Applied Social Psychology*, October 2003, pp. 2053–86; and D. I. Jung and J. J. Sosik, 'Group potency and collective efficacy: examining their predictive validity, level of analysis, and effects of performance feedback on future group performance', *Group & Organization Management*, September 2003, pp. 366–91.

44 A. P. J. Ellis, 'System breakdown: the role of mental models and transactive memory on the relationships between acute stress and team performance', *Academy of Management Journal*, 49, 3 (2006), pp. 576–89.

45 S. W. J. Kozlowski and D. R. Ilgen, 'Enhancing the effectiveness of work groups and teams', *Psychological Science in the Public Interest*, December 2006, pp. 77–124; and B. D. Edwards, E. A. Day, W. Arthur, Jr. and S. T. Bell, 'Relationships among team ability composition, team mental models, and team performance', *Journal of Applied Psychology*, 91, 3 (2006), pp. 727–36.

46 K. A. Jehn, 'A qualitative analysis of conflict types and dimensions in organizational groups', *Administrative Science Quarterly*, September 1997, pp. 530–57. See also R. S. Peterson and K. J. Behfar, 'The dynamic relationship between performance feedback, trust, and conflict in groups: a longitudinal study', *Organizational Behavior and Human Decision Processes*, September–November 2003, pp. 102–12.

47 K. H. Price, D. A. Harrison, and J. H. Gavin, 'Withholding inputs in team contexts: member composition, interaction processes, evaluation structure, and social loafing', *Journal of Applied Psychology*, 91, 6 (2006), pp. 1375–84.

48 See, for instance, B. L. Kirkman and D. L. Shapiro, 'The impact of cultural values on employee resistance to teams: toward a model of globalized self-managing work team effectiveness', *Academy of Management Review*, July 1997, pp. 730–57; and B. L. Kirkman, C. B. Gibson and D. L. Shapiro, ' "Exporting" teams: enhancing the implementation and effectiveness of work teams in global affiliates', *Organizational Dynamics*, 30, 1 (2001), pp. 12–29.

49 G. Hertel, U. Konradt and K. Voss, 'Competencies for virtual teamwork: development and validation of a web-based selection tool for members of distributed teams', *European Journal of Work and Organizational Psychology*, 15, 4 (2006), pp. 477–504.

50 T. D. Schellhardt, 'To be a star among equals, be a team player', *Wall Street Journal*, 20 April 1994, p. B1.

51 T. Schulten (2001) 'Agreements signed on Volkswagen's "5000 × 5000" project'. European Industrial Relations Observatory On-line. Available at: http://www.eurofound.europa.eu/eiro/2001/09/feature/de0109201f.htm.

52 J. S. DeMatteo, L. T. Eby and E. Sundstrom, 'Team-based rewards: current empirical evidence and directions for future research', in Staw and Cummings (eds), *Research in Organizational Behavior*, vol. 20, pp. 141–83.

53 B. Geber, 'The bugaboo of team pay', *Training*, August 1995, pp. 27, 34.

54 C. E. Naquin and R. O. Tynan, 'The team halo effect: why teams are not blamed for their failures', *Journal of Applied Psychology*, April 2003, pp. 332–40.

55 A. B. Drexler and R. Forrester, 'Teamwork – not necessarily the answer', *HRMagazine*, January 1998, pp. 55–58. See also R. Saavedra, P. C. Earley and L. Van Dyne, 'Complex interdependence in task-performing groups', *Journal of Applied Psychology*, February 1993, pp. 61–72; and K. A. Jehn, G. B. Northcraft and M. A. Neale, 'Why differences make a difference: a field study of diversity, conflict, and performance in workgroups', *Administrative Science Quarterly*, December 1999, pp. 741–63.

56 Fourth European Working, Conditions Survey European Foundation for the Improvement of Living and Working Conditions, 2007. Available at http://www.eurofound.europa.eu.

57 R. Vašková (2007) 'Teamwork and high performance work organisation', European Foundation for the Improvement of Living and Working Conditions. Available at: http://www.eurofound.europa.eu/ewco/reports/TN0507TR01/TN0507TR01_2.htm.

58 'Watson Wyatt's global work studies.' *WatsonWyatt.com*, www.watsonwyatt.com/research/featured/workstudy.asp.

59 Nicholls, Lane and Brehm Brechu, 'Taking self-managed teams to mexico'.

60 W. E. Watson, K. Kumar and L. K. Michaelsen, 'Cultural diversity's impact on interaction process and performance: comparing homogeneous and diverse task groups', *Academy of Management Journal*, June 1993, pp. 590–602; P. C. Earley and E. Mosakowski, 'Creating hybrid team cultures: an empirical test of transnational team functioning', *Academy of Management Journal*, February 2000, pp. 26–49; and S. Mohammed and L. C. Angell, 'Surface- and deep-level diversity in workgroups: examining the moderating effects of team orientation and team process on relationship conflict', *Journal of Organizational Behavior*, December 2004, pp. 1015–39.

61 Watson, Kumar and Michaelsen, 'Cultural diversity's impact on interaction process and performance: comparing homogeneous and diverse task groups'.

Communication

After studying this chapter, you should be able to:

1 Identify the main functions of communication.

2 Describe the communication process and distinguish between formal and informal communication.

3 Contrast downward, upward and lateral communication and provide examples of each.

4 Contrast oral, written and nonverbal communication.

5 Contrast formal communication networks and the grapevine.

6 Analyse the advantages and challenges of electronic communication.

7 Show how channel richness underlies the choice of communication channel.

8 Identify common barriers to effective communication.

9 Show how to overcome the potential problems in cross-cultural communication.

The problem with communication . . . is the *illusion* that it has been accomplished.

George Bernard Shaw

Communication: the difference between life and death?

www.dreamstine.com

Can the misunderstandings of a few words literally mean the difference between life and death? They can in the airline business. Consider the following cases:

History's worst aviation disaster occurred in 1977 at foggy Tenerife in the Canary Islands. The captain of a KLM flight thought the air traffic controller had cleared him to take off. But the controller intended only to give departure instructions. Although the language spoken between the Dutch KLM captain and the Spanish controller was English, confusion was created by heavy accents and improper terminology. The KLM Boeing 747 hit a Pan Am 747 at full throttle on the runway, killing 583 people.

In 1990, Colombian Avianca pilots, after several holding patterns caused by bad weather, told controllers as they neared New York Kennedy Airport that their Boeing 737 was running low on fuel. Controllers hear those words all the time, so they took no special action. While the pilots knew there was a serious problem, they failed to use a key phrase – fuel emergency – which would have obligated controllers to direct the Avianca flight ahead of all others and clear it to land as soon as possible. The people at Kennedy never understood the true nature of the pilots' problem. The jet ran out of fuel and crashed 16 miles from Kennedy Airport. Seventy-three people died.

In 1993, Chinese pilots flying a US built MD-80 tried to land in heavy fog at Urumqi, in northwest China. They were baffled by an audio alarm from the jet's ground proximity warning system. Just before impact, the cockpit recorder picked up one crew member saying to the other in Chinese: What does pull up mean? The plane hit power lines and crashed, killing 12.

Bad weather and poor communication paired up again to create another disaster in October 2001, this time at Milano-Linae Airport in Italy. Visibility was poor and tower controllers were not able to establish visual or radar contact with planes. Miscommunications between the controllers and pilots of an SAS commercial jet and a small Citation business jet, combined with the poor visibility, led to the two planes colliding on the runway. One-hundred-and-ten people died.

Communications problems have contributed, directly or indirectly, to some of the most disastrous aviation accidents in history. An analysis of past accidents reveals that common factors associated with poor communication include confusing phraseology, similar call signs, ambiguity, inference problems and a host of other linguistic issues. Examples of aviation disasters caused by communications errors are used to illustrate the variety of elements inherent in this area and most importantly, to help avoid these disasters in the future.

Source: 'Communication failures lead to airline disasters', Professional Communication Conference, 1999.

The preceding examples illustrate the profound consequences of communication. In this chapter, we'll analyse the power of communication and ways in which it can be made more effective. To begin, consider the following self-assessment about your communication style.

SELF-ASSESSMENT LIBRARY

What's my face-to-face communication style?

In the Self-assessment library (available online), take assessment II.A.1 (What's my face-to-face communication style?) and answer the following questions.

1. How did you score relative to your classmates?

2. Why do you think information about your communication style may be useful?

Face-to-face communication style is one communication issue. There are many others. Research indicates that poor communication is probably the most frequently cited source of interpersonal conflict.[1] Because individuals spend nearly 70 per cent of their waking hours communicating – writing, reading, speaking, listening – it seems reasonable to conclude that one of the most inhibiting forces to successful group performance is a lack of effective communication. And good communication skills are very important to your career success. A 2007 study of recruiters found that they rated communication skills as *the* most important characteristic of an ideal job candidate.[2] A cursory glance at the aptitudes required for jobs offered by Europe's largest organizations (for example, Total, Royal Dutch Shell, BP and DaimlerChrysler) emphasises the importance these companies place on a variety of communication skills. Yet, with the new business realities of more diverse workforces and geographically dispersed organizations, effectively communicating has become a difficult challenge.

No individual, group, or organization can exist without communication: the transfer of meaning among its members. It is only through transmitting meaning from one person to another that information and ideas can be conveyed. Communication, however, is more than merely imparting meaning. It must also be understood. In a group in which one member speaks only German and the others do not know German, the individual speaking German will not be fully understood. Therefore, **communication** must include both the *transfer and the understanding of meaning*.

communication
The transfer and understanding of meaning.

An idea, no matter how great, is useless until it is transmitted and understood by others. Perfect communication, if there were such a thing, would exist when a thought or an idea was transmitted so that the mental picture perceived by the receiver was exactly the same as that envisioned by the sender. Although elementary in theory, perfect communication is never achieved in practice, for reasons we shall expand on later in the chapter.

Before making too many generalisations concerning communication and problems in communicating effectively, we need to review briefly the functions that communication performs and describe the communication process.

Functions of communication

1 Identify the main functions of communication.

Communication serves four major functions within a group or organization: control, motivation, emotional expression and information.[3]

Communication acts to *control* member behaviour in several ways. Organizations have authority hierarchies and formal guidelines that employees are required to follow. For instance, when employees are required to communicate any job-related grievance to their immediate boss, to follow their job description, or to comply with company policies, communication is performing a control function. But informal communication also controls behaviour. When work groups tease or harass a member who produces too much (and makes the rest of the group look bad), they are informally communicating with, and controlling, the member's behaviour.

Communication fosters *motivation* by clarifying to employees what is to be done, how well they are doing, and what can be done to improve performance if it's below expectations. We saw this operating in our review of goal-setting and reinforcement theories in Chapter 6. The formation of specific goals, feedback on progress toward the goals, and reinforcement of desired behaviour all stimulate motivation and require communication.

For many employees, their work group is a primary source for social interaction. The communication that takes place within the group is a fundamental mechanism by which members show their frustrations and feelings of satisfaction. Communication, therefore, provides a release for the *emotional expression* of feelings and for fulfilment of social needs.

The final function that communication performs relates to its role in facilitating decision making. It provides the *information* that individuals and groups need to make decisions by transmitting the data to identify and evaluate alternative choices.

The German company, Q-Cells SE, began producing silicon solar cells in 2001 with only 19 employees. By the end of 2007, approximately 1,700 people were employed and the company had grown to be the largest solar cell manufacturer in the world. Communication that at the beginning tended to be centralised, informal and face-to-face became inadequate as the company adapted to a rapid increase of employees, globally dispersed customers, an increasingly diverse workforce (exacerbated with the opening of a new manufacturing plant in Malaysia) and the need for control.

Q-Cells

No one of these four functions should be seen as being more important than the others. For groups to perform effectively, they need to maintain some form of control over members, stimulate members to perform, provide a means for emotional expression, and make decision choices. You can assume that almost every communication interaction that takes place in a group or an organization performs one or more of these four functions.

The communication process

2 Describe the communication process and distinguish between formal and informal communication.

communication process
The steps between a source and a receiver that result in the transfer and understanding of meaning.

formal channels
Communication channels established by an organization to transmit messages related to the professional activities of members.

informal channels
Communication channels that are created spontaneously and that emerge as responses to individual choices.

Before communication can take place, a purpose, expressed as a message to be conveyed, is needed. It passes between a sender and a receiver. The message is encoded (converted to a symbolic form) and passed by way of some medium (channel) to the receiver, who retranslates (decodes) the message initiated by the sender. The result is transfer of meaning from one person to another.[4]

Figure 11.1 depicts this **communication process**. The key parts of this model are: (1) the sender, (2) encoding, (3) the message, (4) the channel, (5) decoding, (6) the receiver, (7) noise and (8) feedback.

The *sender* initiates a message by encoding a thought. The *message* is the actual physical product from the sender's *encoding*. When we speak, the speech is the message. When we write, the writing is the message. When we gesture, the movements of our arms and the expressions on our faces are the message. The *channel* is the medium through which the message travels. It is selected by the sender, who must determine whether to use a formal or informal channel. **Formal channels** are established by the organization and transmit messages that are related to the professional activities of members. They traditionally follow the authority chain within the organization. Other forms of messages, such as personal or social, follow **informal channels** in the organization. These informal channels are spontaneous and emerge as a response to individual choices.[5] The *receiver* is the object to whom the message is directed. But before the message can be received, the symbols in it must be translated into a form that can be understood by the receiver. This step is the *decoding* of the message. *Noise* represents communication barriers that distort the clarity of the message. Examples of possible noise sources include perceptual problems, information overload, semantic difficulties, or cultural differences. The final link in the communication process is a feedback loop. *Feedback* is the check on how successful we have been in transferring our messages as originally intended. It determines whether understanding has been achieved.

Figure 11.1 The communication process

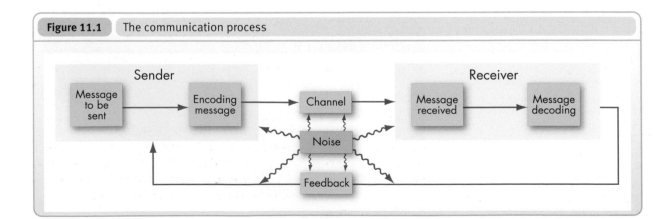

Direction of communication

3 Contrast downward, upward and lateral communication and provide examples of each.

Communication can flow vertically or laterally. The vertical dimension can be further divided into downward and upward directions.[6]

Downward communication

Communication that flows from one level of a group or organization to a lower level is downward communication. When we think of managers communicating with employees, the downward pattern is the one we are usually thinking of. It's used by group leaders and managers to assign goals, provide job instructions, inform employees of policies and procedures, point out problems that need attention and offer feedback about performance. But downward communication doesn't have to be oral or face-to-face contact. When management sends letters to employees' homes to advise them of the organization's new sick leave policy, it's using downward communication. Another example of downward communication is an e-mail from a team leader to the members of her team, reminding them of an upcoming deadline.

When engaging in downward communication, managers must explain the reasons *why* a decision was made. One study found that employees were twice as likely to be committed to changes when the reasons behind them were fully explained. Although this may seem like common sense, many managers feel they are too busy to explain things, or that explanations will open up unwanted debate. Evidence clearly indicates, though, that explanations increase employee commitment and support of decisions.[7]

Another problem in downward communication is its one-way nature; generally, managers inform employees but rarely solicit their advice or opinions. A 2006 study revealed that nearly two-thirds of employees say their boss rarely or never asks their advice. The author of the study noted, 'Organizations are always striving for higher employee engagement, but evidence indicates they unnecessarily create fundamental mistakes. People need to be respected and listened to.' Without feedback, management becomes out of touch with the mood of the people who are responsible for implementing management's vision and plans. There is evidence that across Europe that the degree of feedback managers seek from workers varies. For example, in Finland, Netherlands, and Lithuania this is significantly more common than in Italy or Portugal.[8]

The best communicators are those who explain the reasons behind their downward communications, but also solicit upward communication from the employees they supervise. That leads us to the next direction: upward communication.

Shaun Curry/Getty Images

Michel Tilmant, the former Chief Executive of ING, the Dutch financial giant, used downward communication to announce 7,000 job losses to employees resulting from having recorded significant losses and having to reach an agreement with the Dutch Government over €22 billion of state loan guarantees for its troubled mortgage loan portfolio. Tilmant also announced, through a spokesman, that he would be stepping down as chief executive because of the stress of leading the group through the most turbulent period in living memory.

Source: D. Walsh, Times Online (26 January 2009) 'ING chief "too tired" to go on as losses grow'.

Upward communication

Upward communication flows to a higher level in the group or organization. It's used to provide feedback to higher-ups, inform them of progress toward goals, and relay current problems. Upward communication keeps managers aware of how employees feel about their jobs, co-workers and the organization in general. Managers also rely on upward communication for ideas on how things can be improved. However, a study of a large European health care organization highlighted a fundamental issue with the usefulness of upward communication. The research concluded that not only was upward communication mostly absent, but when it did occur it was almost always inaccurately positive. To acquire influence and secure their performance employees simply agreed with the opinions of their managers when asked for comment. It is argued that for upward communication to be effective, it needs to be critical rather than flattering.[9]

Given that job responsibilities of most managers and supervisors have expanded, upward communication is increasingly difficult because managers are overwhelmed and easily distracted. To engage in effective upward communication, try to reduce distractions (meet in a conference room if you can, rather than your boss's office or cubicle), communicate in headlines not paragraphs (your job is to get your boss's attention, not to engage in a meandering discussion), support your headlines with actionable items (what you believe should happen) and prepare an agenda to make sure you use your boss's attention well.[10]

Lateral communication

When communication takes place among members of the same work group, among members of work groups at the same level, among managers at the same level, or among any other horizontally equivalent personnel, we describe it as lateral communications.

Why would there be a need for horizontal communications if a group or an organization's vertical communications are effective? The answer is that horizontal communication is often necessary to save time and facilitate coordination. In some cases, such lateral relationships are formally sanctioned. More often, they are informally created to short-circuit the vertical hierarchy and expedite action. So lateral communications can, from management's viewpoint, be good or bad. Because strict adherence to the formal vertical structure for all communications can impede the efficient and accurate transfer of information, lateral communications can be beneficial. In such cases, they occur with the knowledge and support of superiors. But they can create dysfunctional conflicts when the formal vertical channels are breached, when members go above or around their superiors to get things done, or when bosses find out that actions have been taken or decisions have been made without their knowledge.

Interpersonal communication

4 Contrast oral, written and nonverbal communication.

How do group members transfer meaning between and among each other? There are three basic methods. People essentially rely on oral, written and nonverbal communication.

Oral communication

The chief means of conveying messages is oral communication. Speeches, formal one-on-one and group discussions, and the informal rumour mill, or grapevine, are popular forms of oral communication.

The advantages of oral communication are speed and feedback. A verbal message can be conveyed and a response received in a minimal amount of time. If the receiver is unsure of the message, rapid feedback allows for early detection by the sender and, hence, allows for early correction. As one professional put it, 'Face-to-face communication on a consistent basis is still the best way to get information to and from employees.'[11]

The major disadvantage of oral communication surfaces whenever a message has to be passed through a number of people. The more people a message must pass through, the greater the potential distortion. Each person interprets the message in their own way. The message's content, when it reaches its destination, is often very different from that of the original. In an organization, where decisions and other communiqués are verbally passed up and down the authority hierarchy, there are considerable opportunities for messages to become distorted.

'PEOPLE ARE GOOD AT CATCHING LIARS AT WORK'   MYTH *OR* SCIENCE?

This statement is essentially false. The core purpose of communication in the workplace may be to convey business-related information. However, in the workplace, we also communicate in order to manage impressions others form of us. Some of this impression management is unintentional and harmless (for example, complimenting your boss on his clothing). However, sometimes people manage impressions through outright lies, such as making up an excuse for missing work or failing to make a deadline.

One of the reasons people lie – in the workplace and elsewhere – is that it works. Although most of us think we're good at detecting a lie, research shows that most people perform no better than chance at detecting whether someone is lying or telling the truth.

A recent review of 108 studies revealed that people detect lies at a rate, on average, only 4.2 per cent better than chance. This study also found that people's confidence in their judgements of whether someone was lying bore almost no relationship to their actual accuracy; we think we're a lot better at catching people lying than we really are. What's even more discouraging is that so-called experts – police officers, parole officers, detectives, judges and psychologists – perform no better than other people. As the authors of this review conclude, 'People are not good detectors of deception regardless of their age, sex, confidence, and experience.'

The point? Don't believe everything you hear and don't place too much weight on your ability to catch a liar based just on your intuition. When someone makes a claim that it's reasonable to doubt, ask her to back it up with evidence.

Source: M. G. Aamodt and H. Custer, 'Who can best catch a liar? A meta-analysis of individual differences in detecting deception', *The Forensic Examiner*, Spring 2006, pp. 6–11.

Written communication

Written communications include memos, letters, fax transmissions, e-mail, instant messaging, organizational periodicals, notices placed on bulletin boards or any other device that is transmitted via written words or symbols.

Why would a sender choose to use written communications? They're often tangible and verifiable. When they're printed, both the sender and receiver have a record of the communication; and the message can be stored for an indefinite period. If there are questions concerning the content of the message, it is physically available for later reference. This feature is particularly important for complex and lengthy communications. The marketing plan for a new product, for instance, is likely to contain a number of tasks spread out over several months. By putting it in writing, those who have to initiate the plan can readily refer to it over the life of the plan. A final benefit of all written communication comes from the process itself. People are usually more careful with the written word than with the oral word. They're forced to think more thoroughly about what they want to convey in a written message than in a spoken one. Thus, written communications are more likely to be well thought out, logical, and clear.

Of course, written messages have drawbacks. They're time-consuming. You could convey far more information to a university instructor in a one-hour oral exam than in a one-hour written exam. In fact, you could probably say the same thing in 10 to 15 minutes that it would take you an hour to write. So, although writing may be more precise, it also consumes a great deal of time. The other major disadvantage is feedback, or lack of it. Oral communication allows the receiver to respond rapidly to what he thinks he hears. Written communication, however, does not have a built-in feedback mechanism. The result is that the mailing of a memo is no assurance that it has been received, and, if received, there is no guarantee the recipient will interpret it as the sender intended. The latter point is also relevant in oral communiqués, except it's easy in such cases merely to ask the receiver to summarise what you've said. An accurate summary presents feedback evidence that the message has been received and understood.

Nonverbal communication

Every time we verbally give a message to someone, we also impart a nonverbal message.[12] Research demonstrates that as much as 93 per cent of the meaning that is transmitted between two people in a face-to-face conversation can come from nonverbal channels. This means that as little as 7 per cent of the meaning we derive from others may come through their words alone.[13] Therefore, no discussion of communication would be complete without consideration of *nonverbal communication* – which includes body movements, the intonations or emphasis we give to words, facial expressions and the physical distance between the sender and receiver.

It can be argued that every *body movement* has a meaning, and no movement is accidental. For example, through body language, we say, 'Come and talk to me, I'm happy' or 'Leave me alone, I'm depressed.' Rarely do we send our messages consciously. We act out our state of being with nonverbal body language. It is important to note that body language varies between, and even within, cultures and is a common cause of misunderstandings. This will be addressed later in the chapter. However, generally speaking, the two most important messages that body language conveys are (1) the extent to which an individual likes another and is interested in their views and (2) the relative perceived status between a sender and receiver.[14] For instance, we're more likely to position ourselves closer to people we like. Similarly, if you feel that you're of higher status than another, you're more likely to display body movements – such as crossed legs or a slouched seated position – that reflect a casual and relaxed manner.[15]

Body language adds to, and often complicates, verbal communication. A body position or movement does not by itself have a precise or universal meaning, but when it is linked with spoken language, it gives fuller meaning to a sender's message.

If you read the verbatim minutes of a meeting, you wouldn't grasp the impact of what was said in the same way you would if you had been there or if you saw the meeting on video. Why? There is no record of nonverbal communication. The emphasis given to words or phrases is missing. Table 11.1 illustrates how *intonations* can change the meaning of a message. *Facial expressions* also convey meaning. A snarling face says something different from a smile. Facial expressions, along with intonations, can show arrogance, aggressiveness, fear, shyness and other characteristics that would never be communicated if you read a transcript of what had been said.

The way individuals space themselves in terms of *physical distance* also has meaning. What is considered proper spacing is largely dependent on cultural norms. For example, what is considered a businesslike distance in some European countries would be viewed as intimate in many parts of North America. If someone stands closer to you than is considered appropriate, it may indicate aggressiveness; if farther away than usual, it may mean disinterest or displeasure with what is being said.

It's important for the receiver to be alert to these nonverbal aspects of communication. You should look for nonverbal cues as well as listen to the literal meaning of a sender's words. You should particularly be aware of contradictions between the messages. Your boss may say she is free to talk to you about a pressing budget problem, but you may see nonverbal signals suggesting that this is not the time to discuss the subject. Regardless of what is being said, an individual who frequently glances at their wristwatch is giving the message that they would prefer to terminate the conversation. We misinform others when we express one message verbally, such as trust, but nonverbally communicate a contradictory message that reads, 'I don't have confidence in you.'

Table 11.1	Intonations: it's the way you say it!

Change your tone, and you change your meaning:

Placement of the emphasis	What it means
Why don't I take **you** to dinner tonight?	I was going to take someone else.
Why don't **I** take you to dinner tonight?	Instead of the guy you were going with.
Why **don't** I take you to dinner tonight?	I'm trying to find a reason why I shouldn't take you.
Why don't I take you to dinner tonight?	Do you have a problem with me?
Why don't I **take** you to dinner tonight?	Instead of going on your own.
Why don't I take you to **dinner** tonight?	Instead of lunch tomorrow.
Why don't I take you to dinner **tonight**?	Not tomorrow night.

Source: Based on M. Kiely, 'When "No" means "Yes"', *Marketing*, October 1993, pp. 7–9. Reproduced from *Marketing* magazine with the permission of the copyright owner, Haymarket Business Publications Ltd.

Organizational communication

5 Contrast formal communication networks and the grapevine.

In this section, we move from interpersonal communication to organizational communication. Our first focus will be to describe and distinguish formal networks and the grapevine. In the following section, we discuss technological innovations in communication.

Formal small-group networks

Formal organizational networks can be very complicated. They can, for instance, include hundreds of people and a half-dozen or more hierarchical levels. To simplify our discussion, we've condensed these networks into three common small groups of five people each (see Figure 11.2). These three networks are the chain, wheel, and all channel. Although these three networks have been extremely simplified, they allow us to describe the unique qualities of each.

The *chain* rigidly follows the formal chain of command. This network approximates the communication channels you might find in a rigid three-level organization. The *wheel* relies on a central figure to act as the conduit for all of the group's communication. It simulates the communication network you would find on a team with a strong leader. The *all-channel* network permits all group members to actively communicate with each other. The all-channel network is most often characterised in practice by self-managed teams, in which all group members are free to contribute and no one person takes on a leadership role.

As Table 11.2 demonstrates, the effectiveness of each network depends on the dependent variable you're concerned about. For instance, the structure of the wheel facilitates the emergence of a leader, the all-channel network is best if you are concerned with having high member satisfaction, and the chain is best if accuracy is most important. Table 11.2 leads us to the conclusion that no single network will be best for all occasions.

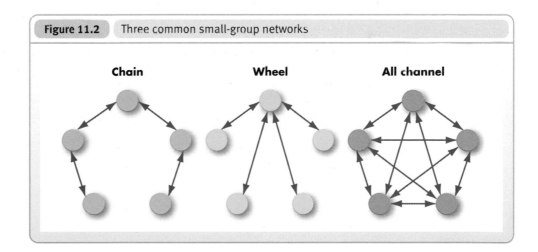

Figure 11.2 Three common small-group networks

Chain   Wheel   All channel

Table 11.2 Small-group networks and effective criteria.

Criterion	Networks		
	Chain	Wheel	All Channel
Speed	Moderate	Fast	Fast
Accuracy	High	High	Moderate
Emergence of a leader	Moderate	High	None
Member satisfaction	Moderate	Low	High

The grapevine

grapevine
An organization's
informal
communication
network.

The formal system is not the only communication network in a group or organization. There is also an informal one, called the **grapevine**.[16] Although the grapevine may be informal, it's still an important source of information. For instance, a survey found that 75 per cent of employees hear about matters first through rumours on the grapevine.[17]

The grapevine has three main characteristics.[18] First, it is not controlled by management. Second, it is perceived by most employees as being more believable and reliable than formal communiqués issued by top management. Finally, it is largely used to serve the self-interests of the people within it.

One of the most famous studies of the grapevine investigated the communication pattern among 67 managerial personnel in a small manufacturing firm.[19] The basic approach used was to learn from each communication recipient how he or she first received a given piece of information and then trace it back to its source. It was found that, while the grapevine was an important source of information, only 10 per cent of the executives acted as liaison individuals (that is, passed the information on to more than one other person). For example, when one executive decided to resign to enter the insurance business, 81 per cent of the executives knew about it, but only 11 per cent transmitted this information to others.

Is the information that flows along the grapevine accurate? The evidence indicates that about 75 per cent of what is carried is accurate.[20] But what conditions foster an active grapevine? What gets the rumour mill rolling?

It's frequently assumed that rumours start because they make titillating gossip. This is rarely the case. Rumours emerge as a response to situations that are *important* to us, when there is *ambiguity*, and under conditions that arouse *anxiety*.[21] The fact that work situations frequently contain these three elements explains why rumours flourish in organizations. The secrecy and competition that typically prevail in large organizations – around issues such as the appointment of new bosses, the relocation of offices, downsizing decisions, and the realignment of work assignments – create conditions that encourage and sustain rumours on the grapevine. A rumour will persist either until the wants and expectations creating the uncertainty underlying the rumour are fulfilled or until the anxiety is reduced.

What can we conclude from the preceding discussion? Certainly the grapevine is an important part of any group or organization communication network and is well worth understanding. It gives managers a feel for the morale of their organization, identifies issues that employees consider important, and helps tap into employee anxieties. The grapevine also serves employees' needs: Small talk serves to create a sense of closeness and friendship among those who share information, although research suggests that it often does so at the expense of those in the 'out' group.[22]

Can management entirely eliminate rumours? No. What management should do, however, is minimise the negative consequences of rumours by limiting their range and impact. Exhibit 11.1 offers a few suggestions for minimising those negative consequences.

6 Analyse the advantages and challenges of electronic communication.

Electronic communications

An indispensable – and in 71 per cent of cases, the primary – medium of communication in today's organizations is electronic. Electronic communications include e-mail, text messaging, networking software, internet or web logs (blogs) and video conferencing. Let's discuss each.

EXHIBIT 11.1	SUGGESTIONS FOR REDUCING THE NEGATIVE CONSEQUENCES OF RUMOURS

1. Announce timetables for making important decisions.

2. Explain decisions and behaviours that may appear inconsistent or secretive.

3. Emphasise the downside, as well as the upside, of current decisions and future plans.

4. Openly discuss worst-case possibilities; they are almost never as anxiety provoking as the unspoken fantasy.

Source: Adapted from L. Hirschhorn, 'Managing rumors', in L. Hirschhorn (ed.), *Cutting Back* (San Francisco, CA: Jossey-Bass, 1983), pp. 54–56. Used with permission.

E-mail

E-mail uses the Internet to transmit and receive computer-generated text and documents. Its growth has been spectacular, and its use is now so pervasive that it's hard to imagine life without it.

As a communication tool, e-mail has a long list of benefits. E-mail messages can be quickly written, edited and stored. They can be distributed to one person or thousands with a click of a mouse. They can be read, in their entirety, at the convenience of the recipient. And the cost of sending formal e-mail messages to employees is a fraction of the cost of printing, duplicating, and distributing a comparable letter or brochure.[23]

E-mail, of course, is not without drawbacks. The following are some of the most significant limitations of e-mail and what organizations should do to reduce or eliminate these problems:

- **Misinterpreting the message.** It's true that we often misinterpret verbal messages, but the potential for misinterpretation with e-mail is even greater. One research team at New York University found that we can accurately decode an e-mail's intent and tone only 50 per cent of the time, yet most of us vastly overestimate our ability to send and interpret clear messages. If you're sending an important message, make sure you reread it for clarity. And if you're upset about the presumed tone of someone else's message, keep in mind that you may be misinterpreting it.[24]

- **Communicating negative messages.** When companies have negative information to communicate, managers need to think carefully. E-mail may not be the best way to communicate the message. A survey of over 2,000 British workers found that 73 per cent of respondents admitted to delegating difficult tasks by e-mail, and worryingly, 2 per cent admitted to firing an employee by e-mail.[25] Employees also need to be careful communicating negative messages via e-mail. Justen Deal, 22, wrote an e-mail critical of some strategic decisions made by his employer, pharmaceutical giant Kaiser Permanente. In the e-mail, he criticised the 'misleadership' of Kaiser CEO George Halvorson and questioned the financing of several information technology projects. Within hours, Deal's computer was seized; he was later fired.[26]

- **Overuse of e-mail.** An estimated 6 trillion e-mails are sent every year, and someone has to answer all those messages! As people become established in their careers and their responsibilities expand, so do their inboxes. A survey of European workers revealed that managers spend at least two hours per day dealing with e-mails, which adds up to a staggering 10 years of a worker's life. Of this, three-and-a-half years are seen as a complete waste of time as 32 per cent of messages read are considered irrelevant. The survey also found that managers are concerned about the extensive use of e-mail because employees tend to discuss long and complex issues over e-mail, which is seen to delay decision making. Philip Vanhoutte, European managing director at headset manufacturer Plantronics who commisioned the study, says managers need to encourage greater use of the telephone and teach people how to effectively use a range of communication technology.[27]

- **E-mail emotions.** We tend to think of e-mail as a sort of sterile, faceless form of communication. But that doesn't mean it's unemotional. As you no doubt know, e-mails are often highly emotional. One CEO said, 'I've seen people not talk to each other, turf wars break out and people quit their jobs as a result of e-mails.' E-mail tends to have a disinhibiting effect on people; senders write things they'd never be comfortable saying in person. Facial expressions tend to temper our emotional expressions, but in e-mail, there is no other face to look at, and so many of us fire away. An increasingly common way of communicating emotions in e-mail is with emoticons. For example, Yahoo!'s e-mail software allows the user to pick from 32 emoticons. Although emoticons used to be considered for personal use only, increasingly adults are using them in business e-mails. Still, some see them as too informal for business use.

  When others send flaming messages, remain calm and try not to respond in kind. Also, when writing new e-mails, try to temper your own tendencies to quickly fire off messages.[28]

- **Privacy concerns.** There are two privacy issues with e-mail. First, you need to be aware that your e-mails may be monitored. The European Union Data Retention Directive requires European companies to keep detailed data about people's e-mail use, although the legality and procedures for monitoring e-mails varies between countries and the interpretations can be confusing. For example, a landmark case in the European Court of Human Rights awarded €3,000 in damages and €6,000 in court costs and expenses to an employee of Carmarthenshire College, based in South Wales after her e-mail, Internet and telephone communications were monitored by one of her bosses. Lynette Copland successfully took the UK government to court claiming the practice contravened European human rights laws.[29] Also, you can't always trust that the recipient of your e-mail will keep it confidential. For these reasons, you shouldn't write anything you wouldn't want made public. Second, you need to exercise caution in forwarding e-mail from your company's e-mail account to a personal, or 'public', (for example, Gmail, Yahoo!, MSN) e-mail account. These accounts often aren't as secure as corporate accounts, so when you forward a company e-mail to them, you may be violating your organization's policy or unintentionally disclosing confidential data.

Instant messaging and text messaging

Like e-mail, instant messaging (IM) and text messaging (TM) use electronic messages. Unlike e-mail, though, IM and TM are either in 'real' time (IM) or use portable communication devices (TM). In just a few years, IM/TM has become pervasive. As you no doubt know from experience, IM is usually sent via desktop or laptop computer, whereas TM is transmitted via mobile phones or handheld devices such as Blackberrys.

The growth of TM has been spectacular. Since the launch of text messaging in the early 1990's, the growth has been phenomenal. More than 80 per cent of Europeans use text messaging and in Britain an average of 4.7 million text messages are sent every hour.[30] Text messaging has also become popular as a means of business communication for generally the same reasons why it has become popular for personal use – it is fast and inexpensive. Managers can stay in touch with employees and employees can stay in touch with each other quickly and cheaply. In an increasing number of cases, this isn't just a luxury, it's a business imperative. For example, Bill Green, CEO of the consulting firm Accenture, doesn't have a permanent office. Since he's on the road all the time, visiting Accenture's 100 locations scattered across the globe, TM is essential for him keep in touch. Although there aren't many other examples so dramatic, the great advantage of TM is that it is flexible; with it, you can be reached almost anywhere, anytime.[31]

Despite their advantages, IM and TM aren't going to replace e-mail. E-mail is still probably a better device for conveying long messages that need to be saved. IM is preferable for one- or two-line messages that would just clutter up an e-mail inbox. On the downside, some IM/TM users find the technology intrusive and distracting. Their continual presence can make it hard for employees to concentrate and stay focused. For example, a survey of managers revealed that in 86 per cent of meetings, at least some participants checked TM. Finally, because instant messages can be intercepted easily, many organizations are concerned about the security of IM/TM.[32]

One other point: It's important to not let the informality of text messaging spill over into business e-mails. Many prefer to keep business communication relatively formal. A survey of employers revealed that 58 per cent rate grammar, spelling and punctuation as 'very important' in e-mail messages.[33] By making sure your professional communications are, well, professional, you'll show yourself to be mature and serious. That doesn't mean, of course, that you have to give up TM or IM; you just need to maintain the boundaries between how you communicate with your friends and how you communicate professionally.

Networking software

Nowhere has communication been transformed more than in the area of networking. You are doubtless familiar with and perhaps a user of social networking platforms such as Facebook and MySpace.

Rather than being one huge site, Facebook, which claims to have over 150 million active users, is actually composed of separate networks based on schools, companies or regions. It might surprise you to learn that individuals over 30 are the fastest-growing users of Facebook.

More than 100 million users have created accounts at MySpace. This site averages more than 40 billion hits per month. MySpace profiles contain two 'blurbs': 'About Me' and 'Who I'd Like to Meet' sections. Profiles can also contain 'Interests' and 'Details' sections, photos, blog entries and other details. Compared to Facebook, MySpace is relatively more likely to be used for purely personal reasons, as illustrated by the 'Friends Space' portion of a user's account.

Amid the growth of Facebook and MySpace, professional networking sites have entered the marketplace and expanded as well. LinkedIn, Ziggs and ZoomInfo are all professional websites that allow users to set up lists of contacts and do everything from casually 'pinging' them with updates to hosting chat rooms for all or some of the users' contacts. Some companies, such as IBM, have their own social networks (IBM's is called BluePages); IBM is selling the BluePages tool to companies and individual users. Microsoft is doing the same thing with its SharePoint tool.

To get the most out of social networks, while avoiding irritating your contacts, use them 'for high-value items only' – not as an everyday or even every-week tool. Also, remember that a prospective employer might check your MySpace or Facebook entry. In fact, some entrepreneurs have developed software that mines such websites for companies (or individuals) that want to check up on a job applicant. So keep in mind that what you post may be read by people other than your intended contacts.[34]

Web logs (blogs)

blog (web log)
A website where entries are written, generally displayed in reverse chronological order, about news, events and personal diary entries.

Sun Microsystems CEO Jonathan Schwartz is a big fan of web logs (**blogs**), websites about a single person or company that are usually updated daily. He encourages his employees to have them and has one himself (http://blogs.sun.com/jonathan). Schwartz's blog averages 400,000 hits per month, and Schwartz, like Apple's managers, allows Sun customers to post comments about the company's products on its website.

Obviously, Schwartz is not the only fan of blogs. Experts estimate that there are over 100 million blogs in over 80 languages. Of these more than 40 per cent are professional bloggers (blog about their industry and profession but not in an official capacity) and around 12 per cent are corporate bloggers (officially blog for their company).[35] BMW, Boeing, Kodak, GM, Dell and many other large organizations have corporate blogs.

So what's the downside? Although some companies have policies in place governing the content of blogs, many don't, and 39 per cent of individual bloggers say they have posted comments that could be construed as harmful to their company's reputation. Many bloggers think their personal blogs are outside their employer's purview, but if someone else in a company happens to read a blog entry, there is nothing to keep them from sharing that information with others, and the employee could be dismissed as a result. Schwartz says that Sun would not fire an employee over any blog entry short of one that broke the law. 'Our blogging policy is "Be authentic". Period,' he says. But most organizations are unlikely to be so forgiving of any blog entry that might cast a negative light on them.

Video conferencing

Video conferencing permits employees in an organization to have meetings with people at different locations. Live audio and video images of members allow them to see, hear, and talk with each other. Video conferencing technology, in effect, allows employees to conduct interactive meetings without the necessity of all being physically in the same location.

In the late 1990s, video conferencing was basically conducted from special rooms equipped with television cameras, located at company facilities. More recently, cameras and microphones are being attached to individual computers, allowing people to participate in video conferences without leaving their desks. As the cost of this technology drops, video conferencing is likely to be increasingly seen as an alternative to expensive and time-consuming travel.

ABUSIVE LANGUAGE IN THE WORKPLACE CAN BE COSTLY — OB IN THE NEWS

Foul language is common in many places of work and it is not always deemed unacceptable. It can, however, pave the way for staff to bring expensive constructive dismissal claims.

Alarm bells rang loud and clear when a senior worker, who was subjected to sustained verbal abuse from the chief executive of his company, was awarded over €1 million. The case of Horkulak v Cantor Fitzgerald International considers where the courts will draw the line on permissible language, and prompts managers to reflect on what they should be doing to avoid such liabilities.

Claims for such language are often defended by arguing that its use is commonplace at work. However, although the use of such language was common at Cantor Fitzgerald, the court found the relationship of trust and confidence between Horkulak and his employer had broken down because of the employer's behaviour, and consequently held that Horkulak had been constructively dismissed.

A number of key points arise from this and other similar cases:

- The use of foul language in the workplace is not necessarily deemed unacceptable, but its use can undermine the relationship of trust and confidence between employer and employee

- The test of whether trust and confidence has broken down is an objective one. This means a court or tribunal will assess how an independent third party would view the situation, rather than how the employer and worker view it

- Regular use of foul and abusive language in the workplace does not sanitise its effect

- The use of foul and abusive language aimed at or concerning the worker in front of other staff is likely to aggravate the undermining of trust and confidence

The message is simple: employers must avoid the use of foul and abusive language when dealing with staff, and must take steps to ensure that all staff – including the most senior – behave accordingly. Horkulak's success and the size of his damages award should give ample warning to employers to take this matter seriously.

Source: Adapted from R. Jeffcott 'Abusive language in the workplace can be costly', *Personnel Today*, 11 November 2003. Available at http://www.personneltoday.com/articles/2003/11/11//21234/abusivelanguage-in-the-workplace-can-be-costly.htm.

Knowledge management

knowledge management (KM)
The process of organising and distributing an organization's collective wisdom so the right information gets to the right people at the right time.

Our final topic under organizational communication is **knowledge management (KM)**. This is a process of organising and distributing an organization's collective wisdom so the right information gets to the right people at the right time. When done properly, KM provides an organization with both a competitive edge and improved organizational performance because it makes its employees smarter. And there is some evidence to support the theoretical value of KM. Return on revenues for the 2008 Europe Most Admired Knowledge Enterprises (MAKE) winners was nearly twice that of the Global Fortune 500 company median. Previous winners of Europe's Most Admired Knowledge Enterprises include BP, Heineken, Nokia, Repsol-YFP, Royal Dutch Shell, SAP and Schlumberger.[36] It can also help control leaks of vital company information so that an organization's competitive advantage is preserved for as long as possible. Despite its importance, KM gets low marks from most business leaders. When consulting firm Bain & Co. asked 960 executives about the effectiveness of 25 management tools, KM ranked near the bottom of the list. One expert concluded, 'Most organizations are still managing as if we were in the industrial era.'[37]

Effective KM begins by identifying what knowledge matters to the organization.[38] Management needs to review processes to identify those that provide the most value. Then it can develop computer networks and databases that can make that information readily available to the people who need it the most. But KM won't work unless the culture supports sharing of information.[39] As we'll show in Chapter 14, information that is important and scarce can be a potent source of power. And people who hold that power are often reluctant to share it with others. So KM requires an organizational culture that promotes, values and rewards sharing knowledge. Finally, KM must provide the mechanisms and the motivation for employees to share knowledge that employees find useful on the job and enables them to achieve better performance.[40] *More* knowledge isn't necessarily *better* knowledge. Information overload needs to be avoided by designing the system to capture only pertinent information and then organising it so it can be quickly accessed by the people whom it can help.

Choice of communication channel

7 Show how channel richness underlies the choice of communication channel.

Accident Group, formerly the UK's largest personal injury claims firm, fired 2,400 employees after its parent firm went into administration. How the firm decided to communicate the message to many of the staff involved – by text message – made national news headlines.[41] What became very clear was that the company erred by selecting the wrong channel for this message. Such an emotional and sensitive message would likely have been better received in a face-to-face meeting.

Why do people choose one channel of communication over another – for instance, a phone call instead of a face-to-face talk? Is there any general insight we might be able to provide regarding choice of communication channel? The answer to the latter question is a qualified 'yes'. A model of media richness has been developed to explain channel selection among managers.[42]

Research has found that channels differ in their capacity to convey information. Some are rich in that they have the ability to (1) handle multiple cues simultaneously; (2) facilitate rapid feedback; and (3) be very personal. Others are lean in that they score low on these three factors. As Figure 11.3 illustrates, face-to-face conversation scores highest in terms of **channel richness** because it provides for the maximum amount of information to be transmitted during a communication episode. That is, it offers multiple information cues (words, postures, facial expressions, gestures, intonations), immediate feedback (both verbal and nonverbal), and the personal touch of 'being there'. Impersonal written media such as formal reports and bulletins rate lowest in richness.

The choice of one channel over another depends on whether the message is routine or nonroutine. The former types of messages tend to be straightforward and have a minimum of ambiguity. The latter are likely to be complicated and have the potential for misunderstanding. Managers can communicate routine messages efficiently through channels that are lower in richness. However, they can communicate nonroutine messages effectively only by selecting rich channels. Referring back to the Accident Group example, it appears that the company used a channel relatively low in richness (text message) to convey a message that, because of its nonroutine nature and complexity, should have been conveyed using a rich communication medium.

channel richness
The amount of information that can be transmitted during a communication episode.

Figure 11.3 | Information richness of communication channels

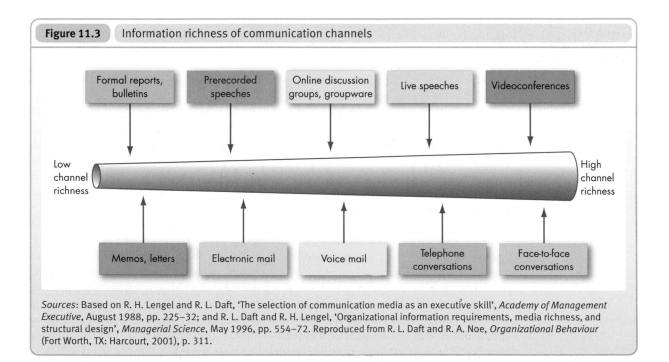

Sources: Based on R. H. Lengel and R. L. Daft, 'The selection of communication media as an executive skill', *Academy of Management Executive*, August 1988, pp. 225–32; and R. L. Daft and R. H. Lengel, 'Organizational information requirements, media richness, and structural design', *Managerial Science*, May 1996, pp. 554–72. Reproduced from R. L. Daft and R. A. Noe, *Organizational Behaviour* (Fort Worth, TX: Harcourt, 2001), p. 311.

Evidence indicates that high-performing managers tend to be more media sensitive than low-performing managers.[43] That is, they're better able to match appropriate media richness with the ambiguity involved in the communication.

The media richness model is consistent with organizational trends and practices of the past decade. It is not just coincidence that more and more senior managers have been using meetings to facilitate communication and regularly leaving the isolated sanctuary of their executive offices to manage by walking around. These executives are relying on richer channels of communication to transmit the more ambiguous messages they need to convey. The past has been characterised by organizations closing facilities, imposing large layoffs, restructuring, merging, consolidating, and introducing new products and services at an accelerated pace – all non-routine messages high in ambiguity and requiring the use of channels that can convey a large amount of information. It is not surprising, therefore, to see the most effective managers expanding their use of rich channels.

COMMUNICATION CHANNELS   FACE THE FACTS

- The top three most effective communication channels, according to the respondents of one study, were team briefings (64 per cent), email (59 per cent) and the intranet (38 per cent).

- In terms of the most effective channels for hearing staff views, 50 per cent mentioned feedback from team briefings and 43 per cent staff attitude surveys.

- Another study revealed that the most used means of direct communication between managers and employees was meeting the entire workforce or team briefings (91 per cent). E-mail was considerably less common (38 per cent), with the least used method being suggestion schemes (30 per cent).

Sources: C. Bingham and P. Suff (2002) 'Internal communication', *Managing Best Practice*, 100, Work Foundation; B. Kersley, C. Alpin, J. Forth, A. Bryson, H. Bewley, G. Dix and S. Oxenbridge, Inside the Workplace: First Findings from the 2004 Workplace Employment Relations Survey.

Barriers to effective communication

8 Identify common barriers to effective communication.

A number of barriers can retard or distort effective communication. In this section, we highlight the most important of these barriers.

Filtering

filtering
A sender's manipulation of information so that it will be seen more favourably by the receiver.

Filtering refers to a sender's purposely manipulating information so it will be seen more favourably by the receiver. For example, when a manager tells his boss what he feels his boss wants to hear, he is filtering information.

The major determinant of filtering is the number of levels in an organization's structure. The more vertical levels in the organization's hierarchy, the more opportunities there are for filtering. But you can expect some filtering to occur wherever there are status differences. Factors such as fear of conveying bad news and the desire to please one's boss often lead employees to tell their superiors what they think those superiors want to hear, thus distorting upward communications.

Selective perception

We have mentioned selective perception before in this book. It appears again here because the receivers in the communication process selectively see and hear based on their needs, motivations, experience, background, and other personal characteristics. Receivers also project their interests and expectations into communications as they decode them. An employment interviewer who expects a female job applicant to put her family ahead of her career is likely to see that in female applicants, regardless of whether the applicants actually feel that way. As we said in Chapter 5, we don't see reality; we interpret what we see and call it reality.

Information overload

information overload
A condition in which information inflow exceeds an individual's processing capacity.

Individuals have a finite capacity for processing data. When the information we have to work with exceeds our processing capacity, the result is **information overload**. And with e-mails, IM, phone calls, faxes, meetings and the need to keep current in one's field, the potential for today's managers and professionals to suffer from information overload is high.

What happens when individuals have more information than they can sort out and use? They tend to select, ignore, pass over or forget information. Or they may put off further processing until the overload situation is over. In any case, the result is lost information and less effective communication.

Emotions

How the receiver feels at the time of receipt of a communication influences how they interprets it. The same message received when you're angry or distraught is often interpreted differently than it is when you're happy. Extreme emotions such as jubilation or depression are most likely to hinder effective communication. In such instances, we are most prone to disregard our rational and objective thinking processes and substitute emotional judgements.

Language

In the current global marketplace, language has been identified as a key enabler of effective business functioning and success. Consequently, language skills are highly sought after. For example, languages such as Mandarin and Spanish help access developing markets and are particularly prized by business. Of all the European countries, language skills have been particularly lamented in the UK. A recent survey by the Confederation of British Industry reported the highest degree of employer's dissatisfaction with graduate skills was foreign languages.[44] However, Britain is not alone. Language is also an issue across Europe, particularly due to the increase of language barriers because of migration from East and Central Europe after EU enlargement.

Paula Bronstein/Getty Images

To effectively work towards achieving the aims of reducing poverty and injustice globally, Oxfam International must deal with formidable language barriers. The charity is a confederation of 13 organizations (from 13 different countries) working together with over 3,000 partner organizations in more than 100 countries.

Even when we're communicating in the same language, words mean different things to different people. Age and context are two of the biggest factors that influence the language a person uses and the definitions he or she gives to words. Most of us will be aware of the influence of age on the meanings of words when talking to those of a generation older than ourselves or to teenagers whose slang we may find mystifying. Rick Woodward, former learning and development director for toiletries maker Kimberly-Clark, provides an example of the importance of context. Woodward, a native of England, began work in the US, where he soon found subtle language differences created communication problems at work. For example, 'fortnight' is not used and 'let's table it' means 'put to one side', instead of 'talk about it', he says. And when people discuss 'seniority', it refers to length of service, rather than position in the company.[45]

The point is that even when people speak a common language, the use of that language is far from uniform. If we knew how each of us modified the language, communication difficulties would be minimised. The problem is that members in an organization usually don't know how those with whom they interact have modified the language. Senders tend to assume that the words and terms they use mean the same to the receiver as they do to them. This assumption is often incorrect.

Communication apprehension

communication apprehension
Undue tension and anxiety about oral communication, written communication, or both.

Another major barrier to effective communication is that some people – an estimated 5 to 20 per cent [46] – suffer from debilitating **communication apprehension**, or anxiety. Lots of people dread speaking in front of a group, but communication apprehension is a more serious problem because it affects a whole category of communication techniques. People who suffer from it experience undue tension and anxiety in oral communication, written communication or both.[47] For example, oral apprehensives may find it extremely difficult to talk with others face-to-face or may become extremely anxious when they have to use the telephone. As a result, they may rely on memos or faxes to convey messages when a phone call would be not only faster but more appropriate.

Studies demonstrate that oral-communication apprehensives avoid situations that require them to engage in oral communication.[48] We should expect to find some self-selection in jobs so that such individuals don't take positions, such as teacher, for which oral communication is a dominant requirement.[49] But almost all jobs require some oral communication. And of greater concern is the evidence that high-oral-communication apprehensives distort the communication demands of their jobs in order to minimise the need for communication.[50] So we need to be aware that there is a set of people in organizations who severely limit their oral communication and rationalise this practice by telling themselves that more communication isn't necessary for them to do their job effectively.

Gender differences

Gender differences are sometimes a barrier to effective communication. Deborah Tannen's research shows that men tend to use talk to emphasise status, whereas women tend to use it to create connections. These tendencies, of course, don't apply to *every* man and *every* woman. As Tannen puts it, her generalisation means 'a larger percentage of women or men *as a group* talk in a particular way, or individual women and men *are more likely* to talk one way or the other'.[51] She has found that women speak and hear a language of connection and intimacy; men speak and hear a language of status, power and independence. So, for many men, conversations are primarily a means to preserve independence and maintain status in a hierarchical social order. For many women, conversations are negotiations for closeness in which people try to seek and give confirmation and support.

For example, men frequently complain that women talk on and on about their problems. Women criticise men for not listening. What's happening is that when men hear a problem, they frequently assert their desire for independence and control by offering solutions. Many women, on the other hand, view telling a problem as a means to promote closeness. The women present the problem to gain support and connection, not to get advice. Mutual understanding is symmetrical. But giving advice is asymmetrical – it sets up the advice giver as more knowledge-able, more reasonable, and more in control. This contributes to distancing men and women in their efforts to communicate.

Global implications

9 Show how to overcome the potential problems in cross-cultural communication.

Effective communication is difficult under the best of conditions. Cross-cultural factors clearly create the potential for increased communication problems. A gesture that is well understood and acceptable in one culture can be meaningless or lewd in another. Unfortunately, as business has become more global, companies' communication approaches have not kept pace. Only 18 per cent of companies have documented strategies for communicating with employees across cultures, and only 31 per cent of companies require that corporate messages be customised for consumption in other cultures. [52]

Cultural barriers
One author has identified four specific problems related to language difficulties in cross-cultural communications.[53]

LOST IN TRANSLATION?   GLOBAL

Multinationals are truly global operations. For example, Daimler AG sells its products in nearly all the countries of the world and has production facilities on five continents. Failing to speak a host country's language can make it tougher for managers to do their jobs well, especially if they are misinterpreted or if they misinterpret what others are saying. Such communication problems make it tougher to conduct business effectively and efficiently and may result in lost business opportunities.

To avoid communication problems, many companies require their managers to learn the local language. For example, Germany-based Siemens requires its managers to learn the language of their host country. Ernst Behrens, the head of Siemens's China operations, learned to speak Mandarin fluently. Robert Kimmett, a former Siemens board member, believes that learning a host country's language gives managers 'a better grasp of what is going on inside a company . . . not just the facts and figures but also texture and nuance'.

However, learning a foreign language can be difficult for managers. The challenge for Western managers is often deepened when the language is Asian, such as Japanese or Mandarin, because it is so different. To compensate, Western managers sometimes rely solely on body language and facial expressions to communicate. The problem? Cultural differences in these nonverbal forms of communication may result in serious misunderstandings. To avoid this pitfall, managers should familiarise themselves with their host country's culture.

Source: Based on K. Kanhold, D. Bilefsky, M. Karnitschnig and G. Parker, 'Lost in translation? Managers at multinationals may miss the job's nuances if they speak only English', *Wall Street Journal*, 18 May 2004, p. B1.

First, there are *barriers caused by semantics*. As we've noted previously, words mean different things to different people. This is particularly true for people from different national cultures. Some words, for instance, don't translate between cultures. Understanding the word *sisu* will help you in communicating with people from Finland, but this word is untranslatable into English. It means something akin to 'guts' or 'dogged persistence'. Similarly, the new capitalists in Russia may have difficulty communicating with their British counterparts because English terms such as *efficiency*, *free market* and *regulation* are not directly translatable into Russian.

Second, there are *barriers caused by word connotations*. Words imply different things in different languages. Negotiations between Americans and Japanese executives, for instance, can be difficult because the Japanese word *hai* translates as 'yes', but its connotation is 'yes, I'm listening' rather than 'yes, I agree'.

Third are *barriers caused by tone differences*. In some cultures, language is formal, and in others, it's informal. In some cultures, the tone changes, depending on the context: People speak differently at home, in social situations and at work. Using a personal, informal style in a situation in which a more formal style is expected can be embarrassing and off-putting.

Fourth, there are *barriers caused by differences among perceptions*. People who speak different languages actually view the world in different ways. Eskimos perceive snow differently because they have many words for it. Thais perceive 'no' differently than do Americans because the former have no such word in their vocabulary.

Cultural context

A better understanding of the cultural barriers just discussed and their implications for communicating across cultures can be achieved by considering the concepts of high- and low-context cultures.[54]

Cultures tend to differ in the importance to which context influences the meaning that individuals take from what is actually said or written in light of who the other person is. Countries such as China, Korea, Japan and Vietnam are **high-context cultures**. They rely heavily on nonverbal and subtle situational cues in communicating with others. What is *not* said may be more significant than what *is* said. A person's official status, place in society and reputation carry considerable weight in communications. In contrast, people from Europe and North America reflect their **low-context cultures**. They rely essentially on words to convey meaning. Body language and formal titles are secondary to spoken and written words (see Figure 11.4).

What do these contextual differences mean in terms of communication? Actually, quite a lot. Communication in high-context cultures implies considerably more trust by both parties. What may appear, to an outsider, as casual and insignificant conversation is important because it reflects the desire to build a relationship and create trust. Oral agreements imply strong commitments in high-context cultures. And who you are – your age, seniority, rank in the organization – is highly valued and heavily influences your credibility. But in low-context cultures, enforceable contracts tend to be in writing, precisely worded, and highly legalistic. Similarly, low-context cultures value directness. Managers are expected to be explicit and precise in conveying intended meaning. It's quite different in high-context cultures, in which managers tend to 'make suggestions' rather than give orders.

A cultural guide

When communicating with people from a different culture, what can you do to reduce misperceptions, misinterpretations, and misevaluations? You can begin by trying to assess the cultural context. You're likely to have fewer difficulties if people come from a similar cultural context to you. In addition, the following four rules can be helpful:[55]

high-context cultures Cultures that rely heavily on nonverbal and subtle situational cues in communication.

low-context cultures Cultures that rely heavily on words to convey meaning in communication.

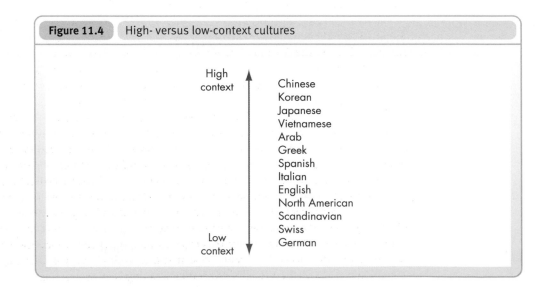

| Figure 11.4 | High- versus low-context cultures |

1. **Assume differences until similarity is proven.** Most of us assume that others are more similar to us than they actually are. But people from different countries are often very different from us. You are therefore far less likely to make an error if you assume that others are different from you rather than assume similarity until difference is proven.

2. **Emphasise description rather than interpretation or evaluation.** Interpreting or evaluating what someone has said or done, in contrast to description, is based more on the observer's culture and background than on the observed situation. As a result, delay judgement until you've had sufficient time to observe and interpret the situation from the differing perspectives of all the cultures involved.

3. **Practice empathy.** Before sending a message, put yourself in the recipient's shoes. What are their values, experiences and frames of reference? What do you know about their education, upbringing and background that can give you added insight? Try to see the other person as they really are.

4. **Treat your interpretations as a working hypothesis.** Once you've developed an explanation for a new situation or think you empathise with someone from a foreign culture, treat your interpretation as a hypothesis that needs further testing rather than as a certainty. Carefully assess the feedback provided by recipients to see if it confirms your hypothesis. For important decisions or communiqués, you can also check with other foreign and home-country colleagues to make sure that your interpretations are on target.

SELF-ASSESSMENT LIBRARY

How good are my listening skills?

In the Self-assessment library (available online), take assessment II.A.2 (How good are my listening skills?).

Summary and implications for managers

A careful review of this chapter yields a common theme regarding the relationship between communication and employee satisfaction: The less the uncertainty, the greater the satisfaction. Distortions, ambiguities and incongruities in communications all increase uncertainty and, hence, they have a negative impact on satisfaction.[56]

The less distortion that occurs in communication, the more that goals, feedback and other management messages to employees will be received as they were intended.[57] This, in turn, should reduce ambiguities and clarify the group's task. Extensive use of vertical, lateral and informal channels will increase communication flow, reduce uncertainty and improve group performance and satisfaction. We should also expect incongruities between verbal and nonverbal communiqués to increase uncertainty and to reduce satisfaction.

Findings in the chapter further suggest that the goal of perfect communication is unattainable. Yet, there is evidence that demonstrates a positive relationship between effective communication (which includes factors such as perceived trust, perceived accuracy, desire for interaction, top-management receptiveness and upward information requirements) and worker productivity.[58] Choosing the correct channel, being an effective listener, and using feedback may, therefore, make for more effective communication. But the human factor generates distortions that can never be fully eliminated. The communication process represents an exchange of messages, but the outcome is meanings that may or may not approximate those that the sender intended. Whatever the sender's expectations, the decoded message in the mind of the receiver represents his or her reality. And it is this 'reality' that will determine performance, along with the individual's level of motivation and degree of satisfaction.

Paying close attention to communication effectiveness is all the more important given the ways in which communication technology has transformed the workplace. Despite the great advantages of electronic communication formats, the pitfalls are numerous. Because we gather so much meaning from how a message is communicated (voice tone, facial expressions, body language), the potential for misunderstandings in electronic communication is great. E-mail, IM and TM, and networking software are vital aspects of organizational communication, but we need to use these tools wisely, or we'll not be as effective as managers as we might be.

Finally, there are a lot of barriers to effective communication, such as language and culture. By keeping these barriers in mind, we can overcome them and increase our communication effectiveness.

POINT/COUNTERPOINT

Keep it a secret

POINT →

We're better off keeping more things to ourselves.[59] Workplace gossip is out of control, and very often, we can't trust people with secrets. Tell a friend never, ever to tell something to someone else, and you've aroused in them an irresistible desire to share the news with others. A good rule of thumb is that if you're sure a confidante has told no one else, that probably means they have told only three other people. You might think this is a paranoid reaction, but research suggests that so-called confidantes rarely keep secrets, even when they swear they will.

Keeping our own secrets is normal, and most children learn to do it at any early age. People survive by protecting themselves, and when someone is keeping a secret, they usually have a good reason for doing so.

Even when we feel like confiding in someone else, it's prudent to keep confidential information to ourselves. Research shows that few of us are able to keep secrets and that if we fear certain negative consequences of telling our secrets (for example, our confidante will think less of us or will tell others), those fears not only don't keep us from blabbing, they are often justified.

Organizational secrets are all the more important to keep quiet. Organizations are rumour mills, and we can permanently damage our careers and the organizations for which we work by disclosing confidential information. Improper disclosure of organizational proprietary information is a huge cost and concern for organizations.

COUNTERPOINT ←

The problem with keeping secrets is that they're expensive to maintain.

One social psychologist found that when people are instructed not to disclose certain information, it becomes more distracting and difficult for them to do so. In fact, the more people are instructed to keep something to themselves, the more they see the secret in everything they do. 'We don't realise that in keeping it secret we've created an obsession in a jar,' he says. So keeping things hidden takes a toll on our psyche – it (usually unnecessarily) adds to the mental burdens we carry with us.

Another psychologist has found that these costs are real. This researcher found that young people who experienced

a traumatic experience often had more health problems later in life. As he researched the topic further, he found out why. Generally, these people conceal the event from others. He even did an experiment which showed that when people who have experienced traumatic events shared them, they later had fewer health problems than people who hadn't shared them. There isn't one identifiable reason why sharing these traumatic events seems to help people, but the result has been found repeatedly.

Thus, for mental and physical health reasons, we're better off not keeping secrets from others.

QUESTIONS FOR REVIEW

1. What are the primary functions of the communication process in organizations?

2. What are the key parts of the communication process, and how do you distinguish formal and informal communication?

3. What are the differences among downward, upward and lateral communication?

4. What are the unique challenges to oral, written and nonverbal communication?

5. How are formal communication networks and the grapevine similar and different?

6. What are the main forms of electronic communication? What are their unique benefits and challenges?

7. Why is channel richness fundamental to the choice of communication channels?

8. What are some common barriers to effective communication?

9. What unique problems underlie cross-cultural communication?

Experiential exercise

AN ABSENCE OF NONVERBAL COMMUNICATION

This exercise will help you to see the value of nonverbal communication to interpersonal relations.

1. The class is to split up into pairs (Party A and Party B).

2. Party A is to select a topic from the following list:
   (a) Managing in the Middle East is significantly different from managing in Europe.
   (b) Employee turnover in an organization can be functional.
   (c) Some conflict in an organization is good.
   (d) Whistle-blowers do more harm than good for an organization.
   (e) An employer has a responsibility to provide every employee with an interesting and challenging job.
   (f) Everyone should register to vote.
   (g) Organizations should require all employees to undergo regular drug tests.
   (h) Individuals who have majored in business or economics make better employees than those who have majored in history or English.
   (i) The place where you get your university degree is more important in determining your career success than what you learn while you're there.

(j) It's unethical for a manager to purposely distort communications to get a favourable outcome.

3. Party B is to choose a position on this topic (for example, arguing *against* the view that 'some conflict in an organization is good'). Party A now must automatically take the opposite position.

4. The two parties have 10 minutes in which to debate their topic. The catch is that the individuals can only communicate verbally. They may *not* use gestures, facial movements, body movements or any other nonverbal communication. It may help for each party to sit on their hands to remind them of their restrictions and to maintain an expressionless look.

5. After the debate is over, form groups of six to eight and spend 15 minutes discussing the following:
   (a) How effective was communication during these debates?
   (b) What barriers to communication existed?
   (c) What purposes does nonverbal communication serve?
   (d) Relate the lessons learned in this exercise to problems that might occur when communicating on the telephone or through e-mail.

Ethical dilemma

DEFINING THE BOUNDARIES OF TECHNOLOGY

You work for a company that has no specific policies regarding non-work-related uses of computers and the Internet. It also has no electronic monitoring devices to determine what employees are doing on their computers. Are any of the following actions unethical? Explain your position on each.

(a) Using the company's e-mail system for personal reasons during the workday

(b) Playing computer games during the workday

(c) Using your office computer for personal use (e.g. to shop online) during the workday

(d) Looking for a mate on an Internet dating service website during the workday

(e) Visiting 'adult' websites on your office computer during the workday

(f) Using your employer's portable communication device for personal use

(g) Conducting any of the above activities at work but before or after normal work hours

(h) For telecommuters working from home, using a computer and Internet access line paid for by your employer to visit online shopping or dating-service sites during normal working hours

CASE INCIDENT 1

Communicating at Go Fly

The history of the Go Fly airline (or simply Go) is hardly extensive. Formed by British Airways to compete in the low cost airline market for an investment of about €40 million, the airline flew for the first time in 1998. Four years later, Go had gone, having been bought by easyJet for close to €500 million. Although brief, the company's success and experiences provide lessons in organizational communication.

When the firm was the subject of a management buyout shortly before its sale, 19 directors and senior managers kept all 750 staff informed by ringing each employee personally. And, according to Dominic Paul, director of people development, that was the culmination of the organization's ongoing approach to employee communications. He explains, 'The idea is to make sure that everyone feels involved. It's a bit like when there's a delay on an aircraft, as long as the pilot advises you why there is a delay and how long you're likely to wait, you feel informed. That's how it works with Go employees, they know what's going on because we keep them informed.'

One of the biggest communications challenges at Go was the fact that many of its staff, such as the ground and aircraft crews, work unsociable hours. The company used a number of ways to keep these staff in the loop. There were regular forums where general management decisions were explained, an overview was given of the state of the business and participants were given the opportunity to ask questions. When employees walked into reception, they had the opportunity to post questions on a whiteboard and receive an answer within the week.

Go also used the latest technology to keep staff up to date with company news. 'Go TV' was broadcast every day on television monitors and was used to supply all sorts of useful information, from the latest share results to more light-hearted news. The company intranet allowed managers to easily post the latest sales figures, the situation regarding the management buyout and general staff gossip, including employees' birthdays.

A day away from the workplace is another less formal way of communicating company values. One of which culmi-

nated in the directors taking 670 staff out to dinner. Paul said, 'We do like to do things informally. It fits into the style of what we do. We have a relaxed approach, and this comes through in the state of mind of our staff, whether young or more mature.'

The then chief executive of Go, Barbara Cassani, also made great efforts to keep in touch with Go employees by recording a weekly message to staff every Friday. This could be accessed via an internal number for office-based staff, with a special external number for crew. And, said Paul, 'She's very direct and honest with staff on what's been happening.'

Paul believes that one of the greatest benefits of the company's proactive communications strategy was in recruitment and retention. The results of a yearly survey of employees showed that 93 per cent understood what Go was trying to achieve, 81 per cent thought Go was a great place to work, and significantly, 83 per cent feel they could contribute to the company's development.

Paul claimed, 'We are a "people business" and our employees are mainly on the front line of that, so it's important we reflect that in how we deal internally. It really is a simple model. We care about our customers and in order to provide a good service we make sure we've got a happy and well-motivated workforce. It's clear where the company is going and everyone will pull together. There is a real energy in the business.'

Questions

1. Which elements of the communication strategy at Go Fly made it successful?

2. How do these link with the topics that have been covered in this chapter?

3. Are there any improvements that you can recommend?

4. Do you think these communication practices would be useful in others firms? Why or why not?

Source: Adapted from 'Go gets to grips with communications', *Employers Law* (1 September 2001).

CASE INCIDENT 2

A common language?

English has increasingly become the common language of multinational firms in an attempt to deal with the language barriers they deal with in their global operations. However, this has not been met with universal approval as the following case demonstrates.

Workers in France protesting against companies who have made English the dominant language in the workplace are successfully invoking a law that mandates the use of their native language in official documents. The law, known as

La loi Toubon after the government minister who piloted it, has led to one firm, General Electric Medical Systems, being fined €580,000 for failing to translate company documents into French.

In another case, an accountant had his complaint upheld that computer programmes were only available in English. The company, Europ Assistance, was ordered to get the programmes translated into French or face a €5,000 fine for each day it failed to comply.

Workers are being supported in their claims by the Right to Work in French in France Collective, a lobby group that is waging a campaign against firms who seek to impose English at firms based in France. Jean-Loup Cuisiniez, a member of the group and an official with the CFTC trade union, said: 'We are not against the English language, but against employers forcing it on their staff.'

Evidence of this sentiment appears at the highest levels. Former President Chirac and his Foreign, Finance and Europe ministers walked out of an EU summit when the leader of a European business lobby, a fellow Frenchman, insisted on speaking in English because it is 'the language of business'.

Questions

1. Is it important that business should have a common language? Why?

2. If a common language is needed, should this be English? Why or why not?

3. What are the potential benefits and problems with predominantly using local languages depending on where the business operates?

Source: Adapted from 'French workers use language law to retain French in the office as firms favour use of English', *Personnel Today* (25 September 2007).

Endnotes

1 See, for example, K. W. Thomas and W. H. Schmidt, 'A survey of managerial interests with respect to conflict', *Academy of Management Journal*, June 1976, p. 317.

2 'Employers cite communication skills, honesty/integrity as key for job candidates', *IPMA-HR Bulletin*, 23 March 2007, p. 1.

3 W. G. Scott and T. R. Mitchell, *Organization Theory: A Structural and Behavioral Analysis* (Homewood, IL: Irwin, 1976).

4 D. K. Berlo, *The Process of Communication* (New York: Holt, Rinehart & Winston, 1960), pp. 30–32.

5 J. Langan-Fox, 'Communication in organizations: speed, diversity, networks, and influence on organizational effectiveness, human health, and relationships', in N. Anderson, D. S. Ones, H. K. Sinangil and C. Viswesvaran (eds), *Handbook of Industrial, Work and Organizational Psychology*, vol. 2 (Thousand Oaks, CA: Sage, 2001), p. 190.

6 R. L. Simpson, 'Vertical and horizontal communication in formal organizations', *Administrative Science Quarterly*, September 1959, pp. 188–96; B. Harriman, 'Up and down the communications ladder', *Harvard Business Review*, September–October 1974, pp. 143–51; A. G. Walker and J. W. Smither, 'A five-year study of upward feedback: what managers do with their results matter', *Personnel Psychology*, Summer 1999, pp. 393–424; and J. W. Smither and A. G. Walker, 'Are the characteristics of narrative comments related to improvement in multirater feedback ratings over time?', *Journal of Applied Psychology*, 89, 3 (June 2004), pp. 575–81.

7 P. Dvorak, 'How understanding the "why" of decisions matters', *Wall Street Journal*, 19 March 2007, p. B3.

8 'Employment in Europe 2007', European Commission. Available at http://ec.europa.eu.

9 D. Tourish (2005) 'Critical upward communication: ten commandments for improving strategy and decision making', *Long Range Planning*, 38, pp.; D. Tourish and P. Robson 'Critical upward feedback in organizations: processes, problems and implications for communications management', *Journal of Communication Management*, 8, 2 (2003).

10 E. Nichols, 'Hyper-speed managers', *HRMagazine*, April 2007, pp. 107–10.

11 L. Dulye, 'Get out of your office', *HRMagazine*, July 2006, pp. 99–101.

12 L. S. Rashotte, 'What does that smile mean? The meaning of nonverbal behaviors in social interaction', *Social Psychology Quarterly*, March 2002, pp. 92–102.

13 S. Robbins and P. Hunsaker (2009) *Training in Interpersonal Skills: Tips for Managing People at Work*, 5th edn. (Upper Saddle River, NJ: Pearson Education); F. Williams, *The New Communications* (Belmont, CA: Wadsworth, 1989).

14 A. Mehrabian, *Nonverbal Communication* (Chicago, IL: Aldine-Atherton, 1972).

15 N. M. Henley, 'Body politics revisited: what do we know today?', in P. J. Kalbfleisch and M. J. Cody (eds), *Gender, Power, and Communication in Human Relationships* (Hillsdale, NJ: Erlbaum, 1995), pp. 27–61.

16 See, for example, N. B. Kurland and L. H. Pelled, 'Passing the word: toward a model of gossip and power in the workplace', *Academy of Management Review*, April 2000, pp. 428–38; and N. Nicholson, 'The new word on gossip', *Psychology Today*, June 2001, pp. 41–45.

17 Cited in 'Heard it through the grapevine', *Forbes*, 10 February 1997, p. 22.

18 See, for instance, J. W. Newstrom, R. E. Monczka and W. E. Reif, 'Perceptions of the grapevine: its value and influence', *Journal of Business Communication*, Spring 1974, pp. 12–20; and S. J. Modic, 'Grapevine rated most believable', *IndustryWeek*, 15 May 1989, p. 14.

19 K. Davis, 'Management communication and the grapevine', *Harvard Business Review*, September–October 1953, pp. 43–49.

20 K. Davis, cited in R. Rowan, 'Where did that rumor come from?' *Fortune*, 13 August 1979, p. 134.

21 R. L. Rosnow and G. A. Fine, *Rumor and Gossip: The Social Psychology of Hearsay* (New York: Elsevier, 1976).

22 J. K. Bosson, A. B. Johnson, K. Niederhoffer and W. B. Swann, Jr., 'Interpersonal chemistry through negativity: bonding by sharing negative attitudes about others', *Personal Relationships*, 13 (2006), pp. 135–50.

23 B. Gates, 'How I work', *Fortune*, 17 April 2006.

24 D. Brady, '*!#?@ the e-mail. can we talk?', *BusinessWeek*, 4 December 2006, p. 109.

25 G. Vorster, 'E-mail and text widely used to duck awkward work confrontations', *Personnel Today*, 23 April 2008.

26 E. Binney, 'Is e-mail the new pink slip?', *HR Magazine*, November 2006, pp. 32–33; and R. L. Rundle, 'Critical case: how an email rant jolted a big HMO', *Wall Street Journal*, 24 April 2007, pp. A1, A16.

27 'Over three years wasted on e-mail', *Strategic Communication Management*, 11, 4 (June–July 2007), p. 9.

28 D. Goleman, 'Flame first, think later: new clues to e-mail misbehavior', *New York Times*, 20 February 2007, p. D5; and E. Krell, 'The unintended word', *HRMagazine*, August 2006, pp. 50–54.

29 T. Espiner, 'Email monitoring may contravene European laws', ZDNet.co.uk. Available at http://news.zdnet.co.uk/itmanagement/0,1000000308,39286674,00.htm. Accessed 2 January 2009.

30 K. Fitchard, 'Advertising by SMS', 24 September 2007. Available at http://www.text.it/mediacentre/facts_figures.cfm.

31 C. Hymowitz, 'Have advice, will travel', *Wall Street Journal*, 5 June 2006, pp. B1, B3.

32 'Survey finds mixed reviews on checking e-mail during meetings', *IPMA-HR Bulletin*, 27 April 2007, p. 1.

33 K. Gurchiek, 'Shoddy writing can trip up employees, organizations', *SHRM Online*, 27 April 2006, pp. 1–2.

34 D. Lidsky, 'It's not just who you know', *Fast Company*, May 2007, p. 56.

35 http://technorati.com/blogging/state-of-the-blogosphere/who-are-the-bloggers/.

36 MAKE study available at http://www.knowledgebusiness.com/knowledgebusiness/templates/TextAndLinksList.aspx?siteId=1&menuItemId=133. Accessed 12 December 2008.

37 P. R. Carlile, 'Transferring, translating, and transforming: an integrative framework for managing knowledge across boundaries', *Organization Science*, 15, 5 (September–October 2004), pp. 555–68; and S. Thurm, 'Companies struggle to pass on knowledge that workers acquire', *Wall Street Journal*, 23 January 2006, p. B1.

38 B. Fryer, 'Get smart', *Inc.*, 21, 13 (14 September 1999), p. 63.

39 E. Truch, 'Managing personal knowledge: the key to tomorrow's employability', *Journal of Change Management*, December 2001, pp. 102–105; and D. Mason and D. J. Pauleen, 'Perceptions of knowledge management: a qualitative analysis', *Journal of Knowledge Management*, 7, 4 (2003), pp. 38–48.

40 J. Gordon, 'Intellectual capital and you', *Training*, September 1999, p. 33.

41 'Bust company sacks workers by text', BBC News, 30 May 2003.

42 See R. L. Daft and R. H. Lengel, 'Information richness: a new approach to managerial behavior and organization design', in B. M. Staw and L. L. Cummings (eds), *Research in Organizational Behavior*, vol. 6 (Greenwich, CT: JAI Press, 1984), pp. 191–233; R. L. Daft and R. H. Lengel, 'Organizational information requirements, media richness, and structural design', *Managerial Science*, May 1986, pp. 554–72; R. E. Rice, 'Task analyzability, use of new media, and effectiveness', *Organization Science*, November 1992, pp. 475–500; S. G. Straus and J. E. McGrath, 'Does the medium matter? the interaction of task type and technology on group performance and member reaction', *Journal of Applied Psychology*, February 1994, pp. 87–97; L. K. Trevino, J. Webster and E. W. Stein, 'Making connections: complementary influences on communication media choices, attitudes, and use', *Organization Science*, March–April 2000, pp. 163–82; and N. Kock, 'The psychobiological model: towards a new theory of computer-mediated communication based on Darwinian evolution', *Organization Science*, 15, 3 (May–June 2004), pp. 327–48.

43 R. L. Daft, R. H. Lengel and L. K. Trevino, 'Message equivocality, media selection, and manager performance: implications for information systems', *MIS Quarterly*, September 1987, pp. 355–68.

44 'Fit for business: employment trends survey 2007', CBI available at cbi.org.uk.

45 'Spotlight on . . . working in the US', *Personnel Today*, 4 July 2006.

46 J. C. McCroskey, J. A. Daly and G. Sorenson, 'Personality correlates of communication apprehension', *Human Communication Research*, Spring 1976, pp. 376–80.

47 See, for instance, B. H. Spitzberg and M. L. Hecht, 'A competent model of relational competence', *Human Communication Research*, Summer 1984, pp. 575–99; and S. K. Opt and D. A. Loffredo, 'Rethinking communication apprehension: a Myers-Briggs perspective', *Journal of Psychology*, September 2000, pp. 556–70.

48 See, for example, L. Stafford and J. A. Daly, 'Conversational memory: the effects of instructional set and recall mode on memory for natural conversations', *Human Communication Research*, Spring 1984, pp. 379–402; and T. L. Rodebaugh, 'I might look ok, but I'm still doubtful, anxious, and avoidant: the mixed effects of enhanced video feedback on social anxiety symptoms', *Behavior Research & Therapy*, 42, 12 (December 2004), pp. 1435–51.

49 J. A. Daly and J. C. McCroskey, 'Occupational desirability and choice as a function of communication apprehension', *Journal of Counseling Psychology*, 22, 4 (1975), pp. 309–13.

50 J. A. Daly and M. D. Miller, 'The empirical development of an instrument of writing apprehension', *Research in the Teaching of English*, Winter 1975, pp. 242–49.

51 D. Tannen, *Talking from 9 to 5: How Women's and Men's Conversational Styles Affect Who Gets Heard, Who Gets Credit, and What Gets Done at Work* (New York: Oxford University Press, 1994), p. 15.

52 R. E. Axtell, *Gestures: The Do's and Taboos of Body Language Around the World* (New York: Wiley, 1991); 'Effective communication: a leading indicator of financial performance', Watson Wyatt 2006, www.watsonwyatt.com; and A. Markels, 'Turning the tide at P&G', *U.S. News & World Report*, 30 October 2006, p. 69.

53 See M. Munter, 'Cross-cultural communication for managers', *Business Horizons*, May–June 1993, pp. 75–76.

54 See E. T. Hall, *Beyond Culture* (Garden City, NY: Anchor Press/Doubleday, 1976); E. T. Hall, 'How cultures collide', *Psychology Today*, July 1976, pp. 67–74; E. T. Hall and M. R. Hall, *Understanding Cultural Differences* (Yarmouth, ME: Intercultural Press, 1990); R. E. Dulek, J. S. Fielden and J. S. Hill, 'International communication: an executive primer', *Business Horizons*, January–February 1991, pp. 20–25; D. Kim, Y. Pan and H. S. Park, 'High- versus low-context culture: a comparison of Chinese, Korean, and American cultures', *Psychology and Marketing*, September 1998, pp. 507–21;

M. J. Martinko and S. C. Douglas, 'Culture and expatriate failure: an attributional explication', *International Journal of Organizational Analysis*, July 1999, pp. 265–93; and W. L. Adair, 'Integrative sequences and negotiation outcome in same- and mixed-culture negotiations', *International Journal of Conflict Management*, 14, 3–4 (2003), pp. 1359–92.

55 N. Adler, *International Dimensions of Organizational Behavior*, 4th edn (Cincinnati, OH: South-Western Publishing, 2002), p. 94.

56 See, for example. R. S. Schuler, 'A role perception transactional process model for organizational communication–outcome relationships', *Organizational Behavior and Human Performance*, April 1979, pp. 268–91.

57 J. P. Walsh, S. J. Ashford and T. E. Hill, 'Feedback obstruction: the influence of the information environment on employee turnover intentions', *Human Relations*, January 1985, pp. 23–46.

58 S. A. Hellweg and S. L. Phillips, 'Communication and productivity in organizations: a state-of-the-art review', in *Proceedings of the 40th Annual Academy of Management Conference*, Detroit, 1980, pp. 188–92. See also B. A. Bechky, 'Sharing meaning across occupational communities: the transformation of understanding on a production floor', *Organization Science*, 14, 3 (May–June 2003), pp. 312–30.

59 Based on E. Jaffe, 'The science behind secrets', *APS Observer*, July 2006, pp. 20–22.

Basic approaches to leadership

I am more afraid of an army of
100 sheep led by a lion than an army
of 100 lions led by a sheep.

Talleyrand

Atomic Anne

Philippe Wojazer/Getty Images

Anne Lauvergeon is one of the most influential figures in the global nuclear power industry. In a world where a Chief Executive Officer's (CEO) tenure may be just months, Lauvergeon has remained CEO at the French multinational firm Areva for nearly ten years. All the more impressive given the uncertain environment firms in this controversial industry find themselves. Although the firm does have other energy interests, Areva could be described as a 'one-stop nuclear shop' because it is most well known for its nuclear activities such as selling uranium, building reactors, reprocessing fuel and storing waste.

Lauvergeon has been credited with breathing life back into the nuclear power industry. Historically, nuclear power has not been universally popular due to environmental and safety concerns, the latter being exacerbated by the Chernobyl disaster in 1986. Governments began to turn their backs on nuclear power and search for other options. However, volatile costs and supply of carbon fuels, along with the need to curb greenhouse gas emissions, has meant attention has once again turned to nuclear energy. And Lauvergeon is at the forefront of espousing the benefits.

Always a high flyer, Lauvergeon previously held positions in the mining industry, investment banking and French civil service before she was appointed to her first CEO position at Cogema (a then French state owned nuclear firm) at the age of 40. She became CEO of Areva two years later when she merged Cogema with other state-owned nuclear units, including the reactor builder Framatome.

Lauvergeon has been ranked the most influential woman in France, #2 in Europe and #8 in the world. But these personal accolades seem to matter little. For Lauvergeon it is Areva that matters, which *Fortune* Magazine has previously recognised as the most admired global company.

The future however, may truly be a test of Lauvergeon's leadership abilities. Two leaks of nuclear fuel in France, one of which tainted drinking water in the south-eastern town where it occurred, raised renewed questions about the safety of nuclear power. Her future may well hinge on her ability to quell fears about the fear of nuclear disaster.

Anne Lauvergeon demonstrates the 'right stuff'. She has successfully led a very large organization and its people in a difficult industry. But what is the right stuff? Personality traits, discussed in Chapter 4 and elsewhere in the text, are only some of the qualities we might associate with effective leadership. To assess yourself on another set of qualities that we'll discuss shortly, take the following self-assessment.

What's my leadership style?

In the Self-assessment library (available online) take assessment II.B.1 (What's my leadership style?) and answer the following questions.

1. How did you score on the two scales?

2. Do you think a leader can be both task-oriented *and* people-oriented? Do you think there are situations in which a leader has to make a choice between the two styles?

3. Do you think your leadership style will change over time? Why or why not?

1 Define *leadership* and contrast leadership and management.

In this chapter, we'll look at the basic approaches to determining what makes an effective leader and what differentiates leaders from nonleaders. First, we'll present trait theories, which dominated the study of leadership up to the late 1940s. Then we'll discuss behavioural theories, which were popular until the late 1960s. Next, we'll introduce contingency theories and interactive theories. But before we review these approaches, let's first clarify what we mean by the term *leadership*.

What is leadership?

The personal qualities of Richard Branson, chairman of Virgin Group, make him a great leader. Branson is described as fun loving, sensitive to the needs of others, hard working, innovative, charismatic, enthusiastic, energetic, decisive, and risk taking. These traits helped the British entrepreneur build one of the most recognised and respected brands in the world. He also commands the admiration of his peers. A survey of UK business chiefs rated Sir Richard Branson above all other British business leaders.[3]

Leadership and *management* are two terms that are often confused. What's the difference between them?

John Kotter argues that management is about coping with complexity.[1] Good management brings about order and consistency by drawing up formal plans, designing rigid organization structures, and monitoring results against the plans. Leadership, in contrast, is about coping with change. Leaders establish direction by developing a vision of the future; then they align people by communicating this vision and inspiring them to overcome hurdles.

Robert House basically concurs when he says that managers use the authority inherent in their designated formal rank to obtain compliance from organizational members.[2] Management consists of implementing the vision and strategy provided by leaders, coordinating and staffing the organization, and handling day-to-day problems.

Although Kotter and House provide separate definitions of the two terms, both researchers and practicing managers frequently make no such distinctions. So we need to present leadership in a way that can capture how it is used in theory and practice.

We define **leadership** as the ability to influence a group toward the achievement of a vision or set of goals. The source of this influence may be formal, such as that provided by the possession of managerial rank in an organization. Because management positions come with some degree of formally designated authority, a person may assume a leadership role simply because of the position he or she holds in the organization. But not all leaders are managers, nor, for that matter, are all managers leaders. Just because an organization provides its managers with certain formal rights is no assurance that they will be able to lead effectively. We find that nonsanctioned leadership – that is, the ability to influence that arises outside the formal structure of the organization – is often as important or more important than formal influence. In other words, leaders can emerge from within a group as well as by formal appointment to lead a group.

leadership
The ability to influence a group toward the achievement of a vision or set of goals.

One last comment before we move on: Organizations need strong leadership *and* strong management for optimal effectiveness. In today's dynamic world, we need leaders to challenge the status quo, to create visions of the future, and to inspire organizational members to want to achieve the visions. We also need managers to formulate detailed plans, create efficient organizational structures and oversee day-to-day operations.

Trait theories

2 Summarise the conclusions of trait theories.

trait theories of leadership
Theories that consider personal qualities and characteristics that differentiate leaders from nonleaders.

Throughout history, strong leaders – Buddha, Napoleon, Mao, Lorenzo de' Medici, de Gaulle, Churchill, Roosevelt – have all been described in terms of their traits. For example, when Margaret Thatcher was prime minister of Great Britain, she was regularly described as confident, iron willed, determined and decisive.

Trait theories of leadership differentiate leaders from nonleaders by focusing on personal qualities and characteristics. Individuals such as Maurice Lévy CEO of Publicis, Virgin Group CEO Richard Branson, Fiat CEO Sergio Marchionne and Apple co-founder Steve Jobs, are recognised as business leaders and often described in terms such as *charismatic, enthusiastic,* and *courageous.* The search for personality, social, physical or intellectual attributes that would describe leaders and differentiate them from nonleaders goes back to the earliest stages of leadership research.

Research efforts at isolating leadership traits resulted in a number of dead ends. For instance, a review in the late 1960s of 20 different studies identified nearly 80 leadership traits, but only five of these traits were common to four or more of the investigations.[4] By the 1990s, after numerous studies and analyses, about the best thing that could be said was that most 'leaders are not like other people', but the particular traits that were isolated varied a great deal from review to review.[5] It was a pretty confusing state of affairs.

A breakthrough, of sorts, came when researchers began organising traits around the Big Five personality framework (see Chapter 4).[6] It became clear that most of the dozens of traits emerging in various leadership reviews could be subsumed under one of the Big Five and that this approach resulted in consistent and strong support for traits as predictors of leadership. For instance, ambition and energy – two common traits of leaders – are part of extraversion. Rather than focus on these two specific traits, it is better to think of them in terms of the more general trait of extraversion.

A comprehensive review of the leadership literature, when organized around the Big Five, has found that extraversion is the most important trait of effective leaders.[7] But results show that extraversion is more strongly related to leader emergence than to leader effectiveness. This is not totally surprising since sociable and dominant people are more likely to assert themselves in group situations. While the assertive nature of extraverts is a positive, leaders need to make sure they're not too assertive – one study found that leaders who scored very high on assertiveness were less effective than those who were moderately high.[8]

Conscientiousness and openness to experience also showed strong and consistent relationships to leadership, though not quite as strong as extraversion. The traits of agreeableness and emotional stability weren't as strongly correlated with leadership. Overall, it does appear that the trait approach does have something to offer. Leaders who are extraverted (individuals who like being around people and are able to assert themselves), conscientious (individuals who are disciplined and keep commitments they make), and open (individuals who are creative and flexible) do seem to have an advantage when it comes to leadership, suggesting that good leaders do have key traits in common.

Recent studies are indicating that another trait that may indicate effective leadership is emotional intelligence (EI), which we discussed in Chapter 8. Advocates of EI argue that without it, a person can have outstanding training, a highly analytical mind, a compelling vision, and an endless supply of terrific ideas but still not make a great leader. This may be especially true as individuals move up in an organization.[9] But why is EI so critical to effective leadership? A core component of EI is empathy. Empathetic leaders can sense others' needs, listen to what followers say (and don't say), and are able to read the reactions of others. As one leader noted, 'The caring part of empathy, especially for the people with whom you work, is what inspires people to stay with a leader when the going gets rough. The mere fact that someone cares is more often than not rewarded with loyalty.'[10]

GOOD LEADERS IN SHORT SUPPLY

OB IN THE NEWS

A Chartered Institute of Personnel and Development (CIPD) study concluded that two-thirds of organizations including many businesses, 'are suffering from a shortage of highly effective leaders'.

It was claimed that more investment in leadership development was needed if employers were to manage organizational changes successfully, deliver business strategies, cope with succession problems and fill internal skills gaps.

Jessica Jarvis, CIPD adviser on learning, training and development, said: 'This leadership deficit could under-mine the ability of organizations to adapt to change and achieve their business strategies. Although many organizations are investing in leadership development, it appears that many leaders lack the skills to successfully lead and manage organizations during times of change.' Among the most frequently reported skills gaps were 'leading people and people management' and 'the ability to think strategically for the business'.

Source: Based on A. Taylor, 'Good leaders in short supply, study finds', *Financial Times*, 29 March 2005, p. 3.

Despite these claims for its importance, the link between EI and leadership effectiveness is much less investigated than other traits. One reviewer noted, 'Speculating about the practical utility of the EI construct might be premature. Despite such warnings, EI is being viewed as a panacea for many organizational malaises with recent suggestions that EI is essential for leadership effectiveness.'[11] But until more rigorous evidence accumulates, we can't be confident about the connection.

Based on the latest findings, we offer two conclusions. First, traits can predict leadership. Twenty years ago, the evidence suggested otherwise. But this was probably due to the lack of a valid framework for classifying and organizing traits. The Big Five seems to have rectified that. Second, traits do a better job at predicting the emergence of leaders and the appearance of leadership than in actually distinguishing between *effective* and *ineffective* leaders.[12] The fact that an individual exhibits the traits and others consider that person to be a leader does not necessarily mean that the leader is successful at getting his or her group to achieve its goals.

'YOU NEED TO BE POPULAR TO BE AN EFFECTIVE LEADER'

MYTH *OR* SCIENCE?

This statement is false. It's not surprising we tend to couple popularity with leadership effectiveness, since most of us tend to attribute various positive qualities to those we like. However, while there may be a link between popularity and leadership, it's not necessarily between effectiveness and the degree to which a leader is liked. For example, a political figure running in an election who is well liked is more likely to become the country's leader, but that has nothing to do with whether the elected official will be worth anything as a leader.

If you consider for a moment, it is often the case that effective leaders need to make decisions that anger people, and that those decisions may be needed by an organization. These 'hard decisions' can result in a leader being unpopular on a personal level, but effective in terms of the organization. As a leader, it is unwise to strive to be 'popular', particularly if in doing so, the leader sacrifices important values, principles and beliefs, and avoids making unpopular decisions when they are necessary.

That isn't to say that leaders should go too far in the opposite direction, and act in obnoxious, offensive or egocentric ways that might, as a by-product, make them unpopular.

Source: 'You need to be popular, or well-liked to be an effective leader', Leader Development Resource Centre. Available at: http://www.work911.com/leadership-development/faq/mythpopular.htm. Accessed 20 January 2009.

Behavioural theories

3 Identify the central tenets and main limitations of behavioural theories.

behavioural theories of leadership
Theories proposing that specific behaviours differentiate leaders from nonleaders.

The failures of early trait studies led researchers in the late 1940s through the 1960s to go in a different direction. They began looking at the behaviours exhibited by specific leaders. They wondered if there was something unique in the way that effective leaders behave. To use contemporary examples, Sir John Browne, former chairman and CEO of BP and Oracle CEO Larry Ellison have been very successful in leading their companies through difficult times.[13] And they both rely on a common leadership style that is tough-talking, intense, and autocratic. Does this suggest that autocratic behaviour is a preferred style for all leaders? In this section, we look at three different **behavioural theories of leadership** to answer that question. First, however, let's consider the practical implications of the behavioural approach.

If the behavioural approach to leadership were successful, it would have implications quite different from those of the trait approach. Trait research provides a basis for *selecting* the 'right' persons to assume formal positions in groups and organizations requiring leadership. In contrast, if behavioural studies were to turn up critical behavioural determinants of leadership, we could *train* people to be leaders. The difference between trait and behavioural theories, in terms of application, lies in their underlying assumptions. Trait theories assume that leaders are born rather than made. However, if there were specific behaviours that identified leaders, then we could teach leadership; we could design programmes that implanted these behavioural patterns in individuals who desired to be effective leaders. This was surely a more exciting avenue, for it meant that the supply of leaders could be expanded. If training worked, we could have an infinite supply of effective leaders.

Ohio State studies

initiating structure
The extent to which a leader is likely to define and structure his or her role and those of subordinates in the search for goal attainment.

consideration
The extent to which a leader is likely to have job relationships characterised by mutual trust, respect for subordinates' ideas, and regard for their feelings.

The most comprehensive and replicated of the behavioural theories resulted from research that began at Ohio State University in the late 1940s.[14] Researchers at Ohio State sought to identify independent dimensions of leader behaviour. Beginning with over 1,000 dimensions, they eventually narrowed the list to two categories that substantially accounted for most of the leadership behaviour described by employees. They called these two dimensions *initiating structure* and *consideration*.

Initiating structure refers to the extent to which a leader is likely to define and structure his or her role and those of employees in the search for goal attainment. It includes behaviour that attempts to organize work, work relationships and goals. A leader characterised as high in initiating structure could be described as someone who 'assigns group members to particular tasks', 'expects workers to maintain definite standards of performance' and 'emphasises the meeting of deadlines'.

Consideration is described as the extent to which a person is likely to have job relationships that are characterised by mutual trust, respect for employees' ideas, and regard for their feelings. We could describe a leader high in consideration as one who helps employees with personal problems, is friendly and approachable, treats all employees as equals, and expresses appreciation and support. A recent survey of employees revealed that when asked to indicate the factors that most motivated them at work, 66 per cent mentioned appreciation. This speaks to the motivating potential of considerate leadership behaviour.[15]

At one time, the results of the Ohio State studies were thought to be disappointing. One 1992 review concluded, 'Overall, the research based on a two-factor conceptualisation of leadership behaviour has added little to our knowledge about effective leadership.'[16] However, a more recent review suggests that this two-factor conceptualisation was given a premature burial. A review of 160 studies found that both initiating structure and consideration were associated with effective leadership. Specifically, consideration was more strongly related to the individual. In other words, the followers of leaders who were high in consideration were more satisfied with their jobs and more motivated and also had more respect for their leader. Initiating structure, however, was more strongly related to higher levels of group and organization productivity and more positive performance evaluations.

Louis Gallois, CEO of aerospace giant European Aeronautic Defence and Space Company (EADS), is an employee-oriented leader. Gallois claims leadership is about trust and doing what you say. He claims, 'I am an employee: if we say we have to save money, then I have to save money. And you have to meet the people – you have to discuss with them, you have to feel them.'

Source: CNBC Europe 'High Flier' An interview with Simon Hobbs, November 2008. Available at http://cnbceb.com/leadership/high-flier/709/.

employee-oriented leader
A leader who emphasises interpersonal relations, takes a personal interest in the needs of employees, and accepts individual differences among members.

production-oriented leader
A leader who emphasises technical or task aspects of the job.

managerial grid
A nine-by-nine matrix outlining 81 different leadership styles.

University of Michigan studies

Leadership studies undertaken at the University of Michigan's Survey Research Center at about the same time as those being done at Ohio State had similar research objectives: to locate behavioural characteristics of leaders that appeared to be related to measures of performance effectiveness.

The Michigan group also came up with two dimensions of leadership behaviour that they labelled *employee-oriented* and *production-oriented*.[17] The **employee-oriented leaders** were described as emphasising interpersonal relations; they took a personal interest in the needs of their employees and accepted individual differences among members. The **production-oriented leaders**, in contrast, tended to emphasise the technical or task aspects of the job; their main concern was in accomplishing their group's tasks, and the group members were a means to that end. These dimensions – employee-oriented and production-oriented – are closely related to the Ohio State dimensions. Employee-oriented leadership is similar to consideration, and production-oriented leadership is similar to initiating structure. In fact, most leadership researchers use the terms synonymously.[18]

The conclusions the Michigan researchers arrived at strongly favoured the leaders who were employee oriented in their behaviour. Employee-oriented leaders were associated with higher group productivity and greater job satisfaction. Production-oriented leaders tended to be associated with low group productivity and lower job satisfaction. Although the Michigan studies emphasised employee-oriented leadership (or consideration) over production-oriented leadership (or initiating structure), the Ohio State studies garnered more research attention and suggested that *both* consideration and initiating structure are important to effective leadership.

Drawing from the Ohio State and Michigan studies, Blake and Mouton proposed a **managerial grid** (sometimes called the *leadership grid*) based on the styles of 'concern for people' and 'concern for production', which essentially represent the Ohio State dimensions of consideration and initiating structure or the Michigan dimensions of employee-oriented and production-oriented.[19]

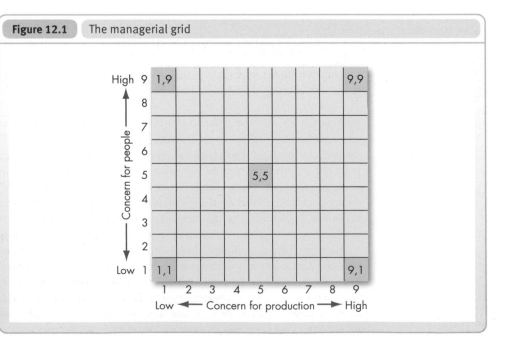

Figure 12.1   The managerial grid

AP Archive/Press Association Images

Sir James Ackers was a successful businessman who nurtured a family business into becoming one of the largest truck-hire companies in the UK. When a recession struck in 1991, he focused on the public sector as a senior UK National Health Service leader. This did not turn out to be as successful. A local newspaper collected 250,000 signatures calling for his resignation over financial controversies. Faced with overwhelming public and political pressure, he resigned in 1993.[22] Predicting the effectiveness of leaders in different contexts, such the public and private sector, illustrates the premise of contingency theories that leadership effectiveness is dependent on situational influences.

The grid, depicted in Figure 12.1, has nine possible positions along each axis, creating 81 different positions in which the leader's style may fall. The grid does not show results produced; rather, it shows the dominating factors in a leader's thinking in regard to getting results. Based on the findings of Blake and Mouton, managers were found to perform best under a 9,9 style, as contrasted, for example, with a 9,1 (authority type) or 1,9 (laissez-faire type) style.[20] Unfortunately, the grid offers a better framework for conceptualising leadership style than for presenting any tangible new information in clarifying the leadership quandary because it doesn't really convey any new information in addition to the Ohio State and the University of Michigan research.[21]

Summary of trait theories and behavioural theories

Judging from the evidence, the behavioural theories, like the trait theories, add to our understanding of leadership effectiveness. Leaders who have certain traits and who display consideration and structuring behaviours, do appear to be more effective. Perhaps trait theories and behavioural theories should be integrated. For example, you would think that conscientious leaders (conscientiousness is a trait) are more likely to be structuring (structuring is a behaviour). And maybe extraverted leaders (extraversion is a trait) are more likely to be considerate (consideration is a behaviour). Unfortunately, we can't be sure there is a connection. Future research is needed to integrate these approaches.

Trait theories and behavioural theories aren't the last word on leadership. Missing is consideration of the situational factors that influence success or failure. Some leaders may have the right traits or display the right behaviours and still fail. For example, Sir Fred Goodwin, a Scottish banker, expanded the Royal Bank of Scotland (RBS) from its Edinburgh base by acquisitions to become a major international bank. However, when a global banking crisis hit, RBS nearly collapsed and Goodwin stood down as CEO soon after. As important as trait theories and behavioural theories are in determining effective versus ineffective leaders, they do not guarantee a leader's success. The context matters, too.

Contingency theories: Fiedler model and situational leadership theory

4 Assess contingency theories of leadership by their level of support.

Some tough-minded leaders seem to gain a lot of admirers when they take over struggling companies and help lead them out of the doldrums. However, these tough-minded leaders don't always seem to 'wear' well. For example, when Michael Armstrong was appointed CEO of the long floundering American telecommunications firm AT&T the announcement was greeted with euphoria. Considered a superman CEO after his highly successful days at IBM, AT&T shares jumped 5 per cent on the day of the announcement. Four years later Armstrong's grand vision to remake AT&T had failed and he subsequently resigned.

This case illustrates that predicting leadership success is more complex than isolating a few traits or preferable behaviours. For Armstrong, what worked at IBM did not work at AT&T. The failure by researchers in the mid-twentieth century to obtain consistent results led to a focus on situational influences. The relationship between leadership style and effectiveness suggested that under condition *a*, style *x* would be appropriate, whereas style *y* would be more suitable for condition *b* and style *z* would be more suitable for condition *c*. But what were the conditions *a*, *b*, *c*, and so forth? It was one thing to say that leadership effectiveness was dependent on the situation and another to be able to isolate those situational conditions. Several approaches to isolating key situational variables have proven more successful than others and, as a result, have gained wider recognition. We shall consider three of these: the Fiedler model, Hersey and Blanchard's situational theory and the path-goal theory.

SELF-ASSESSMENT LIBRARY

What's my LPC score?

In the Self-assessment library (available online) take assessment IV.E.5 (What's my LPC score?).

Fiedler model

The first comprehensive contingency model for leadership was developed by Fred Fiedler.[23] The **Fiedler contingency model** proposes that effective group performance depends on the proper match between the leader's style and the degree to which the situation gives control to the leader.

Identifying leadership style

Fiedler believes a key factor in leadership success is the individual's basic leadership style. So he begins by trying to find out what that basic style is. Fiedler created the **least preferred co-worker (LPC) questionnaire** for this purpose; it purports to measure whether a person is task- or relationship-oriented. The LPC questionnaire contains sets of 16 contrasting adjectives (such as pleasant–unpleasant, efficient–inefficient, open–guarded, supportive–hostile). It asks respondents to think of all the co-workers they have ever had and to describe the one person they *least enjoyed* working with by rating that person on a scale of 1 to 8 for each of the 16 sets of contrasting adjectives. Fiedler believes that based on the respondents' answers to this LPC questionnaire, he can determine their basic leadership style. If the least preferred co-worker is described in relatively positive terms (a high LPC score), then the respondent is primarily interested in good personal relations with this co-worker. That is, if you essentially describe the person you are least able to work with in favourable terms, Fiedler would label you *relationship-oriented*. In contrast, if the least preferred co-worker is seen in relatively unfavourable terms (a low LPC score), the respondent is primarily interested in productivity and thus would be labelled *task oriented*. About 16 per cent of respondents score in the middle range.[24] Such individuals cannot be classified as either relationship oriented or task oriented and thus fall outside the theory's predictions. The rest of our discussion, therefore, relates to the 84 per cent who score in either the high or low range of the LPC questionnaire.

Fiedler assumes that an individual's leadership style is fixed. As we'll show, this is important because it means that if a situation requires a task-oriented leader and the person in that leadership position is relationship oriented, either the situation has to be modified or the leader has to be replaced in order to achieve optimal effectiveness.

Defining the situation

After an individual's basic leadership style has been assessed through the LPC questionnaire, it is necessary to match the leader with the situation. Fiedler has identified three contingency dimensions that, he argues, define the key situational factors that determine leadership effectiveness. These are leader–member relations, task structure and position power. They are defined as follows:

1. **Leader–member relations** is the degree of confidence, trust and respect members have in their leader.

2. **Task structure** is the degree to which the job assignments are procedurised (that is, structured or unstructured).

3. **Position power** is the degree of influence a leader has over power variables such as hiring, firing, discipline, promotions and salary increases.

Fiedler contingency model
The theory that effective groups depend on a proper match between a leader's style of interacting with subordinates and the degree to which the situation gives control and influence to the leader.

least preferred co-worker (LPC) questionnaire
An instrument that purports to measure whether a person is task- or relationship-oriented.

leader–member relations
The degree of confidence, trust, and respect subordinates have in their leader.

task structure
The degree to which job assignments are procedurised.

position power
Influence derived from one's formal structural position in the organization; includes power to hire, fire, discipline, promote, and give salary increases.

| Figure 12.2 | Findings from the Fiedler model |

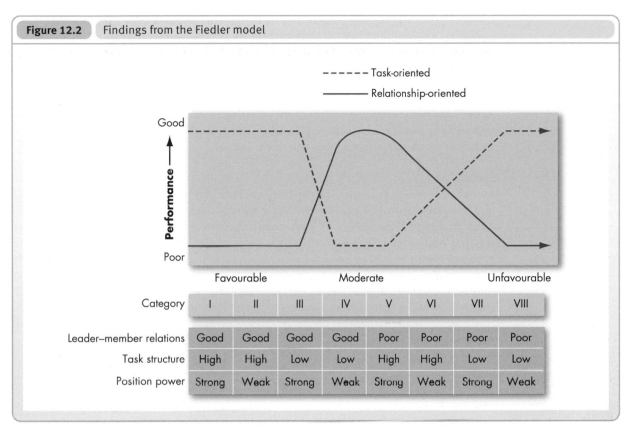

The next step in the Fiedler model is to evaluate the situation in terms of these three contingency variables. Leader–member relations are either good or poor, task structure is either high or low, and position power is either strong or weak.

Fiedler states that the better the leader–member relations, the more highly structured the job, and the stronger the position power, the more control the leader has. For example, a very favourable situation (in which the leader would have a great deal of control) might involve a payroll manager who is well respected and whose employees have confidence in them (good leader–member relations), for which the activities to be done – such as wage computation, cheque writing and report filing – are specific and clear (high task structure), and the job provides considerable freedom for them to reward and punish their employees (strong position power). However, an unfavourable situation might be the disliked chairperson of a voluntary charity fundraising team. In this job, the leader has very little control. Altogether, by mixing the three contingency dimensions, there are potentially eight different situations or categories in which leaders could find themselves (see Figure 12.2).

Matching leaders and situations

With knowledge of an individual's LPC score and an assessment of the three contingency dimensions, the Fiedler model proposes matching them up to achieve maximum leadership effectiveness.[25] Based on his research, Fiedler concluded that task-oriented leaders tend to perform better in situations that were very favourable to them and in situations that were very unfavourable (see Figure 12.2). So Fiedler would predict that when faced with a category I, II, III, VII or VIII situation, task-oriented leaders perform better. Relationship-oriented leaders, however, perform better in moderately favourable situations – categories IV through VI. In recent years, Fiedler has condensed these eight situations down to three.[26] He now says that task-oriented leaders perform best in situations of high and low control, while relationship-oriented leaders perform best in moderate control situations.

How would you apply Fiedler's findings? You would seek to match leaders and situations. Individuals' LPC scores would determine the type of situation for which they were best suited. That 'situation' would be defined by evaluating the three contingency factors of leader–member relations, task structure and position power. But remember that Fiedler views an individual's leadership style as being fixed. Therefore, there are really only two ways in which to improve leader effectiveness.

First, you can change the leader to fit the situation. So, for example, if a group situation rates as highly unfavourable but is currently led by a relationship-oriented manager, the group's performance could be improved by replacing that manager with one who is task-oriented. The second alternative would be to change the situation to fit the leader. That could be done by restructuring tasks or increasing or decreasing the power that the leader has to control factors such as salary increases, promotions and disciplinary actions.

Evaluation

As a whole, reviews of the major studies that have tested the overall validity of the Fiedler model lead to a generally positive conclusion. That is, there is considerable evidence to support at least substantial parts of the model.[27] If predictions from the model use only three categories rather than the original eight, there is ample evidence to support Fiedler's conclusions.[28] But there are problems with the LPC questionnaire and the practical use of the model that need to be addressed. For instance, the logic underlying the LPC questionnaire is not well understood, and studies have shown that respondents' LPC scores are not stable.[29] Also, the contingency variables are complex and difficult for practitioners to assess. It's often difficult in practice to determine how good the leader–member relations are, how structured the task is, and how much position power the leader has.[30]

Cognitive resource theory

cognitive resource theory
A theory of leadership which states that stress unfavourably affects a situation and that intelligence and experience can reduce the influence of stress on the leader.

More recently, Fiedler has reconceptualised his original theory.[31] In this refinement, called **cognitive resource theory**, he focuses on the role of stress as a form of situational unfavourableness and how a leader's intelligence and experience influence his or her reaction to stress.

The essence of the new theory is that stress is the enemy of rationality. It's difficult for leaders (or anyone else, for that matter) to think logically and analytically when they're under stress. Moreover, the importance of a leader's intelligence and experience to effectiveness differs under low- and high-stress situations. Fiedler and associates found that a leader's intellectual abilities correlate positively with performance under low stress but negatively under high stress. And, conversely, a leader's experience correlates negatively with performance under low stress but positively under high stress. So, it's the level of stress in the situation that determines whether an individual's intelligence or experience will contribute to leadership performance.

In spite of its newness, cognitive resource theory is developing a solid body of research support.[32] In fact, a study confirmed that when the stress level was low and the leader was directive (that is, when the leader was willing to tell people what to do), intelligence was important to a leader's effectiveness.[33] And in high-stress situations, intelligence was of little help because the leader was too cognitively taxed to put intellect to good use. Similarly, if a leader is nondirective, intelligence is of little help because the leader is afraid to put intellect to use to tell people what to do. These results are exactly what cognitive resource theory predicts.

Hersey and Blanchard's situational theory

situational leadership theory (SLT)
A contingency theory that focuses on followers' readiness.

Paul Hersey and Ken Blanchard have developed a leadership model that has gained a strong following among management development specialists.[34] This model – called **situational leadership theory (SLT)** – has been incorporated into leadership training programmes at more than 400 of the Fortune 500 companies; and more than 1 million managers per year from a wide variety of organizations have been taught its basic elements.[35]

Situational leadership is a contingency theory that focuses on the followers. Successful leadership is achieved by selecting the right leadership style, which Hersey and Blanchard argue is contingent on the level of the followers' readiness. Before we proceed, we should clarify two points: Why focus on the followers? And what do they mean by the term *readiness*?

The emphasis on the followers in leadership effectiveness reflects the reality that it is the followers who accept or reject the leader. Regardless of what the leader does, effectiveness depends on the actions of the followers. This is an important dimension that has been overlooked or underemphasised in most other leadership theories. The term *readiness*, as defined by Hersey

Patrick Allard/REA/Redux

These researchers at Cytos Biotechnology in Zurich, Switzerland, are developing anti-smoking and anti-obesity vaccines. The biologists and chemists at Cytos use their expertise in immunology and biotechnology in developing vaccines to treat the cause and progression of common chronic diseases that afflict millions of people worldwide. They have a high level of follower readiness. As highly educated, experienced, and responsible employees, they are able and willing to complete their tasks under leadership that gives them freedom to make and implement decisions. This leader–follower relationship is consistent with Hersey and Blanchard's situational leadership theory.

and Blanchard, refers to the extent to which people have the ability and willingness to accomplish a specific task.

SLT essentially views the leader–follower relationship as analogous to that between a parent and a child. Just as a parent needs to relinquish control as a child becomes more mature and responsible, so too should leaders. Hersey and Blanchard identify four specific leader behaviours – from highly directive to highly laissez-faire. The most effective behaviour depends on a follower's ability and motivation. SLT says that if followers are *unable* and *unwilling* to do a task, the leader needs to give clear and specific directions; if followers are *unable* and *willing*, the leader needs to display high task orientation to compensate for the followers' lack of ability and high relationship orientation to get the followers to 'buy into' the leader's desires; if followers are *able* and *unwilling*, the leader needs to use a supportive and participative style; and if the employee is both *able* and *willing*, the leader doesn't need to do much.

SLT has an intuitive appeal. It acknowledges the importance of followers and builds on the logic that leaders can compensate for ability and motivational limitations in their followers. Yet research efforts to test and support the theory have generally been disappointing.[36] Why? Possible explanations include internal ambiguities and inconsistencies in the model itself as well as problems with research methodology in tests of the theory. So despite its intuitive appeal and wide popularity, any enthusiastic endorsement, at least at this time, has to be cautioned against.

Path-goal theory

path-goal theory
A theory which states that it is the leader's job to assist followers in attaining their goals and to provide the necessary direction and/or support to ensure that their goals are compatible with the overall objectives of the group or organization.

Developed by Robert House, path-goal theory extracts elements from the Ohio State leadership research on initiating structure and consideration and the expectancy theory of motivation.[37]

The theory

The essence of **path-goal theory** is that it's the leader's job to provide followers with the information, support or other resources necessary for them to achieve their goals. The term *path-goal* is derived from the belief that effective leaders clarify the path to help their followers get from where they are to the achievement of their work goals and to make the journey along the path easier by reducing roadblocks.

Leader behaviours

House identified four leadership behaviours. The *directive leader* lets followers know what is expected of them, schedules work to be done and gives specific guidance as to how to accomplish tasks. The *supportive leader* is friendly and shows concern for the needs of followers. The *participative leader* consults with followers and uses their suggestions before making a decision. The *achievement-oriented leader* sets challenging goals and expects followers to perform at their highest level. In contrast to Fiedler, House assumes leaders are flexible and that the same leader can display any or all of these behaviours depending on the situation.

Path-goal variables and predictions

As Figure 12.3 illustrates, path-goal theory proposes two classes of contingency variables that moderate the leadership behaviour–outcome relationship: those in the environment that are outside the control of the employee (task structure, the formal authority system, and the work group) and those that are part of the personal characteristics of the employee (locus of control, experience, and perceived ability). Environmental factors determine the type of leader behaviour required as a complement if follower outcomes are to be maximised, while personal characteristics of the employee determine how the environment and leader behaviour are interpreted. So the theory proposes that leader behaviour will be ineffective when it is redundant with sources of environmental structure or incongruent with employee characteristics. For example, the following are illustrations of predictions based on path-goal theory:

- Directive leadership leads to greater satisfaction when tasks are ambiguous or stressful than when they are highly structured and well laid out.

- Supportive leadership results in high employee performance and satisfaction when employees are performing structured tasks.

- Directive leadership is likely to be perceived as redundant among employees with high perceived ability or with considerable experience.

- Employees with an internal locus of control will be more satisfied with a participative style.

- Achievement-oriented leadership will increase employees' expectancies that effort will lead to high performance when tasks are ambiguously structured.

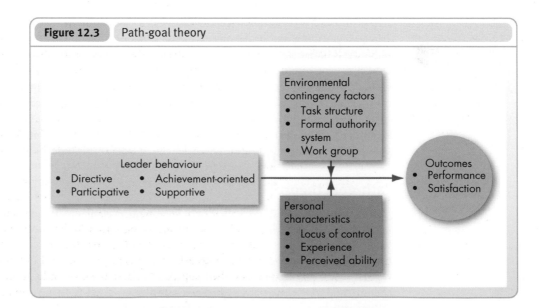

Figure 12.3 Path-goal theory

Evaluation

Due to the complexity of the theory, testing path-goal theory has not proven to be easy. A review of the evidence suggests mixed support. As the authors of this review commented, 'These results suggest that either effective leadership does not rest in the removal of roadblocks and pitfalls to employee path instrumentalities as path-goal theories propose or that the nature of these hindrances is not in accord with the proposition of the theories.' Another review concluded that the lack of support was 'shocking and disappointing.'[38] These conclusions have been challenged by others who argue that adequate tests of the theory have yet to be conducted.[39] Thus, it is safe to say that the jury is still out regarding the validity of path-goal theory. Because it is so complex to test, that may remain the case for some time to come.

Summary of contingency theories

It's fair to say that none of the contingency theories have panned out as well as their developers had hoped. In particular, results for situational leadership theory and path-goal theory have been disappointing. Fiedler's LPC theory has fared better in the research literature.

One limitation of the contingency theories, and indeed of all the theories we've covered so far, is that they ignore the followers. Yet, as one leadership scholar noted, 'leaders do not exist in a vacuum'; leadership is a symbiotic relationship between leaders and followers.[40] But the leadership theories we've covered to this point have largely assumed that leaders treat all their followers in the same manner. That is, they assume that leaders use a fairly homogeneous style with all the people in their work unit. But think about your experiences in groups. Did you notice that leaders often act very differently toward different people? Next we look at a theory that considers differences in the relationships leaders form with different followers.

Leader–member exchange (LMX) theory

5 Contrast the interactive theories path-goal and leader–member exchange.

leader–member exchange (LMX) theory
A theory that supports leaders' creation of in-groups and out-groups; subordinates with in-group status will have higher performance ratings, less turnover, and greater job satisfaction.

Think of a leader you know. Did this leader tend to have favourites who made up his or her 'in-group'? If you answered 'yes', you're acknowledging the foundation of leader–member exchange theory.[41] The **leader–member exchange (LMX) theory** argues that because of time pressures, leaders establish a special relationship with a small group of their followers. These individuals make up the in-group – they are trusted, get a disproportionate amount of the leader's attention and are more likely to receive special privileges. Other followers fall into the out-group. They get less of the leader's time, get fewer of the preferred rewards that the leader controls, and have leader–follower relations based on formal authority interactions.

The theory proposes that early in the history of the interaction between a leader and a given follower, the leader implicitly categorises the follower as an 'in' or an 'out', and that relationship is relatively stable over time. Leaders induce LMX by rewarding those employees with whom they want a closer linkage and punishing those with whom they do not.[42] But for the LMX relationship to remain intact, the leader and the follower must invest in the relationship.

Just precisely how the leader chooses who falls into each category is unclear, but there is evidence that leaders tend to choose in-group members because they have demographic, attitude, and personality characteristics that are similar to the leader's or a higher level of competence than out-group members[43] (see Figure 12.4). For example, leaders of the same gender tend to have closer (higher LMX) relationships than when leaders and followers are of different genders.[44] The key point to note here is that even though it is the leader who is doing the choosing, it is the follower's characteristics that are driving the leader's categorising decision.

Research to test LMX theory has been generally supportive. More specifically, the theory and research surrounding it provide substantive evidence that leaders do differentiate among followers; that these disparities are far from random; and that followers with in-group status will have higher performance ratings, engage in more helping or 'citizenship' behaviours at work and report greater satisfaction with their superior.[45] These positive findings for in-group members shouldn't be totally surprising, given our knowledge of self-fulfilling prophecy (see Chapter 5).

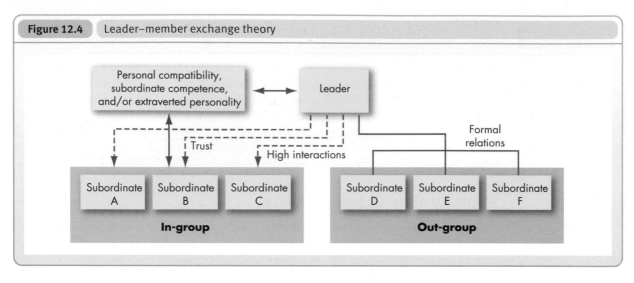

Figure 12.4 Leader–member exchange theory

Leaders invest their resources with those they expect to perform best. And 'knowing' that in-group members are the most competent, leaders treat them as such and unwittingly fulfil their prophecy.[46]

Decision theory: Vroom and Yetton's leader-participation model

6 Identify the situational variables in the leader-participation model.

leader-participation model
A leadership theory that provides a set of rules to determine the form and amount of participative decision making in different situations.

The final theory we'll cover in this chapter argues that *the way* the leader makes decisions is as important as *what* she or he decides. Victor Vroom and Phillip Yetton developed a **leader-participation model** that relates leadership behaviour and participation in decision making.[47] Recognising that task structures have varying demands for routine and nonroutine activities, these researchers argued that leader behaviour must adjust to reflect the task structure. Vroom and Yetton's model is normative – it provides a sequential set of rules that should be followed in determining the form and amount of participation in decision making, as determined by different types of situations. The model is a decision tree incorporating seven contingencies (whose relevance can be identified by making 'yes' or 'no' choices) and five alternative leadership styles. More recent work by Vroom and Arthur Jago has resulted in a revision of this model.[48] The revised model retains the same five alternative leadership styles – from the leader's making the decision completely alone to sharing the problem with the group and developing a consensus decision – but adds a set of problem types and expands the contingency variables to 12. The 12 contingency variables are listed in Exhibit 12.1.

Research testing both the original and revised leader-participation models has not been encouraging, although the revised model rates higher in effectiveness.[49] Criticism has tended to focus on variables that have been omitted and on the model's overall complexity.[50] Other contingency theories demonstrate that stress, intelligence, and experience are important situational variables. Yet the leader-participation model fails to include them. But more important, at least from a practical point of view, is the fact that the model is far too complicated for the typical manager to use on a regular basis. Although Vroom and Jago have developed a computer programme to guide managers through all the decision branches in the revised model, it's not very realistic to expect practicing managers to consider 12 contingency variables, eight problem types and five leadership styles in trying to select the appropriate decision process for a specific problem.

We obviously haven't done justice in this discussion to the model's sophistication. So what can you gain from this brief review? Additional insights into relevant contingency variables. Vroom and his associates have provided us with some specific, empirically supported contingency variables that you should consider when choosing your leadership style.

EXHIBIT 12.1 **CONTINGENCY VARIABLES IN THE REVISED LEADER-PARTICIPATION MODEL**

1. Importance of the decision
2. Importance of obtaining follower commitment to the decision
3. Whether the leader has sufficient information to make a good decision
4. How well structured the problem is
5. Whether an autocratic decision would receive follower commitment
6. Whether followers 'buy into' the organization's goals
7. Whether there is likely to be conflict among followers over solution alternatives
8. Whether followers have the necessary information to make a good decision
9. Time constraints on the leader that may limit follower involvement
10. Whether costs to bring geographically dispersed members together is justified
11. Importance to the leader of minimising the time it takes to make the decision
12. Importance of using participation as a tool for developing follower decision skills

CULTIVATING AN INTERNATIONAL PERSPECTIVE: A NECESSITY FOR LEADERS

GLOBAL

Accounting and consulting firm Pricewaterhouse-Coopers (PwC) is serious about expanding the worldview of its up-and-coming leaders. So the company started the Ulysses Programme, which sends the company's potential leaders to foreign countries to gain knowledge and experience in cultural diversity.

For example, PwC sent one group of managers on an 8-week consulting assignment in the Namibian outback. Their job? To help village leaders deal with the growing AIDS crisis. Without PowerPoint presentations and e-mail, the managers quickly learned to communicate in a more traditional way – face-to-face. The managers were forced to rely less on quick technologies and more on forging connections by cultivating relationships with diverse clients. By experiencing diversity firsthand at what is perhaps its extreme, PwC hopes that its managers will be better equipped to handle issues in any culture in

which they conduct business. The company says that the programme gives its future leaders a broad, international perspective on business issues and makes it more likely that they will find creative, unconventional solutions to complex problems. In addition, participants can realise what they are able to accomplish when they do not have access to their usual resources. In essence, they are forced to become leaders.

The jury is still out on whether the programme is effective at increasing the global leadership skills of those who participate. Nevertheless, participants of the Ulysses Programme tout its benefits, and other companies have taken notice; Johnson & Johnson and Cisco Systems are just two of several companies that have adopted similar programmes.

Source: Based on J. Hempel and S. Porges, 'It takes a village – and a consultant', *BusinessWeek*, 6 September 2004, p. 76.

Leadership across Europe

7 Assess the basic similarities and differences of leadership across Europe.

Leadership in the UK is not the same as leadership in Sweden, France or Spain. To engage in the same behaviours regardless of context is to risk failure and humiliation. To use the same leadership processes without regard to national context is to risk at least mild misunderstanding and private amusement. At worst, it risks a fundamental but unrecognised clash of values which can only rebound to the disadvantage of all parties.[51]

These remarks by Durcan in his book, *Leadership: a Question of Culture*, highlighted an important aspect to further our understanding of leadership, cultural factors. We will deal with global leadership in the next section, but it is worthwhile to focus initially on the European context, as research demonstrates important differences (and similarities) to be aware of.

Research is consistent in demonstrating leadership differences across Europe. For example, studies revealed in Austria and Germany performance-oriented behaviours, such as setting ambitious goals and challenging subordinates, were considered more important to effective leadership than in Finland and Denmark.[52] Most studies detect leadership patterns between European countries characterised by similar values and behaviour. One investigation identified three clusters:

Cluster 1 – The Anglo culture (UK and Ireland) has similar values and expectations to the US. Leadership is seen as achieving results through empowering and motivating people.

Cluster 2 – Scandinavian countries share the same values as the Anglo cluster but differ in one respect that affects their whole approach to leadership. Instead of the competitive individualism of the Anglos, there is a concern for quality of life in general. For this cluster, leadership is more about relationships than results.

Cluster 3 – Mediterranean cluster (Greece, Italy, Spain, Portugal, Turkey, France). In these countries, it is claimed, leaders are seen as and expected to be more powerful.[53]

Other studies have clustered Europe into east and west. It was found that in western Europe equality and achievement is highly prized, so leaders that have humble beginnings and work their way to the top tend to be respected. In eastern Europe power differentials are expected or accepted and leaders that, for example, are born into an influential family are valued. Another study found it was more usual for Western leaders to have a participative style, whereas in the East an autocratic style is more accepted.[54]

Finally, western Europe has been clustered into north and south. Research has found that in the north (e.g. UK, Ireland, Sweden, Denmark) leaders favour greater involvement with subordinates. In the south (e.g. France, Belgium, Spain, Italy, Portugal, Greece) employees prefer to rely more on supervisors. A further study concluded that a coaching leader is preferred in northern Europe and a directing leader in southern Europe.[55]

It must be recognised that these studies invariably involve generalisations, but it is useful to note that for leaders to be effective across Europe, understanding the different cultures is important. For example, a participative style of leadership may not work in southern Europe.

FACE THE FACTS

A cross-cultural study on leadership behaviours identified four clusters of countries with similar cultural profiles: Latin (Italy, France, Spain)/Germanic (Germany and the Netherlands)/Anglo (United Kingdom and the United States)/Nordic (Denmark, Norway and Sweden). A selection of results are presented below:

- In all clusters inspiring followers was rated the most important behaviour to overall leadership effectiveness.

- 77 per cent of Nordic respondents indicated delegating behaviour was important for leadership effectiveness, compared with 51 per cent in the Nordic cluster, 50 per cent Germanic and less than 50 per cent in the Anglo culture.

- Team-building behaviours were valued by 68 per cent, 57 per cent, and 56 per cent of Anglo, Latin and Germanic respondents, respectively. But was less important to Nordic respondents (less than 50 per cent).

Source: 'Different cultures, similar perceptions: stereotyping of western European business leaders', *Catalyst and IMD (Switzerland)* 2006, www.catalyst.org.

Global implications

8 Demonstrate the importance of cultural awareness for global leaders.

You may have noticed that most of the well-known traditional leadership research was conducted in the United States, predominantly by US academics. The American bias is well documented.[56] However, particularly in the last 10 years, global cross-cultural research has developed rapidly and the conclusions indicate, as we saw with the European context, that culture does have a pervasive influence on leadership effectiveness. This does not necessarily mean that the implications of the US theories are not valid in other countries, but does suggest that we need to be aware of cultural influences and potentially adapt accordingly.

Various studies have researched whether there are traits that are globally accepted as positive attributes for a leader to possess. The findings are reasonably consistent – yes and no. The Global Leadership and Organizational Behavior Effectiveness (GLOBE) study found that some traits (e.g. visionary, intelligent, trustworthy and decisive) are endorsed universally as positive attributes for leaders, whereas the endorsement of other traits is more culturally contingent (e.g. compassionate, domineering, orderly and risk taker).[57]

The global relevance of contingency theories, which propose that different leadership styles are suited to different situations, has been questioned. In cultural settings where there is less emphasis on individualism, such as Japan, India and Brazil, the notion of a single effective leadership style for all situations has received some support. However, results from western European countries and from Russia are generally in line with the US, suggesting effective leadership style is a function of the situation.

Hofstede's work on cultural differences provides further evidence for caution. Many US models of leadership advocate involving subordinates in decision making. Workers in a country that is high on power-distance (i.e. it is generally accepted that power is distributed unequally) may feel uncomfortable being involved. Hofstede points to French management writing which pays little attention to participation, but focuses strongly on the exercise of power. Conversely, countries like Sweden and Norway with low power-distance scores are more likely to accept participative leadership models.[58] The implication for leadership practice is that when moving from a low-power distance country to a high-power distance, the leadership style may need to move from democratic to autocratic.

As this type of research increases, we are finding out more about what it takes to be an effective global leader. Although there are various prescriptions, the following Accenture survey provides an example that identifies three competencies of effective global leaders:

- Personal mastery – a high degree of self awareness to monitor their own behaviour, build on their strengths and fill gaps in their competencies

- Provide organizational leadership by creating internal and external networks of influence, including alliances and partnerships as well as formal acquisitions and mergers

- Building organizational and individual competence by seeking and using differences of thought, style and culture around the globe[59]

Summary and implications for managers

Leadership plays a central part in understanding group behaviour, for it's the leader who usually provides the direction toward goal attainment. Therefore, a more accurate predictive capability should be valuable in improving group performance.

The early search for a set of universal leadership traits failed. However, recent efforts using the Big Five personality framework have generated much more encouraging results. Specifically, the traits of extraversion, conscientiousness and openness to experience show strong and consistent relationships to leadership.

The behavioural approach's major contribution was narrowing leadership into task-oriented (initiating structure) and people-oriented (consideration) styles. As with the trait approach, results from the behavioural school were initially dismissed, but recent efforts have confirmed the importance of task- and people-oriented leadership styles.

A major shift in leadership research came when we recognised the need to develop contingency theories that included situational factors. At present, the evidence indicates that relevant situational variables include the task structure of the job; level of situational stress; level of group support; leader's intelligence and experience; and follower characteristics, such as personality, experience, ability and motivation. Although contingency theories haven't lived up to their initial promise, the literature has provided basic support for Fiedler's LPC theory.

Finally, two other theories – leader–member exchange (LMX) theory and the leader-participation model – also contribute to our understanding of leadership. LMX theory has proved influential for its analysis of followers – whether they are included in the leader's 'in-group' or were relegated to the 'out group'. Vroom's leader-participation model focuses on the leader's role as decision maker and considers *how* leaders make decisions (such as whether to involve followers in their decision making).

As a group, these traditional theories have enhanced our understanding of effective leadership. As we'll discover in the next chapter, however, more recent theories have shown even more promise in describing effective leadership.

POINT/COUNTERPOINT

Leaders are born, not made

POINT →

That leaders are born, not made, isn't a new idea. The nineteenth-century historian Thomas Carlyle wrote, 'History is nothing but the biography of a few great men.' Although today we should modify this to include women, his point still rings true: Great leaders are what make teams, companies and even countries great. Can anyone disagree with the political gifts of people like Nelson Mandela and Franklin Roosevelt? Or that Napoleon and Alexander the Great were brilliant and courageous military leaders? Or that Indra Nooyi (PepsiCo), Steve Jobs (Apple), Sergio Marchionne (FIAT) and Rupert Murdoch (News Corp) are gifted business leaders? As one reviewer of the literature put it, 'Leaders are not like other people.' These leaders are great leaders because they have the right stuff – stuff the rest of us don't have, or have in lesser quantities.

If you're not yet convinced, there is new evidence to support this position. A recent study of several hundred identical twins separated at birth found an amazing correlation in their ascendance into leadership roles. These twins were raised in totally different environments – some rich, some poor, some by educated parents, others by relatively uneducated parents, some in cities, others in small towns. But the researchers found that despite their different environments, each pair of twins had striking similarities in terms of whether they became leaders.

Other research has found that shared environment – being raised in the same household, for example – has very little influence on leadership emergence. Despite what we might like to believe, the evidence is clear: A substantial part of leadership is a product of our genes. If we have the right stuff, we're destined to be effective leaders. If we have the wrong stuff, we're unlikely to excel in that role. Leadership cannot be for everyone, and we make a mistake in thinking that everyone is equally capable of being a good leader.[60]

COUNTERPOINT ←

Of course, personal qualities and characteristics matter to leadership, as they do to most other behaviours. But the real key is what you do with what you have.

First, if great leadership were merely the possession of a few key traits – say intelligence and personality – we could simply give people a test and select the most intelligence, extraverted and conscientious people to be leaders. But that would be a disaster. It helps to have these traits, but leadership is much too complex to be reduced to a simple formula of traits. As smart as Steve Jobs is, there are smarter and more extraverted people out there – thousands of them. That isn't the essence of what makes him, or political or military leaders, great. It is a combination of factors – upbringing, early business experiences, learning from failure and driving ambition.

Second, great leaders tell us that the key to their leadership success is not the characteristics they had at birth but what they learned along the way.

Take Warren Buffett, named in 2008 as *Forbes* magazine's richest person in the world, who is admired not only for his investing prowess but also as a leader and boss. Being a great leader, according to Buffett, is a matter of acquiring the right habits. 'The chains of habit are too light to be noticed until they are too heavy to be broken,' he says. Buffett argues that characteristics or habits such as intelligence, trustworthiness and integrity are the most important to leadership – and at least the latter two can be developed. He says, 'You need integrity, intelligence and energy to succeed. Integrity is totally a matter of choice – and it is habit-forming.'

Finally, this focus on 'great men and great women' is not very productive. Even if it were true that great leaders were born, it's a very impractical approach to leadership. People need to believe in something, and one of those things is that they can improve themselves. If we walked around thinking we were just some accumulation of genetic markers and our entire life was just a vessel to play out gene expression, who would want to live that way? People have a choice to think positively (we can become good leaders) or negatively (leaders are predetermined), and it's better to be positive.

Source: M. Pandya, 'Warren Buffett on investing and leadership: I'm wired for this game', *Wharton Leadership Digest*, 3, 7 (April 1999), http://leadership.wharton.upenn.edu/digest/04-99.shtml.

QUESTIONS FOR REVIEW

1. Are leadership and management different from one another? If so, how?

2. What is the premise of trait theories? What traits are associated with leadership?

3. What are the central tenets and main limitations of behavioural theories?

4. What is Fiedler's contingency model? Has it been supported in research?

5. What are the main tenets of path-goal theory? What about leader–member exchange theory?

6. What are the predictions of the leader-participation model?

7. How might a leader from your country be effective across Europe? Globally?

Experiential Exercise

WHAT IS A LEADER?

1. Working on your own, write down 12 adjectives that describe an effective business leader.

2. Break into groups of four or five people each. Appoint a note-taker and spokesperson. Compare your lists, making a new list of adjectives common across two or more persons' list. (Count synonyms – decisive and forceful, for example – as the same.)

3. Each spokesperson should present the group's list to the class.

4. Across the lists, are there many similarities? What does this tell you about the nature of leadership?

Ethical dilemma

REWARDS FOR FAILURE?

Royal Bank of Scotland (RBS) recorded the biggest loss in British corporate history in 2008. The bank had made huge acquisitions at inflated prices, with a depleted capital base and poor risk control. Shareholders saw their holdings almost wiped out. RBS survives owing to a government rescue costing some €25 billion. The UK taxpayer now holds a stake of almost 70 per cent.

Yet RBS still paid annual bonuses to thousands of City staff. The payments ran into hundreds of millions of Euros. Lord Mandelson, the Business Secretary, understandably declared: 'They have got to consider how it looks and how it seems when those mistakes and losses have been made.'

It looks like a reward for grievous failure; and the appearance does not deceive. The real economy suffered from a crisis born in the financial sector. Demand and investment collapsed; household incomes were squeezed. The human costs were hardship, unemployment and eviction.

This is not an isolated example and is not solely the province of the banking industry. Across Europe, political leaders expressed alarm at the soaring pay and bonuses of executives, often in the face of poor performance. French Finance Minister Christine Lagarde branded pay for leaders of poorly performing companies 'perfectly scandalous' and warned of

legislation if companies don't set executive pay to reflect performance. Dutch Finance Minister Wouter Bos proposed a 30 per cent 'fat cat' tax increase on big bonuses and severance packages.

Perhaps business leaders should follow the example of Willie Walsh, CEO at British Airways, who passed up a 2 million euro bonus due him for meeting an earnings target. Walsh was paying penance for the botched opening of the big new BA Terminal 5 at London Heathrow.

Questions

1. If you were an employee of the RBS, would you accept a bonus?

2. Does the fact that Willie Walsh turned down his bonus make him a better leader?

3. How ethical do you believe business leaders are?

4. Is it impossible for leaders to be both ethical *and* successful?

Sources: Based on 'Reward for failure: RBS's bonuses demonstrate that pay and performance must be better aligned',*The Times* (6 February 2009), p. 2; J. Stinson, 'As CEO pay in Europe rises, so does talk of curbing it', *USA Today* (30 June 2008).

CASE INCIDENT 1

Promotion almost as stressful as divorce

The challenge of a major promotion is almost as stressful as a divorce, according to research. Almost 60 per cent of the 600 managers surveyed by global HR consultancy DDI rated promotions as second only to coping with divorce, with both rated as very or extremely challenging. Prioritising key issues, time management, office politics and personal transformation were cited as the most stressful aspects of a promotion. One in three business leaders also said their company provided little or very poor support on how to deal with a promotion.

Steve Newhall, managing director of DDI said: 'It's a familiar story. You work really hard to get that promotion and you're excited about your new role. Then suddenly reality hits home: you are on your own, unsure of what is really expected of you, missing aspects of your previous role that you had finally mastered, without your trusted network of colleagues and politics rife among your new peer group, whom you struggle to engage with.'

This is a familiar story. When workers are promoted into leadership positions they find themselves unprepared for the transition and particularly, the fact that they must now lead their former peers. The importance of getting leadership right is well documented. According to a Monster Poll, 84 per cent of respondents had left a job because of a bad boss. A Gallup survey of more than 1 million employees found that the top reason for leaving was their immediate supervisors. The study also revealed that poorly managed workgroups are, on average, 50 per cent less productive and 44 per cent less profitable than well-managed groups. Most alarmingly, a study of British workers conducted by researchers in Finland found that workers who felt they were being treated fairly had a 30 per cent lower incidence of coronary heart disease.

Sources: G. Fuller 'Promotion "almost as stressful as divorce" says HR survey', *Personnel Today* (25 January 2007); 'Anonymous poll: Canadians blame boss as reason for leaving job', *CMA Management*, 81, 8 (December 2007/January 2008); S. Cullen, (2006) 'Bad bosses: tales from the dark side', *Office Solutions*, 23, 2.

Questions

1. A lot of new managers err in selecting the right leadership style when they move into management. Why do you think this happens?

2. What does this say about leadership and leadership training?

3. Which leadership theories, if any, could help new leaders deal with this type of transition?

4. Do you think it's easier or harder to be promoted internally into a formal leadership position than to come into it as an outsider? Explain.

Source: Based on D. Koeppel, 'A tough transition: friend to supervisor,' *New York Times*, 16 March 2003, p. BU-12.

CASE INCIDENT 2

Who makes the best leaders?

A recent debate at Ashridge business school looked at what makes for successful leadership in European companies and organizations – particularly in comparison to their North American counterparts, from which so many of today's leadership models have emerged. Here are a selection of responses:

Kai Peters, *Chief executive, Ashridge*

European leaders tend to be consultative, patient – working with the organization rather than telling it what to do – and very aware of the environment in which they work. There's a breadth of need to understand, and successful European leaders have a solid grasp of culture in the broader sense – including history and politics – and a good ability to empathise with the audience they are working with. You have to have something of the chameleon about you. The North American leader is driven by the homogeneity of the market.

Erik Swartz, *Managing director, Stockholm Centre for Management Development*

Why focus on commonalities? It goes with the whole idea of the EU. We have an area in Europe that we are trying to organize into some federal system. Compared with federalism in the US, they have 50 states and a lot of forces that make it easy to act together in unity. In Europe, we have to establish that way of thinking.

Atle Jordahl, *Director of international relations, Norwegian School of Economics and Business*

Even if it can be difficult to find a common denominator for European leadership, I think that we have one important thing in common. That is the concern for the US management style. I am particularly thinking of the 'one strong man' approach to leadership that is coming out of US government, companies and business schools; the lack of respect for context that many US companies and leaders communicate to others.

In Europe, we are used to living with multiple realities due to our long history with conflicts over territories, religions, ethnicity and ideologies; and the one-dimensional approach to life and business with a strong focus on profit. As central and eastern European countries move into the market economy, they have to 'choose' between a US or a western European leadership approach.

George Binney, *Co-author, Living Leadership – A Practical Guide for Ordinary Heroes*

European leaders don't 'put it up on the wall'. They don't immediately say: 'These are the values, this is who we are.' It's a more understated, modest way of leading, and there's clearly something very important about a sense of history. The Americans can talk confidently about charismatic leadership in a way that Europeans can't because of that history. So much of what we hear on business and organizations comes out of US business schools. Where's the European voice here? Even though there has been a shift to the 'quiet hero', the focus is still on individuals who 'do' to organizations.

Rick Woodward, *European learning and development director, Kimberly-Clark Europe*

Kimberly-Clark has recently conducted a major survey of all its senior leaders across the world, and found no statistically significant differences between European and North American responses. This year, we launched six global leadership qualities: visionary, building talent, decisiveness, collaboration, inspirational and innovative. We've assessed the top 90 leaders across the globe against these qualities, and designed personal action plans.

Whereas the US has a one-size-fits-all approach, Europe is very much about diversity and difference. US leadership likes simple, big ideas, and they tend to skate over details, whereas in Europe, we tend to think the devil's in the detail. And the whole approach to decision making in the US is very much 'tell and sell', whereas in Europe it is 'argue and agree' – although in the case of the English it's more like 'debate and hesitate'.

Questions

1. Which of the traditional approaches to leadership do you think would be most appropriate for European leaders? Why?

2. On which points do the above contributors agree and disagree about the differences between European and US leaders?

3. Would a successful European leader be successful in the US? Why or why not?

4. What challenges does this present for leadership development in global organizations?

Sources: 'Who makes the best leaders?', *Personnel Today*, 1 June 2005.

Endnotes

1 J. P. Kotter, 'What leaders really do', *Harvard Business Review*, May–June 1990, pp. 103–11; and J. P. Kotter, *A Force for Change: How Leadership Differs from Management* (New York: The Free Press, 1990).

2 R. J. House and R. N. Aditya, 'The social scientific study of leadership: quo vadis?', *Journal of Management*, 23, 3 (1997), p. 445.

3 M. Millar, 'Business chiefs rate Branson "top of the bosses"', *Personnel Today*, 21 June 2004.

4 J. G. Geier, 'A trait approach to the study of leadership in small groups', *Journal of Communication*, December 1967, pp. 316–23.

5 S. A. Kirkpatrick and E. A. Locke, 'Leadership: do traits matter?', *Academy of Management Executive*, May 1991, pp. 48–60; and S. J. Zaccaro, R. J. Foti and D. A. Kenny, 'Self-monitoring and trait-based variance in leadership: an investigation of leader flexibility across multiple group situations', *Journal of Applied Psychology*, April 1991, pp. 308–15.

6 See T. A. Judge, J. E. Bono, R. Ilies and M. Werner, 'Personality and leadership: a review', paper presented at the 15th Annual Conference of the Society for Industrial and Organizational Psychology, New Orleans, 2000; and T. A. Judge, J. E. Bono, R. Ilies and M. W. Gerhardt, 'Personality and leadership: a qualitative and quantitative review', *Journal of Applied Psychology*, August 2002, pp. 765–80.

7 Judge, Bono, Ilies and Gerhardt, 'Personality and leadership'.

8 D. R. Ames and F. J. Flynn, 'What breaks a leader: the curvilinear relation between assertiveness and leadership', *Journal of Personality and Social Psychology*, 92, 2 (2007), pp. 307–24.

9 This section is based on D. Goleman, 'What makes a leader?' *Harvard Business Review*, November–December 1998, pp. 93–102; J. M. George, 'Emotions and leadership: the role of emotional intelligence', *Human Relations*, August 2000, pp. 1027–55; C.-S. Wong and K. S. Law, 'The effects of leader and follower emotional intelligence on performance and attitude: an exploratory study', *Leadership Quarterly*, June 2002, pp. 243–74; and D. R. Caruso and C. J. Wolfe, 'Emotional intelligence and leadership development', in D. David and S. J. Zaccaro (eds), *Leader Development for Transforming Organizations: Growing Leaders for Tomorrow* (Mahwah, NJ: Lawrence Erlbaum, 2004) pp. 237–63.

10 J. Champy, 'The hidden qualities of great leaders', *Fast Company*, 76 (November 2003), p. 135.

11 J. Antonakis, 'Why "emotional intelligence" does not predict leadership effectiveness: a comment on Prati, Douglas, Ferris, Ammeter, and Buckley (2003)', *International Journal of Organizational Analysis*, 11 (2003), pp. 355–61; see also M. Zeidner, G. Matthews and R. D. Roberts, 'Emotional intelligence in the workplace: a critical review', *Applied Psychology: An International Review*, 53 (2004), pp. 371–99.

12 Ibid.; see note 8; R. G. Lord, C. L. DeVader and G. M. Alliger, 'A meta-analysis of the relation between personality traits

and leadership perceptions: an application of validity generalization procedures', *Journal of Applied Psychology*, August 1986, pp. 402–10; and J. A. Smith and R. J. Foti, 'A pattern approach to the study of leader emergence', *Leadership Quarterly*, Summer 1998, pp. 147–60.

13 See S. Hansen, 'Stings like a bee', *INC.*, November 2002, pp. 56–64; J. Greenbaum, 'Is Ghengis on the hunt again?', *internetnews.com*, 14 January 2005, www.internetnews.com/commentary/article.php/3459771.

14 R. M. Stogdill and A. E. Coons (eds), *Leader Behavior: Its Description and Measurement*, Research Monograph no. 88 (Columbus, OH: Ohio State University, Bureau of Business Research, 1951). This research is updated in C. A. Schriesheim, C. C. Cogliser and L. L. Neider, 'Is it "trustworthy"? A multiple-levels-of-analysis reexamination of an Ohio State leadership study, with implications for future research', *Leadership Quarterly*, Summer 1995, pp. 111–45; and T. A. Judge, R. F. Piccolo and R. Ilies, 'The forgotten ones? the validity of consideration and initiating structure in leadership research', *Journal of Applied Psychology*, February 2004, pp. 36–51.

15 D. Akst, 'The rewards of recognizing a job well done', *Wall Street Journal*, January 31, 2007, p. D9.

16 G. Yukl and D. D. Van Fleet, 'Theory and research on leadership in organizations', in M. D. Dunnette and L. M. Hough (eds), *Handbook of Industrial and Organizational Psychology*, vol. 2 (Palo Alto, CA: Consulting Psychologists Press, 1992), pp. 147–97.

17 R. Kahn and D. Katz, 'Leadership practices in relation to productivity and morale', in D. Cartwright and A. Zander (eds), *Group Dynamics: Research and Theory*, 2nd edn (Elmsford, NY: Row, Paterson, 1960).

18 Judge, Piccolo and Ilies, 'The forgotten ones?'

19 R. R. Blake and J. S. Mouton, *The Managerial Grid* (Houston, TX: Gulf, 1964).

20 See, for example, R. R. Blake and J. S. Mouton, 'A comparative analysis of situationalism and 9,9 management by principle', *Organizational Dynamics*, Spring 1982, pp. 20–43.

21 See, for example, L. L. Larson, J. G. Hunt and R. N. Osborn, 'The great hi-hi leader behavior myth: a lesson from Occam's Razor', *Academy of Management Journal*, December 1976, pp. 628–41; and P. C. Nystrom, 'Managers and the hi-hi leader myth', *Academy of Management Journal*, June 1978, pp. 325–31.

22 J. Griffin, '"Scandalous" NHS leader Sir James Ackers dies at 72', *Birmingham Post*, 10 April 2008.

23 F. E. Fiedler, *A Theory of Leadership Effectiveness* (New York: McGraw-Hill, 1967).

24 S. Shiflett, 'Is there a problem with the LPC score in LEADER MATCH?', *Personnel Psychology*, Winter 1981, pp. 765–69.

25 F. E. Fiedler, M. M. Chemers and L. Mahar, *Improving Leadership Effectiveness: The Leader Match Concept* (New York: Wiley, 1977).

26 Cited in House and Aditya, 'The social scientific study of leadership', p. 422.

27 L. H. Peters, D. D. Hartke and J. T. Pohlmann, 'Fiedler's contingency theory of leadership: an application of the meta-analysis procedures of Schmidt and Hunter', *Psychological Bulletin*, March 1985, pp. 274–85; C. A. Schriesheim, B. J. Tepper and L. A. Tetrault, 'Least preferred coworker score, situational control, and leadership effectiveness: a meta-analysis of contingency model performance predictions', *Journal of Applied Psychology*, August 1994, pp. 561–73; and R. Ayman, M. M. Chemers and F. Fiedler, 'The contingency model of leadership effectiveness: its levels of analysis', *Leadership Quarterly*, Summer 1995, pp. 147–67.

28 House and Aditya, 'The social scientific study of leadership', p. 422.

29 See, for instance, R. W. Rice, 'Psychometric properties of the esteem for the least preferred coworker (LPC) scale,' *Academy of Management Review*, January 1978, pp. 106–18; C. A. Schriesheim, B. D. Bannister and W. H. Money, 'Psychometric properties of the LPC scale: an extension of Rice's review', *Academy of Management Review*, April 1979, pp. 287–90; and J. K. Kennedy, J. M. Houston, M. A. Korgaard and D. D. Gallo, 'Construct space of the least preferred coworker (LPC) scale,' *Educational & Psychological Measurement*, Fall 1987, pp. 807–14.

30 See E. H. Schein, *Organizational Psychology*, 3rd edn (Upper Saddle River, NJ: Prentice-Hall, 1980), pp. 116–17; and B. Kabanoff, 'A critique of leader match and its implications for leadership research', *Personnel Psychology*, Winter 1981, pp. 749–64.

31 F. E. Fiedler and J. E. Garcia, *New Approaches to Effective Leadership: Cognitive Resources and Organizational Performance* (New York: Wiley, 1987).

32 See F. E. Fiedler, 'Cognitive resources and leadership performance', *Applied Psychology – An International Review*, January 1995, pp. 5–28; and F. E. Fiedler, 'The curious role of cognitive resources in leadership', in R. E. Riggio, S. E. Murphy and F. J. Pirozzolo (eds), *Multiple Intelligences and Leadership* (Mahwah, NJ: Lawrence Erlbaum, 2002), pp. 91–104.

33 T. A. Judge, A. E. Colbert and R. Ilies, 'Intelligence and leadership: a quantitative review and test of theoretical propositions', *Journal of Applied Psychology*, June 2004, pp. 542–52.

34 P. Hersey and K. H. Blanchard, 'So you want to know your leadership style?', *Training and Development Journal*, February 1974, pp. 1–15; and P. Hersey, K. H. Blanchard and D. E. Johnson, *Management of Organizational Behavior: Leading Human Resources*, 8th edn (Upper Saddle River, NJ: Prentice-Hall, 2001).

35 Cited in C. F. Fernandez and R. P. Vecchio, 'Situational leadership theory revisited: a test of an across-jobs perspective', *Leadership Quarterly*, 8, 1 (1997), p. 67.

36 See, for instance, *Ibid.*, pp. 67–84; C. L. Graeff, 'Evolution of situational leadership theory: a critical review', *Leadership Quarterly*, 8, 2 (1997), pp. 153–70; and R. P. Vecchio and K. J. Boatwright, 'Preferences for idealized styles of supervision', *Leadership Quarterly*, August 2002, pp. 327–42; J. Chen and C. Silverthorne (2005) 'Leadership effectiveness, leadership style and employee readiness', *Leadership & Organization Development Journal*, 26, 3/4, pp. 280–88.

37 R. J. House, 'A path–goal theory of leader effectiveness', *Administrative Science Quarterly*, September 1971, pp. 321–38; R. J. House and T. R. Mitchell, 'Path–goal theory of leadership', *Journal of Contemporary Business*, Autumn 1974, pp. 81–97; and R. J. House, 'Path–goal theory of leadership: lessons, legacy, and a reformulated theory', *Leadership Quarterly*, Fall 1996, pp. 323–52.

38 J. C. Wofford and L. Z. Liska, 'Path–goal theories of leadership: a meta-analysis', *Journal of Management*, Winter 1993, pp. 857–76; P. M. Podsakoff, S. B. MacKenzie and M. Ahearne, 'Searching for a needle in a haystack: trying to identify the illusive moderators of leadership behaviors', *Journal of Management*, 21 (1995), pp. 423–70.

39 J. R. Villa, J. P. Howell, and P. W. Dorfman, 'Problems with detecting moderators in leadership research using moderated multiple regression', *Leadership Quarterly*, 14 (2003), pp. 3–23; C. A. Schriesheim and L. Neider, 'Path–goal leadership theory: the long and winding road', *Leadership Quarterly*, 7 (1996), pp. 317–21; and M. G. Evans, 'R. J. House's "A path–goal theory of leader effectiveness"', *Leadership Quarterly*, 7 (1996), pp. 305–309.

40 W. Bennis, 'The challenges of leadership in the modern world', *American Psychologist*, January 2007, pp. 2–5.

41 R. M. Dienesch and R. C. Liden, 'Leader–member exchange model of leadership: a critique and further development', *Academy of Management Review*, July 1986, pp. 618–34; G. B. Graen and M. Uhl-Bien, 'Relationship-based approach to leadership: development of leader–member exchange (LMX) theory of leadership over 25 years: applying a multi-domain perspective', *Leadership Quarterly*, Summer 1995, pp. 219–47; R. C. Liden, R. T. Sparrowe and S. J. Wayne, 'Leader–member exchange theory: the past and potential for the future', in G. R. Ferris (ed.), *Research in Personnel and Human Resource Management*, vol. 15 (Greenwich, CT: JAI Press, 1997), pp. 47–119; and C. A. Schriesheim, S. L. Castro, X. Zhou and F. J. Yammarino, 'The folly of theorizing "A" but testing "B": a selective level-of-analysis review of the field and a detailed leader–member exchange illustration', *Leadership Quarterly*, Winter 2001, pp. 515–51.

42 R. Liden and G. Graen, 'Generalizability of the vertical dyad linkage model of leadership', *Academy of Management Journal*, September 1980, pp. 451–65; R. C. Liden, S. J. Wayne and D. Stilwell, 'A longitudinal study of the early development of leader–member exchanges,' *Journal of Applied Psychology*, August 1993, pp. 662–74; S. J. Wayne, L. M. Shore, W. H. Bommer and L. E. Tetrick, 'The role of fair treatment and rewards in perceptions of organizational support and leader–member exchange', *Journal of Applied Psychology*, 87, 3 (June 2002), pp. 590–98; S. S. Masterson, K. Lewis and B. M. Goldman, 'Integrating justice and social exchange: the differing effects of fair procedures and treatment on work relationships', *Academy of Management Journal*, 43, 4 (August 2000), pp. 738–48.

43 D. Duchon, S. G. Green and T. D. Taber, 'Vertical dyad linkage: a longitudinal assessment of antecedents, measures, and consequences', *Journal of Applied Psychology*, February 1986, pp. 56–60; Liden, Wayne and Stilwell, 'A longitudinal study on the early development of leader–member exchanges'; and M. Uhl-Bien, 'Relationship development as a key ingredient for leadership development', in S. E. Murphy and R. E. Riggio (eds), *Future of Leadership Development* (Mahwah, NJ: Lawrence Erlbaum, 2003) pp. 129–47.

44 R. Vecchio and D. M. Brazil, 'Leadership and sex-similarity: a comparison in a military setting', *Personnel Psychology*, 60 (2007), pp. 303–35.

45 See, for instance, C. R. Gerstner and D. V. Day, 'Meta-analytic review of leader–member exchange theory: correlates and construct issues', *Journal of Applied Psychology*, December 1997, pp. 827–44; R. Ilies, J. D. Nahrgang and F. P. Morgeson, 'Leader–member exchange and citizenship behaviors: a meta-analysis', *Journal of Applied Psychology*, 92, 1 (2007), pp. 269–77; Z. Chen, W. Lam and J. A. Zhong, 'Leader–member exchange and member performance: a new look at individual-level negative feedback-seeking behavior and team-level empowerment culture', *Journal of Applied Psychology*, 92, 1 (2007), pp. 202–12.

46 D. Eden, 'Leadership and expectations: pygmalion effects and other self-fulfilling prophecies in organizations', *Leadership Quarterly*, Winter 1992, pp. 278–79.

47 See V. H. Vroom and P. W. Yetton, *Leadership and Decision-Making* (Pittsburgh, PA: University of Pittsburgh Press, 1973); and V. H. Vroom and A. G. Jago, 'The role of the situation in leadership', *American Psychologist*, January 2007, pp. 17–24.

48 V. H. Vroom and A. G. Jago, *The New Leadership: Managing Participation in Organizations* (Englewood Cliffs, NJ: Prentice-Hall, 1988); see also V. H. Vroom and A. G. Jago, 'Situation effects and levels of analysis in the study of leader participation', *Leadership Quarterly*, Summer 1995, pp. 169–81.

49 See, for example, R. H. G. Field, 'A test of the Vroom–Yetton normative model of leadership', *Journal of Applied Psychology*, October 1982, pp. 523–32; C. R. Leana, 'Power relinquishment versus power sharing: theoretical clarification and empirical comparison of delegation and participation', *Journal of Applied Psychology*, May 1987, pp. 228–33; J. T. Ettling and A. G. Jago, 'Participation under conditions of conflict: more on the validity of the Vroom-Yetton model', *Journal of Management Studies*, January 1988, pp. 73–83; R. H. G. Field and R. J. House, 'A test of the Vroom–Yetton model using manager and subordinate reports', *Journal of Applied Psychology*, June 1990, pp. 362–66; and R. H. G. Field and J. P. Andrews, 'Testing the incremental validity of the Vroom–Jago versus Vroom–Yetton models of participation in decision making', *Journal of Behavioral Decision Making*, December 1998, pp. 251–61.

50 House and Aditya, 'The social scientific study of leadership', p. 428.

51 J. Durcan (1994) *Leadership: A Question of Culture* (Berkhamsted: Ashridge, 1994), cited in P. Sadler *Leadership* (London: Kogan Page, 2003), pp. 129–31.

52 M. Javidan, 'Performance orientation', in R. House, P. J. Hanges, M. Javidan, P. Dorfman and V. Gupta (eds), *Culture, Leadership and Organizations: The GLOBE studies of 62 Societies* (London: Sage Publications), pp. 239–81.

53 P. Sadler (2003) *Leadership*, 2nd edn (London: Kogan Page), pp. 129–31.

54 P. Smith (1997) Leadership in Europe: Euro-management or the footprint of history? *European Journal of Work and Organizational Psychology*, 6 (1997); A. Jago, G. Reber, W. Bohnisch, J. Maczynski, J. Zavrel and J. Dudorik 'Cultures consequences? A seven nation study of participation', in D. Rogus and A. Raruni (eds) Proceedings of the 24th annual meeting of the Decision Sciences Institute Washington, DC, Decision Science Institute.

55 P. Smith (1997) 'Leadership in Europe: Euro-management or the footprint of history?', *European Journal of Work and Organizational Psychology*, Vol. 6 (1997) pp. 375–86; L. Zander '*The Licence to Lead: an 18 Country Study of the Relationship Between Employees' Preferences Regarding Interpersonal Leadership and National Culture*. Published Doctoral Dissertation (Stockholm: Stockholm School of Economics, 1997).

56 For example, see P. Smith 'Organizational behaviour and national cultures', *British Journal of Management*, 3 (1992), pp. 39–51.

57 R. J. House, P. J. Hanges, M. Javidan, P. W. Dorfman and V. Gupta (eds), *Culture, Leadership, and Organizations.* (Thousand Oaks, CA: Sage, 2004).

58 Based on P. Sadler *Leadership*, 2nd edn (London: Kogan Page, 2003), pp. 129–31.

59 S. Wills (1996) 'European leadership: key issues', *European Management Journal*, 14, 1. pp. 90–97.

60 R. D. Arvey, Z. Zhang and B. J. Avolio, 'Developmental and genetic determinants of leadership role occupancy among women', *Journal of Applied Psychology*, May 2007, pp. 693–706.

Contemporary issues in leadership

Learning Objectives

After studying this chapter, you should be able to:

1 Show how framing influences leadership effectiveness.

2 Define *charismatic leadership* and show how it influences followers.

3 Contrast transformational leadership and transactional leadership and discuss how transformational leadership works.

4 Define *authentic leadership* and show why ethics and trust are vital to effective leadership.

5 Identify the three types of trust.

6 Demonstrate the importance of mentoring, self-leadership and virtual leadership to our understanding of leadership.

7 Identify when leadership may not be necessary.

8 Explain how to find and create effective leaders.

9 Assess whether charismatic and transformational leadership generalise across cultures.

A leader leads by example not by force.

Sun Tsu

An inspirational leader

Born Anita Lucia Perilli and later to become Dame Anita Roddick, the Body Shop founder combined success in business with a passion for environmentalism and social justice. One of the most successful entrepreneurs in history and according to one survey, the second greatest Briton in management and leadership (behind Richard Branson). When the company was sold to L'Oréal in 2006 for close to 1 billion Euros, there were more than 2,000 stores in 55 countries.

After her death in 2007, Prime Minister Gordon Brown called Dame Anita one of the country's 'true pioneers'. He said she campaigned for green issues for many years before it became fashionable and inspired millions to the cause by bringing sustainable products to a mass market. She was also central in inspiring women striving to set up and grow their own companies and to move into senior management positions.

As well as being one of the most lauded businesswomen of her generation, so too was she controversial. Perhaps inevitably for someone who specialised in breaking the rules, there were criticisms. She lambasted the 'pin-striped dinosaurs' of the City, despite the fact that they were financing her and critics questioned whether the vast personal wealth she acquired was incompatible with the ethical message she vociferously advocated. Roddick fans were particularly outraged when the company was sold to L'Oréal, at the time given the lowest rating of any cosmetics firm by *Ethical Consumer* magazine because of the company's record on animal testing and part-owned by Nestlé, notorious for its strategy of selling baby-milk powder to breast-feeding mothers in the Third World.

Roddick simply shrugged at such criticisms. 'If you wear a bullseye on your back saying "I'm doing things in a different way", you're going to get shot at,' she said.

Despite this, it is not possible to miss her commitment to social justice and environmentalism. She was a supporter of Friends of the Earth, Greenpeace, Shelter, the *Big Issue* magazine, the anti-death penalty organization Reprieve and founded the HIV and Aids charity Body and Soul, and the charity Children on the Edge. And this is only a few of her interests.

Those paying tribute to Dame Anita described her as a pioneer, as an inspiration, as an activist, as a champion of the oppressed and as a joy to be with. Many painted a picture of a compassionate campaigner who had been the direct inspiration for many of the socially-conscious organizations now embedded within society.

Sources: P. Valley, 'Dame Anita Roddick: Idealist entrepreneur who with the Body Shop took "cruelty-free" products into the high street', *The Independent*, Wednesday 12 September 2007; 'The Greatest Briton winner', *Personnel Today*, 11 March 2003.

Anita Roddick embodied the qualities of an inspirational leader. One form of inspirational leadership is charismatic leadership. Take the following self-assessment to see how you score on charismatic leadership.

SELF-ASSESSMENT LIBRARY

How charismatic am I?

In the Self-assessment library (available online), take assessment II.B.2 (How charismatic am I?) and answer the following questions.

1. How did you score compared to your classmates? Do you think your score is accurate?

2. Why do you think you scored as you did? Do you think the reason is in your genes? Are your parents charismatic? Or do you think your score has to do with your environment? Were there factors in your upbringing or early life experiences that affected your charisma?

3. Based on the material presented in the chapter, do you think you could become more charismatic? If yes, how might you go about it?

Inspirational approaches to leadership

1 Show how framing influences leadership effectiveness.

framing
A way of using language to manage meaning.

Traditional approaches to leadership – those we considered in Chapter 12 – ignore the importance of the leader as a communicator. **Framing** is a way of communicating to shape meaning. It's a way for leaders to influence how others see and understand events. It includes selecting and highlighting one or more aspects of a subject while excluding others. Framing is especially important to an aspect of leadership ignored in the traditional theories: the ability of the leader to inspire others to act beyond their immediate self-interests.

In this section, we present two contemporary leadership theories with a common theme. They view leaders as individuals who inspire followers through their words, ideas and behaviours. These theories are charismatic leadership and transformational leadership.

Charismatic leadership

2 Define *charismatic leadership* and show how it influences followers.

Mahatma Ghandi, Martin Luther King, Jr., Mustafa Kemal Atatürk and in the business world Sir John Harvey-Jones (ICI), Carlos Ghosn (Nissan and Renault), Paul Polman (Unilever) and Steve Jobs (co-founder of Apple Computer) are individuals frequently cited as being charismatic leaders. So what do they have in common?

What is charismatic leadership?
Max Weber, a sociologist, was the first scholar to discuss charismatic leadership. More than a century ago, he defined *charisma* (from the Greek for 'gift') as,

a certain quality of an individual personality, by virtue of which he or she is set apart from ordinary people and treated as endowed with supernatural, superhuman, or at least specifically

EXHIBIT 13.1	KEY CHARACTERISTICS OF CHARISMATIC LEADERS

1. *Vision and articulation*. Has a vision – expressed as an idealised goal – that proposes a future better than the status quo and is able to clarify the importance of the vision in terms that are understandable to others.

2. *Personal risk*. Willing to take on high personal risk, incur high costs and engage in self-sacrifice to achieve the vision.

3. *Sensitivity to follower needs*. Perceptive of others' abilities and responsive to their needs and feelings.

4. *Unconventional behaviour*. Engages in behaviours that are perceived as novel and counter to norms.

Source: Based on J. A. Conger and R. N. Kanungo, *Charismatic Leadership in Organizations* (Thousand Oaks, CA: Sage, 1998), p. 94.

---

exceptional powers or qualities. These are not accessible to the ordinary person, but are regarded as of divine origin or as exemplary, and on the basis of them the individual concerned is treated as a leader.[1]

charismatic leadership theory
A leadership theory which states that followers make attributions of heroic or extraordinary leadership abilities when they observe certain behaviours.

Weber argued that charismatic leadership was one of several ideal types of authority.

The first researcher to consider charismatic leadership in terms of OB was Robert House. According to House's **charismatic leadership theory**, followers make attributions of heroic or extraordinary leadership abilities when they observe certain behaviours.[2] There have been a number of studies that have attempted to identify the characteristics of the charismatic leader. One of the best reviews of the literature has documented four – they have a vision, they are willing to take personal risks to achieve that vision, they are sensitive to follower needs and they exhibit behaviours that are out of the ordinary.[3] These characteristics are described in Exhibit 13.1.

Are charismatic leaders born or made?

Are charismatic leaders born with their qualities? Or can people actually learn how to be charismatic leaders? The answer to both questions is yes.

It is true that individuals are born with traits that make them charismatic. In fact, studies of identical twins have found that they score similarly on charismatic leadership measures, even if they were raised in different households and had never met. Research suggests that personality is also related to charismatic leadership. Charismatic leaders are likely to be extraverted, self-confident and achievement-oriented.[4]

Although a small minority thinks that charisma is inherited and therefore cannot be learned, most experts believe that individuals also can be trained to exhibit charismatic behaviours and can thus enjoy the benefits that accompany being labelled 'a charismatic leader'.[5] After all, just because we inherit certain tendencies doesn't mean that we can't learn to change. One set of authors proposes that a person can learn to become charismatic by following a three-step process.[6] First, an individual needs to develop an aura of charisma by maintaining an optimistic view; using passion as a catalyst for generating enthusiasm; and communicating with the whole body, not just with words. Second, an individual draws others in by creating a bond that inspires others to follow. Third, the individual brings out the potential in followers by tapping into their emotions.

The three-step approach seems to work, as evidenced by researchers who have succeeded in actually scripting undergraduate business students to 'play' charismatic.[7] The students were taught to articulate an overarching goal, communicate high performance expectations, exhibit confidence in the ability of followers to meet these expectations and empathise with the needs of their followers; they learned to project a powerful, confident and dynamic presence; and they practised using a captivating and engaging voice tone. To further capture the dynamics and energy of charisma, the leaders were trained to evoke charismatic nonverbal characteristics: They alternated between pacing and sitting on the edges of their desks, leaned toward the subjects, maintained direct eye contact and had relaxed postures and animated facial expressions. These researchers found that the students could learn how to project charisma. Moreover, followers of these leaders had higher task performance, task adjustment and adjustment to the leader and to the group than did followers who worked under groups led by noncharismatic leaders.

The Skype company founders Swedish-born Niklas Zennström and Janus Friis from Denmark demonstrate visionary characteristics. 'We are launching Skype as the telecoms company of the future', announced Zennström in self-confident tones at the Skype launch. And Jaanus Friis added: 'We hope that one day, instead of saying "I'll call you", people will say "I'll skype you" and with well over 100 million customers, that's exactly what people are saying'.[8]

vision
A long-term strategy for attaining a goal or goals.

vision statement
A formal articulation of an organization's vision or mission.

How charismatic leaders influence followers

How do charismatic leaders actually influence followers? The evidence suggests a four-step process.[9] It begins by the leader articulating an appealing **vision**. A vision is a long-term strategy for how to attain a goal or goals. The vision provides a sense of continuity for followers by linking the present with a better future for the organization. For example, at Apple, Steve Jobs championed the iPod, noting, 'It's as Apple as anything Apple has ever done.' The creation of the iPod achieved Apple's goal of offering groundbreaking and easy-to-use-technology. Apple's strategy was to create a product that had a user-friendly interface where songs could be quickly uploaded and easily organized. It was the first major-market device to link data storage capabilities with music downloading.

A vision is incomplete unless it has an accompanying vision statement. A **vision statement** is a formal articulation of an organization's vision or mission. Charismatic leaders may use vision statements to 'imprint' on followers an over-arching goal and purpose. Once a vision and vision statement are established, the leader then communicates high performance expectations and expresses confidence that followers can attain them. This enhances follower self-esteem and self-confidence.

Next, the leader conveys, through words and actions, a new set of values and, by his or her behaviour, sets an example for followers to imitate. Finally, the charismatic leader engages in emotion-inducing and often unconventional behaviour to demonstrate courage and convictions about the vision. There is an emotional contagion in charismatic leadership whereby followers 'catch' the emotions their leader is conveying.[10] When you next see a charismatic leader speaking, focus on the reactions of the crowd, and it will bring to light how a charismatic leader can spread their emotion to the followers.

Because the vision is such a critical component of charismatic leadership, we should clarify exactly what we mean by the term, identify specific qualities of an effective vision and offer some examples.[11]

A review of various definitions finds that a vision differs from other forms of direction setting in several ways:

A vision has clear and compelling imagery that offers an innovative way to improve, which recognises and draws on traditions, and connects to actions that people can take to realise change. Vision taps people's emotions and energy. Properly articulated, a vision creates the enthusiasm that people have for sporting events and other leisure-time activities, bringing this energy and commitment to the workplace.[12]

The key properties of a vision seem to be inspirational possibilities that are value centered, realisable, with superior imagery and articulation.[13] Visions should be able to create possibilities that are inspirational and unique and that offer a new order that can produce organizational distinction. A vision is likely to fail if it doesn't offer a view of the future that is clearly and demonstrably better for the organization and its members. Desirable visions fit the times and circumstances and reflect the uniqueness of the organization. People in the organization must also believe that the vision is attainable. It should be perceived as challenging yet doable. Also, visions that have clear articulation and powerful imagery are more easily grasped and accepted.

What are some examples of visions? Rupert Murdoch had a vision of the future of the communication industry by combining entertainment and media. Through News Corporation, Murdoch has successfully integrated a broadcast network, TV stations, movie studio, publishing and global satellite distribution. John Malone of Liberty Media calls News Corporation 'the best run, most strategically positioned vertically integrated media company in the world'.[14] Michael Dell has created a vision of a business that allows Dell Computer to sell and deliver a finished PC directly to a customer in fewer than 8 days. And as the opening vignette demonstrated, Anita Roddick's vision was environmentalism at the heart of business.

Does effective charismatic leadership depend on the situation?

There is an increasing body of research that shows impressive correlations between charismatic leadership and high performance and satisfaction among followers.[15] People working for charismatic leaders are motivated to exert extra work effort and, because they like and respect their leader, express greater satisfaction. It also appears that organizations with charismatic CEOs are more profitable; and charismatic university professors enjoy higher course evaluations.[16] However, there is a growing body of evidence indicating that charisma may not always be generalisable; that is, its effectiveness may depend on the situation. Charisma appears to be most successful when the follower's task has an ideological component or when the environment involves a high degree of stress and uncertainty.[17] This may explain why, when charismatic leaders surface, it's likely to be in politics, religion, wartime or when a business firm is in its infancy or facing a life-threatening crisis. For example, Nissan and Renault Chief Carlos Ghosn won widespread acclaim in the late 1990s for rescuing Nissan from near bankruptcy. However, his reputation was subsequently questioned as the automaker's profit growth failed to keep pace with rivals. It has been suggested his charismatic leadership style is better suited to turning around troubled organizations rather than taking solid performers to the next level.[18]

In addition to ideology and uncertainty, another situational factor limiting charisma appears to be level in the organization. Remember that the creation of a vision is a key component of charisma. But visions typically apply to entire organizations or major divisions. They tend to be created by top executives. Charisma therefore probably has more direct relevance to explaining the success and failures of chief executives than of lower-level managers. So even though an individual may have an inspiring personality, it's more difficult to utilise the person's charismatic leadership qualities in lower-level management jobs. Lower-level managers *can* create visions to lead their units. It's just harder to define such visions and align them with the larger goals of the organization as a whole.

Finally, charismatic leadership may affect some followers more than others. Research suggests, for example, that people are especially receptive to charismatic leadership when they sense a crisis, when they are under stress or when they fear for their lives. More generally, some peoples' personalities are especially susceptible to charismatic leadership.[19] Consider self-esteem. If an individual lacks self-esteem and questions his self-worth, he is more likely to absorb a leader's direction rather than establish his own way of leading or thinking.

The dark side of charismatic leadership

Unfortunately, charismatic leaders who are larger-than-life don't necessarily act in the best interests of their organizations.[20] Many of these leaders used their power to remake their companies in their own image. These leaders often completely blurred the boundary separating their personal interests from their organization's interests. The perils of this ego-driven charisma at its worst are leaders who allow their self-interest and personal goals to override the goals of the organization. Intolerant of criticism, they surround themselves with yes-people who are rewarded for pleasing the leader and create a climate where people are afraid to question or challenge the 'king' or 'queen' when they think he or she is making a mistake. The results at companies such as Enron, Parmalat, Tyco and Worldcom were leaders who recklessly used organizational resources for their personal benefit and executives who broke laws and crossed ethical lines for their own gain.

A study of 29 companies that went from good to great (based on the fact that their cumulative stock returns were all at least three times better than the general stock market over 15 years) found an *absence* of ego-driven charismatic leaders. Although the leaders of these firms were fiercely ambitious and driven, their ambition was directed toward their company rather than themselves. They generated extraordinary results, but with little fanfare. They took responsibility for mistakes and poor results and gave credit for successes to other people. They prided themselves on developing strong leaders inside the firm who could direct the company to greater heights after they were gone. These individuals have been called **level-5 leaders** because they have four basic leadership qualities – individual capability, team skills, managerial competence and the ability to stimulate others to high performance – plus a fifth dimension: a paradoxical blend of personal humility and professional will. Level-5 leaders channel their ego needs away from themselves and into the goal of building a great company. So while level-5 leaders are

level-5 leaders
Leaders who are fiercely ambitious and driven but whose ambition is directed toward their company rather than themselves.

highly effective, they tend to be people you've never heard of and who get little notoriety in the business press – people like Orin Smith at Starbucks and John Whitehead of Goldman Sachs. This study is important because it confirms that leaders don't necessarily need to be charismatic to be effective, especially where charisma is enmeshed with an outsized ego.[21]

We don't mean to suggest that charismatic leadership isn't effective. Overall, its effectiveness is well supported. The point is that a charismatic leader isn't always the answer. Yes, an organization with a charismatic leader at the helm is more likely to be successful, but that success depends, to some extent, on the situation and on the leader's vision. History has numerous examples of charismatic political leaders who were all too successful at convincing their followers to pursue a vision that was disastrous.

Transformational leadership

3 Contrast transformational leadership and transactional leadership and discuss how transformational leadership works.

transactional leaders
Leaders who guide or motivate their followers in the direction of established goals by clarifying role and task requirements.

transformational leaders
Leaders who inspire followers to transcend their own self-interests and who are capable of having a profound and extraordinary effect on followers.

A stream of research has focused on differentiating transformational leaders from transactional leaders.[22] Most of the leadership theories presented in Chapter 12 – for instance, the Ohio State studies, Fiedler's model and path-goal theory – have concerned **transactional leaders**. These kinds of leaders guide or motivate their followers in the direction of established goals by clarifying role and task requirements. **Transformational leaders** inspire followers to transcend their own self-interests for the good of the organization and are capable of having a profound and extraordinary effect on their followers. Jorma Ollila at Nokia, Christopher Gent at Vodafone and Richard Branson of the Virgin Group, are all examples of transformational leaders. They pay attention to the concerns and developmental needs of individual followers; they change followers' awareness of issues by helping them to look at old problems in new ways; and they are able to excite, arouse, and inspire followers to put out extra effort to achieve group goals. Exhibit 13.2 briefly identifies and defines the characteristics that differentiate these two types of leaders.

Transactional and transformational leadership shouldn't be viewed as opposing approaches to getting things done.[23] Transformational and transactional leadership complement each other, but that doesn't mean they're equally important. Transformational leadership builds *on top of* transactional leadership and produces levels of follower effort and performance that go beyond what would occur with a transactional approach alone. But the reverse isn't true. So if you are a good transactional leader, but do not have transformational qualities, you'll likely only be a mediocre leader. The best leaders are transactional *and* transformational.

Full range of leadership model

Figure 13.1 shows the full range of leadership model. Laissez-faire is the most passive and therefore the least effective of the leader behaviours. Leaders using this style are rarely viewed

---

EXHIBIT 13.2 | **CHARACTERISTICS OF TRANSACTIONAL AND TRANSFORMATIONAL LEADERS**

Transactional leader

Contingent Reward: Contracts exchange of rewards for effort, promises rewards for good performance, recognises accomplishments.

Management by Exception (active): Watches and searches for deviations from rules and standards, takes correct action.

Management by Exception (passive): Intervenes only if standards are not met.

Laissez-Faire: Abdicates responsibilities, avoids making decisions.

Transformational leader

Idealised influence: Provides vision and sense of mission, instils pride, gains respect and trust.

Inspirational motivation: Communicates high expectations, uses symbols to focus efforts, expresses important purposes in simple ways.

Intellectual stimulation: Promotes intelligence, rationality and careful problem solving.

Individualised consideration: Gives personal attention, treats each employee individually, coaches, advises.

Source: B. M. Bass, 'From transactional to transformational leadership: learning to share the vision', *Organizational Dynamics*, Vol. 18, No. 3, Winter 1990, p. 22. Copyright 1990, with permission from Elsevier.

Figure 13.1	Full range of leadership model

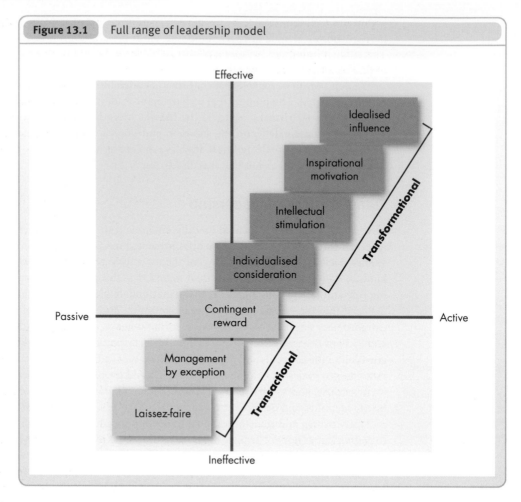

as effective. Management by exception – regardless of whether it is active or passive – is slightly better than laissez-faire, but it's still considered ineffective leadership. Leaders who practise management by exception leadership tend to be available only when there is a problem, which is often too late. Contingent reward leadership can be an effective style of leadership. However, leaders will not get their employees to go above and beyond the call of duty when practising this style of leadership. Only with the four remaining leadership styles – which are all aspects of transformational leadership – are leaders able to motivate followers to perform above expectations and transcend their own self-interest for the sake of the organization. Individualised consideration, intellectual stimulation, inspirational motivation and idealised influence all result in extra effort from workers, higher productivity, higher morale and satisfaction, higher organizational effectiveness, lower turnover, lower absenteeism and greater organizational adaptability. Based on this model, leaders are generally most effective when they regularly use each of the four transformational behaviours.

How transformational leadership works

In the past few years, a great deal of research has been conducted to explain how transformational leadership works. Transformational leaders encourage their followers to be more innovative and creative.[24] For example, Gerard Kleisterlee CEO of the Dutch giant Philips, believes a major growth area for the company is 'green' products. Consequently, to create the products of the future, he has spent a lot of time (and money) communicating the message, empowering talent and drawing on Philips' expertise gained through its enviable record of innovation. Transformational leaders are more effective because they themselves are more creative, but they're also more effective because they encourage those who follow them to be creative too.

Goals are another key mechanism that explains how transformational leadership works. Followers of transformational leaders are more likely to pursue ambitious goals, be familiar with and agree on the strategic goals of the organization and believe that the goals they are pursuing are personally important.[25] VeriSign's CEO, Stratton Sclavos, says, 'It comes down to charting a course – having the ability to articulate for your employees where you're headed and how you're going to get there. Even more important is choosing people to work with who have that same level of passion, commitment, fear, and competitiveness to drive toward those same goals.'

Sclavos's remark about goals brings up vision. Just as research has shown that vision is important in explaining how charismatic leadership works, research has also shown that vision explains part of the effect of transformational leadership. Indeed, one study found that vision was even more important than a charismatic (effusive, dynamic, lively) communication style in explaining the success of entrepreneurial firms.[26] Finally, transformational leadership also engenders commitment on the part of followers and instils in them a greater sense of trust in the leader.[27]

Evaluation of transformational leadership

The evidence supporting the superiority of transformational leadership over transactional leadership is impressive. Transformational leadership has been supported in disparate occupations (for example, school principals, marine commanders, ministers, presidents of MBA associations, union representatives, school teachers, sales reps) and at various job levels. One recent study of R&D firms found, for example, that teams led by project leaders who scored high on transformational leadership produced better-quality products as judged one year later and were more profitable five years later.[28] A review of 87 studies testing transformational leadership found that it was related to the motivation and satisfaction of followers and to the higher performance and perceived effectiveness of leaders.[29]

Transformational leadership theory is not perfect. There are concerns about whether contingent reward leadership is strictly a characteristic of transactional leaders only; and contrary to the full range of leadership model, contingent reward leadership is sometimes more effective than transformational leadership.

In summary, the overall evidence indicates that transformational leadership is more strongly correlated than transactional leadership with lower turnover rates, higher productivity, lower employee stress and burnout and higher employee satisfaction.[30] Like charisma, it appears that transformational leadership can be learned. One study of bank managers found that those managers who underwent transformational leadership training had bank branches that performed significantly better than branches with managers who did not undergo training. Other studies show similar results.[31]

Transformational leadership versus charismatic leadership

There is some debate about whether transformational leadership and charismatic leadership are the same. The researcher most responsible for introducing charismatic leadership to OB, Robert House, considers them synonymous, calling the differences 'modest' and 'minor'. However, the individual who first researched transformational leadership, Bernard Bass, considers charisma to be part of transformational leadership, but argues that transformational leadership is broader than charisma, suggesting that charisma is, by itself, insufficient to 'account for the transformational process'.[32] Another researcher commented, 'The purely charismatic [leader] may want followers to adopt the charismatic's world view and go no further; the transformational leader will attempt to instil in followers the ability to question not only established views but eventually those established by the leader.'[33] Although many researchers believe that transformational leadership is broader than charismatic leadership, studies show that in reality a leader who scores high on transformational leadership is also likely to score high on charisma. Therefore, in practice, measures of charisma and transformational leadership may be roughly equivalent.

Russell Boyce/Reuters

Chairman of the London Organizing Committee for the Olympic Games, Sebastian Coe exemplifies authentic leadership. A former Olympic gold medal winner himself, he clearly believes in and values the Games for London. By being open, approachable, sticking to his ideals and recognising the achievements of others, he has managed to engender trust in what many view as an uncertain endeavour.

Authentic leadership: ethics and trust are the foundation of leadership

4 Define *authentic leadership* and show why ethics and trust are vital to effective leadership.

Although charismatic leadership theories and transformational leadership theories have added greatly to our understanding of effective leadership, they do not explicitly deal with the role of ethics and trust. Some scholars have argued that a consideration of ethics and trust is essential to complete the picture of effective leadership. Here we consider these two concepts under the rubric of authentic leadership.[34]

What is authentic leadership?

authentic leaders
Leaders who know who they are, know what they believe in and value, and act on those values and beliefs openly and candidly. Their followers would consider them to be ethical people.

Douglas R. Conant is not your typical CEO. His style is decidedly understated. When asked to reflect on the strong performance of Campbell Soup, he demurs, 'We're hitting our stride a little bit more [than our peers]'. He regularly admits mistakes and often says, 'I can do better.' Conant appears to be a good exemplar of authentic leadership.[35]

Authentic leaders know who they are, know what they believe in and value and act on those values and beliefs openly and candidly. Their followers would consider them to be ethical people. The primary quality, therefore, produced by authentic leadership is trust. How does authentic leadership build trust? Authentic leaders share information, encourage open communication and stick to their ideals. The result: People come to have faith in authentic leaders.

Because the concept is so recent, there hasn't been a lot of research on authentic leadership. However, we believe it's a promising way to think about ethics and trust in leadership because it focuses on the moral aspects of being a leader. Transformational or charismatic leaders can have a vision, and communicate it persuasively, but sometimes the vision is wrong, or the leader is more concerned with his own needs or pleasures, as in the case with business leaders Calisto Tanzi (ex-CEO of Parmalat) and Jeff Skilling (ex-CEO of Enron).[36]

SELF-ASSESSMENT LIBRARY

Am I an ethical leader?

In the Self-assessment library (available online), take assessment IV.E.4 (Am I an ethical leader?).

Ethics and leadership

The topic of ethics and leadership has received surprisingly little attention. Only recently have ethicists and leadership researchers begun to consider the ethical implications in leadership.[37] Why now? One reason is because ethical lapses by business leaders are never absent from the headlines and these are more rigorously reported than they once were. Some companies, like Boeing, are even tying executive compensation to ethics. They've done so to reinforce the idea that 'there's no compromise between doing things the right way and performance,' in the words of Boeing's CEO Jim McNerney.[38]

Ethics touches on leadership at a number of junctures. Transformational leaders, for instance, have been described by one authority as fostering moral virtue when they try to change the attitudes and behaviours of followers.[39] Charisma, too, has an ethical component. Unethical leaders are more likely to use their charisma to enhance *power over* followers, directed toward self-serving ends. Ethical leaders are considered to use their charisma in a socially constructive way to serve others.[40] There is also the issue of abuse of power by leaders, for example, when they give themselves large salaries, bonuses and share options while, at the same time, they seek to cut costs by laying off long-time employees. Because top executives set the moral tone for an organization, they need to set high ethical standards, demonstrate those standards through their own behaviour and encourage and reward integrity in others.

Leadership effectiveness needs to address the *means* a leader uses in trying to achieve goals, as well as the content of those goals. Recently, scholars have tried to integrate ethical and charismatic leadership by advancing the idea of **socialised charismatic leadership** – leadership that conveys values that are other-centred versus self-centred by leaders who model ethical conduct.[41]

Leadership is not value free. Before we judge any leader to be effective, we should consider both the means used by the leader to achieve goals and the moral content of those goals.

Now let's examine the issue of trust and its role in shaping strong leaders.

What is trust?

Trust, or lack of trust, is an increasingly important leadership issue in today's organizations.[42] In this section, we define *trust* and provide you with some guidelines for helping build credibility and trust.

Trust is a positive expectation that another will not – through words, actions or decisions – act opportunistically.[43] The two most important elements of our definition are that it implies familiarity and risk.

The phrase *positive expectation* in our definition assumes knowledge and familiarity about the other party. Trust is a history-dependent process based on relevant but limited samples of experience.[44] It takes time to form, building incrementally and accumulating. Most of us find it

socialised charismatic leadership
A leadership concept that states that leaders convey values that are other-centred versus self-centred and who role model ethical conduct.

trust
A positive expectation that another will not act opportunistically.

AFP/Getty Images

Organizational relationships with Gerard Kleisterlee, CEO of Philips are founded on knowledge-based trust. Having spent his entire career with Philips his colleagues, some of whom he has worked with for decades, know him well. They describe him as an excellent communicator, respectful of employees' ideas, loyal, serious and a person who delivers results. A former Europe Businessman of the Year, Kleisterlee has been credited with transforming the sleepy electronics company into a consumer-oriented powerhouse.[60]

Interestingly, at the knowledge-based level, trust is not necessarily broken by inconsistent behaviour. If you believe you can adequately explain or understand another's apparent violation, you can accept it, forgive the person and move on in the relationship. However, the same inconsistency at the deterrence level is likely to irrevocably break the trust.

In an organizational context, most manager–employee relationships are knowledge-based. Both parties have enough experience working with each other that they know what to expect. A long history of consistently open and honest interactions, for instance, is not likely to be permanently destroyed by a single violation.

Identification-based trust

The highest level of trust is achieved when there is an emotional connection between the parties. It allows one party to act as an agent for the other and substitute for that person in interpersonal transactions. This is called **identification-based trust**. Trust exists because the parties understand each other's intentions and appreciate each other's wants and desires. This mutual understanding is developed to the point that each can effectively act for the other. Controls are minimal at this level. You don't need to monitor the other party because there exists unquestioned loyalty.

The best example of identification-based trust is a long-term, happily married couple. For example, Timothy comes to learn what's important to his wife Joanne and anticipates those actions. She, in turn, trusts that he will anticipate what's important to her without having to ask. Increased identification enables each to think like the other, feel like the other and respond like the other.

You see identification-based trust occasionally in organizations among people who have worked together for long periods of time and have a depth of experience that allows them to know each other inside and out. This is also the type of trust that managers ideally seek in teams. Team members are so comfortable with and trusting of each other that they can anticipate each other and act freely in each other's absence. In the current work world, it's probably accurate to

identification-based trust
Trust based on a mutual understanding of each other's intentions and appreciation of each other's wants and desires.

say that most large corporations have broken the bonds of identification trust that were built with long-term employees. Broken promises have led to a breakdown in what was, at one time, a bond of unquestioned loyalty. It's likely to have been replaced with knowledge-based trust.

Basic principles of trust

Research allows us to offer some principles for better understanding the creation of both trust and mistrust.[61]

Mistrust drives out trust

People who are trusting demonstrate their trust by increasing their openness to others, disclosing relevant information, and expressing their true intentions. People who mistrust do not reciprocate. They conceal information and act opportunistically to take advantage of others. To defend against repeated exploitation, trusting people are driven to mistrust. A few mistrusting people can poison an entire organization.

Trust begets trust

In the same way that mistrust drives out trust, exhibiting trust in others tends to encourage reciprocity. Effective leaders increase trust in small increments and allow others to respond in kind. By offering trust in only small increments, leaders limit penalty or loss that might occur if their trust is exploited.

Trust can be regained

Once it is violated, trust can be regained, but only in certain situations. When an individual's trust in another is broken because the other party failed to do what was expected of him, it can be restored when the individual observes a consistent pattern of trustworthy behaviours by the transgressor. However, when the same untrustworthy behaviour occurs with deception, trust never fully recovers, even when the deceived is given apologies, promises or a consistent pattern of trustworthy actions.[62]

Mistrusting groups self-destruct

The corollary to the previous principle is that when group members mistrust each other, they repel and separate. They pursue their own interests rather than the group's. Members of mistrusting groups tend to be suspicious of each other, are constantly on guard against exploitation and restrict communication with others in the group. These actions tend to undermine and eventually destroy the group.

Mistrust generally reduces productivity

6 Demonstrate the importance of mentoring, self-leadership and virtual leadership to our understanding of leadership.

Although we cannot say that trust necessarily *increases* productivity, though it usually does, mistrust almost always *reduces* productivity. Mistrust focuses attention on the differences in member interests, making it difficult for people to visualise common goals. People respond by concealing information and secretly pursuing their own interests. When employees encounter problems, they avoid calling on others, fearing that those others will take advantage of them. A climate of mistrust tends to stimulate dysfunctional forms of conflict and retard cooperation.

Contemporary leadership roles

Why are many effective leaders also active mentors? How can leaders develop self-leadership skills in their employees? And how does leadership work when face-to-face interaction is gone? In this section, we briefly address these three leadership role issues.

Mentoring

mentor

A senior employee who sponsors and supports a less-experienced employee, called a protégé.

Many leaders create mentoring relationships. A **mentor** is a senior employee who sponsors and supports a less-experienced employee (a protégé). Successful mentors are good teachers. They can present ideas clearly, listen well and empathise with the problems of their protégés. Mentoring relationships have been described in terms of two broad categories of functions – career functions and psychosocial functions:

Career functions	Psychosocial functions
• Lobbying to get the protégé challenging and visible assignments • Coaching the protégé to help develop their skills and achieve work objectives • Assisting the protégé by providing exposure to influential individuals within the organization • Protecting the protégé from possible risks to their reputation • Sponsoring the protégé by nominating them for potential advances or promotions • Acting as a sounding board for ideas that the protégé might be hesitant to share with their direct supervisor	• Counselling the protégé about anxieties and uncertainty to help bolster their self-confidence • Sharing personal experiences with the protégé • Providing friendship and acceptance • Acting as a role model[63]

Some organizations, such as the Spanish organization Mataró Glassworks, have formal mentoring programmes that officially assign mentors to new or high-potential employees. At Mataró, older employees are assigned to mentor younger workers carrying out the same job. However, in contrast to Mataró's formal system, most organizations rely on informal mentoring – with senior managers personally selecting an employee and taking on that employee as a protégé. Informal mentoring is the most effective mentoring relationship outside the immediate boss–subordinate interface.[64] The boss–subordinate context has an inherent conflict of interest and tension, mostly attributable to managers' directly evaluating the performance of subordinates, limiting openness and meaningful communication.

Why would a leader want to be a mentor? There are personal benefits to the leader as well as benefits for the organization. The mentor–protégé relationship gives the mentor unfiltered access to the attitudes and feelings of lower-ranking employees, and protégés can be an excellent source of early warning signals that identify potential problems. Research suggests that mentor commitment to a programme is key to its effectiveness, so if a programme is to be successful, it's critical that mentors be on board and see the relationship as beneficial to themselves and the protégé. It's also important that the protégé feel that he has contributed to the relationship; if it's something he feels is foisted on him, he'll just go through the motions, too.[65]

Are all employees in an organization equally likely to participate in a mentoring relationship? Unfortunately, the answer is no.[66] Mentors tend to select protégés who are similar to themselves in terms of criteria such as background, education, gender, race, ethnicity and religion. 'People naturally move to mentor and can more easily communicate with those with whom they most closely identify.'[67] In Europe, for instance, upper-management positions in most organizations have been traditionally staffed by white males, so it is hard for minority groups and women to be selected as protégés. There are various European initiatives that aim to help address this balance, for example Norway has passed a law requiring all public companies to allocate 40 per cent of their board seats to women. But clear discrepancies still exist across Europe. Organizations have responded to this dilemma by increasing formal mentoring programmes and providing training and coaching for potential mentors of special groups such as minorities and women.[68]

You might assume that mentoring is important, but the research has been fairly disappointing. Two large-scale reviews suggest that the benefits are primarily psychological rather than tangible. Based on these reviews, it appears that the objective outcomes of mentoring, in terms of career success (compensation, job performance), are very small. One of these reviews concluded, 'Though mentoring may not be properlly labelled an utterly useless concept to careers, neither can it be argued to be as important as the main effects of other influences on career success such as ability and personality.'[69] It may *feel* nice to have a mentor, but it does not appear that having a mentor, or even having a good mentor who provides both support and advice, is important to one's career.

Self-leadership

self-leadership
~~...~~ ~~of processes~~

Is it possible for people to lead themselves? An increasing body of research suggests that many can.[70] Proponents of **self-leadership** propose that there are a set of processes through which individuals control their own behaviour. And effective leaders (or what advocates like to call ...p their followers to lead themselves. They do this by developing leadership ...rs and nurturing followers so they no longer need to depend on formal leaders ...d motivation.

...DERS THAN WOMEN'   **MYTH *OR* SCIENCE?**

...evidence to support
...rs than women;
...nall, evidence

...ory through the
...ding gender and
...en made better
...e was predicated
...tly better skilled for
.../ task focus, lower
...ity to be directive.

...evidence concludes
...ship advantage.
...small, meaning that
...ween men and women
...do have, on average, a
...iew of 45 companies
...ore transformational

than male leaders. The authors concluded, 'These data attest to the ability of women to perform very well in leadership roles in contemporary organizations.'

It is true that men continue to dominate leadership positions. Only 12 of the Fortune Global 500 companies CEO's are women. But being chosen as leader is not the same as performing well once selected. Research suggests that more individuals prefer male leaders. Given the evidence we've reviewed here, those preferences deserve serious reexamination.

Sources: A. H. Eagly, 'Female leadership advantage and disadvantage: resolving the contradictions', *Psychology of Women Quarterly*, March 2007, pp. 1–12; and A. H. Eagly, M. C. Johannesen-Schmidt and M. L. van Engen, 'Transformational, transactional, and laissez-faire leadership styles: a meta-analysis comparing women and men', *Psychological Bulletin*, July 2003, pp. 569–91.

...derlying assumptions behind self-leadership are that people are responsible, capable, ...d ...le to exercise initiative without the external constraints of bosses, rules or regulations. Given the proper support, individuals can monitor and control their own behaviour. The importance of self-leadership has increased with the expanded popularity of teams. Empowered, self-managed teams need individuals who are themselves self-directed. Management can't expect individuals who have spent their organizational lives under boss-centred leadership to suddenly adjust to self-managed teams. Therefore, training in self-leadership is an excellent means to help employees make the transition from dependence to autonomy.

To engage in effective self-leadership: (1) make your mental organizational chart horizontal rather than vertical (although vertical reporting relationships matter, often your most trusted colleagues and people of greatest possible impact are peers); (2) focus on influence and not control (do your job *with* your colleagues, not *for* them or *to* them); and (3) don't wait for the right time to make your mark; create your opportunities rather than wait for them.[71]

Online leadership

How do you lead people who are physically separated from you and with whom your interactions are basically reduced to written digital communications? This is a question that, to date, has received minimal attention from OB researchers.[72] Leadership research has been directed almost exclusively to face-to-face and verbal situations. But we can't ignore the reality that today's managers and their employees are increasingly being linked by networks rather than geographic proximity. Obvious examples include managers who regularly use e-mail to communicate with their staff, managers who oversee virtual projects or teams and managers whose teleworking employees are linked to the office by a computer and an Internet connection.

If leadership is important for inspiring and motivating dispersed employees, we need to offer some guidance as to how leadership might function in this context. Keep in mind, however, that there is limited research on this topic. So our intention here is not to provide definitive guidelines for leading online. Rather, it's to introduce you to an increasingly important issue and get you to think about how leadership changes when relationships are defined by network interactions.

In face-to-face communications, harsh *words* can be softened by nonverbal action. A smile and comforting gesture, for instance, can lessen the blow behind strong words like *disappointed*, *unsatisfactory*, *inadequate* or *below expectations*. That nonverbal component doesn't exist with online interactions. The *structure* of words in a digital communication also has the power to motivate or demotivate the receiver. A manager who inadvertently sends a message in short phrases and in capital letters may get a very different response than if they sent that same message in full sentences using mixed case.

We know that messages convey more than surface information. From a leadership standpoint, messages can convey trust or lack of trust, status, task directives or emotional warmth. Concepts such as task structure, supportive behaviour and vision can be conveyed in written form as well as verbally. It may even be possible for leaders to convey charisma through the written word. But to effectively convey online leadership, managers must recognise that they have choices in the words and structure of their digital communications. They also need to develop the skills of 'reading between the lines' in the messages they receive. In the same way that emotional intelligence taps an individual's ability to monitor and assess others' emotions, effective online leaders need to develop the skill of deciphering the emotional components of messages.

We propose that online leaders have to think carefully about what actions they want their digital messages to initiate. Networked communication is a powerful channel. When used properly, it can build and enhance an individual's leadership effectiveness. But when misused, it has the potential to undermine a great deal of what a leader has been able to achieve through their verbal actions.

In addition, online leaders confront unique challenges, the greatest of which appears to be developing and maintaining trust. Identification-based trust, for instance, is particularly difficult to achieve when there is a lack of intimacy and face-to-face interaction.[73] And online negotiations have also been found to be hindered because parties express lower levels of trust.[74] At this time, it's not clear whether it's even possible for employees to identify with or trust leaders with whom they only communicate electronically.[75]

This discussion leads us to the tentative conclusion that, for an increasing number of managers, good interpersonal skills may include the abilities to communicate support and leadership through written words on a computer screen and to read emotions in others' messages. In this 'new world' of communications, writing skills are likely to become an extension of interpersonal skills.

Challenges to the leadership construct

7 Identify when leadership may not be necessary.

A noted management expert takes issue with the omnipotent role that academicians, practising managers and the general public have given to the concept of leadership. He says, 'In the 1500s, people ascribed all events they didn't understand to God. Why did the crops fail? God. Why did someone die? God. Now our all-purpose explanation is leadership.'[76] He notes that when a company succeeds, people need someone to give the credit to. And that's typically the firm's CEO. Similarly, when a company does poorly, people need someone to blame. CEOs also play this role. But much of an organization's success or failure is due to factors outside the influence of leadership. In many cases, success or failure is just a matter of being in the right or wrong place at a given time.

In this section, we present two perspectives that challenge the widely accepted belief in the importance of leadership. The first argument proposes that leadership is more about appearances than reality. You don't have to *be* an effective leader as long as you *look* like one. The second argument directly attacks the notion that some leadership *will always be effective*, regardless of the situation. This argument contends that in many situations, whatever actions leaders exhibit are irrelevant.

Leadership as an attribution

attribution theory of leadership
A leadership theory which says that leadership is merely an attribution that people make about other individuals.

We introduced attribution theory in Chapter 5. As you may remember, it deals with the ways in which people try to make sense out of cause-and-effect relationships. We said that when something happens, we want to attribute it to something else. The **attribution theory of leadership** says that leadership is merely an attribution that people make about other individuals.[77] The attribution theory has shown that people characterise leaders as having such traits as intelligence, outgoing personality, strong verbal skills, aggressiveness, understanding and industriousness.[78] At the organizational level, the attribution framework accounts for the conditions under which people use leadership to explain organizational outcomes. Those conditions are extremes in organizational performance. When an organization has either extremely negative or extremely positive performance, people are prone to make leadership attributions to explain the performance.[79] As noted earlier, this tendency helps to account for the vulnerability of CEOs (and high-ranking state officials) when their organizations suffer major financial setbacks, regardless of whether they had much to do with it, and it also accounts for why CEOs tend to be given credit for extremely positive financial results – again, regardless of how much or how little they contributed.

One longitudinal study of 128 major corporations provided important support for the attributional approach. Analysing top management team members' perceptions of the charisma of their CEOs and their companies' objective performance, this study found that whereas perceptions of CEO charisma did not lead to objective company performance, company performance did lead to perceptions of charisma.[80]

CULTURAL VARIATION IN CHARISMATIC ATTRIBUTIONS   GLOBAL

Do people from different cultures make different attributions about their leaders' charisma? One study attempted to answer this question.

A team of researchers conducted a study in which individuals from the United States and Turkey read short stories about a hypothetical leader. Each story portrayed the leader's behaviours and the performance of the leader's company differently. In both cultures, individuals believed that the leader possessed more charisma when displaying behaviours such as promoting the company's vision and involving subordinates *and* when the leader's company performed well. However, the participants from the United States, who are more individualistic, focused on the leader's behaviours when attributing charisma. In contrast, the participants from Turkey, who are more collectivistic, focused on the company's performance when attributing charisma.

Why do these differences exist? The researchers speculated that people from individualistic cultures place more emphasis on the person than on the situation and so they attribute charisma when a leader displays certain traits. People from collectivistic cultures, in contrast, place more emphasis on the situation and assume that the leader is charismatic when the company performs well. So, whether others see you as charismatic may, in part, depend on what culture you work in.

Source: Based on N. Ensari and S. E. Murphy, 'Cross-cultural variations in leadership perceptions and attribution of charisma to the leader', *Organizational Behaviour and Human Decision Processes*, September 2003, pp. 52–66.

Following the attribution theory of leadership, we'd say that what's important in being characterised as an 'effective leader' is projecting the *appearance* of being a leader rather than focusing on *actual accomplishments*. Leader-wannabes can attempt to shape the perception that they're smart, personable, verbally adept, aggressive, hardworking and consistent in their style. By doing so, they increase the probability that their bosses, colleagues and employees will *view* them as an effective leader.

Substitutes for and neutralisers of leadership

Contrary to the arguments made throughout this chapter and Chapter 12, leadership may not always be important. A theory of leadership suggests that, in many situations, whatever actions leaders exhibit are irrelevant. Certain individual, job and organizational variables can act as *substitutes* for leadership or *neutralise* the leader's influence on their followers.[81]

WHO WANTS TO BE A CEO MILLIONAIRE? | OB IN THE NEWS

Despite the well publicised 'fat cat' salaries, it would appear that a significant number of workers do not want to rise to the top of the company ranks. Research conducted in 65 countries found that 54 per cent of executives do not want to lead their companies.

In the survey, 64 per cent of respondents who were not already in the top position of their companies said that having a poor work–life balance was their main reason for not wanting to become a corporate bigwig. Some respondents also cited worries over quarterly earnings, stress and intense public scrutiny.

According to Lesley Gaines-Ross, whose firm carried out the research, many younger workers 'are thinking there are a lot of reasons to stop being at the head of their divisions. A lot of this stems from poor leadership development, but there's no chance to be in charge without being in the public spotlight.' As one generation retires from top corporate positions, making those jobs more appealing to younger workers could pose a challenge for companies that really want high-quality leadership.

'The talent pool for the next round of CEOs is much lower than it is now,' Gaines-Ross said. 'To have 54 per cent saying they're going to pass is a real crisis.'

Source: Based on N. Hurst, 'The workplace: who wants to be a CEO millionaire?', *International Herald Tribune*, 22 November 2005. Available at http://www.iht.com/articles/2005/11/22/business/workcol23.php. Accessed 10 February 2009.

Neutralisers make it impossible for leader behaviour to make any difference to follower outcomes. They negate the leader's influence. Substitutes, however, make a leader's influence not only impossible but also unnecessary. They act as a replacement for the leader's influence. For instance, characteristics of employees such as their experience, training, 'professional' orientation or indifference toward organizational rewards can substitute for, or neutralise the effect of, leadership. Experience and training can replace the need for a leader's support or ability to create structure and reduce task ambiguity. Jobs that are inherently unambiguous and routine or that are intrinsically satisfying may place fewer demands on the leadership variable. Organizational characteristics such as explicit, formalised goals, rigid rules and procedures and cohesive work groups can also replace formal leadership (see Table 13.1).

| Table 13.1 | Substitutes for and neutralisers of leadership |

Defining characteristic	Relationship-oriented leadership	Task-oriented leadership
Individual		
Experience/training	No effect on	Substitutes for
Professionalism	Substitutes for	Substitutes for
Indifference to rewards	Neutralises	Neutralises
Job		
Highly structured task	No effect on	Substitutes for
Provides its own feedback	No effect on	Substitutes for
Intrinsically satisfying	Substitutes for	No effect on
Organization		
Explicit formalised goals	No effect on	Substitutes for
Rigid rules and procedures	No effect on	Substitutes for
Cohesive work groups	Substitutes for	Substitutes for

Source: Based on S. Kerr and J. M. Jermier, 'Substitutes for leadership: their meaning and measurement', *Organizational Behavior and Human Performance*, December 1978, p. 378.

This recognition that leaders don't always have an impact on follower outcomes should not be that surprising. After all, we have introduced a number of variables in this text – attitudes, personality, ability and group norms, to name but a few – that have been documented as having an effect on employee performance and satisfaction. Yet supporters of the leadership concept place an undue burden on this variable for explaining and predicting behaviour. It's too simplistic to consider employees as guided to goal accomplishments solely by the actions of their leader. It's important, therefore, to recognise explicitly that leadership is merely another independent variable in our overall OB model. In some situations, it may contribute a lot to explaining employee productivity, absence, turnover, satisfaction, and citizenship behaviour, but in other situations, it may contribute little toward that end.

The validity of substitutes and neutralisers is controversial. One of the problems is that the theory is very complicated: There are many possible substitutes for and neutralisers of many different types of leader behaviours across many different situations. Moreover, sometimes the difference between substitutes and neutralisers is fuzzy. For example, if I'm working on a task that's intrinsically enjoyable, the theory predicts that leadership will be less important because the task itself provides enough motivation. But does that mean that intrinsically enjoyable tasks neutralise leadership effects, or substitute for them, or both? Another problem that this review points out is that substitutes for leadership (such as employee characteristics, the nature of the task and so forth) matter, but it does not appear that they substitute for or neutralise leadership.[82]

8 Explain how to find and create effective leaders.

Finding and creating effective leaders

Djamilla Rosa Cochran/Getty Images

The French couturier Chanel developed an ascension plan for selecting a global CEO, a new position the firm created to manage the intense competition in the luxury-goods business. Selection criteria included a combination of business analytical skills and the ability to think creatively, a requirement for articulating the vision of Chanel's creative leaders. After interviewing 10 executives from the retailing, consumer-goods and luxury-goods industries, Chanel selected Maureen Chiquet. She spent a year in Paris learning Chanel's culture and then served as president of Chanel's US division before she became the firm's global CEO.

We have covered a lot of ground in these two chapters on leadership. But the ultimate goal of our review is to answer this question: How can organizations find or create effective leaders? Let's try to answer that question.

Selecting leaders

The entire process that organizations go through to fill management positions is essentially an exercise in trying to identify individuals who will be effective leaders. Your search might begin by reviewing the specific requirements for the position to be filled. What knowledge, skills and abilities are needed to do the job effectively? You should try to analyse the situation to find candidates who will make a proper match.

Testing is useful for identifying and selecting leaders. Personality tests can be used to look for traits associated with leadership – extraversion, conscientiousness and openness to experience. Testing to find a leadership-candidate's score on self-monitoring also makes sense. High self-monitors are likely to outperform their low-scoring counterparts because the former are better at reading situations and adjusting their behaviour accordingly. You can also assess candidates for emotional intelligence. Given the importance of social skills to managerial effectiveness, candidates with a high EI should have an advantage, especially in situations requiring transformational leadership.[83]

Interviews also provide an opportunity to evaluate leadership candidates. For instance, we know that experience is a poor predictor of leader effectiveness, but situation-specific experience is relevant. You can use an interview to determine whether a candidate's prior experience fits with the situation you're trying to fill. Similarly, the interview is a reasonably good vehicle for identifying the degree to which a candidate has leadership traits such as extraversion, self-confidence, a vision, the verbal skills to frame issues or a charismatic physical presence.

The most important event organizations need to plan for is leadership changes. Nothing lasts forever, so it's always simply a matter of *when* a leader exits, not whether. A lack of planning means organizations have to replace key people quickly and perhaps haphazardly. One survey identified the top concern of international senior HR specialists as 'a terrifying gap between the experience levels of executives and their prospective successors'.[84]

Training leaders

Organizations, in aggregate, spend billions of Euros, dollars and yen on leadership training and development.[85] These efforts take many forms – from executive leadership programmes offered by universities and Business Schools such as Erasmus, INSEAD or Dubai to sailing experiences at the Outward Bound school. Business schools, including some elite programmes, are placing renewed emphasis on leadership development. Some companies, too, place a lot of emphasis on leadership development. For example, Goldman Sachs is well known for developing leaders, so much so that *BusinessWeek* called it the 'Leadership Factory'.[86]

Although much of the money spent on training may provide dubious benefits, our review suggests that there are some things managers can do to get the maximum effect from their leadership-training budgets.[87]

First, let's recognise the obvious. People are not equally trainable. Leadership training of any kind is likely to be more successful with individuals who are high self-monitors than with low self-monitors. Such individuals have the flexibility to change their behaviour.

What kinds of things can individuals learn that might be related to higher leader effectiveness? It may be a bit optimistic to believe that we can teach 'vision creation', but we can teach implementation skills. We can train people to develop 'an understanding about content themes critical to effective visions'.[88] We can also teach skills such as trust building and mentoring. And leaders can be taught situational-analysis skills. They can learn how to evaluate situations, how to modify situations to make them fit better with their style and how to assess which leader behaviours might be most effective in given situations. A number of companies have recently turned to executive coaches to help senior managers improve their leadership skills.[89] For instance, eBay, Pfizer and Unilever have hired executive coaches to provide specific one-on-one training for their top executives to help them improve their interpersonal skills and to learn to act less autocratically.[90]

On an optimistic note, there is evidence suggesting that behavioural training through modelling exercises can increase an individual's ability to exhibit charismatic leadership qualities.[91] Finally, there is accumulating research showing that leaders can be trained in transformational leadership skills that, once learned, deliver bottom-line results. [92]

Global implications

9 Assess whether charismatic and transformational leadership generalise across cultures.

We noted in Chapter 12 that although there is a lack, albeit improving, of cross-cultural research on the traditional theories of leadership there is reason to believe that certain types of leadership behaviours work better in some cultures than in others. What about the more contemporary leadership roles covered in this chapter? Is there cross-cultural research on charismatic/transformational leadership? Does it generalise across cultures? Yes and yes. There has been cross-cultural research on charismatic/transformational leadership, and it seems to suggest that the leadership style works in different cultures.

The GLOBE research programme, which we introduced in Chapter 4, has gathered data on approximately 18,000 middle managers in 825 organizations, covering 62 countries. It's the most comprehensive cross-cultural study of leadership ever undertaken. So its findings should not be quickly dismissed. It's illuminating that one of the results coming from the GLOBE programme is that there *are* some universal aspects to leadership. Specifically, a number of the elements making up transformational leadership appear to be associated with effective leadership, regardless of what country the leader is in.[93] This conclusion is very important because it flies in the face of the contingency view that leadership style needs to adapt to cultural differences.

What elements of transformational leadership appear universal? Vision, foresight, providing encouragement, trustworthiness, dynamism, positiveness and proactiveness. The results led two members of the GLOBE team to conclude that

effective business leaders in any country are expected by their subordinates to provide a powerful and proactive vision to guide the company into the future, strong motivational skills to stimulate all employees to fulfil the vision, and excellent planning skills to assist in implementing the vision.[94]

What might explain the universal appeal of these transformational leader attributes? It's been suggested that pressures toward common technologies and management practices, as a result of global competition and multinational influences, may make some aspects of leadership universally accepted. If that's true, we may be able to select and train leaders in a universal style and thus significantly raise the quality of leadership worldwide.

None of this is meant to suggest that a certain cultural sensitivity or adaptation in styles might not be important when leading teams in different cultures. A vision is important in any culture, but how that vision is formed and communicated may still need to vary by culture.

Summary and implications for managers

Organizations are increasingly searching for managers who can exhibit transformational leadership qualities. They want leaders with vision and the charisma to carry out their vision. And although true leadership effectiveness may be a result of exhibiting the right behaviours at the right time, the evidence is quite strong that people have a relatively uniform perception of what a leader should look like. They attribute 'leadership' to people who are smart, personable, verbally adept and the like. To the degree that managers project these qualities, others are likely to deem them leaders. There is increasing evidence that the effectiveness of charismatic and transformational leadership crosses cultural boundaries.

Effective managers today must develop trusting relationships with those they seek to lead because as organizations have become less stable and predictable, strong bonds of trust are likely to be replacing bureaucratic rules in defining expectations and relationships. Managers who aren't trusted aren't likely to be effective leaders.

For managers concerned with how to fill key positions in their organization with effective leaders, we have shown that tests and interviews help to identify people with leadership qualities. In addition to focusing on leadership selection, managers should also consider investing in leadership training. Many individuals with leadership potential can enhance their skills through formal courses, workshops, rotating job responsibilities, coaching and mentoring.

POINT/COUNTERPOINT

Keep leaders on a short leash

POINT →

A company's leaders need to be managed just like everyone else. Often they cause more harm than good. There is a long list of CEOs who either drove, or practically drove, their companies into the ground: Ola Sundt Ravnestad (Terra-Gruppen), Andy Hornby (HBOS), Raymond Gilmartin (Merck), Calisto Tanzi (Parmalat), Stein Bagger (IT Factory), Henry McKinnell (Pfizer) and the list could go on and on. Although the names always change, this sad fact never does: CEOs are often given the 'run of the house' and are

reined in only after the damage is done. So what happens? A new CEO is hired, and all too often, the same pattern repeats itself.

The key is not who the leader is, but how they are managed. CEOs are given far too much influence and treated with kid gloves by their board of directors (who generally end up selecting and rewarding one another). They're nice while they're being interviewed, but once hired, most turn ▶

into autocrats, running their empires with little room for participation, dissent, and, heaven forbid, any limits on their power. When ex-Pfizer CEO Henry McKinnell was forced out, he complained about the 'war against the corporation'. Actually, the war was against his out-of-control pay package. After he was forced out, Hank Greenberg (AIG) groused, 'If I were starting over, I'd move to China or India.' Poor Hank just didn't have enough room to

run his empire with those darned stakeholders to answer to.

Yes, CEOs need to be hired carefully, but there are limits to how well we can see the 'real' CEO. Much more important is having an autonomous board that will limit the CEO's powers and make him strongly accountable based on performance metrics.

COUNTERPOINT ←

Yes, some CEOs fail, but that's business. If everyone succeeded, why would you need a CEO in the first place? The key to leading companies is to choose wisely.

Select poorly, and you need to put systems in place to manage the leader. But this is a losing game. If you're stuck with a bad CEO, you'll never be able to manage all aspects of their job. Blessed with a good one, and you won't need to worry about managing their performance – the CEO will do that job quite well on her own. Take the example of Boeing's CEO Jim McNerney. He is the first to point out the limits of his own power. 'I'm just one of eleven with a point of view,' he says. 'I have to depend on my power to persuade.'

To treat him as if he were some child to be rewarded and punished at every step is to eliminate any benefits of the

job altogether. Boeing hired well, and though every CEO needs some metrics, mostly the board should stay out of his way and focus on the big picture – strategic planning, meeting long-term objectives and so on. It is fine and good to pay CEOs based on performance, but the devil is often in the details. Link all of a CEO's pay to share price, and what do you think will happen? Some good CEOs won't take the job because they realise they can't perfectly control share price. Others will take the job only to cynically manipulate it to their short-term advantage. Either way, in the long run, the company loses.

There is nothing better than hiring the right CEO. There is nothing worse than hiring the wrong one.[95]

Source: A. Murray, 'After the revolt, creating a new CEO', *Wall Street Journal*, 5 May 2007, pp. A1, A18.

QUESTIONS FOR REVIEW

1. How does framing influence leadership effectiveness?

2. What is charismatic leadership and how does it work?

3. What is transformational leadership? How is it different from transactional and charismatic leadership?

4. What is authentic leadership? Why do ethics and trust matter to leadership?

5. What are the three types of trust?

6. What are the importance of mentoring, self-leadership, and virtual leadership?

7. Are there situations in which leadership is not necessary?

8. How can organizations select and develop effective leaders?

9. Do charismatic and transformational leadership generalise across cultures?

Experiential exercise

YOU BE THE JUDGE: WHICH VISION STATEMENT IS EFFECTIVE

There has been a lot of research about what makes an effective vision statement. A good vision statement is said to have the following qualities:

(a) identifies values and beliefs;
(b) is idealistic or utopian;
(c) represents broad and overarching (versus narrow and specific) goals;
(d) is inspiring;
(e) is future-oriented;
(f) is bold and ambitious;
(g) reflects the uniqueness of the organization; and
(h) is well articulated and easily understood.

Now that you know what makes a good vision statement, you can rate vision statements from actual companies.

1. Break into groups of four or five people each.

2. Each group member should rate each of the following vision statements – based on the eight qualities listed here – on a scale from 1 = very poor to 10 = excellent.

3. Compare your ratings. Did your group agree or disagree?

4. What do you think caused the agreement or disagreement?

5. How would you improve these vision statements?

Vision statements

- **GlaxoSmithKline.** Our vision is to achieve sustainable competitive business advantage through leadership and excellence in environment, health and safety.

- **DuPont.** Our vision is to be the world's most dynamic science company, creating sustainable solutions essential to a better, safer and healthier life for people everywhere.

- **Siemens AG.** Our new vision: Siemens – the pioneer in
  - energy efficiency
  - industrial productivity
  - affordable and personalized healthcare
  - intelligent infrastructure solutions

- **Toshiba.** Toshiba delivers technology and products remarkable for their innovation and artistry – contributing to a safer, more comfortable, more productive life. We bring together the spirit of innovation with our passion and conviction to shape the future and help protect the global environment – our shared heritage. We foster close relationships, rooted in trust and respect, with our customers, business partners and communities around the world.

- **Nissan.** Call us zealous, even overzealous, but at Nissan we know that settling for just any solution is just that. Settling. And, not to mention, the fastest way to go from being an automotive company fuelled by imagination to just another automotive company, period. That's why we think beyond the answer. And ask. Because only through this process of constant challenge can real change occur. One question at a time.

Source: The vision attributes are based on S. A. Kirkpatrick, E. A. Locke and G. P. Latham, 'Implementing the vision: how is it done?', *Polish Psychological Bulletin*, 27 (1996), pp. 93–106.

Ethical dilemma

INTEGRITY, THE ESSENCE OF LEADERSHIP?

Corporate scandals have assumed epidemic proportions. All around the globe, even renowned organizations have been felled from their high pedestals by the misdeeds of their leaders. This raises an intriguing question: How do such resourceful organizations end up with crass 'impostors' as leaders in the first place? The answer perhaps lies in the misplaced emphasis on certain qualities we associate with leadership. True leadership requires a balance among three elemental pre-requisites: Energy, Expertise and Integrity. When they are synchronised, they unleash the latent potential in any organization. Out of these three interacting gears of leadership, it is Integrity that ensures that an organization is run in the right direction – with a view towards collective good rather than selfish motives. Therefore, it is the most non-negotiable of the three elements. Henceforth, leaders ought not to be selected on the basis of the superficial qualities that have blinded us in the past. They must first pass the acid test of Integrity.

The writer of this article strongly suggests that integrity is essential to successful leadership and avoiding corporate scandals. However, is it possible for a leader to be successful without integrity? Can you think of any examples? If you were faced with a situation in which lying about the financial strength of the firm could potentially save the firm from certain collapse, would you do it? (Careful . . . consider what happened to the leaders of Parmalat or Enron.)

Source: J. Singh, 'Impostors masquerading as leaders: can the contagion be contained?', *Journal of Business Ethics*, 82, 3 (2008), 733.

CASE INCIDENT 1

An interview with Maurice Lévy

Simon Hobbs talked to the Chief Executive Officer (CEO) of advertising giant Publicis about fighting fires and how to get ahead in advertising.

Moroccan-born to Spanish parents, Maurice Lévy has spent 35 years positioning French business, Publicis, in an Anglo-Saxon environment, to become the world's fourth-largest advertising conglomerate. The company's agencies include industry giants Saatchi and Saatchi and BBH and media buyer Zenith.

Simon Hobbs: What kind of leader are you?
Maurice Lévy: I think I am no longer a leader; instead, what I wish to be is inspirational. Instead of telling people what to do, it's a journey. In the mid-70s, I was very authoritative. I was young, only 35, and thought I had to impose myself with strong views. Then, I became much more collaborative, with the idea that I had to build the team and grow the company and a view that the group is more important than the individual.
SH: What is the key to good leadership?
ML: Get things right first and the rest will follow. Getting good margins is not the issue – getting good people is. I remember, a long time ago, we had a welcome seminar for newcomers. The founder of Publicis closed it by saying, 'Be happy or leave', which really upset me a lot: We must take care of our people – they are the second most important asset we have. The first are the clients – without them, we would have no people.
SH: What was your first job?
ML: I was in IT when IT was very new. I worked with huge corporations with huge computers and I felt really bored. Then a friend told me there was a small agency looking for someone to run its IT department. I was 24, but said I was 26 as I thought I should be

▶

over 25 to run a department. After three months, I was finishing my IT work in three hours, spending the rest of my day with the creative people and bringing in new business. One day, the chairman offered me the job of CEO. I turned it down saying that if I was CEO at the age of 29, then it was the wrong job for me because I couldn't learn anything more. Two days later, Publicis made me an offer and I'm still there.

SH: You are legendary for having rescued the company's files from a fire.

ML: One day, I was walking on the Champs Élysées and I saw a red blaze: the Publicis building on fire. I said, 'I have people in there!', and tried to run in, but the firemen wouldn't let me. Then I saw a fireman's hat and jacket nearby, put it on and ran in. The lady inside was OK, so I started to rescue the company disks, throwing them out the window to save them from the water. I summoned my team and we entered the building by force and rescued everything we could.

SH: And famously the clients were billed by the end of the month?

ML: Yes. And the clients paid on 2 October.

SH: You once told the *Harvard Review* that you were always arguing with your employer, Publicis founder Marcel Bleustein-Blanchet.

ML: We had some heated conversations. For example, I wanted to go global much earlier.

SH: He thought you should be more cautious?

ML: Yes, he thought that as French people we should not compete with the big US corporations.

SH: So how did you position yourself as a French company, ultimately ending up owning 50 per cent of the US media buying business?

ML: A lot of French operations believe that they have to disguise themselves as Anglo-Saxon, American, etc. I thought that we shouldn't try to be what we are not. I believe – and this is not arrogance – that as French people we are always trying to protect our unique specialisms, and this allows us to understand all the other countries that are trying to do the same. And so we have a different idea to that of homogenisation, the idea of the Americans in the 1990s.

SH: You did 60 deals in your first 10 years. How did you learn to do deals? Especially since the first one, True North, went wrong?

ML: I learned not to get into bed with a partner who doesn't share your values. And that there is no such thing as an equal partner.

SH: In 2003, UK-based advertiser Cordian was on the brink of bankruptcy and you wanted to buy out the

company as cheaply as possible, jumping through many hoops. What kind of leader were you throughout this acquisition?

ML: In terms of leadership, I did a very bad job at managing the price. It was probably the worst experience I had in terms of PR.

SH: You've said that your goal is to invent the blueprint for the digital marketing agency of the future. You said it's not about cosmetic changes but about profound and unsettling changes – so what changes need to be made?

ML: The speed at which society is changing under the influence of digital media and mobility is unprecedented. In advertising, in the past, you were speaking to many individuals. Now, it's a one-to-one. And who is this 'one'? What moves him or her? How far can we be intrusive or emotional?

SH: Let me ask you about Digitas, the American online advertising giant, which you spent $1.3 billion acquiring. Why did you keep it as a separate entity within the group and not put digital into each part of the business.

ML: Because we already have digital in all of our business and we had to move a step further. We believe we can get a disproportional share of the digital business because we are providing our client with the solutions that create value for them, which will connect consumers in a way that no other agency can do. Digitas is bringing this to us.

SH: But isn't it a work in progress?

ML: But since I am here, I am a work in progress! Since 1971, 2 March, starting before 7.00 in the morning, sleeping with Publicis. I am changing every day the way we think.

Questions

1. Would you rate Maurice Lévy as a charismatic or transformational leader?

2. Which parts of the interview give us insights into defining his leadership?

3. Do you think Lévy has developed the trust of his employees? How?

4. Do you think Lévy would be as successful in another industry? In another country?

Source: CNBC European business September 2008. Available at http://cnbceb.com/leadership/maurice-l233vy/518/. Accessed 22 January 2009.

CASE INCIDENT 2

Successful leadership: how would you know?

Was Julius Caesar a successful leader? What about Ghenghis Khan? Simon Bolivar? Or Napoleon? Because we tend to think of these as military leaders, the answers look pretty straightforward. Each achieved major military successes. But then Napoleon was ultimately defeated – does that make him a failure? After all, he won a lot of battles before Waterloo, and his sweeping political and legal reforms have been the basis of French administrative life for nearly 200 years.

Now let's move to the politicians. How do you feel about describing Silvio Berlusconi, Gerhard Schröder? George W. Bush? Tony Blair? Vladimir Putin? as successful leaders? This is altogether more difficult ground. Some of you will have already decided; those of you who have not made up your minds could argue that it is too early to say. The historic verdict on Bush and Blair will probably depend on what happens to Iraq over the next 20 years. Moving next to business territory, with a few exceptions – say Bill Gates and Richard Branson – leaders generally have to be dead to be considered successful.

No problems with Henry Ford and Andrew Carnegie then. But with current CEOs, successful leadership is work in progress. Judgements are particularly hazardous in mid-flight – HBOS, Dexia and Northern Rock were hailed as run by highly successful leaders before the credit crunch.

Questions

1. What criteria can we use to measure successful leadership?

2. Is it possible to label business leaders successful before their careers have ended?

3. Should ethical criteria be used to measure leadership success, or simply financial results?

Source: Based on A. Likierman 'Successful leadership – how would you know?', *Business Strategy Review*, 20, 1 (Spring 2009), pp. 44–49.

Endnotes

1 M. Weber, *The Theory of Social and Economic Organization*, A. M. Henderson and T. Parsons (trans.) (New York: The Free Press, 1947).

2 J. A. Conger and R. N. Kanungo, 'Behavioral dimensions of charismatic leadership', in J. A. Conger, R. N. Kanungo and Associates (eds), *Charismatic Leadership* (San Francisco, CA: Jossey-Bass, 1988), p. 79.

3 J. A. Conger and R. N. Kanungo, *Charismatic Leadership in Organizations* (Thousand Oaks, CA: Sage, 1998); and R. Awamleh and W. L. Gardner, 'Perceptions of leader charisma and effectiveness: the effects of vision content, delivery, and organizational performance', *Leadership Quarterly*, Fall 1999, pp. 345–73.

4 R. J. House and J. M. Howell, 'Personality and charismatic leadership', *Leadership Quarterly*, 3 (1992), pp. 81–108; D. N. Den Hartog and P. L. Koopman, 'Leadership in organizations', in N. Anderson and D. S. Ones (eds), *Handbook of Industrial, Work and Organizational Psychology*, vol. 2 (Thousand Oaks, CA: Sage Publications, 2002), pp. 166–87.

5 See J. A. Conger and R. N. Kanungo, 'Training charismatic leadership: a risky and critical task', *Charismatic Leadership* (San Francisco, CA: Jossey-Bass, 1988), pp. 309–23; A. J. Towler, 'Effects of charismatic influence training on attitudes, behavior, and performance', *Personnel Psychology*, Summer 2003, pp. 363–81; and M. Frese, S. Beimel and S. Schoenborn, 'Action training for charismatic leadership: two evaluations of studies of a commercial training module on inspirational communication of a vision', *Personnel Psychology*, Autumn 2003, pp. 671–97.

6 R. J. Richardson and S. K. Thayer, *The Charisma Factor: How to Develop Your Natural Leadership Ability* (Upper Saddle River, NJ: Prentice-Hall, 1993).

7 J. M. Howell and P. J. Frost, 'A laboratory study of charismatic leadership', *Organizational Behavior and Human Decision Processes*, April 1989, pp. 243–69. See also Frese, Beimel and Schoenborn, 'Action training for charismatic leadership'.

8 A. Thomann, 'Skype – A Baltic success story', *Crédit Suisse Magazine*, 6 September 2006. Available at http://emagazine. credit-suisse.com/app/article/index.cfm?fuseaction= OpenArticle&aoid=163167&coid=7805&lang=EN. Accessed 1 February 2009.

9 B. Shamir, R. J. House and M. B. Arthur, 'The motivational effects of charismatic leadership: a self-concept theory', *Organization Science*, November 1993, pp. 577–94.

10 B. Kark, R. Gan and B. Shamir, 'The two faces of transformational leadership: empowerment and dependency', *Journal of Applied Psychology*, April 2003, pp. 246–55; and P. D. Cherlunik, K. A. Donley, T. S. R. Wiewel and S. R. Miller, 'Charisma is contagious: the effect of leaders' charisma on observers' affect', *Journal of Applied Social Psychology*, October 2001, pp. 2149–59.

11 For reviews on the role of vision in leadership, see S. J. Zaccaro, 'Visionary and inspirational models of executive leadership: empirical review and evaluation', in S. J. Zaccaro (ed.), *The Nature of Executive Leadership: A Conceptual and Empirical Analysis of Success* (Washington, DC: American Psychological Assoc., 2001), pp. 259–78; and M. Hauser and

R. J. House, 'Lead through vision and values', in E. A. Locke (ed.), *Handbook of Principles of Organizational Behavior* (Malden, MA: Blackwell, 2004), pp. 257–73.

12 P. C. Nutt and R. W. Backoff, 'Crafting vision', *Journal of Management Inquiry*, December 1997, p. 309.

13 Ibid., pp. 312–14.

14 J. L. Roberts, 'A mogul's migraine', *Newsweek*, 29 November 2004, pp. 38–40.

15 D. A. Waldman, B. M. Bass and F. J. Yammarino, 'Adding to contingent-reward behavior: the augmenting effect of charismatic leadership', *Group & Organization Studies*, December 1990, pp. 381–94; and S. A. Kirkpatrick and E. A. Locke, 'Direct and indirect effects of three core charismatic leadership components on performance and attitudes', *Journal of Applied Psychology*, February 1996, pp. 36–51.

16 A. H. B. de Hoogh, D. N. den Hartog, P. L. Koopman, H. Thierry, P. T. van den Berg and J. G. van der Weide, 'Charismatic leadership, environmental dynamism, and performance', *European Journal of Work & Organizational Psychology*, December 2004, pp. 447–71; S. Harvey, M. Martin and D. Stout, 'Instructor's transformational leadership: university student attitudes and ratings', *Psychological Reports*, April 2003, pp. 395–402; and D. A. Waldman, M. Javidan and P. Varella, 'Charismatic leadership at the strategic level: a new application of upper echelons theory', *Leadership Quarterly*, June 2004, pp. 355–80.

17 R. J. House, 'A 1976 theory of charismatic leadership', in J. G. Hunt and L. L. Larson (eds), *Leadership: The Cutting Edge* (Carbondale, IL: Southern Illinois University Press, 1977), pp. 189–207; and Robert J. House and Ram N. Aditya, 'The social scientific study of leadership', *Journal of Management*, 23, 3 (1997), p. 441.

18 I. Rowley, 'After huge loss, Nissan plans more layoffs', *Business Week*, 9 February 2009. Available at http://www.businessweek.com/globalbiz/content/feb2009/gb2009029_103868.htm. Accessed 12 February 2009.

19 F. Cohen, S. Solomon, M. Maxfield, T. Pyszczynski and J. Greenberg, 'Fatal attraction: the effects of mortality salience on evaluations of charismatic, task-oriented, and relationship-oriented leaders', *Psychological Science*, December 2004, pp. 846–51; and M. G. Ehrhart and K. J. Klein, 'Predicting followers' preferences for charismatic leadership: the influence of follower values and personality', *Leadership Quarterly*, Summer 2001, pp. 153–79.

20 See, for instance, R. Khurana, *Searching for a Corporate Savior: The Irrational Quest for Charismatic CEOs* (Princeton, NJ: Princeton University Press, 2002); and J. A. Raelin, 'The myth of charismatic leaders', *Training & Development*, March 2003, pp. 47–54.

21 J. Collins, 'Level 5 leadership: the triumph of humility and fierce resolve', *Harvard Business Review*, January 2001, pp. 67–76; J. Collins, 'Good to great', *Fast Company*, October 2001, pp. 90–104; and J. Collins, 'The misguided mix-up', *Executive Excellence*, December 2002, pp. 3–4; and Tosi *et al.*, 'CEO charisma, compensation, and firm performance'.

22 See, for instance, B. M. Bass, B. J. Avolio, D. I. Jung and Y. Berson, 'Predicting unit performance by assessing transformational and transactional leadership', *Journal of Applied Psychology*, April 2003, pp. 207–18; and T. A. Judge and R. F. Piccolo, 'Transformational and transactional leadership: a meta-analytic test of their relative validity', *Journal of Applied Psychology*, October 2004, pp. 755–68.

23 B. M. Bass, 'Leadership: good, better, best', *Organizational Dynamics*, Winter 1985, pp. 26–40; and J. Seltzer and B. M. Bass, 'Transformational leadership: beyond initiation and consideration', *Journal of Management*, December 1990, pp. 693–703.

24 D. I. Jung, C. Chow and A. Wu, 'The role of transformational leadership in enhancing organizational innovation: hypotheses and some preliminary findings', *Leadership Quarterly*, August–October 2003, pp. 525–44; D. I. Jung, 'Transformational and transactional leadership and their effects on creativity in groups', *Creativity Research Journal*, 13, 2 (2001), pp. 185–95; and S. J. Shin and J. Zhou, 'Transformational leadership, conservation, and creativity: evidence from Korea', *Academy of Management Journal*, December 2003, pp. 703–14.

25 J. E. Bono and T. A. Judge, 'Self-concordance at work: toward understanding the motivational effects of transformational leaders', *Academy of Management Journal*, October 2003, pp. 554–71; Y. Berson and B. J. Avolio, 'Transformational leadership and the dissemination of organizational goals: a case study of a telecommunication firm', *Leadership Quarterly*, October 2004, pp. 625–46; and S. Shinn, '21st-century engineer', *BizEd*, January/February, 2005, pp. 18–23.

26 J. R. Baum, E. A. Locke and S. A. Kirkpatrick, 'A longitudinal study of the relation of vision and vision communication to venture growth in entrepreneurial firms', *Journal of Applied Psychology*, February 2000, pp. 43–54.

27 B. J. Avolio, W. Zhu, W. Koh and P. Bhatia, 'Transformational leadership and organizational commitment: mediating role of psychological empowerment and moderating role of structural distance', *Journal of Organizational Behavior*, December 2004, pp. 951–68; and T. Dvir, N. Kass and B. Shamir, 'The emotional bond: vision and organizational commitment among high-tech employees', *Journal of Organizational Change Management*, 17, 2 (2004), pp. 126–43.

28 R. T. Keller, 'Transformational leadership, initiating structure, and substitutes for leadership: a longitudinal study of research and development project team performance', *Journal of Applied Psychology*, 91, 1 (2006), pp. 202–10.

29 Judge and Piccolo, 'Transformational and transactional leadership'.

30 H. Hetland, G. M. Sandal and T. B. Johnsen, 'Burnout in the information technology sector: does leadership matter?', *European Journal of Work and Organizational Psychology*, 16, 1 (2007), pp. 58–75; and K. B. Lowe, K. G. Kroeck and N. Sivasubramaniam, 'Effectiveness correlates of transformational and transactional leadership: a meta-analytic review of the MLQ literature', *Leadership Quarterly*, Fall 1996, pp. 385–425.

31 See, for instance, J. Barling, T. Weber and E. K. Kelloway, 'Effects of transformational leadership training on attitudinal and financial outcomes: a field experiment', *Journal of Applied Psychology*, December 1996, pp. 827–32; and T. Dvir, D. Eden and B. J. Avolio, 'Impact of transformational leadership on follower development and performance: a field experiment', *Academy of Management Journal*, August 2002, pp. 735–44.

32 R. J. House and P. M. Podsakoff, 'Leadership effectiveness: past perspectives and future directions for research', in J. Greenberg (ed.), *Organizational Behavior: The State of the Science* (Hillsdale, NJ: Erlbaum, 1994), pp. 45–82; and B. M. Bass, *Leadership and Performance Beyond Expectations* (New York: The Free Press, 1985).

33 B. J. Avolio and B. M. Bass, 'Transformational leadership, charisma and beyond', working paper, School of Management, State University of New York, Binghampton, 1985, p. 14.

34 See B. J. Avolio, W. L. Gardner, F. O. Walumbwa, F. Luthans and D. R. May, 'Unlocking the mask: a look at the process by which authentic impact follower attitudes and behaviors', *Leadership Quarterly*, December 2004, pp. 801–23; W. L. Gardner and J. R. Schermerhorn, Jr., 'Performance gains through positive organizational behavior and authentic leadership', *Organizational Dynamics*, August 2004, pp. 270–81; and M. M. Novicevic, M. G. Harvey, M. R. Buckley, J. A. Brown-Radford and R. Evans, 'Authentic leadership: a historical perspective', *Journal of Leadership and Organizational Behavior*, 13, 1 (2006), pp. 64–76.

35 A. Carter, 'Lighting a fire under Campbell', *BusinessWeek*, 4 December 2006, pp. 96–101.

36 R. Ilies, F. P. Morgeson and J. D. Nahrgang, 'Authentic leadership and eudaemonic well-being and understanding leader-follower outcomes', *Leadership Quarterly* (in press).

37 This section is based on E. P. Hollander, 'Ethical challenges in the leader–follower relationship', *Business Ethics Quarterly*, January 1995, pp. 55–65; J. C. Rost, 'Leadership: a discussion about ethics', *Business Ethics Quarterly*, January 1995, pp. 129–42; L. K. Treviño, M. Brown and L. P. Hartman, 'A qualitative investigation of perceived executive ethical leadership: perceptions from inside and outside the executive suite', *Human Relations*, January 2003, pp. 5–37; and R. M. Fulmer, 'The challenge of ethical leadership', *Organizational Dynamics*, 33, 3 (2004), pp. 307–17.

38 J. L. Lunsford, 'Piloting Boeing's new course', *Wall Street Journal*, 13 June 2006, pp. B1, B3.

39 J. M. Burns, *Leadership* (New York: Harper & Row, 1978).

40 J. M. Howell and B. J. Avolio, 'The ethics of charismatic leadership: submission or liberation?', *Academy of Management Executive*, May 1992, pp. 43–55.

41 M. E. Brown and L. K. Treviño, 'Socialized charismatic leadership, values congruence, and deviance in work groups', *Journal of Applied Psychology*, 91, 4 (2006), pp. 954–62.

42 See, for example, K. T. Dirks and D. L. Ferrin, 'Trust in leadership: meta-analytic findings and implications for research and practice', *Journal of Applied Psychology*, August 2002, pp. 611–28; the special issue on trust in an organizational context, B. McEvily, V. Perrone, A. Zaheer (guest editors), *Organization Science*, January–February 2003; and R. Galford and A. S. Drapeau, *The Trusted Leader* (New York: The Free Press, 2003).

43 Based on S. D. Boon and J. G. Holmes, 'The dynamics of interpersonal trust: resolving uncertainty in the face of risk', in R. A. Hinde and J. Groebel (eds), *Cooperation and Prosocial Behavior* (Cambridge: Cambridge University Press, 1991), p. 194; D. J. McAllister, 'Affect- and cognition-based trust as foundations for interpersonal cooperation in organizations', *Academy of Management Journal*, February 1995, p. 25; and D. M. Rousseau, S. B. Sitkin, R. S. Burt and C. Camerer, 'Not so different after all: a cross-discipline view of trust', *Academy of Management Review*, July 1998, pp. 393–404.

44 J. B. Rotter, 'Interpersonal trust, trustworthiness, and gullibility', *American Psychologist*, January 1980, pp. 1–7.

45 J. D. Lewis and A. Weigert, 'Trust as a social reality', *Social Forces*, June 1985, p. 970.

46 J. K. Rempel, J. G. Holmes and M. P. Zanna, 'Trust in close relationships', *Journal of Personality and Social Psychology*, July 1985, p. 96.

47 M. Granovetter, 'Economic action and social structure: the problem of embeddedness', *American Journal of Sociology*, November 1985, p. 491.

48 R. C. Mayer, J. H. Davis and F. D. Schoorman, 'An integrative model of organizational trust', *Academy of Management Review*, July 1995, p. 712.

49 C. Johnson-George and W. Swap, 'Measurement of specific interpersonal trust: construction and validation of a scale to assess trust in a specific other', *Journal of Personality and Social Psychology*, September 1982, p. 1306.

50 P. L. Schindler and C. C. Thomas, 'The structure of interpersonal trust in the workplace', *Psychological Reports*, October 1993, pp. 563–73.

51 H. H. Tan and C. S. F. Tan, 'Toward the differentiation of trust in supervisor and trust in organization', *Genetic, Social, and General Psychology Monographs*, May 2000, pp. 241–60.

52 Cited in D. Jones, 'Do you trust your CEO?', *USA Today*, 12 February 2003, p. 7B.

53 D. McGregor, *The Professional Manager* (New York: McGraw-Hill, 1967), p. 164.

54 B. Nanus, *The Leader's Edge: The Seven Keys to Leadership in a Turbulent World* (Chicago: Contemporary Books, 1989), p. 102.

55 See, for instance, Dirks and Ferrin, 'Trust in leadership'; D. I. Jung and B. J. Avolio, 'Opening the black box: an experimental investigation of the mediating effects of trust and value congruence on transformational and transactional leadership', *Journal of Organizational Behavior*, December 2000, pp. 949–64; and A. Zacharatos, J. Barling and R. D. Iverson, 'High-performance work systems and occupational safety', *Journal of Applied Psychology*, January 2005, pp. 77–93.

56 D. E. Zand, *The Leadership Triad: Knowledge, Trust, and Power* (New York: Oxford University Press, 1997), p. 89.

57 Based on L. T. Hosmer, 'Trust: the connecting link between organizational theory and philosophical ethics,' *Academy of Management Review*, April 1995, p. 393; and R. C. Mayer, J. H. Davis and F. D. Schoorman, 'An integrative model of organizational trust', *Academy of Management Review*, July 1995, p. 712.

58 J. M. Kouzes and B. Z. Posner, *Credibility: How Leaders Gain and Lose It, and Why People Demand It* (San Francisco, CA: Jossey-Bass, 1993), p. 14.

59 D. Shapiro, B. H. Sheppard and L. Cheraskin, 'Business on a handshake', *Negotiation Journal*, October 1992, pp. 365–77; R. J. Lewicki, E. C. Tomlinson and N. Gillespie, 'Models of interpersonal trust development: theoretical approaches, empirical evidence, and future directions', *Journal of Management*, December 2006, pp. 991–1022; and J. Child, 'Trust – the fundamental bond in global collaboration', *Organizational Dynamics*, 29, 4 (2001), pp. 274–88.

60 Based on N. D. Schwartz, 'Europe Businessman of the Year: Gerard Kleisterlee', *Fortune Magazine*, 12 January 2007. Available at http://money.cnn.com/magazines/fortune/fortune_archive/2007/01/22/8398023/index.htm. Accessed 12 February 2009.

61 This section is based on Zand, *The Leadership Triad*, pp. 122–34; and A. M. Zak, J. A. Gold, R. M. Ryckman and E. Lenney,

'Assessments of trust in intimate relationships and the self-perception process', *Journal of Social Psychology*, April 1998, pp. 217–28.

62 M. E. Schweitzer, J. C. Hershey and E. T. Bradlow, 'Promises and lies: restoring violated trust', *Organizational Behavior and Human Decision Processes*, 101 (2006), pp. 1–19.

63 See, for example, M. Murray, *Beyond the Myths and Magic of Mentoring: How to Facilitate an Effective Mentoring Process*, rev. edn (New York: Wiley, 2001); K. E. Kram, 'Phases of the mentor relationship', *Academy of Management Journal*, December 1983, pp. 608–25; R. A. Noe, 'An investigation of the determinants of successful assigned mentoring relationships', *Personnel Psychology*, Fall 1988, pp. 559–80; and L. Eby, M. Butts and A. Lockwood, 'Protégés' negative mentoring experiences: construct development and nomological validation', *Personnel Psychology*, Summer 2004, pp. 411–47.

64 J. A. Wilson and N. S. Elman, 'Organizational benefits of mentoring', *Academy of Management Executive*, November 1990, p. 90; and J. Reingold, 'Want to grow as a leader? Get a Mentor?', *Fast Company*, January 2001, pp. 58–60.

65 T. D. Allen, E. T. Eby and E. Lentz, 'The relationship between formal mentoring program characteristics and perceived program effectiveness', *Personnel Psychology* 59 (2006), pp. 125–53; and T. D. Allen, L. T. Eby and E. Lentz, 'Mentorship behaviors and mentorship quality associated with formal mentoring programs: closing the gap between research and practice', *Journal of Applied Psychology*, 91, 3 (2006), pp. 567–78.

66 See, for example, K. E. Kram and D. T. Hall, 'Mentoring in a context of diversity and turbulence', in E. E. Kossek and S. A. Lobel (eds), *Managing Diversity* (Cambridge, MA: Blackwell, 1996), pp. 108–36; B. R. Ragins and J. L. Cotton, 'Mentor functions and outcomes: a comparison of men and women in formal and informal mentoring relationships', *Journal of Applied Psychology*, August 1999, pp. 529–50; and D. B. Turban, T. W. Dougherty and F. K. Lee, 'Gender, race, and perceived similarity effects in developmental relationships: the moderating role of relationship duration', *Journal of Vocational Behavior*, October 2002, pp. 240–62.

67 Wilson and Elman, 'Organizational benefits of mentoring', p. 90.

68 See, for instance, K. Houston-Philpot, 'Leadership development partnerships at Dow Corning Corporation', *Journal of Organizational Excellence*, Winter 2002, pp. 13–27.

69 T. D. Allen, L. T. Eby, M. L. Poteet, E. Lark, E. Lentz and L. Lizzette, 'Career benefits associated with mentoring for protégés: a meta-analysis', *Journal of Applied Psychology*, February 2004, pp. 127–36; and J. D. Kammeyer-Mueller and T. A. Judge, 'A quantitative review of the mentoring literature: test of a model', Working paper, University of Florida, 2005.

70 See C. C. Manz, 'Self-leadership: toward an expanded theory of self-influence processes in organizations', *Academy of Management Review*, July 1986, pp. 585–600; C. C. Manz and H. P. Sims, Jr., *The New Superleadership: Leading Others to Lead Themselves* (San Francisco, CA: Berrett-Koehler, 2001); C. L. Dolbier, M. Soderstrom and M. A. Steinhardt, 'The relationships between self-leadership and enhanced psychological, health, and work outcomes', *Journal of Psychology*, September 2001, pp. 469–85; and J. D. Houghton, T. W. Bonham, C. P. Neck and K. Singh, 'The relationship between self-leadership and personality: a comparison of hierarchical factor structures', *Journal of Managerial Psychology*, 19, 4 (2004), pp. 427–41.

71 J. Kelly and S. Nadler, 'Leading from below', *Wall Street Journal*, 3 March 2007, pp. R4, R10.

72 L. A. Hambley, T. A. O'Neill and T. J. B. Kline, 'Virtual team leadership: the effects of leadership style and communication medium on team interaction styles and outcomes', *Organizational Behavior and Human Decision Processes*, 103 (2007), pp. 1–20; and B. J. Avolio and S. S. Kahai, 'Adding the "E" to e-leadership: how it may impact your leadership', *Organizational Dynamics*, 31, 4 (2003), pp. 325–38.

73 S. J. Zaccaro and P. Bader, 'E-leadership and the challenges of leading e-teams: minimizing the bad and maximizing the good', *Organizational Dynamics*, 31, 4 (2003), pp. 381–85.

74 C. E. Naquin and G. D. Paulson, 'Online bargaining and interpersonal trust', *Journal of Applied Psychology*, February 2003, pp. 113–20.

75 B. Shamir, 'Leadership in boundaryless organizations: disposable or indispensable?', *European Journal of Work and Organizational Psychology*, 8, 1 (1999), pp. 49–71.

76 Comment by Jim Collins and cited in J. Useem, 'Conquering vertical limits', *Fortune*, 19 February 2001, p. 94.

77 See, for instance, J. R. Meindl, 'The romance of leadership as a follower-centric theory: a social constructionist approach', *Leadership Quarterly*, Fall 1995, pp. 329–41; and S. A. Haslam, M. J. Platow, J. C. Turner, K. J. Reynolds, C. McGarty, P. J. Oakes, S. Johnson, M. K. Ryan and K. Veenstra, 'Social identity and the romance of leadership: the importance of being seen to be "doing it for us"', *Group Processes & Intergroup Relations*, July 2001, pp. 191–205.

78 R. G. Lord, C. L. DeVader and G. M. Alliger, 'A meta-analysis of the relation between personality traits and leadership perceptions: an application of validity generalization procedures', *Journal of Applied Psychology*, August 1986, pp. 402–10.

79 J. R. Meindl, S. B. Ehrlich and J. M. Dukerich, 'The romance of leadership', *Administrative Science Quarterly*, March 1985, pp. 78–102.

80 B. R. Agle, N. J. Nagarajan, J. A. Sonnenfeld and D. Srinivasan, 'Does CEO charisma matter?', *Academy of Management Journal*, 49, 1 (2006), pp. 161–74.

81 S. Kerr and J. M. Jermier, 'Substitutes for leadership: their meaning and measurement', *Organizational Behavior and Human Performance*, December 1978, pp. 375–403; J. M. Jermier and S. Kerr, 'Substitutes for leadership: their meaning and measurement – contextual recollections and current observations', *Leadership Quarterly*, 8, 2 (1997), pp. 95–101; and E. de Vries Reinout, R. A. Roe and T. C. B. Taillieu, 'Need for leadership as a moderator of the relationships between leadership and individual outcomes', *Leadership Quarterly*, April 2002, pp. 121–38.

82 S. D. Dionne, F. J. Yammarino, L. E. Atwater and L. R. James, 'Neutralizing substitutes for leadership theory: leadership effects and common-source bias', *Journal of Applied Psychology*, 87 (2002), pp. 454–64; and J. R. Villa, J. P. Howell, P. W. Dorfman and D. L. Daniel, 'Problems with detecting moderators in leadership research using moderated multiple regression', *Leadership Quarterly*, 14 (2002), pp. 3–23.

83 B. M. Bass, 'Cognitive, social, and emotional intelligence of transformational leaders', in R. E. Riggio, S. E. Murphy and F. J. Pirozzolo (eds), *Multiple Intelligences and Leadership* (Mahwah, NJ: Erlbaum, 2002), pp. 113–14.

84 H. Flouch, 'Companies must start to take succession planning seriously', *Personnel Today*, 29 October 2002.

85 See, for instance, P. Dvorak, 'M.B.A. programs hone "soft skills"', *Wall Street Journal*, 12 February 2007, p. B3.

86 J. Weber, 'The leadership factor', *BusinessWeek*, 12 June 2006, pp. 60–64.

87 See, for instance, Barling, Weber and Kelloway, 'Effects of transformational leadership training on attitudinal and financial outcomes'; and D. V. Day, 'Leadership development: a review in context', *Leadership Quarterly*, Winter 2000, pp. 581–613.

88 M. Sashkin, 'The visionary leader', in J. A. Conger, R. N. Kanungo and Associates (eds), *Charismatic Leadership* (San Francisco, CA: Jossey-Bass, 1988), p. 150.

89 D. V. Day, 'Leadership development: a review in context', *Leadership Quarterly*, Winter 2000, pp. 590–93.

90 M. Conlin, 'CEO coaches', *BusinessWeek*, 11 November 2002, pp. 98–104.

91 Howell and Frost, 'A laboratory study of charismatic leadership'.

92 Dvir, Eden and Avolio, 'Impact of transformational leadership on follower development and performance'; B. J. Avolio and B. M. Bass, *Developing Potential Across a Full Range of Leadership: Cases on Transactional and Transformational Leadership* (Mahwah, NJ: Lawrence Erlbaum, 2002); A. J. Towler, 'Effects of charismatic influence training on attitudes, behavior, and performance', *Personnel Psychology*, Summer 2003, pp. 363–81; and Barling, Weber and Kelloway, 'Effects of transformational leadership training on attitudinal and financial outcomes'.

93 R. J. House, M. Javidan, P. Hanges and P. Dorfman, 'Understanding cultures and implicit leadership theories across the globe: an introduction to Project GLOBE', *Journal of World Business*, Spring 2002, pp. 3–10.

94 D. E. Carl and M. Javidan, 'Universality of charismatic leadership: a multi-nation study', paper presented at the National Academy of Management Conference, Washington, DC, August 2001, p. 29.

95 A. Murray, 'After the revolt, creating a new CEO', *Wall Street Journal*, 5 May 2007, pp. A1, A18.

Power and politics

Power is not revealed by striking hard
or often, but by striking true.

Honoré de Balzac

Power and politics at the Volkswagen group: the ousting of Bernd Pischetsrieder

Roland Magunia/Getty Images

Six months after signing a new five-year contract Volkswagen CEO Bernd Pischetsrieder was out, replaced by Martin Winterkorn, the head of Volkswagen's Audi division. No reason was given for the sudden decision by a select committee of its supervisory board, however, fingers were being pointed at Volkswagen's influential chairman, Ferdinand K. Piëch.

Earlier in the year it had come as a surprise to industry analysts when Piëch lobbed a bombshell by telling a newspaper that he doubted the contract of Pischetsrieder would be extended – while Pischetsrieder stood in the media spotlight at the Geneva Auto Show. Piëch claimed he did not have the support of the workers representatives on the board. Perhaps unsurprising as a sex and financial scandal had prosecutors investigating corporate slush funds used to bribe worker representatives with exotic sex trips when Piëch was CEO. However, the undertone of the announcement was clear: an embarrassing attack on Pischetsrieder at a tactical moment.

To understand why Piëch seemed to be manoeuvring to get rid of Pischetsrieder we need to look to the past. Two major events appear to have shaped the relationship. Firstly, Porsche had a considerable shareholding in Volkswagen and Piëch had significant interests in Porsche. He is a grandson of the founder, Ferdinand Porsche, and he and his family control the company. Secondly, he is also Pischetsrieder's forerunner as chief executive of Volkswagen, and had made it very clear how he believed that company should be run.

The new Chief Executive, Winterkorn, analysts said, is a protégé of Mr. Piëch's. 'Pischetsrieder was trying to push through decisions that Piëch was resisting,' said Arndt Ellinghorst, an analyst at Dresdner Kleinwort. 'Winterkorn is someone who will always do everything that Piëch says.'

So who really calls the shots at VW? Probably not the CEO. Most would agree Piëch does.

Sources: Based on M. Landler, 'After power struggle, Volkswagen ousts its chief', *New York Times*, 7 November 2006; and G. Edmonson, 'Can VW's Pischetsrieder survive the Florentine putsch?', *BusinessWeek*, 1 March 2006.

Power and *politics* have been described as the last dirty words. It is easier for most of us to talk about sex or money than it is to talk about power or political behaviour. People who have power deny it, people who want it try not to look like they're seeking it, and those who are good at getting it are secretive about how they do so.[1] To see whether you think your work environment is political, take the following self-assessment.

SELF-ASSESSMENT LIBRARY

Is my workplace political?

In the Self-assessment library (available online), take assessment IV.F.1 (Is my workplace political?); if you don't currently have a job, answer for your most recent job. Then answer the following questions.

1. How does your score relate to those of your classmates? Do you think your score is accurate? Why or why not?

2. Do you think a political workplace is a bad thing? If yes, why? If no, why not?

3. What factors cause your workplace to be political?

A major theme of this chapter is that power and political behaviour are natural processes in any group or organization. Given that, you need to know how power is acquired and exercised if you are to fully understand organizational behaviour. Although you may have heard the phrase 'power corrupts and absolute power corrupts absolutely', power is not always bad. As one author has noted, most medicines can kill if taken in the wrong amount, and thousands die each year in automobile accidents, but we don't abandon chemicals or cars because of the dangers associated with them. Rather, we consider danger an incentive to get training and information that will help us to use these forces productively.[2] The same applies to power. It's a reality of organizational life, and it's not going to go away. Moreover, by learning how power works in organizations, you'll be better able to use your knowledge to become a more effective manager.

A definition of *power*

1 Define *power* and contrast leadership and power.

power
A capacity that *A* has to influence the behaviour of *B* so that *B* acts in accordance with *A*'s wishes.

dependency
B's relationship to *A* when *A* possesses something that *B* requires.

Power refers to a capacity that *A* has to influence the behaviour of *B* so that *B* acts in accordance with *A*'s wishes.[3] This definition implies a *potential* that need not be actualised to be effective, and a *dependency* relationship.

Power may exist but not be used. It is, therefore, a capacity or potential. Someone can have power but not impose it. Probably the most important aspect of power is that it is a function of **dependency**. The greater *B*'s dependence on *A*, the greater is *A*'s power in the relationship. Dependence, in turn, is based on alternatives that *B* perceives and the importance that *B* places on the alternative(s) that *A* controls. A person can have power over you only if he or she controls something you desire. If you want a university degree and have to pass a certain course to get it, and your current instructor is the only faculty member in the college who teaches that course, he or she has power over you. Your alternatives are highly limited, and you place a high degree of importance on obtaining a passing grade. Similarly, if you're attending university on funds totally provided by your parents, you probably recognise the power that they hold over you. You're dependent on them for financial support. But once you're out of university, have a job, and are making a good income, your parents' power is reduced significantly. Who among us, though, has not known or heard of a rich relative who is able to control a large number of family members merely through the implicit or explicit threat of 'writing them out of the will'?

Contrasting leadership and power

A careful comparison of our description of power with our description of leadership in Chapters 12 and 13 reveals that the concepts are closely intertwined. Leaders use power as a means of attaining group goals. Leaders achieve goals, and power is a means of facilitating their achievement.

What differences are there between the two terms? One difference relates to goal compatibility. Power does not require goal compatibility, merely dependence. Leadership, on the other hand, requires some congruence between the goals of the leader and those being led. A second difference relates to the direction of influence. Leadership focuses on the downward influence on one's followers. It minimises the importance of lateral and upward influence patterns. Power does not. Still another difference deals with research emphasis. Leadership research, for the most part, emphasises style. It seeks answers to questions such as: How supportive should a leader be? How much decision making should be shared with followers? In contrast, the research on power has tended to encompass a broader area and to focus on tactics for gaining compliance. It has gone beyond the individual as the exerciser of power because power can be used by groups as well as by individuals to control other individuals or groups.

Bases of power

2 Contrast the five bases of power.

Where does power come from? What is it that gives an individual or a group influence over others? We answer these questions by dividing the bases or sources of power into two general groupings – formal and personal – and then breaking each of these down into more specific categories.[4]

Formal power

Formal power is based on an individual's position in an organization. Formal power can come from the ability to coerce or reward, or it can come from formal authority.

Coercive power

coercive power
A power base that is dependent on fear.

The **coercive power** base is dependent on fear. A person reacts to this power out of fear of the negative results that might occur if she failed to comply. It rests on the application, or the threat of application, of physical sanctions such as the infliction of pain, the generation of frustration through restriction of movement, or the controlling by force of basic physiological or safety needs.

At the organizational level, *A* has coercive power over *B* if *A* can dismiss, suspend, or demote *B*, assuming that *B* values his or her job. Similarly, if *A* can assign *B* work activities that *B* finds unpleasant or treat *B* in a manner that *B* finds embarrassing, *A* possesses coercive power over *B*. Coercive power can also come from withholding key information. People in an organization who have data or knowledge that others need can make those others dependent on them.

Reward power

reward power
Compliance achieved based on the ability to distribute rewards that others view as valuable.

The opposite of coercive power is **reward power**. People comply with the wishes or directives of another because doing so produces positive benefits; therefore, one who can distribute rewards that others view as valuable will have power over those others. These rewards can be either financial – such as controlling pay rates, raises and bonuses; or nonfinancial – including recognition, promotions, interesting work assignments, friendly colleagues and preferred work shifts or sales territories.[5]

Coercive power and reward power are actually counterparts of each other. If you can remove something of positive value from another or inflict something of negative value, you

Sir Liam Donaldson, the Chief Medical Officer for England, has both legitimate power and expert power. As a senior official for the National Health Service he is able to use formal authority to help dictate the operation of the organization to achieve its objective of excellent healthcare. Donaldson is also able to wield power because of his expertise in health issues gained through his background as a surgeon, lecturer, years of experience in the sector and as an author of numerous public health publications.

have coercive power over that person. If you can give someone something of positive value or remove something of negative value, you have reward power over that person.

Legitimate power

legitimate power
The power a person receives as a result of his or her position in the formal hierarchy of an organization.

In formal groups and organizations, probably the most frequent access to one or more of the power bases is one's structural position. This is called **legitimate power**. It represents the formal authority to control and use organizational resources.

Positions of authority include coercive and reward powers. Legitimate power, however, is broader than the power to coerce and reward. Specifically, it includes acceptance by members in an organization of the authority of a position. When school principals, bank presidents or army captains speak (assuming that their directives are viewed to be within the authority of their positions), teachers, tellers and first lieutenants listen and usually comply.

Personal power

You don't have to have a formal position in an organization to have power. Many of the most competent and productive chip designers at Intel, for instance, have power, but they aren't managers and have no formal power. What they have is personal power – power that comes from an individual's unique characteristics. In this section, we look at two bases of personal power – expertise and the respect and admiration of others.

Expert power

expert power
Influence based on special skills or knowledge.

Expert power is influence wielded as a result of expertise, special skill or knowledge. Expertise has become one of the most powerful sources of influence as the world has become more technologically oriented. As jobs become more specialised, we become increasingly dependent on experts to achieve goals. It is generally acknowledged that physicians have expertise and hence expert power – most of us follow the advice that our doctors give us. But it's also important to recognise that computer specialists, tax accountants, economists, industrial psychologists and other specialists are able to wield power as a result of their expertise.

Referent power

Referent power is based on identification with a person who has desirable resources or personal traits. If I like, respect and admire you, you can exercise power over me because I want to please you.

Referent power develops out of admiration of another and a desire to be like that person. It helps explain, for instance, why celebrities are paid millions of dollars to endorse products in commercials. Marketing research shows that people such as David Beckham, Tiger Woods and Roger Federer have the power to influence your choice of, for example, razors and athletic clothes. With a little practice, you and I could probably deliver as smooth a sales pitch as these celebrities, but the buying public doesn't identify with you and me. One of the ways in which individuals acquire referent power is through charisma. Some people have referent power who, while not in formal leadership positions, nevertheless are able to exert influence over others because of their charismatic dynamism, likability and emotional effects on us.

Which bases of power are most effective?

Of the three bases of formal power (coercive, reward, legitimate) and two bases of personal power (expert, referent), which is most important to have? Interestingly, research suggests pretty

Figure 14.1

"I was just going to say 'Well, I don't make the rules.' But, of course, I _do_ make the rules."

Source: Leo Cullum cartoon 1/6/86 *New Yorker*, © Leo Cullum/Condé Nast Publications/ www.cartoonbank.com.

clearly that the personal sources of power are most effective. Both expert and referent power are positively related to employees' satisfaction with supervision, their organizational commitment and their performance, whereas reward and legitimate power seem to be unrelated to these outcomes. Moreover, one source of formal power – coercive power – actually can backfire in that it is negatively related to employee satisfaction and commitment.[6]

Consider Steve Stoute's company, Translation, which matches pop-star spokespersons with corporations that want to promote their brands. Stoute has paired Justin Timberlake with McDonald's, Beyoncé Knowles with Tommy Hilfiger and Jay-Z with Reebok. Stoute's business seems to be all about referent power. As one record company executive commented when reflecting on Stoute's successes, 'He's the right guy for guiding brands in using the record industry to reach youth culture in a credible way.'[7] In other words, using pop stars to market products works because of referent power: People buy products associated with cool figures because they wish to identify with these figures and emulate them.

Dependency: the key to power

Earlier in this chapter we said that probably the most important aspect of power is that it is a function of dependency. In this section, we show how having an understanding of dependency is central to furthering your understanding of power itself.

The general dependency postulate

Let's begin with a general postulate: *The greater B's dependency on A, the greater the power A has over B.* When you possess anything that others require but that you alone control, you make them dependent on you and, therefore, you gain power over them.[8] Dependency, then, is inversely proportional to the alternative sources of supply. If something is plentiful, possession of it will not increase your power. If everyone is intelligent, intelligence gives no special advantage. Similarly, among the superrich, money is no longer power. But, as the old saying goes, 'In the land of the blind, the one-eyed man is king!' If you can create a monopoly by controlling information, prestige, or anything else that others crave, they become dependent on you. Conversely, the more that you can expand your options, the less power you place in the hands of others. This explains, for example, why most organizations develop multiple suppliers rather than give their business to only one. It also explains why so many of us aspire to financial independence. Financial independence reduces the power that others can have over us.

What creates dependency?

Dependency is increased when the resource you control is important, scarce and nonsubstitutable.[9]

Importance

If nobody wants what you have, it's not going to create dependency. To create dependency, the thing(s) you control must be perceived as being important. Organizations, for instance, actively seek to avoid uncertainty.[10] We should, therefore, expect that the individuals or groups who can absorb an organization's uncertainty will be perceived as controlling an important resource. For instance, a study of industrial organizations found that the marketing departments in these firms were consistently rated as the most powerful.[11] The researcher concluded that the most critical uncertainty facing these firms was selling their products. This might suggest that engineers, as a group, would be

Kimberley White/Reuters

Sophie Vandebroek is important at Xerox Corporation. As the company's chief technology officer, she leads the Xerox Innovation Group of 5,000 scientists and engineers at the company's global research centres. The group's mission is 'to pioneer high-impact technologies that enable us to lead in our core markets and to create future markets for Xerox'. Innovation results in products and services customers want to buy and in economic returns for Xerox and its stakeholders.

more powerful at Matsushita than at Procter & Gamble. These inferences appear to be generally valid. An organization such as Matsushita, which is heavily technologically oriented, is highly dependent on its engineers to maintain its products' technical advantages and quality. And, at Matsushita, engineers are clearly a powerful group. At Procter & Gamble, marketing is the name of the game, and marketers are the most powerful occupational group.

Scarcity

As noted previously, if something is plentiful, possession of it will not increase your power. A resource needs to be perceived as scarce to create dependency. This can help explain how low-ranking members in an organization who have important knowledge not available to high-ranking members gain power over the high-ranking members. Possession of a scarce resource – in this case, important knowledge – makes the high-ranking member dependent on the low-ranking member. This also helps to make sense out of behaviours of low-ranking members that otherwise might seem illogical, such as destroying the procedure manuals that describe how a job is done, refusing to train people in their jobs or even to show others exactly what they do, creating specialised language and terminology that inhibit others from understanding their jobs, or operating in secrecy so an activity will appear more complex and difficult than it really is. Ferruccio Lamborghini, the man who created the exotic supercars that continue to carry his name, understood the importance of scarcity and used it to his advantage during the Second World War. Lamborghini was in Rhodes with the Italian army. His superiors were impressed with his mechanical skills, as he demonstrated an almost uncanny ability to repair tanks and cars that no one else could fix. After the war, he admitted that his ability was largely due to having been the first person on the island to receive the repair manuals, which he memorised and then destroyed so as to become indispensable.[12]

The scarcity–dependency relationship can further be seen in the power of occupational categories. Individuals in occupations in which the supply of personnel is low relative to demand can negotiate compensation and benefits packages that are far more attractive than can those in occupations for which there is an abundance of candidates. For example, the market for network systems analysts is extremely tight, with the demand high and the supply limited. The result is that the bargaining power of these analysts is greater than, say, a data input clerk where there is usually an abundant supply.

Nonsubstitutability

The fewer viable substitutes for a resource, the more power the control over that resource provides. Higher education provides an excellent example. At universities in which there are strong pressures for the faculty to publish, we can say that a department head's power over a faculty member is inversely related to that member's publication record. The more recognition the faculty member receives through publication, the more mobile they are; that is, because other universities want faculty who are highly published and visible, there is an increased demand for that person's services. Although the concept of tenure can act to alter this relationship by restricting the department head's alternatives, faculty members who have few or no publications have the least mobility and are subject to the greatest influence from their superiors.

power tactics
Ways in which individuals translate power bases into specific actions.

Power tactics

3 Identify nine power or influence tactics and their contingencies.

What **power tactics** do people use to translate power bases into specific action? That is, what options do individuals have for influencing their bosses, co-workers or employees? And are some of these options more effective than others? In this section, we review popular tactical options and the conditions under which one may be more effective than another.

Research has identified nine distinct influence tactics:[13]

- **Legitimacy.** Relying on one's authority position or stressing that a request is in accordance with organizational policies or rules.

- **Rational persuasion.** Presenting logical arguments and factual evidence to demonstrate that a request is reasonable.
- **Inspirational appeals.** Developing emotional commitment by appealing to a target's values, needs, hopes and aspirations.
- **Consultation.** Increasing the target's motivation and support by involving him or her in deciding how the plan or change will be accomplished.
- **Exchange.** Rewarding the target with benefits or favours in exchange for following a request.
- **Personal appeals.** Asking for compliance based on friendship or loyalty.
- **Ingratiation.** Using flattery, praise, or friendly behaviour prior to making a request.
- **Pressure.** Using warnings, repeated demands and threats.
- **Coalitions.** Enlisting the aid of other people to persuade the target or using the support of others as a reason for the target to agree.

Some tactics are more effective than others. Specifically, evidence indicates that rational persuasion, inspirational appeals and consultation tend to be the most effective. On the other hand, pressure tends to frequently backfire and is typically the least effective of the nine tactics.[14] You can also increase your chance of success by using more than one type of tactic at the same time or sequentially, as long as your choices are compatible.[15] For instance, using both ingratiation and legitimacy can lessen the negative reactions that might come from the appearance of being 'dictated to' by the boss.

To see how these tactics can work in practice, let's consider the most effective way of getting a salary increase. You can start with rational persuasion. That means doing your homework and carefully thinking through the best way to build your case: Figure out how your pay compares to that of peers, or land a competing job offer, or show objective results that testify to your performance. For example, Kitty Dunning, a vice president at Don Jagoda Associates, landed a 16 per cent raise when she emailed her boss numbers showing she had increased sales.[16]

But the effectiveness of some influence tactics depends on the direction of influence.[17] As shown in Table 14.1, studies have found that rational persuasion is the only tactic that is effective across organizational levels. Inspirational appeals work best as a downward-influencing tactic with subordinates. When pressure works, it's generally only to achieve downward influence; and the use of personal appeals and coalitions are most effective with lateral influence attempts. In addition to the direction of influence, a number of other factors have been found to affect which tactics work best. These include the sequencing of tactics, a person's skill in using the tactic and the culture of the organization.

Table 14.1	Preferred power tactics by influence direction	
Upward influence	**Downward influence**	**Lateral influence**
Rational persuasion	Rational persuasion	Rational persuasion
	Inspirational appeals	Consultation
	Pressure	Ingratiation
	Consultation	Exchange
	Ingratiation	Legitimacy
	Exchange	Personal appeals
	Legitimacy	Coalitions

INFLUENCE TACTICS IN CHINA

Researchers usually examine cross-cultural influences in business by comparing two very different cultures, such as those from Eastern and Western societies. However, it is also important to examine differences within a given culture because those differences can sometimes be greater than differences between cultures.

For example, although we might view all Chinese people as being alike due to their shared heritage, China is a big country, housing different cultures and traditions. A recent study examining mainland Chinese, Taiwanese and Hong Kong managers explored how the three cultural subgroups differ according to the influence tactics they prefer to use.

Though managers from all three places believe that rational persuasion and exchange are the most effective influence tactics, managers in Taiwan tend to use inspirational appeals and ingratiation more than managers from either mainland China or Hong Kong. The study also found that managers from Hong Kong rate pressure as more effective in influencing others than do managers in Taiwan or mainland China. Such differences have implications for business relationships. For example, Taiwanese or mainland Chinese managers may be taken aback by the use of pressure tactics by a Hong Kong manager. Likewise, managers from Hong Kong may not be persuaded by managers from Taiwan, who tend to use ingratiating tactics. Such differences in influence tactics may make business dealings difficult. Companies should address these issues, perhaps making their managers aware of the differences within cultures.

Managers need to know what variations exist within their local cultures so they can be better prepared to deal with others. Managers who fail to realise these differences may miss out on opportunities to deal effectively with others.

Source: Based on P. P. Fu, T. K. Peng, J. C. Kennedy and G. Yukl, 'A comparison of Chinese managers in Hong Kong, Taiwan and Mainland China,' *Organizational Dynamics*, February 2004, pp. 32–46.

You're more likely to be effective if you begin with 'softer' tactics that rely on personal power such as personal and inspirational appeals, rational persuasion and consultation. If these fail, you can move to 'harder' tactics (which emphasise formal power and involve greater costs and risks), such as exchange, coalitions and pressure.[18] Interestingly, it's been found that using a single soft tactic is more effective than using a single hard tactic and that combining two soft tactics or a soft tactic and rational persuasion is more effective than any single tactic or a combination of hard tactics.[19]

political skill
The ability to influence others in such a way as to enhance one's objectives.

Recently, research has shown that people differ in their **political skill**, or the ability to influence others in such a way as to enhance their own objectives. Those who are politically skilled are more effective in their use of influence tactics, regardless of the tactics they're using. Political skill also appears to be more effective when the stakes are high – such as when the individual is accountable for important organizational outcomes. Finally, the politically skilled are able to exert their influence without others detecting it, which is a key element in being effective (it's damaging to be labelled political).[20]

Finally, we know that cultures within organizations differ markedly – for example, some are warm, relaxed and supportive; others are formal and conservative. The organizational culture in which a person works, therefore, will have a bearing on defining which tactics are considered appropriate. Some cultures encourage the use of participation and consultation, some encourage reason, and still others rely on pressure. So the organization itself will influence which subset of power tactics is viewed as acceptable for use.

Politics: Power in action

4 Distinguish between legitimate and illegitimate political behaviour.

When people get together in groups, power will be exerted. People want to carve out a niche from which to exert influence, to earn rewards, and to advance their careers.[21] When employees in organizations convert their power into action, we describe them as being engaged in politics. Those with good political skills have the ability to use their bases of power effectively.[22]

Nathalie Koulischer/Reuters

In 1999, Paul van Buitenen, formerly a European Commission auditor, blew the whistle on the commission by making public details of alleged corruption, cronyism and abuse of power. Initially suspended and ordered to face disciplinary action, eventually the entire team of 20 commissioners, headed by then president Jacques Santer, resigned in a symbolic gesture to demonstrate their commitment to cleaning up the commission's act.[23]

Definition of *organizational politics*

There has been no shortage of definitions of *organizational politics*. Essentially, however, they have focused on the use of power to affect decision making in an organization or on behaviours by members that are self-serving and organizationally nonsanctioned.[24] For our purposes, we shall define **political behaviour** in organizations as activities that are not required as part of one's formal role in the organization but that influence, or attempt to influence, the distribution of advantages and disadvantages within the organization.[25] This definition encompasses key elements from what most people mean when they talk about organizational politics. Political behaviour is outside one's specified job requirements. The behaviour requires some attempt to use one's power bases. In addition, our definition encompasses efforts to influence the goals, criteria, or processes used for *decision making* when we state that politics is concerned with 'the distribution of advantages and disadvantages within the organization'. Our definition is broad enough to include varied political behaviours such as withholding key information from decision makers, joining a coalition, whistle-blowing, spreading rumours, leaking confidential information about organizational activities to the media, exchanging favours with others in the organization for mutual benefit and lobbying on behalf of or against a particular individual or decision alternative.

A final comment relates to what has been referred to as the 'legitimate–illegitimate' dimension in political behaviour.[26] **Legitimate political behaviour** refers to normal everyday politics – complaining to your supervisor, bypassing the chain of command, forming coalitions, obstructing organizational policies or decisions through inaction or excessive adherence to rules, and developing contacts outside the organization through one's professional activities. On the other hand, there are also **illegitimate political behaviours** that violate the implied rules of the game. Illegitimate activities include sabotage, whistle-blowing and symbolic protests such as wearing unorthodox dress or protest buttons and groups of employees simultaneously calling in sick.

The vast majority of all organizational political actions are of the legitimate variety. The reasons are pragmatic: The extreme illegitimate forms of political behaviour pose a very real risk of loss of organizational membership or extreme sanctions against those who use them and then fall short in having enough power to ensure that they work.

- A survey of over 600 global managers found leaders at all levels complain that politics is one of their main challenges as they move into more senior positions. At first and mid-levels it ranks top, with almost half of first-level leaders and one-third at level 2 saying that they've been unable to address this challenge effectively.

- A survey of 490 managers found that 60 per cent believe an 'increase in political behaviour in their organization in recent years' was their greatest cause of stress. This figure rises to 77 per cent for those working in the public sector.

- When asked what the most important competencies were for Human Resource professionals, influence and political skills were chosen by 61 per cent of UK HR professionals, compared with only 25 per cent in Norway.

Sources: M. Berry, 'UK HR managers concerned with office politics and influence', *Personnel Today*, 8 December 2004; G. Pitcher, 'Office politics the biggest contributor to workplace stress', *Personnel Today*, 18 January 2007; *Leadership Transitions: Maximising HR's Contribution*, CIPD 2007.

The reality of politics

Politics is a fact of life in organizations. People who ignore this fact of life do so at their own peril. But why, you may wonder, must politics exist? Isn't it possible for an organization to be politics free? It's *possible* but unlikely.

political behaviour
Activities that are not required as part of a person's formal role in the organization but that influence, or attempt to influence, the distribution of advantages and disadvantages within the organization.

legitimate political behaviour
Normal everyday politics.

illegitimate political behaviour
Extreme political behaviour that violates the implied rules of the game.

Organizations are made up of individuals and groups with different values, goals and interests.[27] This sets up the potential for conflict over resources. Departmental budgets, space allocations, project responsibilities and salary adjustments are just a few examples of the resources about whose allocation organizational members will disagree.

Resources in organizations are also limited, which often turns potential conflict into real conflict.[28] If resources were abundant, then all the various constituencies within the organization could satisfy their goals. But because they are limited, not everyone's interests can be provided for. Furthermore, whether true or not, gains by one individual or group are often *perceived* as being at the expense of others within the organization. These forces create competition among members for the organization's limited resources.

Maybe the most important factor leading to politics within organizations is the realisation that most of the 'facts' that are used to allocate the limited resources are open to interpretation. What, for instance, is *good* performance? What's an *adequate* improvement? What constitutes an *unsatisfactory* job? One person's view that an act is a 'selfless effort to benefit the organization' is seen by another as a 'blatant attempt to further one's interest'.[29] In organizations facts can only tell us so much, there is a large and ambiguous middle ground of organizational life – where the facts *don't* speak for themselves – that politics flourish (see Exhibit 14.1).

Because most decisions have to be made in a climate of ambiguity – where facts are rarely fully objective and thus are open to interpretation – people within organizations will use whatever influence they can to taint the facts to support their goals and interests. That, of course, creates the activities we call *politicking*.

Therefore, to answer the earlier question of whether it is possible for an organization to be politics free, we can say 'yes', if all members of that organization hold the same goals and interests, if organizational resources are not scarce, and if performance outcomes are completely clear and objective. But that doesn't describe the organizational world that most of us live in.

EXHIBIT 14.1   **POLITICS IS IN THE EYE OF THE BEHOLDER**

A behaviour that one person labels as 'organizational politics' is very likely to be characterised as an instance of 'effective management' by another. The fact is not that effective management is necessarily political, although in some cases it might be. Rather, a person's reference point determines what he or she classifies as organizational politics. Take a look at the following labels used to describe the same phenomenon. These suggest that politics, like beauty, is in the eye of the beholder.

'Political' label		'Effective management' label
1. Blaming others	vs.	Fixing responsibility
2. 'Kissing up'	vs.	Developing working relationships
3. Apple polishing	vs.	Demonstrating loyalty
4. Passing the buck	vs.	Delegating authority
5. Covering your rear	vs.	Documenting decisions
6. Creating conflict	vs.	Encouraging change and innovation
7. Forming coalitions	vs.	Facilitating teamwork
8. Whistle-blowing	vs.	Improving efficiency
9. Scheming	vs.	Planning ahead
10. Overachieving	vs.	Competent and capable
11. Ambitious	vs.	Career minded
12. Opportunistic	vs.	Astute
13. Cunning	vs.	Practical minded
14. Arrogant	vs.	Confident
15. Perfectionist	vs.	Attentive to detail

Source: Based on T. C. Krell, M. E. Mendenhall and J. Sendry, 'Doing research in the conceptual morass of organisational politics', paper presented at the Western Academy of Management Conference, Hollywood, CA, April 1987.

'POWER BREEDS CONTEMPT'

MYTH *OR* SCIENCE?

This statement appears to be true. When people have power bestowed on them, they appear to be inclined to ignore the perspectives and interests of those without power, according to a recent study.[30]

Researchers made one group of participants feel powerful by asking them to recall and write about a situation in which they had power over another person. Another group of participants was instructed to recall and write about an incident in which someone had power over them. Participants in the powerful group were much more likely to ignore the perspectives of those in the less

powerful group, were less able to accurately read their emotional expressions, and were less interested in understanding how other individuals see things. The authors of this study conclude that power leads to 'the tendency to view other people only in terms of qualities that serve one's personal goals and interests, while failing to consider those features of others that define their humanity'.

So, while power has perks, it also appears to have costs – especially in terms of seeing things from the perspective of those with less of it.

Causes and consequences of political behaviour

Factors contributing to political behaviour

5 Identify the causes and consequences of political behaviour.

Not all groups or organizations are equally political. In some organizations, for instance, politicking is overt and rampant, while in others, politics plays a small role in influencing outcomes. Why is there this variation? Recent research and observation have identified a number of factors that appear to encourage political behaviour. Some are individual characteristics, derived from the unique qualities of the people the organization employs; others are a result of the organization's culture or internal environment. Figure 14.2 illustrates how both individual and organizational factors can increase political behaviour and provide favourable outcomes (increased rewards and averted punishments) for both individuals and groups in the organization.

Individual factors

At the individual level, researchers have identified certain personality traits, needs and other factors that are likely to be related to political behaviour. In terms of traits, we find that employees who are high self-monitors, possess an internal locus of control, and have a high need for power

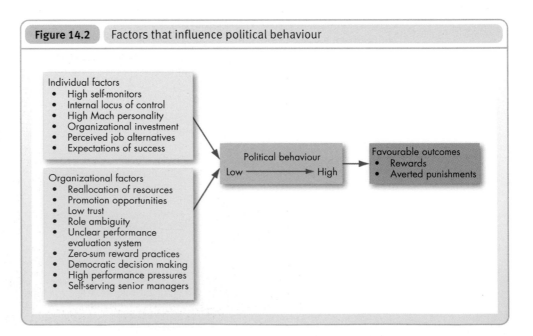

Figure 14.2   Factors that influence political behaviour

are more likely to engage in political behaviour.[31] The high self-monitor is more sensitive to social cues, exhibits higher levels of social conformity, and is more likely to be skilled in political behaviour than the low self-monitor. Individuals with an internal locus of control, because they believe they can control their environment, are more prone to take a proactive stance and attempt to manipulate situations in their favour. Not surprisingly, the Machiavellian personality – characterised by the will to manipulate and the desire for power – is comfortable using politics as a means to further his or her self-interest.

In addition, an individual's investment in the organization, perceived alternatives and expectations of success will influence the degree to which he or she will pursue illegitimate means of political action.[32] The more a person has invested in the organization in terms of expectations of increased future benefits, the more that person has to lose if forced out and the less likely he or she is to use illegitimate means. The more alternative job opportunities an individual has – due to a favourable job market or the possession of scarce skills or knowledge, a prominent reputation or influential contacts outside the organization – the more likely that individual is to risk illegitimate political actions. Finally, if an individual has a low expectation of success in using illegitimate means, it is unlikely that he or she will attempt to do so. High expectations of success in the use of illegitimate means are most likely to be the province of both experienced and powerful individuals with polished political skills and inexperienced and naive employees who misjudge their chances.

Organizational factors

Political activity is probably more a function of an organization's characteristics than of individual difference variables. Why? Because many organizations have a large number of employees with the individual characteristics we listed, yet the extent of political behaviour varies widely.

Although we acknowledge the role that individual differences can play in fostering politicking, the evidence more strongly supports the idea that certain situations and cultures promote politics. Specifically, when an organization's resources are declining, when the existing pattern

Politicking is more likely to surface when organizational resources are declining. In 2007, Deutsche Telekom announced plans to move 50,000 staff at its troubled fixed-line unit T-Com into lower-paying subsidiaries to cut costs. These actions stimulated conflict and increased politicking, such as this strike by thousands of employees.

Torsten Silz/Getty Images

of resources is changing, and when there is opportunity for promotions, politicking is more likely to surface.[33] In addition, cultures characterised by low trust, role ambiguity, unclear performance evaluation systems, zero-sum reward allocation practices, democratic decision making, high pressures for performance and self-serving senior managers will create breeding grounds for politicking.[34]

When organizations downsize to improve efficiency, reductions in resources have to be made. Threatened with the loss of resources, people may engage in political actions to safeguard what they have. But any changes, especially those that imply significant reallocation of resources within the organization, are likely to stimulate conflict and increase politicking.

Promotion decisions have consistently been found to be one of the most political actions in organizations. The opportunity for promotions or advancement encourages people to compete for a limited resource and to try to positively influence the decision outcome.

The less trust there is within the organization, the higher the level of political behaviour and the more likely that the political behaviour will be of the illegitimate kind. So high trust should suppress the level of political behaviour in general and inhibit illegitimate actions in particular.

Role ambiguity means that the prescribed behaviours of the employee are not clear. There are fewer limits, therefore, to the scope and functions of the employee's political actions. Because political activities are defined as those not required as part of one's formal role, the greater the role ambiguity, the more one can engage in political activity with little chance of it being visible.

The practice of performance evaluation is far from a perfect science. The more that organizations use subjective criteria in the appraisal, emphasise a single outcome measure, or allow significant time to pass between the time of an action and its appraisal, the greater the likelihood that an employee can get away with politicking. Subjective performance criteria create ambiguity. The use of a single outcome measure encourages individuals to do whatever is necessary to 'look good' on that measure, but often at the expense of performing well on other important parts of the job that are not being appraised. The amount of time that elapses between an action and its appraisal is also a relevant factor. The longer the time, the more unlikely that the employee will be held accountable for his political behaviours.

The more that an organization's culture emphasises the zero-sum or win/lose approach to reward allocations, the more employees will be motivated to engage in politicking. The zero-sum approach treats the reward 'pie' as fixed so that any gain one person or group achieves has to come at the expense of another person or group. If I win, you must lose! If €15,000 in annual raises is to be distributed among five employees, then any employee who gets more than €3,000 takes money away from one or more of the others. Such a practice encourages making others look bad and increasing the visibility of what you do.

In the past 25 years, there has been a general move among most developed nations toward making organizations less autocratic. Managers in these organizations are being asked to behave more democratically. They're told that they should allow employees to advise them on decisions and that they should rely to a greater extent on group input into the decision process. Such moves toward democracy, however, are not necessarily embraced by all individual managers. Many managers sought their positions in order to have legitimate power so as to be able to make unilateral decisions. They fought hard and often paid high personal costs to achieve their influential positions. Sharing their power with others runs directly against their desires. The result is that managers, especially those who began their careers in the 1960s and 1970s, may use the required committees, conferences and group meetings in a superficial way, as arenas for manoeuvring and manipulating.

The more pressure that employees feel to perform well, the more likely they are to engage in politicking. When people are held strictly accountable for outcomes, this puts great pressure on them to 'look good'. If a person perceives that their entire career is riding on next quarter's sales figures or next month's plant productivity report, there is motivation to do whatever is necessary to make sure the numbers come out favourably.

Finally, when employees see the people on top engaging in political behaviour, especially when they do so successfully and are rewarded for it, a climate is created that supports politicking. Politicking by top management, in a sense, gives permission to those lower in the organization to play politics by implying that such behaviour is acceptable.

How do people respond to organizational politics?

Trish O'Donnell loves her job as a writer on a weekly television comedy series but hates the internal politics. 'A couple of the writers here spend more time kissing up to the executive producer than doing any work. And our head writer clearly has his favourites. While they pay me a lot and I get to really use my creativity, I'm sick of having to be on alert for backstabbers and constantly having to self-promote my contributions. I'm tired of doing most of the work and getting little of the credit.' Are Trish O'Donnell's comments typical of people who work in highly politicised workplaces? We all know of friends or relatives who regularly complain about the politics at their job. But how do people in general react to organizational politics? Let's look at the evidence.

In our discussion earlier in this chapter of factors that contribute to political behaviour, we focused on the favourable outcomes for individuals who successfully engage in politicking. But for most people – who have modest political skills or are unwilling to play the politics game – outcomes tend to be predominantly negative. Figure 14.3 summarises the extensive research on the relationship between organizational politics and individual outcomes.[35] There is, for instance, very strong evidence indicating that perceptions of organizational politics are negatively related to job satisfaction.[36] The perception of politics also tends to increase job anxiety and stress. This seems to be due to the perception that, by not engaging in politics, a person may be losing ground to others who are active politickers; or, conversely, because of the additional pressures individuals feel because of having entered into and competing in the political arena.[37] Not surprisingly, when politicking becomes too much to handle, it can lead to employees quitting.[38] Finally, there is preliminary evidence suggesting that politics leads to self-reported declines in employee performance. This may occur because employees perceive political environments to be unfair, which demotivates them.[39]

In addition to these conclusions, several interesting qualifiers have been noted. First, the politics–performance relationship appears to be moderated by an individual's understanding of the 'hows' and 'whys' of organizational politics. 'An individual who has a clear understanding of who is responsible for making decisions and why they were selected to be the decision makers would have a better understanding of how and why things happen the way they do than someone who does not understand the decision-making process in the organization.'[40] When both politics and understanding are high, performance is likely to increase because the individual will see political actions as an opportunity. This is consistent with what you might expect among individuals with well-honed political skills. But when understanding is low, individuals are more

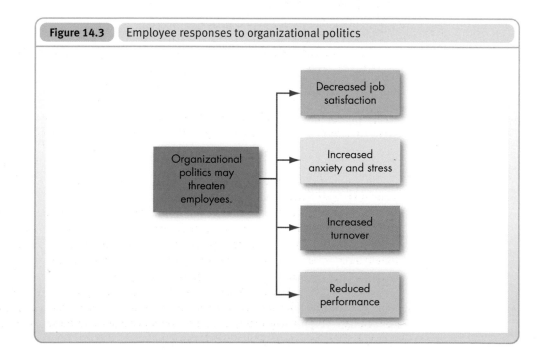

| Figure 14.3 | Employee responses to organizational politics |

EXHIBIT 14.2	DEFENSIVE BEHAVIOURS

Avoiding action

Overconforming. Strictly interpreting your responsibility by saying things like, 'The rules clearly state . . .' or 'This is the way we've always done it.'

Buck passing. Transferring responsibility for the execution of a task or decision to someone else.

Playing dumb. Avoiding an unwanted task by falsely pleading ignorance or inability.

Stretching. Prolonging a task so that one person appears to be occupied – for example, turning a two-week task into a four-month job.

Stalling. Appearing to be more or less supportive publicly while doing little or nothing privately.

Avoiding blame

Buffing. This is a nice way to refer to 'covering your rear'. It describes the practice of rigorously documenting activity to project an image of competence and thoroughness.

Playing safe. Evading situations that may reflect unfavourably. It includes taking on only projects with a high probability of success, having risky decisions approved by superiors, qualifying expressions of judgement and taking neutral positions in conflicts.

Justifying. Developing explanations that lessen one's responsibility for a negative outcome and/or apologising to demonstrate remorse.

Scapegoating. Placing the blame for a negative outcome on external factors that are not entirely blameworthy.

Misrepresenting. Manipulation of information by distortion, embellishment, deception, selective presentation or obfuscation.

Avoiding change

Prevention. Trying to prevent a threatening change from occurring.

Self-protection. Acting in ways to protect one's self-interest during change by guarding information or other resources.

---

defensive behaviours
Reactive and protective behaviours to avoid action, blame, or change.

likely to see politics as a threat, which would have a negative effect on job performance.[41] Second, when politics is seen as a threat and consistently responded to with defensiveness, negative outcomes are almost sure to surface eventually. When people perceive politics as a threat rather than as an opportunity, they often respond with **defensive behaviours** – reactive and protective behaviours to avoid action, blame, or change.[42] (Exhibit 14.2 provides some examples of these defensive behaviours.) And defensive behaviours are often associated with negative feelings toward the job and work environment.[43] In the short run, employees may find that defensiveness protects their self-interest. But in the long run, it wears them down. People who consistently rely on defensiveness find that, eventually, it is the only way they know how to behave. At that point, they lose the trust and support of their peers, bosses, employees, and clients.

Are our conclusions about responses to politics globally valid? The vast majority of research on employee reactions to organizational politics are based on studies conducted in North America. The few studies that have included other countries suggest some minor modifications.[44] One such study compared Israel and Britain and found that these substantially different cultures seem to generally respond as the North Americans do. That is, the perception of organizational politics among employees in these countries is related to decreased job satisfaction and increased turnover.[45] But in countries that are more politically unstable, such as Israel, employees seem to demonstrate greater tolerance of intense political processes in the workplace. This is likely to be because people in these countries are used to power struggles and have more experience in coping with them.[46] This suggests that people from politically turbulent countries in the Middle East or Latin America might be more accepting of organizational politics, and even more willing to use aggressive political tactics in the workplace, than people from countries such as Great Britain or Switzerland.

SELF-ASSESSMENT LIBRARY

How good am I at playing politics?

In the Self-assessment library (available, online), take assessment II.C.3 (How good am I at playing politics?).

Impression management

6 Apply impression management techniques.

We know that people have an ongoing interest in how others perceive and evaluate them. For example, Europeans spend billions of Euros on diets, health club memberships, and cosmetics – often intended to make them more attractive to others. Being perceived positively by others should have benefits for people in organizations. It might, for instance, help them initially to get the jobs they want in an organization and, once hired, to get favourable evaluations, superior salary increases and more rapid promotions. In a political context, it might help sway the distribution of advantages in their favour. The process by which individuals attempt to control the impression others form of them is called **impression management (IM)**.[47] It's a subject that has gained the attention of OB researchers only recently.[48]

> **impression management (IM)**
> The process by which individuals attempt to control the impression others form of them.

Is everyone concerned with IM? No! Who, then, might we predict to engage in IM? No surprise here. It's our old friend, the high self-monitor.[49] Low self-monitors tend to present images of themselves that are consistent with their personalities, regardless of the beneficial or detrimental effects for them. In contrast, high self-monitors are good at reading situations and moulding their appearances and behaviour to fit each situation. If you want to control the impression others form of you, what techniques can you use? Exhibit 14.3 summarises some of the most popular IM techniques and provides an example of each.

Keep in mind that IM does not imply that the impressions people convey are necessarily false (although, of course, they sometimes are).[50] Excuses, for instance, may be offered with sincerity. Referring to the example used in Exhibit 14.3, you can *actually* believe that ads contribute little to sales in your region. But misrepresentation can have a high cost. If the image claimed is false, you may be discredited.[51] If you 'cry wolf' once too often, no one is likely to believe you when the wolf really comes. So the impression manager must be cautious not to be perceived as insincere or manipulative.[52]

EXHIBIT 14.3   IMPRESSION MANAGEMENT (IM) TECHNIQUES

Conformity

Agreeing with someone else's opinion in order to gain their approval.

Example: A manager tells his boss, 'You're absolutely right on your reorganization plan for the western regional office. I couldn't agree with you more.'

Excuses

Explanations of a predicament-creating event aimed at minimising the apparent severity of the predicament.

Example: Sales manager to boss: 'We failed to get the ad in the paper on time, but no one responds to those ads anyway.'

Apologies

Admitting responsibility for an undesirable event and simultaneously seeking to get a pardon for the action.

Example: Employee to boss: 'I'm sorry I made a mistake on the report. Please forgive me.'

Self-promotion

Highlighting one's best qualities, downplaying one's deficits and calling attention to one's achievements.

Example: A salesperson tells his boss, 'Matt worked unsuccessfully for three years to try to get that account. I sewed it up in six weeks. I'm the best closer this company has.'

Flattery

Complimenting others about their virtues in an effort to make oneself appear perceptive and likeable.

Example: New sales trainee to peer: 'You handled that client's complaint so tactfully! I could never have handled that as well as you did.'

Favours

Doing something nice for someone to gain that person's approval.

Example: Salesperson to prospective client: 'I've got two tickets to the theatre tonight that I can't use. Take them. Consider it a thank-you for taking the time to talk with me.'

Association

Enhancing or protecting one's image by managing information about people and things with which one is associated.

Example: A job applicant says to an interviewer, 'What a coincidence. Your boss and I were roommates in college.'

Sources: Based on B. R. Schlenker, *Impression Management* (Monterey, CA: Brooks/Cole, 1980); W. L. Gardner and M. J. Martinko, 'Impression management in organizations', *Journal of Management*, June 1988, p. 332; and R. B. Cialdini, 'Indirect tactics of image management beyond basking', in R. A. Giacalone and P. Rosenfeld (eds), *Impression Management in the Organization* (Hillsdale, NJ: Lawrence Erlbaum, 1989), pp. 45–71.

Are there *situations* in which individuals are more likely to misrepresent themselves or more likely to get away with it? Yes – situations that are characterised by high uncertainty or ambiguity provide relatively little information for challenging a fraudulent claim and reduce the risks associated with misrepresentation.[53]

Most of the studies undertaken to test the effectiveness of IM techniques have related it to two criteria: interview success and performance evaluations. Let's consider each of these.

The evidence indicates that most job applicants use IM techniques in interviews[54] and that, when IM behaviour is used, it works.[55] In one study, for instance, interviewers felt that applicants for a position as a customer service representative who used IM techniques performed better in the interview, and they seemed somewhat more inclined to hire these people.[56] Moreover, when the researchers considered applicants' credentials, they concluded that it was the IM techniques alone that influenced the interviewers. That is, it didn't seem to matter if applicants were well or poorly qualified. If they used IM techniques, they did better in the interview.

Research indicates that some IM techniques work better than others in the interview. Researchers have compared applicants who used IM techniques that focused on promoting one's accomplishments (called *self-promotion*) to applicants who used techniques that focused on complimenting the interviewer and finding areas of agreement (referred to as *ingratiation*). In general, applicants appear to use self-promotion more than ingratiation.[57] What's more, self-promotion tactics may be more important to interviewing success. Applicants who work to create an appearance of competence by enhancing their accomplishments, taking credit for successes, and explaining away failures do better in interviews. These effects reach beyond the interview: Applicants who use more self-promotion tactics also seem to get more follow-up job-site visits, even after adjusting for grade-point average, gender and job type. Ingratiation also works well in interviews, meaning that applicants who compliment the interviewer, agree with their opinions, and emphasise areas of fit do better than those who don't.[58]

In terms of performance ratings, the picture is quite different. Ingratiation is positively related to performance ratings, meaning that those who ingratiate with their supervisors get higher performance evaluations. However, self-promotion appears to backfire: Those who self-promote actually seem to receive *lower* performance evaluations.[59] Another study of 760 boards of directors found that individuals who ingratiate themselves to current board members (express agreement with the director, point out shared attitudes and opinions, compliment the director) increase their chances of landing on a board.[60]

What explains these results? If you think about them, they make sense. Ingratiating always works because everyone – both interviewers and supervisors – likes to be treated nicely. However, self-promotion may work only in interviews and backfire on the job because whereas the interviewer has little idea whether you're being accurate about your accomplishments, the supervisor knows because it's their job to observe you. Thus, if you're going to self-promote, remember that what works in an interview will not always work once you're on the job.

The ethics of behaving politically

7 Determine whether a political action is ethical.

We conclude our discussion of politics by providing some ethical guidelines for political behaviour. Although there are no clear-cut ways to differentiate ethical from unethical politicking, there are some questions you should consider. For example, what is the utility of engaging in politicking? Sometimes we engage in political behaviours for little reason. For example, we may claim to have met famous people we haven't just to become the focus of a group conversation. Outright lies like this may be a rather extreme example of impression management, but many of us have distorted information to make a favourable impression. The point is that before we do so, one thing to keep in mind is whether it's really worth the risk. Another question to ask is an ethical one: How does the utility of engaging in the political behaviour balance out any harm (or potential harm) it will do to others? For example, complimenting a supervisor on their appearance to curry favour is probably much less harmful than grabbing credit for a project that is deserved by others.

Finally, does the political activity conform to standards of equity and justice? Sometimes it is hard to weigh the costs and benefits of a political action, but its ethicality is clear. The department head who inflates the performance evaluation of a favoured employee and deflates the evaluation of a disfavoured employee – and then uses these evaluations to justify giving the former a big raise and nothing to the latter – has treated the disfavoured employee unfairly.

Unfortunately, the answers to these questions are often argued in ways to make unethical practices seem ethical. Powerful people, for example, can become very good at explaining self-serving behaviours in terms of the organization's best interests. Similarly, they can persuasively argue that unfair actions are really fair and just. Our point is that immoral people can justify almost any behaviour. Those who are powerful, articulate and persuasive are most vulnerable because they are likely to be able to get away with unethical practices successfully. When faced with an ethical dilemma regarding organizational politics, try to consider the preceding issues (is playing politics worth the risk and will others be harmed in the process?). If you have a strong power base, recognise the ability of power to corrupt. Remember that it's a lot easier for the powerless than the powerful to act ethically, if for no other reason than they typically have very little political discretion to exploit.

Global implications

8 Show the influence of culture on the uses and perceptions of politics.

Although culture might enter any of the topics we've covered to this point, three questions are particularly important: (1) Does culture influence politics perceptions? (2) Does culture affect the power of influence tactics people prefer to use? and (3) Does culture influence the effectiveness of different tactics?

Politics perceptions

We noted earlier that when people see their work environment as political, negative consequences in their overall work attitudes and behaviours generally result. Although most of the research on politics perceptions has been conducted in the United States, studies seem to suggest that the results may be globally applicable. For example, a study suggested that politics perceptions have the same negative effects in Nigeria. When employees of two agencies in Nigeria viewed their work environments as political, they reported higher levels of job distress and were less likely to help their co-workers. Thus, although developing countries such as Nigeria are perhaps more ambiguous and more political environments in which to work, the negative consequences appear to be the same.[61]

Preference for power tactics

Evidence indicates that people in different countries tend to prefer different power tactics.[62] For instance, a study comparing managers in the United States and China found that US managers prefer rational appeal, whereas Chinese managers preferred coalition tactics.[63] These differences tend to be consistent with the values in these two countries. Reason is consistent with the US preference for direct confrontation and the use of rational persuasion to influence others and resolve differences. Similarly, coalition tactics are consistent with the Chinese preference for using indirect approaches for difficult or controversial requests. Research also has shown that individuals in Western, individualistic cultures tend to engage in more self-enhancement (such as self-promotion) behaviours than individuals in Eastern, more collectivistic cultures.[64]

Effectiveness of power tactics

Unfortunately, while we know people in different cultures seem to have different preferences for the use of power or influence tactics, there is much less evidence as to whether these tactics work better in some cultures than in others. One study of managers in US culture and three Chinese cultures (People's Republic of China, Hong Kong, Taiwan) found that US managers evaluated 'gentle persuasion' tactics such as consultation and inspirational appeal as more effective than did their Chinese counterparts.[65]

Summary and implications for managers

If you want to get things done in a group or an organization, it helps to have power. As a manager who wants to maximise your power, you will want to increase others' dependence on you. You can, for instance, increase your power in relation to your boss by developing knowledge or a skill that they need and for which they perceive no ready substitute. But power is a two-way street. You will not be alone in attempting to build your power bases. Others, particularly employees and peers, will be seeking to make you dependent on them. The result is a continual battle. While you seek to maximise others' dependence on you, you will be seeking to minimise your dependence on others. And, of course, others you work with will be trying to do the same.

Few employees relish being powerless in their job and organization. It has been argued, for instance, that when people in organizations are difficult, argumentative and temperamental, it may be because they are in positions of powerlessness; positions in which the performance expectations placed on them exceed their resources and capabilities.[66]

There is evidence that people respond differently to the various power bases.[67] Expert and referent power are derived from an individual's personal qualities. In contrast, coercion, reward, and legitimate power are essentially organizationally derived. Because people are more likely to enthusiastically accept and commit to an individual whom they admire or whose knowledge they respect (rather than someone who relies on his or her position for influence), the effective use of expert and referent power should lead to higher employee motivation, performance, commitment, and satisfaction.[68] Competence especially appears to offer wide appeal, and its use as a power base results in high performance by group members. The message for managers seems to be, 'Develop and use your expert power base!'

The power of your boss may also play a role in determining your job satisfaction. 'One of the reasons many of us like to work for and with people who are powerful is that they are generally more pleasant – not because it is their native disposition, but because the reputation and reality of being powerful permits them more discretion and more ability to delegate to others.'[69]

An effective manager accepts the political nature of organizations. By assessing behaviour in a political framework, you can better predict the actions of others and use that information to formulate political strategies that will gain advantages for you and your work unit.

Some people are significantly more 'politically astute' than others, meaning that they are aware of the underlying politics and can manage impressions. Those who are good at playing politics can be expected to get higher performance evaluations and, hence, larger salary increases and more promotions than the politically naive or inept.[70] The politically astute are also likely to exhibit higher job satisfaction and be better able to neutralise job stressors.[71] For employees with poor political skills or who are unwilling to play the politics game, the perception of organizational politics is generally related to lower job satisfaction and self-reported performance, increased anxiety and higher turnover.

POINT/COUNTERPOINT

Managing impressions is unethical

POINT ➡

Managing impressions is wrong for both ethical and practical reasons.

First, managing impressions is just another name for lying. Don't we have a responsibility, both to ourselves and to others, to present ourselves as we really are? The Australian philosopher Tony Coady wrote, 'Dishonesty has always been perceived in our culture, and in all cultures but the most bizarre, as a central human vice.' Immanuel Kant's categorical imperative asks us to consider the following: If you want to know whether telling a lie on a particular occasion is justifiable, you must try to imagine what would happen if everyone were to lie. Surely you would agree that a world in which no one lies is preferable to one in which lying is common because in such a world, we could never trust anyone. Thus, we should try to present the truth as best we can. Impression management goes against this virtue.

Practically speaking, impression management generally backfires in the long run. Remember Sir Walter Scott's quote, 'Oh what a tangled web we weave, when first we practise to deceive!' Once we start to distort the facts, where do we stop? One of the world's leading hotel executives was forced to resign with immediate effect from InterContinental Hotels Group (IHG) after being confronted about misleading claims he had made about his academic qualifications when he joined the business. The shock departure of Patrick Imbardelli came just five weeks after IHG announced he was to be promoted to the board in recognition of his fast-growing division's importance within the multinational group.[72]

People are most satisfied with their jobs when their values match the culture of the organizations. If either side misrepresents itself in the interview process, then odds are, people won't fit in the organizations they choose. What's the benefit in this?

This doesn't imply that a person shouldn't put their best foot forward. But that means exhibiting qualities that are good no matter the context – being friendly, being positive and self-confident, being qualified and competent, while still being honest.

COUNTERPOINT ⬅

Oh, come on. Get off your high horse. *Everybody* fudges to some degree in the process of applying for a job. One British survey of 3,000 curriculum vitae's found two-third's of them contained inaccuracies.[73] If you really told the interviewer what your greatest weakness or worst mistake was, you'd never get hired. What if you answered, 'I find it hard to get up in the morning and get to work'?

These sorts of 'white lies' are expected and act as a kind of social lubricant. If we really knew what people were thinking, we'd go crazy. Moreover, you can quote all the philosophy you want, but sometimes it's necessary to lie. You mean you wouldn't lie to save the life of your family? It's naive to think we can live in a world without lying.

Sometimes a bit of deception is necessary to get a job. I know a gay applicant who was rejected from a job he really wanted because he told the interviewer he had written two articles for gay magazines. What if he had told the interviewer a little lie? Would harm really have been done? At least he'd have a job.

As another example, when an interviewer asks you what you earned on your previous job, that information will be used against you, to pay you a salary lower than you deserve. Is it wrong to boost your salary a bit? Or would it be better to disclose your actual salary and be taken advantage of?

The same goes for complimenting interviewers, agreeing with their opinions, and so forth. If an interviewer tells you, 'We believe in community involvement,' are you supposed to tell the interviewer you've never volunteered for anything?

Of course you can go too far. We're not advocating that people totally fabricate their backgrounds. What we are talking about here is a reasonable amount of enhancement. If we can help ourselves without doing any real harm, then impression management is not the same as lying and actually is something we should teach others.

QUESTIONS FOR REVIEW

1. How would you define *power*? How is it different from leadership?

2. What are the five bases of power?

3. What are the nine power or influence tactics?

4. What is political behaviour and how would you distinguish between legitimate and illegitimate political behaviour?

5. What are the causes and consequences of political behaviour?

6. What is impression management and what are the techniques for managing impressions?

7. How can one determine whether a political action is ethical?

8. How does culture influence politics perceptions, preferences for different power or influence tactics and the effectiveness of those tactics?

Experiential exercise

UNDERSTANDING POWER DYNAMICS

Create groups

Each student is to turn in a Euro (or similar value of currency) to the instructor, and students are then divided into three groups, based on criteria given by the instructor, assigned to their workplaces and instructed to read the following rules and tasks. The money is divided into thirds, and two-thirds of it is given to the top group, one-third to the middle group and none to the bottom group.

Conduct exercise

Groups go to their assigned workplaces and have 30 minutes to complete their tasks.

Rules

Members of the top group are free to enter the space of either of the other groups and to communicate whatever they wish, whenever they wish. Members of the middle group may enter the space of the lower group when they wish but must request permission to enter the top group's space (which the top group can refuse). Members of the lower group may not disturb the top group in any way unless specifically invited by the top. The lower group does have the right to knock on the door of the middle group and request permission to communicate with them (which can also be refused).

The members of the top group have the authority to make any change in the rules that they wish, at any time, with or without notice.

Tasks

- **Top group.** To be responsible for the overall effectiveness and learning from the exercise and to decide how to use its money.
- **Middle group.** To assist the top group in providing for the overall welfare of the organization and to decide how to use its money.
- **Bottom group.** To identify its resources and to decide how best to provide for learning and the overall effectiveness of the organization.

Debriefing

Each of the three groups chooses two representatives to go to the front of the class and discuss the following:

1. Summarise what occurred within and among the three groups.
2. What are some of the differences between being in the top group and being in the bottom group?
3. What can we learn about power from this experience?
4. How accurate do you think this exercise is in reflecting the reality of resource allocation decisions in large organizations?

Source: Adapted from L. Bolman and T. E. Deal, *Exchange: The Organizational Behaviour Teaching Journal*, 3, 4 (1979), pp. 38–42. Copyright 1979 Sage Publications, Inc. Journals.

Ethical dilemma

SURVIVING IN TOUGH TIMES

A recent survey revealed IT staff are so desperate to keep their jobs they would resort to haggling, bribery and blackmail. *The Global Recession and its Effect on Work Ethics* survey found that nearly half said they would use their security clearance to find redundancy lists or bribe a friend to do it for them if they feared for their job, and one in 10 said they would consider blackmailing their boss to keep their job.

Adam Bosnian from the company who conducted the survey, Cyber-Ark, warned HR departments to reassess security clearance and access to important documents. 'Employers have a

right to expect loyalty from their workforce, but this works both ways. In these dark days, when everyone is jittery, especially with layoffs at the top of most corporate agendas, the instinct is to look out for number one,' said Bosnian.

When times get tough, such as in a recession, is it more acceptable to be unethical? Do you think people get more political during in these times?

Source: Based on G. Logan, 'IT staff would resort to haggling, bribery and blackmail to keep jobs', *Personnel Today*, 3 December 2008.

CASE INCIDENT 1

'I don't want to fight anymore'

Christiane Kolbus changed her outlook as she moved up through the ranks to a bank executive position. She decided not to fight for her career anymore. In tradition-bound Germany, bucking the tide can be tough. Or so Christiane Kolbus discovered as she tried to build her professional and personal lives simultaneously. She chose to enter one of the country's most profoundly male-dominated industries: banking. And she decided to marry an unemployed machinist, who remained at home and restored antiques while she went out to earn the family's bread.

But things didn't work out the way that Kolbus had anticipated. After beginning her professional career as a Commerzbank trainee in Bremen, she rose quickly through the ranks to become chief of all the bank training programmes in her corporate region. Working long hours and travelling more than three months out of the year, she couldn't even contemplate having children. Slowly, as time went on and her career at the bank developed, she and her husband grew apart from each other. 'We developed in two different directions,' she says. A decade later, when the bank transferred her to Leipzig to develop training programmes for Commerzbank in eastern Germany, Kolbus left her husband behind.

Office politics also had a major influence on her career at Commerzbank. 'The higher up you go, the more political it gets,' she says. 'And the less honest you can be.' Now assistant general manager of training in the Saxony-Anhalt region, Kolbus recently quit Commerzbank's highly

coveted executive-training programme, which grooms selected bank employees for senior management positions. 'I don't want to fight anymore. It takes a lot longer to change things than I thought,' she now admits.

No longer driven and soured by office politics, Kolbus says she now derives much of her satisfaction from friendships, skiing, yoga and motorcycle riding, among other activities. She has decided to remain childless. 'I'm reconciled to the idea of growing old without children. It's no longer necessary for me to depend on other people to be fulfilled,' she says. Still, it's a far cry from the home and work life she envisioned just a decade ago.

Questions

1. Do you think a person's home life contributes to their political behaviours? Does it affect how others will seek to influence them?

2. What type of political behaviours do you think Kolbus needed to engage with to further her career?

3. Kolbus became disillusioned with the constant politics and decided not to fight anymore. Is it possible to 'opt out' of office politics?

4. Do you think Kolbus is correct when she says 'The higher up you go, the more political it gets and the less honest you can be.'?

Source: L. Bernier, 'I don't want to fight anymore', *BusinessWeek*, 15 April 1996, p. 93.

CASE INCIDENT 2

The politics of backstabbing

Scott Rosen believed that he was making progress as an assistant manager of a financial services company – until he noticed that his colleague, another assistant manager, was attempting to push him aside. On repeated occasions, Rosen would observe his colleague speaking with their manager behind closed doors. During these conversations, Rosen's colleague would attempt to persuade the supervisor that Rosen was incompetent and mismanaging his job, a practice that Mr Rosen found out after the fact. Rosen recounts one specific instance of his colleague's backstabbing efforts: When a subordinate asked Rosen a question to which Rosen did not know the answer, his colleague would say to their supervisor, 'I can't believe he didn't know something like that.' On other occasions, after instructing a subordinate to complete a specific task, Rosen's colleague would say, 'I wouldn't make you do something like that.' What was the end result of such illegitimate political tactics? Rosen was demoted, an action that led him to resign shortly after, while his colleague was promoted. 'Whatever I did, I lost,' recounts Rosen.

What leads individuals to behave this way? According to Judith Briles, a management consultant who has extensively studied the practice of backstabbing, a tight job market is often a contributing factor. Fred Nader, another management consultant, believes that backstabbing is the result of 'some kind of character disorder'.

One executive at a technology company admits that blind ambition was responsible for the backstabbing he did. In 1999, he was assigned as an external sales representative, partnered with a colleague who worked internally at their client's office. The executive wanted the internal sales position for himself. To reach this goal, he systematically engaged in backstabbing to shatter his colleague's credibility. Each time he heard a complaint, however small, from the client, he would ask for it in an e-mail and then forward the information to his boss. He'd include a short message about his colleague, such as: 'I'm powerless to deal with this. She's not being responsive and the customer is beating on me.' In addition, he would fail to share important information with her before presentations with their boss, to convey the impression that she did not know what she was talking about. He even went so far as to schedule meetings with their boss on an electronic calendar but then altered her version so that she was late.

Eventually, he convinced his boss that she was overworked. He was transferred to the client's office, while his colleague was moved back to the main office.

Incidents such as these may not be uncommon in the workplace. Given today's competitive work environment, employees may be using political games to move ahead. To guard against backstabbing, Bob McDonald, a management consultant, recommends telling supervisors and other key personnel that the backstabber is not a friend. He states that this may be effective because backstabbers often claim to be friends of their victims and then act as if they are hesitant about sharing negative information with others because of this professed friendship. In any event, it is clear that employees in organizations need to be aware of illegitimate political behaviour. Companies may need to adopt formal policies to safeguard employees against such behaviour; however, it may be the case that behaviours such as backstabbing and spreading negative rumours are difficult to detect. Thus, both employees and managers should try to verify information to avoid the negative repercussions that can come from backstabbing and other illegitimate behaviours.

Questions

1. What factors, in addition to those cited here, do you believe lead to illegitimate political behaviours such as backstabbing?

2. Imagine that a colleague is engaging in illegitimate political behaviour toward you. What steps might you take to reduce or eliminate this behaviour?

3. Do you believe that it is ever justifiable to engage in illegitimate political behaviours such as backstabbing? If so, what are some conditions that might justify such behaviour?

4. In addition to the obvious negative effects of illegitimate political behaviour on victims, such as those described in this case, what might be some negative effects on the perpetrators? on the organization as a whole?

Source: Based on J. Sandberg, 'Sabotage 101: the sinister art of backstabbing', *Wall Street Journal*, 11 February 2004, p. B1.

Endnotes

1 R. M. Kanter, 'Power failure in management circuits', *Harvard Business Review*, July–August 1979, p. 65.

2 J. Pfeffer, 'Understanding power in organizations', *California Management Review*, Winter 1992, p. 35.

3 Based on B. M. Bass, *Bass & Stogdill's Handbook of Leadership*, 3rd edn (New York: The Free Press, 1990).

4 J. R. P. French, Jr. and B. Raven, 'The bases of social power', in D. Cartwright (ed.), *Studies in Social Power* (Ann Arbor, MI: University of Michigan, Institute for Social Research, 1959), pp. 150–67; B. J. Raven, 'The bases of power: origins and recent developments', *Journal of Social Issues*, Winter 1993, pp. 227–51; and G. Yukl, 'Use power effectively,' in E. A. Locke (ed.), *Handbook of Principles of Organizational Behavior* (Malden, MA: Blackwell, 2004), pp. 242–47.

5 E. A. Ward, 'Social power bases of managers: emergence of a new factor', *Journal of Social Psychology*, February 2001, pp. 144–47.

6 P. M. Podsakoff and C. A. Schriesheim, 'Field studies of French and Raven's bases of power: critique, reanalysis, and suggestions for future research', *Psychological Bulletin*, May 1985, pp. 387–411; T. R. Hinkin and C. A. Schriesheim, 'Development and application of new scales to measure the French and Raven (1959) bases of social power', *Journal of Applied Psychology*, August 1989, pp. 561–67; and P. P. Carson, K. D. Carson and C. W. Roe, 'Social power bases: a meta-analytic examination of interrelationships and outcomes', *Journal of Applied Social Psychology*, 23, 14 (1993), pp. 1150–69.

7 J. L. Roberts, 'Striking a hot match', *Newsweek*, 24 January 2005, pp. 54–55.

8 R. E. Emerson, 'Power–dependence relations', *American Sociological Review*, February 1962, pp. 31–41.

9 H. Mintzberg, *Power In and Around Organizations* (Upper Saddle River, NJ: Prentice-Hall, 1983), p. 24.

10 R. M. Cyert and J. G. March, *A Behavioral Theory of the Firm* (Upper Saddle River, NJ: Prentice-Hall, 1963).

11 C. Perrow, 'Departmental power and perspective in industrial firms', in M. N. Zald (ed.), *Power in Organizations* (Nashville, TN: Vanderbilt University Press, 1970).

12 N. Foulkes, 'Tractor boy', *High Life*, October 2002, p. 90.

13 See, for example, D. Kipnis and S. M. Schmidt, 'Upward-influence styles: relationship with performance evaluations, salary, and stress', *Administrative Science Quarterly*, December 1988, pp. 528–42; G. Yukl and J. B. Tracey, 'Consequences of influence tactics used with subordinates, peers, and the boss', *Journal of Applied Psychology*, August 1992, pp. 525–35; G. Blickle, 'Influence tactics used by subordinates: an empirical analysis of the Kipnis and Schmidt subscales', *Psychological Reports*, February 2000, pp. 143–54; and Yukl, 'Use power effectively,' pp. 249–52.

14 G. Yukl, *Leadership in Organizations*, 5th edn (Upper Saddle River, NJ: Prentice-Hall, 2002), pp. 141–74; G. R. Ferris, W. A. Hochwarter, C. Douglas, F. R. Blass, R. W. Kolodinksy and D. C. Treadway, 'Social influence processes in organizations and human resource systems', in G. R. Ferris and J. J. Martocchio (eds), *Research in Personnel and Human Resources Management*, vol. 21 (Oxford, UK: JAI Press/Elsevier, 2003), pp. 65–127; and C. A. Higgins, T. A. Judge and G. R. Ferris, 'Influence tactics and work outcomes: a meta-analysis', *Journal of Organizational Behavior*, March 2003, pp. 89–106.

15 C. M. Falbe and G. Yukl, 'Consequences for managers of using single influence tactics and combinations of tactics', *Academy of Management Journal*, July 1992, pp. 638–53.

16 J. Badal, 'Getting a raise from the boss', *Wall Street Journal*, 8 July 2006, pp. B1, B5.

17 Yukl, *Leadership in Organizations*.

18 Ibid.

19 Falbe and Yukl, 'Consequences for managers of using single influence tactics and combinations of tactics'.

20 G. R. Ferris, D. C. Treadway, P. L. Perrewé, R. L. Brouer, C. Douglas and S. Lux, 'Political skill in organizations', *Journal of Management*, June 2007, pp. 290–320; K. J. Harris, K. M. Kacmar, S. Zivnuska and J. D. Shaw, 'The impact of political skill on impression management effectiveness', *Journal of Applied Psychology*, 92, 1 (2007), pp. 278–85; W. A. Hochwarter, G. R. Ferris, M. B. Gavin, P. L. Perrewé, A. T. Hall and D. D. Frink, 'Political skill as neutralizer of felt accountability–job tension effects on job performance ratings: a longitudinal investigation', *Organizational Behavior and Human Decision Processes*, 102 (2007), pp. 226–39; D. C. Treadway, G. R. Ferris, A. B. Duke, G. L. Adams and J. B. Tatcher, 'The moderating role of subordinate political skill on supervisors' impressions of subordinate ingratiation and ratings of subordinate interpersonal facilitation', *Journal of Applied Psychology*, 92, 3 (2007), pp. 848–55.

21 S. A. Culbert and J. J. McDonough, *The Invisible War: Pursuing Self-Interest at Work* (New York: Wiley, 1980), p. 6.

22 Mintzberg, *Power In and Around Organizations*, p. 26. See also K. M. Kacmar and R. A. Baron, 'Organizational politics: the state of the field, links to related processes, and an agenda for future research', in G. R. Ferris (ed.), *Research in Personnel and Human Resources Management*, vol. 17 (Greenwich, CT: JAI Press, 1999), pp. 1–39; and G. R. Ferris, D. C. Treadway, R. W. Kolokinsky, W. A. Hochwarter, C. J. Kacmar and D. D. Frink, 'Development and validation of the political skill inventory', *Journal of Management*, February 2005, pp. 126–52.

23 BBC News, 'Brussels whistleblower quits in despair', Tuesday, 27 August 2002. Available at http://news.bbc.co.uk/1/hi/world/europe/2219114.stm. Accessed 12 February 2009.

24 S. B. Bacharach and E. J. Lawler, 'Political alignments in organizations', in R. M. Kramer and M. A. Neale (eds), *Power and Influence in Organizations* (Thousand Oaks, CA: Sage Publications, 1998), pp. 68–69.

25 D. Farrell and J. C. Petersen, 'Patterns of political behavior in organizations', *Academy of Management Review*, July 1982, p. 405. For analyses of the controversies underlying the definition of organizational politics, see A. Drory and T. Romm, 'The definition of organizational politics: a review', *Human Relations*, November 1990, pp. 1133–54; and R. S. Cropanzano, K. M. Kacmar and D. P. Bozeman, 'Organizational politics, justice, and support: their differences and similarities', in R. S. Cropanzano and K. M. Kacmar (eds), *Organizational Politics, Justice and Support: Managing Social Climate at Work* (Westport, CT: Quorum Books, 1995), pp. 1–18.

26 Farrell and Peterson, 'Patterns of political behavior in organizations', pp. 406–7; and A. Drory, 'Politics in organization and its perception within the organization', *Organization Studies*, 9, 2 (1988), pp. 165–79.

27 J. Pfeffer, *Power in Organizations* (New York: HarperCollins, 1981).

28 Drory and Romm, 'The definition of organizational politics'.

29 S. M. Rioux and L. A. Penner, 'The causes of organizational citizenship behavior: a motivational analysis', *Journal of Applied Psychology*, December 2001, pp. 1306–14; and M. A. Finkelstein and L. A. Penner, 'Predicting organizational citizenship behavior: integrating the functional and role identity approaches', *Social Behavior & Personality*, 32, 4 (2004), pp. 383–98.

30 A. D. Galinsky, J. C. Magee, M. E. Inesi and D. H. Gruenfeld, 'Power and perspectives not taken', *Psychological Science*, December 2006, pp. 1068–74.

31 See, for example, G. R. Ferris, G. S. Russ and P. M. Fandt, 'Politics in organizations', in R. A. Giacalone and P. Rosenfeld

(eds), *Impression Management in the Organization* (Hillsdale, NJ: Lawrence Erlbaum, 1989), pp. 155–56; and W. E. O'Connor and T. G. Morrison, 'A comparison of situational and dispositional predictors of perceptions of organizational politics', *Journal of Psychology*, May 2001, pp. 301–12.

32 Farrell and Petersen, 'Patterns of political behavior in organizations,' p. 408.

33 G. R. Ferris and K. M. Kacmar, 'Perceptions of organizational politics,' *Journal of Management*, March 1992, pp. 93–116.

34 See, for example, P. M. Fandt and G. R. Ferris, 'The management of information and impressions: when employees behave opportunistically', *Organizational Behavior and Human Decision Processes*, February 1990, pp. 140–58; Ferris, Russ and Fandt, 'Politics in organizations', p. 147; and J. M. L. Poon, 'Situational antecedents and outcomes of organizational politics perceptions', *Journal of Managerial Psychology*, 18, 2 (2003), pp. 138–55.

35 Ferris, Russ and Fandt, 'Politics in organizations'; and K. M. Kacmar, D. P. Bozeman, D. S. Carlson and W. P. Anthony, 'An examination of the perceptions of organizational politics model: replication and extension', *Human Relations*, March 1999, pp. 383–416.

36 W. A. Hochwarter, C. Kiewitz, S. L. Castro, P. L. Perrewé and G. R. Ferris, 'Positive affectivity and collective efficacy as moderators of the relationship between perceived politics and job satisfaction', *Journal of Applied Social Psychology*, May 2003, pp. 1009–35; C. C. Rosen, P. E. Levy and R. J. Hall, 'Placing perceptions of politics in the context of feedback environment, employee attitudes, and job performance', *Journal of Applied Psychology*, 91, 1 (2006), pp. 211–30.

37 G. R. Ferris, D. D. Frink, M. C. Galang, J. Zhou, K. M. Kacmar and J. L. Howard, 'Perceptions of organizational politics: prediction, stress-related implications, and outcomes', *Human Relations*, February 1996, pp. 233–66; E. Vigoda, 'Stress-related aftermaths to workplace politics: the relationships among politics, job distress, and aggressive behavior in organizations', *Journal of Organizational Behavior*, August 2002, pp. 571–91.

38 C. Kiewitz, W. A. Hochwarter, G. R. Ferris and S. L. Castro, 'The role of psychological climate in neutralizing the effects of organizational politics on work outcomes', *Journal of Applied Social Psychology*, June 2002, pp. 1189–207; and M. C. Andrews, L. A. Witt and K. M. Kacmar, 'The interactive effects of organizational politics and exchange ideology on manager ratings of retention', *Journal of Vocational Behavior*, April 2003, pp. 357–69.

39 S. Aryee, Z. Chen and P. S. Budhwar, 'Exchange fairness and employee performance: an examination of the relationship between organizational politics and procedural justice', *Organizational Behavior & Human Decision Processes*, May 2004, pp. 1–14; and K. L. Kacmar, D. P. Bozeman, D. S. Carlson and W. P. Anthony, 'An examination of the perceptions of organizational politics model: replication and extension', *Human Relations*, 52, pp. 383–416.

40 Kacmar, Bozeman, Carlson and Anthony 'An examination of the perceptions of organizational politics model', p. 389.

41 Ibid., p. 409.

42 B. E. Ashforth and R. T. Lee, 'Defensive behavior in organizations: a preliminary model', *Human Relations*, July 1990, pp. 621–48.

43 M. Valle and P. L. Perrewé, 'Do politics perceptions relate to political behaviors? Tests of an implicit assumption and expanded model', *Human Relations*, March 2000, pp. 359–86.

44 See T. Romm and A. Drory, 'Political behavior in organizations: a cross-cultural comparison,' *International Journal of Value Based Management*, 1 (1988), pp. 97–113; and E. Vigoda, 'Reactions to organizational politics: a cross-cultural examination in Israel and Britain,' *Human Relations*, November 2001, pp. 1483–518.

45 E. Vigoda (2001) 'Reactions to organizational politics: a cross-cultural examination in Israel and Britain', *Human Relations*, 54, 11; p. 1483.

46 Ibid., p. 1510.

47 M. R. Leary and R. M. Kowalski, 'Impression management: a literature review and two-component model', *Psychological Bulletin*, January 1990, pp. 34–47.

48 See, for instance, B. R. Schlenker, *Impression Management: The Self-Concept, Social Identity, and Interpersonal Relations* (Monterey, CA: Brooks/Cole, 1980); W. L. Gardner and M. J. Martinko, 'Impression management in organizations', *Journal of Management*, June 1988, pp. 321–38; D. P. Bozeman and K. M. Kacmar, 'A cybernetic model of impression management processes in organizations', *Organizational Behavior and Human Decision Processes*, January 1997, pp. 9–30; M. C. Bolino and W. H. Turnley, 'More than one way to make an impression: exploring profiles of impression management', *Journal of Management*, 29, 2 (2003), pp. 141–60; S. Zivnuska, K. M. Kacmar, L. A. Witt, D. S. Carlson and V. K. Bratton, 'Interactive effects of impression management and organizational politics on job performance', *Journal of Organizational Behavior*, August 2004, pp. 627–40; and W.-C. Tsai, C.-C. Chen and S.-F. Chiu, 'Exploring boundaries of the effects of applicant impression management tactics in job interviews', *Journal of Management*, February 2005, pp. 108–25.

49 M. Snyder and J. Copeland, 'Self-monitoring processes in organizational settings', in R. A. Giacalone and P. Rosenfeld (eds), *Impression Management in the Organization* (Hillsdale, NJ: Lawrence Erlbaum, 1989), p. 11; A. Montagliani and R. A. Giacalone, 'Impression management and cross-cultural adaptation', *Journal of Social Psychology*, October 1998, pp. 598–608; and W. H. Turnley and M. C. Bolino, 'Achieved desired images while avoiding undesired images: exploring the role of self-monitoring in impression management', *Journal of Applied Psychology*, April 2001, pp. 351–60.

50 Leary and Kowalski, 'Impression management', p. 40.

51 Gardner and Martinko, 'Impression management in organizations', p. 333.

52 R. A. Baron, 'Impression management by applicants during employment interviews: the "too much of a good thing" effect', in R. W. Eder and G. R. Ferris (eds), *The Employment Interview: Theory, Research, and Practice* (Newbury Park, CA: Sage Publishers, 1989), pp. 204–15.

53 Ferris, Russ and Fandt, 'Politics in organizations'.

54 A. P. J. Ellis, B. J. West, A. M. Ryan and R. P. DeShon, 'The use of impression management tactics in structural interviews: a function of question type?', *Journal of Applied Psychology*, December 2002, pp. 1200–08.

55 Baron, 'Impression management by applicants during employment interviews'; D. C. Gilmore and G. R. Ferris, 'The effects of applicant impression management tactics on interviewer judgments', *Journal of Management*, December

1989, pp. 557–64; C. K. Stevens and A. L. Kristof, 'Making the right impression: a field study of applicant impression management during job interviews', journal, date, p. xx; and L. A. McFarland, A. M. Ryan and S. D. Kriska, 'Impression management use and effectiveness across assessment methods', *Journal of Management*, 29, 5 (2003), pp. 641–61; and Tsai, Chen and Chiu, 'Exploring boundaries of the effects of applicant impression management tactics in job interviews'.

56 Gilmore and Ferris, 'The effects of applicant impression management tactics on interviewer judgments'.

57 Stevens and Kristof, 'Making the right impression: a field study of applicant impression management during job interviews'.

58 C. A. Higgins, T. A. Judge and G. R. Ferris, 'Influence tactics and work outcomes: a meta-analysis', *Journal of Organizational Behavior*, March 2003, pp. 89–106.

59 Ibid.

60 J. D. Westphal and I. Stern, 'Flattery will get you everywhere (especially if you are a male caucasian): how ingratiation, boardroom behavior, and demographic minority status affect additional board appointments of U.S. companies', *Academy of Management Journal*, 50, 2 (2007), pp. 267–88.

61 O. J. Labedo, 'Perceptions of organizational politics: examination of the situational antecedent and consequences among Nigeria's extension personnel', *Applied Psychology: An International Review*, 55, 2 (2006), pp. 255–81.

62 P. P. Fu and G. Yukl, 'Perceived effectiveness of influence tactics in the United States and China', *Leadership Quarterly*, Summer 2000, pp. 251–66; O. Branzei, 'Cultural explanations of individual preferences for influence tactics in cross-cultural encounters', *International Journal of Cross Cultural Management*, August 2002, pp. 203–18; G. Yukl, P. P. Fu and R. McDonald, 'Cross-cultural differences in perceived effectiveness of influence tactics for initiating or resisting change', *Applied Psychology: An International Review*, January 2003, pp. 66–82; and P. P. Fu, T. K. Peng, J. C. Kennedy and G. Yukl, 'Examining the preferences of influence tactics in Chinese societies: a comparison of Chinese managers in Hong Kong, Taiwan, and mainland China', *Organizational Dynamics*, 33, 1 (2004), pp. 32–46.

63 Fu and Yukl, 'Perceived effectiveness of influence tactics in the United States and China.'

64 S. J. Heine, 'Making sense of East Asian self-enhancement', *Journal of Cross-Cultural Psychology*, September 2003, pp. 596–602.

65 J. L. T. Leong, M. H. Bond and P. P. Fu, 'Perceived effectiveness of influence strategies in the United States and three Chinese societies', *International Journal of Cross Cultural Management*, May 2006, pp. 101–20.

66 R. M. Kanter, *Men and Women of the Corporation* (New York: Basic Books, 1977).

67 See, for instance, Falbe and Yukl, 'Consequences for managers of using single influence tactics and combinations of tactics'.

68 See J. G. Bachman, D. G. Bowers and P. M. Marcus, 'Bases of supervisory power: a comparative study in five organizational settings', in A. S. Tannenbaum (ed.), *Control in Organizations* (New York: McGraw-Hill, 1968), p. 236; M. A. Rahim, 'Relationships of leader power to compliance and satisfaction with supervision: evidence from a national sample of managers', *Journal of Management*, December 1989, pp. 545–56; P. A. Wilson, 'The effects of politics and power on the organizational commitment of federal executives', *Journal of Management*, Spring 1995, pp. 101–18; and A. R. Elangovan and J. L. Xie, 'Effects of perceived power of supervisor on subordinate stress and motivation: the moderating role of subordinate characteristics', *Journal of Organizational Behavior*, May 1999, pp. 359–73.

69 J. Pfeffer, *Managing with Power: Politics and Influence in Organizations* (Boston, MA: Harvard Business School Press, 1992), p. 137.

70 G. R. Ferris, P. L. Perrewé, W. P. Anthony and D. C. Gilmore, 'Political skill at work', *Organizational Dynamics*, Spring 2000, pp. 25–37; K. K. Ahearn, G. R. Ferris, W. A. Hochwarter, C. Douglas and A. P. Ammeter, 'Leader political skill and team performance', *Journal of Management*, 30, 3 (2004), pp. 309–27; and S. E. Seibert, M. L. Kraimer and J. M. Crant, 'What do proactive people do? A longitudinal model linking proactive personality and career success', *Personnel Psychology*, Winter 2001, pp. 845–74.

71 R. W. Kolodinsky, W. A. Hochwarter and G. R. Ferris, 'Nonlinearity in the relationship between political skill and work outcomes: convergent evidence from three studies', *Journal of Vocational Behavior*, October 2004, pp. 294–308; W. Hochwarter, 'The interactive effects of pro-political behavior and politics perceptions on job satisfaction and affective commitment', *Journal of Applied Social Psychology*, July 2003, pp. 1360–78; and P. L. Perrewé, K. L. Zellars, G. R. Ferris, A. Rossi, C. J. Kacmar and D. A. Ralston, 'Neutralizing job stressors: political skill as an antidote to the dysfunctional consequences of role conflict', *Academy of Management Journal*, February 2004, pp. 141–52.

72 S. Bowers and G. Wearden, 'Hotels boss quits after lying on CV', *The Guardian*, Friday 15 June 2007.

73 'CV fibbers warning for employers', BBC News, Friday 14 May 2004. Available at http://news.bbc.co.uk/1/hi/business/3711431.stm. Accessed 15 February 2009.

Conflict and negotiation

Learning Objectives

After studying this chapter, you should be able to:

1 Define *conflict*.

2 Differentiate between the traditional, human relations and interactionist views of conflict.

3 Outline the conflict process.

4 Define *negotiation*.

5 Contrast distributive and integrative bargaining.

6 Apply the five steps of the negotiation process.

7 Show how individual differences influence negotiations.

8 Assess the roles and functions of third-party negotiations.

9 Describe cultural differences in conflict and negotiation.

Truth springs from arguments amongst friends.

David Hume

Easily offended?

UpperCut Images/Alamy

The following is an extract of an interview from a local government employee talking about a situation when a new temporary member of staff started work in the interviewee's office. At the time, another team member, called Anna, was on annual leave.

> *I think one particular day I just sort of said to her, 'I prefer it if you didn't sit at that desk because that's Anna's desk and she's a bit funny about people using her desk.' I said, 'if you could sit at your own desk'. Anyhow she must have really taken offence to it. The next time I had my supervision [appraisal by line manager], fine, brilliant, no problem but then my line manager's manager came in at the end and said that somebody had expressed the opinion that they thought I was bullying. She filled me in on what it was about and I said, 'I asked her not to sit at that desk because I know that that person is quite protective of her own environment.' I said I wasn't really nasty about it at all but she said, 'Well we've had it reported and we've got to mention it to you.'*

The complainant was then prepared to accept an apology and so an apology was made. The interviewee goes on to describe the impact of the situation following this.

> *After that, because of what had been said previously, I was really really paranoid about saying anything that might offend. When I had the next supervision [appraisal], it was mentioned that I was very quiet and I wasn't talking to anybody, I wasn't being part of the team and I said, 'I really do feel uncomfortable.' I was disappointed that my line manager felt that she'd had to bring her line manager in to tell me something like that when really, if she had raised the matter with me I'd have just apologised for what I said.*

This situation continued with a bad atmosphere in the office for the next two or three months.

Source: Based on *Managing Conflict at Work: A Guide for Line Managers*, CIPD 2008.

Often when we consider conflict we think of major arguments, threats and even physical violence. As we see in the opening vignette, conflict is often not so dramatic. It can be created over seemingly very small issues and yet still have lasting effects. At its worst, it can create chaotic conditions that make it nearly impossible for employees to work as a team. However, conflict also has a less-well-known positive side. We'll explain the difference between negative and positive conflicts in this chapter and provide a guide to help you understand how conflicts develop. We'll also present a topic closely akin to conflict: negotiation. But first, gauge how you handle conflict by taking the following self-assessment.

SELF-ASSESSMENT LIBRARY

What's my preferred conflict-handling style?

In the Self-assessment library (available online), take assessment II.C.5 (What's my preferred conflict-handling style?) and answer the following questions.

1. Judging from your highest score, what's your primary conflict-handling style?

2. Do you think your style varies, depending on the situation?

3. Would you like to change any aspects of your conflict-handling style?

A definition of *conflict*

1 Define *conflict*.

There has been no shortage of definitions of *conflict*.[1] Despite the divergent meanings the term has acquired, several common themes underlie most definitions. Conflict must be perceived by the parties to it; whether or not conflict exists is a perception issue. If no one is aware of a conflict, then it is generally agreed that no conflict exists. Additional commonalities in the definitions are opposition or incompatibility and some form of interaction.[2] These factors set the conditions that determine the beginning point of the conflict process.

conflict
A process that begins when one party perceives that another party has negatively affected, or is about to negatively affect, something that the first party cares about.

We can define **conflict**, then, as a process that begins when one party perceives that another party has negatively affected, or is about to negatively affect, something that the first party cares about.[3] This definition is purposely broad. It describes that point in any ongoing activity when an interaction 'crosses over' to become an interparty conflict. It encompasses the wide range of conflicts that people experience in organizations – incompatibility of goals, differences over interpretations of facts, disagreements based on behavioural expectations and the like. Finally, our definition is flexible enough to cover the full range of conflict levels – from overt and violent acts to subtle forms of disagreement.

Transitions in conflict thought

2 Differentiate between the traditional, human relations and interactionist views of conflict.

It is entirely appropriate to say there has been conflict over the role of conflict in groups and organizations. One school of thought has argued that conflict must be avoided – that it indicates a malfunctioning within the group. We call this the *traditional* view. Another school of thought, the *human relations* view, argues that conflict is a natural and inevitable outcome in any group and that it need not be evil but rather has the potential to be a positive force in determining group performance. The third, and most recent, perspective proposes not only that conflict can be a positive force in a group but explicitly argues that some conflict is *absolutely necessary* for a group to perform effectively. We label this third school the *interactionist* view. Let's take a closer look at each of these views.

The traditional view of conflict

traditional view of conflict
The belief that all conflict is harmful and must be avoided.

The early approach to conflict assumed that all conflict was bad. Conflict was viewed negatively, and it was used synonymously with such terms as *violence, destruction* and *irrationality* to reinforce its negative connotation. Conflict, by definition, was harmful and was to be avoided. The **traditional view of conflict** was consistent with the attitudes that prevailed about group behaviour in the 1930s and 1940s. Conflict was seen as a dysfunctional outcome resulting from poor communication, a lack of openness and trust between people and the failure of managers to be responsive to the needs and aspirations of their employees.

The view that all conflict is bad certainly offers a simple approach to looking at the behaviour of people who create conflict. Because all conflict is to be avoided, we need merely direct our attention to the causes of conflict and correct those malfunctions to improve group and organizational performance. Although research studies now provide strong evidence to dispute that this approach to conflict reduction results in high group performance, many of us still evaluate conflict situations using this outmoded standard.

The human relations view of conflict

human relations view of conflict
The belief that conflict is a natural and inevitable outcome in any group.

The **human relations view of conflict** argued that conflict was a natural occurrence in all groups and organizations. Because conflict was inevitable, the human relations school advocated acceptance of conflict. Proponents rationalised its existence: It cannot be eliminated, and there are even times when conflict may benefit a group's performance. The human relations view dominated conflict theory from the late 1940s through the mid-1970s.

The interactionist view of conflict

interactionist view of conflict
The belief that conflict is not only a positive force in a group but that it is also an absolute necessity for a group to perform effectively.

Whereas the human relations view accepted conflict, the **interactionist view of conflict** encourages conflict on the grounds that a harmonious, peaceful, tranquil and cooperative group is prone to becoming static, apathetic, and nonresponsive to needs for change and innovation.[4] The major contribution of the interactionist view, therefore, is encouraging group leaders to maintain an ongoing minimum level of conflict – enough to keep the group viable, self-critical and creative.

functional conflict
Conflict that supports the goals of the group and improves its performance.

dysfunctional conflict
Conflict that hinders group performance.

The interactionist view does not propose that all conflicts are good. Rather, some conflicts support the goals of the group and improve its performance; these are **functional conflict**, constructive, forms of conflict. In addition, there are conflicts that hinder group performance; these are **dysfunctional conflict**, or destructive, forms of conflict. What differentiates functional from dysfunctional conflict? The evidence indicates that you need to look at the *type* of conflict.[5] Specifically, there are three types: task, relationship and process.

task conflict
Conflict over content and goals of the work.

relationship conflict
Conflict based on interpersonal relationships.

Task conflict relates to the content and goals of the work. **Relationship conflict** focuses on interpersonal relationships. **Process conflict** relates to how the work gets done. Studies demonstrate that relationship conflicts are almost always dysfunctional.[6] Why? It appears that the friction and interpersonal hostilities inherent in relationship conflicts increases personality clashes and decreases mutual understanding, which hinders the completion of organizational tasks. Unfortunately, managers spend a lot of their time resolving personality conflicts; one survey indicated that 18 per cent of managers' time is spent trying to resolve personality conflicts among staff members.[7]

process conflict
Conflict over how work gets done.

Unlike with relationship conflict, low levels of process conflict and low to moderate levels of task conflict are functional. For process conflict to be productive, it must be kept low. Intense arguments about who should do what become dysfunctional when they create uncertainty about task roles, increase the time to complete tasks, and lead to members working at cross purposes. Low-to-moderate levels of task conflict consistently demonstrate a positive effect on group performance because it stimulates discussion of ideas that helps groups perform better.

Figure 15.1	The conflict process

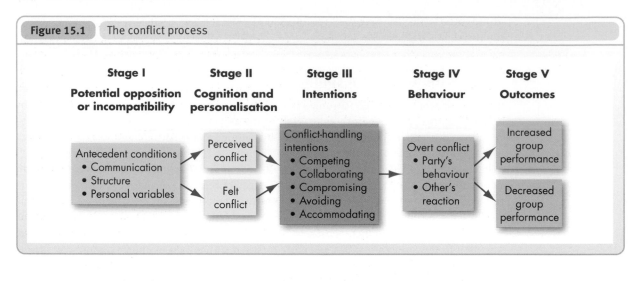

The conflict process

3 Outline the conflict process.

The **conflict process** has five stages: potential opposition or incompatibility, cognition and personalisation, intentions, behaviour and outcomes. The process is diagrammed in Figure 15.1.

> **conflict process**
> A process that has five stages: potential opposition or incompatibility, cognition and personalisation, intentions, behaviour and outcomes.

Stage I: Potential opposition or incompatibility

The first step in the conflict process is the presence of conditions that create opportunities for conflict to arise. They *need not* lead directly to conflict, but one of these conditions is necessary if conflict is to surface. For simplicity's sake, these conditions (which we can also look at as causes or sources of conflict) have been condensed into three general categories: communication, structure and personal variables.

Communication

Katrina had worked in supply-chain management for three years. She enjoyed her work in large part because her boss, Florin, was a great guy to work for. Then Florin got promoted six months ago, and Ardian took his place. Katrina says her job is a lot more frustrating now. 'Florin and I thought alike. It's not that way with Ardian. He tells me something and I do it. Then he tells me I did it wrong. I think he means one thing but says something else. It's been like this since the day he arrived. I don't think a day goes by when he isn't yelling at me for something. You know, there are some people you just find it easy to communicate with. Well, Ardian isn't one of those!'

Katrina's comments illustrate that communication can be a source of conflict.[8] They represent the opposing forces that arise from semantic difficulties, misunderstandings and 'noise' in the communication channels. Much of this discussion can be related to our comments on communication in Chapter 11.

A review of the research suggests that differing word connotations, jargon, insufficient exchange of information, and noise in the communication channel are all barriers to communication and potential antecedent conditions to conflict. Research has further demonstrated a surprising finding: The potential for conflict increases when either too little or too much communication takes place. Apparently, an increase in communication is functional up to a point, whereupon it is possible to overcommunicate, with a resultant increase in the potential for conflict.

Structure

Susanna and Jane both work at the CF Furniture Store – a large discount furniture retailer. Susanna is a salesperson on the floor, and Jane is the company credit manager. The two women have known each other for years and have much in common: They live close to each other, and their oldest daughters attend the same school and are best friends. In reality, if Susanna and Jane had different jobs, they might be best friends themselves, but these two women are consistently fighting battles with each other. Susanna's job is to sell furniture, and she does a very good job. But most of her sales are made on credit. Because Jane's job is to make sure the company minimises credit losses, she regularly has to turn down the credit application of a customer with whom Susanna has just closed a sale. It's nothing personal between Susanna and Jane; the requirements of their jobs just bring them into conflict.

The conflicts between Susanna and Jane are structural in nature. The term *structure* is used, in this context, to include variables such as size, degree of specialisation in the tasks assigned to group members, jurisdictional clarity, member-goal compatibility, leadership styles, reward systems and the degree of dependence between groups.

Research indicates that size and specialisation act as forces to stimulate conflict. The larger the group and the more specialised its activities, the greater the likelihood of conflict. Tenure and conflict have been found to be inversely related. The potential for conflict tends to be greatest when group members are younger and when turnover is high.

The greater the ambiguity in precisely defining where responsibility for actions lies, the greater the potential for conflict to emerge. Such jurisdictional ambiguities increase intergroup fighting for control of resources and territory. Diversity of goals among groups is also a major source of conflict. When groups within an organization seek diverse ends, some of which – like sales and credit at the CF Furniture Store – are inherently at odds, there are increased opportunities for conflict. Reward systems, too, are found to create conflict when one member's gain is at another's expense. Finally, if a group is dependent on another group (in contrast to the two being mutually independent) or if interdependence allows one group to gain at another's expense, opposing forces are stimulated.[9]

Personal variables

Have you ever met someone to whom you took an immediate disliking? You disagreed with most of the opinions they expressed. Even insignificant characteristics – the sound of their voice, the smirk when they smiled, their personality – annoyed you. We've all met people like that.

iStockphoto

Personal variables such as personality differences can be the source of conflict among co-workers. To reduce conflict resulting from personality differences, Vertex Pharmaceuticals teaches employees how to identify other people's personality types and then how to communicate effectively with them. At Vertex, innovation is critical to the company's mission of developing drugs that treat life-threatening diseases. By training employees to work harmoniously in spite of personality differences, Vertex hopes to eliminate unproductive conflict that impedes innovation.

When you have to work with such individuals, there is often the potential for conflict. For example, Philip Hayton, one of the British Broadcasting Corporations longest-serving newscasters quit the corporation after 37 years because of a personality clash with his co-presenter Kate Silverton after working with her for less than three months. Hayton said, 'It boils down to incompatibility. We did four hours of live TV every day and you have to like each other.'[10]

Our last category of potential sources of conflict is personal variables, which include personality, emotions, and values. Evidence indicates that certain personality types – for example, individuals who are highly authoritarian and dogmatic – lead to potential conflict. One global survey found that nearly half of all the employees surveyed cited personality clashes as the primary cause of workplace conflict.[11] Emotions can also cause conflict. For example, an employee who shows up to work irate from her hectic morning commute may carry that anger with her to her 9 A.M. meeting. The problem? Her anger can annoy her colleagues, which may lead to a tension-filled meeting.[12]

Stage II: Cognition and personalisation

If the conditions cited in Stage I negatively affect something that one party cares about, then the potential for opposition or incompatibility becomes actualised in the second stage.

As we noted in our definition of conflict, perception is required. Therefore, one or more of the parties must be aware of the existence of the antecedent conditions. However, because a conflict is **perceived conflict** does not mean that it is personalised. In other words, 'A may be aware that B and A are in serious disagreement . . . but it may not make A tense or anxious, and it may have no effect whatsoever on A's affection toward B.'[13] It is at the **felt conflict** level, when individuals become emotionally involved, that parties experience anxiety, tension, frustration or hostility.

Keep in mind two points. First, Stage II is important because it's where conflict issues tend to be defined. This is the place in the process where the parties decide what the conflict is about.[14] In turn, this 'sense making' is critical because the way a conflict is defined goes a long way toward establishing the sort of outcomes that might settle it. For instance, if I define our salary disagreement as a zero-sum situation (that is, if you get the increase in pay you want, there will be just that amount less for me) I am going to be far less willing to compromise than if I frame the conflict as a potential win/win situation (that is, the euros in the salary pool might be increased so that both of us could get the added pay we want). So the definition of a conflict is important because it typically delineates the set of possible settlements. Our second point is that emotions play a major role in shaping perceptions.[15] For example, negative emotions have been found to produce oversimplification of issues, reductions in trust and negative interpretations of the other party's behaviour.[16] In contrast, positive feelings have been found to increase the tendency to see potential relationships among the elements of a problem, to take a broader view of the situation and to develop more innovative solutions.[17]

Stage III: Intentions

Intentions intervene between people's perceptions and emotions and their overt behaviour. These intentions are decisions to act in a given way.[18]

Intentions are separated out as a distinct stage because you have to infer the other's intent to know how to respond to that other's behaviour. A lot of conflicts are escalated merely by one party attributing the wrong intentions to the other party. In addition, there is typically a great deal of slippage between intentions and behaviour, so behaviour does not always accurately reflect a person's intentions.

Figure 15.2 represents one author's effort to identify the primary conflict-handling intentions. Using two dimensions – *cooperativeness* (the degree to which one party attempts to satisfy the other party's concerns) and *assertiveness* (the degree to which one party attempts to satisfy their own concerns) – five conflict-handling intentions can be identified: *competing* (assertive and uncooperative), *collaborating* (assertive and cooperative), *avoiding* (unassertive and uncooperative), *accommodating* (unassertive and cooperative) and *compromising* (midrange on both assertiveness and cooperativeness).[19]

perceived conflict
Awareness by one or more parties of the existence of conditions that create opportunities for conflict to arise.

felt conflict
Emotional involvement in a conflict that creates anxiety, tenseness, frustration or hostility.

intentions
Decisions to act in a given way.

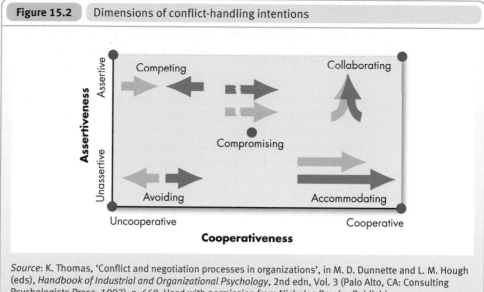

| **Figure 15.2** | Dimensions of conflict-handling intentions |

Source: K. Thomas, 'Conflict and negotiation processes in organizations', in M. D. Dunnette and L. M. Hough (eds), *Handbook of Industrial and Organizational Psychology*, 2nd edn, Vol. 3 (Palo Alto, CA: Consulting Psychologists Press, 1992), p. 668. Used with permission from Nicholas Brealey Publishing.

Competing

When one person seeks to satisfy his or her own interests, regardless of the impact on the other parties to the conflict, that person is **competing**. Competing is when you, for example, win a bet and your opponent loses.

Collaborating

When the parties to conflict each desire to fully satisfy the concerns of all parties, there is cooperation and a search for a mutually beneficial outcome. In **collaborating**, the intention of the parties is to solve a problem by clarifying differences rather than by accommodating various points of view. If you attempt to find a win/win solution that allows both parties' goals to be completely achieved, that's collaborating.

Avoiding

A person may recognise that a conflict exists and want to withdraw from it or suppress it. Examples of **avoiding** include trying to just ignore a conflict and avoiding others with whom you disagree.

Accommodating

When one party seeks to appease an opponent, that party may be willing to place the opponent's interests above his or her own. In other words, in order for the relationship to be maintained, one party needs to be willing to be self-sacrificing. We refer to this intention as **accommodating**. Supporting someone else's opinion despite your reservations about it, for example, would represent accommodating.

Compromising

When each party to a conflict seeks to give up something, sharing occurs, resulting in a compromised outcome. In **compromising**, there is no clear winner or loser. Rather, there is a willingness to ration the object of the conflict and accept a solution that provides incomplete satisfaction of both parties' concerns. The distinguishing characteristic of compromising, therefore, is that each party intends to give up something.

Intentions are not always fixed. During the course of a conflict, they might change because of reconceptualisation or because of an emotional reaction to the behaviour of the other party. However, research indicates that people have an underlying disposition to handle conflicts in certain ways.[20] Specifically, individuals have preferences among the five conflict-handling intentions just described; these preferences tend to be relied on quite consistently, and a person's

---

competing
A desire to satisfy one's interests, regardless of the impact on the other party to the conflict.

collaborating
A situation in which the parties to a conflict each desire to satisfy fully the concerns of all parties.

avoiding
The desire to withdraw from or suppress a conflict.

accommodating
The willingness of one party in a conflict to place the opponent's interests above their own.

compromising
A situation in which each party to a conflict is willing to give up something.

intentions can be predicted rather well from a combination of intellectual and personality characteristics.

Stage IV: Behaviour

When most people think of conflict situations, they tend to focus on Stage IV because this is where conflicts become visible. The behaviour stage includes the statements, actions and reactions made by the conflicting parties. These conflict behaviours are usually overt attempts to implement each party's intentions. But these behaviours have a stimulus quality that is separate from intentions. As a result of miscalculations or unskilled enactments, overt behaviours sometimes deviate from original intentions.[21]

It helps to think of Stage IV as a dynamic process of interaction. For example, you make a demand on me, I respond by arguing, you threaten me, I threaten you back, and so on. Figure 15.3 provides a way of visualising conflict behaviour. All conflicts exist somewhere along this continuum. At the lower part of the continuum are conflicts characterised by subtle, indirect, and highly controlled forms of tension. An illustration might be a student questioning in class a point the instructor has just made. Conflict intensities escalate as they move upward along the continuum until they become highly destructive. Strikes, riots and wars clearly fall in this upper range. For the most part, you should assume that conflicts that reach the upper ranges of the continuum are almost always dysfunctional. Functional conflicts are typically confined to the lower range of the continuum.

conflict management
The use of resolution and stimulation techniques to achieve the desired level of conflict.

If a conflict is dysfunctional, what can the parties do to de-escalate it? Or, conversely, what options exist if conflict is too low and needs to be increased? This brings us to **conflict-management** techniques. Exhibit 15.1 lists the major resolution and stimulation techniques that allow managers to control conflict levels. Note that several of the resolution techniques were described earlier as conflict-handling intentions. This, of course, shouldn't be surprising. Under ideal conditions, a person's intentions should translate into comparable behaviours.

Stage V: Outcomes

The action–reaction interplay between the conflicting parties results in consequences. As our model (see Figure 15.1) demonstrates, these outcomes may be functional in that the conflict results in an improvement in the group's performance or dysfunctional in that it hinders group performance.

Functional outcomes

How might conflict act as a force to increase group performance? It is hard to visualise a situation in which open or violent aggression could be functional. But there are a number of

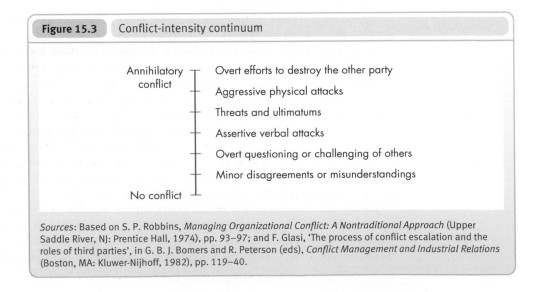

| Figure 15.3 | Conflict-intensity continuum |

Annihilatory conflict — Overt efforts to destroy the other party

— Aggressive physical attacks

— Threats and ultimatums

— Assertive verbal attacks

— Overt questioning or challenging of others

— Minor disagreements or misunderstandings

No conflict

Sources: Based on S. P. Robbins, *Managing Organizational Conflict: A Nontraditional Approach* (Upper Saddle River, NJ: Prentice Hall, 1974), pp. 93–97; and F. Glasl, 'The process of conflict escalation and the roles of third parties', in G. B. J. Bomers and R. Peterson (eds), *Conflict Management and Industrial Relations* (Boston, MA: Kluwer-Nijhoff, 1982), pp. 119–40.

EXHIBIT 15.1	CONFLICT-MANAGEMENT TECHNIQUES

Conflict-resolution techniques

Problem solving	Face-to-face meeting of the conflicting parties for the purpose of identifying the problem and resolving it through open discussion.
Superordinate goals	Creating a shared goal that cannot be attained without the cooperation of each of the conflicting parties.
Expansion of resources	When a conflict is caused by the scarcity of a resource – say, money, promotion, opportunities, office space – expansion of the resource can create a win/win solution.
Avoidance	Withdrawal from, or suppression of, the conflict.
Smoothing	Playing down differences while emphasising common interests between the conflicting parties.
Compromise	Each party to the conflict gives up something of value.
Authoritative command	Management uses its formal authority to resolve the conflict and then communicates its desires to the parties involved.
Altering the human variable	Using behavioural change techniques such as human relations training to alter attitudes and behaviours that cause conflict.
Altering the structural variables	Changing the formal organization structure and the interaction patterns of conflicting parties through job redesign, transfers, creation of coordinating positions and the like.

Conflict-stimulation techniques

Communication	Using ambiguous or threatening messages to increase conflict levels
Bringing in outsiders	Adding employees to a group whose backgrounds, values, attitudes, or managerial styles differ from those of present members.
Restructuring the organization	Realigning work groups, altering rules and regulations, increasing interdependence, and making similar structural changes to disrupt the status quo.
Appointing a devil's advocate	Designating a critic to purposely argue against the majority positions held by the group.

Source: Based on S. P. Robbins, *Managing Organizational Conflict: A Nontraditional Approach* (Upper Saddle River, NJ: Prentice Hall, 1974), pp. 59–89.

instances in which it's possible to envision how low or moderate levels of conflict could improve the effectiveness of a group. A global survey revealed that three-quarters of employees have seen a conflict lead to something positive. Four out of ten found that it led to a better understanding of other people, while a third experienced improved working relationships, and three out of ten even found that conflict led to a better solution to some problem or challenge. Indeed, one in ten say that conflict resulted in the birth of a major innovation or new idea at work.[22]

Conflict is constructive when it improves the quality of decisions, stimulates creativity and innovation, encourages interest and curiosity among group members, provides the medium through which problems can be aired and tensions released, and fosters an environment of self-evaluation and change. The evidence suggests that conflict can improve the quality of decision making by allowing all points, particularly the ones that are unusual or held by a minority, to be weighed in important decisions.[23] Conflict is an antidote for groupthink. It doesn't allow the group to passively agree decisions that may be based on weak assumptions, inadequate consideration of relevant alternatives or other debilities. Conflict challenges the status quo and therefore furthers the creation of new ideas, promotes reassessment of group goals and activities, and increases the probability that the group will respond to change.

For an example of a company that suffered because it had too little functional conflict, you don't have to look further than Samsung, the world's largest conglomerate. In the late 1990s, Kun-Hee Lee, Samsung's chairman and chief executive, invested around 10 billion euros to break into the automotive industry. None of his loyal executives challenged the decision. Not only was Mr Lee a forceful personality, he was also a car buff. After only a year into production,

A lack of functional conflict has been noted as a factor in the global financial crisis. A feature of the recent boom and bust was the breadth of institutions caught up in the crisis. The banks thundered forward en masse and there was too little questioning of this strategy from people within the banks.

Mike Clarke/Getty Images

Samsung Motors folded.[24] Yahoo!'s former CEO Tim Koogle was so conflict averse that a sense of complacency settled in that left managers afraid to challenge the status quo. Even though Yahoo! started out much more successful than Google, it was soon overtaken, and most now believe it will never catch up.

Research studies in diverse settings confirm the functionality of conflict. Consider the following findings. Conflict can positively relate to productivity. For instance, it was demonstrated that, among established groups, performance tended to improve more when there was conflict among members than when there was fairly close agreement. The investigators observed that when groups analysed decisions that had been made by the individual members of that group, the average improvement among the high-conflict groups was 73 per cent greater than that of those groups characterised by low-conflict conditions.[25] Others have found similar results: Groups composed of members with different interests tend to produce higher-quality solutions to a variety of problems than do homogeneous groups.[26]

The preceding leads us to predict that the increasing cultural diversity of the workforce should provide benefits to organizations. And that's what the evidence indicates. Research demonstrates that heterogeneity among group and organization members can increase creativity, improve the quality of decisions, and facilitate change by enhancing member flexibility.[27]

Dysfunctional outcomes

The destructive consequences of conflict on a group's or an organization's performance are generally well known. A reasonable summary might state: Uncontrolled opposition breeds discontent, which acts to dissolve common ties and eventually leads to the destruction of the group. And, of course, there is a substantial body of literature to document how conflict – the dysfunctional varieties – can reduce group effectiveness.[28] Among the more undesirable consequences are a retarding of communication, reductions in group cohesiveness, and subordination of group goals to the primacy of infighting among members. At the extreme, conflict can bring group functioning to a halt and potentially threaten the group's survival.

The demise of an organization as a result of too much conflict isn't as unusual as it might first appear. For instance, the law firm Shea & Gould, closed down solely because the 80 partners just couldn't get along.[29] As one legal consultant familiar with the organization said: 'This was a firm that had basic and principled differences among the partners that were basically irreconcilable.' That same consultant also addressed the partners at their last meeting: 'You don't have an economic problem,' he said. 'You have a personality problem. You hate each other!'

THE DYSFUNCTIONAL OUTCOMES OF CONFLICT ACROSS EUROPE
FACE THE FACTS

- The average number of hours per week employees spent on dealing with workplace conflict was 3.3 in both Germany and Ireland, 1.8 in the UK, France and Denmark and 0.9 in the Netherlands.

- On average, the European worker spends one day a month dealing with conflict in some way (being involved in a disagreement, managing a conflict between co-workers etc.).

- 27 per cent of employees have seen conflict lead to personal attacks, and 25 per cent have seen it result in sickness or absence (in the non-profit sector this figure is 48 per cent). Nearly one in ten have seen conflict lead to a project failure.

Source: Fight, Flight or Face it? Celebrating the Effective Management of Conflict at Work, CIPD/OPP 2008.

Creating functional conflict

If managers accept the interactionist view toward conflict, what can they do to encourage functional conflict in their organizations?[30]

There seems to be general agreement that creating functional conflict is a tough job. As one consultant put it, 'A high proportion of people who get to the top are conflict avoiders. They don't like hearing negatives; they don't like saying or thinking negative things. They frequently make it up the ladder in part because they don't irritate people on the way up.' The degree to which people will engage in creating functional conflict by, for example, playing the 'devil's advocate' can also depend on culture. In Asia the tendency is to avoid questioning and confrontation in comparison to their counterparts in Europe.

Such anticonflict cultures may have been tolerable in the past but are not in today's fiercely competitive global economy. Organizations that don't encourage and support dissent may find their survival threatened. Let's look at some approaches organizations are using to encourage their people to challenge the system and develop fresh ideas.

Hewlett-Packard rewards dissenters by recognising go-against-the-grain types, or people who stay with the ideas they believe in even when those ideas are rejected by management. IBM also has a formal system that encourages dissension. Employees can question their boss with impunity. If the disagreement can't be resolved, the system provides a third party for counsel. Even the UK's Joint Intelligence Committee, a governmental department responsible for directing national intelligence, has an in-house devil's advocate appointed to challenge and probe its assumptions and evidence.

One common ingredient in organizations that successfully create functional conflict is that they reward dissent and punish conflict avoiders. The real challenge for managers, however, is when they hear news they don't want to hear. The news may make their blood boil or their hopes collapse, but they can't show it. They have to learn to take the bad news without flinching. No tirades, no tight-lipped sarcasm, no eyes rolling upward, no gritting of teeth. Rather, managers should ask calm, even-tempered questions: 'Can you tell me more about what happened?' 'What do you think we ought to do?' A sincere 'Thank you for bringing this to my attention', will probably reduce the likelihood that managers will be cut off from similar communications in the future.

Having considered conflict – its nature, causes and consequences – we now turn to negotiation. Negotiation and conflict are closely related because negotiation often resolves conflict.

Negotiation

4 Define
negotiation.

Negotiation permeates the interactions of almost everyone in groups and organizations. There's the obvious: Labour bargains with management. There's the not-so-obvious: Managers negotiate with employees, peers and bosses; salespeople negotiate with customers; purchasing agents negotiate with suppliers. And there's the subtle: An employee agrees to answer a colleague's phone for a few minutes in exchange for some past or future benefit. In today's loosely structured organizations, in which members are increasingly finding themselves having to work with colleagues over whom they have no direct authority and with whom they may not even share a common boss, negotiation skills become critical.

negotiation
A process in which two or more parties exchange goods or services and attempt to agree on the exchange rate for them.

We can define **negotiation** as a process in which two or more parties exchange goods or services and attempt to agree on the exchange rate for them.[31] Note that we use the terms *negotiation* and *bargaining* interchangeably. In this section, we contrast two bargaining strategies, provide a model of the negotiation process, ascertain the role of moods and personality traits on bargaining, review gender and cultural differences in negotiation and take a brief look at third-party negotiations.

Bargaining strategies

5 Contrast
distributive and
integrative
bargaining.

There are two general approaches to negotiation – *distributive bargaining* and *integrative bargaining*.[32] As Table 15.1 shows, distributive and integrative bargaining differ in their goal and motivation, focus, interests, information sharing, and duration of relationship. We now define distributive and integrative bargaining and illustrate the differences between these two approaches.

Distributive bargaining

distributive bargaining
Negotiation that seeks to divide up a fixed amount of resources; a win/lose situation.

fixed pie
The belief that there is only a set amount of goods or services to be divvied up between the parties.

You see a used car advertised for sale in the newspaper. It appears to be just what you've been looking for. You go out to see the car. It's great, and you want it. The owner tells you the asking price. You don't want to pay that much. The two of you then negotiate over the price. The negotiating strategy you're engaging in is called **distributive bargaining**. Its most identifying feature is that it operates under zero-sum conditions. That is, any gain I make is at your expense and vice versa. In the used-car example, every euro you can get the seller to cut from the car's price is a euro you save. Conversely, every euro more the seller can get from you comes at your expense. So the essence of distributive bargaining is negotiating over who gets what share of a fixed pie. By **fixed pie**, we mean that the bargaining parties believe there is only a set amount of goods or services to be divvied up. Therefore, fixed pies are zero-sum games in that every euro in one party's pocket is a euro out of their counterpart's pocket. When parties believe the pie is fixed, they tend to bargain distributively.

Table 15.1	Distributive versus integrative bargaining	
Bargaining characteristic	**Distributive bargaining**	**Integrative bargaining**
Goal	Get as much of the pie as possible	Expand the pie so that both parties are satisfied
Motivation	Win/lose	Win/win
Focus	Positions ('I can't go beyond this point on this issue.')	Interests ('Can you explain why this issue is so important to you?')
Interests	Opposed	Congruent
Information sharing	Low (sharing information will only allow other party to take advantage)	High (sharing information will allow each party to find ways to satisfy interests of each party)
Duration of relationship	Short term	Long term

Trade unions representing workers in the Belgian prison service resorted to strike action when, amongst other demands, a 6% wage increase was not agreed by the Government. Distributive bargaining has led to the industrial relations climate in Belgium's prison service to deteriorate over the past number of years.

Probably the most widely cited example of distributive bargaining is in labour-management negotiations over wages. Typically, labour's representatives come to the bargaining table determined to get as much money as possible out of management. Because every cent more that labour negotiates increases management's costs, each party bargains aggressively and treats the other as an opponent who must be defeated.

The essence of distributive bargaining is depicted in Figure 15.4. Parties *A* and *B* represent two negotiators. Each has a *target point* that defines what he or she would like to achieve. Each also has a *resistance point*, which marks the lowest outcome that is acceptable – the point below which they would break off negotiations rather than accept a less-favourable settlement. The area between these two points makes up each one's aspiration range. As long as there is some overlap between *A*'s and *B*'s aspiration ranges, there exists a settlement range in which each one's aspirations can be met.

When engaged in distributive bargaining, one of the best things you can do is to make the first offer, and to make it an aggressive one. Research consistently shows that the best negotiators are those who make the first offer, and whose initial offer has very favourable terms. Why is this so? One reason is that making the first offer shows power; research shows that individuals

| Figure 15.4 | Staking out the bargaining zone |

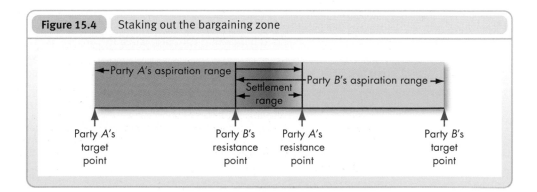

in power are much more likely to make initial offers, speak first at meetings, and thereby gain the advantage. Another reason was mentioned in Chapter 5. Recall that we discussed the anchoring bias, which is the tendency for people to fixate on initial information. Once that anchoring point is set, people fail to adequately adjust it based on subsequent information. A savvy negotiator sets an anchor with the initial offer, and scores of negotiation studies show that such anchors greatly favour the person who sets it.[33]

For example, say you have a job offer, and your prospective employer asks you what sort of starting salary you'd be looking for. You need to realise that you've just been given a great gift – you have a chance to set the anchor, meaning that you should ask for the highest salary that you think the employer could reasonably offer. For most of us, asking for a million euro's is only going to make us look ridiculous, which is why we suggest being on the high end of what you think is reasonable. Too often, we err on the side of caution, being afraid of scaring off the employer and thus settling for too little. It *is* possible to scare off an employer, and it's true that employers don't like candidates to be assertive in salary negotiations, but liking isn't the same as respect or doing what it takes to hire or retain someone.[34] You should realise that what happens much more often is that we ask for less than what we could have gotten.

Another distributive bargaining tactic is revealing a deadline. Consider the following example. Chloe is a human resources manager. She is negotiating salary with Andre, who is a highly sought after new hire. Because Andre knows the company needs him, he decides to ask for an extraordinary salary and many benefits. Chloe tells Ron that the company can't meet his requirements. Andre tells Chloe he is going to have to think things over. Worried the company is going to lose Andre to a competitor, Chloe decides to tell Andre that she is under time pressure and that she needs to reach an agreement with him immediately, or she will have to offer the job to another candidate. Would you consider Chloe to be a savvy negotiator? Well, she is. Why? Negotiators who reveal deadlines speed concessions from their negotiating counterparts, making them reconsider their position. And even though negotiators don't *think* this tactic works, in reality, negotiators who reveal deadlines do better.[35]

Integrative bargaining

A sales representative for a women's sportswear manufacturer has just closed a €10,000 order from a small clothing retailer. The sales rep calls in the order to her firm's credit department. She is told that the firm can't approve credit to this customer because of a past slow-payment record. The next day, the sales rep and the firm's credit manager meet to discuss the problem. The sales rep doesn't want to lose the business. Neither does the credit manager, but he also doesn't want to get stuck with an uncollectible debt. The two openly review their options. After considerable discussion, they agree on a solution that meets both their needs: The credit manager will approve the sale, but the clothing store's owner will provide a bank guarantee that will ensure payment if the bill isn't paid within 60 days. This sales-credit negotiation is an example of **integrative bargaining**. In contrast to distributive bargaining, integrative bargaining operates under the assumption that there are one or more settlements that can create a win/win solution.

In terms of intraorganizational behaviour, all things being equal, integrative bargaining is preferable to distributive bargaining. Why? Because the former builds long-term relationships. It bonds negotiators and allows them to leave the bargaining table feeling that they have achieved a victory. Distributive bargaining, however, leaves one party a loser. It tends to build animosities and deepen divisions when people have to work together on an ongoing basis. Research shows that over repeated bargaining episodes, when the 'losing' party feels positive about the negotiation outcome, he is much more likely to bargain cooperatively in subsequent negotiations. This points to the important advantage of integrative negotiations: Even when you 'win', you want your opponent to feel positively about the negotiation.[36]

Why, then, don't we see more integrative bargaining in organizations? The answer lies in the conditions necessary for this type of negotiation to succeed. These include parties who are open with information and candid about their concerns, a sensitivity by both parties to the other's needs, the ability to trust one another, and a willingness by both parties to maintain flexibility.[37] Because these conditions often don't exist in organizations, it isn't surprising that negotiations often take on a win-at-any-cost dynamic.

integrative bargaining Negotiation that seeks one or more settlements that can create a win/win solution.

There are some ways to achieve more integrative outcomes. For example, individuals who bargain in teams reach more integrative agreements than those who bargain individually. This happens because more ideas are generated when more people are at the bargaining table. So try bargaining in teams.[38] Another way to achieve higher joint-gain settlements is to put more issues on the table. The more negotiable issues that are introduced into a negotiation, the more opportunity there is for 'logrolling' where issues are traded because of differences in preferences. This creates better outcomes for each side than if each issue were negotiated individually.[39]

Finally, you should realise that compromise may be your worst enemy in negotiating a win/win agreement. This is because compromising reduces the pressure to bargain integratively. After all, if you or your opponent caves in easily, it doesn't require anyone to be creative to reach a settlement. Thus, people end up settling for less than they could have obtained if they had been forced to consider the other party's interests, trade off issues, and be creative.[40] Think of the classic example where two sisters are arguing over who gets an orange. Unknown to each other, one sister wants the orange to drink the juice, whereas the other sister wants the orange peel to bake a cake. If one sister simply capitulates and gives the other sister the orange, then they will not be forced to explore their reasons for wanting the orange, and thus they will never find the win/win solution: They could *each* have the orange because they want different parts of it!

The negotiation process

6 Apply the five steps of the negotiation process.

Figure 15.5 provides a simplified model of the negotiation process. It views negotiation as made up of five steps: (1) preparation and planning; (2) definition of ground rules; (3) clarification and justification; (4) bargaining and problem solving; and (5) closure and implementation.[41]

Preparation and planning

Before you start negotiating, you need to do your homework. What's the nature of the conflict? What's the history leading up to this negotiation? Who's involved and what are their perceptions of the conflict? What do you want from the negotiation? What are *your* goals? If you're a supply manager at the hypermarket chain Carrefour, for instance, and your goal is to get a significant cost reduction from a toy supplier, make sure that this goal stays paramount in your discussions and doesn't get overshadowed by other issues. It often helps to put your goals in writing and develop a range of outcomes – from 'most hopeful' to 'minimally acceptable' – to keep your attention focused.

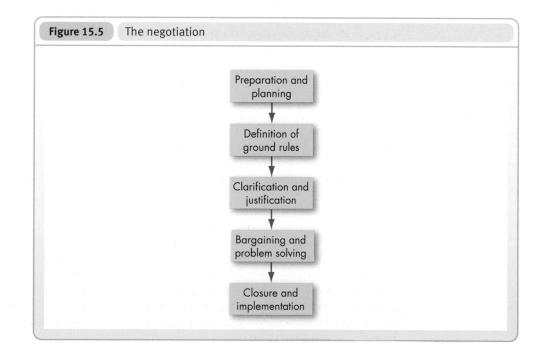

Figure 15.5 The negotiation

You also want to prepare an assessment of what you think the other party's goals are. What are they likely to ask for? How entrenched are they likely to be in their position? What intangible or hidden interests may be important to them? What might they be willing to settle on? When you can anticipate your opponent's position, you are better equipped to counter arguments with the facts and figures that support your position.

Once you've gathered your information, use it to develop a strategy. For example, expert chess players have a strategy. They know ahead of time how they will respond to any given situation. As part of your strategy, you should determine yours and the other side's **b**est **a**lternative **t**o a **n**egotiated **a**greement (**BATNA**).[42] Your BATNA determines the lowest value acceptable to you for a negotiated agreement. Any offer you receive that is higher than your BATNA is better than an impasse. Conversely, you shouldn't expect success in your negotiation effort unless you're able to make the other side an offer they find more attractive than their BATNA. If you go into your negotiation having a good idea of what the other party's BATNA is, even if you're not able to meet theirs, you might be able to get them to change it.

BATNA
The best alternative to a negotiated agreement; the least the individual should accept.

Definition of ground rules

Once you've done your planning and developed a strategy, you're ready to begin defining the ground rules and procedures with the other party over the negotiation itself. Who will do the negotiating? Where will it take place? What time constraints, if any, will apply? To what issues will negotiation be limited? Will there be a specific procedure to follow if an impasse is reached? During this phase, the parties will also exchange their initial proposals or demands.

Clarification and justification

When initial positions have been exchanged, both you and the other party will explain, amplify, clarify, bolster and justify your original demands. This needn't be confrontational. Rather, it's an opportunity for educating and informing each other on the issues, why they are important, and how each arrived at their initial demands. This is the point at which you might want to provide the other party with any documentation that helps support your position.

Bargaining and problem solving

The essence of the negotiation process is the actual give-and-take in trying to hash out an agreement. This is where both parties will undoubtedly need to make concessions.

Closure and implementation

The final step in the negotiation process is formalising the agreement that has been worked out and developing any procedures that are necessary for implementation and monitoring. For major negotiations – which would include everything from labour-management negotiations to bargaining over lease terms to buying a piece of real estate to negotiating a job offer for a senior management position – this requires hammering out the specifics in a formal contract. For most cases, however, closure of the negotiation process is nothing more formal than a handshake.

Individual differences in negotiation effectiveness

7. Show how individual differences influence negotiations.

Are some people better negotiators than others? Though the answer to this question might seem obvious, as it turns out the answers are more complex than you might think. Here we discuss three factors that influence how effectively individuals negotiate: personality, mood/emotions and gender.

Personality traits in negotiation

Can you predict an opponent's negotiating tactics if you know something about his or her personality? It's tempting to answer 'yes' to this question. For instance, you might assume that high-risk takers would be more aggressive bargainers who make fewer concessions. Surprisingly, the evidence hasn't always supported this intuition.[43]

Assessments of the personality–negotiation relationship have been that personality traits have no significant direct effect on either the bargaining process or the negotiation outcomes. However, recent research has started to question the theory that personality and the negotiation process aren't connected. In fact, it appears that several of the Big Five traits are related to negotiation outcomes. For example, negotiators who are agreeable or extraverted are not very successful when it comes to distributive bargaining. Why? Because extraverts are outgoing and friendly, they tend to share more information than they should. And agreeable people are more interested in finding ways to cooperate rather than compete. These traits, while slightly helpful in integrative negotiations, are liabilities when interests are opposed. So, the best distributive bargainer appears to be a disagreeable introvert – that is, someone who is interested in their own outcomes versus pleasing the other party and having a pleasant social exchange. Research also suggests that intelligence predicts negotiation effectiveness, but, as with personality, the effects aren't especially strong.[44]

Though personality and intelligence do appear to have some influence on negotiation, it's not a strong effect. In a sense, that's good news because it means even if you're an agreeable extrovert, you're not severely disadvantaged when it comes time to negotiate. We all can learn to be better negotiators.

Moods/emotions in negotiation

Do moods and emotions influence negotiation? They do, but the way they do appears to depend on the type of negotiation. In distributive negotiations, it appears that negotiators who show anger negotiate better outcomes, because their anger induces concessions from their opponents. This appears to hold true even when the negotiators are instructed to show anger despite not being truly angry.

In integrative negotiations, in contrast, positive moods and emotions appear to lead to more integrative agreements (higher levels of joint gain). This may happen because, as we noted in Chapter 3, positive mood is related to creativity.[45]

Gender differences in negotiations

Do men and women negotiate differently? And does gender affect negotiation outcomes? The answer to the first question appears to be no.[46] The answer to the second is a qualified yes.[47]

AFP/Getty Images

Respected for her intelligence, confident negotiating skills and successful outcomes, Christine Lagarde was appointed by French President Nicholas Sarkozy to the powerful position of minister of finance. As the first female finance minister of a G-8 nation, Lagarde brings to her new post experience as the trade minister of France, where she used her negotiating skills in boosting French exports by 10 per cent.

A popular stereotype is that women are more cooperative and pleasant in negotiations than are men. The evidence doesn't support this belief. However, men have been found to negotiate better outcomes than women, although the difference is relatively small. It's been postulated that this difference might be due to men and women placing divergent values on outcomes. 'It is possible that a few hundred euro's more in salary or the corner office is less important to women than forming and maintaining an interpersonal relationship.'[48]

The belief that women are 'nicer' than men in negotiations is probably due to a confusion between gender and the lower degree of power women typically hold in most large organizations. Because women are expected to be 'nice' and men 'tough', research shows that relative to men, women are penalised when they initiate negotiations.[49] What's more, when women and men actually do conform to these stereotypes – women act 'nice' and men 'tough' – it becomes a self-fulfilling prophecy, reinforcing the stereotypical gender differences between male and female negotiators.[50] Thus, one of the reasons why negotiations favour men is that women are 'damned if they do, damned if they don't'. Negotiate tough and they are penalised for violating a gender stereotype. Negotiate nice and it only reinforces the stereotype (and is taken advantage of).

SELF-ASSESSMENT LIBRARY

What's my negotiating style?

In the Self-assessment library (available online), take assessment II.C.6 (What's my negotiating style?).

In addition to the other party's attitudes and behaviours, the evidence also suggests that women's own attitudes and behaviours hurt them in negotiations. Managerial women demonstrate less confidence in anticipation of negotiating and are less satisfied with their performance after the process is complete, even when their performance and the outcomes they achieve are similar to those for men.[51] This latter conclusion suggests that women may unduly penalise themselves by failing to engage in negotiations when such action would be in their best interests.

NEGOTIATING ACROSS CULTURES — GLOBAL

Obtaining a favourable outcome in a negotiation may in part depend on the cultural characteristics of your opponent. A study of negotiators in the United States, China and Japan found that culture plays an important role in successful negotiation. The study found that, overall, negotiators who had both a self-serving 'egoistic' orientation and a high goal level fared the best overall compared to negotiators with an other-serving 'prosocial' orientation and low goal level. In other words, the strategy combining a self-serving negotiation position, where one is focused only on maximising one's own outcomes, coupled with a strong desire to obtain the best outcomes, led to the most favourable negotiation results.

However, the degree to which this particular strategy resulted in better outcomes depended on the negotiating partner. The results showed that being self-serving and having a high negotiation goal level resulted in higher outcomes (in this case, profits) only when the negotiating opponent was other-serving. Negotiators from the United States are more likely to be self-serving and have high goal

levels. In China and Japan, however, there is a greater likelihood that negotiators are other-serving and thus are more concerned with others' outcomes. Consequently, negotiators from the United States are likely to obtain better outcomes for themselves when negotiating with individuals from China and Japan because American negotiators tend to be more concerned with their own outcomes, sometimes at the expense of the other party.

Though this study suggests that being self-serving can be beneficial in some situations, negotiators should be wary of being too self-serving. US negotiators may benefit from a self-serving negotiation position and a high goal level when negotiating with individuals from China or Japan, but being too self-serving may result in damaged relationships, leading to less favourable outcomes in the long run.

Source: Based on Y. Chen, E. A. Mannix and T. Okumura, 'The importance of who you meet: effects of self- versus other-concerns among negotiators in the United States, the People's Republic of China, and Japan,' *Journal of Experimental Social Psychology*, January, 2003, pp. 1–15.

Third-party negotiations

8 Assess the roles and functions of third-party negotiations.

To this point, we've discussed bargaining in terms of direct negotiations. Occasionally, however, individuals or group representatives reach a stalemate and are unable to resolve their differences through direct negotiations. In such cases, they may turn to a third party to help them find a solution. There are four basic third-party roles: mediator, arbitrator, conciliator, and consultant.[52]

ALL IN A GOOD CAUSE   OB IN THE NEWS

Bristol Mediation, one of the first mediation charities in the UK, was set up in 1987 in response to the riots that had hit the St Paul's area of Bristol two years before. A local Quaker group, looking for a more peaceful way of resolving conflict, decided to import a model of dispute-resolution that had been emerging in the US. This involved a neutral third party helping people find a mutually-agreeable solution themselves. For the next decade or so, it was concerned mostly with disputes between neighbours and in schools but recent changes in funding mean that it has had – for the time being at least – to limit its work to local authority tenants.

'Only about a quarter of the cases referred to us go all the way to face-to-face mediation,' says Teresa Riley, service manager of Bristol Mediation. 'In most cases an agreement can be drawn up much earlier. It's really about getting the stopper out of the bottle, getting it all out into the open.'

Volunteer mediators are trained for between six and ten weekends and are then paired with more experienced mediators in the field. Bristol Mediation currently has about 30 volunteers who deal with over 100 cases each year.

Pauline Harrow, a Bristol resident, made use of the service two years ago when a new tenant moved in to her block of flats and started to leave his bicycle in the narrow hallway.

'I would come home with shopping,' she says, 'and it would be impossible to get upstairs. And I was worried about what would happen if there was a fire.' Harrow suggested he leave the bicycle in the block's back garden but

with limited success. 'I would talk to him nicely about moving it but whenever I brought up the subject he would start shouting. In the end I started moving his bike out the back myself, but that made it worse. He'd come upstairs and bang on my door calling me all sorts of names.'

Harrow complained to the council who called in Bristol Mediation. 'Two people came and spoke to us separately for about half an hour,' says Harrow. 'It turned out that he was terrified of losing his bike. In his previous place he had had to leave his bike in the back yard and it had been stolen more than once. He was a bike courier and if he lost his bike he would have no work and he was desperately trying to pay off his debts.'

Harrow also discovered another side of the story. 'I would usually leave my shopping in the hallway for my husband to bring up when he came home but that meant the courier couldn't get his bike out when he had a job. From his point of view I was the one who was blocking the hall, and that's why he was getting so angry.'

'In the end we signed a contract to keep the hallway clear and we built a metal post in the garden he could chain his bike to. Now, when I come home from shopping, if he's in, he helps me carry my stuff upstairs, and, if he isn't, I carry it up myself.'

Source: D. Baker, 'All in a good cause Bristol mediation. Local authority tenants locked in a dispute are helped to find mutually-agreeable solutions by this charity's volunteers, says David Baker', FT.com (30 March 2007).

---

mediator
A neutral third party who facilitates a negotiated solution by using reasoning, persuasion and suggestions for alternatives.

arbitrator
A third party to a negotiation who has the authority to dictate an agreement.

A **mediator** is a neutral third party who facilitates a negotiated solution by using reasoning and persuasion, suggesting alternatives, and the like. Mediators are widely used in labour-management negotiations and in civil court disputes. The overall effectiveness of mediated negotiations is fairly impressive. The settlement rate is approximately 60 per cent, with negotiator satisfaction at about 75 per cent. But the situation is the key to whether or not mediation will succeed; the conflicting parties must be motivated to bargain and resolve their conflict. In addition, conflict intensity can't be too high; mediation is most effective under moderate levels of conflict. Finally, perceptions of the mediator are important; to be effective, the mediator must be perceived as neutral and noncoercive.

An **arbitrator** is a third party with the authority to dictate an agreement. Arbitration can be voluntary (requested by the parties) or compulsory (forced on the parties by law or contract). The big plus of arbitration over mediation is that it always results in a settlement. Whether or not there is a negative side depends on how 'heavy-handed' the arbitrator appears. If one party is left feeling overwhelmingly defeated, that party is certain to be dissatisfied and unlikely to graciously accept the arbitrator's decision. Therefore, the conflict may resurface at a later time.

conciliator
A trusted third party who provides an informal communication link between the negotiator and the opponent.

consultant
An impartial third party, skilled in conflict management, who attempts to facilitate creative problem solving through communication and analysis.

A **conciliator** is a trusted third party who provides an informal communication link between the negotiator and the opponent. Conciliation does not have the authority to dictate an agreement as arbitration does. Comparing its effectiveness to mediation has proven difficult because the two overlap a great deal. In practice, conciliators typically act as more than mere communication conduits. They also engage in fact-finding, interpreting messages and persuading disputants to develop agreements.

A **consultant** is a skilled and impartial third party who attempts to facilitate problem solving through communication and analysis, aided by a knowledge of conflict management. In contrast to the previous roles, the consultant's role is not to settle the issues, but, rather, to improve relations between the conflicting parties so that they can reach a settlement themselves. Instead of putting forward specific solutions, the consultant tries to help the parties learn to understand and work with each other. Therefore, this approach has a longer-term focus: to build new and positive perceptions and attitudes between the conflicting parties.

Global implications

Conflict and culture

9 Describe cultural differences in conflict and negotiation.

Although there has been relatively little research on cross-cultural differences in how different cultures view, react to, and manage workplace conflict, more studies are beginning to emerge. One major study carried out in 2008 questioned 5,000 full-time employees in nine countries around Europe and the Americas: Belgium, Brazil, Denmark, France, Germany, Ireland, the Netherlands, the United Kingdom and the United States.[53] The results revealed that dealing with conflict was something that a vast majority (85 per cent) of employees in all of these countries had to contend with. There were also some interesting differences between countries; for example, German workers reported the highest levels of conflict: 56 per cent of employees have to deal with conflict 'always' or 'frequently', compared to the overall average of 29 per cent. Here is a selection of the European findings:

Belgium. The incidence of workplace conflict was found to be comparatively low and when there is a conflict a high percentage of employees sought to avoid disagreements. Suggesting a lack of functional conflict, Belgium had one of the highest proportions of workers who fail to experience any positive outcomes from conflict.

France. Although French workers face as much conflict as those in other countries, they experienced fewer negative outcomes than most. They ranked among the lowest for conflicts that led to personal attacks, people leaving or colleagues getting fired. French workers were the most likely to avoid conflict and least likely to seek win/win situations. They are also the least apt to seek advice from colleagues or use a documented process. The research suggested that dealing with workplace conflict is something of a taboo in French organizations and point to the fact that employees had the least training of any country surveyed in how to manage conflict.

Germany. Of all the countries analysed, German employees reported the most workplace conflict and the highest incidence of negative outcomes: almost twice as many say that conflict led to bullying or project failure as anywhere else in the world. A third said that it led to sickness or absence, compared to under a quarter elsewhere. Curiously, Germany is the only country in the study not to rank personality clashes as the most common cause of conflict. In the German workplace, according to employees there, stress is the number one factor underlying disputes.

The Netherlands. Dutch employees experienced the lowest levels of conflict and were the least concerned about it than any other country in the study. By the same token, comparatively few had seen any positive outcomes emerge from a conflict. This suggests that the Dutch tendency to compromise when conflict does occur leads to generally neutral and middling outcomes for both parties.

United Kingdom. Behind only the Dutch, employees in the UK are the next least likely to say they experience conflict. Like the Dutch, UK workers are most likely to deal with the situation by seeking to compromise. The research does suggest that the relatively low figure for experiencing conflict may be due to commonly attributed national characteristics such as a desire to avoid disharmony and a reluctance to get involved in conflict (or even to be aware that it's happening).

Cultural differences in negotiations

Compared to the research on conflict, there is a lot more research on how negotiating styles vary across national cultures.[54] One extensively researched study found negotiation elements that consistently differ in cross-cultural negotiations.

First, negotiators from different cultures may tend to view the purpose of a negotiation differently. For deal makers from some cultures (e.g. Spain), the goal of a business negotiation is a signed contract between the parties. Other cultures (e.g. India) tend to consider that the goal of a negotiation is not a signed contract but rather the creation of a relationship between the two sides. The difference in approach may explain why certain Asian negotiators tend to give more time and effort to negotiation preliminaries.

Second, whether the negotiation process is seen as win/win or win/lose differs across cultures. Win/win negotiators are likely to see deal making as a collaborative, problem-solving process whereas win/lose negotiators are likely to view it as confrontational. For example, the study found that 100 per cent of Japanese respondents claimed that they approached negotiations as a win/win process, whereas only 33 per cent of Spanish executives took that view.

Third, whether the negotiation style is formal or informal differs. It has been observed, for example, that Germans have a more formal style than Americans.

Fourth, there are differences in whether negotiators show or hide emotions. The investigation found that the Germans and English ranked as the least emotional, while among Asian countries the Japanese held that position, but to a lesser degree. Although other differences were found in the review, the final element that will be presented here is risk taking. In deal making, the negotiators' cultures can affect the willingness of one side to take risks – to divulge information, try new approaches and tolerate uncertainties in a proposed course of action. The Japanese are said to be highly risk averse in negotiations, and this tendency was affirmed by the survey. Americans, by comparison, considered themselves to be risk takers, but an even higher percentage of the French, British and Indians claimed to be risk takers.[55]

Summary and implications for managers

Many people automatically assume that conflict is related to lower group and organizational performance. This chapter has demonstrated that this assumption is frequently incorrect. Conflict can be either constructive or destructive to the functioning of a group or unit. As shown in Figure 15.6, levels of conflict can be either too high or too low. Either extreme hinders performance. An optimal level is one at which there is enough conflict to prevent stagnation, stimulate creativity, allow tensions to be released and initiate the seeds for change, yet not so much as to be disruptive or to deter coordination of activities.

What advice can we give managers faced with excessive conflict and the need to reduce it? Don't assume that one conflict-handling intention will always be best! You should select an intention appropriate for the situation. The following are some guidelines:[56]

- Use *competition* when quick, decisive action is vital (in emergencies), on important issues, where unpopular actions need to be implemented (in cost cutting, enforcing unpopular rules, discipline), on issues vital to the organization's welfare when you know you're rights and against people who take advantage of noncompetitive behaviour.

- Use *collaboration* to find an integrative solution when both sets of concerns are too important to be compromised, when your objective is to learn, to merge insights from people with

Figure 15.6   Conflict and unit performance

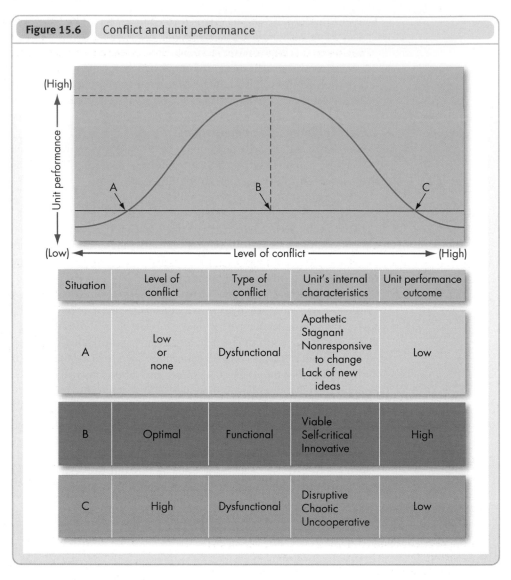

Situation	Level of conflict	Type of conflict	Unit's internal characteristics	Unit performance outcome
A	Low or none	Dysfunctional	Apathetic Stagnant Nonresponsive to change Lack of new ideas	Low
B	Optimal	Functional	Viable Self-critical Innovative	High
C	High	Dysfunctional	Disruptive Chaotic Uncooperative	Low

different perspectives, to gain commitment by incorporating concerns into a consensus, and to work through feelings that have interfered with a relationship.

- Use *avoidance* when an issue is trivial or when more important issues are pressing, when you perceive no chance of satisfying your concerns, when potential disruption outweighs the benefits of resolution, to let people cool down and regain perspective, when gathering information supersedes immediate decision, when others can resolve the conflict more effectively and when issues seem tangential or symptomatic of other issues.

- Use *accommodation* when you find that you're wrong and to allow a better position to be heard, to learn, and to show your reasonableness; when issues are more important to others than to yourself and to satisfy others and maintain cooperation; to build social credits for later issues; to minimise loss when you are outmatched and losing; when harmony and stability are especially important; and to allow employees to develop by learning from mistakes.

- Use *compromise* when goals are important but not worth the effort of potential disruption of more assertive approaches; when opponents with equal power are committed to mutually exclusive goals; to achieve temporary settlements to complex issues; to arrive at expedient solutions under time pressure; and as a backup when collaboration or competition is unsuccessful.

Negotiation is an ongoing activity in groups and organizations. Distributive bargaining can resolve disputes, but it often negatively affects the satisfaction of one or more negotiators because it is focused on the short term and because it is confrontational. Integrative bargaining, in contrast, tends to provide outcomes that satisfy all parties and that build lasting relationships. When engaged in negotiation, make sure you set aggressive goals and try to find creative ways to achieve the goals of both parties, especially when you value the long-term relationship with the other party. That doesn't mean 'giving in' on your self-interest; rather, it means trying to find creative solutions that give both parties what they really want.

POINT/COUNTERPOINT

Conflict benefits organizations

POINT

Let's briefly review how stimulating conflict can provide benefits to the organization:

- **Conflict is a means to solve problems and bring about radical change.** It's an effective device by which management can drastically change the existing power structure, current interaction patterns, and entrenched attitudes. If there is no conflict, it means the real problems aren't being addressed.

- **Conflict facilitates group cohesiveness.** Whereas conflict increases hostility between groups, external threats tend to cause a group to pull together as a unit. Conflict with another group brings together those within each group. Such intragroup cohesion is a

critical resource that groups draw on in good and especially in bad times.

- **Conflict improves group and organizational effectiveness.** Groups or organizations devoid of conflict are likely to suffer from apathy, stagnation, groupthink, and other debilitating diseases. In fact, more organizations probably fail because they have *too little* conflict, not because they have too much. Stagnation is the biggest threat to organizations, but since it occurs slowly, its ill effects often go unnoticed until it's too late. Conflict can break complacency – though most of us don't like conflict, it often is the last best hope of saving an organization.

COUNTERPOINT ←

In general, conflicts are dysfunctional, and it is one of management's major responsibilities to keep conflict intensity as low as humanly possible. A few points support this case:

- **The negative consequences from conflict can be devastating.** The list of negatives associated with conflict is awesome. The most obvious negatives are increased turnover, decreased employee satisfaction, inefficiencies between work units, sabotage, and labour grievances and strikes. Our survey found that in the UK 370 million working days are lost to conflict in some way (i.e. being involved in a disagreement, managing a conflict between co-workers etc). In Germany and

Ireland that figure is an even higher proportion of available working time.[57]

- **Effective managers build teamwork.** A good manager builds a coordinated team. Conflict works against such an objective. When a team works well, the whole becomes greater than the sum of the parts. Management creates teamwork by minimising internal conflicts and facilitating internal coordination.

- **Conflict is avoidable.** It may be true that conflict is inevitable when an organization is in a downward spiral, but the goal of good leadership and effective management is to avoid the spiral to begin with.

QUESTIONS FOR REVIEW

1. What is conflict?

2. What are the differences among the traditional, human relations, and interactionist views of conflict?

3. What are the steps of the conflict process?

4. What is negotiation?

5. What are the differences between distributive and integrative bargaining?

6. What are the five steps in the negotiation process?

7. How do the individual differences of personality and gender influence negotiations?

8. What are the roles and functions of third-party negotiations?

9. How does culture influence negotiations?

36 J. R. Curhan, H. A. Elfenbein and H. Xu, 'What do people value when they negotiate? Mapping the domain of subjective value in negotiation', *Journal of Personality and Social Psychology*, 91, 3 (2006), pp. 493–512.

37 Thomas, 'Conflict and negotiation processes in organizations'.

38 P. M. Morgan and R. S. Tindale, 'Group vs. individual performance in mixed-motive situations: exploring an inconsistency', *Organizational Behavior & Human Decision Processes*, January 2002, pp. 44–65.

39 C. E. Naquin, 'The agony of opportunity in negotiation: number of negotiable issues, counterfactual thinking, and feelings of satisfaction', *Organizational Behavior & Human Decision Processes*, May 2003, pp. 97–107.

40 C. K. W. De Dreu, L. R. Weingart and S. Kwon, 'Influence of social motives on integrative negotiation: a meta-analytic review and test of two theories', *Journal of Personality & Social Psychology*, May 2000, pp. 889–905.

41 This model is based on R. J. Lewicki, 'Bargaining and negotiation', *Exchange: The Organizational Behavior Teaching Journal*, 6, 2 (1981), pp. 39–40.

42 M. H. Bazerman and M. A. Neale, *Negotiating Rationally* (New York: The Free Press, 1992), pp. 67–68.

43 J. A. Wall, Jr., and M. W. Blum, 'Negotiations', *Journal of Management*, June 1991, pp. 278–82.

44 B. Barry and R. A. Friedman, 'Bargainer characteristics in distributive and integrative negotiation', *Journal of Personality & Social Psychology*, February 1998, pp. 345–59.

45 S. Kopelman, A. S. Rosette and L. Thompson, 'The three faces of Eve: strategic displays of positive, negative, and neutral emotions in negotiations', *Organizational Behavior and Human Decision Processes*, 99 (2006), pp. 81–101; and J. M. Brett, M. Olekalns, R. Friedman, N. Goates, C. Anderson and C. C. Lisco, 'Sticks and stones: language, face, and online dispute resolution', *Academy of Management Journal*, 50, 1 (2007), pp. 85–99.

46 C. Watson and L. R. Hoffman, 'Managers as negotiators: a test of power versus gender as predictors of feelings, behavior, and outcomes', *Leadership Quarterly*, Spring 1996, pp. 63–85.

47 A. E. Walters, A. F. Stuhlmacher and L. L. Meyer, 'Gender and negotiator competitiveness: a meta-analysis', *Organizational Behavior and Human Decision Processes*, October 1998, pp. 1–29; and A. F. Stuhlmacher and A. E. Walters, 'Gender differences in negotiation outcome: a meta-analysis', *Personnel Psychology*, Autumn 1999, pp. 653–77.

48 Stuhlmacher and Walters, 'Gender differences in negotiation outcome', p. 655.

49 Bowles, Babcock and Lei, 'Social incentives for gender differences in the propensity to initiative negotiations'.

50 L. J. Kray, A. D. Galinsky and L. Thompson, 'Reversing the gender gap in negotiations: an exploration of stereotype regeneration', *Organizational Behavior & Human Decision Processes*, March 2002, pp. 386–409.

51 C. K. Stevens, A. G. Bavetta and M. E. Gist, 'Gender differences in the acquisition of salary negotiation skills: the role of goals, self-efficacy, and perceived control', *Journal of Applied Psychology*, 78, 5 (October 1993), pp. 723–35.

52 Wall and Blum, 'Negotiations', pp. 283–87.

53 *Fight, Flight or Face it? Celebrating the Effective Management of Conflict at Work*, CIPD/OPP 2008.

54 M. J. Gelfand, M. Higgins, L. H. Nishii, J. L. Raver, A. Dominguez, F. Murakami, S. Yamaguchi and M. Toyama, 'Culture and egocentric perceptions of fairness in conflict and negotiation', *Journal of Applied Psychology*, October 2002, pp. 833–45; and X. Lin and S. J. Miller, 'Negotiation approaches: direct and indirect effect of national culture', *International Marketing Review*, 20, 3 (2003), pp. 286–303.

55 J. *Salacuse* (2005) 'Negotiating: the top ten ways that culture can affect your negotiation', *Ivey Business Journal Online*, London: March–April, p. 1.

56 K. W. Thomas, 'Toward multidimensional values in teaching: the example of conflict behaviors', *Academy of Management Review*, July 1977, p. 487.

57 *Fight, Flight or Face it? Celebrating the Effective Management of Conflict at Work*, CIPD/OPP 2008.

58 K. O'Connor and P. Carnevale, 'A nasty but effective negotiation strategy: misrepresentation of a common-value issue', *Personality and Social Psychology Bulletin*, May 1997, pp. 504–15.

Foundations of organization structure

After studying this chapter, you should be able to:

1 Identify the six elements of an organization's structure.

2 Identify the characteristics of a bureaucracy.

3 Describe a matrix organization.

4 Identify the characteristics of a virtual organization.

5 Show why managers want to create boundaryless organizations.

6 Demonstrate how organizational structures differ and contrast mechanistic and organic structural models.

7 Analyse the behavioural implications of different organizational designs.

8 Show how globalisation affects organizational structure.

Every revolution evaporates and leaves behind only the slime of a new bureaucracy.

Franz Kafka

This organization is disorganization!

Justin Williams/Press Association Images

More than 20 years ago, Lars Kolind and his colleagues built a business model so daring – and so successful – that they conquered new markets and captured the imagination of business innovators around the world that has influenced organizational design to this day.

Lars Kolind arrived at Oticon, a Danish hearing aid manufacturer, in 1988 to revive a deeply troubled company. He cut costs, increased productivity and quickly steered the company back into the black. But he realised that incremental improvements would not be enough to prosper against diversified giants such as Sony, Siemens and Philips. On New Year's Day 1990, Kolind released a four-page memo on reinventing the company. It amounted to a declaration of disorganization.

Oticon needed breakthroughs, Kolind wrote, and breakthroughs 'require the combination of technology with audiology, psychology and imagination. The ability to "think the unthinkable" and make it happen.' In organizations of the future, he continued, 'staff would be liberated to grow, personally and professionally, and to become more creative, action-oriented, and efficient.' What was the enemy of these new organizations? The organization itself.

So Kolind abolished the formal organization. Projects, not functions or departments, became the defining unit of work. Oticon teams formed, disbanded and formed again as the work required. Project leaders (basically, anyone with a compelling idea) competed to attract the resources and people to deliver results. Project owners (members of the company's 10-person management team) provided advice and support, but made few actual decisions. The company had a hundred or so projects at any one time, and most people worked on several projects at once. It was, essentially, a free market in work.

'We want each project to feel like a company, and the project leader to feel like a CEO,' Kolind said. 'We allow a lot of freedom. We don't worry if we use more resources than planned. Deadlines are what really matter.' The company's physical space reflects its logic of work. All vestiges of hierarchy disappeared. Oticon headquarters was transformed into an anti-paper anti-office with uniform mobile workstations consisting of desks without drawers and state-of-the-art networked computers. People are always on the move, their 'office' nothing more than where they choose to park their caddie for the duration of a project – anywhere from a few weeks to several months. It was an environment that maximised walking, talking and acting.

Kolind called it the spaghetti organization, because the place had no fixed structure yet somehow held together. Ideas bubbled up and turned into hits such as a new hearing aid that required less adjustment. Sales and profits soared and the company became a model for management creativity.

Today, although some of the old structures have crept back in as the company has grown and Kolind eventually left, the spaghetti revolution still survives. None of the 500 head-office employees at Oticon even has a cubicle. The latest headquarters features few interior walls. Workers sit around the perimeter of the building at simple desks. They attend meetings on sofas in the middle of each floor. The relaxed atmosphere helps retain top engineers, keeping Oticon at the forefront of innovation. And the company remains very successful.

But some things have clearly changed. Everyone has a boss to whom they report and they no longer have total freedom to choose projects. That seems to suit people fine. A degree of freedom sparks creativity, but Oticon workers also feel comfortable with some formalisation. The trick is striking the right balance.

Sources: P. LaBarre (1996) 'This organization is dis-organization, *Fast Company*, December 18, 2007; J. Ewing 'No-cubicle culture: hearing-aid maker Oticon removed all office boundaries – and has flourished by learning which ones it needs', *Business Week*, 4047 (20 August 2007), p. 60.

Structural decisions are arguably the most fundamental ones a leader, such as Oticon's Lars Kolind, has to make. Before we delve into the elements of an organization's structure and how they can affect behaviour, consider how you might react to one type of organizational structure – the bureaucratic structure – by taking the following self-assessment.

SELF-ASSESSMENT LIBRARY

Do I like bureaucracy?

In the Self-assessment library (available online), take assessment IV.F.2 (Do I like bureaucracy?) and answer the following questions.

1. Judging from the results, how willing are you to work in a bureaucratic organization?

2. Do you think scores on this measure matter? Why or why not?

3. Do you think people who score very low (or even very high) on this measure should try to adjust their preferences based on where they are working?

What is organizational structure?

1 Identify the six elements of an organization's structure.

organizational structure
The way in which job tasks are formally divided, grouped, and coordinated.

An **organizational structure** defines how job tasks are formally divided, grouped, and coordinated. There are six key elements that managers need to address when they design their organization's structure: work specialisation, departmentalisation, chain of command, span of control, centralisation and decentralisation, and formalisation.[1] Table 16.1 presents each of these elements as answers to an important structural question. The following sections describe these six elements of structure.

Work specialisation

Early in the twentieth century, Henry Ford became rich and famous by building automobiles on an assembly line. Every Ford worker was assigned a specific, repetitive task. For instance, one person would just put on the right-front wheel and someone else would install the right-front door. By breaking jobs up into small standardised tasks, which could be performed over and over again, Ford was able to produce cars at the rate of one every 10 seconds, while using employees who had relatively limited skills.

Table 16.1	Key design questions and answers for designing the proper organizational structure	
The key question		**The answer is provided by**
1. To what degree are activities subdivided into separate jobs?		Work specialisation
2. On what basis will jobs be grouped together?		Departmentalisation
3. To whom do individuals and groups report?		Chain of command
4. How many individuals can a manager efficiently and effectively direct?		Span of control
5. Where does decision-making authority lie?		Centralisation and decentralisation
6. To what degree will there be rules and regulations to direct employees and managers?		Formalisation

Work is specialised at the Russian factories that manufacture the wooden nesting dolls called *matryoshkas*. At this factory outside Moscow, individuals specialise in doing part of the doll production, from the craftsmen who carve the dolls to the painters who decorate them. Work specialisation brings efficiency to doll production, as some 50 employees can make 100 *matryoshkas* every two days.

work specialisation
The degree to which tasks in an organization are subdivided into separate jobs.

Ford demonstrated that work can be performed more efficiently if employees are allowed to specialise. Today we use the term **work specialisation**, or *division of labour*, to describe the degree to which activities in the organization are subdivided into separate jobs. The essence of work specialisation is that rather than an entire job being done by one individual, it is broken down into a number of steps, with each step being completed by a separate individual. In essence, individuals specialise in doing part of an activity rather than the entire activity.

By the late 1940s, most manufacturing jobs in industrialised countries were being done with high work specialisation. Because not all employees in an organization have the same skills, management saw specialisation as a means to make the most efficient use of its employees' skills. Managers also saw other efficiencies that could be achieved through work specialisation. Employee skills at performing a task successfully increase through repetition. Less time is spent in changing tasks, in putting away one's tools and equipment from a prior step in the work process, and in getting ready for another. Equally important, training for specialisation is more efficient from the organization's perspective. It's easier and less costly to find and train workers to do specific and repetitive tasks. This is especially true of highly sophisticated and complex operations. For example, could Airbus produce an A380, the world's largest passenger plane, if one person had to build the entire plane alone? Not likely! finally, work specialisation increases efficiency and productivity by encouraging the creation of special inventions and machinery.

For much of the first half of the twentieth century, managers viewed work specialisation as an unending source of increased productivity; and they were probably right. Because specialisation was not widely practised, its introduction almost always generated higher productivity. But by the 1960s, there came increasing evidence that a good thing can be carried too far. The point had been reached in some jobs at which the human diseconomies from specialisation – which surfaced as boredom, fatigue, stress, low productivity, poor quality, increased absenteeism and high turnover – more than offset the economic advantages (see Figure 16.1). In such cases, productivity could be increased by enlarging, rather than narrowing, the scope of job activities. In addition, a number of companies found that by giving employees a variety of activities to do,

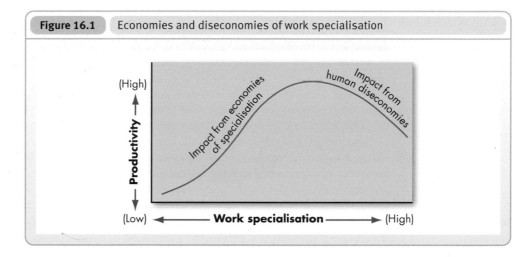

| **Figure 16.1** | Economies and diseconomies of work specialisation |

allowing them to do a whole and complete job, and putting them into teams with interchangeable skills, they often achieved significantly higher output, with increased employee satisfaction.

Most managers today see work specialisation as neither obsolete nor an unending source of increased productivity. Rather, managers recognise the economies it provides in certain types of jobs and the problems it creates when it's carried too far. You'll find, for example, high work specialisation being used by McDonald's to efficiently make and sell hamburgers and fries and by medical specialists in most health organizations. On the other hand, companies such as W.L. Gore have had success by broadening the scope of jobs and reducing specialisation.

Departmentalisation

Once you've divided jobs up through work specialisation, you need to group these jobs together so that common tasks can be coordinated. The basis by which jobs are grouped together is called **departmentalisation**.

departmentalisation
The basis by which jobs in an organization are grouped together.

One of the most popular ways to group activities is by *functions* performed. A manufacturing manager might organize a plant by separating engineering, accounting, manufacturing, personnel, and supply specialists into common departments. Of course, departmentalisation by function can be used in all types of organizations. Only the functions change to reflect the organization's objectives and activities. A hospital might have departments devoted to research, patient care, accounting, and so forth. A professional football franchise might have departments entitled Player Personnel, Ticket Sales and Travel and Accommodations. The major advantage to this type of grouping is obtaining efficiencies from putting like specialists together. Functional departmentalisation seeks to achieve economies of scale by placing people with common skills and orientations into common units.

Jobs can also be departmentalised by the type of *product* the organization produces. Procter & Gamble, for instance, is organized along these lines. Each major product – such as Tide, Pampers, Charmin and Pringles – is placed under the authority of an executive who has complete global responsibility for that product. The major advantage to this type of grouping is increased accountability for product performance, since all activities related to a specific product are under the direction of a single manager. If an organization's activities were service related rather than product related, each service would be autonomously grouped.

Another way to departmentalise is on the basis of *geography* or territory. The sales function, for instance, may have northern, western, eastern and southern European regions. Each of these regions is, in effect, a department organized around geography. If an organization's customers are scattered over a large geographic area and have similar needs based on their location, then this form of departmentalisation can be valuable.

Process departmentalisation can be used for processing customers as well as products. If you've ever been to a motor vehicle office to get a driver's licence, you probably went through several departments before receiving your licence. For example, applicants may go through three steps, each handled by a separate department: (1) validation by motor vehicles division; (2) processing by the licensing department; and (3) payment collection.

A final category of departmentalisation is to use the particular type of *customer* the organization seeks to reach. Microsoft, for instance, is organized around four customer markets: consumers, large corporations, software developers and small businesses. The assumption underlying customer departmentalisation is that customers in each department have a common set of problems and needs that can best be met by having specialists for each.

Large organizations may use all of the forms of departmentalisation that we've described. A major Japanese electronics firm, for instance, organizes each of its divisions along functional lines and its manufacturing units around processes; it departmentalises sales around seven geographic regions and divides each sales region into four customer groupings. Across organizations of all sizes, one strong trend has developed over the past decade. Rigid, functional departmentalisation is being increasingly complemented by teams that cross over traditional departmental lines. As we described in Chapter 10, as tasks have become more complex and more diverse skills are needed to accomplish those tasks, management has turned to cross-functional teams.

Chain of command

Thirty-five years ago, the chain-of-command concept was a basic cornerstone in the design of organizations. As you'll see, it has far less importance today.[2] But contemporary managers should still consider its implications when they decide how best to structure their organizations. The **chain of command** is an unbroken line of authority that extends from the top of the organization to the lowest echelon and clarifies who reports to whom. It answers questions for employees such as 'To whom do I go if I have a problem?' and 'To whom am I responsible?'

You can't discuss the chain of command without discussing two complementary concepts: *authority* and *unity of command*. **Authority** refers to the rights inherent in a managerial position to give orders and expect the orders to be obeyed. To facilitate coordination, each managerial position is given a place in the chain of command, and each manager is given a degree of authority in order to meet their responsibilities. The **unity-of-command** principle helps preserve the concept of an unbroken line of authority. It states that a person should have one and only one superior to whom that person is directly responsible. If the unity of command is broken, an employee might have to cope with conflicting demands or priorities from several superiors.

Times change, and so do the basic tenets of organizational design. The concepts of chain of command, authority and unity of command have substantially less relevance today because of advancements in information technology and the trend toward empowering employees. For instance, a low-level employee today can access information in seconds that 35 years ago was available only to top managers. Similarly, networked computers increasingly allow employees anywhere in an organization to communicate with anyone else without going through formal channels. Moreover, the concepts of authority and maintaining the chain of command are increasingly less relevant as operating employees are being empowered to make decisions that previously were reserved for management. Add to this the popularity of self-managed and cross-functional teams and the creation of new structural designs that include multiple bosses, and the unity-of-command concept takes on less relevance. There are, of course, still many organizations that find they can be most productive by enforcing the chain of command. There just seem to be fewer of them today.

Span of control

How many employees can a manager efficiently and effectively direct? This question of **span of control** is important because, to a large degree, it determines the number of levels and managers an organization has. All things being equal, the wider or larger the span, the more efficient the organization. An example can illustrate the validity of this statement.

Assume that we have two organizations, each of which has approximately 4,100 operative-level employees. As Figure 16.2 illustrates, if one has a uniform span of four and the other a span

chain of command
The unbroken line of authority that extends from the top of the organization to the lowest echelon and clarifies who reports to whom.

authority
The rights inherent in a managerial position to give orders and to expect the orders to be obeyed.

unity of command
The idea that a subordinate should have only one superior to whom he or she is directly responsible.

span of control
The number of subordinates a manager can efficiently and effectively direct.

| Figure 16.2 | Contrasting spans of control |

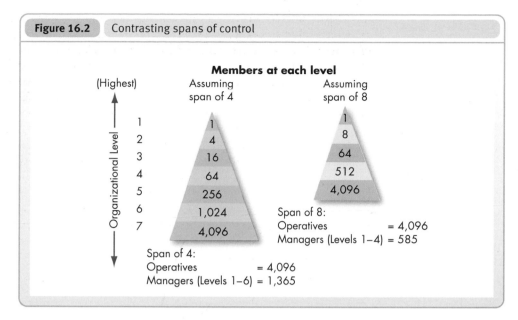

Members at each level

Span of 4:
Operatives = 4,096
Managers (Levels 1–6) = 1,365

Span of 8:
Operatives = 4,096
Managers (Levels 1–4) = 585

of eight, the wider span would have two fewer levels and approximately 800 fewer managers. If the average manager made €50,000 a year, the wider span would save €40 million a year in management salaries! Obviously, wider spans are more efficient in terms of cost. However, at some point, wider spans reduce effectiveness. That is, when the span becomes too large, employee performance suffers because supervisors no longer have the time to provide the necessary leadership and support.

Narrow, or small, spans have their advocates. By keeping the span of control to five or six employees, a manager can maintain close control.[3] But narrow spans have three major drawbacks. First, as already described, they're expensive because they add levels of management. Second, they make vertical communication in the organization more complex. The added levels of hierarchy slow down decision making and tend to isolate upper management. Third, narrow spans of control encourage overly tight supervision and discourage employee autonomy.

The trend in recent years has been toward wider spans of control.[4] They're consistent with recent efforts by companies to reduce costs, cut overheads, speed up decision making, increase flexibility, get closer to customers and empower employees. However, to ensure that performance doesn't suffer because of these wider spans, organizations have been investing heavily in employee training. Managers recognise that they can handle a wider span when employees know their jobs inside and out or can turn to their coworkers when they have questions.

Centralisation and decentralisation

In some organizations, top managers make all the decisions. Lower-level managers merely carry out top management's directives. At the other extreme, there are organizations in which decision making is pushed down to the managers who are closest to the action. The former organizations are highly centralised; the latter are decentralised.

centralisation
The degree to which decision making is concentrated at a single point in an organization.

The term **centralisation** refers to the degree to which decision making is concentrated at a single point in the organization. The concept includes only formal authority – that is, the rights inherent in one's position. Typically, it's said that if top management makes the organization's key decisions with little or no input from lower-level personnel, then the organization is centralised. In contrast, the more that lower-level personnel provide input or are actually given the discretion to make decisions, the more decentralisation there is. An organization characterised by centralisation is an inherently different structural animal from one that is decentralised. In a decentralised organization, action can be taken more quickly to solve problems, more people provide input into decisions and employees are less likely to feel alienated from those who make the decisions that affect their work lives.

Consistent with recent management efforts to make organizations more flexible and responsive, there has been a marked trend toward decentralising decision making. In large companies, lower-level managers are closer to 'the action' and typically have more detailed knowledge about problems than do top managers. For instance, Germany's SMA Technology puts decision making in the hands of employees. 'Reason instead of power' is the motto when decisions are made. This approach leads to employees having a feeling of greater ownership over what they do and makes them more innovative and responsive to customers.

SELF-ASSESSMENT LIBRARY

How willing am I to delegate?

In the Self-assessment library (available online), take assessment III.A.2 (How willing am I to delegate?).

Formalisation

formalisation
The degree to which jobs within an organization are standardised.

Formalisation refers to the degree to which jobs within the organization are standardised. If a job is highly formalised, then the job incumbent has a minimum amount of discretion over what is to be done, when it is to be done and how it is to be done. Employees can be expected always to handle the same input in exactly the same way, resulting in a consistent and uniform output. There are explicit job descriptions, lots of organizational rules, and clearly defined procedures covering work processes in organizations in which there is high formalisation. Where formalisation is low, job behaviours are relatively nonprogrammed, and employees have a great deal of freedom to exercise discretion in their work. Because an individual's discretion on the job is inversely related to the amount of behaviour in that job that is preprogrammed by the organization, the greater the standardisation, the less input the employee has into how the work is to be done. Standardisation not only eliminates the possibility of employees engaging in alternative behaviours but it even removes the need for employees to consider alternatives.

The degree of formalisation can vary widely between organizations and within organizations. Certain jobs, for instance, are well known to have little formalisation. University book sales reps – the representatives of publishers who call on professors to inform them of their company's new publications – have a great deal of freedom in their jobs. They have no standard sales 'spiel', and the extent of rules and procedures governing their behaviour may be little more than the requirement that they submit a weekly sales report and some suggestions on what to emphasise for the various new titles. At the other extreme, there are clerical and editorial positions in the same publishing houses for which employees are required to be at their desks by 8:00 A.M. or be docked a half-hour's pay and, once at that desk, to follow a set of precise procedures dictated by management.

SIEMENS'S SIMPLE STRUCTURE – NOT   OB IN THE NEWS

There is perhaps no tougher task for an executive than to restructure a European organization. Ask former Siemens CEO Klaus Kleinfeld.

Siemens, with €80 billion in revenues in 2006 and branches in 190 countries, is one of the largest electronics companies in the world. Although the company has long been respected for its engineering prowess, it's also derided for its sluggishness and mechanistic structure. So when Kleinfeld took over as CEO, he sought to restructure the company. He has tried to make the structure less bureaucratic so that decisions are made faster. He spun off underperforming businesses. And he simplified the company's structure.

Kleinfeld's efforts drew angry protests from employee groups, with constant picket lines outside his corporate offices. One of the challenges of transforming European organizations is the active participation of employees in executive decisions. Half the seats on the Siemens board of directors are allocated to labour representatives. Not surprisingly, the labour groups did not react positively to Kleinfeld's restructuring efforts. In his efforts to speed those efforts, labour groups alleged, Kleinfeld secretly bankrolled a business-friendly workers' group to try to undermine Germany's main industrial union.

Due to this and other allegations, Kleinfeld was forced out in June 2007 and replaced by Peter Löscher. Löscher has found the same tensions between inertia and the need for restructuring. Only a month after becoming CEO, Löscher was faced with a decision whether to spin off its under-performing €8 billion auto parts unit, VDO. Löscher has to weigh the forces for stability, who wish to protect worker interests, with pressures for financial performance. One of VDO's possible buyers is a US company, TRW, the con-trolling interest of which is held by US private equity firm Blackstone. Private equity firms have been called 'locusts'

by German labour representatives, so, more than most CEOs, Löscher has to balance worker interests with pressure for financial performance.

Source: Based on M. Esterl and D. Crawford, 'Siemens CEO put to early test', *Wall Street Journal*, 23 July 2007, p. A8; and J. Ewing, 'Siemens' culture clash', *BusinessWeek*, 29 January 2007, pp. 42–46.

Common organizational designs

We now turn to describing three of the more common organizational designs found in use: the *simple structure*, the *bureaucracy*, and the *matrix structure*.

The simple structure

What do a small retail store, an electronics firm run by a hard-driving entrepreneur, and an airline in the midst of a companywide pilot's strike have in common? They probably all use the **simple structure**.

The simple structure is said to be characterised most by what it is not rather than by what it is. The simple structure is not elaborate.[5] It has a low degree of departmentalisation, wide spans of control, authority centralised in a single person and little formalisation. The simple structure is a 'flat' organization; it usually has only two or three vertical levels, a loose body of employees and one individual in whom the decision-making authority is centralised.

The simple structure is most widely practised in small businesses in which the manager and the owner are one and the same. This, for example, is illustrated in Figure 16.3, an organization chart for a retail men's store. Jack Gold owns and manages this store. Although he employs five full-time salespeople, a cashier, and extra personnel for weekends and holidays, he 'runs the show'. But large companies, in times of crisis, often simplify their structures as a means of focus-ing their resources. For example, Pat Russo chief executive of Alcatel-Lucent, the Paris based global telecommunications corporation, was given a month to present an emergency restruc-turing plan to simplify the firms organizational structure. The board of Directors believed slow decision-making contributed to a crisis that led to three profit warnings in less than 10 months.

The strength of the simple structure lies in its simplicity. It's fast, flexible and inexpensive to maintain, and accountability is clear. One major weakness is that it's difficult to maintain in any-thing other than small organizations. It becomes increasingly inadequate as an organization grows because its low formalisation and high centralisation tend to create information overload at the top. As size increases, decision making typically becomes slower and can eventually come

simple structure
A structure characterised by a low degree of departmentalisation, wide spans of control, authority centralised in a single person and little formalisation.

Figure 16.3   A simple structure (Jack Gold's men's store)

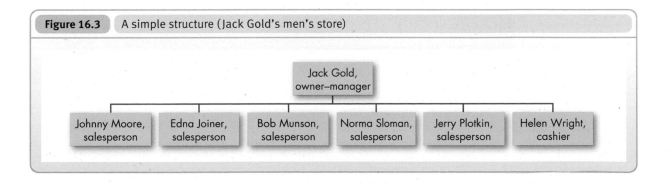

to a standstill as the single executive tries to continue making all the decisions. This often proves to be the undoing of many small businesses. When an organization begins to employ 50 or 100 people, it's very difficult for the owner–manager to make all the choices. If the structure isn't changed and made more elaborate, the firm often loses momentum and can eventually fail. The simple structure's other weakness is that it's risky – everything depends on one person. One person leaving the firm can literally destroy the organization's information and decision-making centre.

The bureaucracy

2 Identify the characteristics of a bureaucracy.

bureaucracy
A structure with highly routine operating tasks achieved through specialisation, very formalised rules and regulations, tasks that are grouped into functional departments, centralised authority, narrow spans of control and decision making that follows the chain of command.

Standardisation! That's the key concept that underlies all bureaucracies. Take a look at the bank where you keep your account, the department store where you buy your clothes, or the government offices that collect your taxes, enforce health regulations, or provide local fire protection. They all rely on standardised work processes for coordination and control.

The **bureaucracy** is characterised by highly routine operating tasks achieved through specialisation, very formalised rules and regulations, tasks that are grouped into functional departments, centralised authority, narrow spans of control and decision making that follows the chain of command. As the opening quote to this chapter attests, *bureaucracy* is a dirty word in many people's minds. However, it does have its advantages. The primary strength of the bureaucracy lies in its ability to perform standardised activities in a highly efficient manner. Putting like specialties together in functional departments results in economies of scale, minimum duplication of personnel and equipment, and employees who have the opportunity to talk 'the same language' among their peers. Furthermore, bureaucracies can get by nicely with less talented – and, hence, less costly – middle- and lower-level managers. The pervasiveness of rules and regulations substitutes for managerial discretion. Standardised operations, coupled with high formalisation, allow decision making to be centralised. There is little need, therefore, for innovative and experienced decision makers below the level of senior executives.

DVLA

The Driver and Vehicle Licensing Agency (DVLA) in the U.K. relies on standardised work processes for coordination and control. DVLA employees follow formalised rules and regulations in performing their routine operating tasks. The bureaucracy of the DVLA enables employees to perform standardised activities in an efficient way. This allows the DVLA, which collects car tax and maintains registers of drivers and vehicles, to process over 95 million vehicle and 17.5 million driver transactions per year.

One of the major weaknesses of a bureaucracy is illustrated in the following dialogue among four executives in one company: 'Ya know, nothing happens in this place until we *produce* something,' said the production executive. 'Wrong,' commented the research and development manager. 'Nothing happens until we *design* something!' 'What are you talking about?' asked the marketing executive. 'Nothing happens here until we *sell* something!' finally, the exasperated accounting manager responded, 'It doesn't matter what you produce, design, or sell. No one knows what happens until we *tally up the results*!' This conversation points up the fact that specialisation creates subunit conflicts. Functional unit goals can override the overall goals of the organization.

The other major weakness of a bureaucracy is something we've all experienced at one time or another when having to deal with people who work in these organizations: obsessive concern with following the rules. When cases arise that don't precisely fit the rules, there is no room for modification. The bureaucracy is efficient only as long as employees confront problems that they have previously encountered and for which programmed decision rules have already been established.

STRUCTURAL CONSIDERATIONS IN MULTINATIONALS | GLOBAL

When bringing out a business innovation in any country, trudging through corporate bureaucracy can cause delays that result in a competitive disadvantage. This is especially true in China, one of the world's fastest-growing economies. Successful multinational corporations operating in China are realising that the optimal structure is decentralised with a relatively high degree of managerial autonomy. Given that more than 1.3 billion people live in China, the opportunity for businesses is tremendous, and as a result, competition is increasing. To take advantage of this opportunity, companies must be able to respond to changes before their competitors.

For example, Tyson Foods gives its vice president and head of the company's China operations, James Rice, the freedom to build the company's business overseas. While walking past a food vendor in Shanghai, Rice got the idea for cumin-flavoured chicken strips. Without the need to obtain approval from upper management, Rice and his team immediately developed the recipe, tested it, and, after receiving a 90 per cent customer-approval rating, began selling the product within two months of coming up with the idea.

Other companies that have implemented more formalised, bureaucratic structures have fared less well. One manager of a consumer electronics company who wanted to reduce the package size of a product to lower its cost and attract lower-income Chinese customers had to send the idea to his boss. His boss, the vice president of Asian operations, then sent the idea to the vice president of international operations, who in turn sent the idea to upper management in the United States. Although the idea was approved, the process took five months, during which a competitor introduced a similarly packaged product.

So, when it comes to innovating in a dynamic, fast-paced economy such as China, decentralisation and autonomy can be major competitive advantages for multinational companies. To gain this competitive advantage, companies like Tyson are empowering their overseas managers to make their own decisions.

Source: Based on C. Hymowitz, 'Executives in China need both autonomy and fast access to boss', *Wall Street Journal*, 10 May 2005, p. B1.

The matrix structure

3 Describe a matrix organization.

matrix structure
A structure that creates dual lines of authority and combines functional and product departmentalisation.

Another popular organizational design option is the **matrix structure**. You'll find it being used in advertising agencies, aerospace firms, research and development laboratories, construction companies, hospitals, government agencies, universities, management consulting firms and entertainment companies.[6] Essentially, the matrix combines two forms of departmentalisation: functional and product departmentalisation.

The strength of functional departmentalisation lies in putting like specialists together, which minimises the number necessary while allowing the pooling and sharing of specialised resources across products. Its major disadvantage is the difficulty of coordinating the tasks of diverse functional specialists so that their activities are completed on time and within budget. Product

Figure 16.4	Matrix structure for a college of business administration

Programmes Academic departments	Undergraduate	Master's	PhD	Research	Executive development	Community service
Accounting						
Finance						
Decision and information systems						
Management						
Marketing						

departmentalisation, on the other hand, has exactly the opposite benefits and disadvantages. It facilitates coordination among specialties to achieve on-time completion and to meet budget targets. Furthermore, it provides clear responsibility for all activities related to a product, but with duplication of activities and costs. The matrix attempts to gain the strengths of each, while avoiding their weaknesses.

The most obvious structural characteristic of the matrix is that it breaks the unity-of-command concept. Employees in the matrix have two bosses – their functional department managers and their product managers. Therefore, the matrix has a dual chain of command.

Figure 16.4 shows the matrix form as used in a college of business administration. The academic departments of accounting, decision and information systems, marketing and so forth are functional units. In addition, specific programmes (that is, products) are overlaid on the functions. In this way, members in a matrix structure have a dual assignment – to their functional department and to their product groups. For instance, a professor of accounting who is teaching an undergraduate course may report to the director of undergraduate programmes as well as to the chairperson of the accounting department.

The strength of the matrix lies in its ability to facilitate coordination when the organization has a multiplicity of complex and interdependent activities. As an organization gets larger, its information-processing capacity can become overloaded. In a bureaucracy, complexity results in increased formalisation. The direct and frequent contact between different specialties in the matrix can make for better communication and more flexibility. Information permeates the organization and more quickly reaches the people who need to take account of it. Furthermore, the matrix reduces 'bureaupathologies' – the dual lines of authority reduce the tendencies of departmental members to become so busy protecting their little worlds that the organization's overall goals become secondary.

There is another advantage to the matrix. It facilitates the efficient allocation of specialists. When individuals with highly specialised skills are lodged in one functional department or product group, their talents are monopolised and underused. The matrix achieves the advantages of economies of scale by providing the organization with both the best resources and an effective way of ensuring their efficient deployment.

The major disadvantages of the matrix lie in the confusion it creates, its propensity to foster power struggles and the stress it places on individuals.[7] When you dispense with the unity-of-command concept, ambiguity is significantly increased, and ambiguity often leads to conflict. For example, it's frequently unclear who reports to whom, and it is not unusual for product managers to fight over getting the best specialists assigned to their products. Confusion and ambiguity also create the seeds of power struggles. Bureaucracy reduces the potential for power

Stephen Dorey/Alamy

Car manufacturers universally outsource production of parts or sections of vehicles and some even contract for the assembly of small numbers of other firms' vehicles. Porsche has taken the notion even further. It has turned to the Finnish firm Valmet Automotive to assemble one of its main product lines, the Cayman and its convertible sibling, the Boxster. This makes Porsche the only major virtual vehicle manufacturer – a company that designs and markets sports cars without actually building them all on its own production line.[8]

grabs by defining the rules of the game. When those rules are 'up for grabs', power struggles between functional and product managers result. For individuals who desire security and absence from ambiguity, this work climate can produce stress. Reporting to more than one boss introduces role conflict, and unclear expectations introduce role ambiguity. The comfort of bureaucracy's predictability is absent, replaced by insecurity and stress.

New design options

4 Identify the characteristics of a virtual organization.

Over the past decade or two, senior managers in a number of organizations have been working to develop new structural options that can better help their firms to compete effectively. In this section, we'll describe two such structural designs: the *virtual organization* and the *boundaryless organization*.

The virtual organization

virtual organization
A small, core organization that outsources major business functions.

Why own when you can rent? That question captures the essence of the **virtual organization** (also sometimes called the *network*, or *modular*, organization), typically a small, core organization that outsources major business functions.[9] In structural terms, the virtual organization is highly centralised, with little or no departmentalisation.

The prototype of the virtual structure is today's movie-making organization. In Hollywood's golden era, movies were made by huge, vertically integrated corporations. Studios such as MGM, Warner Brothers and 20th Century Fox owned large movie lots and employed thousands of full-time specialists – set designers, camera people, film editors, directors, and even actors. Today, most movies are made by a collection of individuals and small companies who come together and make films project by project.[10] This structural form allows each project to be staffed with the talent most suited to its demands, rather than having to choose just from the people employed by the studio. It minimises bureaucratic overheads because there is no lasting organization to maintain. And it lessens long-term risks and their costs because there is no long term – a team is assembled for a finite period and then disbanded.

Ancle Hsu and David Ji run a virtual organization. Their firm, Apex Digital, is one of the world's largest producers of DVD players, yet the company neither owns a factory nor employs an engineer. They contract everything out to firms in China. With minimal investment, Apex has grown from nothing to annual sales of over €400 million in just three years. Virtual organization design is very prevalent in the high-technology industry where concurrent competition and cooperation is rife. For example, Symbian Ltd, a software developer for mobile phones, is a virtual organization set up by a consortium of competitors for handsets, including Nokia, Sony Ericsson, Samsung, Panasonic and Siemens.[11]

Almost all large organizations have increased their outsourcing. For example, companies may outsource their entire information systems to organizations like IBM. Others, such as Aviva and Dell, outsource entire operations – such as customer service or technical support – to other (often overseas) organizations. The Irish airline, Aer Lingus, recently proposed a radical plan to outsource one third of its workforce. Baggage handlers, catering workers, check-in staff and even the cabin crew were targeted.

What's going on here? A quest for maximum flexibility. These virtual organizations have created networks of relationships that allow them to contract out manufacturing, distribution, marketing or any other business function for which management feels that others can do better or more cheaply. The virtual organization stands in sharp contrast to the typical bureaucracy that has many vertical levels of management and where control is sought through ownership. In such organizations, research and development are done in-house, production occurs in company-owned plants, and sales and marketing are performed by the company's own employees. To support all this, management has to employ extra staff, including accountants, human resource specialists and lawyers. The virtual organization, however, outsources many of these functions and concentrates on what it does best.

Figure 16.5 shows a virtual organization in which management outsources all of the primary functions of the business. The core of the organization is a small group of executives whose job is to oversee directly any activities that are done in-house and to coordinate relationships with the other organizations that manufacture, distribute, and perform other crucial functions for the virtual organization. The dotted lines in Figure 16.5 represent the relationships typically maintained under contracts. In essence, managers in virtual structures spend most of their time coordinating and controlling external relations, typically by way of computer-network links.

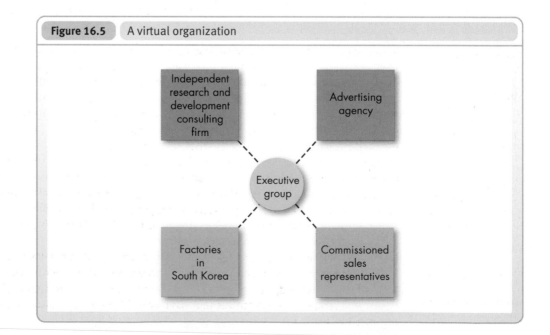

Figure 16.5 A virtual organization

The major advantage to the virtual organization is its flexibility. For instance, it allows individuals with an innovative idea and little money, such as Ancle Hsu and David Ji, to successfully compete against the likes of Sony, Hitachi and Sharp Electronics. The primary drawback to this structure is that it reduces management's control over key parts of its business.

The boundaryless organization

5 Show why managers want to create boundaryless organizations.

General Electric's former chairman, Jack Welch, coined the term **boundaryless organization** to describe his idea of what he wanted GE to become. Welch wanted to turn his company into a 'family grocery store'.[12] That is, in spite of its monstrous size (2008 revenues were €138 billion), he wanted to eliminate *vertical* and *horizontal* boundaries within GE and break down *external* barriers between the company and its customers and suppliers. The boundaryless organization seeks to eliminate the chain of command, have limitless spans of control and replace departments with empowered teams. And because it relies so heavily on information technology, some have turned to calling this structure the *T-form* (or technology-based) organization.[13] Although GE has not yet achieved this boundaryless state – and probably never will – it has made significant progress toward that end. So have other companies, such as Airbus, Nissan, Nestlé and 3M. Let's take a look at what a boundaryless organization would look like and what some firms are doing to try to make it a reality.[14]

boundaryless organization
An organization that seeks to eliminate the chain of command, have limitless spans of control, and replace departments with empowered teams.

By removing vertical boundaries, management flattens the hierarchy. Status and rank are minimised. Cross-hierarchical teams (which include top executives, middle managers, supervisors, and operative employees), participative decision-making practices, and the use of 360-degree performance appraisals (in which peers and others above and below the employee evaluate performance) are examples of what GE is doing to break down vertical boundaries.

6 Demonstrate how organizational structures differ and contrast mechanistic and organic structural models.

Functional departments create horizontal boundaries. And these boundaries stifle interaction between functions, product lines and units. The way to reduce these barriers is to replace functional departments with cross-functional teams and to organize activities around processes. For instance, Xerox now develops new products through multidisciplinary teams that work in a single process instead of around narrow functional tasks. Another way management can cut through horizontal barriers is to use lateral transfers, rotating people into and out of different functional areas. This approach turns specialists into generalists.

Why do structures differ?

mechanistic model
A structure characterised by extensive departmentalisation, high formalisation, a limited information network and centralisation.

In the previous sections, we described a variety of organizational designs ranging from the highly structured and standardised bureaucracy to the loose and amorphous boundaryless organization. The other designs we discussed tend to exist somewhere between these two extremes.

Figure 16.6 reconceptualises our previous discussions by presenting two extreme models of organizational design. One extreme we'll call the **mechanistic model**. It's generally synonymous with the bureaucracy in that it has extensive departmentalisation, high formalisation, a limited information network (mostly downward communication) and little participation by low-level members in decision making. At the other extreme is the **organic model**. This model looks a lot like the boundaryless organization. It's flat, uses cross-hierarchical and cross-functional teams, has low formalisation, possesses a comprehensive information network (using lateral and upward communication as well as downward) and involves high participation in decision making.[15]

organic model
A structure that is flat, uses cross-hierarchical and cross-functional teams, has low formalisation, possesses a comprehensive information network and relies on participative decision making.

With these two models in mind, we're now prepared to address a couple questions: Why are some organizations structured along more mechanistic lines whereas others follow organic characteristics? What are the forces that influence the design that is chosen? In the following pages, we present the major forces that have been identified as causes or determinants of an organization's structure.[16]

Figure 16.6 Mechanistic versus organic models

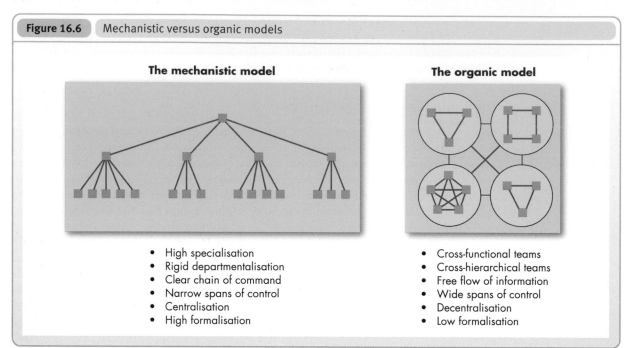

The mechanistic model

- High specialisation
- Rigid departmentalisation
- Clear chain of command
- Narrow spans of control
- Centralisation
- High formalisation

The organic model

- Cross-functional teams
- Cross-hierarchical teams
- Free flow of information
- Wide spans of control
- Decentralisation
- Low formalisation

Strategy

An organization's structure is a means to help management achieve its objectives. Because objectives are derived from the organization's overall strategy, it's only logical that strategy and structure should be closely linked. More specifically, structure should follow strategy. If management makes a significant change in its organization's strategy, the structure will need to be modified to accommodate and support this change.[17]

Most current strategy frameworks focus on three strategy dimensions – innovation, cost minimisation and imitation – and the structural design that works best with each.[18]

To what degree does an organization introduce major new products or services? An **innovation strategy** does not mean a strategy merely for simple or cosmetic changes from previous offerings but rather one for meaningful and unique innovations. Obviously, not all firms pursue innovation. This strategy may appropriately characterise GlaxoSmithKline and Apple, but it's not a strategy pursued by conservative retailer Marks & Spencer.

An organization that is pursuing a **cost-minimisation strategy** tightly controls costs, refrains from incurring unnecessary innovation or marketing expenses, and cuts prices in selling a basic product. This would describe the strategy pursued by Carrefour or the makers of generic grocery products.

Organizations following an **imitation strategy** try to capitalise on the best of both of the previous strategies. They seek to minimise risk and maximise opportunity for profit. Their strategy is to move into new products or new markets only after viability has been proven by innovators. They take the successful ideas of innovators and copy them. Manufacturers of mass-marketed fashion goods that are rip-offs of designer styles follow the imitation strategy. Another example is the camera industry. Sony introduced digital photography in 1981, but it was not until much later when the market had developed and proven itself, that Hewlett-Packard and Nikon entered in the late 1990s.[19]

Table 16.2 describes the structural option that best matches each strategy. Innovators need the flexibility of the organic structure, whereas cost minimisers seek the efficiency and stability of the mechanistic structure. Imitators combine the two structures. They use a mechanistic structure in order to maintain tight controls and low costs in their current activities, while at the same time they create organic subunits in which to pursue new undertakings.

innovation strategy
A strategy that emphasises the introduction of major new products and services.

cost-minimisation strategy
A strategy that emphasises tight cost controls, avoidance of unnecessary innovation or marketing expenses, and price cutting.

imitation strategy
A strategy that seeks to move into new products or new markets only after their viability has already been proven.

Table 16.2	The strategy–structure relationship

Strategy	Structural option
Innovation	Organic: A loose structure; low specialisation, low formalisation, decentralised
Cost minimisation	Mechanistic: Tight control; extensive work specialisation, high formalisation, high centralisation
Imitation	Mechanistic and organic: Mix of loose with tight properties; tight controls over current activities and looser controls for new undertakings

Organization size

There is considerable evidence to support the idea that an organization's size significantly affects its structure.[20] For instance, large organizations – those that typically employ 2,000 or more people – tend to have more specialisation, more departmentalisation, more vertical levels and more rules and regulations than do small organizations. However, the relationship isn't linear. Rather, size affects structure at a decreasing rate. The impact of size becomes less important as an organization expands. Why is this? Essentially, once an organization has around 2,000 employees, it's already fairly mechanistic. An additional 500 employees will not have much impact. On the other hand, adding 500 employees to an organization that has only 300 members is likely to result in a significant shift toward a more mechanistic structure.

Technology

technology
The way in which an organization transfers its inputs into outputs.

The term **technology** refers to how an organization transfers its inputs into outputs. Every organization has at least one technology for converting financial, human and physical resources into products or services. Daimler AG for instance, predominantly uses an assembly-line process

New Line Cinema/Kobal Collection Ltd

The degree of routineness differentiates technologies. The film director Peter Jackson is shown here directing the very successful *Lord of the Rings* trilogy. Nonroutineness characterises the customised work of Jackson who is responsible for creating a vision for the film and guiding the technical crew and actors in the fulfilment of the vision.

to make its cars and trucks. On the other hand, universites may use a number of instruction technologies – the ever-popular formal lecture method, the case-analysis method, the experiential exercise method, the programmed learning method and so forth. In this section we want to show that organizational structures adapt to their technology.

Numerous studies have been carried out on the technology–structure relationship.[21] The details of those studies are quite complex, so we'll go straight to 'the bottom line' and attempt to summarise what we know.

The common theme that differentiates technologies is their *degree of routineness*. By this we mean that technologies tend toward either routine or nonroutine activities. The former are characterised by automated and standardised operations. Nonroutine activities are customised. They include varied operations such as furniture restoring, custom shoemaking, and genetic research.

What relationships have been found between technology and structure? Although the relationship is not overwhelmingly strong, we find that routine tasks are associated with taller and more departmentalised structures. The relationship between technology and formalisation, however, is stronger. Studies consistently show routineness to be associated with the presence of rule manuals, job descriptions, and other formalised documentation. Finally, an interesting relationship has been found between technology and centralisation. It seems logical that routine technologies would be associated with a centralised structure, while nonroutine technologies, which rely more heavily on the knowledge of specialists, would be characterised by delegated decision authority. This position has met with some support. However, a more generalisable conclusion is that the technology-centralisation relationship is moderated by the degree of formalisation. Formal regulations and centralised decision making are both control mechanisms and management can substitute one for the other. Routine technologies should be associated with centralised control if there is a minimum of rules and regulations. However, if formalisation is high, routine technology can be accompanied by decentralisation. So, we would predict that routine technology would lead to centralisation, but only if formalisation is low.

Environment

environment
Institutions or forces outside an organization that potentially affect the organization's performance.

An organization's **environment** is composed of institutions or forces outside the organization that potentially affect the organization's performance. These typically include suppliers, customers, competitors, government regulatory agencies, public pressure groups, and the like.

Why should an organization's structure be affected by its environment? Because of environmental uncertainty. Some organizations face relatively static environments – few forces in their environment are changing. There are, for example, no new competitors, no new technological breakthroughs by current competitors or little activity by public pressure groups to influence the organization. Other organizations face very dynamic environments – rapidly changing government regulations affecting their business, new competitors, difficulties in acquiring raw materials, continually changing product preferences by customers and so on. Static environments create significantly less uncertainty for managers than do dynamic ones. And because uncertainty is a threat to an organization's effectiveness, management will try to minimise it. One way to reduce environmental uncertainty is through adjustments in the organization's structure.[22]

Research has helped clarify what is meant by environmental uncertainty. It's been found that there are three key dimensions to any organization's environment: capacity, volatility, and complexity.[23]

The *capacity* of an environment refers to the degree to which it can support growth. Rich and growing environments generate excess resources, which can buffer the organization in times of relative scarcity.

The degree of instability in an environment is captured in the *volatility* dimension. When there is a high degree of unpredictable change, the environment is dynamic. This makes it difficult for management to predict accurately the probabilities associated with various decision alternatives. Because information technology changes at such a rapid place, more organizations' environments are becoming volatile.

'HIERARCHIES ARE A THING OF THE PAST'   MYTH *OR* SCIENCE?

Mikko Ketokivi argues that this is partly true. He claims that, 'Hierarchies where the subordinate's behaviour is strictly controlled by authority are – or at least should be – a thing of the past for many companies. But "healthy hierarchies" are very much "in". Specifically, there has to be a chain of command in all organizations, and the rules of the hierarchy must be clear. Not all issues can be debated and solved on a peer-to-peer basis and through mutual adjustment, without hierarchy – nothing would get done, we'd sit in meetings all day every day and much of the decision-making would become politicised (some of us already feel this pain in our own organizations). Some decisions must be made by referral to authority.

However, at the same time the top management must understand how to identify and nurture the capabilities that reside in the middle management and the operational level, which is easier said than done.'

Ketokivi's view reflects the notion that hierarchies are not obsolete. They have an important role to play in coordinating and controlling organizations, but hierarchies can also slow decision making causing organizations to become unresponsive in an increasingly volatile environment.

Source: Based on M. Ketokivi, http://www.ketokivi.fi/. Accessed 12 April 2009.

Figure 16.7	Three-dimensional model of the environment

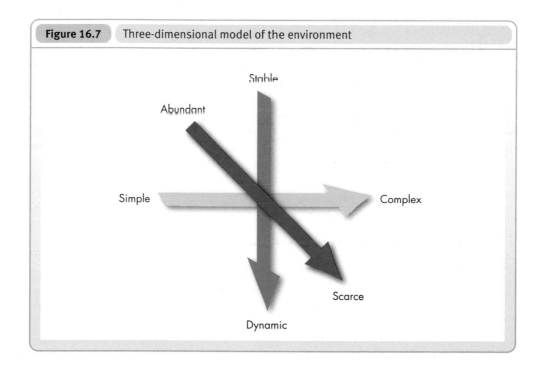

Finally, the environment needs to be assessed in terms of *complexity* – that is, the degree of heterogeneity and concentration among environmental elements. Simple environments – like in the tobacco industry – are homogeneous and concentrated. In contrast, environments characterised by heterogeneity and dispersion – think of companies in the software industry – are called complex, meaning the environment is diverse and the competitors numerous.

Figure 16.7 summarises our definition of the environment along its three dimensions. The arrows in this figure are meant to indicate movement toward higher uncertainty. So organizations that operate in environments characterised as scarce, dynamic and complex face the greatest degree of uncertainty. Why? Because they have little room for error, high unpredictability, and a diverse set of elements in the environment to monitor constantly.

Given this three-dimensional definition of *environment*, we can offer some general conclusions. There is evidence that relates the degrees of environmental uncertainty to different structural arrangements. Specifically, the more scarce, dynamic, and complex the environment, the more organic a structure should be. The more abundant, stable, and simple the environment, the more the mechanistic structure will be preferred.

Organizational designs and employee behaviour

7 Analyse the behavioural implications of different organizational designs.

We opened this chapter by implying that an organization's structure can have significant effects on its members. In this section, we want to assess directly just what those effects might be.

A review of the evidence linking organizational structures to employee performance and satisfaction leads to a pretty clear conclusion – you can't generalise! Not everyone prefers the freedom and flexibility of organic structures. Some people are most productive and satisfied when work tasks are standardised and ambiguity is minimised – that is, in mechanistic structures. So any discussion of the effect of organizational design on employee behaviour has to address individual differences. To illustrate this point, let's consider employee preferences for work specialisation, span of control, and centralisation.[24]

The evidence generally indicates that *work specialisation* contributes to higher employee productivity, but at the price of reduced job satisfaction. However, this statement ignores individual differences and the type of job tasks people do. As we noted previously, work specialisation is not an unending source of higher productivity. Problems start to surface, and productivity begins to suffer, when the human diseconomies of doing repetitive and narrow tasks overtake the economies of specialisation. As the workforce has become more highly educated and desirous of jobs that are intrinsically rewarding, the point at which productivity begins to decline seems to be reached more quickly than in decades past.

Although more people today are undoubtedly turned off by overly specialised jobs than were their parents or grandparents, it would be naive to ignore the reality that there is still a segment of the workforce that prefers the routine and repetitiveness of highly specialised jobs. Some individuals want work that makes minimal intellectual demands and provides the security of routine. For these people, high work specialisation is a source of job satisfaction. The empirical question, of course, is whether this represents 2 per cent of the workforce or 52 per cent. Given that there is some self-selection operating in the choice of careers, we might conclude that negative behavioural outcomes from high specialisation are most likely to surface in professional jobs occupied by individuals with high needs for personal growth and diversity.

A review of the research indicates that it is probably safe to say there is no evidence to support a relationship between *span of control* and employee performance. Although it is intuitively attractive to argue that large spans might lead to higher employee performance because they provide more distant supervision and more opportunity for personal initiative, the research fails to support this notion. At this point it's impossible to state that any particular span of control is best for producing high performance or high satisfaction among employees. Again, the reason is probably individual differences. That is, some people like to be left alone, while others prefer the security of a boss who is quickly available at all times. Consistent with several of the contingency theories of leadership discussed in Chapter 12, we would expect factors such as employees' experiences and abilities and the degree of structure in their tasks to explain when wide or narrow spans of control are likely to contribute to their performance and job satisfaction. However, there is some evidence indicating that a manager's job satisfaction increases as the number of employees supervised increases.

We find fairly strong evidence linking *centralisation* and job satisfaction. In general, organizations that are less centralised have a greater amount of autonomy. And the evidence suggests that autonomy is positively related to job satisfaction. But, again, individual differences surface. While one employee may value their freedom, another may find autonomous environments frustratingly ambiguous.

Our conclusion: To maximise employee performance and satisfaction, individual differences, such as experience, personality and the work task, should be taken into account. As we'll note shortly, culture needs to be taken into consideration, too.

One obvious insight needs to be made before we leave this topic: People don't select employers randomly. There is substantial evidence that individuals are attracted to, selected by and stay with organizations that suit their personal characteristics.[25] Job candidates who prefer predictability, for instance, are likely to seek out and take employment in mechanistic structures, and those who want autonomy are more likely to end up in an organic structure. So the effect of structure on employee behaviour is undoubtedly reduced when the selection process facilitates proper matching of individual characteristics with organizational characteristics.

NATIONAL DIFFERENCES IN ORGANIZATIONAL DESIGN — FACE THE FACTS

A survey of work organization in the EU member states characterised four organizational forms:

Advanced forms

1. **The learning form** (high levels of autonomy, task complexity, learning and problem solving; and by low levels of task monotony, work-rate constraints, teamwork and job rotation)

2. **The lean form** (high levels of teamwork, job rotation, and learning and problem solving; and by low levels of autonomy and tight quantitative production norms)

Conventional forms

1. **The Taylorist form** (Basically the opposite of those defining the learning form)

2. **The Traditional form** (a residual category that cannot be well characterised, although it is associated with high levels of task monotony)

The results

- 67 per cent of EU employees work in organizations characterised as 'advanced forms'

- 64 per cent of Dutch employees work in learning organizations, compared with 19 per cent in Greece

- The learning form is more prevalent in the Netherlands, the Nordic countries and to a lesser extent Germany and Austria. The lean form has a greater presence in the United Kingdom, Spain, Ireland and, to a lesser extent, France.

Source: Employment in Europe 2007, European Commission.

Global implications

8 Show how globalisation affects organizational structure.

When we think about how culture influences how organizations are to be structured, several questions come to mind. First, does culture really matter to organizational structure? Second, do employees in different countries vary in their perceptions of different types of organizational structures? Finally, how do cultural considerations fit with our discussion of the boundaryless organization? Let's tackle each of these questions in turn.

Culture and organizational structure

Does culture really affect organizational structure? The answer might seem obvious – yes! – and there is evidence to support this notion. For example, one major study of 15 western European countries revealed that in all of these countries, apart from Greece, organic structures were more prevalent than mechanistic. However, there were significant variations within these results. The Netherlands (81 per cent) and Denmark (81 per cent) have a particularly high preference for organic structures, whereas, Greece (44 per cent), Italy (54 per cent), and Portugal (54 per cent) less so[26].

National and cultural factors have affected the rate of take-up, but in all of these countries there has been a significant increase in new organizational structures, particularly since the 1990s. Globally influential business models such as those from Japan, US, Germany and the UK tend to be mirrored in other countries. So organizational structure does demonstrate variability across nations, but they all seem to be moving in the same direction. In the age of globalisation the organizations strategy, size, environment and technology are the main drivers of structure rather than culture.

Culture and employee structure preferences

Although there isn't a great deal of research out there, it does suggest that national culture influences the preference for structure, so it, too, needs to be considered.[27] For instance, organizations that operate with people from high power distance cultures, such as those found in Greece, France and most of Latin America, find employees much more accepting of mechanistic structures than where employees come from low power distance countries. So you need to consider cultural differences along with individual differences when making predictions on how structure will affect employee performance and satisfaction.

Culture and the boundaryless organization

When fully operational, the boundaryless organization also breaks down barriers created by geography. Most large companies today see themselves as global corporations, and may well do as much business overseas as in their home countries. As a result, many companies struggle with the problem of how to incorporate geographic regions into their structure. The boundaryless organization provides one solution to this problem because geography is considered more of a tactical, logistical issue than a structural issue. In short, the goal of the boundaryless organization is to break down cultural barriers.

One way to break down barriers is through strategic alliances. Firms such as Shell, Gazprom (Russia's largest company), and Nestlé each have strategic alliances or joint partnerships with dozens of companies. These alliances blur the distinction between one organization and another as employees work on joint projects. And some companies are allowing customers to perform functions that previously were done by management. For instance, some employees receive bonuses based on customer evaluations of their performance. Finally, telecommuting is blurring organizational boundaries. The ThyssenKrupp executive who does his job from his home in Munich or the software designer who works for a Brussels company but does her job in London are just two examples of the millions of workers who are now doing their jobs outside the physical boundaries of their employers' premises.

Summary and implications for managers

The theme of this chapter has been that an organization's internal structure contributes to explaining and predicting behaviour. That is, in addition to individual and group factors, the structural relationships in which people work has a bearing on employee attitudes and behaviour.

What's the basis for the argument that structure has an impact on both attitudes and behaviour? To the degree that an organization's structure reduces ambiguity for employees and clarifies concerns such as 'What am I supposed to do?' 'How am I supposed to do it?' 'To whom do I report?' and 'To whom do I go if I have a problem?' it shapes their attitudes and facilitates and motivates them to higher levels of performance.

Of course, structure also constrains employees to the extent that it limits and controls what they do. For example, organizations structured around high levels of formalisation and specialisation, strict adherence to the chain of command, limited delegation of authority, and narrow spans of control give employees little autonomy. Controls in such organizations are tight, and behaviour tends to vary within a narrow range. In contrast, organizations that are structured around limited specialisation, low formalisation, wide spans of control, and the like provide employees greater freedom and, thus, are characterised by greater behavioural diversity.

Figure 16.8 visually summarises what we've discussed in this chapter. Strategy, size, technology and environment determine the type of structure an organization will have. For simplicity's

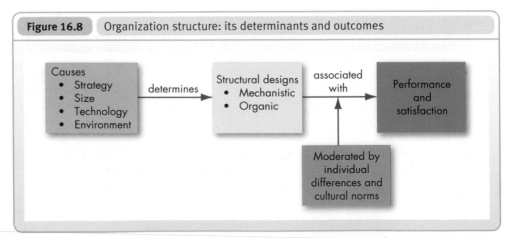

| Figure 16.8 | Organization structure: its determinants and outcomes |

sake, we can classify structural designs around one of two models: mechanistic or organic. The specific effect of structural designs on performance and satisfaction is moderated by employees' individual preferences and cultural norms.

Finally, increasingly, technology is reshaping work such that organizational structures may be increasingly amorphous. This allows a manager the flexibility of taking into account things like employee preferences, experience, and culture so as to design work systems that truly motivate employees.

POINT/COUNTERPOINT

Downsizing improves organizational performance

POINT ➡

There aren't many leaders who like to downsize. Doing so always means inflicting pain on employees and enduring attacks by politicians, labour groups, and the media. But if there is one thing we have learned in the past 20 years, it's that downsizing has been an indispensable factor in making companies more competitive.

In the 1970s and 1980s, most companies in established countries were overstaffed. That made them vulnerable to foreign competition from companies with lower labour costs and a better ability to quickly adapt to new economic conditions and technologies. It's perhaps inevitable that companies do this: Success breeds complacency and, when business is good, companies tend to overstaff and become bloated. Like the patient with a heart condition, they find the remedy is often painful, but fail to address it, and the eventual harm may be much worse.

Nearly all major European and US companies that were around in the 1970s have shrunk their workforces and streamlined their operations. Look at IBM. Once one of the largest employers in the world, it often touted its no-layoff policy. But in the 1980s and 1990s, it became quite clear that IBM was too big, too complex, and spread too thin. Today, IBM is profitable again, but only after it shed nearly 100,000 jobs. Here is what former IBM CEO Lou Gerstner said about the need to restructure the company:

It got stuck because it fell victim to what I call the success syndrome. The more successful enterprises are the more they try to replicate, duplicate, codify what makes us great. And suddenly they're inward thinking. They're thinking how can we continue to do what we've done in the past without understanding that what made them successful is to take risks, to change and to adapt and to be responsive. And so in a sense success breeds its own failure. And I think it's true of a lot of successful businesses.

Layoffs and restructuring are rarely the popular things to do. But without it, most organizations would not survive, much less remain competitive.[28]

COUNTERPOINT ⬅

Downsizing has become a sort of rite of passage for business leaders: You're not a real leader unless you've downsized a company. However, to separate fact from myth, let's look at the evidence. Do companies that have downsized perform better as a result?

To study this, a research team looked at *Standard & Poor's 500* (S&P 500) companies over 20 years. They asked whether reductions in employment at one period of time were associated with higher levels of financial performance at a later period in time.

What did they find? In analysing 6,418 occurrences of changes in employment among the S&P 500, they found that downsizing strategies did *not* result in improved long-term financial performance (as measured by industry-adjusted return on assets). It's important to remember that the results control for prior financial performance and reflect financial performance after the downsizing efforts occurred.

The authors of this study don't argue that downsizing is always a bad strategy. Rather, the upshot is that managers shouldn't assume layoffs are a quick fix to what ails a company. In general, downsizing does *not* improve performance, so the key is to do it only when needed and to do it in the right way.

What are some ways organizations can do this? First, they should use downsizing only as a last resort. Second, and related, they should inform employees about the problem, and give them a chance to contribute alternative restructuring solutions. Third, organizations need to bend over backward to ensure that employees see the layoff process as fair, including making sure the layoff criteria *are* fair (and ideally result from employee involvement), advance notice is given, and job relocation assistance is provided. Finally, make sure downsizing is done to good effect – not just to cut costs, but to reallocate resources to where they can be most effective.

Source: W. F. Cascio, 'Strategies for responsible restructuring', *Academy of Management Executive*, 19, 4 (2005), pp. 39–50.

QUESTIONS FOR REVIEW

1. What are the six key elements that define an organization's structure?

2. What is a bureaucracy, and how does it differ from a simple structure?

3. What is a matrix organization?

4. What are the characteristics of a virtual organization?

5. How can managers create a boundaryless organization?

6. Why do organizational structures differ, and what is the difference between a mechanistic structure and an organic structure?

7. What are the behavioural implications of different organizational designs?

8. How does globalisation affect organizational structure?

Experiential exercise

AUTHORITY FIGURES

Purpose

To learn about one's experiences with and feelings about authority.

Time

Approximately 75 minutes.

Procedure

1. Your instructor will separate class members into groups based on their birth order. Groups are formed consisting of 'only children', 'eldest', 'middle', and 'youngest', according to placement in families. Larger groups will be broken into smaller ones, with four or five members, to allow for freer conversation.

2. Each group member should talk about how he or she 'typically reacts to the authority of others'. Focus should be on specific situations that offer general information about how individuals deal with authority figures (for example, bosses, teachers, parents or coaches). The group has 25 minutes to develop a written list of how the group generally deals with others' authority. Be sure to separate tendencies that group members share and those they do not.

3. Repeat step 2, except this time, discuss how group members 'typically are as authority figures'. Again make a list of shared characteristics.

4. Each group will share its general conclusions with the entire class.

5. Class discussion will focus on questions such as:

   (a) What patterned differences have surfaced between the groups?

   (b) What may account for these differences?

   (c) What hypotheses might explain the connection between how individuals react to the authority of others and how they are as authority figures?

Source: This exercise is adapted from W. A. Kahn, 'An exercise of authority', *Organizational Behavior Teaching Review*, 14, 2 (1989–1990), pp. 28–42. Reprinted with permission.

Ethical dilemma

CAN AN ORGANIZATION'S STRUCTURE CONTRIBUTE TO UNETHICAL BEHAVIOUR?

By December 2008, the biggest corporate scandal in post-war Germany had cost Siemens, a symbol of German engineering excellence and corporate probity, not only its reputation and that of former senior executives but more than €2.5bn in fines and costs. Having been found guilty of corruption and bribery to win lucrative contracts, the company is still being investigated in scores of countries around the world, two ex-board members are under criminal investigation and a senior manager was recently given a suspended two-year sentence.

The first Siemens chief executive to come from outside the company, Austrian Peter Löscher, brought in to clean up the organization, said that a top priority for his first 100 days on the job would be to simplify the byzantine organizational structure that may have contributed to the bribery scandal. The complexity of the company's far-flung operations, which are divided by both product category – like power plant equipment, medical devices and light bulbs – and by geographic region, is believed to have helped employees hide €420 million in suspicious payments.

Mr. Löscher said the business structures and regional divisions would come under scrutiny as he prepared a new organizational plan. 'In the fall, I'll present our conclusions to the supervisory board, with these goals in mind: clear lines of responsibility, a high level of transparency and maximum speed.'

Questions

1. Do you think that it is possible for an organization's structure to influence employees ethics? How?

2. What would an organizational structure that promotes ethical behaviour look like?

3. What restructuring recommendations would you give to Löscher to help promote ethical behaviour at Siemens ?

Sources: Based on C. Dougherty, 'Chief of Siemens pledges to streamline operations', *The New York Times* (6 July 2007): C6(L).; D. Gow, 'Record US fine ends Siemens bribery scandal', *The Guardian* (16 December 2008).

CASE INCIDENT 1

New demands on managers and organizations

The shifting emphasis from vertical designs to horizontal designs to partnership designs has reshaped the roles of managers. The biggest change has been from having direct control over resources required for performance toward dependence on others over whom there is no direct control. Even with more dependence and less control under newer structural designs, managers are still responsible for performance outcomes. For a manager who is used to a traditional top-down approach, it is hard to let go of control. The late business guru Peter Drucker once noted that the problem with large company managers is that they are used to giving orders and not to working with a partner – a totally different proposition.

A nice example is provided by the transition of Strida, a UK-based company that sells lightweight foldable bicycles, from a functional design, vertically integrated manufacturer to a completely new form. In 2001, Strida received a large order from an Italian customer, willing to buy at a price that was below the cost of producing the bicycles in the UK. The CEO of the company, Steedman Bass, immediately began investigating ways of making the organization more efficient. First, he decided to shut down the in-house production plant and identified a manufacturing partner in the Far East who could make the bike at lower cost. He used expert contractors to continue developing new bicycle models, to design the owner's manual, to design the company's website. He used various web-based software services to ensure smooth communication between the designers and the manufacturer, to manage accounts, materials and documents. He then turned to a long-time vendor to take over the back-end operation of the company – including warehouse management, order fulfilment, inventory control, customer service, inbound container management and accounts generation.

The company has low overheads and is now structured to ramp up and down quickly in response to market fluctuations. Bass focuses almost exclusively on managing the various relationships that make up the business. Bass had loved making his own bikes, and therefore the biggest barrier in making the transition was in his willingness to find, trust, and hand over that responsibility to someone else that could do it more efficiently.

Questions

1. How would you describe the new organizational structure at Strida?

2. How has the role of CEO Steedman Bass changed?

3. What new demands are these new organizational structures placing on managers?

4. Do you think these new structures also place new demands on all employees? What might they be?

Source: N. Anand and R. Daft (2007) 'What is the right organization design', *Organizational Dynamics*, 36, 4 pp. 329–44

CASE INCIDENT 2

How have organizational structures changed?

The following is taken from an article written by Stanley Klion and Donald Markstein in 1967.

Organizational structure is essential to perform successfully any activity involving the efforts of numbers of people. It is formal recognition that achieving goals requires a sound dispersion of responsibilities among the management group. Simply stated, the implementation of an organization structure in a business entity involves logically grouping the spectrum of work functions to be performed and assigning them to individuals for execution in a manner designed to meet the entity's objectives.

Organization structure is near to the heart of the management process itself. The management process is a wheel which starts with planning and proceeds sequentially through organization, execution and control. Feedback leads to either continuing or changing the course of action in any phase of the cycle, such as (1) continuing the present plan, (2) modifying the present plan, (3) improving the effectiveness of the execution effort with the present organization structure and resources or (4) assembling a new structure or team of people or new resources to do a better job of meeting the original or modified plan. Effective organization structure is essential to the proper functioning of the overall management process.

These authors go on to propose the following principles of organization:

Objectives

1 The objectives of the enterprise and its component elements should be clearly defined and stated in writing. The organization should be kept simple and flexible.

▶

Activities and grouping of activities

2 The responsibilities assigned to a position should be confined as far as possible to the performance of a single leading function.

3 Functions should be assigned to organizational units on the basis of homogeneity of objective to achieve most efficient and economic operation.

Authority

4 There should be clear lines of authority running from the top to the bottom of the organization, and accountability from bottom to top.

5 The responsibility and authority of each position should be clearly defined in writing.

6 Accountability should always be coupled with corresponding authority.

7 Authority to take or initiate actions should be delegated as close to the scene of action as possible.

8 The number of levels of authority should be kept to a minimum.

Relationships

9 There is a limit to the number of positions that can be effectively supervised by a single individual.

10 Everyone in the organization should report to only one supervisor.

11 The accountability of higher authority for the acts of its subordinates is absolute.

Questions

1. How would you characterise the organizational structure that Klion and Markstein proposed using terms from this chapter?

2. Are these principles of organization still relevant today? Why or why not? What has changed?

3. Can you name any examples of organizations today that seem to follow these organization principles?

4. Would you respond favourably to working in this type of organization? Why or why not?

Source: S. Klion and D. Markstein, 'Organizational structure', *Journal of Accountancy*, 123, 1 (1967), p. 84–86. Copyright 1967. American Institute of Certified Public Accountants, Inc. All rights reserved. Used with permission.

Endnotes

1 See, for instance, R. L. Daft, *Organization Theory and Design*, 8th edn (Cincinnati, OH: South-Western Publishing, 2004).

2 C. Hymowitz, 'Managers suddenly have to answer to a crowd of bosses', *Wall Street Journal*, 12 August 2003, p. B1.

3 See, for instance, L. Urwick, *The Elements of Administration* (New York: Harper & Row, 1944), pp. 52–53; and J. H. Gittell, 'Supervisory span, relational coordination, and flight departure performance: a reassessment of postbureaucracy theory', *Organization Science*, July–August 2001, pp. 468–83.

4 J. Child and R. G. McGrath, 'Organizations unfettered: organizational form in an information-intensive economy', *Academy of Management Journal*, December 2001, pp. 1135–48.

5 H. Mintzberg, *Structure in fives: Designing Effective Organizations* (Upper Saddle River, NJ: Prentice-Hall, 1983), p. 157.

6 L. R. Burns and D. R. Wholey, 'Adoption and abandonment of matrix management programmes: effects of organizational characteristics and interorganizational networks', *Academy of Management Journal*, February 1993, pp. 106–38.

7 See, for instance, S. M. Davis and P. R. Lawrence, 'Problems of matrix organization', *Harvard Business Review*, May–June 1978, pp. 131–42; and T. Sy and S. Cote, 'Emotional intelligence: a key ability to succeed in the matrix organization', *Journal of Management Development*, 23, 5 (2004), pp. 437–55.

8 See, for instance, R. E. Miles and C. C. Snow, 'The new network firm: a spherical structure built on human investment philosophy', *Organizational Dynamics*, Spring 1995, pp. 5–18;

D. Pescovitz, 'The company where everybody's a temp', *New York Times Magazine*, 11 June 2000, pp. 94–96; W. F. Cascio, 'Managing a virtual workplace', *Academy of Management Executive*, August 2000, pp. 81–90; B. Hedberg, G. Dahlgren, J. Hansson and N. Olve, *Virtual Organizations and Beyond* (New York: Wiley, 2001); J. Gertner, 'Newman's own: two friends and a canoe paddle', *New York Times*, 16 November 2003, p. 4BU; and Y. Shin, 'A person–environment fit model for virtual organizations', *Journal of Management*, October 2004, pp. 725–43.

9 J. Bates, 'Making movies and moving on', *Los Angeles Times*, 19 January 1998, p. A1.

10 C. Dougherty, 'Cuts at Porsche's Finnish workshop', *New York Times* (4 April 2009), p. B3(L).

11 N. Anand and R. Daft (2007) 'What is the right organization design?', *Organizational Dynamics*, 36, 4, pp. 329–44.

12 'GE: just your average everyday $60 billion family grocery store', *IndustryWeek*, 2 May 1994, pp. 13–18.

13 H. C. Lucas Jr., *The T-Form Organization: Using Technology to Design Organizations for the 21st Century* (San Francisco, CA: Jossey-Bass, 1996).

14 This section is based on D. D. Davis, 'Form, function and strategy in boundaryless organizations', in A. Howard (ed.), *The Changing Nature of Work* (San Francisco, CA: Jossey-Bass, 1995), pp. 112–38; P. Roberts, 'We are one company, no matter where we are. Time and space are irrelevant', *Fast Company*, April–May 1998, pp. 122–28; R. L. Cross, A. Yan

and M. R. Louis, 'Boundary activities in "boundaryless" organizations: a case study of a transformation to a team-based structure', *Human Relations*, June 2000, pp. 841–68; and R. Ashkenas, D. Ulrich, T. Jick and S. Kerr, *The Boundaryless Organization: Breaking the Chains of Organizational Structure*, revised and updated (San Francisco, CA: Jossey-Bass, 2002).

15 T. Burns and G. M. Stalker, *The Management of Innovation* (London: Tavistock, 1961); and J. A. Courtright, G. T. Fairhurst and L. E. Rogers, 'Interaction patterns in organic and mechanistic systems', *Academy of Management Journal*, December 1989, pp. 773–802.

16 This analysis is referred to as a contingency approach to organization design. See, for instance, J. M. Pennings, 'Structural contingency theory: a reappraisal', in B. M. Staw and L. L. Cummings (eds), *Research in Organizational Behavior*, vol. 14 (Greenwich, CT: JAI Press, 1992), pp. 267–309; J. R. Hollenbeck, H. Moon, A. P. J. Ellis, B. J. West, D. R. Ilgen, L. Sheppard, C. O. L. H. Porter and J. A. Wagner, III, 'Structural contingency theory and individual differences: examination of external and internal person-team fit', *Journal of Applied Psychology*, June 2002, pp. 599–606; and H. Moon, J. R. Hollenbeck, S. E. Humphrey, D. R. Ilgen, B. West, A. P. J. Ellis and C. O. L. H. Porter, 'Asymmetric adaptability: dynamic team structures as one-way streets', *Academy of Management Journal*, October 2004, pp. 681–95.

17 The strategy–structure thesis was originally proposed in A. D. Chandler, Jr., *Strategy and Structure: Chapters in the History of the Industrial Enterprise* (Cambridge, MA: MIT Press, 1962). For an updated analysis, see T. L. Amburgey and T. Dacin, 'As the left foot follows the right? The dynamics of strategic and structural change', *Academy of Management Journal*, December 1994, pp. 1427–52.

18 See R. E. Miles and C. C. Snow, *Organizational Strategy, Structure, and Process* (New York: McGraw-Hill, 1978); D. Miller, 'The structural and environmental correlates of business strategy', *Strategic Management Journal*, January–February 1987, pp. 55–76; D. C. Galunic and K. M. Eisenhardt, 'Renewing the strategy–structure–performance paradigm', in B. M. Staw and L. L. Cummings (eds), *Research in Organizational Behavior*, vol. 16 (Greenwich, CT: JAI Press, 1994), pp. 215–55; and I. C. Harris and T. W. Ruefli, 'The strategy/structure debate: an examination of the performance implications', *Journal of Management Studies*, June 2000, pp. 587–603.

19 E. Valdani and A. Arbore (2007) 'Strategies of imitation: an insight', *Problems and Perspectives in Management*. Available at http://findarticles.com/p/articles/mi_qa5417/is_200701/ai_n21298067/?tag=content;col1. Accessed 12 April 2009.

20 See, for instance, P. M. Blau and R. A. Schoenherr, *The Structure of Organizations* (New York: Basic Books, 1971); D. S. Pugh, 'The Aston program of research: retrospect and prospect', in A. H. Van de Ven and W. F. Joyce (eds), *Perspectives on Organization Design and Behavior* (New York: Wiley, 1981), pp. 135–66; R. Z. Gooding and J. A. Wagner, III, 'A meta-analytic review of the relationship between size and performance: the productivity and efficiency of Organizations and their subunits', *Administrative Science Quarterly*, December 1985, pp. 462–81; and A. C. Bluedorn, 'Pilgrim's progress: trends and convergence in research on Organizational size and environments', *Journal of Management*, Summer 1993, pp. 163–92.

21 See J. Woodward, *Industrial Organization: Theory and Practice* (London: Oxford University Press, 1965); C. Perrow, 'A framework for the comparative analysis of organizations', *American Sociological Review*, April 1967, pp. 194–208; J. D. Thompson, *Organizations in Action* (New York: McGraw-Hill, 1967); J. Hage and M. Aiken, 'Routine technology, social structure, and organizational goals', *Administrative Science Quarterly*, September 1969, pp. 366–77; C. C. Miller, W. H. Glick, Y. Wang and G. P. Huber, 'Understanding technology-structure relationships: theory development and meta-analytic theory testing', *Academy of Management Journal*, June 1991, pp. 370–99; and K. H. Roberts and M. Grabowski, 'Organizations, technology, and structuring', in S. R. Clegg, C. Hardy, and W. R. Nord (eds), *Managing Organizations: Current Issues* (Thousand Oaks, CA: Sage, 1999), pp. 159–71.

22 See F. E. Emery and E. Trist, 'The causal texture of organizational environments', *Human Relations*, February 1965, pp. 21–32; P. Lawrence and J.W. Lorsch, *Organization and Environment: Managing Differentiation and Integration* (Boston, MA: Harvard Business School, Division of Research, 1967); M. Yasai-Ardekani, 'Structural adaptations to environments', *Academy of Management Review*, January 1986, pp. 9–21; Bluedorn, 'Pilgrim's progress'; and M. Arndt and B. Bigelow, 'Presenting structural innovation in an institutional environment: hospitals' use of impression management', *Administrative Science Quarterly*, September 2000, pp. 494–522.

23 G. G. Dess and D. W. Beard, 'Dimensions of organizational task environments', *Administrative Science Quarterly*, March 1984, pp. 52–73; E. A. Gerloff, N. K. Muir and W. D. Bodensteiner, 'Three components of perceived environmental uncertainty: an exploratory analysis of the effects of aggregation', *Journal of Management*, December 1991, pp. 749–68; and O. Shenkar, N. Aranya and T. Almor, 'Construct dimensions in the contingency model: an analysis comparing metric and non-metric multivariate Instruments', *Human Relations*, May 1995, pp. 559–80.

24 See, for instance, L. W. Porter and E. E. Lawler, III, 'Properties of organization structure in relation to job attitudes and job behavior', *Psychological Bulletin*, July 1965, pp. 23–51; L. R. James and A. P. Jones, 'Organization structure: a review of structural dimensions and their conceptual relationships with individual attitudes and behavior', *Organizational Behavior and Human Performance*, June 1976, pp. 74–113; D. R. Dalton, W. D. Todor, M. J. Spendolini, G. J. Fielding and L. W. Porter, 'Organization structure and performance: a critical review', *Academy of Management Review*, January 1980, pp. 49–64; and D. B. Turban and T. L. Keon, 'Organizational attractiveness: an interactionist perspective', *Journal of Applied Psychology*, April 1994, pp. 184–93.

25 See, for instance, B. Schneider, H. W. Goldstein and D. B. Smith, 'The ASA framework: an update', *Personnel Psychology*, 48 (Winter 1995), pp. 747–73.

26 'Employment in Europe 2007' European Commission.

27 See, for example, P. R. Harris and R. T. Moran, *Managing Cultural Differences*, 5th edn (Houston, TX: Gulf Publishing, 1999).

28 'In focus: Lou Gerstner', *CNN World Business*, 2 July 2004, www.cnn.com.

Organizational culture

Learning Objectives

After studying this chapter, you should be able to:

1 Relate institutionalisation culture to organizational culture.

2 Define *organizational culture* and describe its common characteristics.

3 Compare the functional and dysfunctional effects of organizational culture on people and the organization.

4 Explain the factors that create and sustain an organization's culture.

5 Show how culture is transmitted to employees.

6 Demonstrate how an ethical culture can be created.

7 Describe a positive organizational culture.

8 Identify characteristics of a spiritual culture.

9 Show how national culture may affect the way organizational culture is transported to a different country.

A culture of discipline is not a principle of business; it is a principle of greatness.

Jim Collins, Good to Great and the Social Sectors

Culture drives success at Hilti

AFP/Getty Images

When CEO of Hilti, Pius Baschera, accepted the Carl Bertelsmann prize for excellence in corporate culture, beating BMW and Novo Nordisk in the final, he commented:

> *After hearing the details of our approach to corporate culture, you may have the urge to raise your hand and say 'that's your secret to success?!' And I would answer, absolutely. Commitment and continuity are not nice to have but absolute essentials. Our corporate culture is based on the full commitment of top management to a never ending lifestyle of learning and living the core values of our company on every level of the organization.*

The worldwide Hilti Group evolved from modest beginnings. It was founded at the height of the second world war when Martin Hilti and his brother Eugen opened a workshop with just five employees in Liechtenstein, where it remains based. Today the company, which designs, produces and sells products and systems for anything from measuring, positioning and drilling to chiselling, fastening, cutting and sanding, employs close to 20,000 people.

At Hilti integrity, commitment, courage and teamwork are the four cornerstones of their corporate culture. The firm encourages breaking away from habits, questioning the status quo, and trying out new ideas. Karsten Witchman, head of the Latin American region remarks, 'What really keeps me going is the corporate culture. I've never experienced a stronger one. It makes room for other opinions and allows people to admit a weakness. I like it very much here because I can be true, authentic and honest.'

Hilti tries very hard to recruit people who fit with the organization's culture. Michael Hilti, son of the founder, claims that employees who do not share the Hilti values should leave the company. He explains that, 'In a way, it is like team sports, where you also have to play by a set of rules. Suppose a football team hired Roger Federer, the tennis champion, to play offence, but Federer continued to play by the rules of tennis. No matter how superb his technique or how perfect his feel for the ball, he simply wouldn't fit in with the team.'

What is also apparent is that the company does not seek to alter its organizational culture dependent on where it operates. The same cornerstones apply in the more than 120 countries in which it does business.

Sources: A. Thomann, 'Michael Hilti: The steadfast chairman of culture', 3 January 2005, Online Publications *Credit Suisse* available at: http://emagazine.credit-suisse.com/index.cfm?fuseaction=OpenArticle&aoid=78805&lang=EN&coid=120. Accesssed 19 April 2009; www.hilti.com People and Career; *Hilti: Our Culture Journey*, IMD (2006) International Institute of Management Development Lausanne, Switzerland *Case Study* available at www.caseplace.org.

As the chapter-opening example shows, organizational culture is often so strong that it transcends national boundaries. A strong culture provides stability to an organization. But for some organizations, it can also be a major barrier to change. In this chapter, we show that every organization has a culture and, depending on its strength, it can have a significant influence on the attitudes and behaviours of organization members. Before doing so, let's figure out what kind of organizational culture you prefer. Take the self-assessment to find out.

SELF-ASSESSMENT LIBRARY

What's the right organizational culture for me?

In the Self-assessment library (available online), take assessment III.B.1 (What's the right organizational culture for me?) and answer the following questions.

1. Judging from your results, do you fit better in a more formal and structured culture or in a more informal and unstructured culture?

2. Did your results surprise you? Why do you think you scored as you did?

3. How might your results affect your career path?

Institutionalisation: a forerunner of culture

1 Relate institutionalisation culture to organizational culture.

The idea of viewing organizations as cultures – where there is a system of shared meaning among members – is a relatively recent phenomenon. Until the mid-1980s, organizations were, for the most part, simply thought of as rational means by which to coordinate and control a group of people. They had vertical levels, departments, authority relationships and so forth. But organizations are more. They have personalities, too, just like individuals. They can be rigid or flexible, unfriendly or supportive, innovative or conservative. British Airways offices and people *are* different from the offices and people at Virgin Atlantic. Organizational theorists now acknowledge this by recognising the important role that culture plays in the lives of organization members. Interestingly, though, the origin of culture as an independent variable affecting an employee's attitudes and behaviour can be traced back more than 50 years ago to the notion of **institutionalisation.**[1]

institutionalisation
A condition that occurs when an organization takes on a life of its own, apart from any of its members, and acquires immortality.

When an organization becomes institutionalised, it takes on a life of its own, apart from its founders or any of its members. Nokia's origins date back to 1865 when an engineer, Fredrik Idestam, established a mill in southwestern Finland and began manufacturing paper. Today, Nokia bears little resemblance to its past, yet continues to thrive. Sony, Gillette, McDonald's and Disney are examples of organizations that have existed beyond the life of their founder or any one member. When an organization becomes institutionalised, it becomes valued for itself, not merely for the goods or services it produces. It acquires immortality. If its original goals are no longer relevant, it doesn't go out of business. Rather, it redefines itself.

Institutionalisation operates to produce common understandings among members about what is appropriate and, fundamentally, meaningful behaviour.[2] So when an organization takes on institutional permanence, acceptable modes of behaviour become largely self-evident to its members. As we'll see, this is essentially the same thing that organizational culture does. So an understanding of what makes up an organization's culture and how it is created, sustained and learned will enhance our ability to explain and predict the behaviour of people at work.

What is organizational culture?

2 Define *organizational culture* and describe its common characteristics.

A number of years back, an executive was asked what he thought *organizational culture* meant. His answer was, 'I can't define it, but I know it when I see it.' This executive's approach to defining organizational culture isn't acceptable for our purposes. We need a basic definition to provide a point of departure for our quest to better understand the phenomenon. In this section, we propose a specific definition and review several peripheral issues that revolve around this definition.

A definition of *organizational culture*

organizational culture
A system of shared meaning held by members that distinguishes the organization from other organizations.

There seems to be wide agreement that **organizational culture** refers to a system of shared meaning held by members that distinguishes the organization from other organizations.[3] This system of shared meaning is, on closer examination, a set of key characteristics that the organization values. The research suggests that there are seven primary characteristics that, in aggregate, capture the essence of an organization's culture:[4]

1. **Innovation and risk taking.** The degree to which employees are encouraged to be innovative and take risks.
2. **Attention to detail.** The degree to which employees are expected to exhibit precision, analysis, and attention to detail.
3. **Outcome orientation.** The degree to which management focuses on results or outcomes rather than on the techniques and processes used to achieve those outcomes.

The Portugal offices of Cushman and Wakefield, a global real estate firm, has a people-oriented culture. It offers its 50 employees a chance to jump out of an airplane whenever they want. Employees are trained at the company for two days and then get a day off for a parachute jump. It's all in keeping with the company's motto, 'Have Fun', as well as one of its core values, 'Every employee is a team member and contributes to our success.'[5]

Eddie Gerald/Alamy

4. **People orientation.** The degree to which management decisions take into consideration the effect of outcomes on people within the organization.

5. **Team orientation.** The degree to which work activities are organized around teams rather than individuals.

6. **Aggressiveness.** The degree to which people are aggressive and competitive rather than easy-going.

7. **Stability.** The degree to which organizational activities emphasise maintaining the status quo in contrast to growth.

Each of these characteristics exists on a continuum from low to high. Appraising the organization on these seven characteristics, then, gives a composite picture of the organization's culture. This picture becomes the basis for feelings of shared understanding that members have about the organization, how things are done in it, and the way members are supposed to behave. Exhibit 17.1 demonstrates how these characteristics can be mixed to create highly diverse organizations.

Culture is a descriptive term

Organizational culture is concerned with how employees perceive the characteristics of an organization's culture, not with whether they like them. That is, it's a descriptive term. This is important because it differentiates this concept from job satisfaction.

Research on organizational culture has sought to measure how employees see their organization: Does it encourage teamwork? Does it reward innovation? Does it stifle initiative? In contrast, job satisfaction seeks to measure affective responses to the work environment. It's concerned with how employees feel about the organization's expectations, reward practices and the like. Although the two terms undoubtedly have overlapping characteristics, keep in mind that the term *organizational culture* is descriptive, whereas *job satisfaction* is evaluative.

EXHIBIT 17.1	CONTRASTING ORGANIZATIONAL CULTURES

Organization A

This organization is a manufacturing firm. Managers are expected to fully document all decisions, and 'good managers' are those who can provide detailed data to support their recommendations. Creative decisions that incur significant change or risk are not encouraged. Because managers of failed projects are openly criticised and penalised, managers try not to implement ideas that deviate much from the status quo. One lower-level manager quoted an often-used phrase in the company: 'If it ain't broke, don't fix it.'

There are extensive rules and regulations in this firm that employees are required to follow. Managers supervise employees closely to ensure there are no deviations. Management is concerned with high productivity, regardless of the impact on employee morale or turnover.

Work activities are designed around individuals. There are distinct departments and lines of authority, and employees are expected to minimise formal contact with other employees outside their functional area or line of command. Performance evaluations and rewards emphasise individual effort, although seniority tends to be the primary factor in the determination of pay raises and promotions.

Organization B

This organization is also a manufacturing firm. Here, however, management encourages and rewards risk taking and change. Decisions based on intuition are valued as much as those that are well rationalised. Management prides itself on its history of experimenting with new technologies and its success in regularly introducing innovative products. Managers or employees who have a good idea are encouraged to 'run with it'. And failures are treated as 'learning experiences'. The company prides itself on being market-driven and rapidly responsive to the changing needs of its customers.

There are few rules and regulations for employees to follow, and supervision is loose because management believes that its employees are hardworking and trustworthy. Management is concerned with high productivity, but believes that this comes through treating its people right. The company is proud of its reputation as being a good place to work.

Job activities are designed around work teams, and team members are encouraged to interact with people across functions and authority levels. Employees talk positively about the competition between teams. Individuals and teams have goals, and bonuses are based on achievement of these outcomes. Employees are given considerable autonomy in choosing the means by which the goals are attained.

Do organizations have uniform cultures?

Organizational culture represents a common perception held by the organization's members. This was made explicit when we defined culture as a system of *shared* meaning. We should expect, therefore, that individuals with different backgrounds or at different levels in the organization will tend to describe the organization's culture in similar terms.[6]

Acknowledgment that organizational culture has common properties does not mean, however, that there cannot be subcultures within any given culture. Most large organizations have a dominant culture and numerous sets of subcultures.[7] A **dominant culture** expresses the core values that are shared by a majority of the organization's members. When we talk about an organization's culture, we are referring to its dominant culture. It is this macro view of culture that gives an organization its distinct personality.[8] **Subcultures** tend to develop in large organizations to reflect common problems, situations, or experiences that members face. These subcultures are likely to be defined by department designations and geographical separation. The purchasing department, for example, can have a subculture that is uniquely shared by members of that department. It will include the **core values** of the dominant culture plus additional values unique to members of the purchasing department. Similarly, an office or unit of the organization that is physically separated from the organization's main operations may take on a different personality. Again, the core values are essentially retained, but they are modified to reflect the separated unit's distinct situation.

If organizations had no dominant culture and were composed only of numerous subcultures, the value of organizational culture as an independent variable would be significantly lessened because there would be no uniform interpretation of what represented appropriate and inappropriate behaviour. It is the 'shared meaning' aspect of culture that makes it such a potent device for guiding and shaping behaviour. That's what allows us to say, for example, that Microsoft's culture values aggressiveness and risk taking[9] and then to use that information to better understand the behaviour of Microsoft executives and employees. But we cannot ignore the reality that many organizations also have subcultures that can influence the behaviour of members.

dominant culture
A culture that expresses the core values that are shared by a majority of the organization's members.

subcultures
Minicultures within an organization, typically defined by department designations and geographical separation.

core values
The primary or dominant values that are accepted throughout the organization.

Types of organizational culture

A number of authors have attempted to characterise various types of organizational cultures. Having examined hundreds of corporations, Deal and Kennedy noticed that many of the companies fell into four general categories of culture.[10]

1. **Tough-guy, macho culture.** A world of individualists who regularly take high risks and get quick feedback on whether their actions are right or wrong.
2. **The work hard/play hard culture.** Fun and action are the rule here, and employees take few risks, all with quick feedback; to succeed, the culture encourages them to maintain a high level of relatively low-risk activity.
3. **The bet-your-company culture.** Cultures with big stakes decisions, where years pass before employees know whether decisions have paid off. A high-risk, slow feedback environment.
4. **The process culture.** A world of little or no feedback where employees find it hard to measure what they do; instead they concentrate on how it's done. We have another name for this culture when the processes get out of control – bureaucracy!

It is important to note that these authors recognise these classifications are simplistic and companies are not likely to exactly fit any one of these categories. In fact, most companies may be a mix of all four types. For example, the marketing department may be a tough-guy culture and the accounting function a process culture.

The Irish author Charles Handy similarly came up with four types of organizational culture, having been inspired by the rich variety of cultural differences he saw when travelling in Europe. He called them (following earlier work by Roger Harrison) the power, role, task and person culture.

Handy makes it clear that each type can be a good and effective culture. It depends on the organizations purpose and people.

| **Figure 17.1** | Contrasting organizational cultures |

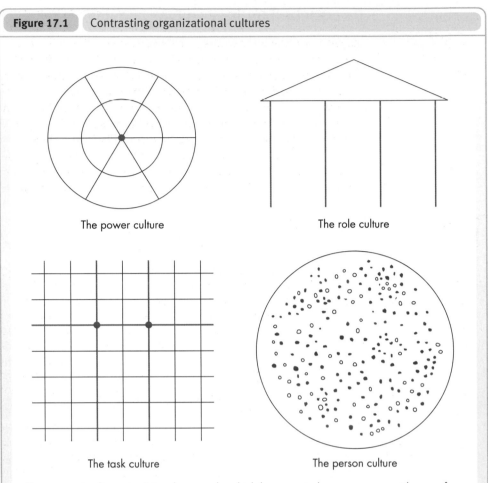

The power culture

The role culture

The task culture

The person culture

The **power culture** is pictured as a web, which has a central power source, with rays of power and influence spreading out from that central figure. They are connected by functional or specialist strings but the power rings are the centres of activity and influence. This type of culture is frequently found in small entrepreneurial organizations.

The **role culture** can be pictured as a Greek temple. The role organization rests its strength in its pillars, its functions and specialities (e.g. the finance department, the purchasing department, and the production facility). They are coordinated at the top by a narrow band of senior management. Similar to a bureaucracy, this culture works by logic and rationality.

The **task culture** is job or project oriented. Its accompanying structure can be best represented as a net. Groups, project teams, or task forces are formed for a specific purpose and can be reformed, abandoned, or continued.

The **person culture** has the individual as the central point. The organization exists to serve the individual. This type of culture is likely to be found at a medical centre, architects' partnerships, or some small consultancy firms. The individuals have banded together for their own needs to, for example, reduce costs by sharing resources.

Source: Adapted from C. Handy, *Understanding Organizations*, Penguin Books 1976, Fourth Edition 1993, p. 183, p. 185, p.187, p. 190.

Many such typologies can now be found in management literature and often they share similar characteristics. The use of these frameworks is to help managers begin to better understand their organization's culture and whether it is appropriate to meeting the company's objectives.

Strong versus weak cultures

It has become increasingly popular to differentiate between strong and weak cultures.[11] The argument here is that strong cultures have a greater impact on employee behaviour and are more directly related to reduced turnover.

strong culture
A culture in which the core values are intensely held and widely shared.

In a **strong culture**, the organization's core values are both intensely held and widely shared.[12] The more members who accept the core values and the greater their commitment to those values is, the stronger the culture is. Consistent with this definition, a strong culture will have a great influence on the behaviour of its members because the high degree of sharedness and intensity creates an internal climate of high behavioural control. For example, the luxury retailer Harrods in London, one of the largest department stores in the world, has a strong service culture. All of Harrods employees (more than 5,000 of them) know in no uncertain terms what is expected of them, and these expectations go a long way in shaping their behaviour.

One specific result of a strong culture should be lower employee turnover. A strong culture demonstrates high agreement among members about what the organization stands for. Such unanimity of purpose builds cohesiveness, loyalty and organizational commitment. These qualities, in turn, lessen employees' propensity to leave the organization.[13]

A GOOD ORGANIZATIONAL CULTURE KNOWS NO BOUNDARIES   GLOBAL

In a study of 230 organizations from different industries around the world, and from regions including Europe, North America, Asia, the Middle East and Africa, having a strong and positive organizational culture was associated with increased organizational effectiveness.

The study, published in the journal *Organizational Dynamics*, found that the strong and positive aspects of organizational culture most critical to success across regions generally included

- Empowering employees
- Having a team orientation
- Having a clear strategic direction and intent
- Possessing a strong and recognisable vision

Though there were similarities when comparing regions in terms of organizational culture and effectiveness, there were some differences when researchers compared individual countries. An organizational culture that stresses empowerment, for example, appears to be more important for performance in countries such as the United States and Brazil and less important in countries such as Japan because of the former two countries' focus on the individual. Also, a focus on creating change within the organization appears to be a strong predictor of organizational effectiveness in South Africa but a relatively weak predictor in Jamaica, but it currently is unclear as to why this is the case.

Overall, the study confirms that having a strong, productive organizational culture is associated with increased sales growth, profitability, employee satisfaction, and overall organizational performance regardless of where the organization is physically located.

Source: Based on D. R. Denison, S. Haaland and P. Goelzer, 'Corporate culture and organizational effectiveness: is Asia different from the rest of the world?', *Organizational Dynamics*, February 2004, pp. 98–109.

FACE THE FACTS

According to research by the Chartered Institute of Personnel and Development (CIPD):

- Organizational culture was a more important predictor of business performance than more traditional predictors such as research and development, technology and quality.
- Companies with strong shared cultures tended to perform better than those with weaker cultures.

- Where strongly shared values were demonstrated, people were more likely to be satisfied, display higher levels of organizational commitment, have lower quit rates, and lower levels of dissent or dissatisfaction over levels of pay.

Source: *Vision and values: Organizational Culture and Values as a Source of Competitive Advantage*, Chartered Institute of Personnel and Development (CIPD).

Culture versus formalisation

A strong organizational culture increases behavioural consistency. In this sense, we should recognise that a strong culture can act as a substitute for formalisation.[14]

In the previous chapter, we discussed how formalisation's rules and regulations act to regulate employee behaviour. High formalisation in an organization creates predictability, orderliness, and consistency. Our point here is that a strong culture achieves the same end without the need for written documentation. Therefore, we should view formalisation and culture as two different roads to a common destination. The stronger an organization's culture, the less management need be concerned with developing formal rules and regulations to guide employee behaviour. Those guides will be internalised in employees when they accept the organization's culture.

What do cultures do?

3 Compare the functional and dysfunctional effects of organizational culture on people and the organization.

We've alluded to the impact of organizational culture on behaviour. We've also explicitly argued that a strong culture should be associated with reduced turnover. In this section, we will more carefully review the functions that culture performs and assess whether culture can be a liability for an organization.

Culture's functions

Culture performs a number of functions within an organization. First, it has a boundary-defining role; that is, it creates distinctions between one organization and others. Second, it conveys a sense of identity for organization members. Third, culture facilitates the generation of commitment to something larger than one's individual self-interest. Fourth, it enhances the stability of the social system. Culture is the social glue that helps hold the organization together by providing appropriate standards for what employees should say and do. Finally, culture serves as a sense-making and control mechanism that guides and shapes the attitudes and behaviour of employees. It is this last function that is of particular interest to us.[15] As the following quote makes clear, culture defines the rules of the game:

> Culture by definition is elusive, intangible, implicit, and taken for granted. But every organization develops a core set of assumptions, understandings, and implicit rules that govern day-to-day behaviour in the workplace . . . Until newcomers learn the rules, they are not accepted as full-fledged members of the organization. Transgressions of the rules on the part of high-level executives or front-line employees result in universal disapproval and powerful penalties. Conformity to the rules becomes the primary basis for reward and upward mobility.[16]

The role of culture in influencing employee behaviour appears to be increasingly important in today's workplace.[17] As organizations have widened spans of control, flattened structures, introduced teams, reduced formalisation and empowered employees, the *shared meaning* provided by a strong culture ensures that everyone is pointed in the same direction.

As we show later in this chapter, who receives a job offer to join the organization, who is appraised as a high performer and who gets a promotion are strongly influenced by the individual – organization 'fit' – that is, whether the applicant's or employee's attitudes and behaviour are compatible with the culture. It's not a coincidence that employees at Disney theme parks appear to be almost universally attractive, clean and wholesome looking, with bright smiles. That's the image Disney seeks. The company selects employees who will maintain that image. And once on the job, a strong culture, supported by formal rules and regulations, ensures that Disney theme-park employees will act in a relatively uniform and predictable way.

Culture as a liability

We are treating culture in a nonjudgemental manner. We haven't said that it's good or bad, only that it exists. Many of its functions, as outlined, are valuable for both the organization and the employee. Culture enhances organizational commitment and increases the consistency of employee behaviour. These are clearly benefits to an organization. From an employee's standpoint, culture is valuable because it reduces ambiguity. It tells employees how things are done and what's important. But we shouldn't ignore the potentially dysfunctional aspects of culture, especially a strong one, on an organization's effectiveness.

Barriers to change

Culture is a liability when the shared values are not in agreement with those that will further the organization's effectiveness. This is most likely to occur when an organization's environment is dynamic.[18] When an environment is undergoing rapid change, an organization's entrenched culture may no longer be appropriate. So consistency of behaviour is an asset to an organization when it faces a stable environment. It may, however, burden the organization and make it difficult to respond to changes in the environment. This helps to explain the challenges that executives at organizations like Marks & Spencer, Lloyds and Yahoo! have had in recent years in adapting to upheavals in their environment. These organizations have strong cultures that worked well for them in the past. But these strong cultures become barriers to change when 'business as usual' is no longer effective.

Barriers to diversity

Hiring new employees who, because of age, gender, culture, disability or other differences, are not like the majority of the organization's members creates a paradox.[19] Management wants new employees to accept the organization's core cultural values. Otherwise, these employees are unlikely to fit in or be accepted. But at the same time, management wants to openly acknowledge and demonstrate support for the differences that these employees bring to the workplace.

Strong cultures put considerable pressure on employees to conform. They limit the range of values and styles that are acceptable. In some instances a strong culture that condones prejudice can even undermine formal corporate diversity policies.[20] Organizations seek out and hire diverse individuals because of the alternative strengths these people bring to the workplace. Yet these diverse behaviours and strengths are likely to diminish in strong cultures as people attempt to fit in. Strong cultures, therefore, can be liabilities when they effectively eliminate the unique strengths that people of different backgrounds bring to the organization. Moreover, strong cultures can also be liabilities when they support institutional bias or become insensitive to people who are different.

Barriers to acquisitions and mergers

Historically, the key factors that management looked at in making acquisition or merger decisions were related to financial advantages or product synergy. In recent years, cultural compatibility has become the primary concern.[21] While a favourable financial statement or product line may be the initial attraction of an acquisition candidate, whether the acquisition actually works seems to have more to do with how well the two organizations' cultures match up.

'PEOPLE SOCIALISE THEMSELVES'   MYTH *OR* SCIENCE?

This statement is true to a significant degree. Although we generally think of socialisation as the process in which a person is shaped by his environment – and indeed that is the major focus of socialisation research – more evidence is accumulating that many people socialise themselves, or at least substantially mould their socialisation experiences.

Research has shown that people with a proactive personality are much better at learning the ropes than are newcomers. (As we noted in Chapter 4, people with a proactive personality identify opportunities, show initiative and take action.) That's because they are more likely to ask questions, seek out help and solicit feedback – in short, they learn more because they seek out more information and feedback.

Research indicates that individuals with a proactive personality are also better at networking when they join an organization, and achieve a closer fit with the culture of their organizations – in short, they build their own 'social capital'. As a result of being more effectively socialised into the organization, proactive people tend to like their jobs more, perform them better, and show less propensity to quit. Proactive people, it seems, do a lot to socialise *themselves* into the culture of an organization.

None of this is meant to deny that socialisation matters. The point is that people are not passive actors in being socialised. It may well be that how well someone is socialised into a new culture depends more on her personality than anything else.

Sources: T. A. Lambert, L. T. Eby, and M. P. Reeves, 'Predictors of networking intensity and network quality among white-collar job seekers', *Journal of Career Development*, June 2006, pp. 351–65; and J. A. Thompson, 'Proactive personality and job performance: a social capital perspective', *Journal of Applied Psychology*, September 2005, pp. 1011–17.

Many acquisitions fail shortly after their consummation. A survey by consulting firm A. T. Kearney revealed that 58 per cent of mergers failed to reach the value goals set by top managers.[22] The primary cause of failure is conflicting organizational cultures. As one expert commented, 'Mergers have an unusually high failure rate, and it's always because of people issues.' For instance, two years after the much heralded merger between of the German car maker Daimler-Benz and the American firm Chrysler, the company had experienced a mass departure of its American talents, an ongoing culture clash, massive financial losses and public derision. Vehicle sales analyst Maryann Keller noted on this merger, '. . . merging corporate culture is the biggest uncertainty. When it comes to the culture of these two companies, they are oil and water'.[23] Organizational cultures can also endure for a long period of time after a merger. Finnish crane producer Kone acquired Norwegian Wisbech Refsum in 1973, yet traces of cultural differences and identities still persisted at the end of the 1990s.[24]

Creating and sustaining culture

4 Explain the factors that create and sustain an organization's culture.

An organization's culture doesn't pop out of thin air. Once established, it rarely fades away. What forces influence the creation of a culture? What reinforces and sustains these forces once they're in place? We answer both of these questions in this section.

How a culture begins

An organization's current customs, traditions and general way of doing things are largely due to what it has done before and the degree of success it has had with those endeavours. This leads us to the ultimate source of an organization's culture: its founders.[26]

The founders of an organization traditionally have a major impact on that organization's early culture. They have a vision of what the organization should be. They are unconstrained by previous customs or ideologies. The small size that typically characterises new organizations further facilitates the founders' imposition of their vision on all organizational members. Culture creation occurs in three ways.[27] First, founders hire and keep only employees who think and feel the same way they do. Second, they indoctrinate and socialise these employees to their way of thinking and feeling. And finally, the founders' own behaviour acts as a role model that encourages employees to identify with them and thereby internalise their beliefs, values, and assumptions. When the organization succeeds, the founders' vision becomes seen as a primary determinant of that success. At this point, the founders' entire personality becomes embedded in the culture of the organization.

The culture at Hyundai, the giant Korean conglomerate, is largely a reflection of its founder Chung Ju Yung. Hyundai's fierce, competitive style and its disciplined, authoritarian nature are the same characteristics often used to describe Chung. Other contemporary examples of founders who have had an immeasurable impact on their organization's culture would include Bill Gates at Microsoft, Ingvar Kamprad at IKEA and Richard Branson at the Virgin Group.

Keeping a culture alive

Once a culture is in place, there are practices within the organization that act to maintain it by giving employees a set of similar experiences.[28] For example, many of the human resource practices we discuss in the next chapter reinforce the organization's culture. The selection process, performance evaluation criteria, training and development activities and promotion procedures ensure that those hired fit in with the culture, reward those who support it, and penalise

Jim Spellman/Getty Images

Roberto Cavalli single-handedly transformed a hand-painted knits business into one of the world's most famous fashion brands over the past four decades. Cavalli is the source and powerful shaper of the company's culture. Within his fashion fiefdom, Mr. Cavalli answers to no one. 'I'm used to always deciding everything myself', the designer says. 'It's a blessing, but also a terrible defect.' Having put the business up for sale, this 'one man show' culture is getting in the way of potential investors as he spurns them as being 'not worthy of my name'.[25]

(and even expel) those who challenge it. Three forces play a particularly important part in sustaining a culture: selection practices, the actions of top management, and socialisation methods. Let's take a closer look at each.

Selection

The explicit goal of the selection process is to identify and hire individuals who have the knowledge, skills, and abilities to perform the jobs within the organization successfully. Typically, more than one candidate will be identified who meets any given job's requirements. When that point is reached, it would be naive to ignore the fact that the final decision as to who is hired will be significantly influenced by the decision-maker's judgement of how well the candidates will fit into the organization. This attempt to ensure a proper match, whether purposely or inadvertently, results in the hiring of people who have values essentially consistent with those of the organization, or at least a good portion of those values.[29] In addition, the selection process provides information to applicants about the organization. Candidates learn about the organization and, if they perceive a conflict between their values and those of the organization, they can self-select themselves out of the applicant pool. Selection, therefore, becomes a two-way street, allowing employer or applicant to abrogate a marriage if there appears to be a mismatch. In this way, the selection process sustains an organization's culture by selecting out those individuals who might attack or undermine its core values.

For instance, W. L. Gore & Associates prides itself on its democratic culture and teamwork. There are no job titles at Gore, nor bosses nor chains of command. All work is done in teams. In Gore's selection process, teams of employees put job applicants through extensive interviews to ensure that candidates who can't deal with the level of uncertainty, flexibility, and teamwork that employees have to deal with in Gore plants are selected out.[30]

Top management

The actions of top management also have a major impact on the organization's culture.[31] Through what they say and how they behave, senior executives establish norms that filter down through the organization as to whether risk taking is desirable; how much freedom managers should give their employees; what is appropriate dress; what actions will pay off in terms of pay raises, promotions and other rewards; and the like.

For example, Ingvar Kamprad, the founder of the flat-pack furniture manufacturer and retailer IKEA avoids wearing suits, flies economy class and frequents cheap restaurants. He has been quoted as saying that his luxuries are the occasional nice cravat and Swedish fish roe. He also claims to furnish his home mostly with his own Ikea products. Does Kamprad need to be so thrifty? No. His wealth is estimated to be around €25 billion. But the man prefers a modest personal lifestyle, and he prefers the same for his company. By acting as a role model for frugality, employees at IKEA have learned to follow his example.[32]

Socialisation

No matter how good a job the organization does in recruiting and selection, new employees are not fully indoctrinated in the organization's culture. Because they are unfamiliar with the organization's culture, new employees are potentially likely to disturb the beliefs and customs that are in place. The organization will, therefore, want to help new employees adapt to its culture. This adaptation process is called **socialisation**.[33]

socialisation
A process that adapts employees to the organization's culture.

At the Greek swimming pool manufacturer, Piscines Ideales, new employees are welcomed by the CEO himself, and receive a welcome book that includes the story of the company, pictures of colleagues, and descriptions of company practices and policies. They are also given the CEO's mobile phone number as soon as they are recruited, and they learn the company's basic values: respect, camaraderie, teamwork, pride, focus on quality and learning and personal development.[34]

For new incoming employees in the upper ranks, companies often put considerably more time and effort into the socialisation process. At the US clothing company Limited Brands, newly hired vice presidents and regional directors go through an intensive one-month programme, called 'onboarding', designed to immerse these executives in the culture of Limited Brands.[35] During this month, they have no direct responsibilities for tasks associated with their

© Michael Christopher Brown/Corbis

New employees at Broad Air Conditioning in Changsha, China, are indoctrinated in the company's military-style culture by going through a 10-day training session of boot camp, where they are divided into platoons and live in barracks. Boot camp prepares new hires for the military formality that prevails at Broad, where employees begin their work week standing in formation during a flag-raising ceremony of two company flags and the flag of China. All employees live in dorms on the company campus and receive free food and lodging. To motivate its workers, Broad has scattered throughout the campus 43 life-size bronze statues of inspirational leaders from Confucius to Jack Welch, the former CEO of General Electric.

new positions. Instead, they spend all their work time meeting with other senior leaders and mentors, working the floors of retail stores, evaluating employee and customer habits, investigating the competition and studying Limited Brands' past and current operations.

As we discuss socialisation, keep in mind that the most critical socialisation stage is at the time of entry into the organization. This is when the organization seeks to mould the outsider into an employee 'in good standing'. Employees who fail to learn the essential or pivotal role behaviours risk being labelled 'nonconformists' or 'rebels', which often leads to expulsion. But the organization will be socialising every employee, though maybe not as explicitly, throughout his or her entire career in the organization. This further contributes to sustaining the culture.

Socialisation can be conceptualised as a process made up of three stages: prearrival, encounter, and metamorphosis.[36] The first stage encompasses all the learning that occurs before a new member joins the organization. In the second stage, the new employee sees what the organization is really like and confronts the possibility that expectations and reality may diverge. In the third stage, the relatively long-lasting changes take place. The new employee masters the skills required for the job, successfully performs the new roles, and makes the adjustments to the work group's values and norms.[37] This three-stage process has an impact on the new employee's work productivity, commitment to the organization's objectives, and eventual decision to stay with the organization. Figure 17.2 depicts this process.

The **prearrival stage** explicitly recognises that each individual arrives with a set of values, attitudes and expectations. These cover both the work to be done and the organization. For instance, in many jobs, particularly professional work, new members will have undergone a considerable degree of prior socialisation in training and in school. One major purpose of a business school, for example, is to socialise business students to the attitudes and behaviours that business firms want. If business executives believe that successful employees value the profit ethic, are loyal, will work hard and desire to achieve, they can hire individuals out of business schools who have been premoulded in this pattern. Moreover, most people in business realise

prearrival stage
The period of learning in the socialisation process that occurs before a new employee joins the organization.

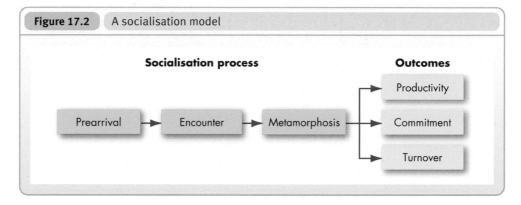

Figure 17.2   A socialisation model

that no matter how well they think they can socialise newcomers, the most important predictor of newcomers' future behaviour is their past behaviour. Research shows that what people know before they join the organization, and how proactive their personality is, are critical predictors of how well they adjust to a new culture.[38]

One way to capitalise on the importance of prehire characteristics in socialisation is to select employees with the 'right stuff' and to use the selection process to inform prospective employees about the organization as a whole. In addition, as noted previously, the selection process also acts to ensure the inclusion of the 'right type' – those who will fit in.

Indeed, the ability of the individual to present the appropriate face during the selection process determines his ability to move into the organization in the first place. Thus, success depends on the degree to which the aspiring member has correctly anticipated the expectations and desires of those in the organization in charge of selection.[39]

encounter stage
The stage in the socialisation process in which a new employee sees what the organization is really like and confronts the possibility that expectations and reality may diverge.

On entry into the organization, the new member enters the **encounter stage**. Here the individual confronts the possible dichotomy between expectations – about the job, the co-workers, the boss and the organization in general – and reality. If expectations prove to have been more or less accurate, the encounter stage merely provides a reaffirmation of the perceptions gained earlier. However, this is often not the case. Where expectations and reality differ, the new employee must undergo socialisation that will detach them from their previous assumptions and replace these with another set that the organization deems desirable. At the extreme, a new member may become totally disillusioned with the actualities of the job and resign. Proper selection should significantly reduce the probability of the latter occurrence. Also, an employee's network of friends and co-workers can play a critical role in helping them 'learn the ropes'. Newcomers are more committed to the organization when their friendship networks are large and diverse. So, organizations can help newcomers socialise by encouraging friendship ties in organizations.[40]

metamorphosis stage
The stage in the socialisation process in which a new employee changes and adjusts to the job, work group, and organization.

Finally, the new member must work out any problems discovered during the encounter stage. This may mean going through changes – hence, we call this the **metamorphosis stage**. The options presented in Exhibit 17.2 are alternatives designed to bring about the desired metamorphosis. Note, for example, that the more management relies on socialisation programmes that are formal, collective, fixed, serial and emphasise divestiture, the greater the likelihood that newcomers' differences and perspectives will be stripped away and replaced by standardised and predictable behaviours. Careful selection by management of newcomers' socialisation experiences can – at the extreme – create conformists who maintain traditions and customs, or inventive and creative individualists who consider no organizational practice sacred.

We can say that metamorphosis and the entry socialisation process is complete when new members have become comfortable with the organization and their job. They have internalised the norms of the organization and their work group, and understand and accept those norms. New members feel accepted by their peers as trusted and valued individuals. They are self-confident that they have the competence to complete the job successfully. They understand the system – not only their own tasks but the rules, procedures and informally accepted practices as

EXHIBIT 17.2	ENTRY SOCIALISATION OPTIONS

Formal vs. informal

The more a new employee is segregated from the ongoing work setting and differentiated in some way to make explicit his or her newcomer's role, the more formal socialisation is. Specific orientation and training programmes are examples. Informal socialisation puts the new employee directly into the job, with little or no special attention.

Individual vs. collective

New members can be socialised individually. This describes how it's done in many professional offices. They can also be grouped together and processed through an identical set of experiences, as in military boot camp.

Fixed vs. variable

This refers to the time schedule in which newcomers make the transition from outsider to insider. A fixed schedule establishes standardised stages of transition. This characterises rotational training programmes. It also includes probationary periods, such as the 8- to 10-year 'associate' status used by accounting and law firms before deciding on whether or not a candidate is made a partner. Variable schedules give no advance notice of their transition timetable. Variable schedules describe the typical promotion system, in which one is not advanced to the next stage until one is 'ready'.

Serial vs. random

Serial socialisation is characterised by the use of role models who train and encourage the newcomer. Apprenticeship and mentoring programmes are examples. In random socialisation, role models are deliberately withheld. New employees are left on their own to figure things out.

Investiture vs. divestiture

Investiture socialisation assumes that the newcomer's qualities and qualifications are the necessary ingredients for job success, so these qualities and qualifications are confirmed and supported. Divestiture socialisation tries to strip away certain characteristics of the recruit. Fraternity and sorority 'pledges' go through divestiture socialisation to shape them into the proper role.

Source: Based on J. Van Maanen, 'People processing: strategies of organizational socialization', *Organizational Dynamics*, Summer 1978, pp. 19–36; and E. H. Schein, 'Organizational culture', *American Psychologist*, February 1990, p. 116.

well. Finally, they know how they will be evaluated; that is, what criteria will be used to measure and appraise their work. They know what is expected of them and what constitutes a job 'well done.' As Figure 17.2 shows, successful metamorphosis should have a positive impact on new employees' productivity and their commitment to the organization and reduce their propensity to leave the organization.

Summary: how cultures form

Figure 17.3 summarises how an organization's culture is established and sustained. The original culture is derived from the founder's philosophy. This, in turn, strongly influences the criteria used in hiring. The actions of the current top management set the general climate of what is acceptable behaviour and what is not. How employees are to be socialised will depend both on the degree of success achieved in matching new employees' values to those of the organization's in the selection process and on top management's preference for socialisation methods.

Figure 17.3	How organization cultures form

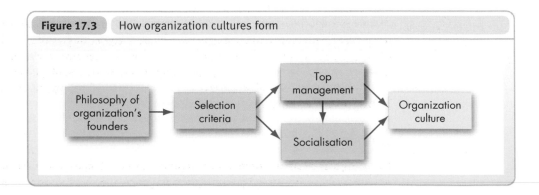

How employees learn culture

5 Show how culture is transmitted to employees.

Culture is transmitted to employees in a number of forms, the most potent being stories, rituals, material symbols and language.

Stories

During the days when Henry Ford II was chairman of the Ford Motor Co., you would have been hard pressed to find a manager who hadn't heard the story about Mr Ford reminding his executives, when they got too arrogant, that 'it's my name that's on the building'. The message was clear: Henry Ford II ran the company.

Hayley Clark, working at the car rental company Hertz at Prestwick Airport in Scotland, took pity on an elderly Australian couple who brought their car back before flying on to Dublin. She noticed they were still at the airport four hours later. They were flying the next day and had been unable to find accommodation because visitors to the nearby Open Golf Championship had taken every available space. So Ms Clark took them home, put them up for the night, then drove them to the airport for their 5a.m. check-in, all before starting her 8a.m. shift. The story is used within Hertz as an illustration of exceptional company service.[41]

Stories such as these circulate through many organizations. They typically contain a narrative of events about the organization's founders, rule breaking, rags-to-riches successes, reductions in the workforce, relocation of employees, reactions to past mistakes and organizational coping.[42] These stories anchor the present in the past and provide explanations and legitimacy for current practices.

Rituals

rituals
Repetitive sequences of activities that express and reinforce the key values of the organization, which goals are most important, which people are important and which are expendable.

Rituals are repetitive sequences of activities that express and reinforce the key values of the organization – what goals are most important, which people are important and which people are expendable.[43] One of the better-known corporate rituals is Wal-Mart's company chant. Begun by the company's founder, Sam Walton, as a way to motivate and unite his workforce, 'Gimme a W, gimme an A, gimme an L, gimme a squiggle, give me an M, A, R, T!' has become a company ritual that bonds Wal-Mart workers and reinforces Sam Walton's belief in the importance of his employees to the company's success. Similar corporate chants are used by IBM, Ericsson, Novell, Deutsche Bank and PricewaterhouseCoopers.[44]

Material symbols

The headquarters of Alcoa doesn't look like your typical head-office operation. There are few individual offices, even for senior executives. It is essentially made up of cubicles, common areas and meeting rooms. This informal corporate headquarters conveys to employees that Alcoa values openness, equality, creativity and flexibility. Some corporations provide their top executives with chauffeur-driven limousines and, when they travel by air, unlimited use of the corporate jet. Others may not get to ride in limousines or private jets, but they might still get a car and air transportation paid for by the company.

The layout of corporate headquarters, the types of automobiles top executives are given, and the presence or absence of corporate aircraft are a few examples of material symbols. Others include the size of offices, the elegance of furnishings, executive perks and attire.[45] These material symbols convey to employees who is important, the degree of egalitarianism desired by top management and the kinds of behaviour (for example, risk taking, conservative, authoritarian, participative, individualistic, social) that are appropriate.

Language

Many organizations and units within organizations use language as a way to identify members of a culture or subculture. By learning this language, members attest to their acceptance of the culture and, in so doing, help to preserve it. The following are examples of terminology used by employees at Knight-Ridder Information, a data redistributor: *accession number* (a number assigned to each individual record in a database), *KWIC* (a set of key-words-in-context), and *relational operator* (searching a database for names or key terms in some order). If you're a new employee at Boeing, you'll find yourself learning a whole unique vocabulary of acronyms, including *BOLD* (Boeing online data), *CATIA* (computer-graphics-aided three-dimensional interactive application), *MAIDS* (manufacturing assembly and installation data system), *POP* (purchased outside production) and *SLO* (service-level objectives).[46]

Organizations, over time, often develop unique terms to describe equipment, offices, key personnel, suppliers, customers or products that relate to its business. New employees are frequently overwhelmed with acronyms and jargon that, after six months on the job, have become fully part of their language. Once assimilated, this terminology acts as a common denominator that unites members of a given culture or subculture.

CHANGE JOBS, AND YOU MAY BE IN FOR A CULTURE SHOCK — OB IN THE NEWS

When Lyria Charles, a project manager, changed jobs, she didn't check her e-mail on weekends. Eventually, a fellow manager pulled her aside and told her that managers were expected to read e-mail over the weekend. 'I didn't know,' Charles said. 'No one told me.'

Employees have to learn the ropes when they change jobs. But unlike many aspects of business, organizational culture has few written rules. Very often, people learn the new culture only after stumbling into barriers and violating unwritten rules. 'It's like going to a different country,' says Michael Kanazawa of Dissero Partners, a management consulting firm.

There are myriad ways in which one organization's culture differs from another. To paraphrase Tolstoy, in certain ways, organizations are all alike, but each develops its culture in its own way.

Some of the differences – such as dress codes – are pretty easy to detect. Others are much harder to discern. In ad-

dition to weekend e-mails, another unwritten rule Charles learned was that she shouldn't have meetings with subordinates in her own office. How did she learn that? When Charles asked to meet with them, her assistant kept scheduling the meetings in the subordinates' cubicles. When Charles asked why, her assistant told her, 'That's how it's done.'

One way to decode the maze is to astutely observe unwritten rules and customs and to ask lots of questions. Some learning of an organization's culture, though, is pure trial and error. When Kevin Hall started a new job as a mortgage banker, he had to make his own travel arrangements because the first person he asked said it wasn't part of her job. When he observed colleagues getting help, though, he asked someone else, who was happy to oblige. 'You feel your way as you go,' Hall said.

Source: Based on E. White, 'Culture shock: learning customs of a new office', *Wall Street Journal*, 28 November 2006, p. B6.

Creating an ethical organizational culture

6 Demonstrate how an ethical culture can be created.

The content and strength of a culture influence an organization's ethical climate and the ethical behaviour of its members.[47] An organizational culture most likely to shape high ethical standards is one that's high in risk tolerance, low to moderate in aggressiveness, and focuses on means as well as outcomes. Managers in such a culture are supported for taking risks and innovating, are discouraged from engaging in unbridled competition, and will pay attention to *how* goals are achieved as well as to *what* goals are achieved.

A strong organizational culture will exert more influence on employees than a weak one. If the culture is strong and supports high ethical standards, it should have a very powerful and positive influence on employee behaviour. Johnson & Johnson, for example, has a strong culture that has long stressed corporate obligations to customers, employees, the community and shareholders, in that order. When poisoned Tylenol (a Johnson & Johnson product) was found on store shelves, employees at Johnson & Johnson across the United States independently pulled the product from these stores before management had even issued a statement concerning the tamperings. No one had to tell these individuals what was morally right; they knew what Johnson & Johnson would expect them to do. On the other hand, a strong culture that encourages pushing the limits can be a powerful force in shaping unethical behaviour. For instance, Enron's aggressive culture, with unrelenting pressure on executives to rapidly expand earnings, encouraged ethical corner-cutting and eventually contributed to the company's collapse.[48]

What can management do to create a more ethical culture? We suggest a combination of the following practices:

- **Be a visible role model.** Employees will look to the behaviour of top management as a benchmark for defining appropriate behaviour. When senior management is seen as taking the ethical high road, it provides a positive message for all employees.

- **Communicate ethical expectations.** Ethical ambiguities can be minimised by creating and disseminating an organizational code of ethics. It should state the organization's primary values and the ethical rules that employees are expected to follow.

- **Provide ethical training.** Set up seminars, workshops and similar ethical training programmes. Use these training sessions to reinforce the organization's standards of conduct, to clarify what practices are and are not permissible, and to address possible ethical dilemmas.

- **Visibly reward ethical acts and punish unethical ones.** Performance appraisals of managers should include a point-by-point evaluation of how their decisions measure up against the organization's code of ethics. Appraisals must include the means taken to achieve goals as well as the ends themselves. People who act ethically should be visibly rewarded for their behaviour. Just as importantly, unethical acts should be conspicuously punished.

- **Provide protective mechanisms.** The organization needs to provide formal mechanisms so that employees can discuss ethical dilemmas and report unethical behaviour without fear of reprimand. This might include creation of ethical counselors, ombudsmen, or ethical officers.

Creating a positive organizational culture

7 Describe a positive organizational culture.

It's often difficult to separate management fads from lasting changes in management thinking, especially early. In this book, we try to keep current while staying away from fads. There is one early trend, though, that we think is here to stay: creating a positive organizational culture.

At first glance, creating a positive culture may sound hopelessly naive, but the one thing that makes us believe this trend is here to stay is that there are signs that management practice and OB research are converging.

A **positive organizational culture** is defined as a culture that emphasises building on employee strengths, rewards more than it punishes and emphasises individual vitality and growth.[49] Let's consider each of these areas.

positive organizational culture
A culture that emphasises building on employee strengths, rewards more than punishes and emphasises individual vitality and growth.

Building on employee strengths

A lot of OB, and management practice, is concerned with how to fix employee problems. Although a positive organizational culture does not ignore problems, it does emphasise showing workers how they can capitalise on their strengths. Management guru Peter Drucker claimed that most people do not know what their strengths are. 'When you ask them, they look at you with a blank stare, or they respond in terms of subject knowledge, which is the wrong answer.' Do you know what your strengths are? Wouldn't it be better to be in an organizational culture that helped you discover those, and learn ways to make the most of them?

Larry Hammond used this approach – finding and exploiting employee strengths – at a time when you'd least expect it: during the darkest days of the business. Hammond is CEO of Auglaize Provico, an agribusiness company. The company was in the midst of its worst financial struggles and had to lay off one-quarter of its workforce. At that nadir, Hammand decided to try a different approach. Rather than dwell on what was wrong, he decided to take advantage of what was right. 'If you really want to [excel], you have to know yourself – you have to know what you're good at, and you have to know what you're not so good at,' says Hammond. With the help of Gallup consultant Barry Conchie, Auglaize Provico focused on discovering and using employee strengths. Hammond and Auglaize Provico turned the company around. 'You ask Larry [Hammond] what the difference is, and he'll say that it's individuals using their natural talents,' says Conchie.[50]

Rewarding more than punishing

There is, of course, a time and place for punishment, but there is also a time and place for rewards. Although most organizations are sufficiently focused on extrinsic rewards like pay and promotions, they often forget about the power of smaller (and cheaper) rewards like praise. Creating a positive organizational culture means that managers 'catch employees doing something right'. Part of creating a positive culture is articulating praise. Many managers withhold praise either because they're afraid employees will coast, or because they think praise is not valued. Failing to praise can become a 'silent killer' like escalating blood pressure. Because employees generally don't ask for praise, managers usually don't realise the costs of failing to do it.

Take the example of Elżbieta Górska-Kołodziejczyk, a plant manager for International Paper's facility in Kwidzyn, Poland. The job environment at the plant is bleak and difficult. Employees work in a windowless basement. Staffing is only roughly one-third of its prior level, while production has tripled. These challenges had done in the previous three managers. So, when Górska-Kołodziejczyk took over, she knew she had her work cut out for her. Although she had many items on her list of ways to transform the organization, at the top of her list was recognition and praise. She initially found it difficult to give praise to those who weren't used to it, especially men, but she found over time that they valued it, too. 'They were like cement at the beginning,' she said, 'like cement.' Górska-Kołodziejczyk has found that giving praise is often reciprocated. One day a department supervisor pulled her over to tell her she was doing a good job. 'This I do remember, yes,' she said.[51]

Emphasising vitality and growth

A positive organizational culture emphasises not only organizational effectiveness, but individuals' growth as well. No organization will get the best out of employees if the employees see themselves as mere tools or parts of the organization. A positive culture realises the difference between a job and a career, and shows an interest not only in what the employee does to contribute to organizational effectiveness, but in what the organization does to facilitate individual growth. An assessment of thousands of organizations revealed one-third felt they were not learning and growing on their job. The figure was even higher in some industries, such as banking, manufacturing, communications and utilities. Although it may take more creativity to encourage employee growth in some types of industries, it can happen in the fast-paced food service industry. Consider the case of Philippe Lescornez and Didier Brynaert.

Philippe Lescornez leads a team of employees at Masterfoods in Belgium. One of his team members is Didier Brynaert, who works in Luxembourg, nearly 150 miles from Masterfoods's Belgian headquarters. Brynaert was considered a good sales promoter who was meeting expectations. Lescornez decided that Brynaert's job could be made more important if he were seen less as just another sales promoter and more as an expert on the unique features of the Luxembourg market. So Lescornez asked Brynaert for information he could share with the home office. He hoped that by raising Brynaert's profile in Brussels, he could create in him a greater sense of ownership for his remote sales territory. 'I started to communicate much more what he did to other people [within the company], because there's quite some distance between the Brussels office and the section he's working in. So I started to communicate, communicate, communicate. The more I communicated, the more he started to provide material,' says Lescornez. As a result, 'Now he's recognised as the specialist for Luxembourg – the guy who is able to build a strong relationship with the Luxembourg clients,' says Lescornez. What's good for Brynaert, of course, is also good for Lescornez, who gets credit for helping Brynaert grow and develop.[52]

Limits of positive culture

Is a positive culture a panacea? Cynics (or should we say realists?) may be sceptical about the benefits of positive organizational culture. To be sure, even though some companies such as Cisco, Microsoft, ConSol, Beaverbrooks and 3M have embraced aspects of a positive organizational culture, it is a new enough area that there is some uncertainty about how and when it works best. Moreover, any OB scholar or manager needs to make sure he is objective about the benefits – and risks – of cultivating a positive organizational culture.

It is important to note that the concept of creating positive cultures largely came from the US. However, not all cultures value being positive as much as US culture does. Further, take the example of Admiral, a British insurance company. The firm has established a Ministry of Fun in its call centres to organize such events as poem writings, table football and fancy dress days. When does the pursuit of a positive culture start to seem coercive or even Orwellian? As one critic notes, 'Promoting a social orthodoxy of positiveness focuses on a particular constellation of desirable states and traits but, in so doing, can stigmatise those who fail to fit the template.'[53]

Our point is that there may be benefits to establishing a positive culture, but an organization also needs to be careful to be objective, and not pursue it past the point of effectiveness.

Spirituality and organizational culture

8 Identify characteristics of a spiritual culture.

What do Windesheim University of Professional Education, Ford, Elcoteq Communications, The Body Shop and the *Times of India* have in common? They're among a growing number of organizations that have embraced workplace spirituality.[54]

What is spirituality?

workplace spirituality
The recognition that people have an inner life that nourishes and is nourished by meaningful work that takes place in the context of community.

Workplace spirituality is *not* about organized religious practices. It's not about God or theology. **Workplace spirituality** recognises that people have an inner life that nourishes and is nourished by meaningful work that takes place in the context of community.[55] Organizations that promote a spiritual culture recognise that people have both a mind and a spirit, seek to find meaning and purpose in their work, and desire to connect with other human beings and be part of a community.

Why spirituality now?

Historical models of management and organizational behaviour had no room for spirituality. As we noted in our discussion of emotions in Chapter 8, the myth of rationality assumed that the well-run organization eliminated feelings. Similarly, concern about an employee's inner life had no role in the perfectly rational model. But just as we've now come to realise that the study of emotions improves our understanding of organizational behaviour, an awareness of spirituality can help you to better understand employee behaviour in the twenty-first century.

Of course, employees have always had an inner life. So why has the search for meaning and purposefulness in work surfaced now? There are a number of reasons. We summarise them in Exhibit 17.3.

EXHIBIT 17.3 | **REASONS FOR THE GROWING INTEREST IN SPIRITUALITY**

- They are looking for a counterbalance to the pressures and stress of a turbulent pace of life. Contemporary lifestyles – single-parent families, geographic mobility, the temporary nature of jobs, new technologies that create distance between people – underscore the lack of community many people feel and increase the need for involvement and connection.

- Formalised religion hasn't worked for many people, and they continue to look for anchors to replace lack of faith and to fill a growing feeling of emptiness.

- Job demands have made the workplace dominant in many people's lives, yet they continue to question the meaning of work.

- They desire to integrate personal life values with their professional lives.

- An increasing number of people are finding that the pursuit of more material acquisitions leaves them unfulfilled.

Characteristics of a spiritual organization

The concept of workplace spirituality draws on our previous discussions of topics such as values, ethics, motivation, leadership, and work/life balance. Spiritual organizations are concerned with helping people develop and reach their full potential. Similarly, organizations that are concerned with spirituality are more likely to directly address problems created by work/life conflicts. What differentiates spiritual organizations from their nonspiritual counterparts? Although research on this question is only preliminary, our review identified four cultural characteristics that tend to be evident in spiritual organizations:[56]

http://www.vanede.nl

The Dutch consultancy firm Van Ede and Partners is a spiritual organization. The company has integrated singing, reflection and meditation into their working environment. National meetings (with 130 colleagues) start with a half hour of singing songs from different cultures around the world including Chorals and Spirituals, Gregorian chants and mantras. Every meeting in all their offices begins with a brief moment of reflection. The company finds that meetings after these moments of reflection and meditation are peaceful, focused and profound, with people speaking their minds freely. Occasionally, employees may meditate on some words of wisdom, which are read out loud several times. Some examples are: 'The Self is One, unmoving it moves, is far away yet near'; 'Only if you put yourself in the Light, can you see your shadow sides'; 'The word of Eternity is only to be heard in silence'.[57]

- **Strong sense of purpose.** Spiritual organizations build their cultures around a meaningful purpose. Although profits may be important, they're not the primary values of the organization. People want to be inspired by a purpose that they believe is important and worthwhile.

- **Trust and respect.** Spiritual organizations are characterised by mutual trust, honesty, and openness. Managers aren't afraid to admit mistakes. The president of Wetherill Associates, a highly successful auto parts distribution firm, says: 'We don't tell lies here, and everyone knows it. We are specific and honest about quality and suitability of the product for our customers' needs, even if we know they might not be able to detect any problem.'[58]

- **Humanistic work practices.** These practices embraced by spiritual organizations include flexible work schedules, group and organization-based rewards, narrowing of pay and status differentials, guarantees of individual worker rights, employee empowerment and job security. Hewlett-Packard, for instance, has handled temporary downturns through voluntary attrition and shortened workweeks (shared by all), and it has handled longer-term declines through early retirements and buyouts.

- **Toleration of employee expression.** The final characteristic that differentiates spiritually based organizations is that they don't stifle employee emotions. They allow people to be themselves – to express their moods and feelings without guilt or fear of reprimand.

SELF-ASSESSMENT LIBRARY

How spiritual am I?

In the Self-assessment library (available online), take assessment IV.A.4 (How spiritual am I?). Note: People's scores on this measure vary from time to time, so take that into account when interpreting the results.

Criticisms of spirituality

Critics of the spirituality movement in organizations have focused on three issues. First is the question of scientific foundation. What really is workplace spirituality? Is it just a new management buzzword? Second, are spiritual organizations legitimate? Specifically, do organizations have the right to impose spiritual values on their employees? Third is the question of economics: Are spirituality and profits compatible?

First, as you might imagine, there is very little research on workplace spirituality. We don't know whether the concept will have staying power. Do the cultural characteristics just identified really separate spiritual organizations? What is a nonspiritual organization, anyway? Do employees of so-called spiritual organizations perceive that they work in spiritual organizations? Although there is some research suggesting support for workplace spirituality (as we discuss later), before the concept of spirituality gains full credence, the questions we've just posed need to be answered.

On the second question, there is clearly the potential for an emphasis on spirituality to make some employees uneasy. Critics might argue that secular institutions, especially business firms, have no business imposing spiritual values on employees. This criticism is undoubtedly valid when spirituality is defined as bringing religion and God into the workplace.[59] However, the criticism seems less stinging when the goal is limited to helping employees find meaning in their work lives. If the concerns listed in Exhibit 17.3 truly characterise a growing segment of the workforce, then perhaps the time is right for organizations to help employees find meaning and purpose in their work and to use the workplace as a source of community.

Finally, the issue of whether spirituality and profits are compatible objectives is certainly relevant for managers and investors in business. The evidence, although limited, indicates that the two objectives may be very compatible. A recent research study by a major consulting firm found that companies that introduced spiritually based techniques improved productivity and significantly reduced turnover.[60] Another study found that organizations that provide their employees with opportunities for spiritual development outperformed those that didn't.[61] Other studies also report that spirituality in organizations was positively related to creativity, employee satisfaction, team performance, and organizational commitment.[62] And if you're looking for a single case to make the argument for spirituality, take a look at Elcoteq, Europe's biggest electronic manufacturing service company.

In 2003, Group Elcoteq Network Corporation, acquired a factory in Offenburg, Germany with about 330 employees. Previously, the plant had been owned by various large telecom companies and went through major restructuring and downsizing during the preceding years as a direct consequence of the collapsing telecom market. Consequently, the firm required a rapid transformation in a very competitive market and with a demoralised workforce. Management decided to manage the turn-around with business practices which were defined in terms of the spiritual values that they emulate. Examples of this were seeing their 360-degree feedback process as supporting trustworthiness, new salary models as supporting justice, and their holiday celebration dinners as promoting service and humility. As a result of their commitment to spiritual virtues, in just over a year the company had achieved outstanding financial results, increased the efficiency of the workforce by 20 per cent, and drastically improved customer satisfaction.[63]

Global Implications

9 Show how national culture may affect the way organizational culture is transported to a different country.

We considered global cultural values (collectivism–individualism, power distance, and so on) in Chapter 4. Here our focus is a bit narrower: How is organizational culture affected by a global context? As the opening vignette suggests, organizational cultures are so powerful that they often transcend national boundaries. But that doesn't mean that organizations should, or could, be blissfully ignorant of local culture.

As we noted in Chapter 4, national cultures differ. Organizational cultures often reflect national culture. For example, the culture at AirAsia, a Malaysian-based airline, emphasises informal dress so as not to create status differences. The carrier has lots of parties, participative management and no private offices. This organizational culture reflects Malaysia's relatively collectivistic culture. However, the culture of British Airways does not reflect the same degree of informality. If British Airways were to merge with AirAsia, it would need to take these cultural differences into account. So when an organization merges with, or acquires, a company from a different country or opens up operations in another country, it ignores the local culture at its own risk.

A hostile takeover bid from the British mobile phone group Vodafone for the German telecoms and engineering group Mannesmann led to a great deal of resistance. Never before had such a large company been taken over by a foreign firm. German political parties, trade unions and the Mannesmann works councils all strongly rejected Vodafone's bid. They believed it could ultimately undermine the German corporate culture which is based on strong employee involvement and co-determination (employees having a role in the management of the company). Vodaphone finally achieved the acquisition after a great deal of negotiation, campaigning and guaranteeing worker's rights to participate.

National cultural differences can also present opportunities 'shake-up' organizational cultures. The German based chemicals group Lanxess appointed a Chinese executive, Liu Zhengrong, as Head of Human Resources to bring some Chinese dynamism to the company. And as the group sought to shift some production to China, it was anticipated that German executives would introduce more rigour to management in China.[64]

Summary and implications for managers

Figure 17.4 depicts organizational culture as an intervening variable. Employees form an overall subjective perception of the organization based on factors such as degree of risk tolerance, team emphasis, and support of people. This overall perception becomes, in effect, the organization's culture or personality. These favourable or unfavourable perceptions then affect employee performance and satisfaction, with the impact being greater for stronger cultures.

Just as people's personalities tend to be stable over time, so too do strong cultures. This makes strong cultures difficult for managers to change. When a culture becomes mismatched to its environment, management will want to change it. But as the Point/Counterpoint demonstrates, changing an organization's culture is a long and difficult process. The result, at least in the short term, is that managers should treat their organization's culture as relatively fixed.

One of the most important managerial implications of organizational culture relates to selection decisions. Hiring individuals whose values don't align with those of the organization is likely to lead to employees who lack motivation and commitment and who are dissatisfied with

| Figure 17.4 | How organizational cultures have an impact on employee performance and satisfaction |

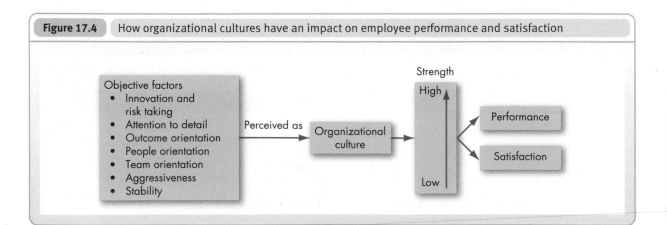

their jobs and the organization.[65] Not surprisingly, employee 'misfits' have considerably higher turnover rates than individuals who perceive a good fit.[66]

We should also not overlook the influence socialisation has on employee performance. An employee's performance depends to a considerable degree on knowing what he should or should not do. Understanding the right way to do a job indicates proper socialisation.

As a manager, you can shape the culture of your work environment. That is particularly the case with some of the cultural aspects we discussed in the latter part of the chapter – all managers can do their part to create an ethical culture, and spirituality and a positive organizational culture should be considered, too. Often you can do as much to shape your organizational culture as the culture of the organization shapes you.

POINT/COUNTERPOINT

Organizational cultures can't be changed

POINT →

An organization's culture is made up of relatively stable characteristics. It develops over many years and is rooted in deeply held values to which employees are strongly committed. In addition, there are a number of forces continually operating to maintain a given culture. These include written statements about the organization's mission and philosophy, the design of physical spaces and buildings, the dominant leadership style, hiring criteria, past promotion practices, entrenched rituals, popular stories about key people and events, the organization's historic performance evaluation criteria and the organization's formal structure.

Selection and promotion policies are particularly important devices that work against cultural change. Employees chose the organization because they perceived their values to be a 'good fit' with the organization. They become comfortable with that fit and will strongly resist efforts to disturb the equilibrium. The terrific difficulties that

organizations such as Marks & Spencer, Volkswagen and the UK's Royal Mail have had in trying to reshape their cultures attest to this dilemma. These organizations historically tended to attract individuals who desired situations that were stable and highly structured. Those in control in organizations will also select senior managers who will continue the current culture. Even attempts to change a culture by going outside the organization to hire a new chief executive are unlikely to be effective. The evidence indicates that the culture is more likely to change the executive than the other way around.

Our argument should not be viewed as saying that culture can *never* be changed. In the unusual case in which an organization confronts a survival-threatening crisis, members of the organization will be responsive to efforts at cultural change. However, anything less than that is unlikely to be effective in bringing about cultural change.

COUNTERPOINT ←

Changing an organization's culture is extremely difficult, but cultures *can* be changed. The evidence suggests that cultural change is most likely to take place when most or all of the following conditions exist:

- **A dramatic crisis.** This is a shock that undermines the status quo and calls into question the relevance of the current culture. Examples are a surprising financial setback, the loss of a major customer, and a dramatic technological breakthrough by a competitor.

- **Turnover in leadership.** New top leadership, which can provide an alternative set of key values, may be perceived as more capable of responding to the crisis.

- **Young and small organizations.** The younger the organization, the less entrenched its culture will be. Similarly, it's easier for management to communicate its new values when the organization is small.

- **Weak culture.** The more widely held a culture is and the higher the agreement among members on its values, the more difficult it will be to change. Conversely, weak cultures are more amenable to change than strong ones.

If all or most of these conditions exist, the following management actions may lead to change: initiating new stories and rituals, selecting and promoting employees who espouse the new values, changing the reward system to support the new values, and undermining current subcultures through transfers, job rotation and terminations.

Under the best of conditions, these actions won't result in an immediate or dramatic shift in the culture. In the final analysis, cultural change is a lengthy process – measured in years rather than in months. But cultures can be changed. The success that new leadership had in turning around the cultures at companies like Oticon, Unipart, 3M and GE attests to this claim.

QUESTIONS FOR REVIEW

1. What is institutionalisation and how does it affect organizational culture?

2. What is organizational culture and what are its common characteristics?

3. What are the functional and dysfunctional effects of organizational culture?

4. What factors create and sustain an organization's culture?

5. How is culture transmitted to employees?

6. How can an ethical culture be created?

7. What is a positive organizational culture?

8. What are the characteristics of a spiritual culture?

9. How does national culture affect how organizational culture is transported to a different country?

Experiential exercise

RATE YOUR CLASSROOM CULTURE

Listed here are 14 statements. Using the 5-item scale (from Strongly Agree to Strongly Disagree), respond to each statement by circling the number that best represents your opinion.

	Strongly Agree	Agree	Neutral	Disagree	Strongly Disagree
1. I feel comfortable challenging statements made by my instructor.	5	4	3	2	1
2. My instructor heavily penalises assignments that are not submitted on time.	1	2	3	4	5
3. My instructor believes that 'it's final results that count.'	1	2	3	4	5
4. My instructor is sensitive to my personal needs and problems.	5	4	3	2	1
5. A large portion of my grade depends on how well I work with others in the class.	5	4	3	2	1
6. I often feel nervous and tense when I come to class.	1	2	3	4	5
7. My instructor seems to prefer stability over change.	1	2	3	4	5
8. My instructor encourages me to develop new and different ideas.	5	4	3	2	1
9. My instructor has little tolerance for sloppy thinking.	1	2	3	4	5
10. My instructor is more concerned with how I came to a conclusion than with the conclusion itself.	5	4	3	2	1
11. My instructor treats all students alike.	1	2	3	4	5
12. My instructor frowns on class members helping each other with assignments.	1	2	3	4	5
13. Aggressive and competitive people have a distinct advantage in this class.	1	2	3	4	5
14. My instructor encourages me to see the world differently.	5	4	3	2	1

Calculate your total score by adding up the numbers you circled. Your score will fall between 14 and 70.

A high score (49 or above) describes an open, risk-taking, supportive, humanistic, team-oriented, easy-going, growth-oriented culture. A low score (35 or below) describes a closed, structured, task-oriented, individualistic, tense, and stability-oriented culture. Note that differences count, so a score of 60 is a more open culture than one that scores 50. Also,

realise that one culture isn't preferable over another. The 'right' culture depends on you and your preferences for a learning environment.

Form teams of five to seven members each. Compare your scores. How closely do they align? Discuss and resolve any discrepancies. Based on your team's analysis, what type of student do you think would perform best in this class?

Ethical dilemma

IS THERE ROOM FOR SNOOPING IN AN ORGANIZATION'S CULTURE?

Although some of the spying Hewlett-Packard performed on some members of its board of directors appeared to violate law, much of it was legal. Moreover, many companies spy on their employees – sometimes with and sometimes without their knowledge or consent. Organizations differ in their culture of surveillance. Some differences are due to the type of business. A Department of Defence contractor has more reason – perhaps even obligation – to spy on its employees than does an orange juice producer.

However, surveillance in most industries is on the upswing. There are several reasons for this, including the huge growth of two sectors with theft and security problems (services and information technology, respectively) and the increased availability of surveillance technology.

Consider the following surveillance actions and, for each action, decide whether it would never be ethical (mark N), would sometimes be ethical (mark S), or would always be ethical (mark A). For those you mark S, indicate on what factors your judgement would depend.

1. Sifting through an employee's trash for evidence of wrongdoing.
2. Periodically reading e-mail messages for disclosure of confidential information or inappropriate use.
3. Conducting video surveillance of workspace.
4. Monitoring websites visited by employees and determining the appropriateness and work-relatedness of those visited.
5. Taping phone conversations.
6. Posing as a job candidate, an investor, a customer or a colleague (when the real purpose is to solicit information).

Would you be less likely to work for an employer that engaged in some of these methods? Why or why not? Do you think use of surveillance says something about an organization's culture?

CASE INCIDENT 1

Which companies have been recognised as among the best places to work in Europe? You would probably guess Google, Microsoft, Cisco or 3M, and you would be right. However, you probably wouldn't guess that on the same list is a small swimming pool manufacturer in Athens. What makes it such a great place to work?

Piscines Ideales treats its 127 employees as if they are part of a big family, in which individuals are nurtured and cared for by the company's leaders, including the chief executive, Stelios Stavridis, who goes by the slogan: 'It is not an employee's right to express themselves, it is an obligation!' Mr Stavridis and other senior managers give their home and mobile phone numbers to employees as soon as they are hired, and managing directors hold dinners with their departmental staffs at least once a year.

'Although the company is growing, it remains a very friendly and human environment,' wrote one employee. 'I consider it as my second family because it makes me feel secure.'

Family life is supported for employees of Piscines Ideales: a number of young mothers are equipped with Internet connections to help them work from home one day a week, and the company provides money and psychological support to new parents. Employees who get married receive a month's salary as a bonus. And the company gives new computers to employees' children when they begin studies at the university. Piscines Ideales also provides employees with a high level of professional support. Through an annual 'job rotation', employees spend a few weeks each year in different departments to gain a more holistic understanding of the company; they follow up by writing a detailed report of their observations and recommendations. Low level employees in all positions are encouraged to develop their skills.

It's no wonder the employees of Piscines Ideales consider it a great place to work.

Questions

1. Would you characterise Piscines Ideales' culture as strong or weak? Why?
2. How would you describe this culture?
3. How do employees learn the company's culture?
4. Do you think this culture is appropriate for a swimming pool manufacturer? Why?
5. Are there any potential problems with Piscines Ideales' culture?

Source: European Special Award – Piscines Ideales, FT.com, special report, 28 May 2008, www.ft.com/bestworkplaces2008.

CASE INCIDENT 2

An odd couple? P&G and Google combine cultures

At Procter & Gamble, the corporate culture is so rigid, employees jokingly call themselves 'Proctoids'. In contrast, Google staffers are urged to wander the halls on company-provided scooters and brainstorm on public whiteboards. Now, this odd couple thinks they have something to gain from one another – so they've started swapping employees. So far, about two-dozen staffers from the two companies have spent weeks dipping into each other's staff training programmes and sitting in on meetings where business plans get hammered out. The initiative has been noticed. Previously, neither company had granted this kind of access to outsiders.

Closer ties are crucial to both sides. P&G, the biggest advertising spender in the world, is waking up to the reality that the next generation of laundry-detergent, toilet-paper and skin-cream buyers now spends more time online than watching TV. And Google craves a bigger slice of P&G's €6.5 billion annual ad budget as its own revenue growth slows.

As the two companies started working together, the gulf between them quickly became apparent. When actress Salma Hayek unveiled an ambitious promotion for P&G's Pampers brand, the Google team was stunned to learn that Pampers hadn't invited any 'motherhood' bloggers – women who run popular websites about child-rearing – to attend the press conference. For their part, P&G employees gasped in surprise during a Tide brand meeting when a Google job-swapper apparently didn't realise that Tide's signature orange-coloured packaging is a key part of the brand's image.

These differences did provide important learning opportunities. Denise Chudy, a Google sales-team leader, caused a stir when she showed a dozen or so P&G employees some Google data indicating that online searches for the word 'coupons' was up about 50 per cent over the previous 12 months. Tracking online searches was 'one of the best learning [experiences] of my first week at Google,' P&G marketing manager Catherine Duval-Russell wrote on an in-house blog.

P&G has a long history as a marketing innovator. Back in the late 1800s, it developed one of the earliest truly national brands – Ivory soap – with saturation advertising in everything from farm journals to religious periodicals. Decades later, radio and TV 'soap operas' famously took their name from the fact that P&G advertised so heavily on them to reach women.

As part of a month-long job swap a mixed group of Google and P&G staffers crowded into P&G's archives to study the 62-year history of Tide. Sessions like these are a key part of P&G's training of up-and-coming brand managers.

Pouring over decades of marketing material – all featuring Tide's bright orange packaging in a starring role – Google employee Jen Bradburn took note. 'It's helpful to know not to mess with the orange too much,' she said. That elicited a chorus of unambiguous 'yesses' from P&G employees in attendance.

Google job-swappers have started adopting P&G's language. During a session on evaluating in-store displays, a P&G marketer described the company's standard method, known as 'stop, hold, close'. Product packaging first needs to 'stop' a shopper. 'Hold' is a pause to read the label, and 'close' is when a shopper puts the product in the cart. 'This is just like our text ads,' Google's Ms. Chudy said. The headline is the 'stop', its description is the 'hold' and the 'close' is clicking through to the website. 'This is going to get so much easier, now that I'm learning their language,' she said.

With mommy-bloggers, Pampers was quick to follow Google's advice. After failing to invite any to its initial Pampers promotion press conference, it invited a dozen or so to visit P&G's baby division. The bloggers claim to have drawn anywhere from 100,000 to 6 million visitors to their websites. The bloggers toured the facilities, met with executives, got a primer on product design and had their hotel and travel costs covered. Their visit was captured on video for other P&G brands to study.

Pampers' sense of discovery of the power of bloggers is apparent in the video. 'This is a very different type of communication than what Procter & Gamble is used to,' Pampers spokesman Bryan McCleary advises viewers of the video. The bloggers 'don't like advertising,' he says in the video. 'What they do like are exciting stories . . . and those things actually can become word-of-mouth advertising, if done in the right way.'

Questions

1. What were Google and P&G trying to achieve by swapping employees?

2. What did they learn from each other?

3. Do you think this method would be effective in changing a company's culture? Why or why not?

4. What risks could there be with this approach?

5. Do you think Google employees would want to work at P&G? Would P&G employees want to work at Google? Explain your answer.

Source: Based on E. Byron, 'A new odd couple: Google, P&G swap workers to spur innovation', *Wall Street Journal*, (Eastern edition), 19 November 2008, p. A.1.

Endnotes

1 P. Selznick, 'Foundations of the theory of organizations', *American Sociological Review*, February 1948, pp. 25–35.

2 See L. G. Zucker, 'Organizations as institutions', in S. B. Bacharach (ed.), *Research in the Sociology of Organizations* (Greenwich, CT: JAI Press, 1983), pp. 1–47; A. J. Richardson, 'The production of institutional behaviour: a constructive comment on the use of institutionalization theory in organizational analysis', *Canadian Journal of Administrative Sciences*, December 1986, pp. 304–16; L. G. Zucker, *Institutional Patterns and Organizations: Culture and Environment* (Cambridge, MA: Ballinger, 1988); R. L. Jepperson, 'Institutions, institutional effects, and institutionalism', in W. W. Powell and P. J. DiMaggio (eds), *The New Institutionalism in Organizational Analysis* (Chicago, IL: University of Chicago Press, 1991), pp. 143–63; and T. B. Lawrence, M. K. Mauws, B. Dyck and R. F. Kleysen, 'The politics of organizational learning: integrating power into the 4I framework', *Academy of Management Review*, January 2005, pp. 180–91.

3 See, for example, H. S. Becker, 'Culture: a sociological view', *Yale Review*, Summer 1982, pp. 513–27; and E. H. Schein, *Organizational Culture and Leadership* (San Francisco, CA: Jossey-Bass, 1985), p. 168.

4 This seven-item description is based on C. A. O'Reilly, III, J. Chatman and D. F. Caldwell, 'People and organizational culture: a profile comparison approach to assessing person–organization fit', *Academy of Management Journal*, September 1991, pp. 487–516; C. A. O'Reilly III, J. Chatman and D. F. Caldwell, 'People and organizational culture: a profile comparison approach to assessing person–organization fit', *Academy of Management Journal*, September 1991, pp. 487–516; and J. A. Chatman and K. A. Jehn, 'Assessing the relationship between industry characteristics and organizational culture: how different can you be?', *Academy of Management Journal*, June 1994, pp. 522–53.

5 '100 best workplaces in Europe 2007', Great place to work institute/Financial Times see http://www.greatplacetowork.com/ and http://www.ft.com/reports/bestwork2007.

6 The view that there will be consistency among perceptions of organizational culture has been called the 'integration' perspective. For a review of this perspective and conflicting approaches, see D. Meyerson and J. Martin, 'Cultural change: an integration of three different views', *Journal of Management Studies*, November 1987, pp. 623–47; and P. J. Frost, L. F. Moore, M. R. Louis, C. C. Lundberg and J. Martin (eds), *Reframing Organizational Culture* (Newbury Park, CA: Sage Publications, 1991).

7 See J. M. Jermier, J. W. Slocum, Jr., L. W. Fry and J. Gaines, 'Organizational subcultures in a soft bureaucracy: resistance behind the myth and facade of an official culture,' *Organization Science*, May 1991, pp. 170–94; and S. A. Sackmann, 'Culture and subcultures: an analysis of organizational knowledge', *Administrative Science Quarterly*, March 1992, pp. 140–61; G. Hofstede, 'Identifying organizational subcultures: an empirical approach', *Journal of Management Studies*, January 1998, pp. 1–12.

8 T. A. Timmerman, 'Do organizations have personalities?', paper presented at the 1996 National Academy of anagement Conference; Cincinnati, OH, August 1996.

9 S. Hamm, 'No letup – and no apologies', *BusinessWeek*, 26 October 1998, pp. 58–64; and C. Carlson, 'Former Intel exec slams Microsoft culture', *eWEEK.com*, 26 March 2002, www.eweek.com/article2/0,1759,94976,00.asp.

10 T. Deal and A. Kennedy, *Corporate Cultures: The Rites and Rituals of Corporate Life* (London: Penguin, 1982. First published by Addison-Wesley publishing).

11 See, for example, G. G. Gordon and N. DiTomaso, 'Predicting corporate performance from organizational culture', *Journal of Management Studies*, November 1992, pp. 793–98; J. B. Sorensen, 'The strength of corporate culture and the reliability of firm performance', *Administrative Science Quarterly*, March 2002, pp. 70–91; and J. Rosenthal and M. A. Masarech, 'High-performance cultures: how values can drive business results', *Journal of Organizational Excellence*, Spring 2003, pp. 3–18.

12 Y. Wiener, 'Forms of value systems: a focus on organizational effectiveness and cultural change and maintenance', *Academy of Management Review*, October 1988, p. 536.

13 R. T. Mowday, L. W. Porter and R. M. Steers, *Employee–Organization Linkages: The Psychology of Commitment, Absenteeism, and Turnover* (New York: Academic Press, 1982); and C. Vandenberghe, 'Organizational culture, person–culture fit, and turnover: a replication in the health care industry', *Journal of Organizational Behavior*, March 1999, pp. 175–84.

14 S. L. Dolan and S. Garcia, 'Managing by values: cultural redesign for strategic organizational change at the dawn of the twenty-first century', *Journal of Management Development*, 21, 2 (2002), pp. 101–17.

15 See C. A. O'Reilly and J. A. Chatman, 'Culture as social control: corporations, cults, and commitment', in B. M. Staw and L. L. Cummings (eds), *Research in Organizational Behavior*, vol. 18 (Greenwich, CT: JAI Press, 1996), pp. 157–200. See also M. Pinae Cunha, 'The "best place to be": managing control and employee loyalty in a knowledge-intensive company', *Journal of Applied Behavioral Science*, December 2002, pp. 481–95.

16 T. E. Deal and A. A. Kennedy, 'Culture: a new look through old lenses', *Journal of Applied Behavioral Science*, November 1983, p. 501.

17 J. Case, 'Corporate culture,' *INC.*, November 1996, pp. 42–53.

18 Sorensen, 'The strength of corporate culture and the reliability of firm performance'.

19 See C. Lindsay, 'Paradoxes of organizational diversity: living within the paradoxes', in L. R. Jauch and J. L. Wall (eds), *Proceedings of the 50th Academy of Management Conference* (San Francisco, CA 1990), pp. 374–78; T. Cox, Jr., *Cultural Diversity in Organizations: Theory, Research & Practice* (San Francisco, CA: Berrett-Koehler, 1993), pp. 162–70; and L. Grensing-Pophal, 'Hiring to fit your corporate culture', *HRMagazine*, August 1999, pp. 50–54.

20 K. Labich, 'No more crude at Texaco', *Fortune*, 6 September 1999, pp. 205–12; and 'Rooting out racism', *BusinessWeek*, 10 January 2000, p. 66.

21 A. F. Buono and J. L. Bowditch, *The Human Side of Mergers and Acquisitions: Managing Collisions between People, Cultures,*

and Organizations (San Francisco, CA: Jossey-Bass, 1989); S. Cartwright and C. L. Cooper, 'The role of culture compatibility in successful organizational marriages', *Academy of Management Executive*, May 1993, pp. 57–70; E. Krell, 'Merging corporate cultures', *Training*, May 2001, pp. 68–78; and R. A. Weber and C. F. Camerer, 'Cultural conflict and merger failure: an experimental approach', *Management Science*, April 2003, pp. 400–12.

22 P. Gumbel, 'Return of the urge to merge', *Time Europe Magazine*, 13 July 2003, www.time.com/time/europe/magazine/article/0,13005,901030721-464418,00.html.

23 J. Badrtalei and D. Bates, 'Effect of organizational cultures on mergers and acquisitions: the case of DaimlerChrysler', *International Journal of Management*, 24, 2 (2007); pp. 303–17.

24 'INTERNATIONAL: culture impacts M&A outcomes', *Oxford Analytica Daily Brief Service*, 8 January 2008, p. 1.

25 S. Meichtry and C. Passariello, 'For Roberto Cavalli, "It's hard to let go of one-man show"; designer seeks an investor but shuns good offers: "Not worthy of my name"', *Wall Street Journal* (Eastern edition), 20 December 2007, p. A1.

26 E. H. Schein, 'The role of the founder in creating organizational culture', *Organizational Dynamics*, Summer 1983, pp. 13–28.

27 E. H. Schein, 'Leadership and organizational culture', in F. Hesselbein, M. Goldsmith, and R. Beckhard (eds), *The Leader of the Future* (San Francisco, CA: Jossey-Bass, 1996), pp. 61–62.

28 See, for example, J. R. Harrison and G. R. Carroll, 'Keeping the faith: a model of cultural transmission in formal organizations', *Administrative Science Quarterly*, December 1991, pp. 552–82; see also G. George, R. G. Sleeth and M. A. Siders, 'Organizational culture: leader roles, behaviors, and reinforcement mechanisms', *Journal of Business & Psychology*, Summer 1999, pp. 545–60.

29 B. Schneider, 'The people make the place', *Personnel Psychology*, Autumn 1987, pp. 437–53; D. E. Bowen, G. E. Ledford, Jr. and B. R. Nathan, 'Hiring for the organization, not the job', *Academy of Management Executive*, November 1991, pp. 35–51; B. Schneider, H. W. Goldstein and D. B. Smith, 'The ASA Framework: an update', *Personnel Psychology*, Winter 1995, pp. 747–73; A. L. Kristof, 'Person–organization fit: an integrative review of its conceptualizations, measurement, and implications', *Personnel Psychology*, Spring 1996, pp. 1–49; D. M. Cable and T. A. Judge, 'Interviewers' perceptions of person–organization fit and organizational selection decisions', *Journal of Applied Psychology*, August 1997, pp. 546–61; and M. L. Verquer, T. A. Beehr and S. H. Wagner, 'A meta-analysis of relations between person–organization fit and work attitudes', *Journal of Vocational Behavior*, December 2003, pp. 473–89.

30 L. Grensing-Pophal, 'Hiring to fit your corporate culture', *HRMagazine*, August 1999, pp. 50–54.

31 D. C. Hambrick and P. A. Mason, 'Upper echelons: the organization as a reflection of its top managers', *Academy of Management Review*, April 1984, pp. 193–206; B. P. Niehoff, C. A. Enz and R. A. Grover, 'The impact of top-management actions on employee attitudes and perceptions', *Group & Organization Studies*, September 1990, pp. 337–52; and H. M. Trice and J. M. Beyer, 'Cultural leadership in organizations', *Organization Science*, May 1991, pp. 149–69.

32 'The worlds billionaires: #4 Ingvar Kamprad and family', 3 August 2007, *Forbes*.com. Available at http://www.forbes.com/lists/2007/10/07billionaires_Ingvar-Kamprad-family_BWQ7.html. Accessed 29 April 2009.

33 See, for instance, J. P. Wanous, *Organizational Entry*, 2nd edn (New York: Addison-Wesley, 1992); G. T. Chao, A. M. O'Leary-Kelly, S. Wolf, H. J. Klein and P. D. Gardner, 'Organizational socialization: its content and consequences', *Journal of Applied Psychology*, October 1994, pp. 730–43; B. E. Ashforth, A. M. Saks and R. T. Lee, 'Socialization and newcomer adjustment: the role of organizational context', *Human Relations*, July 1998, pp. 897–926; D. A. Major, 'Effective newcomer socialization into high-performance organizational cultures', in N. M. Ashkanasy, C. P. M. Wilderom and M. F. Peterson (eds), *Handbook of Organizational Culture & Climate*, pp. 355–68; D. M. Cable and C. K. Parsons, 'Socialization tactics and person-organization fit', *Personnel Psychology*, Spring 2001, pp. 1–23; and K. Rollag, 'The impact of relative tenure on newcomer socialization dynamics', *Journal of Organizational Behavior*, November 2004, pp. 853–72.

34 '100 best workplaces in Europe 2007', Great place to work/ *Financial Times* see http://www.greatplacetowork.com/ and http://www.ft.com/reports/bestwork2007.

35 K. Rhodes, 'Breaking in the top dogs', *Training*, February 2000, pp. 67–74.

36 J. Van Maanen and E. H. Schein, 'Career development', in J. R. Hackman and J. L. Suttle (eds), *Improving Life at Work* (Santa Monica, CA: Goodyear, 1977), pp. 58–62.

37 D. C. Feldman, 'The multiple socialization of organization members', *Academy of Management Review*, April 1981, p. 310.

38 G. Chen and R. J. Klimoski, 'The impact of expectations on newcomer performance in teams as mediated by work characteristics, social exchanges, and empowerment', *Academy of Management Journal*, 46 (2003), pp. 591–607; C. R. Wanberg and J. D. Kammeyer-Mueller, 'Predictors and outcomes of proactivity in the socialization process', *Journal of Applied Psychology* 85 (2000), pp. 373–85; J. D. Kammeyer-Mueller and C. R. Wanberg, 'Unwrapping the organizational entry process: disentangling multiple antecedents and their pathways to adjustment', *Journal of Applied Psychology*, 88 (2003), pp. 779–94; and E. W. Morrison, 'Longitudinal study of the effects of information seeking on newcomer socialization', *Journal of Applied Psychology* 78 (2003), pp. 173–83.

39 Van Maanen and Schein, 'Career development', p. 59.

40 E. W. Morrison, 'Newcomers' relationships: the role of social network ties during socialization', *Academy of Management Journal*, 45 (2002), pp. 1149–60.

41 R. Donkin, 'Work is not everything – especially at the bottom: employees are often told to have positive attitudes, mainly as this makes more money for their bosses', *Financial Times*, 15 December 2005, p. 33.

42 D. M. Boje, 'The storytelling organization: a study of story performance in an office-supply firm', *Administrative Science Quarterly*, March 1991, pp. 106–26; C. H. Deutsch, 'The parables of corporate culture', *New York Times*, 13 October 1991, p. F25; and M. Ricketts and J. G. Seiling, 'Language, metaphors, and stories: catalysts for meaning making in organizations', *Organization Development Journal*, Winter 2003, pp. 33–43.

43 See K. Kamoche, 'Rhetoric, ritualism, and totemism in human resource management', *Human Relations*, April 1995, pp. 367–85.

44 V. Matthews, 'Starting every day with a shout and a song', *Financial Times*, 2 May 2001, p. 11; and M. Gimein, 'Sam Walton made us a promise', *Fortune*, 18 March 2002, pp. 121–30.

45 A. Rafaeli and M. G. Pratt, 'Tailored meanings: on the meaning and impact of organizational dress', *Academy of Management Review*, January 1993, pp. 32–55; and J. M. Higgins and C. McAllaster, 'Want innovation? Then use cultural artifacts that support it', *Organizational Dynamics*, August 2002, pp. 74–84.

46 *DCACronyms*, (Seattle, WA: Boeing, April 1997).

47 See B. Victor and J. B. Cullen, 'The organizational bases of ethical work climates', *Administrative Science Quarterly*, March 1988, pp. 101–25; L. K. Trevino, 'A cultural perspective on changing and developing organizational ethics', in W. A. Pasmore and R. W. Woodman (eds), *Research in Organizational Change and Development*, vol. 4 (Greenwich, CT: JAI Press, 1990); M. W. Dickson, D. B. Smith, M. W. Grojean and M. Ehrhart, 'An organizational climate regarding ethics: the outcome of leader values and the practices that reflect them', *Leadership Quarterly*, Summer 2001, pp. 197–217; and R. L. Dufresne, 'An action learning perspective on effective implementation of academic honor codes', *Group & Organization Management*, April 2004, pp. 201–18.

48 J. A. Byrne, 'The environment was ripe for abuse', *Business Week*, 25 February 2002, pp. 118–20; and A. Raghavan, K. Kranhold and A. Barrionuevo, 'How Enron bosses created a culture of pushing limits', *Wall Street Journal*, 26 August 2002, p. A1.

49 D. L. Nelson and C. L. Cooper (eds), *Positive Organizational Behavior* (London: Sage, 2007); K. S. Cameron, J. E. Dutton and R. E. Quinn (eds), *Positive Organizational Scholarship: Foundations of a New Discipline* (San Francisco, CA: Berrett-Koehler, 2003); and F. Luthans and C. M. Youssef, 'Emerging positive organizational behavior', *Journal of Management*, June 2007, pp. 321–49.

50 J. Robison, 'Great leadership under fire', *Gallup Leadership Journal*, 8 March 2007, pp. 1–3.

51 R. Wagner and J. K. Harter, *12: The Elements of Great Managing* (New York: Gallup Press, 2006).

52 R. Wagner and J. K. Harter, 'Performance reviews without the anxiety', *Gallup Leadership Journal*, 12 July 2007, pp. 1–4; and Wagner and Harter, *12: The Elements of Great Managing*.

53 S. Fineman, 'On being positive: concerns and counterpoints', *Academy of Management Review*, 31, 2 (2006), pp. 270–91.

54 International Centre for Spirit at Work see http://www.spiritatwork.org.

55 D. P. Ashmos and D. Duchon, 'Spirituality at work: a conceptualization and measure', *Journal of Management Inquiry*, June 2000, p. 139. For a comprehensive review of definitions of workplace spirituality, see R. A. Giacalone and C. L. Jurkiewicz, 'Toward a science of workplace spirituality', in R. A. Giacalone and C. L. Jurkiewicz (eds), *Handbook of Workplace Spirituality and Organizational Performance* (Armonk, NY: M. E. Sharpe, 2003), pp. 6–13.

56 This section is based on C. Ichniowski, D. L. Kochan, C. Olson and G. Strauss, 'What works at work: overview and assessment', *Industrial Relations*, 1996, pp. 299–333; I. A. Mitroff and E. A. Denton, *A Spiritual Audit of Corporate America: A Hard Look at Spirituality, Religion, and Values in the Workplace* (San Francisco, CA: Jossey-Bass, 1999); J. Milliman, J. Ferguson, D. Trickett and B. Condemi, 'Spirit and community at South-West Airlines: an investigation of a spiritual values-based model', *Journal of Organizational Change Management*, 12, 3 (1999), pp. 221–33; E. H. Burack, 'Spirituality in the workplace', *Journal of Organizational Change Management*, 12, 3 (1999), pp. 280–91.

57 International Centre for Spirit at Work see http://www.spiritatwork.org.

58 Cited in F. Wagner-Marsh and J. Conley, 'The fourth wave: the spiritually-based firm', *Journal of Organizational Change Management*, 12, 4 (1999), pp. 292–301, p. 295.

59 M. Conlin, 'Religion in the workplace: the growing presence of spirituality in corporate America,' *BusinessWeek*, 1 November 1999, pp. 151–58; and P. Paul, 'A holier holiday season', *American Demographics*, December 2001, pp. 41–45.

60 Cited in Conlin, 'Religion in the workplace', p. 153.

61 C. P. Neck and J. F. Milliman, 'Thought self-leadership: finding spiritual fulfillment in organizational life', *Journal of Managerial Psychology*, 9, 8 (1994), p. 9; for a recent review, see J.-C. Garcia-Zamor, 'Workplace spirituality and organizational performance', *Public Administration Review*, May–June 2003, pp. 355–63.

62 D. W. McCormick, 'Spirituality and management', *Journal of Managerial Psychology*, 9, 6 (1994), p. 5; E. Brandt, 'Corporate pioneers explore spiritual peace', *HRMagazine*, 41, 4 (1996), p. 82; P. Leigh, 'The new spirit at work', *Training and Development*, 51, 3 (1997), p. 26; P. H. Mirvis, 'Soul work in organizations', *Organization Science*, 8, 2 (1997), p. 193; and J. Milliman, A. Czaplewski and J. Ferguson, 'An exploratory empirical assessment of the relationship between spirituality and employee work attitudes', paper presented at the National Academy of Management Meeting, Washington, DC, August 2001.

63 International Centre for Spirit at Work see http://www.spiritatwork.org.

64 G. Dyer, 'A tale of two corporate cultures: the multinational workforce: a Chinese executive's appointment to a German company has prompted an exchange of workplace attitudes', *Financial Times*, 23 May 2006, p. 10.

65 J. A. Chatman, 'Matching people and organizations: selection and socialization in public accounting firms', *Administrative Science Quarterly*, September 1991, pp. 459–84; and A. E. M. Van Vianen, 'Person–organization fit: the match between newcomers' and recruiters preferences for organizational cultures', *Personnel Psychology*, Spring 2000, pp. 113–49.

66 J. E. Sheridan, 'Organizational culture and employee retention', *Academy of Management Journal*, December 1992, pp. 1036–56.

18 Chapter

Human resource policies and practices

After studying this chapter, you should be able to:

1 Define *initial selection* and identify the most useful methods.

2 Define *substantive selection* and identify the most useful methods.

3 Define *contingent selection* and contrast the arguments for and against drug testing.

4 Compare the four main types of training.

5 Contrast formal and informal training methods and contrast on-the-job and off-the-job training.

6 Demonstrate the use of performance evaluation.

7 Show how managers can improve performance evaluations.

8 Explain how diversity can be managed in organizations.

9 Show how human resource policies and practices may need to be adapted across Europe.

10 Show how a global context affects human resource management.

To manage people well, companies should . . . elevate HR to a position of power and primacy in the organization.

Jack Welch

Sack the poor performers!

Iconica/Getty Images

Microsoft chief executive Steve Ballmer caused a stir when he announced to the Institute of Directors conference in 2006 that he sacks one in every 15 employees every year. He suggested that all businesses, large and small, would benefit from such an approach. The idea of culling poor performers is not new in the US, where it is estimated around two-thirds of firms have such a policy. It is far less common in Europe, but will this change as employers seek to focus their training and developing on the best performers and stop wasting money trying to develop the worst?

A survey of 562 executives and senior managers in the UK found 77 per cent believed that a fixed quota for annual staff dismissal would boost financial performance and productivity. The advantages of pursuing this policy were described as ensuring strong team members are not carrying weaker ones, allowing underperforming staff to pursue a fresh challenge more suited to their abilities, and increasing productivity overall.

Stuart Duff, an occupational psychologist, believes that the culling approach is simply the logical conclusion of performance management. 'Why bother to have a performance management system if you don't act at both ends? Most companies, however, just reward the top performers and ignore the poor performers.'

Chris Welford, a director of a talent and assessment firm, believes that culling can even be good for those who get fired.

> *The initial reaction to this idea is horror. However, if you think it through, it's more sensible than it sounds. Most people have skills, but they're not always used in the right way. In any organization, there are about 10 per cent of people who are in the wrong job. It makes sense to have adult conversations with them about their future and then to help them find work that will use their skills. It's much better to do that than to hide behind procedures and rules-based management.*

Despite these many alleged benefits, only 4 per cent of UK companies surveyed dismiss a proportion of their staff. Most companies are quick to dismiss the idea because, as a HR executive explains, 'This is a great idea if you want to manage through fear, retribution and paranoia, and create a general air of unease.'

Implementing this approach is more difficult in some European countries than in the US because of, for example, more stringent employment legislation, stronger trade unions and a tendency towards greater employee involvement in human resource practices. Even in the UK, which has a human resource management model reasonably close to the US, employers are warned that sacking poor performers is likely to lead to a barrage of unfair dismissal claims.

However, Andrew Wileman writes that some European managers tend to be too soft on underperforming staff. He notes of his Spanish CEO friend, 'At his technology centre there was not one single involuntary termination (out of 2,000 staff) in five years. The staff there were pretty committed and hard-working, but they knew that at the end of the day there would be no repercussions if they didn't deliver. So key projects slipped and market opportunities were lost.'

Sources: Adapted from 'Should HR advise managers to sack poor performers or help them improve?', *Personnel Today*, 29 May 2007; Wileman, A. (2008) *Driving Down Cost: How to Manage and Cut Costs Intelligently* (Boston, MA: Nicholas Brealey, 2008), pp. 75–76.

The message of this chapter is that human resource (HR) policies and practices – such as employee selection, training, and performance management – influence an organization's effectiveness.[1] These policies and practices have a direct influence on all employees behaviour and it is important to understand these affects whether you are (or aspire to be) a HR manager or not. For example, I'm sure you can imagine how introducing a policy of firing poor performers (as illustrated in the opining vignette) would affect motivation, teamworking, conflict, politics and the culture of the organization. However, studies show that many managers often don't know which HR practices work, which don't, and what the affects are on employee behaviour. To see how much you know (before learning the right answers in the chapter!), take the self-assessment.

SELF-ASSESSMENT LIBRARY

How much do I know about human resource management (HRM)?

In the Self-assessment library (available online), take assessment IV.G.2 (How much do I know about HRM?) and answer the following questions.

1. How did you score compared to your classmates? Did the results surprise you?

2. How much of effective HRM is common sense?

3. Do you think your score will improve after reading this chapter?

Selection practices

It's been said the most important HR decision you can make is who you hire. That makes sense – if you can figure out who the right people are. The objective of effective selection is to figure out who these right people are, by matching individual characteristics (ability, experience and so on) with the requirements of the job.[2] When management fails to get a proper match, both employee performance and satisfaction suffer.

How the selection process works

Figure 18.1 shows how the selection process works in most organizations. Having decided to apply for a job, applicants go through several stages – three are shown in the exhibit – during

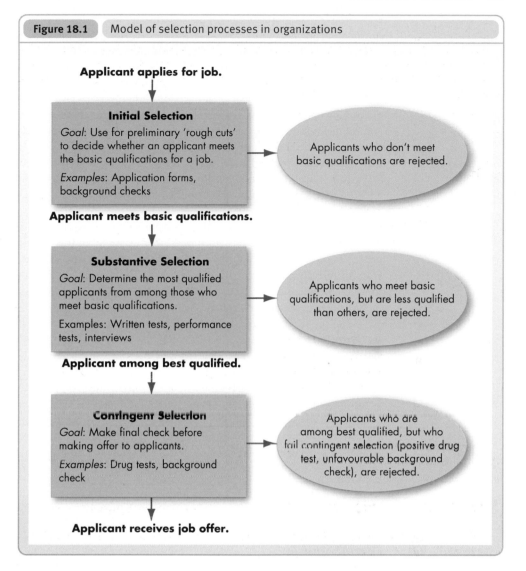

Figure 18.1 | Model of selection processes in organizations

Applicant applies for job.

Initial Selection

Goal: Use for preliminary 'rough cuts' to decide whether an applicant meets the basic qualifications for a job.

Examples: Application forms, background checks

Applicants who don't meet basic qualifications are rejected.

Applicant meets basic qualifications.

Substantive Selection

Goal: Determine the most qualified applicants from among those who meet basic qualifications.

Examples: Written tests, performance tests, interviews

Applicants who meet basic qualifications, but are less qualified than others, are rejected.

Applicant among best qualified.

Contingent Selection

Goal: Make final check before making offer to applicants.

Examples: Drug tests, background check

Applicants who are among best qualified, but who fail contingent selection (positive drug test, unfavourable background check), are rejected.

Applicant receives job offer.

which they can be rejected at any time. In practice, some organizations forgo some of these steps in the interests of time. A meat-packing plant may hire someone who walks in the door (there is not a long line of people who want to 'thread' a pig's intestines for a living). But most organizations follow a process that looks something like this. Let's go into a bit more detail about each of the stages.

Initial selection

1 Define *initial selection* and identify the most useful methods.

Initial selection devices are the first information applicants submit and are used for preliminary 'rough cuts' to decide whether an applicant meets the basic qualifications for a job. Application forms (including letters of recommendation) are initial selection devices. We list background checks as either an initial selection device or a contingent selection device, depending on how the organization does it. Some organizations prefer to check into an applicant's background right away. Others wait until the applicant is about ready to be hired, contingent on everything checking out.

Application forms

You've no doubt submitted your fair share of applications. By itself, the information submitted on an application form is not a very useful predictor of performance. However, it can be a good initial screen. For example, there's no sense in spending time interviewing an applicant for a registered nurse position if he or she doesn't have the proper credentials (education, certification, experience).

Online job applications are now the norm, with many companies no longer accepting paper versions. This method is faster to process because candidate's applications who do not meet the basic requirements can be rejected before even having to be seen by a person. They have also greatly increased the number of applications employers receive because they are easier to fire off and job seekers are less discriminatory to which firms they send them to. For example, telecommunications company O_2 receives about 30,000 applications every year. There have been some unintended consequences in the rise of online job applications. The sheer volume means that most will be rejected and leads to a large group of disaffected people. At O_2, they realised this group is likely to include customers and potential customers. The firm now sends text messages to unsuccessful applicants to help them feel they have had a more personal experience.[3]

It's important that organizations be careful about the questions they ask on applications. Questions about race, gender, sexuality and nationality are disallowed in most European countries. However, there are numerous 'grey areas'. For example, in the UK it is not illegal to ask for a person's age on an application form, but there is some debate whether a minimum number of years of relevant job experience can be asked. The reason being that if an employer specifies more than, for instance, 10 years of experience, then younger workers will be excluded which potentially breaches age discrimination laws.

Background checks

Considering that one survey found some 34 per cent of job applications contain outright lies about experience, education and abilities and 2 per cent of CVs are almost totally fictitious, it is no wonder that background checks are conducted by most companies. And for some jobs, such as those working with children, a background check may be legally required.

There have been some high-profile lapses that illustrate the importance of background checks, such as an English National Health Service Chief Executive being forced to resign after he made up his degree qualifications. But the reasons for thorough checks or applications and references are more generally applicable: firms want to know how an applicant did in past jobs

Alvey & Towers Picture Library/Alamy

NCP (National Car Parks) is the UK's largest commercial car park operator and provider of on-street parking enforcement. NCP conducted background checks to make sure all 150 wardens working for London's Lambeth Council had the right to work in the UK when it took over the contract from another firm. The result was startling. When it became known almost a third of the parking wardens either resigned or just didn't turn up for work.[4]

and whether former employers would recommend hiring the person. The problem is that rarely do former employers provide useful information. In fact, nearly two-thirds of employers refuse to provide detailed reference information on applicants. Why? They are afraid of being sued for saying something bad about a former employee. Although this concern is often unfounded (employers are safe as long as they stick to documented facts) most employers play it safe. The result is a paradox: Most employers want reference information, but few will give it out. There are also other problems. Job applicants may come from anywhere in Europe (or beyond) and there are practical problems such as language, legal variations and cultural differences that often mean getting reliable (or any) information about candidates can be difficult, costly and time consuming.

Letters of recommendation aren't as useful as they may seem. Applicants self-select those who will write good letters, so almost all letters of recommendation are positive. In the end, readers of such letters either ignore them altogether or read 'between the lines' to try to find hidden meaning there.

Substantive selection

2 Define *substantive selection* and identify the most useful methods.

If an applicant passes the initial screens, next are substantive selection methods. These are the heart of the selection process and include written tests, performance tests and interviews.

Written tests

Long popular as selection devices, written tests (traditionally 'paper-and-pencil' tests – though many are now electronic and available online) suffered a general decline in use between the late 1960s and mid-1980s. They were frequently characterised as discriminatory, and many organizations had not validated them as job-related. The past 20 years, however, have seen a resurgence in their use. Testing has evolved significantly. It has become increasingly sophisticated, but easier to use, because of technological advances. Managers have come to recognise that there are valid tests available and they can be helpful in predicting who will be successful on the job.[5] Kimberly-Clark is an enthusiastic advocate of online testing. Having introduced the process in both its graduate and executive recruitment programmes, the company claims to have slashed recruitment and selection costs, streamlined its administrative processes and improved both internal communications and its feedback to job applicants.[6] Applicants, however, tend to view written tests as less valid and fair than interviews or performance tests.[7]

Typical written tests include (1) intelligence or cognitive ability tests, (2) personality tests, (3) integrity tests and (4) interest inventories.

Tests of intellectual ability, spatial and mechanical ability, perceptual accuracy and motor ability have proven to be valid predictors for many skilled, semiskilled and unskilled operative jobs in industrial organizations.[8] Intelligence tests have proven to be particularly good predictors for jobs that include cognitively complex tasks.[9] Many experts argue that intelligence tests are the *single best* selection measure across jobs. A recent review of the literature suggested that intelligence tests are at least as valid in European Economic Community (EEC) nations as in the United States where many of these tests originate.[10]

The use of personality tests has grown significantly in the past decade. Many firms such as 3M and KPMG rely on tests to identify candidates who will be high performers.[11] Organizations use numerous measures of the Big Five traits in selection decisions. The traits that best predict job performance are conscientiousness and positive self-concept.[12] This makes sense in that conscientious people tend to be motivated and dependable, and positive people are 'can-do'-oriented and persistent. Personality tests are relatively inexpensive and simple to use and administer.

As ethical problems have increased in organizations, integrity tests have gained popularity. These are tests that measure factors such as dependability, carefulness, responsibility and honesty. The evidence is impressive that these tests are powerful in predicting supervisory ratings of job performance and counterproductive employee behaviour on the job, such as theft, discipline problems and excessive absenteeism.[13]

You may wonder why applicants would respond truthfully to personality and integrity tests. After all, who would answer 'strongly disagree' to the question 'I always show up on time,' even if they were generally late? Research shows that although applicants can 'fake good' if they are motivated to do so, it doesn't appear that this deception undermines the validity of personality and integrity tests.[14] Why? One speculation is that if faking does exist, those who 'fake well' on selection tests also probably continue to present themselves in a desirable light once on the job. Thus, this sort of impression management not only helps get people hired but it helps them perform better on the job, at least unless taken to pathological degrees.

Performance-simulation tests

What better way to find out whether applicants can do a job successfully than by having them do it? That's precisely the logic of performance-simulation tests.

Although they are more complicated to develop and more difficult to administer than written tests, performance-simulation tests have increased in popularity during the past several decades. This appears to be due to the fact that they have higher 'face validity' than do most written tests.

The two best-known performance-simulation tests are work samples and assessment centres. The former are suited to routine jobs, while the latter are relevant for the selection of managerial personnel and graduate recruitment programmes.

work sample test
A test that is a miniature replica of a job that is used to evaluate the performance abilities of job candidates.

assessment centres
A set of performance-simulation tests designed to evaluate a candidate's managerial potential.

Work sample tests are hands-on simulations of part or all of the job that must be performed by applicants. By carefully devising work samples based on specific job tasks, management determines the knowledge, skills and abilities needed for each job. Then each work sample element is matched with a corresponding job performance element. Work samples are widely used in the hiring of skilled workers, such as welders, machinists, carpenters and electricians. For instance, job candidates for production jobs at BMW's factory have 90 minutes to perform a variety of typical work tasks on a specially built simulated assembly line.[15] Work samples yield validities superior to written aptitude and personality tests.[16]

A more elaborate set of performance-simulation tests, specifically designed to evaluate a candidate's managerial potential, are administered in **assessment centres**. In these tests, line managers, supervisors and/or trained psychologists evaluate candidates as they go through one to several days of exercises that simulate real problems they would confront on the job.[17] For instance, a candidate might be required to play the role of a manager who must decide how to respond to 10 memos in an in-basket within a two-hour period. A recent survey suggests that employers rate the effectiveness of assessment centres. More than 9 out of 10 employers using assessment centres believe they are a very (47 per cent) or fairly (48 per cent) effective means of recruiting staff to fill vacancies.[18]

Interviews

Of all the selection devices organizations around the globe use to differentiate candidates, the interview continues to be the most common.[19] Not only is the interview widely used, it also seems to carry a great deal of weight. That is, the results tend to have a disproportionate amount of influence on the selection decision. The candidate who performs poorly in the employment interview is likely to be cut from the applicant pool regardless of experience, test scores or letters of recommendation. Conversely, 'all too often, the person most polished in job-seeking techniques, particularly those used in the interview process, is the one hired, even though he or she may not be the best candidate for the position'.[20]

These findings are important because of the unstructured manner in which the selection interview is frequently conducted.[21] The unstructured interview – short in duration, casual and made up of random questions – is not a very effective selection device.[22] The data gathered from such interviews are typically biased and often only modestly related to future job performance. Still, managers are reluctant to use structured interviews in place of their favourite pet questions (such as 'If you could be any animal, what would you be, and why?').[23]

Without structure, a number of biases can distort interview results. These biases include interviewers tending to favour applicants who share their attitudes, giving unduly high weight to negative information and allowing the order in which applicants are interviewed to influence evaluations.[24] Using a standardised set of questions, providing interviewers with a uniform method of recording information and standardising the rating of the applicant's qualifications reduce the variability of results across applicants and enhance the validity of the interview as a selection device. The effectiveness of the interview also improves when employers use

Robert Convery/Alamy

In an unusual interview technique, B&Q, the largest retailer in Europe of home improvement tool and supplies, asked applicants for jobs at its Norwich, UK store to dance before answering formal questions. The 'Blame it on the boogie' warm-up outraged trade unions and prompted warnings from legal experts of possible discrimination issues.[25]

behavioural structured interviews.[26] This interview technique requires applicants to describe how they handled specific problems and situations in previous jobs. It's built on the assumption that past behaviour offers the best predictor of future behaviour.

'IT'S FIRST IMPRESSIONS THAT COUNT'

MYTH *OR* SCIENCE?

This statement is true. When we meet someone for the first time, we notice a number of things about that person: physical characteristics, clothes, firmness of handshake, gestures, tone of voice and the like. We then use these impressions to fit the person into ready-made categories. And these first impressions tend to hold greater weight than information received later.

The best evidence about first impressions comes from research on employment interviews. Findings clearly demonstrate that first impressions count. A recent study suggested that interviewers often know whether they will hire someone soon after the opening handshake and small talk.[27]

Research on applicant appearance confirms the power of first impressions.[28] Attractive applicants fare better in interviews and overweight applicants are penalised. Another body of confirming research finds that interviewers' post-interview evaluations of applicants conform, to a substantial degree, to their pre-interview impressions.[29] That is, those first impressions carry considerable weight in shaping the interviewers' final evaluations, assuming that the interview elicits no highly negative information.

In practice, most organizations use interviews for more than a 'prediction-of-performance' device,[30] but also to assess applicant–organization fit. In addition to specific, job-relevant skills, organizations are looking at candidates' personality characteristics, personal values and the like to find individuals who fit with the organization's culture and image.

3 Define *contingent selection* and contrast the arguments for and against drug testing.

Contingent selection

If applicants pass the substantive selection methods, they are basically ready to be hired, contingent on a final check. One contingent method is a drug test. A UK study found 13 per cent of employers carry out pre-employment drug tests and although figures in most other European countries are non-existent, it is generally agreed the practice is increasing. In some countries it is illegal, such as the Netherlands, and in others such as Belgium, pre-employment drug testing can only occur in safety-critical jobs (for example, airline pilots or bus drivers).[31]

Drug testing is controversial. Many applicants think it is unfair or invasive to test them without reasonable suspicion. Such individuals likely believe that drug use is a private matter and applicants should be tested on factors that directly bear on job performance, not lifestyle issues that may or may not be job relevant. Employers might counter this view with the argument that drug use and abuse are extremely costly, not just in terms of financial resources but in terms of people's safety. Despite the controversy over drug testing, it's probably here to stay.

Training and development programmes

Competent employees don't remain competent for ever. Skills deteriorate and can become obsolete and new skills need to be learned. That's why organizations spend billions of euros each year on formal training. One survey found that the average European corporate spends over half a million Euros on training and development each year. Although developing skills is a key objective across Europe, it is important to note that there are national variations. For example, around 60 per cent of UK workers have some kind of formal training, slightly less than 50 per cent in Italy, France and Germany and around 25 per cent in Hungary.[32]

TRAINING TRENDS · FACE THE FACTS

The following results are from a survey that examined training practice trends during 2007. Training managers from 1,000 companies employing more than 500 staff, across the United Kingdom, France, Germany, Italy and Spain took part.

- The survey found the average European corporate spends Euros 580,000 on professional development. France spends the most.

- UK companies topped the list in providing training to 61 per cent of their employees, but they spent 40 per cent less than the European average. In Italy, France and Germany, less than half of their staff received any form of training.

- E-learning and blended learning are most popular in the UK and Spain, with just over 50 per cent of employees using these forms of training.

Source: 'Training survey shows UK PLC leading the way with more innovative practices', *Personnel Today*, 25 June 2008. Available at http://www.personneltoday.com/articles/2008/06/25/46386/training-survey-shows-uk-plc-leading-the-way-with-more-innovative-practices.html.

Types of training

4 Compare the four main types of training.

Training can include everything from teaching employees basic reading skills to conducting advanced courses in executive leadership. Here we discuss four general skill categories – basic literacy and technical, interpersonal and problem-solving skills. In addition, we briefly discuss ethics training.

Basic literacy and numeracy skills

You may be surprised to learn of the scale of this issue. Of the western European countries, the UK ranks particularly poorly. One in three employers has to send staff for remedial training to teach them basic numeracy and maths skills. Two-fifths of organizations had serious concerns about the *basic literacy skills of their employees*, with some staff unable to write in sentences, spell correctly or use accurate grammar.[33] This problem, of course, isn't unique to the United Kingdom. It's a worldwide problem – from the most developed countries to the least.[34] For many undeveloped countries widespread illiteracy means there is almost no hope of competing in a global economy.

Organizations increasingly have to teach basic reading and numeracy skills to their employees. For instance, McDonald's operates seven '*Hamburger Universities*' internationally. Along with

AFP/Getty Images

Technical skills training was undertaken at Carlsberg Bulgaria. When looking at restructuring in the Shoumen factory, the firm realised there was a lack of staff skilled in using the SAP accounting system. Five former accountants, all of whom were over 55 years of age, undertook two months of SAP training and made good progress within a short period of time. The newly SAP skilled workers were sent to the logistics division and immediately improved the functions efficiency.[35]

the leadership, business management and restaurant operations classes are basic skills courses in literacy and maths. Northern Foods also offers basic skills courses including literacy, maths and languages. One reason for doing so is claimed to be that better skilled workers gain confidence in themselves and their work, which ultimately means a better bottom line for business.[36]

Technical skills

Most training is directed at upgrading and improving an employee's technical skills. Technical training has become increasingly important today for two reasons – new technology and new structural designs in the organization.

Jobs change as a result of new technologies and improved methods. For instance, many auto repair personnel have had to undergo extensive training to fix and maintain recent models with computer-monitored engines, electronic stabilising systems, GPS, keyless remote entry and other innovations. Similarly, computer-controlled equipment has required millions of production employees to learn a whole new set of skills.[37]

In addition, technical training has become increasingly important because of changes in organization design. As organizations flatten their structures, expand their use of teams and break down traditional departmental barriers, employees need mastery of a wider variety of tasks and increased knowledge of how their organization operates. For instance, the restructuring of jobs at Miller Brewing Co. around empowered teams has led management to introduce a comprehensive business literacy programme to help employees better understand competition, the state of the beer industry, where the company's revenues come from, how costs are calculated and where employees fit into the company's value chain.[38]

Interpersonal skills

Almost all employees belong to a work unit, and their work performance depends to some degree on their ability to effectively interact with their co-workers and their boss. Some employees have excellent interpersonal skills, but others require training to improve theirs. This includes learning how to be a better listener, how to communicate ideas more clearly and how to be a more effective team player. This type of training is common in organizations because of the obvious importance of these skills. But firms also look to hire people who are effective in interpersonal skills such as communication, negotiation and developing networks. A European graduate survey claims nearly half of all corporate organizations in the EU find it difficult to recruit graduates of the right calibre. The main reasons include a lack of interpersonal skills.[39]

Problem-solving skills

Managers, as well as many employees who perform non-routine tasks, have to solve problems on their jobs. When people require these skills but are deficient in them, they can participate in problem-solving training. This can include activities to sharpen their logic, reasoning and problem-defining skills, as well as their abilities to assess causation, develop and analyse alternatives and select solutions. Problem-solving training has become a basic part of almost every organizational effort to introduce self-managed teams or implement quality-management programmes.

What about ethics training?

Ethics training has increased considerably across Europe over the past decade.[40] Society is now more aware of the impact that business has on the environment. And high profile scandals such as Parmalat, the Siemens bribery case, and the role of banks in the recent global financial crisis have raised the profile of ethical issues. This training may be included in a newly hired employee's orientation programme, made part of an ongoing developmental training programme or provided to all employees as a periodic reinforcement of ethical principles.[41] But the jury is still out on whether you can actually teach ethics.[42]

TRAINING ACROSS CULTURES   GLOBAL

Training across cultures is nothing new, but the growing convergence of markets in Europe and other regions is pushing the issue further up the agenda for many companies. Paul Morris argues that cultural differences between countries can often be underestimated when companies roll out cross-border training programmes. There are major differences between, say, western Europe and the Middle East, he says, but also more subtle variances within Europe itself.

'Recognising cultural differences is much more than acknowledging the different languages a company is dealing with, and sometimes companies seem to take a rather superficial approach,' says Morris, who works with companies such as General Motors and Saab in delivering training across Europe.

When taking into account cultural differences, much will depend on the nature of the training. 'If it's technical training – whether that be automotive, white goods or other sectors – cultural approaches are not that important. Taking a gearbox apart and putting it back together is the same in any country,' he said. For soft skills, however, it may be a different story. For example, a course for middle managers on supervising staff may require a different approach depending on the region.

'In countries like Denmark and Holland there's a similar perception of the role of management, but when you look at eastern Europe, the Middle East or Africa there's much more respect for management hierarchies,' says Morris.

When it comes to training in areas like customer services, parts of central and eastern Europe are radically different from the West, which may require changes in the design of training programmes. 'In Russia it is very difficult to explain the concept of customer care because it's not something that many Russians have experienced,' Morris says.

He argues that the best approach is to develop a central training programme but allow flexibility within that for local trainers to adapt it where necessary to specific cultures. The degree to which training needs to be adapted will depend significantly on the organization. The strong internal culture in some multinationals cuts across many national differences.

Morris says, 'Some companies have a very robust international culture which enables them to roll out training without too many cultural adaptations, but others kid themselves that just because every office has the same colour curtains the company has the same culture across countries.'

Source: Adapted from P. McCurry, 'Untangling the web', *Training and Coaching Today*, 1 March 2001.

Critics argue that ethics are based on values, and value systems are fixed at an early age. By the time employers hire people, their ethical values have already been established. The critics also claim that ethics cannot be formally 'taught', but must be learned by example.

Supporters of ethics training argue that values can be learned and changed after early childhood. And even if they couldn't, ethics training would be effective because it helps employees to recognise ethical dilemmas and become more aware of the ethical issues underlying their actions. Another argument is that ethics training reaffirms an organization's expectations that members will act ethically.

Training methods

5 Contrast formal and informal training methods and contrast on-the-job and off-the-job training.

Training methods are most readily classified as formal or informal and as on-the-job or off-the-job training.

Historically, training meant *formal training*. It's planned in advance and has a structured format. However, recent evidence indicates that 70 per cent of workplace learning is made up of *informal training* – unstructured, unplanned and easily adapted to situations and individuals – for teaching skills and keeping employees current.[43] In reality, most informal training is nothing other than employees helping each other out. They share information and solve work-related problems with one another. Perhaps the most important outcome of this realisation is that many managers are now supportive of what used to be considered 'idle chatter'. At a Siemens plant, for instance, management now recognises that people needn't be on the production line to be working.[44] Discussions around the water cooler or in the cafeteria weren't, as managers thought, about non-work topics such as sports or politics. They largely focused on solving work-related problems. So now Siemens's management encourages such casual meetings.

On-the-job training includes job rotation, apprenticeships, understudy assignments and formal mentoring programmes. But the primary drawback of these on-the-job training methods is that they often disrupt the workplace. *Off-the-job training* includes activities such as classroom lectures, videotapes, public seminars, self-study programmes, Internet courses, satellite-beamed television classes and group activities that use role-plays and case studies.

In recent years, the fastest-growing means for delivering training is probably computer-based training, or e-training.[45] HeidelbergCement, one of the leading global producers of building materials, offer ethics training to over 68,000 employees across 50 countries via e-training. Cisco Systems provides a curriculum of training courses on its corporate intranet, organized by job titles, specific technologies and products.[46] Although many companies now offer all or some of their employee training online, it's unclear how effective it actually is. There also appears to be cultural variations in its acceptance. For example, in parts of southern Europe managers seem to undervalue e-learning and believe it is not as relevant as more traditional classroom training.[47] On the positive side, e-training increases flexibility by allowing organizations to deliver materials anywhere and at any time. It also seems to be fast and efficient. On the other hand, it's expensive to design self-paced online materials, many employees miss the social interaction provided by a classroom environment, online learners are often more susceptible to distractions, and 'clicking through' training is no assurance that employees have actually learned anything.[48]

Individualising formal training to fit the employee's learning style

The way you process, internalise and remember new and difficult material isn't necessarily the same way others do. This fact means that effective formal training should be individualised to reflect the learning style of the employee.[49]

Some examples of different learning styles are reading, watching, listening and participating. Some people absorb information better when they read about it. They're the kind of people who can learn to use computers by sitting in their study and reading manuals. Some people learn best by observation. They watch others and then imitate the behaviours they've seen. Such people can watch someone use a computer for a while and then copy what they've done. Listeners rely heavily on their auditory senses to absorb information. They would prefer to learn how to use a computer, for instance, by listening to an audiotape. People who prefer a participating style learn by doing. They want to sit down, turn on the computer and gain hands-on experience by practising.

You can translate these styles into different learning methods. To maximise learning, readers should be given books or other reading material to review; watchers should get the opportunity to observe individuals modelling the new skills either in person or on video; listeners will benefit from hearing lectures or audiotapes; and participants will benefit most from experiential opportunities in which they can simulate and practice the new skills.

These different learning styles are obviously not mutually exclusive. In fact, good teachers recognise that their students learn differently and, therefore, provide multiple learning methods. They assign readings before class; give lectures; use visual aids to illustrate concepts; and have students participate in group projects, case analyses, role-plays and experiential learning exercises. If you know the preferred style of an employee, you can design a formal training programme to take advantage of this preference. If you don't have that information, it's probably best to design the programme to use a variety of learning styles. Over-reliance on a single style places individuals who don't learn well from that style at a disadvantage.

Evaluating effectiveness

Most training programmes work rather well in that the majority of people who undergo training learn more than those who do not, react positively to the training experience and after the training engage in the behaviours targeted by the programme. Still, some factors make certain programmes work better than others. For example, although lecture styles have a poor reputation, they are surprisingly effective training methods. On the other hand, conducting a needs assessment prior to training was relatively unimportant in predicting the success of a training programme.[50]

The success of training also depends on the individual. If individuals are unmotivated to learn, they will benefit very little. What factors determine training motivation? Personality is important: Those with an internal locus of control, high conscientiousness, high cognitive ability and high self-efficacy learn more in training programmes. The training climate also is important: When trainees believe that there are opportunities on the job to apply their newly learned skills and enough resources to apply what they have learned, they are more motivated to learn and do better in training programmes.[51]

Performance evaluation

Would you study differently or exert a different level of effort for a university course graded on a pass–fail basis than for one that awarded letter grades from A to F? Students typically tell us they study harder when letter grades are at stake. In addition, when they take a course on a pass–fail basis, they tend to do just enough to ensure a passing grade.

This finding illustrates how performance evaluation systems influence behaviour. Major determinants of your in-class behaviour and out-of-class studying effort at university are the criteria and techniques your instructor uses to evaluate your performance. What applies in the university context also applies to employees at work. In this section, we show how the choice of a performance evaluation system and the way it's administered can be an important force influencing employee behaviour.

Purposes of performance evaluation

6 Demonstrate the use of performance evaluation.

Performance evaluation serves a number of purposes.[52] One purpose is to help management make general *human resource decisions*. Evaluations provide input into important decisions such as promotions, transfers and terminations. Evaluations also *identify training and development needs*. They pinpoint employee skills and competencies that are currently inadequate but for which remedial programmes can be developed. Evaluations also fulfil the purpose of *providing feedback to employees* on how the organization views their performance. Furthermore, performance evaluations are the *basis for reward allocations*. Decisions as to who gets merit pay increases and other rewards are frequently determined by performance evaluations.

Each of these functions of performance evaluation is valuable. Yet their importance to us depends on the perspective we're taking. Several are clearly relevant to human resource management decisions. But our interest is in organizational behaviour. As a result, we shall be emphasising performance evaluation as a mechanism for providing feedback and as a determinant of reward allocations.

What do we evaluate?

The criteria that management chooses to evaluate when appraising employee performance will have a major influence on what employees do. The three most popular sets of criteria are individual task outcomes, behaviours, and traits.

Individual task outcomes

If ends count, rather than means, then management should evaluate an employee's task outcomes. Using task outcomes, a plant manager could be judged on criteria such as quantity produced, scrap generated and cost per unit of production. Similarly, a salesperson could be assessed on overall sales volume in the territory, Euro increase in sales, and number of new accounts established.

Behaviours

In many cases, it's difficult to identify specific outcomes that can be directly attributed to an employee's actions. This is particularly true of personnel in advisory or support positions and individuals whose work assignments are intrinsically part of a group effort. We may readily evaluate the group's performance but have difficulty distinguishing clearly the contribution of each group member. In such instances, it's not unusual for management to evaluate the employee's behaviour. Using the previous examples, behaviours of a plant manager that could be used for performance evaluation purposes might include promptness in submitting monthly reports or the leadership style the manager exhibits. Pertinent salesperson behaviours could be the average number of contact calls made per day or sick days used per year.

Note that these behaviours needn't be limited to those directly related to individual productivity.[53] As we pointed out in our previous discussion on organizational citizenship behaviour (see specifically Chapters 1 and 4), helping others, making suggestions for improvements and volunteering for extra duties make work groups and organizations more effective and often are incorporated into evaluations of employee performance.

Traits

The weakest set of criteria, yet one that is still widely used by organizations, is individual traits.[54] We say they're weaker than either task outcomes or behaviours because they're farthest removed from the actual performance of the job itself. Traits such as having a good attitude, showing confidence, being dependable, looking busy or possessing a wealth of experience may or may not be highly correlated with positive task outcomes, but only the naive would ignore the reality that such traits are frequently used as criteria for assessing an employee's level of performance.

Who should do the evaluating?

Who should evaluate an employee's performance? By tradition, the task has fallen to the manager, on the grounds that managers are held responsible for their employees' performance. But that logic may be flawed. Others may actually be able to do the job better.

With many of today's organizations using self-managed teams, teleworking and other organizing devices that distance bosses from their employees, an employee's immediate superior may not be the most reliable judge of that employee's performance. Thus, in more and more cases, peers and even subordinates are being asked to participate in the performance evaluation process. Also, increasingly, employees are participating in their own performance evaluation. For instance, a recent survey found that about half of executives and 53 per cent of employees now have input into their performance evaluations.[55] As you might surmise, self-evaluations often suffer from overinflated assessment and self-serving bias. Moreover, self-evaluations are often low in agreement with superiors' ratings.[56] Because of these drawbacks, self-evaluations are

Sipa Press/Rex Features

Research found that 'warmth' traits such as being caring and likeable strongly correlate to whether the public will vote for a candidate seeking public office. Consequently, demonstrating improvements in these traits are used by political parties to evaluate elected politicians and potential election candidates.[57]

probably better suited to developmental than evaluative purposes and should be combined with other sources of information to reduce rating errors.

In most situations, in fact, it is highly advisable to use multiple sources of ratings. Any individual performance rating may say as much about the rater as about the person being evaluated. By averaging across raters, we can obtain a more reliable, unbiased and accurate performance evaluation.

The latest approach to performance evaluation is the use of 360-degree evaluations.[58] It provides for performance feedback from the full circle of daily contacts that an employee might have, ranging from mailroom personnel to customers to bosses to peers (see Figure 18.2). The number of appraisals can be as few as 3 or 4 or as many as 25, with most organizations collecting 5 to 10 per employee.

More and more employers are using 360-degree programmes. Some of them are Virgin Atlantic, Unipart, Booking.com, JCB, Google and GlaxoSmithKline. What's their appeal? By relying on feedback from co-workers, customers and subordinates, these organizations are hoping to give everyone more of a sense of participation in the review process and gain more accurate readings on employee performance.

The evidence on the effectiveness of 360-degree evaluations, however, is mixed.[59] It provides employees with a wider perspective of their performance. But it also has the potential for being misused. For instance, to minimise costs, many organizations don't spend the time to train evaluators in giving constructive criticism. Some organizations allow employees to choose the peers and subordinates who evaluate them, which can artificially inflate feedback. Problems also arise from the difficulty of reconciling disagreements and contradictions between rater groups.

Methods of performance evaluation

The previous sections explained *what* we evaluate and *who* should do the evaluating. Now we ask: *How* do we evaluate an employee's performance? That is, what are the specific techniques for evaluation?

Figure 18.2	360-degree evaluations

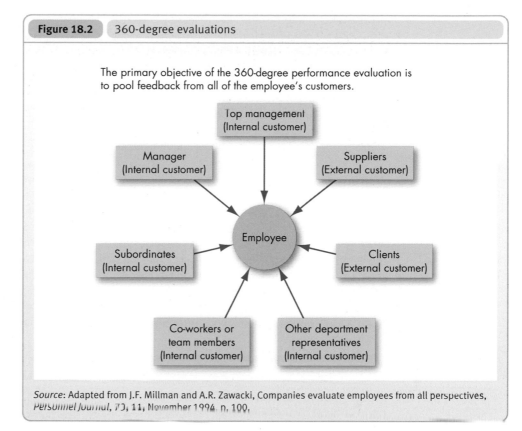

The primary objective of the 360-degree performance evaluation is to pool feedback from all of the employee's customers.

Source: Adapted from J.F. Millman and A.R. Zawacki, Companies evaluate employees from all perspectives, *Personnel Journal*, 73, 11, November 1994, p. 100.

---

critical incidents
A way of evaluating the behaviours that are key in making the difference between executing a job effectively and executing it ineffectively.

graphic rating scales
An evaluation method in which the evaluator rates performance factors on an incremental scale.

behaviourally anchored rating scales (BARS)
Scales that combine major elements from the critical incident and graphic rating scale approaches: The appraiser rates the employees based on items along a continuum, but the points are examples of actual behaviour on the given job rather than general descriptions or traits.

Written essays

Probably the simplest method of evaluation is to write a narrative describing an employee's strengths, weaknesses, past performance, potential and suggestions for improvement. The written essay requires no complex forms or extensive training to complete. But in this method a good or bad appraisal may be determined as much by the evaluator's writing skill as by the employee's actual level of performance.

Critical incidents

Critical incidents focus the evaluator's attention on the behaviours that are key in making the difference between executing a job effectively and executing it ineffectively. That is, the appraiser writes down anecdotes that describe what the employee did that was especially effective or ineffective. The key here is to cite only specific behaviours, not vaguely defined personality traits. A list of critical incidents provides a rich set of examples from which the employee can be shown the behaviours that are desirable and those that call for improvement.

Graphic rating scales

One of the oldest and most popular methods of evaluation is the use of **graphic rating scales**. In this method, a set of performance factors, such as quantity and quality of work, depth of knowledge, cooperation, attendance and initiative, is listed. The evaluator then goes down the list and rates each on incremental scales. The scales may specify five points, so a factor such as *job knowledge* might be rated 1 ('poorly informed about work duties') to 5 ('has complete mastery of all phases of the job'). Although they don't provide the depth of information that essays or critical incidents do, graphic rating scales are less time-consuming to develop and administer. They also allow for quantitative analysis and comparison.

Behaviourally anchored rating scales

Behaviourally anchored rating scales (BARS) combine major elements from the critical incident and graphic rating scale approaches: The appraiser rates the employees based on items along a continuum, but the points are examples of actual behaviour on the given job rather than general descriptions or traits. Examples of job-related behaviour and performance dimensions are found by asking participants to give specific illustrations of effective and ineffective behaviour regarding each performance dimension. These behavioural examples are then translated into a set of performance dimensions, each dimension having varying levels of performance.

Forced comparisons

Forced comparisons evaluate one individual's performance against the performance of another or others. It is a relative, rather than an absolute, measuring device. The two most popular comparisons are group order ranking and individual ranking.

> **group order ranking**
> An evaluation method that places employees into a particular classification, such as quartiles.

> **individual ranking**
> An evaluation method that rank-orders employees from best to worst.

The **group order ranking** requires the evaluator to place employees into a particular classification, such as top one-fifth or second one-fifth. This method is often used in recommending students to graduate schools. Evaluators are asked whether the student ranks in the top 5 per cent of the class, the next 5 per cent, the next 15 per cent and so forth. But in this type of performance appraisal, managers deal with all their subordinates. Therefore, if a rater has 20 employees, only four can be in the top fifth and, of course, four must also be relegated to the bottom fifth. The **individual ranking** approach rank-orders employees from best to worst. If the manager is required to appraise 30 employees, this approach assumes that the difference between the first and second employee is the same as that between the twenty-first and twenty-second. Even though some of the employees may be closely grouped, no ties are permitted. The result is a clear ordering of employees, from the highest performer down to the lowest.

'JOB REVIEW IN 140 KEYSTROKES'   OB IN THE NEWS

In the world of Facebook or Twitter, people love to hear feedback about what they're up to. But sit them down for a performance review, and suddenly the experience becomes traumatic.

Now companies are taking a page from social networking sites to make the performance evaluation process more fun and useful. Accenture has developed a Facebook-style programme called 'Performance Multiplier' in which, among other things, employees post status updates, photos and two or three weekly goals that can be viewed by fellow staffers. Even more immediate: new software from a startup called 'Rypple' that lets people post Twitter-length questions about their performance in exchange for anonymous feedback.

Such initiatives upend the dreaded rite of annual reviews by making performance feedback a much more real-time and ongoing process. Stanford University management professor Robert Sutton argues that performance reviews 'mostly suck' because they're conceived from the top rather than designed with employees' needs in mind. 'If you have regular conversations with people, and they know where they stand, then the performance evaluation is maybe unnecessary,' says Sutton.

What Rypple's and Accenture's tools do is create a process in which evaluations become dynamic – and more democratic. Rypple, for example, gives employees the chance to post brief, 140-character questions, such as 'What did you think of my presentation?' or 'How can I run meetings better?' The queries are e-mailed to managers, peers or anyone else the user selects. Short anonymous responses are then aggregated and sent back, providing a quick-and-dirty 360-degree review.

If having your performance goals posted for the world to see sounds a bit Orwellian, consider this: Rypple reports that some two-thirds of the questions posted on its service come from managers wanting feedback about business questions or their own performance. The biggest payoff of these social network-style tools may prove to be better performance by the boss.

Source: J. McGregor, Performance review takes a page from Facebook, *BusinessWeek*, 12 March 2009 Reprinted from 12 March 2009 issue of Bloomberg BusinessWeek by special permission, copyright © 2009 by Bloomberg.

Suggestions for improving performance evaluations

> 7 Show how managers can improve performance evaluations.

The performance evaluation process is a potential minefield of problems. For instance, evaluators can unconsciously inflate evaluations (positive leniency), understate performance (negative leniency), or allow the assessment of one characteristic to unduly influence the assessment of others (the halo error). Some appraisers bias their evaluations by unconsciously favouring people who have qualities and traits similar to their own (the similarity error). And, of course, some evaluators see the evaluation process as a political opportunity to overtly reward or punish employees they like or dislike. Although there are no protections that will *guarantee* accurate performance evaluations, the following suggestions can significantly help to make the process more objective and fair.

Use multiple evaluators

As the number of evaluators increases, the probability of attaining more accurate information increases. If rater error tends to follow a normal curve, an increase in the number of appraisers will tend to find the majority congregating about the middle. We often see multiple evaluators in competitions in such sports as diving and gymnastics. A set of evaluators judges a performance, the highest and lowest scores are dropped, and the final evaluation is made up of those remaining. The logic of multiple evaluators applies to organizations as well.

If an employee has had 10 supervisors, nine having rated her excellent and one poor, we can safely discount the one poor evaluation. Therefore, by moving employees about within the organization so as to gain a number of evaluations or by using multiple assessors (as provided in 360-degree appraisals), we increase the probability of achieving more valid and reliable evaluations.

Evaluate selectively

Appraisers should evaluate only in areas in which they have some expertise.[60] This precaution increases the interrater agreement and makes the evaluation a more valid process. It also recognises that different organizational levels often have different orientations toward those being rated and observe them in different settings. In general, therefore, appraisers should be as close as possible, in terms of organizational level, to the individual being evaluated. Conversely, the more levels that separate the evaluator and the person being evaluated, the less opportunity the evaluator has to observe the individual's behaviour and, not surprisingly, the greater the possibility for inaccuracies.

Train evaluators

If you can't *find* good evaluators, the alternative is to *make* good evaluators. There is substantial evidence that training evaluators can make them more accurate raters.[61]

Common errors such as halo and leniency have been minimised or eliminated in workshops where managers practice observing and rating behaviours. These workshops typically run from one to three days, but allocating many hours to training may not always be necessary. One case has been cited in which both halo and leniency errors were decreased immediately after exposing evaluators to explanatory training sessions lasting only five minutes.[62] But the effects of training appear to diminish over time.[63] This suggests the need for regular refresher sessions.

Provide employees with due process

The concept of *due process* can be applied to appraisals to increase the perception that employees are being treated fairly.[64] Three features characterise due process systems: (1) Individuals are provided with adequate notice of what is expected of them; (2) all evidence relevant to a proposed violation is aired in a fair hearing so the individuals affected can respond; and (3) the final decision is based on the evidence and free of bias.

There is considerable evidence that evaluation systems often violate employees' due process by providing them with infrequent and relatively general performance feedback, allowing them little input into the appraisal process, and knowingly introducing bias into performance ratings. However, when due process has been part of the evaluation system, employees report positive reactions to the appraisal process, perceive the evaluation results as more accurate, and express increased intent to remain with the organization.

Providing performance feedback

For many managers, few activities are more unpleasant than providing performance feedback to employees.[65] In fact, unless pressured by organizational policies and controls, managers are likely to ignore this responsibility.[66]

Why the reluctance to give performance feedback? There seem to be at least three reasons. First, managers are often uncomfortable discussing performance weaknesses directly with employees. Even though almost every employee could stand to improve in some areas, managers fear a confrontation when presenting negative feedback. This apprehension apparently applies even when people give negative feedback to a computer! Bill Gates reports that Microsoft conducted a project requiring users to rate their experience with a computer.

When we had the computer the users had worked with ask for an evaluation of its performance, the responses tended to be positive. But when we had a second computer ask the same people to evaluate their encounters with the first machine, the people were significantly more critical. Their reluctance to criticise the first computer 'to its face' suggested that they didn't want to hurt its feelings, even though they knew it was only a machine.[67]

Second, many employees tend to become defensive when their weaknesses are pointed out. Instead of accepting the feedback as constructive and a basis for improving performance, some employees challenge the evaluation by criticising the manager or redirecting blame to someone else.[68]

Finally, employees tend to have an inflated assessment of their own performance. Statistically speaking, half of all employees must be below-average performers. But the evidence indicates that the average employee's estimate of their own performance level generally falls around the 75th percentile.[69] So even when managers are providing good news, employees are likely to perceive it as not good enough.

The solution to the performance feedback problem is not to ignore it, but to train managers to conduct constructive feedback sessions. An effective review – one in which the employee perceives the appraisal as fair, the manager as sincere and the climate as constructive – can result in the employee's leaving the interview in an upbeat mood, informed about the performance areas needing improvement and determined to correct the deficiencies.[70] In addition, the performance review should be designed more as a counselling activity than a judgement process. This can best be accomplished by allowing the review to evolve out of the employee's own self-evaluation.

SELF-ASSESSMENT LIBRARY

How good am I at giving performance feedback?

In the Self-assessment library (available online), take assessment III.A.3 (How good am I at giving performance feedback?).

Managing diversity in organizations

8 Explain how diversity can be managed in organizations.

David Morris and his father, Saul, started Habitat International in 1981. The company manufactures a grasslike indoor/outdoor carpet. From the beginning, the Morrises hired refugees from Cambodia, Bosnia and Laos, many of whom didn't speak English. But when a social-service worker suggested in 1984 that the company hire mentally challenged people, Saul balked. Hiring someone with a condition such as Down's syndrome seemed too chancy. But David thought otherwise. He talked his dad into giving it a try.[71]

The first group of eight mentally disabled workers came in with their job coach from the social-services agency and went straight to work boxing mats. Two weeks later, says Saul, employees were coming to him and wondering why the company couldn't 'hire more people like this, who care, do their work with pride, and smile?'

Today, 75 per cent of Habitat's employees have some kind of disability. People with schizophrenia, for instance, are driving forklifts next to employees with autism or cerebral palsy. Meanwhile, the Morris father-and-son team is doing good things both for these people and for themselves. The disabled employees have enhanced self-esteem and are now self-sufficient enough to be off government aid, and the Morrises enjoy the benefits of a dedicated, hard-working labour force. 'We have practically zero absenteeism and very little turnover,' says David.

Habitat International illustrates the role of employee selection in increasing diversity. But effective diversity programmes go well beyond merely hiring a diverse workforce. They also include managing work–life conflicts and providing diversity training. These seem to be common characteristics among major organizations that have developed reputations as diversity leaders – including PwC, AstraZeneca, Goldman Sachs, PepsiCo and Coca-Cola.[72]

Work–life conflicts

We introduced work–life balance in Chapter 1 and discussed the forces that are blurring the lines between work life and personal life. In this section we want to elaborate on this issue – specifically focusing on what organizations can do to help employees reduce conflicts.

Work–life conflicts grabbed management's attention in the 1980s, largely as a result of the growing number of women with dependent children entering the workforce. In response, most major organizations took actions to make their workplaces more family friendly.[73] They introduced programmes such as on-site child care, summer day camps, flexitime, job sharing, leaves for school functions, teleworking and part-time employment. But organizations quickly realised that work–life conflicts were not experienced only by female employees with children. Male workers and women without children were also facing this problem. Heavy work loads and increased travel demands, for instance, were making it increasingly hard for a wide range of employees to meet both work and personal responsibilities. A Harvard study found that 82 per cent of men between the ages of 20 and 39 said a 'family-friendly' schedule was their most important job criterion.[74]

Organizations are modifying their workplaces to accommodate the varied needs of a diverse workforce. This includes providing a wide range of scheduling options and benefits that allow employees more flexibility at work and permit them to better balance or integrate their work and personal lives. For instance, employees at the Swedish office of SAS Institute, a software firm, are provided with flexible scheduling, plus a full array of on-site services, including day care, a fitness facility, weight watchers classes, yoga, Tai Chi, power boxing and other activities. They also have smoking cessation classes, pay for a personal trainer and regularly bring in lecturers to talk about food.[75] Table 18.1 lists some broader examples of initiatives that organizations provide to help their employees reduce work–life conflicts.

Recent research on work–life conflicts has provided new insights for managers into what works and when. For instance, evidence indicates that time pressures aren't the primary problem underlying work–life conflicts.[76] It's the psychological incursion of work into the family domain

Table 18.1	Work–Life initiatives
Strategy	**Programme or policy**
Time-based strategies	Flexitime
	Job sharing
	Part-time work
	Leave for new parents
	Teleworking
	Closing plants/offices for special occasions
Information-based strategies	Intranet work–life website
	Relocation assistance
	Elder-care resources
Money-based strategies	Vouchers for child care
	Flexible benefits
	Adoption assistance
	Discounts for child-care tuition
	Leave with pay
Direct services	On-site child care
	On-site health/beauty services
	Concierge services
	Takeout dinners
Culture-change strategies	Training for managers to help employees deal with work–life conflicts
	Tie manager pay to employee satisfaction
	Focus on employees' actual performance, not 'face time'

Sources: Based on C. A. Thompson, 'Managing the work–life balance act: an introductory exercise', *Journal of Management Education*, April 2002, p. 210; and R. Levering and M. Maskowitz, 'The best in the worst of times', *Fortune*, 4 February 2002, pp. 60–90.

and vice versa. People are worrying about personal problems at work and thinking about work problems at home. So dad may physically make it home in time for dinner, but his mind is elsewhere while he's at the dinner table. This suggests that organizations should spend less effort helping employees with time-management issues and more helping them clearly segment their lives. Keeping work loads reasonable, reducing work-related travel and offering on-site quality child care are examples of practices that can help in this endeavour.

Also, not surprisingly, people have been found to differ in their preference for scheduling options and benefits.[77] Some people prefer organizational initiatives that better segment work from their personal lives. Others prefer initiatives that facilitate integration. For instance, flexitime segments because it allows employees to schedule work hours that are less likely to conflict with personal responsibilities. On the other hand, on-site child care integrates by blurring the boundaries between work and family responsibilities. People who prefer segmentation are more likely to be satisfied and committed to their work when offered options such as flexitime, job sharing and part-time hours. People who prefer integration are more likely to respond positively to options such as on-site child care, gym facilities and company-sponsored family picnics.

Diversity training

The centrepiece of most diversity programmes is training. For instance, a relatively recent survey found that 93 per cent of companies with diversity initiatives used training as part of their programmes.[78] Diversity training programmes are generally intended to provide a vehicle for increasing awareness and examining stereotypes. Participants learn to value individual differences, increase their cross-cultural understanding, and confront stereotypes.[79] For example, the Spanish-based hotel chain NH Hoteles operates 335 hotels in 21 countries. The firm believes that diversity training is essential to success because of the number of people employed from different nationalities and the need to comply with legislation. Included in the diversity training are seminars, usually given by managers and directors from different nationalities, to try to show the importance and the benefit brought by multinational environments as well as the need to avoid prejudices and stereotypes.[80]

Human resource policies and practices in Europe

9 Show how human resource policies and practices may need to be adapted across Europe.

Across Europe HR policies and practices such as selection, training and performance evaluations are commonplace in all countries. But, because of differing legal, political, economic and social environments there are variations in how these practices actually occur. Let's look at a few examples.

In Spain, Portugal, France, the Netherlands, Italy, Greece, Cyprus and the UK interviews are by far the most common method used to select new employees. However, panel interviews are used very infrequently in these countries (preferring individual interviews) except for the Netherlands where panel interviews are used a third of the time and Cyprus where panel interviews are used on almost three-quarters of occasions. The use of psychometric testing to assess potential job candidates is variable. For example, in the Netherlands it is considerably less common than in other parts of western Europe.

Training and Development in France and Belgium is heavily influenced by national legislation. In France 1.5 per cent of a company's wage bill has to be dedicated to training or go to tax. The process is highly regulated and there are two aspects: The company training plan and training initiated by employees. Even the objectives of the company training plan are set out by the government, leaving firm's with far less autonomy than in other countries. Individuals also have a legal right to take leave of absence to train. Consequently, France spends significantly more than other European nations on training. Italy, Greece and particularly Cyprus spend significantly less than the EU average. In terms of providing employees access to training, northern European countries come at the top of the league. More than 50 per cent of workers received training at work in Finland and Sweden. At the other end of the scale are most southern and eastern European countries, where the levels of training are very low, hardly reaching 20 per cent of employees in Spain, Greece, Hungary, Portugal, Romania and 10 per cent of employees in Bulgaria and Turkey.

Implementing HR practices to improve employee's work–life balance will also need to be adjusted depending on the country. For members of the European Union, although the countries must adopt the relevant EU legislation and guidelines, there remain significant variations. The Nordic countries have a well-established track record of governmental intervention in work–life balance. Strict guidelines for establishing flexible working schemes and employee welfare programmes exist. In Germany, implementing family-friendly policies will require collective negotiations to reach agreements. In Poland, there seems to be an unwillingness to actively embrace the notion of flexible working.

As businesses increasingly operate across Europe, have alliances and merge with other European companies, it has become imperative for managers to have a thorough understanding of how HR practices may need to be adapted to positively affect employee's behaviour and ultimately organizational effectiveness.[81]

Global implications

10 Show how a global context affects human resource management.

The previous section focused on variations in HR practices across Europe. The conclusion that many of the human resource policies and practices discussed in this chapter have to be modified to reflect national and cultural differences is far more pronounced when considering the global context.[82] To illustrate this point, let's briefly look at the universality of selection practices and the importance of performance evaluation in different global cultures.

Selection

A study of 300 large organizations in 22 countries demonstrated that selection practices differ by nation.[83] A few common procedures were found. For instance, the use of educational qualifications in screening candidates seems to be a universal practice. For the most part, however, different countries tend to emphasise different selection techniques. Structured interviews, as a case in point, were popular in some countries and nonexistent in others. The authors of the study suggested that 'certain cultures may find structured interviews antithetical to beliefs about how one should conduct an interpersonal interaction or the extent to which one should trust the judgement of the interviewer.'[84]

This study, when combined with earlier research, tells us that there are no universal selection practices. Moreover, global firms that attempt to implement standardised worldwide selection practices can expect to face considerable resistance from local managers. Policies and practices need to be modified to reflect culture-based norms and social values, as well as legal and economic differences.

Performance evaluation

We've looked at the role performance evaluation plays in motivating and affecting behaviour. We must use caution, however, in generalising across cultures. Why? Because many cultures are not particularly concerned with performance appraisal or look at it in different ways.

Let's look at performance evaluation in the context of four cultural dimensions: individualism/collectivism, a person's relationship to the environment, time orientation and focus of responsibility.

Individual-oriented cultures such as the United States emphasise formal performance evaluation systems more than informal systems. They advocate, for instance, written evaluations performed at regular intervals, the results of which managers share with employees and use in the determination of rewards. On the other hand, the collectivist cultures that dominate Asia and much of Latin America are characterised by more informal systems – downplaying formal feedback and disconnecting reward allocations from performance ratings. Japanese technology giant Fujitsu, for instance, introduced a formal, performance-based evaluation system in Japan in the mid-1990s. But the company recently began to dismantle it, recognising that it 'had proved flawed and a poor fit with Japanese [collectivist] business culture'.[85]

US and Canadian organizations hold people responsible for their actions because people in these countries believe they can dominate their environment. In Middle Eastern countries, on the other hand, performance evaluations aren't likely to be widely used because managers in these countries tend to see people as subject to their environment.

Some countries, such as the United States, have a short-term time orientation. Performance evaluations are likely to be frequent in such a culture – at least once a year. In Japan, however, where people hold a long-term time frame, performance appraisals may occur only every 5 or 10 years.

Summary and implications for managers

An organization's human resource policies and practices represent important forces for shaping employee behaviour and attitudes. In this chapter, we specifically discussed the influence of selection practices, training and development programmes and performance evaluation systems.

Selection practices

An organization's selection practices will determine who gets hired. If properly designed, they will identify competent candidates and accurately match them to the job and the organization. The use of the proper selection devices will increase the probability that the right person will be chosen to fill a slot.

Although employee selection is far from a science, some organizations fail to design a selection system that will increase the likelihood of achieving the right person–job fit. When hiring errors are made, the chosen candidate's performance may be less than satisfactory. Training may be necessary to improve the candidate's skills. At worst, the candidate will prove unacceptable and the firm will need to find a replacement. Similarly, when the selection process results in the hiring of less-qualified candidates or individuals who don't fit into the organization, those chosen are likely to feel anxious, tense and uncomfortable. This, in turn, is likely to increase dissatisfaction with the job.

Training and development programmes

Training programmes can affect work behaviour in two ways. The most obvious is by directly improving the skills necessary for the employee to successfully complete the job. An increase in ability improves the employee's potential to perform at a higher level. Of course, whether that potential becomes realised is largely an issue of motivation.

A second benefit of training is that it increases an employee's self-efficacy. As discussed in Chapter 6, self-efficacy is a person's expectation that they can successfully execute the behaviours required to produce an outcome.[86] For employees, those behaviours are work tasks, and the outcome is effective job performance. Employees with high self-efficacy have strong expectations about their abilities to perform successfully in new situations. They're confident and expect to be successful. Training, then, is a means to positively affect self-efficacy because employees may be more willing to undertake job tasks and exert a high level of effort. Or in expectancy terms (see Chapter 6), individuals are more likely to perceive their effort as leading to performance.

Performance evaluation

A major goal of performance evaluation is to assess an individual's performance accurately as a basis for making reward allocation decisions. If the performance evaluation process emphasises the wrong criteria or inaccurately appraises actual job performance, employees will be over-rewarded or under-rewarded. As demonstrated in Chapter 6, in our discussion of equity theory, this can lead to negative consequences such as reduced effort, increases in absenteeism, or a search for alternative job opportunities. In addition, the content of the performance evaluation has been found to influence employee performance and satisfaction.[87] Specifically, performance and satisfaction are increased when the evaluation is based on behavioural, results-oriented criteria, when career issues as well as performance issues are discussed, and when the employee has an opportunity to participate in the evaluation.

POINT/COUNTERPOINT

Teleworking makes good business sense

POINT ➡

More and more companies are turning to flexible work schedules, for good reasons.

The first and most obvious reason is changes in how, and where, work is done. Today's virtual organizations realise that where people work is becoming less and less important.

Second, organizations are realising that offering teleworking and other flexible schedules allows them to attract and retain the best talent. As a head of one government agency noted, 'Telework is not a "nice to have" anymore; it is critical to agencies' business continuity and produc-

tivity, as well as retaining a knowledgeable workforce and appealing to a new generation of employees interested in work/life balance.' Companies such as Ernst & Young have ramped up flexible schedules not only to attract and retain knowledge workers, but to be flexible as a business, such as during tax time.

Third, research shows that while managers are a main source of opposition to telework, when managers are exposed to teleworking, they become much more positive in their attitudes toward it.

COUNTERPOINT ⬅

Teleworking and other flexible schedules are one of those management fads that sounds good but, like most other fads, don't stand up to close scrutiny and logical analysis.

Managers don't view telecommuters very positively. You can agree or disagree with them, but you would have a hard time advising employees to indulge in flexible work schedules when doing so hurts their career. A recent study gave some interesting support to this argument.

When surveyed, more than two-thirds (68 per cent) of employees thought that working at home made them more productive. However, when managers were surveyed, more than one-third (37 per cent) thought that if allowed to work at home, staff would use their so-called working hours for personal activities.

Sure, employees want flexible schedules and rationalise their preferences by arguing that it helps them get more done. But a lot of managers know better – that while some

of 'working at home' does involve work, another part of it involves 'goofing off' doing non-work stuff like washing clothes, cleaning, personal or family activities and so on. That's exactly why employees want it so much.

If you asked employees, 'Would you like to get paid the same for working half as many hours?' most employees would probably say, 'Sure!' But that doesn't mean that management should give employees something for nothing. Effective HRM sometimes means not giving employees what they want.

Source: J. Badal, 'To retain valued women employees, companies pitch flextime as macho', *Wall Street Journal*, 11 December 2006, pp. B1, B3; 'Telework exchange and Federal Managers Association study reveals only 35 per cent of managers believe their agencies support telework', *IPMA-HR Bulletin*, 26 January 2007, pp. 1–2; and R. Scally, '"Working from home today" that's not what your boss thinks', *Workforce Week*, 6 May 2007, p. 1.

QUESTIONS FOR REVIEW

1. What is initial selection and what are the most useful initial selection methods?

2. What is substantive selection and what are the most useful substantive selection methods?

3. What is contingent selection and what are the arguments for and against drug testing?

4. What are the four main types of training?

5. What are the differences between formal and informal training methods and between on-the-job and off-the-job training?

6. What are the main purposes of performance evaluation?

7. How can performance evaluation be improved?

8. How can diversity be managed in organizations?

9. How is human resource management affected by a European and global context?

EVALUATING PERFORMANCE AND PROVIDING FEEDBACK

Objective

To experience the assessment of performance and observe the provision of performance feedback.

Time

Approximately 30 minutes.

Procedure

Select a class leader, either a volunteer or someone chosen by your instructor. The class leader will preside over the class discussion and perform the role of manager in the evaluation review.

Your instructor will leave the room. The class leader is then to spend up to 15 minutes helping the class to evaluate your instructor. Your instructor understands that this is only a class exercise and is prepared to accept criticism (and, of course, any praise you may want to convey). Your instructor also recognises that the leader's evaluation is actually a com-posite of many students' input. So be open and honest in your evaluation and have confidence that your instructor will not be vindictive.

Research has identified seven performance dimensions to the college instructor's job: (1) instructor knowledge; (2) testing procedures; (3) student–teacher relations; (4) organizational skills; (5) communication skills; (6) subject relevance; and (7) utility of assignments. The discussion of your instructor's performance should focus on these seven dimensions. The leader may want to take notes for personal use but will not be required to give your instructor any written documentation.

When the 15-minute class discussion is complete, the leader will invite the instructor back into the room. The performance review will begin as soon as the instructor walks through the door, with the class leader becoming the manager and the instructor playing himself or herself.

When completed, class discussion will focus on performance evaluation criteria and how well your class leader did in providing performance feedback.

IS IT UNETHICAL TO 'SHAPE' YOUR CURRICULUM VITAE (CV)?

When does 'putting a positive spin' on your accomplishments step over the line to become misrepresentation or lying? Does a CV have to be 100 per cent truthful? Apparently, a lot of people don't think so. Studies have found that nearly half of all CV's contain at least one lie.[88] To help clarify your ethical views on this issue, consider the following three situations and answer the questions for each.

1. Aiden left a job for which his title was 'credit clerk'. When looking for a new job, he lists his previous title as 'credit analyst'. He thinks it sounds more impressive. Is this 're-titling' of a former job wrong? Why or why not?

2. About eight years ago, Ella took nine months off between jobs to travel. Afraid that people might consider her unstable or lacking in career motivation, she put down on her CV that she was engaged in 'independent consulting activities' during the period. Was she wrong? How else could she have described this time period on her CV?

3. Hakan is the 46-year-old CEO of a Fortune Global 1000 company. He enrolled in university 20 years ago, but he never got a degree. Just nine months after he was appointed CEO, a local newspaper reported that he had lied on his CV. His CV indicated that he had a bachelor's degree in psychology, but neither he nor the university can produce any evidence of that. Should he be terminated? If yes, why, and if not, what should his employer do about Hakan's missing credentials?

Innovative HRM at Virgin Mobile UK

Innovative HR policies and practices have helped Virgin Mobile UK to become one of the major players on the UK scene.

Recruitment and selection

When asked what she was most proud of in terms of personnel activities, director of HR Lily Lu had no doubt: recruitment. 'I am utterly proud of our recruitment, of how unusual, innovative, eye-catching and fun our campaigns are,' she says. 'They reflect our values of fun, openness and innovation.'

This openness is carried through beyond advertising. Customer service adviser (CSA) selection takes place at an assessment centre and assessors deliberately leave the room so that candidates have carte blanche to ask an existing CSA whatever they wish. The company does not run a conventional management trainee scheme and relies on word-of-mouth and work experience people for its intake. 'We avoid the run-of-the-mill "milk round", with express training, at the end of which people may not be interested,' explains Lu. In the first year, graduate recruits do three or four months in different business areas, making a final choice at the end of the year.

Retention

While Virgin Mobile refuses to disclose staff turnover rate, Lu claims it is low – although higher than she'd like in the customer centres. 'But it is coming down thanks to our culture and the flexibility in working style,' she says.

Employee benefits include four times base salary on death in service, private medical cover, pensions, 25 days holiday, enhanced maternity benefits and paid sick leave up to a maximum of 12 weeks full pay. The company also offers a bonus scheme, subsidised staff restaurant and the popular Virgin 'tribe' discount scheme.

The maternity package consists of the first six weeks of leave at full basic pay, regardless of length of service. For staff who have been with the company for at least two years, maternity pay is enhanced in 20 per cent steps to a maximum of 100 per cent base pay for the full 18 weeks. The company is also investigating non-crèche child-friendly work options.

Flexible working is offered informally to non-customer service staff and the company tries to be as accommodating as possible with shift patterns.

Training and development

One of Virgin Mobile's most innovative initiatives in the training arena is its Trowbridge-based 'learning zone' for which it sets aside about €10,000 a year. The learning zone is rather like a library, with a quiet reading area, fish tank and a variety of training and development resources, including an on-site manager. Training delivery is a mixture of classroom, on-the-job, online and in the learning zone. New recruits receive an average 23 days training. For existing staff, they complete three days training each per year on average.

Performance management

Virgin Mobile's appraisal and development system, the Employee Development Programme (EDP), is Lily Lu's brainchild. Originally a platform for assessing the staff bonus scheme, the EDP links HR strategy to the bottom line and takes into account skills and personal qualities. In the melting pot are customer base, customer satisfaction, personal performance and company financial performance. And each individual has a formal annual assessment with line managers.

Questions

1. Evaluate human resource management (HRM) at Virgin Mobile UK. What is the company doing well? What could be improved?

2. Virgin Mobile has subsidiaries in India, Australia, Canada, South Africa, the United States and France. Do you think these HR practices would work in these countries? Why or why not?

3. Imagine you are working for Virgin Mobile UK. How do you think these HR policies and practices would affect your behaviour at work?

Source: Adapted from L. Hall, 'Innovative recruitment works for Virgin', *Personnel Today*, 16 July 2002.

CASE INCIDENT 2

UBS ordered to pay €20 million for sex discrimination

In 2005, UBS, then Europe's largest bank, was ordered by a New York jury to pay more than €20 million in damages to a former saleswoman who sued the firm for sex discrimination. Laura Zubulake claimed that the bank mistreated her because she was a woman and then fired her after she complained to the Equal Employment Opportunity Commission.

'This sends a message not just to UBS but to everybody,' Ms Zubulake said. 'The message for all senior women on Wall Street is not to be afraid to stand up and speak out when they feel they are being treated differently.'

UBS said it would appeal. 'We are disappointed with the verdict rendered by the jury today,' said a company spokesman, Mark Arena. 'We regard the amount awarded as excessive and will now move to set aside the verdict.' Mr Arena added: 'UBS is committed to its diversity efforts and will continue to ensure that it has an open and diverse work environment.'

In her complaint against UBS, Ms Zubulake said that in late 2000 she was passed over for the job of manager of the Asian equities sales desk in the United States. The position was given instead to Matthew Chapin. Ms Zubulake said Mr Chapin proceeded to undermine her, belittling and ridiculing her in front of co-workers, excluding her from some outings with clients, making sexist remarks and denying her important accounts.

Ms Zubulake, who said she was one of the highest-paid executives on her desk, said the mistreatment extended to the positioning of her desk in the Manhattan office. It was across the aisle from the rest of her colleagues, among the desk assistants.

In August 2001, Ms Zubulake filed a complaint with the employment commission. In October of that year, Mr Chapin sent Ms Zubulake a letter saying her employment had been terminated.

▶

39 'Graduates set to be in demand as Euro firms say they want more', *Personnel Today*, 3 October 2001.

40 For example see L. Oliva, 'Ethics edges on to courses: corporate social responsibility: Business schools are taking the training of ethical managers seriously, says Loredana Oliva', *Financial Times*, 16 February 2004, p. 11; M. Berry, 'Ethics rises up the agenda of UK businesses', *Personnel Today*, 10 March 2008.

41 M. B. Wood, *Business Ethics in Uncertain Times* (Upper Saddle River, NJ: Prentice-Hall, 2004), p. 61.

42 See, for example, D. Seligman, 'Oxymoron 101', *Forbes*, 28 October 2002, pp. 160–64; and R. B. Schmitt, 'Companies add ethics training; will it work?', *Wall Street Journal*, 4 November 2002, p. B1.

43 K. Dobbs, 'The U.S. Department of Labor estimates that 70 per cent of workplace learning occurs informally', *Sales & Marketing Management*, November 2000, pp. 94–98.

44 S. J. Wells, 'Forget the formal training. Try chatting at the water cooler', *New York Times*, 10 May 1998, p. BU-11.

45 See, for instance, K. G. Brown, 'Using computers to deliver training: which employees learn and why?', *Personnel Psychology*, Summer 2001, pp. 271–96; 'The delivery: how U.S. organizations use classrooms and computers in training', *Training*, October 2001, pp. 66–72; and L. K. Long and R. D. Smith, 'The role of web-based distance learning in HR development', *Journal of Management Development*, 23, 3 (2004), pp. 270–84.

46 A. Muoio, 'Cisco's quick study', *Fast Company*, October 2000, pp. 287–95.

47 'Untangling the Web', *Training and Coaching Today*, 1 March 2001.

48 E. A. Ensher, T. R. Nielson and E. Grant-Vallone, 'Tales from the hiring line: effects of the internet and technology on HR processes', *Organizational Dynamics*, 31, 3 (2002), pp. 232–33.

49 D. A. Kolb, 'Management and the learning process', *California Management Review*, Spring 1976, pp. 21–31; and B. Filipczak, 'Different strokes: learning styles in the classroom', *Training*, March 1995, pp. 43–48.

50 W. J. Arthur, Jr., W. Bennett, Jr., P. S. Edens and S. T. Bell, 'Effectiveness of training in organizations: a meta-analysis of design and evaluation features', *Journal of Applied Psychology*, April 2003, pp. 234–45.

51 J. A. Colquitt, J. A. LePine and R. A. Noe, 'Toward an integrative theory of training motivation: a meta-analytic path analysis of 20 years of research', *Journal of Applied Psychology*, October 2000, pp. 678–707.

52 W. F. Cascio, *Applied Psychology in Human Resource Management*, 5th edn (Upper Saddle River, NJ: Prentice-Hall, 1998), p. 59.

53 See W. C. Borman and S. J. Motowidlo, 'Expanding the criterion domain to include elements of contextual performance', in N. Schmitt and W. C. Borman (eds), *Personnel Selection in Organizations* (San Francisco, CA: Jossey-Bass, 1993), pp. 71–98; W. H. Bommer, J. L. Johnson, G. A. Rich, P. M. Podsakoff and S. B. MacKenzie, 'On the interchangeability of objective and subjective measures of employee performance: a meta-analysis', *Personnel Psychology*, Autumn 1995, pp. 587–605; and S. E. Scullen, M. K. Mount and T. A. Judge, 'Evidence of the construct validity of developmental ratings of managerial performance', *Journal of Applied Psychology*, February 2003, pp. 50–66.

54 A. H. Locher and K. S. Teel, 'Appraisal trends', *Personnel Journal*, September 1988, pp. 139–45.

55 Cited in S. Armour, 'Job reviews take on added significance in down times', *USA Today*, 23 July 2003, p. 4B.

56 See review in R. D. Bretz, Jr., G. T. Milkovich and W. Read, 'The current state of performance appraisal research and practice: concerns, directions, and implications', *Journal of Management*, June 1992, p. 326; and P. W. B. Atkins and R. E. Wood, 'Self- versus others' ratings as predictors of assessment center ratings: validation evidence for 360-degree feedback programs', *Personnel Psychology*, Winter 2002, pp. 871–904.

57 M. Shepard and R. Johns, 'Candidate image and electoral preference in Britain', *British Politics*, 3, 3 (2008), pp. 324–49.

58 See, for instance, J. D. Facteau and S. B. Craig, 'Are performance appraisal ratings from different rating sources compatible?', *Journal of Applied Psychology*, April 2001, pp. 215–27; J. F. Brett and L. E. Atwater, '360-Degree feedback: accuracy, reactions, and perceptions of usefulness', *Journal of Applied Psychology*, October 2001, pp. 930–42; F. Luthans and S. J. Peterson, '360 degree feedback with systematic coaching: empirical analysis suggests a winning combination', *Human Resource Management*, Fall 2003, pp. 243–56; and B. I. J. M. van der Heijden and A. H. J. Nijhof, 'The value of subjectivity: problems and prospects for 360-Degree appraisal systems', *International Journal of Human Resource Management*, May 2004, pp. 493–511.

59 Atkins and Wood, 'Self- versus others' ratings as predictors of assessment center ratings'; and B. Pfau, I. Kay, K. M. Nowack and J. Ghorpade, 'Does 360-Degree feedback negatively affect company performance?', *Human Resource Magazine*, 47, 6, pp. 54–59.

60 See, for instance, J. W. Hedge and W. C. Borman, 'Changing conceptions and practices in performance appraisal', in A. Howard (ed.), *The Changing Nature of Work* (San Francisco, CA: Jossey-Bass, 1995), pp. 453–59.

61 See, for instance, T. R. Athey and R. M. McIntyre, 'Effect of rater training on rater accuracy: levels-of-processing theory and social facilitation theory perspectives', *Journal of Applied Psychology*, November 1987, pp. 567–72; and D. J. Woehr, 'Understanding frame-of-reference training: the impact of training on the recall of performance information', *Journal of Applied Psychology*, August 1994, pp. 525–34.

62 H. J. Bernardin, 'The effects of rater training on leniency and halo errors in student rating of instructors', *Journal of Applied Psychology*, June 1978, pp. 301–08.

63 Ibid.; and J. M. Ivancevich, 'Longitudinal study of the effects of rater training on psychometric error in ratings', *Journal of Applied Psychology*, October 1979, pp. 502–08.

64 M. S. Taylor, K. B. Tracy, M. K. Renard, J. K. Harrison and S. J. Carroll, 'Due process in performance appraisal: a quasi-experiment in procedural justice', *Administrative Science Quarterly*, September 1995, pp. 495–523.

65 J. S. Lublin, 'It's shape-up time for performance reviews', *Wall Street Journal*, 3 October 1994, p. B1.

66 Much of this section is based on H. H. Meyer, 'A solution to the performance appraisal feedback enigma', *Academy of Management Executive*, February 1991, pp. 68–76.

67 B. Gates, *The Road Ahead* (New York: Viking, 1995), p. 86.

68 T. D. Schelhardt, 'It's time to evaluate your work, and all involved are groaning', *Wall Street Journal*, 19 November 1996, p. A1.

69 R. J. Burke, 'Why performance appraisal systems fail', *Personnel Administration*, June 1972, pp. 32–40.

70 B. D. Cawley, L. M. Keeping and P. E. Levy, 'Participation in the performance appraisal process and employee reactions: a meta-analytic review of field investigations', *Journal of Applied Psychology*, August 1998, pp. 615–33; and P. E. Levy and J. R. Williams, 'The social context of performance appraisal: a review and framework for the future', *Journal of Management*, 30, 6 (2004), pp. 881–905.

71 N. B. Henderson, 'An enabling work force', *Nation's Business*, June 1998, p. 93.

72 See J. Hickman, '50 best companies for minorities', *Fortune*, 28 June 2004, pp. 136–42; Business in the Community, www.bitc.com.

73 See, for instance, *Harvard Business Review on Work and Life Balance* (Boston, MA: Harvard Business School Press, 2000); and R. Rapoport, L. Bailyn, J. K. Fletcher and B. H. Pruitt, *Beyond Work-Family Balance* (San Francisco, CA: Jossey-Bass, 2002).

74 'On the daddy track', *Wall Street Journal*, 11 May 2000, p. A1.

75 SAS Institute Best workplaces in Europe 2007. Available at http://media.ft.com/cms/8ca0106e-f8c9-11db-a940-00065df10621.pdf.

76 S. D. Friedman and J. H. Greenhaus, *Work and Family – Allies or Enemies?* (New York: Oxford University Press, 2000).

77 N. P. Rothbard, T. L. Dumas and K. W. Phillips, 'The long arm of the organization: work–family policies and employee preferences for segmentation', paper presented at the 61st Annual Academy of Management Meeting, Washington, DC, August 2001.

78 Cited in 'Survey shows 75 per cent of large corporations support diversity programs', *Fortune*, 6 July 1998, p. S14.

79 See, for example, J. K. Ford and S. Fisher, 'The role of training in a changing workplace and workforce: new perspectives and approaches', in E. E. Kossek and S. A. Lobel (eds), *Managing Diversity* (Cambridge, MA: Blackwell Publishers, 1996), pp. 164–93; and J. Barbian, 'Moving toward diversity', *Training*, February 2003, pp. 44–48.

80 Based on EMCC company network: 'Case example of NH Hoteles', *European Foundation for the Improvement of Living and Working Conditions* 2007. Available at http://www.eurofound.europa.eu/emcc/publications/2007/ef07793en.pdf. Accessed 5 May 2009.

81 This section is based on C. Brewster, W. Mayrhofer and M. Morley (eds) *Human Resource Management in Europe: Evidence of Convergence?* (Oxford: Elsevier/Butterworth-Heinemann, 2004); O. Polyacskó (2008) 'Research highlights changes in company training policy', *European Foundation for the Improvement of Living and Working Conditions*, A. Gospodinova (2006) 'Low participation in vocational education and training', *Foundation for the Improvement of Living and Working Conditions*, see http://www.eurofound.europa.eu/; and Fourth European Working, Conditions Survey European Foundation for the Improvement of Living and Working Conditions, 2007.

82 See, for instance, C. Fletcher and E. L. Perry, 'Performance appraisal and feedback: a consideration of national culture and a review of contemporary research and future trends', in N. Anderson, D. S. Ones, H. K. Sinangil and C. Viswesvaran (eds), *Handbook of Industrial, Work, & Organizational Psychology*, vol. 1 (Thousand Oaks, CA: Sage, 2001), pp. 127–44.

83 A. M. Ryan, L. McFarland, H. Baron and R. Page, 'An international look at selection practices: nation and culture as explanations for variability in practice', *Personnel Psychology*, Summer 1999, pp. 359–92.

84 Ibid., p. 386.

85 M. Tanikawa, 'Fujitsu decides to backtrack on performance-based pay', *New York Times*, 22 March 2001, p. W1.

86 P. C. Earley, 'Self or group? Cultural effects of training on self-efficacy and performance', *Administrative Science Quarterly*, March 1994, pp. 89–117.

87 B. R. Nathan, A. M. Mohrman, Jr. and J. Milliman, 'Interpersonal relations as a context for the effects of appraisal interviews on performance and satisfaction: a longitudinal study', *Academy of Management Journal*, 34, 2 (1991), pp. 352–69; and Cawley, Keeping and Levy, 'Participation in the performance appraisal process and employee reactions'.

88 C. Soltis, 'Eagle-eyed employers scour résumés for little white lies', *Wall Street Journal*, 21 March 2006, p. B7.

Organizational change and stress management

After studying this chapter, you should be able to:

1 Identify forces that act as stimulants to change and contrast planned and unplanned change.

2 List the forces for resistance to change.

3 Compare the four main approaches to managing organizational change.

4 Demonstrate two ways of creating a culture for change.

5 Define *stress* and identify its potential sources.

6 Identify the consequences of stress.

7 Contrast the individual and organizational approaches to managing stress.

8 Explain global differences in organizational change and work stress.

Nothing endures but change.

Heraclitus

Successful change at the Slovak Ministry of Finance

STR New/Reuters

Martin Ohlidal enjoyed one of the most rewarding jobs in European consulting: the transformation of the Slovak Ministry of Finance into a state of the art institution.

During his term as Slovak Prime Minister from 1998–2006, Mikulas Dzurinda had recast his post-Soviet state into a bastion of liberal economics, with a flat 19 per cent rate of income tax, corporation tax and value-added tax, and economic take-off as a result.

As part of that overhaul, then Finance Minister Ivan Miklo decided to pursue excellence in the way that the Ministry of Finance delivered its services. Mr Ohlidal, who headed the project stated, 'When we made the final presentation, Mr Miklo . . . paused a few seconds, then said: "That all sounds fine; here's what we will do," and detailed how it would be implemented.'

Slovakia's finance minister was concerned with extending private sector practices into a public institution to optimise its efficiency. That is amply demonstrated by one of the consequences of the overhaul. The number of nominal posts among the ministry's 800 staff fell by 250 but the average pay of remaining employees rose by 30 per cent. That resulted not from across the board increases but from the ministry switching to private sector pay rates and hiring talented lawyers and bankers. Overall, the pay bill was unchanged.

The first part of the project occurred when Mr Ohlidal led a 15-strong team that made a detailed audit 'mapping' the existing procedural and organizational structure of the ministry. Though some things worked well, they found inefficiencies, and even a department serving an abolished tier of local government. Reviewing the results, they identified 19 measures to simplify or supplant operations.

Instead of writing 10-page memos detailing objections to change, there was strong support from ministry management, 'People were focused on showing that they can do it', says Mr Ohlidal. 'The client who is not focused on his improvement is a danger. The Slovak Finance Ministry project was really rather special.'

Thanks to the client and consultant working together, says Mr Ohlidal, the ministry is now widely well regarded throughout Europe for its competence and efficiency.

Source: Adapted from R. Tieman, 'Profile: Slovak success story respected across Europe', FT.com, London, UK, 18 November 2005.

The opening vignette example, the Slovak Ministry of Finance, demonstrates that all organizations, even those in traditionally stable environments, will eventually have to change due to external and/or internal demands. In this chapter we describe environmental forces that require managers to implement comprehensive change programmes. We also consider why people and organizations often resist change and how this resistance can be overcome. We review various processes for managing organizational change. We also discuss contemporary change issues for today's managers. Then we move to the topic of stress. We elaborate on the sources and consequences of stress. Finally, we conclude this chapter with a discussion of what individuals and organizations can do to better manage stress levels.

Before we delve into the subject of change, see how well you handle change by taking the following self-assessment.

SELF-ASSESSMENT LIBRARY

How well do I respond to turbulent change?

In the Self-assessment library (available online), take assessment III.C.1 (How well do I respond to turbulent change?) and answer the following questions.

1. How did you score? Are you surprised by your score?

2. During what time of your life have you experienced the most change? How did you deal with it? Would you handle these changes in the same way today? Why or why not?

3. Are there ways you might reduce your resistance to change?

Forces for change

1 Identify forces that act as stimulants to change and contrast planned and unplanned change.

No company today is in a particularly stable environment. Even traditionally stable industries such as energy and utilities have witnessed – and will continue to experience – turbulent change. Companies that occupy a dominant market share in their industries must change, sometimes radically. When Microsoft was struggling with its controversial operating system – Vista – it was also trying to outflank smaller companies such as Google that are increasingly offering free, web-based software packages. How well Microsoft performs is not simply a function of managing one change but a matter of how well it can manage both short-term and long-term changes.

Thus, the dynamic and changing environments that organizations face today require adaptation, sometimes calling for deep and rapid responses. 'Change or die!' is the rallying cry among today's managers worldwide. Table 19.1 summarises six specific forces that are acting as stimulants for change.

In a number of places in this book, we've discussed the *changing nature of the workforce*. For instance, almost every organization is having to adjust to a multicultural environment. Demographic changes, immigration and outsourcing also have transformed the nature of the workforce.

Technology is changing jobs and organizations. Just about the time an organization adapts to one technological change, other technological challenges and opportunities come to the forefront. It is not hard to imagine the very idea of an office becoming an antiquated concept in the near future.

Economic shocks have continued to impose changes on organizations. In recent years, for instance, low interest rates and the ease of obtaining credit first stimulated a rapid rise in home values, helped sustain consumer spending, and benefited many industries, especially

Table 19.1	Forces for change

Force	Examples
Nature of the workforce	More cultural diversity
	Ageing population
	Many new entrants with inadequate skills
Technology	Faster, cheaper and more mobile computers
	Online music sharing
	Deciphering of the human genetic code
Economic shocks	Rise and fall of dot-com stocks
	Global financial crisis
	Record low interest rates
Competition	Global competitors
	Mergers and consolidations
	Growth of e-commerce
Social trends	Internet chat rooms
	Retirement of Baby Boomers
	Rise in discount and 'big box' retailers
World politics	Major growth of democracy during the 20th century
	Opening of markets in China
	War on terrorism

construction and banking. But when the bubble burst, businesses in these same industries and many others suffered.

Competition is changing. The global economy means that competitors are as likely to come from across the ocean as from across town. Heightened competition means that successful organizations will be the ones that can change in response to the competition. They'll be fast on their feet, capable of developing new products rapidly and getting them to market quickly. They'll rely on short production runs, short product cycles, and an ongoing stream of new products. In other words, they'll be flexible. They will require an equally flexible and responsive workforce that can adapt to rapidly and even radically changing conditions.

Social trends don't remain static. For instance, in contrast to just 15 years ago, people are meeting and sharing information in Internet chat rooms; Baby Boomers have begun to retire; and consumers are increasingly doing their shopping at 'big box' retailers and online. McDonald's has undergone major developments to keep up with changing social trends. Historically a basic hamburger restaurant, the company launched McCafe's in response to the 'coffee culture' and to compete with the likes of Starbucks. The restaurants themselves have also been redesigned. The hard furniture used to ensure customers didn't stay long has been replaced by a 'linger' zone with armchairs, sofas and wi-fi connections. When consumers began becoming more concerned about healthy eating, McDonalds got rid of the supersize meals and introduced salads and bags of fruit. Throughout this book we have argued strongly for the importance of seeing OB in a global context. Business schools have been preaching a global perspective since the early 1980s, but no one – not even the strongest proponents of globalisation – could have imagined how *world politics* would change in recent years. We've seen the breakup of the Soviet Union; the opening up of China and southeast Asia; and political instability in many parts of the world. For example, since the 1990s the fall of the Soviet Union, deregulation in India and the full entry of China into the World Trade Organization doubled the potential global labour force.[1]

WOMEN, HOLOGRAMS AND MIGRANTS TO DOMINATE IN WORKPLACE OF 2028

OB IN THE NEWS

An intriguing vision of the UK's future workforce emerged from a raft of research published last week. It appears that in 20 years' time, the UK will be employing more women, more older people, more migrants – and possibly even holograms.

A study by the Chartered Management Institute (CMI) warned that employers needed to better cater for the changing workforce. Its study, *Management Futures*, found that two-thirds of 1,000 employees surveyed believed work teams would become more multi-generational. A spokesman said: 'HR needs to develop "softer" skills [such as being flexible or creative] to meet the needs of mixing generation Y with baby boomers and to develop workforces that are working more remotely and across borders.'

However, professional services firm KPMG warned that once baby boomers left the workforce, the smaller number of younger staff taking their place would lead to a 'demographic fault line'. It said a much greater flow of labour from overseas would be needed to compensate. Bernard Salt, a partner with KPMG in Australia and primary author of the report, said: 'Without a surge in the annual intake of working-age migrants there will be a slow-down, if not a contraction, in the pool from which the labour force is drawn by the middle of the next decade in the UK.'

And much of this migrant influx is likely to be female. Microsoft research revealed that right-brain thinking – allegedly more prevalent in females and often using skills like flexibility and lateral thinking – would dominate business over the next 25 years. Microsoft mobile working expert Jemma Harris said: 'As these skills and creativity become the currency for tomorrow's economy, we'll see a greater shift towards more equal opportunities for women.'

Finally, some 12 per cent of people surveyed by CMI predicted that companies would implant microchips in employee brains to help them remember information, and a third said holograms would be used to conduct meetings.

It's the future, but not as we know it.

Source: L. Peacock, 'Women, holograms and migrants to dominate in workplace of 2028', *Personnel Today*, 6 October 2008.

Planned change

A group of housekeeping employees who work for a small hotel confronted the owner: 'It's very hard for most of us to maintain rigid 7-to-4 work hours,' said their spokeswoman. 'Each of us has significant family and personal responsibilities. And rigid hours don't work for us. We're going to begin looking for someplace else to work if you don't set up flexible work hours.' The owner listened thoughtfully to the group's ultimatum and agreed to its request. The next day, the owner introduced a flextime plan for these employees.

A major automobile manufacturer spent several billion euros to install state-of-the-art robotics. One area that would receive the new equipment was quality control. Sophisticated computer-controlled equipment would be put in place to significantly improve the company's ability to find and correct defects. Because the new equipment would dramatically change the jobs of the people working in the quality-control area, and because management anticipated considerable employee resistance to the new equipment, executives were developing a programme to help people become familiar with the equipment and to deal with any anxieties they might be feeling.

change
Making things different.

planned change
Change activities that are intentional and goal-oriented.

Both of the previous scenarios are examples of **change**. That is, both are concerned with making things different. However, only the second scenario describes a **planned change**. Many changes in organizations are like the one that occurred at the hotel – they just happen. Some organizations treat all change as an accidental occurrence. We're concerned with change activities that are proactive and purposeful. In this chapter, we address change as an intentional, goal-oriented activity.

What are the goals of planned change? Essentially there are two. First, it seeks to improve the ability of the organization to adapt to changes in its environment. Second, it seeks to change employee behaviour.

If an organization is to survive, it must respond to changes in its environment. When competitors introduce new products or services, government agencies enact new laws, important sources of supplies go out of business, or similar environmental changes take place, the

Antonio Calanni/AP/Press Association Images

Fiat Group Automobiles hired an outsider as a change agent to return the ailing company to profitability. As Fiat's new CEO, Sergio Marchionne led a turnaround by changing a hierarchical, status-driven firm into a market-driven one. Marchionne reduced the layers of Fiat's management and fired 10 per cent of its 20,000 white-collar employees. He improved relationships with union employees, reduced car-development time and introduced new car designs.

organization needs to adapt. Efforts to stimulate innovation, empower employees, and introduce work teams are examples of planned-change activities directed at responding to changes in the environment.

Because an organization's success or failure is essentially due to the things that its employees do or fail to do, planned change also is concerned with changing the behaviour of individuals and groups within the organization. Later in this chapter, we review a number of techniques that organizations can use to get people to behave differently in the tasks they perform and in their interactions with others.

Who in organizations is responsible for managing change activities? The answer is **change agents**.[2] Change agents can be managers or nonmanagers, current employees of the organization, newly hired employees, or outside consultants. A contemporary example of a change agent is Lawrence Summers, former president of Harvard University.[3] When he accepted the presidency in 2001, Summers aggressively sought to shake up the complacent institution by, among other things, leading the battle to reshape the undergraduate curriculum, proposing that the university be more directly engaged with problems in education and public health, and reorganizing to consolidate more power in the president's office. His change efforts generated tremendous resistance, particularly among Harvard faculty. Finally, in 2006, when Summers made comments suggesting that women were less able to excel in science than men, the Harvard faculty revolted, and in a few weeks, Summers was forced to resign. Despite Summer's support among students – a poll shortly before his resignation showed that students supported him by a 3:1 ratio – his efforts at change had ruffled one too many feathers. In 2007, he was replaced with Drew Gilpin Faust, Harvard's first female president, who promised to be less aggressive in instituting changes.[4]

Summers's case shows that many change agents fail because organizational members resist change. In the next section, we discuss resistance to change and what can be done about it.

Resistance to change

2 List the forces for resistance to change.

One of the most well-documented findings from studies of individual and organizational behaviour is that organizations and their members resist change. One recent study showed that even when employees are shown data that suggest they need to change, they latch onto whatever data they can find that suggest they are okay and don't need to change. Our egos are fragile, and we often see change as threatening.[5]

In some ways, resistance to change is positive. It provides a degree of stability and predictability to behaviour. If there weren't some resistance, organizational behaviour would take on the characteristics of chaotic randomness. Resistance to change can also be a source of functional conflict. For example, resistance to a reorganization plan or a change in a product line can stimulate a healthy debate over the merits of the idea and result in a better decision. But there is a definite downside to resistance to change. It hinders adaptation and progress.

Resistance to change doesn't necessarily surface in standardised ways. Resistance can be overt, implicit, immediate or deferred. It's easiest for management to deal with resistance when it is overt and immediate. For instance, a change is proposed and employees quickly respond by voicing complaints, engaging in a work slowdown, threatening to go on strike, or the like. The greater challenge is managing resistance that is implicit or deferred. Implicit resistance efforts are more subtle – loss of loyalty to the organization, loss of motivation to work, increased errors or mistakes, increased absenteeism due to 'sickness' – and hence are more difficult to recognise. Similarly, deferred actions cloud the link between the source of the resistance and the reaction to it. A change may produce what appears to be only a minimal reaction at the time it is

EXHIBIT 19.1	SOURCES OF RESISTANCE TO CHANGE

Individual sources

Habit – To cope with life's complexities, we rely on habits or programmed responses. But when confronted with change, this tendency to respond in our accustomed ways becomes a source of resistance.

Security – People with a high need for security are likely to resist change because it threatens their feelings of safety.

Economic factors – Changes in job tasks or established work routines can arouse economic fears if people are concerned that they won't be able to perform the new tasks or routines to their previous standards, especially when pay is closely tied to productivity.

Fear of the unknown – Change substitutes ambiguity and uncertainty for the known.

Selective information processing – Individuals are guilty of selectively processing information in order to keep their perceptions intact. They hear what they want to hear, and they ignore information that challenges the world they've created.

Organizational sources

Structural inertia – Organizations have built-in mechanisms – such as their selection processes and formalised regulations – to produce stability. When an organization is confronted with change, this structural inertia acts as a counterbalance to sustain stability.

Limited focus of change – Organizations are made up of a number of interdependent subsystems. One can't be changed without affecting the others. So limited changes in subsystems tend to be nullified by the larger system.

Group inertia – Even if individuals want to change their behaviour, group norms may act as a constraint.

Threat to expertise – Changes in organizational patterns may threaten the expertise of specialised groups.

Threat to established power relationships – Any redistribution of decision-making authority can threaten long-established power relationships within the organization.

Threat to established resource allocations – Groups in the organization that control sizeable resources often see change as a threat. They tend to be content with the way things are.

initiated, but then resistance surfaces weeks, months, or even years later. Or a single change that in and of itself might have little impact becomes the straw that breaks the camel's back. Reactions to change can build up and then explode in some response that seems totally out of proportion to the change action it follows. The resistance, of course, has merely been deferred and stockpiled. What surfaces is a response to an accumulation of previous changes.

Exhibit 19.1 summarises major forces for resistance to change, categorised by individual and organizational sources. Individual sources of resistance reside in basic human characteristics such as perceptions, personalities, and needs. Organizational sources reside in the structural makeup of organizations themselves.

Before we move on to ways to overcome resistance to change, it's important to note that not all change is good. Research has shown that sometimes an emphasis on making speedy decisions can lead to bad decisions. Sometimes the line between resisting needed change and falling into a 'speed trap' is a fine one indeed. What's more, sometimes in the 'fog of change', those who are initiating change fail to realise the full magnitude of the effects they are causing or to estimate their true costs to the organization. Thus, although the perspective generally taken is that rapid, transformational change is good, this is not always the case. Some organizations, such as Baring Brothers Bank in the United Kingdom, have collapsed for this reason.[6] Change agents need to carefully think through the full implications.

Overcoming resistance to change

Seven tactics have been suggested for use by change agents in dealing with resistance to change.[7] Let's review them briefly.

Education and communication

Resistance can be reduced through communicating with employees to help them see the logic of a change. Communication can reduce resistance on two levels. First, it fights the effects of misinformation and poor communication: If employees receive the full facts and get any mis-understandings cleared up, resistance should subside. Second, communication can be helpful in 'selling' the need for change. Indeed, research shows that the way the need for change is sold matters – change is more likely when the necessity of changing is packaged properly.[8] A study of German companies revealed that changes are most effective when a company communicates its rationale balancing various stakeholder (shareholders, employees, community, customers) interests versus a rationale based on shareholder interests only.[9]

Participation

It's difficult for individuals to resist a change decision in which they participated. Prior to making a change, those opposed can be brought into the decision process. Assuming that the participants have the expertise to make a meaningful contribution, their involvement can reduce resistance, obtain commitment and increase the quality of the change decision. However, against these advantages are the negatives: potential for a poor solution and great consumption of time.

Building support and commitment

Change agents can offer a range of supportive efforts to reduce resistance. When employees' fear and anxiety are high, employee counselling and therapy, new-skills training or a short paid leave of absence may facilitate adjustment. Research on middle managers has shown that when managers or employees have low emotional commitment to change, they favour the status quo and resist it.[10] So, firing up employees can also help them emotionally commit to the change rather than embrace the status quo.

Implementing changes fairly

Try as managers might to have employees see change positively, most workers tend to react negatively. Most people simply don't like change. But one way organizations can minimise the negative impact of change, even when employees frame it as a negative, is to makes sure the change is implemented fairly. As we learned in Chapter 6, procedural fairness becomes especially important when employees perceive an outcome as negative, so when implementing changes, it's crucial that organizations bend over backwards to make sure employees see the reason for the change, and perceive that the changes are being implemented consistently and fairly.[11]

Manipulation and cooptation

Manipulation refers to covert influence attempts. Twisting and distorting facts to make them appear more attractive, withholding undesirable information and creating false rumours to get employees to accept a change are all examples of manipulation. If corporate management threatens to close down a particular manufacturing plant if that plant's employees fail to accept an across-the-board pay cut, and if the threat is actually untrue, management is using manipulation. *Cooptation*, on the other hand, is a form of both manipulation and participation. It seeks to 'buy off' the leaders of a resistance group by giving them a key role in the change decision. The leaders' advice is sought, not to seek a better decision, but to get their endorsement. Both manipulation and cooptation are relatively inexpensive and easy ways to gain the support of adversaries, but the tactics can backfire if the targets become aware that they are being tricked or used. Once discovered, the change agent's credibility may drop to zero.

Selecting people who accept change

Research suggests that the ability to easily accept and adapt to change is related to personality – some people simply have more positive attitudes about change than others.[12] It appears that people who adjust best to change are those who are open to experience, take a positive attitude toward change, are willing to take risks, and are flexible in their behaviour. One study of managers in Europe, the United States and Asia found that those with a positive self-concept and high risk tolerance coped better with organizational change. The study authors suggested that organizations could facilitate the change process by selecting people who score high on these characteristics. Another study found that selecting people based on a resistance-to-change scale worked well in winnowing out those who tended to react emotionally to change or to be rigid.[13]

Coercion

Last on the list of tactics is coercion; that is, the application of direct threats or force on the resisters. If the corporate management mentioned in the previous discussion really is determined to close a manufacturing plant if employees don't acquiesce to a pay cut, then coercion would be the label attached to its change tactic. Other examples of coercion are threats of transfer, loss of promotions, negative performance evaluations and a poor letter of recommendation. The advantages and drawbacks of coercion are approximately the same as those mentioned for manipulation and cooptation.

The politics of change

No discussion of resistance to change would be complete without a brief mention of the politics of change. Because change invariably threatens the status quo, it inherently implies political activity.[14]

Internal change agents typically are individuals high in the organization who have a lot to lose from change. They have, in fact, risen to their positions of authority by developing skills and behavioural patterns that are favoured by the organization. Change is a threat to those skills and patterns. What if they are no longer the ones the organization values? Change creates the potential for others in the organization to gain power at their expense.

Politics suggests that the impetus for change is more likely to come from outside change agents, employees who are new to the organization (and have less invested in the status quo), or from managers slightly removed from the main power structure. Managers who have spent their entire careers with a single organization and eventually achieve a senior position in the hierarchy are often major impediments to change. Change, itself, is a very real threat to their status and position. Yet they may be expected to implement changes to demonstrate that they're not merely caretakers. By acting as change agents, they can symbolically convey to various constituencies – shareholders, suppliers, employees, customers – that they are on top of problems and adapting to a dynamic environment. Of course, as you might guess, when forced to introduce change, these long-time power holders tend to implement incremental changes. Radical change is too threatening.

Power struggles within the organization will determine, to a large degree, the speed and quantity of change. You should expect that long-time career executives will be sources of resistance. This, incidentally, explains why boards of directors that recognise the imperative for the rapid introduction of radical change in their organizations frequently turn to outside candidates for new leadership.[15]

'CHANGE IS EASIER WHEN YOU ARE IN A CRISIS'   MYTH *OR* SCIENCE?

Not according to consultant Steve Crom. He writes that it is true that a crisis can galvanise people into dramatic action. But, does it bring out the best in the greatest number of people? Under stress, most people become more entrenched and are actually less open to learning.

Granted, renewing a business that is prosperous is difficult because it is easy to become complacent, to lose focus. However, if managers handle change properly, prosperity allows them the time to bring people along with them. That is the key to sustainable change. The challenge is to create a sense of urgency for change during times of success. A sense of urgency pushes people out of their comfort zone into the so-called innovation zone, where they are willing to move into something new and try new behaviours while leaving behind the situation that made them feel comfortable and secure. By contrast, in a crisis, people are always in danger of falling too far out of their comfort zone and into the panic zone, where fear either paralyses them or drives them away.

Source: S. Crom, 'Dispelling several myths about leadership for change'. Available at: http://europe.isixsigma.com/library/content/c060222b.asp. Accessed 10 May 2009.

Approaches to managing organizational change

3 Compare the four main approaches to managing organizational change.

Now we turn to several approaches to managing change: Lewin's classic three-step model of the change process, Kotter's eight-step plan, action research and organizational development.

MANAGING CHANGE

FACE THE FACTS

The following are results from a study of 479 managers

- Two-thirds believed that managing change was their biggest challenge
- More than 80 per cent of the respondent's organizations reported some form of change over the past two years

- Common pitfalls of managing change included a failure to maintain momentum (58 per cent), not consolidating benefits (64 per cent), failing to manage employee motivation (65 per cent), and not learning from any changes (71 per cent).

Source: L. Peacock, 'Change management is human resources' biggest challenge', *Personnel Today*, 11 February 2008.

Lewin's three-step model

unfreezing
Changing to overcome the pressures of both individual resistance and group conformity.

movement
A change process that transforms the organization from the status quo to a desired end state.

refreezing
Stabilizing a change intervention by balancing driving and restraining forces.

driving forces
Forces that direct behaviour away from the status quo.

restraining forces
Forces that hinder movement from the existing equilibrium.

Kurt Lewin argued that successful change in organizations should follow three steps: **unfreezing** the status quo, **movement** to a desired end state, and **refreezing** the new change to make it permanent[16] (see Figure 19.1). The value of this model can be seen in the following example, when the management of a large oil company decided to reorganize its marketing function in the western United States.

The oil company had three divisional offices in the west, located in Seattle, San Francisco and Los Angeles. The decision was made to consolidate the divisions into a single regional office to be located in San Francisco. The reorganization meant transferring more than 150 employees, eliminating some duplicate managerial positions, and instituting a new hierarchy of command. As you might guess, a move of this magnitude was difficult to keep secret. The rumour of its occurrence preceded the announcement by several months. The decision itself was made unilaterally. It came from the executive offices in New York. The people affected had no say whatsoever in the choice. For those in Seattle or Los Angeles, who may have disliked the decision and its consequences – the problems inherent in transferring to another city, pulling youngsters out of school, making new friends, having new co-workers, undergoing the reassignment of responsibilities – their only recourse was to quit. In actuality, fewer than 10 per cent did.

The status quo can be considered to be an equilibrium state. To move from this equilibrium – to overcome the pressures of both individual resistance and group conformity – unfreezing is necessary. It can be achieved in one of three ways (see Figure 19.2). The **driving forces**, which direct behaviour away from the status quo, can be increased. The **restraining forces**, which hinder movement from the existing equilibrium, can be decreased. A third alternative is to combine the first two approaches. Companies that have been successful in the past are likely to encounter restraining forces because people question the need for change.[17] Similarly, research shows that companies with strong cultures excel at incremental change but are overcome by restraining forces against radical change.[18]

| **Figure 19.1** | Lewin's three-step change model |

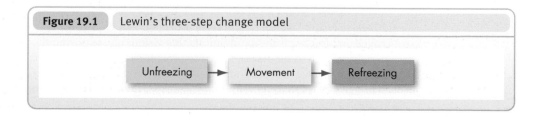

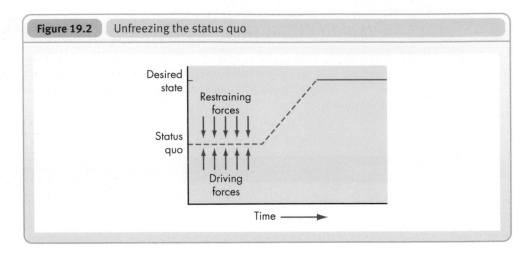

Figure 19.2 Unfreezing the status quo

The oil company's management could expect employee resistance to the consolidation. To deal with that resistance, management could use positive incentives to encourage employees to accept the change. For instance, increases in pay can be offered to those who accept the transfer. Very liberal moving expenses can be paid by the company. Management might offer low-cost mortgage funds to allow employees to buy new homes in San Francisco. Of course, management might also consider unfreezing acceptance of the status quo by removing restraining forces. Employees could be counselled individually. Each employee's concerns and apprehensions could be heard and specifically clarified. Assuming that most of the fears are unjustified, the counsellor could assure the employees that there was nothing to fear and then demonstrate, through tangible evidence, that restraining forces are unwarranted. If resistance is extremely high, management may have to resort to both reducing resistance and increasing the attractiveness of the alternative if the unfreezing is to be successful.

Research on organizational change has shown that, to be effective, change has to happen quickly.[19] Organizations that build up to change do less well than those that get to and through the movement stage quickly.

Once the consolidation change has been implemented, if it is to be successful, the new situation needs to be refrozen so that it can be sustained over time. Unless this last step is taken, there is a very high chance that the change will be short-lived and that employees will attempt to revert to the previous equilibrium state. The objective of refreezing, then, is to stabilise the new situation by balancing the driving and restraining forces.

How could the oil company's management refreeze its consolidation change? By systematically replacing temporary forces with permanent ones. For instance, management might impose a permanent upward adjustment of salaries. The formal rules and regulations governing behaviour of those affected by the change should also be revised to reinforce the new situation. Over time, of course, the work group's own norms will evolve to sustain the new equilibrium. But until that point is reached, management will have to rely on more formal mechanisms.

Kotter's eight-step plan for implementing change

John Kotter built on Lewin's three-step model to create a more detailed approach for implementing change.[20] Kotter began by listing common failures that managers make when trying to initiate change. These included the inability to create a sense of urgency about the need for change, failure to create a coalition for managing the change process, the absence of a vision for change and to effectively communicate that vision, not removing obstacles that could impede the achievement of the vision, failure to provide short-term and achievable goals, the tendency to declare victory too soon, and not anchoring the changes into the organization's culture.

Kotter then established eight sequential steps to overcome these problems. They're listed in Exhibit 19.2.

EXHIBIT 19.2	KOTTER'S EIGHT-STEP PLAN FOR IMPLEMENTING CHANGE

1. Establish a sense of urgency by creating a compelling reason for why change is needed.

2. Form a coalition with enough power to lead the change.

3. Create a new vision to direct the change and strategies for achieving the vision.

4. Communicate the vision throughout the organization.

5. Empower others to act on the vision by removing barriers to change and encouraging risk taking and creative problem solving.

6. Plan for, create, and reward short-term 'wins' that move the organization toward the new vision.

7. Consolidate improvements, reassess changes, and make necessary adjustments in the new programmes.

8. Reinforce the changes by demonstrating the relationship between new behaviours and organizational success.

Source: Reprinted by permission of Harvard Business School Press. From *Leading Change* by J.P. Kotler, Boston, MA 1996. Copyright © 1996 by the Harvard Business School Publishing Corporation; all rights reserved.

Notice how Exhibit 19.2 builds on Lewin's model. Kotter's first four steps essentially extrapolate on the 'unfreezing' stage. Steps 5 through 7 represent 'movement'. And the final step works on 'refreezing'. So Kotter's contribution lies in providing managers and change agents with a more detailed guide for successfully implementing change.

Action research

action research
A change process based on systematic collection of data and then selection of a change action based on what the analysed data indicate.

Action research refers to a change process based on the systematic collection of data and then selection of a change action based on what the analysed data indicate.[21] Its importance lies in providing a scientific methodology for managing planned change. The process of action research consists of five steps: diagnosis, analysis, feedback, action and evaluation. You'll note that these steps closely parallel the scientific method.

The change agent, often an outside consultant in action research, begins by gathering information about problems, concerns and needed changes from members of the organization. This *diagnosis* is analogous to the physician's search to find specifically what ails a patient. In action research, the change agent asks questions, interviews employees, reviews records and listens to the concerns of employees.

Diagnosis is followed by *analysis*. What problems do people key in on? What patterns do these problems seem to take? The change agent synthesises this information into primary concerns, problem areas, and possible actions.

Action research includes extensive involvement of the change targets. That is, the people who will be involved in any change programme must be actively involved in determining what the problem is and participating in creating the solution. So the third step – *feedback* – requires sharing with employees what has been found from steps one and two. The employees, with the help of the change agent, develop action plans for bringing about any needed change.

Now the *action* part of action research is set in motion. The employees and the change agent carry out the specific actions to correct the problems that have been identified.

The final step, consistent with the scientific underpinnings of action research, is *evaluation* of the action plan's effectiveness. Using the initial data gathered as a benchmark, any subsequent changes can be compared and evaluated.

Action research provides at least two specific benefits for an organization. First, it's problem-focused. The change agent objectively looks for problems, and the type of problem determines the type of change action. Although this may seem intuitively obvious, a lot of change activities aren't done this way. Rather, they're solution-centred. The change agent has a favourite solution – for example, implementing flexitime, teams or a process reengineering programme – and then seeks out problems that the solution fits. Second, because action research so heavily involves employees in the process, resistance to change is reduced. In fact, once employees have actively participated in the feedback stage, the change process typically takes on a momentum of its own. The employees and groups that have been involved become an internal source of sustained pressure to bring about the change.

Organizational development at Boehringer Ingelheim, a global research-based pharmaceutical company, involves the Lead and Learn approach to enhance the company's culture and of working together to realise and deliver value through innovation. The core principles of Lead and Learn encourage increased questioning and seizing opportunities while fostering a culture of shared leadership and learning. Initiatives include intensive employee–supervisor dialogue, coaching and access to a vast range of training courses at the company-owned Boehringer Ingelheim Academy.[22]

TopFoto

Organizational development

No discussion of managing change would be complete without including organizational development. **Organizational development (OD)** is not an easily defined single concept. Rather, it's a term used to encompass a collection of planned-change interventions built on humanistic-democratic values that seek to improve organizational effectiveness and employee well-being.[23]

The OD paradigm values human and organizational growth, collaborative and participative processes, and a spirit of inquiry.[24] The change agent may be directive in OD; however, there is a strong emphasis on collaboration. The following briefly identifies the underlying values in most OD efforts:

organizational development (OD)
A collection of planned change interventions, built on humanistic-democratic values, that seeks to improve organizational effectiveness and employee well-being.

1. **Respect for people.** Individuals are perceived as being responsible, conscientious, and caring. They should be treated with dignity and respect.

2. **Trust and support.** An effective and healthy organization is characterised by trust, authenticity, openness, and a supportive climate.

3. **Power equalisation.** Effective organizations deemphasise hierarchical authority and control.

4. **Confrontation.** Problems shouldn't be swept under the rug. They should be openly confronted.

5. Participation. The more that people who will be affected by a change are involved in the decisions surrounding that change, the more they will be committed to implementing those decisions.

What are some of the OD techniques or interventions for bringing about change? In the following pages, we present six interventions that change agents might consider using.

Sensitivity training

sensitivity training
Training groups that seek to change behaviour through unstructured group interaction.

It can go by a variety of names – **sensitivity training**, laboratory training, encounter groups or T-groups (training groups) – but all refer to a method of changing behaviour through unstructured group interaction.[25] Members are brought together in a free and open environment in which participants discuss themselves and their interactive processes, loosely directed by a professional behavioural scientist. The group is process-oriented, which means that individuals learn through observing and participating rather than being told. The professional creates the opportunity for participants to express their ideas, beliefs and attitudes and does not accept – in fact, overtly rejects – any leadership role.

The objectives of the T-groups are to provide the subjects with increased awareness of their own behaviour and how others perceive them, greater sensitivity to the behaviour of others, and increased understanding of group processes. Specific results sought include increased ability to empathise with others, improved listening skills, greater openness, increased tolerance of individual differences, and improved conflict-resolution skills.

Survey feedback

survey feedback
The use of questionnaires to identify discrepancies among member perceptions; discussion follows, and remedies are suggested.

One tool for assessing attitudes held by organizational members, identifying discrepancies among member perceptions and solving these differences is the **survey feedback** approach.[26]

Everyone in an organization can participate in survey feedback, but of key importance is the organizational family – the manager of any given unit and the employees who report directly to him or her. A questionnaire is usually completed by all members in the organization or unit. Organization members may be asked to suggest questions or may be interviewed to determine what issues are relevant. The questionnaire typically asks members for their perceptions and attitudes on a broad range of topics, including decision-making practices; communication effectiveness; coordination between units; and satisfaction with the organization, job, peers and their immediate supervisor.

The data from this questionnaire are tabulated with data pertaining to an individual's specific 'family' and to the entire organization and then distributed to employees. These data then become the springboard for identifying problems and clarifying issues that may be creating difficulties for people. Particular attention is given to the importance of encouraging discussion and ensuring that discussions focus on issues and ideas and not on attacking individuals.

Finally, group discussion in the survey feedback approach should result in members identifying possible implications of the questionnaire's findings. Are people listening? Are new ideas being generated? Can decision making, interpersonal relations or job assignments be improved? Answers to questions like these, it is hoped, will result in the group agreeing on commitments to various actions that will remedy the problems that are identified.

Process consultation

process consultation (PC)
A meeting in which a consultant assists a client in understanding process events with which he or she must deal and identifying processes that need improvement.

No organization operates perfectly. Managers often sense that their unit's performance can be improved, but they're unable to identify what can be improved and how it can be improved. The purpose of **process consultation (PC)** is for an outside consultant to assist a client, usually a manager, 'to perceive, understand and act upon process events' with which the manager must deal.[27] These might include work flow, informal relationships among unit members, and formal communication channels.

PC is similar to sensitivity training in its assumption that organizational effectiveness can be improved by dealing with interpersonal problems and in its emphasis on involvement. But PC is more task-directed than is sensitivity training. Consultants in PC are there to 'give the client "insight" into what is going on around him, within him, and between him and other people.'[28] They do not solve the organization's problems. Rather, the consultant is a guide or coach who advises on the process to help the client solve his or her own problems. The consultant works

An innovative team building experience is provided by Italian Secrets, a self-styled corporate cookery centre. The firm offers groups of business people the opportunity to cook a three course gourmet meal. The main theory that owner Anna Venturi works on is that 'cooking brings together young and old, male and female, secretaries and senior managers'. A family catering company by trade, the Venturis have welcomed teams from Goldman Sachs, Coca-Cola and KPMG.[29]

Foodpix/Getty Images

with the client in *jointly* diagnosing what processes need improvement. The emphasis is on 'jointly' because the client develops a skill at analysing processes within his or her unit that can be continually called on long after the consultant is gone. In addition, by having the client actively participate in both the diagnosis and the development of alternatives, there will be greater understanding of the process and the remedy and less resistance to the action plan chosen.

Team building

team building
High interaction among team members to increase trust and openness.

As we've noted in numerous places throughout this book, organizations are increasingly relying on teams to accomplish work tasks. **Team building** uses high-interaction group activities to increase trust and openness among team members.[30] Team building can be applied within groups or at the intergroup level, at which activities are interdependent. For our discussion, we emphasise the intragroup level and leave intergroup development to the next section. As a result, our interest concerns applications to organizational families (command groups), as well as to committees, project teams, self-managed teams and task groups. Team building is applicable where group activities are interdependent. The objective is to improve coordinative efforts of members, which will result in increasing the team's performance.

The activities considered in team building typically include goal setting, development of interpersonal relations among team members, role analysis to clarify each member's role and responsibilities, and team process analysis. Of course, team building may emphasise or exclude certain activities, depending on the purpose of the development effort and the specific problems with which the team is confronted. Basically, however, team building attempts to use high inter-action among members to increase trust and openness.

It may be beneficial to begin by having members attempt to define the goals and priorities of the team. This will bring to the surface different perceptions of what the team's purpose may be.

Following this, members can evaluate the team's performance – how effective is the team in structuring priorities and achieving its goals? This should identify potential problem areas. This self-critique discussion of means and ends can be done with members of the total team present or, when large size impinges on a free interchange of views, may initially take place in smaller groups followed by the sharing of their findings with the total team.

Team building can also address itself to clarifying each member's role on the team. Each role can be identified and clarified. Previous ambiguities can be brought to the surface. For some individuals, it may offer one of the few opportunities they have had to think through thoroughly what their job is all about and what specific tasks they are expected to carry out if the team is to optimise its effectiveness.

Intergroup development

A major area of concern in OD is the dysfunctional conflict that exists between groups. As a result, this has been a subject to which change efforts have been directed.

intergroup development
OD efforts to change the attitudes, stereotypes and perceptions that groups have of each other.

Intergroup development seeks to change the attitudes, stereotypes, and perceptions that groups have of each other. For example, in one company, the engineers saw the accounting department as composed of shy and conservative types, and the human resources department as having a bunch of 'ultra-liberals who are more concerned that some protected group of employees might get their feelings hurt than with the company making a profit'. Such stereotypes can have an obvious negative impact on the coordination efforts between the departments.

Although there are several approaches for improving intergroup relations,[31] a popular method emphasises problem solving.[32] In this method, each group meets independently to develop lists of its perception of itself, the other group, and how it believes the other group perceives it. The groups then share their lists, after which similarities and differences are discussed. Differences are clearly articulated, and the groups look for the causes of the disparities.

Are the groups' goals at odds? Were perceptions distorted? On what basis were stereotypes formulated? Have some differences been caused by misunderstandings of intentions? Have words and concepts been defined differently by each group? Answers to questions like these clarify the exact nature of the conflict. Once the causes of the difficulty have been identified, the groups can move to the integration phase – working to develop solutions that will improve relations between the groups. Subgroups, with members from each of the conflicting groups, can now be created for further diagnosis and to begin to formulate possible alternative actions that will improve relations.

APPRECIATIVE INQUIRY HELPS RESOLVE TWO GLOBAL FIRMS' DIFFERENCES

GLOBAL

Tim Haynes, an internal consultant at BP, tells the story:

In 1999, BP acquired a leading global lubricants organization, and found itself needing to marry the two company cultures. Employee morale was decreasing, conversations in meetings were rife with confrontation and cynicism, and, most critically, the business' financial results were deteriorating.

I felt the leadership of the business needed to move away from a combative conversation about which of the two organizations' cultures and practices should prevail, to a participative inquiry into those aspects of both cultures that bring inclusion, engagement, collaboration and performance. AI offered a way to do this – an alternative way of looking at change, and a way to build a new organizational culture through the change process itself . . .

The first step was to hold a two-day workshop based on an AI Discovery design with the extended leadership team. The leaders inquired into the factors and values they felt were present at times when the businesses were high-performing, energised and customer-focused. Over the next eight months, the same inquiry was repeated with groups throughout the business and around the world.

The final session back with the leadership team then allowed them to identify four core values that were shared across all employees in the new organization. They were universal values that everyone could identify with. But the conversational process was more important. It was through conversation that things started to change. In the end, articulating the four values was the icing on the cake. Today, BP is seeing employee morale on the increase and financial performance has stabilised.

Source: C. Vanstone, 'Spirit of appreciation', *Personnel Today*, (first appeared in *Training and Coaching*) 1 September 2004.

Appreciative inquiry

appreciative inquiry (AI)
An approach that seeks to identify the unique qualities and special strengths of an organization, which can then be built on to improve performance.

Most OD approaches are problem-centred. They identify a problem or set of problems, then look for a solution. **Appreciative inquiry (AI)** accentuates the positive.[33] Rather than looking for problems to fix, this approach seeks to identify the unique qualities and special strengths of an organization, which can then be built on to improve performance. That is, it focuses on an organization's successes rather than on its problems.

Advocates of AI argue that problem-solving approaches always ask people to look backward at yesterday's failures, to focus on shortcomings, and rarely result in new visions. Instead of creating a climate for positive change, action research and OD techniques such as survey feedback and process consultation end up placing blame and generating defensiveness. AI proponents claim it makes more sense to refine and enhance what the organization is already doing well. This allows the organization to change by playing to its strengths and competitive advantages.

The AI process essentially consists of four steps, often played out in a large-group meeting over a two- or three-day time period and overseen by a trained change agent. The first step is *discovery*. The idea is to find out what people think are the strengths of the organization. For instance, employees are asked to recount times they felt the organization worked best or when they specifically felt most satisfied with their jobs. The second step is *dreaming*. The information from the discovery phase is used to speculate on possible futures for the organization. For instance, people are asked to envision the organization in five years and to describe what's different. The third step is *design*. Based on the dream articulation, participants focus on finding a common vision of how the organization will look and agree on its unique qualities. The fourth stage seeks to define the organization's *destiny*. In this final step, participants discuss how the organization is going to fulfil its dream. This typically includes the writing of action plans and development of implementation strategies.

AI has proven to be an effective change strategy in organizations such as BP, Nokia and the electrical retailer Currys. For instance, during a three-day AI seminar at a logistics firm, workers were asked to recall ideal work experiences – when they were treated with respect, when trucks were loaded to capacity or arrived on time. Assembled into nine groups, the workers were then encouraged to devise money-saving ideas. A team of short-haul drivers came up with 12 cost-cutting and revenue-generating ideas, one of which could alone generate €750,000 in additional profits.[34]

EXHIBIT 19.3 | **PROBLEM SOLVING VS. APPRECIATIVE ENQUIRY**

The challenge

- Falling customer retention rates
- Increased customer complaints
- Increased turnover of customer-facing staff
- Stories of poor service getting into the public domain

Problem-solving view

- Involve your staff and customers in a rigorous analysis of critical incidents of poor customer service
- Get behind the issues and incidents to understand the root causes of failure
- Tell staff to 'raise their game' and make sure they know how urgent and important change is
- Design solutions that eradicate the causes of these failures
- Implement solutions to achieve improvement

Appreciative inquiry view

- Involve your staff and customers in finding past or present incidents that exemplify the best of what is possible, e.g., great customer service, and analyse those incidents rigorously
- Get behind the incidents of great service, to understand the root causes of real success
- Talk about real (not idealised) success, share stories that set new standards and expectations within the culture
- Design new ways of working that support and amplify the causes of success, making it more likely that these will become commonplace
- Implement those changes and continue to assess how it is working

Source: 'Affirmative action', *Training and Coaching Today*, 1 June 2004.

Creating a culture for change

4 Demonstrate two ways of creating a culture for change.

We've considered how organizations can adapt to change. Recently, some OB scholars have focused on a more proactive approach to change – how organizations can embrace change by transforming their cultures. In this section we review two such approaches: stimulating an innovative culture and creating a learning organization.

Stimulating a culture of innovation

How can an organization become more innovative? An excellent model is W. L. Gore, best known as the maker of Gore-Tex fabric.[35] Gore has developed a reputation as one of the world's most innovative companies (and consistently ranks highly in the European Great Place to Work list[36]) by developing a stream of diverse products – including guitar strings, dental floss, medical devices and fuel cells.

What's the secret of Gore's success? What can other organizations do to duplicate its track record for innovation? Although there is no guaranteed formula, certain characteristics surface again and again when researchers study innovative organizations. We've grouped them into structural, cultural and human resource categories. Our message to change agents is that they should consider introducing these characteristics into their organization if they want to create an innovative climate. Before we look at these characteristics, however, let's clarify what we mean by innovation.

Definition of innovation

innovation
A new idea applied to initiating or improving a product, process or service.

We said change refers to making things different. **Innovation** is a more specialised kind of change. Innovation is a new idea applied to initiating or improving a product, process or service.[37] So all innovations involve change, but not all changes necessarily involve new ideas or lead to significant improvements. Innovations in organizations can range from small incremental improvements, such as Coke's extension of its product line to include Diet Coke and Caffeine-Free Coke, up to radical breakthroughs, such as Toyota's battery-powered Prius.

Sources of innovation

Structural variables have been the most studied potential source of innovation.[38] A comprehensive review of the structure-innovation relationship leads to the following conclusions.[39] First, organic structures positively influence innovation. Because they're lower in vertical differentiation, formalisation and centralisation, organic organizations facilitate the flexibility, adaptation and cross-fertilisation that make the adoption of innovations easier. Second, long tenure in management is associated with innovation. Managerial tenure apparently provides legitimacy and knowledge of how to accomplish tasks and obtain desired outcomes. Third, innovation is nurtured when there are slack resources. Having an abundance of resources allows an organization to afford to purchase innovations, bear the cost of instituting innovations, and absorb failures. Finally, inter-unit communication is high in innovative organizations.[40] These organizations are high users of committees, task forces, cross-functional teams and other mechanisms that facilitate interaction across departmental lines.

Innovative organizations tend to have similar *cultures*. They encourage experimentation. They reward both successes and failures. They celebrate mistakes. Unfortunately, in too many organizations, people are rewarded for the absence of failures rather than for the presence of successes. Such cultures extinguish risk taking and innovation. People will suggest and try new ideas only when they feel such behaviours exact no penalties. Managers in innovative organizations recognise that failures are a natural byproduct of venturing into the unknown.

idea champions
Individuals who take an innovation and actively and enthusiastically promote the idea, build support, overcome resistance and ensure that the idea is implemented.

Within the *human resources* category, we find that innovative organizations actively promote the training and development of their members so that they keep current, offer high job security so employees don't fear getting fired for making mistakes, and encourage individuals to become champions of change. Once a new idea is developed, **idea champions** actively and enthusiastically promote the idea, build support, overcome resistance and ensure that the innovation is implemented.[41] The evidence indicates that champions have common personality characteristics: extremely high self-confidence, persistence, energy and a tendency to take risks. Idea champions also display characteristics associated with transformational leadership. They inspire and energise others with their vision of the potential of an innovation and through their strong personal conviction in their mission. They are also good at gaining the commitment of others to support their mission. In addition, idea champions have jobs that provide considerable decision-making discretion. This autonomy helps them introduce and implement innovations in organizations.[42]

Creating a learning organization

Another way organizations can proactively manage change is to make continuous growth part of its culture – to become a learning organization.[43] And this idea is catching on. A recent survey found that 39 per cent of employees in the European Union are considered to be working in a learning organization.[44] In this section, we describe what a learning organization looks like and methods for managing learning.

What's a learning organization?

A **learning organization** is an organization that has developed the continuous capacity to adapt and change. Just as individuals learn, so too do organizations. 'All organizations learn, whether they consciously choose to or not – it is a fundamental requirement for their sustained existence.'[45] However, some organizations just do it better than others.

Most organizations engage in what has been called **single-loop learning**.[46] When errors are detected, the correction process relies on past routines and present policies. In contrast, learning organizations use **double-loop learning**. When an error is detected, it's corrected in ways that involve the modification of the organization's objectives, policies, and standard routines. Double-loop learning challenges deeply rooted assumptions and norms within an organization. In this way, it provides opportunities for radically different solutions to problems and dramatic jumps in improvement.

Exhibit 19.4 summarises the five basic characteristics of a learning organization. It's an organization in which people put aside their old ways of thinking, learn to be open with each other, understand how their organization really works, form a plan or vision that everyone can agree on, and then work together to achieve that vision.[47]

Proponents of the learning organization envision it as a remedy for three fundamental problems inherent in traditional organizations: fragmentation, competition, and reactiveness.[48] First, *fragmentation* based on specialisation creates 'walls' and 'chimneys' that separate different functions into independent and often warring fiefdoms. Second, an overemphasis on *competition* often undermines collaboration. Members of the management team compete with one another to show who is right, who knows more, or who is more persuasive. Divisions compete with one another when they ought to cooperate and share knowledge. Team project leaders compete to show who the best manager is. And third, *reactiveness* misdirects management's attention to problem solving rather than creation. The problem solver tries to make something go away, while a creator tries to bring something new into being. An emphasis on reactiveness pushes out innovation and continuous improvement and, in its place, encourages people to run around 'putting out fires'.

learning organization
An organization that has developed the continuous capacity to adapt and change.

single-loop learning
A process of correcting errors using past routines and present policies.

double-loop learning
A process of correcting errors by modifying the organization's objectives, policies and standard routines.

EXHIBIT 19.4 | CHARACTERISTICS OF A LEARNING ORGANIZATION

1. There exists a shared vision that everyone agrees on.
2. People discard their old ways of thinking and the standard routines they use for solving problems or doing their jobs.
3. Members think of all organizational processes, activities, functions, and interactions with the environment as part of a system of interrelationships.
4. People openly communicate with each other (across vertical and horizontal boundaries) without fear of criticism or punishment.
5. People sublimate their personal self-interest and fragmented departmental interests to work together to achieve the organization's shared vision.

Source: Based on P. M. Senge, *The Fifth Discipline* (New York: Doubleday, 1990).

Managing learning

How do you change an organization to make it into a continual learner? What can managers do to make their firms learning organizations? The following are some suggestions:

- **Establish a strategy.** Management needs to make explicit its commitment to change, innovation and continuous improvement.

- **Redesign the organization's structure.** The formal structure can be a serious impediment to learning. By flattening the structure, eliminating or combining departments, and increasing the use of cross-functional teams, interdependence is reinforced and boundaries between people are reduced.

- **Reshape the organization's culture.** To become a learning organization, managers need to demonstrate by their actions that taking risks and admitting failures are desirable traits. That means rewarding people who take chances and make mistakes. And management needs to encourage functional conflict. 'The key to unlocking real openness at work,' says one expert on learning organizations, 'is to teach people to give up having to be in agreement. We think agreement is so important. Who cares? You have to bring paradoxes, conflicts and dilemmas out in the open, so collectively we can be more intelligent than we can be individually.'[49]

An excellent illustration of a learning organization is what Richard Clark is trying to do at Merck, one of the largest pharmaceutical companies in the world. In addition to changing Merck's structure so that innovation can come from customers (patients and doctors), Merck is also trying to reward researchers for taking risks, even if their risky ideas end in failure. Merck's transformed strategy, structure and culture may or may not succeed, but that's part of the risk of stimulating change through creating a learning organization.

Work stress and its management

5 Define *stress* and identify its potential sources.

Most of us are aware that employee stress is an increasing problem in organizations. Friends tell us they're stressed out from greater work loads and having to work longer hours because of downsizing at their companies. Parents talk about the lack of job stability in today's world and reminisce about a time when a job with a large company implied lifetime security. We read surveys in which employees complain about the stress created in trying to balance work and family responsibilities.[50] Stress is a big problem across Europe. About 1 in 3 workers in the EU report health problems as a result of stress. And in the UK, for example, an estimated 40 per cent of workplace absence in 2007–2008 was due to stress.[51] In this section we'll look at the causes and consequences of stress, and then consider what individuals and organizations can do to reduce it.

What is stress?

stress
A dynamic condition in which an individual is confronted with an opportunity, a demand, or a resource related to what the individual desires and for which the outcome is perceived to be both uncertain and important.

Stress is a dynamic condition in which an individual is confronted with an opportunity, demand, or resource related to what the individual desires and for which the outcome is perceived to be both uncertain and important.[52] This is a complicated definition. Let's look at its components more closely.

Stress is not necessarily bad in and of itself. Although stress is typically discussed in a negative context, it also has a positive value.[53] It's an opportunity when it offers potential gain. Consider, for example, the superior performance that an athlete or stage performer gives in tense situations. Such individuals often use stress positively to rise to the occasion and perform at or near their maximum. Similarly, many professionals see the pressures of heavy work loads and deadlines as positive challenges that enhance the quality of their work and the satisfaction they get from their job.

challenge stressors
Stressors associated with work load, pressure to complete tasks and time urgency.

In short, some stress can be good, and some can be bad. Recently, researchers have argued that **challenge stressors** – or stressors associated with work load, pressure to complete tasks and time urgency – operate quite differently from **hindrance stressors** – or stressors that keep you from reaching your goals (red tape, office politics, confusion over job responsibilities). Although research on challenge and hindrance stress is just starting to accumulate, early evidence suggests that challenge stressors are less harmful (produce less strain) than hindrance stressors.[54]

More typically, stress is associated with **demands** and **resources**. Demands are responsibilities, pressures, obligations and even uncertainties that individuals face in the workplace. Resources are things within an individual's control that can be used to resolve the demands. This demands–resources model has received increasing support in the literature.[55] Let's discuss what it means.

When you take a test at school or you undergo your annual performance review at work, you feel stress because you confront opportunities and performance pressures. A good performance review may lead to a promotion, greater responsibilities and a higher salary. A poor review may prevent you from getting a promotion. An extremely poor review might even result in your being fired. In such a situation, to the extent that you can apply resources to the demands – such as being prepared, placing the exam or review in perspective, or obtaining social support – you will feel less stress.

Research suggests that adequate resources help reduce the stressful nature of demands when demands and resources match. For example, if emotional demands are stressing you, then having emotional resources in the form of social support is especially important. Conversely, if the demands are cognitive – say, information overload – then job resources in the form of computer support or information are more important. Thus, under the demands and resources perspective on stress, having resources to cope with stress is just as important in offsetting stress as demands are in increasing it.[56]

Potential sources of stress

What causes stress? As the model in Figure 19.3 shows, there are three categories of potential stressors: environmental, organizational and personal. Let's take a look at each.[57]

Environmental factors

Just as environmental uncertainty influences the design of an organization's structure, it also influences stress levels among employees in that organization. Indeed, evidence indicates

hindrance stressors
Stressors that keep you from reaching your goals (red tape, office politics, confusion over job responsibilities).

demands
Responsibilities, pressures, obligations and even uncertainties that individuals face in the workplace.

resources
Things within an individual's control that can be used to resolve demands.

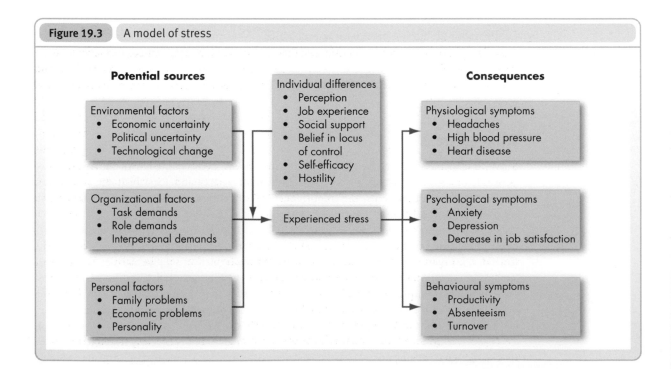

| Figure 19.3 | A model of stress |

that uncertainty is the biggest reason people have trouble coping with organizational changes.[58] There are three main types of environmental uncertainty: economic, political and technological.

Changes in the business cycle create *economic uncertainties*. When the economy is contracting, for example, people become increasingly anxious about their job security. *Political uncertainties* are more pronounced in some countries than others and vary with time. For example the governance of Pakistan, Nepal or Haiti is currently uncertain and leads to stress for people in these countries. Even for countries with relatively stable political systems, such as most European countries, political threats and changes do occur and certainly have in the past, which can induce stress. *Technological change* is a third type of environmental factor that can cause stress. Because new innovations can make an employee's skills and experience obsolete in a very short time, computers, robotics, automation, and similar forms of technological innovation are a threat to many people and cause them stress.

'MEETINGS STRESS PEOPLE OUT' — MYTH *OR* SCIENCE?

As a general rule, this statement is false. A recent investigation revealed that whether you love or hate meetings depends on your work environment, your personality and your attitude about meetings.[59]

In one study of 676 employees, the researchers found that time spent in meetings led to positive reactions (higher job satisfaction, lower depression and intentions to quit) for people whose work was interdependent, but negative reactions for those whose work was independent. This result makes sense in that if you rely on other people to get your work done, meetings are a productive way to exchange information and coordinate efforts. If you do your work independently, however, meetings are likely to simply be interruptions to getting your work done.

Even more interesting were the results of the second study, of 304 employees in the United Kingdom and United States. The researchers found that for accomplishment-oriented people – those who were goal-oriented and hard driving – meetings led to negative reactions. However, for people who scored low on this measure, time spent in meetings was positive.

Finally, the researchers also found in the second study that people's attitudes toward meetings mattered. If people had positive attitudes about meetings, then meetings were more enjoyable and less stressful. For people with negative attitudes, the opposite was true. So, your attitude toward meetings is a bit of a self-fulfilling prophecy: If you think they're a waste of time, they will be.

Organizational factors

There is no shortage of factors within an organization that can cause stress. Pressures to avoid errors or complete tasks in a limited time, work overload, a demanding and insensitive boss, and unpleasant co-workers are a few examples. We've categorised these factors around task, role and interpersonal demands.[60]

Task demands are factors related to a person's job. They include the design of the individual's job (autonomy, task variety, degree of automation), working conditions and the physical work layout. Assembly lines, for instance, can put pressure on people when the line's speed is perceived as excessive. Similarly, working in an overcrowded room or in a visible location where noise and interruptions are constant can increase anxiety and stress.[61] Increasingly, as customer service becomes ever more important, emotional labour is a source of stress.[62] Imagine being a flight attendant for KLM or a hostess at Galeries Lafayette. Do you think you could put on a happy face when you're having a bad day?

Role demands relate to pressures placed on a person as a function of the particular role she plays in the organization. Role conflicts create expectations that may be hard to reconcile or satisfy. Role overload is experienced when the employee is expected to do more than time permits. Role ambiguity is created when role expectations are not clearly understood and the employee is not sure what he or she is to do.

Interpersonal demands are pressures created by other employees. Lack of social support from colleagues and poor interpersonal relationships can cause stress, especially among employees with a high social need.

Personal factors

The typical individual works about 40 to 50 hours a week. But the experiences and problems that people encounter in the other 120-plus nonwork hours each week can spill over to the job. Our final category, then, encompasses factors in the employee's personal life. Primarily, these factors are family issues, personal economic problems and inherent personality characteristics.

National surveys consistently show that people hold *family* and personal relationships dear. Marital difficulties, the breaking off of a relationship and discipline troubles with children are examples of relationship problems that create stress for employees that aren't left at the front door when they arrive at work.[63]

Economic problems created by individuals overextending their financial resources is another set of personal troubles that can create stress for employees and distract their attention from their work. Regardless of income level – people who make €80,000 per year seem to have as much trouble handling their finances as those who earn €18,000 – some people are poor money managers or have wants that always seem to exceed their earning capacity.

Studies in three diverse organizations found that stress symptoms reported prior to beginning a job accounted for most of the variance in stress symptoms reported nine months later.[64] This led the researchers to conclude that some people may have an inherent tendency to accentuate negative aspects of the world in general. If this is true, then a significant individual factor that influences stress is a person's basic disposition. That is, stress symptoms expressed on the job may actually originate in the person's *personality*.

Stressors are additive

A fact that tends to be overlooked when stressors are reviewed individually is that stress is an additive phenomenon.[65] Stress builds up. Each new and persistent stressor adds to an individual's stress level. So a single stressor may be relatively unimportant in and of itself, but if it's added to an already high level of stress, it can be 'the straw that breaks the camel's back'. If we want to appraise the total amount of stress an individual is under, we have to sum up their opportunity stresses, constraint stresses and demand stresses.

Individual differences

Some people thrive on stressful situations, while others are overwhelmed by them. What is it that differentiates people in terms of their ability to handle stress? What individual difference variables moderate the relationship between *potential* stressors and *experienced* stress? At least four variables – perception, job experience, social support and personality – have been found to be relevant moderators.

In Chapter 5, we demonstrated that employees react in response to their perception of reality rather than to reality itself. *Perception*, therefore, will moderate the relationship between a potential stress condition and an employee's reaction to it. For example, one person's fear that they'll lose their job because their company is laying off personnel may be perceived by another as an opportunity to get a large redundancy payment and start their own business. So stress potential doesn't lie in objective conditions; it lies in an employee's interpretation of those conditions.

The evidence indicates that *experience* on the job tends to be negatively related to work stress. Why? Two explanations have been offered.[66] First is the idea of selective withdrawal. Voluntary turnover is more probable among people who experience more stress. Therefore, people who remain with an organization longer are those with more stress-resistant traits or those who are more resistant to the stress characteristics of their organization. Second, people eventually develop coping mechanisms to deal with stress. Because this takes time, senior members of the organization are more likely to be fully adapted and should experience less stress.

There is increasing evidence that *social support* – that is, collegial relationships with co-workers or supervisors – can buffer the impact of stress.[67] The logic underlying this moderating variable is that social support acts as a palliative, mitigating the negative effects of even high-strain jobs.

Personality also affects the degree to which people experience stress and how they cope with it. Perhaps the most widely studied personality trait in stress is *Type A personality*, which we discussed in Chapter 4. Type A – particularly that aspect of Type A that manifests itself in hostility and anger – is associated with increased levels of stress and risk for heart disease.[68] More specifically, people who are quick to anger, maintain a persistently hostile outlook and project a cynical mistrust of others are at increased risk of experiencing stress in situations.

SELF-ASSESSMENT LIBRARY

How stressful is my life?

In the Self-assessment library (available online), take assessment III.C.2 (How stressful is my life?).

Consequences of stress

6 Identify the consequences of stress.

Stress shows itself in a number of ways. For instance, an individual who is experiencing a high level of stress may develop high blood pressure, ulcers, irritability, difficulty making routine decisions, loss of appetite, accident-proneness and the like. These symptoms can be subsumed under three general categories: physiological, psychological, and behavioral symptoms.[69]

Physiological symptoms

Most of the early concern with stress was directed at physiological symptoms. This was predominantly due to the fact that the topic was researched by specialists in the health and medical sciences. This research led to the conclusion that stress could create changes in metabolism, increase heart and breathing rates, increase blood pressure, bring on headaches and induce heart attacks.

The link between stress and particular physiological symptoms is not clear. Traditionally, researchers concluded that there were few, if any, consistent relationships.[70] This is attributed to the complexity of the symptoms and the difficulty of objectively measuring them. More recently, some evidence suggests that stress may have harmful physiological effects. For example, one recent study linked stressful job demands to increased susceptibility to upper respiratory illnesses and poor immune system functioning, especially for individuals who had low self-efficacy.[71]

Psychological symptoms

Stress can cause dissatisfaction. Job-related stress can cause job-related dissatisfaction. Job dissatisfaction, in fact, is 'the simplest and most obvious psychological effect' of stress.[72] But stress shows itself in other psychological states – for instance, tension, anxiety, irritability, boredom and procrastination.

The evidence indicates that when people are placed in jobs that make multiple and conflicting demands or in which there is a lack of clarity about the incumbent's duties, authority, and responsibilities, both stress and dissatisfaction are increased.[73] Similarly, the less control people have over the pace of their work, the greater the stress and dissatisfaction. Although more research is needed to clarify the relationship, the evidence suggests that jobs that provide a low level of variety, significance, autonomy, feedback and identity to incumbents create stress and reduce satisfaction and involvement in the job.[74]

Behavioural symptoms

Behaviour-related stress symptoms include changes in productivity, absence and turnover, as well as changes in eating habits, increased smoking or consumption of alcohol, rapid speech, fidgeting and sleep disorders.[75]

There has been a significant amount of research investigating the stress–performance relationship. The most widely studied pattern in the stress–performance literature is the inverted-U relationship.[76] This is shown in Figure 19.4.

The logic underlying the inverted U is that low to moderate levels of stress stimulate the body and increase its ability to react. Individuals then often perform their tasks better, more intensely,

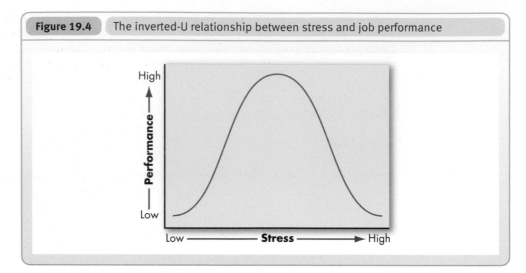

Figure 19.4 The inverted-U relationship between stress and job performance

or more rapidly. But too much stress places unattainable demands on a person, which result in lower performance. This inverted-U pattern may also describe the reaction to stress over time as well as to changes in stress intensity. That is, even moderate levels of stress can have a negative influence on performance over the long term as the continued intensity of the stress wears down the individual and saps energy resources. An athlete may be able to use the positive effects of stress to obtain higher performance during every game, or a sales executive may be able to psych herself up for her presentation at the annual national meeting. But moderate levels of stress experienced continually over long periods, as typified by the emergency room staff in a large urban hospital, can result in lower performance. This may explain why emergency room staffs at such hospitals are frequently rotated and why it is unusual to find individuals who have spent the bulk of their career in such an environment. In effect, to do so would expose the individual to the risk of 'career burnout'.

In spite of the popularity and intuitive appeal of the inverted-U model, it doesn't get a lot of empirical support.[77] At this time, managers should be careful in assuming that this model accurately depicts the stress–performance relationship.

Managing stress

7 Contrast the individual and organizational approaches to managing stress.

From the organization's standpoint, management may not be concerned when employees experience low to moderate levels of stress. The reason, as we showed earlier, is that such levels of stress may be functional and lead to higher employee performance. But high levels of stress, or even low levels sustained over long periods, can lead to reduced employee performance and, thus, require action by management.

Although a limited amount of stress may benefit an employee's performance, don't expect employees to see it that way. From the individual's standpoint, even low levels of stress are likely to be perceived as undesirable. It's not unlikely, therefore, for employees and management to have different notions of what constitutes an acceptable level of stress on the job. What management may consider to be 'a positive stimulus that keeps the adrenalin running' is very likely to be seen as 'excessive pressure' by the employee. Keep this in mind as we discuss individual and organizational approaches toward managing stress.[78]

Individual approaches

An employee can take personal responsibility for reducing stress levels. Individual strategies that have proven effective include implementing time-management techniques, increasing physical exercise, relaxation training and expanding the social support network.

Many people manage their time poorly. The well-organized employee, like the well-organized student, can often accomplish twice as much as the person who is poorly organized. So an understanding and utilisation of basic *time-management* principles can help individuals better cope with tensions created by job demands.[79] A few of the most well-known time-management principles are (1) making daily lists of activities to be accomplished; (2) prioritising activities by importance and urgency; (3) scheduling activities according to the priorities set; and (4) knowing your daily cycle and handling the most demanding parts of your job during the high part of your cycle, when you are most alert and productive.[80]

Physicians have recommended noncompetitive physical exercise, such as aerobics, walking, jogging, swimming and riding a bicycle, as a way to deal with excessive stress levels. These forms of *physical exercise* increase heart capacity, lower the at-rest heart rate, provide a mental diversion from work pressures, and offer a means to 'let off steam'.[81]

Individuals can teach themselves to reduce tension through *relaxation techniques* such as meditation, hypnosis, and biofeedback. The objective is to reach a state of deep relaxation, in which one feels physically relaxed, somewhat detached from the immediate environment, and detached from body sensations.[82] Deep relaxation for 15 or 20 minutes a day releases tension and provides a person with a pronounced sense of peacefulness. Importantly, significant changes in heart rate, blood pressure and other physiological factors result from achieving the condition of deep relaxation.

As we noted earlier in this chapter, having friends, family or work colleagues to talk to provides an outlet when stress levels become excessive. Expanding your *social support network*, therefore, can be a means for tension reduction. It provides you with someone to hear your problems and to offer a more objective perspective on the situation.

Organizational approaches

Several of the factors that cause stress – particularly task and role demands – are controlled by management. As such, they can be modified or changed. Strategies that management might want to consider include improved personnel selection and job placement, training, use of realistic goal setting, redesigning of jobs, increased employee involvement, improved organizational communication and establishment of corporate wellness programmes.

Certain jobs are more stressful than others but, as we learned earlier in this chapter, individuals differ in their response to stressful situations. We know, for example, that individuals with little experience or an external locus of control tend to be more prone to stress. *Selection and placement* decisions should take these facts into consideration. Obviously, management shouldn't restrict hiring to only experienced individuals with an internal locus, but such individuals may adapt better to high-stress jobs and perform those jobs more effectively. Similarly, *training* can increase an individual's self-efficacy and thus lessen job strain.

We discussed *goal setting* in Chapter 6. Based on an extensive amount of research, we concluded that individuals perform better when they have specific and challenging goals and receive feedback on how well they are progressing toward these goals. The use of goals can reduce stress as well as provide motivation. Specific goals that are perceived as attainable clarify performance expectations. In addition, goal feedback reduces uncertainties about actual job performance. The result is less employee frustration, role ambiguity and stress.

Redesigning jobs to give employees more responsibility, more meaningful work, more autonomy and increased feedback can reduce stress because these factors give the employee greater control over work activities and lessen dependence on others. But as we noted in our discussion of work design, not all employees want enriched jobs. The right redesign, then, for employees with a low need for growth might be less responsibility and increased specialisation. If individuals prefer structure and routine, reducing skill variety should also reduce uncertainties and stress levels.

Role stress is detrimental to a large extent because employees feel uncertain about goals, expectations, how they'll be evaluated and the like. By giving these employees a voice in the decisions that directly affect their job performance, management can increase employee control and reduce this role stress. So managers should consider *increasing employee involvement* in decision making.[83]

Increasing formal *organizational communication* with employees reduces uncertainty by lessening role ambiguity and role conflict. Given the importance that perceptions play in moderating the stress–response relationship, management can also use effective communications as a means to shape employee perceptions. Remember that what employees categorise as demands, threats, or opportunities are merely an interpretation, and that interpretation can be affected by the symbols and actions communicated by management.

Our final suggestion is to offer organizationally supported **wellness programmes**. These programmes focus on the employee's total physical and mental condition.[84] For example, they typically provide workshops to help people quit smoking, control alcohol use, lose weight, eat better and develop a regular exercise programme. The assumption underlying most wellness programmes is that employees need to take personal responsibility for their physical and mental health. The organization is merely a vehicle to facilitate this end.

wellness programmes
Organizationally supported programmes that focus on the employee's total physical and mental condition.

Global implications

8 Explain global differences in organizational change and work stress

Organizational change

A number of change issues we've discussed in this chapter are culture bound. To illustrate, let's briefly look at five questions: (1) Do people believe change is possible? (2) If it's possible, how long will it take to bring it about? (3) Is resistance to change greater in some cultures than in others? (4) Does culture influence how change efforts will be implemented? (5) Do successful idea champions do things differently in different cultures?

Do people believe change is possible? Remember that cultures vary in terms of beliefs about their ability to control their environment. In cultures in which people believe that they can dominate their environment, individuals will take a proactive view of change. This, for example, would describe most western European countries. In many other countries, such as Iran and Saudi Arabia, people see themselves as subjugated to their environment and thus will tend to take a passive approach toward change.

If change is possible, how long will it take to bring it about? A culture's time orientation can help us answer this question. Societies that focus on the long term, such as China and Japan, will demonstrate considerable patience while waiting for positive outcomes from change efforts. In societies with a short-term focus, such as Germany, the United Kingdom and the United States, people expect quick improvements and will seek change programmes that promise fast results.

Is resistance to change greater in some cultures than in others? Resistance to change will be influenced by a society's reliance on tradition. Italy, as an example, tends to focus on the past because of strong traditions, whereas in the US, adults tend to emphasise the present. Italians, therefore, may generally be more resistant to change efforts than their US counterparts.

Does culture influence how change efforts will be implemented? Power distance can help with this issue. In high-power-distance cultures, such as Spain or Thailand, change efforts will tend to be autocratically implemented by top management. In contrast, low-power-distance cultures value democratic methods. We'd predict, therefore, a greater use of participation in countries such as Denmark and the Netherlands.

Finally, do successful idea champions do things differently in different cultures? Yes.[85] People in collectivist cultures prefer appeals for cross-functional support for innovation efforts; people in high-power-distance cultures prefer champions to work closely with those in authority to approve innovative activities before work is begun; and the higher the uncertainty avoidance of a society, the more champions should work within the organization's rules and procedures to develop the innovation. These findings suggest that effective managers will alter their organization's championing strategies to reflect cultural values. So, for instance, although idea champions in Russia might succeed by ignoring budgetary limitations and working around confining procedures, champions in Austria, Denmark, Germany or other cultures high in uncertainty avoidance may be more effective by closely following budgets and procedures.

Stress

In considering global differences in stress, there are three questions to answer: (1) Do the causes of stress vary across countries? (2) Do the outcomes of stress vary across cultures? (3) Do the factors that lessen the effects of stress vary by culture? Let's deal with each of these questions in turn.

First, research suggests that the job conditions that cause stress show some differences across cultures. One study of US and Chinese employees revealed that whereas US employees were stressed by a lack of control, Chinese employees were stressed by job evaluations and lack of training. While the job conditions that lead to stress may differ across countries, it doesn't appear that personality effects on stress are different across cultures. One study of employees in Hungary, Italy, the United Kingdom, Israel and the United States found that Type A personality traits (see Chapter 4) predicted stress equally well across countries.[86]

Second, evidence tends to suggest that stressors are associated with perceived stress and strains among employees in different countries. In other words, stress is equally bad for employees of all cultures.[87]

Third, although not all factors that reduce stress have been compared across cultures, research does suggest that whereas the demand to work long hours leads to stress, this stress can be reduced by the resource of social support such as having friends or family to talk to. A recent study found this to be true of workers in a diverse set of countries (Australia, Canada, England, New Zealand, the United States, China, Taiwan, Argentina, Brazil, Colombia, Ecuador, Mexico, Peru and Uruguay).[88]

Summary and implications for managers

The need for change has been implied throughout this text. 'A casual reflection on change should indicate that it encompasses almost all of our concepts in the organizational behaviour literature.'[89] For instance, think about attitudes, motivation, work teams, communication, leadership, organizational structures, human resource practices and organizational cultures. Change was an integral part in the discussion of each.

If environments were perfectly static, if employees' skills and abilities were always up-to-date and incapable of deteriorating, and if tomorrow were always exactly the same as today, organizational change would have little or no relevance to managers. But the real world is turbulent, requiring organizations and their members to undergo dynamic change if they are to perform at competitive levels.

Managers are the primary change agents in most organizations. By the decisions they make and their role-modelling behaviours, they shape the organization's change culture. For instance, management decisions related to structural design, cultural factors and human resource policies largely determine the level of innovation within the organization. Similarly, management decisions, policies and practices will determine the degree to which the organization learns and adapts to changing environmental factors.

We found that the existence of work stress, in and of itself, need not imply lower performance. The evidence indicates that stress can be either a positive or a negative influence on employee performance. For many people, low to moderate amounts of stress enable them to perform their jobs better by increasing their work intensity, alertness and ability to react. However, a high level of stress, or even a moderate amount sustained over a long period, eventually takes its toll, and performance declines. The impact of stress on satisfaction is far more straightforward. Job-related tension tends to decrease general job satisfaction.[90] Even though low to moderate levels of stress may improve job performance, employees find stress dissatisfying.

POINT/COUNTERPOINT

Managing change is an episodic activity

POINT →

Organizational change is an episodic activity. That is, it starts at some point, proceeds through a series of steps and culminates in some outcome that those involved hope is an improvement over the starting point. It has a beginning, a middle and an end.

Lewin's three-step model represents a classic illustration of this perspective. Change is seen as a break in the organization's equilibrium. The status quo has been disturbed, and change is necessary to establish a new equilibrium state. The objective of refreezing is to stabilise the new situation by balancing the driving and restraining forces.

Some experts have argued that organizational change should be thought of as balancing a system made up of five interacting variables within the organization – people, tasks, technology, structure and strategy. A change in any one variable has repercussions on one or more of the others. This perspective is episodic in that it treats organizational change as essentially an effort to sustain equilibrium. A change in one variable begins a chain of events that, if properly managed, requires adjustments in the other variables to achieve a new state of equilibrium.

Another way to conceptualise the episodic view of looking at change is to think of managing change as analogous to captaining a ship. The organization is like a large ship travelling across the calm Mediterranean Sea to a specific port. The ship's captain has made this exact trip hundreds of times before with the same crew. Every once in a while, however, a storm will appear, and the crew has to respond. The captain will make the appropriate adjustments – that is, implement changes – and, having manoeuvred through the storm, will return the ship to calm waters. Like this ship's voyage, managing an organization should be seen as a journey with a beginning and an end, and implementing change as a response to a break in the status quo and needed only occasionally.

COUNTERPOINT ←

The episodic approach may be the dominant paradigm for handling organizational change, but it has become obsolete. It applies to a world of certainty and predictability. The episodic approach was developed in the 1950s and 1960s, and it reflects the environment of those times. It treats change as the occasional disturbance in an otherwise peaceful world. However, it bears little resemblance to today's environment of constant and chaotic change.[91]

If you want to understand what it's like to manage change in today's organizations, think of it as equivalent to permanent white-water rafting.[92] The organization is not a large ship, but more akin to a 40-foot raft. Rather than sailing a calm sea, this raft must traverse a raging river made up of an uninterrupted flow of permanent white-water rapids. To make things worse, the raft is manned by 10 people who have never worked together or travelled the river before, much of the trip is in the dark, the river is dotted by unexpected turns and obstacles, the exact destination is not clear, and at irregular intervals the raft needs to pull to shore, where some new crew members are added and others leave. Change is a natural state and managing change is a continual process. That is, managers never get the luxury of escaping the white-water rapids.

The stability and predictability characterised by the episodic perspective no longer captures the world we live in. Disruptions in the status quo are not occasional, temporary, and followed by a return to an equilibrium state. There is, in fact, no equilibrium state. Managers today face constant change, bordering on chaos. They're being forced to play a game they've never played before, governed by rules that are created as the game progresses.

QUESTIONS FOR REVIEW

1. What forces act as stimulants to change, and what is the difference between planned and unplanned change?

2. What forces act as sources of resistance to change?

3. What are the four main approaches to managing organizational change?

4. How can managers create a culture for change?

5. What is stress and what are the possible sources of stress?

6. What are the consequences of stress?

7. What are the individual and organizational approaches to managing stress?

8. What does research tell us about global differences in organizational change and work stress?

Experiential exercise

POWER AND THE CHANGING ENVIRONMENT

Objectives

1. To describe the forces for change influencing power differentials in organizational and interpersonal relationships.
2. To understand the effect of technological, legal/political, economic and social changes on the power of individuals within an organization.

The situation

Your organization manufactures golf carts and sells them to country clubs, golf courses and consumers. Your team is faced with the task of assessing how environmental changes will affect individuals' organizational power. Read each of the five scenarios and then, for each, identify the five members in the organization whose power will increase most in light of the environmental condition(s).

(m) = male (f) = female

Advertising expert (m)	Accountant–CPA (m)
Chief financial officer (f)	General manager (m)
Securities analyst (m)	Marketing manager (f)
Operations manager (f)	Computer programmer (f)
Industrial engineer (m)	Chemist (m)
Product designer (m)	In-house counsel (m)
Public relations expert (m)	Human resource manager (f)
Corporate trainer (m)	

---

1. New computer-aided manufacturing technologies are being introduced in the workplace during the upcoming 2 to 18 months.

2. New emission standards are being legislated by the government that will essentially make gas-powered golf carts (40 per cent of your current business) obsolete.
3. Sales are way down for two reasons: (a) a decline in the number of individuals playing golf and (b) your competitor was faster to embrace lithium batteries, which allow golf carts to go longer with a charge.
4. Given the growth of golf courses in other countries (especially India, China and Southeast Asia), the company is planning to go international in the next 12 to 18 months.
5. An equal opportunities special interest group is applying pressure to balance the male–female population in the organization's upper hierarchy by threatening to publicise the predominance of men in upper management.

The procedure

1. Divide the class into teams of three to four students each.
2. Teams should read each scenario and identify the five members whose power will increase most in light of the external environmental condition described.
3. Teams should then address the question: Assuming that the five environmental changes are taking place at once, which five members of the organization will now have the most power?
4. After 20 to 30 minutes, representatives of each team will be selected to present and justify their conclusions to the entire class. Discussion will begin with scenario 1 and proceed through to scenario 5 and the 'all at once' scenario.

Source: Adapted from J. E. Barbuto, Jr., 'Power and the changing environment', *Journal of Management Education*, April 2000, pp. 288–96.

Ethical dilemma

IS USING MANIPULATION TO DRIVE CHANGE UNETHICAL?

Manipulation, in the context of managing change, normally involves the very selective use of information and the conscious structuring of events. One common form of manipulation is cooptation. Coopting an individual usually involves giving him or her a desirable role in the design or implementation of the change. Coopting a group involves giving one of its leaders, or someone it respects, a key role in the design or implementation of a change. This is not a form of participation, however, because the initiators do not want the advice of the coopted, merely his or her endorsement.

For example:

A division manager in a large multi-business corporation invited the corporate human relations vice president, a close friend of the president, to help him and his key staff diagnose some problems the division was having. Because of his busy schedule, the corporate vice president was not able to do much of the actual information gathering or analysis himself, thus limiting his own influence on the diagnoses. But his presence at key meetings helped commit him to the

diagnoses as well as the solutions the group designed. The commitment was subsequently very important because the president, at least initially, did not like some of the proposed changes. Nevertheless, after discussion with his human relations vice president, he did not try to block them.

Questions

1. Do you think the corporate human relations vice president has been used by the division manager solely for his own benefit?

2. Do you think this is justified given the fact that the change probably would have been blocked without the vice president's involvement?

3. Would you deal with potential resistance to change by using manipulation techniques such as co-opting? Why or why not?

Source: J. Kotter and L. Schlesinger, 'Choosing strategies for change', *Harvard Business Review*, 57, 2 (1979), pp. 106–14.

CASE INCIDENT 1

Innovating innovation

Executives at Procter & Gamble (P&G) are pretty happy these days. P&G's share price has risen more than 50 per cent over the past five years, and the company's performance has been unusually resistant to the myriad changes that affect all companies.

Many at P&G might point to chief technology officer Gil Cloyd as one of the sources of this success. Although short-term performance is obviously important, Cloyd has been more focused on long-term change, specifically how P&G approaches research and development (R&D). Given the enormous variety of products that P&G offers, including toilet paper, laundry detergents, personal care products, and pet food, the ability to sustain a competitive level of innovation is a tremendous challenge. Says Cloyd,

> One of the challenges we have is serving the needs of a very diverse consumer population, but yet be able to do that quickly and very cost effectively. In the consumer products world we estimate that the required pace of innovation has doubled in the last three years. That means we have less time to benefit from any innovation that we bring into the marketplace.

Cloyd's approach is simple yet complex: Innovate innovation.

What is innovating innovation? As Cloyd explains, 'What we've done is refine our thinking on how we conduct and evaluate research and development. We've made some changes. For example, historically, we tended to put the evaluation emphasis on technical product performance, patents, and other indicators of internal R&D efforts. Now there is more emphasis on perceived customer value.' Cloyd describes P&G's innovation process as holistic, meaning it touches every department of an organization. Holistic innovation includes first setting appropriate financial goals and then implementing an innovation programme for all aspects of the product – from its manufacturing technology to those aspects that the customer experiences directly, such as the product's packaging and appearance.

One of Cloyd's major goals at P&G is to acquire most product ideas from sources external to the organization, which

it is close to doing. As a result, P&G has doubled the number of new products with elements that originated outside the company.

Though P&G is enjoying enormous success due in part to its innovation programme, Cloyd is not resting on his laurels. He emphasises learning as a critical element to continued innovation success. One area he's exploring is computer modelling and simulation. Previously, manufacturing was the main user of computer modelling. Now, Cloyd is using it in the product design process. Explains Cloyd, 'A computational model helps us more quickly to understand what's going on. The simulation capabilities are also allowing us to interact with consumers much more quickly on design options. For example, Internet panels can engage consumers in as little as 24 hours. Digital technology is very important in helping us learn faster. Not only will it accelerate innovation, but the approach will greatly enhance the creativity of our people.' By continually looking for new ways to design, produce, and market products, Cloyd and P&G are indeed 'innovating innovation.'

Questions

1. This book covers the notion of 'idea champions'. What characteristics of Gil Cloyd make him an idea champion?

2. Would you consider P&G to be a 'learning organization'? What aspects of P&G lead you to your answer?

3. Although Cloyd is a major reason for P&G's innovation success, what are some structural features of P&G that might contribute to its ability to innovate so well?

4. The benefits of technological innovations for companies are often short lived because other companies adopt the same technology soon after. What factors do you believe contribute to P&G's ability to continually innovate at such a competitive level?

Source: Based on A. Markels, 'Turning the tide at P&G', *U.S. News & World Report*, 22 October 2006, pp. 1–3; and J. Teresko, 'P&G's secret: innovating innovation,' *IndustryWeek*, December 2004, pp. 26–34.

CASE INCIDENT 2

Creating a learning organization at Tesco

If you're serious about becoming a learning organization, supermarket chain Tesco claimed, then you need a learning director. So the firm charged the task to Kim Birnie back in 2000. It was going to be a challenge. A large proportion of the 220,000 workers across the globe had few qualifications and sometimes unpleasant experiences of learning. Furthermore, whether employees on the shop floor, such as check-out operators and shelf-stackers, wanted to engage with learning was debatable.

The vision to turn Tesco into a learning organization came from the top – chief executive Terry Leahy. 'Everything we do around training, development and learning is to ensure that we reach a high quality and common way of improving the organization's capability,' Birnie says. Tesco had set itself two key, pioneering business tasks: to build its e-commerce business and increase its international presence.

Its international plans were ambitious. Tesco wanted to be one of the first British retailers to succeed in international markets. In 2000, it operated in 10 countries across Europe and Asia and 25 per cent of its business is outside the UK. Developing quality standards and ways of doing things that cross cultural boundaries is a difficult task, especially in an industry such as retailing, which depends so much on individual relationships with customers.

But Birnie believes it is possible to establish a Tesco way of doing things that applies across the board, from senior management to the front line. This does not mean local differences are ignored. 'We can't apply everything in a blanket fashion,' she says. 'flexibility is the key.' Nor does it mean the UK imposes ideas on the rest of the business. The focus is on sharing learning, Birnie insists. 'We want ideas that have portability and can be shared with other parts of the business. So, for example, in central Europe where the stores have a different front we have taken the methodology and adapted it for the rest of our business.'

Creating a learning organization has involved many initiatives. As it will be senior managers who are ultimately responsible, the head office learning team devotes a lot of its time to management development issues. It has developed a leadership programme for its top 1,500 business chiefs. 'That's where we are really focused,' Birnie says. 'This is how we will build our international and dotcom capabilities.'

A major front-line training initiative, called the training framework, is designed to drive up the skills and abilities of Tesco's general sales assistants – again with common standards of behaviour and service in mind. There are three levels – bronze, silver and gold. Bronze has been rolled out across the business and silver is on its way. Meanwhile, Birnie admits, that gold is still aspirational.

'We're looking to see better informed staff doing things in a more effective and efficient way for customers.'

A key to creating the learning organization is the emphasis on knowledge management, the notion of better sharing knowledge throughout the organization (predominantly by using IT systems) which enables people to learn from others and foster innovation. The vision is to link the entire business and give everyone down to the front line sales staff access to 'the knowledge'. The physical aspect of this could see computer terminals in the staffroom or even on the shopfloor. Staff could find out a range of information about products, sales or maybe even their own personnel files. 'This sort of technology would enable us to react to change much more rapidly,' Birnie says. 'It's a must for any organization that has to react quickly to customers.'

Source: Adapted from 'Taking a new direction', *Training and Coaching Today*, 1 October 2000.

Questions

1. Do you think the initiatives Birnie has implemented at Tesco will create a learning organization? What other activities may help?

2. Why is it important for Tesco to become a learning organization?

3. What are the potential sources of resistance to creating a learning organization at Tesco? How might they be overcome?

4. Do you think the learning organization concept is applicable to all organizations? For example, is it equally useful for Google as it is for Tesco?

5. Creating a learning organization at Tesco began in 2000, seek out further information to determine whether the firm has been successful.

Endnotes

1 'Small world', *Foundation Focus*, European Foundation for the Improvement of Living and Working Conditions, May 2008, Issue 5.

2 See, for instance, K. H. Hammonds, 'Practical radicals,' *Fast Company*, September 2000, pp. 162–74; and P. C. Judge, 'Change agents,' *Fast Company*, November 2000, pp. 216–26.

3 J. Taub, 'Harvard radical', *New York Times Magazine*, 24 August 2003, pp. 28–45+.

4 A. Finder, P. D. Healy and K. Zernike, 'President of Harvard resigns, ending stormy 5-year tenure,' *New York Times*, 22 February 2006, pp. A1, A19.

5 P. G. Audia and S. Brion, 'Reluctant to change: self-enhancing responses to diverging performance measures', *Organizational Behavior and Human Decision Processes*, 102 (2007), pp. 255–69.

6 M. T. Hannan, L. Pólos and G. R. Carroll, 'The fog of change: opacity and asperity in organizations', *Administrative Science Quarterly*, September 2003. pp. 399–432.

7 J. P. Kotter and L. A. Schlesinger, 'Choosing strategies for change', *Harvard Business Review*, March–April 1979, pp. 106–14.

8 J. E. Dutton, S. J. Ashford, R. M. O'Neill and K. A. Lawrence, 'Moves that matter: issue selling and organizational change', *Academy of Management Journal*, August 2001, pp. 716–36.

9 P. C. Fiss and E. J. Zajac, 'The symbolic management of strategic change: sensegiving via framing and decoupling', *Academy of Management Journal*, 49, 6 (2006), pp. 1173–93.

10 Q. N. Huy, 'Emotional balancing of organizational continuity and radical change: the contribution of middle managers', *Administrative Science Quarterly*, March 2002, pp. 31–69; D. M. Herold, D. B. Fedor and S. D. Caldwell, 'Beyond change management: a multilevel investigation of contextual and personal influences on employees' commitment to change', *Journal of Applied Psychology*, 92, 4 (2007), pp. 942–51; and G. B. Cunningham, 'The relationships among commitment to change, coping with change, and turnover intentions', *European Journal of Work and Organizational Psychology*, 15, 1 (2006), pp. 29–45.

11 D. B. Fedor, S. Caldwell and D. M. Herold, 'The effects of organizational changes on employee commitment: a multi-level investigation', *Personnel Psychology*, 59 (2006), pp. 1–29.

12 S. Oreg, 'Personality, context, and resistance to organizational change', *European Journal of Work and Organizational Psychology*, 15, 1 (2006), pp. 73–101.

13 J. A. LePine, J. A. Colquitt and A. Erez, 'Adaptability to changing task contexts: effects of general cognitive ability, conscientiousness, and openness to experience', *Personnel Psychology*, Fall, 2000, pp. 563–93; T. A. Judge, C. J. Thoresen, V. Pucik and T. M. Welbourne, 'Managerial coping with organizational change: a dispositional perspective', *Journal of Applied Psychology*, February 1999, pp. 107–22; and S. Oreg, 'Resistance to change: developing an individual differences measure', *Journal of Applied Psychology*, August 2003, pp. 680–93.

14 See J. Pfeffer, *Managing with Power: Politics and Influence in Organizations* (Boston, MA: Harvard Business School Press, 1992), pp. 7 and 318–20.

15 See, for instance, W. Ocasio, 'Political dynamics and the circulation of power: CEO succession in U.S. industrial corporations, 1960–1990', *Administrative Science Quarterly*, June 1994, pp. 285–312.

16 K. Lewin, *Field Theory in Social Science* (New York: Harper & Row, 1951).

17 P. G. Audia, E. A. Locke and K. G. Smith, 'The paradox of success: an archival and a laboratory study of strategic persistence following radical environmental change', *Academy of Management Journal*, October 2000, pp. 837–53.

18 J. B. Sorensen, 'The strength of corporate culture and the reliability of firm performance', *Administrative Science Quarterly*, March 2002, pp. 70–91.

19 J. Amis, T. Slack and C. R. Hinings, 'The pace, sequence, and linearity of radical change', *Academy of Management Journal*, February 2004, pp. 15–39; and E. Autio, H. J. Sapienza and J. G. Almeida, 'Effects of age at entry, knowledge intensity, and imitability on international growth', *Academy of Management Journal*, October 2000, pp. 909–24.

20 J. P. Kotter, 'Leading changes: why transformation efforts fail', *Harvard Business Review*, March–April 1995, pp. 59–67; and J. P. Kotter, *Leading Change* (Boston, MA: Harvard Business School Press, 1996).

21 See, for example, C. Eden and C. Huxham, 'Action research for the study of organizations', in S. R. Clegg, C. Hardy and W. R. Nord (eds), *Handbook of Organization Studies* (London: Sage, 1996).

22 Based on 'Boehringer Ingelheim, Germany: fostering employability', European Foundation for the Improvement of Living and Working Conditions, 25 January 2008. Available at www.eurofound.europa.eu.

23 For a sampling of various OD definitions, see N. Nicholson (ed.), *Encyclopedic Dictionary of Organizational Behavior* (Malden, MA: Blackwell, 1998), pp. 359–61; H. K. Sinangil and F. Avallone, 'Organizational development and change', in N. Anderson, D. S. Ones, H. K. Sinangil and C. Viswesvaran (eds), *Handbook of Industrial, Work and Organizational Psychology*, vol. 2 (Thousand Oaks, CA: Sage, 2001), pp. 332–35.

24 See, for instance, R. Lines, 'Influence of participation in strategic change: resistance, organizational commitment and change goal achievement', *Journal of Change Management*, September 2004, pp. 193–215.

25 S. Highhouse, 'A history of the T-group and its early application in management development', *Group Dynamics: Theory, Research, & Practice*, December 2002, pp. 277–90.

26 J. E. Edwards and M. D. Thomas, 'The organizational survey process: general steps and practical considerations', in P. Rosenfeld, J. E. Edwards and M. D. Thomas (eds), *Improving Organizational Surveys: New Directions, Methods, and Applications* (Newbury Park, CA: Sage, 1993), pp. 3–28.

27 E. H. Schein, *Process Consultation: Its Role in Organizational Development*, 2nd edn (Reading, MA: Addison-Wesley, 1988), p. 9. See also E. H. Schein, *Process Consultation Revisited: Building Helpful Relationships* (Reading, MA: Addison-Wesley, 1999).

28 Schein, *Process Consultation*.

29 R. Bentley, 'The cook, the ape and the Da Vinci code', *Personnel Today* (first appeared in *Training and Coaching Today*) 26 July 2006.

30 W. Dyer, *Team Building: Issues and Alternatives* (Reading, MA: Addison-Wesley, 1994).

31 See, for example, E. H. Neilsen, 'Understanding and managing intergroup conflict', in J. W. Lorsch and P. R. Lawrence (eds), *Managing Group and Intergroup Relations* (Homewood, IL: Irwin-Dorsey, 1972), pp. 329–43.

32 R. R. Blake, J. S. Mouton and R. L. Sloma, 'The union–management intergroup laboratory: strategy for resolving intergroup conflict', *Journal of Applied Behavioral Science*, 1 (1965), pp. 25–57.

33 See, for example, R. Fry, F. Barrett, J. Seiling and D. Whitney (eds), *appreciative Inquiry & Organizational Transformation: Reports From the Field* (Westport, CT: Quorum, 2002); J. K. Barge and C. Oliver, 'Working with appreciation in managerial practice,' *Academy of Management Review*, January 2003, pp. 124–42; and D. van der Haar and D. M. Hosking, 'Evaluating appreciative inquiry: a relational constructionist perspective', *Human Relations*, August 2004, pp. 1017–36.

34 J. Gordon, 'Meet the freight fairy', *Forbes*, 20 January 2003, p. 65.

35 D. Anfuso, 'Core values shape W. L. Gore's innovative culture', *Workforce*, March 1999, pp. 48–51; and A. Harrington, 'Who's afraid of a new product?' *Fortune*, 10 November 2003, pp. 189–92.

36 See Great Place to Work Institute Europe http://www.greatplacetowork-europe.com

37 See, for instance, R. M. Kanter, 'When a thousand flowers bloom: structural, collective and social conditions for innovation in organizations', in B. M. Staw and L. L. Cummings (eds), *Research in Organizational Behavior*, vol. 10 (Greenwich, CT: JAI Press, 1988), pp. 169–211.

38 F. Damanpour, 'Organizational innovation: a meta-analysis of effects of determinants and moderators', *Academy of Management Journal*, September 1991, p. 557.

39 Ibid., pp. 555–90.

40 See P. R. Monge, M. D. Cozzens and N. S. Contractor, 'Communication and motivational predictors of the dynamics of organizational innovation', *Organization Science*, May 1992, pp. 250–74.

41 J. M. Howell and C. A. Higgins, 'Champions of change', *Business Quarterly*, Spring 1990, pp. 31–32; and D. L. Day,

'Raising radicals: different processes for championing innovative corporate ventures', *Organization Science*, May 1994, pp. 148–72.

42 Howell and Higgins, 'Champions of change'.

43 See, for example, T. B. Lawrence, M. K. Mauws, B. Dyck and R. F. Kleysen, 'The politics of organizational learning: integrating power into the 4I framework', *Academy of Management Review*, January 2005, pp. 180–91.

44 'Employment in Europe 2007', European Commission.

45 D. H. Kim, 'The link between individual and organizational learning', *Sloan Management Review*, Fall 1993, p. 37.

46 C. Argyris and D. A. Schon, *Organizational Learning* (Reading, MA: Addison-Wesley, 1978).

47 B. Dumaine, 'Mr. Learning Organization', *Fortune*, 17 October 1994, pp. 147–53, p. 148.

48 F. Kofman and P. M. Senge, 'Communities of commitment: the heart of learning organizations', *Organizational Dynamics*, Autumn 1993, pp. 5–23.

49 Dumaine, 'Mr. Learning Organization', p. 153.

50 See, for instance, K. Slobogin, 'Many U.S. employees feel overworked, stressed, study says', *CNN.com*, 16 May 2001, www.cnn.com; and S. Armour, 'Rising job stress could affect bottom line', *USA Today*, 29 July 2003, p. 1B.

51 See UK Health and Safety Executive http://www.hse.gov.uk/; European Foundation for the Improvement of Living and Working Conditions http://www.eurofound.europa.eu.

52 Adapted from R. S. Schuler, 'Definition and conceptualization of stress in organizations', *Organizational Behavior and Human Performance*, April 1980, p. 189. For an updated review of definitions, see C. L. Cooper, P. J. Dewe and M. P. O'Driscoll, *Organizational Stress: A Review and Critique of Theory, Research, and Applications* (Thousand Oaks, CA: Sage, 2002).

53 See, for instance, M. A. Cavanaugh, W. R. Boswell, M. V. Roehling and J. W. Boudreau, 'An empirical examination of self-reported work stress among U.S. managers', *Journal of Applied Psychology*, February 2000, pp. 65–74.

54 N. P. Podsakoff, J. A. LePine and M. A. LePine, 'Differential challenge-hindrance stressor relationships with job attitudes, turnover intentions, turnover, and withdrawal behavior: a meta-analysis', *Journal of Applied Psychology*, 92, 2 (2007), pp. 438–54; J. A. LePine, M. A. LePine and C. L. Jackson, 'Challenge and hindrance stress: relationships with exhaustion, motivation to learn, and learning performance', *Journal of Applied Psychology*, October 2004, pp. 883–91.

55 N. W. Van Yperen and O. Janssen, 'Fatigued and dissatisfied or fatigued but satisfied? Goal orientations and responses to high job demands', *Academy of Management Journal*, December 2002, pp. 1161–71; and N. W. Van Yperen and M. Hagedoorn, 'Do high job demands increase intrinsic motivation or fatigue or both? The role of job control and job social support', *Academy of Management Journal*, June 2003, pp. 339–48.

56 J. de Jonge and C. Dormann, 'Stressors, resources, and strain at work: a longitudinal test of the triple-match principle', *Journal of Applied Psychology*, 91, 5 (2006), pp. 1359–74.

57 This section is adapted from C. L. Cooper and R. Payne, *Stress at Work* (London: Wiley, 1978); Parasuraman and Alutto, 'Sources and outcomes of stress in organizational settings', pp. 330–50; and P. M. Hart and C. L. Cooper, 'Occupational

stress: toward a more integrated framework', in N. Anderson, D. S. Ones, H. K. Sinangil and C. Viswesvaran (eds), *Handbook of Industrial, Work and Organizational Psychology*, Vol. 2 (London: Sage, 2002), pp. 93–114.

58 A. E. Rafferty and M. A. Griffin, 'Perceptions of organizational change: a stress and coping perspective', *Journal of Applied Psychology*, 71, 5 (2007), pp. 1154–62.

59 S. G. Rogelberg, D. J. Leach, and P. B. Warr, and J. L. Burnfield, '"Not another meeting!" Are meeting time demands related to employee well-being?', *Journal of Applied Psychology*, 91, 1 (2006), pp. 86–96.

60 See, for example, M. L. Fox, D. J. Dwyer and D. C. Ganster, 'Effects of stressful job demands and control of physiological and attitudinal outcomes in a hospital setting', *Academy of Management Journal*, April 1993, pp. 289–318.

61 G. W. Evans and D. Johnson, 'Stress and open-office noise', *Journal of Applied Psychology*, October 2000, pp. 779–83.

62 T. M. Glomb, J. D. Kammeyer-Mueller and M. Rotundo, 'Emotional labor demands and compensating wage differentials', *Journal of Applied Psychology*, August 2004, pp. 700–14; A. A. Grandey, 'When "The show must go on": surface acting and deep acting as determinants of emotional exhaustion and peer-rated service delivery', *Academy of Management Journal*, February 2003, pp. 86–96.

63 V. S. Major, K. J. Klein and M. G. Ehrhart, 'Work time, work interference with family, and psychological distress', *Journal of Applied Psychology*, June 2002, pp. 427–36; see also P. E. Spector, C. L. Cooper, S. Poelmans, T. D. Allen, M. O'Driscoll, J. I. Sanchez, O. L. Siu, P. Dewe, P. Hart, L. Lu, L. F. R. De Moraes, G. M. Ostrognay, K. Sparks, P. Wong and S. Yu, 'A cross-national comparative study of work-family stressors, working hours, and well being: China and Latin America versus the Anglo world', *Personnel Psychology*, Spring 2004, pp. 119–42.

64 D. L. Nelson and C. Sutton, 'Chronic work stress and coping: a longitudinal study and suggested new directions', *Academy of Management Journal*, December 1990, pp. 859–69.

65 H. Selye, *The Stress of Life*, rev. ed. (New York: McGraw-Hill, 1956).

66 S. J. Motowidlo, J. S. Packard and M. R. Manning, 'Occupational stress: its causes and consequences for job performance', *Journal of Applied Psychology*, November 1987, pp. 619–20.

67 See, J. B. Halbesleben, 'Sources of social support and burnout: a meta-analytic test of the conservation of resources model', *Journal of Applied Psychology*, 91, 5 (2006), pp. 1134–45; N. Bolger and D. Amarel, 'Effects of social support visibility on adjustment to stress: experimental evidence', *Journal of Applied Psychology*, 92, 3 (2007), pp. 458–75; and N. A. Bowling, T. A. Beehr and W. M. Swader, 'Giving and receiving social support at work: the roles of personality and reciprocity', *Journal of Vocational Behavior*, 67 (2005), pp. 476–89.

68 R. Williams, *The Trusting Heart: Great News About Type A Behavior* (New York: Times Books, 1989).

69 Schuler, 'Definition and conceptualization of stress', pp. 200–205; and R. L. Kahn and P. Byosiere, 'Stress in organizations', in M. D. Dunnette and L. M. Hough (eds), *Handbook of Industrial and Organizational Psychology*, 2nd edn, Vol. 3, pp. 571–650.

70 See T. A. Beehr and J. E. Newman, 'Job stress, employee health, and organizational effectiveness: a facet analysis, model, and

literature review', *Personnel Psychology*, Winter 1978, pp. 665–99; and B. D. Steffy and J. W. Jones, 'Workplace stress and indicators of coronary-disease risk', *Academy of Management Journal*, September 1988, pp. 686–98.

71 J. Schaubroeck, J. R. Jones and J. L. Xie, 'Individual differences in utilizing control to cope with job demands: effects on susceptibility to infectious disease', *Journal of Applied Psychology*, April 2001, pp. 265–78.

72 Steffy and Jones, 'Workplace stress and indicators of coronary-disease risk', p. 687.

73 C. L. Cooper and J. Marshall, 'Occupational sources of stress: a review of the literature relating to coronary heart disease and mental Ill health', *Journal of Occupational Psychology*, 49, 1 (1976), pp. 11–28.

74 J. R. Hackman and G. R. Oldham, 'Development of the job diagnostic survey', *Journal of Applied Psychology*, April 1975, pp. 159–70.

75 E. M. de Croon, J. K. Sluiter, R. W. B. Blonk, J. P. J. Broersen and M. H. W. Frings-Dresen, 'Stressful work, psychological job strain and turnover: a 2-year prospective cohort study of truck drivers', *Journal of Applied Psychology*, June 2004, pp. 442–54; and R. Cropanzano, D. E. Rupp and Z. S. Byrne, 'The relationship of emotional exhaustion to work attitudes, job performance, and organizational citizenship behaviors', *Journal of Applied Psychology*, February 2003, pp. 160–69.

76 See, for instance, S. Zivnuska, C. Kiewitz, W. A. Hochwarter, P. L. Perrewé and K. L. Zellars, 'What is too much or too little? The curvilinear effects of job tension on turnover intent, value attainment, and job satisfaction', *Journal of Applied Social Psychology*, July 2002, pp. 1344–60.

77 L. A. Muse, S. G. Harris and H. S. Field, 'Has the inverted-U theory of stress and job performance had a fair test?', *Human Performance*, 16, 4 (2003), pp. 349–64.

78 The following discussion has been influenced by J. E. Newman and T. A. Beehr, 'Personal and organizational strategies for handling job stress', *Personnel Psychology*, Spring 1979, pp. 1–38; J. M. Ivancevich and M. T. Matteson, 'Organizational level stress management interventions: a review and recommendations', *Journal of Organizational Behavior Management*, Fall–Winter 1986, pp. 229–48; M. T. Matteson and J. M. Ivancevich, 'Individual stress management interventions: evaluation of techniques', *Journal of Management Psychology*, January 1987, pp. 24–30; J. M. Ivancevich, M. T. Matteson, S. M. Freedman and J. S. Phillips, 'Worksite stress management interventions', *American Psychologist*, February 1990, pp. 252–61; and R. Schwarzer, 'Manage stress at work through preventive and proactive coping', in E. A. Locke (ed.), *Handbook of Principles of Organizational Behavior* (Malden, MA: Blackwell, 2004), pp. 342–55.

79 T. H. Macan, 'Time management: test of a process model', *Journal of Applied Psychology*, June 1994, pp. 381–91; and B. J. C. Claessens, W. Van Eerde, C. G. Rutte and R. A. Roe, 'Planning behavior and perceived control of time at work', *Journal of Organizational Behavior*, December 2004, pp. 937–50.

80 See, for example, G. Lawrence-Ell, *The Invisible Clock: A Practical Revolution in Finding Time for Everyone and Everything* (Seaside Park, NJ: Kingsland Hall, 2002); and B. Tracy, *Time Power* (New York: AMACOM, 2004).

81 J. Kiely and G. Hodgson, 'Stress in the prison service: the benefits of exercise programs', *Human Relations*, June 1990, pp. 551–72.

82 E. J. Forbes and R. J. Pekala, 'Psychophysiological effects of several stress management techniques', *Psychological Reports*, February 1993, pp. 19–27; and M. Der Hovanesian, 'Zen and the art of corporate productivity', *BusinessWeek*, 28 July 2003, p. 56.

83 S. E. Jackson, 'Participation in decision making as a strategy for reducing job-related strain', *Journal of Applied Psychology*, February 1983, pp. 3–19.

84 See, for instance, B. Leonard, 'Health care costs increase interest in wellness programs', *HRMagazine*, September 2001, pp. 35–36; and 'Healthy, happy and productive', *Training*, February 2003, p. 16.

85 See S. Shane, S. Venkataraman and I. MacMillan, 'Cultural differences in innovation championing strategies', *Journal of Management*, 21, 5 (1995), pp. 931–52.

86 J. Chen, C. Silverthorne and J. Hung, 'Organization communication, job stress, organizational commitment, and job performance of accounting professionals in Taiwan and America', *Leadership & Organization Development Journal*, 27, 4 (2006), pp. 242–49; C. Liu, P. E. Spector and L. Shi, 'Cross-national job stress: a quantitative and qualitative study', *Journal of Organizational Behavior*, February 2007, pp. 209–39.

87 H. M. Addae and X. Wang, 'Stress at work: linear and curvilinear effects of psychological-, job- and organization-related factors: an exploratory study of Trinidad and Tobago', *International Journal of Stress Management*, November 2006, pp. 476–93.

88 P. E. Spector, C. L. Cooper, S. Poelmans, T. D. Allen, M. O'Driscoll, J. I. Sanchez, O. L. Sin, P. Dewe, P. Hart and L. Lu, 'A cross-national comparative study of work-family stressors, working hours, and well-being: China and Latin America versus the Anglo world', *Personnel Psychology*, 57 (Spring 2004), pp. 119–42.

89 P. S. Goodman and L. B. Kurke, 'Studies of change in organizations: a status report', in P. S. Goodman (ed.), *Change in Organizations* (San Francisco, CA: Jossey-Bass, 1982), p. 1.

90 Kahn and Byosiere, 'Stress in organizations', pp. 605–08.

91 For contrasting views on episodic and continuous change, see K. E. Weick and R. E. Quinn, 'Organizational change and development', in J. T. Spence, J. M. Darley and D. J. Foss (eds), *Annual Review of Psychology*, vol. 50 (Palo Alto, CA: Annual Reviews, 1999), pp. 361–86.

92 This perspective is based on P. B. Vaill, *Managing as a Performing Art: New Ideas for a World of Chaotic Change* (San Francisco, CA: Jossey-Bass, 1989).

Glossary

Ability An individual's capacity to perform the various tasks in a job.

Absenteeism The failure to report to work.

Accommodating The willingness of one party in a conflict to place the opponent's interests above his or her own.

Action research A change process based on systematic collection of data and then selection of a change action based on what the analysed data indicate.

Adjourning stage The final stage in group development for temporary groups, characterised by concern with wrapping up activities rather than task performance.

Affect A broad range of feelings that people experience.

Affect intensity Individual differences in the strength with which individuals experience their emotions.

Affective commitment An emotional attachment to an organization and a belief in its values.

Affective component of an attitude The emotional or feeling segment of an attitude.

Affective events theory (AET) A model which suggests that workplace events cause emotional reactions on the part of employees, which then influence workplace attitudes and behaviours.

Agreeableness A personality dimension that describes someone who is good natured, cooperative and trusting.

Anchoring bias A tendency to fixate on initial information, from which one then fails to adequately adjust for subsequent information.

Anthropology The study of societies to learn about human beings and their activities.

Appreciative inquiry (AI) An approach that seeks to identify the unique qualities and special strengths of an organization, which can then be built on to improve performance.

Arbitrator A third party to a negotiation who has the authority to dictate an agreement.

Assessment centres A set of performance-simulation tests designed to evaluate a candidate's managerial potential.

Attitudes Evaluative statements or judgements concerning objects, people or events.

Attribution theory An attempt to determine whether an individual's behaviour is internally or externally caused.

Attribution theory of leadership A leadership theory which says that leadership is merely an attribution that people make about other individuals.

Authentic leaders Leaders who know who they are, know what they believe in and value and act on those values and beliefs openly and candidly. Their followers would consider them to be ethical people.

Authority The rights inherent in a managerial position to give orders and to expect the orders to be obeyed.

Autonomy The degree to which a job provides substantial freedom and discretion to the individual in scheduling the work and in determining the procedures to be used in carrying it out.

Availability bias The tendency for people to base their judgements on information that is readily available to them.

Avoiding The desire to withdraw from or suppress a conflict.

BATNA The best alternative to a negotiated agreement; the least the individual should accept.

Behavioural component of an attitude An intention to behave in a certain way toward someone or something.

Behavioural theories of leadership Theories proposing that specific behaviours differentiate leaders from nonleaders.

Behaviourally anchored rating scales (BARS) Scales that combine major elements from the critical incident and graphic rating scale approaches: The appraiser rates the employees based on items along a continuum, but the points are examples of actual behaviour on the given job rather than general descriptions or traits.

Behaviourism A theory which argues that behaviour follows stimuli in a relatively unthinking manner.

Biographical characteristics Personal characteristics – such as age, gender, race and length of tenure – that are objective and easily obtained from personnel records.

Blog (Web log) A website where entries are written, generally displayed in reverse chronological order, about news, events and personal diary entries.

Bonus A pay plan that rewards employees for recent performance rather than historical performance.

Boundaryless organization An organization that seeks to eliminate the chain of command, have limitless spans of control and replace departments with empowered teams.

Bounded rationality A process of making decisions by constructing simplified models that extract the essential features from problems without capturing all their complexity.

Brainstorming An idea-generation process that specifically encourages any and all alternatives while withholding any criticism of those alternatives.

Bureaucracy A structure with highly routine operating tasks achieved through specialisation, very formalised rules and regulations, tasks that are grouped into functional departments, centralised authority, narrow spans of control and decision making that follows the chain of command.

Centralisation The degree to which decision making is concentrated at a single point in an organization.

Chain of command The unbroken line of authority that extends from the top of the organization to the lowest echelon and clarifies who reports to whom.

Challenge stressors Stressors associated with work load, pressure to complete tasks and time urgency.

Change agents Persons who act as catalysts and assume the responsibility for managing change activities.

Change Making things different.

Channel richness The amount of information that can be transmitted during a communication episode.

Charismatic leadership theory A leadership theory which states that followers make attributions of heroic or extraordinary leadership abilities when they observe certain behaviours.

Classical conditioning A type of conditioning in which an individual responds to some stimulus that would not ordinarily produce such a response.

Coercive power A power base that is dependent on fear.

Cognitive component of an attitude The opinion or belief segment of an attitude.

Cognitive dissonance Any incompatibility between two or more attitudes or between behaviour and attitudes.

Cognitive evaluation theory A theory which states that allocating extrinsic rewards for behaviour that had been previously intrinsically rewarding tends to decrease the overall level of motivation.

Cognitive resource theory A theory of leadership which states that stress unfavourably affects a situation and that intelligence and experience can reduce the influence of stress on the leader.

Cohesiveness The degree to which group members are attracted to each other and are motivated to stay in the group.

Collaborating A situation in which the parties to a conflict each desire to satisfy fully the concerns of all parties.

Collectivism A national culture attribute that describes a tight social framework in which people expect others in groups of which they are a part to look after them and protect them.

Command group A group composed of the individuals who report directly to a given manager.

Communication apprehension Undue tension and anxiety about oral communication, written communication or both.

Communication process The steps between a source and a receiver that result in the transfer and understanding of meaning.

Communication The transfer and understanding of meaning.

Competing A desire to satisfy one's interests, regardless of the impact on the other party to the conflict.

Compromising A situation in which each party to a conflict is willing to give up something.

Conceptual skills The mental ability to analyse and diagnose complex situations.

Conciliator A trusted third party who provides an informal communication link between the negotiator and the opponent.

Confirmation bias The tendency to seek out information that reaffirms past choices and to discount information that contradicts past judgements.

Conflict A process that begins when one party perceives that another party has negatively affected or is about to negatively affect, something that the first party cares about.

Conflict management The use of resolution and stimulation techniques to achieve the desired level of conflict.

Conflict process A process that has five stages: potential opposition or incompatibility, cognition and personalisation, intentions, behaviour and outcomes.

Conformity The adjustment of one's behaviour to align with the norms of the group.

Conscientiousness A personality dimension that describes someone who is responsible, dependable, persistent and organized.

Consideration The extent to which a leader is likely to have job relationships characterised by mutual trust, respect for subordinates' ideas and regard for their feelings.

Consultant An impartial third party, skilled in conflict management, who attempts to facilitate creative problem solving through communication and analysis.

Contingency variables Situational factors: variables that moderate the relationship between two or more other variables.

Continuance commitment The perceived economic value of remaining with an organization compared to leaving it.

Continuous reinforcement Reinforcing a desired behaviour each time it is demonstrated.

Contrast effects Evaluation of a person's characteristics that is affected by comparisons with other people recently encountered who rank higher or lower on the same characteristics.

Controlling Monitoring activities to ensure that they are being accomplished as planned and correcting any significant deviations.

Core self-evaluation The degree to which an individual likes or dislikes himself or herself, whether the person sees himself or herself as capable and effective and whether the person feels in control of his or her environment or powerless over the environment.

Core self-evaluations Bottom-line conclusions individuals have about their capabilities, competence and worth as a person

Core values The primary or dominant values that are accepted throughout the organization.

Cost-minimisation strategy A strategy that emphasises tight cost controls, avoidance of unnecessary innovation or marketing expenses and price cutting.

Creativity The ability to produce novel and useful ideas.

Critical incidents A way of evaluating the behaviours that are key in making the difference between executing a job effectively and executing it ineffectively.

Cross-functional teams Employees from about the same hierarchical level, but from different work areas, who come together to accomplish a task.

Decisions Choices made from among two or more alternatives.

Deep acting Trying to modify one's true inner feelings based on display rules.

Defensive behaviours Reactive and protective behaviours to avoid action, blame or change.

Demands Responsibilities, pressures, obligations and even uncertainties that individuals face in the workplace.

Departmentalisation The basis by which jobs in an organization are grouped together.

Dependency B's relationship to A when A possesses something that B requires.

Dependent variable A response that is affected by an independent variable.

Deterrence-based trust Trust based on fear of reprisal if the trust is violated.

Deviant workplace behaviour Voluntary behaviour that violates significant organizational norms and, in so doing, threatens the well-being of the organization or its members. Also called *antisocial behaviour* or *workplace incivility*.

Displayed emotions Emotions that are organizationally required and considered appropriate in a given job.

Distributive bargaining Negotiation that seeks to divide up a fixed amount of resources; a win/lose situation.

Distributive justice Perceived fairness of the amount and allocation of rewards among individuals.

Dominant culture A culture that expresses the core values that are shared by a majority of the organization's members.

Double-loop learning A process of correcting errors by modifying the organization's objectives, policies and standard routines.

Driving forces Forces that direct behaviour away from the status quo.

Dysfunctional conflict Conflict that hinders group performance.

Effectiveness Achievement of goals.

Efficiency The ratio of effective output to the input required to achieve it.

Electronic meeting A meeting in which members interact on computers, allowing for anonymity of comments and aggregation of votes.

Emotional contagion The process by which peoples' emotions are caused by the emotions of others.

Emotional dissonance Inconsistencies between the emotions people feel and the emotions they project.

Emotional intelligence (EI) The ability to detect and to manage emotional cues and information.

Emotional labour A situation in which an employee expresses organizationally desired emotions during interpersonal transactions at work.

Emotional stability A personality dimension that characterises someone as calm, self-confident, secure (positive) versus nervous, depressed and insecure (negative).

Emotions Intense feelings that are directed at someone or something.

Employee engagement An individual's involvement with, satisfaction with and enthusiasm for the work he or she does.

Employee involvement A participative process that uses the input of employees and is intended to increase employee commitment to an organization's success.

Employee stock ownership plan (ESOP) A company-established benefits plan in which employees acquire stock, often at below-market prices, as part of their benefits.

Employee-oriented leader A leader who emphasises interpersonal relations, takes a personal interest in the needs of employees and accepts individual differences among members.

Encounter stage The stage in the socialisation process in which a new employee sees what the organization is really like and confronts the possibility that expectations and reality may diverge.

Environment Institutions or forces outside an organization that potentially affect the organization's performance.

Equity theory A theory which says that individuals compare their job inputs and outcomes with those of others and then respond to eliminate any inequities.

ERG theory A theory that posits three groups of core needs: existence, relatedness and growth.

Escalation of commitment An increased commitment to a previous decision in spite of negative information.

Ethical dilemmas Situations in which individuals are required to define right and wrong conduct.

Evidence-based management (EBM) Basing managerial decisions on the best available scientific evidence.

Evolutionary psychology An area of inquiry which argues that we must experience the emotions we do because they serve a purpose.

Exit Dissatisfaction expressed through behaviour directed toward leaving the organization.

Expectancy theory A theory which says that the strength of a tendency to act in a certain way depends on the strength of an expectation that the act will be followed by a given outcome and on the attractiveness of that outcome to the individual.

Expert power Influence based on special skills or knowledge.

Extraversion A personality dimension that describes someone who is sociable, gregarious and assertive.

Feedback The degree to which carrying out the work activities required by a job results in the individual obtaining direct and clear information about the effectiveness of his or her performance.

Felt conflict Emotional involvement in a conflict that creates anxiety, tenseness, frustration or hostility.

Felt emotions An individual's actual emotions.

Femininity A national culture attribute that has little differentiation between male and female roles, where women are treated as the equals of men in all aspects of the society.

Fiedler contingency model The theory that effective groups depend on a proper match between a leader's style of interacting with subordinates and the degree to which the situation gives control and influence to the leader.

Filtering A sender's manipulation of information so that it will be seen more favourably by the receiver.

Five-stage group-development model The five distinct stages groups go through: forming, storming, norming, performing and adjourning.

Fixed pie The belief that there is only a set amount of goods or services to be divvied up between the parties.

Fixed-interval schedule Spacing rewards at uniform time intervals.

Fixed-ratio schedule Initiating rewards after a fixed or constant number of responses.

Flexible benefits A benefits plan that allows each employee to put together a benefits package individually tailored to his or her own needs and situation.

Flexitime Flexible work hours.

Formal channels Communication channels established by an organization to transmit messages related to the professional activities of members.

Formal group A designated work group defined by an organization's structure.

Formalisation The degree to which jobs within an organization are standardised.

Forming stage The first stage in group development, characterised by much uncertainty.

Framing A way of using language to manage meaning.

Friendship group People brought together because they share one or more common characteristics.

Functional conflict Conflict that supports the goals of the group and improves its performance.

Fundamental attribution error The tendency to underestimate the influence of external factors and overestimate the influence of internal factors when making judgements about the behaviour of others.

Gainsharing A formula-based group incentive plan.

General mental ability (GMA) An overall factor of intelligence, as suggested by the positive correlations among specific intellectual ability dimensions.

Goal-setting theory A theory which says that specific and difficult goals, with feedback, lead to higher performance.

Grapevine An organization's informal communication network.

Graphic rating scales An evaluation method in which the evaluator rates performance factors on an incremental scale.

Group order ranking An evaluation method that places employees into a particular classification, such as quartiles.

Group Two or more individuals, interacting and interdependent, who have come together to achieve particular objectives.

Groupshift A change in decision risk between a group's decision and an individual decision that a member within the group would make; the shift can be toward either conservatism or greater risk.

Groupthink A phenomenon in which the norm for consensus overrides the realistic appraisal of alternative courses of action.

Halo effect The tendency to draw a general impression about an individual on the basis of a single characteristic.

Heredity Factors determined at conception, one's biological, physiological and inherent psychological makeup.

Hierarchy of needs theory A hierarchy of five needs – physiological, safety, social, esteem and self-actualisation – in which, as each need is substantially satisfied, the next need becomes dominant.

High-context cultures Cultures that rely heavily on nonverbal and subtle situational cues in communication.

Higher-order needs Needs that are satisfied internally, such as social, esteem and self-actualisation needs.

Hindrance stressors Stressors that keep you from reaching your goals (red tape, office politics, confusion over job responsibilities).

Hindsight bias The tendency to believe falsely, after an outcome of an event is actually known, that one would have accurately predicted that outcome.

Human relations view of conflict The belief that conflict is a natural and inevitable outcome in any group.

Human skills The ability to work with, understand and motivate other people, both individually and in groups.

Hygiene factors Factors – such as company policy and administration, supervision and salary – that, when adequate in a job, placate workers. When these factors are adequate, people will not be dissatisfied.

Idea champions Individuals who take an innovation and actively and enthusiastically promote the idea, build support, overcome resistance and ensure that the idea is implemented.

Identification-based trust Trust based on a mutual understanding of each other's intentions and appreciation of each other's wants and desires.

Illegitimate political behaviour Extreme political behaviour that violates the implied rules of the game.

Illusory correlation The tendency of people to associate two events when in reality there is no connection.

Imitation strategy A strategy that seeks to move into new products or new markets only after their viability has already been proven.

Impression management (IM) The process by which individuals attempt to control the impression others form of them.

Independent variable The presumed cause of some change in a dependent variable.

Individual ranking An evaluation method that rank-orders employees from best to worst.

Individualism A national culture attribute that describes the degree to which people prefer to act as individuals rather than as members of groups.

Informal channels Communication channels that are created spontaneously and that emerge as responses to individual choices.

Informal group A group that is neither formally structured nor organizationally determined; such a group appears in response to the need for social contact.

Information overload A condition in which information inflow exceeds an individual's processing capacity.

Initiating structure The extent to which a leader is likely to define and structure his or her role and those of subordinates in the search for goal attainment.

Innovation A new idea applied to initiating or improving a product, process or service.

Innovation strategy A strategy that emphasises the introduction of major new products and services.

Institutionalisation A condition that occurs when an organization takes on a life of its own, apart from any of its members and acquires immortality.

Instrumental values Preferable modes of behaviour or means of achieving one's terminal values.

Integrative bargaining Negotiation that seeks one or more settlements that can create a win/win solution.

Intellectual abilities The capacity to do mental activities – thinking, reasoning and problem solving.

Intentions Decisions to act in a given way.

Interacting groups Typical groups in which members interact with each other face-to-face.

Interactional justice The perceived degree to which an individual is treated with dignity, concern and respect.

Interactionlst view of conflict The belief that conflict is not only a positive force in a group but that it is also an absolute necessity for a group to perform effectively.

Interest group People working together to attain a specific objective with which each is concerned.

Intergroup development OD efforts to change the attitudes, stereotypes and perceptions that groups have of each other.

Intermittent reinforcement Reinforcing a desired behaviour often enough to make the behaviour worth repeating but not every time it is demonstrated.

Intuition A gut feeling not necessarily supported by research.

Intuitive decision making An unconscious process created out of distilled experience.

Job characteristics model (JCM) A model that proposes that any job can be described in terms of five core job dimensions: skill variety, task identity, task significance, autonomy and feedback.

Job design The way the elements in a job are organized.

Job enlargement Increasing the number and variety of tasks that an individual performs. Job enlargement results in jobs with more diversity.

Job enrichment The vertical expansion of jobs, which increases the degree to which the worker controls the planning, execution and evaluation of the work.

Job involvement The degree to which a person identifies with a job, actively participates in it and considers performance important to self-worth.

Job rotation The periodic shifting of an employee from one task to another.

Job satisfaction A positive feeling about one's job resulting from an evaluation of its characteristics.

Job sharing An arrangement that allows two or more individuals to split a traditional 40-hour-a-week job.

Knowledge management (KM) The process of organizing and distributing an organization's collective wisdom so the right information gets to the right people at the right time.

Knowledge-based trust Trust based on behavioural predictability that comes from a history of interaction.

Leader–member exchange (LMX) theory A theory that supports leaders' creation of in-groups and out-groups; subordinates with in-group status will have higher performance ratings, less turnover and greater job satisfaction.

Leader–member relations The degree of confidence, trust and respect subordinates have in their leader.

Leader-participation model A leadership theory that provides a set of rules to determine the form and amount of participative decision making in different situations.

Leadership The ability to influence a group toward the achievement of a vision or set of goals.

Leading A function that includes motivating employees, directing others, selecting the most effective communication channels and resolving conflicts.

Learning A relatively permanent change in behaviour that occurs as a result of experience.

Learning organization An organization that has developed the continuous capacity to adapt and change.

Least preferred coworker (LPC) questionnaire An instrument that purports to measure whether a person is task or relationship oriented.

Legitimate political behaviour Normal everyday politics.

Legitimate power The power a person receives as a result of his or her position in the formal hierarchy of an organization.

Level-5 leaders Leaders who are fiercely ambitious and driven but whose ambition is directed toward their company rather than themselves.

Long-term orientation A national culture attribute that emphasises the future, thrift and persistence.

Low-context cultures Cultures that rely heavily on words to convey meaning in communication.

Lower-order needs Needs that are satisfied externally, such as physiological and safety needs.

Loyalty Dissatisfaction expressed by passively waiting for conditions to improve.

Machiavellianism The degree to which an individual is pragmatic, maintains emotional distance and believes that ends can justify means.

Management by objectives (MBO) A programme that encompasses specific goals, participatively set, for an explicit time period, with feedback on goal progress.

Managerial grid A nine-by-nine matrix outlining 81 different leadership styles.

Managers Individuals who achieve goals through other people.

Masculinity A national culture attribute that describes the extent to which the culture favours traditional masculine work roles of achievement, power and control. Societal values are characterised by assertiveness and materialism.

Matrix structure A structure that creates dual lines of authority and combines functional and product departmentalisation.

McClelland's theory of needs A theory which states that achievement, power and affiliation are three important needs that help explain motivation.

Mechanistic model A structure characterised by extensive departmentalisation, high formalisation, a limited information network and centralisation.

Mediator A neutral third party who facilitates a negotiated solution by using reasoning, persuasion and suggestions for alternatives.

Mental models Team members' knowledge and beliefs about how the work gets done by the team.

Mentor A senior employee who sponsors and supports a less-experienced employee, called a protégé.

Merit-based pay plan A pay plan based on performance appraisal ratings.

Metamorphosis stage The stage in the socialisation process in which a new employee changes and adjusts to the job, work group and organization.

Model An abstraction of reality. A simplified representation of some real-world phenomenon.

Moods Feelings that tend to be less intense than emotions and that lack a contextual stimulus.

Motivating potential score (MPS) A predictive index that suggests the motivating potential in a job.

Motivation The processes that account for an individual's intensity, direction and persistence of effort toward attaining a goal.

Movement A change process that transforms the organization from the status quo to a desired end state.

Multi-team systems Systems in which different teams need to coordinate their efforts to produce a desired outcome.

Myers-Briggs Type Indicator (MBTI) A personality test that taps four characteristics and classifies people into 1 of 16 personality types.

Narcissism The tendency to be arrogant, have a grandiose sense of self-importance, require excessive admiration and have a sense of entitlement.

Need for achievement (nAch) The drive to excel, to achieve in relationship to a set of standards and to strive to succeed.

Need for affiliation (nAff) The desire for friendly and close interpersonal relationships.

Need for power (nPow) The need to make others behave in a way in which they would not have behaved otherwise.

Negative affect A mood dimension that consists of emotions such as nervousness, stress and anxiety at the high end and relaxation, tranquillity and poise at the low end.

Neglect Dissatisfaction expressed through allowing conditions to worsen.

Negotiation A process in which two or more parties exchange goods or services and attempt to agree on the exchange rate for them.

Nominal group technique A group decision-making method in which individual members meet face-to-face to pool their judgements in a systematic but independent fashion.

Normative commitment An obligation to remain with an organization for moral or ethical reasons.

Norming stage The third stage in group development, characterised by close relationships and cohesiveness.

Norms Acceptable standards of behaviour within a group that are shared by the group's members.

OB Mod The application of reinforcement concepts to individuals in the work setting.

Openness to experience A personality dimension that characterises someone in terms of imagination, sensitivity and curiosity.

Operant conditioning A type of conditioning in which desired voluntary behaviour leads to a reward or prevents a punishment.

Opportunity to perform Absence of obstacles that constrain the employee. High levels of performance are partially a function of the opportunity to perform.

Organic model A structure that is flat, uses cross-hierarchical and cross-functional teams, has low formalisation, possesses a comprehensive information network and relies on participative decision making.

Organization A consciously coordinated social unit, composed of two or more people, that functions on a relatively continuous basis to achieve a common goal or set of goals.

Organizational behaviour (OB) A field of study that investigates the impact that individuals, groups and structure have on behaviour within organizations, for the purpose of applying such knowledge toward improving an organization's effectiveness.

Organizational citizenship behaviour (OCB) Discretionary behaviour that is not part of an employee's formal job requirements but that nevertheless promotes the effective functioning of the organization.

Organizational commitment The degree to which an employee identifies with a particular organization and its goals and wishes to maintain membership in the organization.

Organizational culture A system of shared meaning held by members that distinguishes the organization from other organizations.

Organizational demography The degree to which members of a work unit share a common demographic attribute, such as age, sex, race, educational level or length of service in an organization and the impact of this attribute on turnover.

Organizational development (OD) A collection of planned change interventions, built on humanistic-democratic values, that seeks to improve organizational effectiveness and employee well-being.

Organizational justice An overall perception of what is fair in the workplace, composed of distributive, procedural and interactional justice.

Organizational structure The way in which job tasks are formally divided, grouped and coordinated.

Organizing Determining what tasks are to be done, who is to do them, how the tasks are to be grouped, who reports to whom and where decisions are to be made.

Participative management A process in which subordinates share a significant degree of decision-making power with their immediate superiors.

Path-goal theory A theory which states that it is the leader's job to assist followers in attaining their goals and to provide the necessary direction and/or support to ensure that their goals are compatible with the overall objectives of the group or organization.

Perceived conflict Awareness by one or more parties of the existence of conditions that create opportunities for conflict to arise.

Perceived organizational support (POS) The degree to which employees believe an organization values their contribution and cares about their well-being.

Perception A process by which individuals organize and interpret their sensory impressions in order to give meaning to their environment.

Performing stage The fourth stage in group development, during which the group is fully functional.

Personality The sum total of ways in which an individual reacts and interacts with others.

Personality traits Enduring characteristics that describe an individual's behaviour.

Personality–job fit theory A theory that identifies six personality types and proposes that the fit between personality type and occupational environment determines satisfaction and turnover.

Physical abilities The capacity to do tasks that demand stamina, dexterity, strength and similar characteristics.

Piece-rate pay plan A pay plan in which workers are paid a fixed sum for each unit of production completed.

Planned change Change activities that are intentional and goal oriented.

Planning A process that includes defining goals, establishing strategy and developing plans to coordinate activities.

Political behaviour Activities that are not required as part of a person's formal role in the organization but that influence or attempt to influence, the distribution of advantages and disadvantages within the organization.

Political skill The ability to influence others in such a way as to enhance one's objectives.

Position power Influence derived from one's formal structural position in the organization; includes power to hire, fire, discipline, promote and give salary increases.

Positive affect A mood dimension that consists of specific positive emotions such as excitement, self-assurance and cheerfulness at the high end and boredom, sluggishness and tiredness at the low end.

Positive organizational culture A culture that emphasises building on employee strengths, rewards more than punishes and emphasises individual vitality and growth.

Positive organizational scholarship An area of OB research that concerns how organizations develop human strength, foster vitality and resilience and unlock potential.

Positivity offset The tendency of most individuals to experience a mildly positive mood at zero input (when nothing in particular is going on).

Power A capacity that A has to influence the behaviour of B so that B acts in accordance with A's wishes.

Power distance A national culture attribute that describes the extent to which a society accepts that power in institutions and organizations is distributed unequally.

Power tactics Ways in which individuals translate power bases into specific actions.

Prearrival stage The period of learning in the socialisation process that occurs before a new employee joins the organization.

Proactive personality People who identify opportunities, show initiative, take action and persevere until meaningful change occurs.

Problem A discrepancy between the current state of affairs and some desired state.

Problem-solving teams Groups of 5 to 12 employees from the same department who meet for a few hours each week to discuss ways of improving quality, efficiency and the work environment.

Procedural justice The perceived fairness of the process used to determine the distribution of rewards.

Process conflict Conflict over how work gets done.

Process consultation (PC) A meeting in which a consultant assists a client in understanding process events with which he or she must deal and identifying processes that need improvement.

Production-oriented leader A leader who emphasises technical or task aspects of the job.

Productivity A performance measure that includes effectiveness and efficiency.

Profiling A form of stereotyping in which a group of individuals is singled out – typically on the basis of race or ethnicity – for intensive inquiry, scrutiny or investigation.

Profit-sharing plan An organization-wide programme that distributes compensation based on some established formula designed around a company's profitability.

Psychological contract An unwritten agreement that sets out what management expects from an employee and vice versa.

Psychological empowerment Employees' belief in the degree to which they affect their work environment, their competence, the meaningfulness of their job and their perceived autonomy in their work.

Psychology The science that seeks to measure, explain and sometimes change the behaviour of humans and other animals.

Punctuated-equilibrium model A set of phases that temporary groups go through that involves transitions between inertia and activity.

Quality circle A work group of employees who meet regularly to discuss their quality problems, investigate causes, recommend solutions and take corrective actions.

Randomness error The tendency of individuals to believe that they can predict the outcome of random events.

Rational Characterised by making consistent, value-maximising choices within specified constraints.

Rational decision-making model A decision-making model that describes how individuals should behave in order to maximise some outcome.

Reference groups Important groups to which individuals belong or hope to belong and with whose norms individuals are likely to conform.

Referent power Influence based on possession by an individual of desirable resources or personal traits.

Reflexivity A team characteristic of reflecting on and adjusting the master plan when necessary.

Refreezing Stabilising a change intervention by balancing driving and restraining forces.

Reinforcement theory A theory which says that behaviour is a function of its consequences.

Relationship conflict Conflict based on interpersonal relationships.

Representative participation A system in which workers participate in organizational decision making through a small group of representative employees.

Resources Things within an individual's control that can be used to resolve demands.

Restraining forces Forces that hinder movement from the existing equilibrium.

Reward power Compliance achieved based on the ability to distribute rewards that others view as valuable.

Rituals Repetitive sequences of activities that express and reinforce the key values of the organization, which goals are most important, which people are important and which are expendable.

Role A set of expected behaviour patterns attributed to someone occupying a given position in a social unit.

Role conflict A situation in which an individual is confronted by divergent role expectations.

Role expectations How others believe a person should act in a given situation.

Role identity Certain attitudes and behaviours consistent with a role.

Role perception An individual's view of how he or she is supposed to act in a given situation.

Selective perception The tendency to selectively interpret what one sees on the basis of one's interests, background, experience and attitudes.

Self-actualisation The drive to become what a person is capable of becoming.

Self-concordance The degree to which a person's reasons for pursuing a goal is consistent with the person's interests and core values.

Self-efficacy An individual's belief that he or she is capable of performing a task.

Self-fulfilling prophecy A situation in which a person inaccurately perceives a second person and the resulting expectations cause the second person to behave in ways consistent with the original perception.

Self-leadership A set of processes through which individuals control their own behaviour.

Self-managed work teams Groups of 10 to 15 people who take on responsibilities of their former supervisors.

Self-monitoring A personality trait that measures an individual's ability to adjust his or her behaviour to external, situational factors.

Self-serving bias The tendency for individuals to attribute their own successes to internal factors and put the blame for failures on external factors.

Sensitivity training Training groups that seek to change behaviour through unstructured group interaction.

Shaping behaviour Systematically reinforcing each successive step that moves an individual closer to the desired response.

Short-term orientation A national culture attribute that emphasises the past and present, respect for tradition and fulfilment of social obligations.

Simple structure A structure characterised by a low degree of departmentalisation, wide spans of control, authority centralised in a single person and little formalisation.

Single-loop learning A process of correcting errors using past routines and present policies.

Situational leadership theory (SLT) A contingency theory that focuses on followers' readiness.

Skill variety The degree to which a job requires a variety of different activities.

Skill-based pay A pay plan that sets pay levels on the basis of how many skills employees have or how many jobs they can do.

Social loafing The tendency for individuals to expend less effort when working collectively than when working individually.

Social psychology An area of psychology that blends concepts from psychology and sociology and that focuses on the influence of people on one another.

Socialisation A process that adapts employees to the organization's culture.

Socialised charismatic leadership A leadership concept that states that leaders convey values that are other-centred versus self-centred and who role model ethical conduct.

Social-learning theory The view that people can learn through observation and direct experience.

Sociology The study of people in relation to their social environment or culture.

Span of control The number of subordinates a manager can efficiently and effectively direct.

Status A socially defined position or rank given to groups or group members by others.

Status characteristics theory A theory which states that differences in status characteristics create status hierarchies within groups.

Stereotyping Judging someone on the basis of one's perception of the group to which that person belongs.

Storming stage The second stage in group development, characterised by intragroup conflict.

Stress A dynamic condition in which an individual is confronted with an opportunity, a demand or a resource related to what the individual desires and for which the outcome is perceived to be both uncertain and important.

Strong culture A culture in which the core values are intensely held and widely shared.

Subcultures Minicultures within an organization, typically defined by department designations and geographical separation.

Surface acting Hiding one's inner feelings and forgoing emotional expressions in response to display rules.

Survey feedback The use of questionnaires to identify discrepancies among member perceptions; discussion follows and remedies are suggested.

Systematic study Looking at relationships, attempting to attribute causes and effects and drawing conclusions based on scientific evidence.

Task conflict Conflict over content and goals of the work.

Task group People working together to complete a job task.

Task identity The degree to which a job requires completion of a whole and identifiable piece of work.

Task significance The degree to which a job has a substantial impact on the lives or work of other people.

Task structure The degree to which job assignments are procedurised.

Team building High interaction among team members to increase trust and openness.

Technical skills The ability to apply specialised knowledge or expertise.

Technology The way in which an organization transfers its inputs into outputs.

Teleworking People who work mainly in their own home or mainly in different places using home as a base, who use both a telephone and a computer to carry out their work

Terminal values Desirable end-states of existence; the goals a person would like to achieve during his or her lifetime.

Theory X The assumption that employees dislike work, are lazy, dislike responsibility and must be coerced to perform.

Theory Y The assumption that employees like work, are creative, seek responsibility and can exercise self-direction.

Three-component model of creativity The proposition that individual creativity requires expertise, creative thinking skills and intrinsic task motivation.

Traditional view of conflict The belief that all conflict is harmful and must be avoided.

Trait theories of leadership Theories that consider personal qualities and characteristics that differentiate leaders from nonleaders.

Transactional leaders Leaders who guide or motivate their followers in the direction of established goals by clarifying role and task requirements.

Transformational leaders Leaders who inspire followers to transcend their own self-interests and who are capable of having a profound and extraordinary effect on followers.

Trust A positive expectation that another will not act opportunistically.

Turnover Voluntary and involuntary permanent withdrawal from an organization.

Two-factor theory A theory that relates intrinsic factors to job satisfaction and associates extrinsic factors with dissatisfaction. Also called motivation-hygiene theory.

Type A personality Aggressive involvement in a chronic, incessant struggle to achieve more and more in less and less time and, if necessary, against the opposing efforts of other things or other people.

Uncertainty avoidance A national culture attribute that describes the extent to which a society feels threatened by uncertain and ambiguous situations and tries to avoid them.

Unfreezing Changing to overcome the pressures of both individual resistance and group conformity.

Unity of command The idea that a subordinate should have only one superior to whom he or she is directly responsible.

Utilitarianism A system in which decisions are made to provide the greatest good for the greatest number.

Value system A hierarchy based on a ranking of an individual's values in terms of their intensity.

Values Basic convictions that a specific mode of conduct or end-state of existence is personally or socially preferable to an opposite or converse mode of conduct or end-state of existence.

Variable-interval schedule Distributing rewards in time so that reinforcements are unpredictable.

Variable-pay programme A pay plan that bases a portion of an employee's pay on some individual and/or organizational measure of performance.

Variable-ratio schedule Varying the reward relative to the behaviour of the individual.

Virtual organization A small, core organization that outsources major business functions.

Virtual teams Teams that use computer technology to tie together physically dispersed members in order to achieve a common goal.

Vision A long-term strategy for attaining a goal or goals.

Vision statement A formal articulation of an organization's vision or mission.

Voice Dissatisfaction expressed through active and constructive attempts to improve conditions.

Wellness programmes Organizationally supported programmes that focus on the employee's total physical and mental condition.

Whistle-blowers Individuals who report unethical practices by their employer to outsiders.

Winner's curse A decision-making dictum which argues that the winning participants in an auction typically pay too much for the winning item.

Work group A group that interacts primarily to share information and to make decisions to help each group member perform within his or her area of responsibility.

Work sample test A test that is a miniature replica of a job that is used to evaluate the performance abilities of job candidates.

Work specialisation The degree to which tasks in an organization are subdivided into separate jobs.

Work team A group whose individual efforts result in performance that is greater than the sum of the individual inputs.

Workforce diversity The concept that organizations are becoming more heterogeneous in terms of gender, age, race, ethnicity, sexual orientation and inclusion of other diverse groups.

Workplace spirituality The recognition that people have an inner life that nourishes and is nourished by meaningful work that takes place in the context of community.

Name index

Organization index

Subject index

360-degree evaluations 498, 499